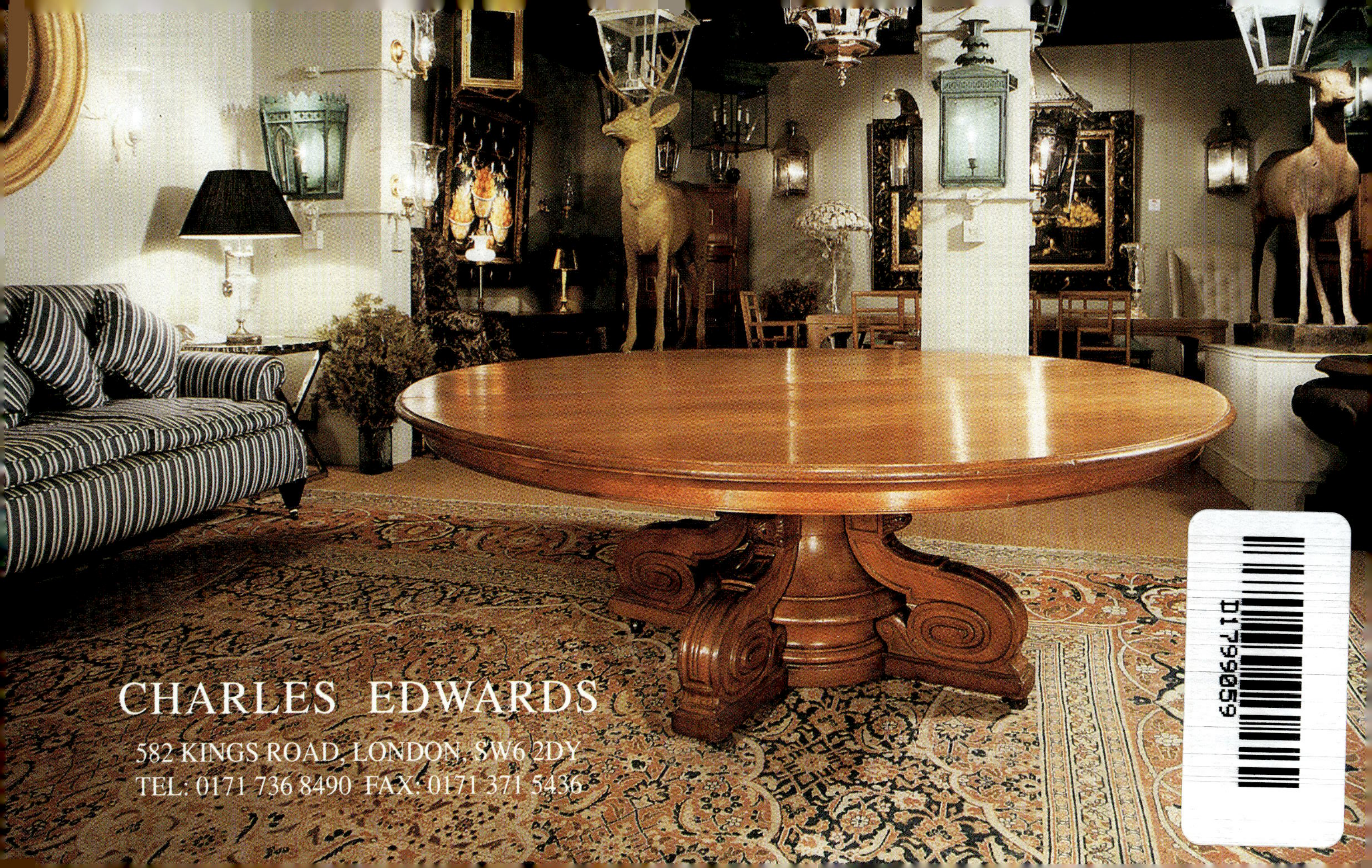
CHARLES EDWARDS
582 KINGS ROAD, LONDON, SW6 2DY
TEL: 0171 736 8490 FAX: 0171 371 5436
D1799059

guide to THE ANTIQUE SHOPS of BRITAIN

1997/8

compiled by Carol Adams

FRONT COVER: Portuguese solid chestnut painted cupboard with Portuguese redondo pots.

ISBN 1 85149 264 X

British Library CIP Data
Guide to the Antique Shops of Britain.
- 1998
(June 1997- June 1998)
1. Great Britain. Antiques trades:
Directories - Serials
I. Antique Collectors' Club
380. 1' 457451'02541

While every resonable care has been exercised in compilation of information contained in this Guide, neither the editors nor The Antique Collector's Club Ltd., or any servants of the company accept any liability for loss, danage or expense incurred by reliance placed on the book or through omissions or incorrect entries howsoever incurred.

Printed in England by The Antique Collectors' Club Ltd., Woodbridge, Suffolk.
Telephone: (01394) 385501

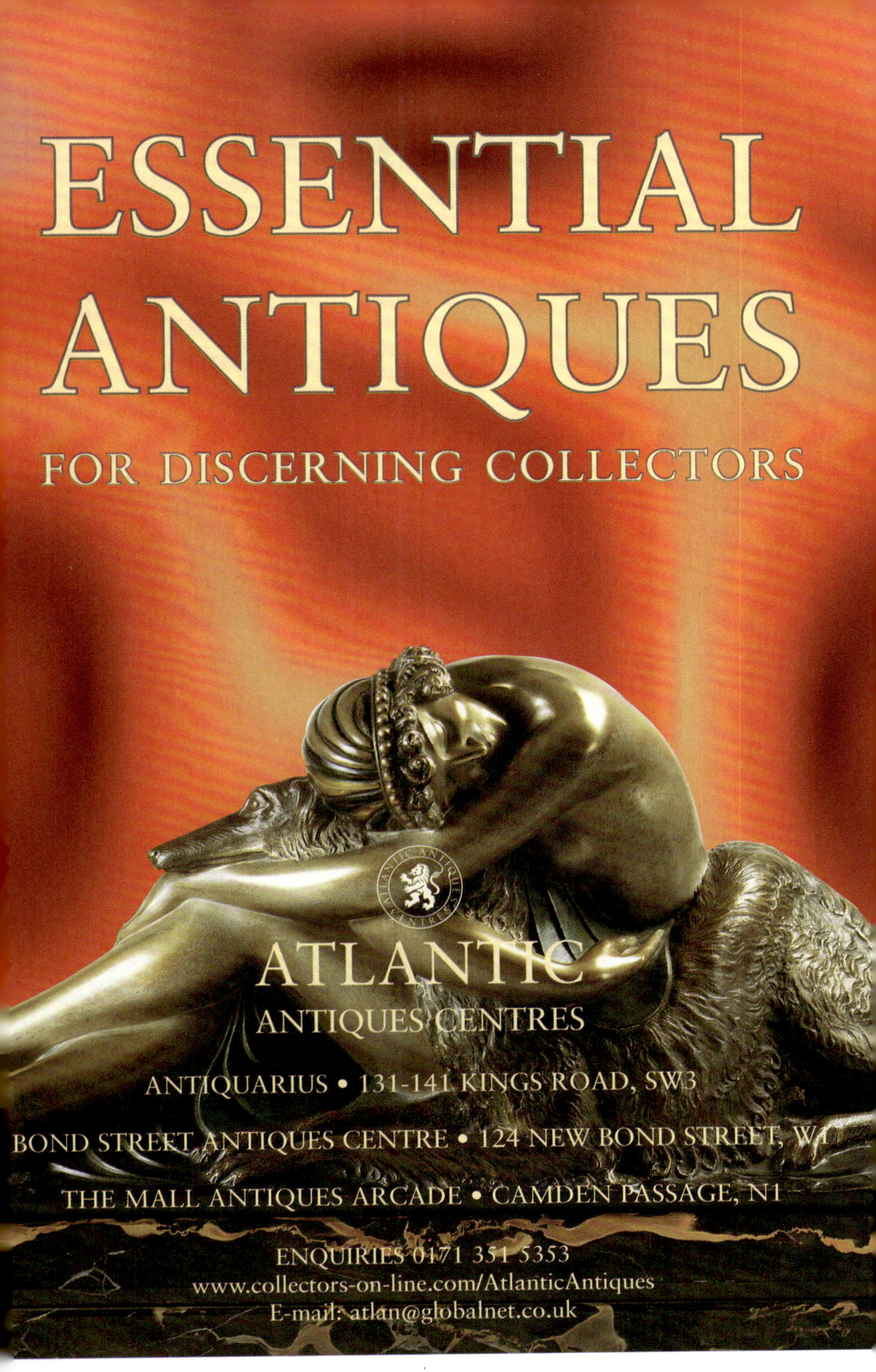
ESSENTIAL ANTIQUES
FOR DISCERNING COLLECTORS
ATLANTIC
ANTIQUES CENTRES
ANTIQUARIUS • 131-141 KINGS ROAD, SW3
BOND STREET ANTIQUES CENTRE • 124 NEW BOND STREET, W1
THE MALL ANTIQUES ARCADE • CAMDEN PASSAGE, N1
ENQUIRIES 0171 351 5353
www.collectors-on-line.com/AtlanticAntiques
E-mail: atlan@globalnet.co.uk

CONTENTS

ACKNOWLEDGEMENTS

Our main sources of information are still the trade magazines but we would like to thank those dealers who provide information about new shops and closures in their area. Without their assistance our job would be far more difficult.

We would also like to thank those dealers who supported us with advertising - without this revenue each copy would cost £30, instead of £14.95 - and those who up-date their entry when we send them the first reminder. Each year we include a form at the end of the Guide which dealers can use to up-date details about their own business. In anticipation of next year's Guide, we are grateful to those dealers who make use of this form.

Finally, thanks must go to the editorial team who carry out the mammoth task of up-dating, compiling and indexing the entries.

C.A.

Editor **Carol Adams**
Advertising Sales **Jean Johnson**
Editorial Team **Judith Neal, Diana Dutson**

INTRODUCTION

This is the 26th edition of the **Guide to the Antique Shops of Britain** which is universally accepted as *the* guide for anybody who wishes to buy antiques in Britain.

This year we have listed nearly 6,000 establishments and, as usual, every one had been confirmed before reprinting. Please help to keep our costs down by returning the first reminder.

We appreciate that quantity without quality is meaningless and the range of information we provide is more detailed and up-to-date than is available in any other publication. We state the obvious facts - name of proprietor, address, telephone number, opening hours and stock and also size of showroom and price ranges (where supplied). Additional information gives details of major trade association members, the date the business was established, the location and also the parking situation, plus street maps for those towns with over 25 shops. Whilst none of these points are decisive in themselves, we feel that they build up to a useful picture of the sort of establishment likely to be found and may well influence a prospective buyer's decision as to whether or not to visit a particular shop. As always, we advise a prior telephone call before making a long trip.

We start preparing the next edition in early 1998. Please let us know if there are any alterations to your entry and, if possible, any changes in your area - openings and closures. We do not print any information given about other dealers without first contacting them, but obviously the more shops in a particular town or village, the more attractive it is to prospective buyers on trips around the country. We would also be grateful for your comments on the Guide and, if you find any information given in the Guide to be incorrect, we would be grateful for your input. We have occasionally had dealers telephoning to say that the stock listed is not what they found when visiting a particular establishment but then refuse to tell us the name of the shop which means we can do nothing about the complaint. Any constructive criticism is welcomed and we look forward to your comments.

HOW TO USE THIS GUIDE

The Guide is set out under six main headings; London, England, Channel Islands, Northern Ireland, Scotland and Wales. Counties are listed alphabetically and within counties the towns are listed alphabetically and within towns the shops are listed, again alphabetically. London is divided into postal districts.

To make route planning easier there is a map at the beginning of each county, coded to show the number of shops in any one town or village. The roads indicated on the map are only a broad intimation of the routes available and it is advisable to use an up-to-date map showing the latest improvements in the road system.

Apart from the six main headings above, there are further helpful lists - an alphabetical list of towns, showing the counties in which they will be found for those not familiar with the location of towns within counties, e.g. Woodbridge is shown in the county of Suffolk. One therefore turns to the Suffolk section to look up Woodbridge. This listing is a valuable aid to the overseas visitor. The second is particularly important to British dealers and collectors - giving an alphabetical list of the name of every shop, proprietor and company director known to be connected with a shop or gallery. Thus, if A. Bloggs and B. Brown own an antique shop called Castle Antiques, there will be entries under Bloggs, A., Brown, B., and Castle Antiques. Listings of specialist dealers, auctioneers, shippers and packers, services, and fairs organisers are also included.

One point that both dealers and collectors constantly seem to miss is that the telephone offers great savings of time and money. Nearly all dealers have to make unscheduled calls during opening hours and the "Back in 5 minutes" notice which has been in the window of a small shop for 20 minutes is a cause of great irritation to the potential buyer. If you have to be a hundred miles along the road in two hours, but there is something at the back of the shop which looks interesting, then the decision to wait or not wait is even more frustrating. A prior telephone call can forstall this. When you telephone, it is usually quite acceptable to describe what you are looking for in terms of Antique Collectors' Club books. Increasingly one sees advertisements referring to page numbers. Most dealers have at least some of the books and use them as a basis for communicating information.

In the main, dealers are factual and accurate in describing their stock to us but there are probably a few who list what they would like to stock rather than as it is. We would appreciate you letting us know of any such anomalies. Please telephone (01394) 385501 or drop us a postcard and help us to ensure that the Guide remains Britain's premier listing of antique shops and galleries.

ABBREVIATIONS IN ENTRIES

In order to cut the bulk of this book as much as possible without curtailing the amount of information, we have made some very simple contractions in the entries.

BADA and LAPADA:	Members are indicated by using a bold type face.
BABADA:	Bath and Bradford on Avon Antique Dealers Association.
EADA:	Essex Antique Dealers Association.
HADA:	Highlands Antique Dealers Association.
TADA:	Tetbury Antique Dealers Association.
TVADA:	Thames Valley Antique Dealers Association.
CADA:	Cotswold Antique Dealers Association.
EST:	Shows the year in which the shop was established or the number of years the dealer or firm has been trading.
CL:	Days when the business is normally closed. It follows the hours of opening. In some small businesses these may prove erratic, as it is often necessary for the dealer to go out at short notice. Unless otherwise stated shops are closed on Sundays. If making a long journey, it is advisable to telephone and make an appointment.
SIZE:	A guide to the size of the showrooms is given to indicate the quantity of stock likely to be seen. Small is under 600 sq. ft. (60 sq. metres), medium between 600 and 1,500 sq. ft. (60 and 150 sq. metres) and large over 1,500 sq. ft. (150 sq.metres).
STOCK:	Dealers are asked to list their stock in order of importance, so that the items listed can be expected to comprise a significant part of the stock. The price range is of very general application and is designed to give some idea to prospective buyers of the type of items to be seen. Not stocked items are indicated after those which are stocked, the items listed are not normally to be found in this shop. Advertisements often give extra information on the size of showrooms, etc.
LOC:	Location of shop. This is a description given by the owner designed to help the would-be caller. Road numbers in the entries are not necessarily shown on the county maps of the Guide, which are merely general aids to direction.
PARK:	This indicates how easy it is for a car to park for 15 minutes outside the shop. Where parking is not easy, alternative suggestions for parking are often given.
TEL:	In addition to their business numbers, some dealers have listed their home telephone numbers so customers can ring for an appointment outside business hours. Clearly callers should use discretion and only make calls out of business hours when they are seriously interested, and in any event not late at night or early in the morning.
SER:	Additional services which the dealer offers. Where "buys at auction" is shown in this section it indicates that if an auction is one which a dealer might normally attend, he may be approached to act as bidder on behalf of someone else. Check the cost of this service, and any others offered, beforehand.
VAT:	Indicates which of the VAT schemes are in operation.

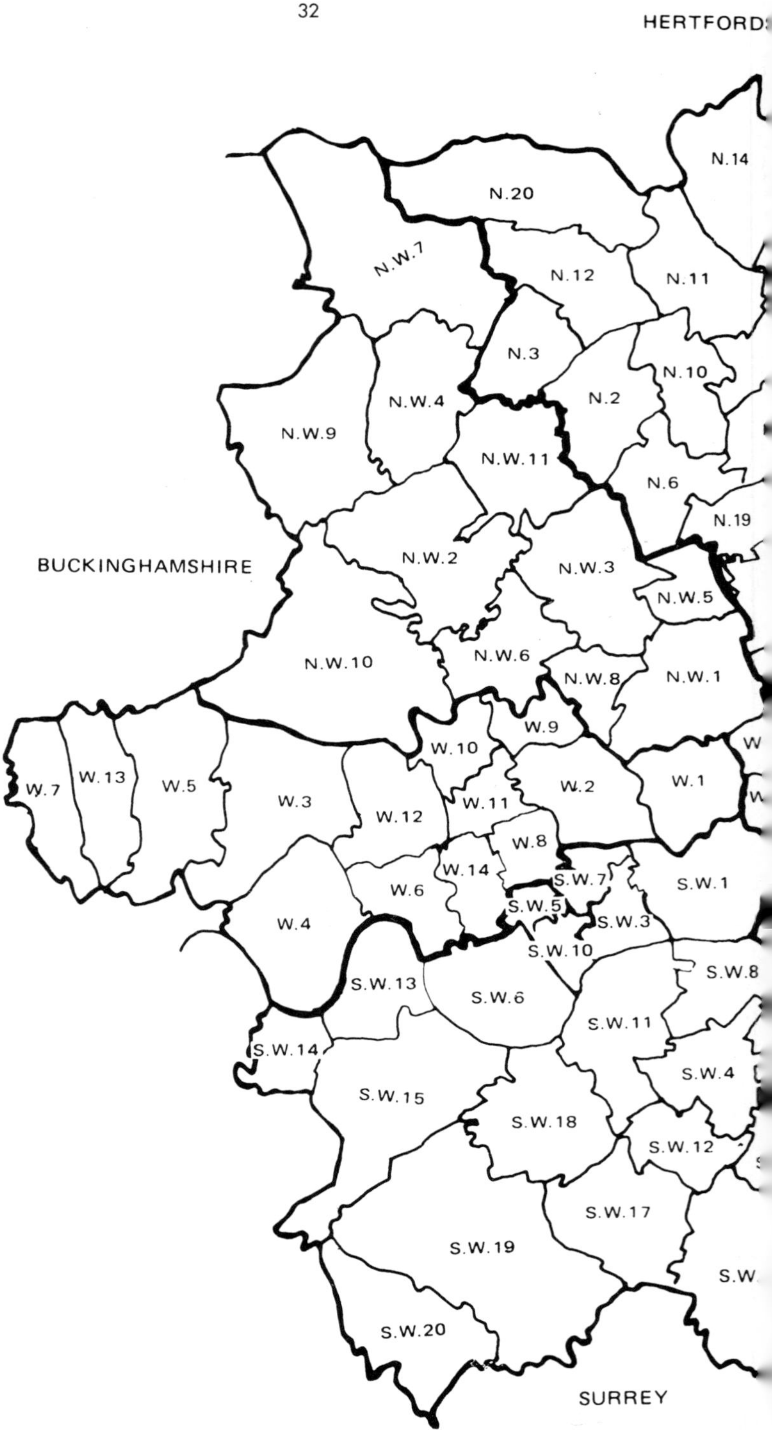
HERTFORD
N.14
N.20
N.W.7
N.12
N.11
N.3
N.10
N.2
N.W.4
N.W.9
N.W.11
N.6
N.19
BUCKINGHAMSHIRE
N.W.2
N.W.3
N.W.5
N.W.10
N.W.6
N.W.8
N.W.1
W.9
W.10
W.7
W.13
W.5
W.3
W.12
W.11
W.2
W.1
W.8
W.14
S.W.7
S.W.1
W.6
S.W.5
W.4
S.W.3
S.W.10
S.W.8
S.W.13
S.W.6
S.W.11
S.W.14
S.W.4
S.W.15
S.W.18
S.W.12
S.W.17
S.W.19
S.W.20
SURREY

London postal districts

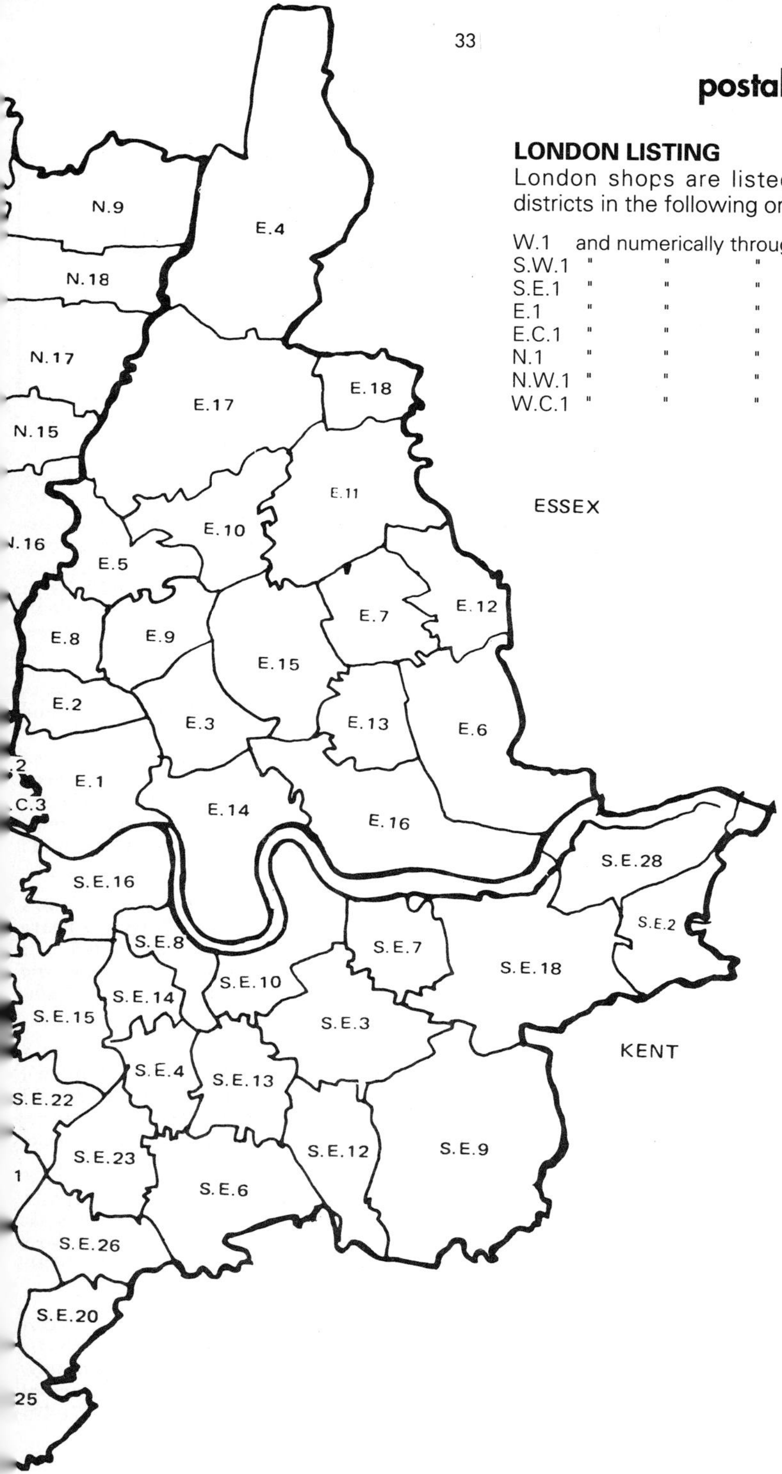

LONDON LISTING

London shops are listed by postal districts in the following order:

W.1	and numerically through to W.14			
S.W.1	"	"	"	" S.W.20
S.E.1	"	"	"	" S.E.26
E.1	"	"	"	" E.18
E.C.1	"	"	"	" E.C.4
N.1	"	"	"	" N.21
N.W.1	"	"	"	" N.W.11
W.C.1	"	"	"	" W.C.2

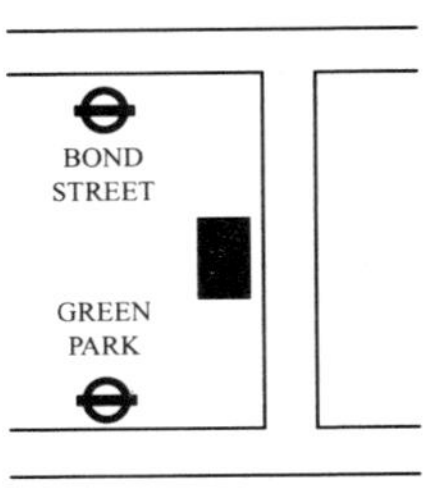

LONDON W1

Aaron Gallery
34 Bruton St.W1X 7DD. (M. and D. Aaron). Est. 1910. Open 10-6, Sat. by appointment. *STOCK: Islamic and ancient art, Oriental carpets.* TEL: 0171 499 9434/5; fax - 0171 499 0072.

Agnew's BADA
43 Old Bond St. and 3 Albemarle St. W1X 4BA. SLAD. Est. 1817. Open 9.30-5.30, Thurs. 9.30-6.30. CL: Sat. SIZE: Large. *STOCK: Paintings, drawings, watercolours, engravings and sculptures of all schools.* TEL: 0171 629 6176; fax - 0171 629 4359. VAT: Spec.

Adrian Alan Ltd BADA LAPADA
66/67 South Audley St. W1Y 5FE. Est. 1963. Open 10-6. CL: Sat. SIZE: Large. *STOCK: English and Continental furniture, especially fine 19th C; sculpture and works of art.* TEL: 0171 495 2324; fax - 0171 495 0204. VAT: Stan/Spec.

Philip Antrobus Ltd
11 New Bond St. W1Y 0SE. Est. 1815. *STOCK: Jewellery.* TEL: 0171 493 4557; fax - 0171 495 2120.

Argyll Etkin Gallery
48 Conduit St., New Bond St. W1R 9FB. (Argyll Etkin Ltd). Est. 1954. Open 9-5.30. CL: Sat. SIZE: Medium. *STOCK: Classic postage stamps, postal history and covers, historical documents and antique letters, 1400-1950, £50-£25,000; stamp boxes and associated writing equipment, 1700-1930, £50-£500.* LOC: Near Oxford Circus. PARK: Savile Row. TEL: 0171 437 7800 (6 lines). SER: Valuations; collections purchased. FAIRS: Major stamp exhibitions worldwide. VAT: Stan.

Armour-Winston Ltd
43 Burlington Arcade. W1V 9AE. Est. 1952. Open 9-5. Sat. 9.30-2. SIZE: Small. *STOCK: Jewellery, especially Victorian; gentlemen's cufflinks.* LOC: Off Piccadilly. Between Green Park and Piccadilly tube stations. PARK: Savile Row. TEL: 0171 493 8937. SER: Valuations; restorations. VAT: Stan/Spec.

W1 continued

Asprey plc BADA
165-169 New Bond St. W1Y 0AR. Est. 1781. Open 9.30-5.30, Sat. 10-5. SIZE: Large. *STOCK: Furniture, works of art, clocks, silver, jewellery, Fabergé and objets de vertu, glass.* PARK: Albemarle St., entrance No.22. TEL: 0171 493 6767; fax - 0171 491 0384. SER: Valuations; restorations (furniture, jewellery, clocks, silver). VAT: Stan/Spec.

Atlantic Bay Carpets BADA
5 Sedley Place. W1R 1HH. (W. Grodzinski and Z. Golebiowski). Est. 1945. Open 9-5, Sat. 9-1. SIZE: Medium. *STOCK: Antique Oriental and European carpets and textiles.* LOC: Near Bond/Oxford St. PARK: Easy. TEL: 0171 355 3301; fax - 0171 355 3760. SER: Valuations; restorations; buys at auction (as stock). VAT: Stan/Spec.

John and Arthur Beare BADA
7 Broadwick St. W1V 1FJ. (J. and A. Beare Ltd). Est. 1892. Open 9-12.15 and 1.30-5. CL: Sat. *STOCK: Violins, violas, cellos, bows and accessories.* TEL: 0171 437 1449. SER: Valuations. VAT: Stan/Spec.

Paul Bennett LAPADA
48A George St. W1H 5RF. (M.J. Dubiner). Open 9.30-6. CL: Sat. SIZE: Large. *STOCK: Silver, 1740-1963, £10-£10,000; Sheffield plate.* PARK: Meters. TEL: 0171 935 1555/486 8836. VAT: Stan/Spec.

Bentley & Co Ltd LAPADA
8 New Bond St. W1Y 9PE. Open 10-5.30. *STOCK: Jewellery, Fabergé, objets d'art.* PARK: Meters. TEL: 0171 629 0651. SER: Valuations; repairs. VAT: Stan/Spec.

Konrad O. Bernheimer Ltd BADA
1 Mount St., Mayfair. W1Y 5AA. CINOA SLAD. Est. 1985. Open by appointment only. *STOCK: Old Master paintings, Continental furniture and Chinese ceramics.* TEL: 0171 495 7028; fax - 0171 495 7027.

W1 continued

Peter Biddulph
34 St George St. W1R 9FA. Open 10-6. CL: Sat. *STOCK: Violins, violas, cellos and bows.* TEL: 0171 491 8621.

H. Blairman and Sons Ltd BADA
119 Mount St. W1Y 5HB. (M.P. and W.Y. Levy and L.G. Hannen). Est. 1884. Open daily. CL: Sat. SIZE: Medium. *STOCK: English and French antiques, mid-18th to early 19th C; works of art, mounted porcelain, Chinese mirror pictures; architect designed furniture, 19th C.* TEL: 0171 493 0444; fax - 0171 495 0766. FAIRS: Grosvenor House. VAT: Spec.

Blunderbuss Antiques
29 Thayer St. W1M 5LJ. (T. Greenaway). Open 9.30-4.30. *STOCK: Arms and armour, militaria.* TEL: 0171 486 2444.

Bond Street Antiques Centre
124 New Bond St. W1. (Atlantic Antique Centres Ltd). Est. 1970. Open 10-5.45. CL: Sat. SIZE: Large - 27 dealers. *STOCK: Wide range of general antiques especially jewellery.* LOC: Bond St. or Green Park tube stations. TEL: Enquiries - 0171 351 5353; fax - 0171 351 5350. Below are listed some of the dealers at this market.

Emmy Abe
Stand 33. *Jewellery.* TEL: 0171 629 1826.

Accurate Trading Co
Stand 1D. (E. Fahimian). *Jewellery.* TEL: 0171 629 0277.

Anita's Antiques
Stand 40. *Jewellery.* TEL: 0171 409 2107.

Anne Bloom Jewellers Ltd
Stand 15. *Antique, period and contemporary jewellery and objet d'art.* TEL: 0171 491 1213. Stan/Margin.

Clayre Armitage
Stand 31. *Jewellery and objects.* TEL: 0171 493 5830.

Astarte Gallery
Stand 14. (A.G. Davies). *Antiquities, works of art, antiques, medallions, ephemera.* TEL: 0171 409 1875; fax - same; URL - http://www.desiderata. com.

N. Bloom & Son (1912) Ltd LAPADA
(I. Harris). *Jewellery, mainly 1860-1960; small silver items, small 19th C decorative furniture.* TEL: 0171 629 5060; fax - 0171 493 2528. SER: Valuations; restorations; repairs; buys at auction. VAT: Stan/Spec.

Rachel Child
Stands 34/35. *Antique jewellery.* TEL: 0171 408 1508.

W1 continued

Mr. Cyrlin
Stand 32. *Antique watches.* TEL: 0171 629 0133.

Adele de Havilland
Stand 18. *Oriental porcelain, netsuke, jade.* TEL: 0171 499 7127.

David Duggan LAPADA
Stands 1A, 1B.*Vintage watches.* TEL: 0171 408 0134; fax - 0171 408 1727.

Elisabeth's Antiques LAPADA
Stands 42-44. (Mrs E. Hage). *Jewellery.*TEL: 0171 491 1723; mobile - 0860 550300.

Matthew Foster
Stand 16 *Antique jewellery.*

N. Foster
Stand 12. *Topographical prints.* TEL: 0171 495 2425.

Lydia Gray
Stand 41. *Antique jewellery.* TEL: 0171 499 9595.

Anthony Green Antiques
Stand 39.*Watches and objects.* TEL: 0171 409 2854; fax - 0171 408 0010.

Massada Antiques LAPADA
Stand 2. (C.B. and C. Yacobi). Est. 1970. *Antique jewellery and silver.* TEL: 0171 493 4792.

Abby Moaven
Stand 22. *Paintings, prints and frames.*

Myra Antiques
Stands 4. *Jewellery, glass, paintings and objects.* TEL: 0171 408 1508/499 1681.

Nonesuch Antiques LAPADA
Stand 3. (Mrs E. Michelson). *Jewellery and objects.* TEL: 0171 629 6783.

P.M.R. Antiques
Stand 25. (Peter Rosen). *Jewellery.* TEL: 0171 495 4406.

Mr. Posner
Stand 17. *Coins, stamps and watches.* TEL: 0171 499 4494.

Resner's BADA LAPADA
Stands 5/6. (S. and G.R. Resner, M.P. Daniels). Est.1918. *Jewellery, £250-£10,000; objets d'art, £200-£1,000; silver, £100-£2,500; all 18th-19th C.* TEL: 0171 629 1413; fax - same; mobile - 0860 704251. SER: Valuations; restorations (jewellery). VAT: Stan/Spec.

Sadi & Sahar
Stand 29/30 & 36/37. (Mrs S. Noorani). *Jewellery, glass and porcelain.* TEL: 0171 491 2081.

W1 continued

Nino Santi
Stand 38. *Antique jewellery and watches.* TEL: 0171 629 3008.

Trianon Antiques and Michael Longmore
Stand 1C. *Antique jewellery.* TEL: 0171 629 6678.

Matsuko Yamamoto
Stand 23. *Antique jewellery and porcelain.* TEL: 0171 491 0983.

Bond Street Silver Galleries

111-112 New Bond St. W1. Open 9-5.30. CL: Sat. PARK: Meters. TEL: 0171 493 6180; fax - 0171 495 3493. Below are listed the dealers at these galleries.

The Antique Jewellery Co Ltd
Fine jewellery. TEL: 0171 491 8969; fax - 0171 491 8949.

Brian Beet
Silver and works of art. TEL: 0171 437 4975; fax - 0171 495 8635.

A. and B. Bloomstein Ltd BADA LAPADA
***Silver, Sheffield plate.* TEL: 0171 493 6180; fax - 0171 495 3493. SER:Valuations; restorations.**

Bruford and Heming LAPADA
NAG. *Domestic silver especially flatware, jewellery.* TEL: 0171 499 7644/629 4289; fax - 0171 493 5879. SER: Valuations; restorations. VAT: Stan/Spec.

Peter Cameron
Silver and old Sheffield plate. TEL: 0171 499 0330.

R. Close Jewellery Restoration
TEL: 0171 495 0287.

Phillip Cull
Silver and Sheffield plate. TEL: 0171 493 2047.

Gavina Ewart BADA
***Silver cutlery and dining table silver, Sheffield plate; furniture and porcelain, 18th and 19th C.* TEL: 0171 491 7266; fax - 01242 526994. VAT: Stan/Spec.**

Adrian Ewart (Gavina Ewart Antiques)
Silver, porcelain, bronze and ormulu. TEL: 0171 491 7266.

O. Frydman
Silver, Sheffield and Victorian plate. TEL: 0171 493 4895. VAT: Stan/Spec.

Graus Antiques
Objets d'art, jewellery and silver. TEL: 0171 629 6680/6651; fax - 0171 629 3361.

W1 continued

M & L Silver Partnership
Silver, old Sheffield and silver plate. TEL: 0171 499 5170; fax - same.

A. Pash & Son
Silver and old Sheffield plate. TEL: 0171 493 5176.

Harry Perovetz
Antique silver; Old Sheffield and Victorian plate. TEL: 0171 954 7780/0181 954 6317; fax - 0181 954 6902.

M. Sedler
Silver and plate. TEL: 0171 839 3131.

N.R. Shaw BADA LAPADA
***Antique silver especially Scottish and Irish provincial.* TEL: 0171 629 1853; fax - same.**

D. P. Stern Jewellery and Silver Restoration
TEL: 0171 629 6292; fax - 0171 355 1427.

E. Swonnell (Silverware) Ltd
Silver, Sheffield plate. TEL: 0171 629 9649. VAT: Stan/Spec.

David Webb
Old silver, plated ware, decorative objects. TEL: 0171 493 1849.

Boodle and Dunthorne Ltd
128-130 Regent St. W1. Open 9-6. *STOCK: Fine English and French jewellery, 19th-20th C, £100-£30,000.* TEL: 0171 437 5050; 0171 584 6363.

Brandt Oriental Art BADA
First Floor, 29 New Bond St. W1Y 9HD. (R. Brandt). Est. 1981. Open by appointment. *STOCK: Oriental works of art, £500-£10,000.* TEL: 0171 499 8835; mobile - 0374 989661. VAT: Spec.

Browse and Darby Ltd
19 Cork St. W1X 2LP. SLAD. Est. 1977. *STOCK: French and British paintings, drawings and sculpture, 19th-20th C.* TEL: 0171 734 7984. VAT: Spec.

John Bull (Antiques) Ltd
JB Silverware LAPADA
139A New Bond St. W1Y 9FB. Open 9-5. CL: Sat. *STOCK: Silver and plate; reproduction silver photo-frames.* TEL: 0171 629 1251; fax - 0171 495 3001. VAT: Global/Margin.

Burlington Gallery Ltd
10 Burlington Gardens. W1X 1LG. (A.S. Lloyd, N.C. Potter and W.M. Lloyd). Est. 1980. Open 9.30-5.30, Sat. 10-5. SIZE: Large. *STOCK: Sporting and decorative prints, 1700 to present day, and works by Cecil Aldin.* LOC: Between Bond St. and Regent St. TEL: 0171 734 9228; fax - 0171 494 3770. SER: Valuations; buys at auction. VAT: Stan/Spec.

W1 continued

Burlington Paintings Ltd BADA
12 Burlington Gardens. W1X 1LG. (A. Lloyd, M. Day and J. Lloyd). Est. 1981. Open 9.30-5.30, Sat. 10-5. SIZE: Small. *STOCK: British and European oil paintings, 19th-20th C, from £1,000.* LOC: Between Old Bond St. and Regent St., facing Savile Row. PARK: NCP Brewer St. TEL: 0171 734 9984. SER: Valuations; restorations (lining, cleaning, reframing oils and watercolours); buys at auction (pictures). VAT: Stan/Spec.

The Button Queen
19 Marylebone Lane. W1M 5FE. (T. and M. Frith). Est. 1953. Open 10-5, Thurs. and Fri. 10-6, Sat. 10-4. SIZE: Large. *STOCK: Antique, old and modern buttons.* LOC: Off Wigmore St. TEL: 0171 935 1505. VAT: Stan.

Carrington and Co. Ltd
170 Regent St. W1R 6BQ. Open 9-5.30. *STOCK: Regimental jewellery and silver, trophies, watches, clocks.* TEL: 0171 734 3727.

Lumley Cazalet Ltd
33 Davies St. W1Y 1FN. SLAD. Est. 1967. Open 10-6. CL: Sat. *STOCK: Late 19th and 20th C original prints including Braque, Chagall, Miro, Matisse, Picasso; drawings by Matisse; drawings and sculpture by Elisabeth Frink.* TEL: 0171 491 4767; fax - 0171 493 8644.

Antoine Cheneviere Fine Arts BADA
27 Bruton St. W1. Open 9.30-6. CL: Sat. *STOCK: 18th-19th C furniture and paintings, objets d'art from Russia, Italy, Austria, Sweden and Germany.* TEL: 0171 491 1007.

Colefax and Fowler
39 Brook St. W1Y 2JE. Est. 1933. Open 9.30-5.30. CL: Sat. SIZE: Large. *STOCK: Decorative furniture, pictures, lamps and carpets, 18th-19th C.* PARK: Meters. TEL: 0171 493 2231. VAT: Stan/Spec.

P. and D. Colnaghi & Co Ltd BADA
15 Old Bond St. W1X 4JL. Est. 1760. Open 9.30-6. SIZE: Large. *STOCK: Master paintings and drawings, 14th-19th C; English paintings, European sculpture.* TEL: 0171 491 7408. SER: Experts and appraisers. VAT: Spec.

Connaught Brown plc
2 Albemarle St. W1X 3HF. (A. Brown). SLAD. Est. 1980. Open 10-6, Sat. 10-12.30. SIZE: Medium. *STOCK: Post Impressionist, Scandinavian and modern works, from £5,000+; contemporary, from £500+.* LOC: Off Piccadilly and parallel to Bond St. PARK: Berkeley Sq. TEL: 0171 408 0362. SER: Valuations; restorations. (paintings, drawings, watercolours and sculpture). FAIRS: Chicago New Pier Art; Islington. VAT: Stan/Spec.

W1 continued

Sandra Cronan Ltd LAPADA
18 Burlington Arcade. W1V 9AB. Est. 1975. Open 10-5.30. *STOCK: Fine and unusual jewels, 18th to early 20th C, £500-£50,000.* LOC: Off Bond St. TEL: 0171 491 4851; fax - 0171 493 2758. SER: Valuations; design commissions. FAIRS: Fine Art & Antiques, Olympia (June). VAT: Stan/Spec.

Anthony d'Offay
9, 21, 23 and 24 Dering St., New Bond St. W1R 9AA. SLAD. Est. 1965. Open 10-5.30, Sat. 10-1. SIZE: Large. *STOCK: Contemporary international paintings, sculpture and drawings.* LOC: Near Oxford Circus and Bond St. tube stations. PARK: Meters in Hanover Sq. TEL: 0171 499 4100; fax - 0171 493 4443. VAT: Stan/Spec.

Barry Davies Oriental Art BADA
1 Davies St. W1Y 1LL. Open 10-6. CL: Sat. *STOCK: Japanese works of art, netsuke, lacquer and bronzes.* TEL: 0171 408 0207.

A. B. Davis Ltd
18 Brook St., (Corner of New Bond St). W1Y 1AA. Est. 1920. Open 10-5. CL: Sat. *STOCK: Antique and secondhand jewellery, small silver items and objets d'art.* TEL: 0171 629 1053; 0171 242 7357 (ansaphone); fax and ansaphone - 0171 499 6454. SER: Valuations; repairs (jewellery and silver). VAT: Stan/Spec.

Richard Day Ltd
173 New Bond St. W1Y 9PB. Open 10-5. CL: Sat. *STOCK: Old Master drawings.* TEL: 0171 629 2991; fax - 0171 493 7569. VAT: Stan.

Jehanne de Biolley Oriental Art
1st Floor, 29 Conduit St. W1R 9TA. Est. 1990. Open by appointment only. *STOCK: Chinese, Korean and Japanese works of art and porcelain; robin's egg blue glazed Chinese porcelain.* LOC: Opposite Westbury Hotel, off New Bond St. TEL: 0171 495 4257. SER: Valuations; restorations.

Demas
31 Burlington Arcade. W1V 9AD. Est. 1953. Open 10-5. CL: Sat. pm. *STOCK: Georgian, Victorian and Art Deco jewellery.* TEL: 0171 493 9496. VAT: Stan.

Charles Ede Ltd
20 Brook St. W1Y 1AD. Est. 1970. Open 12.30-4.30 or by appointment. CL: Mon and Sat. *STOCK: Greek, Roman and Egyptian antiquities, £50-£50,000.* PARK: Meters. TEL: 0171 493 4944; fax - 0171 491 2548. SER: Valuations; buys at auction. VAT: Spec.

Editions Graphiques Gallery
3 Clifford St. (V. Arwas). Est. 1966. Open 10-6, Sat. 10-2. SIZE: Large. *STOCK: Art Nouveau and Art Deco, glass, ceramics, bronzes, sculpture, furniture, jewellery, silver, pewter, books and posters 1880-1940, £25-£50,000; paintings, watercolours and drawings, 1880 to date, £100-£20,000; original graphics, lithographs, etchings, woodcuts, 1890 to date, £5-£10,000.* LOC: Between New Bond St and Savile Row. PARK: 50yds. TEL: 0171 734 3944. SER: Valuations; buys at auction. VAT: Stan/Spec.

Andrew Edmunds
44 Lexington St. W1R 3LH. Open 10-6. CL: Sat. *STOCK: 18th and early 19th C caricature and decorative prints and drawings.* TEL: 0171 437 8594; fax - 0171 439 2551. VAT: Stan/Spec.

Emanouel Corporation (UK) Ltd LAPADA
64 & 64a South Audley St. W1Y 5FD. (E. Naghi). Est. 1974. Open 10-6, Sat. by appointment. *STOCK: Important antiques and fine works of art, 18th-19th C; Islamic works of art.* TEL: 0171 493 4350; fax - 0171 629 3125. VAT: Stan/Spec.

Ermitage Ltd BADA
14 Hay Hill. W1X 7LJ. Est. 1985. Open 10-5. CL: Sat. SIZE: Medium. *STOCK: Fabergé objects, £2,000-£60,000+; Continental silver, 17th-18th C, £1,000-£50,000+; Russian art, 17th-20th C, £800-£25,000+.* LOC: Mayfair area, between Bond St. and Berkeley Sq. PARK: Berkeley Sq. TEL: 0171 499 5459; fax - same. SER: Valuations. FAIRS: Maastricht. VAT: Stan/Spec.

Eskenazi Ltd BADA
10 Clifford St. W1X 1RB. (J.E. Eskenazi and P. Constantinidi). Est. 1960. Open 9.30-6, Sat. by appointment. SIZE: Large. *STOCK: Early Chinese ceramics; bronzes, sculpture, works of art; Japanese netsuke and lacquer.* TEL: 0171 493 5464; fax - 0171 499 3136. VAT: Spec.

John Eskenazi Ltd BADA
15 Old Bond St. W1X 4JL. Open 9-1 and 2-6, Sat. and Sun. by appointment. SIZE: Medium. *STOCK: Oriental art, rugs and textiles.* PARK: Meters. TEL: 0171 409 3001; fax - 0171 629 2146. SER: Rug conservation. FAIRS: International Asian Art, New York (March); Maastricht. VAT: Spec.

Essie Carpets
62 Piccadilly. W1V 9HL. (E. Sakhai). Est. 1766. Open 9.30-6.30, Sun. 10.30-6.30. CL: Sat. SIZE: Large. *STOCK: Persian and Oriental carpets and rugs.* LOC: Opposite St. James St. and Ritz Hotel. PARK: Easy. TEL: 0171 493 7766; home - 0171 586 3388. SER: Valuations; restorations; commissions undertaken. VAT: Stan/Spec.

W1 continued

Brian Fielden BADA
3 New Cavendish St. W1M 7RP. Open 9.30-1 and 2-5.30, Sat. 9.30-1. SIZE: Medium. *STOCK: English walnut and mahogany furniture, 18th to early 19th C; mirrors and barometers.* LOC: 5 minutes walk north of Bond St. PARK: Meters. TEL: 0171 935 6912. VAT: Spec.

The Fine Art Society plc
148 New Bond St. W1Y 0JT. SLAD. Est. 1876. Open 9.30-5.30, Sat. 10-1. SIZE: Large. *STOCK: British fine and decorative arts, 19th-20th C.* PARK: 300yds. TEL: 0171 629 5116. SER: Buys at auction. VAT: Stan/Spec.

Sam Fogg
35 St. George St. W1R 9FA. Est. 1971. Open by appointment. *STOCK: Manuscripts, all periods.* TEL: 0171 495 2333; fax - 0171 409 3326. SER: Valuations; buys at auction.

Fortnum and Mason plc
Piccadilly. W1A 1ER. Open 9.30-6. SIZE: Medium. *STOCK: English furniture, 18th C.* PARK: Meters. TEL: 0171 734 8040.

J.A. Fredericks and Son
Correspondence only to: 72 Elm Park, Stanmore, Middx. (J.A. and C.J. Fredericks). Est. 1938. Open by appointment. *STOCK: English furniture.* TEL: 0181 420 6066. VAT: Spec. *Trade Only.*

H. Fritz-Denneville Fine Arts Ltd
31 New Bond St. W1Y 9HD. SLAD. *STOCK: Paintings, drawings and prints, especially German Romantics, Nazarenes and Expressionists.* TEL: 0171 629 2466; fax - 0171 408 0604. SER: Valuations; restorations; buys at auction.

Deborah Gage. (Works of Art) Ltd
38 Old Bond St. W1X 3AE. Est. 1982. Open 9.30-5.30. CL: Sat. *STOCK: European decorative arts and paintings, 17th-18th C; French and British pictures, late 19th to early 20th C, from £5,000.* TEL: 0171 493 3249; fax - 0171 495 1352. SER: Valuations; cataloguing; buys at auction. VAT: Stan/Spec.

Gallery Zadah Ltd LAPADA
29 Conduit St. W1R 9TA. Est. 1976. Open 9.30-6. *STOCK: Oriental and European carpets, rugs, tapestries and textiles.* TEL: 0171 493 2622/2673.

Garrard & Co. Ltd
(The Crown Jewellers) BADA
112 Regent St. W1A 2JJ. (Richard Jarvis). Est. 1735. Open 9.30-5.30, Sat. 10.30-5.30. SIZE: Large. *STOCK: Jewellery, silver, clocks and watches.* TEL: 0171 734 7020; fax - 0171 734 0711. SER: Valuations; restorations (antique silver and clocks). FAIRS: Maastricht. VAT: Stan.

A Lowestoft bottle vase painted by the Tulip Painter, c.1775, 5in., one of a pair £4,850.

From an article entitled "Factory Fact File: Lowestoft" by David Battie which appeared in the May 1997 issue of **Antique Collecting**

W1 continued

Christopher Gibbs Ltd
8 Vigo St. W1X 1LG. Est. 1960. Open 9.30-5.30. CL: Sat. SIZE: Large. *STOCK: Unusual and decorative paintings, furniture, works of art and sculpture.* TEL: 0171 439 4557. VAT: Spec.

Thomas Gibson Fine Art Ltd
44 Old Bond St. W1X 4HQ. SLAD. Open 10-5. CL: Sat. *STOCK: 19th-20th C Masters and selected Old Masters.* TEL: 0171 499 8572; fax - 0171 495 1924.

Thomas Goode and Co. (London) Ltd
19 South Audley St. W1. Est. 1827. Open 10-6. SIZE: Large. *STOCK: China, glass, silver, tableware, ornamental.* TEL: 0171 499 2823; fax - 0171 629 4230. SER: Restorations. VAT: Spec.

W1 continued

Grays Antique Market
South Molton Lane. W1Y 2LP. Open 10-6. CL: Sat. TEL: 0171 629 7034. Below are listed the dealers at this market.

2nd Time Around Ltd
Stand 105/168/9. (Waite/Kushner). TEL: 0171 499 7442.

AG Antiques
Stand 154/5. (Anthea Geshua). TEL: 0171 493 7564.

Alexanders Cafe
Stand 117. (Elizabeth Anastos). TEL: 0171 629 3223.

Antique Medical Instruments
Stand 374. (Elizabeth Bennion). TEL: 0171 499 5334.

Arca
Stand 351/2/3. (R & E Innocentini). TEL: 0171 629 2729.

Sean Arnold
Stand 316/7/8/28. TEL: 0171 409 7358.

Asian Gallery plc
Stand 107. (Catherine Farrell and David Barrymore). TEL: 0171 629 2935.

W1 continued

Elias Assad
Stand A16/7. *Middle Eastern art.* TEL: 0171 499 4778.

Osman Aytac
Stand 331/2. TEL: 0171 629 7380.

Colin Baddiel
Stand B24/5/C12/3. TEL: 0171 408 1239.

David Baker
Stand H23. TEL: 0171 629 3788.

Rosemary Barnes
Stand 153. *Jewellery.* TEL: 0171 408 0909.

Don Bayney
Stand C24/5. TEL: 0171 629 3644.

Linda Bee
Stand M20/1. *Art Deco.* TEL: 0171 629 5921.

W. Bennett & Co
Stand C31/2. (William Bennett). TEL: 0171 408 1880.

Barbara Berg
Stand 333. TEL: 0171 499 0560.

David Bowden
Stand 319. TEL: 0171 495 1773.

W1 continued

Pauline Boxsey
Stand 136. TEL: 0171 495 0592.

Patrick Boyd-Carpenter
Stand 129/130. TEL: 0171 491 7623.

Sue Brown LAPADA
Stand M14/5/6. TEL: 0171 491 4287.

Helen Buxton Ltd
Stand J23/4/5. (Barbara Crowell). TEL: 0171 409 2685.

Byblos Antiques
Stand K36/7/8. (Ghassan el Haddad). TEL: 0171 495 1327.

Christopher Cavey
Stand 177/8. TEL: 0171 495 1743.

Cekay
Stand 172. (F B L Kay). TEL: 0171 629 5130.

D & J Church
Stand 163. TEL: 0171 499 7936.

Classic Frames
Stand 360/1/322. (Paul Dowling). TEL: 0171 629 4533.

Coins
Stand J30/1. (L. di Lauro). TEL: 0171 355 1565.

Coleman/Sharpe
Stand J12. TEL: 0171 409 2388.

Collections
Stand 329/330. (S. Byron). TEL: 0171 493 2654.

Olivia Collings
Stand 327. TEL: 0171 499 5478.

Continium
Stand 124. (F. and E. Joy). TEL: 0171 493 4909.

Vincente Cortez Llopis
Stand 342. TEL: 0171 629 5011.

Croesus
Stand 323/4. (Phil and Lindy Conyngham-Hynes, A.M. Davies). *Jewellery.* TEL: 0171 493 0624.

Crystalware
Stand L16. (Patricia Angeli). *Jewellery.* TEL: 0171 493 3098.

Beverley Cunningham
Stand 343/4. TEL: 0171 408 1129.

Alan Darer
Stand A22. TEL: 0171 629 3644.

Double Bett
Stand 104. (Dave Bett). TEL: 0171 493 1530.

David Eisler
Stand C22. TEL: 0171 629 2526.

W1 continued

Joanna Elton
Stand 175. TEL: 0171 629 4769.

Rosemary Erbrich
Stand C26. TEL: 0171 629 2526.

Jack First
Stand 310/1. TEL: 0171 409 2722.

Nicola Franks
Stand 343/4. TEL: 0171 408 1129.

French Decorative Art
Stand 367. (Mrs Jain). TEL: 0171 491 0407.

Gallery Diem
Stand 131/143. (Andrew Day). TEL: 0171 629 3206.

Peter Gaunt
Stand 120/1/141/2. TEL: 0171 629 1072.

Trevor Gilbert LAPADA
Stand G10/1. TEL: 0171 408 0028.

The Gilded Lily LAPADA
Stand 132/144/5. (Korin Harvey). TEL: 0171 499 6260.

Golfania
Stand N47. (Sarah Fabian Baddiel). TEL: 0171 408 1239; 01223 357958/445096.

Ora Gordon
Stand J27/K14.

Patrick & Susan Gould
Stand L17. TEL: 0171 408 0129.

R.G. Graham
Stand 112/3/217. TEL: 0171 629 3223.

Peter Greenhalgh
Stand 137. TEL: 0171 491 9178.

Sarah Groombridge LAPADA
Stand 335/6/7. TEL: 0171 629 0225.

Linda Groppi
Stand M20/1. TEL: 0171 629 5921.

Guest & Gray
Stand H25/6/7/8/J10/3. (Anthony Gray). TEL: 0171 408 1252.

Alice Gullersarian
Stand K33. TEL: 0171 629 3788.

Brian Harkins
Stand 126. TEL: 0171 409 2530.

Harrison's Books
Stand J19/20. (Leo Harrison). TEL: 0171 629 1374.

Satoe Hatrell
Stand 156/166. TEL: 0171 629 4296.

Hoffman Antiques
Stand 133. TEL: 0171 499 4340.

W1 continued

David Hogg
Stand 109. TEL: 0171 493 0208.

Lynn and Brian Holmes LAPADA
Stand 304/5/6. *Jewellery*. TEL: 0171 629 7327.

J.L.A.
Stand 123. (Alan Jacobs). TEL: 0171 499 1681.

Jafar
Stand H24/J14. (Jafar Hashtrudi). TEL: 0171 409 7919.

Mohammed Jawad
Stand C33/4. TEL: 0171 629 5270.

Ali Jazi
Stand A30. TEL: 0171 629 6813.

Katie Jones
Stand 126. TEL: 0171 409 2530.

Judson Ltd
Stand 321. (Alpani Kothari). TEL: 0171 493 0804/495 7327.

Junegrove Ltd
Stand 362. (Fiona Williamson). TEL: 0171 495 4889.

K & M Antiques
Stand 340/1. (Martin Harris). TEL: 0171 491 4310.

Andre and Minoo Kaae LAPADA
Stand G22/3. *Jewellery*. TEL: 0171 629 1200.

A.M. Khoei
Stand C33/34. TEL: 0171 629 5270.

Kikuchi Trading Co Ltd LAPADA
Stand 357/8/368. (Konio Kikuchi). TEL: 0171 629 6808.

Louis Laurence
TEL: 0171 493 0043.

Lees de Smet - Aurum
Stand 313. (Paul Lebbitel). TEL: 0171 409 0215.

Monditurn Ltd LAPADA
Stand 345/6/7. (John Joseph). TEL: 0171 629 1140.

Oasis
Stand E14/5/6/7. (Salim Hassbani). TEL: 0171 493 1202.

Oriental Works of Art
Stand K24/5/6/7. (Robert Bouita). TEL: 0171 629 5476.

Paris Smith
Stand K19. (Jackie Hopkins). TEL: 0171 629 3112.

Pars Antiques
Stand A14/5. (Kathy Williams). TEL: 0171 491 9889.

Phoenix
Stand 108. (E. and J. Edwards). TEL: 0171 495 1123.

W1 continued

Pieces of Time LAPADA
Stand M17/8/9. (Johnny Wachsman). TEL: 0171 629 3272.

Pillows of Bond St
Stand 301. (Robin Kumar). TEL: 0171 495 8853.

RBR
Stand 176. (D. Edmunds Brazell). TEL: 0171 495 5635.

RBR Group
Stand 175. (Olivia Gerrish). TEL: 0171 629 4769.

M. Ritchfield Export Ltd
Stand 385. (Musako Kikuchi). TEL: 0171 629 6808.

River Cafe
Stand D17. (Maurizio Businaro). TEL: 0171 408 1831/0181 444 2932.

Rocco
Stand 363. (Jill Barnes). TEL: 0171 409 2743.

Samirami's
Stand E18/9/20. (Hamid Ismail). TEL: 0171 629 1161.

Shadad Antiques
Stand B14. (Farah Hakemi). TEL: 0171 499 0572.

Shiraz Antiques
Stand H10/1. (R.P. Kiadah). TEL: 0171 495 0635.

John Sleight
Stand MF45 41.

Solimani's
Stand A20/1. (Helen Zoakee). TEL: 0171 491 2562.

Solveig & Anita LAPADA
Stand 307/8/9. TEL: 0171 408 1638.

Spa Antiques
Stand 127. (Peter Benjamin). *Oriental items.* TEL: 0171 493 2180.

Spa Antiques
Stand 127. (Ian Conn). TEL: 0171 493 2180.

Spectrum
Stand 372/3. (Sylvia Bedwell). TEL: 0171 629 3501.

Tagore Ltd
Stand 302/3. (Ronald Falloon). TEL: 0171 499 0158.

Tapestries
Stand M108/9. (Kilim Akman). TEL: 0171 491 8806.

Tradewinds
Stand 148/9. (Diane Harby). TEL: 0171 629 5130.

Trianon Ltd LAPADA
Stand 334/378. (Lilliane Flowerdew). TEL: 0171 491 2764.

W1 continued

Trio
Stand L24. (Theresa Clayton). TEL: 0171 629 1184.

Vogue
Stand D15/6 (Danny Anderson). TEL: 0171 629 3668.

Warwick Antiques
Stand 152. (Diane Friedman). TEL: 0171 629 5130.

Watches
Stand 374. (Robert Barany). TEL: 0171 493 7497.

Mary Wellard
Stand 165. TEL: 0171 629 5130.

Westminster Group LAPADA
Stand 138/150. (Paulette Bates and Richard Harrison). TEL: 0171 493 8672.

John Weysom
Stand M14/5/6. TEL: 0171 491 4287.

David Wheatley LAPADA
Stand 106. TEL: 0171 629 1352.

Wheels of Steel
Stand B10. (Jeff Williams). TEL: 0171 629 2813.

Whitehead & Graves
Stand 158. (Robert Barany). TEL: 0171 493 7497.

Aura Williamson
Stand L10/1. TEL: 0171 495 6083.

Wimpole Antiques LAPADA
Stand 348/9. (Freda Hacker). TEL: 0171 499 2889.

Craig Wyncoll
Stand 125. TEL: 0171 409 1498.

Yang
Stand 129/130. TEL: 0171 495 6068.

Yosir
Stand K24/25. TEL: 0171 491 0264.

W1 continued

Richard Green BADA
44 and 39 Dover St. and 4 and 33 New Bond St. W1X 4JQ. SLAD. Open 9.30-6, Sat. 10-12.30. *STOCK: Paintings - Old Master and British; French impressionist and modern British; Victorian sporting and British marine.* PARK: Meters. TEL: 0171 493 3939; fax - 0171 629 2609. VAT: Stan/Spec.

Simon Griffin Antiques Ltd
3 Royal Arcade, 28 Old Bond St. (S.J. Griffin). Est. 1979. Open 10-5, Sat. 10-5.30. *STOCK: Silver, old Sheffield plate.* TEL: 0171 491 7367. VAT: Stan/Spec.

Hadji Baba Ancient Art
34a Davies St. W1Y 1LD. (R.R. Soleimani). Est. 1939. Open 9.30-6, Sat. and Sun. by appointment. SIZE: Medium. *STOCK: Antiquities and Islamic art.* LOC: Next to Claridges Hotel. PARK: Meters. TEL: 0171 499 9363/9384; fax - 0171 493 5504. SER: Valuations.

Hadleigh Jewellers
30A Marylebone High St. W1M 3PF. Open 9.30-5.30. *STOCK: Jewellery, some silver.* TEL: 0171 935 4074. SER: Valuations; repairs; hand-made jewellery. VAT: Stan/Spec.

Hahn and Son Fine Art Dealers
47 Albemarle St. (P. Hahn). Est. 1870. Open 9.45-5.30. CL: Sat. *STOCK: English oil paintings, 18th-19th C.* TEL: 0171 493 9196. VAT: Stan.

Halcyon Days BADA
14 Brook St. W1Y 1AA. (S. Benjamin). Est. 1950. Open 9.15-5.30, Sat. 9.30-5.30. *STOCK: 18th to early 19th C enamels, treen, papier mâché, tôle, objects of vertu, Georgian and Victorian scent bottles.* LOC: Hanover Sq. end of Brook St. PARK: Meters and in Hanover Sq. TEL: 0171 629 8811; fax - 0171 409 0280. FAIRS: Grosvenor House; BADA. VAT: Stan/Spec.

W1 continued

Robert Hall BADA
15c Clifford St. W1X 1RF. Est. 1976. *STOCK: Chinese snuff bottles, Ching dynasty; Oriental works of art, jade carvings, 17th-19th C; all £300-£20,000. Chinese contemporary paintings.* TEL: 0171 734 4008; fax - 0171 734 4408. SER: Valuations; buys at auction. VAT: Stan/Spec.

Hancocks and Co BADA
1 Burlington Gardens. W1X 2HP. Est. 1849. Open 9.30-5.30, Sat. 10.30-3.30. SIZE: Medium. *STOCK: Fine estate jewellery and silver.* LOC: Opposite top of Burlington Arcade. TEL: 0171 493 8904; fax - 0171 493 8905. VAT: Stan/Spec.

Harcourt Antiques
5 Harcourt St. W1 1DS. (J. Christophe). Est. 1961. Open by appointment only. *STOCK: English, Continental and Oriental porcelain, pre-1830.* PARK: Easy. TEL: 0171 723 5919/727 6936. VAT: Stan. *Trade Only.*

S.H. Harris and Son (London) Ltd
17-18 Old Bond St. W1X 3DA. (B.C. and R.H. Harris). Est. 1885. Open 9-5. CL: Sat. SIZE: Small. *STOCK: Jewellery and silver.* LOC: 50yds from Piccadilly. PARK: Burlington St. TEL: 0171 499 0352. SER: Valuations. VAT: Stan/Spec. *Trade Only.*

Harvey and Gore BADA
4 Burlington Gardens. W1X 1LH. (B.E. Norman). Est. 1723. Open 9.30-5. CL: Sat. SIZE: Small. *STOCK: Jewellery, £150-£50,000; silver, £50-£15,000; old Sheffield plate, £65-£6,000; antique paste.* LOC: Near top of Burlington Arcade, off Piccadilly. TEL: 0171 493 2714; fax - 0171 493 0324. SER: Valuations; restorations (jewellery and silver); buys at auction. VAT: Stan/Spec.

Brian Haughton Antiques
3B Burlington Gardens, Old Bond St. W1X 1LE. Est. 1965. Open 10-5.30. SIZE: Large. *STOCK: British and European ceramics, porcelain and pottery, 18th-19th C, £100-£50,000.* PARK: Nearby, Savile Row N.C.P. TEL: 0171 734 5491. SER: Buys at auction. (porcelain and pottery). FAIRS: Organiser - International Ceramics and Seminar, Park Lane Hotel; International Fine Art & Antique Dealers Show, International Fine Art and International Asian Art, New York. VAT: Spec.

Gerard Hawthorn Ltd BADA
104 Mount St., Mayfair. W1Y 5HE. Open 9.30-6, Sat. by appointment. *STOCK: Oriental art - Chinese ceramics, porcelain and pottery; cloisonné and painted enamels, jade, hardstones, lacquer, bronzes, metalwork, paintings, textiles, ivory, works of art including Tibetan and Japanese, 2000 BC to 1916.* LOC: Opposite Connaught Hotel. PARK: Easy. TEL: 0171 409 2888; fax - 0171 409 2777. SER: Valuations; restorations; buys at auction; exhibition yearly. FAIRS: New York.

W1 continued

Hennell of Bond Street Ltd. Founded 1736 (incorporating Frazer and Haws. (1868) and E. Lloyd Lawrence. (1830))
12 New Bond St. W1Y 0HE. Open 9-5.30, Sat. 10-4. SIZE: Medium. *STOCK: Fine jewellery, silver and watches.* PARK: Meters. TEL: 0171 629 6888. SER: Valuations; restorations (silver, jewellery). VAT: Stan/Spec.

G. Heywood Hill Ltd
10 Curzon St. W1Y 7FJ. (J. Saumarez Smith). Open 9-5.30, Sat. 9-12.30. *STOCK: Books, Victorian illustrated, children's and natural history.* TEL: 0171 629 0647; fax - 0171 408 0286.

Holland & Holland
31-33 Bruton St. W1X 8JS. Est. 1835. Open 9.30-5.30, Sat. 10-4. SIZE: Medium. *STOCK: Modern and antique guns, rifles, associated items; sporting prints, pictures and antiquarian books; antique sporting objects.* PARK: Meters in Bruton St. TEL: 0171 499 4411; fax - 0171 499 4544.

Holmes Ltd BADA
24 Burlington Arcade. W1V 9AD. (A.N., B.J. and I.J. Neale). Open 9.30-5. *STOCK: Jewels and silver.* TEL: 0171 493 1396. SER: Valuations; restorations. VAT: Stan.

Howard Antiques
8 Davies St., Berkeley Sq. W1Y 1LJ. Est. 1955. Open 10-6, Sat. by appointment. SIZE: Medium. *STOCK: English and Continental furniture, objects.* PARK: N.C.P. nearby. TEL: 0171 629 2628. SER: Valuations. VAT: Stan/Spec.

Brand Inglis BADA
4th Floor, 5 Vigo St. W1X 1AH. Est. 1960. Open by appointment. SIZE: Small. *STOCK: Silver, 16th-20th C, £1,000-£5,000.* TEL: 0171 439 6604; fax - 0171 439 6605. SER: Valuations; restorations (silver and metalwork); buys at auction (silver). VAT: Spec.

Patrick Jefferson Ltd
94 Mount St.,Mayfair. W1Y 5HG. Est. 1978. Open 9.30-6, Sat. 10-5. SIZE: Large. *STOCK: British furniture, 1700-1830, £5,000-£100,000; works of art and sculpture, 17th-19th C, £500-£25,000.* LOC: Between Berkeley Square and Park Lane, opposite Scotts. PARK: Easy. TEL: 0171 491 4931; fax - 0171 491 4932. SER: Buys at auction.

C. John (Rare Rugs) Ltd BADA
70 South Audley St., Mayfair. W1Y 5FE. Est. 1947. Open 9-5. CL: Sat. *STOCK: Textiles, pre-1800, carpets, tapestries, embroideries.* TEL: 0171 493 5288; fax - 0171 409 7030. VAT: Stan/Spec.

Johnson Walker & Tolhurst Ltd BADA
64 Burlington Arcade. W1V 9AF. Est. 1849. Open 9.30-5.30. *STOCK: Antique and second-hand jewellery, objets d'art, silver.* TEL: 0171 629 2615. SER: Restorations (jewellery, pearl-stringing). VAT: Stan/Spec.

W1 continued

Alexander Juran and Co BADA
74 New Bond St. W1Y 9DD. Est. 1951. Open 9.15-5.30. CL: Sat. *STOCK: Caucasian rugs, nomadic and tribal; carpets, rugs, tapestries.* TEL: 0171 629 2550/493 4484. SER: Valuations; repairs. VAT: Stan/Spec.

Kennedy Carpets LAPADA
9A Vigo St. W1X 1AL. (M. Kennedy). Est. 1974. Open 9.30-6. SIZE: Large. *STOCK: Decorative carpets, collectable rugs and kelims, mid-19th C to new, £500-£50,000.* LOC: Off Regent St., up Sackville St. from Piccadilly, left into Vigo St., shop on left-hand side. PARK: Sackville St. TEL: 0171 439 8873; fax - 0171 437 1201. SER: Valuations; making to order. VAT: Stan.

Lacloche Freres LAPADA
1 Three Kings Yard. W1Y 1FL. Open by appointment only. SIZE: Medium. *STOCK: Fine jewellery.* LOC: Off Davies St. TEL: 0171 355 3471; fax - 0171 355 3473. SER: Valuations; restorations. VAT: Stan/Spec.

Lane Fine Art Ltd
123 New Bond St. W1Y 9AE. (C. Foley). Open 10-6. *STOCK: Oil paintings, 1500-1850 especially English portraits and sporting paintings, landscapes and marines 18th C, £5,000-£500,000.* TEL: 0171 499 5020. VAT: Stan/Spec.

D.S. Lavender (Antiques) Ltd BADA
26 Conduit St. W1R 9TA. Est. 1945. Open 9.30-5. CL: Sat. *STOCK: Jewels, miniatures, works of art.* PARK: Meters. TEL: 0171 629 1782; fax - 0171 629 3106. SER: Valuations. VAT: Stan/Spec.

The Lefevre Gallery
30 Bruton St. W1X 8JD. (Alex Reid and Lefevre Ltd). SLAD. Est. 1871. Open 10-5. CL: Sat. SIZE: Medium. *STOCK: Impressionist paintings, 19th-20th C.* LOC: Between Berkeley Sq. and Bond St. PARK: Meters, Berkeley Sq. TEL: 0171 493 2107. SER: Valuations. VAT: Spec.

Leuchars and Jefferson
94 Mount St., Mayfair. W1Y 5HG. (Patrick Jefferson and Hugh Leuchars). Est. 1978. Open 9.30-6, Sat. 10-5. SIZE: Large. *STOCK: English 18th C furniture and works of art.* LOC: Between Berkeley Square and Park Lane, opposite Scotts. PARK: Easy. TEL: 0171 491 4931; fax - 0171 491 4932. VAT: Spec.

Liberty
Regent St. W1R 6AH. Est. 1875. Open 10-6.30, Thurs. till 7.30. SIZE: Large. *STOCK: British furniture, ceramics, glass and metalware, 1860-1930, Gothic Revival, Aesthetic Movement and Arts & Crafts.* LOC: Regent St. joins Piccadilly and Oxford Circus. PARK: Meters and underground in Cavendish Sq. TEL: 0171 734 1234. VAT: Stan.

W1 continued

Frank Lord
4 Royal Arcade, 12 Albemarle St. Open 10-5.30. SIZE: Small. *STOCK: Vintage watches including Rolex and Cartier.* PARK: Easy. TEL: 0171 495 4882. SER: Valuations.

Maas Gallery
15a Clifford St. W1X 1RF. (R.N. Maas). SLAD. Est. 1960. Open 10-5.30. CL: Sat. SIZE: Medium. *STOCK: Victorian and Pre-Raphaelite paintings, drawings, watercolours and illustrations.* LOC: Between New Bond St. and Cork St. PARK: Easy. TEL: 0171 734 2302; fax - 0171 287 4836. SER: Valuations; buys at auction. VAT: Spec.

MacConnal-Mason Gallery
15 Burlington Arcade, Piccadilly. W1V 9AB. Est. 1893. Open 9-5.30. SIZE: Medium. *STOCK: Pictures, 19th-20th C.* PARK: Meters. TEL: 0171 839 7693. SER: Valuations; restorations. VAT: Spec.

Maggs Bros Ltd BADA
50 Berkeley Sq. W1X 6EL. (J.F., B.D. and E.F. Maggs, P. Harcourt, R. Harding and H. Bett and J. Collins). ABA. Est. 1853. Open 9.30-5. CL: Sat. SIZE: Large. *STOCK: Rare books, manuscripts, autograph letters, and western miniatures.* PARK: Meters. TEL: 0171 493 7160 (6 lines); fax - 0171 499 2007. VAT: Stan/Spec.

Mahboubian Gallery
65 Grosvenor St. W1X 9DB. (H. Mahboubian). Open 10-6. CL: Sat. TEL: 0171 493 9112.

Mallett and Son (Antiques) Ltd BADA
141 New Bond St. W1Y 0BS. Est. 1865. Open 9.15-6, Sat. 11-4. SIZE: Large. *STOCK: English furniture, 1690-1835; clocks, 17th-18th C; china, needlework, decorative pictures, objects and glass.* PARK: Meters in Berkeley Sq. TEL: 0171 499 7411; fax - 0171 495 3179.

Mallett at Bourdon House Ltd
2 Davies St., Berkeley Sq. W1Y 1LJ. Open 9.15-5.30. SIZE: Large. *STOCK: Continental furniture, clocks, objets d'art; garden statuary and ornaments.* PARK: Meters, Berkeley Sq. TEL: 0171 629 2444; fax - 0171 499 2670. VAT: Stan/Spec.

Mallett Gallery BADA
(formerly Christopher Wood Gallery) 141 New Bond St. W1Y 0BS. SLAD. Est. 1977. Open 9.30-6, Sat. 11-4. *STOCK: 19th and early 20th C paintings, watercolours and drawings.* TEL: 0171 499 7411; fax - 0171 495 3179. VAT: Spec.

Mansour Gallery
46-48 Davies St. W1Y 1LD. (M. Mokhtarzadeh). Open 9.30-5.30, Sat. by appointment. *STOCK: Islamic works of art, miniatures; ancient glass and glazed wares; Greek, Roman and Egyptian antiquities.* TEL: 0171 491 7444/499 0510. VAT: Stan.

W1 continued

Marks Antiques LAPADA

49 Curzon St. (Anthony Marks). Est. 1945. Open 9.30-6 including bank holidays. SIZE: Large. *STOCK: Silver, Sheffield plate.* LOC: Green Park tube, opposite Washington Hotel. PARK: Meters. TEL: 0171 499 1788; fax - 0171 409 3183. SER: Valuations; buys at auction. VAT: Stan/Spec.

Marlborough Fine Art (London) Ltd

6 Albemarle St. SLAD. Est. 1946. Open 10-5.30, Sat. 10-12.30. *STOCK: Masters, 19th-20th C.* PARK: Meters or near Cork St. TEL: 0171 629 5161.

Marlborough Rare Books Ltd

144-146 New Bond St. W1Y 9FD. Est. 1946. Open 9.30-5.30. CL: Sat. SIZE: Medium. *STOCK: Illustrated books of all periods; rare books on fine and applied arts and architecture; English literature.* PARK: Meters. TEL: 0171 493 6993. SER: Valuations; buys at auction; catalogues available.

Mayfair Carpet Gallery Ltd

3 Old Bond St. W1R 3TD. *STOCK: Persian, Oriental rugs and carpets.* TEL: 0171 493 0126.

Mayfair Gallery

37 South Audley St. and 36 Davies St. W1Y 5DH. (M. Sinai). Open 10-6, Sat. by appointment. *STOCK: 19th-20th C decorative Continental furniture, clocks, chandeliers, ivories and objets d'art.* TEL: 0171 491 3435/6; fax - 0171 491 3437.

Melton's

27 Bruton Place. W1X 7AB. (C. Neal). Open 9.30-5.30. CL: Sat. *STOCK: Small antiques and decorative accessories: lamps, prints, textiles, English and Continental.* TEL: 0171 409 2938/ 629 3612.

David Messum BADA LAPADA

8 Cork St. W1X 1PD. SLAD. Open 10-6, Sat. 10-4, other times by appointment. *STOCK: British Impressionism, fine English and contemporary paintings.* TEL: 0171 437 5545. SER: Valuations; restorations; framing. VAT: Stan/Spec.

Roy Miles Gallery

29 Bruton St. Open 9.30-5.30, Sat. 9-1. *STOCK: Major art from Russia, also British works.* TEL: 0171 495 4747; fax - 0171 495 6232.

Nigel Milne Ltd

16c Grafton St. W1X 3LF. Est. 1979. Open 9.30-5.30, Sat. by appointment. SIZE: Small. *STOCK: Jewellery, Victorian to 1950's, £200-£100,000; silver frames.* LOC: Corner Grafton St. and Albemarle St., off New Bond St. PARK: Easy. TEL: 0171 493 9646/491 2504. SER: Valuations; buys at auction. VAT: Stan/Spec.

W1 continued

John Mitchell and Son BADA

1st Floor, 160 New Bond St. W1Y 9PA. SLAD. Est. 1931. Open 9.30-5, Sat. by appointment. SIZE: Small. *STOCK: Old Master paintings, drawings and watercolours, especially flower paintings, 17th C Dutch, 18th C English and 19th C French.* LOC: Nearest tube Green Park. PARK: Meters. TEL: 0171 493 7567. SER: Valuations; restorations (pictures); buys at auction.

Paul Mitchell Ltd BADA

99 New Bond St. W1Y 9LF. Open 9.30-5.30. CL: Sat. SIZE: Large. *STOCK: Picture frames.* PARK: Meters. TEL: 0171 493 8732/0860. VAT: Stan.

Bashir Mohamed Ltd

46 Montagu Sq. W1H 1TJ. Open 10-5 by appointment only. CL: Sat. *STOCK: Islamic art, Moghul and south east Asian manuscripts and objects.* TEL: 0171 723 1844. VAT: Spec.

Moira

22-23 New Bond St. Open 9-6. *STOCK: Fine antique and Art Deco jewellery.* TEL: 0171 629 0160. SER: Valuations.

Sydney L. Moss Ltd BADA

51 Brook St. W1Y 1AU. (P.G. and E.M. Moss). Est. 1910. Open 10-6. CL: Sat. SIZE: Large. *STOCK: Chinese and Japanese paintings and works of art; Japanese netsuke and lacquer, 17th-20th C; reference books. (as stock).* LOC: From Grosvenor Sq., up Brook St. to Claridges. PARK: Meters. TEL: 0171 629 4670/493 7374; fax - 0171 491 9278. SER: Valuations and advice; buys at auction. FAIRS: Winter Antiques Fair, New York. VAT: Spec.

Anthony Mould Ltd

1st Floor, 173 New Bond St. W1Y 9PB. SLAD. Open by appointment. *STOCK: British pictures.* TEL: 0171 491 4627.

Paul Nels Ltd LAPADA

6-8 Sedley Place. W1R 1HG. (P.J. Nels). Open 8.30-5. CL: Sat. pm. *STOCK: Rugs, carpets, tapestries and textiles.* TEL: 0171 629 1909.

Noortman

40-41 Old Bond St. W1X 4HP. SLAD. Open 9.30-5.30. *STOCK: Old Masters, French 19th-20th C.* TEL: 0171 491 7284.

Hal O'Nians

44 Grosvenor Hill. W1X 9JE. Open by appointment only. *STOCK: Paintings and watercolours, 16th-20th C.* TEL: 0171 724 3799; fax - same.

The O'Shea Gallery BADA

120a Mount St., Mayfair. W1Y 5HB. ABA. Open 9.30-6, Sat. 9.30-1. *STOCK: Maps, topographical, decorative, natural history,*

W1 continued

sporting and marine prints; rare atlases, illustrated books, 15th-19th C, £5-£25,000. **LOC: Near Berkeley Sq. TEL: 0171 629 1122; fax - 0171 629 1116. SER: Decorative framing; restorations. VAT: Stan/Spec.**

Richard Ogden Ltd BADA

28 and 29 Burlington Arcade, Piccadilly. W1V 0NX. Est. 1948. Open 9.30-5.15, Sat. 9.30-5. SIZE: Medium. *STOCK: Antique jewellery, rings.* LOC: Near Piccadilly Circus. PARK: Meters. TEL: 0171 493 9136/7. SER: Valuations; repairs. VAT: Spec.

Oriental Bronzes Ltd BADA

96 Mount St. W1Y 5HF. Open 10-5.30. CL: Sat. SIZE: Medium. *STOCK: Chinese archaeology, Neolithic to Ming.* LOC: Between Park Lane and Berkeley Sq. PARK: Easy. TEL: 0171 493 0309; fax - 0171 629 2665.

Partridge Fine Arts plc

144-146 New Bond St. W1Y 0LY. SLAD. Est. 1911. Open 9-5.30. CL: Sat. SIZE: Large. *STOCK: English and French furniture, objets d'art and silver, 18th-19th C; English, French and Italian paintings, 18th C.* LOC: North of Bruton St., opposite Sotheby's. PARK: Meters. TEL: 0171 629 0834; fax - 0171 495 6266. SER: Buys at auction. VAT: Spec.

W.H. Patterson Fine Arts Ltd BADA

19 Albemarle St. W1X 3LA. (W.H. and Mrs. P.M. Patterson and J. White). SLAD. Open 9.30-6. SIZE: Large. *STOCK: 19th C and regular exhibitions for contemporary artists, the New English Art Club, Andrew Coates and Willem Dolphyn, Peter Kuhfeld and Paul Brown.* LOC: Near Green Park tube station. PARK: Meters. TEL: 0171 629 4119. SER: Valuations; restorations. VAT: Spec.

Pelham Galleries Ltd BADA

24/25 Mount St., Mayfair. W1Y 5RB. (A. and L.J. Rubin). Est. 1928. *STOCK: Furniture, English and Continental; tapestries, decorative works of art and musical instruments.* TEL: 0171 629 0905; fax - 0171 495 4511. VAT: Spec.

Pendulum of Mayfair Ltd

King House, 51 Maddox St. W1. (K. R. Clements and Dr. H. Specht). Open 10-6 or by appointment. *STOCK: Clocks, mainly longcase, also bracket, mantle and wall; Georgian mahogany furniture.* TEL: 0171 629 6606; fax - 0171 629 6616. SER: Valuations; restorations (clocks). FAIRS: Buxton. VAT: Spec.

Ronald Phillips Ltd BADA

26 Bruton St. W1X 8LH. Est. 1952. *STOCK: English furniture; objets d'art; clocks and barometers.* TEL: 0171 493 2341; fax - 0171 495 0843. VAT: Mainly Spec.

W1 continued

S.J. Phillips Ltd BADA

139 New Bond St. W1A 3DL. (M.S., N.E.L., J.P. and F.E. Norton). Est. 1869. Open 10-5. CL: Sat. SIZE: Large. *STOCK: Silver, jewellery, gold boxes, miniatures.* LOC: Near Bond St. tube station. PARK: Meters. TEL: 0171 629 6261; fax - 0171 495 6180. SER: Restorations; buys at auction. FAIRS: Grosvenor House; Maastricht. VAT: Stan/Spec.

Piccadilly Gallery

16 Cork St. W1X 1PF. SLAD. Est. 1952. Open 10-5.30: Sat. times vary, prior 'phone call advisable. CL: Sat. (Aug. and Sept). *STOCK: Symbolist and Art Nouveau works, 20th C; drawings and watercolours.* PARK: Meters. TEL: 0171 629 2875; fax - 0171 499 0431. VAT: Spec.

Nicholas S. Pitcher Oriental Art

1st Floor, 29 New Bond St. W1Y 9HD. Open 10.30-5 by appointment. CL: Sat. except by appointment. SIZE: Small. *STOCK: Chinese and Japanese ceramics and works of art, early pottery, to 18th C, £200-£5,000.* LOC: Four doors from Sotheby's, above Gordon Scott shoe shop. PARK: Nearby. TEL: 0171 499 6621; home - 0171 731 1975. SER: Valuations; buys at auction. VAT: Spec.

W1 continued

Portal Gallery

16a Grafton St/Bond St. W1X 3LF. (Lionel Levy and Jess Wilder). Est. 1959. Open 10-5.30, Sat. 10-4. SIZE: Medium. *STOCK: Curios, bygones, artefacts, country pieces and objects of virtue, 19th C, £50-£500; contemporary British idiosyncratic paintings, including Beryl Cook.* LOC: Junction of New and Old Bond St. PARK: Easy. TEL: 0171 493 0706; fax - 0171 629 3506.

Jonathan Potter Ltd BADA LAPADA

125 New Bond St. W1Y 9AF. ABA. Est. 1975. Open 10-6, Sat. by appointment. *STOCK: British and World maps, atlases and travel books, 16th-19th C, £50-£10,000.* PARK: Meters nearby. TEL: 0171 491 3520; fax - 0171 491 9754. SER: Valuations; restorations; colouring, framing; buys at auction (maps and prints); catalogue available. VAT: Stan.

Pyms Gallery BADA

9 Mount St., Mayfair. W1Y 5AD. (A. and M. Hobart). Est. 1975. Open 10-6. CL: Sat. *STOCK: British, Irish and French paintings, 19th-20th C.* TEL: 0171 629 2020; fax - 0171 629 2060. SER: Valuations; restorations; buys at auction. VAT: Spec.

Bernard Quaritch Ltd. (Booksellers) BADA

5-8 Lower John St., Golden Sq. W1R 4AU. Est. 1847. Open 9.30-5.30. CL: Sat. SIZE: Large. *STOCK: Rare books and manuscripts.* PARK: Meters, 50 yds. TEL: 0171 734 2983; fax - 0171 437 0967. SER: Buys at auction. VAT: Stan.

Rabi Gallery Ltd

82 Portland Place. (R. and V. Soleymani). Est. 1978. Open 10-6. CL: Sat. *STOCK: Ancient art, antique carpets and works of art.* TEL: 0171 436 0772/580 9064; fax - 0171 436 0772.

William Redford BADA

99 Mount St. W1Y 5HF. Open 10-5. CL: Sat. SIZE: Small. *STOCK: French furniture, works of art, bronzes, some porcelain.* TEL: 0171 629 1165.

David Richards and Sons LAPADA

12 New Cavendish St. W1M 7LJ. (M., H. and E. Richards). Open 9.30-5.30. CL: Sat. SIZE: Large. *STOCK: Silver and plate.* LOC: Off Harley St., at corner of Marylebone High St. PARK: Easy. TEL: 0171 935 3206/0322; fax - 0171 224 4423. SER: Valuations; restorations. VAT: Stan/Spec.

Jonathan Robinson

1st Floor, 29 New Bond St. W1Y 9HD. Est. 1984. Open by appointment. SIZE: Small. *STOCK: Chinese porcelain and works of art, from B.C. to 19th C, £200-£5,000.* LOC: Four doors from Sothebys. PARK: Meters. TEL: 0171 493 0592.

W1 continued

SER: Valuations; consultancy; buys at auction (Oriental items). FAIRS: International Ceramics, Park Lane Hotel. VAT: Spec.

Michael Rose - Source of the Unusual

3 Burlington Arcade, Piccadilly. W1V 9AB. *STOCK: Victorian, antique and period diamonds, jewellery, watches and Fabergé.* TEL: 0171 493 0714.

Russell Rare Books

1st Floor, 81 Grosvenor St. W1X 9DE. (C. Russell). Open 10-5.30. *STOCK: Antiquarian books.* TEL: 0171 629 0532; fax - 0171 499 2983.

Frank T. Sabin Ltd BADA

13 Royal Arcade, Old Bond St. W1X 3HB. (John Sabin). Open 9.30-5.30, Sat. by appointment only. *STOCK: English sporting and decorative prints, 18th-19th C.* TEL: 0171 493 3288; fax - 0171 499 3593.

Alistair Sampson Antiques Ltd BADA

120 Mount St., Mayfair. (Formerly of 156 Brompton Rd). W1Y 5HB. Open 9.30-5.30. SIZE: Large. *STOCK: English pottery, oak and country furniture, metalwork, needlework, primitive pictures, decorative and interesting items,17th-18th C; Chinese works of art.* PARK: Meters. TEL: 0171 409 1799; fax - 0171 409 7717. VAT: Spec.

Robert G. Sawers

PO Box 4QA. W1A 4QA Open by appointment. *STOCK: Books on the Orient, Japanese prints, screens, paintings.* TEL: 0171 409 0863; fax - 0171 409 0817.

Scarisbrick and Bate Ltd

111 Mount St. W1Y 5HE. (A.C. Bate). Est. 1958. Open 9.30-5.30. CL: Sat. SIZE: Medium. *STOCK: Furniture, decorative items, mid-18th C to early 19th C.* Not Stocked: Glass and china. LOC: By Connaught Hotel (off Park Lane). PARK: Meters. TEL: 0171 499 2043/4/5; fax - 0171 499 2897. SER: Restorations (furniture); buys at auction. VAT: Stan.

Thomas E. Schuster

14 Maddox St. Est. 1973. Open 9.30-5.30, Sat. by appointment only. *STOCK: Antique prints, maps, medieval manuscripts, fine and rare colour plate books and atlases.* TEL: 0171 491 2208; fax - 0171 491 9872. FAIRS: ABA, Park Lane.

The Schuster Gallery

14 Maddox St. W1 Open 10-5.30. *STOCK: Decorative and rare prints, maps, 1500-1880; medieval manuscripts, £30-£3,000.* LOC: Near Regent St. TEL: 0171 491 2208; fax - 0171 491 9872. FAIRS: London, New York, Tokyo, San Francisco, Los Angeles.

W1 continued

The Scripophily Shop
Georgian Arcade, Britannia Hotel, Grosvenor Sq. W1A 3AN. (K. Hollender). Est. 1979. Open 10-5, Sat. and Sun. by appointment. SIZE: Large. *STOCK: Old bonds and shares, 1800-1950, £5-£2,000.* TEL: 0171 495 0580. SER: Valuations. VAT: Global.

Seaby Antiquities
14 Old Bond St. W1X 4JL. Est. 1926. Open 10-5. CL: Sat. SIZE: Medium. *STOCK: Antiquities, ancient coins; books on coins, archaeology and history.* LOC: Just off Piccadilly, nearest tube Green Park. TEL: 0171 495 2590; fax - 0171 491 1595.

Shaikh and Son (Oriental Rugs) Ltd
16 Brook St. W1. (M. Shaikh). Open 10-6. CL: Sat. pm. *STOCK: Persian carpets, rugs, £100-£10,000.* TEL: 0171 629 3430. SER: Repairing and cleaning.

Bernard J. Shapero Rare Books
32 St George St. W1R 0EA. Est. 1979. Open 9.30-6.30, Sat. 11-5. SIZE: Large. *STOCK: Antiquarian books - travel, natural history and literature. (old and modern); antiquarian prints and engravings.* LOC: Near Hanover Sq. and Bond St. TEL: 0171 493 0876. SER: Valuations; restorations (antiquarian books); buys at auction. FAIRS: Book - London, Paris, New York, San Francisco.

Christopher Sheppard Ltd
11 St George St. W1R 9DF. Open 10-6. CL: Sat. *STOCK: Ancient and antique glass.* TEL: 0171 629 6489; fax - 0171 495 2905.

The Silver Fund Ltd
2nd Floor, 139A New Bond St. W1Y 9FB. (Alastair Crawford and Michael James). Est. 1977. Open daily, Sat. and Sun. by appointment. SIZE: Large. *STOCK: Silver - English, £200-£20,000; Jensen and Tiffany, £100-£50,000; American, £100-£5,000.* LOC: Opposite Sotheby's. PARK: NCP Mayfair. TEL: 0171 499 8501; fax - 0171 495 4789. SER: Valuations; restorations. FAIRS: Decorative Antiques, London; NEC; Olympia. VAT: Stan/Spec.

W. Sitch and Co. Ltd.
48 Berwick St. W1V 4JD. (R. Sitch). Est. 1776. Open 8-5, Sat. 8-1. SIZE: Large. *STOCK: Edwardian and Victorian lighting fixtures and floor standards.* LOC: Off Oxford St. TEL: 0171 437 3776. SER: Valuations; restorations; repairs. VAT: Stan.

The Sladmore Gallery BADA
32 Bruton Place, Berkeley Sq. W1X 7AA. (E.F. Horswell) Open 10-6. CL: Sat. SIZE: Large. *STOCK: Bronze sculptures, 19th C - Mene, Barye, Fremiet, Bonheur; Impressionist, Bugatti, Troubetzkoy, Pompon; contemporary, Geoffrey Dashwood birds, Mark Coreth African wildlife; sporting, polo.* TEL: 0171 499 0365. SER: Valuations; restorations. VAT: Stan/Spec.

W1 continued

Stephen Somerville Ltd
14 Old Bond St. W1X 3DB. SLAD. Est. 1987. By appointment only. SIZE: Small. *STOCK: Old Master prints and drawings; English paintings, watercolours, prints and drawings, 17th-20th C, £50-£50,000.* LOC: Piccadilly end of Old Bond St. TEL: 0171 493 8363. SER: Buys at auction (as stock). VAT: Spec.

Henry Sotheran Ltd
2/5 Sackville St., Piccadilly. W1X 2DP. Est. 1761. Open 9.30-6, Sat. 10-4. *STOCK: Antiquarian books and prints, including John Gould prints.* TEL: 0171 439 6151. SER: Restorations and binding (books, prints); buys at auction. VAT: Stan.

A & J Speelman Ltd BADA
129 Mount St. W1Y 5HA. Est. 1931. Open 9-5.30. SIZE: Large. *STOCK: Chinese and Japanese works of art, Shang era to 19th C.* TEL: 0171 499 5126. SER: Valuations; buys at auction. VAT: Spec.

Spink Leger Pictures BADA
13 Old Bond St. W1X 4HU. (D.W. Posnett and L.J. Libson). SLAD. Est. 1892. Open 9-5.30, Sat. by appointment. SIZE: Large. *STOCK: Old Masters, English paintings, early English watercolours.* PARK: Meters. TEL: 0171 629 3538; fax - 0171 493 8681. SER: Valuations; restorations.

A distler tinplate and clockwork limousine, 1920, 30.5cm., £825. Sotheby's Sussex.

From the feature "Saleroom Prices" which appeared in the Christmas 1996 issue of **Antique Collecting**

W1 continued

Stair and Company Ltd BADA

14 Mount St. W1Y 5RA. CINOA. Est. 1911. Open 9.30-5.30, Sat. by appointment. SIZE: Large. *STOCK: 18th C English furniture, works of art, mirrors, chandeliers, barometers, needlework, lamps, clocks, prints.* LOC: Past Connaught Hotel, towards South Audley St. PARK: Meters, and Adam's Row. TEL: 0171 499 1784; fax - 0171 629 1050. SER: Restorations; decorations. VAT: Spec.

Stoppenbach and Delestre Ltd

25 Cork St. W1X 1HB. SLAD. Open 10-5.30, Sat. 10-1. *STOCK: French paintings, drawings and sculpture, 19th-20th C.* TEL: 0171 734 3534.

Tessiers Ltd BADA

26 New Bond St. W1Y 0JY. Open 10-5. *STOCK: Silver, jewellery, objets d'art.* TEL: 0171 629 0458; fax - 0171 629 1857. SER: Valuations; restorations. VAT: Spec.

William Thuillier

180 New Bond St. W1Y 9PD. Open by appointment only. *STOCK: Old Master paintings and drawings.* TEL: 0171 499 0106.

Toynbee-Clarke Interiors Ltd

95 Mount St. W1Y 5HG. (G. and D. Toynbee-Clarke). Est. 1953. Open 9-5.30. CL: Sat. SIZE: Medium. *STOCK: Decorative English and Continental furniture and objects, 17th-18th C; Chinese hand painted wallpapers, 18th C; French scenic wallpapers, early 19th C; Chinese and Japanese paintings and screens, 17th-19th C.* LOC: Between north-west corner of Berkeley Sq. and Park Lane. PARK: Meters. TEL: 0171 499 4472; fax - 0171 495 1204. SER: Buys at auction. VAT: Stan/Spec.

Tryon & Swann Gallery

23 Cork St. W1X 1HB. Open 10-6, Sat. by appointment. *STOCK: Sporting, wildlife and marine paintings, bronzes, books, 1900 to contemporary artists, £150-£50,000.* TEL: 0171 734 6961/2256; fax - 0171 287 2480. SER: Valuations; framing; advising; commission buying

M. Turpin Ltd LAPADA

27 Bruton St. W1X 7DB. Open 10-6 or by appointment. CL: Sat. SIZE: Large. *STOCK: English and Continental furniture, mirrors, chandeliers and objets d'art, 18th C.* LOC: Between Berkeley Sq. and Bond St. PARK: Limited and meters. TEL: 0171 493 3275; fax - 0171 408 1869.

Under Two Flags

4 St Christopher's Place. W1M 5HB. (A.C. Coutts). Est. 1973. Open 10-5. CL: Mon. SIZE: Small. *STOCK: Toy soldiers, old and new military prints, books, finely detailed painted models of all periods.* LOC: Off Wigmore St. TEL: 0171 935 6934.

W1 continued

Jan van Beers Oriental Art BADA

34 Davies St. W1Y 1LG. Est. 1978. Open 10-6. CL: Sat. SIZE: Medium. *STOCK: Chinese and Japanese ceramics and works of art, 200BC to 1800 AD.* LOC: Between Berkeley Sq. and Oxford St. PARK: Easy. TEL: 0171 408 0434. SER: Valuations. FAIRS: Cologne. VAT: Spec.

Venners Antiques

7 New Cavendish St. W1M 7RP. (Mrs S. Davis). Open 10.15-4.15, Sat. 10-1. CL: Mon. *STOCK: 18th-19th C English porcelain and pottery.* PARK: Meters. TEL: 0171 935 0184. SER: Valuations; buys at auction. VAT: Spec.

Vigo Carpet Gallery LAPADA

6a Vigo St. W1X 1AH. Open 9-5.30, Fri. 9-5. CL: Sat. *STOCK: Oriental and European rugs and carpets, tapestries and needlework.* TEL: 0171 439 6971; fax - 0171 439 2353. SER: Design.

Walpole Gallery

38 Dover St. W1X 3RB. SLAD. Open 9.30-5.30. CL: Sat. except when exhibitions held. *STOCK: Italian Old Master paintings.* TEL: 0171 499 6626.

Wartski Ltd BADA

14 Grafton St. W1X 4DE. Est. 1865. Open 9.30-5. CL: Sat. SIZE: Medium. *STOCK: Jewellery, 18th C gold boxes, Fabergé, Russian works of art, silver.* PARK: Meters. TEL: 0171 493 1141. SER: Restorations; buys at auction. FAIRS: International Fine Art and Antique Dealers' Show, New York; Tresors; International Fine Art and Antiques for Asia, Singapore. VAT: Stan/Spec.

Waterhouse and Dodd BADA

1st Floor, 110 New Bond St. W1Y 9AA. (R. Waterhouse and J. Dodd). Est. 1987. Open 10-6, Sat. and Sun. by appointment. SIZE: Medium. *STOCK: British and European oil paintings, watercolours and drawings, 1850-1950, £2,000-£50,000.* LOC: Corner of Brook St. and Bond St. - entrance on Brook St. TEL: 0171 491 9293. SER: Valuations; restorations; buys at auction (paintings). FAIRS: City of London Antiques and Fine Art; Olympia. VAT: Spec.

Captain O.M. Watts

7 Dover St., Piccadilly. W1X 3PJ. Open 9-6. SIZE: Small. *STOCK: Nautical antiques and collectables, £30-£2,000.* LOC: Near Bond St. PARK: Meters. TEL: 0171 493 4633; fax - 0171 495 0755. SER: Restorations (scientific instruments); buys at auction (nautical and scientific instruments); hire. VAT: Stan.

The Weiss Gallery

1B Albemarle St. Open 10-6. CL: Sat. *STOCK: Elizabethan, Jacobean and early European portraits.* TEL: 0171 409 0035. SER: Valuations; restorations.

STAIR

& COMPANY ESTABLISHED 1911

A beautifully detailed Regency rosewood Centre or Breakfast Table on a finely detailed square tapered and moulded baluster support above a platform with four outswept scrolled feet embellished with acanthus leaf carving and on castors. The top and frieze supports with brass inlay and the base with ormolu mounts.

ENGLISH, CIRCA 1810

137 cms (54") diameter, 70cms (27½") high

14 MOUNT STREET, LONDON W1Y 5RA

TELEPHONE (0171) 499-1784 FACSIMILE (0171) 629-1050

also at: 942 MADISON AVENUE, NEW YORK, NY 10021, U.S.A.

W1 continued

William Weston Gallery
7 Royal Arcade, Albemarle St. W1X 3HD. SLAD. Est. 1964. Open 9.30-5.30, some Sats. 10.30-2. SIZE: Small. *STOCK: Etchings, lithographs, 1800-1970.* LOC: Off Piccadilly. TEL: 0171 493 0722; fax - 0171 491 9240. VAT: Spec.

Rollo Whately
1st Floor, 9 Old Bond St. W1X 3TA. Est. 1995. Open 9-6. CL: Sat. SIZE: Small. *STOCK: Picture frames, 16th-19th C, £500-£2,000.* LOC: Piccadilly end of Old Bond St. TEL: 0171 629 7861. SER: Valuations; restorations (frames); search; buys at auction. VAT: Stan.

Wildenstein and Co Ltd
147 New Bond St. W1Y 0NY. SLAD. Est. 1934. Open 10-5.30. CL: Sat. SIZE: Large. *STOCK: Impressionist and Old Master paintings and drawings.* PARK: Meters. TEL: 0171 629 0602; fax - 0171 493 3924.

Wilkins and Wilkins
1 Barrett St., St Christophers Pl. W1M 6DN. (M. Wilkins). Est. 1981. Open 10-5. CL: Sat. SIZE: Small. *STOCK: English 17th and 18th C portraits and decorative paintings, £700-£20,000.* LOC: Near Selfridges. TEL: 0171 935 9613; fax - 0171 935 4696. VAT: Stan/Spec.

Wilkinson plc
1 Grafton St. W1X 4LB. Est. 1947. Open 9.30-5. CL: Sat. *STOCK: Glass, especially chandeliers, 18th C and reproduction; art metal work.* LOC: Nearest underground - Green Park. TEL: 0171 495 2477. SER: Restorations and repairs (glass and metalwork).

Williams and Son
2 Grafton St. W1X 3LB. (J.R. Williams). Est. 1931. Open 9.30-6. CL: Sat. SIZE: Large. *STOCK: British and European paintings, 19th C.* LOC: Between Bond St. and Berkeley Sq. TEL: 0171 493 4985/5751; fax - 0171 409 7363. VAT: Stan/Spec.

Linda Wrigglesworth BADA LAPADA
Ground Floor Suite, 34 Brook St. W1Y 1YA. Est. 1978. Open 10-6. CL: Sat. *STOCK: Chinese costume and textiles of the Qing and Ming dynasty, 1398-1911, £200+.* LOC: Corner of South Molton St. PARK: Grosvenor Square. TEL: 0171 408 0177. SER: Valuations; restorations; mounting, framing; buys on commission (Oriental). FAIRS: Maastricht; Olympia.

LONDON W2

Sean Arnold Sporting Antiques
21-22 Chepstow Corner, off Westbourne Grove. W2 4XE. Open 10-6. *STOCK: Sporting antiques and decorative items; golf clubs, 1840-1915, £30-£6,000; tennis racquets, £10-£3,000; vintage luggage.* TEL: 0171 221 2267; fax - 0171 221 5464.

Bayswater Books
27a Craven Terrace, Lancaster Gate. W2 3EL. Est. 1984. Open 11-7. SIZE: Small. *STOCK: Antiquarian books, maps and prints, £5-£500; secondhand books, photographica, ephemera, £1-£500.* LOC: One-way street running south from Craven Rd. to Bayswater Rd. PARK: Meters. TEL: 0171 402 7398. SER: Book search and mail order.

Claude Bornoff BADA
20 Chepstow Corner, Pembridge Villas. W2 4XE. Est. 1949. Open 9.30-5. CL: Sat. SIZE: Medium. *STOCK: English and Continental furniture, china, metalware and unusual items.* PARK: Meters. TEL: 0171 229 8947. VAT: Stan/Spec.

Ruby Buckle (Antique Fireplaces)
18 Chepstow Corner, Pembridge Villas. W2 4XE. Open 10-6. *STOCK: Fireplaces.* TEL: 0171 229 8843; fax - 0171 229 8864.

Connaught Galleries
44 Connaught St. W2 2AA. (M. Hollamby). Est. 1966. Open 10-6.30, Sat. 10-1. SIZE: Medium. *STOCK: Antique and reproduction sporting, historical, geographical and decorative prints.* LOC: Near Marble Arch. PARK: Meters. TEL: 0171 723 1660. SER: Picture framing. VAT: Spec.

Craven Gallery
30 Craven Terrace. W2. (C. and A. Quaradeghini). Est. 1974. Open 11-6, Sat. 3-7, other times by appointment. SIZE: Large and warehouse. *STOCK: Silver and plate, 19th-20th C; furniture, china and glass, Victorian.* LOC: Off Bayswater Rd. PARK: Easy. TEL: 0171 402 2802; home - 0181 998 0769. VAT: Stan. *Trade Only.*

Jacqueline Edge
1 Courtnell St. W2 5BU. Est. 1993. Open Sat. 11-6, other days by appointment. SIZE: Medium. *STOCK: Colonial furniture, early 20th C, £500-£1,000; lacquerware, late 19th to early 20th C; ethnic textiles; urns, pots, ceramics.* LOC: Off Westbourne Grove/Ledbury Rd., on corner with Artesian Rd. PARK: Meters. TEL: 0171 229 1172. SER: Interior/exterior design. VAT: Stan.

Hosains Books and Antiques
25 Connaught St. W2 2AY. Est. 1979. Open 11-5, Sat. by appointment. *STOCK: Secondhand and antiquarian books on India, Middle East, Central Asia; miniatures; prints of India and Middle East.* TEL: 0171 262 7900; fax - same.

W2 continued

Manya Igel Fine Arts Ltd LAPADA
21/22 Peters Court, Porchester Rd. W2 5DR. (M. Igel and B.S. Prydal). Est. 1977. Open 10-5 by appointment only. SIZE: Large. *STOCK: Mainly modern and contemporary British works, £250-£25,000.* LOC: Off Queensway. PARK: Nearby. TEL: 0171 229 1669/8429; fax - 0171 229 6770. VAT: Spec.

Ian Lieber
The Shop, 29 Craven Terrace, Lancaster Gate. W2 3EL. Est. 1965. Open by appointment. SIZE: Medium. *STOCK: Furniture, early 19th C and decorative; porcelain, objets d'art, paintings, costume jewellery.* LOC: Near Bayswater Rd. TEL: 0171 262 5505; fax - 0171 402 4445. SER: Buys at auction. FAIRS: Olympia. VAT: Stan/ Spec.

The Mark Gallery BADA
9 Porchester Place, Marble Arch. W2 2BS. (H. Mark). CINOA. Est. 1969. Open 10-1 and 2-6, Sat. 11-1. SIZE: Medium. *STOCK: Russian icons, 16th-19th C; modern graphics - French school.* LOC: Near Marble Arch. TEL: 0171 262 4906; fax - 0171 224 9416. SER: Valuations; restorations; buys at auction. VAT: Stan/Spec.

M. McAleer
W2 4SN. (Mrs M. McAleer and M.J. McAleer). Est. 1969. Open by appointment. SIZE: Small. *STOCK: Scottish provincial, Irish and small collectable silver.* TEL: 0171 727 7979. SER: Buys at auction (silver).

LONDON W4

The Chiswick Fireplace Co.
68 Southfield Rd., Chiswick. W4 1BD. (Mr Bee). Open 9.30-5.30. SIZE: Medium. *STOCK: Original cast iron fireplaces, late Victorian to early 1900's, £200-£1,000.* LOC: 8 minutes walk from Turnham Green underground. PARK: Easy. TEL: 0181 995 4011. SER: Restorations. VAT: Stan.

J. D. Marshall
38 Chiswick Lane, Chiswick. W4 2JQ. Est. 1985. Open 10-6, Sat. 10-5. CL: Mon. SIZE: Medium. *STOCK: Decorative and unusual objects, furniture, bronzes and chandeliers, £100-£50,000; some garden statuary and furniture, to £10,000.* LOC: Off A4/M4 at the Hogarth roundabout or Chiswick High Rd. PARK: Easy. TEL: 0181 742 8089; fax - same. SER: Valuations; restorations (oil and water gilding; metal patination and non-ferrous casting). VAT: Spec.

W4 continued

The Old Cinema Antique Department Store LAPADA
160 Chiswick High Rd. W4 1PR. Est. 1977. Open 10-6, Sun. 12-5. SIZE: Large. *STOCK: General antiques including furniture, gardenalia, decorative and architectural items, 1800-1940, £100-£6,000.* PARK: Easy. TEL: 0181 995 4166; e-mail - antique@antique.u-net.com; website - www.antiques-uk.co.uk. SER: Restorations. VAT: Stan/Spec.

The Old Dairy
164 Thames Rd., Strand-on-the-Green, Chiswick. W4 3QS. (N.J. Quinn). Est. 1980. Open Tues.-Sun. 10.30-6 and by appointment. SIZE: Medium. *STOCK: 19th C furniture and decorative items including pine, painted and fruitwood armoires, sleighbeds and dressers, £25-£950.* LOC: North side of Thames, east of Kew Bridge, near junction of north and south circulars. PARK: Easy. TEL: 0181 994 3140; home - 0181 742 2395.

Portray Antiques
136 Chiswick High Rd. W4 1PU. (Hratch Bastajian). Est. 1993. Open 8.30-6, Sat. 10-4. SIZE: Medium. *STOCK: Furniture.* PARK: Side streets. TEL: 0181 994 6549; fax - 0181 994 6589. SER: Restorations (repairs, polishing and upholstery); buys at auction (furniture). VAT: Stan/Spec.

Strand Antiques
166 Thames Rd., Strand-on-the-Green, Chiswick. W4 3QS. Est. 1977. Open 12-5 including Sun. or by appointment. SIZE: Large. *STOCK: Books, kitchen items, glass, furniture, jewellery, paintings, prints, fabrics, china, silver, clothes, and collectors' items, £1-£500.* LOC: Behind Bull's Head Public House, about 400yds. from Kew Bridge. PARK: Easy. TEL: 0181 994 1912.

LONDON W5

Aberdeen House Antiques LAPADA
75 St. Mary's Rd. W5 5RH. (N. Schwartz). Est. 1971. Open 10-5.30. SIZE: Medium. *STOCK: Furniture and pictures, £50-£2,000; decorative items and textiles, £25-£2,000; china, glass and silver, £25-£1,000; all 18th-20th C.* LOC: On B455 1 mile north of A4. PARK: Easy and at rear. TEL: 0181 567 5194/1223. SER: Valuations. FAIRS: Olympia. VAT: Stan.

Antique Pine Ltd
16 South Ealing Rd., Ealing. W5 5EX. (L. A. and K. Denwood). Est. 1971. Open 10-6. SIZE: Large. *STOCK: Victorian and Edwardian pine furniture, £50-£1,000.* TEL: 0181 932 0168. SER: Pine stripping and repair; valuations. VAT: Stan.

W5 continued

The Badger
12 St. Mary's Rd. W5 5ES. (M. and E. Aalders). Est. 1967. Open 9.30-6. SIZE: Medium. *STOCK: Furniture, £100-£2,000; clocks, £1,000-£3,000; both 18th-19th C; ceramics, 19th C, £50-£1,000.* PARK: Easy. TEL: 0181 567 5601. SER: Valuations; restorations (furniture and clocks); buys at auction (clocks and watches). VAT: Stan/Spec.

Ealing Gallery
78 St. Mary's Rd., Ealing. W5 5EX. (Mrs N. Lane). Open 10.30-5.30. CL: Mon. and Wed. *STOCK: Oil paintings, £100-£5,000; watercolours, £50-£3,000; both 19th to early 20th C; contemporary paintings, £30-£250.* LOC: Piccadilly Line underground, South Ealing. PARK: Nearby. TEL: 0181 840 7883; fax - same. SER: Valuations; restorations (oils and watercolours); framing. VAT: Spec.

Harold's Place
148 South Ealing Rd. W5 4QJ. (H. Bowman). Est. 1977. Open 10-6. CL: Wed. SIZE: Medium. *STOCK: Wall plates, commemoratives, porcelain, 19th to early 20th C, £5-£100.* LOC: 1/2 mile north of A4/M4 at Ealing. TEL: 0181 579 4825.

Terrace Antiques
10-12 South Ealing Rd. W5 4QA. (N. Schwartz). Est. 1971. Open 10-5.30. SIZE: Medium. *STOCK: Georgian, Victorian and Edwardian furniture, 1780-1920, £50-£1,000; china, glass and pictures, silver and plate, 1850-1950, £10-£200.* LOC: 1 mile north of A4 on B455. PARK: Easy and opposite. TEL: 0181 567 5194/1223. SER: Valuations. FAIRS: Olympia. VAT: Stan.

LONDON W6

Architectural Antiques
351 King St. W6 9NH. (G.P.A. Duc). Est. 1985. Open 9-5, Sat. 10-4. SIZE: Medium. *STOCK: Marble/stone chimney pieces, 18th-19th C, £500-£8,000; gilt/painted overmantles, 19th C, £300-£1,500.* PARK: Easy and Black Lion Lane. TEL: 0181 741 7883; fax - 0181 741 1109. SER: Valuations; cleaning and polishing (marble chimney pieces on site); repair. VAT: Stan. *Trade Only.*

N. Davighi
117 Shepherd's Bush Rd. Est. 1950. Open 9.30-5. SIZE: Medium. *STOCK: Chandeliers, light fittings, general antiques, Georgian and Victorian.* PARK: Easy. TEL: 0171 603 5357. SER: Valuations; restorations (ormolu, chandeliers and brass).

Tony Dixon
121 Shepherds Bush Rd., Hammersmith. W6 7LP. *STOCK: Antiques and objects of desire, English, European and Oriental ceramics and works of art; tribal art, unusual items, £10-£10,000.* TEL: 0171 603 8300; fax - 0171 603 8022.

W6 continued

Paravent
Flat 10, Ranelagh Gardens, Stamford Brook Ave. W6 0YE. (M. Aldbrook). Open by appointment only. *STOCK: Screens, 17th-20th C, £500-£10,000.* TEL: 0181 748 6323; fax - 0181 563 2912. SER: Restorations. VAT: Stan/Spec.

Murray Thomson Ltd
89 Richford St., Shepherds Bush. W6 7HJ. Est. 1966. Open 10-6. SIZE: Large. *STOCK: English furniture, 18th-19th C.* TEL: 0171 727 1727; fax - 0171 727 1825. VAT: Stan/Spec.

LONDON W8

Adrian Alan Ltd BADA LAPADA
219 Kensington Church St. W8 7LX. Open 10-6. *STOCK: English and Continental furniture especially fine 19th C; sculpture and works of art.* TEL: 0171 727 4783; fax - 0171 727 7353. VAT: Stan/Spec.

AntiqueWest Ltd LAPADA
140-142 Kensington Church St. W8 4BN. (Bjorn Gremner). Est. 1969. Open 10-6, Sat. 10-4. SIZE: Small. *STOCK: Chinese pottery and porcelain, neolithic to late 19th C, £200-£12,000; Chinese and Tibetan rugs, early 19th C, £500-£9,000.* LOC: 100 yards south of Notting Hill Gate. PARK: Meters. TEL: 0171 229 4115. FAIRS: Eurantica, Brussels; Stockholm, Alvsjo; International Ceramics, London; Helsingborg, Sweden; Singapore Tresors. VAT: Spec.

Valerie Arieta
97b Kensington Church St. W8 7LN Open 10.30-5, Sat. and other times by appointment. *STOCK: American Indian and Eskimo art; English and Continental antiques.* TEL: 0171 243 1074/794 7613.

Garry Atkins
107 Kensington Church St. W8 7LN. (Garry and Julie Atkins). Est. 1986. Open 10-5.30, Sat. am by appointment. SIZE: Small. *STOCK: English and Continental pottery, to 18th C, £100-£10,000; small furniture, to 19th C, £300-£3,000.* LOC: Between Kensington High St. and Notting Hill Gate. PARK: Meters. TEL: 0171 727 8737; fax - 0171 792 9010. SER: Valuations; buys at auction (English and Continental pottery); annual exhibition (March), catalogues available. FAIRS: International Ceramic. VAT: Spec.

Gregg Baker Oriental Art BADA LAPADA
132 Kensington Church St. W8 4BH. Est. 1985. Open 10-6, weekends by appointment. SIZE: Small. *STOCK: Japanese and Chinese works of art and screens, mainly 18th-19th C, £500-£100,000.* PARK: Meters. TEL: 0171 221 3533; fax - 0171 221 4410. SER: Valuations. VAT: Stan/Spec.

W8 continued

Eddy Bardawil BADA
106 Kensington Church St. W8 4BH. (E.S. Bardawil). Est. 1979. Open 10-1 and 2-5.30, Sat. 10-1.30. SIZE: Medium. *STOCK: English furniture - mahogany, satinwood, walnut; mirrors, brassware, tea-caddies, all pre-1830, £500-£50,000; prints, 18th C.* LOC: Corner premises, Berkeley Gardens/Church St. PARK: Easy. TEL: 0171 221 3967; fax - 0171 221 5124. SER: Valuations; restorations (furniture); polishing. VAT: Stan/Spec.

Barnet Antiques BADA
79 Kensington Church St. W8 4BG. *STOCK: 18th to early 19th C English furniture.* TEL: 0171 376 2817.

Baumkotter Gallery LAPADA
63a Kensington Church St. W8 4BA. (Mrs L. Baumkotter). Est. 1968. Open 9.30-6. CL: Sat. SIZE: Large. *STOCK: 17th-19th C oil paintings.* TEL: 0171 937 5171. VAT: Spec.

Berwald Oriental Art BADA
101 Kensington Church St. W8 7LN. (John R. Berwald). Est. 1986. Open 10-6, Sat. and Sun and other times by appointment. SIZE: Medium. *STOCK: Chinese porcelain, 16th to early 18th C; Chinese pottery, 200BC to 15th C; Oriental works of art; all £1,000-£100,000.* PARK: Meters and nearby. TEL: 0171 229 0800; fax - 0171 229 1101. SER: Valuations; restorations; buys at auction (Oriental). FAIRS: Asian Arts, New York; Arts of Pacific Asia, San Francisco; Park Lane Hotel. VAT: Spec.

David Brower Antiques
113 Kensington Church St. W8 7LN. Est. 1965. Open 10-6. CL: Sat. SIZE: Large. *STOCK: Oriental and Continental decorative porcelain, £100-£5,000; French and Oriental furniture, bronzes and clocks.* PARK: Meters nearby. TEL: 0171 221 4155. SER: Buys at auction. VAT: Stan/Spec.

The Lucy B. Campbell Gallery BADA
123 Kensington Church St. W8 7LP. Est. 1983. Open 10-6, Sat. 10-4. SIZE: Medium. *STOCK: Fine decorative prints, 17th-19th C; contemporary originals.* Not Stocked: Maps and sporting prints. PARK: Meters. TEL: 0171 727 2205; fax - 0171 229 4252. SER: Framing. VAT: Stan.

Anne-Marie Cattanach LAPADA
79 Kensington Church St. W8 4BG. Est. 1977. Open 10-1 and 2-5.30. SIZE: Medium. *STOCK: Furniture, £500-£20,000; boxes and candlesticks, caddies and Oriental porcelain; all 17th-19th C.* PARK: Meters. TEL: 0171 376 2817; home - 0171 727 0460. SER: Valuations; restorations (furniture). FAIRS: Olympia. VAT: Spec.

W8 continued

Church Gallery
77 Kensington Church St. W8 4BG. (A. Spigard). Open 9-6. *STOCK: General antiques and furniture.* TEL: 0171 937 2461; fax - 0171 938 3286. SER: Restorations. VAT: Spec.

Coats Oriental Carpets
4 Kensington Church Walk (off Holland St). W8 4NB. (A. Coats). Est. 1973. Open 11-5, Sat. 11-3 or by appointment. SIZE: Medium. *STOCK: Oriental carpets and rugs, kelims, £50-£2,000; Oriental textiles and embroideries, £10-£100; all 19th C.* LOC: Small pedestrian alleyway just off Holland St., off south end of Kensington Church St. PARK: Easy. TEL: 0171 937 0983; home - 0171 370 2355. SER: Valuations; restorations (reweaving); buys at auction. VAT: Stan/Spec.

Cohen & Cohen BADA
101B Kensington Church St. W8 7LN. Open 10-6. CL: Sat. *STOCK: Chinese porcelain, bronzes, works of art; Japanese prints.* TEL: 0171 727 7677; fax - 0171 229 9653. SER: Valuations; buys at auction. VAT: Stan/Spec.

Garrick D. Coleman
5 Kensington Court. W8 5DL. (G.D. and G.E. Coleman). Est. 1944. Open strictly by appointment only. SIZE: Medium. *STOCK: Chess sets, 1750-1880, £100-£4,000; decorative items, £50-£2,000; glass paperweights, £200-£3,000; conjuring and magic items.* PARK: Easy. TEL: 0171 937 5524; fax - 0171 937 5530. VAT: Stan/Spec.

Mary Cooke Antiques Ltd BADA LAPADA
121A Kensington Church St. W8 7LP. Open 9.30-5.30, Sat. am. by appointment. *STOCK: Silver.* TEL: 0171 792 8077. SER: Valuations; restorations; buys at auction. FAIRS: Chelsea Spring and Autumn; NEC; LAPADA; International; Northern. VAT: Stan/Spec.

Crawley and Asquith Ltd BADA
20 Upper Phillimore Gardens. W8 7HA. Open by appointment. *STOCK: 18th-19th C paintings, watercolours, prints, books.* TEL: 0171 937 9523; fax - 0171 937 2159.

Mrs. M.E. Crick Chandeliers
166 Kensington Church St. W8 4BN. Est. 1897. CL: Sat. *STOCK: English and Continental crystal, glass and ormulu chandeliers, 18th-19th C.* PARK: Meters. TEL: 0171 229 1338; fax - 0171 792 1073.

George Dare
9 Launceston Place, Kensington. W8 5RL. Est. 1980. Open anytime by appointment. SIZE: Medium. *STOCK: English watercolours and oil paintings, mainly 18th-19th C, £100-£2,500.* LOC: Turn left off London bound section of Cromwell Rd., opposite the Forum Hotel. PARK: Easy. TEL: 0171 937 7072; home - same. SER: Restorations; framing; buys at auction (as stock). VAT: Stan.

W8 continued

Davies Antiques LAPADA
40 Kensington Church St. W8 4BX. (H.Q.V. Davies). Est. 1976. Open 10-5.30, Sat. 10-3. ***STOCK: Continental porcelain especially Meissen, 1710-1930.*** **TEL: 0171 937 9216; fax - 0171 938 2032.**

Richard Dennis
144 Kensington Church St. W8 Est. 1967. Open 10-5.30, Sat. 10-2. SIZE: Medium. *STOCK: British studio pottery especially Moorcroft, Martin, Doulton, Pilkington and Parian, 1870-1950, and contemporary.* LOC: Near Notting Hill Gate tube. TEL: 0171 727 2061. VAT: Stan/Spec.

Denton Antiques
156 Kensington Church St. W8 4BN. (M.T. and M.E. Denton). Open 9.30-5.30. CL: Sat. *STOCK: Glass, chandeliers, candelabra, 18th-19th C.* TEL: 0171 229 5866; fax - 0171 792 1073.

H. and W. Deutsch Antiques LAPADA
111 Kensington Church St. W8 7LN Est. 1897. Open 10-5. CL: Tues., Wed. and Sat. SIZE: Large. ***STOCK: 18th-19th C Continental and English porcelain and glassware; silver, plate and enamel ware, miniature portraits; Oriental porcelain, cloisonné, bronzes, £300-£5,000.*** **TEL: 0171 727 5984. VAT: Stan/Spec.**

Michael C. German BADA LAPADA
38B Kensington Church St. W8 4BX. Est. 1954. Open 10-5, Sat. 10-3. ***STOCK: European and Oriental arms and armour; walking stick specialist.*** **TEL: 0171 937 2771.**

Green's Antique Galleries
117 Kensington Church St. W8 7LN. (S. Green). Open 9-5. SIZE: Medium. *STOCK: Jewellery, 18th C to date; pre-1930 clothes and lace; dolls, china, silver, furniture, paintings, masonic, crocodile and leather items.* PARK: Easy. TEL: 0171 229 9618. VAT: Stan/Spec.

Grosvenor Antiques Ltd BADA
27 Holland St., Kensington. W8 4NA. (S.C. and E. Lorie). Est. 1950. ***STOCK: English and Continental porcelain, bronzes and works of art.*** **TEL: 0171 937 8649; fax - 0171 937 7179. VAT: Spec.**

Robert Hales Antiques Ltd
131 Kensington Church St. W8 7LP. Est. 1967. Open 9.30-5.30. CL: Mon. and Sat. SIZE: Small. *STOCK: Islamic, Oriental and ethnographic arms and armour; oceanic art, 16th-19th C.* PARK: Easy. TEL: 0171 229 3887. SER: Valuations; buys at auction. VAT: Spec.

Hampson and Lewis
131E Kensington Church St. (entrance in Peel St). W8 7LP. (Peter Hampson and Sue Lewis). Est. 1981. Open Tues. and Thurs. 10-5, Wed. and Fri. 11-5, Sat. 10-4. SIZE: Small. *STOCK: Silver and jewellery, Arts and Crafts to date, £50-£3,000.* TEL: 0171 229 8173. SER: Restorations (jewellery and silver); buys at auction (silver and jewellery). VAT: Stan/Spec.

W8 continued

Robert Harman Antiques BADA
140-142 Kensington Church St. W8 4BN. (Robert Harman Cannell). Est. 1979. Open 10-6.30. SIZE: Large. ***STOCK: Furniture, £1,000-£30,000; tea caddies, £200-£10,000; works of art, £200-£20,000; all 18th to early 19th C.*** **PARK: Meters and NCP nearby. TEL: 0171 221 6790; home - 01525 402322. SER: Valuations; restorations (furniture); buys at auction (furniture). FAIRS: Olympia, Chelsea and BADA. VAT: Spec.**

Jonathan Harris BADA
Previously at 54 Kensington Church St. CINOA. Open temporarily by appointment only, before moving to new permanent premises. ***STOCK: English, Continental, Oriental furniture; works of art.*** **TEL: 0171 602 6255; fax - 0171 602 0488. VAT: Spec.**

Haslam and Whiteway
105 Kensington Church St. W8 7LN. (T.M. Whiteway). Est. 1969. Open 10-6, Sat. 10-2. SIZE: Small. *STOCK: British furniture, £100-£10,000; British decorative arts, £50-£5,000; Continental and American decorative arts, £50-£500; all 1850-1930.* Not Stocked: Pre-Victorian items. LOC: From Notting Hill Gate tube station, down Kensington Church St. Shop is approx. 300yds. down on right. PARK: Meters. TEL: 0171 229 1145. SER: Valuations; buys at auction. VAT:Stan.

Jeanette Hayhurst Fine Glass BADA
32A Kensington Church St. Open 12-5, Sat. 11-4. ***STOCK: Glass - 18th C English drinking, fine 19th C engraved, table decanters, contemporary art, scent bottles, Roman and Continental.*** **TEL: 0171 938 1539.**

D. Holmes
47c Earls Court Rd. (in Abingdon Villas), Kensington. W8 6EE. Est. 1965. Open Fri. 2-7, Sat. 10-5 or by appointment. *STOCK: Decorative items and furniture, 18th-19th C.* TEL: 0171 937 6961 or 01208 880254. SER: Restorations (furniture). VAT: Stan/Spec.

Hope and Glory
(Royal Commemorative Specialists) 131a Kensington Church St. W8 7LP. Open 10-5. *STOCK: Commemorative china.* TEL: 0171 727 8424.

Jonathan Horne BADA
66b & 66c Kensington Church St. W8 4BY. Est. 1968. Open 9.30-5.30. CL: Sat. and Sun. except by appointment. SIZE: Medium. ***STOCK: Early English pottery, needlework and works of art.*** **TEL: 0171 221 5658; fax - 0171 792 3090. VAT: Stan/Spec.**

W8 continued

Valerie Howard LAPADA
2 Campden St., Off Kensington Church St. W8 7EP. Open 10-5.30, Sat. 10-4. *STOCK: Mason's and English Ironstone china, 1810-1860, £50-£10,000; French faience especially from Quimper and Rouen regions, 1750-1920, £20-£3,000; mirrors, 19th C, £500-£2,000.* TEL: 0171 792 9702. (ansaphone at night). SER: Valuations; restorations (ceramics); buys at auction (as stock). FAIRS: Olympia (June). VAT: Spec.

Iona Antiques BADA
PO Box 285. W8 6HZ. Est. 1974. Open by appointment only. SIZE: Large. *STOCK: 19th C animal paintings, £1,000-£30,000.* LOC: 3 minutes walk from Odeon Cinema, Kensington High St. PARK: Nearby. TEL: 0171 602 1193; fax - 0171 371 2843. FAIRS: Grosvenor House, Olympia.

J.A.N. Fine Art
134 Kensington Church St. (Mrs F.K. Shimizu). Est. 1976. Open 10-6, Sat. by appointment. SIZE: Medium. *STOCK: Japanese and Chinese porcelain, 1st -20th C, from £150; Japanese bronzes and works of art, 15th-20th C, from £150; Japanese paintings and screens, 16th-20th C, from £250; Tibetan thankas and ritual objects, 12th-18th C, from £250.* PARK: Meters. TEL: 0171 792 0736; fax - 0171 221 1380. VAT: Spec.

Japanese Gallery
66d Kensington Church St. W8 4BY. (Mr. and Mrs C.D. Wertheim). Est. 1977. Open 10-6. *STOCK: Japanese wood-cut prints; books, porcelain, netsuke.* TEL: 0171 229 2934. SER: Free authentification; on-the-spot framing for Japanese prints; exhibitions.

Melvyn Jay Antiques and Objets d'Art
64a Kensington Church St. W8 4DB Est. 1960. Open 9-5.45, Sat. 11-2. SIZE: Medium. *STOCK: Mid-19th C French decorative furniture, clocks; Continental porcelain, bronzes and silver, £5-£5,000; English and Continental furniture.* LOC: From Marble Arch to Kensington High St. Bus No.73. PARK: Easy. TEL: 0171 937 6832. SER: Valuations; buys at auction. VAT: Stan/Spec.

Roderick Jellicoe
at Stockspring Antiques, 114 Kensington Church St. W8 4BH. Est. 1974. Open 10-5.30, Sat. 10-1. SIZE: Medium. *STOCK: English porcelain, 18th-19th C, £5-£5,000+.* PARK: Meters. TEL: 0171 727 7995. SER: Valuations; buys at auction (18th C English porcelain). FAIRS: Olympia; London Ceramic. VAT: Spec.

John Jesse
160 Kensington Church St. W8 4BN. Open 10-6, Sat. 11-4. *STOCK: Decorative arts, 1880-1950, especially Art Nouveau and Art Deco silver, glass, bronzes and jewellery.* TEL: 0171 229 0312; fax - 0171 229 4732.

W8 continued

Howard Jones LAPADA
43 Kensington Church St. W8 4BA. (H. Howard-Jones). Est. 1971. Open 10-5. SIZE: Small. *STOCK: Silver, porcelain, bronzes, £20-£5,000.* Not Stocked: Furniture. PARK: Nearby. TEL: 0171 937 4359. VAT: Stan/Spec.

Peter Kemp
170 Kensington Church St. W8 4BN. Est. 1975. Open 10-5. CL: Sat. SIZE: Medium. *STOCK: Porcelain - 10th-19th C Chinese, 17th-19th C Japanese, 18th C Continental; Oriental works of art and porcelain, 18th-19th C.* LOC: 200yds. from Notting Hill tube station. PARK: Meters nearby. TEL: 0171 229 2988. SER: Valuations; restorations (porcelain); buys at auction (Oriental and Continental porcelain). VAT: Spec.

Kensington Church Street Antiques Centre
58-60 Kensington Church St. W8 4DB Open 10-6. Below are listed some of the dealers at this Centre.

Nic Boston
Units 10, 14 & 15. *Majolica (Minton, Wedgwood, George Jones).* TEL: 0171 376 0425; fax - 0171 937 3400. VAT: Stan/Spec.

W8 continued

Didier Antiques
Unit 2. *Jewellery and silver, objets d'art, 1860-1960, £50-£7,000.* TEL: 0171 938 2537. VAT: Stan/Spec.

Freeforms
Unit 6. *20th C decorative arts including post-war design.* TEL: 0171 376 0425.

Gallery 8
Unit 8.

Glass Pyramid
Unit 5.

Graven Images
Unit 7.

Jag
Units 9 & 11. *Art glass, including Loetz, Murano, 1880-1960, pewter, WMF, Liberty; ceramics, bronzes and ivories.* TEL: 0171 938 4404; fax - 0171 937 3400.

M. Lorenzo
Unit 4.

C. Monk
Unit 12.

W8 continued

Noonstar LAPADA
Unit 1. *Cameo glass and decorative items, both 20th C.* TEL: 0171 376 2652. VAT: Stan/Spec.

Zeitgeist
Unit 3. *Liberty metalwork, ceramics and furniture.* TEL: 0171 938 4817; fax - 0171 937 3400.

The Lacquer Chest
71 and 75 Kensington Church St. W8 4BG. (G. and V. Andersen). Est. 1959. Open 9.30-5.30, Sat. 10.30-3. SIZE: Large. *STOCK: Furniture and unusual items.* LOC: Half-way up left-hand side from High St. PARK: Meters. TEL: 0171 937 1306. VAT: Stan/Spec.

Leask Ward LAPADA
79 Kensington Church St. W8 4BG Open 10-1 and 2-5. *STOCK: Oriental and European antiques and paintings.* TEL: 0171 376 2817; home - 0171 435 9781. VAT: Spec.

Lev (Antiques) Ltd
97A&B Kensington Church St. W8 7LN. (Mrs Lev). Est. 1882. Open 10.30-5.30. SIZE: Medium. *STOCK: Jewellery, silver, plate, curios.* PARK: Meters. TEL: 0171 727 9248. SER: Restorations (pictures); repairs (jewellery, silver).

Lewis and Lloyd BADA
65 Kensington Church St. W8 4BA. Est. 1968. Open 10.15-5.30. SIZE: Medium. *STOCK: Furniture and works of art, 18th-19th C, £2,000-£50,000.* PARK: Easy. TEL: 0171 938 3323; fax - 0171 361 0086. VAT: Spec.

Libra Antiques
131d Kensington Church St. *STOCK: Blue and white pottery, lustre ware.* TEL: 0171 727 2990.

London Antique Gallery
66E Kensington Church St. W8 4BY. (Mr. and Mrs. C.D. Wertheim). Open 10-6. *STOCK: London prints; Meissen, Royal Worcester, collectable porcelain.* TEL: 0171 229 2934. SER: Restorations (prints, porcelain and dolls).

C.H. Major (Antiques) Ltd
154 Kensington Church St. W8 4BN. (A.H. Major). Est. 1905. Open 10-6. SIZE: Large. *STOCK: English furniture, from 1760, £200-£25,000.* Not Stocked: China, glass. PARK: Easy. TEL: 0171 229 1162; fax - 0171 221 9676; home - 0181 997 9018. VAT: Stan/Spec.

E. and H. Manners
66a Kensington Church St. W8 4BY. Est. 1986. Open 10-5.30, Sat. and Sun. by appointment. *STOCK: European ceramics, pre-19th C, £100-£20,000.* TEL: 0171 229 5516; fax - same; home - 0181 741 7084. SER: Valuations; restorations; buys at auction (ceramics). FAIRS: International Ceramic. VAT: Spec.

W8 continued

S. Marchant & Son BADA

120 Kensington Church St. W8 4BH. (R.P. Marchant). Est. 1925. Open 9.30-5.30. CL: Sat. *STOCK: Chinese and Japanese pottery and porcelain, jades, cloisonné, Chinese furniture and paintings.* PARK: Easy. TEL: 0171 229 5319/3770; fax - 0171 792 8979. SER: Valuations; restorations (porcelain); buys at auction. VAT: Stan/Spec.

Robert McPherson

at Stockspring Antiques, 114 Kensington Church St. W8 4BH. Est. 1985. Open 10-5.30, Sat. 10-1. *STOCK: Chinese ceramics, 2500 BC to 1800, £5-£4,000.* TEL: 0171 727 7995. SER: FAIRS: Olympia (June). VAT: Spec.

Michael Coins

6 Hillgate St. (off Notting Hill Gate). W8 7SR. (M. Gouby). Est. 1966. Open 10-5. CL: Sat. SIZE: Small. *STOCK: Coins, English and foreign, 1066 A.D. to date; stamps, banknotes and collectors' items.* LOC: From Marble Arch to Notting Hill Gate, turn left at corner of Coronet Cinema. PARK: Easy. TEL: 0171 727 1518; fax - 0171 727 1518. SER: Valuations; buys at auction. VAT: Stan/Spec.

New Century

69 Kensington Church St. W8 4BG. (H.S. Lyons). Est. 1988. *STOCK: Arts and Crafts, aesthetic and Art Nouveau furniture, metal and ceramics, 1870-1920, £20-£3,000.* TEL: 0171 937 2410. SER: Valuations; restorations; buys at auction. VAT: Stan/Spec.

Oliver-Sutton Antiques BADA

34c Kensington Church St. W8 4HA. (P. Sutton). Est. 1967. Open 10-5. CL: Aug. *STOCK: Staffordshire, Walton, Sherratt pottery; 19th C portrait figures, animals, cottages.* TEL: 0171 937 0633. VAT: Spec.

Pruskin Gallery

73 Kensington Church St. W8 4BG. *STOCK: Fine Art Nouveau and Art Deco glass, bronzes, silver, furniture, ceramics, paintings, posters and prints.* TEL: 0171 937 1994; evenings - 0171 938 2892.

Raffety BADA LAPADA

34 Kensington Church St. W8 4HA. Open 10.30-5.30, Sat. 10.30-1.30. *STOCK: Fine English longcase and bracket clocks, 17th-18th C; carriage clocks and barometers.* TEL: 0171 938 1100/229 4947; fax - 0171 938 1100; mobile - 0831 514216. SER: Valuations; buys at auction. VAT: Stan/Spec.

Paul Reeves

32B Kensington Church St. W8 4HA. Est. 1976. Open 10-6. *STOCK: Architect designed furniture and artifacts, 1860-1960.* TEL: 0171 937 1594.

W8 continued

Reindeer Antiques Ltd BADA LAPADA

81 Kensington Church St. W8 4BG. (J.W. Butterworth). Open 9.30-1 and 2-6. *STOCK: Period English and Continental furniture and works of art.* PARK: Meters. TEL: 0171 937 3754; fax - 0171 937 7199. VAT: Stan/Spec.

Roderick Antique Clocks LAPADA

23 Vicarage Gate, Kensington. W8 4AA. (R. Mee). Est. 1975. Open 10-5.15, Sat. 10-3. *STOCK: Clocks - French decorative and carriage, 19th C, £250-£2,000; English longcase and bracket, 18th-19th C, £2,000-£7,500.* LOC: At junction of Kensington Church St. PARK: Easy. TEL: 0171 937 8517. SER: Valuations; restorations (English and French movements and cases). VAT: Spec.

J. Roger (Antiques) Ltd BADA

17 Uxbridge St. W8 7TQ. (J. Roger and C. Bayley). Open by appointment. *STOCK: Late 18th to early 19th C small elegant pieces furniture, mirrors, prints, porcelain and boxes.* TEL: 0171 603 7627/381 2884.

Brian Rolleston Antiques Ltd BADA

104A Kensington Church St. W8 4BU. Est. 1950. Open 10-1 and 2.30-6, Sat. by appointment. SIZE: Large. *STOCK: English furniture, 18th C, £1,500-£50,000.* PARK: Easy. TEL: 0171 229 5892; fax - same. VAT: Spec.

Sabin Galleries Ltd BADA

Campden Lodge, 82 Campden Hill Rd. W8 7AA. (S.F, E.P. and P.G. Sabin). SLAD. Open by appointment only. *STOCK: English paintings and drawings, pre-1830.* TEL: 0171 937 0471.

Patrick Sandberg Antiques BADA

140-142 and 150-152 Kensington Church St. W8 4BN. (P.C.F. Sandberg). Est. 1983. Open 10-6, Sat. 10-4. SIZE: Large. *STOCK: 18th to early 19th C English furniture and accessories - candlesticks, tea caddies, clocks and prints.* TEL: 0171 229 0373; fax - 0171 792 3467. FAIRS: Olympia (Feb., June, Nov). VAT: Spec.

A.V. Santos BADA

1 Campden St. W8 7EP. Open 10-1 and 2-6. CL: Sat. *STOCK: Chinese export porcelain, 17th-18th C.* TEL: 0171 727 4872; fax - 0171 229 4801. VAT: Spec.

M. and D. Seligmann BADA

37 Kensington Church St. W8 4LL. Est. 1948. Open 10.30-5.30, Sat. 11.30-4.30, or by appointment. SIZE: Medium. *STOCK: 17th-18th C English country furniture, pottery, treen, objets d'art.* LOC: Nearest underground Kensington High St. TEL: 0171 937 0400; home - 0171 722 4315; fax - same. FAIRS: Olympia (June and Nov.); Chelsea (Autumn). VAT: Stan/Spec.

W8 continued

Jean Sewell. (Antiques) Ltd BADA
3 Campden St. W8 7EP. (E. and B. Sewell). Est. 1956. Open 10-5.30. SIZE: Medium. *STOCK: Pottery and porcelain, 18th-19th C, £1-£10,000.* Not Stocked: Silver, furniture and china after 1880. LOC: From Notting Hill Gate down Kensington Church St., fourth street on right at Churchill public house. PARK: Easy. TEL: 0171 727 3122; fax - 0171 229 1053. VAT: Stan/Spec.

Sinai Antiques Ltd
221 Kensington Church St. W8 7LX. (E. and M. Sinai). Open 9.30-6. CL: Sat. *STOCK: Carpets, Oriental arts, silver, fine arts.* TEL: 0171 229 6190.

Simon Spero
109 Kensington Church St. W8 7LN. Author of 'The Price Guide to 18th C English Porcelain'. Est. 1964. Open 10-5, Sat. 10-1. CL: Mon. except by appointment. SIZE: Medium. *STOCK: 18th C English ceramics, enamels and watercolours.* PARK: Meters. TEL: 0171 727 7413; fax - 0171 727 7414. SER: Valuations; buys at auction. VAT: Spec.

Constance Stobo
31 Holland St. (off Kensington Church St.). W8 4NA. *STOCK: English lustreware, Staffordshire animals, Wemyss, 18th-19th C pottery.* TEL: 0171 937 6282.

W8 continued

Stockspring Antiques LAPADA
114 Kensington Church St. W8 4BH. (A. Agnew and F. Marno). Open 10-5.30, Sat. 10-1. *STOCK: English, European and Oriental pottery and porcelain.* TEL: 0171 727 7995. VAT: Spec.

Jacob Stodel BADA
116A Kensington Church St. W8 4BH. Est. 1949. *STOCK: Continental furniture, objets d'art, ceramics, English furniture.* TEL: 0171 221 2652; fax - 0171 229 1293. VAT: Spec.

Pamela Teignmouth and Son
108 Kensington Church St. W8 4BH. (Lady Teignmouth and Mr T. Meyer). Est. 1982. Open 10-6, including Sat. in winter only. SIZE: Medium. *STOCK: English and Continental furniture, 18th-19th C, decorative items, £100-£10,000.* TEL: 0171 229 1602; fax - 0171 792 5042. FAIRS: Olympia (June). VAT: Spec.

Through the Looking Glass Ltd
137 Kensington Church St. W8 7LP. (J.J.A. and D.A. Pulton). Est. 1958. Open 10-5.30. SIZE: Large. *STOCK: Mirrors, 19th C, £500-£10,000.* LOC: 200yds. from Notting Hill Gate. PARK: Side roads. TEL: 0171 221 4026. SER: Gilding. VAT: Spec.

Mary Wise BADA
27 Holland St., Kensington. W8 4NA Est. 1959. *STOCK: English porcelain, works of art, bronzes.* Not Stocked: English pottery, jewellery. TEL: 0171 937 8649; fax - 0171 937 7179. SER: Buys at auction (Chinese and English porcelain). VAT: Spec.

LONDON W9

David Bridgwater
at Clifton Little Venice, 3 Warwick Place. W9. *STOCK: Sculptural items, garden ornaments and tools, fountains, metalwork, architectural and decorative items.* TEL: 0171 289 7894.

Fluss and Charlesworth Ltd LAPADA
1 Lauderdale Rd. W9 1LT. (E. Fluss and J. Charlesworth). Est. 1970. Open by appointment. *STOCK: 18th to early 19th C furniture and works of art.* TEL: 0171 286 8339; mobile - 0831 830323. SER: Interior decor. FAIRS: Olympia; LAPADA.

Beryl Kendall, The English Watercolour Gallery
2 Warwick Place, Little Venice. W9 2PX. Est. 1953. Open 2-6, Sat. 11-3.30. CL: Mon. *STOCK: English watercolours, 19th C.* TEL: 0171 286 9902.

Vale Antiques
245 Elgin Ave., Maida Vale. W9 1NJ. (P. Gooley). *STOCK: General antiques.* TEL: 0171 328 4796.

LONDON W11

Michael Aalders
181 Westbourne Grove. W11. Open 10-6. *STOCK: Unusual furniture and furnishings, 17th-18th C; paintings, 19th-20th C.* TEL: 0171 221 4391.

Addison Fine Art
57 Addison Avenue. W11 4ZU. (Mrs D. Geddes). Est. 1978. Open by appointment. SIZE: Small. *STOCK: British and Continental post-impressionist paintings.* TEL: 0171 603 2374. SER: Valuations; restorations; buys at auction (paintings). FAIRS: 20th C British Art (Sept.); Olympia (June). VAT: Spec.

Alice's
86 Portobello Rd. W11. (D. Carter). Est. 1960. Open 9-5. SIZE: Large. *STOCK: General antiques and decorative items.* TEL: 0171 229 8187; fax - 0171 792 2456.

Arbras Gallery
292 Westbourne Grove. W11 2PS Est. 1972. Open Fri. 10-4, Sat. 7-5. SIZE: 2 floors. *STOCK: General antiques - silver, boxes, jewellery, paintings, furniture, books, prints and decorative items.* LOC: 50 yards from Portobello Road. TEL: 0171 229 6772. VAT: Stan/Spec.

Arenski BADA LAPADA
185 Westbourne Grove. W11 2SB. (Jay Arenski). Open 10-5.30. SIZE: Large. *STOCK: Furniture, glass, objects, bronzes and paintings, from 1820, £25-£50,000.* PARK: Easy. TEL: 0171 727 8599. SER: Buys at auction. FAIRS: Olympia, LAPADA. VAT: Stan/Spec.

Sean Arnold Sporting Antiques
Portwine Gallery, 173-175 Portobello Rd. W11 2DY. Open Sat. 8-4. *STOCK: Sporting antiques and decorative items; golf clubs, 1840-1915, £30-£6,000; vintage luggage.* TEL: 0171 221 2267; fax - 0171 221 5464.

Axia Art Consultants Ltd
121 Ledbury Rd. W11 2AQ. Est. 1974. *STOCK: Works of art, icons, textiles, metalwork, wood-work and ceramics, Islamic and Byzantine.* TEL: 0171 727 9724.

B. and T. Antiques LAPADA
79/81 Ledbury Rd. W11 2AG. (Mrs B. Lewis). Open 10-6. *STOCK: Furniture, silver, objets d'art, paintings, 18th C to Art Deco.* TEL: 0171 229 7001; fax - 0171 224 8508.

P.R. Barham
111 Portobello Rd. W11 2QB. Est. 1951. Open 9-5. SIZE: Large. *STOCK: Victorian, Edwardian, Continental furniture, Oriental porcelain, objets d'art, silver, plate and clocks.* TEL: 0171 727 3397. SER: Valuations; buys at auction.

W11 continued

Barham Antiques
83 Portobello Rd. Est. 1954. Open 9.30-5, Sat. 7-5. SIZE: Large. *STOCK: Victorian walnut and inlaid Continental furniture, writing boxes, tea caddies, inkwells and inkstands, glass epergnes, silver plate, clocks, paintings.* TEL: 0171 727 3845; fax - same. SER: Valuations; buys at auction.

Benchmark
184 Westbourne Grove. W11 2RH. (Ben Brierley, Mark Golding and Sandra Keenan Kamen). Est. 1984. Open 10-6, Sun. by appointment. SIZE: Medium. *STOCK: Gothic revival furniture and architect designed objects, especially 19th C designer furniture, also Whitefriars glass, £50-£50,000.* LOC: Near Portobello Rd. PARK: Easy. TEL: 0171 229 4179; home - 0181 968 6625/0161 477 7953; mobile - 0468 058632/058240. SER: Buys at auction.

Daniel Bexfield Antiques LAPADA
Portobello Studios, 101 Portobello Rd. W11 2QB. Est. 1981. Open Sat. 6.30-2.30, Fri. am by appointment. SIZE: Small. *STOCK: Fine silver and objects of virtue, 1700-1940; jewellery, 1800-1920: all £500-£1,000.* TEL: 01582 481930; fax - same; mobile - 0850 681156; internet - www.Bexfield.Co UK; e-mail - antiques@Bexfield.Co.UK. SER: Valuations; buys at auction (silver). FAIRS: LAPADA, London and Birmingham; NEC April, Aug., Nov; Hatfield House. VAT: Spec.

David Black Oriental Carpets BADA
96 Portland Rd., Holland Park. W11 4LN. Est. 1966. Open 11-6. SIZE: Large. *STOCK: Antique and new Oriental room size decorative carpets; tribal rugs, kilims, dhurries, embroideries, £500-£25,000.* LOC: From Notting Hill Gate, second right after Holland Park tube station. PARK: Meters. TEL: 0171 727 2566; fax - 0171 229 4599. SER: Valuations; restorations; cleaning underfelt. VAT: Spec.

Norman Blackburn
32 Ledbury Rd. W11 2AB Est. 1974. Open 10-6, Sat. 10-5. CL: Mon. *STOCK: Framed prints - decorative, stipple and mezzotints, botanical, sporting, marine, portraits and views, pre-1860.* LOC: Two roads east of Portobello. TEL: 0171 229 5316; fax - 0171 229 2269. VAT: Spec.

Books & Things
Arbras Gallery, 292 Westbourne Grove. W11 2PS. (M. Steenson). ABA, PBFA. Est. 1972. Open Sat. 7-4, Fri. by appointment. SIZE: Small. *STOCK: Antiquarian books, £25-£500; posters, £50-£500; both 20th C.* PARK: Meters. TEL: 0171 370 5593 (anytime); fax - 0171 370 5593. SER: Valuations; buys at auction; catalogues issued. FAIRS: PBFA London, Oxford, Bath; ABA, Chelsea.

W11 continued

Britannia Export Antiques

186 Westbourne Grove. W11 2RH. (G. Fiumano). Est. 1973. Open 9.30-6, Sat. 10.30-4. SIZE: Large. *STOCK: Silver and ivory, £300-£10,000; furniture, £500-£20,000; all 18th-20th C.* PARK: Meters. TEL: 0171 221 2011. SER: Valuations; restorations (silver, porcelain, ivory, furniture and pictures); buys at auction (as restorations). VAT: Stan/Spec.

Butchoff Antiques LAPADA

229 and 233 Westbourne Grove. W11 2SE. Est. 1962. Open 10-6, Sat. 10-3.30. SIZE: Large. *STOCK: Furniture and decorative smalls, paintings, 18th-20th C, £500-£30,000.* TEL: 0171 221 8174; fax - 0171 792 8923.

Caelt Gallery

182 Westbourne Grove. W11 2RH. Est. 1967. Open 9.30-6, Sun. 10.30-6. SIZE: Large. *STOCK: Oil paintings, 17th-20th C, £200-£10,000 but mainly £300-£700.* PARK: Easy. TEL: 0171 229 9309; fax - 0171 727 8746. VAT: Spec.

Canonbury

174 Westbourne Grove. W11 2RW. (M. Worster). Est. 1965. Open 10-6, Sat. 10-4.30. SIZE: Large. *STOCK: Dutch, English and French furniture; some porcelain.* LOC: Off Portobello Road. PARK: Easy. TEL: 0171 727 4268; fax - 0171 229 5840. SER: Valuations; restorations. VAT: Stan/Spec.

Jack Casimir Ltd BADA LAPADA

23 Pembridge Rd. W11 3HG. Est. 1933. Open 10-5.30 and by appointment. SIZE: Large. *STOCK: Brass, copper, pewter.* Not Stocked: Silver, china, jewellery. LOC: 2 mins. walk from Notting Hill Gate station. PARK: 100yds. TEL: 0171 727 8643. SER: Exports. VAT: Stan/Spec.

Central Gallery. (Portobello)

125 Portobello Rd. W11 2DY. Open Saturdays only 6-3. SIZE: 32+ dealers. *STOCK: Jewellery, Georgian to 1950's, including rare and unusual pieces, £50-£5,000+.* TEL: 0171 243 8027; fax - same. FAIRS: Olympia; Miami Beach. VAT: Stan/Spec/Global.

The Coach House

189 Westbourne Grove. W11 2SB. (Jay Arenski, Peter Farlow, Peter Petrou and Graham Walpole). Open 9-6. *STOCK: Fine furniture - Regency, Gothic Revival, Arts & Crafts, Aesthetic, Colonial and Campaign, Islamic and Egyptian Revival; oil paintings including maritime, Old Masters and modern, naïve portraits including animal, watercolours and prints; classical and Vienna bronzes, Grand Tour items, ormolu, metalware and treen; decorative glass, silver and plate, pottery including majolica, equestrian objects and tribal art, £200-£200,000.* Not Stocked: Shipping goods and jewellery. PARK: Easy. TEL: 0171 229 8306; fax - 0171 229 4297. SER: Interior decor; shipping arranged. FAIRS: Olympia (June); BADA (May). VAT: Stan/Spec.

W11 continued

Cohen and Pearce (Oriental Porcelain) BADA

84 Portobello Rd. W11 2QD. (M. Cohen). Est. 1974. Open Fri. 10-4, Sat. 8-4 or by appointment. *STOCK: Chinese porcelain, bronzes, works of art; Japanese prints.* TEL: 0171 229 9458; fax - 0171 229 9653. SER: Valuations; buys at auction. VAT: Spec.

Garrick D. Coleman

75 Portobello Rd. Est. 1944. Open 10-4, Sat. 7-5. CL: Mon. *STOCK: Chess sets, 1750-1880, £100-£5,000; works of art £50-£3,000; glass paperweights, £200-£3,000; also conjuring and magic items.* TEL: 0171 937 5524; fax - 0171 937 5530. VAT: Stan/Spec.

Sheila Cook

42 Ledbury Rd. W11 2AB. Est. 1970. SIZE: Small. *STOCK: Textiles and decorative antiques, 1800-1960, £50-£5,000.* PARK: Easy. TEL: 0171 792 8001. SER: Valuations; buys at auction. VAT: Global.

The Corner Portobello Antiques Supermarket

282-290 Westbourne Grove. W11. (B. Lipka & Son Ltd). Open Fri. 12-4, Sat. 7-6. SIZE: 150 dealers. *STOCK: General miniature antiques, silver and jewellery.* TEL: 0171 727 2027. SER: Valuations; restorations.

Crown Arcade

119 Portobello Rd. (Brian King). Est. 1986. Open Sat. 7-5.30. SIZE: Medium. LOC: Near Westbourne Grove. TEL: 0171 229 8797; fax - 0171 243 8774.

Curá Antiques

34 Ledbury Rd. W11 2AB. (G. Antichi). Open 11-6, Sat. 10.30-1. *STOCK: Continental furniture, sculptures, majolica and paintings.* TEL: 0171 229 6880.

Daggett Gallery LAPADA

1st and 2nd Floors, 153 Portobello Rd. W11 2DY. (Caroline Daggett). Est. 1992. Open 10-5. (prior telephone call advisable) and Sat. 9-3.30. SIZE: Medium. *STOCK: Frames, 18th-20th C, from £1.* LOC: 200 yards from Westbourne Grove towards Elgin Crescent. PARK: Meters. TEL: 0171 229 2248. SER: Restoration (frames); gilding; picture plaques; framing; special paint effects. VAT: Stan/Spec.

Charles Daggett Gallery LAPADA

1st and 2nd Floors, 153 Portobello Rd. W11 2DY. (Charles and Caroline Daggett). Est. 1977. Open 10-4, prior telephone call advisable, and Sat. 9-3.30. SIZE: Medium. *STOCK: British pictures, 1740-1840.* LOC: 200 yards from Westbourne Grove, towards Elgin Crescent. PARK: Meters. TEL: 0171 229 2248;

W11 continued

fax - 0171 229 0193. SER: Restorations (pictures and frames); framing. FAIRS: Olympia and NEC, Birmingham. VAT: Stan/Spec.

John Dale

87 Portobello Rd. W11 2QB. Est. 1950. Open 10-4, Sat. 7-5. SIZE: Medium. *STOCK: General antiques.* TEL: 0171 727 1304. VAT: Stan.

Michael Davidson

54 Ledbury Rd., Westbourne Grove. W11 2AJ. Est. 1961. Open 9.45-12.45 and 1.15-5. CL: Sat. pm. in winter. *STOCK: Regency and period furniture, objets d'art.* TEL: 0171 229 6088. SER: Valuations. VAT: Stan/Spec.

Delehar

146 Portobello Rd. W11 2DZ Est. 1919. Open Sat. 9-4. SIZE: Medium. *STOCK: General antiques, works of art.* Not Stocked: Furniture. TEL: 0171 727 9860. VAT: Stan/Spec.

Peter Delehar

146 Portobello Rd. W11 2DZ. Est. 1919. Open Sat. 10-4. SIZE: Medium. *STOCK: Unusual scientific instruments.* TEL: 0171 727 9860 or 0181 866 8659. FAIRS: International Scientific and Medical Instrument (Organiser). VAT: Stan/Spec.

Demetzy Books

113 Portobello Rd. (P. and M. Hutchinson). ABA, PBFA. Est. 1972. Open Sat. 7.30-3.30. SIZE: Medium. *STOCK: Antiquarian leather bound books, 18th-19th C, £5-£1,000; Dickens' first editions and children's and illustrated books, 18th-20th C, £5-£200.* LOC: 20yds. from junction with Westbourne Grove, opposite Earl of Lonsdale public house. PARK: Meters. TEL: 01993 702209. SER: Valuations; buys at auction (books). FAIRS: ABA Park Lane; PBFA Russell Hotel, London (monthly); Randolph Hotel, Oxford; ABAA Los Angeles, San Francisco.

E. and A. Di Michele Antiques

36 Ledbury Rd. W11 2AB. Est. 1973. Open 9.30-1 and 2-5, resident so usually available. *STOCK: Continental furniture and Dutch marquetry.* TEL: 0171 229 1823.

Dodo

288 Westbourne Grove. W11 2PS. (Liz Farrow). Est. 1960. Open Sat. only 7.30-4. *STOCK: British and Continental posters, signs and tins; display figures, showcards, packaging, £1-£600.* LOC: Near Portobello Rd. TEL: Home - 0171 229 3132.

Dolphin Arcade

155-157 Portobello Rd. Open Sat. 7-5.30. SIZE: Large - 34 stalls. *STOCK: Jewellery, silver, Oriental porcelain, English pottery, general antiques.* TEL: 0171 727 4883. VAT: Stan/Spec.

W11 continued

The Facade

196 Westbourne Grove. W11 2RH. Est. 1973. Open Tues.-Sat. 10.30-5. *STOCK: French decorative items and lighting, 1900-1940.* PARK: Easy. TEL: 0171 727 2159. VAT: Stan.

Fairman Carpets Ltd LAPADA

218 Westbourne Grove. W11 2RH. (D.R.J., S.J. and H. Page). Open 9.30-6, Sun. by appointment. *STOCK: Persian and Oriental carpets and rugs; tapestries.* TEL: 0171 229 2262; fax - 0171 229 2263. SER: Valuations; repairs; cleaning. VAT: Stan.

Peter Farlow BADA LAPADA

189 Westbourne Grove. W11 2SB. Est. 1986. Open 9-5.30, Mon. 9-5, evenings by appointment. SIZE: Large. *STOCK: Gothic Revival, 1830-1880, £1,000-£20,000; Arts and Crafts, Aesthetic Movement.* LOC: Near junction with Ledbury Rd. TEL: 0171 229 8306; fax - 0171 229 4297. FAIRS: Olympia (June). VAT: Stan/Spec.

Fleur de Lys Gallery

227a Westbourne Grove. W11 2SE. (H.S. Coronel). Est. 1967. Open 10-5. SIZE: Medium. *STOCK: Oil paintings, 19th C, £1,000-£5,000.* PARK: Easy, but limited. TEL: 0171 727 8595; fax - same; home - 01372 467934.

Judy Fox LAPADA

81 Portobello Rd. and 176 Westbourne Grove. W11. Est. 1970. Open 10-5. SIZE: Large. *STOCK: Furniture and decorative items, 18th-20th C; inlaid furniture, mainly 19th C; pottery and porcelain.* TEL: 0171 229 8130; fax - 0171 229 6998.

J. Freeman LAPADA

85a Portobello Rd. W11 2QB. Est. 1962. Open 9.30-1 and 2-5.30, Sat. 9-6. SIZE: Medium. *STOCK: Victorian silver plate, 1830-1870, £10-£150; Sheffield plate, 1790-1830, £20-£100; Victorian and later silver, £5-£200.* LOC: Nearest tube station Notting Hill Gate. PARK: Easy. TEL: 0171 221 5076; fax - 0171 221 5329. VAT: Stan.

Graham and Green

4 Elgin Crescent. W11 2JA. (A. Graham and R. Harrison). Est. 1974. Open 10-6, Sat. 9.30-6, Sun. 11-5. SIZE: Medium. *STOCK: Turkish kelim rugs, pine and other furniture, re-upholstered Victorian chairs and decorative objects.* LOC: Near Portobello Rd. PARK: Meters nearby. TEL: 0171 727 4594. VAT: Stan.

Gavin Graham Gallery

47 Ledbury Rd. W11 2AA. Est. 1973. *STOCK: Oil paintings.* TEL: 0171 229 4848; fax - 0171 792 9697. VAT: Spec.

W11 continued

Grays Portobello

138 Portobello Rd. Open Sat. 7-4. SIZE: Large. *STOCK: Wide range of general small antiques especially porcelain including Oriental.* TEL: 0171 221 3069; fax - 0171 724 0999.

Henry Gregory

82 Portobello Rd. W11 2QD. (H. and C. Gregory). Est. 1969. Open 10-4, Sat. 8-5. SIZE: Medium. *STOCK: Victorian decorative objects, silver, plate, jewellery, small furniture and sporting items, £2-£2,000.* LOC: Between Westbourne Grove and Chepstow Villas. PARK: Easy. TEL: 0171 792 9221. SER: Export packing and shipping. VAT: Stan/Spec.

Patricia Harbottle

Stand 16, Geoffrey Van Arcade, 107 Portobello Rd. W11 2QB. (Mrs P. Harbottle). Est. 1989. Open Sat. 6.45-3. SIZE: Small. *STOCK: Glass, corkscrews, wine and drink related items, 18th-20th C, £5-£500.* TEL: Home - 0171 731 1972; fax - 0171 731 3663. SER: Valuations; restorations; buys at auction. FAIRS: West London (Jan. and Aug.); Snape; NEC (April, Aug., Dec.); Kensington Antiques (Nov.); Wilton House. VAT: Stan/Spec.

Hirst Antiques

59 Pembridge Rd. W11 3HN. Est. 1963. Open 10-6. SIZE: Medium. *STOCK: Four poster and half-tester beds; decorative furniture and articles.* LOC: End of Portobello Rd., near Notting Hill Gate tube station. TEL: 0171 727 9364. SER: Valuations.

David Ireland

283 Westbourne Grove. Est. 1986. Open Sat. 7-4.30. *STOCK: European and Asian costume and textiles, Paisley shawls, printed cottons, period costume, Chinese court and informal robes.* Not Stocked: Tapestries, cushions and upholstery. TEL: Mobile - 0850 576328; home - 0171 221 4188. SER: Valuations. FAIRS: Antique Textile Society.

J. and B. Antiques LAPADA

Chelsea Galleries, 67 Portobello Rd. W11 2BQ. (J.E. and C.A. Finch). Est. 1978. Open Sat. 7-3 or by appointment. SIZE: Medium. *STOCK: Porcelain and pottery, 18th-19th C, £50-£3,000; objets d'art and vertu, 17th-19th C, £50-£5,000.* TEL: 01295 711689; mobile - 0836 684133. SER: Valuations; buys at auction. VAT: Stan/Spec.

Jones Antique Lighting

194 Westbourne Grove. W11. (Judy Jones). Est. 1978. Open 9.30-6 or by appointment. SIZE: Large. *STOCK: Original decorative lighting, 1860-1960.* Not Stocked: Reproductions. TEL: 0171 229 6866; fax - same. SER: Valuations; repairs; prop hire. VAT: Stan.

W11 continued

Lacy Gallery

203 Westbourne Grove. W11 2AB. Est. 1960. Open Tues.-Fri.10-5, Sat. 10-4. SIZE: Large. *STOCK: Period frames, 1700-1940; decorative paintings and decorative art.* LOC: Two roads east of Portobello Rd. PARK: Easy. TEL: 0171 229 6340; fax - 0171 229 9105. VAT: Stan/Spec.

Patrick Lassalle

139 Portobello Rd. Open Sat. 8-5.30. *STOCK: Prints and maps, 17th to early 20th C, £3-£350.* PARK: Meters nearby. TEL: Mobile - 0956 484786.

Joan Leigh

153 Portobello Rd. Est. 1959. *STOCK: Art Nouveau, Art Deco.* TEL: 0171 727 6848.

M. and D. Lewis

1 Lonsdale Rd., 172 and 193 Westbourne Grove, 83-85 Ledbury Rd. Est. 1960. Open 9.30-5.30, Sat. 9.30-4. *STOCK: Continental and Victorian furniture, porcelain, bronzes.* TEL: 0171 727 3908. VAT: Stan/Spec.

J. Lipitch Ltd BADA

177 Westbourne Grove. W11 2SB. Est. 1955. Open 10-1 and 2-5.30, Sat. 10-1.30. *STOCK: English and Continental furniture, 17th-18th C; bronze, ormolu and porcelain.* TEL: 0171 229 0783. VAT: Spec.

M.C.N. Antiques

183 Westbourne Grove. W11 2SB. Open 9.30-6 or by appointment. *STOCK: Japanese porcelain, cloisonné, Satsuma, bronze, lacquer, ivory.* LOC: Near Portobello Rd. market. PARK: Easy. TEL: 0171 727 3796; fax - 0171 229 8839. SER: Buys at auction. VAT: Stan.

Daniel Mankowitz

208a Westbourne Grove. W11 2RH. Est. 1970. Open 10-6. SIZE: Medium. *STOCK: Furniture, English and Continental, 16th-18th C, £100-£10,000; works of art, English and Continental, 15th-19th C, £50-£5,000; tapestries, 16th-18th C, £200-£3,000.* LOC: Nr. Portobello Road. PARK: Easy. TEL: 0171 229 9270; fax - 0171 229 4687. FAIRS: Olympia. VAT: Spec.

Robin Martin Antiques

44 Ledbury Rd. W11 2AB. (Paul Martin). Est. 1972. Open 10-6. SIZE: Medium. *STOCK: English and Continental furniture and works of art, 17th-19th C.* LOC: Westbourne Grove area. TEL: 0171 727 1301; fax - same; mobile - 0831 544055. VAT: Spec.

Mayflower Antiques

117 Portobello Rd. (J.W. Odgers). Est. 1970. Open Sat. 7-5. SIZE: Medium. *STOCK: Clocks, mechanical music, scientific and marine instruments, general antiques.* TEL: Sat. - 0171

W11 continued

727 0381; office - 01255 504079; fax - same; mobile - 0860 315101/843569; e-mail - mayflower @anglianet.co.uk. VAT: Stan/Spec.

Mercury Antiques BADA

1 Ladbroke Rd. W11 3PA. (L. Richards). Est. 1963. Open 10-5.30. SIZE: Medium. *STOCK: English porcelain, 1750-1850; English pottery and Delft, 1700-1850; glass, 1780-1850.* Not Stocked: Jewellery, silver, plate, Art Nouveau. LOC: Half minute from Notting Hill Gate underground station, turn into Pembridge Rd. and bear left. TEL: 0171 727 5106; fax - 0171 229 3738. VAT: Spec.

Milne and Moller

35 Colville Terrace. W11 2BU. (Mr and Mrs C. Moller). Est. 1976. Open during exhibitions, other times by appointment. SIZE: Small. *STOCK: Watercolours, oils, ceramics and sculpture, 19th C to contemporary, £50-£3,000.* LOC: Near junction of Westbourne Grove and Ledbury Rd. PARK: Easy. TEL: 0171 727 1679; home - same. SER: Portrait commissioning. FAIRS: Olympia. VAT: Spec.

Terence Morse and Son Ltd

197 and 237 Westbourne Grove. W11 2SE. Est. 1947. Open 10-6, Sat. 11-2. SIZE: Large. *STOCK: Furniture, 18th-19th C, £1,000+.* LOC: 200yds. from Portobello Rd. PARK: Easy. TEL: 0171 229 9380/229 4059; fax - 0171 792 3284. VAT: Stan/Spec.

Myriad Antiques

131 Portland Rd., Holland Park Ave. W11 4LW. (S. Nickerson). Est. 1970. Open 11-6. SIZE: Medium. *STOCK: Decorative and unusual furniture (including garden) and objects, mainly 19th C, £10-£1,500.* LOC: Between Notting Hill Gate and Shepherds Bush roundabout. TEL: 0171 229 1709. VAT: Stan.

Nanking Porcelain Co

84 Portobello Rd. W11. (M. Hyams and E. Porter). Est. 1967. Open Fri. 10-4, Sat. 8-4, other times by appointment. *STOCK: Fine Chinese export porcelain, 18th-19th C, £250-£20,000; Orientalia, 18th-19th C, £100-£5,000.* LOC: Near Notting Hill Gate tube station. TEL: Mon.-Fri. 0171 924 2349; Sat. 0171 229 9458. SER: Valuations; buys at auction (Orientalia). VAT: Spec.

Oakstar Ltd LAPADA

Clarendon Rd. W11. (Mrs P. Bromage). Est. 1982. Open by appointment only. SIZE: Small. *STOCK: French and English furniture, 18th-19th C, £200-£10,000; papier mâché trays, £750-£4,000; mirrors, prints and objets d'art, £200-£5,000.* TEL: 0171 630 1822. SER: Restorations (lacquer). FAIRS: Decorative Antiques and Textiles; Olympia Fine Art and Antiques. VAT: Stan/Spec.

W11 continued

Old Father Time Clock Centre

Portobello Studios, 1st Floor, 101 Portobello Rd. W11 2BQ. (John Denvir). Open Fri. 9-2, Sat. 6-4, other times by appointment. *STOCK: Clocks - all types, especially electric (eg. Eureka), mystery, Atmos, novelty, skeleton, carriage, dial and bracket; also spares, books, barometers and glass domes.* TEL: 0181 546 6299; fax - same; 0171 229 2796; mobile - 0836 712088.

Peter Petrou LAPADA

195 Westbourne Grove. W11 2SB. Est. 1972. Open 10-6. *STOCK: European works of art; sculpture of animals in bronze, marble, wood and terracotta; Vienna bronzes, Grand Tour, tribal, Egyptian revival, Oriental, Blue John and Pietra Dura, eccentricities, £200-£100,000.* LOC: 500 yards from Portobello Rd. PARK: Easy. TEL: 0171 229 9575. FAIRS: Olympia. VAT: Stan/Spec.

E.S. Phillips and Sons

99 Portobello Rd. W11 2QB. Est. 1962. Open 10-5. *STOCK: Ecclesiastical antiques and stained glass.* TEL: 0171 229 2113; fax - 0171 229 1963.

Philp BADA

59 Ledbury Rd. W11 2AA. (R. Philp). SLAD. Est. 1961. Open by appointment. *STOCK: Old Master drawings, 16th-17th C English portraiture and Old Master paintings, medieval sculpture, early furniture and 20th C drawings, £50-£40,000.* PARK: Easy. TEL: 0171 727 7915. VAT: Spec.

Piano Nobile Fine Paintings

129 Portland Rd., Holland Park. W11 4LW. (Dr. Robert A. Travers). Est. 1986. Open Tues.-Sat. 10-5.30. SIZE: Medium. *STOCK: Fine 19th C Impressionist and 20th C Post-Impressionist and Modernist British and Continental oil paintings and sculpture, especially Les Petit Maitres of the Paris Schools, £500-£50,000.* PARK: Easy. TEL: 0171 229 1099; fax - same. SER: Valuations; restorations (paintings and sculptures); framing; buys at auction (19th-20th C oil paintings). FAIRS: Grosvenor; 20th C British Art and London Contemporary.

Portobello Antique Co

133 Portobello Rd. W11 2DY. (L. Meltzer and A. Goldsmith). Open Fri. 11-4.30, Sat. 8-4.30, other times by appointment. *STOCK: Porcelain, small furniture, reproduction silver plate and cutlery.* LOC: Off Westbourne Grove. PARK: Easy. TEL: 0171 221 0344; home - 0181 959 8886. VAT: Stan/Spec.

Portobello Antique Store

79 Portobello Rd. W11 2QB. (J.F. Ewing). Est. 1971. Open 10-4, Sat. 8-4.30. SIZE: Large. *STOCK: Silver and plate, £2-£3,000.* LOC: Notting Hill end of Portobello Rd. PARK: Easy weekdays. TEL: 0171 221 1994. SER: Export. VAT: Stan.

W11 continued

Raffety BADA LAPADA
39 Ledbury Rd., Notting Hill Gate. W11 2AA. (Nigel Raffety). Est. 1979. Open by appointment. SIZE: Medium. *STOCK: Clocks, 1680-1880, £1,500-£20,000; barometers, 18th-19th C, £1,000-£5,000.* LOC: Close to Portobello Road Antiques Centre. PARK: Easy. TEL: 0171 229 4947; fax - same. SER: Valuations; restorations (mainly 18th C clocks); buys at auction (antique clocks).

The Red Lion Market. (Portobello Antiques Market)
165/169 Portobello Rd. W11. Est. 1951. Open 5.30-5. SIZE: 200 dealers. *STOCK: General antiques including ethnic antiquities, bronzes, ivory statues, jade, precious metals, dolls, silver and plate, drinking vessels, costumes, Oriental and Western porcelain, furniture, collectables, prints, lace, linen, books, manuscripts, stamps, coins, banknotes, paintings, etchings, sporting memorabilia and curios.* TEL: 0171 221 7638. SER: Valuations; shipping.

A. Rezai Persian Carpets
123 Portobello Rd. W11. Open 9-5. *STOCK: Oriental carpets, kilims, tribal rugs and silk embroideries, £70-£2,000.* TEL: 0171 221 5012.

Roger's Antiques Gallery
65 Portobello Rd. W11. (Bath Antiques Market Ltd). Open Sat. 7-4.30. SIZE: 65 dealers. *STOCK: Wide range of general antiques and collectables with specialist dealers in most fields, especially jewellery.* TEL: Enquiries - 0171 351 5353; fax - 0171 351 5350. SER: Valuations.

Rostrum Antiques
115 Portobello Rd. W11 2DY. (Peter Skupien). Est. 1988. Open Sat. 8.30-5.30, other days by appointment. SIZE: Medium. *STOCK: English and Continental furniture, objets d'art, clocks and paintings, 18th-19th C, £100-£20,000.* LOC: Corner of Westbourne Grove. TEL: 0171 243 0420. SER: Valuations; restorations (quality antique furniture only). VAT: Spec.

Christine Schell LAPADA
Crown Arcade, 119 Portobello Rd. W11. Open Sat. only. *STOCK: Unusual tortoiseshell, silver and enamel objects, late 19th to early 20th C, £150-£2,500.* TEL: 0171 352 5563.

Schredds of Portobello LAPADA
107 Portobello Rd. W11 2QB. (H.J. and G.R. Schrager). Est. 1969. Open Sat. 7.30-3.30. SIZE: Small. *STOCK: Collectors' silver, 17th-19th C, £10-£1,000; Wedgwood, 18th-19th C.* TEL: 0181 348 3314; home - same; fax - 0181 341 5971. SER: Valuations; buys at auction. FAIRS: West Kensington (Jan. and Aug). VAT: Stan/Spec.

W11 continued

The Silver Fox Gallery
121 Portobello Rd. W11 2DY. Open Sat. only 6-3. SIZE: 32+ dealers. *STOCK: Antique jewellery - cameos, hardstone, shell, lava, coral, amber, ivory, jet, tortoiseshell, piqué, micro-mosaics, pietra-dura, Art Nouveau, plique é jour, horn pendants, Arts and Crafts, Art Deco, enamels, Austro-Hungarian, cut-steel, Berlin iron, Scottish, Victorian silver and gold, Alberts, Albertines, longuards, curbs, gates, fobs, seals, intaglios, pocket and vintage wrist watches, cufflinks, fine diamonds, rare gemstones, 18th C to Art Deco, from under £50-£1,000+.*TEL: 0171 243 8027; fax - same. FAIRS: Olympia; Park Lane Hotel. VAT: Stan/Spec/Global.

Justin F. Skrebowski Prints
2nd Floor, 288 Westbourne Grove. W11 2PS. Est. 1985. Open Sat. 9-4, otherwise by appointment. SIZE: Small. *STOCK: Prints, engravings and lithographs, 1700-1850, £50-£500; oil paintings, 1700-1900, £200-£1,500; watercolours, drawings including Old Masters, 1600-1900, £50-£1,000; modern mahogany folio stands and easels; frames - gilt, rosewood, maple, carved, 18th-19th C.* PARK: Meters. TEL: 0171 792 9742; mobile - 0374 612474. SER: Valuations. VAT: Stan/Spec.

David Slater
170 Westbourne Grove. W11 2RW. Est. 1961. Open 9.30-1 and 2-5.30, Sat. 10-1. SIZE: Large. *STOCK: General antiques, decorative items.* PARK: Easy. TEL: 0171 727 3336. VAT: Stan.

Colin Smith and Gerald Robinson Antiques
105 Portobello Rd. W11 2QB. Est. 1979. Open Sat., and Fri. by appointment. SIZE: Large. *STOCK: Tortoiseshell, £100-£2,000; silver, ivory and crocodile items.* TEL: 0181 994 3783/0171 225 1163. FAIRS: Olympia. VAT: Stan.

Louis Stanton BADA
299 and 301 Westbourne Grove. W11 2QA. (L.R. and S.A. Stanton). CINOA. Est. 1965. Open 10-1 and 2-6. SIZE: Medium. *STOCK: Early English oak and walnut furniture, tapestries, sculpture, metalware, objets d'art, pre-1750, £20-£25,000.* PARK: Easy. TEL: 0171 727 9336; fax - 0171 727 5424. SER: Valuations; buys at auction. VAT: Stan/Spec.

Stern Art Dealers LAPADA
46 Ledbury Rd. W11 2AB. (David Stern). Est. 1963. Open 10-6. SIZE: Medium. *STOCK: Oil paintings, 19th-20th C, £500-£6,000.* LOC: Off Westbourne Grove near Portobello. PARK: Easy. TEL: 0171 229 6187. SER: Valuations; restorations. VAT: Stan.

W11 continued

June and Tony Stone Fine Antique Boxes LAPADA

75 Portobello Rd. W11 2BQ. Open 10.30-4.30, Sat. 7-5. CL: Mon. *STOCK: Fine boxes especially tea caddies, 18th-19th C, £200-£10,000.* TEL: 0171 221 1121; office - 01273 500212; mobile - 0468 382424; fax - 01273 500024. FAIRS: Olympia (June and Feb). VAT: Stan/Spec.

Stouts Antiques Market

144 Portobello Rd. W11 2DZ Open Sat. only 6.30-4. TEL: 0171 727 3649; fax - 01923 897618; mobile - 0850 375501. Below are listed some of the dealers at this market.

John M. Cserny

19th-20th C decorative paintings. TEL: 0181 748 7972.

James Forbes Fine Art

Est. 1982. *English works of art, jewellery and silver, from 1700, £50-£5,000.* TEL: 01562 730976; mobile - 0802 291804. VAT: Stan/Spec.

I.S. Jewellery

Antique to Modern jewellery including brooches, rings, gold chains.

Kleanthous Antiques Ltd LAPADA

Est. 1969. *Specially selected pieces for the discerning buyer. Jewellery, Georgian, Victorian, Art Nouveau, Art Deco, to 1950; vintage pocket and wrist watches by Rolex, Cartier, Patek Phillipe, Vacheron and Constantin, Jaeger le Coultre, Longines, I.W.C., Universal and Omega; English and Continental silver, 18th-20th C; boudior, desk, carriage and mantel clocks; objects of vertu. Full guarantee with all purchases.* TEL: 0171 727 3649; fax - 0181 980 1199 and 01923 897618; mobile - 0850 375501/375502. VAT: Stan/Spec.

B.G.L. Lenisa

Antique toys, jewellery and cameras. TEL: 0171 603 3706.

Leon

Pocket, fob and wrist watches, 1700-1950.

S. and G. Antiques

(G. Sirett). *Specialist in miniature porcelain cups and saucers, teasets and vases, £25-£500; English and Continental glass, £25-£1,000; Meissen porcelain and objets d'art, £20-£5,000.* TEL: 0171 229 2178 (Sat.); 0181 907 7140; fax - 0181 909 3277; mobile - 0860 863360. VAT: Stan/Spec.

Silver - Henry

Antique silver flatware, small collectibles including snuff boxes. TEL: 0171 226 9777 (answerphone).

Sirett Antiques Ltd

(Mrs A. M. Sirett). Est. 1976. *Chinese porcelain and objects.* TEL: 0171 229 2178. VAT: Stan.

Chris Yang

Oriental ceramics and works of art. TEL: Mobile - 0956 422846.

W11 continued

Temple Gallery

6 Clarendon Cross. W11 4AP. (R.C.C. Temple). Est. 1959. Open 10-6, weekends and evenings by appointment. SIZE: Large. *STOCK: Icons, Russian and Greek, 12th-16th C, £1,000-£50,000.* PARK: Easy. TEL: 0171 727 3809; fax - 0171 727 1546. SER: Valuations; restorations; buys at auction (icons). VAT: Spec.

Themes and Variations

231 Westbourne Grove. W11 2SE. (L. Fawcett). Open 10-1 and 2-6, Sat 10-6. *STOCK: Post war and contemporary decorative items, furniture, glass, ceramics, carpets, lamps, jewellery.* TEL: 0171 727 5531; fax - 0171 221 6378.

Tomkinson Stained Glass

87 Portobello Rd. W11 2QB. (S. Tomkinson). Open 10-5, Sat. 7-5. SIZE: Medium. *STOCK: Stained glass windows.* LOC: 5 minutes from Notting Hill Gate underground. PARK: Easy. TEL: 0171 267 1669; mobile - 0831 861641. SER: Valuations; restorations (as stock). VAT: Stan.

Christina Truscott

Geoffrey Van Arcade, 105-107 Portobello Rd. W11 2QB. Est. 1967. Open Sat. 6.45-3.30. *STOCK: Lacquer, ivories, tortoiseshell, fans, 18th-19th C, £100-£2,000.* TEL: 01403 730554.

Edric Van Vredenburgh Ltd

105 Portobello Rd. W11 2QB. Est. 1961. Open by appointment only. SIZE: Small. *STOCK: European decorative arts, 1500-1800; sculpture, early objects; Oriental decorative arts, 18th-19th C.* TEL: 0171 727 2739; fax - 0171 792 2092. SER: Valuations; buys at auction. VAT: Stan/Spec.

Victoriana Dolls

101 Portobello Rd. W11 2BQ. (Mrs C. Bond). Open Sat. 8-3 or by appointment. *STOCK: Dolls, toys and accessories.* TEL: Home - 01737 249525.

Virginia

98 Portland Rd., Holland Park. W11 4LQ. (V. Bates). Est. 1971. Open 11-6. SIZE: Medium. *STOCK: Decorative items, £50-£2,000; textiles, clothes and lace, £25-£500; bathroom fittings, £15-£600; all 19th-20th C.* LOC: Holland Park Ave. PARK: Easy. TEL: 0171 727 9908; fax - 0171 229 2198. VAT: Stan.

Johnny Von Pflugh Antiques

286 Westbourne Grove. Est. 1985. Open Sat. 8-5 at Portobello Market or by appointment. SIZE: Small. *STOCK: European works of art, Italian oil paintings, gouaches, 17th-19th C, £300-£1,500; fine ironware, 17th-18th C, £300-£800; medical and scientific instruments, 18th-19th C, £200-£1,000.* LOC: Off Portobello Rd. PARK: Easy. TEL: 0181 740 5306. SER: Valuations; buys at auction (keys, caskets, medical instruments, Italian oil paintings, and gouaches). FAIRS: Olympia (June); Little Chelsea (Scientific and Medical). VAT: Spec.

W11 continued

David and Charles Wainwright
251 Portobello Rd. W11 1LT. Est. 1989. Open 10-6.30, Sun. 11-5. SIZE: Large. *STOCK: Furniture, 15th-20th C including 18th-19th C cupboards, dining tables and architectural pieces, £5-£2000; stonework - urns, mortars, water containers, to 19th C; contemporary wrought iron.* LOC: Corner of Lancaster Rd. PARK: Easy. TEL: 0171 792 1988. FAIRS: Olympia. VAT: Stan.

Graham Walpole LAPADA
187 Westbourne Grove. W11 2RS. Est. 1973. Open 10-5.30. SIZE: Medium. *STOCK: Metalware including brass, bronze, Vienna bronzes, and ormolu; pictures, folk art, lighting, furniture and collectables, £100-£15,000.* LOC: 300 yards off Portobello Rd. PARK: Easy. TEL: 0171 229 0267. FAIRS: Olympia (June). VAT: Stan.

Trude Weaver LAPADA
71 Portobello Rd. Est. 1968. Open 9-5. CL: Mon. and Tues. SIZE: Medium. *STOCK: 18th-19th C furniture, selected objects, textiles.* PARK: Easy. TEL: 0171 229 8738; fax - same. SER: Valuations.

Wolseley Fine Arts plc
12 Needham Rd. W11 2RP. (Rupert Otten and Hannette van der Werf). *STOCK: British and European 20th C drawings and sculpture, works of all description by David Jones, Eric Gill and Edgar Holloway.* TEL: 0171 792 2788; fax - 0171 792 2988. SER: Regular catalogues on subscription.

World Famous Portobello Market
177 Portobello Rd. and 1-3 Elgin Cres. Est. 1951. Open Sat. 5-6. SIZE: 200 dealers. *STOCK: General antiques including ethnic antiquities, bronzes, ivory statues, jade, precious metals, dolls, silver and plate, drinking vessels and costumes; also specialist golf shop.* TEL: 0171 229 8797/328 2320; mobiles - 0831 247215/0850 215131. SER: Valuations; restorations; shipping.

LONDON W13

Quest Antiques
90 Northfields Ave., Ealing. W13 9RT. Est. 1979. Open 10.30-5, Sat. 9.30-4. CL: Mon. and Wed. SIZE: Small. *STOCK: Furniture, 19th C, to £2,000; objects and bric-a-brac, 19th-20th C, £5-£300.* PARK: Easy. TEL: 0181 840 2349; home - same. VAT: Stan.

Rupert's
151 Northfield Ave., Ealing. W13 9QT. (R. Loftus Brigham). Open 10-6 or by appointment. CL: Sat. *STOCK: Early wireless equipment.* TEL: 0181 567 1368.

W13 continued

W.13 Antiques
10 The Avenue, Ealing. W13 8PH Open Tues., Thurs. and Sat. 10-5 or by appointment. SIZE: Medium. *STOCK: Furniture, china and general antiques, 18th-20th C.* LOC: Off Uxbridge Rd., West Ealing. PARK: Easy. TEL: 0181 998 0390. SER: Valuations. VAT: Stan.

LONDON W14

Andy's All Pine
OBQ, 70 Russell Rd., Kensington. W14 8YL. (A. Gibb). Open 9-5, weekends by appointment. *STOCK: Victorian pine.* TEL: 0171 371 1969; fax - 0171 602 8655.

Charleville Gallery
7 Charleville Rd., West Kensington. W14 9JL. (F. King). Est. 1986. Open Wed., Thurs. and Fri. 10-6 or by appointment. *STOCK: Textiles, shawls, cushions, bedspreads, linen, £5-£2,000.* LOC: 2 min. walk from West Kensington station or off M4 onto North End Rd. PARK: Easy. TEL: 0171 385 3795; home - 0171 727 2625.

Stephen Garratt (Fine Paintings)
60 Addison Rd. W14 8JJ. Open by appointment only. *STOCK: Oils and watercolours, 18th-20th C.* TEL: 0171 603 0681.

Marshall Gallery
67 Masbro Rd. W14 0LS. (D. A. and J. Marshall). Resident. Est. 1978. Open 10-6, Sat. 10-5. CL: Mon. SIZE: Medium. *STOCK: French and decorative furniture, £500-£20,000; objects and lighting, £200-£12,000; pictures, from £100; all 18th-20th C.* LOC: Just behind Olympia, off Hammersmith Rd. PARK: Easy. TEL: 0171 602 3317. SER: Restorations (furniture, re-gilding, re-wiring). VAT: Spec.

D. Parikian
3 Caithness Rd. W14 0JB. Open by appointment. *STOCK: Antiquarian books, mythology, iconography, emblemata, Continental books pre-1800.* TEL: 0171 603 8375; fax - 0171 602 1178.

Simpsons - Bespoke Carvings
Blythe Hall, 100 Blythe Rd. W14 0HE. (S. Yardy). Open by appointment. *STOCK: Mirrors - antique including pine and new hand-carved; decorative pieces.* TEL: 0171 603 8625.

LONDON SW1

A.D.C. Heritage Ltd BADA
SW1V 4PB. (F. and T. Raeymaekers and E. Bellord). Open by appointment only. *STOCK: Silver, old Sheffield plate.* TEL: 0171 976 5271; fax - 0171 976 5898. SER: Valuations; restorations; buys at auction.

Didier Aaron (London)Ltd BADA
21 Ryder St., St. James's. SW1Y 6PX. Open 10-6. CL: Sat. SIZE: Large. *STOCK: French furniture, 18th C, £5,000-£500,000; Old Master and 19th C pictures, £5,000-£500,000; objets d'art, £1,000-£50,000.* LOC: 20 yds. from Christie's. TEL: 0171 839 4716. FAIRS: Paris Biennale. VAT: Stan/Spec.

Ackermann & Johnson BADA
27 Lowndes St. SW1X 9HY. Est. 1963. Open 9-5.30, Sat. by appointment. SIZE: Medium. *STOCK: English paintings especially sporting, 18th-20th C.* PARK: Meters. TEL: 0171 235 6464. SER: Valuations; restorations. VAT: Spec.

SW1 continued

Addison-Ross Gallery
40 Eaton Terrace, Belgravia. SW1. (T.C.A. and D.A.A. Ross). *STOCK: Paintings and prints especially sporting and natural history.* TEL: 0171 730 1536. SER: Interior design (pictures).

J. A. Allen & Co. (The Horseman's Bookshop) Ltd
1 Lower Grosvenor Pl. SW1W 0EL. Est. 1926. Open 9-5.30. CL: Sat. pm. *STOCK: Horse books, from 1600.* PARK: Meters. TEL: 0171 834 5606; fax - 0171 233 8001. VAT: Stan.

Verner Åmell Ltd
4 Ryder St., St. James's. SW1Y 6QB. Open 10-5.30. CL: Sat. *STOCK: Dutch and Flemish Old Masters, 16th-17th C; 18th C French and 19th C Scandinavian paintings.* TEL: 0171 925 2759.

Albert Amor Ltd
37 Bury St., St. James's. SW1Y 6AU. Est. 1837. Open 9.30-4.30. CL: Sat. SIZE: Small. *STOCK: 18th C English ceramics, especially first period Worcester and blue and white porcelain.* PARK: Meters. TEL: 0171 930 2444; fax - 0171 930 9067. SER: Valuations; buys at auction. VAT: Spec.

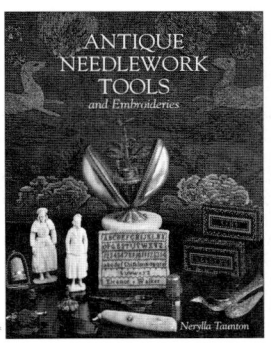

SW1 continued

Anno Domini Antiques BADA
66 Pimlico Rd. SW1W 8LS. (F. Bartman). Est. 1960. Open 10-1 and 2.15-6. CL: Sat. pm. SIZE: Large. *STOCK: Furniture, 17th to early 19th C, £500-£20,000; mirrors, 17th-19th C, £300-£3,000; glass, screens, decorative items and tapestries, £15-£10,000.* Not Stocked: Silver, jewellery, arms, coins. LOC: From Sloane Sq. go down Lower Sloane St., turn left at traffic lights. PARK: Easy. TEL: 0171 730 5496; home - 0171 352 3084. SER: Buys at auction. VAT: Stan/Spec.

Antiquités
227 Ebury St. SW1 8UT. (A. De Cacqueray). Open 10-6, Sat. 11-4. *STOCK: French and Continental furniture, objets d'art.* TEL: 0171 730 5000.

Antiquus
90-92 Pimlico Rd. SW1W 8PL. (E. Amati). Open 9.30-5.30. SIZE: Large. *STOCK: Classical, medieval and Renaissance works of art, paintings, textiles and glass.* LOC: Near Sloane Sq. underground station. PARK: Meters in Holbein Place. TEL: 0171 730 8681; fax - 0171 823 6409.

The Armoury of St. James's Military Antiquarians
17 Piccadilly Arcade, Piccadilly. SW1Y 6NH. Open 9.30-6. SIZE: Small. *STOCK: British and foreign orders, decorations and medals, 18th C to date, £1-£50,000; militaria; toy and hand-painted collectors model soldiers, £4-£4,000.* LOC: Between Piccadilly and Jermyn St. TEL: 0171 493 5082. SER: Valuations. VAT: Stan/Spec.

Artemis Fine Arts Limited LAPADA
15 Duke St., St. James's. SW1Y 6DB. (Adrian Eeles and Katharina Mayer Haunton). SLAD. Open 10-5. CL: Sat. *STOCK: Old Master, 19th C and modern drawings and prints.* TEL: 0171 930 8733.

Astleys
16 Piccadilly Arcade. SW1. Est. 1862. CL: Sat. pm. *STOCK: Meerschaum pipes, 19th C, £30-£1,500; pottery, porcelain, primitive and Oriental pipes, £30-£1,500; smoking accessories, cigar boxes, smoking cabinets, tobacco jars, 19th C, £20-£200.* PARK: Meters. TEL: 0171 499 9950. SER: Valuations; restorations (pipes). VAT: Stan.

Hilary Batstone Decorative Antiques
LAPADA

51 Kinnerton St. SW1. Est. 1983. Open 10-5, Sat. by appointment. SIZE: Small. *STOCK: Painted furniture, £500-£5,000; decorative objects, £50-£1,000; textiles including antique curtains, tassels and tie-backs. Lighting, £50-£3,000; garden statuary, £200-£5,000, both 19th-20th C.* LOC: From Knightsbridge, left into Wilton Place, then right. PARK: Motcomb Street garage. TEL: 0171 259 6070. SER: Restorations (lighting including conversions); shades made to order. FAIRS: Decorative Antiques and Textiles, Chelsea, LAPADA. VAT: Spec.

Chris Beetles Ltd
10 Ryder St., St. James's. SW1Y 6QB. Open 10-5.30, by appointment at weekends. SIZE: Large. *STOCK: English watercolours, paintings and illustrations, 18th-20th C, £500-£50,000.* LOC: 100yds. from Royal Academy. PARK: Meters. TEL: 0171 839 7551. SER: Valuations; framing. VAT: Spec.

Belgrave Carpet Gallery Ltd
91 Knightsbridge. SW1. (A.H. Khawaja). Open 9.30-6.30. *STOCK: Hand knotted Oriental carpets and rugs.* TEL: 0171 235 2541/245 9749.

Blanchard (London) Ltd
86/88 Pimlico Rd. SW1W 8PL. Est. 1990. Open 10-6, Sat. 10-3. SIZE: Medium. *STOCK: English and Continental furniture, lighting and objets d'art.* LOC: Near Sloane Sq. underground station. TEL: 0171 823 6310; fax - 0171 823 6303. SER: Valuations; restorations; buys at auction. VAT: Stan/Spec.

John Bly BADA LAPADA
27 Bury St., St. James's. SW1Y 6AL. (N., J. and V. Bly). Est. 1891. Open 9.30-5, Sat. by appointment. *STOCK: English furniture, silver, glass, porcelain and pictures, 18th-19th C.* TEL: 0171 930 1292.

J.H. Bourdon-Smith Ltd BADA
24 Mason's Yard, Duke St., St. James's. SW1Y 6BU. Est. 1954. Open 9.30-6. CL: Sat. SIZE: Medium. *STOCK: Silver, 1680-1830, £50-£15,000; Victorian and modern silver, 1830 to date, £25-£10,000.* PARK: Meters. TEL: 0171 839 4714. SER: Valuations; restorations (silver); buys at auction. FAIRS: Chelsea; British International (Birmingham); Harrogate; Grosvenor House; BADA; New York; San Francisco; Hong Kong. VAT: Stan/Spec.

Robert Bowman BADA
Est. 1975. Strictly by appointment. SIZE: Medium. *STOCK: Sculpture in bronze, marble and terracotta, early 19th C to early 20th C, £1,000-£200,000.* LOC: Close to Sloane Square. PARK: Metered bays. TEL: 0171 730 8057; fax - 0171 259 9195. SER: Valuations; restorations (bronze, marble and terracotta). FAIRS: Olympia, Maastricht, Singapore, New York. VAT: Spec.

Brisigotti Antiques Ltd
44 Duke St., St. James's. SW1Y 6DD. Open 9.30-5.30. *STOCK: European works of art, Old Master paintings.* TEL: 0171 839 4441; fax - 0171 976 1663.

SW1 continued

Camerer Cuss and Co

17 Ryder St., St. James's. SW1Y 6PY. Est. 1788. Open 9.30-5. CL: Sat. SIZE: Medium. *STOCK: Clocks, 1600-1910, £250-£30,000; watches, 1600-1930, £100-£35,000.* TEL: 0171 930 1941. SER: Valuations; restorations (clocks and watches); buys at auction. VAT: Stan/Spec.

John Carlton-Smith BADA

17 Ryder St., St. James's. SW1Y 6PY. Open 9.30-5.30. CL: Sat. *STOCK: Clocks, barometers, chronometers, 17th-19th C.* TEL: 0171 930 6622. SER: Valuations. VAT: Spec.

David Carritt Limited

15 Duke St., St. James's. SW1Y 6DB. (Timothy Bathurst, Colin Anson, Sebastian Goetz and Adrian Eeles). Open 10-5. CL: Sat. *STOCK: Old Master, 19th C and modern paintings, drawings and prints.* TEL: 0171 930 8733.

Miles Wynn Cato

60 Lower Sloane St. SW1W 8BP. Open Mon.-Fri. 9.30-5.30 and by appointment. *STOCK: English and Welsh pictures and works of art, 1550-1950.* TEL: 0171 259 0306; fax - 0171 259 0305.

Chaucer Fine Arts Ltd

45 Pimlico Rd. SW1W 8NE. Open Mon.-Fri. 10-6, and by appointment. *STOCK: Old Master paintings, sculpture and works of art.* TEL: 0171 730 2972/5872.

Ciancimino Ltd

99 Pimlico Rd. SW1W 8PH. Open 10-6, Sat. by appointment. *STOCK: English and European fine furniture and decorative works of art, early 19th C.* TEL: 0171 730 9950/9959; fax - 0171 730 5365.

Classic Bindings

61 Cambridge St. SW1V 4PS. (Sasha Koziell). Est. 1989. Open 9.30-1 and 2-5.30, Sat. 10.30-1. SIZE: Medium. *STOCK: Bindings, 18th to early 20th C, £8-£150.* LOC: Off Warwick Way, Pimlico. PARK: Easy. TEL: 0171 735 1872; fax - 0171 630 6632. SER: Valuations; restorations (rebinding); buys at auction. VAT: Stan.

Cobra and Bellamy

149 Sloane St. SW1X 9BZ. (V. Manussis and T. Hunter). Est. 1976. Open 10.30-6. SIZE: Medium. *STOCK: Jewellery and designer jewellery, 20th C, £50-£1,000.* TEL: 0171 730 2823. VAT: Stan.

Edward Cohen

40 Duke St., St. James's. SW1. *STOCK: Paintings.* TEL: 0171 839 5180. VAT: Spec.

Cornucopia

12 Upper Tachbrook St. SW1V 1SH. Est. 1967. Open 11-6. SIZE: Large. *STOCK: Jewellery, 20th C clothing and accessories.* PARK: Meters. TEL: 0171 828 5752.

SW1 continued

Cox and Company

37 Duke St., St. James's. SW1Y 6DF. (Mr and Mrs R. Cox). Est. 1972. Open 10-5.30, Sat. by appointment. SIZE: Small. *STOCK: European paintings, 19th-20th C, £1,000-£20,000.* LOC: Off Piccadilly. TEL: 0171 930 1987. SER: Valuations; restorations; buys at auction. VAT: Spec.

Peter Dale Ltd LAPADA

11/12 Royal Opera Arcade, Pall Mall. SW1Y 4UY. Est. 1955. Open 9.30-5. CL: Sat. SIZE: Medium. *STOCK: Firearms, 16th-19th C; edged weapons, armour, 14th-19th C; militaria.* LOC: Arcade behind Her Majesty's Theatre and New Zealand House. PARK: 350yds. Whitcomb St., Public Garage. TEL: 0171 930 3695. SER: Valuations; buys at auction. FAIRS: Arms, spring and autumn. VAT: Spec.

Kenneth Davis (Works of Art) Ltd

15 King St., St. James's. SW1Y 6QU. Open 9-5. CL: Sat. *STOCK: Antique silver and works of art.* TEL: 0171 930 0313; fax - 0171 976 1306.

Shirley Day Ltd BADA

91b Jermyn St. SW1Y 6JB. Est. 1967. *STOCK: Indian, Himalayan and South East Asian sculpture; Japanese screens and paintings.* TEL: 0171 839 2804; fax - 0171 839 3334. VAT: Spec.

Alastair Dickenson Fine Silver Ltd

90 Jermyn St. SW1Y 6JD. Est. 1971. Open 9.30-5.30. CL: Sat. SIZE: Small. *STOCK: Fine English, Irish and Scottish silver, 16th to early 19th C; unusual collectable silver - vinaigrettes, wine labels, card cases, caddy spoons, snuff boxes; Arts and Crafts silver including Omar Ramsden.* LOC: Off Duke St. PARK: Meters. TEL: 0171 839 2808; fax - 0171 839 2809; mobile - 0976 283530. SER: Valuations; restorations (repairs, gilding, re-plating), replacement cruet and ink bottles; buys at auction. VAT: Spec.

Simon Dickinson Ltd

58 Jermyn St. SW1Y 6LX. (Simon Dickinson and David Ker). SLAD. Open 10-5.30, Fri. 10-4.30. CL: Sat. SIZE: Large. *STOCK: Important Old Master and Modern Master paintings.* LOC: 2 mins. from Piccadilly. TEL: 0171 493 0340; fax - 0171 493 0796. SER: Valuations; restorations; buys at auction. VAT: Spec.

Douwes Fine Art Ltd

38 Duke St., St. James's. SW1Y 6DF. SLAD. Est. 1805. Open 9.30-5.30. CL: Sat. SIZE: Medium. *STOCK: Old Master paintings, drawings, watercolours, prints.* PARK: Meters. TEL: 0171 839 5795. VAT: Spec.

Eaton Gallery LAPADA

34 Duke St., St. James's and 9 and 12a Princes Arcade, Jermyn St. SW1Y 6DF. (D. George). Open 10-5.30. *STOCK: English and European paintings, 19th-20th C and contemporary.* TEL: 0171 930 5950; fax - 0171 839 8076.

SW1 continued

Christopher Edwards

63 Jermyn St., St. James's. SW1Y 6LX. Appointment preferred. *STOCK: English literature, to 1900; early Continental books, all subjects.* TEL: 0171 495 4263; fax - 0171 495 4264.

Fernandes and Marche LAPADA

23 Motcomb St. SW1X 8LB. Est. 1956. Open 9.30-5.30. CL: Sat. and Sun. except by appointment. SIZE: Medium. *STOCK: English furniture, giltwood including mirrors and consoles, 18th C.* PARK: Meters. TEL: 0171 235 6773; fax - 0171 823 2234. VAT: Spec.

N. and I. Franklin BADA

11 Bury St., St. James's. SW1Y 6AB. Open 9.30-5.30. CL: Sat. *STOCK: Fine silver and works of art.* TEL: 0171 839 3131; fax - 0171 839 3132.

Victor Franses Gallery BADA

57 Jermyn St., St. James's. SW1Y 6LX. Est. 1948. Open 10-5, Sat. by appointment. *STOCK: 19th C animalier bronzes, rare carpets and rugs.* TEL: 0171 493 6284/629 1144; fax - 0171 495 3668. SER: Valuations; restorations.

S. Franses Ltd

Jermyn St. at Duke St., St. James's. SW1Y 6JD. Est. 1909. Open 9-5. CL: Sat. SIZE: Large. *STOCK: Historic and decorative tapestries, carpets, fabrics and textiles.* TEL: 0171 976 1234. SER: Valuations; restorations; cleaning. VAT: Spec.

Frost and Reed Ltd (Est. 1808) BADA

2-4 King St., St James's. SW1Y 6QP. SLAD. Open 9-5.30. CL: Sat. *STOCK: Fine 19th C British and Continental paintings, marine and sporting pictures, Impressionist drawings and watercolours; works by Sir Alfred Munnings, Montague Dawson, Sir William Russell Flint and Marcel Dyf.* PARK: Meters. TEL: 0171 839 4645. VAT: Stan/Spec.

Galerie Moderne Ltd

10 Halkin Arcade, Motcomb St. SW1X 8JT. Open 9.30-6, Sat. by appointment. *STOCK: René Lalique glass; Sèvres porcelain, 1850-1950; vintage cocktail shakers; antique automobile posters.* TEL: 0171 245 6907.

Gallery '25

6 Halkin Arcade, West Halkin St., Belgravia. SW1. (D. Iglesis). Est. 1969. Open 9.30-5.30, Sat. 10-2. SIZE: Medium. *STOCK: Art glass, £100-£5,000; signed furniture, £1,000-£10,000; decorative fine art, £500-£5,000; all 1900-1930.* LOC: Arcade between Motcomb St and West Halkin St. PARK: Easy. Cadogan Sq. TEL: 0171 235 5178. SER: Valuations; buys at auction (as stock). FAIRS: Park Lane; Olympia. VAT: Stan/Spec.

SW1 continued

General Trading Co Ltd LAPADA

144 Sloane St. SW1X 9BL. (Julian Geach). Est. 1920. Open 9.30-6. SIZE: Medium. *STOCK: English furniture, £100-£6,000; china, prints, £20-£500; all 18th-19th C.* PARK: 50yds., underground garage (Cadogan Place). TEL: 0171 730 0411. VAT: Stan/Spec.

Joss Graham

10 Eccleston St. SW1W 9LT. Open 10-6. *STOCK: Textiles including rugs, kelims, embroideries, tribal costume and shawls; jewellery, metalwork, furniture, masks and primitive art - Indian, Middle Eastern, Central Asian and African.* TEL: 0171 730 4370; fax - same.

Martyn Gregory Gallery BADA

34 Bury St., St. James's. SW1Y 6AU. SLAD. Open 10-6. CL: Sat. SIZE: Medium. *STOCK: Early English watercolours, 18th-20th C; British paintings, both £500-£100,000; specialists in pictures relating to China and the Far East.* TEL: 0171 839 3731. SER: Valuations. VAT: Spec.

Ross Hamilton Ltd LAPADA

95 Pimlico Rd. SW1W 8PH. (Mark Boyce). Est. 1971. Open 9.30-1 and 2-6, Sat. 11-4. SIZE: Large. *STOCK: English and Continental furniture, 17th-19th C, £1,000-£100,000; porcelain and objects, 18th-19th C, £1,000-£3,000; paintings, 17th-19th C, £1,000-£10,000+.* LOC: 2 minutes walk from Sloane Square. PARK: Side streets. TEL: 0171 730 3015. VAT: Stan/Spec.

Harrods Ltd

Brompton Rd., Knightsbridge. SW1X 7XL. Open 10-6, Wed., Thurs. and Fri. 10-7. SIZE: Large. *STOCK: Fine Victorian, Edwardian and period furniture; clocks, oil paintings and objets d'art.* PARK: NCP. TEL: 0171 730 1234, ext. 5940/2759.

Julian Hartnoll

2nd. Floor, 14 Mason's Yard, Duke St., St. James's. SW1Y 6BU. Est. 1968. Open 2.30-5. *STOCK: 19th-20th C British paintings, drawings and prints especially pre-Raphaelite and John Bratby.* TEL: 0171 839 3842. VAT: Spec.

Hawksmoor

9 West Halkin St. SW1X 8JL. (S. Hunter). Est. 1962. Open 9.30-5.30. SIZE: Large. *STOCK: Furniture, 18th-19th C; pictures, 16th-20th; works of art.* LOC: Just off Sloane St., near Harvey Nicholls. PARK: Nearby. TEL: 0171 235 8989. SER: Valuations; restorations (furniture and paintings); buys at auction. VAT: Spec.

Hazlitt, Gooden and Fox Ltd

38 Bury St., St. James's. SW1Y 6BB. SLAD. Open 9.30-5.30. CL: Sat. SIZE: Large. *STOCK: Paintings, drawings and sculpture.* PARK: Meters. TEL: 0171 930 6422; fax - 0171 839 5984. SER: Valuations; restorations. VAT: Spec.

SW1 continued

Thomas Heneage Art Books LAPADA
42 Duke St., St. James's. SW1Y 6DJ. Est. 1975. Open 10-6 or by appointment. CL: Sat. *STOCK: Art reference books.* TEL: 0171 930 9223; fax - 0171 839 9223; e-mail - 100130. 1050@compuserve.com.

Heraz (David Hartwright Ltd)
2 Halkin Arcade, Motcomb St., Belgravia. SW1X 8JT. Est. 1978. Open 10-6, Sat. by appointment. SIZE: Small. *STOCK: Cushions, 17th-19th C; antique Oriental and European carpets and tapestries.* PARK: Easy. TEL: 0171 245 9497. SER: Valuations; restorations (antique textiles and carpets including cleaning). VAT: Stan.

Hermitage Antiques plc
97 Pimlico Rd. SW1W 8PH. (B. Vieux-Pernon). Est. 1967. Open 10-6, Sat. 10-5, Sun. by appointment. SIZE: Large. *STOCK: Biedermeier, Empire and Russian furniture; oil paintings; decorative arts; chandeliers; bronzes.* Not Stocked: Silver and jewellery. LOC: Off Sloane Square. PARK: Easy. TEL: 0171 730 1973; fax - 0171 730 6586. VAT: Stan/Spec.

Carlton Hobbs BADA
46 Pimlico Rd. SW1W 8LP. Est. 1975. Open 9-6, Sat. 10-5, or by appointment. *STOCK: English and Continental furniture, paintings, chandeliers, works of art, £4,000-£850,000.* TEL: 0171 730 3640/3517; fax - 0171 730 6080.

Christopher Hodsoll Ltd BADA
Bennison, 89-91 Pimlico Rd. SW1W 8PH. Open 9-7, Sat. and Sun. by appointment. *STOCK: Furniture, sculpture, pictures and objects.* PARK: Meters. TEL: 0171 730 3370; fax - 0171 730 1516. VAT: Stan/Spec.

William Hotopf Antiques LAPADA
24 Pimlico Rd. SW1. Open 10-6, Sat. and Sun. by appointment. SIZE: Medium. *STOCK: Furniture, 19th C; Anglo-Irish glass, 18th-19th C.* PARK: Multi-storey or meters. TEL: 0171 730 3971; fax - 0171 730 8703. VAT: Stan/Spec.

Hotspur Ltd BADA
14 Lowndes St. SW1X 9EX. (R.A.B. and B.S. Kern). Est. 1924. Open 8.30-6, Sat. 9.30-1. SIZE: Large. *STOCK: English furniture, 1690-1800.* LOC: Between Belgrave Sq. and Lowndes Sq. PARK: 2 underground within 100yds. TEL: 0171 235 1918. VAT: Spec.

How of Edinburgh
41 St. James's Place. SW1A 1NS. (Mrs G.E.P. How). Est. 1930. Open by appointment only. TEL: 0171 495 5481. VAT: Stan/Spec.

Christopher Howe
93 Pimlico Rd. SW1W 8PH. and 36 Bourne St. SW1W 8JA. Est. 1982. Open 9-7, Sat. 10-2.30. SIZE: Large + warehouse nearby. *STOCK: English and European furniture, 16th-20th C, £100-£50,000; decorative objects and lighting.*

SW1 continued

LOC: Near Sloane Square. PARK: Easy. TEL: 0171 730 7987; fax - 0171 730 0157. SER: Valuations. VAT: Stan/Spec.

Christopher Hull Gallery
17 Motcomb St. SW1X 8LB. Open 10-6, Sat. 10-1. *STOCK: Modern British paintings.* TEL: 0171 235 0500.

Humphrey-Carrasco
43 Pimlico Rd. SW1W 8LP. (David Humphrey and Marylise Carrasco). Est. 1987. Open 10-6, Sat. 10-5. *STOCK: English furniture and lighting, architectural objects, 18th-19th C.* LOC: 10 minute walk from Sloane Sq. PARK: Easy. TEL: 0171 730 9911; fax - same. SER: Buys at auction. FAIRS: Olympia. VAT: Stan/Spec

Sally Hunter Fine Art
11/12 Halkin Arcade, Motcomb St. SW1X 8JT. Open 10-6. CL: Sat. *STOCK: British art, 1920 to date.* TEL: 0171 235 0934.

Malcolm Innes Gallery
7 Bury St.,St. James's. SW1Y 6AL. SLAD. Est. 1973. Open 9.30-6 and some Sats. 10-1. *STOCK: Scottish, landscape, sporting and military pictures.* TEL: 0171 839 8083/4; fax - 0171 839 8085. SER: Restorations; framing. VAT: Spec.

Jeremy Ltd BADA
29 Lowndes St. SW1X 9HX. (G.M. and J. Hill). Est. 1946. Open 8.30-6. SIZE: Large. *STOCK: English and French furniture, objets d'art, glass chandeliers, 18th to early 19th C.* PARK: Easy. TEL: 0171 823 2923. FAIRS: Grosvenor House; IAD New York. VAT: Spec.

Jillings of Belgravia LAPADA
8 Halkin Arcade, Motcomb St. SW1X 8JT. (Doro and John Jillings). Est. 1986. Open 10-6, Sat. 10-3. SIZE: Small. *STOCK: Clocks including restored longcase, bracket, bronze ormolu and wall; barometers and small scientific instruments, all 18th-19th C, £500-£25,000.* LOC: 5 minutes from Harrods - Sloane St., left into Cadogan Place, over Lowndes St. into West Halkin St., left into Halkin Arcade. PARK: Meters or Motcomb St. Garage. TEL: 0171 235 8600; fax - 0171 235 9898. SER: Valuations; restorations (hand cleaning and over-hauling of English and French antique clocks and barometers; repairs and case restoration including gilding). FAIRS: LAPADA. VAT: Spec.

Derek Johns Ltd
12 Duke St., St. James's. SW1Y 6BN. SLAD. Open 9.30-6. CL: Sat. *STOCK: Old Master paintings.* TEL: 0171 839 7671; fax - 0171 930 0986.

Lucy Johnson BADA LAPADA
SW1. CINOA. Est. 1982. Open by appointment. SIZE: Medium. *STOCK: Fine furniture; English Delftware; period interiors, 1660-1714.* PARK: Easy. TEL: 0171 465 5743; fax - same. FAIRS: Olympia. VAT: Stan/Spec.

SW1 continued

The Hugh Johnson Collection
68 St. James's St. SW1A 1PH. Open 9.30-5.30. CL: Sat. *STOCK: Antique and modern wine accessories including decanters, glasses, funnels, port tongs.* TEL: 0171 491 4912; fax - 0171 493 0602.

Peter Jones
Sloane Sq. SW1W 8EL. (John Lewis plc). Est. 1945. Open 9.30-6, Wed. 10-7. SIZE: Large. *STOCK: 18th and 19th C furniture, boxes and pictures.* LOC: Fourth floor. TEL: 0171 730 3434.

Keshishian BADA
73 Pimlico Rd. SW1W 8NE. Est. 1978. Open 9.30-6, Sat. 10-5. SIZE: Large. *STOCK: European and Oriental carpets, to late 19th C; Aubussons, mid 19th C; European tapestries, 16th-18th C; Arts and Crafts and Art Deco carpet specialists.* LOC: Off Lower Sloane St. PARK: Easy. TEL: 0171 730 8810; fax - 0171 730 8803. SER: Valuations; restorations. VAT: Stan/Spec.

Knightsbridge Coins
43 Duke St., St. James's. SW1. Open 10-6. CL: Sat. *STOCK: Coins - British, American and South African; medals.* TEL: 0171 930 7597/930 8215.

Kojis Antique Jewellery Ltd
Harrods Fine Jewellery Room, Harrods Ltd., Brompton Rd., Knightsbridge. SW1X 7XL. Open 10-6, Wed., Thurs. and Fri. 10-7. *STOCK: Antique and contemporary jewellery and objects; jade.* TEL: 0171 730 1234 ext. 4062/4072. SER: Valuations; repairs; re-stringing (pearls); designs.

Bob Lawrence Gallery
93 Lower Sloane St. SW1. Est. 1972. Open 10-6. SIZE: Small. *STOCK: Decorative arts – furniture, paintings, objects and furnishings, £50-£10,000.* LOC: 2 minutes Sloane Sq., adjacent Pimlico Rd. PARK: Easy. TEL: 0171 730 5900; fax – 0171 730 5902. SER: Valuations; restorations; buys at auction. VAT: Stan/Spec.

Clare Lawrence Ltd
3 Bury St., St James's. SW1Y 6AB. Est. 1986. Open 11-5. CL: Sat. SIZE: Medium. *STOCK: Chinese snuff bottles and Chinese glass, 18th-19th C.* LOC: Off King St. and Jermyn St., St James's. PARK: St James Sq. TEL: 0171 930 2778. SER: Valuations; restorations; buys at auction. FAIRS: Santa Monica; Miami Beach; Snuff Bottle Convention. VAT: Spec.

Le Pavillon de Sèvres Ltd
9 Halkin Arcade, Motcomb St. SW1X 8JT. Open 9.30-6, Sat. by appointment. *STOCK: 20th C Sèvres porcelain.* TEL: 0171 235 0937.

Lennox Money (Antiques) Ltd
93 Pimlico Rd. SW1W 8PH. (L.B. Money). Est. 1964. Open 9.45-6. CL: Sat. pm. SIZE: Large. *STOCK: Indian colonial and furniture made of unusual woods; chandeliers and textiles.* LOC: 200yds. south of Sloane Sq. TEL: 0171 730 3070. VAT: Spec.

SW1 continued

M. and D. Lewis
84 Pimlico Rd. SW1. Open 9.30-5.30, Sat. 9.30-12, Sun. by appointment. *STOCK: Continental and Victorian furniture, porcelain, bronzes.* TEL: 0171 730 1015; fax - 0171 727 3908 (after 6). VAT: Stan.

Lion, Witch and Lampshade
89 Ebury St. SW1W 9QU. (Mr. and Mrs N. Dixon). Est. 1984. Open 10.30-5.30, Wed. 12.30-5.30, prior telephone call advisable. CL: Sat. *STOCK: Unusual decorative objects, 18th to early 20th C, £5-£150; lamps, wall brackets, chandeliers and candlesticks, £50-£1,000; rocking horses.* PARK: Easy. TEL: 0171 730 1774. SER: Restorations (porcelain and glass). VAT: Stan/Spec.

Longmire Ltd (Three Royal Warrants)
12 Bury St., St. James's. SW1Y 6AB. Open 9.30-5.30, Sat. in Nov. and Dec. only. *STOCK: Individual antique jewellery, cufflink and dress sets: antique, signed, platinum, gold, gem set, hardstone, pearl, carved crystal or enamel - four vices, fishing, polo, golfing, shooting, big game, ladybird and pigs.* LOC: Coming from Piccadilly, down Duke St., right into King St. past Christies, first right into Bury St. PARK: Easy. TEL: 0171 930 8720; fax - 0171 930 1898. SER: Custom hand engraving or enamelling in colour - any corporate logo, initials, crest, coats of arms or tartan, any animal (cat, dog etc.), racing silks, sailing burgees, favourite hobbies or own automobiles.

MacConnal-Mason Gallery
14 and 17 Duke St., St. James's. SW1Y 6DB. Est. 1893. Open 9-6, Sat. 10-2. SIZE: Large. *STOCK: Pictures, 19th-20th C.* PARK: Meters. TEL: 0171 839 7693/409 7323; fax - 0171 839 6797. SER: Valuations; restorations. VAT: Spec.

The Mall Galleries
The Mall. SW1Y 5BD. Open 10-5 seven days. *STOCK: Paintings.* LOC: Near Trafalgar Sq. TEL: 0171 930 6844; fax - 0171 839 7830. SER: Contemporary art exhibitions held.

Paul Mason Gallery BADA
149 Sloane St. SW1X 9BZ. Est. 1969. Open 9-6, Wed. 9-7, Sat. 9-1. *STOCK: Marine, sporting and decorative paintings and prints, 18th-19th C; period and old frames, portfolio stands, ship models.* LOC: Sloane Sq. end of Sloane St. PARK: Easy. TEL: 0171 730 3683/7359. SER: Valuations; restorations (prints, paintings); buys at auction. FAIRS: England and Europe. VAT: Stan/Spec.

Mathaf Gallery Ltd LAPADA
24 Motcomb St. SW1X 8JU. SLAD. Est. 1975. Open 9.30-5.30. *STOCK: Paintings, Middle East subjects, 19th C.* TEL: 0171 235 0010. SER: Valuations.

SW1 continued

Matthiesen Fine Art Ltd.

7-8 Mason's Yard, Duke St., St. James's. SW1Y 6BU. Est. 1978. Open by appointment only. *STOCK: Fine Italian Old Master paintings, 1300-1800; French and Spanish Old Master paintings.* TEL: 0171 930 2437; fax - 0171 930 1387. SER: Valuations; buys at auction.

Mayorcas Ltd BADA

8 Duke St., St. James's SW1Y 6BN. (J.D. and S.M. Mayorcas). Est. 1930. Open 9.30-5.30, Sat. by appointment. SIZE: Medium. *STOCK: Tapestries, textiles, embroideries, needlework, church vestments, European carpets and rugs.* TEL: 0171 839 3100; fax - 0171 839 3223. SER: Valuations; restorations. VAT: Spec.

McCEd

8 Holbein Place. SW1W 8NL. (John McClenaghan). Open 10-6, Sat. 11-5 or by appointment. *STOCK: 19th C architecturally inspired furniture, lighting, objects and mirrors.* LOC: Between Sloane Square and Pimlico Rd. TEL: 0171 730 4025; fax - same. VAT: Stan/Spec.

McClenaghan

69 Pimlico Rd. SW1W 8NE. Open 10-6, Sat. 11-5. SIZE: Medium. *STOCK: English furniture, 19th C, £500-£20,000; objects, lighting, £300-£30,000.* TEL: 0171 730 4187; fax - same. VAT: Stan/Spec.

Christopher Mendez incorporating Craddock and Barnard

58 Jermyn St. SW1Y 6LP. Est. 1966. Open 10-5.30. CL: Sat. SIZE: Small. *STOCK: Old Master prints.* TEL: 0171 491 0015; fax - 0171 495 4949. SER: Valuations; buys at auction. VAT: Stan.

Thomas Mercer (Chronometers) Ltd

32 Bury St., St. James's. SW1Y 6AU. Open Mon.-Fri. 10-5.30, other times by appointment. SIZE: Medium. *STOCK: Marine chronometers.* LOC: Between Jermyn St. and St. James's St. PARK: Meters. TEL: 0171 930 9300; fax - 0171 321 0350. VAT: Stan/Spec.

Mrs Monro Ltd

16 Motcomb St. SW1X 8LB. Est. 1929. Open 9.30-5.30, Fri. 9.30-5. CL: Sat. SIZE: Medium. *STOCK: Small decorative furniture, £500-£1,000+; china, £50-£500+; rugs; prints; pictures and general decorative items, from £50; all 18th-19th C.* LOC: Between Lowndes Sq. and Belgrave Sq. PARK: Garage nearby. TEL: 0171 235 0326; fax - 0171 259 6305. SER: Restorations (furniture and china). VAT: Stan/Spec.

Moreton Street Gallery

40 Moreton St. SW1V 2PB. (W.M. Pearson - Frasco International Ltd). Est. 1972. Open 9-1 and 2-6. CL: Sat. SIZE: Medium. *STOCK: Contemporary oils, watercolours, limited editions, posters; early engravings - Bunbury, Rowlandson, Hogarth,*

SW1 continued

Gilray and Heath. LOC: Off Belgrave Rd. PARK: Easy. TEL: 0171 834 7773/5; fax - 0171 834 7834. SER: Valuations; restorations; buys at auction (originals and engravings). VAT: Stan.

Guy Morrison

91 Jermyn St. SW1Y 6JB. SLAD. Open 9.30-5.30. CL: Sat. *STOCK: British paintings from 1900.* TEL: 0171 839 1454.

Peter Nahum at The Leicester Galleries

5 Ryder St. SW1Y 6PY. Open 9.30-5.30. CL: Sat. and Sun. except by appointment. SIZE: Large. *STOCK: British and European paintings, works on paper and bronzes, including the Pre-Raphaelites and Modern British, 19th-20th C, £1,000-£100,000+.* LOC: 100yds. from Royal Academy. PARK: Meters. TEL: 0171 930 6059; fax - 0171 930 4678. SER: Valuations. VAT: Spec.

Old Maps and Prints

3rd Floor, Harrods, Knightsbridge. SW1X 7XL. Est. 1976. *STOCK: Maps, 16th C to 1890; engravings (all subjects); watercolours.* TEL: 0171 730 1234, ext. 2124.

Ossowski BADA

83 Pimlico Rd. SW1W 8PH. Est. 1960. Open 9-6. CL: Sat. pm. SIZE: Medium. *STOCK: Carved gilt, 18th C; mirrors, consoles, wood carvings.* TEL: 0171 730 3256. SER: Valuations; restorations (gilt furniture). VAT: Stan/Spec.

Pairs Antiques Ltd

202 Ebury St. SW1W 8UN. (Iain M. Brunt). Est. 1994. Open 9-6, Sat. 10-4, or by appointment. SIZE: Medium. *STOCK: Pairs only - 18th-19th C furniture, £500-£10,000; 18th-20th C decorative objects; 19th C paintings, £3,000-£10,000.* PARK: Meters. TEL: 0171 730 1771; fax - 0171 730 1661. SER: Valuations; restorations; buys at auction. VAT: Stan/Spec.

Paisnel Gallery

22 Mason's Yard, Duke St., St James's. SW1Y 6BU. (Stephen Paisnel). Est. 1977. Open 11-6. CL: Sat. SIZE: Small. *STOCK: British and European paintings, especially Newlyn and St. Ives Schools, 19th-20th C, £1,000-£15,000.* LOC: Duke St. runs between Piccadilly and King St. 1 minute from Christies. PARK: St. James Sq. TEL: 0171 930 9293. SER: VAT: Spec.

The Parker Gallery BADA

28 Pimlico Rd. SW1W 8LJ. (Thomas H. Parker Ltd). SLAD. Est. 1750. Open 9.30-5.30, Sat. by appointment. SIZE: Medium. *STOCK: Historical prints, £45-£1,200; English paintings, £1,000-£30,000; ship models, £95-£30,000.* LOC: 5 minutes from Sloane Sq. TEL: 0171 730 6768; fax - 0171 259 9180. SER: Restorations (as stock); mounting; framing. VAT: Stan/Spec.

SW1 continued

Michael Parkin Fine Art Ltd
11 Motcomb St. SW1X 8LB. SLAD. Open 10-6, Sat. 10-1. *STOCK: British paintings, watercolours, drawings and prints, 1860-1960, £50-£10,000.* PARK: Easy. TEL: 0171 235 8144/1845; fax - 0171 245 9846. VAT: Spec.

Trevor Philip and Sons Ltd BADA
75a Jermyn St., St. James's. SW1Y 6NP. (T. and R. Waterman). Est. 1972. Open 9-6, Sat. 10-4. SIZE: Medium. *STOCK: Early scientific instruments, globes, barometers and ships models; silver and vertu.* PARK: At rear. TEL: 0171 930 2954; fax - 0171 321 0212. SER: Valuations; restorations (clocks and scientific instruments); buys at auction. VAT: Stan/Spec.

Pickering and Chatto Ltd
Incorporating Dawsons of Pall Mall, 17 Pall Mall. SW1Y 5NB. Est. 1820. Open Mon.-Fri. 9.30-5.30, or by appointment. SIZE: Large. *STOCK: English literature, economics, politics, philosophy, science, medicine, manuscripts and autographs.* LOC: 300yds. on right from Trafalgar Sq. PARK: Easy. TEL: 0171 930 2515; fax - 0171 930 8627.

Polak Gallery BADA
21 King St., St. James's. SW1Y 6QY. Est. 1854. Open 9.30-5.30. CL: Sat. SIZE: Medium. *STOCK: English and Continental oils and watercolours, 19th-20th C.* PARK: Meters. TEL: 0171 839 2871. SER: Valuations; restorations. VAT: Spec.

Portland Gallery
9 Bury St., St. James's. SW1Y 6AB. SLAD. Est. 1985. Open 10-6. CL: Sat. SIZE: Medium. *STOCK: Scottish pictures, 20th C, £200-£100,000.* TEL: 0171 321 0422. SER: Valuations; buys at auction. VAT: Spec.

Michael Priest Antiques
27a Motcomb St., Belgrave Sq. SW1X 8JU. Est. 1979. Open 9.30-5, Sat. by appointment. SIZE: Medium. *STOCK: Fine mahogany and walnut, paintings - Old Masters and primitives, late 17th C to mid-19th C, £500-£20,000.* TEL: 0171 235 7241. SER: Valuations; restorations (English furniture, oil paintings). VAT: Spec.

Steven Rich & Michael Rich
39 Duke St., St. James's. SW1Y 6DF. Open daily, Sat. by appointment. SIZE: Medium. *STOCK: Master paintings, 16th-19th C; collectors items.* LOC: Just off Piccadilly. PARK: St. James's Sq. TEL: 0171 930 9308; fax - 0171 930 2088. SER: Valuations. FAIRS: Maastricht, Holland. VAT: Spec. *Trade Only.*

SW1 continued

Rogier Antiques
20A Pimlico Rd. SW1W 8LJ. (Miss Lauriance Rogier). Est. 1980. Open 10-6, Sat. 11-4. SIZE: Small. *STOCK: French and Continental painted and country furniture, 18th-19th C, £1,000-£5,000; lamps and wall sconces, 19th C, from £500; decorative antique and reproduction items, from £300.* LOC: 5 minutes walk from Sloane Sq. PARK: Meters. TEL: 0171 823 4780. SER: Restorations (furniture - polishing, painting, lacquering, gilding, copies, decoration, painted effects, murals, trompe l'oeil). VAT: Spec.

Sainsbury & Mason
145 Ebury St. SW1. Est. 1968. Open 10-1 and 2-5.30. *STOCK: Period Oriental and European works of art, especially Chinese and Japanese, bronzes, lacquer, porcelain, glass and pictures.* TEL: 0171 730 3393/8331; home - 0181 874 4173; fax - 0171 730 8334. VAT: Spec.

Gerald Sattin Ltd BADA
14 King St., St. James's. SW1Y 6QU. (G. and M. Sattin). Est. 1966. Open 9-5.30. CL: Sat. pm. SIZE: Medium. *STOCK: English and Continental porcelain, 1720-1900; English glass, 1700-1900; both £55-£2,500; English silver, 1680-1920, £55-£5,000.* Not Stocked: Oriental and post 1920 items. LOC: Close to Christie's. PARK: Meters. TEL: 0171 493 6557; fax - same. SER: Buys at auction. VAT: Stan/Spec.

Seago BADA
22 Pimlico Rd. SW1W 8LJ. (T.P. and L.G. Seago). Open Mon.-Fri. 9.30-5.30 or by appointment. *STOCK: Fine 17th-19th C garden sculpture and ornaments in marble, stone, bronze, lead, terracotta, cast and wrought iron.* TEL: 0171 730 7502; fax - 0171 730 9179.

Sensation Ltd
SW1. (M. Fenwick). Est. 1958. Open by appointment only. *STOCK: Porcelain, decorative objects, painted furniture.* TEL: 0171 581 1533; fax - same.

Julian Simon Fine Art Ltd BADA
70 Pimlico Rd. SW1W 8LS. (M. and J. Brookstone). Open 10-6, Sat. 10-4 or by appointment. *STOCK: Fine English and Continental pictures, 18th-20th C.* TEL: 0171 730 8673; fax - 0171 823 6116.

Sims, Reed Ltd
43a Duke St., St James's. SW1Y 6DD. Open 10-6, Sat. by appointment. *STOCK: Illustrated rare and in-print books on the fine and applied arts; leather-bound literary sets.* TEL: 0171 493 5660; fax - 0171 493 8468.

SW1 continued

Peta Smyth - Antique Textiles LAPADA
42 Moreton St., Pimlico. SW1V 2PB. GMC. Est. 1977. Open 9.30-5.30. CL: Sat. *STOCK: European textiles and needlework, 17th-19th C, £10-£5,000; tapestries and cushions.* PARK: Easy. TEL: 0171 630 9898; fax - 0171 630 5398. SER: Restorations (needlework, tapestries, textiles). FAIRS: Olympia. VAT: Spec.

Somlo Antiques BADA
7 Piccadilly Arcade. SW1Y 6NH. (G. and S. Somlo). Est. 1972. Open 10-5.30 or by appointment. CL: Sat. SIZE: Medium. *STOCK: Pocket and wrist watches, from 17th C, from £500.* LOC: Between Piccadilly and Jermyn St. PARK: Meters. TEL: 0171 499 6526. SER: Valuations; restorations. VAT: Stan/Spec.

Henry Sotheran Ltd
80 Pimlico Rd. SW1W 8PL. Open 10-6, Sat. 10-4. *STOCK: Fine and rare antique prints of architecture, decorative, natural history, travel and topography.* TEL: 0171 730 8756; fax - 0171 823 6090.

Spink and Son Ltd BADA
5 King St., St. James's. SW1Y 6QS. SLAD. Est. 1666. Open 9-5.30. CL: Sat. SIZE: Large. *STOCK: English paintings and watercolours; jewellery; furniture; Chinese, Japanese, Indian, South East Asian, Himalayan and Islamic works of art; textiles; Greek and Roman to present day coins, banknotes, bullion, orders, medals and decorations, militaria, numismatic books.* PARK: Meters. TEL: 0171 930 7888. SER: Valuations; buys at auction; commission sales on behalf of private collectors; coin auctions. VAT: Stan/Spec.

Robin Symes Ltd
3 Ormond Yard, Duke of York St., St. James's. SW1. Open by appointment only. SIZE: Large. *STOCK: Antiquities, ancient art.* PARK: Meters. TEL: 0171 930 9856/7; 0171 930 5300.

Bill Thomson - Albany Gallery BADA
1 Bury St., St. James's. SW1Y 6AB. (W.B. Thomson). Open 8.30-6, Sat. by appointment. *STOCK: British drawings, watercolours and paintings, 1700-1850 and some 20th C.* TEL: 0171 839 6119; fax - 0171 930 4211.

William Tillman Ltd BADA
30 St. James's St. SW1A 1HB. Open 9.30-5.30, Sat. by appointment. *STOCK: English furniture, 18th C.* TEL: 0171 839 2500.

Trafalgar Galleries BADA
35 Bury St., St. James's. SW1Y 6AY. Open 9.30-6. CL: Sat. *STOCK: Old Master paintings.* LOC: Just south of Piccadilly. TEL: 0171 839 6466.

SW1 continued

Rafael Valls Ltd BADA
11 Duke St., St. James's. SW1Y 6BN. SLAD. Est. 1976. Open Mon.-Fri. 9.30-6. *STOCK: Old Master pictures, Dutch and Flemish, 16th-18th C.* TEL: 0171 930 1144; fax - 0171 976 1596. VAT: Spec.

Rafael Valls Ltd BADA
6 Ryder St., St. James's. SW1Y 6BN. SLAD. Open Mon.-Fri. 9.30-6. *STOCK: Decorative European pictures, 18th-19th C.* TEL: 0171 930 0029; fax - 0171 976 1596. VAT: Spec.

Johnny Van Haeften Ltd BADA
13 Duke St., St. James's. SW1Y 6DB. (J. and S. Van Haeften). SLAD. TEFAF. Est. 1978. Open 10-6, Sat. and Sun. by appointment. SIZE: Medium. *STOCK: Dutch and Flemish Old Master paintings, 16th-17th C, £5,000-£5m.* LOC: Middle of Duke St. TEL: 0171 930 3062/3; fax - 0171 839 6303. SER: Valuations; restorations (Old Masters); buys at auction (paintings including Old Masters). VAT: Spec.

Rupert Wace Ancient Art Ltd
1st Floor, 107 Jermyn St. SW1Y 6EE. Open Mon.-Fri. 10-5. *STOCK: Egyptian, Classical and near Eastern antiquities.* TEL: 0171 495 1623.

Dick Reid's workshop in York at work on the replica chimneypieces for Spencer House.

From an article entitled "Conservation Matters" by Julie Targett which appeared in the July/August 1996 issue of **Antique Collecting**

SW1 continued

Waterman Fine Art Ltd
74A Jermyn St., St. James's. SW1Y 6NP. Open 9-6, Sat. 10-4. *STOCK: 20th C paintings and watercolours.* TEL: 0171 839 5203; fax - 0171 321 0212.

Westenholz Antiques Ltd
76-78 Pimlico Rd. SW1W 8LP. Open 10-6, Sat. by appointment. *STOCK: 18th-19th C furniture, pictures, objects, lamps, mirrors.* TEL: 0171 824 8090.

Whitford Fine Art
6 Duke St., St. James's. SW1Y 6BN. (Adrian Mibus). Open 10-6. CL: Sat. *STOCK: Oil paintings and sculpture, late 19th to 20th C; Post War abstract and pop art.* TEL: 0171 930 9332; fax - 0171 930 5577.

Philip Whyte
32 Bury St., St. James's. SW1Y 6AU. Est. 1972. Open Mon.-Fri. 10-5.30, other times by appointment. SIZE: Medium. *STOCK: Clocks, watches, marine chronometers and other horological items.* LOC: Between Jermyn St. and St. James's St. PARK: Meters. TEL: 0171 321 0353; fax - 0171 321 0350. VAT: Stan/Spec.

Arnold Wiggins and Sons Ltd BADA
4 Bury St., St. James's. SW1Y 6AB. (M. Gregory). Open Mon.-Fri 9-5.30. *STOCK: Picture frames, 16th-19th C.* TEL: 0171 925 0195.

Thomas Williams (Fine Art) Ltd
P O Box 909. SW1. Open by appointment only. *STOCK: Old and modern Master drawings, £300-£150,000.* TEL: 0171 930 7818; fax - 0171 930 7815. SER: Valuations; buys at auction (paintings and drawings).

LONDON SW3

Norman Adams Ltd BADA
8/10 Hans Rd., Knightsbridge. SW3 1RX. Est. 1923. Open 9-5.30, Sat. and Sun. by appointment. SIZE: Large. *STOCK: English furniture, 18th C, £650-£250,000; objets d'art (English and French) £500-£50,000; mirrors, glass pictures, 18th C; clocks and barometers.* LOC: 30yds. off the Brompton Rd., opposite west side entrance to Harrods. TEL: 0171 589 5266; fax - 0171 589 1968. FAIRS: Grosvenor House; BADA. VAT: Spec.

After Noah
261 King's Rd. SW3 5EL. (M. Crawford and Z. Candlin). *STOCK: Arts and Craft oak and similar furniture, 1880's to 1950's, £1-£1,000; iron, iron and brass beds; decorative items, bric-a-brac including candlesticks, mirrors, lighting, kitchenalia and jewellery.* TEL: 0171 351 2610. SER: Restorations. VAT: Stan.

SW3 continued

Maria Andipa & Son Icon Gallery
LAPADA

162 Walton St. SW3 2JL. Est. 1969. Open 11-6. *STOCK: Icons from Greece, Russia, Byzantium, Egypt, Ethiopia, the Middle East and North Africa, 15th-19th C.* TEL: 0171 589 2371. SER: Valuations; restorations; research; collections; represented in the USA.

Antiquarius
131/141 King's Rd. SW3. (Atlantic Antiques Centres Ltd). Est. 1970. Open 10-6. LOC: On the corner of King's Rd. and Flood St., next to Chelsea Town Hall. TEL: Enquiries - 0171 351 5353; fax - 0171 351 5350. Below are listed some of the many specialist dealers at this market.

Jaki Abbott
Stand M11/12. *Jewellery.* TEL: 0171 352 7980.

Giovanna Accossato
Stand K1/6. *Silver, walking sticks and canes.* TEL: 0171 352 7989.

Valeria Alessandri
Stand V26. *Jewellery and ivory.* TEL: 0171 352 4690.

Trevor Allen
Stand V36. *Antique jewellery.* TEL: 0171 352 7061.

AM-PM
Stands V35. (Mr. Ghini). *Vintage watches.* TEL: 0171 352 7989.

Amato Antiques LAPADA
Stand V9. *Antique glass, porcelain and ormolu.* TEL: 0171 352 3666.

S. Arena
Stand E5. *General antiques, silver plate.* TEL: 0171 352 7989.

S. Aritake
Stand E3/4., *Watches, pens and lighters, general.* TEL: 0171 376 5394.

Baptista Arts LAPADA
Stand V10. (John Cox). *Decorative antiques, silver, Art Deco and Art Nouveau.* TEL: 0171 352 5793.

Bernice Barker
Stand R7/8. *Brass and copper.* TEL: 0171 352 8882.

Beauty & The Beast
Stand Q9-10. (E. Bradwin). *Costume jewellery, Art Deco, beauty and the beast, bronze animals.* TEL: 0171 351 5149.

Alexandra Bolla
Stand J1. *Jewellery.* TEL: 0171 352 7989.

Sean Bolster
Stand D1/D2. *Jewellery and objects.* TEL: 0171 376 7348.

SW3 continued

Miss E. Bradwin
Stand T5/6. *Jewellery, Art Deco and bronze animals.* TEL: 0171 351 5149.

Margaret Bristow
Stand T1/2. *Antique silver and plate.* TEL: 0171 352 1285.

Brown & Kingston
Stand V6. *Staffordshire porcelain, Imari, blue and white.* TEL: 0171 376 8881

Derek Brunwin
Stand V25. *Antique jewellery and silver.* TEL: 0171 352 4690.

Miss T. Buchinger
Stand Q2. *Jewellery and silver scent bottles.* TEL: 0171 352 8734.

C. Butterworth
Stand B2/3,C1. *Decorative antiques including lighting.* TEL: 0171 352 3583.

Jasmin Cameron
Stand J6. *Vintage fountain pens, £35-£600; silver ink stands and writing implements, £165-£400; 19th C paint boxes, £190-£1,100; 19th C drinking glasses and decanters, £8-£140.* TEL: 0171 351 4154; fax - 0171 351 5350. SER:Valuations; restorations (fountain pens).

Mrs V. Carroll
Stand N1. *Jewellery and small items.* TEL: 0171 352 8734.

W. Chapman
Stand L1/10. *Corkscrews, general antiques, tortoiseshell.* TEL: 0171 352 7989.

Chelsea Antiques Rug Gallery
Stand V15. (N. Somnez). *Oriental carpets.* TEL: 0171 351 6611.

Chelsea Clocks
Stand H3-4, R1-2. *Clocks and general.* TEL: 0171 352 8646.

SW3 continued

Classic Frames
Stand A7/8. (Paul Dowling). *Antique decorative prints and frames.* TEL: 0171 376 5056.

Claude & Martine
Stand V16. (C. and M. Latreville) *Fine silver and jewellery.* TEL: 0171 352 5964.

Adrian Cohen
Stand M1/16. *Antique silver and silver plate.*

Eli Cohen
Stand Q5. *Jade, netsuke and Oriental art.* TEL: 0171 351 7038.

J. Cowan
Stand N12. *Jewellery.* TEL: 0171 352 1750.

Luigi Cutolo
Stands V30/33. *Period costume jewellery.* TEL: 0171 349 0519.

Jesse Davis **LAPADA**
Stand A9-A11. *Majolica, china, silver.* TEL: 0171 352 4314.

Glen Dewart
Stand P7/8. *Antique prints and paintings.* TEL: 0171 352 4777.

Amber Donnovan
Stand V18. *Vintage watches, gold jewellery.* TEL: 0171 376 7808.

Donald Edge **LAPADA**
Stand V17. *Decorative items, pictures, antique and period jewellery.* TEL: 0171 352 2660.

Mrs. P. Evans
Stand N6/7. *Dolls and accessories.* TEL: 0171 376 4419.

Flight of Fancy
Stand A9-A11. (Davis and Fawkes). *General antiques.* TEL: 0171 352 4314.

SW3 continued

Fothergill & Crowley
Stand J2/3. *Period clothing and textiles.* TEL: 0171 351 0011.

French Glasshouse
Stand P14/15/16. (Mr and Mrs M. Bach). *Art Deco and Art Nouveau, glass and china.* TEL: 0171 376 5394.

S. A. Geris
Stand M2. *Watches.* TEL: 0171 352 6604.

Liliana Giardini
Stand V37. *Jewellery, silver and collectables.*

Mrs E. Gibbons
Stand N15/16. *Antique trextiles, embroideries, lace and samplers.*

C. Gibson
Stand M10. *Silver and plate, general antiques.* TEL: 0171 352 4690.

Brian Gordon LAPADA
Stand G1. *Antique silver and plate.* TEL: 0171 352 5808.

Mrs B. Gunn
Stand M3-4. *Fans, small silver.* TEL: 0171 352 4690.

Stuart Hands
Stand V11. *Antique textiles, small furniture.* TEL: 0171 376 7776.

Jackie Harrison
Stand P5. *Country style antiques.* TEL: 0171 352 8734.

Hayman & Hayman
Stands K2/3/4/5. *Photo frames/scent bottles.* TEL: 0171 351 6568.

Peter A. Jeffs - Aesthetics BADA LAPADA
Stand V3. *Silver, ceramics and decorative arts, 1860-1960, £50-£5,000.* TEL: 0171 352 0395. VAT: Stan/Spec.

Mrs P. A. Kaskimo
Stand C2. *General antiques, paintings.* TEL: 0171 352 7989.

Martin Kaye
Stands V27/28. *Watches, jewellery and silver.*

D. Kelly
Stand L3, M13. *Books.* TEL: 0171 352 4690.

King and Country
Stand V5. (M. Fantham) *Decorative furniture and accessories.* TEL: 0171 376 8781.

Vivika Krell
Stand P6. *Silver and general antiques.* TEL: 0171 352 8734.

SW3 continued

Miss Kukielska
Stand P1. *Antique jewellery, china.* TEL: 0171 352 8734.

Mrs Lapari
Stand L2. *Antique jewellery.* TEL: 0171 352 5592.

Bob Lawrence
Shop U137. *Decorative art, furniture and pictures. Art Nouveau and Art Deco.* TEL: 0171 351 7172.

Mrs L. Lehane
Stand A6. *Antique luggage.*

M. Lexton
Stand N8-11. *Silver.* TEL: 0171 351 5980.

Sam Lindsay
Stand V21. *Antique jewellery.* TEL: 0171 351 7378.

Sylvia Llewelyn
Stands A12/13/E2. *Antique dolls, ceramics, period costume jewellery.* TEL: 0171 351 4981.

Fay Lucas LAPADA
Stand B4/5. *Jewellery and silver.* TEL: 0171 351 6004.

Henry Mann
Stand V14. *Art Deco/Art Nouveau.* TEL: 0171 352 4690.

Mariad Antiques
Stand N13/14. (Mrs M. McClean). *Jewellery and Vienna bronzes.* TEL: 0171 351 9526.

M. Markov
Stand V8. *Jewellery, Clarice Cliff pottery and decorative art.* TEL: 0171 352 4545.

Mrs. J. Martin
Stand A3. *General antiques.* TEL: 0171 352 7989.

Ms. Martinez-Negrilo
Stand P2/3. *Jewellery, porcelain, glass and paintings.* TEL: 0171 352 8734.

G. S. Mathias
Stand R5-6. *Victorian, Edwardian furniture, general, clocks.* TEL: 0171 351 0484.

May Avenue
Stand V13. (Zoe Bajcer). *Art Deco ceramics including Clarice Cliff, Keith Murray.* TEL: 0171 351 5757.

Mrs N. McDonald-Hobley
Stand A4. *Jewellery.* TEL: 0171 351 0154.

William McLeod-Brown
Stand L5-7. *Prints especially botanicals, books.* TEL: 0171 352 4690.

Mrs P. Miller
Stand J4/5. *Jewellery.* TEL: 0171 352 4690.

SW3 continued

Mrs Teresa Molloy
Stand E6. *Oil paintings.* TEL: 0171 352 7989.

Mrs. D. Mousavi
Stand D4. *Gold and silver.* TEL: 0171 352 8734.

Ruth Muggleton
Stand L9. *Silver and plate.* TEL: 0171 376 8449.

R.S. and S. Necus
Stand A18-19. *Silver, plate, objets de vertu.* TEL: 0171 352 2405.

June Newman
Stand Q3/4. *Small inlaid furniture and decorative objects.* TEL: 0171 376 5112.

Sue Norman
Stand L4. *Blue and white transfer ware.* TEL: 0171 352 7217.

Miss J. Palmer
Stand M8/9. *Jewellery and silver.* TEL: 0171 352 0431.

Maria Perez
Stand V22/23. *Jewellery.* TEL: 0171 351 1986.

Linda Perkins
Stand V7. *Antique tiaras and hair accessories.* TEL: 0171 376 5212.

Joanna Piotrowska
Stand Q7/8. *Mirrors and boxes.* TEL: 0171 352 2704.

Miss E. Pollock
Stand G4-6. *General antiques, small silver, jewellery and glass.* TEL: 0171 352 8734.

The Purple Shop
Stand J9-11. (Gardner and Becker). *Antique and period jewellery and Art Nouveau, Art Deco.* TEL: 0171 352 1127.

Mrs Victoria Quiroz
Stand Q14/15. *General antiques.*

Abdul Rabi
Stand P4. *Jewellery and watch repairs.*

Robert Raymond LAPADA
Stand V19. *Antique jewellery.* TEL: 0171 349 0809.

K. Reilly
Stand V4. *Art Nouveau, Art Deco.* TEL: 0171 352 2099.

Mrs Gwen Riley
Stand D5. *Porcelain and china.* TEL: 0171 352 7989.

A. Ronco
Stand V1. *Bronzes and curiosities.* TEL: 0171 376 8116.

SW3 continued

Michelle Rowan
Stand V38. *Jewellery and silver.* TEL: 0171 352 8744.

Salamanca
Stand M14/15. (Mrs D. Martin). *Moorcroft porcelain.* TEL: 0171 351 5829.

Miss Jerri Scott
Stand P9-P11. *General antiques and jewellery.* TEL: 0171 352 2366/352 9471.

M. Simpson
Stand E1. *Antique ivory.* TEL: 0171 352 7989.

Sybarites
Stand V18. *Watches and jewellery.* TEL: 0171 376 7808.

John Szwarc
Stand G2/3. *Jewellery and cuff-links.* TEL: 0171 352 8201.

A. Thompson
Stand V13A. *Antique silver.* TEL: 0171 352 8680.

S. & A. Thompson LAPADA
Stand V12. *Antique silver and small furniture.* TEL: 0171 352 8680.

Simon Thorpe LAPADA
Stand T3-4. *Silver.* TEL: 0171 351 2911; fax - 0171 351 6690.

Brian Tipping
Stand P12. *Antique pipes.* TEL: 0171 352 3315.

Mr. Vidich
Stand A14-17. *Prints, etchings and lithographs.* TEL: 0171 376 4252.

G. Walters
Stand F2-5. *Antique porcelain and silver.* TEL: 0171 376 5467.

West Country Jewellery
Stand M6/7. (David Billing). *Jewellery.* TEL: 0171 376 8252.

XS Baggage
Stand A7/8, B1/6. (Mr and Mrs Lehane) *Antique travel requisites and sporting memorabilia.* TEL: 0171 352 7989.

Miss E. Zakoji
Stand V20. *Antique jewellery.*

Apter Fredericks Ltd BADA
265-267 Fulham Rd. SW3 6HY. (B. and Mrs. C Apter and H. Apter). Open 9.30-5.30, Sat. and evenings by appointment. *STOCK: English furniture, 17th to early 19th C.* TEL: 0171 352 2188; fax - 0171 376 5619. VAT: Stan/Spec.

SW3 continued

Boodle and Dunthorne Ltd
58 Brompton Rd. SW3 1BW. Open 9.30-6. *STOCK: Fine English and French jewellery, 19th-20th C, £100-£30,000.* TEL: 0171 584 6363; 0171 437 5050.

Joanna Booth BADA
247 King's Rd., Chelsea. SW3 5EL. Est. 1963. Open 10-6. SIZE: Medium. *STOCK: Wood carvings, oak furniture, 17th C, £50-£5,000; Old Master drawings, textiles, tapestry.* Not Stocked: Silver, glass, pottery, clocks. PARK: Meters. TEL: 0171 352 8998; fax - 0171 376 7350. SER: Buys at auction. VAT: Spec.

Butler and Wilson
189 Fulham Rd. SW3 6JN. *STOCK: Jewellery, Art Deco, crocodile and leather accessories.* TEL: 0171 352 3045.

John Campbell Picture Frames Ltd
164 Walton St. SW3 2JL. Open 9.30-5.30. *STOCK: 20th C impressionist and modern British oils and watercolours.* TEL: 0171 584 9268; fax - 0171 581 3499. SER: Master framing, carving, gilding and restorations.

Chelsea Antique Market
245A and 253 King's Rd. SW3 5EL. Est. 1965. Open 10-6. SIZE: Large - 30 dealers. *STOCK: General antiques, antiquarian books and prints, jewellery.* LOC: From Sloane Sq. directly along Kings Rd. From South Kensington underground along Sidney St. to Kings Rd., turn right. TEL: 0171 352 5689/1720; stall-holders - 0171 352 1424/5581. VAT: Stan.

Chelsea Rare Books
313 King's Rd. SW3 5EP. (L.S. Bernard). Est. 1968. Open 10-6. *STOCK: Antiquarian books, prints and watercolours.* TEL: 0171 351 0950. VAT: Stan.

Richard Courtney Ltd BADA
112-114 Fulham Rd. SW3 6HU. Est. 1959. Open 9.30-1 and 2-6. CL: Sat. SIZE: Large. *STOCK: English furniture, 18th C, £500-£20,000.* PARK: Easy. TEL: 0171 370 4020. VAT: Spec.

Colin Denny Ltd
18 Cale St. SW3 3QU. Est. 1968. Open 10-6. *STOCK: Marine works of art, 19th C.* TEL: 0171 584 0240. VAT: Stan/Spec.

Robert Dickson and Lesley Rendall Antiques BADA
263 Fulham Rd. SW3 6HY. Est. 1969. Open 10-6, Sat. 10.30-4. SIZE: Medium. *STOCK: Late 18th to early 19th C furniture and works of art, £500-£100,000.* PARK: Easy. TEL: 0171 351 0330. VAT: Spec.

SW3 continued

Dragons of Walton St. Ltd
23 Walton St. SW3 2HX. (R. Fisher). *STOCK: Mainly painted and decorated furniture; hand decorated children's furniture, decorative items.* LOC: Close to Harrods. PARK: Hasker St. or First St. TEL: 0171 589 3795; fax - 0171 584 4570.

Michael Foster BADA
118 Fulham Rd., Chelsea. SW3 6HU. Open 9.30-5.30, Sat. by appointment. *STOCK: 18th C English furniture and works of art.* TEL: 0171 373 3636/3040. SER: Valuations; restorations.

C. Fredericks and Son BADA
92 Fulham Rd. SW3 6HR. (R.F. Fredericks). Open 9.30-5.30, Sat. by appointment. SIZE: Large. *STOCK: Furniture, 18th C, £500-£15,000.* LOC: Near to South Kensington underground station. PARK: Easy. TEL: 0171 589 5847. VAT: Stan/Spec.

Gallery Lingard
Walpole House, 35 Walpole St. SW3 4QS. SLAD. Open by appointment only. *STOCK: Architectural drawings, watercolours, paintings and prints.* TEL: 0171 730 9233; fax - 0171 730 9152.

Gallery Yacou LAPADA
127 Fulham Rd. SW3 6RT. Open 10.30-6, Sat. 11-6. *STOCK: Decorative and antique Oriental and European carpets (room-size and over-size).* LOC: Walking distance from Bibendum. TEL: 0171 584 2929; fax - 0171 584 3535.

David Gill LAPADA
60 Fulham Rd. SW3 6HH. Est. 1986. Open 10-6. SIZE: Medium. *STOCK: Decorative and fine arts, Picasso, Cocteau ceramics and drawings, 1900 to present day.* PARK: Onslow Sq. TEL: 0171 589 5946; fax - 0171 584 9184. VAT: Stan.

Godson and Coles BADA
310 King's Rd. SW3 5UH. Est. 1978. Open 9.30-5.30 and by appointment. *STOCK: Fine 18th to early 19th C English furniture, especially lacquer and painted, and related works of art.* TEL: 0171 352 8509.

Green and Stone
259 Kings Rd. SW3 5EL. (R.J.S. Baldwin). Est. 1927. Open 9-5.30, Sat. 9.30-6. *STOCK: Writing and artists' materials, watercolours, 18th-19th C, drawings, 19th C.* LOC: At junction of King's Rd and Old Church St. PARK: Meters. TEL: 0171 352 0837/6521. SER: Restorations (pictures). VAT: Stan.

James Hardy and Co
235 Brompton Rd. SW3 2EP. Open 10-5.30. *STOCK: Silver including tableware, and jewellery.* PARK: Meters. TEL: 0171 589 5050; fax - 0171 823 8769. SER: Valuations.

SW3 continued

Stephanie Hoppen Ltd
17 Walton St. SW3 2HX. Est. 1962. Open 10-6, Sat. 12-5. *STOCK: Decorative picture specialist - watercolours, oils, drawings and prints, antique and modern.* TEL: 0171 589 3678.

Anthony James and Son Ltd BADA
88 Fulham Rd. SW3 6HR. Est. 1949. Open 9.30-5.45, Sat. by appointment. SIZE: Large. *STOCK: Furniture, 1700-1880, £200-£50,000; mirrors, bronzes, ormolu and decorative items, £200-£20,000.* PARK: Easy. TEL: 0171 584 1120; fax - 0171 823 7618. SER: Valuations; buys at auction. VAT: Spec.

John Keil Ltd BADA
154 Brompton Rd. SW3 1HX. Est. 1959. Open 9-6. CL: Sat. except by appointment. SIZE: Large. *STOCK: English furniture, 18th to early 19th C, from £500.* LOC: Near Knightsbridge underground station. PARK: 200 yds. TEL: 0171 589 6454; fax - 0171 823 8235. SER: Restorations (fine pieces). VAT: Spec.

Stanley Leslie
15 Beauchamp Place. SW3 1NQ. Open 9-5. *STOCK: Silver and Sheffield plate.* PARK: Meters. TEL: 0171 589 2333.

Michael Lipitch Ltd BADA
98 Fulham Rd. SW3 6HS. *STOCK: 18th to early 19th C English furniture, decoration and works of art.* TEL: 0171 589 7327; fax - 0171 823 9106.

Peter Lipitch Ltd BADA
120/124 Fulham Rd. SW3 6HU. Est. 1954. Open 9.30-5.30. SIZE: Large. *STOCK: Fine English furniture and mirrors.* TEL: 0171 373 3328; fax - 0171 373 8888. VAT: Spec.

The Map House
54 Beauchamp Place. SW3 1NY. (P. Curtis and P. Stuchlik). Est. 1907. Open 9.45-5.45, Sat. 10.30-5 or by appointment. *STOCK: Antique and rare maps, atlases, engravings and globes.* TEL: 0171 589 4325/584 8559; fax - 0171 589 1041. VAT: Stan.

McKenna and Co LAPADA
28 Beauchamp Place. SW3 1NJ. (C. Macmillan and M. McKenna). Est. 1982. Open 10-6. SIZE: Medium. *STOCK: Fine jewellery, Georgian to post war, £50-£10,000; some silver and objects.* Not Stocked: Pictures and furniture. LOC: Off Brompton Rd., near Harrods. PARK: Meters. TEL: 0171 584 1966; fax - 0171 225 2893. SER: Valuations; restorations. FAIRS: Olympia. VAT: Stan/Spec.

SW3 continued

Merola
178 Walton St. SW3 2JL. (M. Merola). Open 10-6. *STOCK: Jewellery, handbags, hats and accessories, 1900-1960.* TEL: 0171 589 0365; fax - 0171 373 4297.

No. 12
12 Cale St., Chelsea Green. SW3 3QU. Open 10-6. *STOCK: French country furniture and accessories.* TEL: 0171 581 5022; fax - 0171 581 3966.

Old Church Galleries
320 King's Rd., Chelsea. SW3 5UH. (Mrs M. Harrington). Open 10-6. *STOCK: Maps and engravings, from 16th C; sporting and decorative prints.* TEL: 0171 351 4649; fax - 0171 351 4449. SER: Framing.

Jacqueline Oosthuizen LAPADA
23 Cale St., (Off Sydney St.), Chelsea Green. SW3 3QR. Est. 1960. Open 10-6, Sat. and Sun. by appointment. SIZE: Medium. *STOCK: Staffordshire figures, animals, cottages and toby jugs, 18th-19th C, £50-£10,000; jewellery, 19th-20th C, £15-£5,000; decorative ceramics including Poole pottery, 19th-20th C, £20-£1,000.* LOC: Near King's Rd. and Fulham Rd. PARK: Easy. TEL: 0171 352 6071. VAT: Stan/Spec.

SW3 continued

Perez LAPADA
199 Brompton Rd. SW3 1LA. (Mr Tyran). Est. 1983. Open 10-6. SIZE: Large. *STOCK: Antique carpets, rugs, tapestries and Aubussons.* LOC: 50 yards from Harrods. PARK: Easy. TEL: 0171 589 2199 (ansaphone). SER: Valuations; restorations; buys at auction. VAT: Stan/Spec.

David Pettifer Ltd BADA
219 King's Rd. SW3 5EJ. Est. 1963. Open Mon.-Fri. 9.30-5.30. SIZE: Large. *STOCK: English furniture and works of art, 18th-19th C.* LOC: From Sloane Sq., 11, 19 or 22 bus. PARK: Easy. TEL: 0171 352 3088; fax - same. SER: Buys at auction. VAT: Spec.

Prides of London
15 Paultons House, Paultons Sq. SW3 5DU. Open by appointment only. *STOCK: Fine 18th-19th C English and Continental furniture; objets d'art.* TEL: 0171 586 1227. SER: Interior design.

The Purple Shop
15 Flood St., Chelsea. SW3 5ST. (A.J. Gardner and O.M. Becker). Est. 1967. Open 10-6. *STOCK: Antique and period jewellery especially Art Nouveau and Art Deco; studio pottery.* LOC: Near Chelsea Town Hall. PARK: Meters and nearby. TEL: 0171 352 1127. SER: Valuations. VAT: Stan.

SW3 continued

Rogers de Rin LAPADA
76 Royal Hospital Rd., Chelsea. SW3 4HN. (V. de Rin). Est. 1950. Open 10-5.30, Sat. 10-1, Sun. 11-5. SIZE: Small. *STOCK: Wemyss pottery, objets d'art, decorative furnishings (Regency taste), collectors' specialities, 18th-19th C, £50-£10,000.* LOC: Just beyond Royal Hospital, corner of Paradise Walk. PARK: Easy. TEL: 0171 352 9007; fax - 0171 351 9407. SER: Buys at auction; free catalogue on request. VAT: Stan/Spec.

Charles Saunders Antiques
255 Fulham Rd. SW3 6JA. Open 9.30-5.30, Sat. 10-5. *STOCK: Decorative furniture, objects and lamps, 18th-19th C.* TEL: 0171 351 5242. VAT: Spec.

Christine Schell LAPADA
15 Cale St. SW3 3QS. (B. King and C. Davies). Est. 1971. Open 10-5.30. SIZE: Small. *STOCK: Unusual tortoiseshell, silver and enamel objects, late 19th to early 20th C, £150-£2,500.* LOC: North of King's Rd., between Sloane Ave. and Sydney St. PARK: Easy. TEL: 0171 352 5563. SER: Valuations; restorations (tortoiseshell, ivory, shagreen, crocodile, leather, enamels, silver and hairbrush re-bristling). FAIRS: Olympia. VAT: Stan/Spec.

SW3 continued

Robert Stephenson LAPADA
1 Elystan St., Chelsea Green. SW3 3NT. Open 9.30-5.30, Sat. 10.30-2. *STOCK: Decorative and Oriental carpets; Oriental and European kilims; needlepoints, kilim-upholstered furniture, cushions and textiles.* TEL: 0171 225 2343; fax - same.

Gordon Watson Ltd LAPADA
50 Fulham Rd. SW3 6HH. Est. 1977. Open 11-6. *STOCK: Art Deco and 1940's glass, jewellery and furniture, £500-£10,000; silver by Jensen and Jean E. Puiforcat, 1920's, £500-£30,000.* LOC: At junction with Sydney St. PARK: Sydney St. TEL: 0171 589 3108/584 6328. SER: Valuations; buys at auction (Art Nouveau and Art Deco). VAT: Stan/Spec.

O.F. Wilson Ltd BADA LAPADA
Queens Elm Parade, Old Church St. (corner Fulham Rd.), Chelsea. SW3 6EJ. (P. and V.E. Jackson, M.E. Briscoe-Knight and R.G. White). Est. 1935. Open 9.30-5.30, Sat. 10.30-1. *STOCK: English and French furniture, mantelpieces, objets d'art.* TEL: 0171 352 9554; fax - 0171 351 0765. SER: Valuations. VAT: Spec.

SW3 continued

Clifford Wright Antiques Ltd BADA
104-106 Fulham Rd. SW3 6HS. Est. 1964. Open Mon.-Fri. 9-5.30, or by appointment. *STOCK: Furniture, period giltwood, looking glasses and consoles, 18th to early 19th C.* TEL: 0171 589 0986; fax - 0171 589 3565. VAT: Spec.

LONDON SW5

Antique and Modern Furniture Ltd
160 Earls Court Rd. SW5 9QQ. Est. 1941. Open 9.30-1 and 2.30-6. CL: Thurs. *STOCK: Furniture, mainly 18th-19th C.* TEL: 0171 373 2935.

Beaver Coin Room
Beaver Hotel, 57 Philbeach Gdns. SW5 9ED. (J. Lis). Est. 1971. Open by appointment. SIZE: Small. *STOCK: European coins, 10th-18th C; commemorative medals, 15th-20th C; all £5-£5,000.* LOC: 2 mins. walk from Earls Court Rd. PARK: Easy. TEL: 0171 373 4553; fax - 0171 373 4555. SER: Valuations; buys at auction (coins and medals). FAIRS: London Coin and Coinex. VAT: Stan.

LONDON SW6

20th Century Gallery
821 Fulham Rd. SW6 5HG. (E. Brandl and H. Chapman). Open 10-6, Sat. 10-1. SIZE: Small. *STOCK: Post impressionist and modern British oils and watercolours; original prints.* LOC: Near Munster Rd. junction. PARK: Easy. TEL: 0171 731 5888. SER: Restorations (paintings); framing. VAT: Spec.

275 Antiques
275 Lillie Rd., Fulham. SW6. (David Fisher). Open 10-5.30. SIZE: Medium. *STOCK: English and Continental decorative furniture, £200-£1,500; decorative objects, £25-£300; unique table lamps, £100-£700; mirrors, £400-£1,500; garden furniture, £50-£800.* PARK: Easy. TEL: 0171 386 7382; home - 0171 381 5094.

(55) For Decorative Living
55 New King's Rd., Chelsea. SW6 4SE. (Mrs J. Rhodes). Open 10.30-5.30. *STOCK: Furniture, lighting and decorative items.* TEL: 0171 736 5623. SER: Design.

And So To Bed Limited
638/640 King's Rd. SW6. Est. 1970. Open 10-6. SIZE: Large. *STOCK: Brass, lacquered and wooded beds.* LOC: End of King's Rd., towards Fulham. PARK: Easy. TEL: 0171 731 3593/4/5. SER: Restorations; spares; interior design. VAT: Stan.

SW6 continued

Arabesque Antiques
313 Lillie Rd., Fulham. SW6 7LL. (John Wea and Alexandra Fane). Est. 1986. Open 11-5.30 *STOCK: Furniture, 18th-19th C, £150-£2,500, decorative smalls, candlesticks, lamps and chandeliers, £50-£1,000; pictures and mirrors, 18th-20th C, £50-£1,250. Textiles, costumes, curtains, table and bed covers, tie backs, £40-£500; French and English decorative furniture, £100-£10,000; decorative smalls and prints, plant holders, photo frames, £20-£300.* LOC: From Old Brompton Rd., west for half a mile after crossing Northend Rd. PARK: Easy and nearby. TEL: 0171 610 2380; fax - same; mobile - 0973 321530 (Weal). SER: Shipping arranged. FAIRS: Vincent Sq.; Kensington Town Hall, Brocante; Mainwarings; Newark; Ardingly; NEC.

Christopher Bangs BADA LAPADA
P O Box 6077, London SW6 7XS. SW6 7XS. CINOA. Est. 1971. Open by appointment only. *STOCK: Domestic metalwork and metalware, works of art, decorative objects.* TEL: 0171 381 3532 (24 hrs); fax - 0171 381 2192 (24 hrs); mobile - 0836 333532. SER: Valuations; research; commission buys at auction; finder. VAT: Stan/Spec.

SW6 continued

Barclay Samson Ltd
39 Inglethorpe St. SW6 6NS. Open by appointment only. *STOCK: Pre 1950 original lithographic posters: French, German, Swiss, American, British and Russian Constructivist schools.* TEL: 0171 381 4341; fax - 0171 610 0434; mobile - 0385 306401. VAT: Spec.

Robert Barley Antiques
48 Fulham High St. SW6 3LQ. (R.A. Barley). Est. 1965. Open 9.30-5.30, Sat. 10-1. SIZE: Medium. *STOCK: Unusual decorative objects, furniture, lighting.* LOC: Near Putney Bridge. PARK: Easy. TEL: 0171 736 4429; fax - same. VAT: Stan/Spec.

Baroque 'n' Roll
291 Lillie Rd., Fulham. SW6 7LL. SIZE: Large. *STOCK: Highly decorative antiques, Gothic style and 18th C splendour; mirrors, garden statuary and textiles.* TEL: 0171 381 5008. SER: Lavish interior design.

Big Ben Antique Clocks
5 Broxholme House, New King's Rd. SW6 4AA. (R. Lascelles). Est. 1978. Open 10-4. *STOCK: Clocks especially longcase, from £1,000.* LOC: At junction of Wandsworth Bridge Rd. and New King's Rd. TEL: 0171 736 1770; fax - 0171 384 1957. SER: Buys at auction.

SW6 continued

Bishops Park Antiques
53-55 Fulham High St. SW6 3JJ. Open 10-6. *STOCK: Pine especially English and Continental, 18th-19th C.* TEL: 0171 736 4573.

Bookham Galleries
164 Wandsworth Bridge Rd. SW6. (J.H. and J. Rowe). Est. 1969. Open 10-5.30. CL: Mon. and Thurs. *STOCK: Furniture, 18th-19th C; Oriental rugs.* TEL: 0171 736 5125.

Julia Boston LAPADA
The Old Stores, The Gasworks, 2 Michael Rd. SW6 2AD. CINOA. Est. 1976. Open Tues., Wed. and Thurs. 10-6, other days by appointment. SIZE: Large. *STOCK: Tapestry cartoons, 18th-19th C; prints and works of art, 16th-19th C; furniture, 18th-19th C.* LOC: King's Rd. towards Fulham, left Waterford Rd., straight over roundabout, through industrial gates. PARK: Own. TEL: 0171 610 6783; fax - 0171 610 6784. SER: Restorations (pictures and prints). FAIRS: Olympia (June and Nov.); Decorative (Jan., March and Sept.). VAT: Spec.

CHARLES EDWARDS
582 KINGS ROAD, LONDON, SW6 2DY TEL. 0171 736 8490 FAX. 0171 371 5436

SW6 continued

I. and J.L. Brown Ltd
632-636 King's Rd. SW6 2DU. Open 9-5.30. *STOCK: English country and French provincial furniture including tables and country chairs; metalware and decorative items.* TEL: 0171 736 4141; fax - 0171 736 9164. SER: Restorations.

Rupert Cavendish Antiques
610 King's Rd. SW6 2DX. Est. 1980. Open 10-6. SIZE: Large. *STOCK: Empire and Biedermeier furniture and oil paintings.* LOC: Just before New King's Rd. PARK: Easy. TEL: 0171 731 7041; fax - 0171 731 8302. SER: Valuations. VAT: Spec.

John Clay
263 New King's Rd., Fulham. SW6 4RB. Est. 1974. Open 8.30-6, Sat. 10-6. SIZE: Medium. *STOCK: Furniture, £50-£5,000; objets d'art and animal objects, silver and clocks, £10-£1,500; all 18th-19th C.* Not Stocked: Pine. LOC: Close to Parsons Green, A3. PARK: Easy. TEL: 0171 731 5677. SER: Restorations (furniture, objets d'art). VAT: Stan/Spec.

Fergus Cochrane Antiques
570 King's Rd. SW6 2DY. (F.V. Cochrane and L. Warren). Est. 1981. Open 10-5. SIZE: Medium. *STOCK: Decorative lighting, furniture and objects, 1700-1930, £100-£3,000.* PARK: Easy. TEL: 0171 736 9166.

SW6 continued

Cooper Fine Arts Ltd
768 Fulham Rd. SW6 5SJ. (J. Hill-Reid). Est. 1976. Open 10-6.30. SIZE: Medium. *STOCK: Oils and watercolours, £200-£5,000; bronzes, £200-£1,000; all 1850-1950.* LOC: Putney Bridge end of Fulham Rd. PARK: Easy. TEL: 0171 731 3421; home - same. SER: Valuations; restorations; framing; buys at auction. VAT: Stan/Spec.

J. Crotty and Son Ltd
74 New King's Rd., Parsons Green. SW6 4LT. Est. 1945. Open 9.30-5. CL: Sat. pm. SIZE: Medium. *STOCK: Fire grates, fenders, 18th-19th C; marble and pine mantelpieces, fire irons and screens, period lighting.* PARK: In adjacent side street. TEL: 0171 731 4209. SER: Restorations (antique metal fireplace equipment); buys at auction. VAT: Stan.

Charles Edwards BADA
582 King's Rd. SW6 2DY. Open 9.30-6. *STOCK: Antique and reproduction light fixtures; furniture, 18th-19th C; architectural and decorative items, mirrors, British oil paintings, garden furniture and statuary.* TEL: 0171 736 8490; fax - 0171 371 5436.

SW6 continued

Christopher Edwards
The Old Stores, The Gasworks, 2 Michael Rd. SW6 2AD. Est. 1982. Open Tues., Wed. and Thurs. 10-6 or by appointment. SIZE: Large. *STOCK: Architecturally inspired furniture, works of art, lighting, 19th C, £100-£10,000.* LOC: King's Rd. towards Fulham, left Waterford Rd., straight over roundabout, through industrial gates. PARK: Own. TEL: 0171 610 6836; fax - 0171 610 6847; mobile - 0831 707043. SER: Valuations; buys at auction. FAIRS: Olympia (June and Nov). VAT: Stan/Spec.

Nicole Fabre Antiques LAPADA
592 King's Rd. SW6 2DX. Est. 1989. Open 10.30-6, Sat. 11-6, Sun. by appointment only. SIZE: Medium. *STOCK: French furniture, provincial style, French textiles, decorative objects, some English country furniture, to 1870.* PARK: Meters. TEL: 0171 384 3112; fax - 0171 610 6410. FAIRS: Olympia. VAT: Spec.

Fairfax Antiques and Fireplaces
568 King's Rd. SW6 2DY. Open 11-5.30. *STOCK: Cast iron and pine fireplaces, architectural items, decorative furniture.* TEL: 0171 736 5023.

SW6 continued

George Floyd Ltd
592 Fulham Rd. SW6 5UA. Open 8.30-5.30. SIZE: Large. *STOCK: 18th to early 19th C furniture and accessories.* TEL: 0171 736 1649. VAT: Stan/Spec.

Fulham Cross Antiques
318-320 Munster Rd., Fulham. SW6 6BH. (Michael G. Jones). SIZE: Large - 10 dealers. *STOCK: English and French antique and decorative furniture and related objects including lighting and mirrors.* TEL: 0171 610 3644.

George d'Epinois
793 Fulham Rd. SW6. (A. George). Est. 1979. Open 9.30-5.30. *STOCK: English furniture, 1690-1820, £250-£30,000.* PARK: Easy. TEL: 0171 736 2387. SER: Valuations; restorations. FAIRS: Harrogate; Olympia; Brugge, Belgium. VAT: Spec.

Judy Greenwood
657 Fulham Rd. SW6 5PY. Est. 1978. Open 10-5. *STOCK: French decorative furniture, lighting, quilts and textiles.* TEL: 0171 736 6037.

Robin Greer
29 Oxberry Ave. SW6 5SP. Est. 1965. Open by appointment. *STOCK: Children's and illustrated books, original illustrations.* TEL: 0171 736 3707; fax - 0171 731 8353. SER: Catalogues issued.

SW6 continued

Gregory, Bottley and Lloyd
13 Seagrave Rd. SW6 1RP. Est. 1850. SIZE: Medium. *STOCK: Mineral specimens, £1-£5,000; fossils, £5-£500.* PARK: Easy. TEL: 0171 381 5522; fax - 0171 381 5512. SER: Valuations. VAT: Stan.

Guinevere Antiques
574/580 King's Rd. SW6 2DY. Open 9.30-6, Sat. 10-6. SIZE: Large. *STOCK: Period and decorative antiques and accessories.* TEL: 0171 736 2917; fax - 0171 736 8267.

Gutlin Clocks and Antiques
616 King's Rd. SW6. Est. 1990. Open 9.30-7. SIZE: Medium. *STOCK: Longcase clocks, £2,000-£8,000; mantle clocks, £300-£6,000; furniture and lighting, £500-£3,000; all 18th-19th C.* LOC: 200 yards from beginning of New King's Rd. PARK: Maxwell Rd. TEL: 0171 384 2439; fax - same; home - 0181 740 6830. SER: Valuations; restorations (clocks and clock cases); buys at auction (clocks).

Nicholas Harris BADA LAPADA
564 King's Rd. SW6 2DY. Est. 1971. Open 10.30-6 - appointment highly recommended. *STOCK: Silver and decorative arts, 19th-20th C.* TEL: 0171 371 9711; fax - 0171 371 9537. VAT: Stan/Spec.

Hollingshead and Co
56 Tasso Rd., Fulham. SW6. (D. Hollingshead). Est. 1946. Open 8.30-5, Sat. 9-1. SIZE: Medium. *STOCK: Marble and wood mantelpieces, grates, fenders, fire irons, chandeliers, £50-£20,000.* Not Stocked: Furniture. TEL: 0171 385 8519. SER: Valuations; restorations (marblework and wood mantelpieces). VAT: Stan.

House of Mirrors
597 King's Rd. SW6 2EL. (G. Witek). Est. 1960. Open 10-6. *STOCK: Mirrors.* TEL: 0171 736 5885.

HRW Antiques (London) Ltd LAPADA
26 Sulivan Rd. SW6 3DT. Open 9-5, Sat. 10-1. SIZE: Large. *STOCK: Furniture and objects of art, 18th-19th C.* TEL: 0171 371 7995; fax - 0171 371 9522.

Peter Hurford Antiques
618-620 King's Rd. SW6 2DU. Open 10-5.30. *STOCK: Continental and British decorative objects and furniture, screens and mirrors, 18th-19th C, £500-£10,000.* TEL: 0171 731 4655. VAT: Spec.

P.L. James
590 Fulham Rd. SW6 5NT. Open 7-5. CL: Sat. *STOCK: Gilded mirrors, English and Oriental lacquer, period objects and furniture.* TEL: 0171 736 0183. SER: Restorations (painted and lacquer furniture, gilding, carving). VAT: Stan/Spec.

SW6 continued

Eric King Antiques
11 Crondace Rd. SW6 4BB. Est. 1966. Open by appointment. *STOCK: Decorative furniture and accessories, 18th-20th C.* PARK: Easy. TEL: 0171 731 2554.

King's Court Galleries
951/953 Fulham Rd. SW6 5HY. (Mrs J. Joel). Open 9.30-5.30. *STOCK: Antique maps, engravings, decorative and sporting prints.* TEL: 0171 610 6939. SER: Framing (on site).

L. and E. Kreckovic
559 King's Rd. SW6. Open 10-6. *STOCK: 18th-19th C furniture.* TEL: 0171 736 0753; fax - 0171 731 5904.

The Lamp Gallery
355 New King's Rd. SW6 4RJ. (G. Jones). Est. 1986. Open 10-5.30. SIZE: Medium. *STOCK: Interior lighting including Art Nouveau and Art Deco lamps, 1840-1940, £10-£5,000+.* LOC: 400yds. from Putney Bridge. PARK: Easy - pay and display. TEL: 0171 736 6188; fax - 0171 731 2632. SER: Valuations; restorations (metal polishing, re-wiring). VAT: Stan/Spec.

Lewin
638 Fulham Rd. SW6 5RT. (David, Matthew and Harriett Lewin). Open 10-5.30, Sun. 11-4.30. SIZE: Medium. *STOCK: Dutch colonial furniture, 1900-1930; contemporary Indonesian furniture, textiles and gifts.* TEL: 0171 731 1616. VAT: Stan.

Lunn Antiques
86 New King's Rd. SW6 4LU. (S. Lunn). Est. 1975. Open 10-6. *STOCK: Victorian and Edwardian hand worked linens, sheets, bedspreads, pillowcases, tablecloths, Oriental embroidery, pre-war clothing, some early lace and costume.* TEL: 0171 736 4638. VAT: Stan.

Magpies
152 Wandsworth Bridge Rd., Fulham. SW6 2UH. Open 10-5. SIZE: 4 dealers. *STOCK: China, glass, kitchenalia, collectables, cutlery, door furniture, lighting, silver plate, fireplace accessories and small furniture.* TEL: 0171 736 3738.

Michael Marriott Ltd
588 Fulham Rd. SW6 5NT. Est. 1979. Open 10-5.30. CL: Sat. pm. and Sun. except by appointment. SIZE: Large. *STOCK: English furniture, 1700-1850, £400-£15,000; leather upholstery, £250-£4,500; framed prints, £45-£800.* LOC: Junction of Fulham Rd. and Parsons Green Lane. PARK: Easy. TEL: 0171 736 3110/736 0568. SER: Valuations; restorations. VAT: Stan/Spec.

SW6 continued

David Martin-Taylor Antiques LAPADA
558 King's Rd. SW6 2DZ. Open 10-6, Sat. 11-5. SIZE: Medium. *STOCK: Classic and decorative furniture and unusual objects, 18th-19th C; 19th C American wickers.* PARK: Easy. TEL: 0171 731 4135; fax - 0171 371 0029; internet - Http:// www.all-about-antiques.co.uk. SER: Hire. VAT: Stan/Spec.

Megan Mathers Antiques LAPADA
571 Kings Rd. SW6 2EB. Open 10-6. *STOCK: 18th-19th C English and Continental furniture and decorative objects.* TEL: 0171 371 7837.

Mark Maynard Antiques
651 Fulham Rd. SW6 5PU. Est. 1977. Open 10-5, Sun. by appointment. SIZE: Medium. *STOCK: Decorative items, £25-£300.* LOC: Near Fulham Broadway underground. PARK: Easy. TEL: 0171 731 3533; home - 0171 373 4681. VAT: Stan/Spec.

Mora & Upham
584 King's Rd. SW6 2DX. (Matthew Upham and Ricardo Mora). Est. 1976. Open 10-6, Sat. 10.30-5. SIZE: Medium. *STOCK: Furniture, pictures and decorative objects, 18th-19th C.* LOC: Corner premises. PARK: Easy. TEL: 0171 731 4444; fax 0171 736 0440. SER: Valuations; restorations (pictures, china and furniture); buys at auction (furniture and jewellery). VAT: Spec.

Sylvia Napier Ltd
554 King's Rd. SW6 2DZ. Est. 1972. Open 10-6. SIZE: Large. *STOCK: Furniture - decorative European, 18th-19th C, £100-£15,000; decorative Oriental, 17th-19th C, £200-£7,000; garden, 19th C, £150-£7,000; objets d'art; unusual chandeliers.* LOC: Near junction with Lots Rd. PARK: Easy. TEL: 0171 371 5881. SER: Restorations. VAT: Spec.

Old Pine and Painted Furniture
594 King's Rd. SW6 2DX. (S. and R. Rippingale). Open 10-5.30. *STOCK: Painted and pine furniture.* TEL: 0171 736 5999. VAT: Stan.

Old World Trading Co
565 King's Rd. SW6. (R.J. Campion). Est. 1970. Open 9.30-6. *STOCK: Fireplaces, chimney pieces and accessories, chandeliers, mirrors, furniture including decorative, works of art.* TEL: 0171 731 4708; fax - 0171 731 1291.

Paul Orssich
117 Munster Rd., Fulham. SW6 6DH. Open 10-6, Sat. and other times by appointment. *STOCK: Antiquarian maps and books, especially on Hispanic studies, 16th-19th C, from £25; Art Deco illustrations, 1898-1935, £15-£500.* TEL: 0171 736 3869; fax - 0171 371 9886; e-mail - orssich@cityscape.co.uk.

SW6 continued

Ossowski
595 King's Rd. SW6 2EL. Est. 1960. Open 9.30-5.30. SIZE: Large. *STOCK: Furniture, 18th C.* TEL: 0171 731 0334. SER: Valuations; restorations. VAT: Stan/Spec.

M. Pauw Antiques
606 King's Rd. SW6 2DX. Est. 1985. SIZE: Medium. *STOCK: English and Continental furniture, 18th-19th C; decorative items, lighting fixtures, cast iron and lead planters, £500-£20,000.* PARK: Easy. TEL: 0171 731 4022; fax - 0171 731 7356. VAT: Stan/Spec.

Perez Antique Carpets Gallery
150 Wandsworth Bridge Rd., Fulham. SW6 2UH (R. Tyran). Est. 1984. Open 10-6.30, Wed. 10-7.30. SIZE: Large. *STOCK: Carpets, 19th C £400-£40,000; rugs, 18th-20th C, £300-£3,000 textiles, 19th C, £70-£1,500.* PARK: Easy. TEL 0171 371 9619/9620. SER: Valuations; restorations; buys at auction (Oriental and European carpets, rugs and textiles, tapestries). VAT Stan/Spec.

The Pine Mine (Crewe-Read Antiques)
100 Wandsworth Bridge Rd., Fulham. SW6 2TF (D. Crewe-Read). Est. 1971. Open 9.45-5.45, Sat till 4.30. SIZE: Large. *STOCK: Georgian and Victorian pine, Welsh dressers, farmhouse tables chests of drawers, boxes and some architectural items.* LOC: From Sloane Sq., down King's Rd. into New King's Rd., left into Wandsworth Bridge Rd. PARK: Outside. TEL: 0171 736 1092 SER: Furniture made from old wood; stripping export.

Peter Place Antiques
632-636 King's Rd. SW6. Usually open 9.30-5.30. *STOCK: 18th-19th C metalware, decorative items, paintings, folk art.* TEL: 0171 736 9945.

Daphne Rankin and Ian Conn
608 King's Rd. SW6 2DX. Est. 1979. Open 10.30-6. SIZE: Medium. *STOCK: Oriental porcelain including Chinese, Japanese, Imari Cantonese, Satsuma, Nanking, Famille Rose £500-£25,000.* PARK: Maxwell Rd. adjacent to shop. TEL: 0171 384 1847; fax - 0171 352 0218 SER: Valuations; buys at auction (as stock) FAIRS: Olympia (June). VAT: Stan/Spec.

Reffold
572 King's Rd. SW6 2DY. (K. Jackson, Shield & Allen). Est. 1968. Open Mon.-Fri. 10-5. SIZE Medium. *STOCK: Early furniture, works of art and paintings.* PARK: Easy. TEL: 0171 736 7145 fax - 0171 736 0029. VAT: Spec.

SW6 continued

Richardson and Kailas Icons BADA LAPADA
65 Rivermead Court, Ranelagh Gardens. SW6 3RY. (C. Richardson and M. Kailas). Open by appointment. *STOCK: Icons and frescoes.* TEL: 0171 371 0491.

Rogers & Co LAPADA
604 Fulham Rd. SW6 5RP. (M. and C. Rogers). Est. 1971. Open 10-5.30. SIZE: Large. *STOCK: Furniture, 18th-19th C, £100-£3,000; upholstered and boardroom furniture, Tillman dining tables.* LOC: Near Fulham library, Parsons Green Lane. PARK: Side streets. TEL: 0171 731 3504; fax - 0171 610 6040. SER: Valuations; interior design. VAT: Stan/Spec.

George Sherlock Antiques
588 King's Rd. SW6 2DX. Est. 1968. Open 9.30-5.30. SIZE: Large. *STOCK: General antiques, decorative furniture and upholstery, 1650-1900, £20-£15,000.* PARK: Easy. TEL: 0171 736 3955; fax - 0171 371 5179. VAT: Stan/Spec.

Simon Horn Furniture Ltd
117-121 Wandsworth Bridge Rd. SW6 2TP. IDDA. Est. 1981. Open 8.30-5.30, Sat. 9.30-5.30, Sun. by appointment. SIZE: Large. *STOCK: Wooden classical style bedframes, £500-£5,000; bedside tables, £150-£650; all 1790-1910 or recent larger copies.* LOC: South from New King's Rd., towards river down Wandsworth Bridge Rd., premises on left at first zebra crossing. PARK: Easy. TEL: 0171 731 1279; fax - 0171 736 3522. SER: Restorations (as stock). FAIRS: Decorex; Paris Furniture Show; Index Dubai. VAT: Stan.

John Spink
14 Darlan Rd., Fulham. SW6 5BT. Open by appointment. *STOCK: Fine English watercolours and selected oils, 1720-1920.* TEL: 0171 731 8292; fax - 0171 731 6955.

Thornhill Galleries Ltd
76 New King's Rd. SW6 4LT. Est. 1880. Open 10-5, Sat. 10-3. SIZE: Large. *STOCK: English and French marble, stone and wood chimney-pieces, panelled rooms, architectural features and wood carvings, fire grates and fenders, all 17th-19th C; decorative iron interiors and other fire accessories, 17th-20th C.* LOC: Continuation of King's Rd. Coming from Sloane Sq. shop is on right-hand side. PARK: Easy. TEL: 0171 736 5830. SER: Valuations; restorations (architectural items); buys at auction (architectural items). VAT: Stan/Spec.

Through the Looking Glass Ltd
563 King's Rd. SW6 2EB. (J.J.A. and D.A. Pulton). Est. 1966. Open 10-5.30. SIZE: Large. *STOCK: Mirrors, 18th-19th C.* TEL: 0171 736 7799. SER: Restorations. VAT: Spec.

SW6 continued

Ferenc Toth
598A King's Rd. SW6 2DX. (F.I. Toth). Est. 1978. Open 9.30-5.30. SIZE: Medium. *STOCK: Mirrors, furniture and decorative items, 18th-19th C.* LOC: Fulham end of King's Rd., Chelsea. PARK: Easy. TEL: 0171 731 2063; fax - same; home - 0171 602 1771. SER: Valuations; buys at auction. VAT: Spec.

Trowbridge Gallery LAPADA
555 King's Rd. SW6 2EB. (M. Trowbridge). Est. 1980. Open 9.30-6, Sat 9.30-5. SIZE: Large. *STOCK: Decorative prints, 17th-19th C, £35-£3,000.* LOC: Near Christopher Wray Lighting. PARK: Easy. TEL: 0171 371 8733. SER: Valuations; restorations; buys at auction (antiquarian books and prints); hand-made frames; decorative mounting. FAIRS: Decorative Antiques and Textiles, Olympia, LAPADA, City of London. VAT: Stan.

Tulissio De Beaumont LAPADA
283 Lillie Rd. SW6 7LL. (David Tulissio and Dominic De Beaumont). Est. 1987. Open 10-6. SIZE: Medium. *STOCK: Chandeliers, wall lights and lamps, 18th-20th C, £100-£1,500; bronzes and sculpture, 19th C, £50-£1,500; general decorative antiques, 18th-20th C, £50-£2,500; furniture, 18th-19th C, £50-£5,000.* LOC: 10 minutes from New King's Road, next to Fulham Cross. PARK: Easy. TEL: 0171 385 0156; fax - 0171 610 0455; mobiles - 0973 186305/176047. VAT: Stan/Spec.

François Valcke
610 King's Rd. SW6 2DX. Est. 1982. Open 10-6. SIZE: Medium. *STOCK: 20th C oil paintings and drawings.* LOC: Past World's End. PARK: Easy. TEL: 0171 736 6024; fax - 0171 731 8302. VAT: Spec.

Vaughan
156-160 Wandsworth Bridge Rd. SW6 2UH. (Vaughan Ltd). Est. 1980. Open 10-5. CL: Sat. SIZE: Large. *STOCK: Decorative furniture and objects, 18th-19th C; lamps and light fittings.* PARK: Easy. TEL: 0171 731 3133. VAT: Stan/Spec.

Whiteway and Waldron Ltd
305 Munster Rd., Fulham. SW6 6BJ. (M. Whiteway and G. Kirkland). Est. 1976. Open 10-6, Sat. 11-4. SIZE: Large. *STOCK: Religious antiques including candlesticks, statuary, gothic and carved church woodwork.* LOC: At junction with Lillie Rd. PARK: On forecourt for loading, or Strode Rd. TEL: 0171 381 3195; fax - same. SER: Buys at auction (religious items). VAT: Stan.

SW6 continued

Christopher Wray's Lighting Emporium

600 King's Rd. SW6 2DX. Est. 1964. Open 10-6. SIZE: Large. *STOCK: Decorative light fittings of 1880s, brass, antiques, decorative objects.* LOC: From Sloane Sq. over Stanley Bridge. PARK: Own. TEL: 0171 736 8434; fax - 0171 731 3507. VAT: Stan.

LONDON SW7

Anglo Persian Carpet Co

6 South Kensington Station Arcade. SW7 2NA. Est. 1910. Open 9.30-6. *STOCK: Carpets and rugs.* TEL: 0171 589 5457. SER: Valuations; restorations (carpets and rugs); cleaning.

Aubrey Brocklehurst BADA

124 Cromwell Rd. SW7 4ET. Est. 1946. Open 9-1 and 2-5.30 (or later by arrangement), Sat. 10-1. SIZE: Medium. *STOCK: English clocks and barometers.* TEL: 0171 373 0319. SER: Valuations; restorations, furniture and clock repairs; buys at auction. VAT: Spec.

Julie Collino

15 Glendower Place, South Kensington. SW7 3DR. Est. 1971. Open 11-6, Sat. 2-6, Sun. by appointment. *STOCK: Watercolours, oils, etchings, £25-£1,000; china, £25-£500; both 19th-20th C; furniture, £50-£2,000.* LOC: Off Harrington Rd. TEL: 0171 584 4733; home - 0171 373 5353. FAIRS: Olympia. VAT: Stan/Spec.

M.P. Levene Ltd BADA

5 Thurloe Place. SW7 2RR. Est. 1926. Open 9.30-6. CL: Sat. pm. *STOCK: Silver, old Sheffield plate, various, all prices.* LOC: Few minutes past Harrods near South Kensington Station. PARK: Easy. TEL: 0171 589 3755. SER: Valuations; buys at auction. VAT: Stan/Spec.

A. & H. Page

66 Gloucester Rd. SW7 4QT. Est. 1840. Open 9-5.45, Sat. 10-2. *STOCK: Silver, jewellery, watches.* TEL: 0171 584 7349. SER: Valuations; repairs; silversmith.

Period Brass Lights

9a Thurloe Place, Brompton Rd. SW7. (M. Beattie). Est. 1967. *STOCK: Brass reproduction and antique light fittings; suits of armour.* PARK: Meters. TEL: 0171 589 8305.

The Taylor Gallery

1 Bolney Gate. SW7 1QW. (J. Taylor). Est. 1986. Open by appointment only. *STOCK: Irish, British and marine Paintings, 19th-20th C.* TEL: 0171 581 0253.

SW7 continued

The Wyllie Gallery

44 Elvaston Place. SW7 5NP. (J.G. Wyllie). Open by appointment. *STOCK: 19th-20th C marine paintings and etchings, especially works by the Wyllie family.* TEL: 0171 584 6024.

LONDON SW8

Nicholas Beech Antiques

789 Wandsworth Rd. SW8 3JQ. (N.A. Beech). Est. 1981. Open 9.30-1 and 2-5.30, Sat. 10-5, Sun by appointment. SIZE: Medium. *STOCK: English and Continental pine furniture, Georgian, Victorian and Edwardian, £20-£3,000; decorative items.* LOC: Over Chelsea Bridge (south side) straight over roundabout. At 3rd set of traffic lights turn left, shop 100yds. on right. PARK: Easy. TEL: 0171 720 8552. SER: Restoration (pine); pine stripping. VAT: Stan.

Heskia BADA

SW8 5BP. Est. 1877. Open by appointment only. *STOCK: Oriental carpets, rugs and tapestries.* TEL: 0171 373 4489. SER: Valuations; cleaning and repairs.

H.W. Newby (A.J. & M.V. Waller)

At C.F.A.S.S. Ltd, 42 Ponton Rd. SW8 5BP. Est. 1949. Open by appointment. SIZE: Small. *STOCK: Porcelain, faience, pottery, pre-1830, £50-£5,000; English and Continental glass.* Not Stocked: Silver, jewellery. PARK: Easy. TEL: 0181 974 8659; mobile - 0836 294523. SER: Valuations; buys at auction.

LONDON SW10

Alasdair Brown Antiques

24 Chelsea Wharf, 15 Lots Road. SW10 0QJ. Est. 1986. Open 10-6, Sat. and Sun. by appointment. SIZE: Large. *STOCK: Furniture, to £10,000; decorative items, to £5,000; upholstery, lighting and unusual items.* LOC: On the river next to Chelsea Harbour. PARK: Easy. TEL: 0171 35[illegible] 1477; fax - 0171 351 1577. SER: Valuations; restorations; finder service. FAIRS: Olympia (Feb., June and Nov). VAT: Stan/Spec.

Jonathan Clark & Co

18 Park Walk, Chelsea. SW10 0AQ. Open 10-6.30, Sat. 11-5. *STOCK: Modern British and European paintings and sculpture.* TEL: 0171 35[illegible] 3555; fax - 0171 823 3187.

Collins and Hastie Ltd

5 Park Walk, Chelsea. SW10 0AJ. (Caroline Hastie and Diana Collins). Open 10-6, Sat. by appointment only. SIZE: Medium. *STOCK: British oils - sporting, animal and country scenes, 19th C, £500-£30,000; watercolours - sporting, animal including*

SW10 continued

dogs, 19th-20th C. LOC: Park Walk runs between King's Rd. and Fulham Rd. PARK: Easy. TEL: 0171 351 4292. SER: Restorations (pictures); buys at auction.VAT: Spec.

The Furniture Cave

533 King's Rd. SW10 0TZ. Est. 1967. Open 10-6, Sun. 11-4. SIZE: Large. LOC: Corner of Lots Rd. PARK: Meters. TEL: 0171 352 4229/5478. SER: Shipping; forwarding. VAT: Stan/Spec. All dealers specialise in antique furniture and decorative objects.

Paul Andrews Antiques

Basement. *English and Continental decorative antique furniture; sculpture, Old Master paintings, prints and drawings.* TEL: 0171 352 4584; fax - 0171 351 78165.

Brown's Antique Furniture

First Floor. *Library and dining, and decorative objects, from early 18th C.* TEL: 0171 352 2046; fax - 0171 352 3654.

Stuart Duggan

First Floor. *Georgian and Victorian furniture especially 19th-20th C pianos.* TEL: 0171 352 2046; fax - 0171 352 3654.

Ronald Harman

Ground Floor. *Early 19th C and Regency furniture.* TEL: 0171 352 3775; fax - 0171 352 3759.

Kenneth Harvey LAPADA

Ground Floor. *Decorative furniture, mirrors, chandeliers, light fittings.* TEL: 0171 352 8645; fax - 0171 376 3225.

Simon Hatchwell Antiques

Ground Floor. Est. 1961. *English and Continental decorative furniture and objets d'art.* TEL: 0171 351 2344; fax - 0171 351 3520.

MSM Antiques

Basement., *Town and country furniture.* TEL: 0171 352 7305; fax - 0171 351 0480.

Anthony Outred BADA

Ground Floor. *English and Continental furniture, 18th-19th C; works of art.* TEL: 0171 352 8840; fax - 0171 376 3627.

Phoenix Trading Company

Furniture including Indian, porcelain, bronzes. TEL: 0171 351 6543; fax - 0171 352 9803.

Mark Ransom Limited

First Floor. *Continental furniture especialising French Empire; antiquarian books, maps and prints.* TEL: 0171 376 7653; fax - 0171 352 3654.

SW10 continued

Anthony Redmile

Basement. *Marble resin neo-classical Grand Tour objects.* TEL: 0171 351 3813; fax - 0171 352 8131.

Steve Thomas

First Floor. *Georgian and Victorian furniture: pedestal desks, writing tables, library, bureaux.* TEL: 0171 352 2046; fax - 0171 352 3654.

Jim Weatherall

First Floor. *Georgian, Victorian and Edwardian furniture.* TEL: 0171 352 2046; fax - 0171 352 3654.

York Whiting LAPADA

Ground Floor. *17th-20th C furniture, English and Continental, paintings, carpets and textiles.* TEL: 0171 376 8530; fax - 0171 352 7994.

Gallery on Lots Road

10 The Plaza, 535 Kings Road. SW10 0SZ. Open 11-7, Sat. 11-6, Sun. 12-5. SIZE: Large. *STOCK: Oil paintings and watercolours, 1850-1990.* TEL: 0171 349 8771; fax - 0171 349 8772. SER: Valuations; restorations (oils and watercolours); re-gilding frames; framing; buys at auction (19th-20th C paintings).

Rupert Hastie

5 Park Walk, Chelsea. SW10 0AJ. Open 10-6, Sat. 11-4. *STOCK: Continental and English furniture and works of art, 18th-19th C.* TEL: 0171 351 6820; fax - 0171 351 7929. VAT: Spec.

Hollywood Road Gallery

12 Hollywood Rd., Chelsea. SW10 9HY. (P. and C. Kennaugh). Open 10.30-7, Fri. and Sat. 10.30-3. *STOCK: Oils, watercolours, prints, 19th-20th C, £200-£3,000.* TEL: 0171 351 1973.

Hünersdorff Rare Books

P.O. Box 582. SW10 9RU. ABA. Est. 1969. Open by appointment only. *STOCK: Continental books in rare editions, early printing, science and medicine, illustrated books, Latin America, horticulture.* TEL: 0171 373 3899; fax - 0171 370 1244.

Thomas Kerr Antiques Ltd

at L'Encoignure, 517 King's Rd. SW10 0IX. Est. 1977. Open 10-6. SIZE: Large. *STOCK: French country furniture, paintings, mirrors and decorative items.* TEL: 0171 351 6465; fax - 0171 351 4744. VAT: Stan/Spec.

Langford's Marine Antiques BADA LAPADA

The Plaza, 535 King's Rd. SW10 0SZ. (L.L. Langford). Est. 1941. *STOCK: Ships models, antique and marine objects, stationary steam engine models.* TEL: 0171 351 4881; fax - 0171 352 0763. SER: Valuations; restorations. VAT: Stan/Spec.

SW10 continued

Stephen Long
348 Fulham Rd. SW10 9UH. Est. 1966. Open 9-1 and 2.15-5.30. CL: Sat. pm. and Sun. except by appointment. SIZE: Small. *STOCK: English pottery, 18th-19th C, to £400; English painted furniture, 18th to early 19th C; toys and games, household and kitchen items, chintz, materials and patchwork, to £500.* Not Stocked: Stripped pine, large brown furniture, fashionable antiques. LOC: From South Kensington along road on right between Ifield Rd. and Billing Rd. PARK: Easy. TEL: 0171 352 8226. VAT: Stan/Spec.

Mallord Street Antiques
Lower Floor, 498 King's Rd. SW10. (Ginny Mejia). Est. 1987. Open 10-5. SIZE: Small. *STOCK: Decorative furniture and objets d'art, 18th-19th C.* LOC: Near World's End. PARK: Easy. TEL: 0171 351 1442; home/fax - 0171 352 9659. SER: Valuations; buys at auction (furniture). FAIRS: Decorative (Mar. and Sept.). VAT: Stan/ Spec.

McVeigh & Charpentier
498 King's Rd. SW10. (Maggie Charpentier and Pam McVeigh). Est. 1979. Open 10.30-5.30, Sat. 11-3. SIZE: Medium. *STOCK: Continental furniture, £600-£6,000; objets d'art, £200-£2,000, all 17th-19th C.* LOC: Two blocks down from Earls Court. PARK: In cul de sac adjacent. TEL: 0171 351 1442/352 6084; fax - 0171 937 1506; home - 0171 937 6459. SER: Restorations. FAIRS: Olympia (Nov. and June); Harvey (Sept., Jan. and Mar.). VAT: Spec.

McWhirter
22 Park Walk, Chelsea. SW10 0AQ. (A.J.K. McWhirter). Open 10-6, Sat. by appointment. SIZE: Medium. *STOCK: Unusual furniture, objects and works of art.* LOC: Near Fulham Road Cinema. PARK: Easy. TEL: 0171 351 5399; fax - 0171 352 9821. SER: Valuations; buys at auction. VAT: Spec.

Offer Waterman and Co. Fine Art
20 Park Walk. SW10 0AQ. Est. 1986. Open 9-6.30, Sat. 10-4, Sun. by appointment. SIZE: Small. *STOCK: Modern and Contemporary British paintings, 1900-1996, £500-£5,000.* LOC: Off Fulham Rd. PARK: Easy. TEL: 0171 351 0068; fax - 0171 351 2269. SER: Valuations; restorations (as stock); framing; buys at auction (Modern British paintings). FAIRS: Art '97; 20th C British Art. VAT: Stan/Spec.

Park Walk Gallery
20 Park Walk, Chelsea. SW10 0AQ. (J. Cooper). Est. 1988. Open 10-6.30, Sat. 11-4. SIZE: Medium. *STOCK: Paintings, £250-£100,000; watercolours, £250-£20,000; drawings, £200-£15,000; all 19th-20th C English and Continental.* LOC: Off Fulham Rd. PARK: Easy. TEL: 0171 351 0410; fax - same. SER: Valuations; restorations. FAIRS: 20th C British, Olympia. VAT: Spec.

SW10 continued

Pawsey and Payne BADA
PO Box No. 11830 SW10 9FE. (Hon. N.V.B. and L.N.J. Wallop). SLAD. Est. 1910. Open by appointment. *STOCK: English oils and watercolours, 18th-19th C.* TEL: 0171 930 4221; fax - 0171 370 0959. SER: Valuations; restorations. VAT: Stan/Spec.

H.W. Poulter and Son
279 Fulham Rd. SW10 9PZ. Est. 1946. Open 9.30-5. CL: Sat. pm. SIZE: Large. *STOCK: English and French marble chimney pieces, grates, fenders, fire-irons, brass, chandeliers.* PARK: Meters. TEL: 0171 352 7268. SER: Restorations (marble work). VAT: Stan/Spec.

Rare Carpets Gallery
496 King's Rd., Chelsea. SW10. Est. 1963. Open 10-6. SIZE: Large. *STOCK: European and Oriental decorative carpets, tapestries.* TEL: 0171 351 3296; fax - 0171 376 4876. SER: Valuations; restorations; cleaning; part exchange. VAT: Stan.

Rendlesham Antiques
498 King's Rd. SW10. Est. 1970. Open 10-6, Sat. 11-2. SIZE: Medium. *STOCK: English and Continental furniture, objets d'art.* TEL: 0171 351 1442.

John Thornton
455 Fulham Rd. SW10 9UZ. Open 10-5.30. *STOCK: Antiquarian books especially theology.* TEL: 0171 352 8810.

LONDON SW11

Antiques and Things
91 Eccles Rd. SW11 1LX. (Mrs V. Crowther). Est. 1986. Open 10-5, Sat. 10-6. SIZE: Medium. *STOCK: Decorative curtain furniture and fittings, linen, lace, textiles, Victorian to Edwardian, £1-£500; china, glass, kitchenalia, 18th-19th C, £5-£500; English and French furniture, decorative items, 19th C, £20-£2,000.* LOC: Off Lavender Hill, near Clapham junction. TEL: 0171 350 0597.

John Bloxham (Fine Art) Ltd
117 St John's Hill, Battersea. SW11 1SZ. Est. 1978. Open Tues.-Sat. 10-5, other times by appointment. SIZE: Medium. *STOCK: Watercolours and oils, 19th-20th C, £200-£3,000; decorative and antiquarian prints, 18th-20th C, £20-£500.* LOC: Just off South Circular, near Wandsworth Common. PARK: Easy. TEL: 0171 924 7500 (ansaphone). SER: Valuations; restorations (works on paper and oils, frames); buys at auction (as stock); conservation mounting and framing. VAT: Stan.

SW11 continued

Eccles Road Antiques

60 Eccles Rd., Battersea. SW11. (H. Rix). Open 10-5. *STOCK: General antiques, pine furniture and smalls.* TEL: 0171 228 1638.

The English Room

SW11 4PY. (Mrs Val Cridland). Est. 1985. By appointment only. *STOCK: 19th C furniture and decorative items.* TEL: 0171 720 6655; fax - 0171 978 2397. SER: Search and courier (trade and private), London and country - shipment of goods purchased arranged. VAT: Stan/Spec.

Keith Gretton Old Advertising

Unit 14, Northcote Rd. Antiques Market, 155A Northcote Rd., Battersea. SW11 6EG. Open 10-6, Sun. 12-5. *STOCK: Advertising, signs, bottles, packaging and display.* LOC: Near Clapham Junction. PARK: Easy. TEL: 0171 228 6850; home - 0171 228 0741. SER: Valuations.

Northcote Road Antiques Market

155A Northcote Rd., Battersea. SW11 6QB. (H. Rix). Open 10-6, Sun. 12-5. SIZE: 30 dealers. *STOCK: Victoriana and Art Deco collectables, silver, glass, furniture, lighting, textiles, jewellery, old advertising.* TEL: 0171 228 6850.

SW11 continued

Overmantels

66 Battersea Bridge Rd. SW11 3AG. (Seth Taylor). BCFA. Est. 1980. Open 9.30-5.30. SIZE: Medium. *STOCK: English giltwood mirrors, £400-£3,000; French giltwood mirrors, £700-£3,000; both 18th-19th C. Furniture, 19th C, £200-£2,000.* LOC: 200m south of Battersea Bridge. PARK: Nearby. TEL: 0171 223 8151; fax - 0171 924 2283. SER: Valuations; restorations (gesso work and gilding). VAT: Stan/Spec.

Robert Young Antiques

68 Battersea Bridge Rd. SW11 3AE. Est. 1974. Open 10-6, Sat. 10-5. CL: Mon. SIZE: Medium. *STOCK: English oak and country furniture, 17th-18th C, £500-£20,000; English and European treen and objects of folk art, £20-£10,000; English and European provincial pottery and metalwork, £20-£2,500.* LOC: Turn off King's Rd. or Chelsea Embankment into Beaufort St., cross over Battersea Bridge Rd., 9th shop on right. PARK: Opposite in side street. TEL: 0171 228 7847; fax - 0171 585 0489. SER: Valuations; buys at auction (treen and country furniture). FAIRS: Olympia, Chelsea. VAT: Stan/Spec.

LONDON SW12

The Kilim Warehouse Ltd

28A Pickets St. SW12 8QB. (J. Luczyc-Wyhowska). Est. 1982. Open 10-5.30, Sat. 10-4. SIZE: Medium. *STOCK: Kilims from Eastern Europe, Asia Minor and beyond, £50-£8,000.* LOC: Near Clapham South tube station and Nightingale Lane. PARK: Easy. TEL: 0181 675 3122; fax - 0181 675 8494; internet - http://www.kilim-warehouse.co.uk/kilim/; e-mail - info@kilim-warehouse.co.uk. SER: Restorations; cleaning. VAT: Stan.

Twentieth Century

SW12 8BN. (M. Taylor). Est. 1986. By appointment only. *STOCK: Art Deco, Art Nouveau, Arts and Crafts, decorative arts items, £50-£500.* PARK: Easy. TEL: 0181 675 6351. FAIRS: Battersea Art Deco; Kensington Decorative Arts; Loughborough Art Deco; Manchester; Birmingham. VAT: Stan.

LONDON SW13

Alton Gallery

2a Suffolk Road, Barnes. SW13 9PH. Open by appointment only. *STOCK: 19th-20th C British art.* TEL: 0181 748 0606. SER: Framing.

SW13 continued

The Barnes Gallery

(formerly The Wykeham Galleries), 51 Church Rd., Barnes. SW13. Est. 1989. Open 10-5. CL: Mon. *STOCK: Paintings, sculptures, prints, 20th C, £100-£1,000.* LOC: From Hammersmith Bridge down Castlenau. PARK: Easy. TEL: 0181 741 1277.

Christine Bridge LAPADA

78 Castelnau, Barnes. SW13 9EX. Est. 1972. Open anytime by appointment only. SIZE: Medium. *STOCK: Glass - 18th C collectors and 19th C coloured, engraved and decorative, £50-£15,000; small decorative items - papier mâché, bronzes, needlework, ceramics.* LOC: Main road from Hammersmith Bridge. PARK: Easy. TEL: 0181 741 5501; fax - same; mobile - 0831 126668; e-mail - cbridge.antiques@dial.pipex.com; internet - http://dialspace.dial.pipex.com/cbridge.antiques/. SER: Valuations; restorations (glass - cutting, polishing, declouding); buys at auction; shipping. FAIRS: Olympia; LAPADA; West London; Brussels; Tokyo; Melbourne; Singapore; California. VAT: Stan/Spec.

SW13 continued

Campion
71 White Hart Lane, Barnes. SW13 0PP. (J. Richards). Est. 1983. Open 10-1 and 2-5.30. SIZE: Small. *STOCK: Interesting lights, kilims, small furniture, coffee tables.* LOC: Along river from Barnes High St., turn left at White Hart public house. PARK: Easy. TEL: 0181 878 6688; home - same. SER:

Simon Coleman Antiques
40 White Hart Lane, Barnes. SW13. Est. 1974. SIZE: Large. *STOCK: Country furniture, oak, fruitwood, pine, French and English farm tables, 18th-19th C.* PARK: Easy. TEL: 0181 878 5037. VAT: Stan/Spec.

The Dining Room Shop
62/64 White Hart Lane, Barnes. SW13 0PZ. (K. Dyson). Est. 1985. Open 10-5.30, Sun. by appointment. SIZE: Medium. *STOCK: Formal and country dining room furniture, 18th-19th C; glasses, china especially dinner services; cutlery, damask and lace table linen, 19th C; associated small and decorative items.* LOC: Near Barnes railway bridge, turning opposite White Hart public house. PARK: Easy. TEL: 0181 878 1020; home - 0181 876 5212. SER: Valuations; restorations; finder; interior decorating. VAT: Stan/Spec.

Marilyn Garrow LAPADA
6 The Broadway, White Hart Lane, Barnes. SW13 0NY. Open 10-5.30, Sat. 10-1. *STOCK: European, Ottoman and Asian textiles.* TEL: 0181 392 1655.

Joy McDonald
50 Station Rd., Barnes. SW13 0LP. Resident. Est. 1966. SIZE: Small. *STOCK: Furniture, 18th-19th C; oak, fruitwood, unusual items, large mirrors especially 19th C French gilt; some china and glass.* PARK: Easy. TEL: 0181 876 6184. SER: Restorations (furniture, gilt mirrors).

New Grafton Gallery
49 Church Rd., Barnes. SW13 9HH. (D. Wolfers). Est. 1968. Open 10-5.30. CL: Mon. SIZE: Medium. *STOCK: British paintings and drawings, £150-£3,000.* LOC: Off Castelnau which runs from Hammersmith Bridge. PARK: Easy. TEL: 0181 748 8850; home - 0181 876 6294. SER: Valuations; restorations; buys at auction. VAT: Stan/Spec.

Remember When
6 and 7 Rocks Lane, Barnes. SW13 0DB. Est. 1973. Open 9.30-7 including Sun. *STOCK: Pine furniture.* TEL: 0181 878 2817; fax - 0181 876 6934.

SW13 continued

Jeremy Seale Antiques
56 White Hart Lane, Barnes. SW13 0PZ. Est. 1988. Open 10-1 and 2-5.30, Sat. 10-5.30, evenings by appointment. SIZE: Medium. *STOCK: Furniture, 18th-19th C, £300-£6,000; decorative items, 19th C; pictures and prints, 18th-19th C; both £50-£500.* LOC: From M3 into London, just off A316 (sign to Mortlake and Barnes), White Hart Lane on right on Barnes approach. PARK: Easy. TEL: 0181 876 1041; fax - 0181 296 0717; mobile - 0956 457795. SER: Finder; valuations; interior design consultant. VAT: Stan/Spec.

Tobias and The Angel
68 White Hart Lane, Barnes. SW13 0PZ. (A. Hughes). Est. 1985. Open 10-6. SIZE: Large. *STOCK: Quilts, textiles, furniture, country and painted beds, decorative objects, from 1800.* LOC: Parallel to Barnes High St. PARK: Easy. TEL: 0181 878 8902; home - 01206 391003. SER: Interior design. VAT: Stan/Spec.

LONDON SW14

Paul Foster's Bookshop
119 Sheen Lane, East Sheen. SW14 8AE. PBFA. Est. 1983. Open 10.30-6. SIZE: Medium. *STOCK: Books - antiquarian, 17th-19th C, £100-£1,000; out of print, 19th-20th C, £1-£500; general, 50p-£100.* LOC: 20 yards from South Circular. PARK: Easy. TEL: 0181 876 7424. FAIRS: Hotel Russell, PBFA monthly.

Yesterday's Antiques
315 Upper Richmond Rd. West. SW14 8QR. (H. Rau). Open 9.30-6, Sun. 9.30-5. *STOCK: Old pine and country furniture.* TEL: 0181 876 7536.

LONDON SW15

R.A. Barnes Antiques LAPADA
26 Lower Richmond Rd., Putney. SW15. Open 10-5. CL: Sat. SIZE: Large. *STOCK: English, Oriental and Continental porcelain, antiques and collectables; Wedgwood, ironstone, china, brass, copper, 19th C; Bohemian and art glass, Regency, Victorian and some 18th C small furniture, primitive paintings.* TEL: 0181 789 3371. VAT: Stan/Spec.

The Clock Clinic Ltd LAPADA
85 Lower Richmond Rd., Putney. SW15 1EU. (R.S. Pedler). FBHI. Est. 1971. Open 9-6, Sat. 9-1. CL: Mon. *STOCK: Clocks and barometers.* TEL: 0181 788 1407; fax - 0181 780 2838. SER: Valuations; restorations (as stock); buys at auction. VAT: Stan/Spec.

SW15 continued

Han-Shan Tang Books
42 Westleigh Ave., Putney. SW15 6RL. Open by appointment only. *STOCK: Secondhand and antiquarian books and periodicals on Chinese, Japanese, Korean and central Asian art and culture.* TEL: 0181 788 4464; fax - 0181 780 1565.

Harwood Antiques
24 Lower Richmond Rd., Putney. SW15 1JP. (G. M. Harwood). Est. 1962. SIZE: Medium. *STOCK: Decorative items and furniture, £150-£1,500; textiles, £30-£500; mirrors, oils, watercolours and prints, £100-£550; all 18th-19th C.* LOC: Continuation of King's Rd., over Putney Bridge. PARK: Nearby. TEL: 0181 788 7444.

Jorgen Antiques
40 Lower Richmond Rd., Putney. SW15 1JP. (A.J. Dolleris). Est. 1960. Open 11-5. CL: Mon. and Sat. SIZE: Large. *STOCK: English and Continental furniture, 18th to early 19th C, £50-£5,000.* LOC: Between Putney Bridge and Putney Common. PARK: Easy. TEL: 0181 789 7329. VAT: Spec.

A.V. Marsh and Son
Vale House, Kingston Vale. SW15 3RN. Est. 1960. Open 9-6. *STOCK: Furniture, 18th to early 19th C.* TEL: 0181 546 5996.

Thornhill Galleries Ltd. in association with A. & R. Dockerill Ltd
Rear of 78 Deodar Rd., Putney. SW15 2NJ. Est. 1880. Open 9-5.15, Sat. 10-12.30. SIZE: Large. *STOCK: English and French marble, stone and wood chimney-pieces, English and French panelled rooms, architectural features and wood carvings, fire grates and fenders, 17th-19th C; decorative iron interiors and other fire accessories, 17th-20th C.* LOC: Off Putney Bridge Rd. PARK: Easy. TEL: 0181 874 2101/5669. SER: Valuations; restorations (architectural items); buys at auction (architectural items). VAT: Stan/Spec.

LONDON SW16

H.C. Baxter and Sons BADA LAPADA
40 Drewstead Rd. SW16 1AB. (T.J., J. and G.J Baxter). Est. 1928. Open Wed. and Thurs. 8.30-5.15, or by appointment. SIZE: Medium. *STOCK: English furniture, 1730-1830, £1,000-£35,000.* LOC: Near Streatham Hill station. PARK: Easy. TEL: 0181 769 5869/5969; fax - 0181 769 0898.

A. and J. Fowle
542 Streatham High Rd. SW16 3QF. Est. 1962. Open 9.30-7. SIZE: Large. *STOCK: General antiques, Victorian and Edwardian furniture.* LOC: From London take A23 towards Brighton. PARK: Easy. TEL: 0181 764 2896.

SW16 continued

Rapscallion Antiques Ltd
25 Shrubbery Rd., Streatham. SW16 2AS. (Mrs P. Barry). Open 10-5. CL: Mon. and Thurs. *STOCK: General antiques and bric-a-brac.* TEL: 0181 769 8078.

William Reeves Bookseller Ltd
1a Norbury Crescent. SW16 4JR. Est. 1871. Open by appointment. SIZE: Medium. *STOCK: Books about music, 1800-1970, £1-£100.* LOC: From station under railway bridge, first left. PARK: Easy. TEL: 0181 764 2108.

LONDON SW17

Ted Few
97 Drakefield Rd. SW17 8RS. Resident. Est 1975. Open by appointment. SIZE: Medium *STOCK: Paintings and sculpture, 1700-1940 £500-£5,000.* LOC: 5 mins. walk from Tooting Bec underground station. TEL: 0181 767 2314 SER: Valuations; buys at auction. VAT: Spec.

LONDON SW18

International Arts Group
436 Garratt Lane, Wandsworth. SW18 4DP. Open 9-6. CL: All day Mon. and Wed. p.m. except by appointment. *STOCK: Oils, watercolours etchings, limited edition prints, 19th-20th C.* TEL 0181 944 1404; fax - 0181 947 8174.

Mr Wandle's Workshop
202 Garratt Lane, Wandsworth. SW18 4ED. (S Zoil). Open 9-5.30. *STOCK: Victorian an Edwardian fireplaces and surrounds especiall cast iron.* TEL: 0181 870 5873. SER: Shot blasting.

Woodentops Country Furniture
537/539 Garratt Lane, Earlsfield. SW18 4SR. (C R. Smith). Est. 1987. Open 10-7, Sun. 10.30-5 SIZE: Large. *STOCK: Pine furniture, mainly reproduction.* LOC: Main road between Wandsworth an Tooting. PARK: Easy. TEL: 0181 947 6124. SER Restorations (pine). VAT: Stan.

LONDON SW19

Acanthus Antiques
171 Arthur Rd., Wimbledon Park. SW19 8AD (Isabella von Lobkowitz and Jerry Pol). Est. 198 Open 9.30-5.30, Sat. 9.30-2. CL: Mon. SIZE Small. *STOCK: Furniture and general antique Arts and Crafts, Art Nouveau, £20-£2,000.* LOC 50yds. from Wimbledon Park underground station. PARK: Easy. TEL: 0181 944 8404 (24 hrs SER: Vaulations; restorations (furniture); buys at auction.

SW19 continued

Adams Room Antiques LAPADA
18-20 Ridgway, Wimbledon Village. SW19 4LN. Est. 1971. Open 9.30-5. SIZE: Large. *STOCK: 18th-19th C English and French furniture especially dining; decorative Regency chairs, silver.* LOC: 4 miles from King's Rd., Chelsea; 1 mile off Kingston by-pass, M3. TEL: 0181 946 7047/947 4784. SER: Export orders arranged. VAT: Spec.

Allegra's Lighthouse Antiques LAPADA
75-77 Ridgway, Wimbledon Village. SW19 4ST. (Mrs E. Kingston). Est. 1969. Open 12-5.30, Sat. 10-5.30. *STOCK: Antique lighting, brass and glass chandeliers, sets of wall lights, table lights; period mirrors; 19th C furniture, £600-£6,000.* PARK: Easy. TEL: 0181 946 2050.

Chelsea Bric-a-Brac Shop Ltd
16 Hartfield Rd., Wimbledon. SW19 3TA. (P. and C. Wirth). Est. 1960. Open 10-5 or by appointment. CL: Wed. SIZE: Medium. *STOCK: Furniture - antique, Victorian, pine and shipping, 1800-1930, £20-£5,000; brass, copper, steel, £1-£500; bric-a-brac, £1-£250; all from Victorian.* Not Stocked: Jewellery, weapons. LOC: Left from Wimbledon station, first turning on right, shop 100yds. on left. PARK: 100yds. TEL: 0181 946 6894; home - 0181 542 5509. SER: Restorations (wood and upholstery); Continental export. VAT: Stan.

Clunes Antiques
9 West Place, Wimbledon Common. SW19 4UH. Est. 1973. Open 10-4.30. CL: Mon. *STOCK: General small and country antiques, Staffordshire figures, theatrical ephemera.* TEL: 0181 946 1643.

Coromandel
P.O Box 9772. SW19 3ZG. (P. Lang and B. Leigh). Resident. Open at any time by appointment. SIZE: Small. *STOCK: Boxes and table cabinets veneered in ivory, horn or tortoiseshell, sadeli (micro-mosaic work) or from solid exotic woods (sandalwood, amboyna, ebony, coromandel, etc) - Anglo-Indian, Vizagapatam, Indo-Portuguese, Dutch East Indies, Sri Lanka, 17th-19th C, £250-£5,000.* PARK: Easy. TEL: 0181 543 9115; fax - 0181 543 6255.

The David Curzon Gallery
35 Church Rd., Wimbledon Village. SW19. Open 10-6. CL: Mon. SIZE: Medium. *STOCK: Paintings and watercolours, from 1900, £350-£10,000.* LOC: 7 min. walk from Wimbledon Underground/BR. PARK: Reasonable. TEL: 0181 944 6098. VAT: Spec.

SW19 continued

Richard Maryan and Daughters
177 Merton Rd. SW19 1EE. Est. 1966. Open 10-5. CL: Wed. pm. and Mon. SIZE: Large. *STOCK: General antiques.* PARK: Reasonable. TEL: 0181 542 5846.

Mark J. West - Cobb Antiques Ltd BADA
39B High St., Wimbledon Village. SW19 5BY. Open 10-5.30, other times by appointment. SIZE: Large. *STOCK: Antique glass, £5-£5,000.* PARK: Easy. TEL: 0181 946 2811/540 7982. SER: Valuations; buys at auction. FAIRS: Olympia.

LONDON SW20

W.G.T. Burne (Antique Glass) Ltd BADA
PO Box 9465. (Formerly of Elystan St.) SW20 9ZD. (Mrs G. and A.T.G. Burne). Est. 1936. *STOCK: English and Irish glassware, Georgian and Victorian decanters; chandeliers, candelabra and lustres.* TEL: 0181 543 6319 (answerphone); fax - same; mobile - 0374 725834. SER: Valuations; restorations. VAT: Stan/Spec.

Hamilton's Corner
407A Kingston Rd. SW20 8JS. (P. and W Hamilton). Est. 1972. Open 10-5. CL: Wed. SIZE: Medium. *STOCK: Edwardian furniture; stripped pine, shipping goods, £25-£500.* LOC: From A3 at New Malden follow A298 Merton for 1 mile. PARK: Easy. TEL: 0181 540 1744. VAT: Stan.

Kensington Sporting Paintings Ltd LAPADA
2 The Downs, Wimbledon. SW20 8HN. (J.S. Bates). Open by appointment only. *STOCK: Oil paintings especially sporting; animalier bronzes, 19th C.* TEL: 0181 947 7772. SER: Valuations; restorations.

LONDON SE1

Antique Trade Warehouse
155 Tower Bridge Rd., Bermondsey. SE1 3LW. (Margaret McCarthy). Est. 1983. Open 9.30-5. SIZE: Warehouse. *STOCK: General antiques and shipping goods.* PARK: Easy. SER: Valuations.

Antique Warehouse
175D Bermondsey St., Newhams Row. SE1 3UW. (Waterloo Trading Co. and Micallef Antiques). Open Mon.-Fri. 8-6. SIZE: Large. *STOCK: Victorian, Edwardian and shipping furniture.* TEL: 0171 357 7168; fax - 0171 357 7179. SER: Robert Boys Shipping; packing.

SE1 continued

The Antiques Pavilion

175 Bermondsey St. SE1 3UW. (Capital City Investments Ltd). Est. 1966. Open 9.30-6, Fri. 7-6, Sat. 9-2. SIZE: Large. *STOCK: Furniture, Georgian to 1930's, £25-£25,000.* LOC: Near Bermondsey Market, close to Tower Bridge. PARK: Easy. TEL: 0171 403 2021. SER: Restorations (re-leathering, French polishing); buys at auction. VAT: Stan.

Nigel A. Bartlett BADA

67 St. Thomas St. SE1 3QX. Open 9.30-5.30. CL: Sat. *STOCK: Marble, pine and stone chimney pieces.* TEL: 0171 378 7895/6; fax - 0171 378 0388.

Bermondsey Antique Traders LAPADA

158 Bermondsey St. SE1. (R. Bush and B. Hawkins). Open 9.30-5. SIZE: Large. *STOCK: Furniture.* TEL: 0171 378 1000; fax - same.

Bermondsey Antiques Market

Corner of Long Lane and Bermondsey St. SE1. (Atlantic Antiques Centres Ltd). Est. 1959. Open Fri. 5 am-2 pm. *STOCK: Wide range of general antiques and collectables including specialist dealers in most fields especially silver.* LOC: Borough, Tower Hill or London Bridge tube stations. TEL: Enquiries - 0171 351 5353; fax - 0171 351 5350. SER: Valuations; book binding.

Victor Burness Antiques and Scientific Instruments

241 Long Lane, Bermondsey. SE1 4PR. (V.G. Burness). Est. 1975. Open Fri. 6am-1pm or by appointment. SIZE: Small. *STOCK: Scientific instruments, marine items, 19th C, £20-£1,500.* PARK: Easy. TEL: Home - 01732 454591. SER: Valuations. FAIRS: Portman Hotel.

Euro Antiques Warehouse

Royal Oak Yard, Bermondsey St. SE1. (Ian Wilson). Est. 1975. Open 9-6, Fri. 7-6. SIZE: Large. *STOCK: Furniture, including 1930's and secondhand reproduction, £500-£6,000.* PARK: Own. TEL: 0171 403 0765; home - 01732 885527. VAT: Stan.

The Old Cinema Antique Warehouse LAPADA

157 Tower Bridge Rd., Bermondsey. SE1 3LW. Open 10-6, Sun. 12-5. SIZE: Very large. *STOCK: Furniture - antique, architectural, garden and shop including replica, £100-£20,000.* PARK: Easy. TEL: 0171 407 5371; fax - 0171 403 0359; internet - www.antiques-uk.co.uk. VAT: Stan/Spec.

SE1 continued

Oola Boola Antiques London

166 Tower Bridge Rd. SE1 3LS. (R. and S. Scales). Est. 1968. Open 9-5.30. Sat.10-5. SIZE: Large. *STOCK: Furniture, £5-£3,000; mahogany, oak, some walnut, Victorian, Arts & Crafts, Art Nouveau, Edwardian, Art Deco and shipping goods.* TEL: 0171 403 0794; home - 0181 693 5050; fax - 0171 403 8405.

Penny Farthing Antiques

177 Bermondsey St. SE1. Est. 1976. Open 10-5. CL: Sat. SIZE: Medium. *STOCK: Furniture including shipping, £25-£1,000; longcase clocks, £200-£1,000; general small antiques and shipping items, £5-£200.* LOC: 5 mins. from Tower Bridge. PARK: Usually easy. TEL: 0171 407 5171. VAT: Stan.

Tower Bridge Antiques

159/161 Tower Bridge Rd. SE1 3LW. Open 9-5, Sat. 9.30-5, Sun. 10-4. SIZE: Large. *STOCK: Victorian, Georgian and Edwardian furniture, shipping goods.* TEL: 0171 403 3660. VAT: Stan.

Giovanni Viventi

173 Bermondsey St. SE1 3UW. Est. 1976. Open 9.30-6.30. CL: Sat. and Sun. except by appointment. SIZE: Large. *STOCK: Furniture and general antiques.* TEL: 0171 407 2566/403 0022; fax - 0171 403 6808.

George S. Wissinger Antiques

166 Bermondsey St. SE1 3TQ. Open 7-5.30. CL: Sat. SIZE: Large. *STOCK: Furniture and paintings.* TEL: 0171 407 5795; fax - same.

LONDON SE3

Michael Silverman

PO Box 350. SE3 0LZ. *STOCK: Manuscripts, autograph letters, historical documents.* TEL: 0181 319 4452; fax - 0181 856 6006. SER: Catalogue available. *Postal Only.*

Vale Stamps and Antiques

21 Tranquil Vale, Blackheath. SE3 0BU. (H.J. and R.P. Varnham). Est. 1952. Open 10-5.30. CL: Thurs. SIZE: Small. *STOCK: Roman bronze and silver artefacts, £25-£200; Georgian and Victorian jewellery, £25-£250.* LOC: Village centre, 100yds. from station. PARK: Nearby. TEL: 0181 852 9817. SER: Valuations; buys at auction (antiquities). VAT: Stan/Spec.

Wallace Antiques Ltd

56 Tranquil Vale, Blackheath. SE3 0BD. Open 9.30-5.30. *STOCK: Furniture including reproduction.* TEL: 0181 852 2647.

LONDON SE5

Franklin's Camberwell Antiques Market
161 Camberwell Rd. SE5. (R. Franklin). Est. 1968. Open 10-6, Sun. 1-6. SIZE: Large - five floors. *STOCK: French and English mirrors and beds, furniture, lighting, prints, architectural and garden items.* LOC: 1 mile from Elephant and Castle via Walworth Rd. PARK: 50yds. behind building, outside premises on Sunday. TEL: 0171 703 8089. VAT: Stan/Spec.

Robert E. Hirschhorn BADA
SE5 8JA. Est. 1979. Open by appointment. *STOCK: English and Continental furniture, mainly oak, walnut and fruitwood, and works of art, 18th C and earlier.* TEL: 0171 703 7443; mobile - 0831 405937. FAIRS: BADA (March); Olympia (June and Nov.); Chelsea (Sept.); Grosvenor House (June).

LONDON SE6

Wilkinson plc
5 Catford Hill. SE6 4NU. Est. 1947. Open 9-5. CL: Sat. SIZE: Medium. *STOCK: Glass especially chandeliers, 18th C and reproduction, art metal work.* LOC: Opposite Catford Bridge railway station. Entrance through Wickes D.I.Y. car park. PARK: Easy. TEL: 0181 314 1080. SER: Restorations and repairs (glass, metalwork).

LONDON SE7

Ward Antiques
267 Woolwich Rd., Charlton. SE7. (T. and M. Ward). Est. 1981. Open 9.30-5.30, Sun. 10-2. SIZE: Medium. *STOCK: Victorian fireplaces, Victorian and Edwardian furniture, £50-£1,000.* LOC: From A102 M take Woolwich/Woolwich ferry turn, 100yds. from roundabout, immediately under railway bridge across the road. PARK: Easy. TEL: 0181 305 0963; home - 0181 698 0771/591 3451.

LONDON SE8

Antique Warehouse
9-14 Deptford Broadway. SE8 4PA. Est. 1986. Open 10-6, Sun. 11-4. SIZE: Large. *STOCK: Fine furniture, 1750 to 20th C; sofas, chairs, mirrors and oleographs.* TEL: 0181 691 3062. VAT: Stan.

LONDON SE9

The Fireplace
257 High St., Eltham. SE9 1TY. (A. Clark). Est. 1978. Open daily. SIZE: Medium. *STOCK:*

SE9 continued

Fireplaces, 19th-20th C, £100-£1,000. PARK: Adjacent side streets. TEL: 0181 850 4887. SER: Restorations (fireplaces). VAT: Stan.

R.E. Rose FBHI
731 Sidcup Rd., Eltham. SE9 3SA. Est. 1976. Open 9-5. CL: Thurs. SIZE: Small. *STOCK: Clocks and barometers, 1750-1930, £50-£5,000.* LOC: A20 from London, shop on left just past fiveways traffic lights at Green Lane. PARK: Easy. TEL: 0181 859 4754. SER: Restorations (clocks and barometers); spare parts for antique clocks and barometers. VAT: Stan/Spec.

LONDON SE10

Creek Antiques
23 South St., Greenwich. SE10 8NW. Est. 1986. Open 11-5, appointment advisable Mon. and Tues. SIZE: Small. *STOCK: Jewellery and silver, from Victorian, £5-£500.* LOC: 200 yards from British Rail station. PARK: Easy. TEL: 0181 293 5721; mobile - 0378 427521. SER: Valuations; restorations (jewellery and watch repairs, silversmithing)

Greenwich Antiques Market
Greenwich High Rd. SE10. Est. 1972. Open Sun. 7.30-4.30, and Sat. (June-Sept.). SIZE: 80 stalls. *STOCK: General antiques and bric-a-brac.* LOC: Almost opposite railway station. PARK: Adjacent.

The Greenwich Gallery
9 Nevada St. SE10 9JL. (R.F. Moy). Est. 1965. Open 10-5.30 including Sun. *STOCK: Mainly English oil paintings and watercolours, 18th C to 1950.* TEL: 0181 305 1666. SER: Restorations; framing; exhibitions. VAT: Spec.

The Junk Shop
9 Greenwich South St. SE10 8NW. (T.B. de C. Moy). Est. 1985. Open 10-5.30, including Sun. SIZE: Large. *STOCK: Larger antique and decorative items, 18th C to 1950s; furniture, architectural antiques, bric-a-brac.* LOC: A202. From London follow A2, then turn left at Deptford - or follow riverside road from Tower Bridge. PARK: Meters. TEL: 0181 305 1666, ext. 25. SER: Restorations (furniture). VAT: Stan/Spec.

SE10 continued

Lamont Antiques Ltd LAPADA
Tunnel Avenue Antique Warehouse, Tunnel Avenue Trading Estate, Greenwich. SE10 0QH. (N. Lamont and F. Llewellyn). Open 9-5.30. CL: Sat. SIZE: Large. *STOCK: Architectural fixtures and fittings, bars, stained glass, pub mirrors and signs, shipping furniture, £5-£25,000.* PARK: Own. TEL: 0181 305 2230; fax - 0181 305 1805. SER: Container packing.

Peter Laurie Antiques
28 Greenwich Church St. SE10 9BQ. Open 10-5 including Sun. CL: Fri. am. *STOCK: Nautical items, navigational instruments, maritime curiosities, weapons and photographic items.* TEL: 0181 853 5777.

The Warwick Leadlay Gallery
5 Nelson Rd., Greenwich. SE10 9JB. Est. 1974. Open 9.30-5.30, Sun. and Bank Holidays 11-5.30. SIZE: Large. *STOCK: Antiquarian prints, maps, illustrated books and Nelsoniana, 17th-19th C.* LOC: 2 mins. walk from Cutty Sark. PARK: Nearby. TEL: 0181 858 0317; fax - 0181 853 1773; home - 0181 293 5032. SER: Valuations; restorations, cleaning, colouring, mounting, framing. VAT: Stan.

SE10 continued

Main Street Antiques
24 Woolwich Rd. SE10 0JU. (B. Sessacar). Open 10-6 including Sun. CL: Thurs. *STOCK: Victorian pine and fireplaces.* TEL: 0181 305 1971.

Relcy Antiques
9 Nelson Rd., Greenwich. SE10. (R. Challis). Est. 1958. Open 10-6. CL: Sun. except by appointment. SIZE: Large. *STOCK: English furniture, especially bureaux and bookcases, £50-£15,000; English and Continental pictures, especially marine and sporting, £20-£5,000; instruments and marine items, ships' heads, sextants, telescopes, models, £20-£15,000; all 18th-19th C.* Not Stocked: Reproduction and Art Deco. LOC: ¾ mile off A2 towards River Thames. TEL: 0181 858 2812. SER: Valuations, restorations (furniture and pictures); buys at auction (Georgian and Victorian furniture, pictures). VAT: Stan/Spec.

Rogers Turner Books
22 Nelson Rd., Greenwich. SE10 9JB. Est. 1975. Open Thurs.-Sun. 10-6. *STOCK: Antiquarian books especially on clocks and scientific instruments.* TEL: 0181 853 5271; fax - same; Paris - 0033 13912 1191. SER: Buys at auction (British and European); catalogues available.

SE10 continued

Spread Eagle Antiques
8 Nevada St. SE10 9JL. (R.F. Moy). Est. 1954. Open 10-5.30 including Sun. SIZE: Large. *STOCK: Books, period costume, curios, china, bric-a-brac, prints, postcards.* Not Stocked: Furniture. LOC: A202. From London follow A2, then turn left at Deptford - or follow riverside road from Tower Bridge. PARK: Easy. TEL: 0181 305 1666. SER: Valuations; restorations (furniture, china, pictures). VAT: Stan/Spec.

Spread Eagle Antiques
1 Stockwell St. SE10 9JL. (R.F. Moy). Est. 1954. Open 10-5.30 including Sun. SIZE: Large. *STOCK: Furniture, pictures and decorative items, 18th-19th C.* PARK: Easy. TEL: 0181 305 1666; home - 0181 692 1618. SER: Valuations; restorations (pictures, furniture). VAT: Stan/Spec.

Robert Whitfield Antiques LAPADA
Tunnel Avenue Antique Warehouse, Tunnel Avenue Trading Estate, Greenwich. SE10 0QH. Open 10-5. CL: Sat. *STOCK: Edwardian, Victorian and secondhand furniture, especially bentwood chairs.* TEL: 0181 305 2230; fax - 0181 305 1805. SER: Container packing.

LONDON SE13

Robert Morley and Co Ltd BADA
34 Engate St., Lewisham. SE13 7HA. Est. 1881. Open 9-5. *STOCK: Pianos, harpsichords, clavichords, spinets, virginals.* PARK: Own. TEL: 0181 318 5838; fax - 0181 297 0720. SER: Restorations (musical instruments). VAT: Stan.

LONDON SE15

Peter Allen Antiques Ltd. World Wide Antique Exporters LAPADA
17-17a Nunhead Green, Peckham. SE15 3QQ. Est. 1966. Open 8-4. CL: Sat. SIZE: Large. *STOCK: Fine Victorian furniture.* TEL: 0171 732 1968.

A. Fagiani
30 Wagner St. SE15. Est. 1965. Open 8-1 and 2-6, Sat. 8-1. *STOCK: Bookcases, pedestal desks.* LOC: Off Kent Rd. and Ilderton Rd. TEL: 0171 732 7188. SER: Valuations; restorations (furniture); French polishing. VAT: Stan.

LONDON SE20

The Black Cat
202 High St. SE20 7QB. (Brian and Cindy Aust). Open by appointment only. *STOCK: Furniture, 19th C; general and decorative antiques.* LOC: Opposite Kent House Rd., Beckenham, Kent. TEL: 0181 466 9996.

LONDON SE21

Acorn Antiques
111 Rosendale Rd., West Dulwich. SE21 8EZ. (Mrs G. Kingham). Open 10-6, Sat. 10-5.30. *STOCK: Jewellery, china, glass, silver and plate, fire irons and fenders.* TEL: 0181 761 3349.

LONDON SE23

Oddiquities
61 Waldram Park Rd. and 20 Sunderland Rd., Forest Hill. SE23 2PW. (Mrs S.A. Butler). Est. 1966. Open 10-6, Sat. 10-4. CL: Sun. except by appointment and Thurs. SIZE: Medium. *STOCK: Oil lamps, gas and electric light fitments, 1800-1930; fire furnishings, 1780-1920; all £20-£500; general antiques, 1800-1920, £15-£1,000.* Not Stocked: Coins, stamps, medals, jewellery. LOC: On South Circular Rd., between Catford and Forest Hill. PARK: Opposite. TEL: 0181 699 9574.

LONDON SE24

Under Milkwood
379-381 Milkwood Rd., Herne Hill. SE24 0HA. (Nick and Sue Williams). Est. 1988. Open 10-5, Mon. 9-5.30, Sat. 9.30-5.30, Wed. by appointment. SIZE: Small. *STOCK: Victorian and Edwardian fireplaces, £150-£1,000; Victorian pine furniture, £100-£600.* LOC: At rear of Herne Hill station. PARK: Easy. TEL: 0171 733 3921; home - 0181 244 8562. SER: Valuations; restorations; fireplace-fitting. FAIRS: Ardingly, Newark.

LONDON SE25

Engine 'n' Tender
19 Spring Lane, Woodside Green. SE25 4SP. (Mrs Joyce M. Buttigieg). Est. 1957. Open Thurs. 12-6, Fri. 12-6.30, Sat. 10-6. SIZE: Small. *STOCK: Model railways, mainly pre 1939; Dinky toys, to 1968; old toys, mainly tinplate.* LOC: Near Woodside station. PARK: Easy. TEL: 0181 654 0386. FAIRS: Local toy.

North London Clock Shop Ltd
Rear of 60 Saxon Rd. SE25 5EH. (D.S. Tomlin). Est. 1960. Open 9-6. CL: Sat. SIZE: Medium. *STOCK: Clocks, longcase, bracket, carriage, skeleton, 18th-19th C.* PARK: Easy. TEL: 0181 664 8089. SER: Restorations (clocks and barometer); wheel cutting, hand engraving, dial painting, clock reconversions. FAIRS: Olympia. VAT: Stan.

LONDON SE26

Abbott Antiques and Country Pine
109 Kirkdale. SE26 4QJ. Est. 1972. Open 10-5.30, Sat. 10-5, Sun. 11-3. *STOCK: Victorian and Edwardian furniture including pine, and bric-a-brac.* LOC: 1/2 mile from South Circular Rd. at Forest Hill. TEL: 0181 699 1363.

T.A. Hillyer Antiques
301 Sydenham Rd. SE26 5EW. Est. 1952. Open 9.30-4, Sat. 9.30-2. CL: Wed. SIZE: Small. *STOCK: Furniture, silver, plate, porcelain, glass, books, bric-a-brac.* PARK: Easy. TEL: 0181 778 6361; home - 0181 777 2506. SER: Valuations.

Vintage Cameras Ltd
256 Kirkdale, Sydenham. SE26 4NL. (J. Jenkins). Est. 1968. Open 9-5. SIZE: Large. *STOCK: Vintage cameras, 1840-1950, £50-£5,000; general photographica, 1840-1950, £5-£50.* LOC: Near South Circular Rd. PARK: Nearby. TEL: 0181 778 5416; fax - 0181 778 5841. SER: Valuations. VAT: Stan.

LONDON E2

George Rankin Coin Co. Ltd
325 Bethnal Green Rd. E2. Open 10-5. *STOCK: Coins, medals, medallions and jewellery.* TEL: 0171 739 1840/729 1280; fax - 0171 729 5023.

St. Peters Organ Works
St. Peters Close, Warner Pl. E2 7AF. (J.P. Mander and D. Frostick). Est. 1935. CL: Sat. SIZE: Large. *STOCK: Antique pipe organs.* LOC: Opposite children's hospital, Hackey Rd. PARK: Own. TEL: 0171 739 4747. SER: Valuations; restorations. VAT: Stan.

LONDON E4

Record Detector
3 & 4 Station Approach, Station Rd., Chingford. E4 6AL. (N. Salter). Est. 1992. Open 10-6. CL: Thurs. SIZE: Small (2 shops). *STOCK: Secondhand and collectable records, L.P's, E.P's, singles and CD's.* LOC: In forecourt of North Chingford railway station. PARK: Easy. TEL: 0181 529 6361/2938.

LONDON E8

Boxes and Musical Instruments
2 Middleton Rd., Hackney. E8 4BL. (A. and J. O'Kelly). Est. 1974. Open any time by appointment. SIZE: Medium. *STOCK: Boxes - caddies, sewing, writing, snuff, vanity, jewellery and desk, £50-£3,000; musical instruments, plucked string, £250-£1,500; all 18th-19th C.* LOC: Off Kingsland Rd., continuation of Bishopsgate. PARK: Easy. TEL: 0171 254 7074; home - same; e-mail - boxes@global net.co.uk. SER: Valuations;

E8 continued

restorations (exceptional instruments only). Registered with the Conservation Unit of the Museums and Galleries Commission.

LONDON E11

P. Blake - Old Cottage Antiques
8 High St., Wanstead. E11 2AJ. Est. 1920. Open Thurs. and Fri. 10.30-5.30. SIZE: Medium. *STOCK: Furniture, paintings, 19th-20th C.* LOC: Near Wanstead station and Snaresbrook. TEL: 0181 989 2317/504 9264. SER: Valuations; buys at auction. VAT: Stan/Spec.

LONDON E17

Collectors Centre - Antique City
98 Wood St. E17. Est. 1978. Open 9.30-5.30. CL: Thurs. SIZE: Large. *STOCK: Antiques, collectables, 40's, 50's, 60's, £1-£500.* PARK: Opposite. TEL: 0181 520 4032. *Trade Only.*

Georgian Village Antiques Market
100 Wood St., Walthamstow. E17 3HX. Est. 1972. Open 10-5. CL: Thurs. SIZE: 10 shops. *STOCK: Clocks, barometers, postcards, collectables, jewellery, brass, copper, stamps, silver, silver plate, crafts.* LOC: 50yds. from Dukes Head. PARK: Adjacent. TEL: 0181 520 6638.

Georgina's Antiques
134 Palmerston Rd., Walthamstow. E17 6PY. (G.P. Webb). Open Thurs., Fri. and Sat. 10-5. *STOCK: Victorian and Edwardian furniture and china; decorative items.* TEL: 0181 520 7015.

LONDON E18

Rupert's Antiques
33 Victoria Rd., South Woodford. E18. Open 10-6. *STOCK: Pine including reproduction, satinwood; Victorian fireplaces, surrounds, smalls.* TEL: 0181 530 6229. SER: Installations (fireplaces).

LONDON EC1

City Clocks
31 Amwell St. EC1R 1UN. (J. Rosson). FBHI. Est. 1960. Open 9-5, Sat. 9.30-1.30 or by appointment. CL: Mon. SIZE: Medium. *STOCK: Clocks, watches, some furniture, 18th-19th C, £100-£7,000.* PARK: Easy. TEL: 0171 278 1154. SER: Valuations; restorations (clocks and watches); buys at auction. VAT: Stan.

Eldridge London
99-101 Farringdon Rd. EC1R 3DT. (B. Eldridge). Est. 1953. Open 10-5, Sat. 10-1. SIZE: Large. *STOCK: Furniture and items of social and historical importance.* PARK: Easy. TEL: 0171 837 0379. VAT: Spec.

EC1 continued

Finecraft Workshop Ltd
10 Greville St. EC1 8SB. (Martyn J. Pummell). NAG. Est. 1955. Open 10.15-5, Sat. 10.15-4.30, Sun. 10.15-2. SIZE: Medium. *STOCK: Jewellery, 19th-20th C, £100-£8,000+.* LOC: Between Farringdon Rd. and Hatton Garden. PARK: Nearby. TEL: 0171 242 3825; fax - 0171 404 0170. SER: Valuations; restorations; re-making and repairing; insurance claims undertaken; buys at auction. FAIRS: Europe and USA. VAT: Stan.

C.R. Frost and Son Ltd
60-62 Clerkenwell Rd. EC1M 5PX. BCWMG; BHI. *STOCK: Quality vintage watches, clocks and barometers.* TEL: 0171 253 0315; fax - 0171 253 7454. SER: Repairs; clock and watch materials; batteries; clock glasses and bevelling to order.

Jonathan Harris (Jewellery) Ltd
63-66 Hatton Garden (office). EC1N 8LE. (E.C. and D. Harris). Est. 1958. Open 9.30-4.30. CL: Sat. *STOCK: Antique and secondhand rings, brooches, pendants, bracelets and other jewellery, from £100.* PARK: Nearby. TEL: 0171 242 9115/242 1558; fax - 0171 831 4417. SER: Valuations; export. FAIRS: Basle, Switzerland and Munich, Germany. VAT: Stan/Spec.

Hirsh Ltd
10 Hatton Garden. EC1N 8AH. (A. Hirsh). Open 10-6, Sun. 10-3. *STOCK: Fine jewellery, silver and objets d'art.* TEL: 0171 405 6080; fax - 0171 430 0107. SER: Valuations; jewellery designed and remodelled.

R. Holt and Co. Ltd
98 Hatton Garden. EC1N 8NX. Est. 1948. Open 9.30-5.30. CL: Sat. *STOCK: Gemstone specialists.* TEL: 0171 405 5286/0197; fax - 0171 430 1279. SER: Valuations; restorations (gem stone cutting and testing; bead stringing; inlaid work).

House of Buckingham (Antiques)
113-117 Farringdon Rd. EC1R 3BT. (B.B. White). Est. 1970. Open 9-6. *STOCK: Boxes, clocks, furniture, brass, nautical goods.* TEL: 0171 278 2013. VAT: Stan/Spec.

Joseph and Pearce Ltd LAPADA
63-66 Hatton Garden. EC1. Est. 1896. Open by appointment. *STOCK: Jewellery, 1800-1960, £100-£2,500.* TEL: 0171 405 4604/7; fax - 0171 242 1902. VAT: Stan/Spec. *Trade Only.*

R.I. McKay
88/90 Hatton Garden. EC1N 8PN. Est. 1951. Open by appointment only. SIZE: Small. *STOCK: Jewellery, all periods, from £100.* LOC: Centre of Hatton Garden. PARK: Easy and multi-storey nearby. TEL: 0171 405 7544; fax - 0171 404 5586. VAT: Stan/Spec. *Trade Only.*

EC1 continued

A.R. Ullmann Ltd
10 Hatton Garden. EC1N 8AH. (J.S. Ullmann). Est. 1939. Open 9-5, Sat. 9.30-5. SIZE: Small. *STOCK: Jewellery, gold, silver and diamond; silver and objets d'art.* LOC: Very close to Farringdon and Chancery Lane tube stations. PARK: Multi-storey in St. Cross St. TEL: 0171 405 1877; fax - 0171 404 7071; home - 0181 346 2546. SER: Valuations; restorations. VAT: Stan/Spec.

LONDON EC2

The London Architectural Salvage & Supply Co. (LASSCo) LAPADA
St. Michael's Church, Mark St. (off Paul St.). EC2A 4ER. Est. 1977. Open 10-5 including Sun. *STOCK: Architectural antiques including panelled rooms, chimney pieces, lighting, statuary, garden ornaments, fountains, church and door furniture, stained glass, new and antique flooring, columns and capitals, architectural stonework, relics and curiosities.* TEL: 0171 739 0448; fax - 0171 729 6853.

Westland & Company
St. Michael's Church, Leonard St. EC2A 4ER. Est. 1986. Open 9-6. SIZE: Large. *STOCK: Unusual architectural items including fireplaces;*

EC2 continued

panelling, panelled rooms, light-fittings, turret clocks, stonework ceilings and garden elements; English and Continental furniture and clocks; all £100-£100,000. LOC: Off Gt. Eastern St. PARK: Easy. TEL: 0171 739 8094; fax - 0171 729 3620.

LONDON EC3

Ash Rare Books

25 Royal Exchange. EC3V 3LP. (L. Worms). Est. 1946. Open 10-5.30. CL: Sat. SIZE: Small. *STOCK: Books, 1550-1980, £20-£10,000; maps, 1550-1850, £25-£2,000; prints, 1650-1900, £20-£1,000.* LOC: On the Threadneedle St. side of the Royal Exchange, opposite Bank of England. TEL: 0171 626 2665; fax - 0171 623 9052. SER: Buys at auction (books and maps); picture framing and mount cutting. VAT: Stan.

Halcyon Days BADA

4 Royal Exchange. EC3V 3LL. (S. Benjamin). Est. 1950. Open 10-5.30. *STOCK: 18th to early 19th C enamels, Georgian and Victorian scent bottles, papier mâché, tôle, objects of vertu, treen, unusual small Georgian furniture.* TEL: 0171 626 1120; fax - 0171 283 1876. FAIRS: Grosvenor House; BADA. VAT: Stan/Spec.

Nanwani and Co

2 Shopping Arcade, Bank Station, Cornhill. EC3V 3LA. Est. 1958. CL: Sat. *STOCK: Precious and semi-precious stones, Oriental items, objets d'art.* TEL: 0171 623 8232; fax - 0171 283 2548. VAT: Stan.

Royal Exchange Art Gallery

14 Royal Exchange. EC3V 3LL. Est. 1974. Open 10.30-5.15. CL: Sat. *STOCK: Oil paintings, watercolours and etchings, especially marine and landscape, 18th-20th C.* TEL: 0171 283 4400.

Searle and Co Ltd

1 Royal Exchange, Cornhill. EC3V 3LL. Est. 1893. Open 9-5.30. SIZE: Medium. *STOCK: Georgian, Victorian and secondhand silver; Victorian, Edwardian and secondhand jewellery.* LOC: Near Bank underground. PARK: Meters. TEL: 0171 626 2456. SER: Valuations; restorations; repairs; engraving. VAT: Stan/Spec.

LONDON EC4

J. Clarke-Hall Ltd

22 Bride Lane. EC4Y 8DX. ABA. Est. 1934. Open Mon.-Fri. 12-4. SIZE: Small. *STOCK: 19th C prints, maps and ephemera.* LOC: Off bottom of Fleet St., near Ludgate Hill. PARK: Meters. TEL: 0171 353 5483/4116. SER: Bookbinding; framing. VAT: Stan.

J. Clarke-Hall Ltd

5 Bride Court, Fleet St. EC4Y 8DX. ABA. Est. 1934. Open Mon.-Fri. 10.30-6. SIZE: Small. *STOCK: English literature, specialising in Samuel*

EC4 continued

Johnson, Lewis Carroll; illustrated books, modern first editions, £5-£750. TEL: 0171 353 4116/5483. SER: Bookbinding; framing; quarterly catalogue.

LONDON N1

After Noah

121 Upper St., Islington. N1 1QP. (M. Crawford and Z. Candlin). Est. 1990. Open 10-6, Sun. 12-5. SIZE: Medium. *STOCK: Arts and Craft oak and similar furniture, 1880's to 1950's, £1-£1,000; iron, iron and brass beds; decorative items, bric-a-brac including candlesticks, mirrors, lighting, kitchenalia and jewellery.* PARK: Side streets. TEL: 0171 359 4281; fax - same. SER: Restorations. VAT: Stan.

Angel Arcade

116-118 Islington High St., Camden Passage. N1 8EG. Open Wed. and Sat. Other days access available to the shops. SIZE: Large. *STOCK: General antiques.*

Annie's Antique Clothes

10 Camden Passage, Islington. N1. (A. Moss). Open 11-5. CL: Mon. TEL: 0171 359 0796.

The Antique Trader

The Millinery Works, 85/87 Southgate Rd. N1 3JS. (B. Thompson and D. Rothera). Est. 1968. Open at any time by appointment. SIZE: Large. *STOCK: Arts & Crafts and art furniture, £100-£15,000.* LOC: Close to Camden Passage Antiques Centre. PARK: Free. TEL: 0171 359 2019; fax - 0171 226 9446. VAT: Stan/Spec.

At the Sign of the Chest of Drawers

281 Upper St., Islington. N1 2TZ. (A. Harms). Open 10-6 including Sun. *STOCK: Pine, country furniture.* TEL: 0171 359 5909.

Ian Auld

1 Gateway Arcade, Camden Passage, Islington. N1 0PG. Est. 1968. Open Wed. and Sat. 10-5. SIZE: Small. *STOCK: Tribal art, mainly African; antiquities, mainly pottery, some Pre-Colombian, £25-£1,000.* Not Stocked: Victoriana. LOC: Near Angel tube station. PARK: Easy. TEL: 0171 359 1440.

Banbury Fayre

6 Pierrepont Arcade, Camden Passage, Islington. N1. (N. Steel). Est. 1984. Open Wed., Fri. and Sat. SIZE: Small. *STOCK: Collectables including commemoratives, shipping, Boy Scout movement, Boer War, air line travel.* PARK: 200yds. TEL: Home - 0181 852 5675.

William Bedford plc LAPADA

The Merchants Hall, 46 Essex Rd., Islington. N1 8LN. (John Bedford and Noel Corrigan). Est. 1959. Open 9.30-5.30. SIZE: Large. *STOCK: English period furniture and accessories.* LOC: 100yds. Camden Passage. PARK: Easy. TEL: 0171 226 9648; fax - 0171 226 6225. VAT: Stan/Spec.

N1 continued

Boutique Fantasque
13 Pierrepont Row, Camden Passage, Islington. N1. (Mrs M.A.B. Gates). Est. 1962. Open Wed. and Sat. SIZE: Small. *STOCK: Watercolours and prints, general antiques, porcelain, jewellery, small collectors' items.* LOC: From Piccadilly, No.19 bus. Tube to Angel station. PARK: 200yds.

Bushwood Antiques LAPADA
317 Upper St., Islington. N1 2XQ. (A. Bush). Est. 1967. Open 9.30-5.30 or by appointment. SIZE: Large. *STOCK: 18th-19th C furniture, decorators' items, works of art and clocks.* LOC: 100yds. from Camden Passage. PARK: 50yds. TEL: 0171 359 2095; fax - 0171 704 9578. VAT: Stan.

Camden Passage Antiques Centre
12 Camden Passage. N1 8ED. (S. Lemkow). Est. 1960. Open weekdays 10.30-5.30. Also 100 stalls open Wed. 8-3 and Sat. 9-5 - general antiques; Thurs. 9-4 - books. SIZE: 400 shops and boutiques some of which are listed in this section. LOC: Behind the Angel, Islington. TEL: 0171 359 0190.

Patric Capon BADA
350 Upper St., Islington. N1 0PD. Est. 1970. Open Wed. and Sat. or by appointment. SIZE: Medium. *STOCK: Unusual carriage clocks, 19th C, £450-£6,000; 8-day and 2-day marine chronometers, 19th C, £850-£4,500; clocks and barometers, 18th-19th C, £400-£6,500.* LOC: Adjacent Camden Passage. PARK: Easy. TEL: 0171 354 0487; fax - 0181 295 1475; home - 0181 467 5722. SER: Valuations; restorations. FAIRS: Olympia. VAT: Stan/Spec.

Chancery Antiques Ltd
357a Upper St., Islington. N1 0PD. (R. and D. Rote). Est. 1950. Open 10.30-5 or by appointment. CL: Mon. and Thurs. SIZE: Medium. *STOCK: Oriental works of art especially Japanese Meiji period.* TEL: 0171 359 9035. VAT: Stan/Spec.

Peter Chapman Antiques LAPADA
10 Theberton St., Islington. N1 0QX. (P.J. Chapman). CPTA. Est. 1971. Open 9.30-1 and 2-6. CL: Sun. and public holidays except by appointment. SIZE: Medium. *STOCK: Furniture and decorative objects, 1700-1900; paintings, drawings and prints, 17th to early 20th C; stained glass.* LOC: 5 mins. walk from Camden Passage down Upper St. PARK: Easy. TEL: 0171 226 5565; mobile - 0831 093662; fax - 0181 348 4846. SER: Valuations; restorations (furniture and period objects); buys at auction. VAT: Stan/Spec.

Chapter One
2 Pierrepont Arcade, Camden Passage. N1 9ES. (Yvonne Gill). Est. 1993. Open Wed. 9-3, Sat. 9-5 or by appointment.SIZE: Small. *STOCK: Handbags, costume jewellery, vintage accessories, fabrics, bric-a-brac, 1880-1960, £5-£300.* TEL: 0171 359 1185. SER: Jewellery repairs.

N1 continued

Charlton House Antiques
7 Charlton Place, Camden Passage, Islington. N1 8AQ. Open Wed. and Sat. 8-5, Tue. and Fri. 10-4. SIZE: Large. *STOCK: European and Scandinavian furniture, 1840-1930, £100-£5,000; general antiques.* LOC: Near Angel underground station. PARK: Easy. TEL: 0171 226 3141; fax - same. VAT: Stan/Spec.

Carlton Davidson Antiques
33 Camden Passage, Islington. N1 8EA. Est. 1981. Open Wed.-Sat. 10-4. SIZE: Medium. *STOCK: Lamps, chandeliers, mirrors and decorative items, £100-£3,000.* LOC: Near Charlton Place. PARK: Meters. TEL: 0171 226 7491. FAIRS: Decorative Antiques, Chelsea. VAT: Stan.

Dean's Antiques
25 Camden Passage, Islington. N1. Open Wed. and Sat. 9.30-5. *STOCK: Decorative items.* TEL: 0171 354 9940.

Dome Antiques (Exports) Ltd LAPADA
75 Upper St., Islington. N1 0NU. (A.D. Woolf). Est. 1961. Open 9.30-5.30. SIZE: Large. *STOCK: English furniture, 1700-1900, £500-£10,000; desks, library and dining tables, sets of chairs.* LOC: Opposite Islington Green. PARK: At rear. TEL: 0171 226 7227; mobile - 0831 805888; fax - 0171 704 2960. SER: Valuations. VAT: Stan/Spec.

Donay Antiques
35 Camden Passage, Islington. N1 8EA. (D.C. and C.E. Goddard). Est. 1980. Open Wed. and Sat. 9-5. SIZE: Large. *STOCK: Games and puzzles, £10-£2,000; chess sets, £50-£2,000; artists' colour boxes, £200-£800; stationery and letter boxes; amusement arcade machines.* LOC: Near Angel tube station. PARK: Charlton Place nearby. TEL: 0171 359 1880; fax - 0171 704 0488.

Eclectica
2 Charlton Place. N1. (E. Wilson). Open Wed. and Sat. 9-5.30, Thurs. and Fri. 12-5, or by appointment. *STOCK: Antique costume jewellery.* TEL: 0171 226 5625.

Feljoy Antiques
Shop 3, Angel Arcade, Camden Passage. N1 8EA. Open Wed. and Sat. 8-4. *STOCK: Decorative antiques and textiles.* TEL: 0171 354 5336.

Michael Finney Antique Prints and Books
11 Camden Passage, Islington. N1 8EA. Open 10-5. CL: Mon. *STOCK: Prints, 17th-19th C; plate books, watercolours especially David Roberts, Egypt, Holy Land and Spain, £1-£1,000.* PARK: Meters. TEL: 0171 226 9280; fax - 0171 359 0321.

The Fleamarket
7 Pierrepont Row, Camden Passage, Islington. N1 8EE. Open 9.30-6. CL: Mon. SIZE: Large. 26 stand-holders. *STOCK: Jewellery, furniture,*

N1 continued

objets d'art, militaria, guns, swords, pistols, porcelain, coins, medals, stamps, 18th-19th C, £1-£500; antiquarian books, prints, fine art, china, silver, glass and general antiques. PARK: Easy. TEL: 0171 226 8211. SER: Valuations; buys at auction; weapon repairs.

Vincent Freeman
1 Camden Passage, Islington. N1 2UD. Est. 1966. Open 10-5. CL: Mon. and Thurs. SIZE: Large. *STOCK: Music boxes, furniture and decorative items, from £100.* TEL: 0171 226 6178; fax - 0171 226 7231. VAT: Stan/Spec.

Furniture Vault
50 Camden Passage, Islington. N1 8AE. Open Tues.-Sat. 9.30-4.30. *STOCK: Furniture, 18th-20th C; decorative bronzes.* TEL: 0171 354 1047.

Georgian Village
Islington Green. N1. Open 10-4, Wed. and Sat. 7-5. PARK: Nearby. TEL: 0171 226 1571.

"Get Stuffed"
105 Essex Rd., Islington. N1 2SL. Est. 1975. Open 12-5, Mon. 1-5, Sat. 12-3. CL: Thurs. *STOCK: Stuffed birds, fish, animals, trophy heads; rugs; butterflies, insects.* TEL: 0171 226 1364; fax - 0171 359 8253. SER: Restorations; taxidermy; glass domes and cases supplied.

The Graham Gallery — LAPADA
104 Islington High St., Camden Passage, Islington. N1 8EG. Est. 1973. Open 10-5. SIZE: Large. *STOCK: Silver, 1750-1930, £250-£50,000; Victorian silver plate, £250-£50,000; Sheffield plate, £250-£25,000; Victorian oil paintings, £2,000-£50,000; late Victorian fine marquetry and painted furniture, £1,000-£50,000.* LOC: 2 mins. from Angel Underground. PARK: Easy. TEL: 0171 354 2112; fax - 0171 704 0728. VAT: Stan.

Gordon Gridley
28 & 41 Camden Passage, Islington. N1 8EA. Est. 1968. CL: Mon. SIZE: Large + warehouse at rear. *STOCK: English and Continental furniture, paintings, decorative objects, metalwork, glass and ceramics, statuary and garden furniture, 17th-19th C, £50-£20,000.* PARK: Business Design Centre or Charlton Place. TEL: 0171 226 0643. SER: Valuations; restorations. VAT: Stan/Spec.

Linda Gumb — LAPADA
9 Camden Passage, Islington. N1. Est. 1981. Open 9.30-4.30, Wed. 7.30-5, Sat. 9-5. SIZE: Medium. *STOCK: Textiles, 18th-19th C; decorative objects, 19th C; all £10-£5,000.* PARK: Easy. TEL: 0171 354 1184. SER: Buys at auction. FAIRS: Olympia. VAT: Stan.

Rosemary Hart
4 Gateway Arcade, 355 Upper St., Camden Passage. N1 0PG. Est. 1980. Open Wed. and Sat. 9-5, Tues. and Fri. 11-4. SIZE: Small. *STOCK:*

N1 continued

Silver plated tableware and decorative serving pieces, £5-£500; small silver gifts, from £50. LOC: Near Angel tube station. TEL: 0171 359 6839.

Hart and Rosenberg
2 and 3 Gateway Arcade, Camden Passage, Islington. N1 0PD. (E. Hart and H. Rosenberg). Est. 1968. Open 10-5, Wed. 9-5. CL: Mon. and Thurs. SIZE: Medium. *STOCK: Chinese, Japanese and European porcelain, works of art, decorative items, some furniture, £25-£5,000.* LOC: Near Angel tube station. PARK: Nearby. TEL: 0171 359 6839; fax - 0181 676 8984. SER: Valuations; buys at auction. VAT: Stan/Spec.

Sherry Hatcher
5 Gateway Arcade, Camden Passage, Upper St., Islington. N1 0PG. Est. 1966. Open 10-5. SIZE: Small. *STOCK: Perfume bottles, sugar shakers, silver, boxes and interesting silver items.* LOC: Near Angel tube station. PARK: Easy. TEL: 0171 226 5679.

Heritage Antiques — LAPADA
112 Islington High St., Camden Passage. N1 8EG. (A. Daniel). Est. 1975. Open Wed. 8.30-5 and Sat. 9.30-5 or by appointment. SIZE: Large. *STOCK: Metalware, £25-£3,000; some furniture and decorative items.* TEL: 0171 226 7789 or 01273 326850; fax - 01273 326850. VAT: Stan/Spec.

House of Steel Antiques
400 Caledonian Rd. N1 1DN. (J. Cole). Est. 1974. Open 10.30-5.30, Sat. by appointment. SIZE: Warehouse. *STOCK: Metal items - fireplaces, 18th-19th C, £50-£1,000; spiral staircases, £300-£1,000; balconies, railings, garden furniture, £50-£500; all 19th C.* LOC: Near King's Cross. PARK: Own. TEL: 0171 607 5889. SER: Valuations; restorations (welding, polishing, sandblasting); steel furniture manufactured, items made to order. VAT: Stan.

Diana Huntley — LAPADA
8 Camden Passage, Islington. N1 3ED. Est. 1970. Open Tues. and Fri. 10-4, Wed. 7.30-5, Thurs. by appointment, Sat. 9-5. *STOCK: European porcelain, £50-£10,000; objets d'art; all 19th C.* TEL: 0171 226 4605; fax - 0171 359 0240. SER: Valuations. VAT: Stan/Spec.

Inheritance
8-10 Gateway Arcade, Camden Passage, Islington. N1 8EG. (A. Pantelli). Est. 1969. Open 10.30-5. CL: Mon. SIZE: Small. *STOCK: Victorian paintings, Old Masters, 18th-19th C furniture, clocks, Oriental porcelain, silver.* TEL: 0171 226 8305. SER: Valuations. VAT: Stan/Spec.

Intercol London
Gallery, 114 Islington High St. (within Camden Passage). Correspondence - 43 Templars Crescent, N3 3QR.. (Y. Beresiner). Est. 1977. Open Wed.-Sat. 9-5, other times by appointment. SIZE: Large. *STOCK: Playing cards, maps and banknotes and related literature, £5-£1,000+.* PARK: Easy. TEL:

N1 continued

0181 349 2207; fax - 0181 346 9539. SER: Valuations; restorations (maps including colouring); buys at auction (playing cards, maps, banknotes and books). FAIRS: Major specialist European, U.S.A. and Far Eastern. VAT: Stan/Spec.

Islington Antiques

12-14 Essex Rd. N1 8LN. (R.A. Bent). Est. 1984. Open 9-6. SIZE: Large. *STOCK: Original pine furniture, English and Continental.* TEL: 0171 226 6867.

Japanese Gallery

23 Camden Passage, Islington. N1 8EA. Open 9.30-4.30. *STOCK: Japanese woodcut prints; books, porcelain, screens, kimonos, scrolls, furniture.* TEL: 0171 226 3347; fax - 0171 229 2934. SER: Framing; free authentification.

Jubilee Photographica

10 Pierrepont Row, Camden Passage, Islington. N1 8E. (Beryl Vosburgh). Est. 1970. Open Wed. and Sat. 10.30-4 or by appointment. SIZE: Small. *STOCK: Photographica - apparatus, images, daguerreotypes, ambrotypes, tintypes, vintage paper prints, stereoscopic cards and viewers, magic lanterns and slides, topographical and family-albums, cabinet cards and cartes de visite, 10p-£1,000.* LOC: From Piccadilly Circus, take 19 bus to Angel, Islington. PARK: Meters. TEL: Home - 0171 607 5462. SER: Buys at auction.

N1 continued

Julian Antiques LAPADA

54 Duncan St. N1. Est. 1964. Open by appointment only. ***STOCK: French clocks, fireplaces, bronzes, fenders, mirrors.*** **TEL: 0171 833 0835.**

Carol Ketley Antiques LAPADA

4-5 Pierrepoint Arcade, Camden Passage. N1 8EF. Est. 1979. Open Wed. 8-3.30, Sat. 9.30-4.30, other days by appointment. SIZE: Medium. ***STOCK: Mirrors, decanters, drinking glasses, English pottery, furniture and decorative objects, 1780-1900, £10-£2,000.*** **PARK: Nearby. TEL: 0171 359 5529; mobile - 0831 827284; fax - 0171 226 4589. FAIRS: Olympia; Little Chelsea; Decorative Antiques and Textile. VAT: Spec.**

Judith Lassalle

7 Pierrepont Arcade, Camden Passage, Islington. N1 8EF. Est. 1765 Cornhill. Open Wed. 7.30-4, Sat. 9.30-4, other times by appointment. *STOCK: Books, maps, children's games, optical toys and rocking horses, 17th to early 20th C, £25-£5,000.* PARK: Nearby. TEL: 0171 607 7121; shop - 0171 354 9344. SER: Valuations; restorations; buys at auction. FAIRS: Ephemera.

N1 continued

John Laurie (Antiques) Ltd LAPADA
351/352 Upper St., Islington. N1 0PD. (J. Gewirtz). Est. 1962. Open 9.30-5. SIZE: Large. *STOCK: Silver, Sheffield plate.* TEL: 0171 226 0913/6969; fax - 0171 226 4599. SER: Restorations; packing; shipping. VAT: Stan.

Sara Lemkow
12 Camden Passage. N1. Open 10-5. *STOCK: Oil lamps, brass, iron, copper, kitchen utensils.* TEL: 0171 359 0190.

Michael Lewis Antiques LAPADA
16 Essex Rd., Islington. N1 8LN. Est. 1977. Open 9-6, Sun. by appointment. SIZE: Large. *STOCK: Pine and country furniture, British and Irish, 18th-19th C, £100-£6,500.* LOC: 100yds. north of Camden Passage. PARK: Easy. TEL: 0171 359 7733. VAT: Stan/Spec.

Wan Li
7 Gateway Arcade, 355 Upper St., Camden Passage, Islington. N1 0PD. Est. 1969. *STOCK: Mainly Chinese ceramics, works of art and silver; English ceramics, glass, small objects and paintings.* VAT: Stan/Spec.

London Militaria Market
Angel Arcade, Camden Passage, Islington. N1. (S. Bosley and M. Warren). Est. 1987. Open Sat. 8-2. SIZE: Large. 35 dealers. *STOCK: Militaria, 1800 to date.* LOC: Near Angel tube station. PARK: Meters and nearby. TEL: 01628 822503 or 01455 556971.

Finbar MacDonnell
17 Camden Passage, Islington. N1 8EA. Open 10-6. *STOCK: Decorative prints, mainly pre-1850.* TEL: 0171 226 0537.

The Mall Antiques Arcade
359 Upper St., Islington. N1. (Atlantic Antiques Centres Ltd). Est. 1979. Open 10-5, Wed. 7.30-5, Sat. 9-6. CL: Mon. LOC: 5 mins. from Angel tube station. PARK: Meters. TEL: 0171 354 2839; enquiries - 0171 351 5353. Below are listed the dealers at this Arcade.

N1 continued

S. and J. Afford
Stand G21. *Art Nouveau, Art Deco, glass, ceramic[s]* TEL: Mobile - 0831 114909.

Alexandra Alfandary LAPAD[A]
Stand G9. *Meissen porcelain.* TEL: 0171 35[4] 9762: fax - 0171 727 4352.

Alice Springs
Stand G28. (Mrs H. Dumbrell). *Antique jewellery and collectables.*

Alma Antiques
Stand G17. (T. and A. Goldstrom). *Miniatures objects, watercolours and jewellery.* TEL: 0171 35 9045.

Antique Clocks - Terence Plank LAPAD[A]
Stand G23. *Antique clocks.* TEL: 0171 226 2426.

Audley Art Ltd
Stand G20. (A. Singer). *Meissen porcelain and o[il] paintings.* TEL: 0171 704 9507.

Louise Bannister
Stand G27. *Decorative items.* TEL: 0171 226 6665.

David Bowden
Stand G12. *Oriental and European works of ar[t]* TEL: 0171 226 3033.

John Carnie
Stand B5. *Barometers, scientific instruments related accessories and small furniture.* TEL: 017 226 4992.

Tony Coakley
Stand G2. *Art Deco and Art Nouveau.* TEL: 017 354 3349.

P. Collingridge
Stand G6. *Lighting items, brasss and furniture* TEL: 0171 354 9189.

Coperffelde
Stand G21. (Frank Bench). *Small antique furniture porcelain.* TEL: 01367 240078.

N1 continued

J. Donovan
Stand G10. *Art Nouveau and Art Deco china and objets d'art.* TEL: 0171 359 8416.

Chris Dunn St. James
Stand G7. *Vintage jewellery.* TEL: 0171 704 0127.

Hallmark Antiques
Stand G15. *Antique silver and jewellery.*

Heather Antiques
Stand G25. (Mrs. Cohen). *Silver.* TEL: 0171 226 2412.

Patricia Kleinman LAPADA
Stand G3. *English watercolours, 19th to early 20th C.* TEL: 0171 704 0798.

Andrew Lineham BADA
Stand G19. *Glass and porcelain.* TEL: 0171 704 0195.

London Barometer Company
Stand B5. (Carnie & Grummit). *Antique barometers, scientific instruments.* TEL: 0171 226 4992.

Monika
Stand G16. (M. Jartelius). *Fine period costume jewellery and accessories, 1920's-1950's.* TEL: 0171 354 3125.

Linda Morgan Antiques
Stand G26. *Antique jewellery.* TEL: 0171 359 0654.

D. L. Murphy
Stand G4/5. *Antique silver.* TEL: 0171 345 1204.

Nadine Okker LAPADA
Stand G8. *Porcelain, glass and bronzes.* TEL: 0171 354 9496.

Original Photgraphic Prints
Stand G14. (Manuela Höfer). *Photographs and prints.* TEL: 0171 930 1904; fax - 0171 839 7509.

John Pearman
Stand G24. *China, glass, bronzes and objects.* TEL: 0171 359 0591.

Mrs Sylvia Powell LAPADA
Stand G18. *Decorative arts, art pottery, 1870-1940.* TEL: 0171 354 2977.

Robin Quy
Stand G11. *Antique silver and Georgian glass.* TEL: 0171 359 8671.

Gad Sassower
Stand G13. *Bakelite items, £10-£2,000; radios, early 20th C, £500-£1,000.* TEL: 0171 354 4473.

Sonia Shea
Stand G1. *Silver, glass and jewellery.* TEL: 0171354 2839.

Michael Young
Stand G22. *Decorative items.* TEL: 0171 226 2225.

N1 continued

Lower Mall

The Clock Studio
Stand B1. (George Riley). *Antique clocks and furniture.* TEL: 0171 354 1719.

Peter Lehmann
Stand B8. *Furniture.* TEL: 0171 704 0701.

Mrs C. Sidoli
Stand B4. *18th-19th C furniture, paintings and decorative accessories.*

Malcolm D. Stevens LAPADA
Stand B2/3. *Furniture.* TEL: 0171 359 1020.

Alex Woodage
Stand B6/7. *Furniture, clocks and accessories.* TEL: Mobile - 0836 332921.

Collingridge & Allen
Stand B9/10. *Furniture, 1800-1900; pictures and prints.* TEL: 0171 354 9189; mobile - 0860 581858.

Mallard Billiards
134 Liverpool Rd. N1 1LA. (Jeffrey Walkden). Est. 1985. Open 9.30-6, Sat. and Sun. by appointment. SIZE: Medium. *STOCK: Billiard tables, 19th C, £1,000-£15,000; billiards accessories, early 20th C.* LOC: 5 minutes from Angel underground station.At junction with Islington High St. PARK: Easy. TEL: 0171 700 5600; fax - same. SER: Valuations; restorations (as stock); buys at auction. VAT: Stan.

Laurence Mitchell Antiques Ltd
LAPADA
13 Camden Passage, Islington. N1 8EA. (L.P.J. Mitchell). Est. 1972. Open 10-5, Wed. 8-5, Mon. by appointment. *STOCK: 19th C Meissen specialist; Oriental, English and other European porcelain, pottery and works of art.* TEL: 0171 359 7579; fax - 0171 226 1738; e-mail - L.mitchell@mail.bogo.co.uk; x-url - http://www.bogo.co.uk/l.mitchell/. VAT: Stan/Spec.

Chris Newland Antiques
357 Upper St., Islington. N1. Est. 1964. Open 10-6. SIZE: Large. *STOCK: Mahogany furniture, 19th C, £300-£1,000; office furniture, 19th-20th C; shipping furniture, marble, works of art.* PARK: NCP 100 yards. TEL: 0171 359 9805. SER: Valuations; restorations (furniture, French polishing). VAT: Stan/Spec.

Number Nineteen
19 Camden Passage, Islington. N1 8EA. (D. Griffith and J. Wright). Open 10-5. *STOCK: Decorative antiques including military and campaign furniture, leather chairs, pub accessories, club fenders and other fittings from hotels and gentlemen's clubs; quality vintage luggage.* TEL: 0171 226 1126.

N1 continued

The Old Tool Chest
41 Cross St., Islington. N1 2BB. (E.J. Maskell). Open 10-6. *STOCK: Woodworking tools.* TEL: 0171 359 9313.

Jacqueline Oosthuizen
1st Floor, Georgian Village, Camden Passage, Islington. N1. Est. 1960. Open Wed. and Sat. 8-4. SIZE: Medium. *STOCK: Staffordshire figures, 18th-19th C, £50-£10,000; jewellery, European and English ceramics, 18th-20th C.* PARK: Nearby. TEL: 0171 226 5393/352 6071. VAT: Stan/Spec.

Pieter Oosthuizen t/a de Verzamelaar
1st Floor, Georgian Village, Camden Passage. N1. Est. 1992. Open Wed. and Sat. 8-4. SIZE: Medium. *STOCK: Dutch Art Nouveau ceramics, 1880-1930, £30-£8,000; Boer War memorabilia, 1899-1902, £5-£2,000.* PARK: Nearby. TEL: 0171 359 3322; 0171 376 385; fax - same. SER: Buys at auction. VAT: Spec.

Kevin Page Oriental Art LAPADA
2, 4 and 6 Camden Passage, Islington. N1 8ED. Est. 1968. Open 10-4. CL: Mon. SIZE: Large. *STOCK: Oriental porcelain and furniture, cloisonné, bronzes, ivories.* LOC: 1 min. from Angel tube station. PARK: Easy. TEL: 0171 226 8558. SER: Valuations. VAT: Stan.

Sue Pottle
9 Georgian Village, 30-31 Islington Green, Islington. N1. Open Wed. and Sat. 7-3. SIZE: Small. *STOCK: Pine, majolica, decorative items.* LOC: Junction of Upper St. and Essex Rd. PARK: Nearby. TEL: 0171 226 9907 and 0181 348 5801.

Relic Antiques
21 Camden Passage, Islington. N1. (Malcolm Gliksten). Est. 1968. Open 10-5. CL: Mon and Thurs. *STOCK: Näive art, figureheads and trade signs; fairground art; boat and plane models; toys and games, especially Noah's Arks, rocking horses, child's washstands; decorative items, French brocante and country furniture; original tea canisters and period shopfittings, £40-£6,000.* PARK: Meters. TEL: 0171 388 2691; fax - same; 0171 359 2597; mobile - 0831 785059. SER: Valuations; annual auction. VAT: Stan.

N1 continued

Restall Brown and Clennell Ltd
Adelaide Wharf, 120 Queensbridge Rd., E2 8PD. (S. Brown). Open Mon.-Fri. 9-5.30 appointment advisable. *STOCK: English furniture, 17th-19th C.* TEL: 0171 739 6626; fax - 0171 739 6123. VAT: Stan/Spec.

Rookery Farm Antiques
12 Camden Passage, Islington. N1 8ED. *STOCK: Pine and country furniture.* TEL: 0171 359 0190.

Marcus Ross Antiques
14/16 Pierrepont Row, Camden Passage, Islington. N1 8EF. Est. 1972. Open 10.30-4.30 CL: Mon. *STOCK: Oriental porcelain, general antiques, Victorian walnut furniture.* TEL: 0171 359 8494.

Keith Skeel Antique Warehouse LAPADA
7-9 Elliotts Place. N1 8HX. SIZE: Large. *STOCK: Interesting and unusual furniture.* TEL: 0171 226 7012. *Trade Only.*

Keith Skeel Antiques and Eccentricities LAPADA
94/98 Islington High St. N1 8EG. Est. 1969. Open 9-6. SIZE: Large. *STOCK: Interesting and unusual decorative items.* LOC: 1 min. from the Angel underground station. TEL: 0171 359 9894/226 7012. VAT: Stan. *Trade and Export Only.*

Style
1 Ground Floor, Georgian Village, Camden Passage. N1. (M. Webb and P. Coakley). Open Wed. and Sat. 9.30-4 or by appointment. *STOCK: Art Nouveau, WMF and Liberty pewter, Art Deco bronzes, ceramics and glass.* TEL: 0171 359 7867; private - 0181 449 2588; fax - same; mobile - 0831 229640.

N1 continued

Sugar Antiques

8-9 Pierrepont Arcade, Camden Passage, Islington. N1 8EF. (Elayne and Tony Sugarman). Est. 1980. Open Wed. 6.30-4, Sat. 9-4, other times by appointment. SIZE: Medium. *STOCK: Wrist and pocket watches, 19th-20th C, £25-£2,000; fountain pens and lighters, early 20th C to 1960's, £15-£1,000; costume jewellery and collectables, 19th-20th C, £5-£500.* PARK: Meters. TEL: 0171 354 9896 (answerphone). SER: Repairs (as stock); buys at auction (as stock). VAT: Stan.

Swan Fine Art

120 Islington High St., Camden Passage. N1 8EG. (P. Child). Open 10-5, Wed. and Sat. 9-5 or by appointment. SIZE: Medium. *STOCK: Paintings, fine and decorative sporting and animal, portraits, 17th-19th C, £500-£25,000+.* PARK: Easy, except Wed. and Sat.. TEL: 0171 226 5335; fax - 0171 359 2225; mobile - 0860 795336. VAT: Spec.

Tadema Gallery BADA LAPADA

10 Charlton Place, Camden Passage, Islington. N1. (S. and D. Newell-Smith). Est. 1978. Open Wed. and Sat. 10-5, or by appointment. SIZE: Medium. *STOCK: 20th C abstract art and jewellery, from Art Nouveau to 1960's artist designed pieces.* PARK: Reasonable. TEL: 0171 359 1055; fax - same. SER: Valuations. VAT: Spec.

Tapsell Antiques

At Christopher House, 5 Camden Passage, Islington. N1 8EH. (Christopher Tapsell). Est. 1969. Open 10.30-5.30, Wed. and Sat. 9-5.30, Mon. by appointment. SIZE: Medium. *STOCK: English and Continental furniture, mid 18th C to 1900, £400-£15,000; Oriental porcelain, 17th C to 1900, £50-£10,000; decorative bronzes, mirrors and lighting, 17th C to 1900, £300-£4,000.* PARK: Opposite. TEL: 0171 354 3603; fax - 0171 226 4326. SER: Valuations; restorations; buys at auction (European furniture and Oriental porcelain). FAIRS: Olympia. VAT: Stan/Spec.

The Textile Company

P.O Box 2800, London N1 4DQ. (Judy Wentworth). Est. 1982. Open by appointment only. *STOCK: 18th C silks, British and French printed cottons, patchworks, lace, 1600-1850; Paisley and Kashmir shawls, period costume and accessories.* Not Stocked: Tapestries, upholstery and cushions. TEL: 0171 254 3256. SER: Buys at auction; hire; photographic archive.

Titus Omega

Shop 18, Ground Floor, Georgian Village, Camden Passage. N1. (John Featherstone-Harvey). Est. 1986. Open Wed. 8-3, Sat. 9-4. SIZE: Small. *STOCK: Art Nouveau, 1890-1910, £100-£3,000.* LOC: Islington Green. TEL: 0171 704 8003; home - 0171 607 8996. SER: Valuations.

N1 continued

Turn On Lighting

116/118 Islington High St., Camden Passage. N1 8EG. Est. 1976. *STOCK: Lighting, 1840-1940.* TEL: 0171 359 7616; fax - same.

Vane House Antiques

15 Camden Passage, Islington. N1 8EH. (M. Till and B. Snyder). Est. 1950. Open 10-5. *STOCK: 18th to early 19th C furniture.* TEL: 0171 359 1343. VAT: Stan/Spec.

Yesterday Child LAPADA

Angel Arcade, 118 Islington High St. N1. (D. and G. Barrington). Est. 1970. Open Wed. and Sat. 8.30-3. SIZE: Small. *STOCK: Dolls, 1800-1925, £25-£5,000.* PARK: Easy. TEL: 0171 354 1601; home and fax - 01908 583403. SER: Valuations; restorations. VAT: Stan/Spec.

York Arcade

80 Islington High St., Camden Passage. N1 8EQ. Open Wed. and Sat. 8-5. SIZE: 16 dealers. LOC: 1 min. from Angel tube - Northern Line. PARK: Duncan St. TEL: 0171 833 2640. Below are listed the dealers at this arcade.

Franco Baldini

19th C jewellery, silver and plate. TEL: 0171 503 8246.

Catherine Braithwaite

19th-20th C pictures and Doulton ware. TEL: Mobile - 0973 462957.

Cat Box

Unit 9. *Cat antiques and collectibles, some dog items.* TEL: 0181 744 9277.

Ginette Fiandarca

19th-20th C china, glassware, silver and decorative items.

Keith Harmer

18th-19th C paintings, mirrors and decorative items.

Hollywood Deco

Unit 11. *Vintage film posters and Art Deco items.* TEL: 0181 445 1781.

Inge

Unit 3. *20th C costume jewellery and decorative items.* TEL: 0181 452 8133.

Inspirations

Unit 4. *Costume jewellery, collectibles and accessories.*

Raesmith Cartoons

Unit 10. *Original cartoon artwork and 20th C childrens' book illustrations.* TEL: 0181 348 6569.

N1 continued

Templar Antiques
Unit 12. *Fine 18th-19th C glassware and porcelain.* TEL: 01621 819737.

William Wain
Unit 2. *20th C costume jewellery and fashion accessories.* TEL: 0181 291 4027; fax - 0181 693 1814.

LONDON N2

Amazing Grates - Fireplaces Ltd
61-63 High Rd., East Finchley. N2. (T. Tew). Resident. Est. 1971. Open 10-6. SIZE: Large. *STOCK: Mantelpieces, grates and fireside items, £200-£5,000; Victorian tiling, £2-£20; early ironwork, all 19th C.* LOC: 100yds. north of East Finchley tube station. PARK: Own. TEL: 0181 883 9590/6017. SER: Valuations; restorations (ironwork, welding of cast iron and brazing, polishing); installations. VAT: Stan.

The Antique Shop (Valantique)
9 Fortis Green. N2 9JR. (Mrs V. Steel). Open Tues.-Sat. 11-6. SIZE: Medium. *STOCK: General antiques especially original lighting and fenders; small furniture, pottery, porcelain, glass, oil paintings, watercolours, prints, mirrors, copper, brass, unusual items, £5-£500.* LOC: 2 mins. from East Finchley tube station. PARK: Side street. TEL: 0181 883 7651. SER: Buys at auction.

Martin Henham (Antiques)
218 High Rd., East Finchley. N2 9AY. Open 10-6. SIZE: Medium. *STOCK: Furniture and porcelain, 1710-1920, £5-£1,700; paintings, 1650-1900, £10-£1,000.* PARK: Easy. TEL: 0181 444 5274. SER: Valuations; restorations (furniture and paintings); buys at auction.

Lauri Stewart - Fine Art
36 Church Lane. N2 8DT. Open 10-5. CL: Mon. *STOCK: Modern British oils and watercolours.* TEL: 0181 883 7719. SER: Restorations (oils, watercolours, porcelain); framing.

LONDON N4

Joseph Lavian LAPADA
Building E, Ground Floor, 105 Eade Rd. N4 1TJ. Est. 1950. Open 9.30-5.30. SIZE: Large. *STOCK: Oriental carpets, rugs, kelims, tapestries and needlework, Aubusson, Savonnerie and textiles, 17th-19th C.* TEL: 0181 800 0707; fax - 0181 800 0404. SER: Valuations; restorations.

Teger Trading and Bushe Antiques
318 Green Lanes. N4 1BX. *STOCK: Antique and reproduction garden statuary, lamps, Art Deco, Art Nouveau, animalier, Oriental and classical style figures.* TEL: 0181 802 0156; fax - 0181 802 4110. SER: Restorations; film hire. *Trade Only.*

LONDON N5

Strike One (Islington) Ltd BAD
48a Highbury Hill. N5 1AP. (J. Mighell). Es 1968. Open by appointment. SIZE: Mediun *STOCK: Clocks, pre-1870, especially earl English wall and Act of Parliament, £2,000 £15,000; English longcase, 1675-1820, £3,000 £40,000; English bracket, lantern, skeleton an French carriage; Vienna regulators; barometer music boxes, horological books.* PARK: Easy TEL: 0171 354 2790; fax - same. SER: Valu ations; restorations (clocks, barometers) catalogue available. VAT: Stan/Spec.

Walford's - Nicholas Goodyer
15 Calabria Rd., Highbury Fields. N5 1JB. Es 1951. Open 9.30-5. CL: Sat. *STOCK: Antiquaria books especially illustrated.* TEL: 0171 226 568 fax - 0171 354 4716.

LONDON N6

Centaur Gallery
82 Highgate High St., Highgate Village. N6 (J. and D. Wieliczko). Est. 1960. Open 11- *STOCK: 18th to early 19th C oil paintings, water colours, prints, sculpture, ethnic and folk ar unusual items.* TEL: 0181 340 0087.

Fisher and Sperr
46 Highgate High St. N6 5JB. (J.R. Sperr). Es 1945. Open daily 10.30-6. SIZE: Large. *STOCK Books, 15th C to date.* LOC: From centre o Highgate Village, nearest underground station Archway (Highgate), Highgate. PARK: Easy TEL: 0181 340 7244; fax - 0181 348 4293. SER Valuations; restorations (books); buys at auction VAT: Stan.

Betty Gould and Julian Gonnermann Antiques
408-410 Archway Rd., Highgate. N6 5AT. Es 1964. Open 10-5.30, Sat. 9.30-5.30. CL: Mon. an Thurs. SIZE: Medium. *STOCK: Furniture, 18th 20th C, £50-£5,000.* LOC: On A1, just belo Highgate tube station (corner of Shepherds Hill PARK: Highgate Ave. TEL: 0181 340 4987. SER Restorations; French polishing; upholstery.

Highgate Antiques BADA LAPAD
P O Box 10060, Highgate. N6 5JH. (Jea Horsman and Enid Thomas). Est. 198 *STOCK: English and Welsh porcelain and glas 18th to early 19th C, £100-£3,000.* TEL: 018 340 9872/348 3016; fax - 0181 340 1621. SER Valuations. FAIRS: Olympia, BADA, NEC Cumberland Ceramic. VAT: Spec.

Home to Home
355c Archway Rd. N6 4EJ. Open 9.30-6.30, Sa 10-5. *STOCK: Mainly Victorian, Edwardian an some Georgian furniture; Victorian pine.* TEL 0181 340 8354.

N6 continued

D.M. and P. Manheim (Peter Manheim) Ltd BADA
P.O. Box 1259. N6 4TR. (P. Manheim). Est. 1926. Open by appointment only. *STOCK: English porcelain, pottery and enamels, 1680-1820.* TEL: 0181 340 9211. VAT: Spec.

LONDON N7

Tsar Architectural
487 Liverpool Rd. N7. (R. Quinn). Open 9.30-7. *STOCK: Fireplaces and associated items.* TEL: 0171 609 4238. SER: Restorations.

LONDON N8

Crouch End Antiques
47 Park Rd., Crouch End. N8 8TE. (M.V. Kairis). Est. 1979. Open 10-6. SIZE: Medium. *STOCK: Furniture, 19th C, £100-£1,000.* LOC: Corner of Shanklin Rd. TEL: 0181 348 7652. SER: Valuations; restorations; renovation materials supplied. FAIRS: Alexandra Palace. VAT: Stan/Spec.

Sandra Lummis Fine Art
Flat 7, 17 Haslemere Rd. N8 9QP. (Mrs. S. Lummis and Dr T. Lummis). Est. 1985. Viewing by appointment. CL: Aug. *STOCK: British art (Modernist school), 20th C from Sickert to contemporary, especially Bloomsbury painters, £500-£50,000.* LOC: From Highgate Hill, along Hornsey Lane, left at 'T' junction, then 1st right. PARK: Easy. TEL: 0181 340 2293; home - same. SER: Commissions; valuations; advice on restoration and framing. VAT: Spec.

Solomon
49 Park Rd., Crouch End. N8 8SY. (Solomon Salim). Est. 1984. Open 9.30-6. SIZE: Medium

N8 continued

STOCK: Furniture including upholstered, £200-£2,000; decorative items, £100-£500; all 1800-1920. LOC: 2 minutes off North Circular at Muswell Hill turn-off. PARK: Easy. TEL: 0181 341 1817. SER: Valuations; restorations (furniture including upholstery); buys at auction (furniture). VAT: Spec.

LONDON N10

M.E. Korn
47 Tetherdown, Muswell Hill. N10 1NH. (E. Korn). ABA, PBFA. Est. 1971. Open by appointment. *STOCK: Books - natural history, medical, science, art and literature, 16th-19th C, £10-£1,000.* TEL: 0181 883 5251 (answerphone); fax - same. SER: Valuations; buys at auction (antiquarian books). FAIRS: PBFA, Russell Hotel monthly; York, Oxford, Cambridge; ABAA in California, Boston, New York and Toronto.

LONDON N12

Finchley Fine Art Galleries
983 High Rd., North Finchley. N12 8QR. (S. Greenman). Est. 1972. Open 1-7, including Sun., Wed. by appointment. SIZE: Large. *STOCK: 18th-20th C watercolours, paintings, etchings, prints, mostly English, £25-£10,000; Georgian, Victorian, Edwardian furniture, to £4,000; china and porcelain - Moorcroft, Doulton, Worcester, Clarice Cliff, £5-£2,000; musical and scientific instruments, bronzes, early photographic apparatus, fire-arms, shotguns.* LOC: Off M25, junction 23, take Barnet road. Gallery on right 3 miles south of Barnet church, opposite Britannia Road. PARK: Easy. TEL: 0181 446 4848. SER: Valuations; restorations; picture re-lining, cleaning and framing.

LONDON N13

Palmers Green Antiques Centre
472 Green Lanes, Palmers Green. N13 5PA. (Michael Webb). Est. 1976. Open 10-5.30, Sun. 11-5. CL: Tues. SIZE: Medium. *STOCK: General antiques and collectables.* PARK: Nearby. TEL: 0181 350 0878. SER: Valuations; restorations. FAIRS: Alexandra Palace; Kempton Park.

Trader Antiques
484 Green Lanes, Palmers Green. N13 5XD. (M. Webb). Open 10.30-5. *STOCK: Stripped pine, glass, furniture and general antiques.* TEL: 0181 886 9552.

LONDON N14

C.J. Martin (Coins) Ltd LAPADA
85 The Vale, Southgate. N14 6AT. Open by appointment. *STOCK: Ancient and medieval coins and ancient artefacts.* TEL: 0181 882 1509/4359.

Southgate Antiques & Collectables
46 Chase Side, Southgate. N14 5PA. Open 10-5.30. SIZE: Medium - 4 dealers. *STOCK: Wide range of general small antique and collector's items, including named porcelain and glass, china tableware, silver and jewelery; period furniture.* LOC: Near Southgate underground station. TEL: 0181 447 8017. VAT: Stan.

LONDON N16

W. Forster
83a Stamford Hill. N16 5TP. Est. 1952. Open by appointment. *STOCK: Bibliography and books about books.* LOC: Nearest station Manor House (Piccadilly Line) or 253 bus to Stamford Hill Broadway. PARK: Easy. TEL: 0181 800 3919.

LONDON N19

Curios
130c Junction Rd., Archway. N19. Open 12-7 including Sun. *STOCK: Decorative objects especially unusual items; general antiques, pictures, taxidermy and fireplaces.* TEL: 0171 272 5603.

LONDON N20

The Totteridge Gallery
61 Totteridge Lane. N20 0HD. Est. 1979. Open daily, Sun. by appointment. SIZE: Small. *STOCK: Oil paintings, £1,000-£25,000; watercolours, £300-£10,000; both 18th to early 20th C. Limited edition Russell Flint prints, 20th C, £500-£3,000.* LOC: Opposite Totteridge and Whetstone tube station. PARK: Easy. TEL: 0181 446 7896. SER: Valuations; restorations; frame repairs. VAT: Stan/Spec.

LONDON N21

Dolly Land
862/864 Green Lanes, Winchmore Hill. N21 2R[illegible] Est. 1987. Open 9.30-4.30. CL: Mon. and We[illegible] *STOCK: Dolls, teddies, trains, die-cast limite[illegible] editions.* PARK: Easy. TEL: 0181 360 105[illegible] SER: Restorations; part exchange; dolls' hospita[illegible] FAIRS: Doll and Bear.

The Little Curiosity Shop
24 The Green, Winchmore Hill. N21. (Mrs H[illegible] Freedman). Est. 1967. Open 1-5. CL: We[illegible] *STOCK: Clocks, porcelain, general antique[illegible] mostly Victorian, bronzes, silver, music boxe[illegible] jewellery and diamond items.* LOC: Neare[illegible] stations - Winchmore Hill (Eastern Region), an[illegible] Southgate (Piccadilly Line underground). PAR[illegible] Easy. TEL: 0181 886 0925. VAT: Stan.

Winchmore Antiques
14 The Green, Winchmore Hill. N21 1AY. (Dav[illegible] Hicks and Stewart Christian). Open 10-6. SIZ[illegible] Medium. *STOCK: General antiques, £1-£50[illegible] architectural brass fittings, vintage lamps an[illegible] spare parts; all 18th-20th C.* LOC: Junction of [illegible] roads, at east end of Broad Walk. PARK: Eas[illegible] TEL: 0181 882 4800. SER: Valuations; restoratio[illegible] (metal polishing, silver plating, oil lamps).

LONDON NW1

Art Furniture
158 Camden St. NW1 9PA. Open 12-5 includin[illegible] Sun. SIZE: Warehouse. *STOCK: Decorative ar[illegible] 1851-1951, Arts & Crafts furniture by Heal'[illegible] Liberty and others; Art Deco furniture includin[illegible] Aalto, P.E.L.* LOC: Under railway bridge o[illegible] Camden St. going south. PARK: Easy. TEL: 017[illegible] 267 4324. SER: Export; hire. VAT: Stan.

Barkes and Barkes
76 Parkway. NW1 7AH. (J.N. and P. R. Barkes[illegible] Est. 1976. Open Thurs. 12-7.30, Fri. and Sat. 1[illegible] 6, and every day during exhibitions. *STOC[illegible] Post-war Russian paintings; British artists - Ni[illegible] Botting and Mark Pearson.* LOC: Just north [illegible] Regents Park. PARK: Next street. TEL: 0171 28[illegible] 1550. VAT: Spec.

Collectors Arch
Old Time Square, The Stables Market, Chalk Far[illegible] Road, Camden. NW1 8AH. Open Sat. and Sun. [illegible] 5.30. SIZE: Large - over 200 dealers. *STOC[illegible] Wide range of antiques, including smalls, lightin[illegible] furniture and classic motor cycles.* LOC: Off Cha[illegible] Farm Road almost opposite Ferdinand St. TE[illegible] 0171 267 6632/0181 445 7685.

Ian Crispin Antiques
95 Lisson Grove. NW1 6UP. Est. 1971. Open 1[illegible] 5. *STOCK: General antiques and shipping good[illegible]* TEL: 0171 402 6845. VAT: Stan. *Trade Only.*

NW1 continued

East-Asia Co

103 Camden High St. NW1. Est. 1972. Open 10-6. *STOCK: Oriental antiquarian books on history and culture; Japanese and Chinese paintings and prints; jade, netsuke, objets d'art; books on Oriental art.* TEL: 0171 388 5783; fax - 0171 387 5766.

W.R. Harvey & Co (Antiques) Ltd.

BADA

70 Chalk Farm Rd. NW1 8AN. GMC. Open by appointment only. SIZE: Medium. *STOCK: Fine English furniture, £500-£50,000; clocks, mirrors, objets d'art, £250-£20,000; all 1680-1830.* LOC: 100 yards from The Roundhouse Theatre; 300 yards from Camden High St. PARK: Easy. TEL: 01993 76501; fax - 01993 906601. SER: Valuations; restorations. FAIRS: BADA, Chelsea (March and Sept). VAT: Stan/Spec.

Laurence Corner

62-64 Hampstead Rd. NW1 2NU. Est. 1955. Open 9.30-6. SIZE: Large. *STOCK: Uniforms, helmets, militaria, theatrical costumes, props, fancy dress, flags.* LOC: From Tottenham Court Rd. - Warren St. end - continue into Hampstead Rd., then Drummond St. is first turning on right by traffic lights. PARK: Easy. TEL: 0171 813 1010; fax - 0171 813 1413. SER: Hire.

Regent Antiques

9-10 Chester Court, Albany St. NW1 4BU. (T. Quaradeghini). Est. 1983. Open 10-5.30, Sat. by appointment. SIZE: Large and warehouse. *STOCK: Furniture, 18th C to Edwardian, £100-£20,000; decorative items and bric-a-brac, 19th-20th C.* LOC: 1/4 mile from Gt. Portland St. station towards Camden Town. PARK: Easy. TEL: 0171 935 6944; fax - 0171 935 7814. SER: Restorations (furniture); gilding. VAT: Stan. *Trade Only.*

Relic Antiques Trade Warehouse

127 Pancras Rd. NW1 1UN. (Malcolm Gliksten). Est. 1968. Open 10-5.30, Sat. 11-5. *STOCK: Original pond yacht models; ornate French mirrors; small decorative items and brocante; French posters.* PARK: Meters. TEL: 0171 387 6039; fax - 0171 388 2691; mobile - 0831 785059. SER: Valuations; London office for annual Brillscote Farm Auction (Lea, Wilts.). VAT: Stan.

This and That (Furniture)

50 and 51 Chalk Farm Rd. NW1 8AN. (R.P. Schanzer). Est. 1974. Open 10.30-6 including Sun. SIZE: Medium. *STOCK: Country furniture, stripped pine, oak and walnut, 1890-1930.* LOC: Between Roundhouse and Camden Lock. PARK: Easy. TEL: 0171 267 5433. VAT: Stan.

Victorian Fireplace Co

53 Camden Lock Place, Chalk Farm Rd., Camden Town. NW1 8AF. (Geoffrey Moore). Est. 1984. Open Sat. and Sun. 10-6. SIZE: Small. *STOCK: Fireplaces, £95-£695; fireplace accessories, £10-*

NW1 continued

£165; all 1770's-1910. LOC: West yard, Camden Lock Market. TEL: 0171 482 2543. SER: Restorations (cast-iron refurbishment, repair and welding); fireparts. VAT: Stan.

David J. Wilkins

27 Princess Rd., Regents Park. NW1 8JR. Est. 1974. Open 9.15-5. CL: Sat. SIZE: Large. *STOCK: Oriental rugs.* LOC: Off Regent's Park Rd., near St Mark's church. PARK: Easy. TEL: 0171 722 7608; home - 01279 726149. SER: Valuations; restorations; Oriental rug broker. VAT: Stan.

LONDON NW2

The Corner Cupboard

679 Finchley Rd. NW2 2JP. (M. Fry and R. Fischelis). Est. 1950. Open 9.30-5.30. SIZE: Small. *STOCK: Jewellery, 18th-19th C, from £5; silver, china, glass.* LOC: Number 2 or 13 bus from Central London. PARK: Easy. TEL: 0171 435 4870. VAT: Stan.

G. and F. Gillingham Ltd

LAPADA

62 Menelik Rd. NW2 3RH. Est. 1960. Open by appointment. *STOCK: Furniture, 1750-1950.* TEL: 0171 435 5644; fax - same. *Export Trade Only.*

Gunter Fine Art

4 Randall Ave. NW2 7RN. (G.A. and A.M. Goodwin). Est. 1977. Open by appointment only. SIZE: Small. *STOCK: Watercolours, 18th-20th C, £150-£3,000; oil paintings, 19th-20th C £200-£3,000.* LOC: North Circular Rd., near Brent Cross shopping centre. PARK: Easy. TEL: 0181 452 3997. SER: Buys at auction.

Soviet Carpet and Art Centre

303-305 Cricklewood Broadway. NW2 6PG. (R. Rabilizirov). Est. 1983. Open 10.30-5, Sun. 10.30-5.30. CL: Sat. SIZE: Large. *STOCK: Hand-made rugs, 19th-20th C, £500-£1,000; fine and applied art, 20th C, £100-£500.* LOC: A5. PARK: Side road. TEL: 0181 452 2445. SER: Valuations; restorations (hand-made rugs). VAT: Stan.

LONDON NW3

Patricia Beckman Antiques

LAPADA

NW3 7SN. (Patricia Beckman and Peter Beckman). Est. 1968. Open by appointment. *STOCK: Furniture, 18th-19th C.* TEL: 0171 435 5050/0500. VAT: Spec.

Tony Bingham

LAPADA

11 Pond St. NW3 2PN. Est. 1964. *STOCK: Musical instruments, books, music, oil paintings, engravings of musical interest.* TEL: 0171 794 1596; fax - 0171 433 3662. VAT: Stan/Spec.

NW3 continued

P.G. de Lotz
20 Downside Cres., Hampstead. NW3 2AP. Est. 1967. *STOCK: Antiquarian books on history warfare - naval, military and aviation.* TEL: 0171 794 5709; fax - 0171 284 3058. SER: Catalogue available; search.

Dolphin Coins
2c England's Lane, Hampstead. NW3 4TG. (R. Ilsley). BNTA. Est. 1966. Open 9.30-5. SIZE: Medium. *STOCK: British and world coins, early and medieval, from 100BC, £20-£50,000.* LOC: Off Haverstock Hill. PARK: Easy. TEL: 0171 722 4116; fax - 0171 483 2000. SER: Valuations; catalogues; buys at auction (coins). VAT: Spec.

Bridget Farrelley
152 Fleet Rd. NW3 2QX. Est. 1948. Open 10-5. Cl: Thurs. *STOCK: Pictures, furniture, porcelain, general antiques.*

Keith Fawkes
1-3 Flask Walk, Hampstead. NW3 1HJ. Est. 1970. Open 10-5.30. *STOCK: Antiquarian and general books.* TEL: 0171 435 0614.

Otto Haas (A. and M. Rosenthal)
49 Belsize Park Gardens. NW3 4JL. Est. 1866. Open 9.30-5 by appointment. CL: Sat. *STOCK: Manuscripts, printed music, autographs, rare books on music.* TEL: 0171 722 1488; fax - 0171 722 2364.

Hampstead Antique and Craft Market
12 Heath St., Hampstead. NW3 6TE. Est. 1967. Open 10.30-5, Sat. 10-6, Sun. 11.30-4.30. CL: Mon. SIZE: 24 units. *STOCK: General antiques.* LOC: 2 mins. walk from Hampstead underground. TEL: 0171 794 3297. SER:

Klaber and Klaber BADA
PO Box 9445. NW3 1WD. (Mrs B. Klaber and Miss P. Klaber). Est. 1968. Open by appointment. *STOCK: English and Continental porcelain and enamels, 18th-19th C.* TEL: 0171 435 6537; fax - 0171 435 9459. SER: Buys at auction (porcelain, enamels). FAIRS: Grosvenor House. VAT: Spec.

Duncan R. Miller Fine Arts BADA
17 Flask Walk, Hampstead. NW3 1HJ. SLAD. Open 10-6, Sat. 11-5, Sun. 2-5. SIZE: Small. *STOCK: Modern British and European paintings, drawings and sculpture, especially Scottish Colourist paintings.* LOC: Off Hampstead High St., near underground station. PARK: Nearby. TEL: 0171 435 5462. SER: Valuations; conservation and restoration (oils, works on paper and Oriental rugs); buys at auction. FAIRS: Grosvenor House; BADA. VAT: Spec.

NW3 continued

Frederick Mulder
83 Belsize Park Gardens. NW3. Open by appointment. *STOCK: Old Master and modern original prints; modern illustrated books.* TEL 0171 722 2105; fax - 0171 483 4228.

Newhart (Pictures) Ltd
PO Box 1608. NW3 3LB. (Ann and Bernard Hart). Open by appointment only. *STOCK: Oil paintings and watercolours, 1850-1930, from £500.* TEL 0171 722 2537; fax - 0171 722 4335. SER: Valuations; restorations; framing. VAT: Spec.

David and Charles Wainwright
28 Rosslyn Hill. NW3 1NH. Est. 1989. Open 10-6, Sun. 11-5. SIZE: Large. *STOCK: Furniture, 15th-20th C including 18th-19th C cupboards, dining tables and architectural pieces, £5-£2,000; stonework - urns, mortars and water containers, to 19th C; contemporary ironwork.* LOC: Hampstead on corner of Downshire Hill. PARK: Easy. TEL 0171 431 5900. FAIRS: Olympia. VAT: Stan.

LONDON NW4

Talking Machine
30 Watford Way, Hendon. NW4 3AL. Open 10-5, Sat. 9.30-1.30. *STOCK: Mechanical music, old gramophones, phonographs, vintage records and 78's, needles and spare parts, early radios and televisions, typewriters, sewing machines, juke boxes, early telephones.* TEL: 0181 202 3473; fax - same; mobile - 0374 103139. SER: Buys at auction. VAT: Stan.

LONDON NW5

Acquisitions (Fireplaces) Ltd
24-26 Holmes Rd., Kentish Town. NW5. (K. Kennedy). Est. 1970. Open 9.30-5. SIZE: Medium. *STOCK: Fireplaces, Georgian, Victorian, Edwardian reproduction, fire-side accessories, £195-£595.* LOC: 3 mins. walk from Camden Town tube station (Camden High St.). PARK: Easy. TEL: 0171 485 4955. VAT: Stan.

Game Advice
23 Holmes Rd. NW5 3AA. (S. Elithorn). Est. 1976. Open by appointment only. SIZE: Small. *STOCK: Games, puzzles, jigsaws, cards, educational toys, chess sets; chess, cookery and children's books, £25-£100; ephemera, £5-£50, all 18th-19th C.* LOC: Just off Kentish Town Rd. PARK: Easy. TEL: 0171 485 4226. SER:

Barrie Marks Ltd
11 Laurier Rd. NW5 1SD. ABA. Open by appointment only. *STOCK: Antiquarian books - illustrated, private press, colourplate, colour printing; modern first editions.* TEL: 0171 48[illegible] 5684; fax - 0171 284 3149.

NW5 continued

Orientalist LAPADA

74 Highgate Rd. NW5 1PB. (E. and H. Sakhai). Est. 1885. SIZE: Large. *STOCK: Rugs and carpets including reproduction.* PARK: Easy and nearby. TEL: 0171 482 0555; fax - 0171 267 9603. SER: Valuations; restorations (cleaning and repairing rugs, carpets and tapestries); buys at auction (Oriental carpets, rugs and textiles). VAT: Stan/Spec.

LONDON NW6

H. Baron

76 Fortune Green Rd. NW6 1DS. Open Fri. and Sat. 1-6. *STOCK: Antiquarian music, books on music and iconography, autograph music and letters.* TEL: 0171 794 4041; office and fax - 0181 459 2035.

John Denham Gallery

50 Mill Lane, West Hampstead. NW6 1NJ. Open 10-5. CL: Sat. *STOCK: Paintings, drawings and prints, 17th-20th C, £5-£5,000.* TEL: 0171 794 2635. SER: Restorations; conservation; re-framing. VAT: Spec.

Gallery Kaleidoscope

66 Willesden Lane. NW6 7SX. (K. Barrie). Est. 1965. Open 10-6. SIZE: Medium. *STOCK: Oils, watercolours, prints, pottery and sculpture, 19th-20th C.* LOC: 10 mins. from Marble Arch. PARK: Easy. TEL: 0171 328 5833. SER: Restorations; framing. VAT: Stan/Spec.

Milne Henderson BADA

15 Greville Place. NW6 5JE. (S. Milne Henderson). Est. 1970. Open by appointment. *STOCK: Japanese, Chinese and Korean paintings and screens.* TEL: 0171 328 2171; fax - 0171 624 7274. SER: Valuations; buys at auction. VAT: Stan.

Scope Antiques

64-66 Willesden Lane. NW6 7SX. (K. Barrie). Est. 1966. Open 10-6. SIZE: Large. *STOCK: Furniture, general antiques, decorative items, silver, bric-a-brac.* PARK: Easy. TEL: 0171 328 5833. SER: Restorations (silver). VAT: Stan/Spec.

LONDON NW7

Gerald Clark Antiques

1 High St., Mill Hill Village. NW7 1QY. (G.J. Clark). Est. 1976. Open by appointment. SIZE: Medium. *STOCK: Early English and Victorian Staffordshire pottery, small furniture, watercolours and plaques, 18th-19th C.* PARK: Easy. TEL: 0181 958 4295. SER: Valuations; buys at auction. FAIRS: Olympia. VAT: Spec.

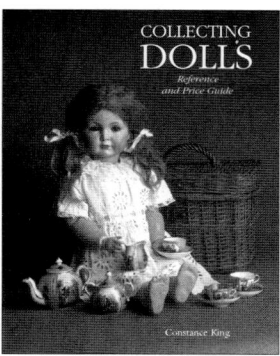

LONDON NW8

Alfies Antique Market
13-25 Church St. NW8. (B. Gray). Open 10-6. CL: Mon. SIZE: 300 stands with 180+ dealers on 5 floors. TEL: 0171 723 6066. Below are listed the dealers at this market.

20th Century Design
Stand G89/90. (Simon Alderson). *Art Deco.* TEL: 0171 723 0449.

Michael Abrahams
Stand F117. *Oils and watercolours, 19th-20th C, from £30.* TEL: 0171 724 4041.

Accurate Trading Co Ltd
Stand G30. *Antique and fine gem jewellery, 1780-1960, £1-£10,000, Victorian, Edwardian, Art Deco, 1930 to 1960, £45-£5,000.* TEL: 0171 723 1513; mobile - 0956 272490; fax - 0171 629 0277.

Beth Adams
Stand G43/44. *Decorative arts, 1860-1950's, £8-£750.* TEL: 0171 723 5613; fax - 0171 262 1576.

Mike Amey
Stand F21. *Paintings, furniture and objets d'art.* TEL: 0171 723 0678

NW8 continued

Mavis Axe
Stand G112. *Gold, glass, costume jewellery and bric-a-brac, 1920's to 1960's, £15-£500.*

David Bennett Antiques
Stand G104/5. *Boxes, scent bottles, small furniture, silver inkwells, fish servers, clocks, brass scales, glasses, decanters, wooden watch stands, 1800-1900, £20-£300.* TEL: 0171 723 0564.

Bibliopola
Stand F17. (Jo Del-Grosso). *Antiquarian illustrated, childrens books; modern first editions, 1600-1940.* TEL: 0171 724 7231.

M. J. Black
Stand F59/61. *Decorative and unusual objects.* TEL: 0171 723 0687.

Bloomsbury Antiques
Stand G14. (Maggie Miall). *Decorative lamps and ceiling light bowls, late 18th C.* TEL: 0171 706 3254; fax - same.

Everton & Marilyn Bookal Antiques
Stand F74/76/80/82. *Decorative and French country furniture, light fitting, bric-a-brac, 18th C to 1920's, £200-£5,000.* TEL: 0171 723 0429; mobile - 0468 997687; fax - 01227 720602.

NW8 continued

G. Brooks
Stand G103. *Jewellery, figures, mugs and objets d'art, Georgian to 1960, £25-£1,500.* TEL: 0171 723 0564; mobile - 0385 786395.

Bernie Bruno
Stand G115. *Clocks and watches.* TEL: 0171 723 0564

S. Brunswick
Stand F1-12. *House and garden furnishings, from 18th C.* TEL: 0171 724 9097; fax - 0181 902 5656.

Ursula Burnstock
Stand S121/133/134. *French and English chandeliers, wall lights, mirrors, small furniture, decorative items, 19th C.*

Vincenzo Cafferella
Stand G108/9, G118/9. *Oil paintings.* TEL: 0171 723 0564.

David Casolani
Stand F107/8. *Oil paintings and watercolours, 19th-20th C, from £30.* TEL: 0171 724 4041.

Marsia Cauicchio
Stand G132. *Art Deco.* TEL: 0171 723 0564.

Linda Chan
Stand G120. *Jewellery.* TEL: 0171 723 0564.

Classical Casts
Stand G49. (Tina Art). *Greek and Roman plaster casts of mythological figures and scenes, copied from originals, £8-£160.* TEL: 0171 723 5613; mobile - 0956 243784.

Collectors World
Stand G101, G130/143. (Jo Khan). *Toys including tin plate, Dinky, Meccano, lead soldiers; clocks, watches, cameras, film and TV memorabilia.* TEL: 0171 723 0564; mobile - 0860 791588.

Susie Cooper Ceramics
Stand G70-4, G93-5. (Nick Jones). *Susie Cooper ceramics, from £10.* TEL: 0171 723 0449; fax - 01634 405325.

Country Furniture and Decorative Antiques
Stand S126-129. (Wendy A. Carmichael). *Decorative antiques, 18th-20th C, £20-£1,000.* TEL: 0171 723 5731.

Cristobal
Stand G125-7. (Steve Miners). *Period costume, jewellery and accessories, 1920's to 1960's, £14-£2,000.* TEL: 0171 724 7789; fax - same; mobile 0956 388194.

Frances Cundy
Stand S6. *Costume and textiles, hats, shoes, linen and lace, beaded bags, small upholstered furniture, exquisite and unusual objects, 1900's-1960's, £5-£750.* TEL: 0171 723 6105; mobile - 0973 479057.

NW8 continued

Dalmoak Fine Art
Stand F46/7. (W. Simpson). *Decorative items, 18th-20th C, £50-£2,000.* TEL: 0171 723 0678.

Ruth Davis
Stand F77/78. *Glass, silver collectables and porcelain, 1760-1920, £30-£500+.* TEL: 0171 723 0429; mobile - 0831 717587.

Ruth Delany Antiques
Stand S111/2/9, S120. *General antiques and objets d'art, 18th-20th C, £10-£5,000.* TEL: Mobile - 0973 751351.

Dodo
Stand F73, F83/84. (Liz Farrow). *Posters, tins and advertising signs, 1890-1940.* TEL: 0171 706 1545.

Gerald Dougall
Stand F16. *Decorative antiques, 18th-20th C, £20-£1,000.* TEL: 0171 723 0678.

Michael Druks
Stand 050/51. *Collectables, unusual and curious items, 19th-20th C, £5-£250.* TEL: 0171 723 2548; fax - 0171 209 2764.

East-West Antiques
Stand G113/4, G117. (Colin Thompson). *Books and Oriental objects, from 1800, £5-£500.* TEL: 0171 723 0564.

Eastgates Antiques
Stand 7/9. (Joan Latford). *China teasets, wall plates, cups and saucers; Victorian coloured and Art Deco pressed glass; oil lamps and silver, 19th-20th C, £15-£1,500.* TEL: 0171 258 0312.

Paul Evans
Stand G54/55. *20th C design, art jewellery, books, £50-£1,000.* TEL: Mobile - 0378 791216.

Fashion in Print
Stand G5. (Katie Tilleke). *Fashion engravings and prints, 17th-20th C, £5-£500.* TEL: 0171 724 3722.

Fine Arts
Stand F48, F71/2. (Shoshi Preiss). *Fine arts.* TEL: 0171 723 0678.

Julia Foster
Stand F56. (J. Foster Fogle). *19th C decorative antiques.* TEL: 0171 723 0678; mobile - 0973 146610.

Furniture and Design
Stand B16-21. (Roger Schneider). *English Arts and Crafts furniture, 1860-1960, £20-£2,000.* TEL: 0171 724 9761.

Furniture and Design
Stand B3-8, B13-15. (Fiona Wicks). *English Arts and Crafts furniture, 1860-1960, £20-£2,000.* TEL: 0171 724 9761.

NW8 continued

Robin Gardiner
Stand G45/6. *Prints.* TEL: 0171 723 0449.

Gardiner and Gardiner
Stand F13/24. (Helen Gardiner). *Ornamental antiques, 18th-19th C.* TEL: 0171 723 5595.

Gatti's Works of Art
Stand F105. *Carvings, objects and paintings, 15th-18th C, £300+.* TEL: 0171 724 2892.

Genie
Stand 057/8. (E. Deimbacher). *Collectables and cutlery, 1900-1970, £2-£100.* TEL: 0171 723 2548.

Brenda Gerwat-Clark
Stand G2/4. *Dolls and teddy bears.* TEL: 0171 724 5650.

Richard Gibbon
Stand G82/86. *Costume jewellery, 20th C decorative arts, lighting, £10-£2,000.* TEL: 0171 723 0449.

Glassworks
Stand S2/4. (Paola Di Lorenzo). *1950's Italian glass.* TEL: 0171 723 6105.

Jocelyn Glenn Antiques
Stand F22. *Furniture and objects, Edwardian and Victorian.* TEL: 0171 723 0678.

Goldsmith and Perris — LAPADA
Stand G59-62. *Silver and plate.* TEL: 0171 724 7051.

Anne Gormley-Greene
Stand S104. *Pictures, prints, samplers, English porcelain, small decorative furniture, 18th-19th C, £5-£1,000.* TEL: 0171 723 5731.

Patricia Gould
Stand F70. *Textiles, 1400-1900, £5-£1,500.* TEL: 0171 723 0429.

L. Greco
Stand G26/7. *Jewellery, silver and plate, 1920's, 30's, 50's, £20-£350.* TEL: 0171 262 0766; mobile - 0802 965493.

Guillou-Emary
Stand G40/1. (Jean Gillou). *General decorative antiques, 18th-20th C, £25-£800.* TEL: 0171 723 5613.

Annie Hartnett and Ann Davey
Stand G35/6. *Textiles, beaded bags, embroidery, period costume, quilts, linen and lace, wedding veils, stoles and collars, 18th C to 1940's, £3-£500.* TEL: 0171 706 4123; fax - 01273 749860.

Victoria Harvey
Stand F19. *General decorative antiques.* TEL: 0171 723 0678.

NW8 continued

Henry Hay
Stand S54. *Art Deco, chrome and brass lamps, bakelite telephones, 20th C, £25-£500.* TEL: 0171 723 2548.

George Hepburn
Stand B43/4. *Paintings, 18th-20th C, £50-£2,000.* TEL: 0171 723 3437; mobile - 0421 598487.

Noel Hickey
Stand F54/5. *Decorative antiques.* TEL: 0171 72[illegible] 0678.

Edward Holden - Old Paintings & Drawings
Stand F122-5, F130. (Holden & Li). *Oils and water colours, drawings, 17th to early 20th C, £10-£2,000.* TEL: 0171 723 1370; fax 0171 609 0864.

Frances Houlding
Stand G121-4. *Silver and jewellery.* TEL: 0171 72[illegible] 1513.

John Howard
Stand S53. *Jewellery, china and textiles, 19th-20th C.* TEL: 0171 723 6105.

Dudley R. Howe
Stand S55/6, S67. *Collectables, 1900-1970, £5-£50[illegible]* TEL: 0171 723 2548.

V. Hoyer-Millar
Stand F57/8. *Decorative antiques.* TEL: 0171 72[illegible] 0678.

Huxtable's Old Advertising
Stand S3/5. (David Huxtable). *Advertising, collectables, tins, signs, bottles, commemoratives, old packaging, from late Victorian, 50p to £1,000.* TEL: 0171 724 2200; fax - 01727 833445.

International Antiques
Stand F127/8, F139/40. (Anthony Lask). *Silver and plate, English and American quilts.* TEL: 0171 72[illegible] 4648.

Peter Jacques
Stand S59/60. *Brass and architectural fittings.* TEL: 0171 723 6105.

Jay and Gee
Stand B35/6. (Ms and Jacob Fefer). *Bronzes, glass and collectables, Victorian to Art Deco, £10-£2,000.* TEL: 0171 724 3437.

Roger Jennings
Stand B41/2. *Georgian to 20th C bedsteads, £50[illegible]-£10,000.* TEL: 0171 724 3439.

Jeremiah Fine Art
Stand G12/13, G145. (Jeremy Sewell). *Prints, 17th-20th C.* TEL: 0171 723 1513.

NW8 continued

Rod Jones and Bill Campbell
Stand B28-32. *Period picture framer, original frames cut to size, 18th-20th C, £20-£1,000.* TEL: 0171 724 3437.

Jaydev Judeo
Stand F115. *Scientific and nautical instruments.* TEL: 0171 723 1370.

F. Kemp
Stand G116/129. *General decorative antiques including ornaments.* TEL: 0171 724 2114.

Mrs Khawaja
Stand G31. *Gold jewellery, 1940's to 1960's, £50-£1,200.* TEL: 0171 723 1513; mobile - 0956 272490.

Kitchen Bygones
Stand B51-53. (N. Oakley). *Kitchen antiques - working and decorative, 1800-1940's, £1.50-£500.* TEL: 0171 258 3045; fax - 01923 260453.

Bea Kornicky
Stand G64/65a. *General antiques and Oriental items, 19th C.* TEL: 0171 723 0449.

Lamb Silverware
Stand F106. (Jacob Bannin). *Silver, 1750 to 20th C, from £5.* TEL: 0171 723 2203.

Barry Landsman
Stand F103/4. *Watercolours, 18th-19th C, £50-£1,000.* TEL: 0171 723 1370.

Michael Lassere
Stand F40-45. *19th C general antiques, £20-£1,000.* TEL: 0171 723 2688.

Legacy
Stand G50/1. (J. Rosser and W. Garraway) *Postcards, old tins, ephemera, commemoratives, decorative and miniature objects.* TEL: 0171 723 0449.

Diane Levitt
Stand G102. TEL: 0171 723 0564. SER: Jewellery repair

Sarah Lewis
Stand S40. *Textiles - cushions, curtains, tapestries and embroideries; trims, tassels, prints, linen and lace, silk, shawls and clothes, 19th-20th C, £10-£10,000.* TEL: 0171 723 6105.

P. Ley
Stand G13. *Decorative items, 1850-1920, £15-£160.* TEL: 0171 723 0564.

Libra Designs
Stand B37/9, B45/6. (Marie Gottlieb). *Art Deco furniture, 20th C, £50-£5,000.* TEL: 0171 402 1976; fax - 0171 637 5210.

Aidan Lindsay
Stand B58/9. *Upholstery.* TEL: 0171 784 3439.

NW8 continued

Mark Andrew Lock Antiques
Stand S113-118. *Decorative antiques, 19th to early 20th C, £200-£2,000.* TEL: 0171 723 0678; mobile - 0589 540789.

Per Lundell
Stand G16-22. *Carpets, furnishing fabrics, Oriental porcelain, satsuma, clocks and pictures.*

Connie Margrie
Stand F50/1. *Soft furnishings and decorative objects, 1830-1930.* TEL: 0171 723 0678.

Marie Antiques
Stand G107, G136/9. (Marie Warner). *Victorian jewellery, Glens silver plate, small furniture, 18th-19th C.* TEL: 0171 723 0564.

Nigel Martin
Stand F100. *Textiles.* TEL: 0171 723 1370.

Francesca Martire
Stand F131-7. *Arts and Crafts, 20th C paintings costume jewellery, decorative arts.* TEL: 0171 723 1370.

Maryam
Stand G25. (R. Fatemi). *Jewellery, 1920- 1960's, £35-1,000.* TEL: 0171 723 1513.

The Maze
Stand G133/4. (S. Thammachote). *Costume jewellery and accessories, 1920's to 1960's, £14-£2,000.* TEL: 0171 724 7789; fax - same; mobile 0956 388194.

Robert McCoy
Stand F20. *Paintings, 19th-20th C, £50-£500.* TEL: 0171 723 0678.

Nigel McDonald
Stand F23. *Decorative antiques.* TEL: 0171 723 0678.

Margaret Miall
Stand G19. *English and Continental porcelain, glass and furniture, to mid 20th C.*

Mike Miller
Stand G37. *Art Nouveau, Art Deco fittings and lighting, £25-£500.* TEL: 0171 723 5613.

Modus Vivendi
Stand G79/80. (Helga Wellingham). *Antique and decorative prints.* TEL: 0171 723 0449.

Murray
S48/49. (John Beck). *Pottery - Torquay, North Devon, Honiton and Elton.* TEL: 0171 723 6105.

Bruna Naufal
Stand B1/2. *Modernist furniture, from 1920.* TEL: 0171 724 3437.

NW8 continued

Dean Nicholson
Stand S11. *General antiques.* TEL: 0171 723 6105.

Noe & Chiesa
Stand G87-8. *Art Deco and bakelite, 20th C, from £4.* TEL: 0171 723 0449.

Teresa Norton-Gore
Stand S10. *Buttons.* TEL: 0171 723 6105.

K. Norton-Grant
Stand F113/126. *Brass, pewter, pottery and china, 16th-20th C, £1-£250.* TEL: 0171 723 1370.

NS Watches
Stand G1. (M. Heidarieh). *Watches, clocks, prints, pens and silver, from 1850, from £10.* TEL: 0171 724 5650.

G. Payder
Stand G24. TEL: 0171 723 1513.

Gary Pe
Stand S12. *Decorative arts.* TEL: 0171 723 6105.

Stevie Pearce
Stand G144, T105. *Costume jewellery, fashion accessories, 1900-1970, from £10.* TEL: 0171 723 1513.

Mateo Picasso
Stand B47/8, B50. *Silver and plate, furniture.* TEL: 0171 724 3439.

Planet Bazaar
Stand G56/57. (A. C. Campbell). *20th C furniture, glass, art and collectables, £5-£5,000.* TEL: 0171 224 0833; mobile - 0956 326301; fax - 0171 224 0833.

Laraine Plummer Antiques
Stand S131/2. *Country furniture and decorative antiques, 18th-19th C, £10-£500.* TEL: 0171 723 5731.

Katharine Pole
Stand S105. *Textiles and decorative antiques, 18th-19th C, £5-£500.* TEL: 0171 723 5731.

Angela Pullan-Wells
Stand G140/2. (A. J. Futerman and D. Partleton). *Decorative furniture, art, glass, porcelain and cushions, jewellery, perfume bottles, collectables, 1780-1950, £20-£4,000.* TEL: 0171 723 0564.

Quality Artefacts
Stand S13/14. (Frank Ainsworth). *Fine glass, ceramics, collectibles, Royal Lancastrian glazes, fine silver, 18th-20th C, £30-£1,800.* TEL: Mobile - 0973 462997; fax - 0171 372 7901.

John Rastall
Stand G47/8. *20th C ceramics.* TEL: 0171 723 0449.

NW8 continued

Rayner & Chamberlin
Stand S1. *Post-war design, £20-£1,000.* TEL: 018 293 9439.

Angela Regana
Stand S110. TEL: 0171 723 5731. SER: Restor ations.

Geoffrey Robinson
Stand G75-78, G91/2. *Glass, lighting, chrome, Ar Deco, 1925-1960's.* TEL: 0171 723 0449; fax 0171 706 3254.

Albert Rockman
Stand G28/9. *China.* TEL: 0171 723 1513.

Rojeh Antiques
Stand B22-27, B33/4. (I. Fayez). *Art Deco furnitur £20-£7,000.* TEL: 0171 724 6960; mobile - 086 156390; fax - 0181 964 5959.

Alvin Ross
Stand G9/11. *Toys, games, dolls, teddy bears, min atures, ephemera, collectables, Victorian to 198(* TEL: 0171 723 1513.

Hoshang Samii
Stand S102/3, S125/130. *French decorati antiques, 18th-19th C, £10-£600.* TEL: 0171 72 5731.

Patrick Scola
Stand G63. *Collectables and memorabilia.* TEI 0171 723 0449

Michael Scott
Stand G38/9. *Furniture.* TEL: 0171 723 5613.

Yousef Shavleyan
Stand F109/11. *Ceramics and glass.* TEL: 0171 72 1370.

Gloria Sinclair
Stand F118/21. *Porcelain and jewellery, 18th-19 C.* TEL: 0171 724 7118.

Derek Smith
Stand G52/3. *Lamps, china, bakelite and glas 1920's to 1930's, £60-£350.* TEL: 0171 723 0449.

Kelvin Spooner
Stand S107/8. *Prints.* TEL: 0171 723 5731.

Elise Taylor
Stand G135. *Jewellery and handbags, 1860-193* TEL: 0171 723 0564.

Eugene Tiernan
Stand F14. *Decorative antiques, 19th-20th C, £5 £1,500.* TEL: 0171 723 8964; fax - same.

David Tilleke - Antiques, Prints & Engravings
Stand G6-8. *Prints and engravings, 17th-20th C, £ £500.* TEL: 0171 724 3722.

NW8 continued

The Toy Boy
Stand G23. (Paul Mulvey). *TV and film related dolls, toys and autographs, 1960's to 1980's, £1-£2,000.* TEL: 0171 723 1513; mobile - 0973 135906.

Travers Antiques
Stand G33/4. (Paula and S. Kluth). *Furniture and decorative objects, mainly 19th C, £250-£2,000.* TEL: 0171 258 0662.

Doris Urquhart
Stand F79. *Primitive and country objects, 19th C.* TEL: 0171 723 0429.

June Victor
Stand S42-47. *Decorative textiles and antique linen, 17th-20th C, £5-£500.* TEL: 0171 723 6105.

G. Viventi
Stand G128. *Silver and plate, jewellery, 1820 to 1950, £15-£500.* TEL: 0171 723 0564.

Catherine Wallis
Stand F52/3. *Decorative items, French furniture.* TEL: 0171 723 0429.

D. F. Wallis
Stand F15. *Medical and scientific items, cork-screws, 19th C, £1-£500.* TEL: 0171 402 1038; fax - same.

Martin Wallis
Stand S106. *Paintings, prints and frames, 18th-20th C, £50-£2,000.* TEL: 0171 723 5731; fax - 01322 446443.

Jessica Ward
Stand S100/1. *Decorative antiques, 18th-20th C, £5-£1,000.* TEL: 0171 723 5731.

Stephen Watson
Stand G66-8. *Decorative glass including Lalique.* TEL: 0171 723 0449.

Dean Williams
Stand G100. *Commemoratives, Toby jugs, British ceramics - Doulton, Wedgewood, Kevin Francis, 19th-20th C, £30-£2,000.* TEL: Mobile - 0410 226820.

Nick Wright
Stand B55/7. *Furniture.* TEL: 0171 724 3439.

All In One Antiques
Church St. NW8 8EE. (H. Freeman). Open .30-5, Mon. 10-3. *STOCK: General antiques ncluding upholstered items.* TEL: 0171 724 746. SER: Restorations; upholstery.

Beverley
0 Church St., Marylebone. NW8 8EP. Open 11- or by appointment. *STOCK: Art Nouveau, Art Deco, decorative objects.* TEL: 0171 262 1576.

NW8 continued

D. and A. Binder
34 Church St. NW8 8EP. Open 10-6. *STOCK: Traditional shop-fittings, counters, cabinets, vitrines and display stands.* LOC: Near Lisson Grove. TEL: 0171 723 0542; fax - 0171 724 0837.

Bizarre
24 Church St., Marylebone. NW8 8EP. (A. Taramasco and V. Conti). Open 10-5. *STOCK: Art Deco and Art Nouveau.* TEL: 0171 724 1305; fax - 0171 724 1316.

Camden Art Gallery
22 Church St. NW8 8EP. (Allen and Anne Silver). Est. 1968. Open 10-5. SIZE: Medium. *STOCK: Oil paintings and furniture, 18th-19th C, £300-£10,000.* LOC: Off Edgware Rd. PARK: Easy. TEL: 0171 262 3613; fax - 0171 723 2333. SER: Valuations; restorations (furniture, picture framing and cleaning). FAIRS: Barbican. VAT: Spec.

The Collector
9 Church St., Marylebone. NW8 8EE. (Tom Power). Est. 1973. Open 9.30-5.30, Sun. 10-2. SIZE: Large. *STOCK: Royal Doulton, from 1900, £50-£3,000; Beswick, from 1920, £40-£1,000; Moorcroft, £150-£750.* LOC: 500 yards from Edgware Road underground station, 1/2 mile from Marble Arch. PARK: Easy (Not Sat.). TEL: 0171 706 4586; fax - 0171 706 2948. SER: Valuations. FAIRS: Specialist Decorative Art, mainly Royal Doulton. VAT: Stan.

Nicholas Drummond/Wrawby Moor Art Gallery Ltd
6 St. John's Wood Rd. NW8 8RE. (J.N. Drummond). Est. 1972. Open by appointment only. *STOCK: English and European oils, £250-£30,000; works on paper.* LOC: Pass Lords entrance and next lights, house last bow front on left, facing down Hamilton Terrace. TEL: 0171 286 6452; home - same; fax - 0171 266 9070. SER: Valuations; restorations (oils); buys at auction. VAT: Spec.

Robert Franses and Sons
NW8. Est. 1969. Open by appointment only. *STOCK: European and Oriental carpets, tapestries, needlework, Turkish village and early Chinese rugs.* TEL: 0171 328 0949. SER: Restorations. VAT: Stan/Spec.

Gallery of Antique Costume and Textiles
2 Church St., Marylebone. NW8 8ED. Open 10-5.30. *STOCK: Curtains, needleworks, paisley shawls, original clothing up to 1940's and English quilts, 19th-20th C; tassles, decorative borders, silk panels, velvets and brocades, £5-£20,000.* LOC: 500yds. from Marylebone tube and 1/2 mile from Marble Arch. PARK: Easy. TEL: 0171 723 9981 (ansaphone).

NW8 continued

The Gallery on Church Street
12 Church St. NW8 8EP. (E. Phillips). Open 10-5.30. SIZE: Small. *STOCK: Posters, Art Nouveau and Art Deco, watercolours, oils and decorative prints.* PARK: Easy. TEL: 0171 723 3389; fax - 0171 723 3389.

Patricia Harvey Antiques and Decoration LAPADA
42 Church St., Marylebone. NW8 8EP. Est. 1961. Open 10-6, Sat. 11-4. SIZE: Medium. *STOCK: Decorative furniture, objets, accessories and paintings, £100-£20,000.* LOC: Between Lisson Grove and Edgware Rd., shop is near Alfies Antique Market. TEL: 0171 262 8989; home - 0171 624 1787; fax - 0171 262 9090. SER: Valuations; buys at auction; interior decoration. FAIRS: Decorative Antiques and Textiles. VAT: Stan.

Just Desks
20 Church St. NW8 8EP. (G. Gordon and N. Finch). Est. 1967. Open 9.30-6 or by appointment. *STOCK: Victorian, Edwardian and reproduction desks, writing tables, davenports, bureaux, chairs, filing cabinets and roll tops.* PARK: Meters. TEL: 0171 723 7976; fax - 0171 402 6416. VAT: Stan.

Lenson Smith LAPADA
11 Church St., Lisson Grove. NW8. *STOCK: Decorative items, Vienna bronzes, early brass, animalia, French furniture.* TEL: 0171 724 7763.

Magus Antiques
4 Church St. NW8 8ED. (D.A. Robinson). Est. 1973. Open 10-6. CL: Mon. SIZE: Medium. *STOCK: Porcelain and glass, European and Oriental, £10-£15,000; bronzes, furniture, £100-£15,000.* LOC: Left off Edgware Rd., 200yds. north of Marylebone flyover. PARK: Easy. TEL: 0171 724 1278. SER: Valuations; buys at auction. FAIRS: Olympia. VAT: Stan.

NW8 continued

Risky Business
44 Church St. NW8 8EP. (P.R. John and Mrs C.M. Dobson). Est. 1976. Open 10-6. SIZE: Medium. *STOCK: Decorative furnishings, 1900-1950; vintage sporting paraphernalia, luggage; cane, rattan, club style furniture and one-off original pieces.* LOC: Near Lisson Grove. PARK: Easy. TEL: 0171 724 2194. VAT: Stan.

Silver Belle
48 Church St. NW8 8EP. Est. 1986. Open 9.30-5.30, Sun. and Mon. by appointment. SIZE: Medium. *STOCK: Silver and Sheffield plate, china including tea sets.* PARK: Easy. TEL: 0171 723 2908; fax - same. SER: Valuations; restorations (re-plating).

The Studio
18 Church St. NW8 8EP. Open 10-6, Sat. 10-5. *STOCK: British Arts and Crafts, Gothic and Art Deco, especially furniture, 1830-1960's.* TEL: 0171 258 0763. SER: Valuations; buys at auction.

Tara Antiques
6 Church St. NW8 8ED. (G. Robinson). Est. 1971. Open 10-6. CL: Mon. SIZE: Medium. *STOCK: Unusual marble and bronze statuary, Vienna bronzes, silver, furniture, paintings, ivory and tortoiseshell.* PARK: Easy. TEL: 0171 724 2405. SER: Buys at auction. VAT: Stan.

Townsends
81 Abbey Rd., St. John's Wood and 106 Boundary Rd. NW8 0AE. (M. Townsend). Est. 1972. Open 10-6. SIZE: Large. *STOCK: Fireplaces, £100-£3,000; stained glass, £30-£200; architectural items, £10-£300; all mainly 19th C.* LOC: Corner of Abbey Rd. and Boundary Rd. PARK: Easy. TEL: 0171 624 4756; fax - 0171 372 3005. SER: Valuations. VAT: Stan.

Wellington Gallery LAPADA
1 St John's Wood High St. NW8 7NG. (Mrs K. Barclay). Open 10.30-6. *STOCK: Fine furniture, 18th-19th C; paintings, Georgian*

NW8 continued

***glass, porcelain, silver and Sheffield plate, general antiques.* TEL: 0171 586 2620; fax - 0171 722 4242. SER: Valuations; restorations; curtain making, upholstery.**

LONDON NW9

B.C. Metalcrafts Ltd LAPADA

69 Tewkesbury Gardens. NW9 0QU. Est. 1946. Open by appointment only. *STOCK: Lighting, ormolu and marble lamps; Oriental and European vases; clocks, pre-1900, £5-£500.* Not Stocked: Silver. TEL: 0181 204 2446; fax - 0181 206 2871. SER: Restorations and conversions; buys at auction. VAT: Stan/Spec. *Trade Only.*

LONDON NW10

David Malik and Son Ltd

5 Metro Centre, Britannia Way, Park Royal. NW10 7PA. Open 9-5. CL: Sat. *STOCK: Chandeliers, wall lights.* PARK: Easy. TEL: 0181 965 4232; fax - 0181 965 2401. VAT: Stan.

LONDON NW11

Delieb Antiques

31 Woodville Rd. NW11 9TP. (E. Delieb). Est. 1953. Open by appointment only. CL: Sat. *STOCK: Collectors' silver and rarities.* TEL: 0181 458 2083. SER: Valuations.

Christopher Eimer

P.O. Box 352. NW11 7RF. *STOCK: Commemorative and historical medals.* TEL: 0181 458 9933; fax - 0181 455 3535.

LONDON WC1

Abbott and Holder

30 Museum St. WC1A 1LH. Est. 1938. Open 9.30-6, Thurs. till 7. *STOCK: Pictures, especially watercolours.* TEL: 0171 637 3981. VAT: Spec

Atlantis Bookshop

49a Museum St. WC1 1LY. Open 10-5.30, Sat. 11-5. *STOCK: Antiquarian books on the occult and paranormal.* TEL: 0171 405 2120

Austin/Desmond Fine Art

Pied Bull Yard, 68/69 Great Russell St. WC1B 3BN. (J. Austin). SLAD. Open 10.30-5.30. *STOCK: Modern and contemporary British paintings and prints.* TEL: 0171 242 4443; fax - 0171 404 4480.

WC1 continued

Cinema Bookshop

13-14 Great Russell St. WC1B 3NH. (F. Zentner). Est. 1969. Open 10.30-5.30. SIZE: Small. *STOCK: Books, magazines, posters and stills.* LOC: First right off Tottenham Court Rd. PARK: Easy. TEL: 0171 637 0206. SER: Mail order. VAT: Stan.

Classic Collection

2 Pied Bull Yard, Bury Place. WC1A 2JR. Open 9-5.30. SIZE: Medium. *STOCK: Classic and collectors' cameras, 1850-1960, from £10; daguerreotypes, optical toys and steroscopes.* LOC: Near Great Russell St. and Bloomsbury. PARK: Easy. TEL: 0171 831 6000; fax - 0171 831 5424. SER: Valuations; restorations. FAIRS: Camera Collectors, U.K. and Europe. VAT: Stan.

George and Peter Cohn

Unit 21, 21 Wren St. WC1X 0HF. Est. 1947. Open 9-5, Sat. and Fri. pm. by appointment. *STOCK: Decorative lights.* PARK: Forecourt. TEL: 0171 278 3749. SER: Restorations (chandeliers and wall-lights). *Trade Only.*

Sebastian D'Orsai Ltd

39 Theobalds Rd. WC1X 8NW. (A. Brooks). Open 9-5. CL: Sat. *STOCK: Framed watercolours.* TEL: 0171 405 6663. SER: Restorations (paintings and prints); framing; gilding. VAT: Stan.

J.A.L. Franks

7 New Oxford St. WC1A 1BA. Est. 1947. *STOCK: Stamps, maps, postcards, cigarette cards.* TEL: 0171 405 0274; fax - 0171 430 1259.

Robert Frew Ltd

106 Gt. Russell St. WC1B 3NA. (Robert Frew and Chantziaras Panagiotis). ABA, PBFA. Open 10-6, Sat. 10-2. *STOCK: Books, 15th-20th C, £5-£25,000; maps and prints, 15th-19th C, £5-£5,000.* LOC: Turn right off Tottenham Court Rd. to British Museum, shop on left past YMCA. PARK: Easy. TEL: 0171 580 2311. FAIRS: ABA Grosvenor House, Chelsea; PBFA, Hotel Russell; various USA. VAT: Stan.

Jessop Classic Photographica

67 Great Russell St. WC1 3BN. Open 9-5.30. *STOCK: Classic photographic equipment, cameras and optical toys.* TEL: 0171 831 3640; fax - 0171 831 3956.

London Antiquarian Book Arcade

37 Great Russell St. WC1. (Ronald Morris and Myrna Adolph-Morris). ABA. Open 10-6, Sun. 12-5. SIZE: Large. *STOCK: Antiquarian books, 17th-19th C, £30-£2,000; modern first editions, £10-£6,000; maps and prints, 18th-19th C, £10-£500; modern prints, £10-£500.* LOC: Near British Museum. TEL: 0171 436 2054; home - same; fax - 0171 436 2057. SER: Valuations; book search. VAT: Stan.

WC1 continued

Marchmont Bookshop
39 Burton St. WC1H 9AL. (D. Holder). Open 11-6.30. CL: Sat. *STOCK: Literature, including modern first editions.* TEL: 0171 387 7989.

The Museum Bookshop
36 Gt. Russell St. WC1B 3PP. (Ashley Jones). Est. 1982. Open 10-5.30. *STOCK: Books on antiquities - Egyptian, Middle Eastern, classical; glass, ceramics, conservation.* LOC: 3 minutes from Tottenham Court Rd. underground station. PARK: Easy. TEL: 0171 580 4086; fax - 0171 436 4361.

Nortonbury Antiques LAPADA
BCM Box 5345. WC1N 3XX. Open by appointment. *STOCK: Silver, 17th-19th C.* TEL: 01984 631668; fax - same; mobile - 0374 174092.

The Print Room
37 Museum St. WC1A 1LP. (A. Balfour-Lynn and K. Surya). Est. 1984. Open 10-6, Sat. 10-4, other times by appointment. *STOCK: Prints including natural history, views of London, costume plates and caricatures, 1580-1850, £10-£3,000.* LOC: Off Gt. Russell St., opposite British Museum. PARK: N.C.P. Bloomsbury Sq. TEL: 0171 430 0159; fax - 0171 831 2874. SER: Valuations; buys at auction (antiquarian books and prints).

Rennies
13 Rugby St. WC1. (Paul and Karen Rennie). Open Tues.-Sat. *STOCK: Decorative arts, 1880-1960; vintage posters, mainly British.* TEL: 0171 405 0220.

S.J. Shrubsole Ltd
43 Museum St. WC1A 1LY. (C.J. Shrubsole). Est. 1918. Open 9-5.30. CL: Sat. SIZE: Medium. *STOCK: Silver, late 17th to mid-19th C, £50-£25,000; Sheffield plate, mid-18th to mid-19th C, £10-£5,000.* LOC: 1 min. from British Museum. PARK: Easy. TEL: 0171 405 2712. SER: Valuations; restorations (silver); buys at auction. VAT: Stan/Spec.

Skoob Books Ltd
11a-15 Sicilian Ave., Southampton Row, Holborn. WC1A 2QH. Est. 1978. Open 10.30-6.30. SIZE: Large. *STOCK: Secondhand books specialising in philosophy, cultural strudies, literature, science and technology.* LOC: In pedestrian arcade, near Holborn Underground. PARK: Easy. TEL: 0171 404 3063; fax - 0171 404 4398. SER: Publishers of Skoob Seriph and Skoob Pacifica series; catalogues for philosophy, anthropology and economics.

WC1 continued

Skoob Two
17 Sicilian Avenue. WC1A 2QH. Open 10.30-6.30. SIZE: Medium. *STOCK: Secondhand books on anthropology, the sciences, classics, psychology, esoterica and new age; used classical and jazz CDs.* TEL: 0171 405 0030; fax - 0171 404 4398. SER: Publishers of Skoob Esoterica Anthropology catalogue.

LONDON WC2

Anchor Antiques Ltd
26 Charing Cross Rd. WC2H 0DG. (K.B. Embden and H. Samne). Est. 1964. Open by appointment. *STOCK: Continental and Oriental ceramics, European works of art and objets de vertu.* TEL: 0171 836 5686. VAT: Spec. *Trade Only.*

Apple Market Stalls
Covent Garden Market. WC2E 8RF. Open every Monday. SIZE: 48 stalls. *STOCK: General antiques and quality collectables.* TEL: 0171 836 9136.

At the Movies
2 Cecil CourtWC2. Open 11-6, Sat. 11.30-6. *STOCK: Film posters and memorabilia, including books and stills.* TEL: 0171 240 7221.

A.H. Baldwin and Sons Ltd BADA
11 Adelphi Terrace. WC2N 6BJ. IAPN, BNTA. Est. 1872. Open 9-5. CL: Sat. SIZE: Medium. *STOCK: Coins, 600 BC to present; commemorative medals, 16th C to present, numismatic literature.* LOC: Off Robert St., near Charing Cross. TEL: 0171 930 6879/839 1310; fax 0171 930 9450. SER: Valuations; auction agents for selling and purchasing. VAT: Stan/Spec.

Bell, Book and Radmall
4 Cecil Court. WC2N 4HE. Est. 1974. Open 10-5.30, Sat. 11-4. *STOCK: First editions of 19th-20th C English and American literature including detective fiction.* TEL: 0171 240 2161.

Blackwell's
100 Charing Cross Rd. WC2. SIZE: Small. *STOCK: Antiquarian and rare modern books.*

M. Bord (Gold Coin Exchange)
16 Charing Cross Rd. WC2H 0HR. Est. 196- Open 9.30-6. SIZE: Small. *STOCK: Gold, silver and copper coins, Roman to Elizabeth II, all prices.* LOC: Near Leicester Sq. underground station. TEL: 0171 836 0631/240 0479. SER: Valuations; buys at auction. FAIRS: All major coin. VAT: Stan/Spec.

WC2 continued

Covent Garden Flea Market

Jubilee Market, Covent Garden. WC2E 8RB. (Sherman and Waterman Associates Ltd). Est. 1975. Open Mon. and Bank Holidays 5-5. SIZE: 200 stalls. *STOCK: General antiques.* LOC: South side of piazza, just off The Strand, via Southampton St. PARK: Easy and N.C.P. Drury Lane. TEL: 0171 836 2139/240 7405.

Deco Inspired

67 Monmouth St. WC2H 9DG. (Stanley and Nicole Chaman). Est. 1984. Open 11-7. SIZE: Small. *STOCK: American Art Deco, 1920-1960.* PARK: Easy. TEL: 0171 240 5719. FAIRS: Italy, France and USA. VAT: Stan.

David Drummond at Pleasures of Past Times

11 Cecil Court, Charing Cross Rd. WC2N 4EZ. Est. 1962. Open 11-2.30 and 3.30-5.45 and usually 1st Sat. monthly, other times by appointment. SIZE: Medium. *STOCK: Scarce and out-of-print books of the performing arts; early juvenile and illustrated books; vintage postcards, valentines, entertainment ephemera.* Not Stocked: Coins, stamps, medals, jewellery, maps, cigarette cards. LOC: In pedestrian court between Charing Cross Rd. and St. Martin's Lane. TEL: 0171 836 1142. VAT: Stan.

W. and G. Foyle Ltd

113-119 Charing Cross Rd. WC2. Est. 1904. *STOCK: Antiquarian books.*

Stanley Gibbons

399 Strand. WC2R 0LX. Est. 1856. Open 8.30-6, Sat. 9.30-5.30. SIZE: Large. *STOCK: Popular and specialised stamps, postal history, catalogues, albums, accessories; autographs and memorabilia.* LOC: Opposite Savoy Hotel. TEL: 0171 836 8444; fax - 0171 836 7342. SER: Valuations. VAT: Stan/Spec.

Gillian Gould at Ocean Leisure

Embankment Place, 11-14 Northumberland Avenue. WC2N 5AQ. Est. 1988. Open 9.30-6, Thurs. 9.30-7, Sat. 9.30-5.30 or by appointment. SIZE: Small. *STOCK: Marine antiques and collectables, scientific instruments, £30-£1,000.* PARK: Meters. TEL: 0171 930 5050; fax - 0171 930 3032; home - 0171 433 1747; fax - 0171 431 7716; mobile - 0831 150060. SER: Valuations; restorations; hire; sources gifts for personal and corporate presentation; buys at auction. VAT: Stan.

Grosvenor Prints

28/32 Shelton St., Covent Garden. WC2H 9HP. Est. 1975. Open 10-6, Sat. 11-4. SIZE: Large. *STOCK: 18th-19th C topographical and decorative prints, specialising in portraits, dogs and British field sports.* LOC: One street north of

WC2 continued

Covent Garden tube. PARK: Easy. TEL: 0171 836 1979; fax - 0171 379 6695. SER: Valuations; restorations; buys at auction. VAT: Stan/Spec.

Lee Jackson

2 Southampton St., Covent Garden. WC2E 7HA. PBFA. Est. 1996. Open 10-6. SIZE: Large. *STOCK: Maps and views of the world, 16th-19th C, £10-£3,000.* LOC: Off the Strand, opposite the Savoy Hotel. PARK: Meters. TEL: 0171 240 1970. VAT: Stan.

S. and H. Jewell Ltd

26 Parker St. WC2B 5PH. Est. 1830. Open 9-5.30, Sat. by appointment. SIZE: Large. *STOCK: Furniture.* TEL: 0171 405 8520. SER: Valuations; restorations. VAT: Stan/Spec.

Thomas Kettle Ltd

53a Neal St. WC2. Est. 1974. Open 10-7. SIZE: Medium. *STOCK: Wrist watches, 1910-1950, £350-£5,000; contemporary designer jewellery, £40-£2,000.* LOC: Near Covent Garden tube. PARK: Leicester Sq. TEL: 0171 379 3579. SER: Valuations; restorations (wrist watches). VAT: Stan.

The London Silver Vaults

Chancery House, 53-65 Chancery Lane. WC2. Est. 1892. Open 9-5.30, Sat. 9-1. SIZE: 34 shops. *STOCK: Antique and modern silver, plate, jewellery, objets d'art, clocks, watches, collectors' items.* TEL: 0171 242 3844. The following are some of the dealers at these vaults.

A. M. W. Silverware

Vault 52. TEL: 0171 242 3620; fax - 0171 831 3923.

Argenteus Ltd — LAPADA

Vault 2. TEL: 0171 831 3637; fax - 0171 430 0126. VAT: Stan/Spec.

Benjamin Jewellery Ltd ~ — LAPADA

Vault 46. TEL: 0171 831 1380; fax - 0171 831 4629.

Lawrence Block

Vault 28 and 65. Est. 1959. *Silver especially flatware; jewellery.* TEL: 0171 242 0749. SER: Valuations; restorations; buys at auction.

A. Bloom

Vault 27. TEL: 0171 242 6189.

Luigi Brian Antiques

Vault 17. TEL: 0171 405 2484; fax - same.

B.L. Collins

Vault 20. TEL: 0171 404 0628; fax - 0171 404 1451.

P. Daniels

Vault 51. TEL: 0171 430 1327.

WC2 continued

B. Douglas LAPADA
Vault 12/14. TEL: 0171 242 7073.

M.J. Dubiner
Vault 38.

R. Feldman Ltd LAPADA
Vault 4/6. TEL: 0171 405 6111; fax - 0171 430 0126.

I. Franks LAPADA.
Vault 9/11. Est. 1926. TEL: 0171 242 4035.

Hamilton
Vault 25. TEL: 0171 831 7030; fax - 0171 831 5483.

S. Kalms LAPADA
Vault 31/32. TEL: 0171 430 1254; fax - 0171 405 6206.

B. Lampert
Vault 19. TEL: 0171 242 4121.

Langfords LAPADA
Vault 8/10. Est. 1940. *Silver and plate especially cutlery*. TEL: 0171 242 5506; fax - 0171 405 0431. SER:Valuations. VAT: Stan/Spec.

Nat Leslie Ltd
Vault 21/22/23. Est. 1940. *Silver and plate, especially cutlery.* TEL: 0171 242 4787; fax - 0171 242 4504. VAT: Stan/Spec.

Linden and Co. (Antiques) Ltd
Vault 7. (H, F, H.M. and S. C. Linden). TEL: 0171 242 4863; fax - 0171 405 9946. VAT: Stan/Spec.

C. and T. Mammon
Vault 31 & 64. TEL: 0171 405 2397.

J. Mammon Antiques
Vault 30. TEL: 0171 242 4704. *Trade Only.*

I. Nagioff (Jewellery)
Vault 63 and 69. (I. and R. Nagioff). Est. 1955. *Jewellery, 18th-20th C, £5-£2,000+; objets d'art, 19th C, to £200.* TEL: 0171 405 3766. SER: Valuations; restorations (jewellery). VAT: Stan.

Percy's LAPADA
Vault 16. *Candelabra, candlesticks, flatware and collectables.* TEL: 0171 242 3618.

Rare Art
Vault 15. TEL: 0171 405 9968.

Saunders
Vault 60.

David S. Shure and Co
Vault 1. (S. Bulka). Est. 1900. Author. *Silver and plate.* TEL: 0171 405 0011; fax - same. SER: Valuations. VAT: Stan.

WC2 continued

Silstar
Vault 29. (B. Stern). Est. 1955. TEL: 0171 242 6740. VAT: Stan/Spec.

B. Silverman BADA
Vault 26/33. (S. and R. Silverman). Est. 1927. TEL: 0171 242 3269. SER:Valuations; buys at auction. VAT: Stan/Spec.

Jack Simons (Antiques) Ltd LAPADA
Vault 35 and 37. Est. 1955. TEL: 0171 242 3221. VAT: Stan/Spec.

S. and J. Stodel
Vault 24. TEL: 0171 405 7009; fax - 0171 242 6366.

A. Urbach
Vault 50.

William Walter Antiques Ltd BADA LAPADA
Vault 3/5. (R.W. Walter). Est. 1927. TEL: 0171 242 3248; fax - 0171 404 1280. SER:Valuations; restorations (silver, plate).

A. and G. Weiss
Vault 42/44. TEL: 0171 242 8100. VAT: Stan.

Peter K. Weiss
Vault 18. Est. 1955. *Watches, clocks.* TEL: 0171 242 8100; fax - 0171 242 7310. VAT: Stan.

Wolfe (Jewellery)
Vault 41. TEL: 0171 405 2101; fax - same. VAT: Stan/Spec.

Arthur Middleton
12 New Row, Covent Garden. WC2N 4LF. Est. 1968. Open 10-6, Sat. by appointment only. SIZE: Medium. *STOCK: Globes, 1720-1950, from miniatures to large library pairs; scientific instruments - navigation, astronomy, surveying, microscopes, 18th-19th C, £100-£50,000.* LOC: New Row runs between Leicester Sq. and Covent Garden. Shop 300yds. east from Leicester Sq. TEL: 0171 836 7042/7062; fax - 0171 497 2486. SER: Valuations; buys at auction; prop hire. VAT: Stan.

Pearl Cross Ltd
35 St. Martin's Court. WC2N 4AL. Est. 189[illegible] Open 9.30-4.45. CL: Sat. *STOCK: Jewellery, silver, clocks, watches.* PARK: Meters. TEL: 0171 836 2814/240 0795; fax - 0171 240 273[illegible] SER: Valuations; restorations (jewellery, silver). VAT: Stan/Spec.

Henry Pordes Books Ltd
58-60 Charing Cross Rd. WC2H 0BB. Open 10-[illegible] *STOCK: Secondhand and remainder books on most subjects including antiques.* TEL: 0171 83[illegible] 9031; fax - 0181 886 2201.

WC2 continued

Reg and Philip Remington
18 Cecil Court, Charing Cross Rd. WC2N 4HE. ABA. Est. 1979. Open 10-5, Sat. by appointment. SIZE: Medium. *STOCK: Voyages and travels, 17th-20th C, £5-£1,000.* LOC: Near Trafalgar Sq. TEL: 0171 836 9771. SER: Buys at auction. FAIRS: London Book, Grosvenor House. VAT: Stan.

Bertram Rota Ltd
1st Floor, 31 Long Acre. WC2E 9LT. Est. 1923. Open 9.30-5.30. CL: Sat. *STOCK: Antiquarian and secondhand books, especially first editions, private presses, English literature, and literary autographs.* TEL: 0171 836 0723.

The Silver Mouse Trap
56 Carey St. WC2A 2JB. (A. Woodhouse). Est. 1690. Open 10-5. CL: Sat. SIZE: Medium. *STOCK: Jewellery, silver.* LOC: South of Lincoln's Inn Fields. TEL: 0171 405 2578. SER: Valuations; restorations. VAT: Spec.

Justin F. Skrebowski Prints
9 Cecil Court. WC2. Est. 1985. Open 11-6, Sat. 11.30-6. *STOCK: 18th-19th C decorative prints, watercolours, oil paintings and old frames.* TEL: 0171 240 7221; mobile - 0374 612474. SER: Valuations. VAT: Stan/Spec.

Stage Door Prints
1 Cecil Court, Charing Cross Rd. WC2N 4EZ. (A. Reynold). Open 11-6. *STOCK: Prints of performing arts, sports and topographical; signed photographs, maps, Victorian cards, valentines; performing arts book room and bargain basement.* TEL: 0171 240 1683.

Storey's Ltd
3 Cecil Court, Charing Cross Rd. WC2 4EZ. (T. Kingswood). Est. 1929. Open 10-6. *STOCK: Prints, especially naval and military; antiquarian books.* LOC: Between Charing Cross Rd. and St. Martin's Lane. PARK: Trafalgar Square garage. TEL: 0171 836 3777; fax - same.

Tooley Adams & Co.
13 Cecil Court, Charing Cross Rd. WC2N 4EZ. (D. Adams and S. Luck). ABA. Est. 1964. Open 9-5. SIZE: Large. *STOCK: Antiquarian maps, atlases; travel and map related reference books.* LOC: Between St. Martin's Lane and Charing Cross Rd. PARK: St. Martin's Lane. TEL: 0171 240 4406; fax - 0171 240 8058; e-mail - 101661.2730@compuserve.com. SER: Valuations; restorations. FAIRS: Bonnington Map; Imcos Map. VAT: Stan.

WC2 continued

Trafalgar Square Collectors Centre
7 Whitcomb St. WC2H 7HA. (D.C. Pratchett and R.D. Holdich). Est. 1979. Open 10-5. CL: Sat. *STOCK: Coins and military medals, bonds, banknotes, badges and militaria, 18th-20th C, £5-£10,000.* LOC: Next to National Gallery. PARK: NCP. TEL: 0171 930 1979; fax - 0171 930 1152. SER: Valuations; buys at auction (coins and military medals). VAT: Stan/Spec.

Travis and Emery
17 Cecil Court, Charing Cross Rd. WC2N 4EZ. (V. Emery). ABA. Est. 1960. Open 10-6. SIZE: Medium. *STOCK: Musical literature, music and prints.* LOC: Between Charing Cross Rd. and St. Martin's Lane opposite Odeon. PARK: Meters. TEL: 0171 240 2129; fax - 0171 497 0790. VAT: Stan.

Watkins Books Ltd
19 Cecil Court, Charing Cross Rd. WC2N 4EZ. Est. 1880. Open 10-6, Wed. 10.30-6. *STOCK: Mysticism, occultism, Oriental religions, astrology, psychology, complementary medicine and a wide selection of books in the field of mind, body and spirit - both new and secondhand.* TEL: 0171 836 2182; fax - 0171 836 6700.

The Witch Ball
2 Cecil Court, Charing Cross Rd. WC2. (R. Glassman). Resident. Est. 1969. Open 10.30-6. SIZE: Small. *STOCK: Prints relating to the performing arts, from 17th C, topographical prints, 20th C posters.* LOC: 2 mins. from Leicester Sq. tube station. PARK: NCP nearby. TEL: 0171 836 2922. VAT: Stan.

Zeno Booksellers and Publishers
6 Denmark St. WC2H 8LP. Est. 1944. Open 9.30-6, Sat. till 5. SIZE: Medium. *STOCK: Antiquarian books on Greece, Cyprus, Byzantium, Turkey, Middle East and the Balkans.* LOC: From Tottenham Court Rd., into Charing Cross Rd., first turning on left. TEL: 0171 240 1968; 0171 836 2522; fax - same.

Zwemmer
24 Litchfield St. WC2H 9NJ. Est. 1921. Open 10-6.30, Sat. 10-6. SIZE: Large. *STOCK: Books on art and fine art; rare and out-of-print catalogue raisonnés.* LOC: Just south of Cambridge Circus, Leicester Sq. underground. TEL: 0171 379 7886.

AVON

This county no longer exists. Towns and villages previously listed in this section will either be found under Gloucestershire (Bristol) or Somerset (Bath).

In case of difficulty please refer either to the Towns and Villages Index or, if you are looking for a particular dealer, the Dealers Index where they will be listed with the name of the new county under which they appear.

Bedfordshire

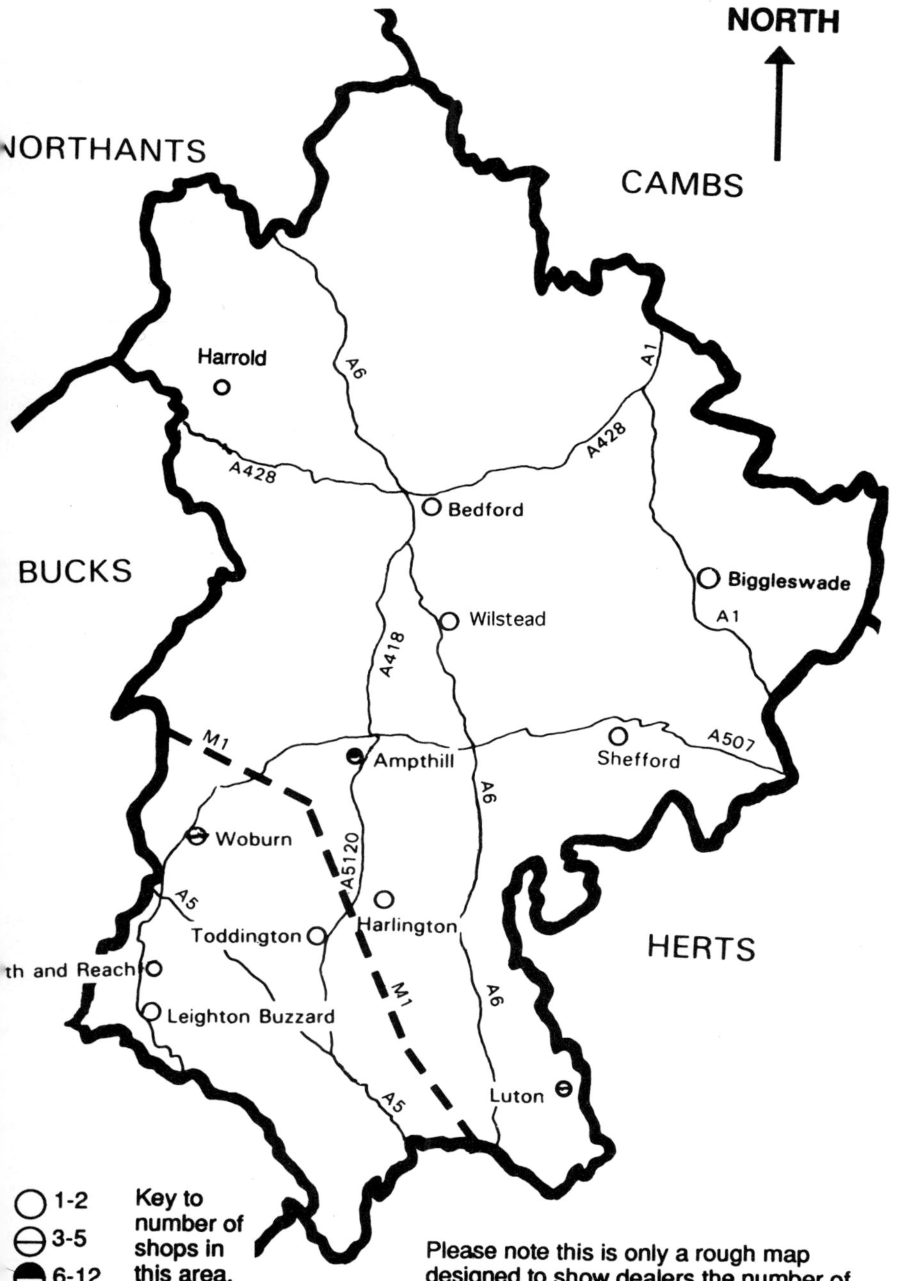

1-2
3-5
6-12
13+

Key to number of shops in this area.

Please note this is only a rough map designed to show dealers the number of shops in the various towns, and is not necessarily totally accurate.

AMPTHILL

Ampthill Antiques
Market Sq. MK4 5ZP. (A. Olney). Est. 1980. Open 10-5, Sun. 2-5. CL: Mon. SIZE: Large. *STOCK: Furniture, collectables, jewellery, Clarice Cliff, clocks.* LOC: Town centre. PARK: Easy and at rear. TEL: 01525 403344.

Ampthill Emporium
6 Bedford St. MK45 2NB. Est. 1979. Open 10-5.30 including Sun. SIZE: Large - 25 dealers. *STOCK: Antique and secondhand furniture.* LOC: 5 mins. from junction 13, M1. PARK: Easy. TEL: 01525 402131.

House of Clocks
106 Dunstable St. (John Ginty). Resident. Est. 1957. Open 9-5, Sun. 1-5. SIZE: Medium. *STOCK: Clocks including longcase, bracket, carriage and wall, £150-£12,000.* PARK: Behind Market Sq. TEL: 01525 403136; fax - same. SER: Valuations; restorations (clocks). FAIRS: Manchester; Birmingham: Uxbridge: Kettering: Luton. VAT: Stan/Spec.

Paris Antiques
97B Dunstable St. MK45 2NG. (Paul and Elizabeth Northwood). Est. 1985. Open 9.30-5. CL: Mon. SIZE: Medium. *STOCK: Furniture, 18th to early 20th C, £250-£4,000; brass and copper, silver and plate, pictures and smalls.* LOC: Off junction 12, M1. PARK: Opposite. TEL: 01525 840488; home - 01525 861420; mobile - 0402 274558. SER: Valuations; restorations (mainly furniture, some metal); buys at auction.

Pilgrim Antiques
11 Dunstable St. MK45 1BY. (Gary Lester). Est. 1982. Open 10-5.30, including Sun. SIZE: Large. *STOCK: Furniture including dining tables, bookcases, chairs and upholstery, 18th-20th C, £500-£5,000.* LOC: Town centre. PARK: Rear of premises. TEL: 01525 633023; home - 01525 752460. SER: Restorations.

The Pine Parlour
82a Dunstable St. MK45 2LF. (Lynn Barker). Est. 1989. Open 10-5 including Sun. CL: Mon. SIZE: Small. *STOCK: Pine furniture, 19th C, £200-£800; kitchenalia, £5-£60.* PARK: Easy. TEL: 01525 403030; home - same. SER: Valuations.

Guy Roe Antiques
20 Dunstable St. MK45 2JT. Est. 1990. Open 9.30-5, appointment preferred. CL: Sat. and Sun. except by appointment. SIZE: Small. *STOCK: Fine furniture, 18th to early 19th C, £500-£5,000; tea caddies, associated objects.* LOC: Near council offices on Flitwick road. PARK: Easy, opposite. TEL: 01525 404795; fax - same; mobile - 0374 808347. VAT: Stan/Spec. *Mainly Trade.*

Ampthill continued

S. and S. Timms Antiques Ltd LAPADA
Rear of 20 Dunstable St. MK45 2JT. Est. 1976. Open Mon.-Fri. 9.30-5 and any time by appointment. SIZE: Large. *STOCK: Furniture, 1700-1900, £500-£15,000; copper, brass.* LOC: A5120. PARK: Easy. TEL: 01525 403067; home - 01525 718829; mobile - 0860 482995 and 0585 458541. FAIRS: LAPADA, Guildford and provincial; Chelsea Decorative. VAT: Stan/Spec.

Transatlantic Antiques & Fine Art
101 Dunstable St. (I.J. and D. M. Higgins). Est. 1995. Open 10.30-5 including Sun. CL: Mon. SIZE: Large. *STOCK: 19th C furniture, £150-£4,000; glass, ceramics, silver and metalware, 19th C, £5-£3,000; pictures and interesting objects, 18th-19th C, £50-£1,000.* LOC: Main street. PARK: Off Market Square. TEL: 01525 403346; fax - same. SER: Restorations; buys at auction. FAIRS: NEC. VAT: Spec.

BEDFORD

Architectural Antiques - Bedford
70 Pembroke St. MK40 3RQ. (Paul and Linda Hoare). Est. 1989. Open 12-5, Sat. 10-5. SIZE: Medium. *STOCK: Early Georgian to early 20th C fireplaces, £500-£1,000; sanitary ware, from late Victorian, £100-£500; doors, panelling, pews, chimney pots and other architectural items, Georgian and Victorian, £50-£100.* LOC: Follow signs to town centre, turn on The Embankment on Castle Rd., shop is off Castle Rd., near Post Office. PARK: Easy. TEL: 01234 213131/343421. SER: Valuations; restorations; installations.

BIGGLESWADE

Shortmead Antiques
46 Shortmead St. SG18 0AP. (S.E. Sinfield). Open 10.30-4. CL: Thurs. SIZE: Small. *STOCK: Furniture, £50-£1,000; boxes, porcelain, silver, bronzes, copper and brass, all pre-1930.* LOC: ½ mile from A1. TEL: 01767 601780 (ansaphone).

HARLINGTON

Willow Farm Pine Centre
Willow Farm. LU5 6LJ. (M. and A. Price). Est. 1974. Open 10-5 daily. SIZE: Large. *STOCK: Good reclaimed and antique pine.* LOC: Off Barton Rd., near kennels. PARK: Easy. TEL: 01525 872052; home - same.

HARROLD

Harrold Antique Centre
Chepstow Place, High St. (Geoff and Shirley Knight). Open 10-6 including Sun; Wed. 1-5. SIZE: 20 dealers. *STOCK: Pine and period furniture, linen, clocks, china, dolls and collectables.* LOC: Off A428 Bedford-Northampton road. TEL: 01234 720666. SER: Pine stripping.

HEATH AND REACH, Nr. Leighton Buzzard

Baroq at Brindleys
Woburn Rd. LU7 0AR. (Brian Dawson and M.J. Spencer - Consultant). Open 10-5, Sun. 12-4. SIZE: 20 dealers. *STOCK: Pottery and porcelain, £10-£500; paintings and watercolours, 18th-20th C, £100-£1,000; furniture, £100-£2,500.* LOC: A418, off A5. PARK: Easy and Red Lion. TEL: 01525 237750; restoration - 01525 237831; home - 01234 240448.

Charterhouse Gallery Ltd LAPADA
26 Birds Hill. LU7 0AQ. Open 10-5. CL: Fri. *STOCK: 19th to early 20th C watercolours.* PARK: Easy - next door. TEL: 01525 237379. SER: Restoration (pictures and frames).

LEIGHTON BUZZARD

David Ball Antique Furnisher
59 North St. LU7 7EQ. (D. and J. Ball). Est. 1968. Open Mon. 10-5 or by appointment. STOCK: *Furniture, general antiques and watercolours, 17th-20th C, £3-£2,000.* LOC: A418 to Woburn. PARK: Easy. TEL: 01525 382954; home - 01525 210753. SER: Valuations; restorations. FAIRS: Luton. VAT: Stan/Spec.

LUTON

Bargain Box
4 & 6a Adelaide St. LU1 5BB. Open 9-6, Wed. 9-1. *STOCK: General antiques.* TEL: 01582 423809.

Bernadette's Antiques & Collectables
19a Adelaide St. LU1 5BB. Open 9-6, Wed. 9-1. *STOCK: General antiques.* TEL: 01582 423809.

J. Denton (Antiques)
Rear of 440 Dunstable Rd. LU4 8DJ. Est. 1979. Open 10.15-4 or by appointment. CL: Sat. SIZE: Medium. *STOCK: Furniture and small items, Victorian and Edwardian; shipping goods, bric-a-brac.* LOC: Corner of Arundel Rd. and Dunstable Rd. PARK: Easy. TEL: 01582 582726; home - 01296 661471.

Foye Gallery
15 Stanley St. LU1 5AL. Est. 1960. Open 9.30-5 or by appointment. *STOCK: Engravings, etchings, drawings, watercolours, paintings, maps, books.* TEL: 01582 38487. VAT: Stan.

Luton continued

Knight's Gallery
41 Mill St. LU1 2NA. (J.C. Knight). Est. 1973. Open 9-5, Sat. 10-1. SIZE: Small. *STOCK: Watercolours, 19th-20th C, £50-£2,000.* PARK: Easy. TEL: 01582 36266; home - 01582 615495. SER: Valuations; restorations; framing; buys at auction (watercolours).

SHEFFORD

Secondhand Alley
2-4 High St. SG17 5DG. Open Mon., Fri. and Sat. 9-5, Sun. and Bank Holidays 12-5. *STOCK: Shipping furniture, bric-a-brac.* PARK: Easy. TEL: 01462 814747. VAT: Spec.

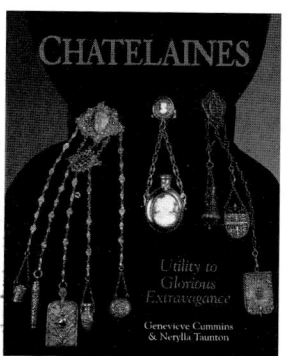

TODDINGTON, Nr. Dunstable

Cobblers Hall Antiques

119/121 Leighton Rd. LU5 6AR. (A.G. Huckett). Est. 1974. Open by appointment only. *STOCK: English porcelain, mid-18th to mid-19th C, £25-£1,000. Georgian and early Victorian writing boxes and slopes, treen, Tunbridgeware, period brass and copper.* PARK: Easy. TEL: 01525 872890. FAIRS: Worcester; Petersfield; Derby; Felbridge; Oatland Park and Worksop; NEC; Kenilworth; Luton; Solihull; Wilton; Bristol.

WILSTEAD (WILSHAMSTEAD) Nr. Bedford

Manor Antiques

The Manor House, Cottonend Rd. MK45 3BT. (Mrs S. Bowen). Est. 1976. Open 10-5, Sun. by appointment. SIZE: Large. *STOCK: Furniture, especially dining, 19thC to Edwardian, £100-£5,000; lighting and oil lamps, Victorian to 1940's; general antiques.* LOC: Just off A6, 4 miles south of Bedford. PARK: Own. TEL: 01234 740262; home - same. SER: Restorations (furniture); buys at auction. FAIRS: London Decorative. VAT: Stan/Spec.

WOBURN

Questor

13/14 Market Place. MK17 9PZ. (P. Parkinson-Large). Open 10-1 and 2-5.30, Sun. 11-1 and 2-5. *STOCK: Furniture including painted, £50-£1,000; porcelain, jewellery, small antiques, original works of art.* TEL: 01525 290658.

Christopher Sykes Antiques

The Old Parsonage. MK17 9QL. (C. and M. Sykes). Est. 1949. Open 9-5. SIZE: Large. *STOCK: Collectors' items - attractive, early brass, copper and pewter; scientific and medical instruments; specialist in rare corkscrews, £10-£800; silver decanter labels, tastvins and funnels, pottery barrels and bin labels, glass decanters and tantalus.* LOC: In main street opposite Post Office on A50. PARK: Easy. TEL: 01525 290259/290467; fax - 01525 290061. SER: 130 page illustrated mail order catalogue on corkscrews and wine related antiques available £7 each. VAT: Stan/Spec.

Town Hall Antiques

Market Place. MK17 9PZ. Open 10-5.30, Sun. 11-5.30. SIZE: Medium. *STOCK: Furniture, £50-£5,000; lighting, ceramics, glass, silver and plate, £10-£2,000; prints and pictures, £5-£2,000; all 18th to early 20th C; mirrors, 17th-20th C; dolls; domestic metalware; antiquities - Bronze Age, Iron Age and Roman.* LOC: Off A5 and off junction 12 or 13, M1. PARK: Easy. TEL: 01525 290950. SER: Valuations; restorations (pictures, furniture and ceramics).

The Woburn Abbey Antiques Centre

MK43 0TP. Est. 1967. Open every day (including Bank Holidays) 11-5 Nov. to Easter; 10-6 Easter to Oct. CL: 24th-26th Dec. 1996. SIZE: Over 50 shops and showcases on two floors. *STOCK: English and Continental furniture, porcelain, mirrors, clocks, engravings, silver, oils and watercolours, etc.* LOC: Exits 12 and 13, M1. On A5 follow signs to Woburn Abbey and after entering grounds, follow signs, The Antiques Centre is in the South Courtyard. PARK: Easy. TEL: 01525 290350; fax - 01525 290271. SER: Carriage for large items; worldwide shipping.

Woburn Fine Arts

12 Market Place. MK17 9PZ. (Z. Bieganski). Est. 1983. Open 2-5.30, Sat. and Sun. 11-1 and 2-5.30 or by appointment. CL: Thurs. SIZE: Medium. *STOCK: Post-impressionist paintings, 1880-1940; European paintings, 17th-18th C; British paintings, 20th C.* PARK: Easy. TEL: 01525 290624. SER: Restorations (oils and watercolours); framing.

Woburn Abbey Antiques Centre

One of the largest Antiques Centres under one roof in Great Britain and the most original — with 40 independent shops and 12 showcases comprising 50 established dealers, some of whom are members of L.A.P.A.D.A. and B.A.D.A. — is situated in the magnificent South Court of Woburn Abbey.

We are pleased to offer the dealer and private collector a wide range of Antiques: Clocks, Lamps, Porcelain and Glass, Paintings, Prints, Georgian and Victorian Furniture, Jewellery, Georgian Silver, Painted Furniture, Works of Art, etc., at competitive prices.

One of the streets on the ground floor

Within one hour's drive of Oxford, Cambridge, Birmingham and London (via M1, Exit 12 or 13 signposted Woburn Abbey). Trains from St. Pancras to Flitwick or Euston to Bletchley can be met by prior arrangement. Dealers admitted free and their park entrance refunded at the Antiques Centre. Visiting dealers' car park adjacent to the Antiques Centre.

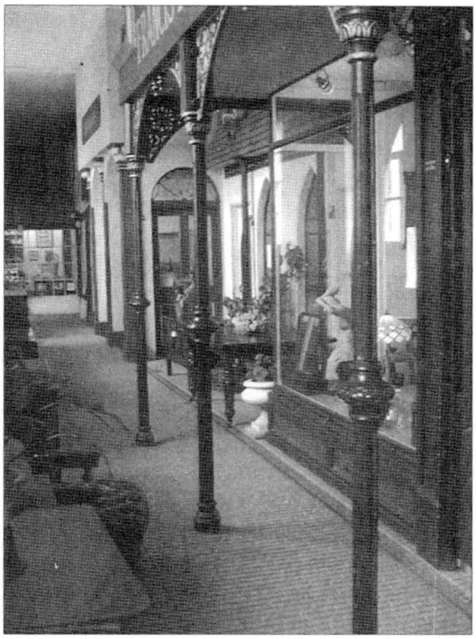

One of the streets on the ground floor

OPEN EVERY DAY OF THE YEAR EXCEPT
24th-26th DECEMBER 1997

Easter Sunday to October 10-6 p.m. November to Easter 11-5 p.m.

WOBURN ABBEY ANTIQUES CENTRE, WOBURN ABBEY
BEDFORDSHIRE MK43 0TP

Telephone Woburn (01525) 290350 Fax (01525) 290271

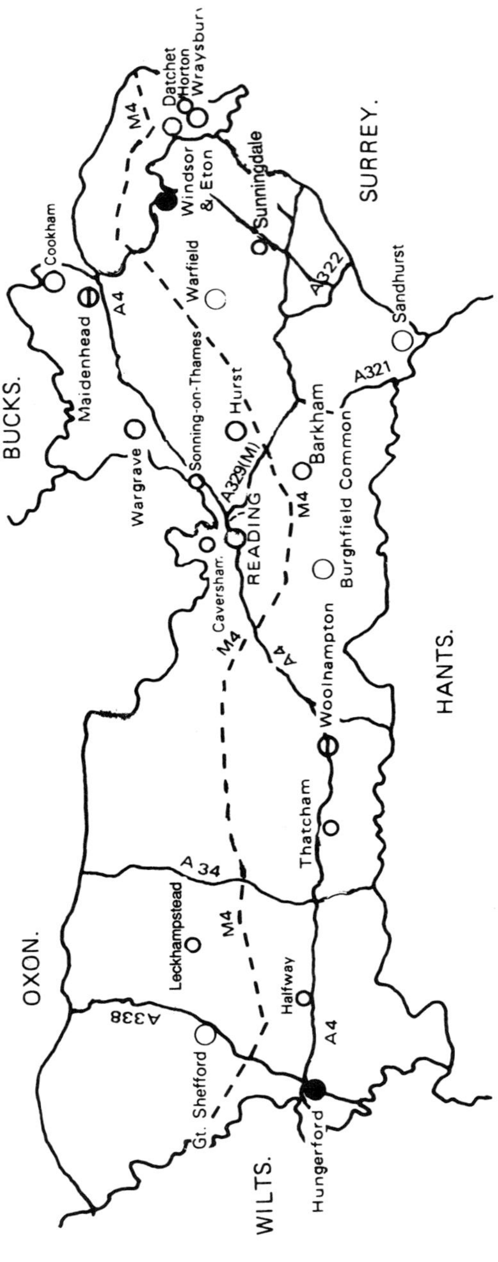

NORTH

Key to number of shops in this area.

- 1-2
- 3-5
- 6-12
- 13+

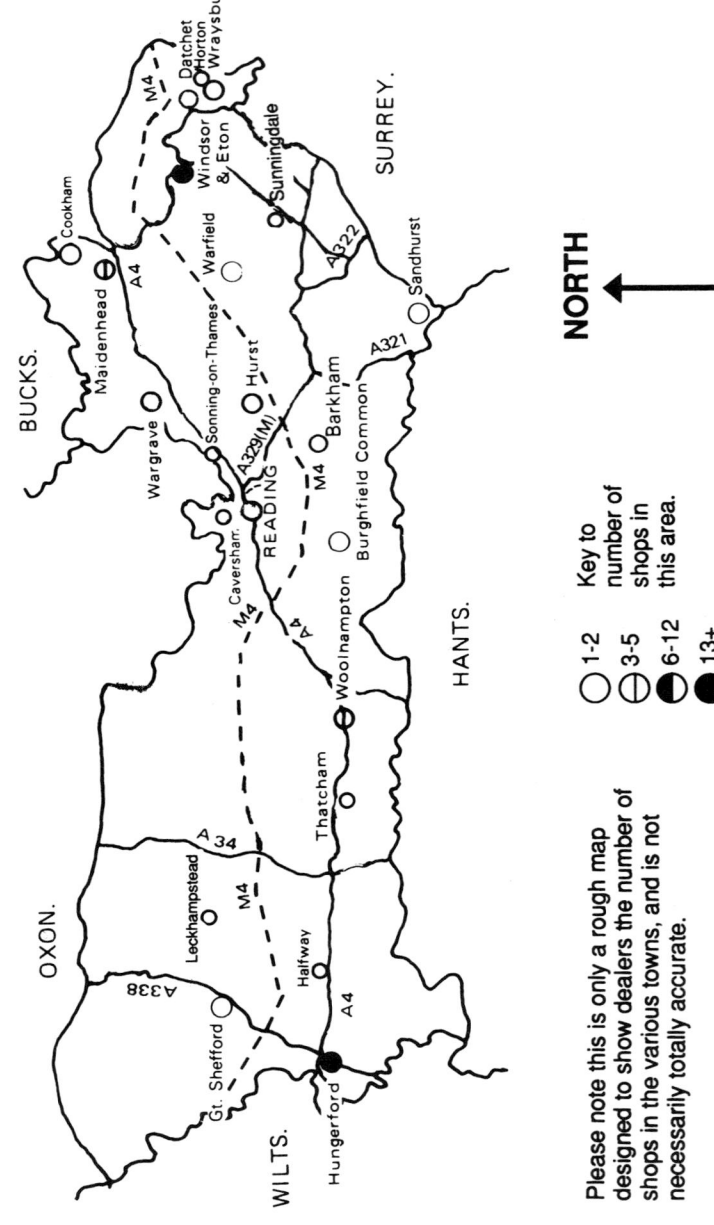

Please note this is only a rough map designed to show dealers the number of shops in the various towns, and is not necessarily totally accurate.

BARKHAM, Nr. Wokingham

Barkham Antique Centre

Barkham St. RG11 4PL. (Eileen and Ken Lowes). Open 10.30-5 including Sun. SIZE: Large - 50+ dealers. *STOCK: Tables, chairs, chests, 18th-20th C, £100-£3,500; sofas, Victorian lady's chairs, collectables, kitchenalia, Dinky toys, model cars, porcelain, stamps, metalware, lamps and bric-a-brac.* LOC: Off M4 junction 10, A329M to Wokingham, over station crossing to Barkham (B3349), left at Bull public house. PARK: Easy. TEL: 01734 761355; home - 01734 783705. SER: Valuations; restorations (china, French polishing, upholstery, cabinet making); courtesy car from Wokingham station on request.

BURGHFIELD COMMON, Nr. Reading

Graham Gallery

Highwoods. RG7 3BG. (J. Steeds). Est. 1976. Open by appointment at any time. SIZE: Medium. *STOCK: English watercolours, £50-£1,500; English oil paintings, £200-£8,000; English prints, £25-£200; all 19th to early 20th C.* LOC: 4 miles from Reading on Burghfield road. PARK: Easy. TEL: 01734 832320; fax - 01734 831070. SER: Valuations; restorations (cleaning, framing).

CAVERSHAM, Nr. Reading

The Clock Workshop LAPADA

17 Prospect St. RG4 8JB. (J. M. Yealland). FBHI, TVADA. Est. 1980. Open 9.30-5.30, Sat. 10-1. SIZE: Small. *STOCK: Clocks, late 17th to late 19th C, £350-£60,000; barometers, 18th-19th C, £500-£8,000.* LOC: Prospect St. is the beginning of main Reading to Henley road. PARK: North St. TEL: 01734 470741. SER: Valuations; restorations (clocks and barometers); buys at auction. FAIRS: TVADA; LAPADA. VAT: Stan/Spec.

COOKHAM

Phillips and Sons

The Dower House. SL6 9SN. Open by appointment. *STOCK: British impressionist paintings by the Staithes group, late 19th to early 20th C, £200-£10,000.* TEL: 01628 529337. SER: Valuations; restorations (pictures); framing. VAT: Spec.

DATCHET

The Studio Gallery

The Old Bank, The Green, SL3 9JH. (Julian Bettney). Open 11-7, until 6 Sun. CL: Tues. am. and Fri. *STOCK: Fine paintings and prints, 1740-1940; architectural fittings; decorative furniture and fittings, garden items.* LOC: Off junction 5, M4, opposite Manor Hotel. TEL: 01753 544100;

Datchet continued

mobile - 0836 330566. SER: New age furniture designed and manufactured; framing; restorations (oil paintings and frames) ; garden design.

GREAT SHEFFORD, Nr. Hungerford

Alan Hodgson

No 2 Ivy House, Wantage Rd. RG16 7DA. *STOCK: Country and pine furniture, boxes, collectors' items.* LOC: A338, 10 minutes from Hungerford towards Wantage. TEL: 01488 648172.

Ivy House Antiques

Wantage Rd. RG17 7DA. (J. Hodgson). Est. 1972. Open 10-5. *STOCK: Country and pine furniture, kitchenalia, collectors' items, Victoriana.* LOC: 2 miles from J14 M4; A338, 10 minutes from Hungerford towards Wantage. TEL: 01488 648549.

HALFWAY, Nr. Newbury

Walker and Walker BADA

Halfway Manor. RG20 8NR. (Alan and Kym Walker). TVADA. Open by appointment. *STOCK: Fine barometers and weather instruments.* TEL: 01488 658693; mobile - 0831 147480. SER: Restorations.

Queenly robes. This elaborate Elizabethan-style costume, reputed to have been worn by Glenda Jackson as Elizabeth I, expects £200-£250 at Phillips Bayswater sale of costumes on 15 April.

From an Auction Review which appeared in the July/August 1996 issue of **Antique Collecting**

HORTON, Nr. Windsor

John A. Pearson Antiques BADA
Horton Lodge, Horton Rd. SL3 9NU. (Mrs J.C.Sinclair Hill). Est. 1902. Open by appointment only. SIZE: Large. *STOCK: English furniture, 1700-1850, £50-£30,000; oil paintings, 17th-19th C, £50-£50,000; decorative objects.* Not Stocked: Items after 19th C. LOC: From London turn off M4, exit 5, past London Airport; from M25 take exit 14. 10 mins from Heathrow. PARK: Easy. TEL: 01753 682136.

HUNGERFORD

Below Stairs of Hungerford
103 High St. RG17 0NB. (S. Hofgartner). Est. 1974. Open 10-6, including Sun. SIZE: Large. *STOCK: Kitchen and decorative garden items, bedroom furniture, lighting, collectables, interior fittings and taxidermy, mainly 19th C English, £20-£2,500.* Not Stocked: Reproductions. LOC: Main street. PARK: Easy. TEL: 01488 682317. SER: Valuations. VAT: Stan.

Sir William Bentley Billiards (Antique Billiard Table Specialist Company)
Standen Manor Farm. RG17 0RB. Open by appointment seven days a week. SIZE: Large. *STOCK: Billiard tables, billiard/dining tables; antique and modern accessories including*

Hungerford continued

panelling and brass lights. TEL: 01488 681711; 0181 9401152; fax - 01488 685197. SER: Restorations; removals and storage.

Bow House Antiques
3-4 Faulkner Sq., Charnham St. RG17 0ER. (L.R. Herrington). Open 10.30-4. CL: Mon. SIZE: Medium. *STOCK: Small period and Victorian furniture.* LOC: A4. PARK: Easy, own. TEL: 01488 683198; home - 01488 684319.

Dolls and Toys of Yesteryear at Bow House Antiques
3-4 Faulkner Sq., Charnham St. RG17 0HH. (D.M. Herrington). Open 10.30-4. CL: Mon. SIZE: Medium. *STOCK: Dolls' houses, £150-£3,000; dolls' house furniture and accessories, £1-£300; rocking horses, £500-£1,500; all 19th to early 20th.* PARK: Easy. TEL: 01488 683198; home - 01488 684319. FAIRS: Toy and Doll, Kensington Town Hall; London Victoria International Doll Shows.

The Fire Place (Hungerford) Ltd
Hungerford Old Fire Station, Charnham St. RG17 0EP. (E.B. and E.M. Smith). Est. 1976. Open 10-1.30 and 2.15-5. SIZE: Large. *STOCK: Fireplace furnishings and metalware especially fenders; paintings.* LOC: On A4. PARK: Opposite. TEL: 01488 683420. VAT: Stan/Spec.

Robert and Georgina Hastie LAPADA
35a High St. RG17 0NF. Est. 1987. Open 9.30-5, Sun. by appointment. SIZE: Medium. *STOCK: Decorative items, 1750-1920, £50-£6,000; furniture and clocks, 18th-19th C, £200-£6,000; textiles, 19th C, £50-£1,000.* Not Stocked: Silver, porcelain and dolls. LOC: A338. PARK: Easy. TEL: 01488 682873; fax - 01264 731289; mobile - 0860 641560. VAT: Stan/Spec.

Hungerford Arcade
High St. RG17 0NF. (Wynsave Investments Ltd). Est. 1972. Open 9.30-5.30, Sun. 11-5. SIZE: Over 80 stallholders. *STOCK: General antiques and period furniture.* PARK: Easy. TEL: 01488 683701.

Roger King Antiques
111 High St. RG17 0NB. (Mr and Mrs R.F King). Est. 1974. Open 9.30-5. SIZE: Large. *STOCK: Furniture, 1750-1880, £50-£1,500, china, 19th C; oil paintings.* Not Stocked: Silver jewellery. LOC: Opposite Hungerford Arcade. PARK: Easy. TEL: 01488 682256. VAT: Spec.

Marlborough Sporting Gallery and Bookshop
127a High St.RG17 0EY. Est. 1977. Open 10-6 Sun. 11-5. SIZE: Medium. *STOCK: Sporting oils watercolours, £100-£10,000; sporting prints, £20 £5000; all 1800-1975; books, 1750 to date, £10 £500.* LOC: Industrial estate. PARK: Easy. TEL 01488 686921; fax - 01488 686143. SER: Valuations; restorations (oils, watercolours, prints) buys at auction. FAIRS: Major equestrian events VAT: Spec.

Hungerford continued

Medalcrest Ltd
Charnham House, 29/30 Charnham St. RG17 0EJ. (D.H. Farrow). Est. 1981. Open 9.30-5.30, Sat. 10-6, Sun. by appointment. SIZE: Large. *STOCK: 18th-19th C furniture; barometers, metalware, small items.* TEL: 01488 684157; fax - same. VAT: Spec.

The Old Malthouse BADA
15 Bridge St. RG17 0EG. (P.F. Hunwick). CINOA. Est. 1963. Open 10-5.30. SIZE: Large. *STOCK: 18th to early 19th C walnut and mahogany furniture, clocks, barometers, glass, mirrors, decorative items, tôleware and brass.* Not Stocked: Orientalia. LOC: A338, left at Bear Hotel, shop is approx. 120 yds. on left, just before bridge. PARK: In front of shop. TEL: 01488 682209; fax - same. SER: Valuations. VAT: Spec.

Riverside Antiques LAPADA
Charnham St. RG17 0EP. (M. Stockland). Est. 1976. Open 10-5.30. SIZE: Large. *STOCK: General antiques including furniture and decorative items.* LOC: On A4 just before The Bear Hotel. PARK: Easy. TEL: 01488 682314. VAT: Stan/Spec.

Styles Silver LAPADA
12 Bridge St. RG17 0EH. (P. and D. Styles). Est. 1974. Open Sat. and any time by appointment. SIZE: Medium. *STOCK: Antique, Victorian and secondhand silver including cutlery.* PARK: Easy. TEL: 01488 683922; home - same; fax - 01488 683488. SER: Repairs; finder.

Youll's Antiques
27 and 28 Charnham St. RG17 0EJ. (B. Youll). Open 10.30-5.30 including Sun. *STOCK: French and English furniture and decorative items.*

HURST, Nr. Reading

Peter Shepherd Antiques
Penfold, Lodge Rd. RG10 0EG. Est. 1962. Open by appointment only. *STOCK: Glass, rarities and books.* TEL: 01734 340755.

LECKHAMPSTEAD
Nr. Newbury

Hill Farm Antiques
Hill Farm, Shop Lane. RG20 8QG. (Mike Beesley). Open 9-5, Sun. by appointment. *STOCK: 19th C dining tables, chairs and library furniture.* LOC: Off B4494 between Stag public house and church. PARK: Own at rear. TEL: 01488 638541/638361. SER: Restorations; shipping arranged; buys at auction.

MAIDENHEAD

Jaspers Fine Arts Ltd
36 Queen St. SL6 1HZ. (D. N. Johnson). Open 9-6. *STOCK: Victorian watercolours and paintings; maps and prints.* TEL: 01628 36459. SER: Restorations; framing.

Miscellanea
71 St. Marks Rd. SL6 2DP. (J. Davidson). Open 10-5.30. SIZE: Large. *STOCK: Furniture, books, bric-a-brac, collectors' items.* LOC: 1/2 mile off A4. PARK: Easy. TEL: 01628 23058.

Widmerpool House Antiques
Boulters Lock. Open by appointment only. *STOCK: English furniture, 18th-19th C; oil paintings, watercolours, prints; porcelain, glass, silver, 19th C.* TEL: 01628 23752.

READING

P.D. Leatherland Antiques
68 London St. RG1 4SQ. TVADA. Est. 1970. Open 9-5. *STOCK: Furniture, 18th C to 1920's; decorative china, clocks, metalware, mirrors and pictures, £5-£4,000.* PARK: Easy. TEL: 01734 581960. VAT: Stan/Spec.

Reading Emporium
1a Merchants Place (off Friar St). RG1 1DT. Est. 1972. Open 10-5. SIZE: 11 stalls. *STOCK: General antiques including Victoriana, advertising items, jewellery and bottles.* TEL: 01734 590290.

SANDHURST

Antiques - Sheila White
Sandhurst Farmhouse, 207 Yorktown Rd., College Town. GU47 0RT. *STOCK: General antiques.* LOC: Barn at rear of premises. TEL: 01252 873290.

Berkshire Metal Finishers Ltd
Swan Lane Trading Estate. GU47 9DD. (J.A. and Mrs. J. Sturgeon). Est. 1957. Open 8-1 and 2-6, Sat. 8-1 and 2-4, Sun. 9-1. SIZE: Large. *STOCK: Brass, copper and steel metalware; silver plate.* LOC: Off A30 towards Wokingham on A321, after 1.25 miles turn left into Swan Lane, estate 1st turning right, last factory near car park. PARK: Easy. TEL: 01252 873475; fax - 01252 875434. SER: Restorations (metalware polishing and lacquering).

SONNING-ON-THAMES

Cavendish Fine Arts - Janet Middlemiss LAPADA
The Dower House. RG4 6UL. TVADA. Open by appointment only. *STOCK: Fine Queen Anne and English Georgian furniture, glass and porcelain.* TEL: 01189 691904; mobile - 0831 295575. VAT: Stan/Spec.

Sonning-on-Thames continued

Csaky's Antiques
RG4 0TW. Open by appointment only. *STOCK: Early English and Continental furniture; carvings, works of art.* TEL: 01734 697608.

SUNNINGDALE

The Coworth Gallery
9 Coworth Rd. SL5 0NX. (Stephen Paddon). Est. 1985. Open most times, subject to a 'phone call. SIZE: Small. *STOCK: 19th C English and French country furniture, paintings, carpets, decorative items.* LOC: Turn right into Bedford Lane off A30 from London, after Planet Pizza. PARK: Easy. TEL: 01344 26532; mobile - 0831 182076. SER: Restorations.

THATCHAM, Nr. Newbury

Jackdaw Antiques
Bluecoat School. (D. Johnson). Open 10-4.30. CL: Mon. and Tues. *STOCK: General antiques.* PARK: Easy. TEL: 01635 865901.

WARFIELD

Moss End Antique Centre
Moss End Garden Centre. RG12 6EJ. TVADA. Open 10.30-5. CL: Mon. SIZE: Large - 25 dealers. *STOCK: General antiques and collectables.* LOC: A3095. PARK: Own. TEL: 01344 861942.

WARGRAVE

John Connell - Wargrave Antiques
66 High St. RG10 8BY. Open Wed.-Sun. other times by appointment. SIZE: Large - several dealers. *STOCK: Furniture, Georgian-Edwardian; small items, china, glass, metal.* PARK: Nearby. TEL: 01734 402914. SER: Restorations (furniture); silver plating; metal polishing.

WINDSOR AND ETON

Addrison Bros
25 King's Rd. Windsor. SL4 2AD. (Mr and Mrs Addrison). Est. 1980. Open 11-6 and occasional Sun. SIZE: Small. *STOCK: Furniture, pine, oak, mahogany and walnut, Victorian to 1930, £1-£800.* LOC: Close to castle. PARK: Easy. TEL: 01753 863780; home - same.

Antiquus
17 High St., Eton. (Mrs C. Casier). Open 10-5. *STOCK: Furniture, objets d'art, porcelain and textiles.* TEL: 01753 831039; home - 01753 840848.

Roger Barnett Antiques
91 High St., Eton. SL4 6AF. Est. 1975. TEL: 01753 867785.

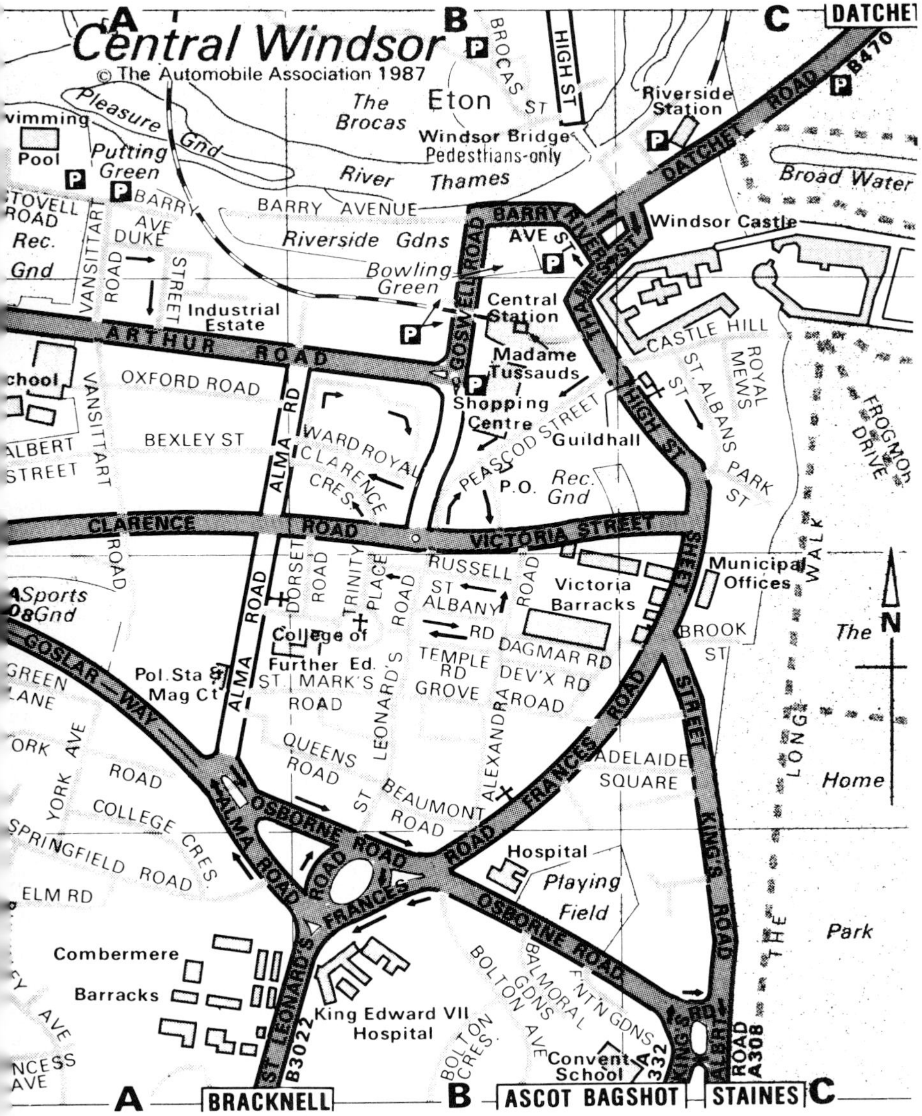

Key to Town Plan

AA Recommended roads	Car Parks (P)
Other roads	Parks and open spaces
Restricted roads	AA Service Centre (AA)
Buildings of interest	© Automobile Association 1988.

Windsor and Eton continued

Berkshire Antiques Co Ltd
42 Thames St., Windsor. SL4 1YY. Open 10.30-5.30, Sun. by appointment. SIZE: Large. *STOCK: Antique and modern designer jewellery; general antiques, china, porcelain and glass, silver and silverplate, Royal commemoratives, toys and dolls, £10-£25,000.* TEL: 01753 830100; fax - 01753 832278. SER: Valuations; repairs.

Country Furniture
79 St. Leonards Rd., Windsor. SL4 3BZ. (Jan Hicks and Austin Maude). TVADA. Open 9.30-5.30. *STOCK: French provincial furniture and unusual decorative items.* TEL: 01753 830154; fax - same.

Eton Antique Bookshop
88 High St., Eton. SL4 6AF. TEL: 01753 855534.

Eton Antiques Partnership
80 High St., Eton. SL4 6AF. (Mark Procter). Est. 1967. Open 10-5, Sun. 11-5.30. SIZE: Large. *STOCK: Mahogany and rosewood furniture, 18th-19th C.* LOC: Slough East exit from M4 westbound. PARK: Nearby. TEL: 01753 860752; home - same. SER: Exporting; interior design consultants. VAT: Stan/Spec.

Windsor and Eton continued

Grove Gallery
89 Grove Rd., Windsor. *STOCK: Oils, watercolours, prints.* TEL: 01753 865954/853658.

Shirley Hayden Antiques
79 High St., Eton. SL4 6AF. TVADA. Est. 1980. Open 10-5.30, Sun. 11.30-5. SIZE: Small. *STOCK: English mahogany furniture, 18th-19th C, £350-£4,500; decorative items - pictures, mirrors, lamps and porcelain.* LOC: First antiques shop on left over the bridge from Windsor. PARK: Meadow Lane. TEL: 01753 833085; home - 01753 540203. FAIRS: TVADA. VAT: Spec.

J. Manley
27 High St., Eton. SL4 6AX. Est. 1891. Open 9-5. *STOCK: Watercolours, old prints.* TEL: 01753 865647. SER: Restorations; framing, mounting.

Peter J. Martin
40 High St., Eton. SL4 6BD. TVADA. Est. 1963. Open 9-1 and 2-5. CL: Sun. SIZE: Large and warehouse. *STOCK: Period, Victorian and decorative furniture and furnishings, £50-£5,000; metalware, £10-£500, all from 1800.* PARK: 50yds. opposite. TEL: 01753 864901; home - 01753 863987. SER: Restorations; shipping arranged; buys at auction. VAT: Stan/Spec.

Morgan Stobbs
17 High St., Eton. SL4 6AX. (Glenn Morgan). TVADA. Open 10.30-5.30, Sun. 1-5. *STOCK: Arts & Crafts, Art Deco furniture and objects, 1880-1940.* TEL: 01753 840631.

Mostly Boxes
93 High St., Eton. SL4 6AF. (G.S. Munday). Est. 1977. Open 9.30-6.45. SIZE: Small. *STOCK: Wooden, mother of pearl, and tortoiseshell boxes.* PARK: 100 yds. TEL: 01753 858470. SER: Restorations (boxes). VAT: Spec.

O'Connor Brothers
Trinity Yard, 59 St. Leonards Rd., Windsor. SL4 3BX. *STOCK: Furniture and general antiques.* TEL: 01753 866732; freephone - 0500 030405. VAT: Stan.

Oriental Rug Gallery Ltd
115-116 High St., Eton. SL4 6AQ. (Richard Mathias and Julian Blair). TVADA, BORDA. Open 10-5.30. *STOCK: Russian, Afghan, Turkish and Persian carpets, rugs and kelims; Oriental objets d'art.* PARK: Behind showroom. TEL: 01753 623000; fax - same.

Ulla Stafford Antiques **BADA**
41 High St., Eton. SL4 6BD. SIZE: Large. *STOCK: Georgian and Continental furniture, Chinese export porcelain, 18th C; works of art and ceramics, 17th-18th C.* PARK: Easy. TEL: 01753 859625; home - 01734 343208; fax - same. VAT: Spec.

Windsor and Eton continued

Studio 101

101 High St., Eton. SL4 6AF. (Anthony Cove). Est. 1959. SIZE: Medium. *STOCK: Mahogany furniture, some 18th C, mainly 19th C, £50-£1,000; brass, silver plate, 19th C, £10-£200.* LOC: Walk over Windsor Bridge from Windsor and Eton Riverside railway station. PARK: Public, at rear of premises. TEL: 01753 863333.

T.L.O. Militaria

Longclose House, Common Rd., Eton Wick. SL4 6QY. (Tony L. Oliver). Est. 1959. Open 9-5 by appointment only. *STOCK: Militaria, medals, badges, insignia especially German 1914-1990; civilian and military vehicles, 1914-1955.* TEL: 01753 862637; fax - 01753 841998.

Times Past Antiques

59 High St., Eton. SL4 6BL. (P. Jackson). MBHI. Est. 1970. Open 10-6, Sun. 12-5. SIZE: Medium. *STOCK: Clocks and music boxes, £100-£3,000; furniture, all 18th-19th C; silver, 19th C, £5-£500.* PARK: Reasonable. TEL: 01753 857018; home - same. SER: Valuations; restorations (clocks and watches); buys at auction (clocks). VAT: Stan/Spec.

Turks Head Antiques

98 High St., Eton. SL4 6AF. Open 10-5. CL: Wed. *STOCK: Silver and plate, porcelain, glass and interesting collectables.* TEL: 01753 863939.

WOOLHAMPTON, Nr. Reading

The Bath Chair

Woodbine Cottage, Bath Rd. RG7 5RT. (J.A. Lewzey). Est. 1980. Usually open 10-6 and by appointment. SIZE: Small. *STOCK: Furniture and decorative items, £5-£5,000.* LOC: A4. PARK: Easy. TEL: 01734 712225. SER: Valuations; buys at auction.

Woolhampton continued

The Old Bakery

Bath Rd. RG7 5RE. (S. Everard). Resident. Est. 1969. *STOCK: Furniture, objets d'art, collectors' items, general antiques.* TEL: 01734 712116.

Old Post House Antiques

Bath Rd. RG7 5RE. (V. A. Liddiard). Est. 1975. Open 10-6. SIZE: Small. *STOCK: Furniture, 18th-19th C, £50-£300; bric-a-brac and brassware, £2-£100.* LOC: On A4. PARK: Easy. TEL: 01734 712294; home - 01734 713460.

WRAYSBURY

Clive Rogers Oriental Rugs

66 Staines Rd. TW19 5BS.. Est. 1974. Open by appointment. SIZE: Medium. *STOCK: Oriental rugs, carpets, textiles; Oriental and Islamic works of art.* LOC: On B376, 5 minutes from Heathrow Airport. PARK: Easy. TEL: 01784 481177/481100; fax - 01784 481144. SER: Valuations; restorations (as stock); historical analysis commission agents; buys at auction. VAT: Stan/Spec.

Wyrardisbury Antiques

23 High St. TW19 5DA. (C. Tuffs). Est. 1978. Open 10-5. CL: Mon. and Thurs. except by appointment. SIZE: Small. *STOCK: Clocks, £25-£2,000; small furniture, tea caddies, boxes and watercolours, £10-£500; porcelain, £30-£500.* LOC: A376 from Staines by-pass (A30) or from junction 5 M4/A4 via B470, then B376. PARK: Easy. TEL: 01784 483225. SER: Restorations (clocks).

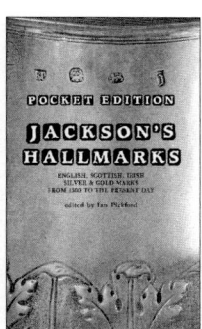

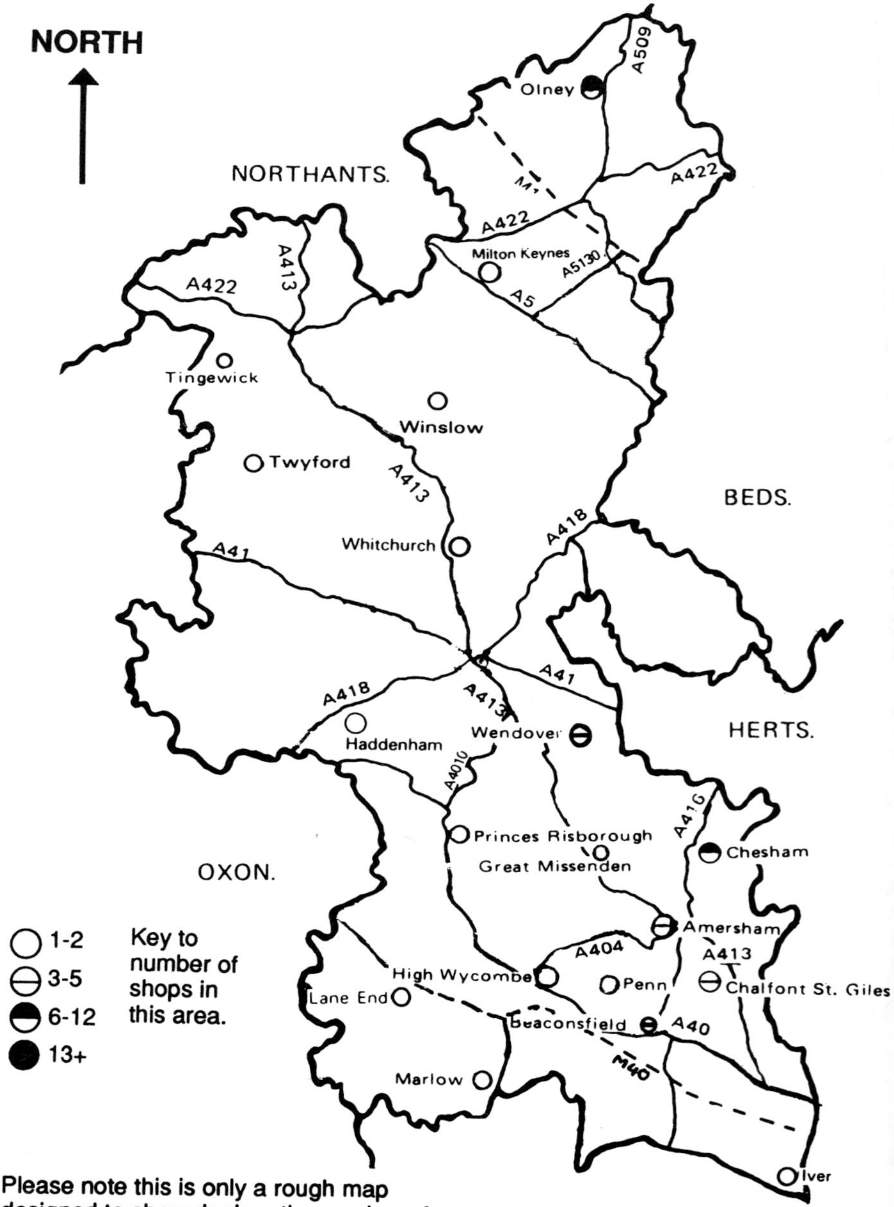

Please note this is only a rough map designed to show dealers the number of shops in the various towns, and is not necessarily totally accurate.

AMERSHAM

Amersham Antiques and Collectors Centre
20-22 Whielden St., Old Amersham. HP7 0HT. Open 9.30-5.30. SIZE: 35-40 dealers. *STOCK: Antiques and collectables.* TEL: 01494 431282.

The Cupboard Antiques LAPADA
30 High St., Old Amersham. HP7 0DS. (N. Lucas). TVADA. Open 10-5. CL: Fri. SIZE: 4 showrooms. *STOCK: Georgian, Regency and early Victorian furniture and decorative items.* PARK: Easy. TEL: 01494 722882.

Partridges
57 High St., Old Amersham. HP7 0DT. (Mrs Diana Krolle). Est. 1976. Open 10.30-5. CL: Mon. and Fri. *STOCK: Antique and decorative items.* PARK: Easy. TEL: Home - 01753 882331.

Michael and Jackie Quilter
38 High St. HP7 0DJ. Est. 1970. Open 10-5. *STOCK: General antiques, stripped pine, copper, brass, unusual objects.* PARK: Easy. TEL: 01494 433723. VAT: Stan.

Sundial Antiques
19 Whielden St. HP7 0HU. (A. and Mrs M. Macdonald). Est. 1970. Open 9.30-5.30. CL: Thurs. SIZE: Small. *STOCK: English and European brass, copper, metalware, fireplace furniture, 18th-19th C, £5-£500; small period furniture, 1670-1910, £25-£1,500; oil lamps, 1840-1914, £25-£500; decorative items, 1750-1910, £5-£500; weapons, 1600-1860, £25-£1,000; pottery, porcelain, curios, pre-1914, £10-£750.* Not stocked: Jewellery, clocks, coins, oil paintings, stamps, books, silver, firegrates. LOC: On A404, in Old Town 200yds. from High St. on right; from High Wycombe, 500yds. from hospital on left. PARK: Easy. TEL: 01494 727955.

BEACONSFIELD

Buck House Antique Centre
47 Wycombe End, Old Town. HP9 1LZ. (C. and B. Whitby). Est. 1979. Open 10-5, Sun. 12-5. CL: Wed. SIZE: Medium - 10 dealers. *STOCK: Wide variety of general antiques including English and Oriental porcelain, clocks, barometers, oak and mahogany furniture, stripped pine, boxes and beds, to 1930's, £5-£1,000.* LOC: A40. TEL: 01494 670714. SER: Valuations.

June Elsworth - Beaconsfield Ltd
Clover House, 16 London End. HP9 2JH. (Mrs J. Elsworth). Est. 1983. CL: Mon. SIZE: Small. *STOCK: Fine English furniture, 18th-19th C; decorative accessories and silver,19th C.* LOC: In old town, on A40. PARK: Easy. TEL: 01494 675611; fax - 01494 671273. VAT: Spec.

Beaconsfield continued

Grosvenor House Interiors
51 Wycombe End, Beaconsfield Old Town. HP9 1LX. (T.I. Marriott). Est. 1970. Open 9-1 and 2-5.30. CL: Wed. SIZE: Large. *STOCK: 18th-19th C furniture, especially upholstered and mid-19th C walnut; fireplaces and accessories; 19th C watercolours.* PARK: Easy. TEL: 01494 677498. SER: Interior architectural design, fireplace specialists. VAT: Stan/Spec.

Period Furniture Showrooms
49 London End. HP9 2HW. (R.E.W. Hearne and N.J. Hearne). TVADA. Est. 1965. Open 9-5.30. SIZE: Large. *STOCK: Furniture, 1700-1900, £50-£3,000.* LOC: A40 Beaconsfield Old Town. PARK: Own. TEL: 01494 674112; fax - 01494 681046. SER: Restorations (furniture). VAT: Stan/Spec.

The Spinning Wheel
86 London End. HP9 2JD. (Mrs M. Royle). Est. 1945. Open 10-5. CL: Wed. *STOCK: English furniture, 18th-19th C, mahogany and oak items, porcelain, glass.* TEL: 01494 673055; home - 01494 3294. VAT: Stan/Spec.

CHALFONT ST. GILES

Gallery 23 Antiques
High St. HP9 4QH. (Mrs A. Vollaro). Est. 1991. Open 10-5. *STOCK: Furniture, silver, Continental and English porcelain, glass, paintings, prints and watercolours.* TEL: 01494 871512.

Images in Watercolour LAPADA
(E. and D. Parkinson). TVADA. Est. 1968. *STOCK: Watercolours, drawings and some oils, 1800-1930.* TEL: 01494 875592. SER: Restorations (oils and watercolours). FAIRS: Various. VAT: Spec.

T. Smith
The Furniture Village, London Rd. HP8 4NN. Est. 1982. Open 10-5 including Sun. SIZE: Medium. *STOCK: Antique pine and architectural items.* LOC: Opposite Pheasant public house. PARK: Easy. TEL: 01494 873031. SER: Valuations; restorations (including upholstery); buys at auction (furniture).

CHESHAM

Albert Bartram
177 Hivings Hill. HP5 2PN. Est. 1968. Open by appointment.*STOCK: Metalwork, 16th-17th C; pewter, £100-£5,000.* LOC: 1 mile from town centre on the Bellingdon road. PARK: Easy. TEL: 01494 783271; fax - same. VAT: Spec.

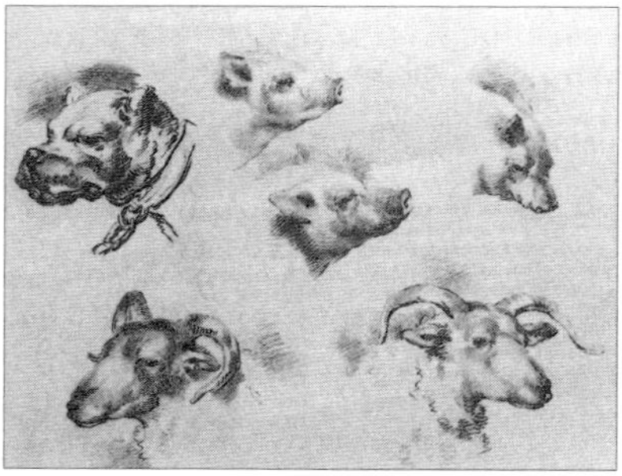

After George Morland. Stipple engraving, c.1790-1800, sold with eleven similar and 33 further prints in a folio for £460 in May 1995. A good indication of the excellent value for money to be found in mixed folios.

From an article entitled "Decorative Prints for the New Collector" by Richard Kay of Phillips which appeared in the November 1996 issue of **Antique Collecting**

Chesham continued

Chess Antiques LAPADA

85 Broad St. HP5 3EF. (M.P. Wilder). Est. 1966. Open 9-5, Sat. 10-5. SIZE: Small. *STOCK: Furniture and clocks.* PARK: Easy. TEL: 01494 783043. SER: Valuations; restorations. VAT: Stan/Spec.

For Pine

340 Berkhampstead Rd. HP5 3HF. (D. Hutchin). Open 10-5. CL: Thurs. *STOCK: Pine furniture.* Not Stocked: Reproduction. TEL: 01494 776119.

Omniphil Prints

Germains Lodge, Fullers Hill. HP5 1LR. (Ross Muddiman). Est. 1953. Open 9-5.30 or by appointment. CL: Sat. SIZE: Warehouse. *STOCK: Rare prints on all subjects and Illustrated London News from 1842.* TEL: 01494 771851.

Queen Anne House

57 Church St. HP5 1HY. (Miss A.E. Jackson). Est. 1918. Open Wed., Fri. and Sat. 9.30-5, other times by appointment. SIZE: Large. *STOCK: Furniture, decorative and furnishing pieces, porcelain figures, other china, glass, silver plate, copper, brass, Victoriana, Persian rugs.* Not Stocked: Silver, weapons, jewellery. PARK: Easy. TEL: 01494 783811. SER: Buys at auction. VAT: Stan/Spec.

Chesham continued

M.V. Tooley, CMBHI

at Chess Antiques, 85 Broad St. HP5 3EF. Est. 1960. Open 9-6, Sat. 10-5. SIZE: Small. *STOCK: Clocks and barometers.* TEL: 01494 783043. SER: Valuations; restorations; spare parts.

GREAT MISSENDEN

The Pine Merchants

52 High St. HP16 0AU. (Mrs J. Peters). Open 10-5. CL: Mon. SIZE: Medium. *STOCK: Stripped pine and Victorian bedsteads.* TEL: 01494 862002.

Peter Wright Antiques

(Incorporating Missenden Restorations and Abbey Clocks & Repairs), 36b High St. HP16 0AU. Est. 1992. Open 10-6 or any time by appointment. SIZE: Small. *STOCK: General antiques, curios and collectors' items.* LOC: A413. TEL: 01494 891330. SER: Restorations (clocks, furniture and ceramics).

HADDENHAM

H.S. Wellby Ltd

The Malt House, Church End. HP17 8AH. (C.S. Wellby). Est. 1820. Open by appointment 9-6. *STOCK: 18th-19th C paintings.* TEL: 01844 290036. SER: Restorations. VAT: Spec.

HIGH WYCOMBE

Browns' of West Wycombe

Church Lane, West Wycombe. HP14 3AH. Est. Pre 1900. Open 8-5.30. CL: Sat. *STOCK: Furniture.* LOC: On A40 approximately 3 miles west of High Wycombe on Oxford Rd. PARK: Easy. TEL: 01494 524537; fax - 01494 439548. SER: Restorations and hand-made copies of period chairs.

Windmill Fine Art

Widmer End. (Ray and Carol White). TVADA. Open by appointment only. *STOCK: Fine Victorian and early 20th C watercolours.* TEL: 01494 713757; fax - same; mobile - 0585 370408. SER: Valuations; commissions search. FAIRS: Most major.

IVER

"Yester-year"

12 High St. SL0 9NG. (P.J. Frost). Resident. Est. 1969. Open 10.30-6. SIZE: Small. *STOCK: Furniture, porcelain, pottery, glass, metalwork, 18th to early 20th C.* PARK: Easy. TEL: 01753 652072. SER: Valuations; restorations (furniture, pictures); framing; buys at auction.

NE END, Nr. High Wycombe

Bach Antiques
Essex House, Finings Rd. HP14 3EY. (C. and Mrs. B. Whitby). Est. 1982. Open Thurs., Fri. and Sat. 12-4. SIZE: Small. *STOCK: Furniture including pine, general antiques, pre 1920.* LOC: B482 between Marlow and Stokenchurch, Finings Rd. is extension of High St. PARK: Easy. TEL: 01494 882683. SER: Valuations; restorations (furniture).

MARLOW

Glade Antiques
(Sonia Garry). TVADA. Open by appointment only. *STOCK: Fine Oriental ceramics, bronzes and jades; Chinese items from Han, Tang, Song, Ming and Quing periods; Japanese items - mainly Kakiemon, Nabeshima, Kutani, Satsuma and Imari; also Korean Koryo, Yi and Choson periods.* TEL: 01628 487255; fax - 01628 476601; mobile - 0976 159669.

Jack Harness Antiques
Westfield Farm, Henley Rd., Medmenham. SL7. Est. 1981. Open 9-5 or by appointment. SIZE: Large warehouse. *STOCK: Pine and country furniture, especially period pine and original painted French provincial furniture.* PARK: Easy. TEL: 01491 410691; fax - same; mobile - 0468 666833; home - 01628 471775. SER: Restorations; courier. VAT: Stan/Spec. *Mainly Trade.*

Angela Hone Watercolours LAPADA
SL7 1QB. Open by appointment only. *STOCK: Watercolours, 1850-1920.* TEL: 01628 484170.

Marlow Antiques Centre
35 Station Rd. SL7 1NW. (Kay Darby and Keith Hill). TVADA. SIZE: 30+ dealers. *STOCK: Wide range of general antiques and collectables including Georgian, Victorian and Edwardian furniture, country pine, silver, glass, china, bedsteads, clocks, old tools and garden items, cameras, books, jewellery.* TEL: 01628 473223; fax - 01628 778834.

MILTON KEYNES

Temple Lighting (Jeanne Temple Antiques)
Stockwell House, Wavendon. MK17 8LS. Est. 1968. SIZE: Medium. *STOCK: Victorian, Edwardian and 1930's light fittings; 19th C furniture; decorative items.* LOC: Just off main Woburn Sands to Newport Pagnell road. TEL: 01908 583597.

OLNEY

Courtyard Antiques
4 Rose Court. MK46 0ED. (Trisha Sharp). Est. 1993. Open 10-4.30, Sat. 10-5, Sun. 2-5. SIZE: Medium. *STOCK: Pine and country furniture, 18th-19th C, £50-£1,000; china, glass, figures and silver, 18th C to Art Deco, £5-£300; prints, watercolours, framed cigarette cards, 18th-20th C, £10-£500+.* LOC: Off Market Sq., down alleyway. PARK: Rear access to traders car park. TEL: 01234 712200.

Fenlan
17B Stilebrook Rd.,Yardley Road Industrial Estate. Est. 1982. Open 8-5, Sat. 9-1. SIZE: Medium. *STOCK: Mahogany, rosewood, walnut, oak and pine furniture, 18th to early 20th C.* PARK: Easy. TEL: 01234 711799; fax - 01234 711799. SER: Restorations; cabinet making; restoration products and sundries; French polishing. FAIRS: Newark. VAT: Stan/Spec.

Market Square Antiques
MK46 4BA. (J.D. and H. Vella). Open 10-5, Sun. 1.30-5. *STOCK: Furniture, clocks, china, silver, glass, copper, brass, pine.* TEL: 01234 712172. SER: Restorations.

Olney Antique Centre
Rose Court. MK46 4BA. (J.D. and H. Vella). Open 10-5, Sun. 1.30-5. *STOCK: China, furniture, jewellery, linen, pine, postcards.* TEL: 01234 712172.

John Overland Antiques
Rose Court, Market Place. MK46 4BY. Est. 1977. Open 10-5 including Sun. SIZE: Medium. *STOCK: 18th-19th C mahogany and oak furniture, clocks, writing boxes, smalls, brass, copper.* PARK: Market Sq. TEL: 01234 712351. SER: Valuations; restorations (furniture, clocks). VAT: Stan/Spec.

Pine Antiques
10 Market Place. MK46 4EA. (Linda Wilkinson). Open 10-5, Sat. 9.30-5.30, Sun. 12-5. *STOCK: Pine furniture.* TEL: 01234 711065; 01908 510226.

Robin Unsworth Antiques
1 Weston Rd. (R. and Z. M. Unsworth). Est. 1971. Open 10-5, Sun. 1-5. SIZE: Small. *STOCK: Longcase and wall clocks, £500-£4,000; period and Victorian furniture, £200-£4,000; objects of art, £50-£1,000.* LOC: 6 miles from junction 14, M1. PARK: Easy. TEL: 01234 711210; home - 01908 617193. SER: Valuations; buys at auction (clocks).

PENN, Nr. High Wycombe

Country Furniture Shop LAPADA

3 Hazlemere Rd., Potters Cross. HP10 8AA. (M. and V. Thomas). Est. 1955. Open 9.30-1 and 2-5.30. SIZE: Large. *STOCK: Furniture, Georgian, £100-£5,000; Victoriana, £5-£2,500; large Victorian dining tables, Victorian dining chairs.* LOC: B474. PARK: Easy. TEL: 01494 812244; home - same. SER: Valuations. VAT: Stan/Spec.

Penn Barn

By the Pond, Elm Rd. HP10 8LB. (P. J. M. Hunnings). ABA. Est. 1968. Open 9.30-1 and 2-5, Sun. by appointment. SIZE: Medium. *STOCK: Antiquarian books, maps and prints, 19th C, £5-£250; watercolours and oils, 19th-20th C, £50-£1,000.* LOC: B474. PARK: Easy. TEL: 01494 815691. SER: Restorations; cleaning and repairs. VAT: Stan/Spec.

PRINCES RISBOROUGH

Pine Reflections

15 Park St. HP27 9AH. (M. Duda). Est. 1978. By appointment only. *STOCK: Furniture, period and Continental pine, English country oak.* SER: Export. *Trade Only.*

Well Cottage Antiques Centre

20-22 Bell St. HP27 0AD. Open 9.30-5.30, Sun. and Bank Holidays 1-5. SIZE: Medium. *STOCK: Furniture including pine; silver, jewellery, china, glass, brass, copper, silhouettes, miniatures, treen, pictures and collectables.* LOC: A4010. TEL: 01844 342002.

TINGEWICK, Nr. Buckingham

Tim Marshall Antiques

Main St. MK18 4NL. Resident. Open 9.30-6, Sun. 12-6. SIZE: Medium. *STOCK: Early oak and country furniture; longcase clocks.* TEL: 01280 848546.

Tingewick Antiques Centre

Main St. MK18 4NN. (B.J. and R. Smith). Est. 1982. Open 10-5.30, Sun. 11-4.30. CL: Fri. SIZE: Medium. *STOCK: Furniture including desks, mainly pine and oak, 19th to early 20th C, £5-£1,000; clocks, 18th-19th C, £20-£2,000; collectables, kitchenalia, Art Deco, pottery, pictures, £1-£1,500.* LOC: On A421. TEL: 01280 848219; home - same. SER: Valuations; restorations (copper, brass, spelter); upholstery; French polishing.

TWYFORD, Nr. Buckingham

Adrian Hornsey Ltd

Three Bridge Mill. MK18 4DY. Open 8-6, other times by appointment. SIZE: Large - 25 dealers.

Twyford continued

STOCK: General antiques, accessories and architectural. TEL: 01296 738373; fax - 01296 738322.

WENDOVER

Antiques at ...Wendover Antiques Centre

The Old Post Office, 25 High St. HP22 6DU. (N. Gregory). Open 10-5.30, Sun. and Bank Holidays 11-5.30. SIZE: Large - 30 dealers. *STOCK: General antiques including town and country furniture, flatware, kitchenalia, pottery and porcelain, silver, lamps and lighting, clocks, barometers, telescopes, scientific and medical instruments, beds and bathroom fittings, decorative items, glass, metalware, lace, linen and architectural salvage for interior and exterior renovation, dateline 1930.* PARK: Own. TEL: 01296 625335; evenings - 01296 624633.

Sally Turner Antiques LAPADA

Hogarth House, High St. HP22 6DU. Open 10-5.30. SIZE: 7 showrooms + barn. *STOCK: Decorative and period furniture, general antiques.* PARK: At rear of shop. TEL: 01296 624402; fax - same.

Wendover Antiques LAPADA

1 South St. HP22 6EF. (R. and D. Davies). Est. 1979. Open 9-5.30, prior telephone call advisable. SIZE: Medium. *STOCK: Furniture, oils, 17th-19th C; decorative prints; 18th C silk embroideries, silhouettes, miniatures, Georgian decanters, some silver and Sheffield plate; all £50-£5,000.* LOC: Near village centre on Wendover-Amersham road. PARK: 100yds. TEL: 01296 622078. VAT: Stan/Spec.

WHITCHURCH

Deerstalker Antiques

28 High St. HP22 4JT. (R.J. and L.L. Eichler). Open 10-5.30. CL: Mon. SIZE: Small. *STOCK: General antiques.* TEL: 01296 641505.

WINSLOW

Medina Antiquarian Maps and Prints

8 High St. MK18 3HF. (P. Williams). Open 9.30-5.30. CL: Thurs. pm. *STOCK: Maps, prints and watercolours.* TEL: 01296 712468.

Winslow Antiques Centre

15 Market Sq. MK18 3AB. Est. 1992. Open 10-5 or by appointment. SIZE: 20 dealers. *STOCK: Furniture, English pottery, silver and jewellery, general antiques.* LOC: A413. TEL: 01296 714540; fax - 01296 714556.

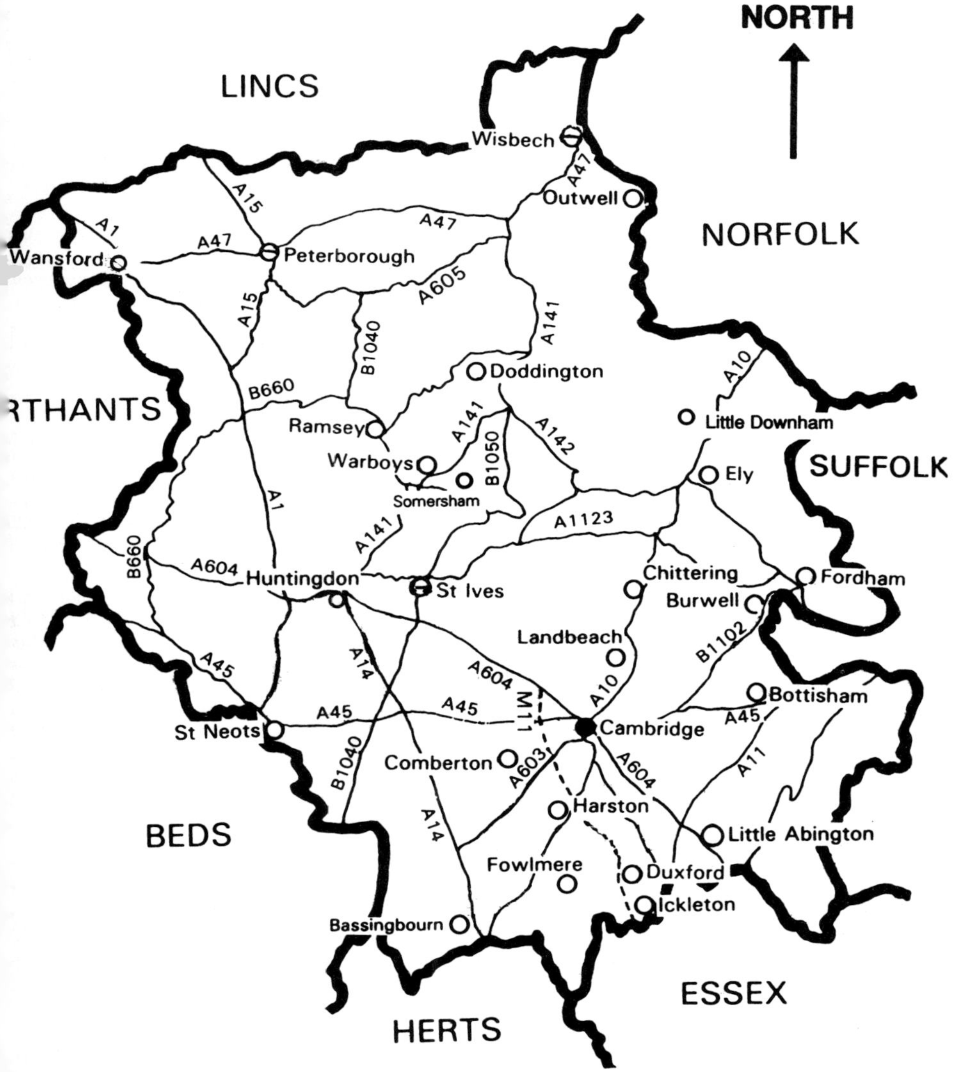

Please note this is only a rough map designed to show dealers the number of shops in the various towns, and is not necessarily totally accurate.

Key to number of shops in this area.

- 1-2
- 3-5
- 6-12
- 13+

BASSINGBOURN, Nr. Royston

David Bickersteth
4 South End. SG8 5NG. Est. 1967. Open by appointment. *STOCK: Antiquarian books.* TEL: 01763 245619; fax - 01763 242969.

BOTTISHAM, Nr. Cambridge

Cambridge Pine
Hall Farm, Lode Rd. CB5 9DN. (Mr and Mrs D. Weir). Est. 1980. Open seven days. SIZE: Large. *STOCK: Pine, 18th-19th C and reproduction, £25-£1,400.* LOC: Midway between Bottisham and Lode, near Anglesey Abbey. PARK: Easy. TEL: 01223 811208; home - same. SER: Fitted farmhouse kitchens.

BURWELL

Peter Norman Antiques and Restorations
Sefton House, 57 North St. CB5 0BA. (P. Norman and A. Marpole). Est. 1975. Open 9-12.30 and 2-5.30. SIZE: Medium. *STOCK: Furniture, clocks, arms and Oriental rugs, 17th-19th C, £250-£10,000.* PARK: Easy. TEL: 01638 742197. SER: Valuations; restorations (furniture, oil paintings, clocks, arms). VAT: Stan/Spec.

CAMBRIDGE

20th Century
169 Histon Rd. CB4 3JD. (S. Charles). Open Wed., Thurs., and Fri. 12-5, Sat. 10-5. *STOCK: Decorative arts, 1880-1980.* TEL: 01223 359482.

Jess Applin Antiques BADA
8 Lensfield Rd. CB2 1EG. Est. 1968. Open 10-5.30. *STOCK: Furniture, 17th-19th C; works of art.* LOC: At junction with Hills Rd., opposite church. PARK: Pay and display nearby. TEL: 01223 315168. VAT: Spec.

John Beazor and Sons Ltd BADA
78-80 Regent St. CB2 1DP. Est. 1875. Open 9.15-5, Sat. 10-4 or by appointment. *STOCK: English furniture, late 17th to early 19th C; clocks, barometers and decorative items.* TEL: 01223 355178; fax - same. SER: Valuations. VAT: Spec.

Benet Gallery
26 Long Road. CB2 2PS. (G.H. and J. Criddle). Est. 1965. Open by appointment. SIZE: Large. *STOCK: Maps and prints of Cambridge, all periods.* TEL: 01223 248739. VAT: Stan.

Buckies LAPADA
31 Trinity St. CB2 1TB. (G. McClure-Buckie). NAG, GMC. Est. 1972. Open 9.45-5. CL: Mon. SIZE: Medium. *STOCK: Jewellery, silver, objets d'art.* PARK: Multi-storey, nearby. TEL: 01223 357910. SER: Valuations; restorations and repairs. VAT: Stan/Spec.

Cambridge continued

Cambridge Fine Art Ltd LAPAD
Priesthouse, 33 Church St., Little Shelford. CB 5HG. (R. and J. Lury). Resident. Est. 197 Open daily 10-6, Sun. by appointment. SIZE Large. *STOCK: British and European painting 1780-1900; modern British paintings, 1880-194 British prints by J.M. Kronheim to the Baxte Process.* LOC: Next to church. PARK: Eas TEL: 01223 842866/843537. SER: Valuation restorations; buys at auction. VAT: Stan/Spec.

Collectors Centre
Hope St. Yard, Hope St. CB1 3NA. Est. 197 Open 10-5. SIZE: Medium. *STOCK: Strippe pine and oak, Victorian walnut and mahogan Victoriana, wind-up gramophones and gener items, 19th-20th C.* LOC: Off Mill Rd., Romse Town. PARK: Own. TEL: 01223 211632. SE Restorations (paintings, frames); carver an gilder; gramophone repairs.

Collectors' Market
Dales Brewery, Gwydir St (off Mill Rd), (Mrs E.M Highmoor). Est. 1976. Open 10-5, Sat. 9.30-5.3 SIZE: 8 units. *STOCK: Collectors' items fro £1.50-£750, including bygones, prints, pine, bric-a brac, kitchenalia, sofas and chairs.* TEL: 0122 300269.

Gabor Cossa Antiques
34 Trumpington St. CB2 1QY. (M. Edgell and D Theobaldy). Est. 1948. Open 10-5.30. *STOCK English ceramics, Delftware, English glas Oriental ceramics, bijouterie.* LOC: Opposit Fitzwilliam Museum. PARK: 400yds. TEL 01223 356049. VAT: Global.

Cottage Antiques
16-18 Lensfield Rd. CB2 1EG. (Mrs A. Owen an Mrs A. Yandell). Est. 1981. Open 10-5.30, Su by appointment. SIZE: Medium. *STOCK: 18t 19th C pottery, porcelain, blue and whit Staffordshire figures, glass, country furnitur brass, copper; general antiques and antiquitie rugs.* LOC: Opposite Catholic Church. PARK Nearby. TEL: 01223 316698.

Peter Ian Crabbe
3 Pembroke St. CB2 3QY. Open 10-4.3 *STOCK: Furniture and porcelain.* TEL: 0122 357117. VAT: Spec.

G. David
16 St. Edward's Passage. CB2 3PJ. ABA, PBF Est. 1896. Open 9-5. *STOCK: Antiquarian book fine bindings, secondhand and out of print book selected publishers remainders.* TEL: 0122 354619.

Deighton Bell and Co
13 Trinity St. CB2 1TD. (Heffers Booksellers ABA, PBFA. Est. 1794. Open 9-5.30. SIZ Large. *STOCK: Antiquarian, rare and fine o books, most subjects; also bibliography, ty ography and illustrated books.* PARK: Mul storey, 300yds. TEL: 01223 568585; fax - 012 354936. SER: Buys at auction. VAT: Stan.

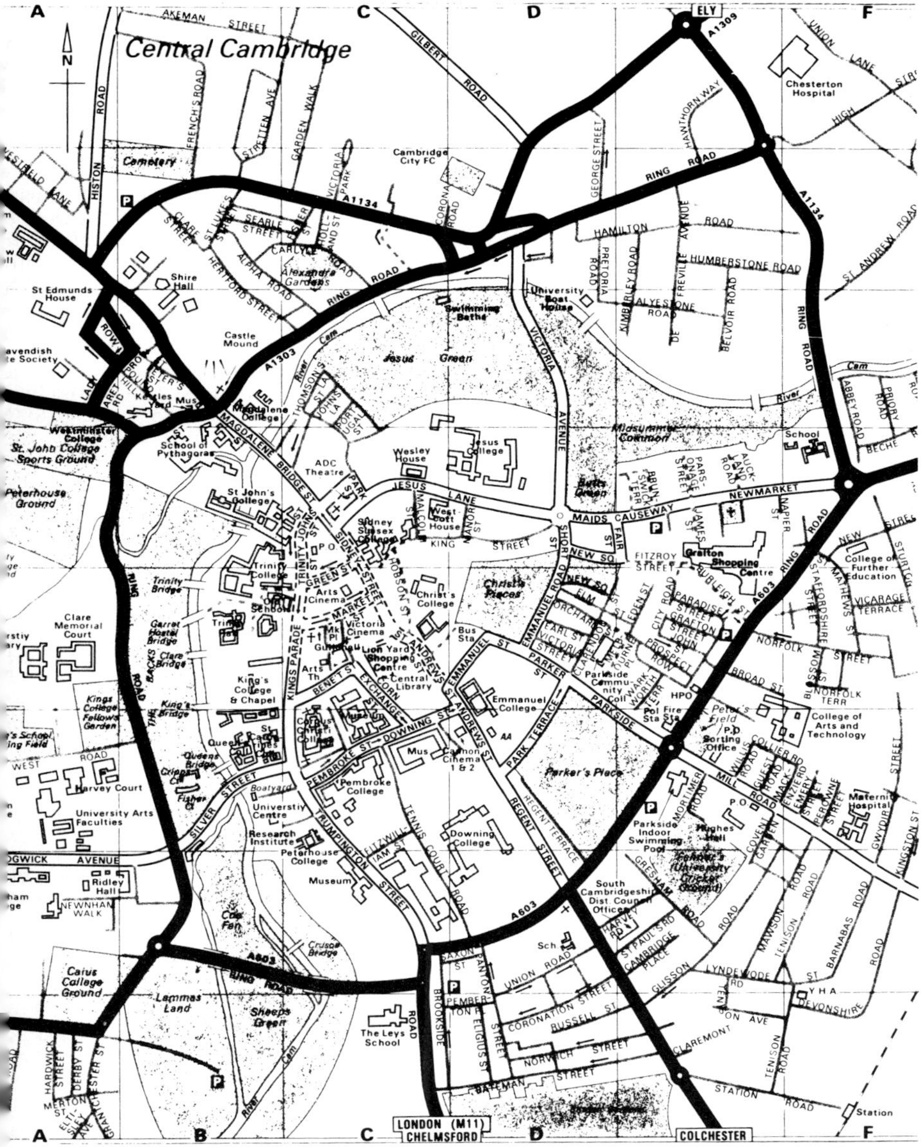

Key to Town Plan

AA Recommended roads		Car Parks	P
Other roads		Parks and open spaces	
Restricted roads		AA Service Centre	AA
Buildings of interest			

Cambridge continued

Galloway and Porter Ltd
30 Sidney St., and 3 Green St. CB2 3HS. ABA. Est. 1900. *STOCK: Antiquarian and secondhand books.* TEL: 01223 67876.

Gwydir Street Antiques Centre
Units 1 & 2 Dales Brewery, Gwydir St. CB1 2LJ. Open 10-5, Sat. 9.30-5.30, Sun. 11-5. *STOCK: Victorian and Edwardian furniture in mahogany, walnut, pine, satinwood and oak; upholstered arm chairs and sofas; lamps, mirrors and other decorative items.* LOC: Off Mill Rd. PARK: Opposite. TEL: 01223 356391.

W. Heffer
CB4 3EJ. Est. 1970. Open by appointment only. *STOCK: General furniture, silver, china, clocks, watches.* TEL: Home - 01223 363634. SER: Valuations; restorations (wood, metalware, silver, china, mother-of-pearl).

Hyde Park Corner Antiques (Antiques Centre)
12 Lensfield Rd. CB2 1EG. (S.J. Cope-Brown). Open 10-5. SIZE: 8 dealers. *STOCK: Pre-1830 English ceramics; glass, silver, furniture, early metalware, pot-lids and Prattware, treen, jewellery and early prints.* TEL: 01223 353654. SER: Valuations; restorations (pottery, porcelain and furniture).

Sarah Key
The Haunted Bookshop, 9 St. Edward's Passage. CB2 3PJ. Est. 1987. Open 10-5. *STOCK: Childrens' and illustrated books, antiquarian and literature.* TEL: 01223 312913.

The Lawson Gallery
7-8 King's Parade. CB2 1SJ. Est. 1967. Open 9.30-5. SIZE: Medium. *STOCK: Local and fine art; reproduction railway posters of '30s, '40s and '50s; prints.* LOC: Opposite King's College. PARK: Lion's Yard. TEL: 01223 313970. VAT: Stan.

Sebastian Pearson Paintings Prints and Works of Art
3 Pembroke St. CB2 3QY. Est. 1989. Open 10.30-5.30. CL: Mon. SIZE: Medium. *STOCK: Oil paintings and watercolours, £300-£3,500; 20th C British prints (etchings and wood engravings), £60-£600.* LOC: City centre. PARK: Nearby. TEL: 01223 323999; home - 01438 871364. SER: Valuations; picture framing. VAT: Spec.

Pembroke Antiques
7 Pembroke St. CB2 3QY. (K.N. and R.M. Galey). Open 10-5. CL: Mon. SIZE: Small. *STOCK: Silver, furniture, 18th-19th C; jewellery, 18th-20th C.* LOC: 100 yards off Trumpington St., opposite Pembroke College. PARK: 100 yards. TEL: 01223 363246. VAT: Stan/Spec.

Solopark Plc
The Old Railway Station, Station Rd., Nr. Pampisford. CB2 4HB. (R.J. Bird). Open Mon.-

Cambridge continued

Thur. 8-5, Fri. and Sat. 8-4, Sun. 9-1. *STOCK: Recycled and traditional building materials an[d] period architectural items.* TEL: 01223 83466[3] fax - 01223 834780.

CHITTERING, Nr. Cambridge

Simon and Penny Rumble Antiques
Causeway End Farmhouse. CB5 9PW. Open b[y] appointment. *STOCK: Early oak and countr[y] furniture, some decorative items.* LOC: 6 mile[s] north of Cambridge, off A10. TEL: 01223 861831.

COMBERTON

Comberton Antiques
5a West St. CB3 7DS. (Mrs M. McEvoy). Est. 198[0] Open Mon., Fri. and Sat. 10-5, Sun. 2-5. SIZE: Medium. *STOCK: Furniture, 1780-1920, £50-£2,000; bric-a-brac, 1830-1920, £5-£100; hand made Turkish kelims; shipping goods.* LOC: 6 mile[s] west of Cambridge, 2 miles west of M11. PARK: Easy. TEL: 01223 262674; home - 01223 263457.

DODDINGTON

Doddington House Antiques
2 Benwick Rd. PE15 0TG. (B.A. Frankland). Es[t.] 1974. *STOCK: Furniture, mirrors, clocks, baro[-] meters, pictures and interesting items.* LOC: A[t] Clocktower. PARK: Easy. TEL: 01354 74075[5] SER: Restorations (chair caning and rushing[;] barometers).

DUXFORD

Riro D. Mooney
4 Moorfield Rd. CB2 4PS. Est. 1946. Open 9-[7] SIZE: Medium. *STOCK: General antiques, 178[0-] 1920, £5-£1,200.* LOC: 1 mile from M11. PARK: Easy. TEL: 01223 832252. VAT: Stan/Spec.

ELY

Mrs Mills Antiques
1a St. Mary's St. CB7 4ER. Open 10-1 and 2-[5] CL: Tues. *STOCK: China, jewellery, silver.* N[ot] Stocked: Furniture. TEL: 01353 664268.

Waterside Antiques
The Wharf. CB7 4AU. (G. Peters). Est. 198[6] Open 9.30-5.30 including Bank Holidays, Sun. [1-] 5.30. SIZE: Large. *STOCK: General antique[s]* LOC: Waterside area. PARK: Easy. TEL: 0135[3] 667066. SER: Valuations.

FORDHAM

Phoenix Antiques
1 Carter St. CB7 5NG. Est. 1966. Open b[y] appointment only. SIZE: Medium. *STOCK: Ear[ly] European furniture, domestic metalwork, potte[ry]*

Fordham continued

and delft, carpets, scientific instruments, treen and bygones. LOC: Centre of village. PARK: Own. TEL: 01638 720363.

FOWLMERE, Nr. Royston

Mere Antiques

High St. SG8 7SU. (R.W. Smith). Est. 1979. Open 10-1 and 2-6, including Sun. SIZE: Medium. *STOCK: Furniture, porcelain and clocks, 18th-19th C, to £5,000.* PARK: Easy. TEL: 01763 208477; home - 01763 208495. SER: Valuations. VAT: Spec.

HARSTON

Antique Clocks

1 High St. CB2 5PX. (C.J. Stocker). Open every day. LOC: On A10, 5 miles south of Cambridge. PARK: Easy. TEL: 01223 870264.

HUNTINGDON

Adams Furniture Centre

The Old Post Office, George St. PE18 6AW. (Stephen Copsey). Est. 1977. Open 9.30-5.30. CL: Thurs. SIZE: Large. *STOCK: Mainly furniture.* LOC: Off Huntingdon ring road. PARK: Easy. TEL: 01480 435100; fax - 01480 454387. SER: Valuations; buys at auction. VAT: Stan/Spec.

ICKLETON

Abbey Antiques

18 Abbey St. CB10 1SS. (K. Wilson). Est. 1974. Open 10-5, Sun. 2-5. SIZE: Large. *STOCK: General antiques, 17th-20th C, £1-£1,000.* LOC: Turn off at Stumps Cross at Gt. Chesterford, 1 mile to Ickleton, shop is in main street. PARK: Easy. TEL: 01799 530637. SER: Valuations; restorations (furniture); French polishing.

LANDBEACH

P.R. Garner Antiques

104 High St. CB4 4DT. Est. 1966. Open by appointment only. SIZE: Medium. *STOCK: China, glass, brass, copper, pewter, unrestored furniture, Victorian and earlier; automobilia and collectors cars; shipping goods.* LOC: Off A10. PARK: Easy. TEL: 01223 860470. SER: Valuations. VAT: Stan/Spec.

J.V. Pianos and Cambridge Pianola Company

The Limes. CB4 4DR. (F.T. Poole). Est. 1972. Open Mon.-Fri., evenings and weekends by appointment. SIZE: Medium. *STOCK: Pianos, pianolas and pianola rolls.* LOC: First building on right in Landbeach from A10. PARK: Easy. TEL: 01223 861348/861507; home - same; fax - 01223 441276. SER: Valuations; restorations. VAT: Stan.

LITTLE ABINGTON, Nr. Cambridge

Abington Books

29 Church Lane. CB1 6BQ. (J. Haldane). Est. 1971. By appointment only. SIZE: Small. *STOCK: Books on Oriental rugs, from 1877, £1-£5,000; books on classical tapestries, from 17th C, £1-£3,000.* PARK: Easy. TEL: 01223 891645; fax - 01223 893724. SER: Valuations; book binding.

LITTLE DOWNHAM, Nr. Ely

The Old Bishop's Palace Antique Centre

Tower Rd. CB6 2TD. (Elaine Griffin-Singh). Est. 1992. Open every day, incl. Bank Holidays. SIZE: 60 dealers. *STOCK: Furniture, paintings, glass, silver, jewellery, golf clubs, fishing tackle, sporting prints, kelims, china, mainly 18th-19th C, £5-£5,000.* LOC: A10 Ely by-pass, then B1411 to Little Downham. PARK: Own. TEL: 01353 699177; home - same. SER: Restorations. VAT: Stan/Spec.

OUTWELL, Nr. Wisbech

A.P. and M.A. Haylett

Glen-Royd, 393 Wisbech Rd. PE14 8PG. Open 9-6 including Sun. *STOCK: Country furniture, pottery, treen and metalware, 1750-1900, £5-£500.* Not Stocked: Firearms. LOC: A1101. PARK: Easy. TEL: 01945 772427; home - same. SER: Buys at auction.

PETERBOROUGH

Fitzwilliam Antiques Centre

Fitzwilliam St. PE1 2RX. (Watkins and Stafford Ltd). Open 10-5, Sun. 12-5. SIZE: 50 dealers. *STOCK: General antiques.* TEL: 01733 65415.

Ivor and Patricia Lewis Antique and Fine Art Dealers LAPADA

Westfield, 30 Westwood Park Rd. PE3 6JL. Open by appointment. ***STOCK: Furniture - fine 19th C ormolu mounted French, painted and inlaid Edwardian satinwood; bronzes and porcelain.*** **TEL: 01733 344567.**

Old Soke Books

68 Burghley Rd. PE1 2QE. (Peter and Linda Clay). Open Tues.-Sat. 10.30-5.30. *STOCK: Antiquarian and secondhand books, small general antiques including furniture, paintings, prints and postcards.* TEL: 01733 64147.

G. Smith and Sons (Peterborough) Ltd

1379 Lincoln Rd., Werrington. PE4 6LT. (Mike Groucott). Est. 1902. Open 9-5. SIZE: Medium. *STOCK: General antiques, furniture and clocks.* LOC: Old Lincoln Road, Werrington village. PARK: Easy. TEL: 01733 571630. SER: Restorations.

RAMSEY, Nr. Huntingdon

Abbey Antiques
63 Great Whyte. PE17 1HL. (R. and J. Smith). Est. 1977. Open 10-5 including Sun. CL: Mon. SIZE: Small. *STOCK: Furniture including pine, 1850-1930, £50-£500; porcelain, Goss and crested china, 1830-1950, £3-£500; Beswick, Wade and Fen pottery and small collectables, Mabel Lucie Attwell.* PARK: Easy. TEL: 01487 814753. SER: Museum and Collectors' Club - Memories UK (Enesco figurines sold). FAIRS: Alexandra Palace, Harrow.

SOMERSHAM, Nr. Huntingdon

T. W. Pawson - Clocks
31A High St. PE17 3JA. Est. 1981. Open 9.30-6, Sat. 10-1 but appointment advisable. SIZE: Small. *STOCK: Antique clocks, £150-£5,000; mercury barometers, mid to late 19th C.* LOC: Main road through village. PARK: Easy. TEL: 01487 841537; home - same. SER: Valuations; restorations (clock and barometer repairs and overhauls); buys at auction.

ST IVES

Hyperion Antique Centre
Station Rd. PE17 4BH. (Colin Gunter and Pat Bernard). Est. 1996. Open 9.30-5. SIZE: Medium. *STOCK: Furniture, 18th-20th C, £30-£3,000; ceramics and pictures, silver and plate, £5-£200; linen and lace, £2-£100; all 19th-20th C.* LOC: Turn right into Station Rd. at far end of car park. PARK: Nearby. TEL: 01480 464140; home - 01954 203227. VAT: Stan/Spec.

B.R. Knight and Sons
Quay Court, Bull Lane, Bridge St. PE17 4AU. (M. Knight). Est. 1972. Open Mon., Wed., Fri. 11-2, Sat. 10.30-4.30 or by appointment. SIZE: Medium. *STOCK: Porcelain, pottery, jewellery, paintings, watercolours, prints, decorative arts.* LOC: Off Bridge St. PARK: Nearby. TEL: 01480 468295/300042.

Quayside Antiques
3 The Quay. PE17 4AR. (H.S. Northwood). Est. 1960. Open 10-5.30 including Sun. SIZE: Large. *STOCK: Fine English furniture, to 1820, from £1,000.* LOC: 30 yards from historic 17th C bridge over River Ouse. PARK: Easy. TEL: 01480 495181. SER: Valuations; restorations. VAT: Stan/Spec.

ST. NEOTS

Tavistock Antiques
Cross Hall Manor, Eaton Ford. PE19 4AH. Open by appointment. *STOCK: Period English furniture.* TEL: 01480 472082. *Trade Only.*

WANSFORD, Nr. Peterborough

Starlight
16 London Rd. PE8 6JB. Resident. Open Tues.-Fri. and usually Sat. 10-1 and 2-5 or by appointmen[t]. *STOCK: Period and new lighting, candles, o[il] lamps and parts.* LOC: On A1 near A47 junctio[n]. PARK: Easy. TEL: 01780 783999; fax - same.

Sydney House Antiques
14 Elton Rd. PE8 6JD. (G. and R. Hancox). Es[t]. 1972. Open 10-5 including Sun., Mon. 2-5.30, oth[er] times by appointment. SIZE: Large. *STOCK: Furniture, including marquetry, 19th-20th C, £15[0]-£2,000; Minton, 1850-1920, £100-£2,000; Doult[on] and Lambeth, £50-£1,000; Royal Worcester, 186[0]-1940, £100-£1,500.* PARK: Easy. TEL: 0178[0] 782786. SER: Valuations; buys at auction (Minto[n], Doulton, Royal Worcester, 19th C furniture).

Paul Warrington
Bridge House, Old North Rd. Open b[y] appointment. *STOCK: Period and decorativ[e] furniture, architectural items and garden statuar[y].* TEL: 01780 481534.

WARBOYS

Warboys Antiques
Old Church School, High St. PE17 2SX. (Lambden and E. Godfrey). Est. 1986. Open Tues-Sat. 11-5. SIZE: Medium. *STOCK: Decorativ[e] smalls, 18th-20th C; sports equipment, advertisin[g] items, 19th-20th C; all £1-£1,500.* LOC: Off A14[1]. PARK: Easy. TEL: 01487 823686; fax - 0148[7] 496296. SER: Valuations. FAIRS: Alexandr[a] Palace.

WISBECH

Attic Gallery
88 Elm Rd. PE13 2TB. (B.G. Ransome). Es[t]. 1980. Open by appointment. SIZE: Smal[l]. *STOCK: Georgian and Victorian silver.* PAR[K]: Easy. TEL: 01945 583734.

Peter A. Crofts BAD[A]
Briar Patch, High Rd., Elm. PE14 0DN. Es[t]. 1949. CL: Sat. *STOCK: General antique furniture, porcelain, silver, jewellery.* LO[C]: A1101. TEL: 01945 584614. VAT: Stan/Spec.

Walpole Highway Antiques Centre
Walpole Highway. PE14 7RN. (D. Bayley). Op[en] 10.30-5 including Sun. SIZE: Large - 35 deale[rs]. *STOCK: General antiques - furniture includin[g] pine, china and bygones. £1-£1,500.* LOC: A4[7] between Wisbech and King's Lynn. PARK: Ow[n]. TEL: 01945 880733/881033.

R. Wilding
Lanes End, Gadds Lane, Leverington. PE13 5B[?]. *STOCK: Walnut chests, bureau bookcase[s], serving tables, mahogany and gilt console table[s], mahogany, walnut and gilt mirrors.* TEL: 019[45] 588204; fax - 01945 476558. SER: Veneerin[g]; polishing; (compo) gilding; conversions; cabin[et] making. Trade Only.

Cheshire

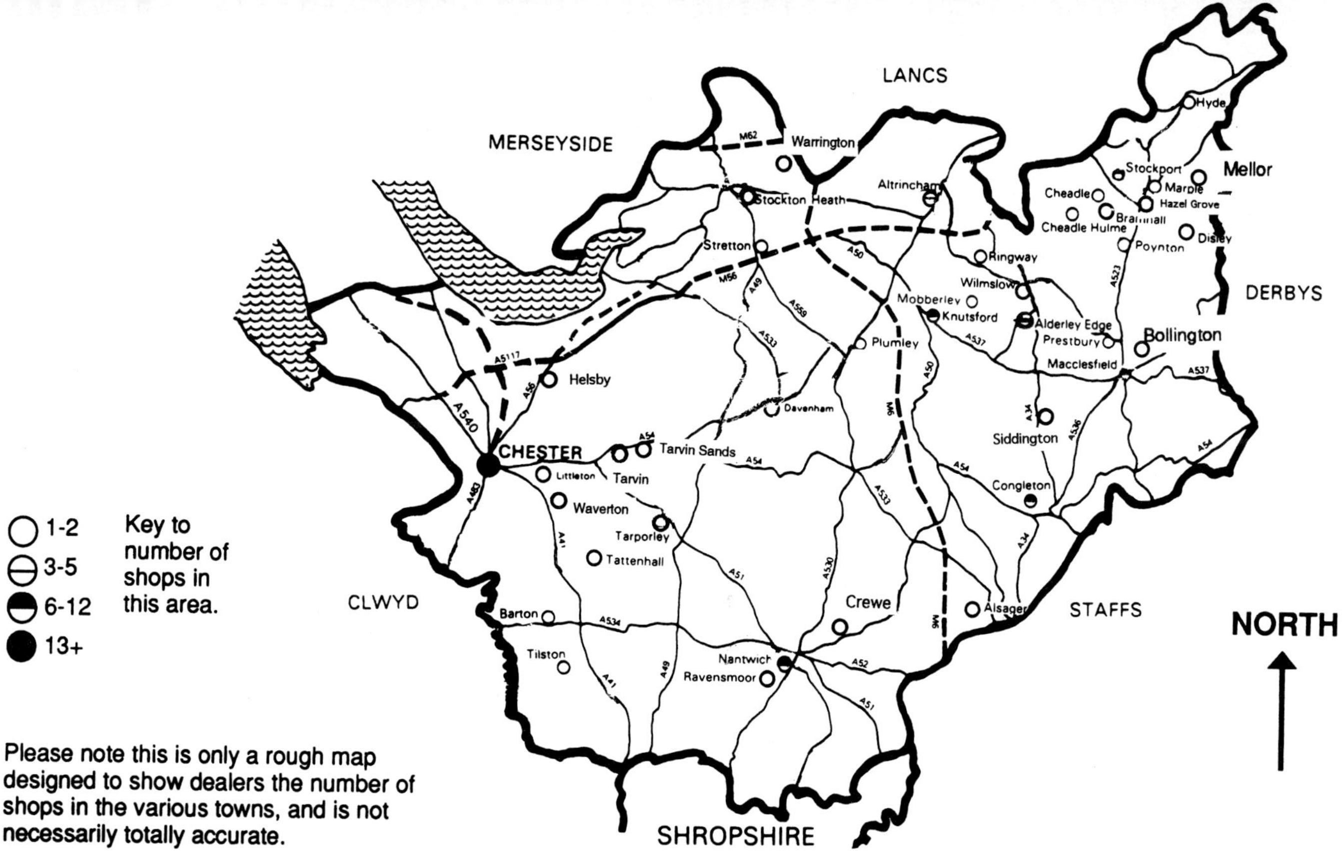

Please note this is only a rough map designed to show dealers the number of shops in the various towns, and is not necessarily totally accurate.

ALDERLEY EDGE

Anthony Baker Antiques LAPADA

14 London Rd. SK9 7JS. (G.D.A. Price). Est. 1974. Open 11-5.30. CL: Mon. and Wed. SIZE: Medium. *STOCK: Furniture and clocks, 17th-19th C, £50-£2,000; glass, pottery and collectors items.* Not Stocked: Jewellery, weapons. LOC: A34, village centre. PARK: Easy. TEL: 01625 582674. VAT: Stan/Spec.

Brook Lane Antiques

93 Brook Lane. SK9 7SD. (G.M. Broadbridge). Est. 1983. Open 9-5. SIZE: Small. *STOCK: Furniture especially wardrobes.* TEL: 01625 584896.

The Edge Antiques

8 Trafford Rd. SK9 7HZ. (Vivienne and Andrew Smith). Est. 1977. Open 10-12.30 and 2-4.30, Sat. 10-1, Sun. and Sat. pm. by appointment. CL: Mon. and Wed. SIZE: Small. *STOCK: Victorian light fittings, gas brackets, £100-£500; Victorian pine.* LOC: Parallel to London Rd. (A34). PARK: Easy. TEL: 01625 582176; home - 01625 584089.

Sara Frances Antiques

2 West St. SK9 7EG. (Mrs. F.S. Waterworth). Est. 1990. Open Thurs.-Sat. 10-1 and 2-5. SIZE: Small. *STOCK: Furniture, 17th-19th C, £100-£3,500; silver, 19th-20th C, £50-£500; decorative items, 17th-20th C, £100-£2,500.* LOC: A34 from Congleton. Off London Rd., shop next to Barclays Bank. PARK: Easy. TEL: 01625 585549; home - 01625 861268. SER: Valuations; restorations (furniture and silver).

D.J. Massey and Son

51a London Rd. SK9 7DY. Est. 1900. Open 9-5.30, Wed. 9-5. SIZE: Large. *STOCK: Gold and diamond jewellery; silver, all periods.* LOC: On A34. PARK: Easy. TEL: 01625 583565. VAT: Stan/Spec.

ALSAGER, Nr. Crewe

Forest Books of Cheshire

The Bookshop Upstairs, 14b Lawton Rd. ST7 2AF. (Mrs E. Mann). Open Mon. and Wed.11-5, Tues. and Sat. 11-5.30, Thurs.and Fri. 11-7. *STOCK: Books including new and secondhand, antiquarian, humanities; pictures, ephemera, collectables.* TEL: 01270 882618.

Trash 'n' Treasure

48 Sandbach Rd. South. ST7 2LP. (G. and D. Ogden). Est. 1979. Open 10-12 and 1-5, Fri. and Sat. 10-12 and 1-5.30. CL: Wed. SIZE: Medium. *STOCK: Ceramics, furniture and pictures, Victorian, Edwardian and 1930's, £5-£1, 000.* LOC: 10 minutes junction 16, M6. PARK: Nearby. TEL: 01270 872972/873246. SER: Valuations.

ALTRINCHAM

Altrincham Antiques

39 Hale Rd. and 15 & 23 Tipping St. WA14 2EY Open 10-6 including Sun. SIZE: Medium *STOCK: General antiques, £5-£6,500.* LOC A538 Hale road. PARK: Own. TEL: 0161 94 3554; fax - same; mobile - 0836 316366.

Bizarre Decorative Arts North West

116 Manchester Rd. WA14 4PY. (Malcolm C and Rebecca Lamb). Resident. Est. 1986. Ope 10-6, Sun. by appointment. SIZE: Large. *STOCK Furniture and lighting, £100-£15,000; figurine bronzes, ceramics including Clarice Cliff, an jewellery, £5-£2,000; all Art Nouveau and A Deco.* LOC: A56. PARK: Own. TEL: 0161 92 8895; home - same; fax - 0161 929 8310. SEI Valuations; restorations (furniture and lightin silver and chrome plating, pewter polishing FAIRS: NEC Aug; Loughborough Art Dec Kensington Decorative Arts. VAT: Stan/Spec.

Lostock Antiques

23 Oxford Rd. WA14 2ED. (Timothy and Car Lawlor). Est. 1988. Open 10-5. CL: Wed. p.r SIZE: Medium. *STOCK: Furniture, 18th-19th £70-£1,5000; pottery, Wemyss, china, Worceste books, glass, textiles.* TEL: 0161 929 8696. SEI Restoration (excluding upholstery); Frenc polishing; furniture made to order; own range furniture products - pure beeswax. FAIR Cheshire Show and local.

Robert Redford Antiques & Interior

48 New St. WA14 2QS. (S. and R. Redford Open 10-6. CL: Mon. and Wed. *STOCK: Gener antiques, furniture, small silver, porcelain, glas* PARK: Easy. TEL: 0161 929 8171; home - 01 928 4827/926 8232.

Squires Antiques

25 Regent Rd. WA14 1RX. (V. Phillips). E 1977. Open 10-5. CL: Mon. and Wed. SIZ Medium. *STOCK: Small furniture, 1800-193 £60-£1,500; small silver, 1850-1970, £20-£40 brass, copper and bric-a-brac, 1850-1940, £1 £400; jewellery, porcelain, fire accessories, lig fittings and interior design items.* Not Stocke Large furniture, coins and badges. LOC: Adjace hospital, and large car park. PARK: Easy. TE 0161 928 0749. SER: Valuations.

BARTON, Nr. Malpas

Derek and Tina Rayment Antiques

BADA LAPAI

Orchard House, Barton Rd. SY14 7HT. (D.J. a K.M. Rayment). Est. 1960. Open by appointme every day. *STOCK: Barometers, 18th-20th from £100.* LOC: A534. PARK: Easy. TE 01829 270429; home - same. SER: Valuatio restorations (barometers only); buys at aucti (barometers). FAIRS: NEC; LAPADA; BAD Olympia; Chelsea. VAT: Stan/Spec.

BOLLINGTON, Nr. Macclesfield

Corner House Antiques

59/61 High St. SK10 5PH. (Mr and Mrs R. G. Wright). Resident. Est. 1988. Open 10.30-6, Sun. 12-6. CL: Tues. SIZE: Medium. *STOCK: Decorative and unusual furniture and furnishings, 18th to early 20th C, £50-£2,500; prints, etchings and engravings, watercolours and oils, 19th-20th C, £50-£400; collectables, 18th-20th C, £50-£200.* PARK: Easy. TEL: 01625 576362; home - same. SER: Finder; courier; buys at auction. FAIRS: Local. VAT: Stan/Spec.

Yesterdays

8 Palmerston St. SK10 5PW. (Mrs Olive Kershaw). Est. 1989. Open 9.30-1 and 2-5.30, Wed. 9.30-1, Sat. 10-4, Sun. 12-4. SIZE: Small. *STOCK: China and glass, Victorian to Art Deco; small mahogany and pine furniture; Victoriana, all £5-£1,000.* LOC: 4 miles from Macclesfield, through village, opposite car park. PARK: Opposite. TEL: 01625 573222; fax - 01625 576976. SER: Valuations; restorations (fine furniture); buys at auction. VAT: Stan.

BRAMHALL

David H. Dickinson

P.O. Box 29. SK7 2EJ. Est. 1976. Open by appointment only. *STOCK: Fine antique furniture and extraordinary works of art.* TEL: 0161 440 688. SER: Valuations.

CHEADLE

Malcolm Frazer Antiques

9 Brooklyn Crescent. SX8 1DX. Open by appointment. *STOCK: Marine, scientific and decorative antiques.* TEL: 0161 428 3781.

CHEADLE HULME

Allan's Antiques and Reproductions

0 Ravenoak Rd. SK8 7DL. (S. Allan and D. Lloyd). Est. 1979. CL: Wed. *STOCK: Furniture, general antiques, metalware, including silver, especially flatware/cutlery.* TEL: 0161 485 132/486 6368 (ansaphone).

CHESTER

Adams Antiques LAPADA

5 Watergate Row. CH1 2LE. (B. and T. Adams). Est. 1973. Open 10-5. CL: Sun. except by appointment. SIZE: Medium. *STOCK: English and Continental furniture, £200-£4,000; English and French clocks, £150-£4,000; objets d'art, £10-£1,000; all 18th-19th C.* PARK: Nearby. TEL: 01244 319421. SER: Valuations; restorations (furniture, clocks, and porcelain). VAT: Stan/Spec.

Chester continued

Aldersey Hall Ltd

Town Hall Sq., 47 Northgate St. CH1 2HQ. (Kim Wilding-Welton). Est. 1990. Open 8.30-5.30. SIZE: Medium. *STOCK: Art Deco and general British ceramics, £5-£500; small furniture, £50-£200; all 1880-1940.* LOC: Between library and Odeon cinema. PARK: Own 100 yards. TEL: 01244 324885. SER: Valuations; buys at auction (Art Deco ceramics). FAIRS: Alexandra Palace, Loughborough, Ardingly, Newark and Birmingham. VAT: Stan/Spec.

Angela Antiques

32 Christleton Rd. CH3 5UG. (Angela Jones). Est. 1977. CL: Wed. and Fri. except by appointment. SIZE: Small. *STOCK: Small furniture, pine, china and collectables, 19th-20th C, £50-£100.* LOC: Off A41, 1/2 mile from city centre. PARK: Opposite. TEL: 01244 351562; home - 01244 329312. SER: Valuations; buys at auction. VAT: Stan/Spec.

Antique Exporters of Chester

CH3 7RZ. Open by appointment only. SIZE: Warehouse. *STOCK: Furniture.* TEL: 01829 741001; home - 01244 570069. SER: Packing. *Export Only.*

The Antique Shop

40 Watergate St. CH1 2LA. (Peter Thornber). Est. 1985. Open 10-5.30, Sat. 10-6, Sun. (May-Dec.) 1-5, other times by appointment. SIZE: Small. *STOCK: Metalware - brass, pewter, copper, iron, etc, 1700-1900, £35-£350; Doulton - character jugs, figures and series ware, 1890-1960, £35-£350; blue and white transfer printed ware; Prattware pot lids, British Army cap badges; fountain pens; boxes and treen; cranberry glass, etc.* LOC: Off Bridge St. PARK: Nearby. TEL: 01244 316286; home - 0151 327 1725. SER: Restorations (metalwork). FAIRS: Cheshire.

Avalon Post Card and Stamp Shop

1 City Walls, Rufus Court, Northgate St. CH1 2JG. (G.E. Ellis). *STOCK: Postcards, stamps and collectables.* TEL: 01244 318406.

Baron Fine Art LAPADA

68 Watergate St. CH1 2LA. (S. and R. Baron). Est. 1984.Open 10-5.15. *STOCK: Watercolours and oils, some etchings, late 19th to early 20th C, some contemporary, £50-£25,000.* PARK: Easy. TEL: 01244 342520. SER: Restorations; framing. FAIRS: Tatton Park; World of Watercolours; LAPADA (Jan.); NEC (April and Aug.). VAT: Stan/Spec.

Olwyn Boustead Antiques LAPADA

59-61 Watergate Row. CH1 2LE. (Mrs O.L. Boustead). Open 10-5.30. *STOCK: 17th-19th C town and country furniture; portraits, clocks, metalware, pottery, porcelain and lighting.* TEL: 01244 342300/350366.

Chester continued

Cameo Antiques

19 Watergate St. CH1 2LB. Est. 1994. Open 9-5, Sat. 9-5.30. SIZE: Small. *STOCK: Jewellery and silver, 1800-1990, £10-£2,000; English and Continental porcelain, 1750-1950.* LOC: Off Bridge St. PARK: Easy. TEL: 01244 311467; fax - same. SER: Valuations; restorations. VAT: Stan/Spec.

Chester Drawers Antique Centre

26 Watergate Row. CH1 2LD. (Alan Bailey). Open 10-5. SIZE: 12 rooms - 20 cabinets. *STOCK: Wide range of general antiques including furniture, pictures, ceramics, clocks, jewellery and collectables.* PARK: Under Moat House Hotel. TEL: 01244 311600. SER: Valuations; restorations; buys at auction. FAIRS: Robert Bailey (Chester Racecourse); Reg Cooper (Arley); NEC.

Farmhouse Antiques

21-23 Christleton Rd., Boughton. CH3 5UF. (K. Appleby). Est. 1973. Open 9-5. SIZE: Large. *STOCK: Farmhouse furniture, longcase clocks, Staffordshire pottery, country bygones, mechanical music.* LOC: 1 mile from City centre on A41. PARK: Easy. TEL: 01244 322478; evenings - 01244 318391. SER: Export. VAT: Stan/Spec.

Guildhall Fair - Chester

Watergate St. Open Thurs. 10-4. SIZE: 40 dealers. *STOCK: General antiques.*

Jamandic Ltd

22 Bridge St. Row. CH1 1NN. Est. 1975. Open 9.30-5, Sat. by appointment except during Nov. and Dec. SIZE: Medium. *STOCK: Decorative furniture, porcelain, pictures and prints.* TEL: 01244 312822. SER: Interior design; export. VAT: Stan/Spec.

Kayes of Chester

9 St. Michaels Row. CH1 1EF. (A.M. Austin-Kaye and N.J. Kaye). NAG. Est. 1948. Open 9-5.30. SIZE: Medium. *STOCK: Diamond rings and jewellery, 1850-1950, £20-£20,000; silver and plate, 1700-1930, £20-£8,000; small objects and ceramics, 19th to early 20th C, £50-£1,000.* PARK: Nearby. TEL: 01244 327149. SER: Valuations; restorations (silver, jewellery and plate); buys at auction. VAT: Stan/Spec.

Lowe and Sons

11 Bridge St. Row. CH1 1PD. Est. 1770. *STOCK: Jewellery and silver, Georgian, Victorian and Edwardian; unusual collectors' items.* TEL: 01244 325850. VAT: Stan/Spec.

Made of Honour

11 City Walls. CH1 1LD. (E. Jones). Open 10-5. *STOCK: General antiques, Staffordshire figures, British ceramics, books, woolworks, samplers, tapestries, beadworks and textiles.* LOC: Next to Eastgate clock, wall level. TEL: 01244 314208.

Chester continued

Melody's Antique Galleries LAPAD

30-32 City Rd. CH1 3AE. (M. Melody). Est 1977. Open 10-5.30 or by appointment. SIZE Large. *STOCK: 18th-20th C oak, mahogany walnut and pine furniture; porcelain, silver plate, lighting, decorative items.* LOC: 400yds from station. TEL: 01244 328968; fax - 0124 341818. SER: Courier; container packing VAT: Stan/Spec.

Moor Hall Antiques

27 Watergate Row. CH1 2LE. (John Murphy Resident. Est. 1992. Open 10-5.30, Mon., Fri. an Sat. 10.30-5.30.SIZE: Large. *STOCK: Furniture 18th-19th C, £1,000-£2,000; prints, 19th C, £5 £200; modern decorative items, £20-£100.* LOC City centre. PARK: Easy. TEL: 01244 34009 SER: Restorations (oils, watercolours an furniture). VAT: Stan/Spec.

Richard A. Nicholson

25 Watergate St. CH1 2LB. Est. 1961. Open 1 1.30 and 2.15-5. SIZE: Large. *STOCK: Map 1540-1840, £1-£2,000; prints, 1650-1890, £ £300; watercolours and drawings, £4-£200.* LO Town centre 100yds. from The Cross. PARK 200yds. at bottom of street behind church. TE 01244 326818; home - 01244 336004; fax - 0124 336138; internet - http://www.u-net.com/map VAT: Stan/Spec.

On the Air

The Broadcasting Museum, 42 Bridge St. Ro CH1 1NN. (Steve Harris). Est. 1990. Open 10- Sun. 11-4.30. CL: Sun. and Mon. Christmas Easter. SIZE: Small. *STOCK: Vintage wireles gramophones and telephones, £50-£500.* LOC: yards from The Cross. PARK: Rear of premise TEL: 01244 348468; fax - 01244 348468. SE Valuations; restorations (vintage wireless ar gramophones). FAIRS: National Vinta Communications, NEC and Wembley.

Richmond Galleries

Watergate Building, New Crane St. CH1 4J (Mrs M. Armitage). Est. 1970. Open 10-5.3 SIZE: Large. *STOCK: Pine and country furnitu including Spanish and French; decorative iten* LOC: Direction of Sealand Rd. PARK: Ow TEL: 01244 317602; home - 01244 324285.

St. Peters Art Gallery

14 Nicholas St. CH1 2NX. (D. Hellon). Est. 198 Open 10-5. CL: Sat. SIZE: Medium. *STOC Victorian watercolours, £500-£15,000.* PARK: rear in Nicholas St. Mews. TEL: 01244 3455 VAT: Spec.

Stothert - Antiquarian Books

4 Nicholas St. CH1 8JG. (T. and E. Stother GADAR. Est. 1957. Open 9.30-1 and 2-5.3 SIZE: Medium. *STOCK: Books, 16th-20th C, £ £1,000.* LOC: At junction with Watergate TEL: 01244 340756. VAT: Stan/Spec.

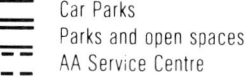

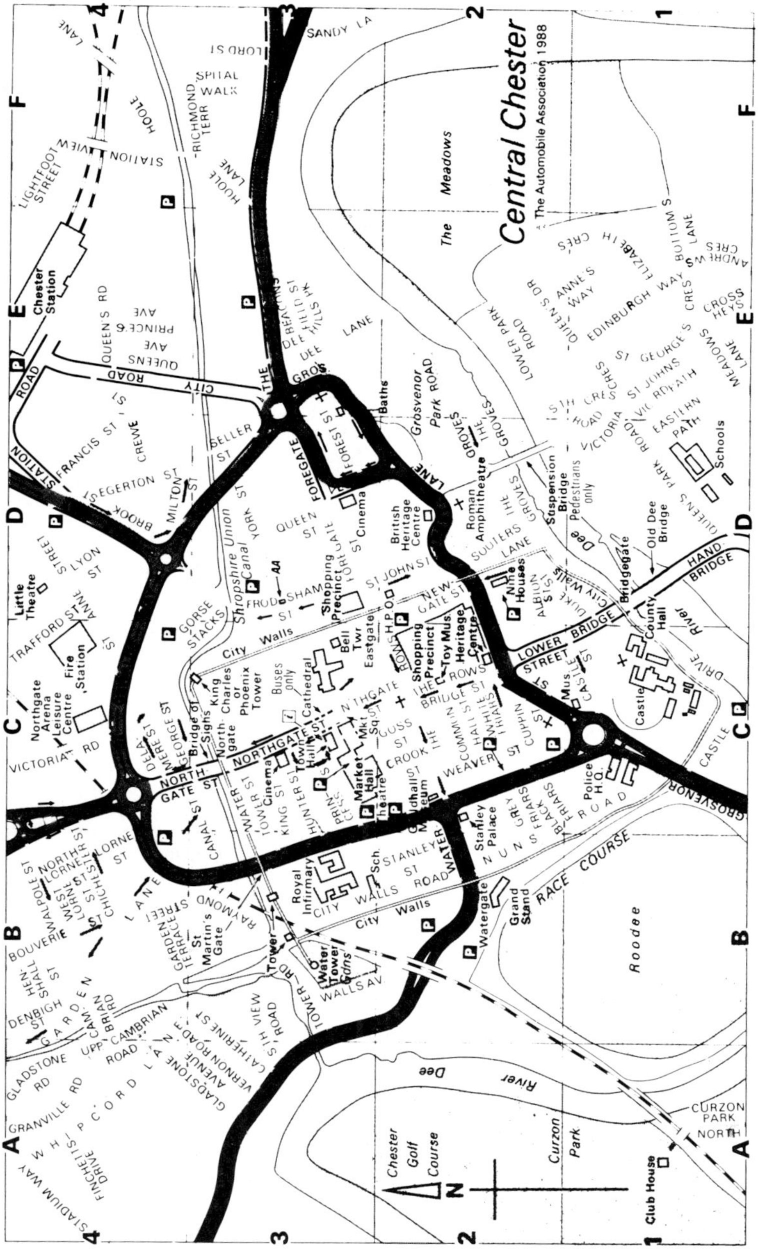

Key to Town Plan

AA Recommended roads		Car Parks	P
Other roads		Parks and open spaces	
Restricted roads		AA Service Centre	AA
Buildings of interest		© Automobile Association 1988.	

Chester continued

John Titchner & Sons LAPADA
67 Watergate Row. Open 10-5.30. *STOCK: Furniture, 18th-19th C.* TEL: 01244 326535.

Veevers
55 Watergate St. (Mr and Mrs A. C. Spicer). Est. 1986. Open 9.30-5. SIZE: Medium. *STOCK: Jewellery and silver, 18th-20th C, £5-£5,000; clocks, 19th-20th C, £50-£1,500.* PARK: Limited and nearby. TEL: 01244 400616. SER: Valuations; restorations (jewellery and clocks). FAIRS: Newark. VAT: Stan/Spec.

Watergate Antiques
56 Watergate St. CH1 2LD. (A. Shindler). Est. 1968. Open 9.30-5.30. SIZE: Medium. *STOCK: Porcelain and pottery, jewellery; specialist in silver and silver plate to the Trade.* LOC: From Liverpool first set of traffic lights past Waterfall Roundabout, turn left. PARK: At rear. TEL: 01244 344516; fax - 01244 320350. VAT: Stan.

Joyce and Rod Whitehead
11 City Walls. CH1 1LD. Open 10-5. *STOCK: Fine art, woolworks, samplers, tapestries, beadwork, textiles, books and decorative items.* LOC: Next to the Eastgate Clock. TEL: 01244 314208.

CONGLETON

W. Buckley Antiques Exports
35 Chelford Rd. CW12 4QA. Open 7 days by appointment. *STOCK: Mainly shipping and Victorian furniture.* TEL: 01260 275299. SER: Shipping.

Little Collectables
8/10 Little St. CW12 3RY. (L.C. and C. Turner). Est. 1989. CL: Wed. SIZE: Medium. *STOCK: Pottery and glass, Doulton, £5-£1,000.* LOC: Town centre. PARK: Nearby. TEL: 01260 299098.

Pine Too
8/10 Rood Hill. CW12 1LG. (Mrs J.P. Tryon). Open 9.30-5.30. *STOCK: Antique and reproduction furniture.* LOC: Just off A34. PARK: Nearby. TEL: 01260 279228; mobile - 0468 508750.

R. and M. Antiques
7-9 Kinsey St. CW12 1ES. (Mr and Mrs M.D. Peters). Est. 1973. Open 10-5. CL: Wed. SIZE: Small. *STOCK: General antiques including small furniture, brass, ceramics and silver, mainly 19th C, £10-£600.* LOC: Just off A34, shop adjacent to town hall. PARK: Limited and nearby. TEL: 01260 280404. SER: Valuations; restorations (French polishing, clocks). FAIRS: Grasmere. VAT: Stan/Spec.

Chester continued

Ann Roberts Antiques
22 Mill St. CW12 1AB. Est. 1983. Open Tues., Thurs., Fri. and Sat., 11.30-4.30. SIZE: Medium. *STOCK: Copper and brass fenders, Georgian and Victorian, £50-£300; wood fire surrounds, £100-£650; cast iron fires, Georgian-Victorian, £95-£500; clocks (all guaranteed); oak, pine and mahogany furniture; oil lamps.* LOC: Adjacent to pedestrian area town centre. PARK: Opposite. TEL: 01260 298942; home - 01260 299033. SER: Restorations (clocks, brass cleaning).

CREWE

Steven Blackhurst
102 Edleston Rd. CW2 7HD. Est. 1988. Open 9.30-5, Sat. 10-5, Sun. by appointment. CL: Wed. SIZE: Small. *STOCK: Stripped pine, 19th to early 20th C, £25-£600; satinwood furniture, 1900, £100-£500.* LOC: Turn off Nantwich Rd. (A534), shop 250 yards on left. TEL: 01270 258617; home - 01270 665991.

DAVENHAM, Nr. Northwich

Davenham Antique Centre
461 London Rd. CW9 8NA. Est. 1985. Open 10-5. CL: Wed. SIZE: 9 dealers. *STOCK: General antiques including furniture, country items, pictures, plated ware, china, brass and copper.* LOC: A533, off A556.TEL: 01606 44350.

DISLEY

Crescent Antiques
7 Buxton Rd. SK12 2DZ. (J.P. Cooper). Est. 1972. Open 11.30-6.30, Sun. 1.30-6.30. CL: Wed. SIZE: Small. *STOCK: General antiques including furniture, pottery, silver, 19th C, £20-£500.* PARK: Opposite Co-op. TEL: 01663 765677.

Mill Farm Antiques
50 Market St. SK12 2DT. (F.E. Berry). Est. 196[illegible]. Open every day. SIZE: Medium. *STOCK: Pianos, clocks, mechanical music, shipping goods, general antiques, £50-£5,000.* LOC: A6 7 miles south of Stockport. PARK: Easy. TEL: 0166[illegible] 764045 (24hrs). SER: Valuations; restorations (clocks, watches, barometers, music boxes). VAT: Stan/Spec.

HAZEL GROVE

The Clock House
14 Buxton Road. SK7 6AD. (A.W. Thom). LBH[illegible] Resident. Est. 1975. Open 10-6 including Sun. SIZE: Small. *STOCK: Prestige and vintage wri[illegible] and pocket watches, clocks, barometers, jewellery.* LOC: Turn off A6 at town by-pass. PARK: Easy. TEL: 0161 456 5752; fax - same. SER: Restorations and repairs; producer [illegible] instructional horology videos.

IELSBY

weetbriar Gallery

obin Hood Lane. WA6 9NH. (Mrs A. Metcalfe). st. 1986. Open 9-5.30, or by appointment to see ıll stock. *STOCK: Antique and modern paper-eights, £5-£3,500.* LOC: Off M56, junction 14. irst left at traffic lights, first right after Elf arage, past three right turns. Premises on hillside ith long, low sandstone wall in front. PARK: asy. TEL: 01928 723851; home - same; fax - 1928 724153; mobile - 0860 907532. SER: aluations; buys at auction (paperweights). AIRS: Glass (May and Nov.); National otorcycle Museum (Birmingham); NEC (Aug.), hepton Mallet; Newark; Ardingly. VAT: Stan/pec.

YDE

eter Bunting Antiques BADA LAPADA

erneth Low. SK14 5LW. Est. 1980. Open by ppointment. SIZE: Medium. *STOCK: Early ık, country furniture, portraits and period coration.* LOC: Off A560 between Hyde and omiley just outside Gee Cross. PARK: Easy. EL: 0161 368 5544; fax - 0161 368 1488; obile - 0860 540870. VAT: Stan/Spec.

KNUTSFORD

Arts and Antiques Centre

113 King St. WA16 6EH. (David and Patricia McLeod). Est. 1995. Open 10-5.30, Sun. 12-5.30. CL: Mon. SIZE: 20+ dealers plus contemporary art gallery. *STOCK: Furniture, 18th C, £100-£2,000; pine, £200-£600; ceramics and collectables, £10-£300; clocks, 18th C, £300-£2,000; radios, £30-£1,000; costume jewellery, £5-£1,000.* LOC: Main street, 5 minutes from junction 19, M6. PARK: Easy. TEL: 01565 654092. SER: Valuations; restorations (ceramics).

B.R.M. Coins

3 Minshull St. WA16 6HG. (Brian Butterworth). Est. 1968. Open 10-5, Sat. 10-1. SIZE: Small. *STOCK: Coins, medals and banknotes, worldwide, BC to date, from 5p; money boxes, scales and weights.* LOC: A50. PARK: Nearby. TEL: 01565 651480; home - 01606 74522. SER: Valuations; buys at auction (as stock).

Cranford Clocks

at Arts and Antiques Centre, 113 King St. WA16 6EH. (Mr and Mrs M.E. Uppink). Est. 1988. Open Tues.-Sun. 10-5.30. SIZE: Small. *STOCK: Clocks, 1800-1920, £200-£3,000; small furniture.* LOC: Off M6, junction 19. PARK: Nearby. TEL: 01565 633331. SER: Valuations; restorations (clock movements).

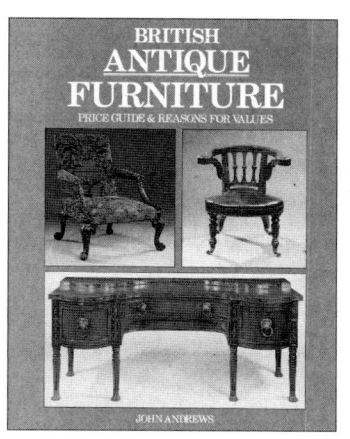

Knutsford continued

Cranford Galleries
10 King St. WA16 6DL. (M.R. Bentley). Est. 1964. Open 11-5. CL: Wed. SIZE: Small. *STOCK: Pictures, prints and Victoriana.* Not Stocked: Glass. LOC: Main St. PARK: Easy. TEL: 01565 633646. SER: Framing and mounting. VAT: Stan.

Glynn Interiors
92 King St. WA16 6ED. Est. 1963. Open 9-1 and 2-5. CL: Wed. SIZE: Large. *STOCK: Furniture, 1750-1900, £50-£2,000; Victorian chairs, £50-£650.* Not Stocked: Porcelain. LOC: 10 mins. drive after leaving M6 at Exit 19. PARK: Own. TEL: 01565 634418. SER: Restorations (re-upholstery) and cabinet repairs. VAT: Stan/Spec.

Lion Gallery and Bookshop
15a Minshull St. WA16 6HG. (R.P. Hepner). Est. 1964. Open Fri. 10.30-4.30, Sat. 10-4.30. *STOCK: Antiquarian maps, prints and books, watercolours and oils, 16th-20th C; O.S. maps and early directories.* LOC: King St. 3 mins. M6. PARK: Nearby. TEL: 01565 652915; mobile - 0850 270796; fax - 01565 750142. SER: Restorations; binding, cleaning, framing and mounting. VAT: Stan.

LITTLETON, Nr. Chester

John Titchner and Sons LAPADA
Littleton Old Hall, Little Heath Rd. CH3 7DW. Open 9-5. CL: Sat. *STOCK: Furniture, 18th-19th C.* TEL: 01244 336986.

MACCLESFIELD

Gatehouse Antiques
72 Chestergate. (W.H. Livesley). Est. 1973. Open 9-5. CL: Sun. except by appointment and Wed. pm. *STOCK: Small furniture, silver and plate, glass, brass, copper, pewter, jewellery, 1650-1880.* PARK: At rear. TEL: 01625 426476; home - 01625 612841.

Hidden Gem
1,3,5 and 7 Chester Rd. SK10 5SY. (Mrs P. Tilley). Usually open 11-5 or by appointment. *STOCK: Victorian paintings and general antiques.* TEL: Home - 01625 828348.

Hills Antiques
Indoor Market, Grosvenor Centre. SK11 6SY. (D. Hill). Est. 1968. Open 9.30-5.30. *STOCK: Small furniture, jewellery, collectors' items, stamps, coins, postcards.* LOC: Town Centre. PARK: Easy. TEL: 01625 420777/420467.

D.J. Massey and Son
47 Chestergate. SK11 6QQ. Est. 1900. Open 9-5.30. *STOCK: Jewellery, gold and diamonds, all periods.* TEL: 01625 616133.

MARPLE BRIDGE, Nr. Stockport

The Mulberry Bush
20 Town St. SK6 5AA. (David M. Brookes). Est 1983. Open 9-5, Wed 9-1. SIZE: Small. *STOCK: Furniture, 18th-20th C, £50-£1,000; ceramics, collectables, 19th-20th C, £5-£500.* LOC: By the river on New Mills road, just off A626. PARK: Easy. TEL: 0161 427 8825; home - same. SER: Valuations; buys at auction.

MELLOR, Nr. Stockport

Town House Antiques
Cold Wall Farm, Cobden Edge. (Paul Buxcey). Usually open, prior telephone call essential. *STOCK: Furniture including decorative; associated items.* TEL: 0161 427 1343.

MOBBERLEY

David Bedale
WA16 7HR. Est. 1977. By appointment. SIZE: Medium. *STOCK: 18th-19th C furniture, unusual and decorative items.* TEL: 01565 872270. VAT: Stan/Spec.

NANTWICH

Adams Antiques LAPADA
Weaver House, 57 Welsh Row. CW5 5EW. (Sandi Summers). Resident. Est. 1975. Open 10-5 or by appointment. SIZE: Large. *STOCK: Mainly oak country furniture, dressers, corner cupboards, tables and chairs; bureaux, longcase clocks, paintings for investment and interior decoration; Mason's Ironstone and Staffordshire figures.* LOC: Chester road out of Nantwich. PARK: Easy. TEL: 01270 625643; fax - same; mobile - 0468 622980. SER: Valuations. FAIRS: LAPADA; NEC; Harrogate. VAT: Stan/Spec.

Tim Armitage
99 Welsh Row. CW5 5ET. (T.J. Armitage). Est. 1967. Open by appointment. SIZE: Small. *STOCK: Tin toys, steam models and early advertising.* LOC: Main road into town from Chester. PARK: Easy. TEL: 01270 626608; home - same. SER: Valuations; buys at auction (toys and models).

Rex Boyer Antiques LAPADA
Townwell House, 52 Welsh Row. CW5 5E[illegible]. Resident. Est. 1958. Open 9-5.30. SIZE: Large. *STOCK: 17th-19th C oak, mahogany and walnut furniture.* LOC: Main Chester road. PARK: Easy. TEL: 01270 625953. VAT: Stan/Spec.

Chapel Antiques
47 Hospital St. CW5 5RL. (Miss D.J. Atkin). Est. 1983. Open 9.30-5.30, Wed. 9.30-1, or by appointment. CL: Mon. SIZE: Medium. *STOCK: Oak, mahogany and pine furniture, Georgian and*

Nantwich continued

Victorian, £100-£3,000; longcase clocks, pre-1830, £1,000-£3,000; copper, brass, silver, glass, porcelain, pottery and small items, 19th C, £10-£500. LOC: Enter town via Pillory St., turn right nto Hospital St. PARK: Easy. TEL: 01270 529508; home - 01270 811437. SER: Valuations; estorations (furniture, clocks).

Roderick Gibson

70-72 Hospital St. CW5 5RP. Open 9-5, Thurs. 9-7. *STOCK: Furniture and decorative collectors' pieces.* TEL: 01270 625301. VAT: Stan/Global.

Lions and Unicorns

Kiltearn House, 33 Hospital St. CW5 5RL. (J. Pearson). Open by appointment. SIZE: Small. *STOCK: Commemoratives - pottery, porcelain, extiles, glass, tins, metals, books and postcards, 5-£350.* LOC: Town centre, near church. PARK: Easy. TEL: 01270 628892/613830; fax - 01270 624666. SER: Buys at auction; catalogue issued nd constantly updated; parcel post worldwide.

Love Lane Antiques

Love Lane. CW5 5BH. (M. Simon). Open 10-5. CL: Wed. SIZE: Small. *STOCK: General antiques, 19th-20th C, £5-£500.* LOC: Two minutes walk rom town square. PARK: Nearby. TEL: 01270 626239.

Nantwich Art Deco and Decorative Arts

7 Welsh Row. CW5 5ET. (M. J. Poole and P. M. avill). Est. 1987. Open Thurs.-Sat. 10-5. SIZE: mall. *STOCK: Art Deco and decorative arts, pottery, china, cabinets, £5-£250.* PARK: Easy. TEL: 01270 624876; home - 01270 811541. FAIRS: Loughborough Art Deco; Birmingham 'Wednesday' Rag Market Fair; Alexandra Palace; Warwick and Chester Art Deco.

Pillory House

8 Pillory St. CW5 5BD. (D. Roberts). Est. 1968. Open 9-5. CL: Wed. *STOCK: Hand-carved chimney pieces and oak.* TEL: 01270 623524.

Richardson Antiques

Victoria Warehouse, Pall Mall. CW5 5RU. (Terry Richardson). Est. 1981. Open daily, Sun. by appointment. SIZE: Medium. *STOCK: Furniture, collectables and china.* PARK: Opposite. TEL: 01270 625963; home - 01270 628348. SER: Valuations; restorations (cleaning oil paintings, cabinet making, French polishing, upholstery, clocks).

Wyche House Antiques

Est. 1976. Open by appointment only. SIZE: Medium. *STOCK: 18th-19th C oak and mahogany furniture, china, brass, copper.* TEL: 01270 628474; mobile - 0374 831698. SER: Valuations.

PLUMLEY

Coppelia Antiques

Holford Lodge, Plumley Moor Rd. WA16 9RS. (V. and R. Clements). Resident. Est. 1970. Open every day by appointment. SIZE: Medium. *STOCK: Over 500 clocks (mainly longcase and wall, £1,000-£30,000); tables - Georgian mahogany, wine, oak gateleg and side; bureaux, desks, chests of drawers, lowboys, coffers, Victorian suites.* LOC: 4 miles junction 19, M6. PARK: Easy. TEL: 01565 722197; fax - 01565 722744. SER: Valuations. FAIRS: Buxton (May). VAT: Spec.

POYNTON, Nr. Stockport

Harper Fine Paintings

"Overdale", Woodford Rd. SK12 1ED. (P.R. Harper). Est. 1967. Open by appointment. SIZE: Large. *STOCK: Watercolours, £100-£35,000; oils including European, £250-£60,000; prints, British, £20-£1,000; all mainly 19th-20th C.* LOC: From A523 centre of Poynton lights, turn into Chester Rd., over railway. After ¼ mile turn right, 1st drive on left after railway bridge. PARK: Easy. TEL: 01625 879105; home - same. SER: Valuations; restorations; buys at auction (as stock). VAT: Stan/Spec.

Poynton continued

Recollections

73 Park Lane. SK12 1RD. (Angela Smith). Open 10-5. SIZE: Medium. *STOCK: Decorative collectables, small furniture, waxed pine, old costume jewellery and amber and antique linens.* PARK: Easy - Civic Centre (free). TEL: 01625 859373.

PRESTBURY, Nr. Macclesfield

Prestbury Antiques

The Spindle, Rear of The White House, The Village. SK11 4DG. (P. Ginsberg). Open 10-5 seven days. *STOCK: Furniture, pictures, silver, glass ceramics, decorative items and collectables, 18th-20th C.* TEL: 01625 827966. VAT: Stan/Spec.

RAVENSMOOR, Nr. Nantwich

Antiques and Curios

Swanley Lane. CW5 8PZ. (Mrs R.A. Booth). Resident. Est. 1971. SIZE: Small. *STOCK: Furniture including country pine and oak; copper brass, iron and china, 18th-19th C, £50-£10,000.* PARK: Easy. TEL: 01270 624774; home - same. SER: Restorations (pine stripping). FAIRS: Nantwich.

RINGWAY, Nr. Altrincham

Cottage Antiques

Hasty Lane. WA15 8UT. (J. and J. M. Gholam). Est. 1967. SIZE: Medium. *STOCK: Furniture, metalware, ceramics, glass, early 18th-mid 19th C.* Not Stocked: Jewellery, jade and ivory. LOC: Off junction 6, M56, off A538, very close to airport. PARK: Easy. TEL: 0161 980 7961. SER: Valuations.

SIDDINGTON, Nr. Macclesfield

G. Bagshaw Antiques

The Old Smithy, Capesthorne Hall Estate Yard. SK11 9JX. Est. 1971. Open 10-5.30. SIZE: Small. *STOCK: General antiques.* LOC: On A34 Congleton Road, near Monks Heath. PARK: Easy. TEL: 01625 860909. SER: Valuations; restorations (ceramics, clock dials re-painted, paintings and prints); ceramic restoration course (postal and residential).

STOCKPORT

Antique Furniture Warehouse

Units 3/4 Royal Oak Buildings, Cooper St. SK1 3QJ. Open 9.30-5.30. SIZE: Large. *STOCK: English and Continental furniture, paintings, bronzes, clocks, shipping goods, Art Deco, pottery, porcelain and curios, decorative items, architectural, radios and televisions, silver and silver plate.* LOC: 2 mins. off M56 towards town centre. PARK: Easy. TEL: 0161 429 8590. VAT: Stan.

Stockport continued

Antiques Import Export UK
Hole in the Wall Antique Warehouse, Hadfield House, Lancashire Hill. SK4 1RR. Open 10-5.30. SIZE: Large. *STOCK: Victorian and Edwardian mahogany, to £1,000.* PARK: Easy. TEL: 0161 476 4013; fax - 0161 477 2684. SER: Valuations; restorations. FAIRS: Newark.

E. R. Antiques Centre
122 Wellington St., off Wellington Rd. South. SK1 1YH. (E. Warburton). Est. 1979. Open 12-5.30. SIZE: Medium - 6 dealers. *STOCK: Victorian and cut glass, perfume bottles, blue and white china, pottery, curios, jewellery, pictures, linen, £5-£200.* LOC: Turn into Edwards St. by the Town Hall, at 'T' junction turn left, shop 500yds. on left at bollards. PARK: Easy. TEL: 0161 429 6646; home - 0161 480 5598.

Flintlock Antiques
28 and 30 Bramhall Lane. SK2 6HR. (F. Tomlinson and Son). Est. 1968. SIZE: Large. *STOCK: Furniture, clocks, pictures, scientific instruments.* TEL: 0161 480 9973. VAT: Stan/Spec.

Halcyon Antiques
435/437 Buxton Rd., Great Moor. SK2 7HE. (Mrs Jill A. Coppock). Est. 1980. Open 10-5. SIZE: Large. *STOCK: Porcelain and glass, 1750-1940, £1-£5,000; furniture, 1750-1940, £50-£2,000; jewellery, silver and plate, linen and lace.* LOC: A6, 2 miles south of town. PARK: Easy. TEL: 0161 483 5038; home - 0161 439 3524. SER: Valuations.

Highland Antiques
7 Wellington Rd. North. SK4 2LP. (E. Todd). Est. 1970. SIZE: Medium. *STOCK: Silver and plate; Chinese and Japanese pottery, porcelain and furniture, 18th-19th C.* LOC: A6. PARK: Easy. TEL: 0161 476 6660; fax - 0161 476 6669. SER: Valuations; restorations; buys at auction. FAIRS: Manchester. VAT: Stan/Spec.

Hole in the Wall Antiques
370 Buxton Rd., Great Moor. SK2 7BY; warehouse Hadfield House, Lancashire Hill. SK4 1RR. (M. and A. Ledger). Est. 1960. Open 10-5, Sun. by appointment. SIZE: Large. *STOCK: Furniture, 18th-20th C, pine, smalls, £50-£5,000.* LOC: A6. PARK: Easy. TEL: 0161 483 6603; warehouse - 0161 476 4013. SER: Restorations; import and export; courier.

Imperial Antiques LAPADA
295 Buxton Rd., Great Moor. SK2 7NR. (A. Todd). Est. 1972. Open 10-5.30, Sun. by appointment. SIZE: Large. *STOCK: Silver and plate, 19th-20th C; porcelain especially Japanese and Chinese, 18th-19th C; both £10-£1,000.* LOC: 296 Buxton Rd., 1.5 miles south of town centre. PARK: Easy. TEL: 0161 483 3322; home - 0161 428 4152. SER: Buys at auction (as stock). VAT: Stan/Spec.

Stockport continued

Limited Editions
35 King St. East. SK1 1XJ. (C.W. Fogg). Est. 1978. Open 9.45-6, Sat. 9.30-5.30. CL: Thurs. except by appointment. SIZE: Large. *STOCK: Furniture, 19th C, especially dining tables and chairs, £100-£1,000; arm chairs and couches for re-upholstery.* LOC: Off Warren St., next to Sainsbury's. PARK: Own at rear. TEL: 0161 480 1239; workshops - 0161 474 7255. SER: Valuations; restorations (furniture). VAT: Stan/Spec.

Nostalgia Architectural Antiques
Holland's Mill, Shaw Heath. SK3 8BH. (D. and E. Durrant). Est. 1975. Open 10-6, Sat. 10-5. CL: Mon. SIZE: Large. *STOCK: Fireplaces, £200-£15,000; bathroom fittings and architectural items, £50-£2,000; all 18th-19th C.* PARK: At rear. TEL: 0161 477 7706; fax - 0161 477 2267. SER: Valuations. VAT: Stan/Spec.

Oak Room
(Nigel Pitceathly). Open by appointment. *STOCK: Oak and country furniture including primitive, 16th-19th C.* TEL: 0161 432 5976; mobile - 0831 476316.

Page Antiques
424 Buxton Rd., Great Moor. SK2 7JQ. Open Mon.-Sat. SIZE: Large. *STOCK: Georgian to Edwardian furniture, brass, copper, silver, plate, stripped pine especially for Australian and German markets.* LOC: A6. TEL: 0161 483 9202; home - 01663 732358. SER: Courier. VAT: Stan/Spec.

STOCKTON HEATH, Nr. Warrington

Victoriana Antiques
85a Walton Rd. WA4 6NW. (Mrs J. Taylor). Est. 1976. Open 1-5 or by appointment. CL: Mon. and Thurs. SIZE: Small. *STOCK: Furnishings, to 1930, £50-£2,800; metalware and fireside furniture, to 1910, £30-£800; antique and decorative lighting, to 1930, £15-£500.* LOC: A56 towards Chester, 400yds. from village centre. PARK: Own. TEL: Mobile - 0370 454443; home - 01925 261035. SER: Valuations; restorations (furniture, metalware). FAIRS: Cumberland Hotel and Deanwater Hotel, Wilmslow (monthly).

STRETTON, Nr. Warrington

Antiques Etc.
Shepcroft House, London Rd. WA4 5PJ. (Mr M. Clare). Est. 1978. Resident, usually available. SIZE: Medium. *STOCK: Furniture, pine, barometers, clocks, instruments and items of interest, £5-£2,000.* LOC: A49, towards Warrington, through Stretton traffic lights, next turning on left. PARK: Easy. TEL: 01925 730431; mobile - 0836 570663.

TARPORLEY

Marie José Burke
The Pavillion, High St. CW6 0DX. ADA. Est. 1959. Open 10-5, appointment advisable. CL: Sat. STOCK: Period English furniture. VAT: Spec.

Maria Hopwood Antiques
Hulgrave Hall, Tiverton. CW6 9UQ. Resident. Est. 1992. Open daily including Sun. SIZE: Medium. STOCK: Pine and country furniture, rural bygones, sporting goods and architectural antiques, kitchenalia and domestic paraphernalia, from 1750, £1-£2,000. LOC: A49 south from Tarporley, 1 mile from Beeston market. PARK: Own. TEL: 01829 732427; home - 01829 733313; mobile - 0831 246151; fax - 01829 733802. SER: Valuations; restorations (furniture).

Milestone Antiques
67 High St. CW6 0DP. (D. Perry). Open 10-5. STOCK: General antiques and reproduction. TEL: 01829 733026.

Tarporley Antique Centre
76 High St. Open 10-5, Sun. 11-4. SIZE: 9 dealers on two floors. STOCK: Furniture, ceramics, commemoratives, treen, Studio pottery, glass, oils, watercolours, prints, framing, etc. LOC: Main road, near Crown public house. PARK: In front of premises and opposite. TEL: 01829 733919. SER: Framing; caning; buys at auction.

TARVIN, Nr. Chester

Antique Fireplaces
The Manor House, Church St. (Mrs G. O'Toole). Est. 1979. Open Fri., Sat. and Sun. 10-5 or by appointment. SIZE: Medium. STOCK: Fireplaces and ranges, 18th-19th C, £150-£3,000. LOC: At junction of A556 and A51. PARK: Easy. TEL: 01829 740936; home - 01606 46717. SER: Valuations; restorations; installations (fireplaces and ranges); new tiles and fenders ordered from suppliers on request. FAIRS: Tatton Park, Knutsford.

TARVIN SANDS, Nr. Chester

Cheshire Brick and Slate Co
Brook House Farm, Salters Bridge. CH3 8HL. (Malcolm Youde). Est. 1978. Open 8-5.30, Sat. 8-4.30, Sun. 10-4. SIZE: Large. STOCK: Reclaimed conservation building materials, 16th-20th C; architectural antiques - garden statuary, stonework, lamp posts, gates, fireplaces, bathroom suites, chimney pots and ironwork, 18th-20th C, £50-£1,000; furniture, pews, leaded lights, pottery, 18th-20th C, £5-£1,000. LOC: Directly off A54 just outside Tarvin. PARK: Own. TEL: 01829 740883. SER: Valuations; restorations (fireplaces, timber treatment); building/construction and demolition; renovations. VAT: Stan.

TATTENHALL, Nr. Chester

The Great Northern Architectural Antique Company Ltd
New Russia Hall, Chester Rd. CH3 9AH. Open 9.30-4.30 including Sun. SIZE: Large. STOCK. Period doors, fire surrounds, stained glass, sanitary ware, garden statuary, furniture and curios. LOC: Off A41. PARK: Easy. TEL: 0182● 770796; fax - 01829 770971. VAT: Stan.

TILSTON, Nr. Malpas

Well House Antiques
The Well House. SY14 7DP. (S. French Greenslade). Est. 1968. Open by appointment only. SIZE: Small. STOCK: Collectors' items china, glass, silver. LOC: From Whitchurch or A41, take B5395 signposted Malpas. PARK Easy. TEL: 01829 250332.

WARRINGTON

A. Baker and Sons
10 Cairo St. WA1 1ED. (A.R. Baker). NAG. Est 1907. Open 9.30-5, Sat. 9.30-4. SIZE: Small STOCK: Silver and jewellery, 18th-20th C, from £100. LOC: Off M6, junction 9, take A50 into town Cairo St. off Sankey St. between Co-op and Barclay Bank. PARK: Easy. TEL: 01925 633706; fax - same SER: Valuations; restorations (as stock). VAT: Stan.

The Rocking Chair Antiques
Unit 3, St. Peter's Way. WA2 7BL. (N., M. and J Barratt). Est. 1971. Open 9-5.30. SIZE: Large STOCK: Furniture and bric-a-brac. LOC: O● Orford Lane. PARK: Easy. TEL: 01925 65240● fax - same; mobile - 0374 492891. SER: Valu ations; shipping; packing. VAT: Stan.

WAVERTON

J. Alan Hulme
Antique Maps & Old Prints, 52 Mount Way. CH 7QF. Open Mon.-Sat. by appointment. STOCK Maps, 16th-19th C; prints, 18th-19th C. TEL 01244 336472.

WILMSLOW

Peter Bosson Antiques
10B Swan St. SK9 1HE. Est. 1965. Open 10-12.● and 2.15-5, or by appointment. CL: Mon. and We● SIZE: Small. STOCK: Clocks, 1675-1900, £● £2,000; barometers, unusual items. Not Stocke● Porcelain, silver. LOC: On A34. PARK: 50yd● away. TEL: 01625 525250; home - 01625 52785 SER: Restorations (clock repair); buys at auction.

Celebrations Past and Present
59 Chapel Lane. SK9 5JH. (S. Fisher). Est. 197● Open 9.30-5.30, Sun. 9.30-1. SIZE: Mediu● STOCK: General small antiques including glass a● pottery. LOC: From Manchester - past town cent● on Knutsford road, Chapel Lane second righ● PARK: Easy. TEL: 01625 548061. SER: Valuation●

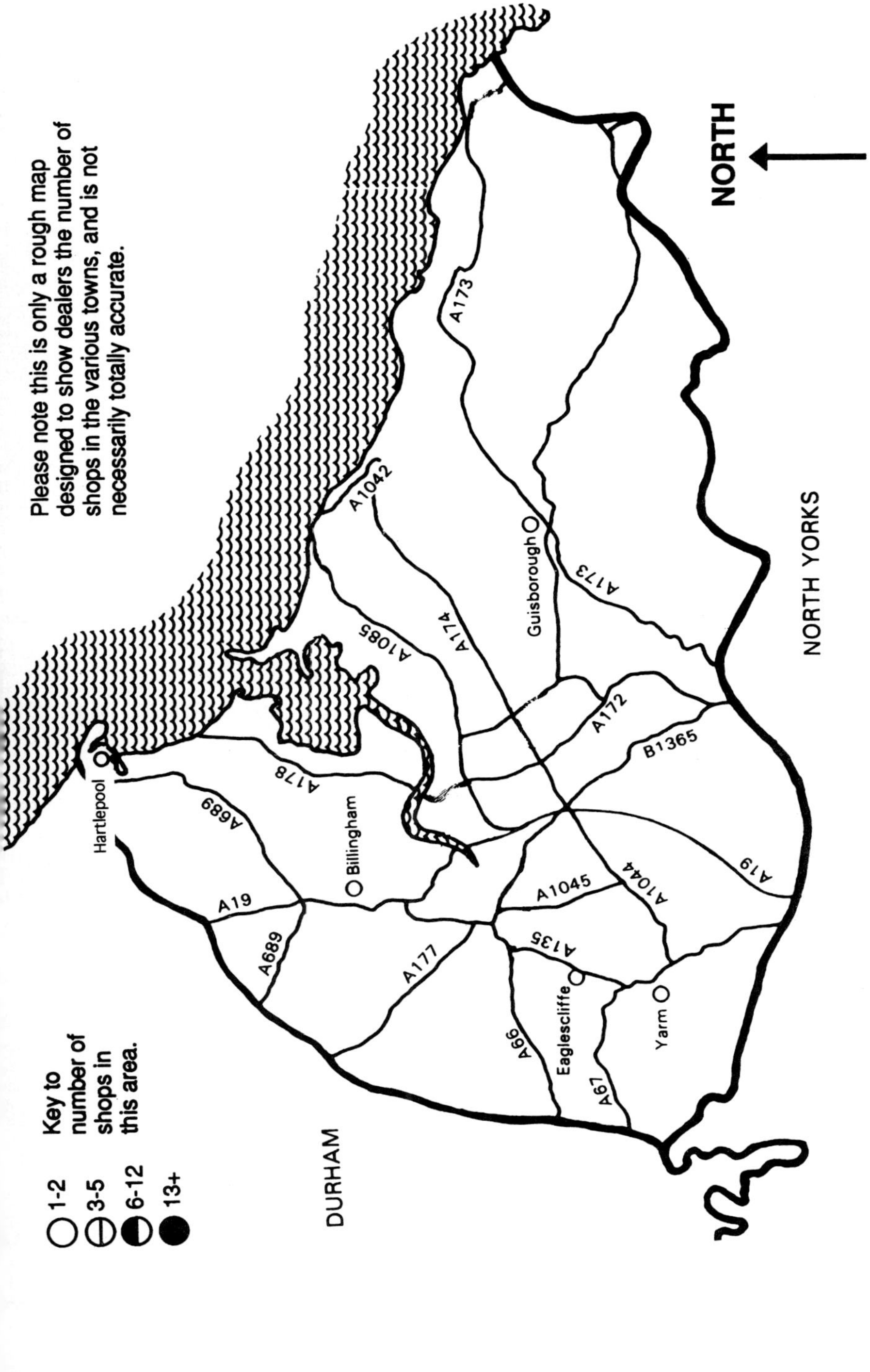
Please note this is only a rough map designed to show dealers the number of shops in the various towns, and is not necessarily totally accurate.
NORTH
NORTH YORKS
DURHAM
Key to number of shops in this area.
1-2
3-5
6-12
13+
Hartlepool
Billingham
Guisborough
Eaglescliffe
Yarm
A19
A66
A67
A135
A177
A689
A178
A1045
A1044
A1085
A174
A172
B1365
A173
A1042

BILLINGHAM

Margaret Bedi Antiques LAPADA
5 Station Rd. TS23 1AG. Est. 1976. Open by appointment. ***STOCK: Mainly English period furniture, 1720-1920; oils and watercolours, 19th-20th C.*** **LOC: 300yds. off A19, by village green. PARK: Easy. TEL: 01642 782346; mobile - 0860 577637. VAT: Stan/Spec.**

EAGLESCLIFFE, Nr. Stockton-on-Tees

T.B. and R. Jordan (Fine Paintings) LAPADA
Aslak. TS16 0QN. Est. 1974. Open by appointment. ***STOCK: Oil paintings and watercolours, 19th-20th C, £200-£5,000.*** **LOC: Village centre. PARK: Easy. TEL: 01642 782599; fax - 01642 780473. SER: Framing; restorations; commissions. VAT: Spec.**

GUISBOROUGH

Atrium Antiques
(W.L. and M.G. Richardson). Est. 1967. Open by appointment. *STOCK: Furniture, silver, pottery, jewellery, clocks, general items.* PARK: Easy. TEL: 01287 632777.

HARTLEPOOL

Antique Fireplace Centre
Units, 6, 7 & 8 Newburn Bridge Industrial Estate. TS24 7AH. (D.J. Crowther). Est. 1983. Open 9-5. CL: Wed. SIZE: Large. *STOCK: Victorian and Edwardian fireplaces, Victorian 4-panel pine doors, architectural antiques.* TEL: 01429 279007/222433; mobile - 0374 639754.

YARM

Ruby Snowden Antiques
20 High St. TS15 9AE. (R.H. Snowden). Est. 1977. Open 9-5.30, Wed. 9-5, Sun. by appointment. SIZE: Medium. *STOCK: Furniture, 1700-1930s, £50-£2,000; porcelain and Staffordshire, £5-£200; jewellery, silver, glass, copper and brass.* LOC: Opposite library. PARK: Easy. TEL: 01642 785363; home - 01642 819918. SER: Valuations. VAT: Stan/Spec.

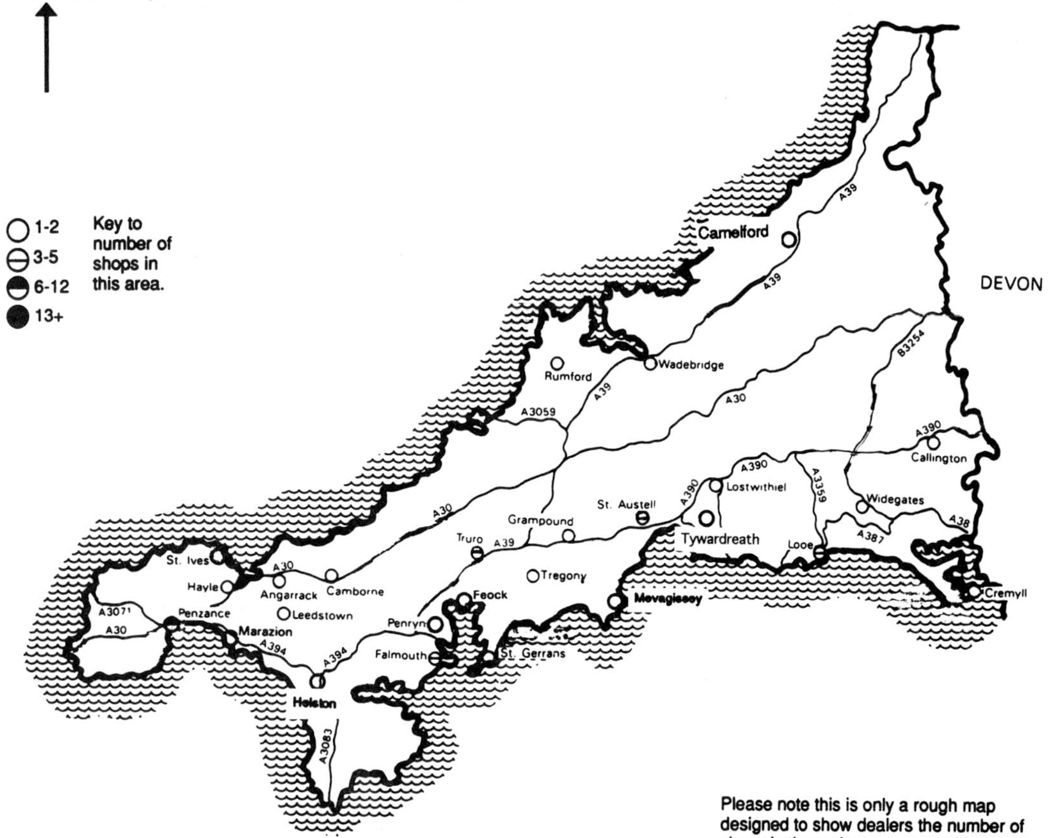

Please note this is only a rough map designed to show dealers the number of shops in the various towns, and is not necessarily totally accurate.

ANGARRACK, Nr. Hayle

Paul Jennings Antiques

Millbrook House. TR27 5HY. Est. 1974. Open by appointment. SIZE: Small. *STOCK: Clocks, furniture, £100-£3,000.* LOC: ½ mile from A30. TEL: 01736 754065. VAT: Stan/Spec. *Trade Only.*

BOSCASTLE

Newlyfe Antiques

The Old Mill. PL35 0AQ. (Harry Ruddy). Open seven days a week May-Sept. - prior phone call advisable at other times. *STOCK: Collectables, small furniture, French beds.* TEL: 01840 250230.

Old Mill Antiques

PL35 0AQ. (B. Hedges). Open seven days a week May-Sept. - prior phone call advisable at other times. *STOCK: Collectables, small furniture, French beds.* TEL: 01840 250230.

CALLINGTON

Country Living Antiques

Weston House, Haye Rd. PL17 7JJ. (Ian Baxter). Resident. Est. 1990. Open 10-6. SIZE: Large - incl. barn. *STOCK: 19th C oak and pine country furniture, general antiques, £1-£2,000.* LOC: Town centre. PARK: Own car park. TEL: 01579 382245; fax - same. SER: Valuations; buys at auction. FAIRS: China Fleet Club (quarterly); Liskeard (monthly).

CAMBORNE

Victoria Gallery

28 Cross St. TR14 8EX. (J.P. Maker). Open Mon. 1-5.15, Tues., Wed., Fri. 11-5.15, other times by appointment. CL: Thurs. and Sat. *STOCK: Books, pictures, general antiques, furniture, silver and jewellery.* TEL: 01209 719268.

CAMELFORD

Bridge Antiques

1 Market Place. PL32 9PB. (Paul Smith). Open 10-5, Sat. 10-1. CL: Mon. SIZE: Small. *STOCK: Brown furniture, 18th-20th C, £100-£2,000; china, glass and metalware, 18th-20th C, £20-£500; watercolours and prints, 19th-20th C, £20-£200.* LOC: Town centre, on A39. PARK: Free, 1 minute walk. TEL: 01840 213701 (24 hrs). SER: Valuations; restorations (furniture); French polishing. FAIRS: Ardingly, Westpoint, Newark.

CREMYLL

Cremyll Antiques

The Cottage, Cremyll Beach, Torpoint. PL10 1HX. *STOCK: Clocks and watches, small items, jewellery.* TEL: 01752 823490. SER: Repairs (barometers, barographs, watches, clocks, jewellery).

FALMOUTH

E. Cunningham Antiques

5 Webber St. Open 10.30-5.30. *STOCK: Genera antiques.* TEL: 01326 313207.

John Maggs

54 Church St. TR11 3DS. (C.C. Nunn). Est. 1900 Open 10-5. SIZE: Medium. *STOCK: Antiquaria prints and maps, exclusive limited editions.* LOC Main street. PARK: At rear of shop. TEL: 0132 313153; fax - same. SER: Restorations; framing binding.

Rosina's

4 High St. TR11 2AB. (Mrs R. Gealer). Open 11 4.30. *STOCK: Old dolls, bears, incl. limite edition, Steiff and artist bears, toys, linen and lace clothes; modern miniatures.* TEL: 01326 31140 home - 01326 317739. SER: Restorations.

Waterfront Antiques Market

1st Floor, 4 Quay St. Open 10-5. SIZE: 20 dealer *STOCK: Furniture, pottery, porcelain, glass silver, metalware, kitchenalia, pictures, book clocks, jewellery, decorative and collectors' item* TEL: 01326 311491.

FEOCK, Nr. Truro

Strickland and Dorling

Come-to-Good. TR3 6QS. (P. Strickland and Dorling). Est. 1950's. Usually open. *STOCK Small furniture, pottery, porcelain, silve pictures, maps of Cornwall, bijouterie an collectors' items.* TEL: 01872 862394.

GRAMPOUND, Nr. Truro

Pine and Period Furniture

Fore St. TR2 4QT. (S. Payne). Open 10-5. Cl Sat. *STOCK: Pine and period furniture.* TEI 01726 883117.

Radnor House

Fore St. TR2 4QT. (P. and G. Hodgson). Es 1972. Open 10-5. SIZE: Medium. *STOCK Furniture and accessories, pre-1900.* N Stocked: Jewellery, coins and weapons. LO A390. PARK: Easy. TEL: 01726 882921; home same. SER: Valuations; buys at auction. VA Stan/Spec.

HAYLE

Copperhouse Gallery - W. Dyer & Sons

14 Fore St. TR27 4DX. (A.P. Dyer). Est. 190 Open 9-1 and 2-5.30, Wed. 9-1. SIZE: Mediu *STOCK: Watercolours, some oils, includi Newlyn and St. Ives Schools, 19th to early 20th £25-£1,000.* LOC: Main road. PARK: Easy. TE 01736 752787; home - 01736 753362. SE Restorations (watercolours and oils).

HELSTON

Humphreys Antiques
45 Meneage St. TR1 38RH. (Norman Boyes). SIZE: Medium. *STOCK: General antiques.* TEL: 01326 564286.

LEEDSTOWN, Nr. Hayle

A.W. Glasby and Son Antiques
TR27 6DA. (D.E. Glasby). Est. 1936. Open 10.15-12.45 and 2.15-5. CL: Sat. and Mon. SIZE: Large. *STOCK: Furniture, porcelain and clocks, £10-£5,000.* Not Stocked: Coins, medals, scientific instruments. LOC: On main road half-way between Hayle and Helston. PARK: Easy. TEL: 01736 850303.

LOOE

Dowling and Bray
Fore St. PL13 1AE. Est. 1920. *STOCK: General antiques, furniture, pictures.* TEL: 01503 262797. VAT: Stan.

Looe Antiques
1 Seafront Court, The Quay, East Looe. (Miss G. Jones). Est. 1986. Open daily from 10, Sun. from 12. SIZE: Medium. *STOCK: General antiques and collectors' items, mainly 19th-20th C, £5-£1,000.* PARK: Easy in winter, otherwise nearby car parks. TEL: 01503 265495. SER: Valuations.

Tony Martin
Fore St. PL13 1AE. Est. 1965. Open 9.30-1 and 2-5 appointment advisable. CL: Thurs. pm. SIZE: Medium. *STOCK: Porcelain, 18th C; silver, 18th-19th C, both £20-£200; glass, furniture, oils and watercolours.* LOC: Main street. TEL: 01503 262734; home - 01503 262228. VAT: Stan/Spec.

LOSTWITHIEL

John Bragg Antiques
35 Fore St. PL22 0BN. Open 10-5. *STOCK: Furniture, mainly period mahogany and Victorian.* LOC: 100yds. off A390. TEL: 01208 872827.

Old Palace Antiques
Old Palace, Quay St. PL22 0BS. (D. Bryant). Open 10-1 and 2-5. CL: Wed. pm. *STOCK: Pine, general antiques, postcards and collectors' items.* TEL: 01208 872909.

MARAZION

Antiques
The Shambles, Market Place. TR17 0AR. (Andrew S. Wood). Est. 1988. Open 10-5.30, Sun by appointment. SIZE: Medium. *STOCK: General antiques and collectors' items, especially 19th to early 20th C pottery and porcelain including Staffordshire figures; Victorian and early 20th C decorative and pressed glass; Art Deco ceramics*

Marazion continued

especially Shelley; Goss and crested china, Devon and commemorative ware, postcards and bottles. Not Stocked: Weapons and large furniture. LOC: Main street. PARK: Easy. TEL: 01736 711381; home - same.

MEVAGISSEY, Nr. St. Austell

Granny's Attic
18 Church St. PL26 6SP. (Heather and David Wetzel). Resident. Est. 1988. Open April-Sept. 10-6 including Sun; Oct.-Mar. prior telephone call advisable. SIZE: Small. *STOCK: Collectables, stamps, postcards and militaria, 50p to £50.* LOC: A390. PARK: Adjacent. TEL: 01726 843818; fax - same. SER: Buys at auction.

PENRYN

Duchy Antiques
7 The Praze. TR10 8DH. (Leon Robertson). Est. 1972. *STOCK: Furniture, paintings and general antiques.* TEL: 01326 372767.

West Country Antiques
15 Church Rd. (J.D. Gavin). Open 8.30-6. *STOCK: General antiques.* TEL: 01326 375092.

PENZANCE

Ken Ashbrook Antiques
Leskinnick Place. Est. 1973. Open Wed. 10-1, Thurs. and Fri. 10-1 and 2.15-5, Sat. 10.30-1, other times by appointment. SIZE: Large. *STOCK: Furniture, 18th-20th C, £100-£5,000.* LOC: 1 min. from railway station. PARK: Nearby. TEL: 01736 330914; home - 01736 65477. SER: Valuations; restorations (cabinet work); buys at auction (furniture). VAT: Stan/Spec.

Kishere (Mortlake) pint and quart hunting mugs of about 1800, with silver rims (the pint hall-marked for 1798), heights 5⅛in. and 6⅞in.

From an article entitled "Tavern Mugs" by Robin Hildyard of the Victoria and Albert Museum which appeared in the September 1996 issue of **Antique Collecting**

Penzance continued

James Buchanan Antiques

Captain Cutter's House, 52 Chapel St. Open 10-4.30. *STOCK: Furniture and interesting items, 1700 to modern, including town and country furniture, pictures, metalware, glass, china and rugs.* LOC: Town centre. PARK: Easy. TEL: 01736 756579; mobile - 0421 678826.

Chapel Street Antiques Market

61/62 Chapel St. Open 9.30-5. SIZE: 20 dealers. *STOCK: Furniture, pottery, porcelain, glass, silver, metalware, kitchenalia, pictures, books, clocks, jewellery, decorative and collectors' items.* TEL: 01736 63267.

Daphne's Antiques

17 Chapel St. TR18 4AW. Est. 1976. Open 9-5. SIZE: Medium. *STOCK: Early country and 18th-19th C mahogany furniture, Georgian glass, Delft, pottery and decorative objects.* TEL: 01736 61719.

Brian Humphrys Antiques

1 St. Clare St. TR18 2PB. Est. 1964. SIZE: Medium. *STOCK: Furniture, clocks, silver, jewellery, 18th-19th C, £25-£4,000.* PARK: Easy opposite. TEL: 01736 65154. SER: Valuations; buys at auction. VAT: Stan/Spec.

Little Jem's

Antron House, 55 Chapel St. TR18 5AE. (J. Lagden). Open 9.30-5. *STOCK: Antique and modern jewellery (specialising in opal and amber), gem stones, objets d'art, paintings, clocks and watches.* TEL: 01736 51400. SER: Repairs; commissions.

New Street Books

4 New St. TR18 2LZ. (B.J. Maker). Open 10-5. *STOCK: Books and pictures.* TEL: 01736 62758.

Penzance Antiques and Furnishings

1/2 Old Brewery Yard, Bread St. TR18 2SL. (Catherine Farnes and Nick Everard). Open 10-5. *STOCK: Furniture, textiles, linen and lace, jewellery, clocks, mirrors and lamps, period clothing.* TEL: 01736 51053. SER: Film hire.

Pinewood Studios

46 Market Jew St. (R. Aby). Open 9.30-5.30. *STOCK: Pine furniture.* Not Stocked: Reproductions. TEL: 01736 68793.

Tony Sanders Penzance Gallery and Antiques

14 Chapel St. TR18 4AW. Est. 1972. Open 9-5.30. SIZE: Medium. *STOCK: Oils and watercolours including Newlyn and St. Ives schools, 19th-20th C, £50-£5,000; contemporary paintings and sculpture; glass, silver, china and small furniture.* TEL: 01736 66620/68461. VAT: Stan.

RUMFORD

Henley House Antiques

PL27 7SS. (P. Neale). *STOCK: Juvenilia, small antiques, bric-a-brac.* TEL: 01841 540322.

ST. AUSTELL

Ancient and Modern

32-34 Polkyth Rd. PL25 4LW. (P.J. Watts). Est. 1965. Open 10-5. *STOCK: General antiques, paintings, clocks, jewellery, bric-a-brac.* TEL: 01726 73983.

Mrs. Margaret Chesterton

33 Pentewan Rd. PL25 5BU. Est. 1965. Open 10-5.30, appointment advisable. CL: Sat. pm. *STOCK: Victoriana, Edwardiana, 1800-1915, some furniture, porcelain, glass, £1-£500; brass, copper, pewter, jewellery, clocks, watercolours.* LOC: Coming from Plymouth, travel direct to St. Austell. Keep on main by-pass until roundabout for Mevagissey and Pentewan Rd. House is 100yds. on left down this road. PARK: Easy. TEL: 01726 72926.

St. Austell Antiques Centre

37/39 Truro Rd. PL25 5JE. (Roger Nosworthy). Est. 1972. Open 10-5. SIZE: Large - several dealers. *STOCK: Wide range of antiques and collectables.* LOC: Town centre, just off A390. PARK: Easy. TEL: 01726 63178; home - 0128 81548. SER: Valuations; restorations (furniture). VAT: Stan/Spec.

ST. GERRANS, Nr. Portscatho

Turnpike Cottage Antiques and Tearooms

The Square. TR2 5EB. (T. and S. Green). Est. 1988. Open 11-1.30 and 3-6, Sun. and wintertime 3-6. CL: Thurs. SIZE: Medium. *STOCK: General antiques, furniture, porcelain, bric-a-brac, £5-£4,000.* LOC: Near church. PARK: Easy, at rear. TEL: 01872 580853; home - same. SER: Valuations; restorations (furniture, watercolours).

ST. IVES

Mike Read Antique Sciences

"Ayia Napa", Wheal Whidden, Carbis Bay. TR26 2QX. Est. 1974. Open by appointment. SIZE: Small. *STOCK: Scientific instruments - navigational, surveying, mining, barometers, telescopes and microscopes, medical, 18th-19th C, £10-£5,000; maritime works of art and nautical artifacts.* LOC: Turn right at St. Ives end of Carbis Bay, 100yds. on right. PARK: Easy. TEL: 01736 798219; home - same. SER: Valuations; restorations.

TREGONY, Nr. Truro

Clock Tower Antiques

57 Fore St. TR2 5RW. (The Warne Family). Open 10-6, (extended in summer), evenings and Sun. by appointment. SIZE: Medium. *STOCK: Ceramics, including Doulton stoneware, Mason's Ironstone, 19th C blue and white transferware, £10-£500; paintings and prints, 19th to early 20th C, £50-£1,000; furniture, 18th to early 20th C, £75-£3,000; brass, copper and treen, £10-£300.* Not Stocked: Silver and jewellery. LOC: Village centre, B3287. PARK: Easy. TEL: 01872 530225; home - same.

TRURO

Alan Bennett

24 New Bridge St. TR1 2AA. Est. 1954. Open 9-5.30. SIZE: Large. *STOCK: Furniture, £50-£5,000; jewellery and porcelain, to 1900, £5-£1,000; paintings and prints, £20-£2,000.* LOC: Eastern side of cathedral. PARK: 100yds. from shop. TEL: 01872 73296. VAT: Stan/Spec.

Blackwater Pine Antiques

Blackwater. TR4 8ET. (J.S. Terrett). Open 9-6. *STOCK: Pine and country furniture.* TEL: 01872 560919. SER: Restorations; stripping; furniture made to order.

Bric-a-Brac

16A Walsingham Place. TR1 2RP. (Lynne and Richard Bonehill). Est. 1971. SIZE: Small. *STOCK: Militaria, £5-£2,000; small furniture, £20-£1,000; commemorative and crested china, £5-£150; collectors' items and bric-a-brac, 50p-£2,000; all 19th-20th C.* LOC: Town centre, just off Victoria Sq. PARK: Multi-storey nearby. TEL: 01872 225200; home - 01736 793213. SER: Buys at auction. FAIRS: Lostwithiel.

Pydar Antiques and Pine

Peoples Palace, Pydar St. TR1 2AZ. (D. Severn and J. Poole). Est. 1968. Open 10.30-5 and by appointment. SIZE: Medium. *STOCK: Furniture - English 18th and 19th C, £50-£2,500; Victorian and Edwardian, £50-£2,000; pine, £10-£1,500; silver, plate, porcelain, glass, prints and watercolours, £5-£500.* PARK: Easy. TEL: 01872 223516; home - 01872 510485 or 01637 872034.

TYWARDREATH, Nr. Par

Myles Varcoe

Treverran Barton. PL24 2TZ. Est. 1971. Open by appointment only. *STOCK: Pictures, mainly 19th and 20th C marine watercolours and oils, £50-£5,000.* LOC: Telephone for instructions. TEL: 01208 873410; fax - 01208 872956.

WADEBRIDGE

St. Breock Gallery

St. Breock Churchtown. PL27 7JS. (R.G.G. Haslam-Hopwood). Open 10-5. *STOCK: Watercolours, 19th-20th C; furniture, general antiques and objets d'art.* LOC: Near Royal Cornwall Showground. PARK: Own. TEL: 01208 812543; fax - 01208 814671. SER: Restorations; buys at auction.

Victoria Antiques

21 Molesworth St. PL27 7DQ. (M. and S. Daly). Open Mon.-Sat. SIZE: Large. *STOCK: Furniture, 17th-19th C, £25-£10,000.* LOC: On A39 between Bude and Newquay. PARK: Nearby. TEL: 01208 814160. SER: Valuations; restorations.. VAT: Stan/Spec.

WIDEGATES, Nr. Looe

Pink Cottage Antiques

PL13 1QL. (I. and B. Barrett). Est. 1981. Open 9.30-5, Sun 2-4.30, longer hours in summer. SIZE: Medium. *STOCK: Furniture, £50-£2,500; brass and copper, £5-£250; china and glass, £2-£300; oil lamps and clocks; all mainly Victorian and Edwardian, some Georgian.* Not Stocked: Clothing, militaria, jewellery, silver. LOC: A387 from Plymouth, 4 miles before Looe. PARK: At rear. TEL: 01503 240258; home - same. SER: Restorations (furniture).

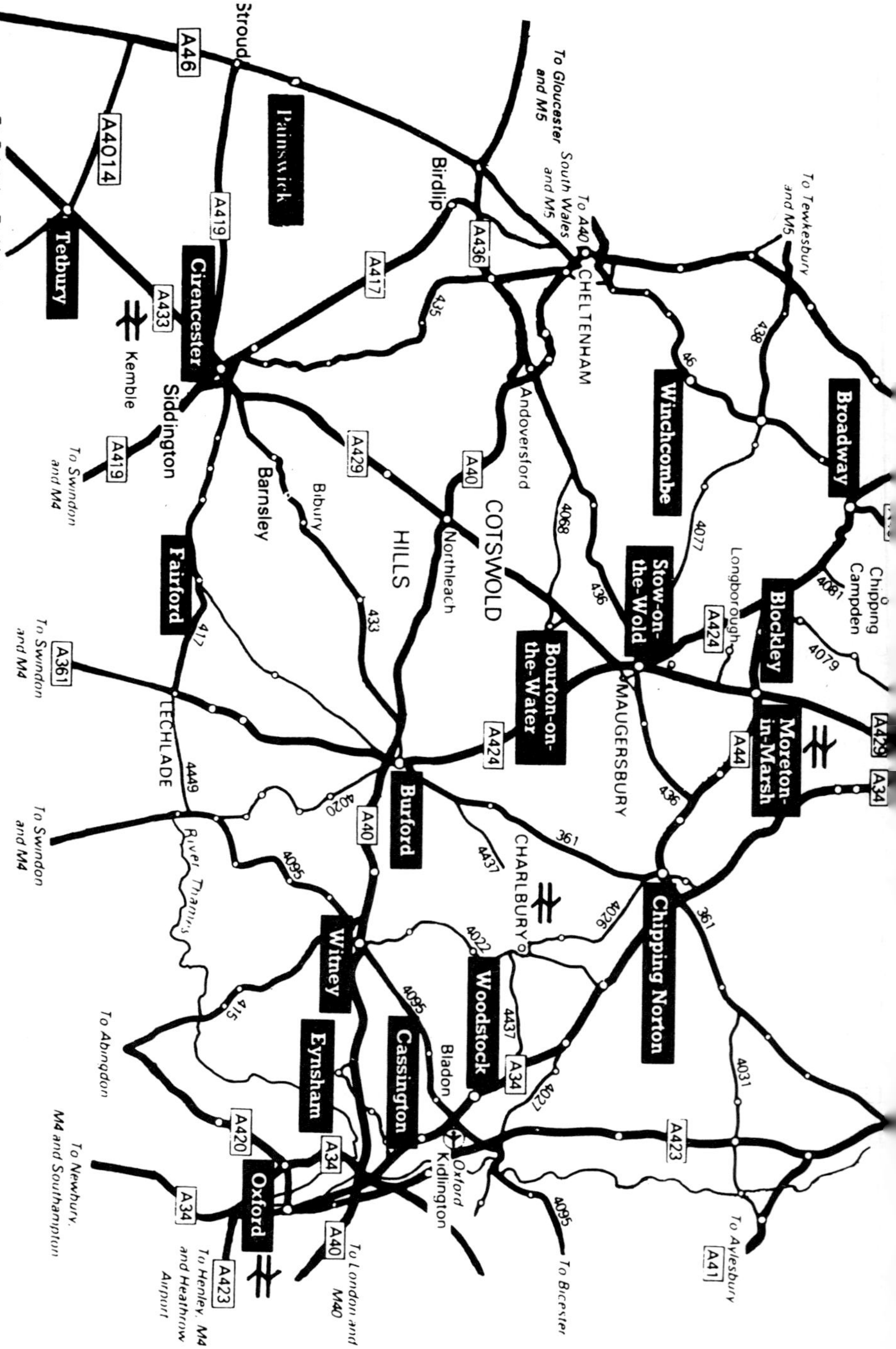

Railway Stations at Oxford, Charlbury, Kemble (for Tetbury, Cirencester), Moreton-in-Marsh (fast trains from London Paddington)

THE COTSWOLD ANTIQUE DEALERS' ASSOCIATION

Buy Fine Antiques and Works of Art at provincial prices in England's lovely and historic countryside

The Cotswolds, one of the finest areas of unspoilt countryside in the land, have been called "the essence and the heart of England." The region has a distinctive character created by the use of honey-coloured stone in its buildings and dry stone walls. Within the locality the towns and villages are admirably compact and close to each other and the area is well supplied with good hotels and reasonably priced inns. The Cotswolds are within easy reach of London (1½ hour by road or rail) and several major airports.

Cotswold sheep – which inspired the logo for the Cotswold Antique Dealers' Association – a quatrefoil device with a sheep in its centre – have played an important part in the region's history with much of its wealth created by the woollen industry. As for antiques, shops and warehouses of the CADA offer a selection of period furniture, pictures, porcelain, metalwork, and collectables unrivalled outside London.

With the use of the CADA directory on the following pages, which lists the names of its members, their specialities and opening times, visitors from all over the world can plan their buying visit to the Cotswolds. CADA members will assist all visiting collectors and dealers in locating antiques and works of art. They will give you advice on where to stay in the area, assistance with packing, shipping and insurance and the exchange of foreign currencies. They can advise private customers on what can realistically be bought on their available budgets, and if the first dealer does not have the piece which you are selecting he will know of several other members who will. The CADA welcomes home and overseas buyers in the certain knowledge that there are at least fifty dealers with a good and varied stock, a reputation for fair trading and an annual turnover in excess of £15,000,000.

BARNSLEY, Nr. Cirencester

Denzil Verey
Barnsley House. GL7 5EE. CADA. Resident. Est. 1980. Open 9.30-5.30, Sat. 10-5.30, other times by appointment. SIZE: Large. *STOCK: Country furniture, including pine, 18th-19th C; brass, country and kitchen bygones, unusual and decorative items.* LOC: 4 miles from Cirencester on B4425 to Burford, 1st large house in village, set back off road on the right. PARK: Easy. TEL: 01285 740402; fax - 01285 740628. VAT: Stan/Spec.

BROADWAY

Fenwick and Fenwick Antiques
88-90 High St. WR12 7AJ. CADA. Est. 1980. Open 10-6, and by appointment. SIZE: Large. *STOCK: Furniture, oak, mahogany and walnut, 17th to early 19th C; samplers, boxes, treen, Tunbridgeware, Delft, decorative items and corkscrews.* TEL: 01386 853227; after hours - 01386 858502; fax - 01386 858504.

H.W. Keil Ltd BADA
Tudor House. WR12 7DP. (V.M. Keil). CADA. Est. 1925. Open 9-5.30. CL: Thurs. pm. SIZE: Large. *STOCK: Walnut, oak, mahogany and rosewood furniture; early pewter, brass and copper, tapestry, glass and works of art, 17th-18th C.* LOC: By village clock. TEL: 01386 852408; fax - 01386 852069. VAT: Spec.

John Noott Galleries BADA LAPADA
14 Cotswold Court, The Green and at The Lygon Arms, High St. WR12 7AA. CADA. Est. 1972. Open 9.30-1 and 2-5, also by appointment only at The Manor House, West End, Broadway. SIZE: Large. *STOCK: Paintings and watercolours, 19th C to Contemporary.* PARK: Easy. TEL: 01386 852787/858969; fax - 01386 858348. SER: Valuations; restorations; framing. VAT: Stan/Spec.

BURFORD

Jonathan Fyson Antiques
50 High St. OX18 4QF. (J.R. Fyson). CADA. Est. 1970. Open 9.30-1 and 2-5.30. SIZE: Medium. *STOCK: English and Continental furniture, decorative brass and steel including lighting and fireplace accessories; papier mâché, tôle, treen, porcelain, glass, jewellery.* LOC: At junction of A40/A361 between Oxford and Cheltenham. PARK: Easy. TEL: 01993 823204; fax - same; home - 01367 860223. SER: Valuations. VAT: Spec.

Burford continued

Gateway Antiques
Cheltenham Rd., Burford Roundabout. OX8 4JA (M.C. Ford and P. Brown). CADA. Est. 1986 Open 10-5.30 and Sun. pm. SIZE: Large. *STOCK English and Continental furniture, 18th-19th C, decorative accessories.* LOC: On roundabou (A40) Oxford/Cheltenham road. PARK: Easy TEL: 01993 823678. SER: Valuations. VAT Stan/Spec.

David Pickup BADA
115 High St. OX18 4RG. CADA. Est. 1977 Open 9.30-1 and 2-5.30, Sat. 10-1 and 2-4 SIZE: Medium. *STOCK: Fine furniture, from £1,000+; works of art, £500-£10,000; decorative objects, from £100+; all late 17th-19th C* PARK: Easy. TEL: 01993 822555. FAIRS New York International; BADA. VAT: Spec.

Richard Purdon BADA
158 High St. OX18 4QY. CADA. Open 9.30 5.30. SIZE: Medium. *STOCK: Antique Eastern and European carpets, village and tribal rugs needlework, textiles and related items.* TEL: 01993 823777; fax - 01993 823719. SER: Valuations; restorations. VAT: Stan/Spec.

Manfred Schotten Antiques
109 High St. OX18 4RH. CADA. Est. 1974. Open 9-5.30 or by appointment. *STOCK: Sporting antiques and library furniture.* TEL: 01993 822302; fax - 01993 822055. SER: Restorations.

Swan Gallery LAPADA
High St. OX18 4RE. (D. Pratt). CADA. Est 1966. Open 9.30-5.30. SIZE: Large. *STOCK Country furniture in oak, yew, walnut and fruitwood, 17th-19th C, £300-£9,000; oil paintings Staffordshire figures and small decorative items 18th-20th C, £50-£800.* PARK: Easy. TEL 01993 822244. VAT: Mainly Spec.

CHIPPING NORTON

Bugle Antiques LAPADA
9 Horsefair. OX7 5AL. (M. and D. Harding Hill). CADA. Est. 1971. Open 9.30-6. *STOCK Windsor chairs, including sets; English country furniture in oak, elm and fruitwood; dressers bureaux and large tables.* TEL: 01608 643322 fax - same. VAT: Stan/Spec.

Key Antiques BADA
11 Horse Fair. OX7 5AL. (D. and M. Robinson) CADA. Resident. Open 9.30-5.30 or by appointment. SIZE: Medium. *STOCK: Period oak and country furniture, domestic metalware including lighting and downhearth equipment, early carvings, firemarks, keys.* LOC: On main road PARK: Easy. TEL: 01608 643777. VAT: Spec.

IRENCESTER

Villiam H. Stokes BADA
The Cloisters, 6/8 Dollar St. GL7 2AJ. (W.H. stokes and P.W. Bontoft). CADA. Est. 1968.)pen 9.30-5.30, Sat. 9.30-4.30. ***STOCK: Early ak furniture, £1,000-£30,000; brassware, £150- 5,000; all 16th-17th C.*** **TEL: 01285 653907; ax - same. VAT: Spec.**

Rankine Taylor Antiques LAPADA
4 Dollar St. GL7 2AN. CADA. Est. 1969.)pen 9-5.30, Sun. by appointment. SIZE: arge. ***STOCK: Furniture, 17th to early 19th C, 300-£35,000; glass, 18th-20th C, £8-£350; ilver, rare interesting objects and decorative tems, 17th-20th C, £20-£4,000.*** **Not Stocked: /ictoriana. LOC: From church, turn right nto West Market Place, via Gosditch St. into)ollar St. PARK: Own - private opposite. TEL: 01285 652529. VAT: Spec.**

Bernard Weaver Antiques
:8 Gloucester St. GL7 2DH. CADA. Open 9.30- , Sat. 9.30-1. SIZE: Medium. *STOCK: urniture, mahogany and oak, 18th-19th C; Art Jouveau and Arts and Crafts.* LOC: Continuation f Dollar St. PARK: Easy. TEL: 01285 652055; ome - same. SER: Valuations.

AIRFORD

Blenheim Antiques
Aarket Place. GL7 4AB. (N. Hurdle). CADA. Resident. Est. 1972. Open 9.30-6.30. *STOCK: 8th-19th C furniture.* TEL: 01285 712094. VAT: Stan/Spec.

Gloucester House Antiques Ltd
Aarket Place. GL7 4AB. (Mrs Scilla Chester-Aaster). CADA. Est. 1972. Open 9-5.30. SIZE: arge. *STOCK: English and French country urniture in oak, elm, fruitwood, pine; pottery, aiënce and decorative items.* PARK: Easy. TEL: 1285 712790; home - 01285 653066; fax - 1285 713324. VAT: Spec.

MORETON-IN-MARSH

Astley House - Fine Art LAPADA
Astley House, High St. GL56 0LL. (D. and N. Glaisyer). CADA. Est. 1974. Open 9-5.30. CL: Wed. SIZE: Medium. ***STOCK: Oil paintings nd botanical watercolours, 19th-20th C, £200- 10,000.*** **LOC: Main street. PARK: Easy. TEL: 01608 650601; fax - 01608 651777. SER: Restorations (oils and watercolours); framing. VAT: Spec.**

Moreton-on-Marsh continued

Astley House - Fine Art LAPADA
Astley House, London Rd. GL56 0LE. (D. and N. Glaisyer). CADA. Est. 1974. Open 10-1 and 2-5. CL: Wed. SIZE: Large. ***STOCK: Oil paintings, 19th-20th C; large decorative paintings and portraits.*** **LOC: Town centre. PARK: Easy. TEL: 01608 650601; fax - 01608 651777. SER: Restorations (oils and watercolours); porcelain framing. VAT: Spec.**

STOW-ON-THE-WOLD

Duncan J. Baggott LAPADA
Woolcomber House, Sheep St. GL54 1AA. CADA. Est. 1967. Open 9-5.30 or by appointment. SIZE: Large. ***STOCK: 17th-20th C English furniture, paintings, domestic metalwork and decorative items; garden statuary and ornaments.*** **PARK: Sheep St. or Market Sq. TEL: 01451 830662; fax - 01451 832174.**

Baggott Church Street Ltd BADA
Church St. GL54 1BB. (D.J. and C.M. Baggott). CADA. Est. 1978. Open 9.30-5.30 or by appointment. SIZE: Large. ***STOCK: English furniture, 17th-19th C; portrait paintings, metalwork, pottery, treen and decorative items.*** **LOC: South-west corner of market square. PARK: In market square. TEL: 01451 830370; fax - 01451 832174.**

A pair of Chelsea sweetmeat figures of 'The Bun Sellers', c.1765, 9in., gold anchor marks, with a few chips and slight restoration.

From an article entitled "Factory Fact File: Chelsea" by David Battie which appeared in the April 1997 issue of **Antique Collecting**

Stow-on-the-Wold continued

Christopher Clarke Antiques Ltd
The Fosse Way. GL54 1JS. (C.J. Clarke). CADA. Est. 1961. Open 9.30-6. SIZE: Medium. *STOCK: Furniture, 17th-19th C, £300-£15,000; walnut, mahogany, metalware, 16th-18th C, £200-£5,000.* Not Stocked: Silver, glass, medals, coins, prints. LOC: Corner of the Fosse Way and Sheep St. PARK: Easy. TEL: 01451 830476; fax - 01451 830300.

Cotswold Galleries
GL54 1AB. (Richard and Cherry Glaisyer). CADA. Est. 1961. Open 9-5.30 or by appointment. SIZE: Large. *STOCK: Oil paintings, especially 19th-20th C landscape.* TEL: 01451 870567; fax - 01451 870678. SER: Restorations; framing.

The John Davies Gallery
Church St. GL54 1BB. CADA. Est. 1977. Open 9.30-1.30 and 2.30-5.30. SIZE: Large. *STOCK: Contemporary and late period paintings; limited edition bronzes.* PARK: In square. TEL: 01451 831698; fax - 01451 832477. SER: Restoration and conservation to museum standard.

Fosse Way Antiques
Ross House, The Square. GL54 1AF. (M. Beeston). CADA. Est. 1969. Open 10-5. SIZE: Large. *STOCK: Furniture and oil paintings, £300-£8,000; bronzes, Sheffield plate, caddies, boxes and decorative objects, £50-£1,000; all 18th-19th C.* LOC: East side of the Square, behind the Town Hall. PARK: Easy. TEL: 01451 830776. SER: Valuations; buys at auction. VAT: Spec.

Keith Hockin (Antiques) Ltd BADA
The Square. GL54 1AF. CADA. Est. 1968. Open 9-6. CL: Sun. except by appointment. SIZE: Medium. *STOCK: Oak furniture, 1600-1750; country furniture in oak, fruitwoods, yew, 1700-1850; pewter, copper, brass, ironwork, all periods.* Not Stocked: Mahogany. PARK: Easy. TEL: 01451 831058. SER: Buys at auction (oak, pewter, metalwork). VAT: Stan/Spec.

Stow-on-the-Wold continued

Huntington Antiques Ltd LAPADA
The Old Forge, Church St. GL54 1BE. (M.F. and S.P. Golding). CADA. CINOA. TEFAF Resident. Est. 1974. Open 9.30-5.30 or by appointment. *STOCK: Early period and fine country furniture, metalware, treen and textiles, tapestries and works of art.* TEL: 01451 830842; fax - 01451 832211. SER: Valuations; buys at auction. FAIRS: Maastricht; Madrid; Basel. VAT: Spec.

Roger Lamb Antiques & Works of Art LAPADA
The Square. GL54 1AB . CADA. Open 10-5. *STOCK: 18th-early 19th C furniture, especially small items, lighting, decorative accessories, oils and watercolours.* TEL: 01451 831371. SER: Search.

Antony Preston Antiques Ltd BADA
The Square. GL54 1AB. CADA. Est. 1965. Open 9.30-5.30 or by appointment. *STOCK: 18th-19th C English and Continental furniture and objects; barometers and period lighting.* TEL: 01451 831586; fax - 0171 581 5076. VAT: Stan/Spec.

Queens Parade Antiques Ltd BADA
The Square. GL54 1AB. (Antony Preston Antiques Ltd). CADA. Est. 1965. Open 9.30-5.30. SIZE: Large. *STOCK: 18th-19th C furniture, papier mâché, tôle peinte, needlework and period lighting.* LOC: Off Fosse Way. PARK: Easy. TEL: 01451 831586. VAT: Stan/Spec.

Samarkand Galleries LAPADA
8 Brewery Yard, Sheep St. GL54 1AA. (Brian MacDonald). CADA. CINOA. Est. 1980. Open 10-5.30, Sun. by appointment. SIZE: Medium. *STOCK: Tribal and village rugs and artefacts, 19th C, £100-£10,000; fine decorative carpets, 19th-20th C, £1,000-£10,000+; kelims, 19th-20th C, £200-£2,000.* LOC: Street adjacent to Market Sq. PARK: Easy. TEL: 01451 832322; fax - same; home - 01451 831173. SER: Exhibitions; valuations; restorations; cleaning. VAT: Stan/Spec.

Stow-on-the-Wold continued

Stow Antiques LAPADA
The Square. GL54 1AF. (Mr and Mrs J. Hutton-Clarke). CADA. Resident. Est. 1969. Open Mon.-Thurs. 2-5.30, Sat. 11-1 and 2-5.30, other times by appointment. SIZE: Large. *STOCK: Furniture, mainly Georgian, £500-£30,000; decorative items, gilded mirrors, £50-£10,000.* PARK: Easy. TEL: 01451 830377; fax 01451 870018. SER: Shipping worldwide.

STRETTON-ON-FOSSE, Nr. Moreton-in-Marsh

Astley House – Fine Art LAPADA
The Old School. GL56 9SA. (D. and N. Glaisyer). CADA. Est. 1974. Open by appointment. SIZE: Large. *STOCK: Large decorative oil paintings, 19th-20th century.* LOC: Village centre. PARK: Easy. TEL: 01608 650601; fax – 01608 651777. ER: Valuations; restorations; framing; exhibitions; mailing list. VAT: Spec.

TADDINGTON, Nr. Cutsdean

Architectural Heritage
Taddington Manor. GL54 5RY. CADA. Est. 1978. Open 9.30-5.30, Sat. 10.30-4.30. SIZE: Large. *STOCK: Period panelling, oak, mahogany and pine; chimney pieces in marble, stone, oak and mahogany; garden statuary, fountains, seats and urns.* PARK: Easy. TEL: 01386 584414; fax - 1386 584236. VAT: Stan.

TETBURY

Breakspeare Antiques LAPADA
6 and 57 Long St. GL8 8AQ. (M. and S. Breakspeare). CADA. Resident. Est. 1962. Open 10-5 or by appointment. CL: Thurs. pm. IZE: Medium. *STOCK: English period furniture - early walnut, 1690-1740, mahogany, 1750-1835.* PARK: Own car park. TEL: 01666 503122; fax - same. VAT: Stan/Spec.

Day Antiques
New Church St. GL8 8DS. CADA. Est. 1975. Open 9-6. SIZE: Medium. *STOCK: Oak and country furniture, early pottery, metalware, treen, some period mahogany.* TEL: 01666 502413. VAT: Stan/Spec.

WINCHCOMBE, Nr. Cheltenham

Prichard Antiques
5 High St. GL54 5LJ. (K.H. and D.Y. Prichard). CADA. Est. 1979. Open 9-5.30, Sun. by appointment. SIZE: Large. *STOCK: Period and decorative*

Winchcombe continued

furniture, £10-£10,000; treen and metalwork, £5-£500; interesting and decorative accessories. LOC: On main Broadway to Cheltenham road. PARK: Easy. TEL: 01242 603566. VAT: Spec.

WITNEY

W.R. Harvey & Co (Antiques) Ltd BADA
86 Corn St. OX8 7BU. CADA. GMC. Open 9.30-5.30, and by appointment. SIZE: Large. *STOCK: Fine English furniture, £500-£50,000; clocks, mirrors, objets d'art, £250-£20,000; all 1680-1830.* LOC: 100 yds. from Market Place. TEL: 01993 706501; fax - 01993 706601. SER: Valuations; restorations; consultancy. FAIRS: BADA; Chelsea (March & Sept.) VAT: Stan/Spec.

Witney Antiques BADA LAPADA
96/100 Corn St. OX8 7BU. (L.S.A. and C.J. Jarrett and R.R. Jarrett-Scott). CADA. Est. 1962. Open 10-5. SIZE: Large. *STOCK: English furniture, 17th-18th C; bracket and longcase clocks, mahogany, oak and walnut, metalware, needleworks and works of art.* LOC: From Oxford on old A40 through Witney via High St., turn right at T-junction, 400yds. on right. PARK: Easy. TEL: 01993 703902/703887; fax - 01993 779852. SER: Restorations. FAIRS: BADA; Grosvenor House. VAT: Spec.

TETBURY ANTIQUE DEALERS' ASSOCIATION

Philip Adler Antiques
4 The Chipping. TADA. Open 10-5 or by appointment. *STOCK: Eclectic and general decorative and period antiques.* TEL: 01666 505759.

The Antique and Interior Centre
51A Long St. TADA. Open 10-5, Sun. 11-5 and most Bank Holidays. SIZE: 8 dealers. *STOCK: Furniture, porcelain, silver and pictures; interior design items.* TEL: 01666 505083.

The Antiques Emporium
The Old Chapel, Long St. GL8 8AA. (C. and D. Sayers). TADA. Est. 1993. Open 10-5, Sun. 1-5. SIZE: Large - 38 dealers. *STOCK: Fruitwood and country furniture, fine oak and mahogany, china, porcelain, treen, copper and brass, jewellery, silver, kitchenalia, militaria, £1-£15,000.* Not Stocked: Reproductions. PARK: Nearby. TEL: 01666 505281. SER: Export. VAT: Stan/Spec.

Art-Tique
18 Long St. GL8 8AQ. (George Bristow). TADA. Open 9.30-6. CL: Mon. *STOCK: Interiors, textiles, carpets and kelims and objets d'art from the Orient.* TEL: 01666 503597.

Ball and Claw Antiques
45 Long St. GL8 8AA. (Chris and Nick Kirkland). TADA. Est. 1985. Open 10-1 and 2-5. SIZE: Medium. *STOCK: Furniture, 18th-19th C, £100-£3,000; decorative items, objects and prints, some country items.* PARK: Easy. TEL: 01666 502440; internet - http://www.all-about-antiques.co.uk/ballc.html. SER: Valuations; buys at auction. VAT: Stan/Spec.

Balmuir House Antiques — LAPADA
14 Long St. GL8 8AQ. (P. Whittam). TADA. Est. 1946. Open 9.30-5.30, Sun. by appointment. SIZE: Large. *STOCK: Furniture, paintings, mirrors, 19th C, £500-£5,000.* LOC: Town centre. PARK: Easy. TEL: 01666 503822; home - same. SER: Valuations; restorations (furniture, upholstery, paintings). VAT: Spec.

The Chest of Drawers
24 Long St. GL8 8AQ. (A. and P. Bristow). TADA. Resident. Est. 1969. Open 9.30-6 or by appointment. CL: Thurs. am. SIZE: Medium. *STOCK: Late Georgian, Regency and Victorian furniture; country pieces, 17th-18th C; china and brass.* LOC: On A433. PARK: Easy. TEL: 01666 502105; home - same. VAT: Spec.

The Coach House Bookshop
4 The Chipping. (Philip Gibbons). TADA. Ope 10-6, Sun. 11-5. *STOCK: Secondhand an antiquarian titles including A & C Black colou plate books; prints, antique furniture and smal items.* TEL: 01666 504330; e-mail - gibbons@ books.i-way.co.uk. SER: Book search.

Country Homes
61 Long St. GL8 8AA. (C. and D. Sayers) TADA. Est. 1984. Open 9-5.30, Sun. 1-5.30 SIZE: Medium. *STOCK: Pine furniture, 19th C £100-£1,500; treen.* PARK: Nearby. TEL: 0166 502342. SER: Import/export. VAT: Stan/Spec.

Day Antiques
5 New Church St. GL8 8DS. CADA. TADA. Es 1975. Open 9-6. SIZE: Medium. *STOCK: Oa and country furniture, early pottery, metalware treen, some period mahogany.* TEL: 0166 502413. VAT: Stan/Spec.

The Decorator Source
39a Long St. GL8 8AA. (Colin Gee). TADA. Ope 10-5 or by appointment. SIZE: Large. *STOCK French provincial furniture - armoires, farm tables buffets; decorative items and accessories of interes to interior decorators.* PARK: Easy. TEL: 0166 505358. VAT: Stan/Spec.

Dolphin Antiques
48 Long St. GL8 8AQ. (P. and L. Davis). TADA Est. 1986. Open 10-5.30. CL: Thurs. SIZE: Small *STOCK: Mainly 19th C decorative porcelain including Meissen, Dresden, Royal Worcester Samson, Coalport and Sitzendorf; general antiques all 1750-1930, £20-£2,000.* Not Stocked: Furniture PARK: Nearby. TEL: 01666 504242; home - same.

Fifty-One Antiques Et Cetera
51 Long St. (Sylvia Powell). TADA. Est. 1977 Open 10-5, Sun. by appointment. SIZE: Small *STOCK: English and French country furniture £50-£5,000; decorative items.* PARK: Easy. TEL 01666 505026.

Anne Fowler
35 Long St. GL8 8AA. TADA. Est. 1971. Ope 10-5.30, Sun. by appointment. SIZE: Medium *STOCK: Mainly French painted and decorativ items including garden furniture and accessorie mirrors, faience and pots, wirework, lighting an prints, £20-£2,000.* PARK: Easy. TEL: 0166 504043; home - same; fax - 01666 504900. VAT Stan/Spec.

;ales Antiques

2 Long St. GL8 8AQ. (M.R. Mathews). TADA. ;st. 1979. Open 10-5.30. SIZE: Medium. *STOCK: ;nglish and French country furniture and 'ecorative items, 17th-19th C, £5-£5,000.* PARK: ;asy. TEL: 01666 502686. VAT: Stan/Spec.

Iester Antiques

2 Church St. (Lorna Coles and Peter Bairstow). 'ADA. Open 10-5.30 including Sun. *STOCK: 'urniture, decorative items, lamps, lanterns, iirrors, clocks, memorabilia, curios, pictures, opper and brass, Oriental items.* TEL: 01666 05125.

3obbie Middleton

8 Long St. TADA. Open 10-1 and 2-5, Sun. by ppointment. *STOCK: 18th-19th C mahogany, ak and fruitwood furniture, mirrors, upholstery nd decorative items.* TEL: 01666 502761; mobile 0374 192660. VAT: Spec.

Iorpheus - Elgin House

New Church St. GL8 8DT. (B. Symes). TADA.)pen every day 9-5.30. *STOCK: 18th-19th C oak, iahogany and pine furniture; restored wood, rass and upholstered beds, 4-posters, half-testers nd lit bateau styles.* TEL: 01666 504068; fax - 1666 503352.

Old Mill Market Shop

12 Church St. GL8 8JG. (Mr and Mrs M. Green). TADA. Open 10-5.30, Thurs. 10-1. *STOCK: General antiques, collectables and bric-a-brac.* TEL: 01666 503127.

Porch House Antiques

40/42 Long St. GL8 8AQ. TADA. Open 10-5. *STOCK: 17th-20th C furniture and decorative items.* TEL: 01666 502687.

Tetbury Gallery

18 Market Place. (Jane Maile and Helen Joyner). FATG. TADA. Open every day. *STOCK: Original and limited edition prints, from Victorian watercolours and oils to contemporary artists including Russell Flint, David Shepherd and Ben Maile.* TEL: 01666 503412.

Westwood House Antiques

29 Long St. (Richard Griffiths and Lynne Petersen). TADA. Open 10-5.30 or by appointment. *STOCK: Oak, elm and ash country furniture especially dressers, dresser bases and tables, 17th-19th C; occasional French fruitwood items; decorative pottery, pewter and treen.* TEL: 01666 502338.

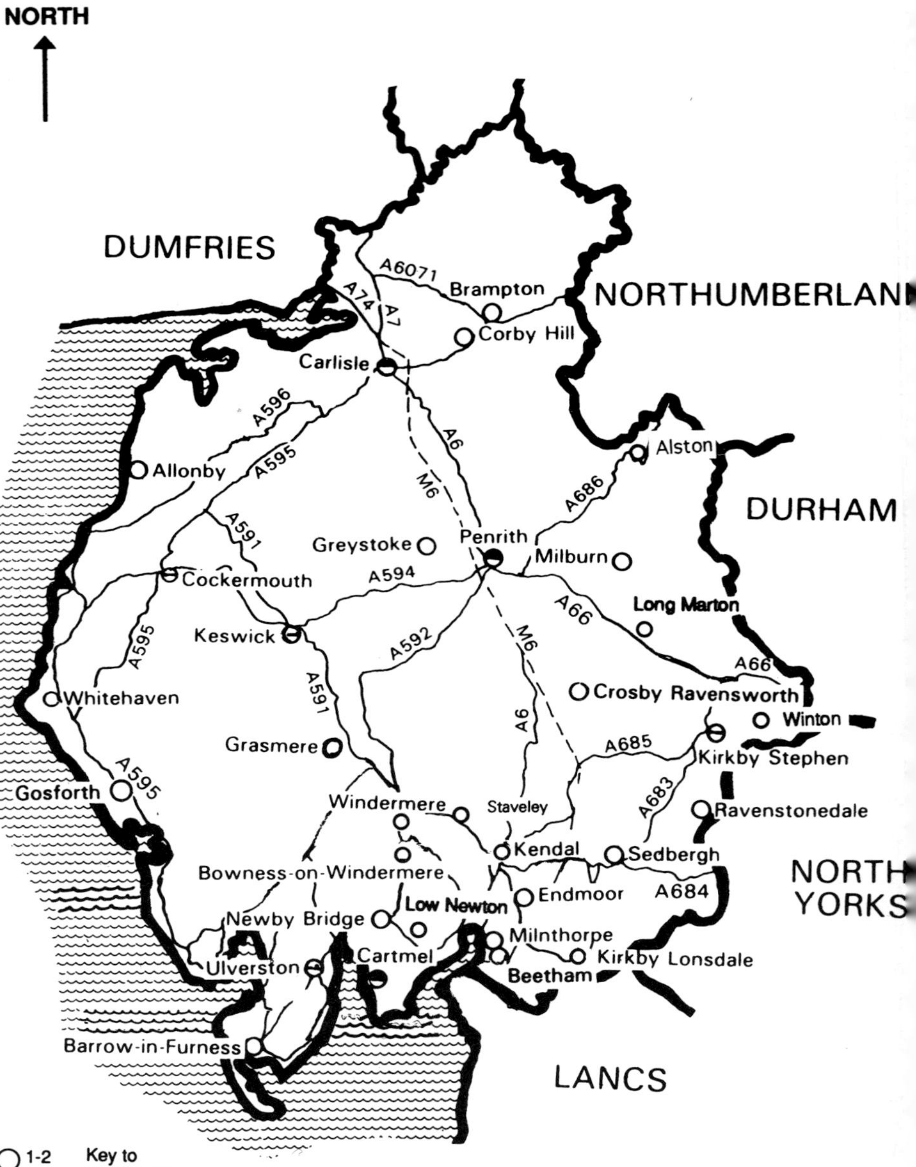

1-2
3-5
6-12
13+

Key to number of shops in this area.

Please note this is only a rough map designed to show dealers the number shops in the various towns, and is not necessarily totally accurate.

ALLONBY

Cottage Curios
Main St. CA15 6PX. (B. Pickering). Est. 1965. Open daily from 2 pm.

ALSTON

Brownside Coach House
CA9 3BP. (M.J. Graham). Est. 1987. Open 11-5, May to end Sept. CL: Mon. and Tues. *STOCK: Glass, 1780-1920's, to £800.* LOC: 1.5 miles outside Alston on Penrith road. PARK: Easy. TEL: 01434 381263. FAIRS: Windermere; Holker Hall.

BARROW-IN-FURNESS

Antiques
237 Rawlinson St. LA13 0AD. (H. Vincent). Est. 1965. *STOCK: Jewellery, furniture, paintings, weapons, clocks, brass, copperware, silver, bric-a-brac.* LOC: Off A590 (A6). PARK: Easy. TEL: 01229 823432.

BEETHAM, Nr. Milnthorpe

Peter Haworth
Temple Bank. LA7 7AL. Open by appointment. *STOCK: English and Scottish paintings and watercolours, 1850-1950, £100-£25,000.* LOC: 2 miles south of Milnthorpe on A6 to Lancaster. PARK: Easy. TEL: 015395 62352; fax - 015395 63438. SER: Valuations; restorations; commissions.

BOWNESS-ON-WINDERMERE

J.W. Thornton Antiques Supermarket
North Terrace. LA23 3AU. SIZE: Large. *STOCK: Fine art, general antiques, furniture, shipping and architectural items, pine, bric-a-brac, paintings, decorators items.* TEL: 015394 42930/45183 or 01229 869745/580284. SER: Valuations; buys at auction. VAT: Stan/Spec.

White Elephant Antiques
16 Quarry Rigg, Lake Rd. (Mrs J.C. Barlow). Est. 1987. Open 9.30-5.30 including Sun. SIZE: Medium. *STOCK: General antiques, 18th-19th C, £5-£1,000; copper, brass, mahogany reproduction furniture, scrimshaw, curios.* LOC: Far end of Quarry Rigg precinct. PARK: Easy. TEL: 015394 46962; home - 015394 88685. SER: Buys at auction.

BRAMPTON

Mary Fell Antiques
Collectors' Corner, 32-34 Main St. CA8 1RS. Est. 1960. Open Tues., Wed., Fri. and Sat. 11-6, other times by appointment. *STOCK: Sheraton and Victorian furniture, porcelain, china, glass, silver and plate, bric-a-brac, early Victorian oil*

Brampton continued

paintings, pictures, prints, jewellery, pot-lids. Not Stocked: Coins, armour and swords. LOC: Town centre, beside public car park. PARK: Easy. TEL: Home - 01228 22224. SER: Valuations; restorations (furniture); buys at auction.

CARLISLE

Carlisle Antique and Craft Centre
Cecil Hall, Cecil St. CA1 1NT. Open 9.30-5. SIZE: Large plus trade warehouse. LOC: Off Warwick Rd. PARK: Easy. TEL: 01228 36910; fax - same. Below are listed the dealers at this centre.

AGM Antiques
(A. Mawer). *Old and new pine, mahogany and oak furniture.*

Cumbria Country Pine
(W. Kraft). *Pine furniture to order. French oak furniture.*

Cumbria Fine Pine
Stripped pine furniture; mahogany and oak bedroom suites, large furniture, china, quilts.

It's About Time
(B. and W. Mitton). Est. 1985.*Longcase, bracket and carriage clocks, watches; Royal Worcester fine porcelain, jewellery, textiles.* TEL: 01228 36910.

Logwood Antiques
(Philip Dent). *Oak and mahogany furniture.*

Maureen Morano
Cane and rush seating. SER: Restorations (as stock).

Mr and Mrs J. Sharp
Small Victorian furniture.

Warwick Antiques
(J. Wardrope). CMBHI. *Period furniture, wall and bracket clocks.* SER: Valuations; restorations (clocks).

Yesterday's Pine
(J. Conway). *Pine furniture.* SER: Pine stripping.

James W. Clements
19 Fisher St. CA3 8RF. Est. 1887. Open 9.30-5. CL: Thurs. *STOCK: Silver, jewellery, porcelain and glass.* TEL: 01228 25565. VAT: Global/margin.

Maurice Dodd Books
44 Cecil Street. CA1 1NT. (R.J. McRoberts). Est. 1945. CL: Sat. pm. *STOCK: Antiquarian books.* TEL: 01228 22087; fax - same. VAT: Stan/Spec.

Saint Nicholas Galleries (Antiques) Ltd
28 London Rd. CA1 2EL. (J., C. and F.E. Carruthers). Open 9.30-5. CL: Thurs. SIZE: Medium. *STOCK: General antiques, 18th C, £5-£500.* LOC: City centre. PARK: Nearby. TEL: 01228 34425.

Carlisle continued

Saint Nicholas Galleries Ltd. (Antiques and Jewellery)

39 Bank St. CA3 8HJ. (C.J. Carruthers). Open 10-5. CL: Mon. SIZE: Medium. *STOCK: Jewellery, silver, plate, Rolex and pocket watches, clocks; collectables; Royal Doulton; Dux, Oriental vases; pottery, porcelain; watercolours, oil paintings; pine furniture; brass and copper.* LOC: City centre. PARK: Nearby. TEL: 01228 34459.

Souvenir Antiques

Treasury Court, Fisher St. CA3 8RF. (J. Higham). Open 10-5. SIZE: Small. *STOCK: Porcelain and pottery, Victorian to Art Deco, £5-£500; coronation ware, crested china, local prints, maps, postcards, Roman and medieval coins, costume jewellery.* Not Stocked: Textiles. LOC: City centre between Fisher St. and Scotch St. PARK: Nearby. TEL: 01228 401281.

CARTMEL

Anthemion - The Antique Shop

BADA LAPADA

LA11 6QD. (J. Wood). Est. 1982. Open 10-5 including Sun. SIZE: Large. *STOCK: English period furniture, 17th to early 19th C, £100-£30,000; decorative items, 17th-19th C,*

Cartmel continued

***£20-£2,000.* Not Stocked: Victoriana, bric-a-brac. LOC: Village centre. PARK: Easy. TEL: 01539 536295; mobile - 0468 443757. FAIRS: BADA; NEC; Olympia; Chester; West London. VAT: Stan/Spec.**

Anvil Antiques

Cavendish St. LA11 6PU. (J. Wood). Est. 199 Open 10-5 including Sun. SIZE: Large. *STOCK: Oak and country furniture, brass, copper, tree and decorative items, 17th-19th C.* LOC: From the village square, under the archway and past the Cavendish Arms. PARK: Easy. TEL: 0153 536362. VAT: Stan/Spec.

Bacchus Antiques - In the Service of Wine

Longlands. LA11 6HG. (Mrs J.A. Johnson). Est. 1979. Open by appointment only. *STOCK: Fine corkscrews.* TEL: 01539 536475.

Norman Kerr - Gatehouse Bookshop

The Square. LA11 6PX. Open by appointment only. *STOCK: Antiquarian books.* TEL: 01539 536247.

Peter Bain Smith (Bookseller)

Bank Court, Market Sq. LA11 6QB. In season open every day 10.30-6. CL: Mon. and Tues. from mid Nov. to Easter. Open 1.30-4.30. *STOCK: Books including antiquarian, especially children's and local topography.* LOC: A590 from Lever Bridge, off roundabout at Lindale by-pass through Grange-over-Sands. PARK: Nearby. TEL: 0153 536369. SER: Valuations.

Maggie Tallentire Antiques

at Anvil Antiques, Cavendish St. LA11 6PU. Open 10-5 including Sun. SIZE: Small. *STOCK: Oak and country furniture, 17th-19th C; country pottery, treen, needlework and decorative accessories.* TEL: 01539 536362; mobile - 058 764151. VAT: Stan/Spec.

COCKERMOUTH

Cockermouth Antiques

5 Station St. CA13 9QW. (E. Bell and G. Davies). Est. 1983. Open 10-5. SIZE: Large. *STOCK: General antiques especially ceramics, furniture, pictures, glass, books, metalware, quilts.* LOC: Just off A66, in town centre. PARK: Easy. TEL: 01900 826746.

Cockermouth Antiques Market

Courthouse, Main St. CA15 5XM. Est. 197 Open 10-5. SIZE: Large - 7 stallholders. *STOCK: Victorian, Edwardian and Art Deco items, furniture, printed collectables, postcards, books, linen, china, glass, textiles, jewellery and pictures.* LOC: Town centre, just off A66. PARK: 50 yds. TEL: 01900 824346. SER: Restorations (furniture), stripping (pine). VAT: Stan/Spec.

Cockermouth continued

Holmes Antiques
1 Market Place. CA13 9NH. (C. and S. Holmes). Est. 1972. Open 10-5. CL: Thurs. SIZE: Medium. *STOCK: Furniture, paintings, prints, small antiques, collectors' items.* PARK: Rear of premises. TEL: 01900 826114; home - 017687 78364.

CORBY HILL, Nr. Carlisle

Langley Antiques
The Forge. CA4 8PL. (Mrs P. Mather). Est. 1976. Open 10.30-5. CL: Thurs. SIZE: Medium. *STOCK: Country oak, period and Edwardian furniture and especially clocks.* LOC: 5 miles from Carlisle on A69. PARK: Easy. TEL: 01228 560899.

CROSBY RAVENSWORTH, Nr. Penrith

Jennywell Hall Antiques
CA10 3JP. (Mrs M. Macadie). Resident. Est. 1975. Open weekends 10-6, also most weekdays but phone call advisable. SIZE: Medium. *STOCK: Oak and mahogany furniture, paintings, interesting objects.* LOC: 5 miles from junction 39, M6. PARK: Easy. TEL: 01931 715288; home - same.

ENDMOOR, Nr. Kendal

Calvert Antiques
Sycamore House. LA8 0ET. (N.A. Hutchinson-Shire). Est. 1986. Open 9.30-5.30, Sun. 10.30-4, other times by appointment. SIZE: Medium. *STOCK: Furniture, 17th to early 19th C; clocks, 17th-19th C.* Not Stocked: China, silver, treen and jewellery. LOC: On A65. Leave M6 at junction 36 on to Skipton/Kirby Lonsdale road, first exit left to Endmoor. PARK: Easy. TEL: 0153 956 7597; home - same. SER: Restorations (furniture); replica furniture made to order; upholstery.

GOSFORTH

Archie Miles Bookshop
Beck Place. CA20 1AT. (Mrs C.M. Linsley). Open 10-5.30, Sun. 1-5.30, out of season opening times may vary. CL: Mon. *STOCK: Secondhand, antiquarian and out-of-print books, maps and prints.* TEL: 0194 67 25792.

GRASMERE, Nr. Ambleside

The Stables
College St. LA22 9SW. (J.A. and K.M. Taalmans). Est. 1971. Open daily 10-6 Easter-November, other times telephone call advisable. SIZE: Small. *STOCK: Brass and copper items, oil lamps, domestic bygones; pottery, silver, prints, books.* Not Stocked: Weapons, coins. LOC: By the side of Moss Grove Hotel. PARK: Easy. TEL: 015394 35453; home - same.

GREYSTOKE, Nr. Penrith

Pelican Antiques
Church Rd. CA11 0TW. (Mrs J. Kirkby). Est. 1897. Open daily but prior telephone call advisable. *STOCK: General small antiques, £5-£300.* PARK: Easy. TEL: 01768 483477.

Roadside Antiques
Watsons Farm, Greystoke Gill. CA11 0UQ. (K. and R. Sealby). Resident. Est. 1988. Open 10-6 including Sun. SIZE: Medium. *STOCK: Ceramics, longcase clocks, glass, Staffordshire figures, pot-lids,furniture, small collectables, jewellery, mainly 19th C, £5-£2,000.* LOC: B5288 Penrith/ Keswick road to Greystoke, through village, first left then left again, premises second on right. PARK: Easy. TEL: 01768 483279.

KENDAL

Below Stairs
125 Stricklandgate. (S. and T. Ritchie). Open 10-4. *STOCK: China, brass, copper, coloured glass, silver and collectables.* LOC: Main street on road towards Windermere. TEL: 01539 741278.

Brian Blakemore - Dower House Antiques
40 Kirkland. LA9 5AD. Open 9.15-6, Thurs. 9.15-1. *STOCK: Pottery, porcelain, paintings, furniture.* TEL: 01539 722778.

Kendal Studios Antiques
2/3 Wildman St. LA9 6EN. (Mr. R. Aindow). Est. 1950. Open 10.30-4, prior telephone call advisable. CL: Fri. SIZE: Medium. *STOCK: Ceramics, maps and prints, paintings, oak furniture, art pottery.* LOC: Leave M6 at junction 37, follow one-way system, shop on left. PARK: Nearby. TEL: 01539 723291 (24 hrs. answering service). SER: Finder; shipping. VAT: Stan/Spec.

The Silver Thimble
39 All Hallows Lane. (V. Ritchie). Est. 1980. Open 10-4. SIZE: Large. *STOCK: Jewellery, silver, glass, linen and lace, porcelain, copper and brass.* LOC: Turn left at second set of traffic lights on main road into Kendal from south, shop 200yds. on right. PARK: Easy. TEL: 01539 731456.

KESWICK

And So To Bed
Lake Rd. CA12 5BZ. (W.I. Raw). Est. 1981. Open 9.30-5. *STOCK: Brass beds, iron and brass beds, mattress and base sets for antique beds, mirrors, linen, quilts, £150-£2,000.* LOC: Top of Main St. TEL: 0176 87 74881. VAT: Stan.

Keswick continued

Cat in the Window

29 Station St., (Beneath Ravensworth Hotel). CA12 5HH. (E. Fell). Est. 1980. Open 10-12.30 and 1.30-4.30, Fri. 12-5, Mon. and Wed. by appointment. SIZE: Small. *STOCK: Porcelain and pottery, copper, brass and pewter, small furniture.* LOC: Near Fitz Park. PARK: Easy and nearby. TEL: 017687 71234. SER: Valuations; buys at auction. FAIRS: Colin Caygill in Cumbria.

John Young and Son (Antiques)

LAPADA

12-14 Main St. CA12 5JD. Est. 1890. Open 9-5.30. SIZE: Large. *STOCK: 17th-20th C. furniture, clocks and decorative items for the home and garden.* LOC: Town centre. PARK: At rear. TEL: 017687 73434. VAT: Stan/Spec.

KIRKBY LONSDALE

Alexander Adamson LAPADA

Tearnside Hall. LA6 2PU. (N.J.G., D. and P.A. Adamson). Est. 1863. Open 9.30-5.30, Sun. by appointment. *STOCK: Furniture, 17th to early 19th C; glass and porcelain.* PARK: Easy. TEL: 015242 71989. SER: Valuations; restorations (furniture). VAT: Spec.

Kirkby Lonsdale continued

Architus Antiques

14 Main St. (J. Pearson and B. Rigby). Est. 199 Open 10-4.30, Sat. 10-5.30. SIZE: Mediur *STOCK: Victorian oil lamps, £100-£250; chi and glass, jewellery and silver, Victorian to ear 20th C.* LOC: First antique shop on left in villa from A65 towards Kendal. TEL: 015242 7240 home - 015242 71517. SER: Valuations.

KIRKBY STEPHEN

Archway Antiques

1 Walton's Yard, Market Sq. CA17 4QT. (Al and Beatrice Stocks). Est. 1993. Open Fri., Sa Sun. and Mon.10.30-5.30. CL: Bank Holidays a Christmas to end Jan. SIZE: Small. *STOC Ceramics, glass and metalware, £5-£250; sm furniture, £50-£500; all 18th-19th C.* LOC: To centre, behind war memorial. PARK: Easy. TE 017683 71905; fax - same; home - 015396 2122 SER: Buys at auction; commission sales.

Haughey Antiques LAPAD

28/30 Market St. CA17 4QW. (D.M. Haughey Est. 1969. Open 10-5, Sun. by appointmen SIZE: Large. *STOCK: Furniture, 17th-19th garden furniture and statuary.* PARK: Ow TEL: 0176 83 71302; fax - 0176 83 72423. SE Valuations. VAT: Stan/Spec.

Kirkby Stephen continued

David Hill

36 Market Sq. CA17 4QT. Est. 1965. Open 9.30-4. SIZE: Medium. *STOCK: Longcase clocks, £350-£1,500; country furniture, £10-£1,000; both 18th-19th C; curios, £5-£50; shipping goods, kitchenalia, iron and brassware.* LOC: On A685. PARK: Easy. TEL: 0176 83 71598. VAT: Stan/Spec.

Mortlake Antiques

32-34 Market St. CA17 4QW. (C.J. and J.A. Bate). Est. 1946. Open 10-5, Mon.-Sat. in summer and Mon, Fri. and Sat. in winter. SIZE: Medium. *STOCK: Furniture, period, Victorian, Edwardian and country including stripped pine; treen, kitchenalia, bygones, bric-a-brac and metalware.* Not Stocked: Silver, glass, porcelain. LOC: On A685, 12 miles east of junction 38, M6. PARK: Easy. TEL: 017683 71666 (ansaphone).

LONG MARTON, Nr. Appleby

Ben Eggleston Antiques

The Dovecote. CA16 6BJ. (Ben and Kay Eggleston). Est. 1976. Open strictly by appointment. SIZE: Large. *STOCK: Antiques pine furniture, unstripped and unrestored for the trade, £5-£2,500.* LOC: 2 miles east of A66 between Appleby and Penrith. PARK: Easy. TEL: 017683 61849; home and fax - same. SER: Valuations; buys at auction. VAT: Stan/Spec. *Strictly Trade Only.*

LOW NEWTON, Nr. Grange-over-Sands

Utopia Antiques Ltd

Yew Tree Barn. LA11 6JP. (P.J. and Mrs J. Wilkinson). Open 10-5. *STOCK: Pine and country furniture, decorative accessories.* PARK: Easy. TEL: 015395 30065. VAT: Stan.

W.R.S. Architectural Antiques

Yew Tree Barn. LA11 6JP. (Clive Wilson). Open 10-5, Sun. 12-6 (winter 11-5). *STOCK: General architectural antiques including fireplaces; period furniture.* TEL: 01539 531498.

MILBURN, Nr. Penrith

Netherley Cottage Antiques

CA10 1TN. (J. Heelis). Est. 1970. Usually open 9.30-8 but appointment advisable. SIZE: Small. *STOCK: Country cottage pottery, porcelain and ornaments, 18th-19th C, £1-£70; kitchen and dairy items, interesting bygones, brass, watercolours, £1-£85; treen, some Oriental items.* Not Stocked: Silver and clocks. TEL: 0176 83 61403. SER: Buys at auction.

MILNTHORPE

The Antique Shop

Park Rd. LA7 7PW. Open 10-4.30. SIZE: Medium. *STOCK: General antiques, books, furniture.* LOC: From A6, left at traffic lights in village, opposite Post Office. TEL: 01524 781718.

NEWBY BRIDGE

Shire Antiques

The Post House, High Newton, Newton-in-Cartmel. LA11 6JQ. (B. and Mrs J. Shire). Open every day except Tues. SIZE: Medium. *STOCK: Early oak furniture, 16th-18th C; Georgian copper, brass, treen.* Not Stocked: Silver and jewellery. LOC: On A590 to Barrow, house is 50yds. from main road in High Newton. PARK: Easy. TEL: 0153 95 31431; home - same. SER: Valuations; restorations (furniture). VAT: Stan/Spec.

Townhead Antiques LAPADA

LA12 8NP. (E.M. and C.P. Townley). Est. 1960. Open 9-5, other times by appointment. SIZE: Large. *STOCK: 18th-19th C furniture, silver, porcelain, glass, decorative pieces; clocks, pictures, garden furniture.* LOC: A592. 1 mile from Newby Bridge on the Windermere road. PARK: Easy. TEL: 0153 95 31321; fax - 0153 95 30019. SER: Valuations. VAT: Stan/Spec.

PENRITH

Antiques of Penrith

4 Corney Sq. CA11 7PX. (L. Mildwurf and Partners). Est. 1964. Open 10-12 and 1.30-5, Sat. 10-12.30. CL: Wed. SIZE: Large. *STOCK: Early oak and mahogany furniture, clocks, brass, copper, glass, china, silver plate, metal, Staffordshire figures, curios.* Not Stocked: Jewellery, paintings, rugs. LOC: Near Town Hall. PARK: Easy. TEL: 01768 862801. VAT: Stan/Spec/Global.

The Gallery

54 Castlegate. CA11 7HY. (K.G. Plant). Est. 1969. Open by appointment only. SIZE: Small. *STOCK: Paintings and watercolours, 17th-20th C, £50-£20,000.* LOC: From town centre towards the railway station. TEL: 01768 865538; home - same. SER: Valuations; buys at auction (paintings). VAT: Stan/Spec.

Hearth and Home

6 Brunswick Rd. CA11 7LU. Open 9-5. *STOCK: Antique and reproduction furniture and decorative accessories, fireplaces, multi-fuel and gas stoves.* TEL: 01768 867200.

Penrith continued

Joseph James Antiques

Corney Sq. CA11 7PX. (G.R. Walker). Est. 1970. Open 9-5.30. CL: Wed. SIZE: Medium. *STOCK: Furniture and upholstery, 18th C and Victorian, £10-£3,000; porcelain and pottery, £5-£1,000; silver and plate, pictures, £2-£800; all 18th-19th C.* LOC: On the one-way system in the town, 100yds. from the main shopping area (Middlegate), 50yds. from the town hall. PARK: Easy and 100yds. TEL: 01768 862065. SER: Re-upholstery; soft furnishings. VAT: Stan.

Market Place Antiques

22 Cornmarket. CA11 0UQ. (R.H. and A.M. Sealby). Est. 1995. Open Tues., Thurs., Fri. and Sat. 10-4.30. *STOCK: Ceramics, clocks, glass, Staffordshire figures, pot lids, furniture and small collectables, mainly 19th C, £1-£1,500.*PARK: Gt Dockray or Southend. TEL: 01768 899579.

Penrith Coin and Stamp Centre

37 King St. CA11 7AY. (Mr and Mrs A. Gray). Resident. Est. 1974. Open 9-5.30. CL: Wed. Sept.-May. SIZE: Medium. *STOCK: Coins, B.C. to date, 1p-£500; jewellery, secondhand, £5-£500; Great Britain and Commonwealth stamps.* LOC: Just off town centre. PARK: Behind shop. TEL: 01768 864185; fax - same. SER: Valuations; jewellery repairs. FAIRS: Many coin. VAT: Stan.

Penrith continued

Jane Pollock Antiques LAPADA

4 Castlegate. CA11 7HZ. Open 9.30-5. CL: Wed. SIZE: Medium. *STOCK: Georgian and Victorian silver, some 20th C small items; Victorian pottery, blue and white lustre; wooden boxes, some small furniture.* LOC: One-way street from town centre towards station. PARK: Easy. TEL: 01768 867211. SER: Valuations; restorations (silver, blue glass liners); buys at auction (silver, pottery). FAIRS: Olympia, Kensington, Chester and Harrogate. VAT: Global/margin.

RAVENSTONEDALE, Nr. Kirkby Stephen

The Book House

Grey Garth. CA17 4NQ. (C. and M. Irwin). PBFA. Est. 1963. Open 9-5. CL: Tues. *STOCK: Books, mainly 19th-20th C, £1-£1,000; some postcards, 20th C, 25p-£10.* LOC: Off A685. Square house across road triangle from village school. PARK: Easy. TEL: 015396 23634; home - same; fax - 015396 - 23434. SER: Valuations. FAIRS: Northern PBFA. VAT: Stan.

SEDBERGH

R. F. G. Hollett and Son

6 Finkle St. LA10 5BZ. (R. F. G. and C. G. Hollett). Est. 1951. Open 10-12 and 1.15-5. SIZE: Large. *STOCK: Antiquarian books, 15th-20th C, £20-£20,000+; maps, prints and paintings, 17th-19th C, £10-£5,000.* LOC: Town centre. PARK: Free nearby. TEL: 015396 20298; fax - 015396 21396; e-mail - hollett@sedbergh.demon.co.uk SER: Valuations. VAT: Stan.

Stable Antiques

Wheelwright Cottage, 15-16 Back Lane. LA10 5AQ. Est. 1970. Open 10-6 or by appointment. *STOCK: Small furniture, brass, copper, silver, china, prints, small collectors' items, treen.* LOC: 5 miles from exit 37, M6. TEL: 015396 20251.

STAVELEY

Staveley Antiques

27/29 Main St. LA8 9LU. (P. John Corry). Est. 1991. Open 10-5, Sun. by appointment. SIZE: Large. *STOCK: Brass and iron bedsteads, 183[illegible]-1930, £200-£1,200; lighting, 1880-1935, from £5[illegible]; fire-irons, kerbs and metalware, from 1850, from £50.*LOC: Between Kendal and Windermere on A591 (now bypassed). PARK: Easy. TEL: 015[illegible] 821393; home - 01539 821123. SER: Valuations; restorations (brass and iron bedsteads, metalware).

JLVERSTON

\1A Antiques
·9B Market St. (J.W. Thornton). Est. 1960. Open ·y appointment. SIZE: Large. *STOCK: Bric-a-·rac, clocks, furniture, shipping items, pictures, 'ecorators items.* PARK: Easy. TEL: 01229 ·69745/580284 or 015394 42930/45183. SER: 'aluations; restorations; buys at auction. VAT: ;tan/Spec.

;lizabeth and Son
1arket Hall. (J.R. Bevins). Est. 1960. Open 9-5. :L: Wed. SIZE: Medium. *STOCK: Victorian and :dwardian glass, silver, brass and copper, gold nd silver jewellery, books.* LOC: Town centre. 'ARK: Easy. TEL: 01229 582763.

;mith's Court Antiques
.ower Brook St. (David Wood). Est. 1988. Open 1on. and Fri. 11-4, Tues. 10-4, Thurs. and Sat. 0-4.30. SIZE: Small.*STOCK: Silver, brass and opper, china and glass, small furniture, 18th-9th C, £20-£900.* LOC: Town centre. TEL: 1229 581324; home - 01229 869252. FAIRS: Iarrogate.

VHITEHAVEN

1ichael Moon
1-43 Roper St. CA28 7BS. (M. and S. Moon). BA, PBFA. Est. 1969. Open 9.30-5. SIZE: arge. *STOCK: Antiquarian books including 'umbrian topography.* PARK: Nearby. TEL: 1946 62936. FAIRS: PBFA Northern. VAT: tan.

VINDERMERE

'he Birdcage Antiques
ollege Rd. LA23 1BX. (Mrs T.A. Griffiths). st. 1983. Open Wed., Fri. and Sat. 10-5, or by ppointment. SIZE: Small. *STOCK: General ntiques, glass, brass, copper, pre-1920's ;hting, country bygones, Staffordshire, 18th C 1920; 19th C pottery.* LOC: From A591 rough village, past end of one-way system, turn ;ht after 50yds. PARK: Alongside shop. TEL: 5394 45063; home - 015394 43041/43310. AT: Global/Stan.

oseph Thornton Antiques
Victoria St. LA23 1AB. (J.W. Thornton). Est. 71. Open 10-4.30 or by appointment. SIZE: rge. *STOCK: General antiques, art, archi-:tural and decorators' items, clocks, bric-a-brac.*)C: 50yds. from railway station. PARK: Easy. :L: 015394 42930/45183 or 01229 869745/ 0284. SER: Valuations; buys at auction. VAT: an/Spec.

WINTON, Nr. Kirkby Stephen

Winton Hall Antiques
The Manor House. (Mr. S. Baldwick). Resident. Est. 1975. Open 9-5 including Sun. SIZE: Large. *STOCK: Oak and country furniture, 1600-1800, £100-£7,000; mahogany, 1750-1830, £100-£4,000.* LOC: One mile through Kirkby Stephen on A685, take 2nd right to Winton, approx 200yds on - large Georgian house overlooking village green. PARK: Easy. TEL: 017683 72194; home - 017683 72194. SER: Valuations; buys at auction. VAT: Stan/Spec.

Derbyshire

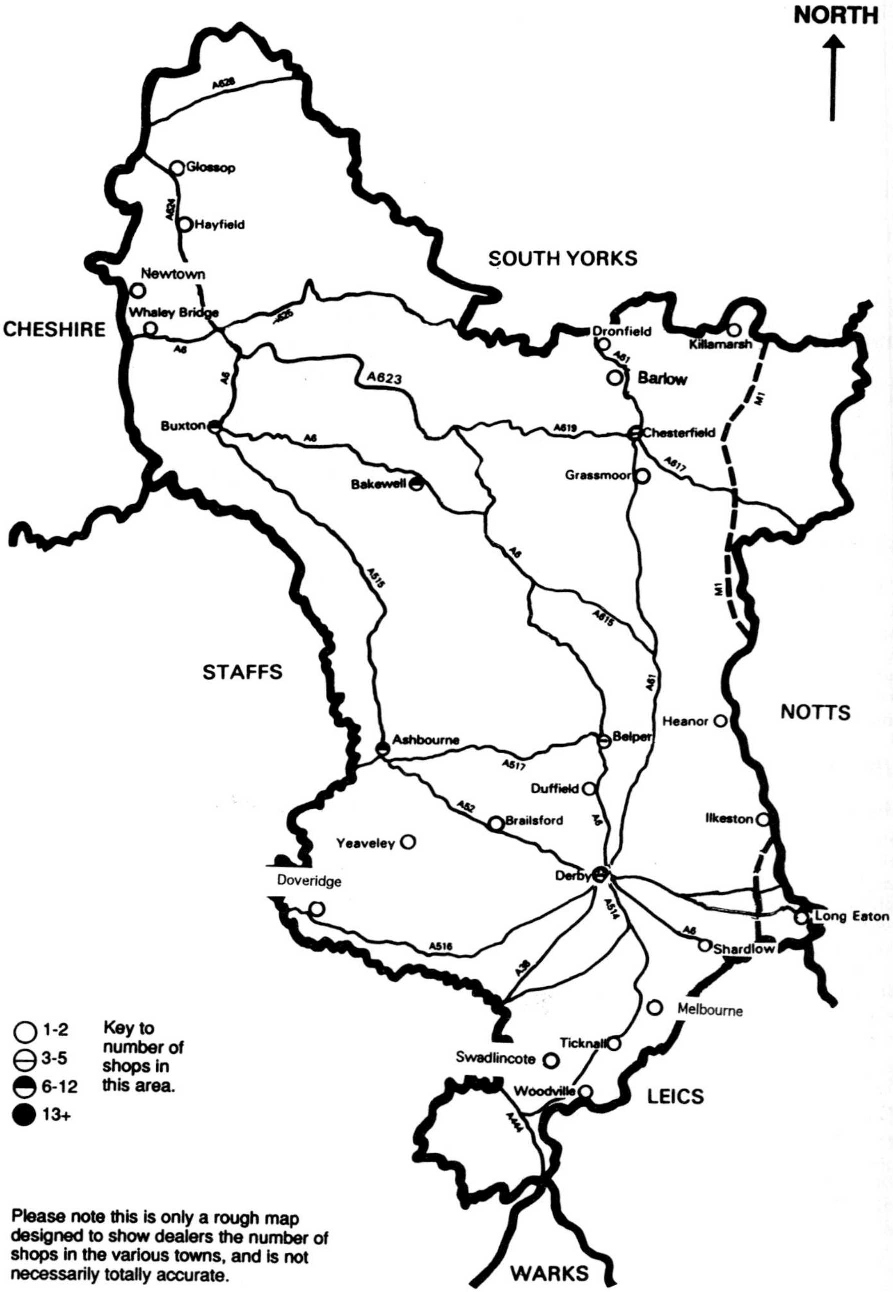

○ 1-2	Key to number of shops in this area.
⊖ 3-5	
◓ 6-12	
● 13+	

Please note this is only a rough map designed to show dealers the number of shops in the various towns, and is not necessarily totally accurate.

ASHBOURNE

Cavendish House Gallery
9 Church St. DE6 1AE. Open 10-5. CL: Wed. *STOCK: Victorian oils and watercolours, Contemporary works of art by local artists and French Impressionist works.* TEL: 01335 344606.

Pamela Elsom - Antiques
5 Church St. DE6 1AE. Est. 1963. Open 10-5. CL: Mon. and Wed. SIZE: Medium. *STOCK: Furniture, £20-£5,000, metalware, both 17th-19th C; period smalls, general antiques, treen, pottery, glass, secondhand books.* Not Stocked: Coins, militaria. LOC: On A52. PARK: Easy. TEL: 01335 343468. SER: Valuations. VAT: Spec.

Manion Antiques
23 Church St. DE6 1AE. (Mrs V.J. Manion). Est. 1984. Open Thurs., Fri. and Sat. 10-5, other times by appointment. SIZE: Small. *STOCK: Porcelain, silver, jewellery, small furniture, £50-£100+.* PARK: Easy. TEL: 01335 343207; home - same. SER: Valuations.

Rose Antiques
37 Church St. DE6 1AJ. Est. 1982. Open 10-5. SIZE: Medium. *STOCK: Furniture, silver, porcelain, jewellery, copper, brass and pine.* LOC: A52. PARK: Easy. TEL: 01335 343822; home - 01283 575301.

Spurrier-Smith Antiques LAPADA
38, 39 and 41 Church St. DE6 1AJ. (I. Spurrier-Smith). Est. 1973. Open 10-5, Wed. and Sun. by appointment. SIZE: Large (8 showrooms) + warehouse. *STOCK: Furniture, oils, watercolours, porcelain, pottery, metalware, instruments, oriental bronzes, collectables, pine, decorative items. Warehouse - pine and American export goods.* TEL: 01335 343669/342198; home - 01629 822502. SER: Valuations. VAT: Stan/Spec.

Kenneth Upchurch
30B Church St. Est. 1972. *STOCK: Oil paintings and watercolours, mainly 19th C; pottery and porcelain.* TEL: 01332 754499.

BAKEWELL

Bakewell Antiques and Collectors' Centre
King St. DE45 1DZ. Est. 1992. Open 10-5, Sun. 11-5. *STOCK: General antiques and collectables.* TEL: 01629 812496; fax - 01629 814531.

Beedham Antiques Ltd
PO Box 4. DE45 1ZU. (W.H. Beedham). Open by appointment only. *STOCK: English oak furniture, 16th-17th C; objects and works of art.* LOC: Off 619. TEL: 01629 58475/01433 630079. SER: Valuations; buys at auction. VAT: Spec.

Chappell's Antiques & Fine Art
BADA LAPADA

**King St. DE45 1DZ. Est. 1940. Open 9.30-5.30. *STOCK: 17th-19th C English furniture, oil*

Bakewell continued

***paintings, porcelain, pottery, metalwork, clocks and decorative items.* TEL: 01629 812496; fax - 01629 814531. VAT: Stan/Spec.**

De-Vine Antiques LAPADA
Bakewell Antiques Centre, King St. DE45 1DZ. (Mr and Mrs P. A. Vine.). Est. 1994. Open 10-5, Sun. 10.30-5. SIZE: Small. *STOCK: British pottery and porcelain including Moorcroft, Worcester, Wedgwood fairyland lustre, Doulton, late 19th to early 20th C, £500-£1,000.* LOC: A6 from Derby. PARK: Easy. TEL: Mobile - 0585 212684; fax - 01733 390451; home - 01733 223119. SER: Buys at auction. FAIRS: NEC (April, Aug., Nov.) VAT: Stan/Spec.

Michael Goldstone BADA
Avenel Court. DE45 1DZ. Est. 1927. Open 9-5.30 or by appointment, prior telephone call advisable. SIZE: Large. *STOCK: Oak furniture, 16th-18th C, from £100; walnut furniture, brass, 18th C, from £500.* PARK: Easy. TEL: 01629 812487; home - same. VAT: Spec.

Martin and Dorothy Harper Antiques
LAPADA

King St. DE45 1DZ. Est. 1973. Open 10-5.30, Sun. and other times by appointment. CL: Thurs. SIZE: Medium. *STOCK: Furniture, £100-£5,000; metalware, £30-£300; glass, £15-£150; all 17th to late 19th C; needlework, 19th C.* PARK: Easy. TEL: 01629 814757. SER: Valuations; restorations (re-upholstery); buys at auction. VAT: Stan/Spec.

Lewis Antiques LAPADA
King St. (Les Lewis). Est. 1977. Open most days 10-5. SIZE: Small. *STOCK: Town and country furniture, clocks, barometers, pictures and porcelain, 18th-19th C, £50-£5,000.* LOC: Follow Monyash Rd. near town centre. PARK: Nearby. TEL: 01629 813141. VAT: Stan/Spec.

Water Lane Antiques
Water Lane. DE45 1EU. (M. and L. Pembery). Est. 1967. Open 9.30-1 and 1.30-5.30. SIZE: Medium. *STOCK: Furniture, £500-£4,000; metalware, £100-£1,000; objets d'art, £100-£1,500; all 18th-19th C.* LOC: Off Market Sq. PARK: Nearby. TEL: 01629 814161. SER: Valuations; restorations. VAT: Stan/Spec.

BARLOW, Nr. Chesterfield

Byethorpe Furniture (Brian Yates Antiques)
Shippen Rural Business Centre, Church Farm. , Est. 1977. Open 10-5. SIZE: Medium. *STOCK: Country furniture, mainly 17th-18th C, £100-£5,000; boxes, £50-£500; porcelain, copper and brass, £10-£300.* PARK: Easy. TEL: 0114 2899111; fax - same. SER: Restorations (furniture); specialist woodwork; upholstery; handmade reproductions. VAT: Stan/Spec.

BELPER

Belper Antiques Centre
2 Queen St. DE56 1NR. (R. Briggs). Est. 1973. SIZE: Medium. *STOCK: Pre 1950 smalls and 19th-20th C jewellery, £5-£500; furniture, clocks and pictures, 18th-19th C, £50-£2,000.* LOC: Turn right towards Market Place at Safeway island on A6 north of Derby. PARK: Nearby. TEL: 01773 823002. SER: Valuations; restorations (clocks, gilding, furniture); buys at auction. FAIRS: Newark, Birmingham. VAT: Stan.

Sweetings (Antiques 'n' Things)
1 & 1a The Butts. DE56 1HX. (K.J. and J.L. Sweeting). Est. 1971. Open daily. SIZE: Large. *STOCK: Pre 1940's furniture including stripped pine, oak, mahogany, satinwood, £20-£1,000.* LOC: Off A6, near Market Place. PARK: Easy. TEL: 01773 825930/822780. SER: Valuations; restorations (pine and satinwood); shipping. VAT: Stan.

Neil Wayne "The Razor Man"
The Cedars (rear of 55 Field Lane), DE56 1DD. Resident. Est. 1969. Open every day 9.30-6, prior telephone call essential. SIZE: Medium. *STOCK: Razors and shaving items, 18th to early 19th C, £20-£300.* PARK: Easy. TEL: 01773 824157; fax - 01773 825573; e-mail - neil-wayne@freedmus.demon.co.uk.

BRAILSFORD

Antique Exporters U.K
The Estate Yard, Post Office Lane. DE6 3BT. Est. 1977. Open by appointment. SIZE: Large. *STOCK: Special orders only - English furniture, 17th-19th C and reproduction.* LOC: A52 Ashbourne/Derby. PARK: Easy. TEL: 01335 360005; fax - 01335 360121. SER: Restorations; cabinet makers; interior design; packers and shippers. VAT: Stan. *Trade Only.*

BUXTON

The Antiques Warehouse
25 Lightwood Rd. SK17 7BJ. (N.F. Thompson). Est. 1983. Open 10.30-4.30 or by appointment. SIZE: Large. *STOCK: Furniture, mainly mahogany, 17th-20th C; paintings, smalls, Victorian brass and iron beds.* LOC: Off A6. PARK: Own. TEL: 01298 72967; home - 01298 871932. SER: Valuations; restorations; buys at auction.

The Barn
Wainwright Yard, Ashwood Rd. SK17 7EL. (Roger and Lucy Judd). Est. 1986. Open 9.30-5 and by appointment Sun. p.m. CL: Mon. and Sun. a.m. SIZE: Medium. *STOCK: Pine robes and furniture, 1840-1920, £200-£800; Victorian kitchenalia and chairs, £10-£200.* LOC: From A6 southbound, turn left after golf course - 5th turning on right. PARK: Easy. TEL: 01298 71680; home - same. SER: Valuations; restorations; pine stripping; buys at auction (country chairs).

Buxton continued

Lewis Antiques
64 Fairfield Rd. SK17 7DW. (J. and S. Lewis Resident. Open 10.30-5, other times by appoin ment. CL: Mon. and Wed. *STOCK: Genera antiques, furniture, smalls, linen, collectable* TEL: 01298 78648.

Maggie Mays
Unit 10, Cavendish Arcade. (Mrs. J. Wild). Es 1993. Open 10.30-5. CL: Mon. *STOCK: Victoria furniture and effects, £35-£800; Art Dec glassware, mirrors, pottery, £20-£500; Edwardia furniture, £100-£800.* LOC: Opposite Turne Memorial on Terrace Road. PARK: Easy. TE Mobile - 0831 606003; home - 01663 73393 SER: Valuations; buys at auction.

The Penny Post Antiques
9 Cavendish Circus. SK17 6AT. (D. and Hammond). Est. 1978. Open 10-4.30, Sat. 10- SIZE: Small. *STOCK: Furniture, 18th to ear 20th C, £100-£1,000; commemoratives ar crested china, £5-£150; collectables; gener antiques.* LOC: Town centre, opposite Pala Hotel. PARK: Easy. TEL: Home - 01298 25965.

West End Galleries
8 Cavendish Circus. SK17 6AT. (A. and Needham). Est. 1955. Open 9-5. CL: Sat. p. SIZE: Large. *STOCK: French, Dutch, Engli furniture; clocks, paintings, works of art, bronz* LOC: A6. PARK: Easy. TEL: 01298 2454 VAT: Stan/Spec.

What Now Antiques
Cavendish Arcade, The Crescent. SK17 9BQ. (Carruthers). Open 10.30-5, Sun. 2-5. CL: Mc *STOCK: General antiques and collectabl including 19th-20th C pottery, silver and pla jewellery, die-cast toys, textiles, watercolou Victorian and Edwardian furniture, £1-£1,0(* TEL: 01298 27178/23417. SER: Export; guic tours for foreign trade; valuations.

CHESTERFIELD

Polly Coleman Antiques
424 Chatsworth Rd., Brampton. S40 3BD. E 1981. Open Fri. and Sat. 11-5. SIZE: Sma *STOCK: Pictures, prints and watercolou etchings, £50-£350; small furniture, unus chairs, £150-£250; porcelain, £100-£150; all l 19th C to 1930's.* LOC: A619 to Chatswo House from Chesterfield. PARK: Adjacent, do Old Chapel Lane. TEL: 01246 202225; mobi 0585 934664. SER: Valuations; restoratic (upholstery); picture framing; buys at auct (pictures and prints).

Anthony D. Goodlad
26 Fairfield Rd. Brockwell. S40 4TP. Est. 19 Open by appointment only. *STOCK: Gene militaria, WWI and WWII.* LOC: Close to to centre. PARK: Easy. TEL: 01246 204004.

Chesterfield continued

Hackney House Antiques
Hackney Lane, Barlow. S18 5TQ. (Mrs J.M. Gorman). Resident. Est. 1984. *STOCK: Furniture, 18th-19th C; prints, clocks, linen, silver.* TEL: 01142 890248.

Ian Morris
479 Chatsworth Rd. S40 3AD. Est. 1967. Open 9-5, Sat. 12-5. SIZE: Medium. *STOCK: Furniture, 18th-20th C, £50-£2,000; pictures, small items.* LOC: Main road A619, to Baslow and Chatsworth House. TEL: 01246 235120. SER: Valuations. VAT: Stan/Spec.

DERBY

Abbey House
115 Woods Lane. DE22 3UE. (Shirley White). Resident. Est. 1959. Open by appointment. *STOCK: Dolls, teddy bears and all things juvenile.* TEL: 01332 331426; fax - same. SER: Repairs (dolls and teddies); restorations (furniture).

Friargate Pine and Antiques Centre
The Pump House, Friargate Wharf, Stafford St. Entrance. DE1 1JL. (N. J. Marianski). Open 9-5. *STOCK: Antique and reproduction pine furniture.* TEL: 01332 341215.

Tanglewood
Tanglewood Mill, Coke St. DE1 1NE. (R. Beech). Est. 1979. Open 10-5. CL: Sat. (Trade anytime). SIZE: Large + warehouse. *STOCK: Country pine from Britain and Eire, 18th-19th C.* LOC: Off A52. PARK: Own. TEL: 01332 346005; fax - same. VAT: Stan.

Charles H. Ward
2 Friar Gate. DE1 1BU. (M.G. Ward). CL: Wed. pm. *STOCK: Oil paintings, 19th-20th C; watercolours.* TEL: 01332 342893. SER: Restorations.

DOVERIDGE

Pine Antiques Workshop
Bell Farm, Yelt Lane. DE6 5JU. (M.A. and A. Groves). Open Tues.-Sat. 9-5.30, other times by appointment. *STOCK: English and Welsh pine, pottery, linen and kitchenalia.* TEL: 01889 64898; fax - same.

DRONFIELD

Bardwell Antiques
1 Chesterfield Rd. S18 6XA. (S. Bardwell). Open 9-5. *STOCK: General antiques.* TEL: 01246 12183; fax - same.

DUFFIELD, Nr. Derby

Dragon Antiques
1 Tamworth St., (J.A. Palfree). Est. 1991. Open 9.30-5.30, Sat. 10-6, Wed. and Sun. by appointment. SIZE: Medium. *STOCK: Furniture, late 18th to early 20th C, £350-£2,000; mantel, wall and longcase clocks, 18th-19th C, £100-£6,000; decorative pictures, porcelain and books, 19th C, £5-£500.* LOC: Just off A6 in village centre. PARK: Easy. TEL: 01332 842332. VAT: Spec.

Wayside Antiques
62 Town St. DE6 4GG. (Mrs J. Harding). Est. 1975. *STOCK: Furniture, 18th-19th C, £50-£5,000; porcelain, pictures, boxes and silver.* TEL: 01332 840346. VAT: Stan/Spec.

GLOSSOP

Derbyshire Clocks
104 High St. West. SK13 8BB. (J.A. and T.P. Lees). Est. 1975. CL: Tues. *STOCK: Clocks.* TEL: 01457 862677. SER: Restorations (clocks and barometers).

GRASSMOOR, Nr. Chesterfield

N. and C.A. Haslam
220 Chesterfield Rd. S42 5EZ. Open by appointment. *STOCK: 17th-19th C furniture and decorative items.* TEL: 01246 853672 (24 hrs). SER: Buys at auction and on commission. VAT: Stan/Spec.

HAYFIELD, Nr. New Mills

Michael Allcroft Antiques
1 Church St. Open Sat. and Sun. 12-5, other times by appointment. *STOCK: Pine furniture and decorative items.* TEL: 01663 742684.

HEANOR

Bygones
23c Derby Rd. DE7 7QG. (Mrs P. Buttifant). Open 10-5. CL: Mon. and Wed. *STOCK: Furniture, porcelain, objets d'art, paintings and prints.* TEL: 01773 768503. SER: Framing.

ILKESTON

Matsell Antiques Ltd
DE7 5JQ. Est. 1945. Open by appointment only. *STOCK: Decorative objects, works of art, Oriental ceramics.* LOC: Close to M1, junction 25 or 26. TEL: 01159 302446; fax - same. SER: Specialist photography for antiques/art; buys on commission. VAT: Stan/Spec.

KILLAMARSH

Havenplan's Architectural Emporium

The Old Station, Station Rd. S31 8EN. Est. 1972. Open Tues.-Sat. 10-4. SIZE: Large. *STOCK: Architectural fittings and decorative items, church interiors and furnishings, fireplaces, doors, decorative cast ironwork, masonry, bygones, garden ornaments, 18th to early 20th C.* LOC: M1, exit 30. Take A616 towards Sheffield, turn right on to B6053, turn right on to B6058 towards Killamarsh, turn right between two railway bridges. PARK: Easy. TEL: 01142 489972; fax - 01142 511057; home - 01246 433315. SER: Hire.

LONG EATON

Goodacre Engraving Ltd

Thrumpton Ave. (off Chatsworth Ave.), Meadow Lane. NG10 2GB. Est. 1948. *STOCK: Longcase and bracket clock movements, parts and castings.* TEL: 01159 734387; fax - 01159 461193. SER: Hand engraving, movement repairs, silvering and dial repainting. VAT: Stan.

Miss Elany

2 Salisbury St. NG10 1BA. (D. and Mrs Mottershead). Est. 1977. Open 9-5. SIZE: Medium. *STOCK: Pianos, 1900 to date, £50-£500; general antiques, Victorian and Edwardian, £25-£200.* PARK: Easy. TEL: 0115 9734835. VAT: Stan.

MELBOURNE

The Spindles

DE73 1BA. (Mrs C. Reynolds). Est. 1972. Resident. Usually available but telephone call advisable. SIZE: Large. *STOCK: Clocks, watches, 17th-19th C.* LOC: 0.5 miles from junction 14, M42. PARK: Easy. TEL: 01332 862609. VAT: Stan.

NEWTOWN, Nr. New Mills

Michael Allcroft Antiques

203 Buxton Rd. SIZE: Large. *STOCK: Shipping furniture and decorative pine.* TEL: 01663 742684; mobile - 0831 588613.

SHARDLOW, Nr. Derby

Shardlow Antiques Warehouse

24 The Wharf. DE7 2GH. Open 10.30-5, Sun. 12-5. CL: Fri. SIZE: Large. *STOCK: Furniture, Georgian to shipping.* LOC: Off M1, junction 24. PARK: Own. TEL: 01332 792899/662899.

SWADLINCOTE

G.K. Hadfield

Rock Farm, Chilcote. DE12 8DQ. (G.K. and J.V Hadfield and D.W. and N.R. Hadfield-Tilly). Est 1972. Open Tues.-Sat. 9-5. *STOCK: Clocks - longcase, dial, Act of Parliament, skeleton, Black Forest, American and carriage; secondhand and rare horological books.* LOC: Between Ashby-de la-Zouch and Tamworth, 3 miles from Junc. 11 A42/M42. TEL: 01827 373466; fax - 0182 373699. SER: Restoration materials (antique clocks); valuations (clocks and horologica books). VAT: Stan/Spec.

TICKNALL

Sam Savage Antiques

The Old Coach House, Hayes Farm, Main St DE73 1JZ. (S. Savage). Resident. Est. 1969. Open by appointment only. *STOCK: Early period furniture, 17th-19th C; decorative items, Oriental rugs, paintings.* LOC: Centre of Ticknall, on A514, 4 miles from Ashby-de-la-Zouch, 10 mile west from exit 24, M1 and 6 miles east of Ashb turn-off on M42. PARK: Easy. TEL: 0133 862195. SER: Valuations.

WHALEY BRIDGE

Nimbus Antiques

Chapel Rd. , (L.M. and H.C. Brobbin). Est. 1978 Open 9-5.30, Sun. 2-5.30. SIZE: Large. *STOCK Furniture, mainly mahogany, desks, dining table chairs and clocks, 18th-19th C.* LOC: A6. PARK Easy. TEL: 01663 734248; home - 01663 73333 SER: Valuations; restorations. VAT: Stan/Spec.

WOODVILLE

Wooden Box Antiques

32 High St. DE11 7EH. (Mrs R. Bowler). Es 1982. Open 10-5 including some Sun. SIZE Medium. *STOCK: Furniture, Georgian-Edwardian £75-£400; original cast-iron fireplace surrounds, £50-£600; Victorian tiles, country pine furniture, pine doors.* LOC: A50, between Ashby de-la-Zouch and Burton-on-Trent. PARK: Eas TEL: 01283 212014; home - same. SER: Restor ations (furniture).

YEAVELEY, Nr. Ashbourne

Gravelly Bank Pine Antiques

DE6 2DT. (A. Brassington). Open every da including evenings. *STOCK: Mahogany, oak an pine furniture, 18th-19th C, £50-£500.* PARK Easy. TEL: 01335 330237; home and fax same.SER: Valuations; restorations (pine); buys auction.

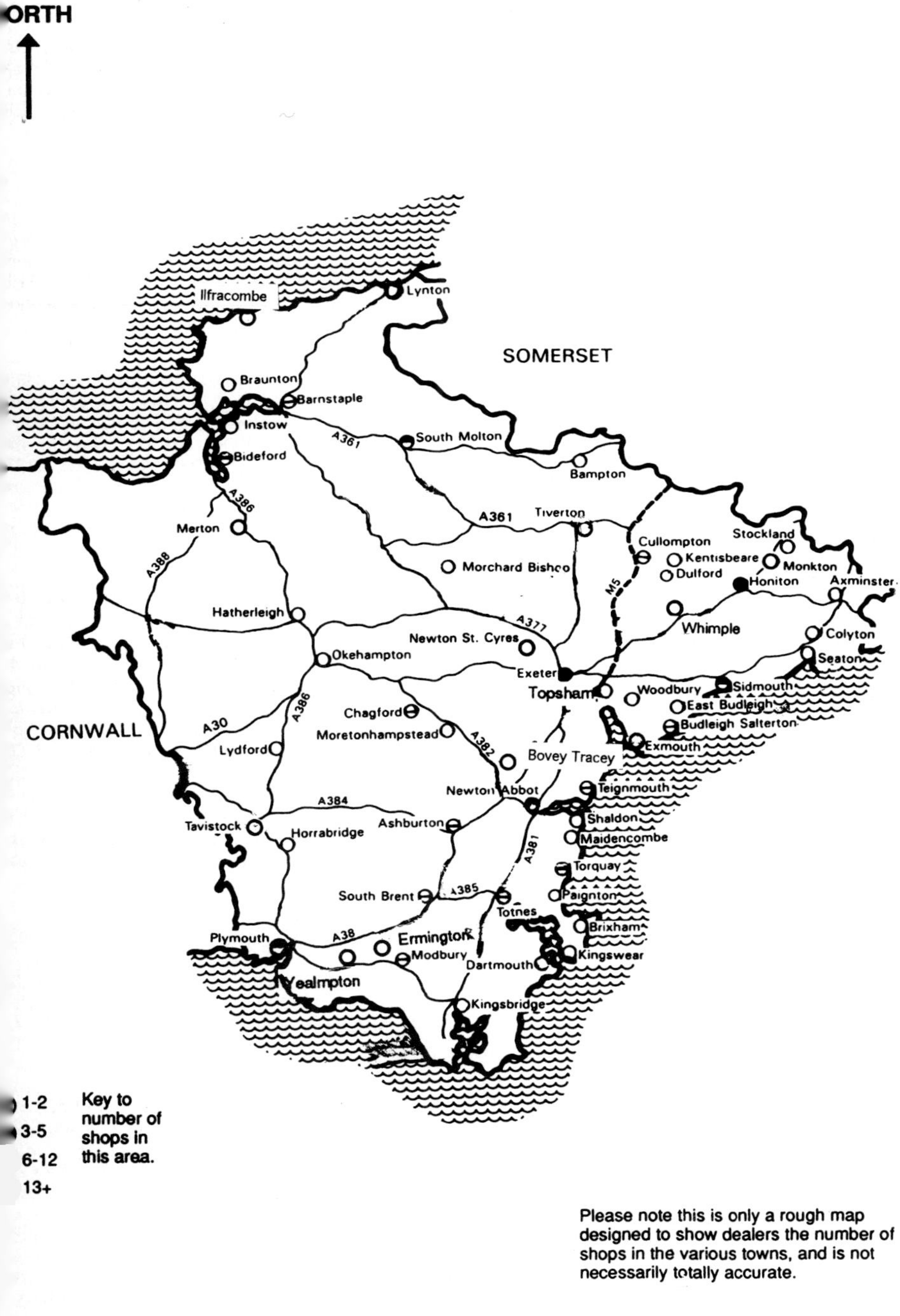

1-2
3-5
6-12
13+

Key to number of shops in this area.

Please note this is only a rough map designed to show dealers the number of shops in the various towns, and is not necessarily totally accurate.

ASHBURTON

Ashburton Marbles
Great Hall, North St. TQ13 7DU. (Adrian Ager). Est. 1976. Open 8-5, Sat. 10-5. SIZE: Warehouse and showroom. *STOCK: Marble and wooden fire-surrounds, decorative cast iron inserts; scuttles, fenders, overmantels, 1790-1910; architectural decorative antiques, garden statuary and related items, chandeliers, soft furnishings and furniture.* PARK: Easy. TEL: 01364 653189; fax - same.

M. W. Dunscombe Antiques
6 East St. TQ13 7AA. Est. 1980. Open Thurs. and Fri. 9.30-5, Sat. 9.30-1, other times by appointment. SIZE: Large. *STOCK: Furniture, 18th C to Edwardian, £150-£2,000.* LOC: Just off A38 town centre. PARK: Easy. TEL: 01364 654144; fax - same; home - same. VAT: Spec.

Moor Antiques
19a North St. TQ13 7QH. (T. and Mrs E. Gatland). Est. 1984. CL: Wed. pm. SIZE: Small. *STOCK: Small furniture, 1780-1900, £200-£1,500; clocks, 1830-1910, £100-£1,000; silver and china, 1800-1900, £25-£500.* LOC: A38 town centre, 100 yards past town hall. PARK: Nearby. TEL: 01364 653767. SER: Valuations.

The Shambles
22 North St. TQ13 7QD. Est. 1982. Open 10-5, Sat. 10-1. SIZE: 8 dealers. *STOCK: Country and general antiques and decorative items, £5-£1,500.* LOC: Town centre. PARK: Opposite. TEL: 01364 653848. SER: Valuations. FAIRS: Little Chelsea, Sandown, Kensington Brocante, Westpoint Exeter. VAT: Stan/Spec.

AXMINSTER

W.G. Potter and Son
1 West St. EX13 5HS. Est. 1863. Open 9-5. CL: Sat. pm. SIZE: Medium. *STOCK: Pine including, 19th-20th C; some mahogany and oak.* LOC: In main street (A35) opposite church. PARK: Easy. TEL: 01297 32063. SER: Restorations (furniture); buys at auction. VAT: Stan/Spec.

BAMPTON, Nr. Tiverton

Bampton Antiques
9 Castle St. EX16 9LN. (J.M. Yendell). Est. 1983. Open 10.30-5. CL: Mon. SIZE: Medium. *STOCK: Furniture including country, porcelain, glass, collectables, fine art.* LOC: B3227 from Taunton. PARK: Easy. TEL: 01398 331197; home - 01884 860575. SER: Valuations.

Robert Byles
7 Castle St. Est. 1966. Open by chance, knocking or appointment. *STOCK: Early oak, local farmhouse tables and settles, metalwork, pottery, unstripped period pine, architectural items.* TEL: 01398 331515. SER: Restoration materials. VAT: Stan/Spec.

BARNSTAPLE

Medina Gallery
80 Boutport St. EX31 1SR. (R. Jennings). Es[t.] 1972. Open 9.30-5. CL: Wed. pm. SIZE: Smal[l.] *STOCK: Maps, prints, photographs, oils an[d] watercolours, £1-£500.* TEL: 01271 71025. SE[R:] Picture framing, mounting. VAT: Stan.

Mark Parkhouse Antiques and Jewellery
106 High St. EX31 1HP. Est. 1976. CL: We[d.] *STOCK: Jewellery, furniture, silver, painting[s,] clocks, glass, porcelain, small collectors' item[s,] 18th-19th C, £100-£10,000.* PARK: Nearby. TE[L:] 01271 74504. SER: Valuations; buys at auctio[n.] VAT: Stan/Spec.

Tudor House
115 Boutport St. (C. and D. Pilon). Est. 198[.] Open 9.30-3.30,Wed. 9.30-1. SIZE: Larg[e.] *STOCK: Furniture and bric-a-brac, late 18th [...] and reproduction.* LOC: Off M5, Tiverton li[nk] road to town centre. PARK: Easy. TEL: 012[..] 75370; home - 01271 71750. SER: Valuation[s;] restorations (furniture).

BIDEFORD

J. Collins and Son **BADA LAPADA**
The Studio, 28 High St. EX39 2AN. (J. and [.] Biggs). CINOA. Est. 1953. Open Mon.-Fr[i.] 9.30-5, Sat., Sun., evenings and trade b[y] appointment. SIZE: Large. *STOCK: Georgia[n] and Regency furniture; general antiqu[es] including framed and restored 19th-20th C o[ils] and watercolours.* LOC: From Bideford O[ld] Bridge turn right, then first left into the Hi[gh] St. PARK: Easy. TEL: 01237 473103; fax 01237 475658; home - 01237 476485. SE[R:] Valuations; restorations (period furnitur[e,] paintings and watercolours); cleaning a[nd] framing; buys at auction. VAT: Spec.

Medina Gallery
20 Mill St. EX39 2JR. (R. Jennings). Est. 19[..] Open 9.30-5. CL: Wed. pm. SIZE: Mediu[m.] *STOCK: Maps and prints, photographs, oils, wat[er]colours, £1-£500.* PARK: Easy. TEL: 012[..] 476483. SER: Picture framing, mounting. VA[T:] Stan.

Petticombe Manor Antiques
Petticombe Manor, Monkleigh. EX39 5JR. ([...] Wilson). Est. 1971. Open daily until 7 pm. SIZ[E:] Large. *STOCK: Furniture including dining tab[les] and chairs, desks and bureaux, bookcases a[nd] display cabinets, Pembroke and Sutherla[nd] tables; china, glass, brass and copper, oils a[nd] watercolours, prints and mirrors, hand-stripp[ed] pine, mainly 19th to early 20th C.* LOC: La[rge] manor house on A388 Bideford to Holswort[hy] road. PARK: Own. TEL: 01237 475605; hom[e -] same. SER: Restorations (re-upholstery, Fre[nch] polishing, cabinet work). VAT: Stan.

J. Collins and Son

(Established 1953)

ANTIQUES AND FINE PAINTINGS

The Studio • 28 High Street • Bideford • North Devon • EX39 2AN
Tel: Bideford (01237) 473103 • Fax: (01237) 475658

Opening hours - Monday-Friday 9.30am-5pm
SATURDAY, SUNDAY & EVENINGS BY APPOINTMENT
TRADE BY APPOINTMENT PLEASE

With the opening of the North Devon Link Road (A361) we are now 40 minutes from the M5 motorway. Take Exit 27 to Bideford Bridge, at roundabout go left, follow road to the quayside, turn right up High Street with National Westminster Bank on the corner, three quarters to the top, parking outside premises for 30 minutes or in long term car park, 3 minutes walk.

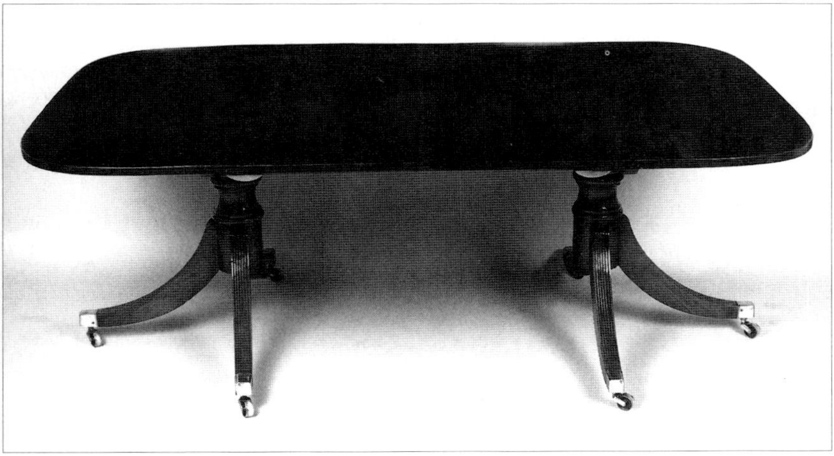

REGENCY MAHOGANY TWO PILLAR DINING TABLE. ENGLISH C.1810.

Extensive showroom specialising in Georgian and Regency furniture with associated items. Also Victorian oil paintings and watercolours.
Our entire stock is on photographic record.
Colour photographs are available for clients requiring that 'specific item'.
Why not give us a phone call!

Skilled Restoration of Period Furniture , Oil Paintings and Watercolours Undertaken

Our workshop is a member of U.K.I.C. and is also included on the register maintained by the Conservation Unit of the Museums and Galleries Commission

BOVEY TRACEY, Nr. Newton Abbot

Frank's Antiques
10 Town Hall Place. TQ13 9EH. (F.G. Tedd). Est. 1974. Open 10-5, prior telephone call advisable. SIZE: Small. *STOCK: Furniture, 17th-20th C; mechanical music including gramophones, 19th-20th C; clocks, 18th-20th C.* LOC: 5 minutes from A38. PARK: 100 yards. TEL: 01626 833325; home - same. SER: Valuations; restorations (gramophones, furniture including French polishing). FAIRS: National Vintage Communications (NEC).

BRAUNTON

Timothy Coward Fine Silver LAPADA
Marisco, Saunton. EX33 1LG. Open by appointment. *STOCK: Antique and early 20th C silver.* TEL: 01271 890466.

BRIXHAM

John Prestige Antiques
1 and 2 Greenswood Court. TQ5 9HN. Est. 1971. Open 8.45-6. CL: Sat. and Sun. except by appointment. SIZE: Large + warehouse. *STOCK: Period and Victorian furniture; shipping goods.* TEL: 01803 856141; home - 01803 853739; fax - 01803 851649. VAT: Stan/Spec.

BUDLEIGH SALTERTON

Alison Gosling Antiques
46a High St. Est. 1983. Open 12.30-5, other times by appointment. CL: Mon. and Thurs. SIZE: Medium. *STOCK: Furniture, 18th C to Edwardian, £150-£3,000; porcelain and decorative items, late 18th C to 1930's, £10-£400.* LOC: Next to Barclay's Bank. PARK: Easy. TEL: 01395 443737; home - 01395 271451. SER: Valuations.

New Gallery
Abele Tree House, 9 Fore St. EX9 6NG. (Mrs P. Hull). Est. 1968. Open Jan.-Easter by appointment only, Easter-Christmas 10-5. CL: Sun. and Mon. except by appointment. SIZE: Large. *STOCK: Fine art, oil paintings, watercolour drawings, prints.* PARK: Adjacent. TEL: 01395 443768. SER: Valuations; framing.

Quinney's
High St. EX9 6LQ. (Miss A. Fearfield). Est. 1947. Open Mon., Wed. and Fri. 9.30-12.30, other times by appointment only. *STOCK: Furniture, porcelain, silver, glass.* PARK: Easy. TEL: 01395 442793. SER: Valuations; minor restorations. VAT: Spec.

Budleigh Salterton continued

David J. Thorn
2 High St. EX9 6LQ. Est. 1950. Open Tues. an Fri. 10-1 and 2.15-5.30, Sat. 10-1. SIZE: Smal *STOCK: English, Continental and Orienta pottery and porcelain, 1620-1850, £5-£5,000 English furniture, 1680-1870, £20-£5,000 paintings, silver, jewellery, £1-£1,000.* PARK Easy. TEL: 01395 442448. SER: Valuations VAT: Stan/Spec.

CHAGFORD

Mary Payton Antiques
The Old Market House. TQ13 8AB. (Mrs M Essex). Est. 1968. Open 10-1 and 2.30-5. CL Wed. and Mon. SIZE: Small. *STOCK: Englis pottery and porcelain especially Staffordshir English glass, 18th-19th C; maps and prints (We Country), 17th-19th C.* Not Stocked: Jeweller firearms, coins, silver, pewter. LOC: Comin from Whiddon Down (A30) by A382, turn right Easton Court. Shop in the town square. PARK Easy. TEL: 01647 432428; home - 01647 43238

Rex Antiques
The Old Cinema. TQ13 8AB. (John Meredith Est. 1979. Open every day 9-1 and 2-5 or b appointment. SIZE: Large. *STOCK: Country oa 16th-19th C, £5-£2,000; Oriental brass an copper, weapons, large unusual items, granit architectural items, old iron work.* PARK: Eas TEL: 01647 433405. SER: Buys at auction. VA Stan/Spec. Trade only.

Whiddons Antiques and Tearooms
6 High St. TQ13 8AJ. (D. Meldrum). Est. 197 Open 10.30-5.30. SIZE: Medium. *STOCK: Gener and country items - furniture including pine, clock prints, paintings, copper, brass, books ar collectables.* LOC: Opposite church. PARK: Eas TEL: 01647 433406; home - 01647 433303.

COLYTON

Colyton Antique Centre
Dolphin St. EX12 2UR. Open 10-5. SIZE: 3 dealers. *STOCK: General antiques and collec ables.* PARK: Easy. TEL: 01297 552339.

CULLOMPTON

Cobweb Antiques
The Old Tannery, Exeter Rd. EX15 1DT. (Holmes). Est. 1980. Open 10-5.30 including Su SIZE: Large. *STOCK: Pine and country furnitu painted, decorative and mahogany items, £ £2,000.* LOC: Half a mile from junction 28, M PARK: Easy. TEL: 01884 38207. SER: Strippir restorations; packing; courier. VAT: Stan/Spec.

Cullompton continued

Cullompton Old Tannery Antiques
Exeter Rd. EX15 1DT. (Cullompton Antiques Ltd). Est. 1989. Open 10-5.30 including Sun. SIZE: Large. *STOCK: Pine, oak, mahogany and fruitwood country furniture; china and decorative items.* LOC: Off M5, junction 28, through town centre, premises on right, approximately 1 mile. PARK: Easy. TEL: 01884 38476; fax - same. VAT: Stan/Spec.

Francis de Aguilar Furniture
The Old Tannery, Exeter Rd. EX15 1DT. *STOCK: Country and period French and English furniture.*

Mills Antiques
The Old Tannery, Exeter Rd. Est. 1979. Open 10-5.30, Sat. and Sun. 10-5. *STOCK: 17th C to Edwardian furniture and decorative items.* PARK: Easy. TEL: 01884 32462.

DARTMOUTH

Chantry Bookshop and Gallery
1 Higher St. TQ6 9RB. (M.P. Merkel). Est. 1969. Open 10.30-5. CL: 15th Jan.-20th Mar. SIZE: Small. *STOCK: Antiquarian books and watercolours; decorative maps, town plans, prints, sea charts and battle plans.* LOC: Next to 'The Cherub' public house. PARK: Nearby. TEL: 01803 832796; home - 01803 834208.

DULFORD, Nr. Cullompton

G. Mounter
Bakers Farm. EX14 2DJ. Usually open, prior telephone call advisable. *STOCK: Painted country and formal furniture, early and primitive Windsor chairs; unstripped pine.* TEL: 01884 266358. *Trade Only.*

EAST BUDLEIGH

Antiques at Budleigh House
Budleigh House. EX9 7ED. (W. Cook). Est. 1982. Open 10-5, Sat. 10-1. CL: Mon. and Wed. SIZE: Small. *STOCK: 18th-19th C small furniture and decorative objects, porcelain, glass, silver and metalware, £5-£1,000.* LOC: Opposite Sir Walter Raleigh public house. PARK: Easy. TEL: 01395 445368; home - same. SER: Valuations; buys at auction.

ERMINGTON, Nr. Ivybridge

Mill Gallery
(Christopher Trant). Resident. Est. 1984. CL: Sat. SIZE: Small. *STOCK: Oils and watercolours, 18th-20th C, £300-£1,000.* LOC: From A38 take Ivybridge exit, follows signs, 1st premises in village. PARK: Easy. TEL: 01548 830172. SER: Valuations; restorations (oils); buys at auction (as stock). VAT: Spec.

EXETER

The Antique Centre on the Quay

The Quay. EX2 4AP. Open 10-5 winter, 10-6 summer including Sun. SIZE: 20+ dealers. *STOCK: Antiques, collectables, books, records, tools and jewellery.* TEL: 01392 493501.

Exeter Rare Books

Guildhall Shopping Centre. EX4 3HG. (R.C. Parry). ABA. Est. 1965. Open 10-1 and 2-5. SIZE: Small. *STOCK: Books, antiquarian, secondhand, out-of-print, 17th-20th C, £5-£500.* LOC: City centre. PARK: Easy. TEL: 01392 436021. SER: Valuations; buys at auction. FAIRS: ABA Chelsea, Bath and Edinburgh.

Fagins Antiques

The Old Whiteways Cider Factory, Hele. EX5 4PW. (C.J. Strong). Open 9.15-5, Sat. 11-5. *STOCK: Furniture, decorative items, architectural and shipping items.* TEL: 01392 882062/01395 279660; fax - 01392 882194.

Gold and Silver Exchange

Eastgate House, Princesshay. EX4 3JT. *STOCK: Jewellery, watches including Rolex.* TEL: 01392 217478.

The House that Moved

24 West St. (L. Duriez). Open 10-5. *STOCK: Lace, shawls, babywear, linen, 1920's costume, Victorian and Edwardian bridal wedding dresses.* TEL: 01392 432643.

McBains of Exeter LAPADA

Exeter Airport, Clyst Honiton. EX5 2BA. SIZE: Large warehouse complex. *STOCK: Furniture.* LOC: A30, 2 miles from exit 30, M5. Below are listed the dealers who are trading from this address. TEL: 01392 366261; fax - 01392 365572. *Trade Only.*

Ash Brothers Antiques

Art deco, unstripped pine, shipping goods. TEL: 01392 364483. VAT: Stan.

McBains of Exeter

(I.S., G., R. and M. McBain). Est. 1963. *Furniture, period and Victorian; decorative and shipping goods.* TEL: 01392 366261; fax - 01392 365572.

Miscellany Antiques

Shipping goods. TEL: 01392 366261.

Leon Robertson Antiques

Furniture. TEL: 01392 366261.

Tredantiques

Georgian, Victorian and Edwardian furniture. TEL: 01392 366261.

Exeter continued

The Meeting

38 South St. EX1 1ED. (L. Emanuel). Open 10-5.30. SIZE: Large - 30 dealers. *STOCK: Furniture and clocks, 18th-19th C, £100-£3,000; porcelain, glass, silver, jewellery, rugs and textiles, fine art, books, boxes, treen, 19th-20th C, £20-£1,500.* LOC: City centre, opposite White Hart. PARK: Opposite and 150 metres. TEL: 01392 412260. SER: Valuations.

Micawber Antiques

New Buildings Lane, 25-26 Gandy St. EX4 3LS. (Penny Standing). Est. 1984. Open 10-5. SIZE: Small. *STOCK: China, pottery and clocks, 1840-1940, £10-£300; costume jewellery, oil lamps, metalware, general antiques, £3-£200.* LOC: City centre. PARK: Nearby. TEL: 01392 52200. SER: Picture framing; clock and barometer repairs.

Brian Mortimer

87 Queen St. EX4 3RP. *STOCK: General antiques, jewellery, silver, Victoriana.* TEL: 01392 79994. VAT: Stan/Spec.

John Nathan Antiques

153/154 Cowick St., St. Thomas. EX4 1AS. (J. Doble). Est. 1950. Open 9-5.30. SIZE: Small. *STOCK: Silver and jewellery, £5-£5,000; clocks including Georgian and Victorian, £25-£3,000.* LOC: From Exeter inner by-pass over new Exe Bridge, take A30 Okehampton Rd. under railway arch, shop on right. PARK: Easy. TEL: 01392 278216. SER: Valuations; restorations (silver and jewellery); buys at auction. VAT: Stan.

Pennies

Pennies Furniture Centre, Unit 2, Wessex Estate, Station Rd., Exwick. EX4 4NZ. (Penelope and Michael Clark). Est. 1982. Open 9-6. SIZE: Medium. *STOCK: Furniture, from Victorian; china, glass and bric-a-brac, books.* LOC: Behind St. David's Station, over railway lines. PARK: Easy. TEL: 01392 71928/76532/216238. SER: Valuations. VAT: Stan/Spec.

Phantique

47 The Quay. EX2 4AN. SIZE: 14 dealers. *STOCK: General antiques.* TEL: 01392 49899[illegible]. SER: Restorations.

The Quay Gallery Antiques Emporium

43 The Quay. EX2 4AP. (A. Nebbett). Est. 198[illegible]. Open 10-5 including Sun. SIZE: Large - [illegible] dealers. *STOCK: 18th-20th C oak and mahogany furniture, marine items, porcelain, silver, plate, glass and decorative items.* LOC: Next to Old Customs House. PARK: Easy. TEL: 01392 213283; fax - 01392 490585.

:XMOUTH

3oase Antiques
5 High St. EX8 1NN. Open 10-5. *STOCK: Jewel- 'ery, silver, Victorian collectables.* LOC: Town :entre. PARK: Easy. TEL: 01395 271528.

Lilians
32 Exeter Rd. (L. Treasure). Open 9-5. *STOCK: ;eneral antiques.* TEL: 01395 279512.

ɪATHERLEIGH

Iatherleigh Antiques BADA
5 Bridge St. EX20 3JS. (S. and M. Dann).)pen 9-1 and 2-5, anytime by appointment. :L: Wed. and Thurs. SIZE: Medium. *STOCK: :ollectors' furniture and works of art, pre-1700.* 'ARK: Easy. TEL: 01837 810159/01837 ·10500. VAT: Spec.

ɪONITON

Che Antique Centre Abingdon House
36 High St. EX14 8JP. (M.V. Melliar-Smith and .J. Butler). Est. 1985. Open 10-5. SIZE: Large - 5 dealers. *STOCK: Arts and Crafts and general ntiques including furniture, country and sporting 'ems, luggage and early metalwork.* LOC: Exeter nd of High St. PARK: Nearby. TEL: 01404 2108.

'ane Barnes Antiques & Interiors
9 High St. EX14 8PW. Open 10-4. CL: Thurs. IZE: Medium. *STOCK: General antiques and ountry pine, glass, clocks.* LOC: Main St. PARK: asy. TEL: 01404 41712. SER: Furniture copies ıade to order.

. Barrymore and Co
3-75 High St. EX14 8PG. (J. and M. Ogden). Est. 979. Open 10-5, Thurs. by appointment only. IZE: Medium. *STOCK: Silver, 17th-20th C, £100- 15,000; Old Sheffield plate, Victorian electro- 'ate, £100-£4,000; jewellery, £150-£5,000; all 9th C to early 20th C.* LOC: Main st. PARK: asy. TEL: 01404 42244. VAT: Stan/Spec.

3ramble Cross Antiques LAPADA
xeter Rd. EX14 8AL. Open 10-5.30. *STOCK: 8th-19th C furniture, clocks and decorative ems.* TEL: 01404 47085. VAT: Stan/Spec.

.oderick Butler BADA
Iarwood House. EX14 8PY. Est. 1948. Open 30-5. SIZE: Large. *STOCK: 17th-18th C and egency furniture, curiosities, unusual items, ırly metalwork.* LOC: Adjacent to roundabout : eastern end of High St. PARK: In courtyard. 'EL: 01404 42169. VAT: Spec.

: & S Antiques
59 High St. EX14 8LJ. (I. Crackston and H. edge). Est. 1986. Open 10-5. SIZE: Medium.

Honiton continued

STOCK: Period country antiques, copper, brass, ceramics, 19th C and earlier. PARK: Nearby. TEL: 01404 43436.

Fountain Antiques
132 High St. EX14 8JP. (J. Palmer and G. York). Open 9.30-5.30. *STOCK: General antiques including pictures, books and linen.* TEL: 01404 42074.

Honiton Antique Toys
38 High St. EX14 8PJ. (L. and S. Saunders). Est. 1986. Open 10.30-5. CL: Mon. and Thurs. *STOCK: Toys, dolls and teddies.* PARK: Easy. TEL: 01404 41194.

Honiton Clock Clinic
167 High St. EX14 8LQ. (David Newton). Est. 1992. Open 10-4. SIZE: Small. *STOCK: Clocks and barometers.* LOC: Exeter end of High St. PARK: Nearby. TEL: 01404 47466.

Honiton Fine Art
189 High St. EX14 8LQ. (C.B. and P.R. Greenberg). Est. 1974. Open 9.30-5. SIZE: Medium. *STOCK: English watercolours and oil paintings, 18th-19th C, £300-£5,000; Old Master drawings, Dutch, Italian and French, 16th-18th C, £300-£1,500.* LOC: Town centre. PARK: Easy. TEL: 01404 45942. SER: Valuations; restorations (oil paintings and watercolours).

Honiton continued

The Honiton Lace Shop
44 High St. EX14 8PJ. Open 9.30-1 and 2-5. *STOCK: Lace including specialist and collectors; quilts, shawls and other textiles, bobbins and lace making equipment.* TEL: 01404 42416; fax - 01404 47797.

Honiton Old Bookshop
Felix House, 51 High St. EX14 8PW. (R. Collicott). Est. 1991. Open 10-5.30. *STOCK: Books - travel, childrens' illustrated; plate books and bindings; all £5-£500.* LOC: Main street. PARK: Easy. TEL: 01404 47180. SER: Catalogues available (3 per annum). FAIRS: London PBFA. VAT: Stan.

House of Antiques
195 High St. EX14 8LQ. (Kevin Wheeler-Johns and Ian Baum). Est. 1992. Open 10-5. SIZE: Large. *STOCK: Edwardian and Victorian furniture, general antiques.* LOC: Exeter end of High St. PARK: Nearby. TEL: 01404 41648; home - 01752 560711.

L.J. Huggett and Son
Stamps Building, King St. EX14 8AG. Open 9.30-5, Sat 9.30-4. SIZE: Large. *STOCK: Furniture, 18th-19th C.* TEL: 01404 42043; home - 01404 47117.

Lombard Antiques
14 High St. EX14 8PU. Est. 1984. Open 10-5.30. SIZE: Small. *STOCK: 18th-19th C English furniture, porcelain and decorative items.* PARK: Easy. TEL: 01404 42140.

The Old Dairy - Antiques & Bygones
Vine Passage, High St. EX14 8NN. (Miss N. J. Symes). Est. 1993. Open Tues.-Sat. 10-5 or by appointment. SIZE: Small. *STOCK: 19th-20th C country pine and oak furniture, £25-£1,000.* LOC: Off High St., opposite Vine Inn. PARK: Easy and at rear. TEL: 01404 44876. SER: Restorations (furniture including pine stripping).

Otter Antiques
69 High St. EX14 8PW. (G.F. Wilkin). Open 9-5, Thurs. by appointment only. *STOCK: Silver and plate including cutlery and flatware.* TEL: 01404 42627.

Pilgrim Antiques
145 High St. EX14 8LJ. (G. and J.E. Mills). Est. 1970. Open 9-5.30. SIZE: Large - trade warehouse. *STOCK: Period English and Continental furniture.* PARK: Easy. TEL: 01404 41219/45316; fax - 01404 45317. SER: Packing and shipping. VAT: Stan/Spec.

Upstairs, Downstairs
12 High St. EX14 8PU. Open 10-5.30. SIZE: Large. *STOCK: 18th-19th C furniture, porcelain, metalware, pictures and clocks.* PARK: Easy. TEL: 01404 44481/42140.

Wickham Antiques
191 High St. EX14 8LQ. (J. and E. Waymouth). Est. 1986. Open 9.30-5. SIZE: Medium. *STOCK:*

Honiton continued

Mahogany and oak country furniture, decorativ items. PARK: Easy. TEL: 01404 44654.

Geoffrey M. Woodhead
53 High St. EX14 8PW. Est. 1950. Open 9.3(5.30. SIZE: Medium. *STOCK: Books and unusu items.* Not Stocked: Coins, stamps, silver, plat LOC: A30 opposite largest tree in street. PARK Easy. TEL: 01404 42969. VAT: Stan/Spec.

HORRABRIDGE

Ye Olde Saddlers Shoppe
PL20 7RF. (R. Howes). Est. 1970. SIZE: Smal *STOCK: General antiques, furniture, clocks an watches, collectors' items.* LOC: 4 miles fro Tavistock on A386. PARK: Easy - opposite or rear of shop. TEL: 01822 852109.

ILFRACOMBE

Relics
113 High St. (Nicola D. Bradshaw). Resident. Es 1977. Open 10-1 and 2-5, Thurs. 10-1. SIZE: Sma *STOCK: General antiques and small collectable Victorian and Edwardian.* LOC: Opp. The Bunch Grapes. PARK: Nearby. TEL: 01271 865486; hon - same. SER: Valuations. VAT: Stan.

INSTOW, Nr Bideford

Porcupines Bookroom
EX39 4JZ. (Sue Lowe). Est. 1963. Open b appointment only. *STOCK: Books, 16th-20th special editions, Lear, coin/medal books, Dev topography.* TEL: 01271 861158.

KENTISBEARE, Nr. Cullompton

Sextons
Dulford Cottage. EX15 2DX. (B.A. and F. Ward-Smith). Est. 1979. Open 9-6, Sat. and Su by appointment. SIZE: Medium. *STOCK: Engli and French country furniture, 1720-1900, £10 £3,000.* LOC: Telephone for directions. PAR Easy. TEL: 01884 266429; home - same. VA Stan. *Trade Only.*

KINGSBRIDGE

Avon House Antiques/Hayward's Antiques
13 Church St. TQ7 1BT. (D.H. and M. Hayward). Open 10-1 and 2-5. *STOCK: Gener antiques.* TEL: 01548 853718.

KINGSWEAR, Nr. Dartmouth

David L.H. Southwick Rare Art **BA**
Beacon Lodge, Beacon Lane. TQ6 0BU. Op by appointment. *STOCK: Chinese a Japanese works of art.* TEL: 01803 752533; f - 01803 752535.

LYDFORD, Nr. Okehampton

Skeaping Gallery
Townend House. EX20 4AR. Est. 1972. Open by appointment. *STOCK: Oils and watercolours.* TEL: 01822 820383; fax - same. VAT: Spec

LYNTON

Vendy Antiques
29A Lee Rd. EX35 6BS. (D.R. and T.W. Vendy). Est. 1964. Open 10-1 and 2-4, Sat. by appointment. *STOCK: General antiques including furniture and smalls, mainly Victorian, £10-£2,000.* PARK: Easy. TEL: 01598 752722; home - 01598 753227.

MAIDENCOMBE, Nr. Torquay

G.A. Whiteway-Wilkinson
Sunsea, Teignmouth Rd. TQ1 4TP. Est. 1943. Open by appointment only. *STOCK: General antiques, fine art and jewellery.* LOC: Approximately halfway on main Torquay/Teignmouth road. TEL: 01803 329692. VAT: Spec.

MERTON, Nr. Okehampton

Barometer World (Barometers)
Quicksilver Barn. EX20 3DS. (P.R. Collins). Est. 1979. Open 8-5. SIZE: Medium. *STOCK: Mercurial wheel and stick barometers, 1780-1800, £450-£3,500; aneroid barometers, 1850-1930, £70-£1,200.* LOC: Between Hatherleigh and Torrington on A386. PARK: Easy. TEL: 01805 603443; fax - 01805 603344. SER: Valuations; restorations (barometers). VAT: Stan/Spec.

MODBURY, Nr. Ivybridge

Fourteen A
14A Broad St. PL21 0PU. (Bridget Kirke). Est. 1986. Open 10-5. SIZE: Small. *STOCK: Lighting, door furniture, brass fire irons, copper, kitchenalia, old and new linen, 19th C boxes, new blue and white china and oriental rugs.* LOC: Next to Post Office. PARK: Nearby. TEL: 01548 831136; home - 01458 560055.

Quality Box Antiques
at Fourteen A, 14a Broad St. (Marjorie Ridsdill). Est. 1982. Open 10-5, Sun. by appointment. SIZE: Small. *STOCK: White linen and quilts, 19th to early 20th C, £5-£500; coloured embroidered linen, early 20th C, £2-£100; jewellery, silver and flatware, 19th-20th C, £5-£300; small furniture, 19th-20th C, £50-£500.* LOC: Shop next to Post Office. PARK: Nearby. TEL: 01548 831136; home - 01364 72376. FAIRS: Ardingly.

Wild Goose Antiques
34 Church St. PL21 0QR. (Mr and Mrs E. Christopher-Walsh). Open 10-5 and by appointment. CL: Mon. *STOCK: General antiques, pictures, porcelain, chandeliers, silver, jewellery.* TEL: 01548 830715; home - 01548 830238. VAT: Stan.

Modbury continued

Ye Little Shoppe
1B Broad St. PL21 0PS. (Eric W. Ridsdill). Est. 1990. Open 10-5. CL.Wed. SIZE: Small. *STOCK: Tea, writing and jewellery boxes, 19th C, £40-£350; woodworkers and saddlers tools, 19th C to early 20th C, £10-£150; small furniture and china, to £300; oil lamps, 19th-20th C, £18-£300.* LOC: Main street. PARK: Nearby. TEL: 01548 830732. SER: Restorations (writing boxes, including embossed and gilded leathers). FAIRS: Ardingly.

MONKTON, Nr. Honiton

Pugh's Farm Antiques
Pugh's Farm. EX14 9QH. (G. Garner and C. Cherry). Est. 1974. Open 9.30-5.30, Sun. am. by appointment. SIZE: Large. *STOCK: General antiques including Victorian and Edwardian furniture, beds and country farmhouse tables imported from France.* LOC: A30 2 miles from Honiton. PARK: Easy. TEL: 01404 42860; home - same; fax - 01404 47792. VAT: Stan.

MORCHARD BISHOP, Nr. Crediton

Morchard Bishop Antiques
Meadowbank. EX17 6PD. (J.C. and E.A. Child). Resident. Open by appointment. *STOCK: Mainly metalware boxes and pottery.* LOC: 8 miles west of Crediton, off A377 at Morchard Rd. PARK: Easy. TEL: 01363 877456.

MORETONHAMPSTEAD

The Old Brass Kettle

2-4 Ford St. TQ13 8LN. (H. Clark). Est. 1950. Open 9.30-1 and 2.15-5.30. CL: Sun. except by appointment, and Thurs. SIZE: Medium. *STOCK: Pottery, porcelain and furniture, 19th C.* LOC: A382 from Newton Abbot, B3212 from Exeter. TEL: 01647 440334. SER: Buys at auction. VAT: Spec.

NEWTON ABBOT

The Attic

9 Union St. TQ12 2JX. (G.W. Gillman). Est. 1976. CL: Mon. and Thurs., prior telephone call advisable. SIZE: Medium. *STOCK: General antiques, to £1,000.* LOC: Town centre. PARK: Easy. TEL: 01626 55124. SER: Valuations.

Newton Abbot Antiques Centre

55 East St. TQ12 2JP. (P. and D. Stockman). Est. 1973. Open every Tues. 9-3. LOC: 200yds. from clock tower. PARK: Through arch. TEL: 01626 54074. Below are listed some of the dealers at this centre.

Mrs Adams
China, glass, small furniture.

Blockley
Decorative objects and furniture.

Bobs
Oak and mahogany furniture.

Caunter
Victoriana, 19th C china and pottery.

Curio Corner
Plate, china, glass, jewellery.

Mrs Forster
Plate, pottery and porcelain.

Vyvyan Goode
Furniture and silver, pictures, objets d'art, glass, plate.

Hendrika
General antiques and china.

Jo Hicks
Furniture, curios, pictures, silver, jewellery, Staffordshire.

H. Hill
Costume, china, glass, fabrics, lace.

B. Hunt
Silver and china, furniture, period tools.

Mrs Jones
China, glass, brass and copper, small furniture.

John Lawrence
Furniture and china, metal toys.

Mrs Lock
General antiques, china and pottery.

Newton Abbot continued

M. Morrell
Small china, collectables.

G. Mosdell
Antiquarian books and prints.

P. & D. Antiques
Victorian and shipping furniture; Staffordshire, 18th-19th C.

Mrs Peddie
Silver, jewellery, furniture, china and pottery including Staffordshire.

Prints Etc.
Prints, pictures.

P. Shearman
Furniture, china, brass and copper.

Paul and Dorothy Stockman
Pottery and period porcelain, furniture, flat back Stafffordshire.

Sylvia
Shipping goods and china.

Tony's
Clocks.

Village Antiques
Silver, china and furniture.

Liz Wheeleker
General antiques, decor, china, silver, jewellery.

Derick Wilson
Jewellery, shipping goods and furniture.

P. Winchester
Postcards, china.

Winckworth
Clocks, small furniture, jewellery and china, bottles, plate, Goss.

P. Wright
General antiques, small items.

Mavis Young
Small general antiques, pictures.

NEWTON ST. CYRES, Nr. Exeter

Gordon Hepworth Fine Art

Hayne Farm, Sand Down Lane. EX5 5DE. (C.G. and I.M. Hepworth). Est. 1990. Open Wed.-Sat. during exhibitions or by appointment. SIZE: Large barn - 2 floors. *STOCK: Modern British paintings, post-war and contemporary especially West Country - West Cornwall and St. Ives School, £150-£3,000.* LOC: A377, 3 miles N.W. of Exeter turn left by village sign, into Sand Down Lane, farm entrance on left, after last white house. PARK: Easy. TEL: 01392 851351; home - same.

OKEHAMPTON

Alan Jones Antiques

Fatherford Farm. EX20 1QQ. Est. 1971. Open any-time by appointment. SIZE: Large - warehouse and showroom. *STOCK: Furniture, oak, walnut and mahogany, some pine; copper, brass, barometers, clocks.* LOC: On A30, one mile from Okehampton. PARK: Easy. TEL: 01837 52970; home - 01409 231428. SER: Valuations. VAT: Stan/Spec.

PLYMOUTH

Annterior Antiques

22 Molesworth Rd., Millbridge. PL1 5LZ. (A. Tregenza and R. Mascaro). Est. 1982. Open 9.30-5.30, Sat. 9.30-5, or by appointment. SIZE: Small. *STOCK: Stripped pine, 18th-19th C, £50-£3,000; some painted, mahogany and decorative furniture; brass and iron beds, 19th C, £250-£1,500; decorative small items.* LOC: Follow signs to Torpoint Ferry from North Cross roundabout, turn left at junction of Wilton St. and Molesworth Rd. PARK: Easy. TEL: 01752 558277; home - 01752 562774. SER: Buys at auction; finder. VAT: Stan/Spec.

Antique Fireplace Centre

30 Molesworth Rd., Stoke. PL1 5NA. (Brian Taylor). Est. 1988. Open 10-5 or by appointment. *STOCK: Fire surrounds - timber, marble, slate, cast iron, £100-£3,500; Georgian and Victorian fire grates, £100-£1,500; original accessories including scuttles, coal boxes, fire irons and overmantels, lamps and lanterns.* LOC: 50yds. from Victoria Park, map sent on request. PARK: Easy. TEL: 01752 559441/569061; fax - 01752 605964. SER: Valuations. VAT: Stan/Spec.

Barbican Antiques Centre

82-84 Vauxhall St., Barbican. PL4 0EX. (T. Cremer-Price). Open 9.30-5 every day. SIZE: 60+ dealers. *STOCK: Silver and plate, art pottery, porcelain, glass, jewellery, coins, stamps, clocks, collectables.* PARK: Own. TEL: 01752 201752; fax - same.

Alan Jones Antiques

Applethorn Slade Farm, Near Plympton. PL7 5AS. Resident. Est. 1965. Open by appointment. SIZE: Small. *STOCK: Maritime and scientific items, navigational instruments, telescopes, optical toys and collectors items.* LOC: Off A38, near Plymouth. TEL: 01752 338188.

M. and A. Antique Exporters

44 Breton Side. PL4 0AY. (M. Antonucci). Open 9-5. *STOCK: General antiques.* TEL: 01752 665419; fax - 01752 228058. SER: Imports; exports.

New Street Antique Centre

27 New St., The Barbican. (Turner Properties). Est. 1980. Open 10-5. SIZE: Medium. *STOCK: Clocks, silver, jewellery, weapons, general antiques.* PARK: Nearby. TEL: 01752 661165. VAT: Stan/Spec.

Plymouth continued

Anne-Marie Scott-Masson

Mount Stone House, Devil's Point. PL1 3RW. *STOCK: Small period pieces, prints, furnishing fabrics and wallpaper.* TEL: 01752 664413. SER: Interior design.

Brian Taylor Antiques

24 Molesworth Rd., Stoke. PL1 5LZ. Est. 1975. Open 10-5 Fri. and Sat., or by appointment. SIZE: Medium. *STOCK: Gramophones, phonographs, mechanical music, radios, 1840-1940, £50-£5,000+; Oriental items including buddhas and thankas, £50-£2,000; clocks, 18th-19th C, £50-£4,000.* LOC: 50yds. from Victoria Park, map sent on request. PARK: Easy. TEL: 01752 569061; home - same; fax - 01752 605964. SER: Valuations; restorations (clocks and gramophones).

Michael Wood Fine Art

Island House, The Barbican. PL1 2LS. Est. 1971. Private view gallery, open by appointment only. SIZE: Medium. *STOCK: Oils and watercolours - contemporary, £150-£5,000; modern British, £1,000-£2,500; Newlyn, St. Ives and Victorian, £350-£15,000.* LOC: On first floor, above Tourist Information. PARK: Opposite. TEL: 01752 225533; home - 01752 787444. SER: Valuations; restorations (paintings, watercolours, prints, picture frames); buys at auction (paintings, watercolours and prints, 1850 to present day). VAT: Stan/Spec.

SEATON

Etcetera Etc Antiques

12 Beer Rd. EX12 2PA. (B. Warren and M. Rymer). Est. 1969. Open 10-1 and 2-5. CL: Thurs. SIZE: Medium. *STOCK: General antique furniture, ceramics, glass, brass and decorative items.* PARK: Own. TEL: 01297 21965.

SHALDON, Nr. Teignmouth

Tempus Fugit

16c Fore St. TQ14 0DF. (R.C. Walkley). Est. 1982. Open 10-5, Sat. 10-1, Sun. am. by appointment. CL: Thurs. pm. SIZE: Small. *STOCK: Clocks, 18th-19th C, £25-£6,000; watches, furniture, paintings, jewellery and porcelain.* LOC: From A379 take left turn over bridge to Shaldon. On bend turn left into Fore St., shop on right. PARK: Easy. TEL: 01626 872752. SER: Valuations; restorations (clocks); buys at auction; export facilities.

W. J. Woodhams

28 Fore St. TQ14 0DE. Resident. Est. 1970. Open 10-5.30. SIZE: Small. *STOCK: Furniture, £5-£5,000; silver and porcelain, bric-a-brac, £5-£200; all 18th-19thC.* PARK: Easy. TEL: 01626 872630. SER: Valuations; restorations (furniture); buys at auction (furniture). VAT: Stan/Spec.

SIDMOUTH

Gainsborough House Antiques

Libra Court, Libra House, Fore St. EX10 8AJ. (K.S. Scratchley). Est. 1935. Open 9.15-1 and 2.15-5, Thurs. 9.15-12.45, Sat. 9.15-1, Thurs. pm. by appointment. SIZE: Small. *STOCK: Small general antiques, 1750-1950, £1-£1,000; medals and militaria, 1700 to date, £1-£1,500.* LOC: Down Fore St., 50 yds from seafront, left down York St., entrance to premises on left. PARK: 100 yds. TEL: 01395 514394; home - 01395 515112. SER: Valuations.

Dorothy Hartnell Antiques and Victoriana

At Gallery 21, 21 Fore St. EX10 8AL. Est. 1974. Open 10-1 and 2-5, Sun. by appointment. CL: Thurs. in winter. SIZE: Medium. *STOCK: Porcelain and pottery, small furniture, brass, pictures, interesting items, £5-£2,500.* LOC: Town centre. TEL: 01395 515291.

The Lantern Shop

4 New St. EX10 8AP. (Miss J.M. Creeke). Est. 1974. Open 10-4.45. SIZE: Medium. *STOCK: Period table lighting, 1750-1950, £45-£2,000; English porcelain, 1800-1915, £5-£1,000; watercolours and oils, 1800-1950, £15-£1,000; small furniture, 1750-1920, £25-£850.* LOC: Town centre, between Market Sq. and Fore St., behind sea front. PARK: Nearby. TEL: 01395 516320. SER: Valuations; restorations (lamps, oil paintings); framing; silk lampshade re-covering and making. VAT: Stan/Spec.

The Lantern Shop Gallery

5 New St. EX10 8AP. (Miss J.M. Creeke). Est. 1974. Open 10-4.45. SIZE: Medium. *STOCK: Topographical prints, especially East Devon and adjacent counties, 1750-1900, £5-£450; decorative prints and engravings, 1750-1960, £5-£300; maps, especially south-west England, West Midlands and Home Counties, 1600-1850, £10-£400.* LOC: Town centre between Market Sq. and Fore St., behind the sea front. PARK: Nearby. TEL: 01395 578462. SER: Valuations; restorations (cleaning and re-framing prints). VAT: Stan.

Sidmouth Antiques and Collectors Centre

All Saints Rd. SIZE: 20 dealers. *STOCK: Furniture, antiquarian books, collectors' records, linen and lace, Oriental rugs, china, glass, pictures.*

The Vintage Toy and Train Museum Shop

Sidmouth Antique Centre, All Saints Road. EX10 8ES. (R.D.N., M.E. and J.W. Salisbury). Open 10-5. *STOCK: Hornby Gauge 0 and Dublo trains, Dinky toys, Meccano and other die-cast and tinplate toys, wooden jig-saw puzzles.* TEL: 01395 512588; home - 01395 513399.

SOUTH BRENT

Philip Andrade BADA LAPADA

White Oxen Manor, Rattery. TQ10 9JX. Usually open 9-5.30, Sat. 9-1, but a prior 'phone call is advisable. ***STOCK: English town furniture, 18th-early 19th C, and interesting objects, £100-£10,000.*** **TEL: 01364 72454; fax 01364 73061.**

P.M. Pollak

Moorview, Plymouth Rd. TQ10 9HT. (Dr. P.M. Pollak). ABA. Est. 1973. Open by appointment. SIZE: Small. *STOCK: Antiquarian books especially medicine and science; prints, some instruments, £50-£5,000.* LOC: On edge of village, near London Inn. PARK: Own. TEL: 01364 73457; fax - 01364 72918. SER: Valuations; buys at auction; catalogues issued, computer searches.

L.G. Wootton Clocks and Watches

2 Church St. TQ10 9AB. Est. 1948. Open by appointment only. *STOCK: Clocks and watches, all periods; small antiques, unusual curios.* LOC: Just off A38. PARK: Easy. TEL: 01364 72553. SER: Valuations; repairs and restorations (clocks).

SOUTH MOLTON

Cobbs Curiosity Shop

24 East St. Est. 1984. Open 10-4. SIZE: Small. *STOCK: Small furniture, curios, jewellery and silver, interesting items, £5-£1,000.* PARK: Easy. TEL: 01769 574104.

The Furniture Market

14a Barnstaple St. EX36 3BQ. (R.M. and V.J. Golding). Est. 1971. Open 10-1 and 2-5, Wed 10-1. SIZE: Large - 20 dealers. *STOCK: Furniture, collectables, silver and glass, to early 20th C, £5-£2,000.* LOC: On old A361, 100 yards from town centre. PARK: Nearby. TEL: 01769 573401. SER: Valuations; buys at auction.

The Lace Shop

Bay House, 33 East St. EX36 3DF. (Fenela Sadler). Est. 1985. *STOCK: Lace, 17th-20th C, £5-£1,000; linens, patchwork, bridal veils, head dresses and dresses, 19th-20th C, £10-£4,000.* PARK: Easy. TEL: 01769 573184; home - same. SER: Valuations; restorations (handmade lace and embroidery); bridal gowns to order. VAT: Stan/Spec.

Memory Lane Antiques

100 East St. EX36 3DF. (D. Mason). Open 10-5. SIZE: 3 showrooms. *STOCK: General antiques, including china, glass, silver, jewellery, plate, brass, copper and furniture.* TEL: 01769 574288.

Treasure Trove Antiques

101 East St. EX36 3DF. (D. Mason). Open 10-5. SIZE: 2 small showrooms. *STOCK: China, glass, clocks, kitchenalia and all small items.* TEL: 01769 574288.

PHILIP ANDRADE

WHITE OXEN MANOR

RATTERY

NEAR SOUTH BRENT, DEVON TQ10 9JX

TELEPHONE 01364 72454

FAX: 01364 73061

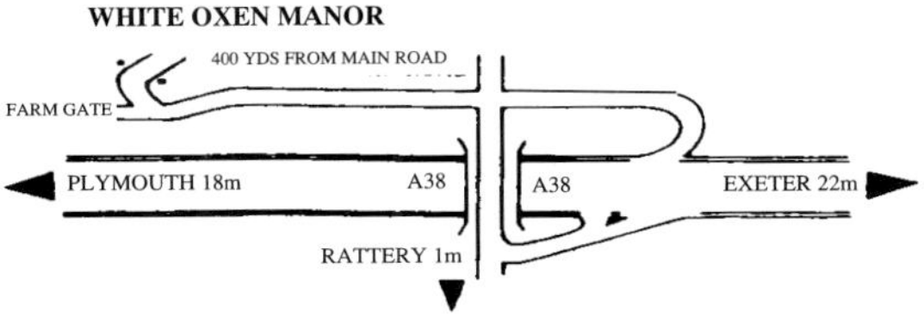

LAPADA MEMBER

Quality Antique Furniture & Objects

MEMBER OF THE BRITISH ANTIQUE DEALERS' ASSOCIATION

South Molton continued

J.R. Tredant
50/50a South St. EX36 4AG. Usually open. *STOCK: General antiques.* TEL: 01769 573006; home - 01769 572416. SER: Valuations.

STOCKLAND, Nr. Honiton

Colystock Antiques
Rising Sun Farm. EX14 9NH. (D.C. McCollum). Est. 1975. Open seven days. SIZE: Large. *STOCK: Pine and oak including English, Irish and Continental, 18th-19th C.* TEL: 01404 861271. SER: Container packing and documentation; courier.

TAVISTOCK

King Street Curios
5 King St. PL19 0DS. (T. and P. Bates). Est. 1979. Open 9-5. SIZE: Medium. *STOCK: Pine furniture, postcards, cigarette cards, china, glass, general collectables, jewellery, to £100.* LOC: Town centre.

TEIGNMOUTH

Charterhouse Antiques
1B Northumberland Place. TQ14 8DD. (A. and S. Webster). Est. 1974. Open 11-1 and 2.15-4, Sat. 10-1 and 2-4. CL: Mon. and Thurs. SIZE: Small. *STOCK: Pottery and porcelain, especially commemoratives, 18th C to 1930s, £1-£200; Victorian jewellery and small silver, 1800-1930, £5-£400; weapons, small furniture, paintings, 1780-1900, £10-£500.* LOC: If facing sea, turn right at Post Office, third left, shop round corner on left. PARK: Easy and nearby. TEL: 01626 54592.

Leigh C. Extence
2 Wellington St. TQ14 8HH. Open 9.30-1 and 2-5. *STOCK: Clocks, 1750-1880; barometers, 1770-1860.* PARK: Limited or in car park. TEL: 01626 773353; mobile - 0585 319226. SER: Buys at auction; clock finding service (for dealers and collectors). VAT: Spec.

Extence Antiques
2 Wellington St. TQ14 8HH. (T.E. and L.E. Extence). Est. 1928. Open 9.30-1 and 2-5.30. SIZE: Medium. *STOCK: Furniture, 18th to early 19th C; jewellery, silver, objets d'art, clocks.* PARK: Limited. TEL: 01626 773353. VAT: Stan/Spec.

The Old Passage
13a Bank St. TQ14 8AW. (G. and R.H. Doel). Est. 1981. Open 11-1 and 2.30-4.30. CL: Mon. and Thurs. SIZE: Small. *STOCK: Porcelain, pottery, glass, treen and silver, mainly 19th-20th C, £5-£200.* LOC: Main street. PARK: Nearby. TEL: 01626 772634; home - 01626 776196. SER: Restorations (furniture repair, French polishing). FAIRS: Livestock Market, Exeter.

Teignmouth continued

Timepiece
125 Bitton Park Rd. TQ14 9BZ. (Clive and Willo Pople). Est. 1988. Open 9.30-5.30, Sat. 9.30-6. CL Mon. SIZE: Medium. *STOCK: Country furnitur antique pine and clocks, 19th C, £25-£2,000 kitchenalia and collectables, 19th-20th C, £1-£10* LOC: On main Newton Abbot road, next to Bitto Park. PARK: Easy. TEL: 01626 770275.

TIVERTON

Barrington Antiques
8-10 Barrington St. EX16 6PU. Est. 1967. Open 10 5. CL: Thurs. p.m. SIZE: Large. *STOCK: Perio furniture.* PARK: Easy. TEL: 01884 256141. SER Oak furniture made to order. VAT: Stan/Spec.

Bygone Days Antiques
40 Gold St. EX16 6PY. (N. Park). Open 10-1 an 2-5. CL: Thurs. *STOCK: Furniture, Victorian an Georgian; watercolours and oils.* TEL: 0188 252832; home - 01884 243615.

TOPSHAM, Nr. Exeter

The Ark Antiques & Design
76 Fore St. EX3 0HQ. (M. and C. Bowyer). Es 1985. Open daily, Sun. by appointment. SIZE Large. *STOCK: Country and decorative furnitur* LOC: Centre of Fore St., next to Lloyds Ban PARK: Easy. TEL: 01392 874301/873561; fax 01392 873738. SER: Large breakfronts made t order; valuations; restorations (country furniture VAT: Stan/Spec. Export and Trade.

Mere Antiques
13 Fore St. EX3 0HF. (Marilyn Hawkins). Residen Est. 1986. Open 9.30-5.30, Sat. 10-4.30, Sun. b appointment. SIZE: Small. *STOCK: English an Continental porcelain, 19th C, £50-£5,00 Japanese satsuma, 19th-20th C, £350-£5,00 furniture, 18th-19th C, £200-£5,000.* PARK: Eas and nearby. TEL: 01392 874224; fax - same. SE Valuations; buys at auction (as stock). FAIR NEC; Barbican; Earls Court. VAT: Spec.

Mulberry House
6 & 7 Fore St. EX3 0HF. (J. G. and M. J. Sellers Est. 1989. Open 10-5.30. SIZE: Large (7 units *STOCK: 19th C dining tables, £1,000-£2,00 desks, bookcases, £500-£1,000; occasion furniture, porcelain and smalls, £25-£400.* LOC Off junction 30, M5. PARK: Public at rear. TE 01392 876321; home - 01392 876297. SE Valuations; restorations (furniture). FAIRS: We Point, Exeter.

Pennies
40 Fore Street. (Penelope and Michael Clark Open 10-5. *STOCK: Collectables and antique* TEL: 01392 877020. VAT: Stan/Spec.

TORQUAY

Birbeck Gallery
45 Abbey Rd. TQ2 5NQ. Est. 1952. Open by appointment. SIZE: Medium. *STOCK: Paintings and prints, 19th to early 20th C, to £10,000; general antiques.* LOC: 200yds. up Abbey Rd. from main street roundabout at Torquay G.P.O. PARK: Easy. TEL: 01803 291658/297144 /324449. SER: Valuations; restorations; buys at auction.

Great Western Antiques
Torre Station, Newton Rd. TQ2 5DD. (J. Jefferies). Est. 1975. Open 10.30-5.30, including Sun. SIZE: Large. *STOCK: Victorian and Edwardian furniture, architectural and marine items, £1-£40,000.* LOC: Railway station on main road into town. PARK: Easy. TEL: 01803 200551; fax - 01803 295115; e-mail - antiques@gwa.zynet.co.uk. VAT: Stan/Spec.

Sheraton House Antiques
Sheraton House, 1 Laburnum Row, Torre. TQ2 5QX. (I.S. Hutton). Open 9.45-4.45. CL: Wed. pm. *STOCK: General antiques.* TEL: 01803 293334.

Spencers Antiques
187 Union St., Torre. TQ1 4BY. *STOCK: General antiques.* TEL: 01803 296598.

Torre Antique Traders
266 Higher Union St. TQ2 5QU. (Mrs R. Curtis). Open 10-5. SIZE: Medium. *STOCK: General antiques.* LOC: Continuation of main shopping area (Union St). PARK: Easy. TEL: 01803 292184.

TOTNES

Collards Books
4 Castle St. TQ9 5NU. (B. Collard). Est. 1970. Open 10-5, restricted opening in winter. *STOCK: Antiquarian and secondhand books.* LOC: Opposite castle. PARK: Nearby. TEL: Home - 01548 550246.

Fine Pine Antiques
Woodland Rd., Harbertonford. TQ9 7SX. Est. 1973. Open 9.30-5. *STOCK: Stripped pine and country furniture.* TEL: 01803 732465. SER: Restorations; stripping.

Past and Present
94 High St. TQ9 5SN. (James Sturges). CL: Lunch-times. SIZE: Large. *STOCK: Furniture, £100-£2,000; smalls, bygones, £5-£300; all 18th-20th C.* LOC: A38. PARK: 150 yards. TEL: 01803 866086. FAIRS: Sandown Park.

WHIMPLE, Nr. Exeter

Anthony James Antiques
Brook Cottage, The Square. EX5 2SL. Open by appointment. *STOCK: 17th-19th C furniture and works of art.* LOC: A30 between Exeter and Honiton. PARK: Easy. TEL: 01404 822146. SER: Valuations. VAT: Spec.

WOODBURY, Nr. Exeter

Pink Cottage Antiques
at Woodbury Antiques, Church St. EX5 1HN. (Verity Rawlings). Open 10-5. *STOCK: Porcelain, glass, jewellery, silver and collectibles.* PARK: Easy. TEL: 01395 232856.

Woodbury Antiques
Church St. EX5 1HN. (H. Jarman). Est. 1966. Open 10-5, Sat. 10-1. SIZE: Large. *STOCK: Victorian and Edwardian furniture and items.* PARK: Easy. TEL: 01395 232727. VAT: Stan/Spec.

YEALMPTON, Nr. Plymouth

Colin Rhodes Antiques LAPADA
15 Fore St. PL9 2JN. Est. 1969. *STOCK: 17th to early 19th C furniture, paintings and objets d'art.* TEL: 01752 881170/862232. SER: Valuations. VAT: Spec.

Torr Bridge Antiques
Ford Rd. PL8 2NA. (W.J. and D.C. Foster). Est. 1994. Open Sat. 10-5.30, other times by appointment or ring doorbell. SIZE: Small. *STOCK: Porcelain, mainly 18th C Chinese and English: books and engravings, £1-£1,000.* LOC: Off Plymouth-Kingsbridge road (B3186), towards Newton Ferrers. PARK: Easy. TEL: 01752 880954; home - same. SER: Valuations.

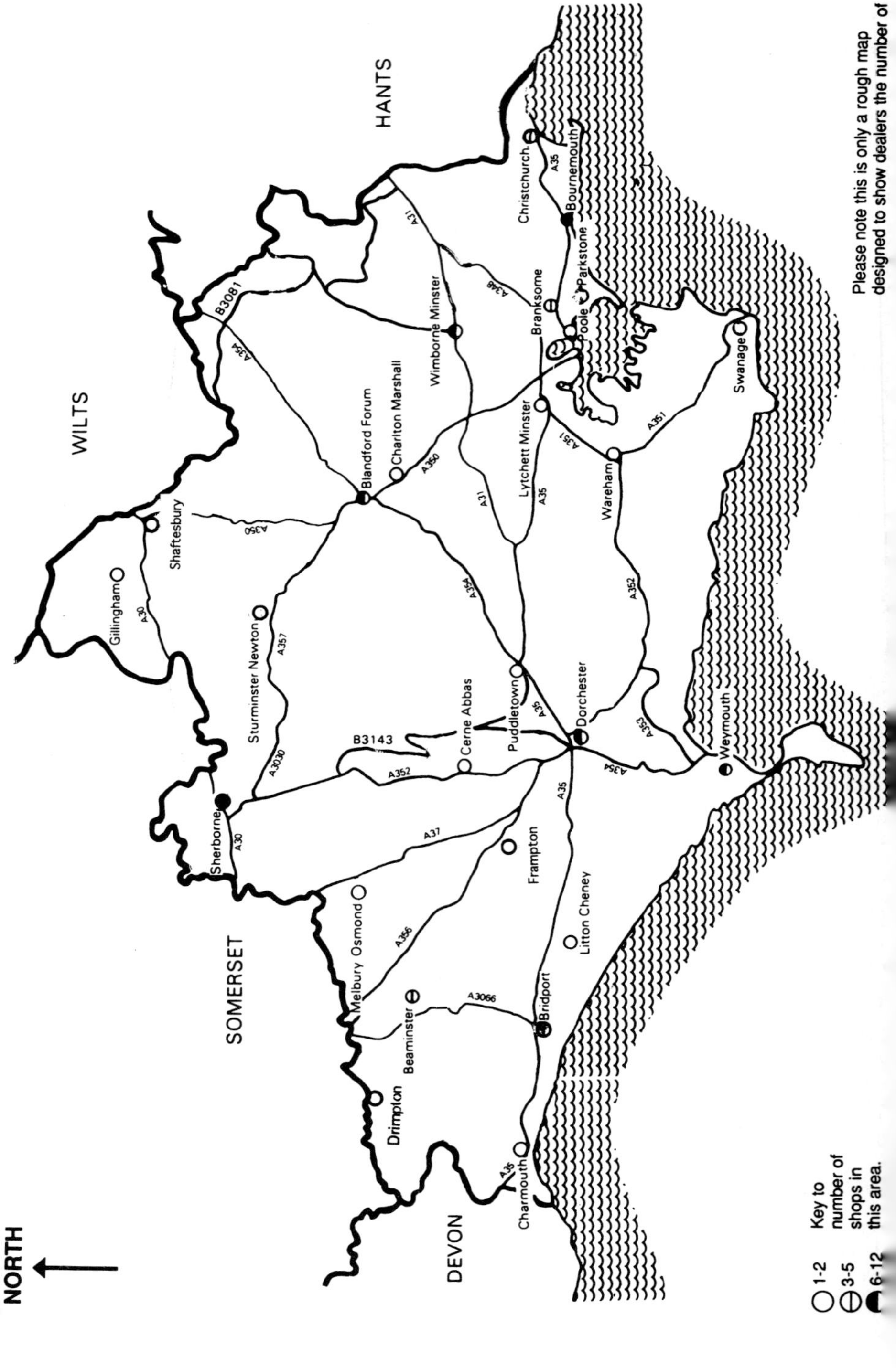

Please note this is only a rough map designed to show dealers the number of

EAMINSTER

eaminster Antiques
Church St. DT8 3JA. (Mrs T.P.F. Frampton). st. 1982. Open 9.30-5.30. CL: Wed. SIZE: mall. *STOCK: Small furniture, £20-£1,400; lver, £10-£800; objets d'art, porcelain, boxes, 8th C to Art Deco, £5-£1,400; brass and ictures, 18th C to 1920s, £1-£1,000; thimbles nd sewing objects, collectables.* Not Stocked: oins and medals. LOC: Just off square. PARK: asy. TEL: 01308 862591; home - 01935 891395.

ottage Antiques
7 The Square. DT8 3AU. Open 10-5.30 or by ppointment. CL: Wed. *STOCK: Furniture, aintings, clocks, prints, decorative items.* LOC: 3066. TEL: 01308 862136.

ood Hope Antiques
Hogshill St. DT8 3AE. (D. Beney). Est. 1980. pen 9.30-1 and 2-5. CL: Tues. and Wed. SIZE: ledium. *STOCK: Clocks especially longcase, racket and wall, barometers, £500-£5,000; rniture, £200-£2,500; all 18th-19th C.* LOC: own square. PARK: Easy. TEL: 01308 862119. ER: Valuations; restorations (clocks, including als; barometers). VAT: Spec.

LANDFORD FORUM

& D Antiques
1 East St. DT11 7DU. (A. and D. Edgington). Est. 981. Open 10-5, Sun. by appointment. CL: Mon. nd Wed. pm. SIZE: Small. *STOCK: Drinking lasses, 18th C, £50-£1,000; decanters, 19th C, 15-£100; Lalique, £100-£5,000.* LOC: Town entre on main east-west route (one-way system). ARK: Easy. TEL: 01258 455643; home - same. ER: Valuations (glass); buys at auction (18th C inking glasses and decanters). VAT: Spec.

ncient and Modern Bookshop ncluding Garret's Antiques)
4 Salisbury St. DT11 7QE. (Mrs P. Davey). pen 9.30-12.30 and 1.30-5. CL: Wed. *STOCK: ooks and small antiques.* TEL: 01258 455276.

he Dorset Bookshop
East St. DT11 7DX. (D.G. Edmondson and E. aly). Open 9.30-5, Wed. 9.30-2. SIZE: Small. *TOCK: 19th and 20th C books, some antiuarian.* LOC: Town centre, near Market Place. ARK: Nearby. TEL: 01258 452266.

ilton Antiques
larket Place. DT11 7HU. Open 9-5. CL: Wed. ZE: Medium. *STOCK: Furniture, 18th-19th C, 50-£2,000; decorative items, 18th-20th C, £5-200.* LOC: Opposite parish church, adjacent to wn museum. PARK: Easy - Market Square. EL: 01258 450100. SER: Valuations; restorions (polishing, etc).

Blandford Forum continued

Stour Gallery
28 East St. DT11 7DR. (R. Butler). Est. 1966. Open 10-1 and 2-4, Sun. by appointment. CL: Mon. and Wed. pm. SIZE: Medium. *STOCK: Watercolours, oils and pastels, early 19th to 20th C, £50-£3,000.* LOC: On right-hand side of High St., on one way system. PARK: Opposite. TEL: 01258 456293; home - 01258 453174. SER: Restorations (oil, watercolours, wash line mounts); framing.

Strowger of Blandford
13 East St. DT11 7DU. Est. 1962. Open 10.30-1 and 2-5.30, or by appointment. SIZE: Medium. *STOCK: Period furniture.* LOC: A354. PARK: Easy. TEL: 01258 454374/860103.

BOURNEMOUTH

Antiques and Furnishings
339 Charminster Rd. BH8 9QR. (P. Neath). Open 10-5.30. *STOCK: Furniture including Victorian stripped pine; brass, copper, china, textiles and decorative objects.* TEL: 01202 527976.

Arcade Antiques
6 Westbourne Arcade, Westbourne. BH4 9AY. (Richard Samuel). Est. 1984. Open 10-4.30, Wed. 10-2, Fri. and Sat. 9.30-5. SIZE: Medium. *STOCK: General antiques, furniture, collectors' items, Poole pottery.* LOC: Just off A35 between Bournemouth and Poole. PARK: Easy. TEL: 01202 764800; fax - 01202 769537. SER: Valuations. VAT: Spec.

The Artist Gallery
1086 Christchurch Rd., Boscombe East. BH7 6BQ. Open 9.30-5. CL: Wed. *STOCK: Limited edition prints and original works of art - David Shepherd, Sir William Russell Flint, E.R. Sturgeon, Lowry, Gordon King and others.* PARK: Forecourt. TEL: 01202 417066.

Blade and Bayonet
884 Christchurch Rd., Boscombe. BH7 6DJ. (L.M. Martin). Resident. Est. 1982. Open 10-12 and 1-5. CL: Mon. SIZE: Medium. *STOCK: Militaria, mid 17th to 20th C, £75-£485.* LOC: Near Pokesdown station. PARK: Easy. TEL: 01202 429891. SER: Valuations; restorations (mainly cleaning weapons). FAIRS: Bournemouth, Southsea, Bovington Tank Museum, Midhurst, Dorking, Farnham.

Boscombe Militaria
86 Palmerston Rd., Boscombe. BH1 4HU. (E.A. Browne). Est. 1981. Open 10-1 and 1.45-5. CL: Wed. *STOCK: German militaria, £10-£500; British and American militaria, £5-£300, all 1914-1918 and 1939-1945.* LOC: Just off Christchurch Rd. PARK: Easy. TEL: 01202 304250 (answerphone); fax - 01202 733696. FAIRS: Farnham; Cheshunt; major South of England Arms.

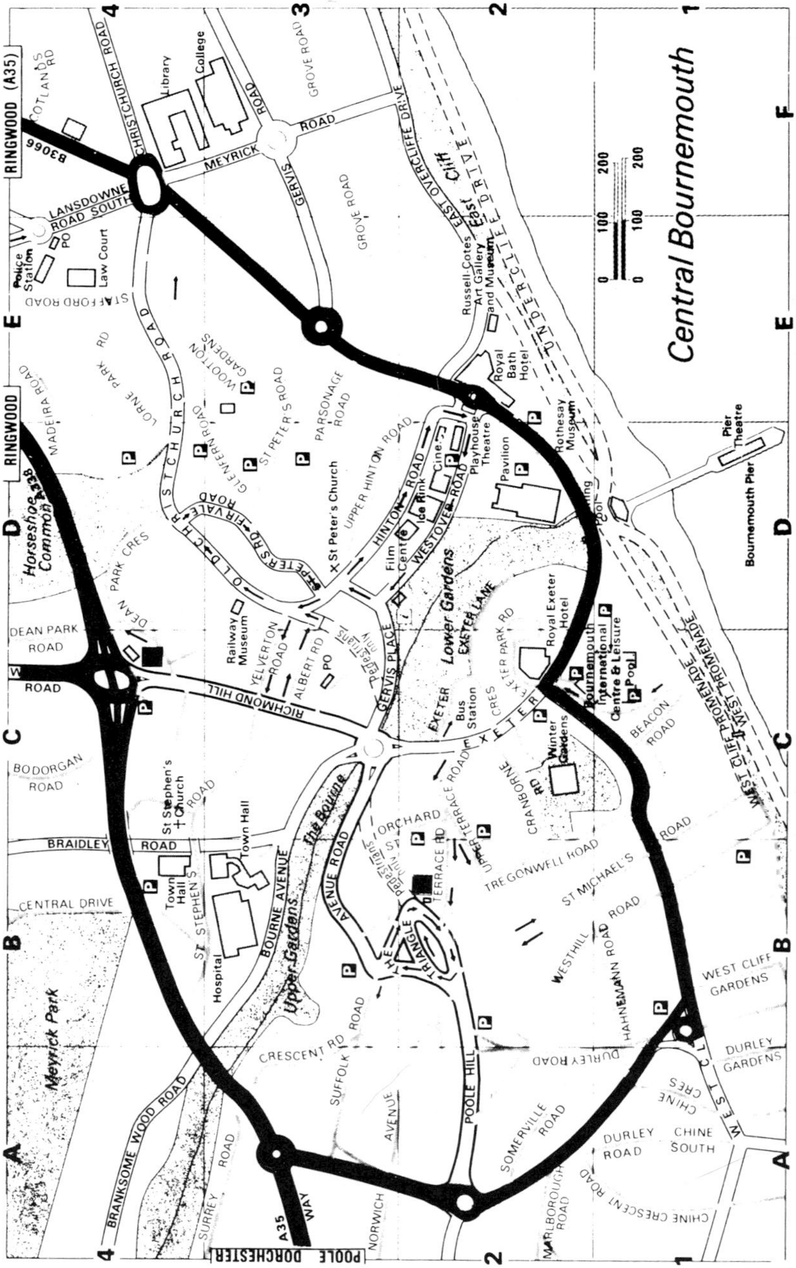
Central Bournemouth
RINGWOOD (A35)
B3066
RINGWOOD
A338
POOLE DORCHESTER
A35
WAY
Horseshoe Common
Meyrick Park
Upper Gardens
Lower Gardens
The Bourne
CHRISTCHURCH ROAD
LANSDOWNE
ROAD SOUTH
MEYRICK ROAD
GERVIS ROAD
GROVE ROAD
EAST OVERCLIFFE DRIVE
UNDERCLIFF DRIVE
East Cliff
Library
College
Police Station
PO
Law Court
STAFFORD ROAD
LORNE PARK RD
MADEIRA ROAD
WOOTTON GARDENS
ST PETER'S ROAD
PARSONAGE ROAD
GLENFERN ROAD
OLD CHRISTCHURCH ROAD
FIRVALE ROAD
ST PETER'S RD
St Peter's Church
UPPER HINTON ROAD
HINTON ROAD
WESTOVER ROAD
Ice Rink
Cine
Film Centre
Playhouse Theatre
Pavilion
Royal Bath Hotel
Russell-Cotes Art Gallery and Museum
Rothesay Museum
Pier Theatre
Bournemouth Pier
DEAN PARK CRES
DEAN PARK ROAD
RICHMOND HILL
Railway Museum
YELVERTON ROAD
ALBERT RD
GERVIS PLACE
EXETER LANE
EXETER PARK RD
Royal Exeter Hotel
Bournemouth International Centre & Leisure Pool
EXETER ROAD
EXETER CRES
Bus Station
Winter Gardens
BEACON ROAD
WEST CLIFF PROMENADE
WEST PROMENADE
BODORGAN ROAD
BRAIDLEY ROAD
St Stephen's Church
ST STEPHEN'S ROAD
Town Hall
CENTRAL DRIVE
Hospital
BOURNE AVENUE
AVENUE ROAD
ORCHARD ST
TERRACE RD
UPPER TERRACE ROAD
CRANBORNE RD
TREGONWELL ROAD
ST MICHAEL'S ROAD
WESTHILL ROAD
HAHNEMANN ROAD
TRIANGLE
WEST CLIFF GARDENS
DURLEY ROAD
DURLEY GARDENS
CHINE CRES
WEST CLIFF
CRESCENT RD
SUFFOLK ROAD
AVENUE
POOLE HILL
SOMERVILLE ROAD
DURLEY ROAD
CHINE SOUTH
MARLBOROUGH ROAD
CHINE CRESCENT ROAD
BRANKSOME WOOD ROAD
SURREY ROAD
NORWICH
0 100 200

Key to Town Plan

AA Recommended roads		Car Parks	P
Other roads		Parks and open spaces	
Restricted roads		AA Service Centre	AA
Buildings of interest			

Bournemouth continued

Boscombe Models and Collectors Shop

802c Christchurch Rd., Boscombe. BH7 6DD. (Sylvia Hart). Open 10-1 and 2-4.30. CL: Wed. *STOCK: Collectors' toys, 19th-20th C, £1-£1,000.* LOC: On Somerset Rd. TEL: 01202 398884.

Peter Denver Antiques

36 Calvin Rd., Winton. BH9 1LN. (P. Denver-White). Est. 1961. Open 10-5. CL: Mon. SIZE: Small. *STOCK: Furniture, porcelain, pictures, glass, Georgian-Edwardian, £5-£800.* LOC: Off main Wimborne Rd. PARK: Easy. TEL: 01202 532536; home - 01202 513911.

Richard Dunton Antiques LAPADA

914 and 920 Christchurch Rd., Boscombe. BH7 6DL. (R.D. Dunton). Resident. Est. 1980. Open 9-5.30, Sat. and Sun. by appointment. SIZE: Large. *STOCK: Antiques and decorative accessories - Staffordshire, majolica, glass, paintings, brass, oak and pine, sculpture and garden furniture, £20-£50,000.* PARK: Easy. TEL: 01202 425963; fax - 01202 418456. SER: Valuations. VAT: Stan/Spec. *Trade Only.*

Lionel Geneen Ltd LAPADA

781 Christchurch Rd., Boscombe. BH7 6AW. BDADA. Est. 1902. Open 9-5, Sat. 9-12, other times by appointment. CL: Lunchtimes. SIZE: Large. *STOCK: English, Continental and Oriental furniture, china and works of art including bronzes, enamels, ivories, jades, Art Nouveau and Art Deco, all 17th C to early 20th C.* LOC: Main road through Boscombe. PARK: Easy. TEL: 01202 422961; home - 01202 520417. SER: Valuations. VAT: Stan/Spec.

H.L.B. Antiques

139 Barrack Rd. BH23 2AW. (H.L. Blechman). Est. 1969. SIZE: Large. *STOCK: Collectable items.* PARK: Easy. TEL: 01202 429252/482388.

Hampshire Gallery LAPADA

18 Lansdowne Rd. BH1 1SD. Est. 1971. *STOCK: Paintings and watercolours, 17th to early 20th C.* TEL: 01202 551211. SER: Valuations; restorations. VAT: Spec.

Hardy's Clobber

874 Christchurch Road, Boscombe. BH7 6DQ. (J.W. Hardy). Open 10-5. *STOCK: Clothing and fabrics, from Victorian.* TEL: 01202 429794.

Hardy's Collectables

862 Christchurch Rd., Boscombe. BH7 6DQ. (J. Hardy). Open 10-5. SIZE: 20 dealers. *STOCK: Art Deco and Art Nouveau glass and 50's collectables especially Poole pottery.* TEL: 01202 422407/303030.

Bournemouth continued

Libra Antiques

916 Christchurch Rd. Est. 1967. Open 10-5.30. CL: Wed. pm. SIZE: Medium. *STOCK: Furniture, Art Nouveau, silver and plate, copper, brass, shipping goods.* PARK: Opposite. TEL: 01202 427615. VAT: Stan.

G.B. Mussenden and Son Antiques, Jewellery and Silver

24 Seamoor Rd., Westbourne. BH4 9AR. Est. 1948. Open 9-5. CL: Wed. SIZE: Medium. *STOCK: Antiques, jewellery, silver.* LOC: Central Westbourne, corner of R.L. Stevenson Ave. PARK: Easy. TEL: 01202 764462. SER: Valuations. VAT: Stan/Global/Spec.

Geo. A. Payne and Son Ltd

742 Christchurch Rd., Boscombe. BH7 6BZ. (H.G. and N.G. Payne). FGA. Est. 1946. Open 9-5.30. SIZE: Small. *STOCK: Jewellery, 19th-20th C, £10-£3,000; silver, 18th-20th C, £30-£1,000; plate, £10-£200.* LOC: Opposite Browning Ave. and Chessel Ave. PARK: Browning Ave. TEL: 01202 394954. SER: Valuations; gemstone testing; restorations (silver, jewellery, clocks, watches). VAT: Stan/Spec.

R.E. Porter

2-6 Post Office Rd. BH1 1BA. Est. 1934. Open 9.30-5. SIZE: Medium. *STOCK: Silver (including early antique spoons up to modern), Georgian, £20-£5,000; jewellery, pot lids, Baxter and Le Blond prints, clocks including second-hand.* Not Stocked: Furniture, arms, armour, carpets. LOC: Walking from the Square, take the Old Christchurch Rd., then the first turning on the left. PARK: 300yds. at top of Richmond Hill. TEL: 01202 554289. SER: Valuations. VAT: Stan/Spec.

Portique

15/16/17 Criterion Arcade. BH1 1BU. Est. 1971. *STOCK: Silver, jewellery, Derby china, glass paperweights, cloisonné, clocks.* LOC: Coming from the square take the Old Christchurch Rd. from roundabout, arcade entrance is between first and second turnings on left. TEL: 01202 552979. VAT: Stan/Spec.

Sainsburys of Bournemouth Ltd LAPADA

23-25 Abbott Rd. BH9 1EU. Est. 1918. Open 8-1 and 2-6. CL: Sat. pm. *STOCK: Furniture especially bookcases and dining tables, 18th C, to £15,000.* PARK: Own. TEL: 01202 529271; home - 01202 763616; fax - 01202 510028. VAT: Stan/Spec.

Sandy's Antiques

790 Christchurch Rd., Boscombe. BH7 6DD. BDADA. SIZE: Shop+warehouse. *STOCK: Oriental items, general antiques; shipping goods, pre-1930.* TEL: 01202 301190; evenings - 01202 470787. VAT: Stan/Spec.

Bournemouth continued

Peter Stebbing
7 Post Office Rd. BH1 1BB. (P.M. Stebbing). Est. 1960. Open 9.30-5. SIZE: Small. *STOCK: Furniture, £25-£1,000; glass, silver, £1-£100; metalware, jewellery; all 18th-19th C.* LOC: Next to Head Post Office. PARK: 200yds. TEL: 01202 552587. SER: Valuations.

Sterling Coins and Medals
2 Somerset Rd., Boscombe. BH7 6JH. (W.V. Henstridge). Est. 1969. Open 9.30-4. CL: Wed. pm. SIZE: Small. *STOCK: Coins, medals, militaria, World War II German items.* LOC: Next to 806 Christchurch Rd. TEL: 01202 423881. SER: Valuations. VAT: Stan.

D.C. Stuart Antiques
34-40 Poole Hill. BH2 5PS. Open 9-5.30. *STOCK: General antiques, hand-carved reproduction furniture.* TEL: 01202 555544.

M.C. Taylor
995 Christchurch Rd., Boscombe East. BH7 6BB. (Mark Taylor). CMBHI, BDADA. Est. 1982. SIZE: Small. *STOCK: Clocks, barometers and music boxes, 19th C, £500-£1,000.* LOC: Opposite St. James' School and Kings Park entrance. PARK: Easy. TEL: 01202 429718. SER: Valuations; restorations. VAT: Stan/Spec.

Victorian Chairman
883 Christchurch Rd., Boscombe. BH7 6AU. (M. Leo). Open 9.30-5. *STOCK: Furniture especially chairs, sofas and tables.* TEL: 01202 420996. SER: Upholstery restoration.

Victorian Parlour
874 Christchurch Rd., Boscombe. BH7 6DJ. (D.S. Lloyd). Est. 1984. Open 9.30-5.30. SIZE: Large. *STOCK: Georgian, Victorian and Edwardian stripped pine; unusual country bygones.* PARK: Easy. TEL: 01202 433928. SER: Restorations (cane and rush seating).

Yesterday Tackle and Books
42 Clingan Rd., Boscombe East. BH6 5PZ. (David and Alba Dobbyn). Open by appointment. *STOCK: Fishing tackle and associated items including taxidermy; books.* TEL: 01202 476586. SER: Catalogues issued.

BRANKSOME

Allen's (Branksome) Ltd
447/449 Poole Rd. BH12 1DH. (D.L and P.J. D'Ardenne). Est. 1948. Open 9-5.30. SIZE: Large. *STOCK: Furniture.* TEL: 01202 763724; fax - 01202 763724. VAT: Stan/Spec.

Branksome Antiques
370 Poole Rd. BH12 1AW. (B.A. Neal). Est. 1973. Open 10-5. CL: Wed. and Sat. SIZE: Medium. *STOCK: Scientific and marine items, furniture and general small items.* PARK: Easy. TEL: 01202 763324; home - 01202 679932. SER: Buys at auction (as stock). VAT: Stan/Spec.

Branksome continued

David Mack Antiques
434-436 Poole Rd. and 43a Langley Rd. BH12 1DF. Est. 1963. Open 9-5.30 or by appointment. SIZE: Large. *STOCK: 18th-19th C tables, chairs, display cabinets, desks, bureaux, bookcases; later furniture and shipping goods.* LOC: 2 doors from Branksome rail station. PARK: Own. TEL: 01202 760005; fax - 01202 765100. SER: Restorations. VAT: Stan/Spec.

BRIDPORT

Batten's Jewellers
26 South St. DT6 3NQ. (R. Batten). Open 9.30-5. *STOCK: Jewellery and silver.* TEL: 01308 456910. SER: Valuations; repairs.

Bridport Antiques Centre
5 West Allington. DT6 5BJ. Open 9-5. SIZE: 1[illegible] dealers. *STOCK: Pine and country furniture, lace, linen, porcelain, glass, books, prints, water colours, oils, postcards, jewellery, classical garden ornaments, taxidermy.* TEL: 01308 425885.

Hobby Horse Antiques
29 West Allington. DT6 5JB. (J. Rodber). Resident. Est. 1948. Open mornings and all day Fri. and Sat. SIZE: Medium. *STOCK: Mechanical antiques, toys, trains, porcelain, brass, copper, bygones, silver, jewellery.* LOC: West Bridport on south side of A35 between Dorchester and Exeter. PARK: Nearby. TEL: 01308 422801.

PIC's Bookshop
11 South St. DT6 3NR. CL: Thurs. pm. *STOCK: Books, engravings and prints.* TEL: 01308 425689.

Tudor House Antiques **LAPADA**
88 East St. DT6 3LL. (P. Knight and D. Burton). Est. 1940. Open 9-1 and 2-5.30, Sun. by appointment. SIZE: Small. *STOCK: General antiques.* LOC: Left hand side of main street from Dorchester. PARK: Easy. TEL: 01308 427200; home - same. VAT: Stan/Spec.

CERNE ABBAS

Cerne Antiques
DT2 7LA. (I. Pulliblank). Est. 1972. Open 10-1 and 2-5, Sun. 2-5. CL: Mon. and Fri. SIZE: Medium. *STOCK: Silver, porcelain, furniture including unusual items, mainly 19th C, £1-£400.* LOC: A352. PARK: Easy. TEL: 01300 341490; home - same.

:HARLTON MARSHALL, Nr. Blandford

:ona Dawson Antiques
he Old Clubhouse. DT11 9PA. Est. 1958. Open 0-6. CL: Mon. *STOCK: Mainly furniture, clocks, 8th-19th C.* TEL: 01258 453146.

:HARMOUTH, Nr. Bridport

:harmouth Antique Centre
'he Street. DT6 6QH. (S.R. Dodd). Open 10-5. 'L: Sun. and Mon. SIZE: Medium - 10 dealers. *TOCK: General antiques; Shelley a speciality.* EL: 01297 560122; mobile - 0378 107994.

:HRISTCHURCH

.L. Arditti
8 Bargates. BH23 1QP. (A. and J.L. Arditti). Est. 964. Open 9-5.30. CL: Sun. except by appoint-ıent. SIZE: Medium. *STOCK: Oriental carpets nd rugs, 18th to early 20th C, £500-£8,000.* OC: From town centre take road towards Hurn irport, left side on corner of Bargates and wynham Avenue. PARK: Twynham Avenue. EL: 01202 485414. SER: Valuations; restor-tions; cleaning (Persian rugs). VAT: Stan/Spec.

:hristchurch Carpets
5/57 Bargates. BH23 1QE. (J. Sheppard). Est. 963. Open 9-5.30. SIZE: Large. *STOCK: Persian arpets and rugs, 19th-20th C, £100-£1,000.* LOC: lain road. PARK: Adjacent. TEL: 01202 482712. ER: Valuations. VAT: Stan/Spec.

Iamptons
2 Purewell. BH23 1EP. (G. Hampton). Open 10-. CL: Sat. am. SIZE: Large. *STOCK: Furniture, 8th-19th C; general antiques, clocks, china, ıstruments, metalware, oil paintings, Chinese nd Persian carpets and rugs.* PARK: Easy. TEL: 1202 484000.

I. & R. Lankshear Antiques
49 Barrack Rd. BH23 2AP. (M.I. Lankshear). pen 9.30-6. *STOCK: General antiques, especially ilitaria and swords; collectables, postcards, igarette cards, medals and paintings.* PARK: orecourt. TEL: 01202 473091. SER: Valuations.

'he Old Stores
/est Rd., Bransgore. BH23 8BQ. (W. and Mrs J. 'ollier). Open Thurs. and Fri. 9-7 or by arrange-ıent. *STOCK: General antiques.* TEL: 01425 72616; fax - same.

:RANBORNE, Nr.Wimborne

'ower Antiques
he Square. BH21 5PR. (P.W. Kear and P. White). st. 1975. Open 8.30-5.30. CL: Sat. *STOCK: eorgian and Victorian furniture.* TEL: 01725 17552.

DORCHESTER

Box of Porcelain
51d Icen Way. DT1 1EW. (R.J. and Mrs. S.Y. Lunn). Est. 1984. Open 10-5. *STOCK: Porcelain including Worcester, Doulton, Belleek.* LOC: Close town centre, near Dinosaur Museum. TEL: 01305 250856. SER: Valuations; Beswick & Doulton collectors' finder service.

Colliton Antique and Craft Centre
Colliton St., North Sq. Open daily, Sun. by appointment. SIZE: 14 dealers. *STOCK: 18th-20th C furniture, £25-£5,000; brass, bric-a-brac, pictures, china, pine, clocks, jewellery and silver, toys.* LOC: By town clock. PARK: Easy. TEL: 01305 269398/260115. SER: Restorations (cabinet work and metalware). VAT: Stan/Spec.

Michael Legg Antiques
15 High East St (Showrooms) and Old Malt House, Bottom-o-Town. DT1 1HH. (E.M.J. Legg). Open 9-5.30 or any time by appointment. SIZE: Medium. *STOCK: 17th-19th C furniture, porcelain, pictures, silver, glass.* TEL: 01305 264596. VAT: Stan/Spec.

Legg of Dorchester
Regency House, 51 High East St. DT1 1HU. (W. and H. Legg). Est. 1930. *STOCK: General antiques, Regency and decorative furniture, stripped pine.* TEL: 01305 264964. VAT: Stan/Spec.

John Walker Antiques BADA
52 High West St. DT1 1UT. Open 9.30-5 or by appointment. SIZE: Small. *STOCK: Early furniture, textiles, metalwork, ceramics, wood carvings, 16th-18th C; British folk art, 16th-19th C.* LOC: Main street. PARK: Easy. TEL: 01305 260324. SER: Valuations; buys at auction. VAT: Spec.

Words Etcetera
2 Cornhill. DT1 1BA. (Julian Nangle). PBFA, ABA. Est. 1970. Open 9.30-5.30. SIZE: Medium. *STOCK: Antiquarian and quality second-hand books and prints.* LOC: Close to museum. TEL: 01305 251919; fax - 01258 820618; home - 01258 820415. SER: Buys at auction (books). FAIRS: PBFA London (June).

DRIMPTON, Nr. Crewkerne

Drimpton Antiques
The Old Barn, Netherhay. DT8 3RH. (C. A. Gibbs). Est. 1982. Open 10-5 including Sun. SIZE: Medium. *STOCK: General antiques and collectables.* PARK: Easy. TEL: 01308 867597. SER: Valuations; restorations; French polishing; buys at auction.

FRAMPTON

Georgina Ryder LAPADA
Frampton House. DT2 9NH. Resident. Est. 1977. Open by appointment only. SIZE: Medium. *STOCK: 17th-18th C tapestries; 18th-19th C Continental furniture; decorative objects, all £200-£20,000.* LOC: From Dorchester take A37 towards Yeovil, turn off towards Crewkerne, Frampton first village. PARK: Easy. TEL: 01300 320308; fax - same. SER: Valuations; restorations (upholstery). FAIRS: Olympia; Decorative; LAPADA. VAT: Spec.

GILLINGHAM

Talisman LAPADA
The Old Brewery, Wyke. SP8 4NW. Open 9-5, Sat. 10-4. SIZE: Large. *STOCK: Unusual and decorative items, garden furniture, architectural fittings, 18th-19th C; English and Continental furniture.* TEL: 01747 824423/824222; fax - 01747 823544. VAT: Stan/Spec.

LITTON CHENEY, Nr. Dorchester

F. Whillock
Court Farm. DT2 9AU. Open by appointment. *STOCK: Maps and prints.* TEL: 01308 482457. SER: Framing.

LYTCHETT MINSTER

Old Button Shop Antiques
BH16 6JF. (T. Johns). Est. 1970. Open 2-5, Sat. 11-1, other times by appointment. CL: Mon. *STOCK: Small antiques, brass, copper, curios, unusual items, and antique Dorset buttons.* TEL: 01202 622169.

MELBURY OSMOND, Nr. Dorchester

Hardy Country
Holt Mill Farm. DT2 0JR. Est. 1980. SIZE: Large. *STOCK: Stripped pine country furniture, Edwardian and Victorian, £50-£800.* LOC: Off A37. PARK: Easy. TEL: 01935 873361; home - 01935 83440.

PARKSTONE, Nr. Poole

Ashley Antiques
176 Ashley Rd. BH14 9BY. (M. Hodson). Open 10-3.30, Sat. 10-4. *STOCK: General antiques.* TEL: 01202 744347.

D.J. Burgess
116-116a Ashley Rd. BH14 9BN. Open 9.30-5.30. CL: Wed. and Thurs. *STOCK: Clocks, watches, some furniture.* TEL: 01202 730542. SER: Restorations (clocks and watches).

Parkstone continued

D. J. Jewellery
166-168 Ashley Rd. BH14 9BY. (D. J. and P. M O'Sullivan). BWCG. Est. 1978. Open 9-5.30 SIZE: Large. *STOCK: Jewellery, £5-£1,000 silver and plate, £5-£600; clocks, watches, objets d'art.* Not Stocked: Furniture. PARK: Easy. TEL 01202 745148. SER: Valuations; repairs and restorations (jewellery, clocks, watches) - postal service; gem testing. VAT: Stan.

The Emporium
Mansfield Rd., Upper Parkstone. BH14 0DD. (I Saunders). Est. 1976. Open daily, Wed., Sat. and Sun. by appointment. SIZE: Small. *STOCK: Collectables including stamps, postcards, railway and transport memorabilia, books and ephemera.* LOC: Opposite Victoria Cross public house. PARK: Nearby. TEL: 01202 743742. FAIRS: Collectors.

Wiffen's Antiques
95/101 Bournemouth Rd. (C. A. Wiffen). Est. 1960. Open 9-5.30. SIZE: Large. *STOCK: Furniture including shipping; porcelain, pictures, silver and plate, clocks, brass and copper, jewellery, statuary and garden items.* TEL: 0120 736567. SER: Valuations; restorations.

Christopher Williams Antiquarian Bookseller
19 Morrison Ave. BH12 4AD. *STOCK: Books especially antiques, art, bibliography, cookery, wine, topography.* TEL: 01202 743157. FAIRS: Various book and craft fairs. *Postal only.*

POOLE

G.D. and S.T. Antiques
(G.D. and S.T. Brown). Open by appointment. *STOCK: General antiques.* TEL: 01202 676340.

Overhill Antique and Old Pine Warehouse
Wareham Rd., Holton Heath. BH16 6JW. (Michael Johnson). Est. 1975. Open 10-6, Sun. 11-4. SIZE: Large. *STOCK: Continental pine including German and East European, 1750-1930, £10-£1,500.* LOC: From A35 Bakers Arms roundabout, on to A35 towards Wareham, premises 1 mile. PARK: Own. TEL: 01202 621818. SER: Restorations (pine stripping and finishing).

PUDDLETOWN, Nr. Dorchester

Antique Map and Bookshop
32 High St. DT2 8RU. (C.D. and H.M. Proctor). Open 9-5. *STOCK: Antiquarian and secondhand books, maps, prints and engravings.* TEL: 0130 848633; fax - 01305 848992. SER: Postal.

;HAFTESBURY

1r. Punch's Antique Market
3 Bell St. SP7 8AE. IPSA. Est. 1971. Open 10-6. 'L: Mon. SIZE: Large. *STOCK: Wide variety of eneral antiques, fine art and collectables. Also 'unch and Judy collection.* LOC: On corner with 1uston's Lane. PARK: Easy and 100 yards. TEL: 1747 855775; fax - same. SER: Valuations; estorations; buys at auction. *Trade Only.*

'haston Antiques
6A Bell St. SP7 8AE. (J. D. Hine). Resident. Est. 997. Open 9.30-1 and 2-5, Wed. 9.30-1. SIZE: mall.*STOCK: Furniture, 18th-19th C, £300-5,000.* LOC: From town centre, turn right pposite Grosvenor Hotel into Bell St. TEL: 1747 850405; home - same. SER: Restorations urniture).

;HERBORNE

▲bbas Antiques
7 Newlands. DT9 3JG. Open 9-5. *STOCK: Small ollectables and furniture.*

▲ntiques of Sherborne
The Green. DT9 3HZ. (C. and L. Greenslade).)pen 10-5. *STOCK: Furniture, upholstery, decor-tive items, linen, rugs and collectables.* TEL: 1935 816549; home - 01963 210737. SER: estorations (furniture); buys at auction; ommission sales.

asper Burton Antiques
3 Cheap St. DT9 3PU. Est. 1964. Open 9-1 and -5. CL: Wed. SIZE: Medium. *STOCK: General ntiques, especially furniture.* PARK: Easy. TEL: 1935 814434. VAT: Stan/Spec.

)odge and Son LAPADA
8-33 Cheap St. DT9 3PU. (S. Dodge). Open 9-.30. SIZE: Large. *STOCK: Furniture from all eriods, mainly Georgian.* PARK: At rear. 'EL: 01935 815151. VAT: Stan/Spec.

;reystoke Antiques
wan Yard, Off Cheap St. DT9 3AX. (F.L. and 1.E. Butcher). Est. 1970. Open 10-4.30. *STOCK: ilver, Georgian, Victorian and later; some 19th : pottery and porcelain.* LOC: Off main street. 'ARK: Car park adjacent to Swan Yard, or utside shop. TEL: 01935 812833. VAT: Stan/ 1argin/Global.

Ieygate Browne Antiques
outh St. DT9 3NG. (M. and W.Heygate rowne). Open 9.30-5.30. SIZE: Large. *STOCK: 8th-19th C furniture, pottery and porcelain.* ,OC: Off Cheap St. towards station. PARK: ;asy. TEL: 01935 815487. SER: Valuations; estorations. VAT: Stan/Spec.

Sherborne continued

The Nook
South St. DT9 3LX. (H.B. Bruton). *STOCK: General antiques - furniture, china, glass, brass and copper.* TEL: 01935 813987.

Pine on the Green
The Green. DT9 4EW. (S. Dodge). Open 9-5.30. SIZE: Medium. *STOCK: Restored antique pine furniture; period oak dressers and tables, elm furniture, walnut, fruitwood and chestnut pieces, antique and reconstituted, English and continental.* LOC: Off A30, 1st shop on left hand side at the top of the town. PARK: Easy. TEL: 01935 815216.

Sherborne Antique Centre
Mattar Arcade, 17 Newlands. DT9 3JG. Est. 1965. Open 9-5. SIZE: 5 shops. *STOCK: Fine arts, painting, furniture, rugs, objets d'art, jewellery, gold, silver.* LOC: From A30 via Greenhill. PARK: Easy. TEL: 01935 813464.

The Swan Gallery
51 Cheap St. DT9 3AX. (S. and Mrs K. Lamb). Est. 1977. Open 9.30-5, Wed. 10-1. SIZE: Large. *STOCK: Watercolours, 18th to early 20th C; prints, maps, antiquarian and secondhand books.* PARK: Easy, at rear. TEL: 01935 814465; fax - 01308 868195. SER: Valuations; restorations (paintings, watercolours and prints); framing. VAT: Stan/Spec.

Richard White Antiques
The Music House, The Green. DT9 3HX. Est. 1984. Open 10-1 and 2-5. SIZE: Medium. *STOCK: Furniture, vernacular and country, £300-£5,000; ceramics and folk art, 18th-19th C.* LOC: Just off A30. PARK: Easy. TEL: 01935 815209; fax - 01963 220019. VAT: Spec.

Henry Willis (Antique Silver)
38 Cheap St. DT9 3PX. Est. 1973. Open 10-5. SIZE: Small. *STOCK: Silver, 17th-19th C, £15-£1,500.* LOC: Town centre, just off A30. PARK: Nearby. TEL: 01935 816828. SER: Valuations; restorations (silver); buys at auction (silver). FAIRS: Olympia (June). VAT: Stan/Spec.

STURMINSTER NEWTON

Quarterjack Antiques
Bridge St. DT10 1BZ. (A.J. Neilson). Est. 1969. SIZE: Small. *STOCK: 18th-19th C glassware, country oak and mahogany furniture, pictures, walking sticks and horse brasses.* TEL: 01258 472558; home - same.

Tom Tribe and Son
Bridge St. DT10 1BZ. CMBHI. Resident. Open 9-5, Sat. 9-1 and by appointment. *STOCK: Longcase and mantle clocks, barometers.* PARK: At side of shop. TEL: 01258 472311. VAT: Stan/Spec.

SWANAGE

Georgian Gems Antique Jewellers

28 High St. BH19 2NU. (Brian Barker). NAG. Est. 1971. Open 9.30-1 and 2.30-5 or by appointment. SIZE: Small. *STOCK: Jewellery, £5-£2,000; silver, £5-£500; both from 1700.* LOC: Town centre. PARK: Nearby. TEL: 01929 424697. SER: Valuations; repairs; gem testing; special search.

Reference Works

12 Commercial Rd. BH19 1DF. (B. Lamb). Open by appointment. *STOCK: Reference books on ceramics, all subjects, new and out-of-print, £5-£600; some small British porcelain £10-£400.* TEL: 01929 424423; fax - 01929 422597. SER: Mail order, catalogue available; six newsletters each year; ceramic research and consultancy. FAIRS: Details on request.

WAREHAM

Heirlooms Antique Jewellers and Silversmiths

21 South St. BH20 4LR. (Mr. M. and Mrs G. Young). FGA, DGA, RJDip. Est. 1986. Open 9.15-5. CL: Wed. SIZE: Medium. *STOCK: Jewellery, £30-£1,000; silver, £20-£500; both Georgian to Edwardian.* LOC: On main thoroughfare. PARK: At rear. TEL: 01929 554207. SER: Valuations; restorations; repairs; gem testing.

Watercolour before treatment with the old window mount removed. The watercolour is attached to a poor quality backboard with animal glue, both the glue and backboard are very discoloured and can be seen to have caused deterioration to the watercolour paper due to their close association. The watercolour is discoloured and slightly foxed; this is primarily due to the acid produced in the materials that have in turn transferred to the watercolour paper. The watercolour can also be seen to have received a history of abuse where the edges of the paper are torn and skinned. This clearly shows what can be hiding beneath a seemingly decent mount.

From an article entitled "Restoring Watercolours" by Julie Targett which appeared in the October 1996 issue of **Antique Collecting**

WEYMOUTH

Books Afloat

66 Park St. DT4 7DE. (J. Ritchie). Open 9.3 5.30. *STOCK: Rare and secondhand boo especially nautical; maritime ephemera, sh models, paintings, prints.* LOC: Near railw station. PARK: Nearby. TEL: 01305 779774.

Books & Bygones

Great George St. DT4 7AR. (Mrs Denise Nash Est. 1981. Open 11-5.30, Sun. 12-5. SIZ Medium. *STOCK: Books including antiquaria 50p to £1,000; antiques and collectables, fro 18th C, £1-£750; ephemera, from 50p.* LOC: Ne King's statue, on esplanade. PARK: Easy. TE 01305 777231; home - 01305 771529. SE Valuations; buys at auction.

Finesse Fine Art

9 Coniston Crescent. DT3 5HA. (T. Wraight a W. Flint). Open by appointment only. *STOCK: Pr war motoring accessories - metal mascots a Lalique glassware, including mascots, fine bronz picnic hampers, £500-£20,000.* TEL: 013 854286; fax - 01305 852888; mobile - 0973 8693

Nautical Antique Centre

3a Hope Square. DT4 8TR. (D.C. Warwick). E 1989. Open 10-1 and 2-5.30 - prior 'phone c advisable, Sat., Sun. and Mon. by appointmer SIZE: Medium. *STOCK: Exclusively nautica including sextants, logs, clocks, flags, blocks, o sails, rope, bells, ship models, telescopes, sh badges, portholes and memorabilia, al restaurant/pub decorative items, 19th-20th C, £ £2,000.* LOC: Off Brewers Quay, adjacent harbo PARK: Nearby. TEL: 01305 777838; home - 013 783180. SER: Buys at auction (nautical items).

North Quay Collector's Centre

North Quay. (R.A. Shorey). Open 10-5. SIZE: dealers. *STOCK: General antiques and collec ables.* TEL: 01305 779313.

Park Antiquities

37 Park St. DT4 7DF. (F. and Mrs. J.R. Ballar *STOCK: General antiques, porcelain, small fu niture, treen, advertising items.* LOC: Near railw station. PARK: Nearby. TEL: 01305 787666.

The Treasure Chest

29 East St. DT4 8BN. (P. Barrett). Open 10- CL: Wed. pm. *STOCK: Maps, prints, gener antiques, coins, medals, silver, china.* PAR Next door. TEL: 01305 772757.

WIMBORNE MINSTER

Antiquatat Antiques LAPA

The Old Civic Centre, Hanham Rd. BH21 1A (D.W. Schwier). Est. 1973. Open 9-4.30. SIZ Large. *STOCK: Period furniture, silver, cloc containers.* PARK: Own. TEL: 01202 887496.

'imborne Minster continued

he Curio Company

\ Mill Lane. BH21 1JQ. (Mrs Nina Spencer). t. 1987. Open 10-4. CL: Wed. SIZE: Small. *'OCK: General antiques especially unusual and rious.* LOC: Opposite side of Square to King's ad hotel. PARK: 100 yards. TEL: Home – 202 889430.

our Seasons Gallery

West Borough. BH21 1NF. (Nigel and Maria x). Est. 1996. Open Wed.- Sat. 10-5.30. SIZE: nall. *STOCK: Small 18th-19th furniture, intings, collectables; contemporary art gallery th regular exhibitions.* LOC: Near minster. RK: Easy and nearby. TEL: 01202 882204; fax 1202 881105.

B. Antiques

A West Row. (J. and Mrs. G. Beckett). Est. 78. Open 10-4, Fri. and Sat. 9.30-4. CL: Wed. ZE: Small. *STOCK: Copper, £5-£360; brass, -£350; furniture, £30-£1,200; all 18th-20th C.* C: 2 mins. from Sq. PARK: Nearby. TEL: me - 01202 882522. SER: Valuations; restor-ons (metalware); buys at auction (copper).

Wimborne Minster continued

Quercus

27 Leigh Rd. (Bryan Chew). Est. 1985. Open 10.30-4.30, Sun. and Mon. by appointment. SIZE: Small. *STOCK: Oak and country furniture and clocks, £1,000-£5,000; treen, £100-£500; metalware, £50-£500; all 17th-19th C.* LOC: From A31 follow signs to town centre, left after cricket ground and pub, premises 100 yards on left, opposite car park. PARK: Easy and opposite. TEL: 01202 886275. SER: Valuations; restorations (oak and country furniture); buys at auction (oak and country furniture). FAIRS: Petworth, Harrogate, Snape, Arley Hall, Hoghton Tower. VAT: Spec.

Victoriana Antiques

3 Leigh Rd. (Mrs P. Hammer). Open Tues., Thurs. and Fri. 10-1 and 2.30-4. *STOCK: General small antiques, glass, jewellery, silver, brass, objets d'art.* PARK: Easy. TEL: 01202 886739.

Wimborne Antiques and Collectables Centre

21 Newborough, Off Poole Rd. BH21 1RB. (J. Spendier). Est. 1990. Open Thurs.-Sun. 9-5 and Bank Holidays. SIZE: Large. *STOCK: Victorian furniture, collectables and bric-a-brac.* LOC: Corner of Grove Rd and Newborough. PARK: Nearby. TEL: 01202 841251.

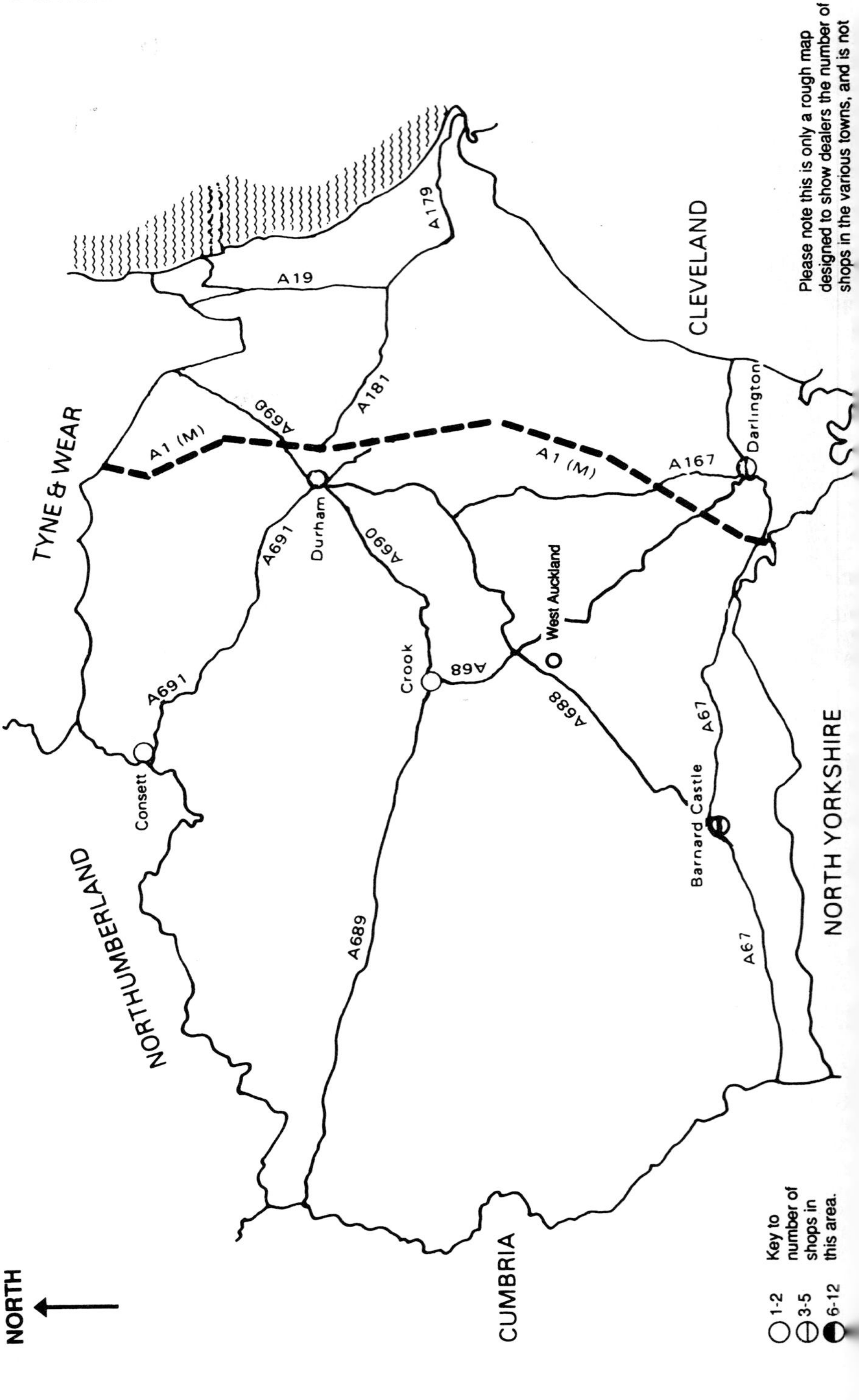
NORTH
TYNE & WEAR
NORTHUMBERLAND
CUMBRIA
CLEVELAND
NORTH YORKSHIRE
A19
A179
A181
A690
A1 (M)
A1 (M)
A167
A691
A691
A690
A68
A688
A67
A67
A689
Durham
Darlington
Consett
Crook
West Auckland
Barnard Castle
1-2
3-5
6-12
Key to number of shops in this area.
Please note this is only a rough map designed to show dealers the number of shops in the various towns, and is not

ARNARD CASTLE

rown's Antiques LAPADA
4 The Bank. DL12 8PN. (Philip and Judy rown). Resident. Est. 1978. Open 10-5, Sun. nd Mon. by appointment only. SIZE: Medium. *TOCK: Georgian mahogany, 18th-19th C oak, 500-£1,000+; pottery and paintings, 19th C, 100-£1,000.* LOC: A66 off A1M at Scotch orner heading west. PARK: Easy. TEL: 1833 637891. SER: Valuations; restorations furniture, pictures, pottery and porcelain, arpets and tapestries). VAT: Spec.

he Collector
ouglas House, The Bank. DL12 8PH. (R.A. rdan and P.R. Hunter). Est. 1970. Open 10-5, rior telephone call advisable. SIZE: Large. *TOCK: Country furniture, especially early oak, eriod mahogany; Persian and Turkish rugs; arden furnishings.* TEL: 01833 637783. SER: estorations (especially metal work and early rniture). VAT: Spec.

rant's Antiques
he Ancient Manor House, The Bank. DL12 8PN. arl and Stephanie Grant). Resident. Est. 1976. pen 10-5, sometimes on Sun., any other time by pointment. SIZE: Small. *STOCK: Oak furniture, 00-£5,000; pottery, £20-£500; rugs, £50-£1,000; l 17th C; interesting items.* LOC: Main road. ARK: Nearby. TEL: 01833 637437. SER: Valuions; restorations; buys at auction. VAT: Stan.

oan and David White Antiques
eville House, 10 The Bank. Est. 1975. Open hurs.-Sat. 11-5. *STOCK: Georgian, Victorian d export furniture and decorative items.* LOC: 0yds. from Market Cross. TEL: 01833 638329; me - 01325 374303. VAT: Stan/Spec.

ONSETT

arry Raine Antiques
elvinside House, Villa Real Rd. DH8 6BL. ppointment advisable. SIZE: Large. *STOCK: eneral antiques.* TEL: 01207 503935.

ROOK

Patterson Antiques
L15 0LZ. Est. 1968. Open by appointment ly. SIZE: Small. *STOCK: Furniture and smalls, th-20th C.* LOC: 6 miles from A68. TEL: 388 746586.

DARLINGTON

S. Brown and Sons 'The Popular Mart'
26 Hollyhurst Rd. DL3 6HT. Est. 1976. Open 9.30-5. CL: Wed. pm. and Sat. pm., except by appointment. SIZE: Large. *STOCK: General antiques, from late 19th C, £5-£500.* LOC: From town centre, along Woodlands Rd. to Hollyhurst Rd., shop adjacent to Memorial Hospital. PARK: Easy. TEL: 01325 354769; home - 01325 355490. SER: Valuations; buys at auction.

Robin Finnegan (Jeweller)
83 Skinnergate. DL3 7LX. Est. 1974. Open 10-5.30. SIZE: Medium. *STOCK: Jewellery, general antiques, coins and medals, £1-£2,000.* TEL: 01325 489820. SER: Valuations. VAT: Stan.

Nichol and Hill
20-22 Grange Rd. DL1 5NG. Open 10-5. *STOCK: Victorian and Edwardian furniture.* TEL: 01325 357431. SER: Restorations, upholstery, interior decoration.

Alan Ramsey Antiques LAPADA
Unit 10 Dudley Rd, Yarm Road Industrial Estate. DL1 4GG. Est. 1973. Open Tues., Thurs. and Fri. 10-3. SIZE: Warehouse. *STOCK: Victorian, Edwardian and Georgian furniture.* PARK: Easy. TEL: 01325 361679; home - 01642 711311. VAT: Stan/Spec. *Trade Only.*

DURHAM

J. Shotton Antiquarian Books, Prints and Coins
89 Elvet Bridge. DH1 3AG. Est. 1967. Open 9.30-5. CL: Mon. *STOCK: Antiquarian books, coins, prints, maps and paintings.* TEL: 0191 386 4597.

WEST AUCKLAND

Eden House Antiques
10 Staindrop Rd. DL14 9JX. (Chris and Margaret Metcalfe). Est. 1978. Open daily including Sun. SIZE: Small. *STOCK: Clocks, 18th-19th C, £50-£1,500; furniture, 18th-20th C, £250-£750; bric-a-brac, 19th-20th C, £25-£75; good quality oak, walnut, pine and mahogany reproduction furniture.* LOC: A68, approx.7 miles west of A1M. PARK: Easy. TEL: 01388 833013; home - same. SER: Valuations; restorations (clocks and furniture); buys at auction (clocks and furniture).

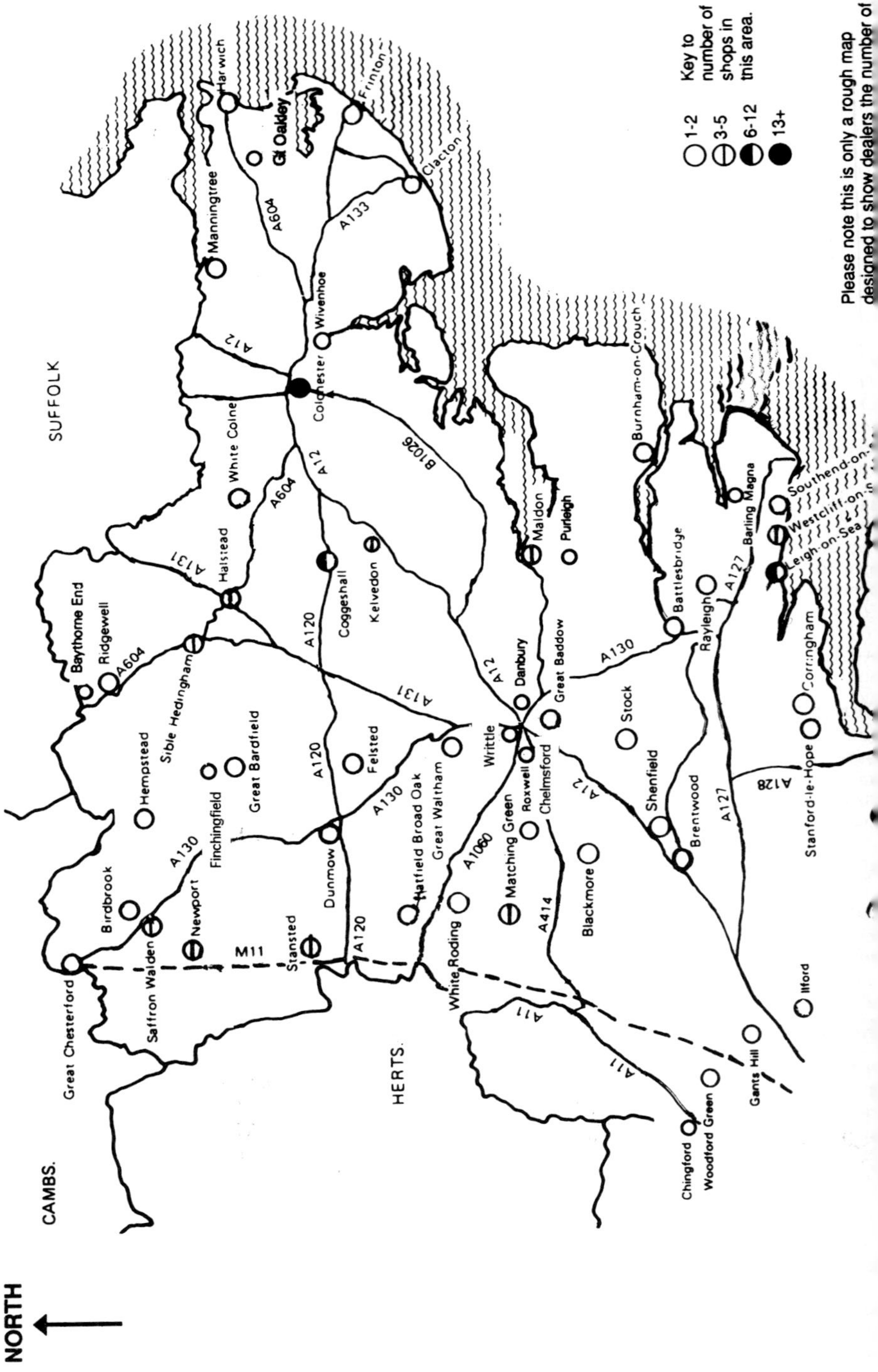
NORTH
CAMBS.
SUFFOLK
HERTS.
Key to number of shops in this area.
1-2
3-5
6-12
13+
Please note this is only a rough map designed to show dealers the number of
Harwich
Gt Oakley
Frinton
Clacton
Manningtree
Wivenhoe
Colchester
White Colne
Halstead
Coggeshall
Kelvedon
Maldon
Purleigh
Burnham-on-Crouch
Barling Magna
Southend-on-
Westcliff-on-
Leigh-on-Sea
Battlesbridge
Rayleigh
Corringham
Stanford-le-Hope
Baythorne End
Ridgewell
Sible Hedingham
Hempstead
Finchingfield
Great Bardfield
Felsted
Dunmow
Great Waltham
Hatfield Broad Oak
Writtle
Danbury
Great Baddow
Roxwell
Chelmsford
Matching Green
Stock
Shenfield
Brentwood
Blackmore
Birdbrook
Newport
Saffron Walden
Great Chesterford
Stansted
White Roding
Ilford
Gants Hill
Woodford Green
Chingford
A12
A604
A133
A131
A120
B1026
A130
A127
A128
A414
A1060
A11
M11

·BRIDGE

·evival

·oach House, Market Place, RM4 1UA. (R. Y. ·fferson). Est. 1988. Open 11-5.30 including ·in. CL: Fri. SIZE: Large. *STOCK: Furniture, ·eorgian to Deco, £20-£3,000; china and glass, ·lver, 1800-1960, £5-£500.* LOC: From London - ·f M11, junction 5, turn right then left on to ·113. From M25, junction 26 follow A121, then ·172. PARK: Opposite. TEL: 01992 814000; fax ·01992 814300. SER: Valuations; restorations ·urniture and upholstery).

·ARLING MAGNA

·omino Antiques

·otash Cottage, Barling Rd. SS3 0LY. (S. ·arish). Resident. By appointment only. *STOCK: ·oyal Worcester porcelain, £100-£4,000; ·atercolours, £300-£2,500; English porcelain.* ·EL: 01702 218691; fax - same. FAIRS: ·akefield Ceramic.

·ATTLESBRIDGE

·attlesbridge Antique Centre

·S11 7RF. SIZE: Over 60 units within adjacent ·emises (see below). *STOCK: Wide range from ·rge furniture to jewellery, all periods with ·ecialist dealers for most items.* LOC: A130,

Battlesbridge continued

mid-way between Chelmsford and Southend. Junction 29, M25, east on A127 to A130, then north for 3 miles. By rail: Liverpool St.-Southend-on-Sea, change at Wickford for Battlesbridge. PARK: Own. SER: Restorations (furniture); container facilities; nationwide and overseas delivery service.

Cromwell House Antique Centre
TEL: Management : Jim Gallie - 01268 575000; ground floor dealers - 01268 762612; first floor dealers - 01268 734030.

Haybarn and Bridgebarn Antique Centres
(J. P. Pettitt). TEL: 01268 763500/735884.

Muggeridge Farm Warehouse
(Jim Gallie). TEL: 01268 575000.

The Old Granary Antique and Craft Centre
(Jim Gallie). TEL: Office - 01268 575000; showrooms - 01268 764197.

Farmhouse Antiques

Maltings Rd. SS11 7RF. (Ian F. Vince). EADA. Open Wed.-Sun. 10-5. *STOCK: Furniture and smalls.* LOC: Battlesbridge Antique Centre A130. TEL: 01268 561586 or 01245 400046.

BAYTHORNE END

Swan Antiques
The Swan. CO9 4AF. (Mr and Mrs K. Mercado). Est. 1983. Open 9.30-6 including Sun. SIZE: Medium. *STOCK: Furniture, 18th-19th C and some Edwardian, £50-£2,000; porcelain, 19th C, £5-£1,000; small silver and collectables, 19th-20th C, £5-£500.* LOC: A604 at Clare/Long Melford junction. PARK: Easy. TEL: 01440 785306; home - same. SER: Valuations; restorations. FAIRS: Newark and Ardingly.

BIRDBROOK, Nr. Halstead

I. Westrope
The Elms. CO9 4AB. Est. 1958. Open 9-5, Sat. 10-1, or by appointment. *STOCK: Furniture; dolls' furniture; china; garden ornaments including statues and birdbaths.* LOC: A604. TEL: 01440 785365; evenings - 01440 785426.

BLACKMORE, Nr. Ingatestone

Hay Green Antiques
Hay Green Farmhouse. CM4 0QE. (T. Harding). Open 9.30-5.30. CL: Mon. *STOCK: Pine, some mahogany and Victorian furniture.* TEL: 01277 821275.

Megarry's and Forever Summer
Jericho Cottage, The Duckpond Green. CM4 0RR. (Peter and Judi Wood). EADA. Est. 1986. Open 10-6 including Sun.; winter - open 11-5 including Sun. CL: Wed. SIZE: Medium.*STOCK: Furniture, mainly 18th-19th C, some 20th C, £60-£3,500; ceramics, glass, treen and metalware, 19th-20th C, £5-£200; small silver and plate, jewellery and collectables, 19th-20th C, £5-£100; pine, 19th to early 20th C, £75-£1,000.* LOC: From A12, turn left at war memorial, premises behind Bull garden. PARK: Own. TEL: 01277 821031; home - 01277 822170. SER: Valuations; restorations (furniture including French polishing, clocks and jewellery).

BRENTWOOD

Brandler Galleries
1 Coptfold Rd. CM14 4BM. (J. Brandler). Est. 1973. Open 10-5.30, Sun. by appointment. CL: Mon. SIZE: Medium. *STOCK: British pictures, 20th C, £100-£30,000.* LOC: Near Post Office. PARK: Own at rear. TEL: 01277 222269 (24 hrs); fax - 01277 222786. SER: Valuations (photographs); restorations (picture cleaning, relining, framing); buys at auction (pictures); 2-3 free catalogues annually.

Brentwood continued

Neil Graham Gallery
11 Ingrave Rd. CM15 8AP. EADA. FATG. Es[illegible] 1977. CL: Mon. SIZE: Large. *STOCK: 19th [illegible] early 20th C watercolours, oils and prints, £5[illegible] £1,000; Victorian and Edwardian occasion[illegible] furniture, £100-£1,500; silver, pottery a[illegible] porcelain, 19th-20th C, £25-£500.* LOC: Ne[illegible] junction of Wilson's Corner, town centre. PAR[illegible] Easy and High St. TEL: 01277 215383; fax same. SER: Valuations; restorations (painting[illegible] buys at auction. FAIRS: NEC Spring a[illegible] Summer. VAT: Stan/Spec.

BURNHAM ON CROUCH

Quay Antiques
28 High St. CM0 8AA. (C. McMullan). Est. 19[illegible] Open 10-5 or by prior appointment. CL: We[illegible] *STOCK: Paintings, prints, china, glass, Victoria[illegible] jewellery, small furniture.* TEL: Home - 01[illegible] 782468.

CHELMSFORD

Hutchison Antiques
163 Main Rd., Broomfield. (G. Hutchison). EAD[illegible] Est. 1980. Open 11-5.30, Sun. by appointment. C[illegible] Mon. SIZE: Medium. *STOCK: Furniture, 18[illegible] 19th C, £300-£1,000+; china, mainly 19th C, fr[illegible] £50; paintings, from 19th C, from £100.* LOC: [illegible] main road, near Broomfield hospital. PAR[illegible] Easy.TEL: 01245 441184. SER: Valuatio[illegible] restorations (as stock); buys at auction (as stock).

CHINGFORD

Nicholas Salter Antiques
8 Station Approach, Station Rd. E4 7AZ. E[illegible] 1971. Open 9.30-5, Fri. and Sat. 9.30-6. C[illegible] Thurs. SIZE: Large. *STOCK: Furniture, 18[illegible] 1930, £150-£1,500; china and linen, 1870-19[illegible] £30-£150.* LOC: Next door to North Chingf[illegible] station. PARK: Easy. TEL: 0181 529 2938.

CLACTON-ON-SEA

L.R. Sharman
80B Rosemary Rd. CO15 1TG. Est. 1973. O[illegible] 9.30-5.15. CL: Wed. SIZE: Small. *STOC[illegible] Furniture, 19th C decorative arts, £100-£5,0[illegible] jewellery, bronzes, clocks, music boxes, milita[illegible]* LOC: Town centre. PARK: Own. TEL: 01[illegible] 424620. SER: Valuations; jewellery repairs.

COGGESHALL

Antique Metals
9A East St. CO6 1SH. (M.C. Chaplin). Est. 1959. Open 9-5, Sun. 12-5. *STOCK: Brass, copper and polished steel, especially fenders and fireside equipment; lighting including oil lamps.* TEL: 01376 562252.

Argentum Antiques
1 Church St. CO6 1TU. (Mrs. Dianne M. Carr). EADA. Open 10-5. CL: Tues. and Wed. SIZE: Medium. *STOCK: Silver and Old Sheffield plate, 19th-20th C, £100-£1,000; furniture, 19th C, £200-£2,000; decorative items, 19th C.* LOC: Between A120 and A12, town centre. PARK: Easy. TEL: 01376 561365. VAT: Spec.

Coggeshall Antiques
Doubleday Corner. CO6 1NJ. Open 10-5, Sun. 2-5. SIZE: Large. *STOCK: Furniture, paintings and decorative items, 18th-19th C.* LOC: A120 opposite White Hart Hotel. PARK: At rear. TEL: 01376 562646; home - 01245 256027.

Elkin Mathews
16 Stoneham St. CO6 1TT. (D.C. Muir). Est. 1887. Open 9.30-1 and 2-4.30, Sat. 10-1 and 2-5. CL: Wed. SIZE: Medium. *STOCK: Antiquarian and secondhand books, 50p-£1,000.* LOC: Just off A120 between Colchester and Braintree. PARK: Own, at rear. TEL: 01376 561730. SER: Valuations; restorations; buys at auction. FAIRS: Major London. VAT: Stan.

English Rose Antiques
7 Church St. CO6 1TU. (Mark J. Barrett). Est. 1983. Open 10-1 and 2-5.30 including Sun., Wed. by appointment. SIZE: Medium. *STOCK: English and Continental pine including dressers, chests, tables and wardrobes, 19th C, £50-£500; fruitwood, ash and elm country furniture and kitchenalia.* LOC: In village centre. PARK: Loading or 50 yds. TEL: 01376 562683; home - same. SER: Valuations; restorations (cabinet work, small repairs, stripping and finishing).

Lindsell Chairs
11 Market Hill. CO6 1TS. (T.J.L. and A.M. Martin). Est. 1982. Open 10.30-6. SIZE: Large. *STOCK: Chairs and other seating, some tables, mid-18th C to 1914, £100-£4,000+.* Not Stocked: Windsor, caned, rush seated or commode chairs. LOC: Town centre. PARK: Nearby. TEL: 01376 562766; home - 01371 870222. SER: Restorations. VAT: Stan/Spec.

Mark Marchant (Antiques)
3 Market Sq. CO6 1TS. Resident. Est. 1960. Open 11-5, Sun. 2.30-5.30. SIZE: Small. *STOCK: Clocks, barometers and music boxes only.* LOC: A120. PARK: Easy. TEL: 01376 561188. SER: Valuations; restorations; buys at auction. VAT: Spec.

Coggeshall continued

Partners in Pine
63/65 West St. CO6 1NS. (W.T. Newton). Resident. Open 7 days 10-6. *STOCK: Victorian stripped pine.* TEL: 01376 561972.

Times Past
5A Church St. CO6 1TU. (Victoria Waine). Est. 1981. Open 10-5. CL: Mon. and Wed. SIZE: Medium. *STOCK: Art Deco and Art Nouveau, glass, china, metalware, lighting and small furniture, £5-£1,000; Clarice Cliff, Cooper, Shelley, figurines, Lalique, Sabino, Vasart, Monart, etc.* TEL: 01376 563600.

COLCHESTER

101 Antiques
101 Crouch St. CO3 3HA. (Mrs. S.P. Edwards). Est. 1969. Open 9.30-4. CL: Thurs. SIZE: Small. *STOCK: Glass, china, metalware and furniture, 19th-20th C, £1-£500.* LOC: Almost opposite the old Essex County Hospital on Lexden Rd. PARK: Easy. TEL: 01206 549150. FAIRS: Ipswich Moathouse.

Badger Antiques
The Old House, The Street, Elmstead Market. CO7 7AA. (A. Johnson). Resident. Est. 1977. Open 9.30-5.30, Sun. by appointment. SIZE: Medium. *STOCK: Furniture, pine, ceramics, glass, lace, linen and unusual bygones.* LOC: 4 miles from Colchester on old A133 Clacton road. PARK: Easy. TEL: 01206 822044. SER: Valuations; restorations (furniture and clocks).

Barntiques
Lampitts Farm, Turkeycock Lane, Stanway. CO3 5ND. (A. Jones and S. Doubleday). Resident. Est. 1978. Open weekends. SIZE: Medium. *STOCK: General antiques and pine.* LOC: Turn left at Eight Ash Green from A604. PARK: Easy. TEL: 01206 210486; home - 01206 212421.

S. Bond and Son
14/15 North Hill. CO1 1DZ. (R. Bond). Open 9-5.30. SIZE: Large. *STOCK: Furniture and pictures.* TEL: 01206 572925. SER: Restorations. VAT: Stan/Spec.

Elizabeth Cannon Antiques
85 Crouch St. CO3 3EZ. Open 9-5.30. *STOCK: General antiques including jewellery, silver, glass, porcelain, engravings and furniture.* PARK: Easy. TEL: 01206 575817.

Castle Bookshop
37 North Hill. CO1 1QR. (R.J. Green). *STOCK: Antiquarian and secondhand books, maps & prints.* TEL: 01206 577520. VAT: Stan.

Colchester continued

Dean Antiques
Mill Farm, Harwich Rd., Gt. Bromley. CO7 7JQ. Est. 1947. Open 9-5, including Sun. SIZE: Medium. *STOCK: Mahogany, country and pine furniture, 18th-19th C.* Not Stocked: Reproductions. LOC: 6 miles from Colchester. 1½ miles off A120 Harwich road, follow signs for Mill Farm camping. PARK: Own. TEL: 01206 250485; home - same; fax - 01206 252040. SER: Valuations.

Essex Antiques Centre
Priory St., (Scalpay Securities Ltd). Est. 1969. Open 10-5.30. SIZE: Large - 52 dealers. *STOCK: General antiques and collectables.* LOC: Near town centre, off Queen St. Next to St. Botolph's Priory. PARK: Easy. TEL: 01206 871150. SER: Restorations (jewellery, furniture, paintings).

Grahams of Colchester
19 Short Wyre St. CO1 1LN. Open 9-5.30. *STOCK: Jewellery and silver.* TEL: 01206 576808. SER: Valuations; restorations.

Richard Iles Gallery
10a, 10 and 12 Northgate St. CO1 1HA. (R. and C. Iles). Est. 1970. Open 10-1 and 2-4, Thurs. 10-1. SIZE: Small. *STOCK: Watercolours, 19th to early 20th C, £75-£700.* LOC: Off North Hill. PARK: NCP nearby. TEL: 01206 577877. SER: Restorations (oils, engravings and watercolours); framing.

Mayflower Antiques
14/15 North Hill. CO1 1DZ. Est. 1970. Open 9-5.30. *STOCK: 19th C furniture, clocks, decorative antiques, paintings.* PARK: Easy. TEL: 01206 572925; mobile - 0860 315101; e-mail - mayflower@anglianet.co.uk. VAT: Stan/Spec.

Anthony Rush Antiques
85 High St., Earls Colne. CO6 2QX. *STOCK: Furniture, china, glass, jewellery, pictures, prints and bric-a-brac.* TEL: 01787 223348.

Stock Exchange
The Old Saleroom, 4 North Station Rd. CO1 1RD. (J. Mellish and G. Dean). Open 10-5. *STOCK: General antiques.* TEL: 01206 561997.

Trinity Antiques Centre
7 Trinity St. CO1 1JN. Est. 1976. Open 9.30-5. SIZE: 7 dealers + cabinets. *STOCK: General antiques - small furniture, copper, clocks, brass, porcelain, silver, jewellery, collectors' items, Victoriana, maps and prints, linen, pine furniture.* TEL: 01206 577775.

CORRINGHAM, Nr. Stanford-le-Hope

Bush House
Church Rd. SS17 9AP. (F. Stephens). Est. 1976. Open by appointment. *STOCK: Staffordshire*

Corringham continued

animals, portrait figures, 1770-1901, £50-£5,00 LOC: Opposite the church. PARK: Own. TEL 01375 673463; home - same. FAIRS: Park Lar Hotel; NEC, Birmingham; K.M. Ceramic.

DANBURY

Danbury Antiques
Eves Corner (by the Village Green). CM3 4Q (Mrs Pam Southgate). Est. 1983. Open 10-5, We 10-1, Sun. 10.30-1. SIZE: Medium. *STOCK Jewellery and silver, ceramics, metalwar furniture, 18th to early 20th C, £5-£1,800.* LOC Off M25, take A12, then A414. PARK: Eas TEL: 01245 223035. SER: Valuations; resto ations (jewellery, upholstery, furniture). FAIR Furzehill, Margaretting, Billericay. VA Stan/Spec.

DUNMOW

Julia Bennet (Antiques) **LAPAD**
Flemings Hill Farm, Gt. Easton. CM6 2E Open by appointment. *STOCK: 18th mahogany, 17th-19th C oak and country fu niture, decorative and garden pieces.* TE 01279 850279.

Simon Hilton
Flemings Hill Farm, Gt. Easton. CM6 2E Resident. Est. 1937. Open by appointmen *STOCK: Oil paintings, watercolours a drawings, £100-£10,000; fine prints a sculpture, £50-£5,000; all 17th-20th C.* TE 01279 850107/850279. SER: Valuations; resto ations (oil paintings, watercolours and drawing buys at auction. VAT: Spec.

FELSTED, Nr. Great Dunmow

Argyll House Antiques
Argyll House, Station Rd. CM6 3DG. (J. Howa and C. Downing). EADA. Est. 1978. CL: We SIZE: Medium. *STOCK: Furniture, Victorian a Edwardian, £25-£1,000; porcelain, 19th C to mi 20th C, £5-£500; collectors' items and epheme £1-£250.* LOC: Village centre. PARK: Easy. TE 01371 820682; home - same.

FINCHINGFIELD

Finchingfield Antiques Centre
The Green. CM7 4JX. (Peter Curry). Est.199 Open 10-6, including Sun., Mon. by appointme SIZE: Large - 25 dealers. *STOCK: Wide range general antiques, to £1,000.* LOC: From M A120 to Gt. Dunmow, then B1057. PARK: Ea TEL: 01371 810258; fax - same; home - sar SER: Buys at auction.

FRINTON-ON-SEA

Dickens Curios
151 Connaught Ave. CO13 9AH. (Miss M. Wilsher). Est. 1970. Open 9.45-1 and 2.15-5.30, Sat. 9.45-5. CL: Wed. pm. SIZE: Small. *STOCK: Victoriana and earlier items, £5-£200; furniture, 18th-20th C, £5-£300; jewellery, £5-£25; cigarette cards.* Not Stocked: Firearms, watches and clocks. LOC: From Frinton Station quarter of mile down Connaught Ave., opposite Hammond's Garage. PARK: Easy. TEL: 01255 674134.

Frinton Antiques
CO13 9BT. (Mrs. G.M. Pethick). Est. 1952. Open by appointment. *STOCK: Small decorative furniture; fine porcelain, silver, glass and pottery.* TEL: 01255 671894. VAT: Stan/Spec.

GANTS HILL

Antique Clock Repair Shoppe
26 Woodford Ave. IG2 6XG. (K. Ashton). Est. 1971. Open 10-5. *STOCK: Clocks, pictures, bric-a-brac.* TEL: 0181 550 9540.

GRAYS

Kendons and Atticus Books
10 London Rd. RM17 5XY. Open Mon., Thurs., Fri. and Sat. 9.30-5. SIZE: 25+ dealers. *STOCK: Collectables - jewellery, clocks, watches, children's books and comics, toys, silver, Goss/crested china, military items, furniture, pictures, antiquarian and Essex books.* LOC: Town centre, mins from station, 10 mins from M25. TEL: 01375 371200. SER: Framing; jewellery repairs; medal mounting.

GREAT BADDOW

Baddow Antique Centre
The Bringy, Church St. CM2 7JW. Est. 1969. Open 10-5, Sun. 11-5. SIZE: 22 dealers. *STOCK: Furniture, general antiques, Victorian brass bedsteads, bric-a-brac and shipping goods.* PARK: Easy. TEL: 01245 476159. SER: Restorations; upholstery.

GREAT BARDFIELD

Golden Sovereign
The Old Police House, High St. CM7 4SP. (C. and W. Leitch). EADA. Est. 1969. Open Mon., Tues. and Thurs. 10-6 and Wed., Fri. and Sat. afternoons. SIZE: Small. *STOCK: Glass, silver, small furniture, small items, 18th-19th C, from £5.* LOC: B1057. From Dunmow, 100yds. beyond Thaxted turning, 2nd shop on left. PARK: Easy. TEL: 01371 810507; home - same.

GREAT CHESTERFORD, Nr. Saffron Walden

C. and J. Mortimer and Son
School St. CB10 1NN. Est. 1962. Open Thurs., Sat. and Sun. 2.30-5 or by appointment. SIZE: Medium. *STOCK: Oak furniture, 16th-17th C, from £400; portrait paintings, 16th-17th C, from £1,500.* LOC: From London on B1383. PARK: Easy. TEL: 01799 530261.

GREAT OAKLEY, Nr. Harwich

John Burls
1 The Plains. CO12 5AS. (John and Jonathan Burls). Est. 1960. Open in summer 10-1 and 2-4, Sun. 11-1 and 2-4; prior telephone call advisable in winter. SIZE: Small. *STOCK: Pottery and porcelain, 18th-20th C, £2-£300; furniture, £40-£500; paintings, £20-£350; both 19th-20th C. Clocks, silver, brass and copper, jewellery and prints.* LOC: 3 miles from A120 Colchester to Harwich road. PARK: Easy. TEL: 01255 880141; home - same. SER: Valuations; restorations (furniture); buys at auction.

GREAT WALTHAM, Nr. Chelmsford

The Stores
CM3 1DE. (M. Webster). Est. 1974. Open 10-5. CL: Sun. and Tues. SIZE: Large. *STOCK: Pine furniture.* LOC: On A130. PARK: At rear. TEL: 01245 360277; home - 01376 26997. VAT: Stan.

HALSTEAD

Antique Bed Shop
Napier House, Head St. CO9 2BT. (Veronica McGregor). EADA. Est. 1977. Open Wed.-Sat., Sun., Mon. and Tues. by appointment. SIZE: Large. *STOCK: Antique wooden beds in mahogany, rosewood, walnut, chestnut, oak, bergere, 19th-20th C, £1,295-£2,795 including new base, mattress and UK delivery.* Not Stocked: Brass, iron or pine beds. LOC: On A131 to Sudbury, 200 yds from Halstead High Street. PARK: Own. TEL: 01787 477346; fax - 01787 478757. SER: Worldwide delivery. VAT: Spec.

Causeway Antiques
The Forecourt, Townsford Mill Antiques Centre, The Causeway. CO9 1ET. (Mr and Mrs L.W. Stevens-Wilson). Est. 1966. Open Sat. 10-5, Sun. 11-5, other times by appointment. SIZE: Small. *STOCK: Furniture, £50-£1,500; porcelain and glass, £10-£500; general antiques and metalware, £10-£1,000.* LOC: Off A604 in town centre. PARK: Easy. TEL: 01787 478931; home - same. SER: Valuations; lectures.

Halstead continued

Halstead Antiques
71 Head St. CO9 2AU. (P. Earl). Est. 1973. *STOCK: Small general antiques, glass, bric-a-brac.* TEL: 01787 473265.

Townsford Mill Antiques Centre
The Causeway. CO9 1ET. (M.T. Stuckey). Open 10-5, Sun. and Bank Holidays 11-5. SIZE: 70 dealers. *STOCK: General antiques and collectables.* LOC: On A131 Braintree/Sudbury road. TEL: 01787 474451.

HARWICH

Mayflower Antiques
105 High St., Dovercourt. CO12 3AP. (J.W. Odgers). Est. 1970. Open 10-6. CL: Sat. SIZE: Medium. *STOCK: Clocks, mechanical music, scientific and marine instruments, collectors' items.* LOC: Main road. PARK: Easy. TEL: 01255 504079; mobiles - 0860 315101/843569; e-mail - mayflower@anglianet.co.uk. VAT: Stan/Spec.

HATFIELD BROAD OAK

Tudor Antiques
CM22 7HF. (R.M. and P.A. Wood). Est. 1977. Open 10-4. *STOCK: Furniture, porcelain, glass, unusual items.* LOC: B183, close to M11 and A120. TEL: 01279 718557.

HEMPSTEAD, Nr. Saffron Walden

Michael Beaumont Antiques
Hempstead Hall. CB10 2PR. Open Sat., Sun., Mon. and Wed. 10.30-5. SIZE: Large. *STOCK: Furniture - oak, mahogany, walnut, rosewood, 17th-19th C, £50-£4,000.* LOC: On B1054 between Hempstead and Steeple Bumpstead. PARK: Easy. TEL: 01440 730239. SER: Restorations (furniture). VAT: Stan/Spec.

ILFORD

Belgrave Antiques and Bric-a-Brac
77 Belgrave Rd. IG1 3AL. (Mrs M.M. Germain). Est. 1969. Open 10-2 and 3.30-6.30. *STOCK: Furniture, paintings, bric-a-brac, books.* TEL: 0181 554 8032.

Flowers Antiques
733 High Rd., Seven Kings. IG3 8RL. (J.C. and A.D. Meeson). Est. 1988. Open 9.30-5.30. *STOCK: Furniture, Edwardian, Victorian; glass, china.* PARK: Easy. TEL: 0181 599 9959.

KELVEDON, Nr. Colchester

Colton Antiques
Station Rd. CO5 9NP. (G. Colton). Est. 1993 Open 8.30-4.30, Sun. by appointment. SIZE Medium. *STOCK: Furniture, 19th C, £100 £5,000.* PARK: Own. TEL: 01376 571504. SER Restorations. VAT: Stan/Spec.

Kelvedon Art and Antiques
2 High St. CO5 9AG. (Sarah Mabey). Open 10-5 SIZE: Large. *STOCK: Furniture, paintings an decorative items, 18th-19th C.* PARK: Easy - ow car park. TEL: 01376 573065; home - 0124 256027.

Millers Antiques Kelvedon
46 High St. CO5 9AG. Est. 1920. Open 9-5.3 Sat. 10-4 or by appointment. SIZE: Large *STOCK: 17th-19th C mahogany, walnu fruitwood, oak, English and French furniture* PARK: Own. TEL: 01376 570098; fax - 0137 572186. VAT: Stan/Spec.

G.T. Ratcliff Ltd
Greys Mill. (W.D. Boyd Ratcliff and F.D Campbell). Est. 1935. Open 9-5, Sat. and Sun. b appointment. SIZE: Large. *STOCK: Furnitur and smalls, mainly 18th-19th C.* LOC: A12 PARK: Easy. TEL: 01376 570234; fax - 0137 571764. VAT: Stan. *Trade Only.*

Thomas Sykes Antiques LAPAD
16 High St. CO5 9AG. (T.W. Sykes and O.I Folkard). Est. 1983. Open 10-5, Sun. b appointment. SIZE: Large. *STOCK: 18th-19t C furniture and Victorian pictures, £50 £35,000.* LOC: Off A12. PARK: Own. TEL 01376 571969; fax - 01376 571063. SER: Bu at auction. VAT: Spec.

LEIGH-ON-SEA

K.S. Buchan
135 The Broadway. SS9 1PJ. Open 10-5. *STOC Furniture and general antiques.* TEL: 017 79440.

Castle Antiques
PO Box 1911, 72 Broadway. SS9 1JG. (B.L. ar J.A. Gair). Open strictly by appointment onl *STOCK: 18th-19th C English pottery includir Mason's Ironstone; Staffordshire figures, trib edged weapons, ethnic weapons, cased birds a fish.* TEL: 01702 711390; fax - 01702 7573 mobile - 0973 674355.

Collectors' Paradise
993 London Rd. SS9 3LB. (H.W. and P.E. Smith Est. 1967. Open 10-5.30. CL: Fri. SIZE: Sma *STOCK: Clocks, 1830-1930, from £85; bric- brac; postcards, 1900-1930s; cigarette card 1889-1939.* LOC: On A13. PARK: Easy. TE 01702 73077.

Leigh-on-Sea continued

Pall Mall Antiques
104c/104d Elm Rd. SS9 1SQ. (M. Sherman). EADA. Open 10-5. *STOCK: Porcelain, glass, metalware and collectables.*TEL: 01702 77235.

Penny Farthing
104 Elm Rd. SS9 1SQ. (R. and N. Cameron). Open 10-5. CL: Mon. and Wed. *STOCK: Furniture, clocks and jewellery.* TEL: 01702 79796.

John Stacey and Sons
86-90 Pall Mall. SS9 1RG. Est. 1946. Open 9-5.30. CL: Sat. pm. *STOCK: General antiques.* TEL: 01702 77051. SER: Valuations; exporters; auctioneers. VAT: Stan.

J. Streamer Antiques
86 Broadway and 212 Leigh Rd. SS9 1AE. Est. 1965. Open 9.30-5.30. CL: Wed. *STOCK: Jewellery, silver, bric-a-brac, small furniture.* TEL: 01702 72895/711633.

Tilly's Antiques
1801 London Rd. SS9 2ST. (S.T. and R.J. Austen). Est. 1972. Open 10-5. CL: Wed. SIZE: Medium. *STOCK: Furniture, 19th C, £100-£500+; Victorian and Edwardian dolls, £100-£500; general antiques, 19th-20th C, £5-£200.* LOC: A13. PARK: Easy. TEL: 01702 557170. SER: Valuations; restorations (furniture and dolls).

Richard Wrenn Antiques
113/115 Broadway West. SS9 2BU. Est. 1950. Open 10.30-5.30. CL: Mon., Wed. and Fri. pm. SIZE: Large. *STOCK: Furniture, £250-£5,000; porcelain, glass, £30-£1,000; jewellery, silver, objets d'art, £40-£2,000; metalware, brass, copper, £20-£500.* LOC: 250yds. west of Leigh Church. TEL: 01702 710745. VAT: Stan/Spec.

MALDON

Abacus Antiques
105 High St. CM9 7EP. (Mrs J. Davidson). Open 10-4.30. CL: Mon. and Wed. SIZE: Medium. *STOCK: Jewellery, 19th to early 20th C, £10-£500; porcelain, pottery, glass, small silver and collectors' items, 1800-1930, £5-£500; furniture, 19th C and Edwardian, £20-£2,000.* Not Stocked: firearms, coins, stamps, books. LOC: Town centre. PARK: Easy. TEL: 01621 850528; home - same. SER: Valuations.

The Antique Rooms
3D High St. CM9 7EB. (Mrs E. Hedley). Est. 1966. Open 10-4. CL: Wed. SIZE: Medium. *STOCK: Furniture, pottery, porcelain, glass and silver, costume, linen and lace, jewellery, lace-making equipment, collectors' items.* LOC: Just off High St. PARK: Nearby. TEL: 01621 856985.

Maldon continued

Clive Beardall Antiques
104B High St. CM9 7ET. BAFRA, EADA. Est. 1982. Open 8-5.30, Sat 8-4.30. SIZE: Medium. *STOCK: Furniture, 18th-19th C, £100-£5,000.* LOC: Off High St. up alleyway between Pollards and Peter Foulkes. PARK: Easy. TEL: 01621 857890. SER: Restorations (furniture). VAT: Stan/Spec.

Maldon Antiques and Collectors Market
All Saints Church Hall, London Rd. , Est. 1975. Open first Sat. every month 9-4. LOC: Top of High St., opposite Police Station. PARK: Own. TEL: 01702 230746.

MANNINGTREE

Forty Nine
High St. CO11 1AH. (A. Patterson). Open 10-1 and 2-5. *STOCK: General and country antiques.* PARK: Easy. TEL: 01206 396170.

F. Freestone
Kiln Tops, 29 Colchester Rd. Open 9-6, appointment advisable. *STOCK: General antiques, furniture, clocks.* TEL: 01206 392998.

MATCHING GREEN, Nr. Harlow

Old Barn Antiques
Downhall Rd. CM17 0RA. Est. 1971. Open 9-5.30, Sat. and Sun. by appointment. SIZE: Warehouse. *STOCK: French, English and Continental furniture and smalls, 17th-19th C, £20-£5,000.* LOC: Turning off A1060 at Hatfield Heath. PARK: Own. TEL: 01279 731440. VAT: Stan.

A collection of H.M. silver hatpins, £20-£130 each. Black Horse Agencies, Locke & England.

From a feature entitled "Saleroom Prices" which appeared in the April 1997 issue of **Antique Collecting**

Matching Green continued

Stone Hall Antiques
Downhall Rd. CM17 ORA. Est. 1971. Open 9-5.30, Sat. and Sun. by appointment. SIZE: Warehouse. *STOCK: Furniture, 17th-19th C, £50-£10,000.* LOC: Turning off A1060 at Hatfield Heath. PARK: Own. TEL: 01279 731440; home - same. VAT: Stan.

West Essex Antiques
Downhall Rd. CM17 0RA. Est. 1982. Open 9-5.30, Sat and Sun. by appointment. SIZE: Large warehouse. *STOCK: English furniture, 17th-19th C, £50-£5,000.* LOC: Turning off A1060 at Hatfield Heath. PARK: Own. TEL: 01279 730607. SER: Restorations. VAT: Stan.

NEWPORT, Nr. Saffron Walden

Brown House Antiques
High St. CO11 3QY. (B.E. and J. Hodgkinson). Est. 1978. Open 10-5. SIZE: Medium. *STOCK: Furniture, from 18th C, £50-£2,500.* LOC: B1383, off M11 at Stansted interchange. PARK: Easy. TEL: 01799 540238; home - same. SER: Valuations; restorations; buys at auction (furniture). VAT: Stan/Spec.

Gostick Hall Antiques
CB11 3PP. Est. 1979. Open by appointment. *STOCK: Victorian and Edwardian jewellery, silver, porcelain, glass.* TEL: 01799 540633.

Newport continued

Newport Gallery
High St., CB11 3QZ. (W. Kemp and E.C. Hitchcock). Open 9.30-5. CL: Mon. *STOCK: Watercolours, prints and oils.* LOC: On B1383, two miles from Saffron Walden. PARK: At rear. TEL: 01799 540623.

PURLEIGH, Nr. Chelmsford

David Lloyd Gallery
The Studio, Turnstone, The Street. CM3 6QL. Open by appointment. *STOCK: 19th-20th C watercolours and oils.* TEL: 01621 828093.

RAYLEIGH

F.G. Bruschweiler (Antiques) Ltd

LAPADA

41-67 Lower Lambricks. SS6 7EN. Est. 1963. Open 9-5, Sat. by appointment. SIZE: Warehouses. *STOCK: Furniture, 18th-19th C.* LOC: A127 to Weir roundabout through Rayleigh High St. and Hockley Rd., first left past cemetery, then second left, warehouse round corner on left. PARK: Easy. TEL: 01268 773761/773932; home - 0162 182 8152; fax 01268 773318. VAT: Stan. *Trade Only.*

F. G. BRUSCHWEILER (Antiques) LTD.

41-67 LOWER LAMBRICKS, RAYLEIGH
ESSEX SS6 7EN

35 miles from London & 1 hour by car from the airport

3500 sq metres of antique furniture

Always a minimum 10,000 items in stock

Bars always in stock from 6-25 feet long

Bars built to customer's dimensions

We have a stock of very important antique furniture which allows us to sell to USA, Japan, Australia, Italy, Spain, Portugal, Belgium, etc...

To receive our catalogue & brochure

Tel. (01268) 773 761
(01268) 773 932
Fax. (01268) 773 318

ESTABLISHED 1963

MEMBER OF LAPADA

RIDGEWELL, Nr. Halstead

Ridgewell Crafts and Antiques
CO9 4SG. (C.M.J. Godsell). Est. 1952. Open 10-6.30 including Sun. CL: Wed. SIZE: Medium. *STOCK: Clocks and watches, 19th C, £5-£500; china, brass, copper, some furniture.* LOC: On A604, 6 miles from Haverhill towards Colchester. PARK: Easy. TEL: 01440 785272.

ROXWELL, Nr. Chelmsford

Freemans Antiques
CM1 4NJ. By appointment only. *STOCK: 17th-18th C oak, especially coffers.* TEL: 01245 231286.

SAFFRON WALDEN

Bush Antiques
26-28 Church St. CB10 1JQ. (Mrs. B.E. Bush and Mrs. J.M. Hosford). EADA. Est. 1962. Open 10.30-4.30. CL: Thurs. SIZE: Medium. *STOCK: English ceramics including blue and white transfer printed pottery, copper lustre and pink lustre, £25-£250; mahogany and country furnitutre, to £1,000; copper and brass, to £250; all 1800-1860.* LOC: 300 yards north of Market Sq., on crossroads with Museum St. PARK: Nearby. TEL: 01799 523277. FAIRS: Bury St. Edmunds (Spring and Autumn).

The Interior Design Shop
4 & 5 Rose & Crown Walk. CB10 1JH. (Peter Mileham). Est. 1981. Open 10-5. CL: Mon. *STOCK: Victorian mahogany, £200-£3,000; upholstered items, Georgian to 1930's, £300-£2,000; oak and early mahogany, 1790-1900, £300-£2,000.* TEL: 01799 516456; fax - 01799 516699SER: Valuations; restorations; interior design. VAT: Stan/Spec.

Lankester Antiques and Books
Old Sun Inn, Church St., and Market Hill. CB10 1HQ. (P. Lankester). Est. 1965. Open 9.30-5.30. SIZE: Large. *STOCK: Furniture, porcelain, pottery, metalwork, general antiques, books, prints and maps.* TEL: 01799 522685. VAT: Stan

Saffron Walden continued

Littlebury Antiques - Littlebury Restorations Ltd
58/60 Fairycroft Rd. CB10 1LZ. (N.H. D'Oyly). Est. 1962. Open 9-5. CL: Sat. and Sun. except by appointment. SIZE: Medium. *STOCK: Barometers, marine antiques, chess sets, walking sticks and curios.* PARK: Easy. TEL: 01799 527961; fax - same; home - 01279 771530. SER: Valuations; restorations; buys at auction. VAT: Stan/Spec.

Maureen Morris LAPADA
CB11 4TA. Open by appointment. *STOCK: Samplers, needleworks, textiles and small country furniture.* TEL: 01799 521338; fax - 01799 522802.

SHENFIELD

The Chart House
33 Spurgate, Hutton Mount. CM13 2JS. (C.C. Crouchman). Est. 1974. Open by appointment only. SIZE: Small. *STOCK: Nautical items.* PARK: Easy. TEL: 01277 225012; home - same. SER: Hire of nautical items and equipment; buys at auction.

SIBLE HEDINGHAM, Nr. Halstead

Churchgate Antiques
Prayors Farm, Prayors Hill. CO9 3LE. (B. Wilkinson). Est. 1979. Open 10-5, Sun. by appointment. CL: Mon. SIZE: Large. *STOCK: English and Irish period pine, £75-£1,800.* PARK: Easy. TEL: 01787 462269; home - 01787 461311. SER: Valuations; restorations (stripping). VAT: Stan.

Hedingham Antiques
100 Swan St. CO9 3HP. (P. Patterson). EADA. Open 10-12.30 and 1.30-5 or by appointment. SIZE: Medium and warehouse. *STOCK: Shop - furniture, 1790-1910; china, glass, silver plate, Victorian to Art Deco, bric-a-brac. Warehouse - old and modern furniture and effects.* LOC: A604, village centre. PARK: Easy. TEL: 01787 460360; home - same. SER: Restorations.

Sible Hedingham continued

Lennard Antiques LAPADA

c/o W.A. Pinn & Sons, 124 Swan St. CO9 3HP. Est. 1978. *STOCK: Oak and country furniture, English Delftware, 18th to early 19th C.* LOC: On A604 opposite Shell garage in middle of village. TEL: 01787 461127. FAIRS: Chelsea; West London; Olympia (June); Harrogate (Feb.); Buxton.

W.A. Pinn and Sons BADA LAPADA

124 Swan St. CO9 3HP. (K.H. and W.J. Pinn). Est. 1943. CL: Sun. except by appointment. SIZE: Medium. *STOCK: Furniture, 17th to early 19th C, £100-£5,000; clocks, 18th to early 19th C, £500-£6,000; Chinese export porcelain, £25-£1,000; interesting items, prior to 1830, £10-£1,500.* LOC: On A604 opposite Shell Garage. PARK: On premises. TEL: 01787 461127. FAIRS: Chelsea Spring and Autumn. VAT: Stan/Spec.

SOUTHEND-ON-SEA

Lonsdale Antiques

86 Lonsdale Rd, Southchurch. SS2 4LR. (H.M. Clark). Open 9-5.30. CL: Wed. *STOCK: Jewellery, pictures, porcelain, general small antiques.* TEL: 01702 462643.

Reddings Art and Antiques

98 London Rd. SS1 1PG. (F.H. Redding). Resident. *STOCK: Oils and watercolours, general antiques.* TEL: 01702 354647.

STANFORD-LE-HOPE

Barton House Antiques

Wharf Rd. SS17 0DY. (L. and J. Pigney). Est. 1973. Open all times but appointment advisable. SIZE: Medium. *STOCK: 17th-19th C furniture; 18th-19th C English porcelain, including English 18th C blue and white, copper, brass and glass.* LOC: Turn off A13 to centre of town, 200yds. on right hand side. PARK: Easy. TEL: 01375 672494. SER: Valuations; buys at auction. VAT: Spec. *Mainly Trade.*

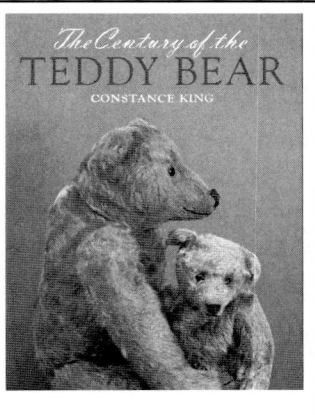

STANSTED

Harris Antiques (Stansted)

40 Lower St. CM24 8LR. (F.A.D. and B.D.A. Harris, and E.V. Bradshaw). Resident. EADA. Est. 1956. Open 9.30-5.30, Sun. by appointment only. SIZE: Medium. *STOCK: Quality period furniture, porcelain and silver, 17th-19th C, £2,000-£6,000.* LOC: Near M11 and Stansted Airport. PARK: Easy. TEL: 01279 812233; home - same. SER: Valuations; restorations (furniture and porcelain). FAIRS: Anglia Arts and Antiques; Crown. VAT: Spec.

Linden House Antiques

3 Silver St. CM24 8HA. (A.W. and K.M. Sargeant). Est. 1961. Open 9-5.30. CL: Sun. except by appointment. SIZE: Large. *STOCK: English furniture, 18th-19th C, £100-£10,000; small decorative items, including library and dining room furniture.* LOC: A11. TEL: 01279 812372. VAT: Spec.

Valmar Antiques LAPADA

Croft House, High Lane. CM24 8LQ. (John and Marina Orpin). Resident. Est. 1960. Open by appointment. SIZE: Large. *STOCK: Furniture and decorative items, £50-£10,000.* TEL: 01279 813201; fax - 01279 816962; mobile - 0831 093701. FAIRS: Major British.

STOCK

Sabine Antiques

38 High St. CM4 9BW. (C.E. Sabine). EADA. Est. 1974. Open 10-5 or by appointment. CL: Mon. *STOCK: Furniture, from £50; china and glass, from £5.* LOC: Village centre on B1007. PARK: Easy. TEL: 01277 840553. SER: Valuations; restorations (furniture); silver plating; framing.

WESTCLIFF-ON-SEA

David, Jean and John Antiques

Lincoln House Gallery, 587 London Rd. SS0 9PQ. Est. 1963. Open 10-5. CL: Wed. SIZE: Large. *STOCK: Clocks, furniture, £25-£3,000; porcelain, bronzes, weapons, objets d'art, some shipping goods.* LOC: Opposite Jewsons. TEL: 01702 339106; fax - 01268 560536; home - 01268 733330; evenings - 01268 785815. SER: Valuations; restorations (clocks, barometers and small furniture). VAT: Stan/Spec.

It's About Time

863 London Rd. SS0 9SZ. (R. and V. Alps). EADA. Est. 1980. Open 9-5.30. CL: Wed. SIZE: Large. *STOCK: Clocks, 18th-19th C, £200-£4,000; barometers, Victorian and Edwardian furniture.* LOC: A13. PARK: Easy. TEL: 01702 72574; fax - same; home - 01702 205204.

Westcliff-on-Sea continued

Ridgeway Antiques

66 The Ridgeway. SS0 8NU. (Trevor Cornforth and Charles Jackson). EADA. Est. 1987. Open 10.30-5. SIZE: Small. *STOCK: General antiques, £5-£1,000.* LOC: A13 London road, right at Chalkwell Ave., right to The Ridgway. PARK: Easy. TEL: 01702 710383. SER: Valuations. FAIRS: Ridgeway and Hallmark.

WHITE COLNE, Nr. Colchester

Fox and Pheasant Antique Pine

CO6 2PS. (J. and J. Kearin). Est. 1978. Open 8-6 SIZE: Large. *STOCK: Stripped pine.* LOC: A604 PARK: Easy. TEL: 01787 223297. SER: Pine stripping; restorations; kitchens; joinery.

WHITE RODING

White Roding Antiques

'Ivydene', Chelmsford Rd. CM6 1RG. (F. and J Neill). Est. 1971. Open by appointment. SIZE Medium. *STOCK: Furniture and shipping goods 18th-19th C, £10-£1,500.* LOC: A1060 between Bishops Stortford and Chelmsford. PARK: Easy TEL: 01279 876376; home - same. VAT Stan/Spec.

WOODFORD GREEN

P. Blake - Lanehurst Antiques LAPADA

403 High Rd. IG8 0XG. Est. 1952. Open by appointment only. SIZE: Medium. *STOCK Furniture, general antiques.* LOC: A11, close to Castle public house. TEL: 0181 504 9264; fax same; mobile - 04100 31079SER: Valuations buys at auction. VAT: Stan/Spec.

Galerie Lev

1 The Broadway. Open 10-5. *STOCK: Oils watercolours, collectors' items, silver plate porcelain.* LOC: Near Woodford underground station. TEL: 0181 505 2226. SER: Framing (Trade only).

WRITTLE, Nr. Chelmsford

Whichcraft Jewellery

54-56 The Green. CM1 3DU. (A. Turner). EADA Est. 1967. Open 9.30-5.30. CL: Mon. SIZE: Small *STOCK: Jewellery, silver and watches, 19th C £30-£100.* PARK: Easy. TEL: 01245 420183 SER: Valuations; restorations (jewellery). VAT Stan/Spec.

Gloucestershire

○ 1-2 ⊖ 3-5 ◐ 6-12 ● 13+ Key to number of shops in this area.

Please note this is only a rough map designed to show dealers the number of shops in the various towns, and is not necessarily totally accurate.

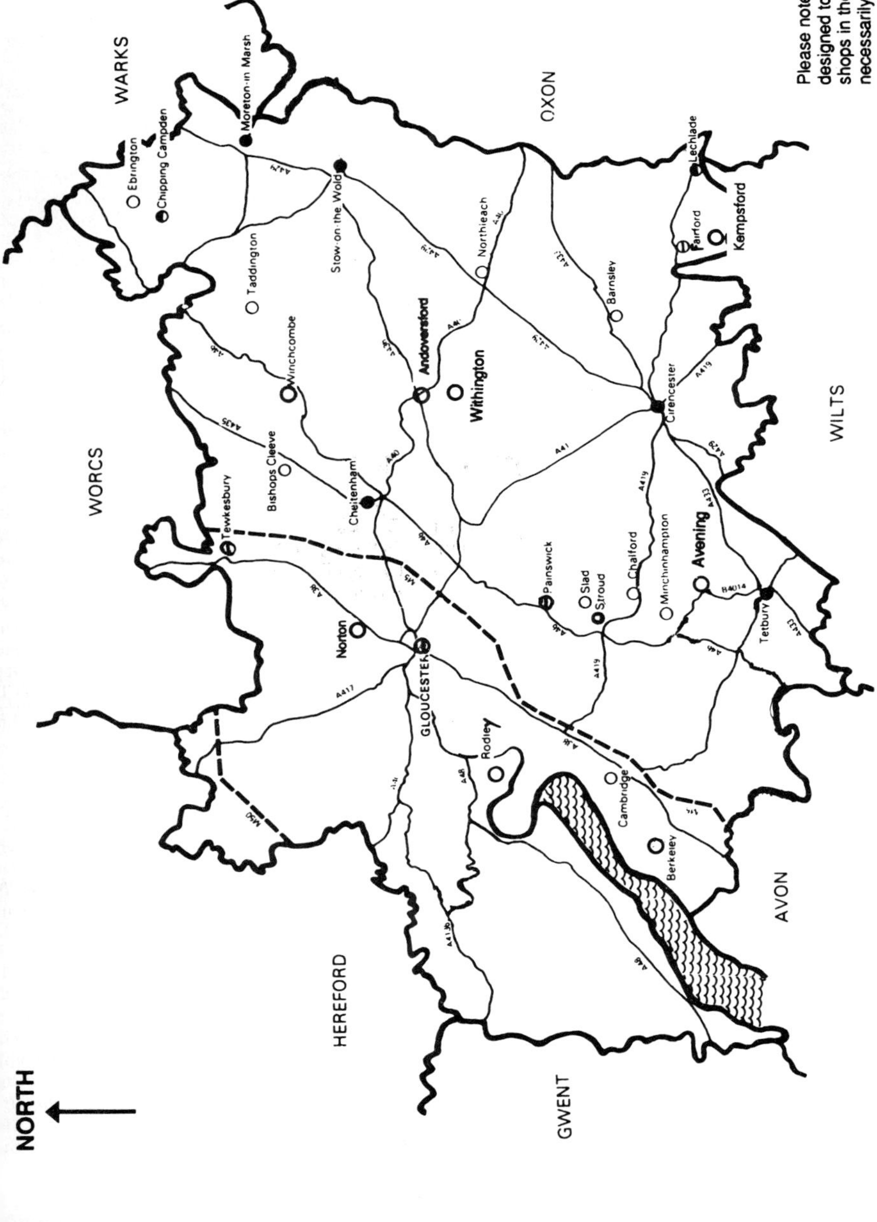

ANDOVERSFORD, Nr. Cheltenham

Julian Tatham-Losh

Brereton House, Stow Rd. GL54 4JN. (Julian and Patience Tatham-Losh). Resident. Est. 1980. Open Mon.-Fri. 8-6, at any other time by appointment. SIZE: Large. *STOCK: 19th C decorative smalls, bamboo and interesting furniture, majolica, flow blue, Staffordshire figures and animals, boxes and caddies, candlesticks and decorative glass, primitive and folk art items, £5-£2,000.* Not Stocked: Reproductions. LOC: From A40 Oxford to Cheltenham road take A436 to Stow-on-the-Wold, premises first house on left. PARK: Own large. TEL: 01242 820646; mobile - 0850 574924. SER: Antique and decorative items supplied to order, especially repeat bulk shipping items. FAIRS: Newark; NEC; Earls Court. VAT: Stan/Spec. *Trade Only.*

AVENING, Nr. Tetbury

Andrew Lelliott

Avening Park Workshop, West End. GL8 8LT. BAFRA. Open Mon.-Fri. 8.30-1 and 2-5 (appointment advisable), other times by appointment. SIZE: Small. *STOCK: 17th-19th C chests of drawers, bureaux and occasional tables, mainly English oak and mahogany.* LOC: Map available. TEL: 01453 835783; home - 01453 832652. SER: Restorations (furniture).

BARNSLEY, Nr. Cirencester

Denzil Verey

Barnsley House. GL7 5EE. CADA. Resident. Est 1980. Open 9.30-5.30, Sat. 10-5.30, other time by appointment. SIZE: Large. *STOCK: Countr furniture, including pine, 18th-19th C; brass country and kitchen bygones, unusual an decorative items.* LOC: 4 miles from Cirenceste on B4425 to Burford, 1st large house in village set back off road on the right. PARK: Easy. TEL 01285 740402; fax - 01285 740628. VAT Stan/Spec.

BERKELEY

Berkeley Antiques Market

GL13 9BP. Open 9.30-1 and 2-5. CL: Mon SIZE: Large - 10 dealers. *STOCK: Genera antiques, oak, mahogany, pine, linen and smalls £1-£1,000.* LOC: Village centre, 1 mile fror A38. PARK: Easy. TEL: 01453 511032.

The Stuffed Dog Antiques

The White Hart Court, 6 High St. (Mrs S.L Giddens). Est. 1995. Open Tues. and Thurs 10.30-1 and 2-4.30, Sat. afternoon in summe (prior telephone call advisable), and by appoint ment. SIZE: Small. *STOCK: Samplers, quilts folk art and naive paintings, decorative countr items and small furniture, 18th-19th C, £10 £1,000.* LOC: From A38 turn left into High St

erkeley continued

ast Berkeley Arms Hotel, shop 50 yards on right. 'ARK: Easy. TEL: 01453 810024; home - same. 'AIRS: NEC, Newark and Ardingly.

ISHOPS CLEEVE, Nr. Cheltenham

Cleeve Picture Framing
'hurch Rd. GL52 4LR. (J. Gardner). Open 9-1 nd 2-5.30, Sat. 9-1. *STOCK: Prints and pictures.* 'EL: 01242 672785. SER: Framing, cleaning, estoring (oils, watercolours and prints).

'he Priory Gallery
'he Priory, Station Rd. GL52 4HH. (R.M. and E. ames). Est. 1977. SIZE: Large. *STOCK: British nd European watercolours and oils, late 19th-0th C, £500-£50,000.* LOC: A435. PARK: Easy. 'EL: 01242 673226. SER: Buys at auction (as tock). VAT: Stan/Spec.

RISTOL

lexander Gallery
22 Whiteladies Rd. BS8 2RP. (P.J. Slade and .S. Evans). Open 9-5.30, Wed. 9-1. *STOCK: 9th-20th C paintings, watercolours and prints.* EL: 0117 9734692; fax - 0117 9466991.

'he Antique Centre Bristol
rewitt St., Redcliffe. BS1 6BB. (Sharon Aiken). pen 10-5.30, Sun. 1-4. SIZE: 50 units. *STOCK: eneral antiques, fine art, collectors' items.* TEL: 117 983 8868.

ntique Corner with A & C Antique Clocks
5 Bryants Hill, Hanham. BS5 8QT. (D.A. and P. Andrews). Est. 1985. Open 10-5. CL: Mon. nd Wed. SIZE: Large - 2 floors. *STOCK: urniture, clocks, ceramics (incl. Suzi Cooper and larice Cliff), 18th-20th C, £5-£3,000.* LOC: Next The Trooper public house, A431 Bristol to Bath oad. PARK: Easy. TEL: 0117 9476141. SER: lock and watch repairs.

ntique Four-Poster Beds
3 Richmond Hill. BS8. (Val Dewdney). Est. 1973. pen at all times but appointment advisable. SIZE: arge. *STOCK: Four-poster beds and bedposts, 8th-19th C, £950-£6,500.* LOC: Near suspension idge. PARK: Easy. TEL: 0117 9744450; home - ame; fax - same.

u Temps Perdu
Stapleton Rd., Easton. BS5 0QR. (Peter C. hapman). Open 10-6. SIZE: Large + yard. *TOCK: Period fireplaces, bathroom ware and oors; traditional building materials.* LOC: On lge of Old Market. PARK: Easy. TEL: 0117 555223.

Bristol continued

Bizarre Antiques
210 Gloucester Rd., Bishopston. BS7 8NZ. (E.J. Parkin). Open 8.15-5. *STOCK: General antiques.* TEL: 0117 9427888; home - 0117 9503498.

The Bristol Antiques Centre
Broad Plain. BS20 9HR. Open 10-4.30, Sun. 12-4. *STOCK: General antiques including furniture, decorative and collectors' items, jewellery.* TEL: 0117 9297739.

Bristol Guild of Applied Art Ltd
68/70 Park St. BS1 5JY. Est. 1908. Open 9-5.30, Mon. and Sat. 9.30-5.30. *STOCK: Furniture, late 19th-20th C.* TEL: 0117 9265548.

Bristol Trade Antiques
192 Cheltenham Rd. BS6 5RB. (L. Dike). Est. 1970. SIZE: Large and warehouse. *STOCK: General antiques.* TEL: 0117 9422790.

Robin Butler BADA
20 Clifton Rd. BS8 1AQ. Est. 1978. Open 9.30-5.30, Sat. 10-3. SIZE: Medium. *STOCK: Fine furniture, silver, wine antiques, glass and works of art, 1600-1850, from £50.* Not Stocked: Victoriana, weapons, carpets, shipping goods. LOC: Map showing location sent on request. PARK: Easy, in drive to left of shop. TEL: 0117 9733017. SER: Valuations. VAT: Spec.

Cleeve Antiques
282 Lodge Causeway, Fishponds. BS16 3RD. (T. and S.E. Scull). Est. 1978. Open 9.30-5.30. CL: Wed. *STOCK: Furniture and bric-a-brac.* TEL: 0117 9658366; home - 0117 9567008.

Cotham Galleries
22 Cotham Hill, Cotham. BS6 6LF. (D. Jury). Est. 1960. Open 9-5.30. SIZE: Small. *STOCK: Furniture, glass, metal.* LOC: From city centre up Park St. into Whiteladies Rd. Turn right at Clifton Down station. PARK: Easy. TEL: 0117 9736026. SER: Valuations.

Cotham Hill Bookshop
39A Cotham Hill, Cotham. BS6 6JY. (R. Plant and M. Garbett). Open 9.30-5.30. *STOCK: Antiquarian and secondhand books especially fine art; antiquarian prints.* TEL: 0117 9732344.

David Cross (Fine Art)
7 Boyces Ave., Clifton. BS8 4AA. Est. 1969. Open 9.30-6. *STOCK: British paintings, especially marine and landscape, Bristol school; related drawings, prints and watercolours.* LOC: Between Victoria Sq. and Regent St. PARK: Easy. TEL: 0117 9732614. SER: Valuations; restorations (oils, watercolours, frames); buys at auction; framing. VAT: Spec.

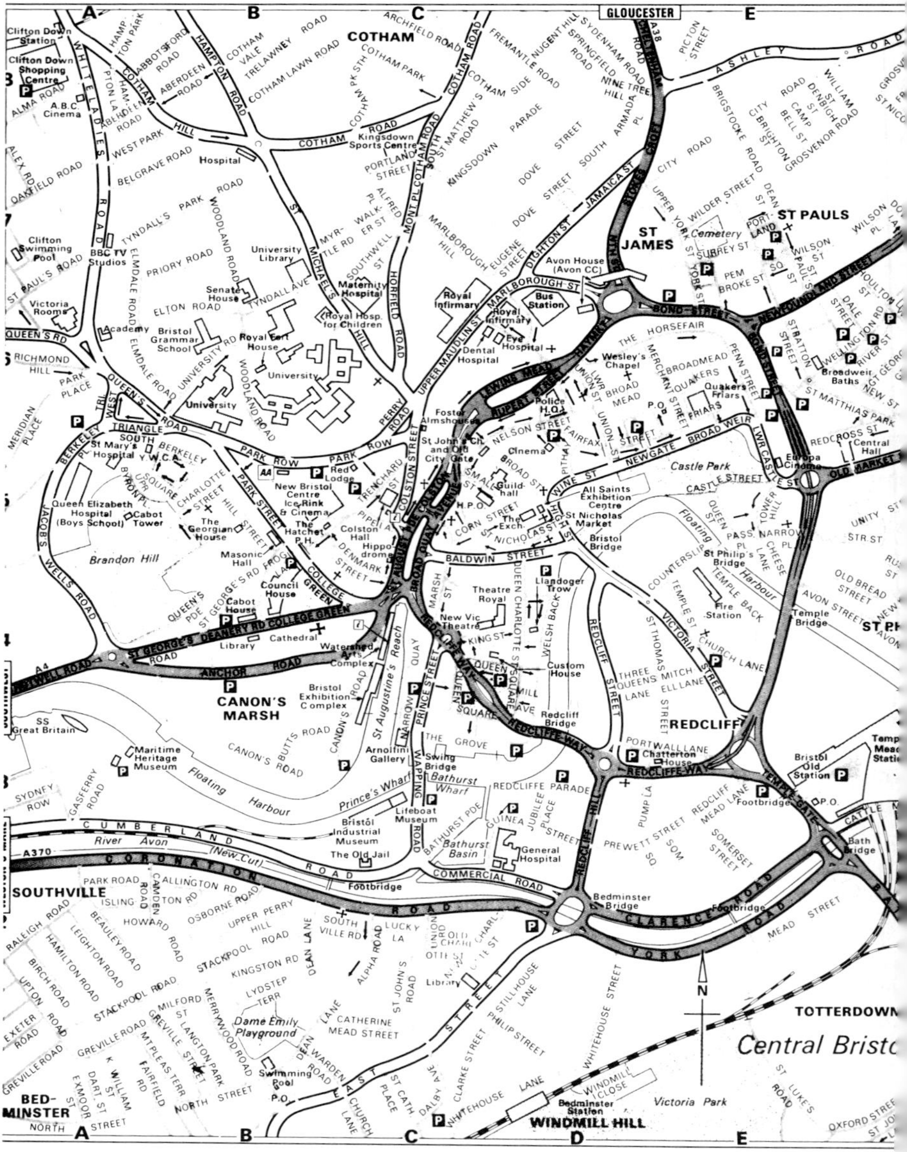

Key to Town Plan

AA Recommended roads	Car Parks
Other roads	Parks and open spaces
Restricted roads	AA Service Centre
Buildings of interest	

istol continued

ichard Essex Antiques
318 7BP. Est. 1969. *STOCK: General antiques m mid-18th C.* TEL: 01934 863302.

lame and Grate
9 Hotwells Rd., Hotwells. BS8 4RU. Open 9-5. *OCK: Original cast-iron fireplaces, marble rrounds and fireplace accessories.* PARK: asy. TEL: 0117 9252560/9292930.

rey-Harris and Co
Princess Victoria St., Clifton. BS8 4BP. Est. 63. Open 9.30-5.30. *STOCK: Jewellery, ctorian; silver, old Sheffield plate.* TEL: 0117 37365. SER: Valuations. VAT: Stan/Spec.

hris Grimes Militaria
Lower Park Row. BS1 5BN. Open 11-5.30. *OCK: Militaria, scientific instruments, nautical ms.* TEL: 0117 9298205.

.R. Heath
Pembroke Rd., Clifton. BS8 3DX. Open by pointment only. *STOCK: Rare books, pamphlets, oadsides, pre-1850.* TEL: 0117 9741183; fax - 17 9732901.

emps
Carlton Court, Westbury-on-Trym. BS9 3DF. M. Kemp). Open 9-5.30. *STOCK: Jewellery.* L: 0117 9505090.

ichael's Antiques
) Wells Rd. (M. Beese). Resident. TEL: 0117 13943.

obert Mills Architectural Antiques d
rroways Rd., Eastville. BS2 9XB. Est. 1969. en 9.30-5. CL: Sat. SIZE: Large. *STOCK: chitectural items, panelled rooms, shop eriors, Gothic Revival, stained glass, church odwork, bar and restaurant fittings, 1750-20, £50-£30,000.* LOC: Half mile from Junction M32. PARK: Easy. TEL: 0117 9556542; fax - 17 9558146. VAT: Stan.

. 74 Antiques and Collectables
Alma Rd., Clifton. (Mrs S.J. Wilson). Est. 1989. en Tues.-Sat. 10.30-5.30. SIZE: Medium. *OCK: English walnut and mahogany furniture, h-19th C, £100-£4,000+; English and Conti-ital porcelain, 19th C, £20-£500+.* LOC: rning off Whiteladies Rd., main road from city ntre to M4/M5. PARK: Easy. TEL: 0117 3821; home - 0117 9730351. SER: Restorations luding upholstery. VAT: Stan/Spec.

dwoods
Colston Yard. BS1 5BD. (S. Duck). Open 11-0, Sat. 11-4. *STOCK: Victorian and Edwardian niture, pine and other woods.* TEL: 0117 9023. SER: Restorations.

Bristol continued

Period Fireplaces
The Old Station, Station Rd., Montpelier. BS6 5EE. (John Ashton and Martyn Roberts). Est. 1987. Open daily. SIZE: Small. *STOCK: Fireplaces, originals and reproduction, £100-£500.* LOC: Just off Gloucester Rd. PARK: Easy. TEL: 0117 9444449. SER: Valuations; restorations; fitting. VAT: Stan.

Potter's Antiques and Coins
60 Colston St. BS1 5AZ. (B.C. Potter). Est. 1965. Open 10.30-5.30. SIZE: Small. *STOCK: Antiquities, 500 B.C. to 1600 A.D., £5-£500; commemoratives, 1770-1953, £4-£300; coins, 500 B.C. to 1967, £1-£100; drinking glass, 1770-1953, £3-£200; small furniture, from 1837, £10-£200.* LOC: Near top of Christmas Steps, close to city centre. PARK: N.C.P. Park Row. TEL: 0117 9262551. SER: Valuations; buys at auction. VAT: Stan/Spec.

Relics - Pine Furniture
109 St. George's Rd., College Green. BS1 5UW. (R. Seville and S. Basey). Est. 1972. Open 10-6. SIZE: Large. *STOCK: Victorian style pine furniture, £25-£700.* LOC: Near cathedral, 1/2 mile from city centre. PARK: Easy. TEL: 0117 9268453. VAT: Stan.

Something Old, Something New
115 Coldharbour Rd., Redland. BS6 7SD. (Z. Bouyamourn). Open 10-5.30. *STOCK: General antiques and French furniture.* TEL: 0117 9247479.

St. Nicholas Markets
The Exchange Hall, Corn St. BS1 1JQ. (Steve Morris). Est. 1975. Open 9.30-5. *STOCK: Wide range of general antiques and collectors' items.* TEL: 0117 9224014.

John and Sheila Symes
93 Charlton Mead Drive, Westbury-on-Trym. BS10 6LW. Open by appointment. *STOCK: Postcards, ephemera and autographs.* TEL: 0117 9501074.

Triangle Books (inc. John Roberts Bookshop Est. 1955)
43 Triangle West, Clifton. BS8 1ES. Open 10-5.30. SIZE: Large. *STOCK: Secondhand and antiquarian books and prints.* LOC: Just off Queens Rd. PARK: Meters or nearby multi-storey. TEL: 0117 9268568; fax - 0117 9226653. VAT: Spec.

The Wise Owl Bookshop
26 Upper Maudlin St. BS2 8DJ. Open 10.30-5.30. *STOCK: Antiquarian and secondhand books, all subjects including music and the performing arts; sheet music, records, tapes and CDs.* TEL: 0117 9262738; evenings - 0117 9246936.

CAMBRIDGE, Nr. Gloucester

Bell House Antiques
Bell House. GL2 7BD. (G. and J. Hawkins). Resident. Open 10-1 and 2-5. SIZE: Medium. *STOCK: Furniture, shipping goods, stripped pine, small items, bygones, £5-£500.* LOC: Near Slimbridge, on main A38. PARK: Easy. TEL: 01453 890463. SER: Valuations.

CHALFORD

J. and R. Bateman Antiques
Green Court, High St. , Est. 1975. Open 9-6 or by appointment. *STOCK: Furniture, oak and country, 17th-19th C; decorative items.* PARK: Easy. TEL: 01453 883234. SER: Restorations; cabinet making, rushing and caning. VAT: Stan/Spec.

CHELTENHAM

Art and Antiques LAPADA
17 Montpellier Walk. GL50 1SD. (Joy Turner). Est. 1950. Open 10-4.30. CL: Wed. *STOCK: General antiques.* TEL: 01242 522939. VAT: Stan/Spec.

Art et Maison
Clarence Parade. GL50 3PA. (Sue and Kate Chate). Open Wed.-Sat. 10-5.30, Mon. and Tues. by appointment. SIZE: Small. *STOCK: Antique pine and other furniture, £50-£750; decorative items including ceramics, metals, prints, etc.* LOC: On the main inner ring road above the bus station. PARK: Loading only, nearest parking Jessop Ave. TEL: 01242 222554; home - same. SER: Valuations; restoration (French polishing, veneer repairs, minor construction repairs). FAIRS: CAF, Three Counties Showground, Malvern.

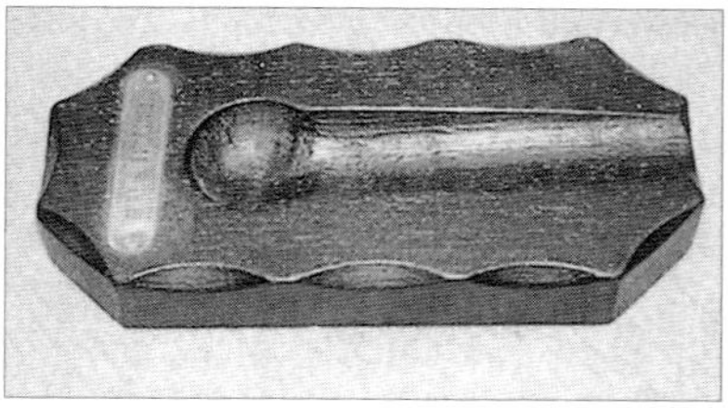

A pipe stand form H.M.S. Terrible.

From an article entitled "Ship Timber Souvenirs" by Richard A. Price which appeared in the September 1996 issue of **Antique Collecting**

Cheltenham continued

David Bannister FRGS
26 Kings Rd. GL52 6BG. PBFA. Est. 1963. Ope by appointment only. SIZE: Medium. *STOCK Early maps and prints, 1480-1850, from £2 decorative and topographical prints; atlases an colour plate books.* TEL: 01242 514287; fax 01242 513890. SER: Valuations; restoration lectures; buys at auction. FAIRS: Organiser Antique Map and Print (Bonnington Hotel). VAT Stan.

Bed of Roses
12 Prestbury Rd. GL52 2PW. (Martin Losh). Es 1978. Open Tues.-Fri. 10-1 and 2-5, Sat. 9.3 5.30. SIZE: Large. *STOCK: Fine stripped pin* LOC: 200 metres on town side of roundabou B4632, close to Pittville Circus. PARK: Eas TEL: 01242 231918. VAT: Stan/Spec.

Edward Bradbury and Son
32 High St. GL50 1DZ. (O. Bradbury). Resider Est. 1986. Open by appointment. SIZE: Sma *STOCK: Works of art, tribal art, furniture, 18t 19th C; books on art reference, monographs artists and photographers, manuscripts.* PARK Nearby. TEL: 01242 254952. SER: Valuation VAT: Spec.

Butler and Co
111 Promenade. GL50 1NW. (D.J. Butler). Es 1968. Open Sat. only. SIZE: Small. *STOCK English coins, 1st to 20th C; world coins, 19th both £5-£25; British campaign medals, 19th-20 C, £50-£100.* PARK: Easy. TEL: 01242 52227 home - 01242 234439. SER: Valuations. FAIR Cheltenham.

Charlton Kings Antiques Centre
199 London Rd., Charlton Kings. GL52 6HU. Es 1984. Open 9.30-5.30. SIZE: Large - 11 dealer *STOCK: General antiques, including furnitur china, glass and pictures, £5-£1,000.* LOC: C A40. PARK: Easy. TEL: 01242 510672.

Cheltenham Antique Market
54 Suffolk Rd. GL50 2AQ. (K.J. Shave). Es 1970. Open 9.30-5.30. SIZE: 14 dealers. *STOCK General antiques.* TEL: 01242 529812.

Cocoa
7 Queens Circus. GL50 1RX. (Cara Wagstaff). E 1973. Open 10-5. SIZE: Small. *STOCK: Lac antique wedding dresses and accessories, 19th-20 C, £1-£2,000.* LOC: Rear of Montpellier, ne Queens Hotel. PARK: Easy. TEL: 01242 23358 SER: Re-creations; restorations (period textiles VAT: Stan.

Government House
Suffolk Rd. GL50 2AQ. Open Sat. 10.30-6, oth times by appointment. *STOCK: Antique and pr war lighting and accessories.* LOC: In antiq area. PARK: Private. TEL: 01242 255897. SE Spare parts stocked.

:heltenham continued

;reens of Cheltenham Ltd
5 Montpellier Walk. GL50 1SD. Est. 1946. Open -5. CL: Wed. pm. SIZE: Large. *STOCK: Vic- orian and diamond set jewellery, porcelain, ilver, glass and some furniture.* LOC: Con- inction of Promenade and main shopping centre. ARK: Easy. TEL: 01242 512088. SER: Buys at uction. VAT: Stan/Spec.

Ieydens Antiques and Militaria
20 High St. GL50 3JA. (R.E.J. Heyden). Open 0-5.30. *STOCK: Bric-a-brac and militaria.* TEL: 1242 690909.

avid Howard
2 Moorend Crescent. GL53 0EL. Est. 1983. pen by appointment. *STOCK: Fine oil paintings, atercolours and drawings, 19th-20th C, £500- 5,000.* PARK: Easy. TEL: 01242 243379; home same. SER: Valuations; buys at auction; search (pictures). VAT: Spec.

I.W. Keil (Cheltenham) Ltd BADA
29-131 Promenade. GL50 1NW. Est. 1953. IZE: Large. *STOCK: Furniture, paintings, 7th-18th C; metalwork, chandeliers.* LOC: pposite Queens Hotel, at top of Promenade. ARK: Easy. TEL: 01242 522509. SER: pholstery. VAT: Spec.

atchford Antiques
15 London Rd., Charlton Kings. GL52 6HY. (K. nd R. Latchford). Est. 1985. Open 10-5. SIZE: mall. *STOCK: Furniture, china, glass and objets 'art, 18th-19th C, £5-£1,000.* LOC: 2 miles from heltenham, on A40 towards London at Sixways hopping Centre, on right. PARK: Easy. TEL: 1242 226263. VAT: Stan/Spec.

Ianor House Antiques LAPADA
2 Suffolk Rd. GL50 2AQ. (J.G. Benton). Est. 972. Open Fri. and Sat. 10-5.30, other times y appointment only. SIZE: Large. *STOCK: urniture, 18th-19th C; general antiques, 19th C nd Victorian, all £50-£5,000; paintings and ramics.* Not Stocked: Small items, china and wellery. LOC: A40. PARK: Nearby. TEL: 1242 232780 and 01278 760159.

Ianor House Gallery
5 Royal Parade, Bayshill Rd. GL50 3AY. (Geoff assell). Resident. Open anytime by appointment. IZE: Small. *STOCK: Oils and watercolours, 250-£500; prints, under £100; all 20th C.* LOC: entral. PARK: Easy. TEL: 01242 228330; home same; fax - 01242 228328. SER: Valuations; storations (oils); buys at auction (as stock). AT: Stan/Spec.

Iartin and Co. Ltd
) The Promenade. GL50 1LP. (I.M. and N.C.S. immer). Est. 1890. *STOCK: Silver, Sheffield ate, jewellery, objets d'art.* TEL: 01242 522821; x - 01242 570430. VAT: Stan/Spec.

Cheltenham continued

Montpellier Clocks BADA
13 Rotunda Terrace, Montpellier. GL50 1SW. (B. Bass and T. Birch). Open 9-5.30. *STOCK: Clocks, 17th-19th C; barometers.* LOC: Close to Queens Hotel. PARK: Easy. TEL: 01242 242178; fax - same. SER: Repairs and restorations by West Dean/BADA Dip. conservator.

Patrick Oliver LAPADA
4 Tivoli St. GL50 2UW. Est. 1896. SIZE: Large. *STOCK: Furniture and shipping goods.* PARK: Easy. TEL: 01242 519538. VAT: Stan/Spec.

Past & Present
31 Suffolk Parade. (Melanie Trundle). Est. 1992. Open daily. SIZE: Small. *STOCK: Edwardian and Victorian furniture, mirrors and prints.* PARK: Easy. TEL: 01242 511100. SER: Valuations.VAT: Stan.

Eric Pride Oriental Rugs
44 Suffolk Rd. GL50 2AQ. Est. 1980. Open Wed.-Fri. 10-6, other times by appointment. SIZE: Medium. *STOCK: Rugs and carpets, £100-£4,000; kilims, £300-£2,000; saddle-bags and horse covers, £150-£800; all 19th to early 20th C.* LOC: A40 near Cheltenham College. PARK: Nearby. TEL: 01242 580822 (answerphone). SER: Valuations; restorations (cleaning and repairs).

Michael Rayner
11 St. Luke's Rd. GL53 7JQ. Open 10-6, other times by appointment. CL: Mon. and Tues. *STOCK: Books, antiquarian and secondhand.* TEL: 01242 512806.

Robson Antiques
New Barn Farm, Farmington. Est. 1982. Open daily by appointment. *STOCK: Furniture, from 18th C, £50-£5,000.* PARK: Easy. TEL: 01451 861006.

Scott-Cooper Ltd BADA
52 The Promenade. GL50 1LY. Est. 1912. *STOCK: Silver, plate, jewellery, clocks, ivory, enamel, objets de vertu.* TEL: 01242 522580. SER: Restorations and repairs (silver and jewellery). VAT: Stan/Spec.

Tapestry
33 Suffolk Parade. GL50 2AE. Open 10-5.30. SIZE: Medium. *STOCK: Antique and decorative furniture and objects, including brass and iron beds, soft furnishings and garden items.* LOC: 10 mins. walk from The Promenade. PARK: Easy. TEL: 01242 512191.

John P. Townsend
Ullenwood Park Farm, Ullenwood. GL53 9QX. Est. 1969. Open 9-5. CL: Sat. SIZE: Medium. *STOCK: Furniture - stripped pine, country and shipping, to 1940's; books.* TEL: 01242 870223.

Cheltenham continued

Triton Gallery
27 Suffolk Parade. GL50 2AE. (L. Bianco). Resident. Open 9-5.30, other times by appointment. *STOCK: Period furniture, 18th C paintings, mirrors and lighting.* TEL: 01242 510477.

CHIPPING CAMPDEN

Antique Heritage
High St. GL55 6AT. (D.B. Smith). Est. 1981. Open 10-5, Sun. 11-4. SIZE: Small. *STOCK: Small items, china, porcelain, tables, boxes, Georgian and Victorian, £15-£400.* LOC: Village centre. PARK: Easy. TEL: 01386 840727.

Campden Country Pine Antiques
High St. GL55 6HN. (Jane and Frank Kennedy). Est. 1988. Open 10-12 and 2-5 including Sun. SIZE: Large. *STOCK: 17th-19th C English pine.* LOC: On village green at Leasebourne end of High St. PARK: Easy. TEL: 01386 840315; home - same; fax - 01386 841740. SER: National and international delivery.

Pedlars
Lower High St. GL55 6AL. (A. Yates). Open 10-5. *STOCK: General antiques.* TEL: 01386 840680.

Saxton House Gallery LAPADA
High St. GL55 6HQ. (S.D. and J. Coy). Open 9-5.30. CL: Thurs. SIZE: Medium. *STOCK: Fine English clocks and barometers, unusual carriage clocks, jewellery, Georgian furniture, paintings and watercolours.* LOC: Village centre. PARK: Easy. TEL: 01386 840278. VAT: Stan/Spec.

School House Antiques LAPADA
School House, High St. GL55 6HB. (G. Hammond). Open 9.30-5 including Sun.(June-Sept.). CL: Thurs. (Oct.-May). *STOCK: Clocks, 18th-19th C; furniture including oak and shipping, 17th-19th C; works of art, oils and watercolours.* TEL: 01386 841474; fax - 01386 841367. SER: Restorations.

Stuart House Antiques
High St. GL55 6HB. (J. Collett). Est. 1985. Open 10-1 and 2-5.30 including Sun. SIZE: Large. *STOCK: China, 19th C; general antiques, from 18th C; all £1-£1,000.* LOC: Opposite market hall. PARK: Easy. TEL: 01386 840995. SER: Valuations; china search; restorations (ceramics).

Swan Antiques
High St. GL55 6HB. (J. Stocker). Est. 1960. Open 10-1 and 2-4.45, Thurs. and Sun. by appointment. SIZE: Medium. *STOCK: Silver, George II to 1920; jewellery including Victorian; porcelain; furniture, 17th C oak to 1860 mahogany; decorative items.* LOC: Village centre. PARK: Easy. TEL: 01386 840759. SER: Gemmologist.

CHIPPING SODBURY, Nr. Bristol

Sodbury Antiques
70 Broad St. (Millicent Brown). Est. 1986. C Wed. SIZE: Small. *STOCK: Porcelain and chin mainly 18th-19th C; antique and secondha jewellery, £5-£1,000.* PARK: Easy. TEL: 014 273369. SER: Buys at auction.

CIRENCESTER

Jonathan Beech Antique Clocks
Nurses Cottage, Ampney Crucis. GL7 5RY. E 1985. Open 9.30-5.30. SIZE: Medium. *STOC Longcase, wall and bracket clocks, 1700-188 £500-£7,000.* LOC: A417 2 miles from Cirencest left at The Crown of Crucis, then 300yds. on le PARK: Easy. TEL: 01285 851495.

Walter Bull and Son (Cirencester) Lt
10 Dyer St. GL7 2PF. Est. 1815. Open 9-5. SIZ Small. *STOCK: Silver, from 1700, £50-£3,00 objets d'art.* LOC: Lower end of Market Plac PARK: At rear. TEL: 01285 653875; fax - 012 641751. VAT: Stan/Spec.

Cirencester Antique Market
Market Place. GL7 2PP. (Antique Forum Lt Open Fri. SIZE: 60 dealers. *STOCK: Gener antiques.* TEL: 01225 765586.

Corner Cupboard Curios
2 Church St. GL7 1LE. (P. Larner). *STOC General antiques and gramophonalia.* TE 01285 655476.

Forum Antiques
Springfield Farm, Perrotts Brook. (W. Mitche Est. 1986. Open Mon.-Fri. 8.30-5.30 by appoi ment only. SIZE: Small. *STOCK: Period fu niture, pre-1850.* TEL: 01285 831821. SE Valuations; restorations. VAT: Spec.

Hares
4 Black Jack St. Est. 1972. Open 10-5.30, Sun. appointment. SIZE: Large. *STOCK: Furnitu especially dining tables and long sets of chai 18th to early 19th C, £100-£50,000; upholstery a decorative objects.* LOC: Near Market Squa PARK: Own. TEL: 01285 640077; mobile - 08 350097; e-mail - hares@star.co.uk. SER: Rest ations; traditional upholstery. VAT: Spec.

Thomas and Pamela Hudson
At the Sign of the Herald Angel, 17 Park St. G 2BX. Resident. Est. 1959. Open by appointme only. *STOCK: Work boxes, needlework tools a needleworks.* TEL: 01285 652972. SER: Mail ord

E.C. Legg and Son
3 College Farm Workshops, Tetbury Rd. G 6PY. Est. 1902. Open 9-5. CL: Sat. *STOCK: 1 C furniture.* PARK: Easy. TEL: 01285 6506 SER: Restorations (furniture, gilt frames); canir re-leathering desk tops.

Cirencester continued

Silver Street Antiques and Things
) Silver St. GL7 2BS. (S.A. Tarrant). Resident. Est. 1992. Open 10-5.30. SIZE: Medium. *STOCK: General antiques including small furniture, £5-£800.* LOC: Between Corn Hall and museum. PARK: Nearby. TEL: 01285 641600.

William H. Stokes BADA
The Cloisters, 6/8 Dollar St. GL7 2AJ. (W.H. Stokes and P.W. Bontoft). CADA. Est. 1968. Open 9.30-5.30, Sat. 9.30-4.30. *STOCK: Early oak furniture, £1,000-£30,000; brassware, £150-£5,000; all 16th-17th C.* TEL: 01285 653907; fax - same. VAT: Spec.

Rankine Taylor Antiques LAPADA
34 Dollar St. GL7 2AN. CADA. Est. 1969. Open 9-5.30, Sun. by appointment. SIZE: Large. *STOCK: Furniture, 17th to early 19th C, £300-£35,000; glass, 18th-20th C, £8-£350; silver, rare interesting objects and decorative items, 17th-20th C, £20-£4,000.* Not Stocked: Victoriana. LOC: From church, turn right into West Market Place, via Gosditch St. into Dollar St. PARK: Own - private opposite. TEL: 01285 652529. VAT: Spec.

Patrick Waldron Antiques
18 Dollar St. GL7 2AN. Resident. Est. 1965. Open 9.30-1 and 2-6, Sun. by appointment. SIZE: Medium. *STOCK: Furniture, 18th-19th C.* LOC: In street behind church. PARK: Easy and public behind shop. TEL: 01285 652880; home - same; workshop - 01285 643479. SER: Restorations (furniture); buys at auction.

P.J. Ward Fine Paintings
11 Gosditch St. GL7 2AG. Open 9-5. *STOCK: 17th-19th C paintings.* TEL: 01285 658499. SER: Valuations; restorations; framing. VAT: Spec.

Waterloo Antiques
0 The Waterloo. GL7 2PZ. (Philip A. Ruttleigh). Est. 1990. Open 9.30-5.30 including Sun. SIZE: Medium. *STOCK: Furniture - 18th-19th C mahogany, 17th-18th C oak, elm and country, 19th C English and Continental pine, all £50-£3,000; ceramics, from 1700, £10-£2,000.* LOC: Left at traffic lights after Market Place or right from London Rd. PARK: Opposite. TEL: 01285 644887; home - same. SER: Restorations (furniture including paint stripping); upholstery.

Bernard Weaver Antiques
3 Gloucester St. GL7 2DH. CADA. Open 9.30-5, Sat. 9.30-1. SIZE: Medium. *STOCK: Furniture, mahogany and oak, 18th-19th C; Art Nouveau and Arts and Crafts.* LOC: Continuation of Dollar St. PARK: Easy. TEL: 01285 652055; home - same. SER: Valuations.

Cirencester continued

Woodminster Antiques
14 Dollar St. GL7 2AJ. (M. Sharpe). Resident. Est. 1988. Open 10-6. SIZE: Medium. *STOCK: Oak and country furniture, 17th-18th C, £100-£10,000; Staffordshire and faience pottery, 18th-19th C, £25-£500.* LOC: From church, turn right up West Market Place via Gosditch St. PARK: Easy. TEL: 01285 644485; mobile - 0802 877738. SER: Valuations; restorations (pottery); buys at auction. VAT: Spec.

EBRINGTON, Nr. Chipping Campden

John Burton Natural Craft Taxidermy
21 Main St. GL55 6NL. Est. 1973. Open by appointment. SIZE: Medium. *STOCK: Taxidermy - Victorian and Edwardian cased fish, birds and mammals, from £40-£2,500; glass domes, sporting trophies.* LOC: Village centre. PARK: Easy. TEL: 01386 593231; home - same. SER: Valuations; restorations (taxidermy); buys at auction (taxidermy). VAT: Stan.

FAIRFORD

Blenheim Antiques
Market Place. GL7 4AB. (N. Hurdle). CADA. Resident. Est. 1972. Open 9.30-6.30. *STOCK: 18th-19th C furniture.* TEL: 01285 712094. VAT: Stan/Spec.

Mark Carter Antiques
5 Macaroni Wood, Eastleach. GL7 3NF . Est. 1979. SIZE: Large - warehouse. *STOCK: English mahogany, oak and fruitwood furniture, 17th-19th C, £300-£5,000.* LOC: Telephone for directions. PARK: Own. TEL: 01367 850483; mobile - 0836 260567. SER: Valuations. VAT: Spec.

Gloucester House Antiques Ltd
Market Place. GL7 4AB. (Mrs Scilla Chester-Master). CADA. Est. 1972. Open 9-5.30. SIZE: Large. *STOCK: English and French country furniture in oak, elm, fruitwood, pine; pottery, faiënce and decorative items.* PARK: Easy. TEL: 01285 712790; home - 01285 653066; fax - 01285 713324. VAT: Spec.

Anthony Hazledine
Antique Oriental Carpets, High St. GL7 4AD. Est. 1976. Mon., Fri. and Sat. 9-5, other days by appointment. SIZE: Small. *STOCK: Oriental carpets and textiles, 18th-19th C, £150-£4,000.* PARK: Easy. TEL: 01285 713400; home and fax - same. SER: Valuations; restorations; buys at auction (as stock). VAT: Stan/Spec.

GLOUCESTER

Steven D. Bartrick
The Antique Centre, Severn Rd. GL1 2LE. Es 1985. Open 9-5, Sat. 9-4.30, Sun. 1-4.30. *STOCK Topographical prints and some maps.* LOC Gloucester dock area. PARK: At side of buildin TEL: 01452 529716; home - 01242 231691.

Gloucester Antique Centre
1 Severn Rd. GL1 2LE. Est. 1949. Open 10- Sun. 1-5. SIZE: 110 dealers. 50p admissio charge - Trade free. *STOCK: General antiques furniture, jewellery, silver, clocks, ceramic collectables.* LOC: Within the Dock area. PARK Easy. TEL: 01452 529716; fax - 01452 307161.

Arthur S. Lewis LAPAD
Est. 1969. By appointment. *STOCK: Antiqu clocks and mechanical music.* TEL: 014 780258.

Military Curios, HQ84
(The Curiosity Shop), Southgate. GL1 2DX. (Williams). Est. 1964. Open 10-6, including Su *STOCK: Medals, badges, (3rd Reich specialitie militaria, blazer badges, Govt. surplus, edg weapons, replicas, air weapons; Jaguar - spare mascots.* LOC: A38, city centre. PARK: 100 y (Docks). TEL: 01452 527716; fax - same. SE Valuations; medal find and mounting; costu hire; badge-making; mail order.

Gloucester continued

A.J. Ponsford Antiques
Decora, Northbrook Rd., off Eastern Avenue. GL4 3DP. (A.J. and R.L. Ponsford). Est. 1962. Open 8-5.30. CL: Sat. SIZE: Large. *STOCK: Furniture, 1800-1880, £25-£4,000; furniture, 1650-1800, £200-£15,000; copper, brass.* LOC: 1 mile from M5, Wall's roundabout, south into Eastern Ave. ring road, past Royal Mail on right, 400 yds. turn right into Northbrook Rd. 150 yds. on left. PARK: Own. TEL: 01452 307700. SER: Valuations; restorations (furniture and oil paintings); rushing, caning, upholstery, picture framing; manufacturers of false books and decorative accessories. VAT: Stan/Spec.

KEMPSFORD, Nr. Fairford

Outhouse Antiques
Cross Tree Cottage. GL7 2EU. (R. W. King). Resident. Est. 1981. Open 8.30-5.30 including Sun. SIZE: Small. *STOCK: Country furniture, 18th-19th C; decorative items, kitchenalia, china and glass.* LOC: A417 to Fairford, Kempsford 4 miles south past air base. PARK: Easy. TEL: 01285 810318. FAIRS: Stoneleigh, Cheltenham.

LECHLADE-ON-THAMES

Aspley House Antiques Centre
Market Place. GL7 3AD. (Ian Smith). Est. 1979. Open 10-5.30, Sun. 11.30-4.30. SIZE: Large. *STOCK: Town and country furniture, silver, brass, copper, glass, porcelain, tools and kitchenalia, Oriental rugs.* LOC: A361 midway between Cirencester and Burford. PARK: Easy. TEL: 01367 253697. SER: Valuations; restorations.

Gerard Campbell BADA
Maple House, Market Pl. GL7 3AB. (J. and G. Campbell). Est. 1980. Open by appointment. SIZE: Large. *STOCK: Clocks especially Biedermeier Vienna regulators, 18th-19th C, £1,500-15,000; oils, 20th C, £200-£5,000.* PARK: Easy. TEL: 01367 252267; home - same. SER: Valuations; buys at auction. VAT: Spec.

Lechlade-on-Thames continued

D'Arcy Antiques
High St. GL7 3AE. (J.W. and Mrs. M.A. Corbey). Est. 1986. Open 10-5. SIZE: Medium. *STOCK: Furniture, 1800-1960, £50-£1,800; china, 1800-1960, £1-£100; brass, 1780-1960, £2-£100.* LOC: A361, town centre. PARK: Easy. TEL: 01367 252471; home - 01793 852792.

Greystones Antiques and Interiors
High St. GL7 3AE. (S.J. and M.E. Sheppard). Resident. Open 10.30-5.30 including Sun. SIZE: Large - 4 showrooms. *STOCK: Furniture, smalls, Oriental rugs, decorators items, 19th and 20th C, £10-£3,500.* PARK: Easy, next to shop. TEL: 01367 253140 (24 hours).

Jubilee Hall Antiques Centre
Oak St. GL7 3AY. Open 10-5 Mon.-Sat., Sun. 11-5. SIZE: Large. PARK: Own. LOC: On left 350yds. from town centre going north towards Burford. TEL: 01367 253777. Listed below are the dealers at this centre:

Mandy Barnes
Georgian and Victorian furniture and decorative objects.

John Calgie
Period furniture, mirrors, copper, brass and interesting objects.

Collingridge & Allen
18th and 19th C furniture and mirrors, architectural items and prints.

Cooke & Dunn
Porcelain, glass, silver and objects of art.

Caroline Haillay
Furniture, pottery, glass, small silver and objects of art.

Julian Homer
Clarice Cliff, antique rugs and country objects.

Peter Gibbons
Period pewter, treen, brass, arms and armour and country furniture.

John & Sally Gormley
18th and 19th C furniture and decorative objects.

Lechlade-on-Thames continued

Colin Morris
Country furniture, Staffordshire, brass, copper and period objects.

Cathy Nix
Moorcroft and other art deco ceramics and early British telephones.

Oak Antiques
(David and Vicky Wilson). *Period country oak furniture and metalware.*

Oakleigh Antiques
(Gill Abraham and John Wright). *18th and 19th C mahogany and upholstered furniture, pictures and satsuma.*

Mary Pennel
Porcelain, small silver and jewellery.

Keith Robinson
18th and 19th C English furniture, engravings, ceramics, lighting and Japanese and English objects of art.

David Spurling
19th C Staffordshire pottery, glass and period porcelain and pottery.

Fiona Taylor
Sporting antiques, golf, cricket, rowing etc., and antique luggage.

Fred & Margaret Taylor
Small period silver, period glass and porcelain and objects of art.

Unicorn Antiques
(John Ward). *18th and 19th C furniture, period metalware and country objects.*

Lechlade Antiques Arcade
5, 6 and 7 High St. GL7 3AD. (J. Dickson). Open 10-6 including Sun. SIZE: 40+ dealers. *STOCK: General antiques, collectables, books, bric-a-brac.* TEL: 01367 252832.

Riverside Marina Arcade
Park End Wharf. GL7 3AQ. (B. Fontaine). Est. 1995. Open 7 days 8-5, April-Oct. 8-8. SIZE: Medium. *STOCK: General antiques and collectables, gifts and crafts, £5-£500.* PARK: Easy. TEL: 01367 252955; home - same. SER: Restorations. VAT: Stan.

Mark A. Serle (Antiques and Restoration)
6 Burford St. GL7 3AP. Est. 1978. Open 9.30-5.30. SIZE: Small. *STOCK: Collectables, £5-£100; woodworking tools, £5-£50; furniture, £50-£1,000; all 19th C; militaria, £5-£150.* LOC: A361. PARK: Easy. TEL: 01367 253145; home - 01993 851664. SER: Restorations (furniture).

Lechlade-on-Thames continued

The Swan Antiques and Crafts Centr
Burford St. (Cilla and Ivor Littleton). Est. 198 Open 10.30-4.30 including Sun. SIZE: 50 dealer *STOCK: General antiques including furnitur collectables, books and pictures, jewellery an ceramics, 19th to early 20th C, £5-£850.* PARK Own. TEL: 01367 252944; home - 01367 25212

Town & Country Antiques
3 Burford St. (T. Mendham). Open 10-5. SIZ Small. *STOCK: Pine, oak and decorative item £10-£1,000.* PARK: Easy. TEL: 01367 253753.

MINCHINHAMPTON, Nr. Stroud

J.V. Vosper
20 High St. GL6 9BN. Est. 1952. *STOC Furniture, glass, china, silver, brass, plate, bri a-brac, 18th-20th C.* TEL: 01453 882480.

Mick and Fanny Wright
'The Trumpet', West End. GL6 9JA. Open 10.3 5.30. CL: Mon. and Tues. SIZE: Mediu *STOCK: Watches, clocks, furniture, china, silv and plate, 50p-£1,500.* LOC: 200 yards fro crossroads at bottom of High St. PARK: Nearb TEL: 01453 883027.

MORETON-IN-MARSH

Antique Centre
London House, High St. GL56 OAH. Est. 197 Open 10-5 including Sun. SIZE: Large. *STOC Furniture, paintings, watercolours, print pottery, porcelain, domestic artifacts, clock silver, jewellery and plate, mainly 17th-19th £5-£3,000.* LOC: Centre of High St. (A429 PARK: Easy. TEL: 01608 651084. VAT: Sta Spec.

Astley House - Fine Art LAPAD
Astley House, High St. GL56 0LL. (D. and Glaisyer). CADA. Est. 1974. Open 9-5.30. C Wed. SIZE: Medium. *STOCK: Oil paintin and botanical watercolours, 19th-20th C, £20 £10,000.* LOC: Main street. PARK: Easy. TE 01608 650601; fax - 01608 651777. SE Restorations (oils and watercolours); framin VAT: Spec.

Astley House - Fine Art LAPA
Astley House, London Rd. GL56 0LE. (D. a N. Glaisyer). CADA. Est. 1974. Open 10-1 a 2-5. CL: Wed. SIZE: Large. *STOCK: O paintings, 19th-20th C; large decorati paintings and portraits.* LOC: Town cent PARK: Easy. TEL: 01608 650601; fax - 016 651777. SER: Restorations (oils a watercolours); porcelain framing. VAT: Spec

Moreton-in-Marsh continued

Berry Antiques LAPADA.
High St. GL56 0AH. (Chris Berry). Est. 1989. Open 10-5.30, Sun. 11-5.30. CL: Tues. SIZE: Medium. *STOCK: Furniture, late 18th to 19th C, 1,000-£10,000; porcelain, £50-£500; paintings, 200-£5,000; both 19th C.* LOC: Near junction with Broadway road. PARK: Easy. TEL: 01608 52929; home - same. SER: Valuations. FAIRS: NEC, LAPADA (NEC). VAT: Spec.

Simon Brett BADA
reswyke House, High St. GL56 0LH. Est. 972. Open 10-5.30. *STOCK: Antique and ollectors' fishing tackle and carved wood fish odels; portrait miniatures.* TEL: 01608 50751; fax - 01608 651791. VAT: Spec.

Chandlers Antiques
ligh St. GL56 0AD. (I. Kellam and P. Grout). pen 9.30-1 and 2-5.30. *STOCK: Pottery, orcelain, glass, silver, jewellery, small furniture nd general antiques.* TEL: 01608 651347.

Cox's Architectural Reclamation Yard
nit 5, Fosseway Industrial Estate. GL55 6AZ . (P. Watson). Est. 1991. Open 8.30-6, Sat. 9.30-5, Sun. y appointment. SIZE: Large. *STOCK: Architectural antiques, fire surrounds and places, £250-500; doors, £50-£100, all 19th C.* LOC: Just off osseway on northern end of Moreton in Marsh. ARK: Easy. TEL: 01608 652505; fax - same. ER: Valuations. FAIRS: Newark. VAT: Stan.

Europa Antiques
he Old Dairy, Fosse Way Industrial Estate. L55 6AZ. (Graham Gadsby and Trevor Vosket). Est. 1994. Open 9-5. SIZE: Large. *TOCK: Pine, 19th C, £50-£500; stripped pine; nglish mahogany and oak, 18th-19th C.* LOC: 429 Fosse Way. PARK: Easy. TEL: 01608 52241; fax - 01608 652250; home - 01386 41504. SER: Restorations and stripping; buys at uction. FAIRS: Newark; Archenliesh. VAT: tan.

Jeffrey Formby Antiques LAPADA
rchard Cottage, East St. GL56 0LQ. Resident. st. 1994. Open by appointment. SIZE: Small. *TOCK: Fine English clocks, pre 1850, £2,000-10,000; horological books, old and new, £5-£500.* OC: 100 yards from High St. PARK: Easy. EL: 01608 650558. SER: Restorations (clock ovements and cases); buys at auction (English locks, pre 1850). FAIRS: NEC, Kenilworth, hester. VAT: Spec.

Grimes House Antiques & Fine Art
igh St. GL56 0AT. (S. and V. Farnsworth). Est. 978. Open 9.30-1 and 2-5, other times by ppointment. *STOCK: Specialist dealers in old anberry glass, plus furniture, boxes and fine aintings.* TEL: 01608 651029.

Moreton-in-Marsh continued

Lemington House Antiques
Oxford St. GL56 0LA. (K.W. and Y. Heath). Open 10.30-5.30. *STOCK: Early walnut, satinwood, mahogany and oak furniture, 17th-19th C.* LOC: Close to junction with High St. PARK: Own. TEL: 01608 651443.

Mrs M.K. Nielsen
Seaford House, High St. GL56 0AD. Est. 1965. Open Thurs., Fri. and Sat. 9.30-1 and 2-5 or by appointment. SIZE: Medium. *STOCK: Derby porcelain, £45-£5,000; Worcester, £65-£5,000; furniture, £150-£4,500.* LOC: A429 Fosseway. PARK: Easy. TEL: 01608 650448. VAT: Stan/Spec.

Oriental Gallery
High Barn, Longborough. (Patricia Cater). Open by appointment only. *STOCK: Oriental ceramics and works of art.* TEL: 01451 830944; fax - 01451 870126.

Elizabeth Parker
High St. GL56 0LL. (P.J. and T.M. King-Smith). Est. 1975. Open 9-6. SIZE: Medium. *STOCK: 18th and 19th C furniture, £500-£10,000; clocks, silver, boxes, porcelain, brass and copper.* LOC: Opposite Manor House Hotel, on Fosseway junction of A44 from Broadway. TEL: 01608 650917. SER: Buys at auction. VAT: Stan/Spec.

Anthony Sampson
Dale House. GL56 0AD. Est. 1967. Open 9-1 and 2-5.30, Sun. by appointment. SIZE: Medium. *STOCK: Town and country furniture, to 1830; decorative items.* Not Stocked: Reproductions. LOC: Main street. PARK: Easy. TEL: 01608 650763; fax - 01608 652424. VAT: Spec.

Southgate Gallery
Fosse Manor Farm. GL56 9NQ. (J. Constable and N. Collins). Est. 1968. Open by appointment only. *STOCK: Modern British paintings.* TEL: 01608 650051. SER: Restorations (oils).

Windsor House Antiques Centre
High St. GL56 0AD. Open 10-5.30, Sun. 12-5.30. SIZE: 40 dealers. *STOCK: General antiques.* TEL: 01608 650993.

NORTHLEACH, Nr. Cheltenham

The Doll's House
Market Place. GL54 3EJ. (Miss Michal Morse). Est. 1971. Open Thurs. Fri. and Sat. 10-5 and some Sun. 11-4, other times prior telephone call advisable. SIZE: Small. *STOCK: Handmade doll's houses and minature furniture in one twelfth scale.* LOC: A40. PARK: Easy. TEL: 01451 860431; home and fax - same. SER: Restorations (as stock). VAT: Stan.

Northleach continued

Keith Harding's World of Mechanical Music

The Oak House, High St. GL54 3ET. (K. Harding, FBHI and C.A. Burnett, CMBHI). Est. 1961. Articles on clocks, musical boxes. Open 10-6 including Sun. *STOCK: Clocks, musical boxes and automata.* TEL: 01451 860181; fax - 01451 861133. SER: Guided tours and demonstrations; valuations; restorations (musical boxes, clocks); buys at auction. VAT: Stan/Spec.

NORTON, Nr. Gloucester

Ronson's Architectural Effects

Norton Barn, Wainlodes Lane. GL2 9LN. (A.P. Jones). Est. 1988. Open 8-5, Sat. 8-1. SIZE: Large. *STOCK: Architectural items including garden ornaments and architectural effects, £25-£1,000; antique pine, £50-£1,000.* LOC: A38 between Gloucester and Tewkesbury. PARK: Easy. TEL: 01452 731236. SER: Buys at auction (garden ornaments and statues). FAIRS: Restorex Period Living, Olympia. VAT: Stan.

PAINSWICK

Craig Carrington Antiques

Pincot House, Pincot Lane. GL6 7QP. Est. 1970. Open by appointment. *STOCK: English and Continental furniture and works of art.* TEL: 01452 813248. SER: Buys at auction. VAT: Spec.

Painswick Antique Centre

New St. GL6 6XH. (R.J.B. Short). Open 10-5, Sat. 10-5.30, Sun. 10.30-5.30. *STOCK: General antiques from jewellery to period furniture.* LOC: A46, near Painswick church. PARK: Easy. TEL: 01452 812431.

Nina Zborowska BADA

Damsels Mill, Paradise. GL6 6UD. Est. 1980. By appointment, except during exhibitions (May-June and Oct.-Nov) 11-5 including Sun. SIZE: Medium. *STOCK: Modern British paintings and drawings, St Ives, Newlyn, NEAC and Bloomsbury schools, 1900-1970, £500-£20,000.* LOC: From Cheltenham towards Stroud on A46, take

Painswick continued

first turning on left to Sheepscombe. PARK Easy. TEL: 01452 812460; fax - 01452 812912 SER: Valuations; restorations. FAIRS: World of Watercolours; 20th C British Art.

RODLEY, Nr. Westbury on Severn

Kelly Antiques

Landeck, Upper Rodley Rd. GL14 1QZ. (G Kelly). Resident. Always open. *STOCK: Antique pine.* TEL: 01452 760315.

SLAD, Nr. Stroud

Ian Hodgkins and Co. Ltd

Upper Vatch Mill, The Vatch. GL6 7JY. Open by appointment only. *STOCK: Antiquarian books including pre-Raphaelites and associates, the Brontës, Jane Austen; 19th C illustrated, children's art and literature books, European royalty.* TEL 01453 764270; fax - 01453 764270.

STOW-ON-THE-WOLD

Acorn Antiques

Sheep St. GL54 1AA. (Maggie Masters). Est. 1987. Open 9.30-1 and 2.15-5, Sat. 9.30-1 and 2.30-5. CL: Wed. pm. SIZE: Medium. *STOCK: 19th C Staffordshire figures and animals; small furniture, Georgian, Victorian and Edwardian collectables.* PARK: Easy. TEL: 01451 831519.

Ashton Antiques

7a Talbot Court. GL54 1BQ. Est. 1966. Open 11-5. SIZE: Large - 2 floors. *STOCK: Fine English furniture including dining, china and pictures.* PARK: Easy. TEL: 01451 870067. VAT: Spec.

Duncan J. Baggott LAPADA

Woolcomber House, Sheep St. GL54 1AA CADA. Est. 1967. Open 9-5.30 or by appointment. SIZE: Large. *STOCK: 17th-20th C English furniture, paintings, domestic metalwork and decorative items; garden statuary and ornaments.* PARK: Sheep St. or Market Sq. TEL: 01451 830662; fax - 01451 832174.

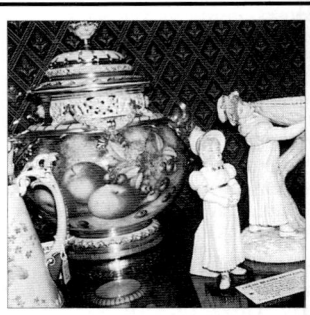

tow-on-the-Wold continued

;aggott Church Street Ltd BADA

hurch St. GL54 1BB. (D.J. and C.M. aggott). CADA. Est. 1978. Open 9.30-5.30 or y appointment. SIZE: Large. *STOCK: English ırniture, 17th-19th C; portrait paintings, etalwork, pottery, treen and decorative items.* OC: South-west corner of market square. ARK: In market square. TEL: 01451 830370; ıx - 01451 832174.

:olin Brand Antiques

udor House, Sheep St. GL54 1AA. Est. 1985. pen 10-1 and 2-5, Sun. by appointment. CL: 'ed. SIZE: Medium. *STOCK: Clocks, small rniture, £200-£4,000; porcelain, £30-£600, all re-1900.* LOC: Opposite Post Office. PARK: ain square. TEL: 01451 831760; fax and home same. VAT: Spec.

. and J. Caspall Antiques

ıeep St. GL54 1AA. Author of "Fire and Light in e Home pre-1820". Est. 1971. Open 9.30-5.30 or / appointment. *STOCK: Period oak, 16th C to 760; early metalwork, especially lighting and arth, early woodcarvings, period domestic and corative items.* PARK: Nearby. TEL: 01451 31160. SER: Valuations. VAT: Spec.

nnarella Clark Antiques

Park St. GL54 1AQ. Est. 1968. Open by pointment any time. SIZE: Medium. *STOCK: icker and garden, English and French country ıd painted furniture, needlework, pottery, quilts ıd decorative objects.* LOC: Park St. leads from ıeep St., 1st right at lights leading into town. ARK: Easy. TEL: 01451 830535; home - same.

hristopher Clarke Antiques Ltd

ıe Fosse Way. GL54 1JS. (C.J. Clarke). CADA. st. 1961. Open 9.30-6. SIZE: Medium. *STOCK: ırniture, 17th-19th C, £300-£15,000; walnut, ahogany, metalware, 16th-18th C, £200-£5,000.* ot Stocked: Silver, glass, medals, coins, prints. OC: Corner of the Fosse Way and Sheep St. ARK: Easy. TEL: 01451 830476; fax - 01451 30300.

Stow-on-the-Wold continued

Cotswold Galleries

GL54 1AB. (Richard and Cherry Glaisyer). CADA. Est. 1961. Open 9-5.30 or by appointment. SIZE: Large. *STOCK: Oil paintings, especially 19th-20th C landscape.* TEL: 01451 870567; fax - 01451 870678. SER: Restorations; framing.

Country Life Antiques

Grey House, The Square. GL54 1AF. Open 10-5. *STOCK: Scientific instruments, decorative accessories, pewter, brass, copper, furniture.* PARK: Easy. TEL: 01451 831564; fax - same.

The John Davies Gallery

Church St. GL54 1BB. CADA. Est. 1977. Open 9.30-1.30 and 2.30-5.30. SIZE: Large. *STOCK: Contemporary and late period paintings; limited edition bronzes.* PARK: In square. TEL: 01451 831698; fax - 01451 832477. SER: Restoration and conservation to museum standard.

Durham House Antiques Centre

Sheep St. GL54 1AA. Open 10-5, Sun. 11-5. SIZE: 30+ dealers. PARK: Easy. TEL: 01451 870404; fax - same. SER: Buys at auction. FAIRS: NEC (Aug); Newark; Ardingly. Below are listed the dealers at this market.

Aston Antiques
Arts and Crafts, Victorian and decorative objects, fabrics, pillows, crystal and porcelain.

John Benson-Wilson
Continental porcelain and cabinet pieces, Meissen, Samson.

Judi Bland Antiques
Toby jugs, Staffordshire, oak furniture, metalware and decorative items.

Bread and Roses
19th and 20th C kitchen, dairy, laundry, garden and outdoor objects.

Castle Antiques
Art, small furniture, brass, copper and period metalware, crystal, pottery and treen.

Stow-on-the-Wold continued

Victoria Charles Antiques
Furniture, clocks, silverware, ceramics, glass and metalware.

Brian Collyer
English pottery and Staffordshire figures; cork-screws and wine related items.

Crockwell Antiques
(Philip Dawes). *Longcase clocks, 18th C oak and country furniture, brass, copper and Ironstone china.*

Jane Fairfield
Elegant silver and plate, Continental porcelain and objet d'art.

Tony and Jane Finnegan
Traditional furniture, interesting home accessories and comforts.

John and Sally Gormley
General antique furniture and decorative objects, 18th and 19th C.

Beryl and Brian Harrison
Linen, lace, tableware and fabrics.

Erna Hiscock
Samplers, country furniture and interesting objects.

Harry Horner
Silver and silver plated flatware and cutlery including classical designs.

Dorothy and Christopher Hyatt
Glass, 18th-20th C early English porcelain and pottery.

Lineage Antiques
Small silverware, jewellery, Mauchline ware, portrait miniatures and interesting small objects.

Little Nells
(Helen Middleton). *Antiques and collectables, 18th-20th C cabinet pieces and collectables.*

Audrey McConnell
Silver, picture frames, jewellery, china and pottery.

Colin Morris
Treen, early metalware, glass and pewter.

Peggy Nichols
Silver and plate, jewellery, glass and ceramics.

Outram Antiques
(Philip and Dorothy Lipman). *Oak and country furniture and collectables.*

Paper Moon Books
Fine leather bindings, 19th and early 20th C, English poetry, prose,history, etc.

Pauline Parkes
Sewing ephemera, Mauchline ware, treen and interesting objects.

Stow-on-the-Wold continued

Edith Prosser Antiques
English furniture, 18th-20th C, mirrors and peric accesories.

Quartz & Clay
Deco, Arts & Crafts, pottery, ceramics and glass Clarice Cliff, Whitefriar (Powell), Denby.

Jack Robinson
Continental and English porcelain and glass.

Samarkand Galleries
(Brian MacDonald). *Eastern rugs and carpe especially antique tribal rugs and carpets.* SEI Valuations; restorations; lecturer.

Betty Thornley Antiques
Tôle, glassware, decorative prints, late 18th-ear 19th C, objects of merit.

Margaretha and David Walter-Ellis
Small furniture and decorative objects, 18th-20th C

Paul Wright Antiques
Georgian and Victorian furniture, fine jewellery ar silver. SER: Restorations; stones supplied ar matched.

Yorca Antiques
(P. and P. Hughes). *18th-20th C porcelain ar objets d'art.*

The Fosse Gallery

The Square. Est. 1979. Open 10-5.30. SIZI Large. *STOCK: English and Scottish painter many RA, RSA and Royal Glasgow Institu members, including Gore, Howard, War Dunstan, Spear, Weight, Morrocco, Donaldso McClure, Haig, Devlin and Boyd.* LOC: O Fosseway, A429. PARK: Easy. TEL: 0145 831319. SER: Valuations; buys at auction. VA Spec.

Fosse Way Antiques

Ross House, The Square. GL54 1AF. (M Beeston). CADA. Est. 1969. Open 10-5. SIZI Large. *STOCK: Furniture and oil painting £300-£8,000; bronzes, Sheffield plate, caddie boxes and decorative objects, £50-£1,000; a 18th-19th C.* LOC: East side of the Square, behir the Town Hall. PARK: Easy. TEL: 0145 830776. SER: Valuations; buys at auction. VA Spec.

Fox Cottage Antiques

Digbeth St. GL54 1BN. (Sue London). Est. 198 Open 10-5. SIZE: 7 dealers. *STOCK: Wide varie of general antiques including pottery an porcelain, silver and plate, metalware, print small furniture, country and decorative item mainly pre 1900, £5-£500.* LOC: Left hand side bottom of narrow street, running down from Th Square. PARK: Nearby. TEL: 01451 870307.

;tow-on-the-Wold continued

ˆeith Hockin (Antiques) Ltd BADA
'he Square. GL54 1AF. CADA. Est. 1968.)pen 9-6. CL: Sun. except by appointment. ;IZE: Medium. ***STOCK: Oak furniture, 1600-750; country furniture in oak, fruitwoods, yew, 700-1850; pewter, copper, brass, ironwork, all ·eriods.*** **Not Stocked: Mahogany. PARK: Easy. 'EL: 01451 831058. SER: Buys at auction oak, pewter, metalwork). VAT: Stan/Spec.**

Iuntington Antiques Ltd LAPADA
'he Old Forge, Church St. GL54 1BE. (M.F. nd S.P. Golding). CADA. CINOA. TEFAF. tesident. Est. 1974. Open 9.30-5.30 or by ppointment. ***STOCK: Early period and fine ountry furniture, metalware, treen and textiles, ıpestries and works of art.*** **TEL: 01451 830842; ax - 01451 832211. SER: Valuations; buys at uction. FAIRS: Maastricht; Madrid; Basel. 'AT: Spec.**

ˆenulf Fine Arts LAPADA
·igbeth St. GL54 1BN. (E. and J. Ford). Est. 978. Open 9.30-1 and 2-5.30. ***STOCK: 19th to arly 20th C oils, watercolours and prints; ecorative items and 20th C ceramics; small ırniture.*** **TEL: 01451 870878 or 01242 603204. ·ER: Valuations; restorations (oils and water-olours, period framing).**

Roger Lamb Antiques & Works of ırt LAPADA
'he Square. GL54 1AB. CADA. Open 10-5. ***TOCK: 18th-early 19th C furniture, especially nall items, lighting, decorative accessories, oils nd watercolours.*** **TEL: 01451 831371. SER: earch.**

ˌittle Elms Antiques
he Square. GL54 1AF. (Michael Rowland). ·pen 11-5. SIZE: Small. *STOCK: Furniture ıcluding dressers, ladder and spindle back 'hairs, gateleg and side tables, 17th-18th C, 100-£5,000.* PARK: Easy. TEL: 01451 870089; ome - same. SER: Valuations. VAT: Spec.

Iartin House Antiques
heep St. GL54 1AA. (G. Finney). Resident. pen 10.30-5.30. CL: Fri. *STOCK: 18th-19th C orcelain and pottery.* TEL: 01451 831217.

ark House Antiques
ark St. GL54 1AQ. (G. and B. Sutton). Est. 986. Open 10-5. CL: Tues. and all of May. SIZE: ɑrge. *STOCK: Early dolls, teddy bears, toys, 'ctorian linen and lace, porcelain, collectables, nall furniture and pictures.* PARK: Easy. TEL: 451 830159; home - same. SER: Museum of olls, teddies, toys, textiles and collectables. AT: Stan/Spec.

Stow-on-the-Wold continued

Antony Preston Antiques Ltd BADA
The Square. GL54 1AB. CADA. Est. 1965. Open 9.30-5.30 or by appointment. ***STOCK: 18th-19th C English and Continental furniture and objects; barometers and period lighting.*** **TEL: 01451 831586; fax - 0171 581 5076. VAT: Stan/Spec.**

Priests Antiques
The Malt House, Digbeth St. GL54 1BN. (A.C. Priest). Est. 1979. Open 10-5, Sat. 10.30-5. SIZE: Large. *STOCK: Mahogany, 18th to early 19th C; oak, walnut, and fruitwood, 17th-18th C.* PARK: Easy. TEL: 01451 830592. SER: Valuations. VAT: Spec.

Queens Parade Antiques Ltd BADA
The Square. GL54 1AB. (Antony Preston Antiques Ltd). CADA. Est. 1965. Open 9.30-5.30. SIZE: Large. ***STOCK: 18th-19th C furniture, papier mâché, tôle peinte, needlework and period lighting.*** **LOC: Off Fosse Way. PARK: Easy. TEL: 01451 831586. VAT: Stan/Spec.**

Ruskin Antiques
5 Talbot Court. GL54 1DP. (Anne and William Morris). Est. 1990. Open 9.30-1 and 2-5.30, Sun. 11-1 and 2-4.30. SIZE: Small. *STOCK: Interesting and unusual decorative objects - Arts and Crafts movement and Art Deco glass and pottery, 1700-1930.* LOC: Between The Square and Sheep Street. PARK: Nearby. TEL: 01451 832254; home - 01993 831880. SER: Valuations.

Samarkand Galleries LAPADA
8 Brewery Yard, Sheep St. GL54 1AA. (Brian MacDonald). CADA. CINOA. Est. 1980. Open 10-5.30, Sun. by appointment. SIZE: Medium. ***STOCK: Tribal and village rugs and artefacts, 19th C, £100-£10,000; fine decorative carpets, 19th-20th C, £1,000-£10,000+; kelims, 19th-20th C, £200-£2,000.*** **LOC: Street adjacent to Market Sq. PARK: Easy. TEL: 01451 832322; fax - same; home - 01451 831173. SER: Exhibitions; valuations; restorations; cleaning. VAT: Stan/Spec.**

Arthur Seager Antiques
50 Sheep St. Open 10-5.30. SIZE: Medium. *STOCK: Fine 16th-18th C oak furniture, carvings, metalware, paintings, pewter and period accessories, £200-10,000.* PARK: Easy. TEL: 01451 831605. SER: Valuations (furniture). VAT: Spec.

Geoffrey Stead BADA
1 Waddington Warehouses, Bourton Industrial Park, Bourton-on-the Water. GL54 2HQ. Est. 1963. Open by appointment only. ***STOCK: English and Continental furniture, decorative objects and paintings.*** **LOC: 3 miles from Stow-on-the-Wold, on A429. TEL: 01608 674364; fax - 01608 674533.**

Stow-on-the-Wold continued

Stow Antiques LAPADA

The Square. GL54 1AF. (Mr and Mrs J. Hutton-Clarke). CADA. Resident. Est. 1969. Open Mon.-Thurs. 2-5.30, Sat. 11-1 and 2-5.30, other times by appointment. SIZE: Large. *STOCK: Furniture, mainly Georgian, £500-£30,000; decorative items, gilded mirrors, £50-£10,000.* PARK: Easy. TEL: 01451 830377; fax - 01451 870018. SER: Shipping worldwide.

Styles of Stow

The Little House, Sheep St. GL54 1AA. (Mr and Mrs W.J. Styles). Est. 1981. Open 9.15-1 and 2-5.30, Sat. 9.15-1 and 1.30-5.30, other times by appointment. SIZE: Medium. *STOCK: Longcase (40+) and bracket clocks, and barometers, 18th-19th C, £400-£30,000; fine furniture, 18th-19th C, £250-£15,000; paintings and collectables, 19th-20th C, £25-£10,000.* LOC: Opposite post office. PARK: Easy. TEL: 01451 830455; home and fax - same. SER: Valuations; restorations; buys at auction (longcase and bracket clocks). VAT: Margin.

Talbot Court Galleries

Talbot Court. GL54 1BQ. (J.P. Trevers). Est. 1988. Open 9.30-1 and 2-5.30, Sun. by appointment. SIZE: Medium. *STOCK: Prints and maps, 1600-1900, £5-£500; restrike engravings, £25-£150.* LOC: Behind Talbot Hotel in precinct between the Square and Sheep St. PARK: Nearby. TEL: 01451 832169; fax - 01451 832167. SER: Valuations; restorations (cleaning, colouring); framing; buys at auction (engravings). VAT: Stan.

Vanbrugh House Antiques

Park St. GL54 1AQ. (J. and M.M. Sands). Resident. Est. 1972. Open 10-6 or by appointment. *STOCK: Furniture and decorative items, 17th to early 19th C; early maps, music boxes, square pianos, clocks and barometers.* LOC: Opposite the Bell Inn. PARK: Easy. TEL: 01451 830797; fax - same. SER: Valuations. VAT: Stan/Spec.

STROUD

Gnome Cottage Antiques

55 Middle St. GL5 1DZ. (G.I. Fry). Est. 1961. Open 10.30-5.30. SIZE: Bookshop attached. *STOCK: Antique and modern furniture, collectables, curios and militaria.* TEL: 01453 755788.

Shabby Tiger Antiques

18 Nelson St. GL5 2HN. (S. Krucker). Est. 1975. Open 11-6. *STOCK: 19th C furniture, pictures, jewellery, silver and plate, china, glass, metalware, decorative items.* LOC: Nelson St. is adjacent to Parliament St. car park. PARK: Opposite. TEL: 01453 759175.

TADDINGTON, Nr. Cutsdean

Architectural Heritage

Taddington Manor. GL54 5RY. CADA. Es 1978. Open 9.30-5.30, Sat. 10.30-4.30. SIZI Large. *STOCK: Period panelling, oak, mahogan and pine; chimney pieces in marble, stone, oa and mahogany; garden statuary, fountains, sea and urns.* PARK: Easy. TEL: 01386 584414; fax 01386 584236. VAT: Stan.

TETBURY

Philip Adler Antiques

4 The Chipping. TADA. Open 10-5 or by appoir ment. *STOCK: Eclectic and general decorative ar period antiques.* TEL: 01666 505759.

The Antique and Interior Centre

51A Long St. TADA. Open 10-5, Sun. 11-5 ar most Bank Holidays. SIZE: 8 dealers. *STOC Furniture, porcelain, silver and pictures; interi design items.* TEL: 01666 505083.

The Antiques Emporium

The Old Chapel, Long St. GL8 8AA. (C. and Sayers). TADA. Est. 1993. Open 10-5, Sun. 1- SIZE: Large - 38 dealers. *STOCK: Fruitwood a country furniture, fine oak and mahogany, chir porcelain, treen, copper and brass, jeweller silver, kitchenalia, militaria, £1-£15,000.* N Stocked: Reproductions. PARK: Nearby. TE 01666 505281. SER: Export. VAT: Stan/Spec.

Art-Tique

18 Long St. GL8 8AQ. (George Bristow). TAD Open 9.30-6. CL: Mon. *STOCK: Interior textiles, carpets and kelims and objets d'art frc the Orient.* TEL: 01666 503597.

Ball and Claw Antiques

45 Long St. GL8 8AA. (Chris and Nick Kirklan TADA. Est. 1985. Open 10-1 and 2-5. SIZ Medium. *STOCK: Furniture, 18th-19th C, £1C £3,000; decorative items, objects and prints, so country items.* PARK: Easy. TEL: 01666 5024 internet - http://www.all-about-antiques.c uk/ballc.html. SER: Valuations; buys at aucti VAT: Stan/Spec.

Balmuir House Antiques LAPA

14 Long St. GL8 8AQ. (P. Whittam). TAD Est. 1946. Open 9.30-5.30, Sun. by appointme SIZE: Large. *STOCK: Furniture, paintin mirrors, 19th C, £500-£5,000.* LOC: Town cent PARK: Easy. TEL: 01666 503822; home - sa SER: Valuations; restorations (furnitu upholstery, paintings). VAT: Spec.

Breakspeare Antiques LAPA

36 and 57 Long St. GL8 8AQ. (M. and Breakspeare). CADA. Resident. Est. 19 Open 10-5 or by appointment. CL: Thurs. p SIZE: Medium. *STOCK: English peri furniture - early walnut, 1690-1740, mahoga 1750-1835.* PARK: Own car park. TEL: 01 503122; fax - same. VAT: Stan/Spec.

etbury continued

/I. J. Bristow Antiques
8 Long St. GL8 8AQ. Est. 1964. Open Fri. and at. 9.30-1 and 2-5, but any time by appointment. IZE: Small. *STOCK: Longcase, bracket and ntern clocks; barometers, 17th-18th C; furniture.* ot Stocked: Victoriana, bric-a-brac. LOC: In ain street. PARK: Easy. TEL: 01666 502222. AT: Spec.

'he Chest of Drawers
4 Long St. GL8 8AQ. (A. and P. Bristow). ADA. Resident. Est. 1969. Open 9.30-6 or by ppointment. CL: Thurs. am. SIZE: Medium. *TOCK: Late Georgian, Regency and Victorian rniture; country pieces, 17th-18th C; china and ass.* LOC: On A433. PARK: Easy. TEL: 01666 02105; home - same. VAT: Spec.

'he Coach House Bookshop
The Chipping. (Philip Gibbons). TADA. Open)-6, Sun. 11-5. *STOCK: Secondhand and antiarian titles including A & C Black colour plate ooks; prints, antique furniture and small items.* EL: 01666 504330; e-mail - gibbons@ books.iay.co.uk. SER: Book search.

:ountry Homes
Long St. GL8 8AA. (C. and D. Sayers). ADA. Est. 1984. Open 9-5.30, Sun. 1-5.30. IZE: Medium. *STOCK: Pine furniture, 19th C, 00-£1,500; treen.* PARK: Nearby. TEL: 01666)2342. SER: Import/export. VAT: Stan/Spec.

ay Antiques
New Church St. GL8 8DS. CADA. TADA. Est. 75. Open 9-6. SIZE: Medium. *STOCK: Oak d country furniture, early pottery, metalware, een, some period mahogany.* TEL: 01666)2413. VAT: Stan/Spec.

he Decorator Source
a Long St. GL8 8AA. (Colin Gee). TADA. pen 10-5 or by appointment. SIZE: Large. *'OCK: French provincial furniture - armoires, rm tables, buffets; decorative items and :cessories of interest to interior decorators.* \RK: Easy. TEL: 01666 505358. VAT: Stan/ ec.

olphin Antiques
Long St. GL8 8AQ. (P. and L. Davis). TADA. t. 1986. Open 10-5.30. CL: Thurs. SIZE: Small. *'OCK: Mainly 19th C decorative porcelain, cluding Meissen, Dresden, Royal Worcester, mson, Coalport and Sitzendorf; general tiques; all 1750-1930, £20-£2,000.* Not ocked: Furniture. PARK: Nearby. TEL: 01666 4242; home - same.

ifty-One Antiques Et Cetera
Long St. (Sylvia Powell). TADA. Est. 1977. pen 10-5, Sun. by appointment. SIZE: Small. *'OCK: English and French country furniture, 0-£5,000; decorative items.* PARK: Easy. TEL: 666 505026.

Tetbury continued

Anne Fowler
35 Long St. GL8 8AA. TADA. Est. 1971. Open 10-5.30, Sun. by appointment. SIZE: Medium. *STOCK: Mainly French painted and decorative items including garden furniture and accessories, mirrors, faience and pots, wirework, lighting and prints, £20-£2,000.* PARK: Easy. TEL: 01666 504043; home - same. VAT: Stan/Spec.

Gales Antiques
52 Long St. GL8 8AQ. (M.R. Mathews). TADA. Est. 1979. Open 10-5.30. SIZE: Medium. *STOCK: English and French country furniture and decorative items, 17th-19th C, £5-£5,000.* PARK: Easy. TEL: 01666 502686. VAT: Stan/Spec.

Hampton Gallery
8 Tetbury Upton. GL8 8LP. (P. Downey). Resident. Est. 1969. Open by appointment. SIZE: Large. *STOCK: Weapons, arms and armour, 1700-1800, £50-£5,000.* LOC: Off junction 17, M4. PARK: Easy. TEL: 01666 502971. SER: Valuations; buys at auction (arms). FAIRS: All major. VAT: Spec.

Jester Antiques
22 Church St. (Lorna Coles and Peter Bairstow). TADA. Open 10-5.30 including Sun. *STOCK: Furniture, decorative items, lamps, lanterns, mirrors, clocks, memorabilia, curios, pictures, copper and brass, Oriental items.* TEL: 01666 505125.

Bobbie Middleton
58 Long St. TADA. Open 10-1 and 2-5, Sun. by appointment. *STOCK: 18th-19th C mahogany, oak and fruitwood furniture, mirrors, upholstery and decorative items.* TEL: 01666 502761; mobile - 0374 192660. VAT: Spec.

Morpheus - Elgin House
1 New Church St. GL8 8DT. (B. Symes). TADA. Open every day 9-5.30. *STOCK: 18th-19th C oak, mahogany and pine furniture; restored wood, brass and upholstered beds, 4-posters, half-testers and lit bateau styles.* TEL: 01666 504068; fax - 01666 503352.

Old Mill Market Shop
12 Church St. GL8 8JG. (Mr and Mrs M. Green). TADA. Open 10-5.30, Thurs. 10-1. *STOCK: General antiques, collectables and bric-a-brac.* TEL: 01666 503127.

Porch House Antiques
40/42 Long St. GL8 8AQ. TADA. Open 10-5. *STOCK: 17th-20th C furniture and decorative items.* TEL: 01666 502687.

Tetbury Gallery
18 Market Place. (Jane Maile and Helen Joyner). FATG. TADA. Open every day. *STOCK: Original and limited edition prints, from Victorian watercolours and oils to contemporary artists including Russell Flint, David Shepherd and Ben Maile.* TEL: 01666 503412.

Tetbury continued

Westwood House Antiques

29 Long St. (Richard Griffiths and Lynne Petersen). TADA. Open 10-5.30 or by appointment. *STOCK: Oak, elm and ash country furniture especially dressers, dresser bases and tables, 17th-19th C; occasional French fruitwood items; decorative pottery, pewter and treen.* TEL: 01666 502338.

TEWKESBURY

Abbey Antiques

62 Church St. GL20 5RZ. Est. 1945. CL: Thurs. pm. *STOCK: General antiques, Victoriana, trade and shipping goods.* TEL: 01684 292378.

Berkeley Antiques

132 High St. GL20 5JR. (P. & S. Dennis). Open 9.30-5.30. CL: Thurs. pm. SIZE: Large. *STOCK: Mahogany, oak, walnut and pine, 17th-19th C, £50-£2,000; brass, copper, silver, china and glass.* TEL: 01684 292034. SER: Restorations. VAT: Stan/Spec.

Gainsborough House Antiques

81 Church St. GL20 5RX. (A. and B. Hilson). Open 9.30-5. *STOCK: Furniture, 18th to early 19th C; glass, porcelain.* TEL: 01684 293072. SER: Restorations; conservation.

Tewkesbury Antique & Curio Centre

Tolsey Hall, Tolsey Lane. Open 10-5, including Sun. SIZE: 10+ units. *STOCK: General antiques, toys, books, collectables.* LOC: Town centre. TEL: 01684 294091. SER: Restorations.

WICKWAR

Bell Passage Antiques LAPADA

38 High St. GL12 8NP. (Mrs D.V. Brand). Est 1966. Open 9-5. CL: Mon. and Thurs. SIZE: Large. *STOCK: Furniture, glass, porcelain, some pictures.* LOC: On B4060. PARK: Easy. TEL: 01454 294251; fax - same. SER: Valuations; restorations; upholstery.

WINCHCOMBE, Nr. Cheltenham

Muriel Lindsay

Queen Anne House. GL54 5LJ. Resident. Est 1965. Open 10-1 and 2.15-5. CL: Sun. and Mon except to Trade by appointment. *STOCK: Staffordshire, metalwork, glass, small items.* TEL: 01242 602319. VAT: Spec.

Prichard Antiques

16 High St. GL54 5LJ. (K.H. and D.Y. Prichard). CADA. Est. 1979. Open 9-5.30, Sun. by appointment. SIZE: Large. *STOCK: Period and decorative furniture, £10-£10,000; treen and metalwork, £5-£500; interesting and decorative accessories.* LOC: On main Broadway to Cheltenham road. PARK: Easy. TEL: 0124[illegible] 603566. VAT: Spec.

WITHINGTON, Nr. Cheltenham

Brian Sinfield - Compton Cassey Gallery

GL54 4DE. Open Sat. 10-5, other times by appointment. *STOCK: Mainly contemporary, but some Victorian and Edwardian paintings and sculptures.* TEL: 01242 890500; fax - 0124[illegible] 890599. SER: Commission sales.

(Left to right). Pastimes; Alice in Wonderland; Bunnykins; Little Tommy Tucker; Pip, Squeak and Wilfred. All by Royal Doulton, c.1900 to 1939.

From an article entitled "Gifts for Good Children" by Maureen Batkin which appeared in the May 1997 issue of **Antique Collecting**

Hampshire

Please note this is only a rough map designed to show dealers the number of shops in the various towns, and is not necessarily totally accurate.

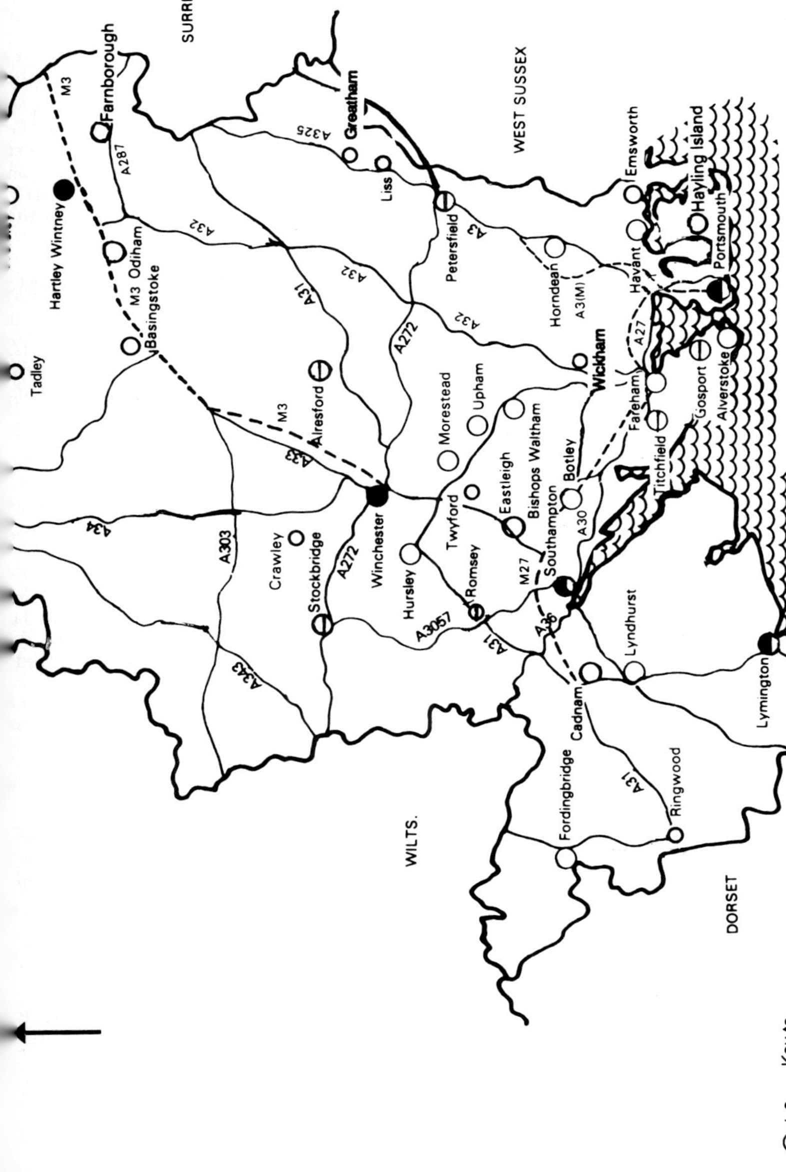

○ 1-2
⊖ 3-5
◐ 6-12
● 13+

Key to number of shops in this area.

ALRESFORD, Nr. Winchester

Alresford Antiques

49 West St. SO24 9AB. (Mr and Mrs C. Carpenter). Est. 1992. Open Wed. and Sat. 10-4.30. SIZE: Small. *STOCK: Small curios, china and glass, 18th-20th C, £5-£200; Oriental items, 18th-19th C, £25-£300.* LOC: A31, next to garage. PARK: Easy. TEL: 01962 735959; home - 01962 733160; mobile - 0860 590647. SER: Probate valuations. FAIRS: Sandown Park; Alexandra Palace.

Artemesia LAPADA

16 West St. SO24 9AT. (D.T.L. Wright). Est. 1972. Open 9.30-5. SIZE: Medium. *STOCK: English and Continental furniture, English, Continental and Oriental porcelain and works of art, £20-£6,000.* LOC: A31. PARK: Nearby. TEL: 01962 732277. SER: Valuations. VAT: Spec.

Close Antiques BADA

SO24 9EG. (C. Baron). Open by appointment only. SIZE: Medium. *STOCK: 17th-18th C oak, fruitwood, and walnut country furniture; samplers, Delftware, early brass, copper, iron and treen.* PARK: Easy. TEL: 01962 732189. VAT: Spec.

Evans and Evans LAPADA

40 West St. SO24 9AU. (D. and N. Evans). Est. 1953. Open Fri. and Sat. or by appointment. SIZE: Medium. *STOCK: Clocks, watches, 1680-1900, £250-£50,000; musical boxes, 19th C, £500-£12,000; Regency and Victorian barometers, £200-£2,000. Stock only as listed.* LOC: A31. Shop on left going east. PARK: Easy. TEL: 01962 732170. SER: Valuations; buys at auction. VAT: Stan/Spec.

Studio Bookshop and Gallery

17 Broad St. SO24 9AW. (L. Oxley). ABA. Est. 1951. Open 9-5. SIZE: Large. *STOCK: Antiquarian books, £5-£2,500; topographical prints, £2-£250; maps, £5-£800; watercolours, £75-£9,000.* LOC: B3046. PARK: Easy. TEL: 01962 732188. SER: Valuations; restorations (oil paintings, prints, books); framing; book-binding. FAIRS: USA, London ABA. VAT: Stan.

ALVERSTOKE, Nr. Gosport

Alverstoke Antiques

47 Village Rd. (Dyer and Follett Ltd). Est. 1960. Open 9-12.45 and 2.15-5.30. SIZE: Small. *STOCK: Furniture.* PARK: Easy. TEL: 01705 582204; fax - 01705 588499. SER: Restorations. VAT: Stan/Spec.

Olive Antiques

2A Church Rd. PO12 2LB. Est. 1976. Open 8.15-5. SIZE: Medium. *STOCK: Gold, silver, diamonds, jewellery, clocks, barometers, mirrors and porcelain, £10-£1,000.* LOC: Main road from

Alverstoke continued

Fareham to Gosport and then to Alverstok PARK: Easy. TEL: 01705 522812. SER: Val ations; gem stone testing.

BASINGSTOKE

Squirrel Collectors Centre

9 New St. RG21 1DF. (A.H. Stone). Est. 198 Open 10-5.30. SIZE: Small. *STOCK: Jewelle and silver, Victorian and Edwardian, £5-£1,50 books, cigarette and post cards, watche collectors' and small items, toys and recor* LOC: Near traffic lights at junction wi Winchester St. PARK: Nearby. TEL: 012 464885. SER: Valuations. FAIRS: Farnha Maltings monthly. VAT: Stan.

BISHOPS WALTHAM, Nr. Southampto

Pinecrafts

4 Brook St. (A. Robinson). Open 10-5. SIZ Large. *STOCK: Pine furniture.* TEL: 014 892878. SER: Restorations; stripping. VAT: Sta

BOTLEY, Nr. Southampton

Butterfly Pine

Old Flour Mills, High St. S03 2GB. (K.J. Sha Est. 1986. Open 10-5.30, Thurs. 10-1, Sun. 5.30. SIZE: Medium. *STOCK: Pine, £500-£1,0 darkwood furniture, £250-£1,500; associa items, porcelain and prints, £50-£500; all 18 19th C.* LOC: Off M27, exit 7. PARK: Easy. T 01489 788194; fax - 01489 784626. SER: Va ations; restorations (clocks, furniture includi upholstery, caning and French polishing); buys auction; finder; furniture made to order from and new pine. VAT: Stan.

CADNAM

C.W. Buckingham

Twin Firs, Southampton Rd. SO4 2NP. Resid Open 9-6 or by appointment. CL: Thurs. *STO Mainly pine, some period and Victorian furnit* TEL: 01703 812122.

CRAWLEY, Nr. Winchester

Bakers Country Furniture

Folly Farm. (T. R. Baker). Open 9-5. *STO General antiques especially pine.* TEL: 01 776687.

EASTLEIGH

Tappers Antiques

186 Southampton Rd. SO5 5QW. (P.A. Pass Open 10-5. *STOCK: General collectables curios.* LOC: 1 mile off M27. TEL: 01 643105.

EMSWORTH

Clockwise
10 South St. PO10 7EH. (D. Judge). AHS. GMC. Est. 1976. Open daily. SIZE: Small. *STOCK: Longcase, wall, mantle, bracket and carriage clocks, 18th-19th C, £300-£6,000; barometers, books and tools.* LOC: A259 off A27, head for harbour. PARK: Easy. TEL: 01243 377558; 01962 842331. SER: Valuations; restorations (clocks and barometers). VAT: Margin.

Dolphin Quay Antique Centre
Queen St. PO10 7BU. (Mac and Nancy Farmer). Est. 1997. Open 10-5, Sun. 10-4. SIZE: Large - several dealers. *STOCK: English, French and country furniture, 18th C to 1939, £50-£3,000; marine paintings, prints, porcelain, clocks, textiles, period costume, etc, £25-£1,000.* PARK: Easy, in square. TEL: 01243 379994.

Tiffins Antiques
12 Queen St. PO10 7BL. (Mrs P. Hudson). Est. 1987. Open 10-5. SIZE: Small. *STOCK: General antiques, oil lamps and clocks.* TEL: 01243 372497; home - same. SER: Restorations (clocks).

EVERSLEY, Nr. Wokingham

Kingsley Barn Antique Centre
Church Lane. RG27 0PX. (G. Bazely). Est. 1988. Open 10.30-5. CL: Mon. SIZE: Large. *STOCK: Furniture, china and bric-a-brac.* LOC: 1.5 miles from Blackbush airport. PARK: Easy. TEL: 01734 328518.

FAREHAM

Elizabethans
58 High St. PO16 7BG. (E.J. Keeble). Est. 1961. Open Mon., Thurs. and Sat. 10-4. *STOCK: Small general antiques including furniture.* TEL: 01329 234964 (answerphone).

FARNBOROUGH

Martin and Parke LAPADA
97 Lynchford Rd. (J. Martin and J. Warde). Est. 1971. Open 9-5. SIZE: Large. *STOCK: Furniture, shipping goods and books.* TEL: 01252 515311. VAT: Stan.

FORDINGBRIDGE

Mark Collier BADA
54 High St. SP6 1AX. *STOCK: Period and decorative antiques.* Not Stocked: Coins, medals and stamps. TEL: 01425 652555; fax - 01425 656886.

Fordingbridge continued

Quatrefoil

Burgate. SP6 1LX. (C.D. and Mrs I. Aston). Resident. Est. 1972. Always open. SIZE: Large. *STOCK: Early oak furniture, 16th-18th C, £50-£15,000; carvings and sculpture, 13th-17th C, £20-£20,000; antiquities and coins, £50-£10,000.* LOC: On A338, adjacent Tudor Rose Inn. PARK: Easy. TEL: 01425 653309. VAT: Stan/Spec.

GOSPORT

E.T. Cooper

20 Stoke Rd. PO12 1JB. Est. 1972. Open 9.30-12.30 and 1.30-5. CL: Wed. pm. SIZE: Medium. *STOCK: Silver, china, glass, furniture, mechanical music, fairground equipment.* LOC: Main road from Lee-on-Solent through Gosport. PARK: In side road. TEL: 01705 585032. SER: Valuations; buys at auction.

Peter Pan's Bazaar

87 Forton Rd. PO12 4TG. (S.V. Panormo). Est. 1960. CL: Mon., Tues. and Wed. *STOCK: Vintage cameras, early photographica, images, 1850-1950, £5-£1,500.* LOC: Main road into town. PARK: Easy. TEL: 01705 524254. FAIRS: Main south of England.

Peter Pan's of Gosport

87 Forton Rd. PO12 4TG. (J. McClaren). Est. 1965. CL: Mon., Tues. and Wed. *STOCK: Jewellery, dolls, toys and miniatures.* LOC: Main road into town. PARK: Easy. TEL: 01705 524254. FAIRS: Main south of England.

GREATHAM, Nr. Liss

Jardinique

Kemps Place, Selborne Rd. GU33 6HG. (Edward and Sarah Neish). Est. 1994. Open 10-5. CL: Mon. SIZE: Very large. *STOCK: Garden ornaments, urns, statuary and furniture, £100-£3,000.* LOC: West of A3 roundabout at Liss, turn left after 750 yards onto B3006, premises 200 yards on left. PARK: Easy. TEL: 01420 538000; fax - 01420 538700. SER: Valuations; buys at auction (as stock). VAT: Stan/Spec.

HARTLEY WINTNEY

Nicholas Abbott LAPADA

High St. RG27 8NY. (C.N. Abbott). Est. 1962. Open 9.30-5.30. *STOCK: English furniture, 18th to early 19th C.* LOC: A30. PARK: Easy. TEL: 01252 842365.

Airdale Antiques

at Deva, High St. RG27 8NY. (E.J. Andreae). Est. 1972. *STOCK: Country furniture, 17th-19th C; polished pine.* TEL: 01252 843538.

Andwells LAPADA

High St. RG27 8NY. Est. 1967. Open 9-5.30, Sat. 9.30-5.30. SIZE: Large. *STOCK: Georgian and Regency furniture, mainly mahogany.* LOC: Main street. PARK: Easy. TEL: 01252 842305; fax - 01252 845149. VAT: Stan/Spec.

Antique House

22 High St. RG27 8NY. (R.M. Campbell and F. Weaver). Open 9.30-5.30, Sun. by appointment. *STOCK: Furniture in walnut, mahogany, rosewood, oak and fruitwoods, 1710-1910; inlaid Edwardian furniture, mirrors, oils, watercolours and prints, £50-£5,000.* PARK: Easy. TEL: 01252 844499; fax - 01252 845270. SER: Restorations (furniture and porcelain).

The Antiques Centre

Primrose House, London Road. (Mrs. Shelagh Lister). Open 10-5 including some Sun. SIZE: Large - 15+ dealers. *STOCK: Pine, Georgian and Victorian furniture, £50-£5,000; prints, brass, copper, silver, 19th-20th C china including Art Deco; general decorative items, all £5-£500.* PARK: Easy. TEL: 01252 843393; mobile - 083 734838.

Cedar Antiques Limited

High St. RG27 8NY. (Derek and Sally Green). Est. 1964. Open 9-5.30. SIZE: Large. *STOCK: Fine English oak, walnut and country furniture, 17th-18th C, £50-£10,000; French provincial furniture, 1680-1780, £800-£5,000; steel and brasswork, £30-£1,000.* Not Stocked: China, glass, silver. LOC: A30. PARK: Opposite. TEL: 01252 843252; fax - 01252 845235. SER: Valuations; restorations (period furniture); interior design and furnishing. VAT: Stan/Spec.

'artley Wintney continued

'ryan Clisby Antique Clocks

Andwells Antiques, High St. RG27 8NY. Est. 976. Open 9.30-5.30. SIZE: Large. *STOCK: ongcase clocks, 1700-1830, £1,500-£15,000; arometers, 1770-1850, £350-£3,000; bracket, all and mantel clocks.* LOC: A30 village centre. ARK: Easy. TEL: 01252 716436. SER: Valu-ions; restorations (clocks and barometers). AT: Spec.

eva Antiques

igh St. RG27 8NY. (A. Gratwick). Open 9-5.30. IZE: Large. *STOCK: 18th-19th C English*

Hartley Wintney continued

mahogany and walnut furniture. PARK: Easy. TEL: 01252 843538/843656; fax - 01252 842946. VAT: Stan/Spec.

Colin Harris Antiques

at Deva, High St. Est. 1966. Open 9-5.30. *STOCK: General antiques, mainly furniture and small decorative items, 18th-19th C, £20-£3,000.* LOC: A30. PARK: Easy. TEL: 01252 843538; home - 01734 732580. FAIRS: NEC (April and August). VAT: Spec.

Hartley Wintney continued

David Lazarus Antiques BADA

High St. RG27 8NS. Resident. Est. 1973. Open 9.30-5.30; some Sundays, other times by appointment. SIZE: Medium. *STOCK: 17th to early 19th C English and Continental furniture; objets d'art.* LOC: Main street. PARK: Own. TEL: 01252 842272. VAT: Stan/Spec.

Millon Antiques

Corner House, London Rd., Phoenix Green. RG27 8RT. (J.D. Millon-Milovanovich). Open 9.30-5. SIZE: Medium. *STOCK: English furniture, 1700-1850.* TEL: 01252 845442. VAT: Spec.

Old Forge Cottage Antiques

The Green. RG27 8PG. (Sue Carpenter). Open Tues., Thurs., Fri. and Sat. 10-4, other days by appointment. SIZE: Medium. *STOCK: Country and general antiques.* LOC: A30. PARK: Easy. TEL: 01252 842916.

Phoenix Green Antiques

London Rd. RG27 8RT. (J. Biles). Open 9.30-5.30, Sat. 10-5 or by appointment. SIZE: Large. *STOCK: English and Continental country furniture, Georgian mahogany, 18th-19th C.* TEL: 01252 844430.

Hartley Wintney continued

A.W. Porter and Son

High St. RG27 8NY. (M.A. Porter). Est. 184 Open 9-5.30, Sat. 9-5. *STOCK: Clocks, silve jewellery, glass.* LOC: Opposite Lloyds Ban TEL: 01252 842676. SER: Restorations (clocks VAT: Stan/Spec.

Sheila Revell Antiques

at Deva, High St. RG27 8NY. Open 9-5.3 *STOCK: 18th-19th C decorative objects, sma furniture and collectors' items especially te caddies and boxes.* TEL: 01252 843538.

HAVANT

Antiques and Nice Things

40 North St. PO9 1PT. (M.T. Davis-Shaw). E 1965. Open 10-5. *STOCK: Paintings, prints, po celain, copper, brass, silver, Sheffield plate, sma furniture, maps, clocks, jewellery, glass.* LO Near station. PARK: Own. TEL: 01705 48493 home - 01243 372551. SER: Restorations.

HAYLING ISLAND

J. Morton Lee BAD

Cedar House, Bacon Lane. PO11 0DN. E 1984. Open by appointment. *STOCK: Wate colours, 18th-20th C, £50-£10,000.* PAR Easy. TEL: 01705 464444. SER: Valuation buys at auction; exhibitions in April and Se FAIRS: World of Watercolours, Harrogat BADA; Buxton; Olympia (June); NEC (Au Northern; Kensington; Barbican. VA Stan/Spec.

HORNDEAN

Goss and Crested China Centre and Goss Museum

62 Murray Rd. PO8 9JL. (N.J. Pine). Est. 19 SIZE: Medium. *STOCK: Goss, 1860-1930, £ £1,000; other heraldic china, Art Deco pott including Carlton ware, Charlotte Rhea Chamelion, 1890-1930, £1-£1,000.* PARK: Ea TEL: 01705 597440. SER: Valuations; buys auction (Goss). VAT: Stan.

HURSLEY, Nr. Winchester

Hursley Antiques

SO21 2JY. (S. Thorne). Coppersmith. Est. 19 Open 10-6. *STOCK: Pine.* LOC: 4 miles fr Winchester on Romsey Rd. PARK: Easy. T 01962 775488. SER: Restorations and repa (metalware).

LISS

Plestor Barn Antiques
Farnham Rd. GU33 6JQ. Open 9-5. SIZE: Large. *STOCK: Furniture, including upholstered, Victorian and Edwardian, shipping goods, pine; china and glass, copper and brass.* LOC: A325, 2 mins from A3 roundabout. TEL: 01730 893922.

LYMINGTON

Corfields Ltd
120 High St. SO41 9AQ. Open 9.15-5.30. SIZE: Large. *STOCK: English furniture, porcelain, English School watercolours and oil paintings.* TEL: 01590 673532; fax - 01590 678855. SER: Restorations. VAT: Stan/Spec.

Hughes and Smeeth Ltd
Gosport St. SO41 9BG. (P. Hughes and S. Smeeth). ABA. Est. 1976. Open 9.30-5. SIZE: Small. *STOCK: Antiquarian and secondhand books, maps and prints.* LOC: At bottom of High St. PARK: Nearby. TEL: 01590 676324. SER: Valuations; binding; framing. VAT: Stan.

Lymington Antiques Centre
76 High St. SO41 9AL. Open 10-5, Sat. 9-5. SIZE: 30 dealers. *STOCK: General antiques and books.* TEL: 01590 670934.

Barry Papworth
8 St. Thomas St. SO41 9NE. Est. 1960. Open 9-. SIZE: Small. *STOCK: Diamond jewellery, £50-4,000; silver, £25-£1,500; both 18th-19th C. Watches, 19th C, £50-£1,000.* LOC: A337 into town, bay window on left. TEL: 01590 676422. SER: Valuations; restorations. VAT: Stan/Spec.

Robert Perera Fine Art
9 St. Thomas St. SO41 9NB. (R.J.D. Perera). Open 10-1 and 2-5, lunch-times and Sun. by appointment. SIZE: Small. *STOCK: British paintings, 19th-20th C, £100-£5,000; occasional ceramics and sculpture, 19th-20th C, £50-£1,500.* LOC: Top (west) end of main shopping area. PARK: Easy. TEL: 01590 678230; home - 01590 73190.

Charles Wallrock - Wick Antiques
ath Rd. SO41 8NE. (Mr and Mrs C. Wallrock). Est. 1985. Open 10-1 and 2-5, including Sun. in summer. CL: Sat. pm in winter. SIZE: Medium. *STOCK: French and English furniture, 19th C, 1,000-£5,000; small 19th C, £300-£800; late 9th to early 20th C items, £70-£150.* LOC: On road at bottom of High St. towards yacht club and marina. PARK: Limited. TEL: 01590 677558; home - 01590 672515. SER: Valuations; restorations (furniture polishing, repairs, upholstery and -gilding); buys at auction. FAIRS: Olympia. VAT: Spec.

LYNDHURST

Lita Kaye of Lyndhurst
13 High St. SO43 7BB. (S. and S. Ferder). Est. 1947. Open 9.30-1 and 2.15-5. SIZE: Large. *STOCK: Furniture, clocks, 1690-1820; decorative porcelain, 19th C.* LOC: A35. PARK: 100yds. in High St. TEL: 01703 282337. VAT: Stan/Spec.

MORESTEAD, Nr. Winchester

Burgess Farm Antiques
SO21 1LZ. (N. Spencer-Brayn). Est. 1970. Open 9-5. SIZE: Large. *STOCK: Furniture, especially pine and country, 18th-19th C, £25-£5,000; architectural items - doors, panelling, fire-places.* LOC: 2 miles south of Winchester, off Corehampton road at Jackmans Hill corner. PARK: Easy. TEL: 01962 777546. SER: Stripping; export. VAT: Stan/Spec.

ODIHAM

Monaltrie Antiques
76 High St. RG25 1LN. (Mrs W. Helmore). Est. 1972. Open 10-12.30 Tues.-Sat. and 2.30-4 Tues., Thurs. and Fri. SIZE: Medium. *STOCK: Furniture, £250-£1,500; copper and brass, £50-£250; silver and collectables, £50-£300; all 18th-19th C.* LOC: 1.5 miles junction 5, M3. PARK: Easy. TEL: 01256 702660; home - same. SER: Valuations; buys at auction.

The Odiham Gallery LAPADA
78 High St. (I. Walker). Open 10-5, Sat. 10-1. *STOCK: Decorative and Oriental rugs and carpets.* TEL: 01256 703415.

PETERSFIELD

The Barn
Station Rd. GU31 4AH. (P. Gadsden). Est. 1956. Open 9-5. *STOCK: Victoriana, bric-a-brac; also large store of trade and shipping goods.* TEL: 01730 262958. VAT: Stan.

Cull Antiques LAPADA
62 Station Rd. GU32 3ES. (J. Cull). Est. 1978. Open 10-5.30 (closed lunchtimes) or by appointment. *STOCK: 18th C English furniture and metalwork.* TEL: 01730 263670.

The Folly Antiques Centre
Folly Market, College St. GU31 4AD. (Philip Rose Ltd). Est. 1980. Open 9.30-5.30. SIZE: Medium. *STOCK: Furniture, 17th-20th C, £100-£1,000; ceramics and silver, 18th-20th C, £5-£100; clocks, 19th-20th C, £50-£1,000; pictures, general.* LOC: Town centre. PARK: Nearby. TEL: 01730 265937; home - 01730 269370.

Petersfield continued

The Petersfield Bookshop **BADA**
16a Chapel St. GU32 3DS. (F. Westwood). ABA. Est. 1918. Open 9-5.30. SIZE: Large. *STOCK: Books, old and modern, £1-£500; maps and prints, 1600-1859, £1-£200; oils and watercolours, 19th C, £20-£1,000.* LOC: Chapel St. runs from the Square to Station Rd. PARK: Opposite. TEL: 01730 263438. SER: Restorations and rebinding of old leather books; picture-framing and mount-cutting. FAIRS: Buxton and London ABA. VAT: Stan.

PORTSMOUTH

Affordable Antiques
89 Albert Rd., Southsea. PO5 2SG. (Max Gosling). Est. 1987. Open 10.30-3, Sat. 9.30-5. SIZE: Medium. *STOCK: Furniture, Victorian, Edwardian and 1930's, £2-£5,000.* LOC: Near Kings Theatre. PARK: Easy. TEL: 01705 293344/ 421993. SER: Valuations.

Affordable Pine
52 Albert Rd., Southsea. PO5 2SJ. (Una Gosling). Est. 1995. Open 10.30-3, Sat. 9.30-5. SIZE: Medium. *STOCK: Victorian pine and satinwoods, teapots, £5-£1,000.* Not Stocked: Reproduction. LOC: Nr. King's Theatre. PARK: Easy. TEL: 01705 340044/421993.

A. Fleming (Southsea) Ltd
The Clock Tower, Castle Rd. PO5 3DE. Est. 1905. Open 9.30-5. CL: Sat. pm. *STOCK: Furniture, silver, china, general antiques, jewellery.* TEL: 01705 822934. SER: Restorations. VAT: Stan/Spec.

The Gallery
11 and 19 Marmion Rd., Southsea. PO5 2AT. (I. Murphy). Open 10-5. *STOCK: At No.19 - Victorian chairs and chesterfields; at No.11 - furniture, mainly Victorian and Edwardian.* PARK: Nearby. TEL: 01705 822016.

Oldfield Gallery
76 Elm Grove, Southsea. PO5 1LN. Est. 1970. Open 10-5. CL: Mon. SIZE: Large. *STOCK: Maps and engravings, 16th-19th C, £5-£1,000; decorative prints and some paintings, 19th-20th C, £5-£1,000.* PARK: Easy. TEL: 01705 838042; fax - 01705 838042. SER: Valuations; restorations (maps and prints); framing. FAIRS: Bonnington Hotel Map (monthly). VAT: Stan.

Portsmouth Stamp Shop
184 Chichester Rd., North End. PO2 0AX. (G. Coast). Est. 1967. Open 9.15-5.30. *STOCK: Stamps, coins, cigarette cards, banknotes.* TEL: 01705 663450. VAT: Stan.

Portsmouth continued

Times Past
141 Highland Rd., Southsea. PO4 9EY. (S. New) Open 10-4, Wed. by appointment. *STOCK: General antiques and shipping goods.* TEL: 01705 822701; mobile - 0831 418488.

Wessex Medical Antiques
77 Carmarthen Ave. PO6 2AG. (Dr. D.J. Warren) Est. 1984. Open by appointment. SIZE: Medium *STOCK: Medical items, 17th-19th C, £50-£10,000.* LOC: Off Havant Rd., Drayton. PARK: Easy. TEL: 01705 376518; home - same; fax 01705 201479. SER: Free catalogue; valuations; buys at auction (as stock). FAIRS: Scientific and Medical, Portman Hotel, London. VAT: Stan.

RINGWOOD

Millers of Chelsea Antiques Ltd
LAPADA
Netherbrook House, 86 Christchurch Rd. BH24 1DR. BDADA. Est. 1897. Open 9-5.30, Sat. 10-4, other times by appointment. SIZE: Large. *STOCK: Furniture - English and Continental country, mahogany and gilt, military, decorative items, treen, majolica and fäience, 18th-19th C, £25-£3,000.* LOC: On B3347 towards Christchurch. PARK: Own. TEL: 01425 472062; fax - 01425 47272[illegible] FAIRS: Decorative Antiques; Kensington Antique Fairs. VAT: Stan/Spec.

Smith & Sons
104 Christchurch Rd. BH24 1DR. (D.R. and G.[illegible] Smith). Est. 1978. Open 9.30-5.30. SIZE: Large and warehouse. *STOCK: Pine and other woods, 18th-19th C, £30-£1,000; model railways, 19th-20th C, from £5; Chinese furniture.* Not Stocked: Silver, fine china, bric-a-brac. LOC: Almost opposite fire station. PARK: Own. TEL: 0142[illegible] 476705; home - same. SER: Restorations. VAT: Stan.

ROMSEY

Bell Antiques
8 Bell St. SO51 8GA. (M. and B.M. Gay). FGA. Est. 1979. Open 9.30-5.30. CL: Wed. pm (winter). SIZE: Large. *STOCK: Jewellery and silver, glass, pottery, porcelain, small furniture, prints and maps, mainly 19th and 20th C.* LOC: Near market place. PARK: Town centre. TEL: 01794 514719. VAT: Global/Stan/Spec.

Cambridge Antiques **LAPADA**
5 Bell St. SO51 8GY. Open 8.30-5.30. SIZE: Large. *STOCK: Furniture, small china, jewellery, paintings.* LOC: From the West, Romsey by-pass, left into Palmerston St., first left then first right, 100yds. on left. PARK: Nearby. TEL: 01794 512885/523089/512069. VAT: Stan/Spec.

Romsey continued

Lacewing Fine Art Gallery
4 Tee Court, Bell St. SO51 8GY. (N. James). Open 10-5. CL: Wed. *STOCK: Paintings, watercolours and sculpture, 16th-20th C, £200-£10,000.* TEL: 01794 523443; fax - same.

"Old Cottage Things"
Broxmore Park, Sherfield English. SO5 6FU. (R. Comport). Est. 1970. *STOCK: Original building, architectural and garden materials; old pine country kitchens and furniture.* LOC: A27. TEL: 01794 884538.

Romsey Medal and Collectors Centre
5 Bell St. SO51 8GY. (T. Cambridge, OMRS). Est. 1980. Open 9-5.30. *STOCK: Medals, badges, militaria, and commemorative china.* LOC: From the west, Romsey by-pass, left into Palmerston St., first left then first right, 100yds. on left. PARK: Nearby. TEL: 01794 512069/512885; fax 01794 830332.

SOUTHAMPTON

Mr. Alfred's "Old Curiosity Shop" and The Morris Gallery (Fine Art Dealer, Valuer, Curator & Restorer)
280 Shirley Rd., Shirley. SO15 3HL. Est. 1952. Open 9-6, including Sun. *STOCK: Furniture, 18th-20th C; paintings, porcelain, bronzes, brass, glass, books, silver, jewellery and general antiques.* LOC: On left of main Shirley road, 3/4 mile from Southampton central station. PARK: Easy. TEL: 01703 774772.

Meg Campbell
10 Church Lane, Highfield. SO17 1SZ. Est. 1967. Open by appointment only. *STOCK: English, Scottish and Irish silver, collectors' pieces, Old Sheffield plate, portrait miniatures.* TEL: 01703 557636. SER: Mail order; catalogues available. VAT: Spec.

H.M. Gilbert and Son
2 1/2 Portland St. SO1 0EB. (R.C. and A.M. Gilbert). ABA. Est. 1859. Open 9-5. *STOCK: Antiquarian and secondhand books, £1-£500.* PARK: Easy. TEL: 01703 226420. SER: Valuations; bookbinding; repairs.

J. Moody
0 Bedford Place. SO15 2DS. (J. and A.H. Gubb). Est. 1905. Open 9-5. CL: Wed. pm. SIZE: Large. *STOCK: Furniture, 1650-1910; silver, porcelain, to 1900.* LOC: Half mile north of Civic Centre. PARK: 50yds. in next block. TEL: 01703 333720. SER: Valuations. VAT: Stan/Spec.

Parkhouse and Wyatt Ltd
6 Above Bar. SO9 4FF. Est. 1794. SIZE: Small. *STOCK: Silver, jewellery.* LOC: City centre. PARK: Pay & display and multi-storey. TEL: 01703 226653 ext. 25. SER: Valuations; repairs.

Southampton continued

Relics Antiques
54 Northam Rd. (R.M. Simmonds). Open 9-5. *STOCK: General antiques.* TEL: 01703 221635.

STOCKBRIDGE

George Hofman Antiques at the Sign of the Black Cat
Brookside, High St. SO20 6EY. Est. 1973. Open 10-5.30, Wed. 10-3, or by appointment. SIZE: Medium. *STOCK: General antiques, furniture, soft furnishings, fabrics and decorative items.* LOC: A30. PARK: At rear. TEL: 01264 810570; home - same. VAT: Stan/Spec.

Lane Antiques
High St. SO20 6EU. (E.K. Lane). Est. 1981. Open 10-5. CL: Wed. SIZE: Small. *STOCK: English and Continental porcelain, 18th-19th C; silver and plate, decorative items, glass, small furniture.* PARK: Easy. TEL: 01264 810435.

Stockbridge Antique Centre
Old London Rd. SO20 6EJ. (Peter Rogers). Est. 1962. Open 10-5.30. SIZE: Large. *STOCK: Furniture - mahogany, oak and pine, 18th-20th C, £50-£2,000; decorative items, silver and plate.* LOC: On White Hart public house roundabout. PARK: Easy. TEL: 01264 810632; fax - same. SER: Restorations (silver and jewellery). VAT: Stan/Spec.

Elizabeth Viney BADA
Jacob's House, High St. SO20 6HF. (Miss E.A. Viney MBE). Est. 1967. Open 9-5, appointment advisable Mon. and Wed. CL: Sun except by appointment. SIZE: Small. *STOCK: Period furniture - mahogany, walnut, oak and country; treen, brass and copper, especially candlesticks.* Not Stocked: Victoriana. LOC: A30. Opposite old Post Office. PARK: Easy. TEL: 01264 810761. VAT: Stan/Spec.

TADLEY

Gasson Antiques and Interiors LAPADA
P O Box 7225. RG26 5IY. Open by appointment. *STOCK: Georgian, Victorian and Edwardian furniture, clocks, porcelain and decorative items.* TEL: 01189 813636; mobile - 0860 827651.

TITCHFIELD, Nr. Fareham

Alexanders
13 South St. PO14 4DL. Open Thurs.-Sat. 10-6. *STOCK: General antiques including Art Nouveau and Art Deco.* PARK: Easy. TEL: 01329 315962. SER: Restorations (furniture); silver and chrome plating.

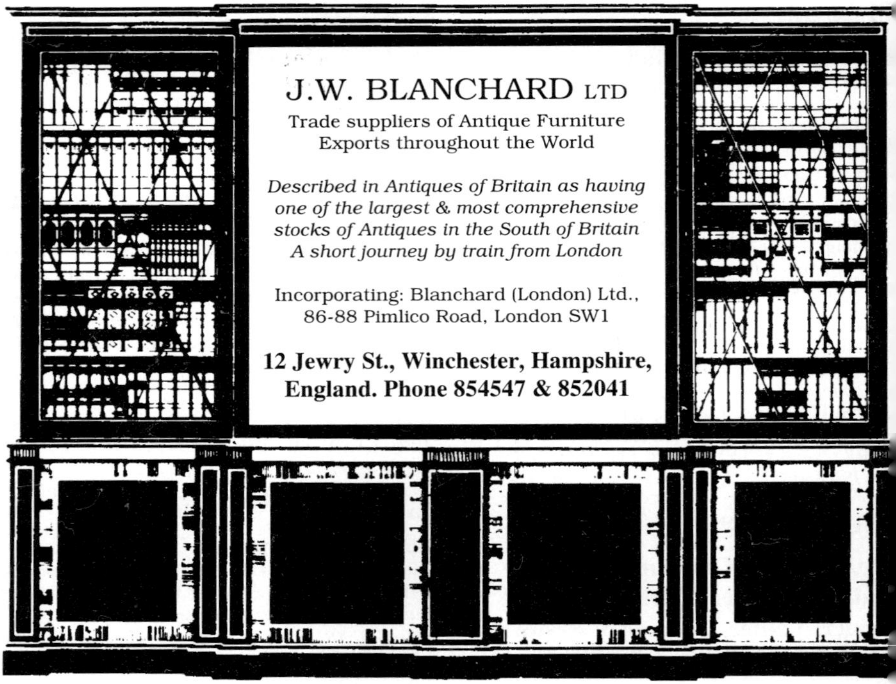

Titchfield continued

Gaylords

75 West St. PO14 4DG. (I. Hebbard). Est. 1970. Open 9.30-5.30. SIZE: Large. *STOCK: Furniture, from 18th C; clocks, £50-£10,000.* LOC: Junc. 9 off M27. PARK: Easy. TEL: 01329 843402; home - 01329 847134. SER: Valuations. VAT: Stan/Spec.

Robin Howard Antiques

6 & 8 South St. PO14 4DJ. Open Tues.-Sat. SIZE: Small. *STOCK: Antique and modern jewellery, silver and plate, boxes and small collectables, £10-£500.* LOC: ¼ mile from A27. PARK: Easy. TEL: 01329 842794. SER: Valuations.

TWYFORD, Nr. Winchester

Twyford Antiques

High St. SO21 1NH. Open 9.30-5.30. SIZE: Large. *STOCK: Clocks, furniture.* TEL: 01962 713484. SER: Valuations; restorations (clocks).

UPHAM, Nr. Southampton

Susanna Fisher

Spencer. SO3 1JD. Est. 1971. Open by appointment only. *STOCK: Navigational charts and sailing directions, 16th-19th C.* TEL: 01489 860291; fax - 01489 860638. SER: Buys at auction; catalogues available. *Mainly Postal.*

WICKHAM, Nr. Fareham

Bridge House Antique Centre

Bridge St. PO17 5JH. (Barry and Jan Mapson Est. 1995. Open 10.30-5.30 including Sun. Cl Mon. SIZE: Large - several dealers. *STOCK Wide variety of general antiques includin furniture, clocks, paintings, porcelain, silver an jewellery, Art Deco, kitchenalia, collectable from Georgian to Edwardian and later.* LOC: In Bridge St. from A32, premises 50 yards, adjace to river. PARK: Wickham Sq. TEL: 0132 833079; fax - same. VAT: Stan/Spec.

WINCHESTER

Bell Fine Art

67b Parchment St. SO23 8AT. (K.E. and B. Bel Open 9.30-5.30. *STOCK: Victorian watercolou and oils, prints, £5-£5,000.* TEL: 01962 86043 fax - same; home - 01962 733556. SER: Val ations; restorations (oils and watercolours); bu at auction. VAT: Spec.

J.W. Blanchard Ltd LAPAD

12 Jewry St. SO23 8RZ. Est. 1940. Open 9- SIZE: Large. *STOCK: 18th and 19th C boo cases and dining room furniture.* PARK: Ow TEL: 01962 854547/852041; fax - 019 842572. VAT: Stan/Spec.

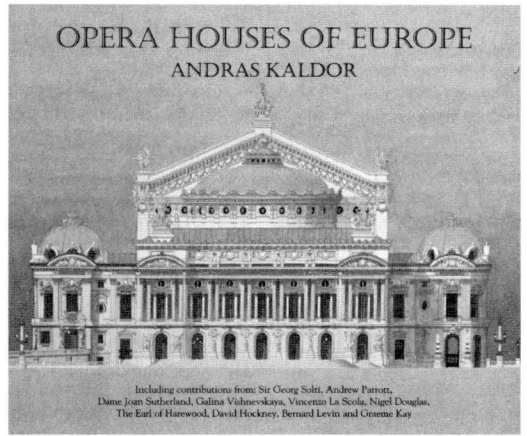

Winchester continued

Burns and Graham

27 St. Thomas St. SO23 9HJ . (M. and G. Rollitt). Est. 1971. Open 9.30-5.30, or by appointment. *STOCK: English furniture, mirrors, period decorative items, 1680-1840.* LOC: Town centre. PARK: At rear. TEL: 01962 853779. SER: Valuations. VAT: Stan/Spec.

Cabbages & Kings

20a Jewry St. SO23 8RZ. Open 9.30-5. SIZE: Large. *STOCK: 18th, 19th C, and some later furniture, pine, pictures, old woodworking tools, architectural artefacts, unusual and decorative items, porcelain, weapons, collectors items, smalls, shipping goods.* TEL: 01962 852363; fax - 01962 855763.

Clockwise

69 Parchment St. SO23 8AT. (D. Judge). AHS. GMC. Est. 1976. Open daily. SIZE: Medium. *STOCK: Longcase, wall, mantle, bracket and carriage clocks, 18th-19th C, £300-£6,000; barometers, books and tools.* LOC: Central, off main pedestrian precinct, near Smiths. PARK: Easy. TEL: 01962 842331; 01243 377558. SER: Valuations; restorations (clocks and barometers).

Peter M. Daly

Rear of Cabbages and Kings, 20a Jewry St. SO23 8RZ. PBFA. Open Wed., Fri. and Sat. 10-5. *STOCK: Rare and secondhand books; some pictures and prints, maps.* TEL: Home - 01962 867732.

H.M. Gilbert

19 The Square. SO23 9EY. (R.C. and A.M. Gilbert). ABA. Open 9-5.30. *STOCK: Antiquarian and secondhand books, £1-£1,000.* TEL: 01962 852832. SER: Valuations; repairs; rebinding.

G.E. Marsh Antique Clocks Ltd BADA

32a The Square. SO23 9EX. Est. 1947. Open 9.30-5, Sat. 9.30-1 and 2-5. *STOCK: English clocks, watches and barometers c1680-1880, including longcase, bracket, French and Continental.* LOC: Near Cathedral. PARK: Easy. TEL: 01962 844443; fax - same. SER: Saleroom valuations; restorations; commissions.

The Pine Cellars

39 Jewry St. and 7 Upper Brook St. SO23 8RY. (N. Spencer-Brayn). Est. 1970. Open 10-5. SIZE: Large and warehouses. *STOCK: Pine and country furniture, 18th-19th C, £10-£5,000; painted furniture, architectural items, panelled rooms.* LOC: One way street, a right turn from top of High St. or St. Georges St., shop 100yds. on right. Brook St. premises - opposite Brooks Shopping Centre. PARK: Nearby. TEL: 01962 867014/ 777546/870102. SER: Stripping and export. VAT: Stan/Spec.

Winchester continued

Printed Page

2/3 Bridge St. SO23 9BH. CL: Mon. SIZE Small. *STOCK: Maps and prints, 17th-19th C, £5 £500.* LOC: Bottom of High St., cross over rive and shop is on left. PARK: Chesil St. car par close to shop. TEL: 01962 854072; fax - 0196 862995. SER: Framing (pictures, tapestries medals, etc). VAT: Stan.

Mary Roofe Antiques

1 Stonemason's Court, 67 Parchment St. SO2 8AT. (R. and M. Roofe). Est. 1983. Open 10-5 Mon. by appointment. SIZE: Small. *STOCK 18th-19th C furniture, boxes, Tunbridgeware treen, small collectors' items, £5-£2,500.* LOC 200yds. from High St. and Buttercross. TEL 01962 840613; home - 01962 862619.

Samuels Spencers Antiques and Decorative Arts Emporium

39 Jewry St. SO23 8RY. (N. Spencer-Brayn). Ope 10-5. SIZE: 31 dealers. *STOCK: General antique* LOC: One way street, right turn from top of Hig St. or St. George St., shop 100yds. on right. PARK Nearby. TEL: 01962 867014/777546.

SPCK Bookshops

24 The Square. SO23 9EX. Open 9-5.30. *STOCK Books including antiquarian.* TEL: 0196 866617.

Todd and Austin Antiques of Winchester

2 Andover Rd. SO23 7BS. (G. Austin). Est. 196 Open by appointment only. SIZE: Mediun *STOCK: 19th C paperweights, silver tea caddie boxes, objets d'art and decorative items.* LOC: minute from Winchester Station. PARK: Eas TEL: 01962 869824. SER: Selected range o view at Lainston House Hotel, Sparsholt, N Winchester; finder service.

Webb Fine Arts

38 Jewry St. SO23 8RY . (D.H. Webb). Est. 195 Open 9-5, Sat. 9-1. SIZE: Large - 4 floor *STOCK: Oil paintings and furniture.* PARK Own. TEL: 01962 842273. SER: Valuation restorations (oil paintings); lining and framin buys at auction (paintings). VAT: Stan/Spec.

Herefordshire

○	1–2	Key to number of shops in this area.
⊖	3–5	
◒	6–12	
●	13+	

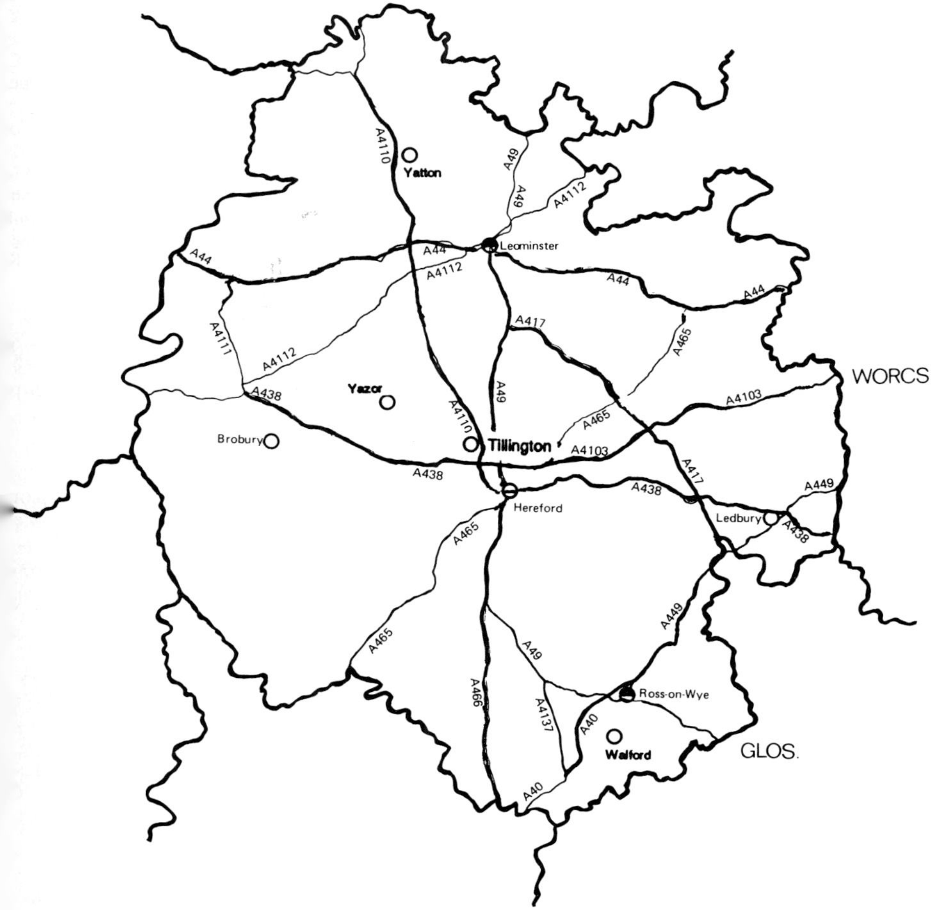

N

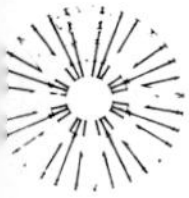

Please note this is only a rough map designed to show dealers the number of shops in the various towns, and is not necessarily totally accurate.

BROBURY, Nr. Hay-on-Wye

Brobury House Gallery

HR3 6BS. (E. Okarma). Resident. Est. 1972. Open 9-4.30, 9-4 in winter. *STOCK: Old prints, 17th-20th C; watercolours, 19th-20th C.* PARK: Easy. TEL: 01981 500229. SER: Restorations (framing). VAT: Stan.

HEREFORD

I. and J.L. Brown Ltd

58-59 Commercial Rd. HR1 2BP. Open 8-5.30. SIZE: Large. *STOCK: Matched sets of period country chairs, £500-£4,000; English country and French provincial furniture, decorative items.* LOC: A465, 300 metres from railway station, 100 metres from city ring road. PARK: 2 minutes walk from shop. TEL: 01432 358895; fax - 01432 275338; home - 01432 840674. SER: Restorations; re-rushing chairs. VAT: Stan/Spec.

Great Brampton House Antiques Ltd

LAPADA

Great Brampton House, Madley. HR2 9NA. (Lady Pidgeon). Est. 1969. Open 9-5 or by appointment. SIZE: Large. *STOCK: English and French furniture and fine art.* TEL: 01981 250244; fax - 01981 251333.

Hereford Antique Centre

128 Widemarsh St. HR4 9HN. (L. F. Mitchell). Est. 1991. Open 9-5, Sun. 1-5. SIZE: 30 dealers. *STOCK: General antiques and collectables.* PARK: Easy. TEL: 01432 266242. SER: Restorations; shipping.

Warings of Hereford Antiques

47 St. Owen St. HR1 2JB. (R. Waring). Open 9-6 including Sun. *STOCK: Fine 19th C furniture, farmhouse pine; gold and silver.* TEL: 01432 276241.

LEDBURY

John Nash Antiques and Interiors

LAPADA

Tudor House, 17c High St. HR8 1DS. (J. Nash and L. Calleja). Est. 1972. Open 10-5.30, Sun. by appointment. SIZE: Medium. *STOCK: Mahogany, oak and walnut furniture, 18th-20th C, £300-£10,000; decorative items, fabrics and wallpapers.* TEL: 01531 635714; fax - 01531 635050; home - 01684 540432. SER: Valuations; restorations; buys at auction (furniture, silver). VAT: Stan/Spec.

Ledbury continued

Serendipity

The Tythings, Preston Court. HR8 2LL. (Mrs R Ford). Open 9-5 or by appointment. SIZE: Large *STOCK: 17th-20th C furniture and genera antiques.* LOC: Take A449 for 3 miles fror Ledbury, at roundabout turn left on B4215 premises 500yds. on left behind half-timbere house. TEL: 01531 660245/660380. SER: Restor ations (furniture); buys at auction. FAIRS Kensington; Olympia. VAT: Stan/Spec.

LEOMINSTER

Barometer Shop

New St. HR6 8BT. (R. Cookson). Est. 1965. Ope 9-5 or by appointment. *STOCK: Barometers barographs, clocks, scientific instruments, perio furniture.* LOC: Corner of A49 and Broad S PARK: Easy. TEL: 01568 613652/610200. SER Valuations; restorations (workshop on th Register of the Conservation Unit of the Museum and Galleries Commission); barometers and cloc spares.

Coltsfoot Gallery

Hatfield. HR6 0SF. (Edwin Collins). Est. 197 SIZE: Medium. *STOCK: Sporting and wildlif watercolours and prints, £20-£2,000.* PARK Easy. TEL: 01568 760277; home - same. SER Restoration and conservation of works of art o paper; mounting; framing.

Courts Miscellany

48A Bridge St. Open 10.30-5. *STOCK: Genera curios including corkscrews, social and politica history, police, fire brigade and sporting items tools, horse brasses, enamel signs - advertising military, brewery; studio pottery and commemo atives.* TEL: 01565 612995.

P. and S.N. Eddy

22 Etnam St. HR6 8AQ. Resident. Est. 195 Open 9-6. CL: Sun. except by appointment. SIZE Small. *STOCK: Oak and mahogany furniture saltglaze stoneware, 18th C brass and coppe early metalware, treen and bygones.* Not Stocke Arms, armour, coins, medals, jewellery. LOC A44. PARK: Easy. TEL: 01568 612813; home same.

Farmers Gallery

1 High St. SIZE: 6 galleries. *STOCK: 18th-19th furniture, paintings, prints, maps, frames, needl work, porcelain and decorative items.* LOC Town centre. PARK: Easy. TEL: 01568 61141 fax - 01568 611141. SER: Exhibition galler available.

eominster continued

effery Hammond Antiques LAPADA
Shaftesbury House', 38 Broad St. HR6 8BS. J. and E. Hammond). Resident. Est. 1970.)pen 9-6, Sun. by appointment. SIZE: Medium. *TOCK: Furniture and works of art, 18th to arly 19th C.* LOC: Town centre. PARK: Own. 'EL: 01568 614876; fax - same; internet - ttp://www.entrepreneurs.net/ creative-ye/jhshop.htm. SER: Valuations; buys at uction (furniture). VAT: Stan/Spec.

Iubbard Antiques LAPADA
'he Golden Lion, Bridge St. HR6 8DU. (D. T. nd P. Saunders). Resident. Open 9-5, other-'ise ring door bell. *STOCK: 16th-18th C oak urniture, especially dressers and coffers; opper, 18th-19th C; patchwork quilts.* LOC: orth side of town, just off by-pass. PARK: wn. TEL: 01568 614362.

,eominster Antiques Market
4 Broad St. Open 10-5. SIZE: 15 traders - 3 oors. *STOCK: General antiques including 'ountry and painted furniture, mahogany, oak, ine, treen, Staffordshire, pottery, porcelain, xtiles, pictures, metalware, jewellery, clocks, rchitectural antiques and shipping items.* TEL: 1568 612189.

OSS-ON-WYE

aileys Architectural Antiques
'he Engine Shed, Ashburton Industrial Estate. R9 7BW. (M. and S. Bailey). Est. 1978. Open 9-. SIZE: Medium. *STOCK: Garden tools and rniture, French and English lighting, pews, apel chairs, ironwork, dressers, tables, cast on fireplaces, marble and wood surrounds, irrors, tiles, bathroom taps, baths and basins, tchen sinks, buckets, apple boxes, flower pots, ugs, pictures and planters.* LOC: Gloucester de of Ross, just off A40. TEL: 01989 563015; x - 01989 768172.

ritz Fryer Antique Lighting
2 Brookend St. HR9 7EG. (F. Fryer and J. raham). Est. 1981. Open 10-5.30, Sun. by ppointment. SIZE: Large. *STOCK: Decorative ghting, original shades, Georgian to Art Deco.* EL: 01989 567416; fax - 01989 567742. SER: estorations; lighting scheme design.

obin Lloyd Antiques
3/24 Brookend St. HR9 7EE. Est. 1970. Open 30-5.30. SIZE: Large. *STOCK: Country oak, 7th-19th C, especially dressers, gatelegs, 'indsors; farmhouse tables, longcase clocks, ndlesticks, metalware, blue & white pottery; moires, £5-£10,000.* LOC: 100yds. downhill

Ross-on-Wye continued

from Market Hall. PARK: Nearby. TEL: 01989 562123; fax - same. SER: Restorations (furniture, oil paintings, metalware and long case clocks). VAT: Global/Spec.

Relics
19 High St. HR9 5BZ. (Mr and Mrs I. Power). Open 10-5. CL: Wed. *STOCK: Jewellery, linen, silver, clocks, smalls and furniture.* TEL: 01989 564539. SER: Restorations and repairs (clocks and jewellery).

Ross Old Book and Print Shop
51 and 52 High St. HR9 5HH. Open 10-5. *STOCK: Antiquarian and secondhand books, prints and maps.* TEL: 01989 567458.

Singleton Antiques
29-30 Brookend St. HR9 7EF. (J.W. & A.A. Chapman). Est. 1994. Open 9.30-5.30. SIZE: Medium. *STOCK: Oak, 17th-19th C, £500-£5,000; country furniture, 18th-19th C, £100-£2,000; decorative items and pictures, 19th-20th C, £10-£2,000.* LOC: Main shopping street. PARK: Easy. TEL: 01989 763400; fax - 01989 763200. SER: Valuations. VAT: Stan/Spec.

Ross-on-Wye continued

Trecilla Antiques
36 High St. HR9 5HD. (Lt. Col. and Mrs I.G. Mathews). Est. 1969. Open 9.30-5. CL: Sun. and Wed pm., except by appointment. SIZE: Large. *STOCK: Furniture, longcase clocks, all periods; arms and armour, £50-£7,500; silver, china, glass, metalware, £10-£3,000; prints, maps, militaria and bygones, £1-£500.* LOC: A40. PARK: Private. TEL: 01989 563010; home - 01981 540274. SER: Valuations; restorations; buys at auction. VAT: Stan/Spec.

TILLINGTON, Nr. Hereford

Chatelain Antique Beds and Mirrors
Whitmore Cross. HR4 8LE. (J. R. Jennings and R. Kingsley-Taylor). Est. 1970. Open Wed.-Sat. 10-5 or by appointment. SIZE: Medium. *STOCK: 17th-20th C beds and giltwood mirrors, £500-£3,000.* PARK: Easy. TEL: 01432 760034; fax - 01432 350389. SER: Valuations; restorations. VAT: Stan/Spec.

WALFORD, Nr. Ross-on-Wye

Old Pine Shop
Warryfield Barn. HR9 5QW. Open 10-5 or by appointment. SIZE: Large. *STOCK: Pine furniture, especially dressers, chests, tables, desks,*

Walford continued

blanket boxes, wardrobes, linen presses; Vic torian brass and iron bedsteads. LOC: Approx. miles from Ross town. TEL: 01989 566331 workshop - 01989 768278. SER: Restorations.

Robson Antiques
Little Howle Farm, Howle Hill. HR9 5SL. (Robson). Est. 1982. Open daily including Sun SIZE: Large. *STOCK: Furniture, from 18th C £50-£5000.* PARK: Easy. TEL: 01989 768128 home - same. SER: Valuations; buys at auction.

YATTON, Nr. Leominster

Moreden Prints
(B. Croxton). Open by appointment. *STOCK Antiquarian and collectable prints and maps* TEL: 01568 770549. SER: Book and print search mount cutting.

YAZOR

M. and J. Russell
The Old Vicarage. HR4 7BA. Est. 1969. Usuall open Fri. to Mon. and evenings, other time appointment advisable. *STOCK: English perio oak and country furniture, some garden antiques* LOC: 7 miles west of Hereford on A480. TEL 01981 590674. *Mainly Trade.*

Hertfordshire

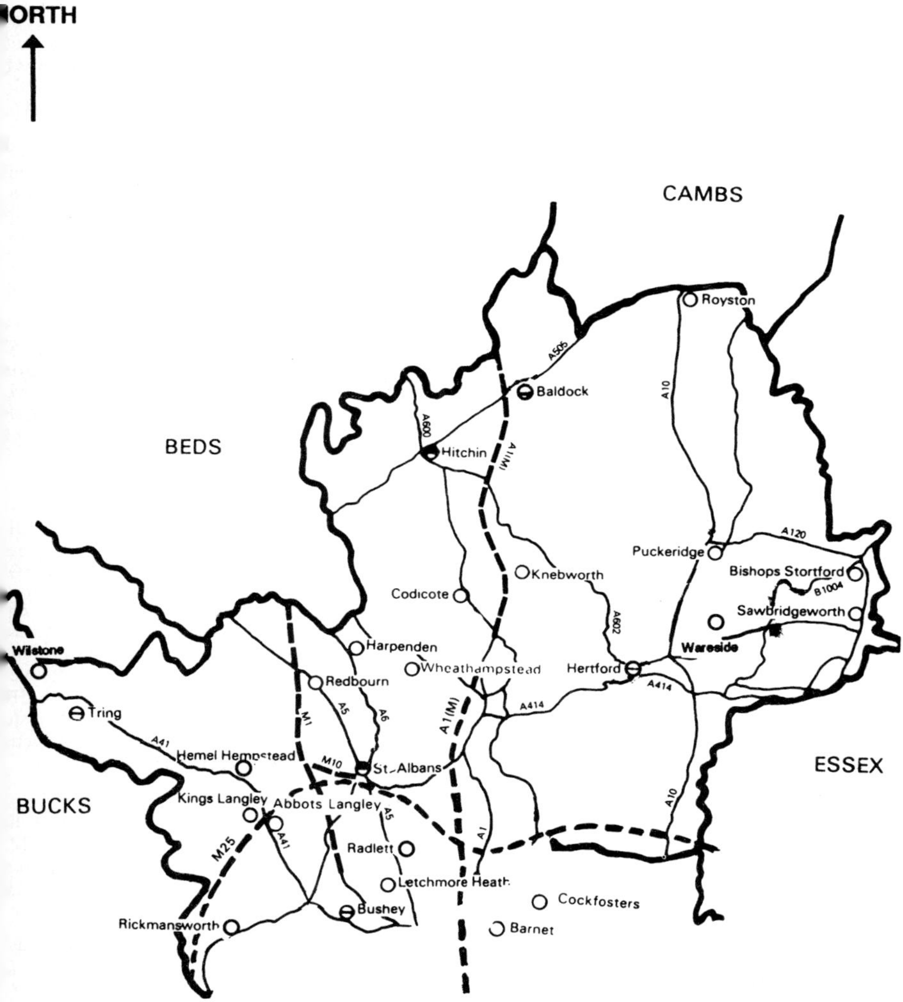

2 , 5, 12, 4+ Key to number of shops in this area.

Please note this is only a rough map designed to show dealers the number of shops in the various towns, and is not necessarily totally accurate.

ABBOTS LANGLEY, Nr. Watford

Dobson's Antiques
53 High St. WD5 0AA. Est. 1926. Open 8.30-5.30. CL: Tues. pm. *STOCK: Carved oak, stripped pine, shipping goods, bric-a-brac, £5-£2,000.* LOC: 4 miles north of Watford. TEL: 01923 263186. VAT: Stan/Spec.

BALDOCK

The Attic
20 Whitehorse St. SG7 6QN. (P. Sheppard). Est. 1977. CL: Thurs. SIZE: Small. *STOCK: Small furniture, china, brass and copper, dolls and teddy bears, £5-£100.* LOC: 3 minutes from A1(M). PARK: Easy. TEL: 01462 893880.

Anthony Butt Antiques
7/9 Church St. SG7 5AE. Resident. Usually open. *STOCK: English furniture, 17th-19th C, £200-£3,000; works of art and objects of interest.* Not Stocked: Bric-a-brac, shipping goods. PARK: Easy. TEL: 01462 895272. SER: Valuations. VAT: Spec.

Howards
33 Whitehorse St. SG7 6QF. (D.N. Howard). Est. 1970. Open 9.30-5.00. CL: Mon. *STOCK: Clocks, 18th-19th C, £200-£5,000.* PARK: Easy. TEL: 01462 892385. SER: Valuations; restorations and repairs (clocks). VAT: Spec.

Ralph and Bruce Moss
26 Whitehorse St. SG7 6QQ. (R.A. and B.A. Moss). Est. 1973. Open 9-6. SIZE: Large. *STOCK: Furniture, £100-£10,000; general antiques, £5-£5,000.* LOC: A505, in town centre. PARK: Own. TEL: 01462 892751. VAT: Stan/Spec.

The Wheelwright
1 Mansfield Rd. SG7 6EB. (E. and L. Hurst). Resident. Est. 1976. Open 9.30-5.30. CL: Thurs. SIZE: Medium. *STOCK: Small porcelain and china, jewellery, small furniture, bric-a-brac, 19th C, £5-£500.* LOC: Off A1. PARK: Easy. TEL: 01462 893876.

BARNET

C. Bellinger Antiques
91 Wood St. EN5 4BX. Est. 1974. Open Thurs., Fri. and Sat. 10-4 or by appointment. SIZE: Medium. *STOCK: Furniture, silver and plate, smalls.* LOC: Opposite Ravenscroft Park. PARK: Within 100yds. TEL: 0181 449 3467. VAT: Stan/Spec.

BERKHAMSTED

Gossoms End Antiques
Entreat, Gossoms End. (David White). Est. 1970. Open 10-6 including Sun. SIZE: Small. *STOCK:*

Berkhamsted continued

Furniture and decorative items, £50-£2,00 mirrors, books, pine, china, glass, toys, sporti relics and collectibles, £5-£2,000; oil painting watercolours and prints, £25-£2,000; all 18t 20th C. LOC: From junction 20, M25 onto A41 junction 8, M1 onto A414; through town Gossoms End. PARK: Easy. TEL: 01442 87878 home - same. SER: Valuations; restorations; bu at auction. FAIRS: Kensington Brocant Sandown Park. VAT: Stan/Spec.

BISHOP'S STORTFORD

The Windhill Antiquary
4 High St. CM23 2LT. (G.R. Crozier). Est. 195 Open 10-1 and 2-4, appointment advisable. C Wed. pm. SIZE: Medium. *STOCK: Engli furniture, 18th C; carved and gilded wall mirro 17th-19th C.* Not Stocked: Shipping goods. LO Next to George Hotel. PARK: Up hill - first rig TEL: 01279 651587; home - 01920 821316.

BUSHEY, Nr. Watford

Bushey Antique Centre
39 High St. WD2 1NB. (Graham Lindsay). E 1983. Open 9.30-5.30, Sun. 10-4.30. SIZE: dealers. *STOCK: Furniture, 18th-20th C, £5 £500; smalls, collectables, clocks, dolls a jewellery, £5-£250; fireplaces and chimn pieces, 18th-19th C, £160-£800.* LOC: Betwe Harrow and Watford. PARK: At rear. TEL: 01 950 5040; home - same. SER: Valuations; rest ations (woodwork and furniture); buys at aucti (furniture and fires). VAT: Spec.

Circa Antiques
43 High St., Bushey Village. (K. Wildman). E 1978. Open 9.30-5.30 or by appointment. SIZ Medium. *STOCK: General antiques, furnitu porcelain, silver and clocks.* TEL: 0181 950 923

Country Life Antiques
33a High St. WD2 1BDA. (Peter Myers). E 1981. Open 9-5. SIZE: Large. *STOCK: Victori and Edwardian, European and Scandinavi original pine, French country oak; kitchenal watercolours, china and Art Deco.* PARK: Ea TEL: 0181 950 8576. VAT: Stan.

Thwaites and Co
33 Chalk Hill, Oxhey. WD1 4BL. Est. 1971. Op 9-5, Sat. 9.30-12.30. *STOCK: Stringed instr ments, from violins to double basses.* TEL: 019 232412. SER: Restorations.

COCKFOSTERS

H. Pordes Ltd
383 Cockfosters Rd. EN4 0JS. *STOCK: An quarian books including scientific and learne remainders.* TEL: 0181 449 2524; fax - 0181 4 9595. *Postal Only.*

:ODICOTE

Vheldon and Wesley Ltd
,ytton Lodge. SG4 8TE. Est. 1921. Open by ppointment only. *STOCK: Antiquarian books on 'atural History.* TEL: 01438 820370; fax - 1438 821478. SER: Buys at auction. *Mail Order nly.*

IARPENDEN

Ieg Andrews
3 Cowper Rd. AL5 5NF. Est. 1982. Open by ppointment. *STOCK: Worldwide collectable, angable and wearable antique costume and xtiles including Chinese embroideries and oven fabrics, robes, shoes, hats, large hangings, Iorris and Arts and Crafts embroideries and oven cloths, Paisley shawls, samplers, silkwork ictures; European costumes and textiles.* TEL: 1582 460107; home - same; fax - same. SER: aluations; advice; buys at auction.

IEMEL HEMPSTEAD

bbey Antiques - Fine Jewellery & ilver
7 High St., Old Town. HP1 3AH. (L., E., S. and C. ames). Est. 1962. Open 9.30-5.30. CL: Wed. pm. IZE: Medium. *STOCK: Silver, plate, jewellery, 5-£5,000.* LOC: M1, junction 8, M25, junction 20, rough main shopping centre to old town. PARK: asy. TEL: 01442 64667. SER: Valuations; wellery design and repair. VAT: Stan/Global.

:herry Antiques
)1-103 High St. HP1 3AH. (A. and R.S. ullen). Open 9.30-4.30. CL: Wed. pm. SIZE: ledium. *STOCK: Victorian, Edwardian, and me period furniture, pine, general antiques, ollectors' and decorative items, bric-a-brac, edlework tools, dolls, linens, some silver, plate, wellery, glass, pottery, porcelain, brass, pper, some shipping items.* PARK: Easy. TEL: 442 64358. VAT: Stan/Spec.

ERTFORD

eckwith and Son
. Nicholas Hall, St. Andrew St. SG14 1HZ. .C.M. Gray). Est. 1904. Open 9-1 and 2-5.30. ZE: Large. *STOCK: General antiques, furniture, ver, pottery, porcelain, prints, weapons, clocks, atches, glass.* Not Stocked: Fabrics. LOC: 502/B158. PARK: Adjacent. TEL: 01992 582079. R: Valuations; restorations (fine porcelain, rniture, upholstery, silver, clocks). VAT: Spec.

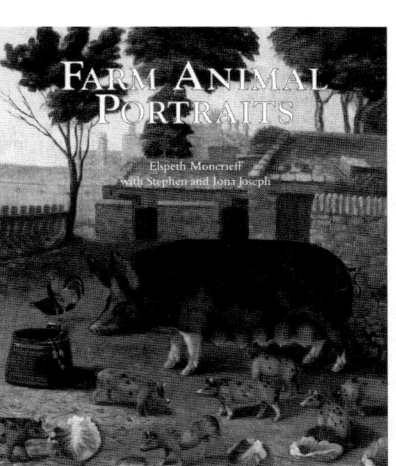

Hertford continued

Hertford Antiques

51 St Andrew St. SG14 1HZ. (S.D. Garratt and R.F. Norris). Est. 1994. Open 10-5.30 including Sun. SIZE: Large - 50+ dealers. *STOCK: Furniture, jewellery, porcelain, silver, glass, books, £5-£4,000.* LOC: Next to St Andrew's Church. PARK: Easy. TEL: 01992 504504.

Robert Horton Antiques

13 Castle St. SG14 1ER. Est. 1972. Open 9-5. *STOCK: Clocks, barometers, furniture.* TEL: 01992 587546. VAT: Stan/Spec.

Michael Rochford

25 St. Andrew St. SG14 1JA. Open 10-5. *STOCK: Trade goods including general antiques, furniture.* TEL: 01992 584385.

HITCHIN

Bexfield Antiques

13 and 14 Sun St. SG5 1AH. (A.B. Bexfield). Est. 1962. Open 9.30-5. *STOCK: Jewellery, silver, porcelain, copper, pewter and furniture.* PARK: Nearby. TEL: 01462 432641; fax - 01462 631555; e-mail - arthur@bex-field.demon.co.uk. SER: Valuations (probate and insurance).

Countrylife Gallery

41-43 Portmill Lane. SG4 7SH. (David and Monica Moor). Open by appointment only. SIZE: Small. *STOCK: Watercolours - botanical, flower and natural history, 1780-1930, £50-£500; oils - flowers and natural history, 1850-1930, £500-£5,000.* LOC: Town square. PARK: 50yds. TEL: 01462 433267; home - same. SER: Valuations; restorations; buys at auction (English watercolours and pictures). FAIRS: Royal Horticultural Socy. VAT: Spec.

Michael Gander

10 Bridge St. SG5 2DE. Est. 1973. Open 9-6. *STOCK: Period furniture, metalware.* TEL: 01462 432678.

Hanbury Antiques

86 Tilehouse St. SG5 2DU. (Mrs M.D. Hanbury). Est. 1988. CL: Mon. and Wed afternoons. SIZE: Small. *STOCK: English furniture, £25-£2,000; porcelain and decorative objects, silver, £5-£500; all 18th-20th C.* LOC: Continuation of Bridge St. PARK: 100 yards. TEL: 01462 420487; home - same. SER: Valuations.

Eric T. Moore

24 Bridge St. SG5 2DF. Open 9.30-1 and 2.15-5.30, Wed. 9-12.30, Sat. 9.30-5.30. *STOCK: Antiquarian books, maps and prints.* TEL: 01462 450497. SER: Picture framing, mount cutting.

Hitchin continued

Phillips of Hitchin (Antiques) Ltd

BAD

The Manor House. SG5 1JW. (M. and Phillips). Est. 1884. Open 9-5.30. SIZE: Larg *STOCK: Furniture, walnut and mahogany, 18 to early 19th C, £500-£20,000.* LOC: Bancroft, main street of Hitchin. PARK: Eas TEL: 01462 432067; fax - 01462 441368. SE Restorations (furniture); books on collectin FAIRS: Specialist antique exhibitions at t Manor House. VAT: Spec.

Tom Salusbury Antiques

9A Bridge St. Est. 1963. SIZE: Small. *STOC Furniture, 18th-19th C, £100-£3,000; accessori 18th-20th C, £10-£500.* LOC: 3 miles from A junction 8. PARK: At rear. TEL: 01462 45427 fax - same. SER: Valuations; restorations; buys auction. FAIRS: Luton. VAT: Stan/Spec.

Carole Thomas (Fine Arts)

28 Bridge St. SG5 1DF. Est. 1976. Open 10-5. appointment advisable on Wed. *STOCK: Engl watercolours, 1800-1950, £100-£4,000; paintings, drawings, etchings from £60.* LO Near town centre. PARK: Own. TEL: 014 436077. SER: Valuations; cleaning; restorin framing. VAT: Stan.

KING'S LANGLEY

Frenches Farm Antiques

Tower Hill, Chipperfield. WD4 9LN. (I. Cros Est. 1972. Open 2-6 or by appointment. SIZ Large. *STOCK: Furniture including pine, £ £700; porcelain, Victoriana, copper, brass, £100; mainly 18th-19th C.* Not Stocked: Silv jewellery, firearms, paintings. LOC: Fr Chipperfield take Bovingdon Rd. On rig 500yds. from Royal Oak public house. PAR Easy. TEL: 01923 265843.

KNEBWORTH

Hamilton Billiards & Games Co.

Park Lane. SG3 6PJ. (H. Hamilton). Est. 19 Open 9-5, weekends and evenings by appoi ment. SIZE: Large. *STOCK: Victorian a Edwardian billiard tables, £3,000-£18,000; 1 C convertible billiard/dining tables a accessories, £30-£5,000; indoor and outd games.* LOC: Near railway station. PARK: Ea TEL: 01438 811995. SER: Valuations; rest ations (billiard tables and furniture); buys auction (as stock). VAT: Stan.

LETCHMORE HEATH, Nr. Watford

Anne Barlow Antiques
1 Letchmore Cottages. WD2 8EE. (Mrs Barlow). Est. 1952. Open 2.30-6.30. CL: Mon. SIZE: Small. *STOCK: Continental and unusual items especially Quimper pottery, country furniture, faience porcelain, toys, clocks, collectors' items, £1-£500.* PARK: Easy. TEL: 01923 855270. SER: Valuations.

PUCKERIDGE

St. Ouen Antiques LAPADA
Vintage Corner, Old Cambridge Rd. SG11 1SA. (J., J. and S.T. Blake and Mrs P.B. Francis). Est. 1918. Open 10.30-5. SIZE: Large. *STOCK: English and Continental furniture, decorative items, silver, porcelain, pottery, glass, clocks, barometers, paintings.* TEL: 01920 821336. SER: Valuations; restorations.

RADLETT

Hasel-Britt Ltd
157 Watling St. WD7 7NQ. (Mrs Britton). Est. 1962. Open 10-5.30. CL: Wed. pm. *STOCK: General antiques, 19th C; pottery and porcelain.* TEL: 01923 854477.

REDBOURN, Nr. St. Albans

J.N. Antiques
86 High St. AL3 7BD. (M. and J. Brunning). Est. 1975. Open 9-6. SIZE: Medium. *STOCK: Furniture, 18th-20th C, £5-£3,000; brass and copper, porcelain, 19th C, £5-£100; pictures, 19th-20th C.* PARK: 50 yds. TEL: 01582 793603; fax - same. SER: Valuations. VAT: Spec.

Tim Wharton Antiques LAPADA
24 High St. AL3 7LL. Est. 1970. Open 10-5.30, Sat. 10-4. CL: Mon. and usually Thurs. *STOCK: Oak and country furniture, 17th-19th C; some mahogany, 18th to early 19th C; copper, brass, ironware and general small antiques.* LOC: On left entering village from St. Albans on A5183. PARK: Easy. TEL: 01582 794371. VAT: Stan/Spec.

RICKMANSWORTH

Clive A. Burden
Elmcote House, The Green, Croxley Green. WD3 3HN. Est. 1966. Open 9-5, appointment preferred. SIZE: Medium. *STOCK: Maps, 1500-1860, £5-£1,500; natural history, botanical and Vanity Fair prints, 1720-1870, £1-£1,000; antiquarian books, pre-1870, £10-£5,000.* TEL: 01923 778097; fax - 01923 896520; home - 01923 772387. SER: Valuations; buys at auction (as stock). VAT: Stan.

Rickmansworth continued

Galliard Antiques
2 Station Road. WD3 2DE. (Ellen Harriman Open 10-5.30. CL: Mon. *STOCK: Furnitur clocks, decorative antiques.* TEL: 01923 778087

ROYSTON

Royston Antiques
29 Kneesworth St. SG8 5AB. (J. and M Newnham). Est. 1965. Open 10-5, Sat. 9.30- CL: Thurs. SIZE: Medium. *STOCK: Furnitu 1750-1930, £50-£2,500; porcelain, books, £ £500; collectors' items, pine, metalware, bygon* TEL: 01763 243876.

SAWBRIDGEWORTH

The Herts and Essex Antiques Cent
The Maltings, Station Rd. CM21 9JX. Est. 19 Open 10-5, Sat. and Sun. 10.30-6. CL: Mo SIZE: Large - over 100 dealers. *STOCK: Gener antiques and collectables, £1-£2,000.* LO Opposite B.R. station. PARK: Easy. TEL: 012 722044. SER: Restorations.

ST. ALBANS

By George! Antiques Centre
23 George St. Open 10-5, Sun. 1-5. SIZE: dealers. *STOCK: A wide range of gener antiques, jewellery and collectables.* LO 100yds. from Clock Tower. PARK: Intern courtyard (loading) and Christopher Place C Park (NCP) nearby. TEL: 01727 853032. SE Restorations.

The Clock Shop - Philip Setterfield St. Albans
161 Victoria St. AL1 3TA. Est. 1974. Open 11 Sat. 11-4. CL: Thurs. *STOCK: Clocks a watches.* LOC: City station bridge. TEL: 017 856633; fax - same. SER: Restorations; repa (clocks, watches, barometers). VAT: Stan/Spec.

Forget-me-Knot Antiques
at Over the Moon, 27 High St. AL3 4E (Heather Sharp). Est. 1987. Open 9.30-5.30, S by appointment. *STOCK: Mainly Victori jewellery and collectables, specializing in sil name brooches.* TEL: 01727 848907. SE Valuations. VAT: Stan.

James of St Albans
11 George St. AL3 4ER. (S.N. and W. Jame Est. 1957. Open 10-5, Thurs. 10-1. *STOC Furniture including reproduction; smalls, br and copper; topographical maps and prints Hertfordshire.* TEL: 01727 856996. VA Stan/Spec.

t. Albans continued

lagic Lanterns
t By George! Antiques Centre, 23 George St. .L3 4ES. (Josie A. Marsden). Est. 1987. Open 0-5, Thurs. 11-5, Sat. 10-5.30, Sun. 1-5. SIZE: ledium. *STOCK: Lighting - candle, gas and arly electric, 1800-1950's, £35-£1,000; small rniture, prints, mirrors, china, metalware, fire ccessories, 1850-1950, £25-£500.* LOC: Near the bbey. PARK: Multi-storey nearby. TEL: 01727 53032; home - 01727 865680.

riental Rug Gallery Ltd
2 Verulam Rd. AL3 4DQ. (R. Mathias and J. lair). Open 9-6, Sun. 10.30-4. *STOCK: Russian, fghan, Turkish and Persian carpets, rugs and lims; Oriental objets d'art.* TEL: 01727 841046.

t. Albans Antique Market
own Hall, Chequer St. AL4 0XS. Est. 1978. pen Mon. 9.30 (8.30 trade)-4, some Bank olidays. SIZE: 30 stands. *STOCK: A wide ariety of antiques.* TEL: 01727 844957.

tuart Wharton
George St. AL3 4ER. FGA DGA. Est. 1967. pen 9-5.30. SIZE: Medium. *STOCK: Silver, 8th-20th C, £20-£2,000; jewellery, mainly odern, £20-£5,000.* LOC: Near clock tower. ARK: Multi-storey, city centre. TEL: 01727 59489; fax - 01727 855474. SER: Registered aluer (jewellery and silver); goldsmithing, gem sting; buys at auction (silver). VAT: Stan.

RING

ohn Bly BADA
ear of 50 High St. HP23 5AG. Est. 1891. pen 9-5. SIZE: Large. *STOCK: English rniture.* TEL: 01442 823030.

ountry Clocks
Pendley Bridge Cottages, Tring Station. HP23 QU. (T. Cartmell). Resident. Est. 1976. Open aily, prior 'phone call advisable. SIZE: Small. *OCK: Clocks, 18th-19th C.* LOC: One mile om A41 in village, cottage nearest canal bridge. ARK: Easy. TEL: 01442 825090. SER: Restorons (clocks).

arrelly Antiques
e Long Barn, 50 High St. (P. Farrelly). Open 4. *STOCK: Furniture.* TEL: 01442 891905. R: Restorations. VAT: Spec.

ew England House Antiques
High St. HP23 5AG. (Jennifer and Suj unjee). Est. 1990. Open 10-5. SIZE: Large. *OCK: Fine Georgian and Victorian furniture, 00-£5,000; paintings, glass, silver, decorative rnishings.* LOC: A41 towards Aylesbury. ARK: Next to shop. TEL: 01442 827262; home - 462 431914. SER: Valuations; restorations aintings, metalwork and furniture); searches dertaken. FAIRS: Luton. VAT: Stan/Spec.

Tring continued

Tring Triangle Antiques Centre
15 Western Rd. HP23 4BQ. (M. Chase). Est. 1994. Open Wed.-Sun. 11-5. SIZE: Large - 20 dealers. *STOCK: General antiques, 19th C, £5-£800; Susie Cooper, Art Deco, clocks, cigarette cards, Victorian and Edwardian furniture, porcelain and collectors' items.* LOC: Town centre. PARK: Side street. TEL: 01442 825060. SER: Restorations (furniture, china, barometers and clocks).

WARESIDE

Wareside Antiques
SG12 7QY. (David Broxup). Est. 1983. Open by appointment only. SIZE: Medium. *STOCK: Furniture, dining tables, sets of chairs, etc.* LOC: On Ware to Much Hadham road. PARK: Easy. TEL: 01763 281234.

WHEATHAMPSTEAD

Collins Antiques (F.G. and C. Collins Ltd.)
Corner House. AL4 8AP. (S.J. and M.C. Collins). Est. 1907. Open 9-1 and 2-5. SIZE: Large. *STOCK: Furniture, mahogany, 1730-1920, £100-£8,000; oak, 1600-1800, £50-£5,000; walnut, 1700-1740, £75-£3,000.* Not Stocked: Silver. LOC: London, A1(M) junction 4 to B653. PARK: Easy. TEL: 01582 833111. VAT: Stan/Spec.

WILSTONE, Nr. Tring

Michael Armson (Antiques) Ltd
The Old Post Office, 34 Tring Road. HP23 4PB. Open 8.30-5.30. CL: Wed pm. SIZE: Large. *STOCK: Furniture, 17th-19th C.* TEL: 01442 890990; fax - 01442 891167; mobile - 0860 910034.

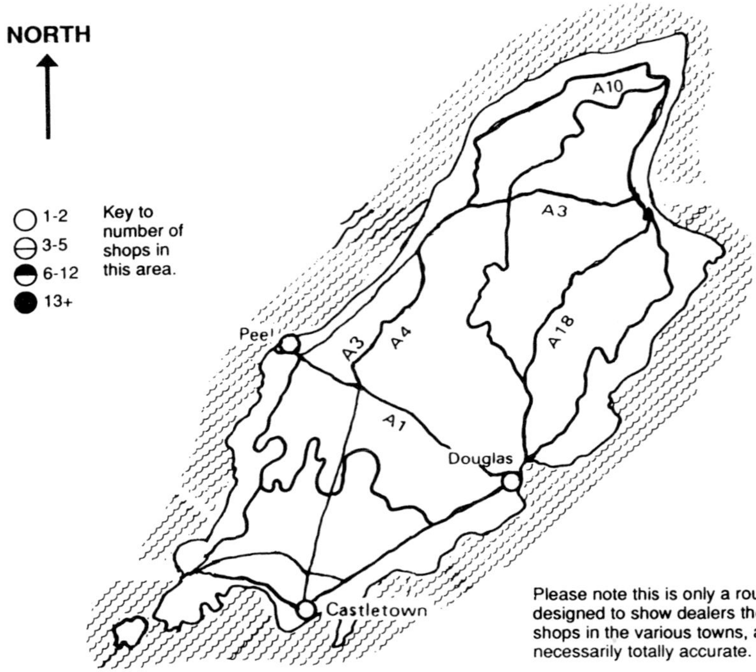

Please note this is only a rough map designed to show dealers the number c shops in the various towns, and is not necessarily totally accurate.

CASTLETOWN

J. and H. Bell Antiques

22 Arbory St. IM9 1LJ. Est. 1965. Open Wed., Fri. and Sat. 10-5. SIZE: Medium. *STOCK: Jewellery, silver, china, early metalware, furniture, 18th-20th C, £5-£5,000.* TEL: 01624 823132 or 01624 822414. VAT: Stan/Spec.

DOUGLAS

John Corrin Antiques

73 Circular Rd. IM1 1AZ. Est. 1972. Open Sat. 9-5.30 otherwise by appointment. SIZE: Medium. *STOCK: Furniture, 18th-19th C, £100-£6,000; clocks, barometers, 19th C.* LOC: From the promenade, travel up Victoria St., this becomes Prospect Hill and Circular Rd. is on left. PARK: Easy. TEL: 01624 629655; home - 01624 621382.

PEEL

Dorothea Horn At The Golden Past

18A Michael St. Est. 1982. Open 10.30-4.30. Cl Mon. am. and Thurs. Oct.-Mar. SIZE: Mediun *STOCK: Jewellery, porcelain, silver, glass, bool and paintings, 1840-1940, £5-£100.* LOC: Mai shopping street. PARK: Easy. TEL: 0162 842170; home - 01624 843839.

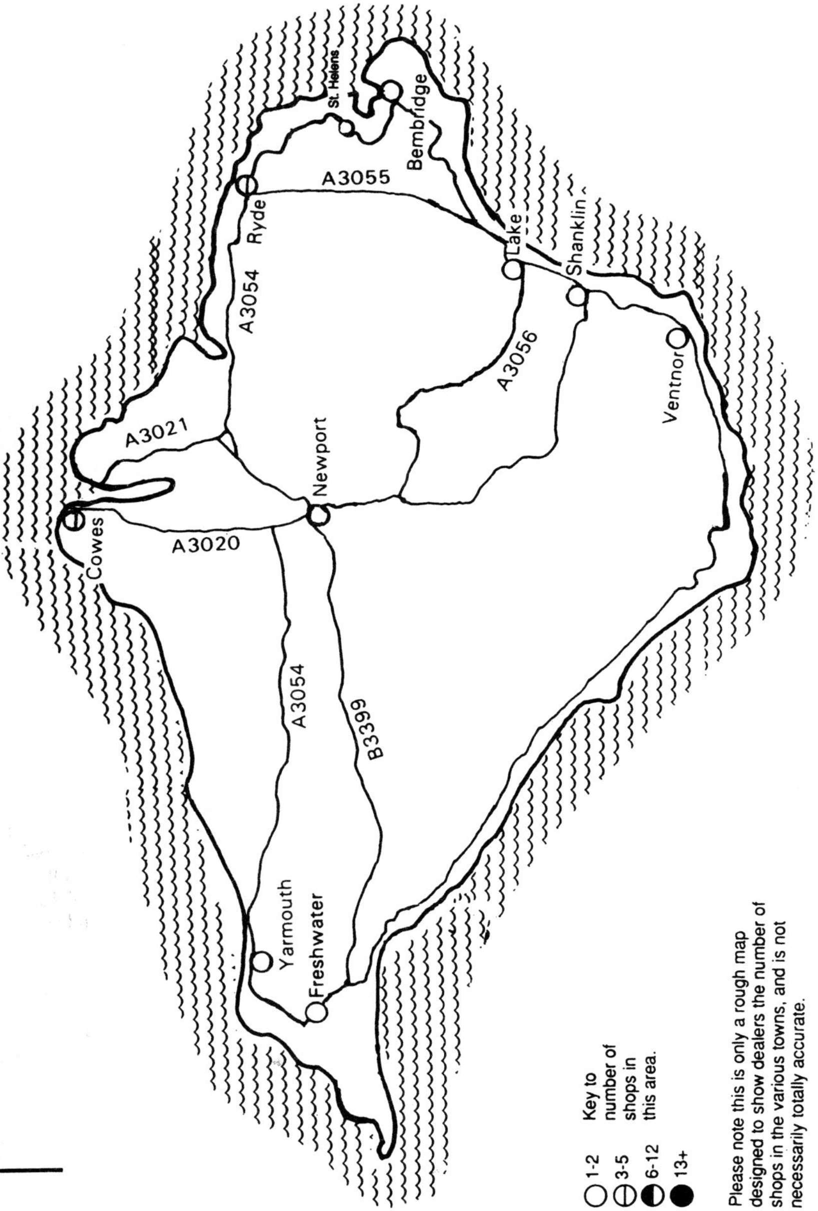

○ 1-2 Key to
⊖ 3-5 number of
◐ 6-12 shops in
● 13+ this area.

Please note this is only a rough map designed to show dealers the number of shops in the various towns, and is not necessarily totally accurate.

BEMBRIDGE

Windmill Antiques LAPADA

1 Foreland Rd. PO35 5XN. (E.J. de Kort). Est. 1970. CL: Thurs. pm. SIZE: Medium. *STOCK: Furniture, silver, porcelain, jewellery.* TEL: 01983 873666. SER: Valuations; buys at auction. VAT: Stan/Spec.

COWES

Julia Margaret Cameron Gallery

90B High St. PO31 7AW. (J. Flynn). *STOCK: Antiquarian books, maps and prints especially local, postcards.* TEL: 01983 290404.

Charles Dickens Bookshop

65 High St. PO31 7RL. *STOCK: Antiquarian and secondhand books, especially 19th C English literature, nautical and children's.* TEL: 01983 293598/280586.

Galerias Segui

75 High St. PO31 7AJ. Est. 1976. Open 10-5. SIZE: Medium. *STOCK: Pine furniture, £60-£600; prints and watercolours, £15-£200; bric-a-brac.* LOC: Between Midland and Lloyds Bank, near Red Funnel Pier. PARK: 200yds. TEL: 01983 292148.

Royal Standard Antiques

70-72 Park Rd. PO31 7LY. (Dennis and Caroline Bradbury). Resident. Est. 1992. Open 10.30-5.30, or any time by appointment. SIZE: Medium. *STOCK: Victorian, Edwardian and French provincial furniture, £100-£1,000; architectural items, £50-£800; pictures, commemoratives, breweriana, £5-£500.* LOC: 5 mins. walk from hydrofoil terminus; corner of Park Rd. and Victoria Rd. PARK: Own, behind premises. TEL: 01983 281672; home - same.

FRESHWATER

Aladdin's Cave

147/149 School Green Rd. PO40 9BB. (Mrs Dunn). Est. 1984. Open 9.30-4.30, including Su SIZE: Medium. *STOCK: China, collectors' item glass, linen, old pine, furniture, memorabili books, 19th-20th C, £5-£500.* PARK: Easy. TE 01983 752934; home - 01983 753846.

LAKE

Lake Antiques

Sandown Rd. PO36 9JP. (P. Burfield). Est. 198 Open 10-4. CL: Wed. *STOCK: General antique Victorian and Edwardian furniture, clocks.* LO On the main Sandown-Shanklin Rd. PARK: C forecourt. TEL: 01983 406888/865005; mobile 04100 67678.

NEWPORT

Mike Heath Antiques

3-4 Holyrood St. PO30 5AU. (M. and B. Heat Est. 1974. Open 9.30-5. CL: Thurs. SIZ Medium. *STOCK: General antiques and bric-brac, 19th-20th C, £5-£500.* LOC: Off High PARK: Nearby. TEL: 01983 525748; home same. SER: Restorations (copper and brass).

RYDE

Hayter's

18-20 Cross St. PO33 2AD. (R.W. and F. Hayter). Est. 1956. Open 9-1 and 2-5.30. C Thurs. SIZE: Large. *STOCK: Furniture includi Victorian.* LOC: Through main traffic flow fr sea front to town centre. TEL: 01983 5637 VAT: Stan/Spec.

:yde continued

łoyal Victoria Arcade
Jnion St. Open 9-5.30; basement market open 'hurs., Fri. and Sat. in summer. TEL: 01983 64661. Below are listed some of the dealers in ıis Arcade.

Crocus
Collectables, art deco to 1950's.

Echoes
Costume jewellery, militaria and general antiques.

Uriah's Heap
Jewellery, writing equipment, instruments, china, glass and collectables.

Jriah's Heap
Royal Victoria Arcade, Union St. PO33 2LQ. F. Cross). Open Wed., Fri. and Sat. 10-5. *TOCK: Small antiques, china, silver, collect-bles, linen, lace, fountain pens, jewellery.* TEL: 1983 564661.

HANKLIN

'he Shanklin Gallery
7 Regent St. PO37 7AE. Open 9-5. SIZE: 1edium. *STOCK: Oils, watercolours, engravings, ·ints, maps, 17th-20th C, £10-£2,000.* LOC: Town entre near railway station. PARK: Easy. TEL: 1983 863113. SER: Valuations; restorations (oils, atercolours and prints); framing.

T. HELENS, Nr. Bembridge

t. Helens Antiques
) Lower Green Rd. PO33 1UB. Open daily in ımmer 10-1 and 2.30-5.30; winter - Mon., Wed., i. and Sat. 10-1 and 2.30-5. *STOCK: General ıtiques, ceramics, furniture, textiles, glass, ictorian jewellery, prints and violins.* TEL: .983 874896.

ENTNOR

eter Goodall
) Pier St. PO38 1SX. Est. 1965. Open by ›pointment only. SIZE: Medium. *STOCK: ıgravings, etchings, lithographs and aquatints, 'th-20th C, £5-£1,000.* TEL: 01983 856116. ER: Valuations.

entnor Rare Books
Pier St. PO38 1ST. (N.C.R. and T.A. Traylen). 3A. *STOCK: Antiquarian and secondhand books, ints.* TEL: 01983 853706; fax - 01983 853357.

ARMOUTH

arlborough House Antiques
James Sq. PO41 0NS. (P.A. Webb). Est. 1972. *'OCK: Local prints and maps, silver, jewellery, ttery, glass and furniture.* TEL: 01983 760498.

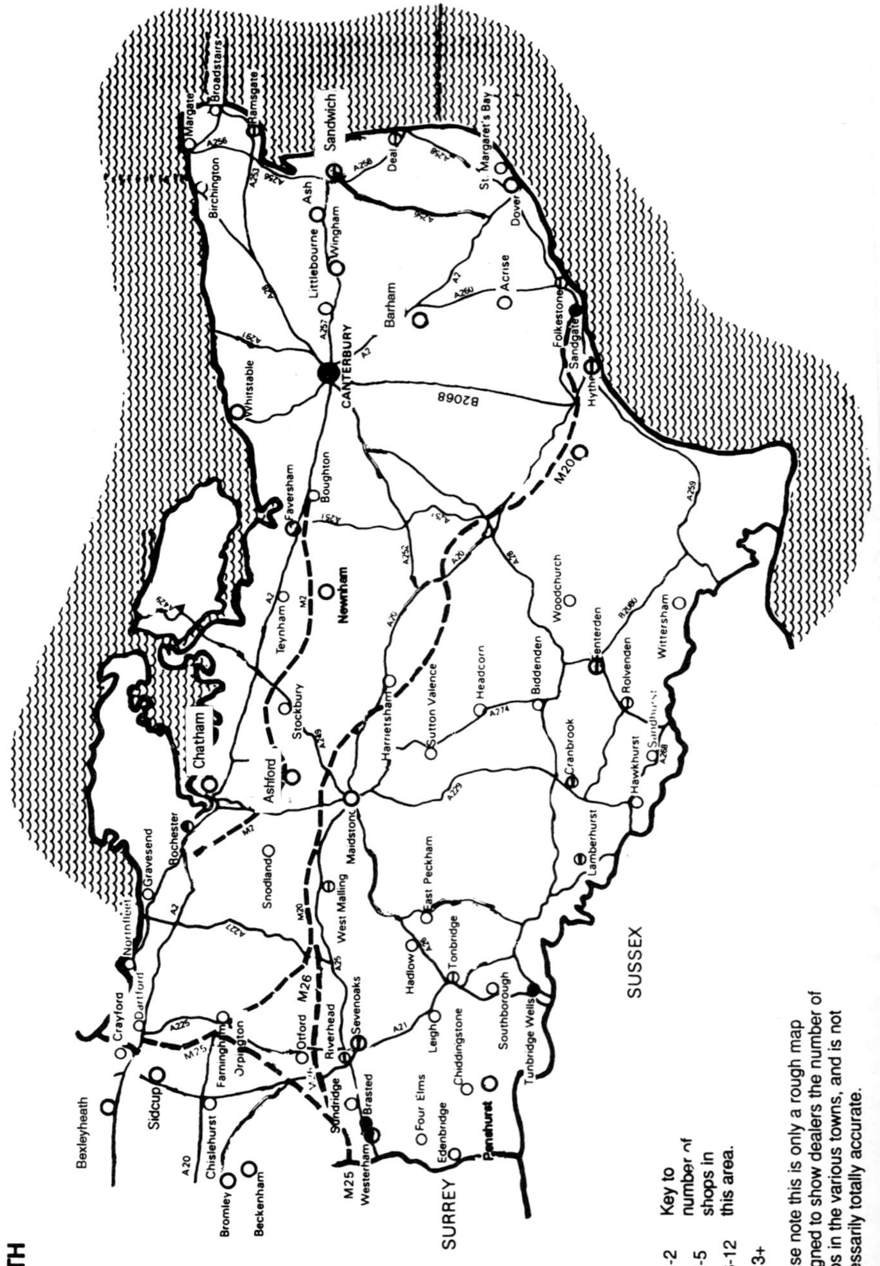

○ 1-2
⊖ 3-5
◐ 6-12
● 13+

Key to number of shops in this area.

Please note this is only a rough map designed to show dealers the number of shops in the various towns, and is not necessarily totally accurate.

\CRISE, Nr. Folkestone

∖. Kirby Antiques

:aroline Cottage, Ridge Row. Open by appointment only. CL: Mon. *STOCK: Early period oak.* 'EL: 01303 893230.

\SH, Nr. Canterbury

Ienry's of Ash

1 The Street. CT3 2EN. (P.H. Robinson). Est. 988. Open 10-12 and 2-5. CL: Tues. pm and Ved. SIZE: Small. *STOCK: General antiques, 'ictorian and Art Deco, £5-100; small furniture, 50-£500.* LOC: Main street. PARK: Outside. 'EL: 01304 812600. SER: Buys at auction (small ems). FAIRS: Copthorne; Ashford; Great Danes.

\SHFORD

:ounty Antiques

ld Mill Cottage, Kennett Lane, Stanford North. 'N25 6DG. (B. Nilson). Open by appointment. *TOCK: General antiques.* TEL: 01303 813039.

ARHAM

tablegate Antiques

Mrs. G. Giuntini). Open nearly every day, but rior 'phone call advisable. SIZE: Large. *STOCK: 'eorgian and Victorian dining tables, chairs, deboards, etc.* LOC: Village just off the A2 to over. PARK: Easy. TEL: 01227 831639.

ECKENHAM

eckenham Antique Market

ld Council Hall, Bromley Rd. Est. 1979. Open 'ed. only 9.30-2. SIZE: 20 stalls. *STOCK: eneral antiques.* TEL: 0181 777 6300.

epys Antiques

Kelsey Park Rd. BR3 2LH. (S.P. Elton). Est. 69. Open 10 a.m. CL: Wed. *STOCK: Furniture, intings, clocks, silver, porcelain, copper, brass.* OC: Central Beckenham. TEL: 0181 650 0994.

EXLEYHEATH

exleyheath Antiques Centre

1 Broadway. DA6 8DB. (Jackie Marriott-nith). Est. 1977. Open 10-5, Sat. 9.30-5.30, Sun. -4. SIZE: Large. *STOCK: Furniture, £20-,000+; jewellery, china and glass, collectables, -£1,000+.* LOC: Main road. PARK: Loading d nearby. TEL: 0181 303 5147; fax - same. ER: Valuations; monthly auctions held. FAIRS: dingly; Newark.

BIDDENDEN, Nr. Ashford

Harriet Ann Sleigh Beds

Standen Farm, Smarden Rd. TN27 8JT. (Mr and Mrs Body). Est. 1987. Open 9.30-5.30 including Sun. SIZE: Medium. *STOCK: Eastern European and Scandinavian sleigh beds; French fruitwood doubles or singles; European pine armoires, chests and cabinets; bedside lights, bedroom decorative accessories especially childrens.* LOC: Off M25 to M20, exit after Maidstone at Leeds Castle, take A274. PARK: Easy. TEL: 01580 291220; fax - same; home - same. SER: Mattresses available to order; reproduction beds in certain styles. FAIRS: Penshurst Castle; Olympia; Earls Court.

Two Maids Antiques

6 High St. TN27 8AH. (J. Thornley). Est. 1979. Open 10-5 and by appointment. CL: Mon. and Wed. SIZE: Medium. *STOCK: 17th-18th C metalwork, lace bobbins, Victorian picture frames, wood carvings, treen, miniatures and small furniture.* LOC: A262. PARK: Opposite. TEL: 01580 291807; home - same.

BIRCHINGTON, Nr. Margate

John Chawner

36 Station Approach. CT7 9RD. Open 10.30-12.30 and 1.30-5. *STOCK: Clocks, barometers, smalls and bureaux.* PARK: Easy. TEL: 01843 843309. SER: Repairs (clocks and barometers).

BOUGHTON, Nr. Faversham

Clockshop

187 The Street. ME13 9BH. (S.G. Fowler). LBHI. Resident. Est. 1968. Open 10-6. SIZE: Small. *STOCK: Clocks.* PARK: Easy. TEL: 01227 751258. SER: Repairs (clocks).

Jean Collyer Antiques

194 The Street. ME13 9AL. (Mrs J.B. Collyer). Est. 1977. Open Tues. and Fri. 2-5, Sat. 10-5. SIZE: Small. *STOCK: Porcelain, glass, furniture, general antiques, 18th to mid-19th C.* PARK: Easy. TEL: 01227 751454; home - same. SER: Valuations. VAT: Stan/Spec.

BRASTED, Nr. Westerham

David Barrington

The Antique Shop. TN16 1JA. Est. 1947. Open 9-6. SIZE: Medium. *STOCK: Furniture, 18th C.* LOC: A25. PARK: Easy. TEL: 01959 562537. VAT: Stan/Spec.

Brasted Antiques and Interiors

High St. TN16 1JJ. (Mrs R.B. Rowlett). Open 10-5.30. *STOCK: Furniture, paintings and bric-a-brac.* TEL: 01959 564863. SER: Interior design.

Brasted continued

Courtyard Antiques

High St. TN16 1JE. (H. La Trobe). Open 10-5.30. *STOCK: General antiques including silver, jewellery, furniture especially extending Victorian dining tables and sets of chairs.* PARK: Easy. TEL: 01959 564483. SER: Valuations; restorations (furniture); French polishing and re-leathering.

Peter Dyke

Kentish House, High St. Est. 1977. Open 10-5, Sat. 1-5. SIZE: Small. *STOCK: Furniture, 18th-19th C, £500-£10,000; paintings, 19th-20th C, £500-£1,000+; decorative objects, 19th C, £150-£1,000.* LOC: A25. PARK: Easy. TEL: 01959 565020. SER: Valuations; buys at auction. VAT: Spec.

Ivy House Antiques

High St. TN16 1JA. (R. Throp and P. Welsh). Open 10-6. SIZE: Medium. *STOCK: Furniture, porcelain, paintings, decorative items.* LOC: A25. PARK: Easy. TEL: 01959 564581; home - same. VAT: Stan/Spec.

Keymer Son & Co. Ltd

Swaylands Place, The Green. TN16 1JY. Est. 1977. Open 10-1 and 2.30-5. CL: Sat. SIZE: Small. *STOCK: 18th-19th C furniture, £100-£3,000.* LOC: A25. PARK: Easy. TEL: 01959 564203; fax - 01959 561138.

Roy Massingham Antiques LAPADA

The Coach House. TN16 1JJ. Open 9-5 or by appointment. *STOCK: 18th-19th C furniture, pictures and decorative items.* TEL: 01959 562408; mobile - 0860 326825.

Old Bakery Antiques

High St. TN16 1JA. Open 9.30-5. *STOCK: Country furniture and decorative items.* TEL: 01959 562994.

Old Manor House Antiques

The Old Manor House, The Green. TN16 1JL. Open daily. *STOCK: Clocks, barometers, lighting, copper and brass, mirrors, furniture and general antiques.* TEL: 01959 562536.

Southdown House Antique Galleries

High St. TN16 1JE. (R. and D. Thomas). Est. 1978. Open 9.30-5.30. *STOCK: Furniture, porcelain, glass, metalware, tapestries, 18th-19th C; oils and watercolours, 19th C.* TEL: 01959 563522.

Graham Stead Antiques and Reference Books

Southdown House, High St. Open 9.30-5.30. *STOCK: Furniture, mainly 19th C mahogany, decorative items, £50-£3,000; reference books on antiques and collectables.* PARK: Own. TEL: 01959 563522.

Brasted continued

Dinah Stoodley

High St. TN16 1JE. (Mrs D. Stoodley). Est. 196 Open 9.30-5.30. SIZE: Medium. *STOCK: Oa and country furniture, 1600-1800; pottery, meta ware and pewter.* Not Stocked: Victorian jewellery, silver. LOC: A25. PARK: Easy. TE 01959 563616. VAT: Spec.

Tilings Antiques

High St. TN16 1JA. (H. Loveland and Fawcett). Est. 1974. Open 10-5.30 or by appoin ment. SIZE: Medium. *STOCK: Furnitur ceramics, decorative items, 18th-19th C, £2 £2,000.* LOC: Village centre on A25. PARI Easy. TEL: 01959 564735. VAT: Stan/Spec.

The Village Antique Centre

4 High St. (Ms K. Phillips). Est. 1983. Open 10- including Sun. SIZE: Large. *STOCK: Furnitur ceramics, silver, jewellery, glass, decorative a collectibles, 15th-20th C, £5-£10,000.* LOC: A between Sevenoaks and Westerham. PARK: Ow TEL: 01959 564545; home - 01293 824173. SE Valuations; restorations (furniture).

W.W. Warner (Antiques) Ltd

The Green. TN16 1JL. (Mrs C.U. Warner). E 1957. Open 10-1 and 2-5. SIZE: Mediu *STOCK: English pottery, porcelain, glass a mahogany furniture, 18th-19th C, £100-£1,0* Not Stocked: Silver, Victoriana. LOC: A2 PARK: Easy. TEL: 01959 563698. SER: Buys London auctions. VAT: Spec.

BROADSTAIRS

Broadstairs Antiques and Collectable

49 Belvedere Rd. CT10 1PF. (P. Edwards). E 1980. Open winter 10-4.30, summer 10-5. C Wed. *STOCK: General antiques, linen, la china and small furniture.* LOC: Road oppos Lloyds Bank. TEL: 01843 861965.

BROMLEY

Antica

Rear of 35-41 High St. BR1 1LE. (L. and Muccio). Open 10-5.30. *STOCK: Gener antiques.* LOC: Opposite Habitat. TEL: 0181 4 7661. VAT: Stan.

Bromley Antique Market

Widmore Rd. Est. 1968. Open Thursday 7.30 SIZE: 70 stalls. *STOCK: General antiqu jewellery, books, bric-a-brac, copper, brass a clocks, collectors' items, coins, furs, stam postcards.* VAT: Stan.

:ANTERBURY

\ntique and Design
'he Old Oast, Hollow Lane. (Steve Couchman). :st. 1988. Open 9-6, Sun. 10-4. SIZE: Large. *TOCK: Pine furniture, decorative items, 1800-950, £5-£1,500.* LOC: M2 from London, :anterbury exit, straight at first roundabout, right t second and third roundabouts, left at second edestrian lights, shop 500 yds. TEL: 01227 62871. SER: Restorations; buys at auction; nport and export. VAT: Stan/Spec.

ℝ. J. Baker
5 Palace St. CT1 2DZ. Est. 1971. Open 9.30-30. CL: Thurs. SIZE: Small. *STOCK: Silver and wellery, 18th-19th C, £500-£2,000; handmade odern silverware, modern jewellery.* LOC: 5 inutes from cathedral, opposite The King's chool. PARK: Easy. TEL: 01227 463224. SER: aluations; restorations; gold and silversmiths; anufacturers. VAT: Stan/Spec.

urgate Antique Centre
)c Burgate. CT1 2HG. (Mr and Mrs Winterflood). st. 1986. Open 10-5. SIZE: 12 dealers. *STOCK: urniture, silver, porcelain, Art Deco, paintings, ints, books, militaria, lead soldiers and toys, 9th-20th C.* LOC: City Wall overlooking athedral Gardens. TEL: 01227 456500. SER: aluations.

he Canterbury Bookshop
Palace Street. CT1 2DZ. (David Miles). Open -5. *STOCK: Antiquarian and children's books, ctures and prints.* TEL: 01227 464773; fax - 227 780073.

haucer Bookshop
Beer Cart Lane. CT1 2NY. (R. Sherston-Baker). BA, PBFA. Est. 1977. Open 10-5. SIZE: edium. *STOCK: Books and prints, 18th-20th C, -£150; maps, 18th-19th C, £50-£250.* LOC: 5 nutes walk from cathedral, via Mercery Lane d St. Margaret's St. PARK: Castle St. TEL: 227 453912. SER: Valuations; restorations ook binding); buys at auction (books, maps and nts). VAT: Stan.

oach House Antiques
Duck Lane, St. Radigunds. CT1 2AE. Est. 75. Open daily. SIZE: Large. *STOCK: General tiques, small furniture, ceramics, glass, linen, oks, collectors' items and bygones.* Not ocked: Jewellery. TEL: 01227 463117.

onquest House Antiques
Palace St. CT1 2DZ. (C.C. Hill and D.A. agee). Open 10-5. *STOCK: 18th-19th C niture and decorative items.* TEL: 01227 4587; fax - 01227 451375.

Canterbury continued

H.S. Greenfield and Son, Gunmakers (Est. 1805)
4/5 Upper Bridge St. CT1 2NB. (T.S. Greenfield). *STOCK: English sporting guns, in pairs and singles; Continental sporting guns, firearms.* TEL: 01227 456959. SER: Valuations; restorations (antique firearms). VAT: Stan.

R. and J. L. Henley Antiques
37a Broad St. CT1 2LR. Open 9-6. *STOCK: General antiques, Victorian brass beds.* TEL: 01227 769055. VAT: Stan/Spec.

Leadenhall Gallery
12 Palace St. CT1 2DZ. (D.L. Greenaway). Open 10-5.30. *STOCK: Prints and maps.* TEL: 01227 457339.

Nan Leith's Brocanterbury
Errol House, 68 Stour St. CT1 2NZ. Open afternoons only. *STOCK: Art Deco, Victoriana, pressed glass, costume jewellery.* LOC: Close to Heritage Museum. TEL: 01227 454519.

Michael Pearson Antiques
2 The Borough, Northgate. CT1 2DR. Open 10-6. *STOCK: 17th and 18th C furniture, including early oak, clocks and country furniture; wood carvings.* TEL: 01227 459939. SER: Valuations; restorations (clocks and furniture).

Pine and Things
Oast Interiors, Wincheap Rd. CT1 3TY. Est. 1977. Open 9-5.30. SIZE: Large. *STOCK: Pine furniture, 19th C and reproduction, £100-£500; ornaments and collectors' items.* LOC: A28 towards Ashford, 1 mile from city centre. PARK: Easy. TEL: 01227 470283. VAT: Stan.

Rastro Antiques
44a High St. CT1 2SA. (J. Coppage). Est. 1981. Open 10-5. SIZE: 8 dealers. *STOCK: Bric-a-brac, vintage clothing, books, stamps, ephemera, etc.* LOC: Up narrow lane off High St. PARK: Nearby. TEL: 01227 463537.

The Saracen's Lantern
8-9 The Borough. CT1 2DR. (W.J. Christophers). Est. 1970. *STOCK: General antiques, silver, jewellery, clocks, watches, Victorian bottles and pot-lids, Georgian, Victorian and Edwardian furniture.* LOC: Near Cathedral opposite King's School. PARK: At rear, by way of Northgate and St. Radigun's St. TEL: 01227 451968.

Stablegate Antiques
19 The Borough, Palace St. CT1 2DR. (Mrs G. Giuntini). Est. 1989. Open 10-5.30. SIZE: Small. *STOCK: General antiques, furniture and porcelain, Georgian, Victorian and Edwardian, £5-£4,000; jewellery, glass, objets d'art, collectables.* LOC: Between Mint Yard Gate and King's School. PARK: Nearby. TEL: 01227 764086; home - 01227 831639.

Canterbury continued

Town and Country Furniture
141 Wincheap. CT1 3SE. (V. Keen). Est. 1986. Open 9-5. SIZE: Medium. *STOCK: Furniture, country collectables, 50p-£1,000.* LOC: A28 Wincheap road. PARK: Nearby. TEL: 01227 762340. SER: Paint and metal stripping; restoration (furniture); French polishing; lead light repairs; reclaimed pine furniture made to order.

Victorian Fireplace
Thanet House, 92 Broad St. CT1 2LU. (J.J. Griffith). Est. 1980. Open 10-5.30. CL: Mon. SIZE: Medium. *STOCK: Georgian to Victorian fireplaces.* LOC: Town centre. PARK: Nearby. TEL: 01227 767723. SER: Restorations; fitting. VAT: Stan/Spec.

CHATHAM

P. Farmer
The Chaplain's House, Chatham Historic Dockyard. ME4 4SX. Est. 1989. Open by appointment only. SIZE: Small. *STOCK: Chandeliers and wall lights, mainly 19th C, £100-£5,000; etchings and engravings, mainly 15th-17th C, £2,000-£4,000.* LOC: Follow signs from junction 3, M2. PARK: Easy. TEL: 01634 828076; fax - same. SER: Restorations (chandeliers); commission manufacture of chandeliers.

CHIDDINGSTONE, Nr. Edenbridge

Barbara Lane Antiques
Tudor Cottage. TN8 7AH. (Mrs E.B. Avery). Est. 1967. Open 10-5. *STOCK: General antiques, furniture, silver and plate, porcelain and 20th C collectables.* LOC: Behind Castle Inn. PARK: Easy. TEL: 01892 870577.

CHISLEHURST

Chislehurst Antiques LAPADA
7 Royal Parade. BR7 6NR. (Mrs M. Crawley). Est. 1976. Open 10-5. SIZE: Large. *STOCK: Furniture, 1760-1910; lighting - oil, gas, electric, 1850-1910; decorative antiques.* LOC: Half mile from A20, 3 miles from M25. PARK: Easy. TEL: 0181 467 1530; mobile - 0468 081577. VAT: Spec.

Michael Sim
1 Royal Parade. BR7 5PG. Open 9-6 including Sun. SIZE: Medium. *STOCK: English furniture, Georgian and Regency, £500-£50,000; clocks, barometers, globes and scientific instruments, £500-£50,000; Oriental works of art, £50-£5,000; pictures, Victorian, £100-£10,000; portrait miniatures, £300-£5,000; animalier bronzes, £1,000-£10,000.* LOC: 50yds. from War Memorial at junction of Bromley Rd. and Centre Common Rd. PARK: Easy. TEL: 0181 467 7040; home - same; fax - 0181 467 4352. SER: Valuations; restorations; buys at auction. VAT: Spec.

CRANBROOK

Douglas Bryan BADA LAPAD
The Old Bakery, St. David's Bridge. TN1 3HN. (Douglas and Catherine Bryan). Es 1971. Open 9.30-5, Wed. 9.30-1 and by appoin ment. SIZE: Medium. *STOCK: Mainly Englis oak furniture, 17th-18th C; woodcarvings, som metalware.* LOC: Adjacent Tanyard car park off road towards Windmill. PARK: Adjacen TEL: 01580 713103; fax - 01580 712407.

Cranbrook Antique Centre
15 High St. (Mr. and Mrs R. Bisram). Open 10- SIZE: 7 dealers - 2 floors. *STOCK: 19th C fu niture, collectables and silver.* TEL: 015 712173.

Cranbrook Gallery
21B Stone St. TN17 3HE. (P.A. Donovan). Op 9.15-5, Sat. 9.15-4. CL: Mon. *STOCK: Wate colours, prints and maps, 18th-19th C.* TE 01580 713021.

Swan Antiques
Stone St. (R. White). Est. 1982. Open 10-5, We 10-1. SIZE: Medium. *STOCK: Country furnitu 17th-19th C, from £500+; folk art and nai paintings.* LOC: Town centre. PARK: Easy. TE 01580 712720; home - 01580 291864. SER: Va ations; buys at auction. FAIRS: Olympia; Batters Decorative and Fine Art. VAT: Spec.

The Wooden Chair Antiques Centre
Waterloo Rd. TN17 3JQ. (Mrs G. Evans). Op 9.30-5.30. *STOCK: General antiques, furnitu and collectables.* LOC: Opposite Cranbro Public School. PARK: Easy. TEL: 01580 7136 SER: Upholstery and soft furnishings.

CRAYFORD

Watling Antiques
139 Crayford Rd. DA1 4AS. Open 10-6. *STOCK: General antiques and shipping goo* TEL: 01322 523620.

DARTFORD

Dartford Antiques
27 East Hill. (M. Skudder). Est. 1976. Open 10 SIZE: Medium. *STOCK: Furniture, 19th-20th £25-£100; collectors' items.* LOC: On hill i town from tunnel. PARK: Easy. TEL: 01 291350. SER: Valuations.

DEAL

Decors
67 Beach St. CT14 6HY. (N. Loftus-Potter). 1973. Open 9.30-7 including Sun; open in wi Fri.-Mon. or by appointment. *STOCK: Decora items, general antiques and fabrics (includ modern).* PARK: Easy. TEL: 01304 3680 home - same.

)eal continued

Che Print Room Gallery

5a Beach St. CT14 6DS. (M. McKenna). Open Mon., Fri. and Sat. 10-1 and 2.30-5.30, other imes by appointment. *STOCK: Antiquarian and Continental prints and maps.* TEL: 01304 68904.

)uill Antiques

2 Alfred Sq. CT14 6LR. (A.J. and A.R. Young).)pen 9-5.30. *STOCK: General antiques, porcelain, ostcards.* TEL: 01304 375958.

ierendipity

68 High St. CT14 6BQ. (M. and K. Short). Est. 976. Open 10-12.30 and 2-4.30, Sat. 9.30-5, or y appointment. CL: Thurs. SIZE: Medium. *TOCK: Staffordshire figures, ceramics, pictures, ırniture, etc.* PARK: Easy. TEL: 01304 369165; ome - 01304 366536. SER: Valuations; restortions (ceramics, oil paintings).

)OVER

. and L. Saunders

96/197 London Rd. CT17 0TF. Est. 1980. Open .30-5.30. *STOCK: General antiques.* TEL: 1304 214003.

EAST PECKHAM, Nr. Tonbridge

Desmond and Amanda North

The Orchard, Hale St. TN12 5JB. Est. 1971. Open daily, appointment advisable. SIZE: Medium. *STOCK: Oriental rugs, runners, carpets and cushions, 1800-1939, £60-£3,500.* LOC: On A228 (was B2015), 150yds. south of junction with B2016. PARK: Easy. TEL: 01622 871353; home - same. SER: Valuations; restorations (reweaving, re-edging, patching, cleaning).

EDENBRIDGE

Chevertons of Edenbridge Ltd LAPADA

Taylour House, 67-71 High St. TN8 5AL. (D. Adam). Open 9-5.30. SIZE: Large. *STOCK: Furniture and accessories, £250-£25,000.* LOC: From Westerham, on B2026 to Edenbridge. PARK: Own. TEL: 01732 863196/863358; fax - 01732 864298. VAT: Stan/Spec.

FARNINGHAM

P.T. Beasley

Forge Yard, High St. DA4 0DB. (P.T. and R. Beasley). Est. 1964. CL: Tues. *STOCK: English furniture, some pewter, brass, Delft, woodcarvings.* LOC: Opposite Social Club. TEL: 01322 862453.

FAVERSHAM

Collectors' Corner
East St/Crescent Rd. ME13 8AD. Est. 1952. Open 10-3. CL: Sat. SIZE: Small. *STOCK: Collectors' items - coins and medals, stamps, cigarette and post cards, badges, ceramics and silver, jewellery, prints, oils and watercolours, copper and brass, 18th-20th C, £1-£20,000.* LOC: Opposite P.O., at only set of traffic lights. PARK: Easy and at rear of shop by arrangement. TEL: 01795 539721; home - 01795 536642. SER: Valuations.

Squires Antiques (Faversham)
3 Jacob Yard, Preston St. ME13 8NY. (A. Squires). Est. 1985. Open 10-5. CL: Wed. and Thurs. *STOCK: General antiques.* TEL: 01795 531503.

FOLKESTONE

Richard Amos
37 Cheriton High St. CT19 4EY. Open 9.30-12 and 2-5. CL: Wed. pm. *STOCK: General antiques.* TEL: 01303 275449.

Lawton's Antiques
26 Canterbury Rd. CT19 5NG. (Ian Lawton). Resident. Open 9-5.30. CL: Wed. SIZE: Small. *STOCK: Paintings, Victorian furniture, silver and china, general antiques.* LOC: Off Dover road. PARK: Easy. TEL: 01303 246418; home - 01303 255431; mobile - 0850 333136. SER: Valuations; restorations (paintings and furniture); buys at auction. VAT: Stan/Spec.

Alan Lord Antiques
71 Tontine St. CT20 1JR. (A.G., J.A. and R.G. Lord). Est. 1956. Open 9-1 and 2-5. CL: Sat. pm. SIZE: Large. *STOCK: Period and Victorian furniture, china, silver, etc. Rear warehouse - trade and shipping goods.* LOC: Road up from harbour. PARK: Easy. TEL: 01303 253674 anytime. VAT: Stan/Spec.

G. and D.I. Marrin and Sons
149 Sandgate Rd. CT20 2DA. ABA. Est. 1949. Open 9.30-1 and 2.30-5.30. SIZE: Large. *STOCK: Maps, early engravings, topographical and sporting prints, paintings, drawings, books, engravings.* TEL: 01303 253016; fax - 01303 850956. SER: Restorations; framing. VAT: Stan.

FOUR ELMS, Nr. Edenbridge

Treasures
The Cross Roads. (B. Ward-Lee). Open 10-5. *STOCK: Copper, brass, glass, porcelain, silver, jewellery, linen, books, toys, pine, small furniture and collectables.* TEL: 01732 700363.

Yew Tree Antiques
The Cross Roads. TN8 7NH. (G. Nixon). Est. 1984. Open 9-5. SIZE: Medium. *STOCK: Porcelain and copper, 19th-20th C, £5-£500;*

Four Elms continued

glass, jewellery, linen, small furniture an collectables. LOC: Off A25 - B269. PARK: Eas TEL: 01732 700215.

GRAVESEND

Copperfield Antiques
33 Darnley Rd. DA11 9QH. (Mrs J. Wade an Mrs C. Frid). Est. 1989. Open 10-4.30. CL: We SIZE: Small. *STOCK: Mainly Victorian mahogany and satin walnut furniture, som smalls, £5-£500.* LOC: Near railway statio PARK: Nearby. TEL: 01474 535200; home 01474 569982. SER: Restorations.

Alan Wood
Open by appointment. *STOCK: Specialist i Staffordshire Portrait figures.* TEL: 01474 533722

HADLOW, Nr.Tonbridge

The Pedlar's Pack
The Square. TN11 0DA. (Mrs Nina Joy). Es 1976. Open 10-5.30, Wed. 10-1. CL: Mon. SIZ Medium. *STOCK: Country furniture, £50-£60 brass, copper, glass and china, £25-£300; a 18th-19th C; small interesting items, 19th-20th C jewellery, £40-£600.* LOC: On Tonbridge Maidstone Rd. PARK: Easy. TEL: 01732 85129 home - same.

Rosewood Gallery
High St. (R. and G. King). Est. 1969. *STOC Oriental carpets, general antiques and curio* LOC: A26. PARK: Easy. TEL: 01732 852359; f enquiries re. carpets - 01732 850228. SE Repairs and hand cleaning (carpets). VAT: Stan.

HARRIETSHAM, Nr. Maidstone

Judith Peppitt
Chegworth Manor Farm, Chegworth. ME17 1D Open by appointment. *STOCK: English wate colours, 19th-20th C.* LOC: 1 mile from Lee Castle. PARK: Easy. TEL: 01622 859313.

HAWKHURST

Septimus Quayles Emporium
Ockley Rd. TN18 4NG. (Mrs M.R. Martin). E 1971. Open 9.30-5, Sat. 9.30-4. CL: Wed. p *STOCK: General small antiques.* TEL: 015 752222.

HEADCORN, Nr. Ashford

Penny Lampard
31-33 High St. TN27 9NE. (Mrs P. Lampar Est. 1981. Open 9.30-5.30. SIZE: Large. *STOC Stripped pine and dark wood furniture.* PAR Easy. TEL: 01622 890682. FAIRS: Sutt Valence. VAT: Stan.

HYTHE

John Jackson LAPADA
99 North Rd. CT21 4AS . (J.H. Jackson). Open by appointment. *STOCK: Formal and decorative furniture, 17th-19th C, related accessories.* TEL: 01303 266732. FAIRS: London.

Malthouse Arcade
High St. CT21 5BW. (Mr and Mrs R.M. Maxtone Grahame). Est. 1974. Open Fri., Sat. and Bank Holiday Mon. 9.30-5.30. SIZE: Large - 37 stalls. *STOCK: Furniture, jewellery and collectors' items.* LOC: West end of High St. PARK: 50yds. TEL: 01303 260103; home - 01304 613270.

Owlets
99 High St. CT21 5JH. Open 9-4.45. *STOCK: Antique and secondhand jewellery, silver, Staffordshire pottery, Swatch watches.* TEL: 01303 230333.

Samovar Antiques
158 High St. CT21 5JR. (Mrs F. Rignault). Open 9.30-5, Wed. 9.30-1. *STOCK: 19th C furniture, French Provincial furniture, Oriental carpets and rugs and general antiques.* PARK: Own. TEL: 01303 264239.

Traditional Pine Furniture
248 Seabrook Rd., Seabrook. CT21 5RQ. (M. Hannant). Est. 1977. Open daily. SIZE: Large. *STOCK: Pine, 19th C, £50-£500.* LOC: 1.5 miles from end of M20 on A259. PARK: Easy. TEL: 01303 239931. VAT: Stan.

LAMBERHURST

The China Locker
TN3 8HN. (G. Wilson). Open by appointment only. SIZE: Small. *STOCK: Prints, 18th-19th C, £5-£40.* TEL: 01892 890555. FAIRS: Penshurst Village Hall; Sutton Valence School; Spa Hotel, Tunbridge Wells.

LEIGH, Nr. Tonbridge

Clive Marsden
TN11 8RL. Open by appointment only. *STOCK: Furniture and clocks.* TEL: 01732 833794. SER: Restorations (furniture and clocks); furniture and clock cases made to order.

Anthony Woodburn BADA LAPADA
Orchard House, High St. TN11 8RH. Est. 1975. Open daily, Sun. by appointment. SIZE: Medium. *STOCK: Clocks and barometers, 17th to early 19th C.* LOC: Off A21. PARK: Easy. TEL: 01732 832258; fax - 01732 838023. SER: Valuations; buys at auction (clocks). VAT: Spec.

LITTLEBOURNE, Nr. Canterbury

Jimmy Warren Antiques
Cedar Lodge, 28 The Hill. CT3 1TA. Est. 1969. Open 9-6 including Sun. *STOCK: Decorative antiques, 18th-19th C; garden ornaments.* LOC: A257. PARK: Own. TEL: 01227 721510; fax - 01227 722431. SER: Valuations; restorations. VAT: Stan/Spec.

MAIDSTONE

Charles International Antiques
LAPADA
Unit 2 Phoenix Park, Coldred Rd., Parkwood Industrial Estate. (Mr and Mrs C. Bremner). Est. 1968. Open 9-4.30. *STOCK: Victorian, Edwardian and shipping goods.* TEL: 01622 682882. SER: Valuations; full container and documentation facilities.

Newnham Court Antiques
Newnham Court Shopping Village, Bearsted Rd. (Mr and Mrs Draper). Est. 1991. Open 9-5.45, Sun. 10.30-4.30. SIZE: Medium. *STOCK: Dining furniture including sideboards and cabinets, late Victorian to 1930's, £300-£2,500; collectables, £1-£250.* PARK: Easy. TEL: 01622 631526. VAT: Stan/Spec.

Sutton Valence Antiques LAPADA
Unit 4 Haslemere Parkwood Estate, Sutton Rd. ME15 9NL. (T. and N. Mullarkey). Est. 1971. Open 9-5.30, Sun. 11-4. SIZE: Large warehouse. *STOCK: Antique and shipping furniture.* LOC: Approx. 3 miles south of Maidstone town centre, just off A274. PARK: Easy. TEL: 01622 675332; fax - 01622 692593. SER: Container packing and shipping; courier; buys at auction.

MARGATE

Furniture Mart
Grotto Hill. CT9 2BU. (R.G. Scott). Est. 1971. CL: Wed. SIZE: Large. *STOCK: General antiques £1-£1,500; shipping goods.* LOC: Corner of Bath Place. TEL: 01843 220653. SER: Restorations; stripping; restoration materials supplied. VAT: Global/Stan.

NEWNHAM, Nr. Sittingbourne

Periwinkle Press
47 The Street. ME9 0LN. (A.L. and C. Swain). Est. 1967. Open 10.30-6, Sun. 12.30-6. *STOCK: Antiquarian books and prints, maps, watercolours.* LOC: Village centre. PARK: Easy. TEL: 01795 890388. SER: Restorations (prints and oils); framing.

NORTHFLEET

Northfleet Hill Antiques
36 The Hill. DA11 9EX. (Mrs M. Kilby). Est. 1986. Open Tues., Fri. and Sat. 9.30-5. SIZE: Small. *STOCK: Furniture, 19th to early 20th C, £50-£800; bygones and collectables, £1-£100.* LOC: A226 near junction with B261 and B2175. PARK: Easy (behind Ye Olde Coach and Horses Inn). TEL: 01474 321521.

ORPINGTON

Antica
48 High St., Green Street Green. Open 10-5.30. *STOCK: General antiques.* TEL: 01689 851181.

OTFORD

Ellenor Antiques and Tea Shop
11a High St. (Ellenor Hospice Care). Open 10-5. SIZE: Medium. *STOCK: Furniture, ceramics, glass, 19th to early 20th C, £5-£1,500.* LOC: Towards Sevenoaks, 3 miles south of junction 4, M25. PARK: Nearby. TEL: 01959 524322. SER: Items sold on donation or commission basis for hospice charity.

PENSHURST, Nr. Tonbridge

Buxton House Stores
TN11 8BT. (Sali Morant and Jonny Farringdon). Est. 1972. Open Thurs., Fri., Sat. 12-5, Sun. 2-5. *STOCK: Furniture, textiles, linens and decorative items, £2-£250.* LOC: Main road. PARK: Easy. TEL: 01892 870220; home - same; internet - http://www.wizzo.demon.co.uk/.

RAMSGATE

De Tavener Antiques
24 Addington St. CT11 9JJ. (Mr and Mrs I.E. Gregg). Est. 1983. Open 9.30-5.30, Wed. 9.30-12.30. SIZE: Small. *STOCK: Clocks and barometers, bric-a-brac.* LOC: End of A299, above Sally Line berth. PARK: Easy. TEL: 01843 582213; home - same. SER: Valuations; restorations (clocks and barometers). FAIRS: Great Danes Hotel, Maidstone; Inn on the Lake Hotel, Gravesend.

Granny's Attic
2 Addington St. CT11 9JL. (Penelope J. Warn). Est. 1987. Open 10-5. CL: Thurs. pm. SIZE: Medium. *STOCK: Pre-1940's items, £2-£500.* LOC: Left off harbour approach road or right off Westcliffe Rd. PARK: Easy. TEL: 01843 588955; home - 01843 596288.

Thanet Antiques Trading Centre
45 Albert St. CT11 9EX. (Mr and Mrs R. Fomison). Est. 1971. Open 9-5, Sun. by appointment. SIZE: Large. *STOCK: Furniture and*

Ramsgate continued

a-brac, 18th-20th C, £1-£5,000. LOC: From London Rd. right to seafront. With harbour on right turn first left down Addington St., then last right. PARK: Own. TEL: 01843 597336; home - 01843 597540.

RIVERHEAD

Amherst Antiques LAPADA
23 London Rd. TN13 2BU. (D. Brick). Est. 1985. Open 9.30-5. CL: Wed. SIZE: Small. *STOCK: Furniture, £500-£3,000; porcelain, £50-£2,000; silver, £50-£3,000; Tunbridge ware £50-£1,500.* LOC: A25. PARK: Nearby. TEL: 01732 455047. FAIRS: Olympia; NEC; Buxton; Guildford; West London; Chester; Snape; Barbican. VAT: Stan/Spec.

Mandarin Gallery
32 London Rd. TN13 2DE. (J. and Mrs. M.C Liu). Est. 1984. Open 9.30-5. CL: Wed. SIZE Medium. *STOCK: Chinese rosewood and lacque furniture, 18th-19th C, £200-£4,000; Orienta porcelain, £35-£3,500; Oriental paintings on sil and paper, £15-£500; both 19th-20th C; jade stone, ivory and wood carvings.* Not Stocked Non-Oriental items. LOC: A21. PARK: Easy TEL: 01732 457399; home - same. SER: Restorations (Chinese furniture); framing.

Roundabout Antiques
28a London Rd. TN13 2DE. (Mrs C. Ledamu and Mrs L. López Fonseca). Est. 1991. Ope 9.30-5. CL: Wed. SIZE: Small. *STOCK: Collectables, china, glass, smalls, including Victoria and Art Deco, £5-£100; furniture, to £300; lace linen and embroideries, £1-£200, Victorian t 1930's.* LOC: A25, then take London Rd. toward Dunton Green, shop 50 yards from mini roundabout. PARK: Easy. TEL: 01732 741873.

ROCHESTER

Baggins Book Bazaar - The Largest Secondhand Bookshop in England
19 High St. ME1 1QB. Open 10-6 including Su *STOCK: Secondhand and antiquarian book* TEL: 01634 811651.

Cottage Style Antiques
24 Bill Street Rd. ME2 4RB. (W. Miskimmin Open 9.30-5.30. *STOCK: General and architectural antiques.* TEL: 01634 717623.

Deo Juvante Antiques
43 High St. ME1 1LN. (Lorraine and Margar Petrie). Est. 1969. SIZE: Medium. *STOCK Furniture, 1650-1930's, £100-£500; smalls, 180 1950's, £5-£100; gold and silver, 1750-1950' £20-£100.* LOC: A2 into town, turn right in High St, then first right again. PARK: Limite and nearby. TEL: 01634 843750. SER: Val ations; restorations. VAT: Stan/Spec.

Rochester continued

Droods
62 High St. (A.J. Stewart and C. Morgan). Open 10-5.30. *STOCK: General antiques.* TEL: 01634 829000.

Gem Antiques
88 High St. ME1 1JT. (Jason Hunt). Est. 1980. Open 9-5.30, Sun. 12-6. SIZE: Medium. *STOCK: General antiques including jewellery.* LOC: A20, centre of High St. PARK: Nearby. TEL: 01634 814129. SER: Valuations; restorations (jewellery). FAIRS: Barbican, Olympia, Kenilworth, Goodwood, NEC (Aug), Café Royal. VAT: Stan/Spec.

Francis Iles
Rutland House, La Providence, High St. ME1 1LX. (The Family Iles). Est. 1960. Open 9.30-5.30. SIZE: Large. *STOCK: Watercolours and oils, mainly 20th C, £50-£10,000.* LOC: Off central High St. PARK: 40yds. TEL: 01634 843081; fax - 01634 846681. SER: Restorations (cleaning and relining); framing. VAT: Stan/Spec.

Langley Galleries
143 High St. ME1 1EL. (K.J. Cook). Est. 1978. Open 9-5.30. *STOCK: Prints, watercolours, oils, 19th-20th C.* TEL: 01634 811802. SER: Restorations and cleaning (watercolours and oils); framing.

Memories
128 High St. ME1 1JT. (Mrs V.A. Lhermette). Est. 1985. Open 9-5. SIZE: Medium. *STOCK: Small furniture, £50-£500; china, £5-£75; both 1900-1950; pictures, late Victorian to Edwardian, £20-£70; collectables, bric-a-brac, linen.* PARK: Opposite. TEL: 01634 811044.

Rochester Antique Centre
93 High St. ME1 1LX. (Jane Staff and Jim Field). Est. 1990. Open 10-5, including Sun. in summer. SIZE: Large - 3 floors. *STOCK: Smalls, clocks, silver, furniture and dolls.* LOC: Near the cathedral. PARK: Easy (loading only). TEL: 01634 846144. SER: Valuations; restorations (clocks and dolls). VAT: Stan/Spec.

ROLVENDEN, Nr. Cranbrook

Falstaff Antiques
63-67 High St. TN17 4LP. (C.M. Booth). Est. 1964. Open 9-6, Sun. by appointment. SIZE: Medium. *STOCK: English furniture, £5-£700; china, metal, glass, silver, £1-£200.* Not Stocked: Paintings. LOC: On A28, 3 miles from Tenterden, 1st shop on left in village. PARK: Easy. TEL: 01580 241234. SER: Valuations. VAT: Stan/Spec.

Kent Cottage
39 High St. TN17 4LP. (Mrs R. Amos). Open by appointment. *STOCK: Porcelain - Continental*

Rolvenden continued

including Meissen, and English; English scent bottles, silver and small furniture. LOC: A28, 3 miles S.E of Tenterden. PARK: Easy. TEL: 01580 241719.

J.D. and R.M. Walters
10 Regent St. TN17 4PE. Est. 1977. Open 8-6. SIZE: Small. *STOCK: Mahogany furniture, 18th-19th C.* LOC: A28 turn left in village centre onto B2086, shop on left. PARK: Easy. TEL: 01580 241563; home - same. SER: Handmade copies of period furniture including chairs; restorations (GMC). VAT: Stan/Spec.

SANDGATE, Nr. Folkestone

Beaubush House Antiques LAPADA
95 High St. CT20 3BY. (J. Winikus). Open 9.30-5, Sat. 10-4. *STOCK: British and Continental porcelain and pottery, 18th to early 19th C.* TEL: 01303 249099/265567.

Christopher Buck Antiques BADA LAPADA
56-60 High St. CT20 3AP. Est. 1983. Open 10-5. CL: Wed. SIZE: Medium. *STOCK: English furniture, 18th C, £500-£30,000; decorative items, 18th-19th C, £100-£2,000.* LOC: 5 mins. from M20. PARK: Easy. TEL: 01303 221229. SER: Valuations; restorations (furniture); buys at auction. FAIRS: Olympia, Chelsea. VAT: Stan/Spec.

Dench Antiques
Cromwell House, 32 High St. CT20 3AP. (Mr and Mrs J.W.G. Elcombe). Est. 1980. Open 10-6. SIZE: Medium + warehouse. *STOCK: 18th-19th C Continental and English furniture, decorators' items and statuary.* PARK: Easy. TEL: 01303 240824; fax - 01303 257346. VAT: Stan/Spec.

Michael File Antiques
13 Sandgate High St. CT20 3BA. Est. 1972. Open 9.30-5.30. *STOCK: Furniture, silver plate, Victoriana, decorator's items and collectables.* TEL: 01303 249574.

Finch Antiques
40 High Street. CT20 3AP. (Robert and Sylvia Finch). Est. 1978. Open 9.30-6, Sun. 11-5. SIZE: Medium. *STOCK: Furniture, 1800-1920, £150-£3,000; silver plate and writing items, £5-£400.* PARK: Easy. TEL: 01303 240725. SER: Restorations (furniture, French polishing).

Michael Fitch Antiques LAPADA
99 High St. CT20 3BY. Open 10-5.30, Sun. by appointment. *STOCK: Georgian, Victorian and Edwardian furniture and clocks.* TEL: 01303 249600; fax - same; evenings - 01303 230839.

Sandgate continued

Freeman and Lloyd Antiques BADA LAPADA

44 High St. CT20 3AP. (K. Freeman and M.R. Lloyd). Est. 1968. Open 10-5.30, Mon. and Wed. by appointment only. SIZE: Medium. *STOCK: Fine Georgian and Regency English furniture; clocks, paintings and other period items.* LOC: On main coast road between Hythe and Folkestone (A259). PARK: Easy. TEL: 01303 248986; fax - same; mobile - 0860 100073. SER: Valuations. FAIRS: Chelsea (Sept); BADA(March); Olympia(Gold Section-June, BADA Pavilion-Nov). VAT: Spec.

David Gilbert Antiques

30 High St. CT20 3AP. Est. 1975. Open 9-5. SIZE: Medium. *STOCK: Furniture, smalls, glass, 1790-1930, £5-£1,000.* LOC: A259. PARK: Easy. TEL: 01303 850491; home - 01304 812237. SER: Valuations.

Robin Homewood Antiques

59a Sandgate High St. CT20 3AH. (R.A. Homewood). Est. 1984. Open 9.30-5.30, Sun. by appointment. *STOCK: General antiques.* TEL: 01303 249466.

Sandgate continued

Hyron Antiques

86 High St. CT20 3BY. (R. Welsh). Open 9.30-5.30. *STOCK: General antiques.* TEL: 01303 240698. SER: Buys at auction.

Nordens

43/43a High St. CT20 3AH. Est. 1946. Open 10-1 and 2.30-5.30 or by appointment. *STOCK: General antiques, Victoriana, bric-a-brac.* LOC: Main Folkestone to Hythe Rd. TEL: 01303 248443.

Old English Oak

102 High St. CT20 3BY. (A. Martin). *STOCK: Oak furniture and interesting items.* TEL: 01303 248560.

Old English Pine

100 High St. CT20 3BY. (A. Martin). Open 10-6. *STOCK: Pine furniture and interesting items.* TEL: 01303 248560.

J.T. Rutherford and Son

55 High St. CT20 3AH. Est. 1963. Open 9-6, Sun. 9-2 or by appointment. SIZE: Medium. *STOCK: Furniture and longcase clocks; weapons - flintlock percussion pistols, muskets, edged weapons, swords including dress.* LOC: A295. PARK: Easy. TEL: 01303 249515; home - 01303 260822. SER: Restorations (furniture); buys at auction. VAT: Stan/Spec.

Sandgate continued

Sandgate Antiques Centre
61-63 High St. CT20 3AH. (Jonathan Greenwall Antiques). Est. 1964. Open 9.30-5.30. SIZE: Large. LOC: Folkestone-Brighton road. PARK: Easy. TEL: 01303 248987. SER: Valuations.

SANDHURST

Forge Antiques and Restorations
Rye Rd. TN18 5JG. (J. Nesfield). Open 9-6. *STOCK: Victoriana, ceramics, glass, furniture including pine, £1-£5,000.* LOC: A268. PARK: Own. TEL: 01580 850308/850665. SER: Restorations (furniture). VAT: Spec.

SANDWICH

Delf Stream Gallery
14 New St. CT13 9AB. (N. Rocke). Est. 1985. Open Mon., Thurs., Fri. and Sat. 10-5, other days by appointment. SIZE: Small. *STOCK: Art pottery, 19th-20th C, £25-£2,000.* LOC: Main one-way road in town centre, around corner from Guildhall. PARK: Easy. TEL: 01304 617684; home - same; fax - 01304 615479. SER: Valuations (art pottery); restorations (as stock); buys at auction. FAIRS: Ardingly; Newark; Kensington Decorative Arts.

Noah's Ark Antique Centre
King St. CT13 9BT. (Mr and Mrs R.M. Maxtone Graham). Est. 1978. Open 10-4. CL: Wed. SIZE: Medium. *STOCK: Staffordshire figures, china, porcelain, antiquarian books, watercolours, oil paintings, prints, small furniture, silver, jewellery, copper and brass.* PARK: Guildhall. TEL: 01304 611144; home - 01304 613270.

James Porter Antiques
5 Potter St. CT13 9DR. Est. 1948. Open 9.30-5.30. CL: Wed. *STOCK: Period furniture, brass and copper.* TEL: 01304 612218.

Nancy Wilson
Monken Quay, Strand St. CT13 9HP. Open 11-5, other times by appointment. SIZE: Large. *STOCK: Period furniture, longcase clocks, £100-£5,000.* LOC: 100yds. from King's Arms public house. PARK: Easy. TEL: 01304 612345; home - same.

SEVENOAKS

The Antiques Centre
120 London Rd., Tubs Hill. TN13 1BA. (Ruth Harrison). Est. 1964. Open 10-1 and 2-4.30, Wed. and Sat. 10-1, other times by appointment. SIZE: Large. *STOCK: Furniture, 17th-19th C; interesting and decorative items.* LOC: Near station, on left side of hill. PARK: Opposite or in driveway. TEL: 01732 452104. VAT: Stan/Spec.

Sevenoaks continued

Bradbourne Gallery
4 St. John's Hill. TN13 3NP. (Jane Ross Antiques and Decoration). Open 9.30-5, Sat. 9-1. SIZE: Several dealers. *STOCK: Silver, furniture, ceramics, jewellery, glass, prints and paintings, treen, 18th C to Edwardian.* LOC: 1 mile from town centre, continuation of High St./Dartford Rd. PARK: Easy. TEL: 01732 460756; fax - same.

Peppercorns Antique and Craft Centre
57/59 High St. TN13 1JF. (Miss M.A. Hubert). Open 10.15-5.30. SIZE: Large. *STOCK: Wide variety of general antiques and collectables including furniture, 1850-1920, £5-£200.* LOC: Town centre. PARK: Nearby. TEL: 01732 740329. SER: Valuations; restorations (pictures).

SIDCUP

Sidcup Antique and Craft Centre
Elm Parade, Main Rd. DA14 6NF. (M.H. and G.M. Tripp). Est. 1993. Open 10-5 including Sun. SIZE: 90+ dealers. *STOCK: Wide range of antiques and craft items.* LOC: M25, junction 3 then A20 to Sidcup (Queen Mary's Hospital). Premises near traffic lights, opposite police station. PARK: Easy. TEL: 0181 300 7387.

SNODLAND

Aaron Antiques
90 High St. ME6 5AL. (R.J. Goodman). Open 10-5 or by appointment. *STOCK: Clocks and pocket watches, paintings and prints, period and shipping furniture, English, Continental and Oriental porcelain; antiquarian books, postcards, coins and medals.* TEL: 01634 241748. VAT: Stan.

SOUTHBOROUGH, Nr. Tunbridge Wells

Henry Baines **LAPADA**
14 Church Rd. TN4 0RX. Est. 1968. Open Tues.-Fri. 9.30-5, Sat. 10-4.30, prior telephone call advisable. *STOCK: Early oak and country furniture especially tables and sets of chairs; French provincial furniture and decorative items.* PARK: Easy. TEL: 01892 532099. VAT: Stan/Spec.

ST. MARGARET'S BAY, Nr. Dover

Alexandra's Antiques
1-2 The Droveway. CT15 6DY. (J. Cox-Freeman). Est. 1979. Open 10-1 and 2.15-4.30, Wed. and Sat. pm. by appointment only. SIZE: Small. *STOCK: Paintings by Victorian and local artists; furniture, porcelain and jewellery.* LOC: Between Dover and Deal at top of hill. PARK: Easy. TEL: 01304 853102; fax - 01304 853306; home - 01304 852682.

STOCKBURY

Steppes Hill Farm Antiques BADA
The Hill Farm, South St. ME9 7RB. (W.F.A. Buck). Est. 1965. Always open, appointment advisable. SIZE: Medium. *STOCK: English porcelain, pottery, pot-lids, 18th-20th C, £5-£5,000; small silver; caddy spoons, wine labels, silver boxes, 18th-19th C, to £1,000; furniture, 18th-19th C, £10-£5,000.* LOC: 5 mins. from M2 on A249. Enquire in village for Steppes Hill Antiques. PARK: Easy. TEL: 01795 842205. SER: Valuations; buys at auction. FAIRS: BADA; Chelsea; International Ceramics. VAT: Spec.

SUNDRIDGE, Nr. Sevenoaks

Sundridge Gallery
9 Church Rd. TN14 6DT. (T. and M. Tyrer). Open 10-5.30. *STOCK: Watercolours and oils, 19th-20th C; some Oriental rugs.* TEL: 01959 564104.

Colin Wilson Antiques
99-103 Main Rd. TN14 6EQ. Open 10-6. *STOCK: Victorian mahogany and inlaid Edwardian furniture.* TEL: 01959 562043. SER: Repairs; restorations. VAT: Stan/Spec.

SUTTON VALENCE, Nr. Maidstone

Sutton Valence Antiques LAPADA
North St. ME17 3AP. (T. and N. Mullarkey). Est. 1971. Open 9.30-5, Sun. 11-4. SIZE: Large. *STOCK: Furniture, porcelain, clocks, silver, metalware, shipping items, 18th-19th C.* LOC: On A274 Maidstone/Tenterden Rd. PARK: Side of shop. TEL: 01622 843333; fax - 01622 843499. SER: Valuations.

TENTERDEN

Flower House Antiques
90 High St. TN30 6JB. (Barry Rayner and Quentin Johnson). Est. 1965. Open 9.30-5.30, Sun. by appointment. SIZE: Medium. *STOCK: English and Continental furniture, 18th to early 19th C; Oriental works of art, 16th-19th C; pictures, lighting, mirrors, objets d'art.* LOC: A28. PARK: Easy and private. TEL: 01580 763764. SER: Valuations; restorations. VAT: Spec.

Garden House Antiques
116-118 High St. TN30 6HT. (H. Kirkham) Resident. Always open. *STOCK: Mainly 18th-19th C furniture, paintings and porcelain; old fishing reels and rods.* PARK: Easy. TEL: 01580 763664. SER: Valuations; interior design.

The Lace Basket
at Garden House, 116 High St. TN30 6HD. (C Walls). Open 10.30-5. *STOCK: Textiles, Victorian linen and lace, samplers and quilts.* PARK Opposite. TEL: 01580 763664. SER: Valuations.

Sparks Antiques
4 Manor Row, High St. TN30 6HP. (Patrick Robbins and Philip Ingham). Est. 1967. Open 9-5.30, Sun. by appointment. SIZE: Medium. *STOCK: English and Continental furniture, 17th-19th C, £200-£8,000; paintings and prints, 18th-19th C, £200-£5,000; pottery and metalwork 18th-19th C, £50-£1,000.* LOC: A28. PARK Easy. TEL: 01580 766696; home - 01424 43123 or 01797 362276. SER: Valuations; restoration (furniture). VAT: Spec.

Tenterden Antiques Centre
66 High St. TN30 6AU. (B.M. Jackson). Open 10-5 including Sun. SIZE: 20 dealers. *STOCK: Wide range of general antiques.* TEL: 01580 765885 765655.

TEYNHAM, Nr. Sittingbourne

Jackson-Grant Antiques
The Old Chapel, 133 London Rd. ME9 9QJ (D.M. Jackson-Grant). Est. 1966. Open 10-5, Sun 1-5. SIZE: Large. *STOCK: Country furniture oak, 17th-19th C, £50-£2,000; period walnu £450-£1,500; mahogany, £100-£1,000; some pine; smalls, 18th C to Art Deco, £5-£500.* LOC A2 between Faversham and Sittingbourne

Teynham continued

PARK: Easy. TEL: 01795 522027; home - same; mobile - 0831 591881. FAIRS: Newark; Ardingly. VAT: Stan/Spec.

TONBRIDGE

Barden House Antiques
1-3 Priory St. TN9 2AP. (Mrs B.D. Parsons). Open 10-5. SIZE: 5 dealers. *STOCK: General antiques and collectables.* TEL: 01732 350142; evenings - 01732 355718.

Lawsons
165 High St. TN9 1BX. (M.P. Baldwin). Est. 1966. Open 10-5.30. SIZE: Large. *STOCK: Furniture, smalls and pictures, £5-£1,000.* LOC: North end of High St. PARK: Public at rear. TEL: 01732 367606. VAT: Stan/Spec.

Derek Roberts Fine Antique Clocks, Music Boxes, Barometers BADA
25 Shipbourne Rd. TN10 3DN. Author of several books on clocks. Est. 1968. Open 9.30-5.30 or by appointment. SIZE: Medium. *STOCK: Fine restored clocks, mostly £1,000-£80,000; music boxes.* LOC: A227. From London A21 Tonbridge North turnoff, left 20 yds before first lights, left again and 50 yds up on right. PARK: Easy. TEL: 01732 358986; fax - 01732 771842. SER: Cabinet and clock making. VAT: Spec.

B. Somerset
Stags Head, 9 Stafford Rd. TN9 1HT. Est. 1948. Open 11-6.30. *STOCK: Clocks, £500-£5,000.* LOC: Off High Street beside castle. TEL: 01732 352017. SER: Valuations; restorations (cabinets, gilt and French polishing); buys at auction (longcase and bracket clocks). VAT: Stan.

TUNBRIDGE WELLS

Aaron Antiques
77 St. Johns Rd. TN4 9TT. (R.J. Goodman). Open 9-5. *STOCK: Clocks and pocket watches, paintings and prints; period and shipping furniture; English, Continental and Oriental porcelain; antiquarian books, postcards, coins and medals.* TEL: 01892 517644. VAT: Stan/Spec.

Amadeus Antiques
32 Mount Ephraim. TN3. (P.A. Davies). Open 10-5, Sun. by appointment. SIZE: Medium. *STOCK: Unusual furniture, to Art Deco, £50-£5,000; china and bric-a-brac, £25-£500; chandeliers, £100-£1,000.* LOC: Near hospital. PARK: Easy. TEL: 01892 544406; 01892 864884. SER: Valuations.

Baskerville Books
13 Nevill St. TN2 5RU. (Mike Banwell). Est. 1982. Open 10-5. CL: Wed. SIZE: Small. *STOCK:*

Tunbridge Wells continued

Antiquarian and secondhand books; small collectible antiques and occasional period and shipping furniture. LOC: 50 yards from entrance to Pantiles. PARK: Nearby. TEL: 01892 526776. SER: Valuations.

Nicholas Bowlby
9 Castle St. TN1 1XJ. Est. 1981. Open 10-5.30. CL: Mon. and Wed. SIZE: Large. *STOCK: English paintings, watercolours and drawings, 18th-20th C, £50-£20,000.* LOC: Near The Pantiles. TEL: 01892 510880. SER: Valuations; restorations; buys at auction (watercolours and drawings). VAT: Spec.

Chapel Place Antiques
9 Chapel Place. TN1 1YQ. (J. and A. Clare). Open 9-6. *STOCK: Antique and modern silver, old watches, jewellery, carriage clocks; some porcelain and dolls.* TEL: 01892 546561.

Claremont Antiques
6 Chapel Place. TN1 1YQ. (Anthony Broad). Open 10-5.30, other times by appointment. SIZE: Medium. *STOCK: Irish, Eastern European, French, etc pine, hardwood and painted country furniture, 18th-19th C; decorative items, all £10-£3,000.* LOC: Pedestrian precinct, lower end of High St. PARK: Nearby. TEL: 01892 511651. SER: Restorations (furniture). VAT: Spec.

Tunbridge Wells continued

Corn Exchange Antiques Centre
64 The Pantiles. TN2 5TN. (B. Henderson). Open 9.30-5. *STOCK: Furniture, clocks, books, prints, ceramics and silver.* TEL: 01892 539652.

County Antiques
94 High St. TN1 1YF. (Mrs. I. Hale). Open 10-5, Wed. 10-1. *STOCK: Small antiques and decorative items.* TEL: 01892 530767.

Cowden Antiques
24 Mount Ephraim Rd. TN1 1ED. (A. Linstead). Est. 1970. Open 10-5. CL: Wed. SIZE: Medium. *STOCK: Period oak and mahogany, decorative items and curtains.* PARK: Reasonable. TEL: 01892 520752. SER: Interiors. VAT: Stan/Spec.

Glassdrumman Antiques
at Pantiles Spa Antiques,4/6 Union Sq., The Pantiles. TN4 8LX. (G. and A. Dyson Rooke). Open 9.30-5, Sat. 9.30-5.30. SIZE: Large. *STOCK: Jewellery, silver, furniture, glass, china and collectables, 18th-19th C.* PARK: Nearby. TEL: 01892 541377.

Graham Gallery
1 Castle St. TN1 1XJ. (Joyce Graham). Est. 1987. Open 10.30-5, Sat. 10-5.30. CL: Mon. and Wed. *STOCK: 19th-20th C watercolours and Modern British paintings, £200-£5,000.* LOC: Off High St. PARK: Nearby. TEL: 01892 526695. VAT: Spec.

Tunbridge Wells continued

Hadlow Antiques
P.O Box 134. TN2 5YA. (M. and L. Adler). Est. 1966. Open by appointment only. SIZE: Small. *STOCK: Clocks, watches, 17th-20th C; dolls and accessories, automata, 18th-20th C; scientific and medical instruments, music boxes, singing birds, gramophones and collectors' items.* TEL: 01825 830368; fax - same. SER: Valuations; restorations; buys at auction. VAT: Stan/Spec.

Hall's Bookshop
20 Chapel Place. TN1 1YQ. Est. 1898. Open 9.30-5. *STOCK: Antiquarian and secondhand books.* TEL: 01892 527842.

Kentdale Restorations
Forge Rd., Eridge Green. TN3 9LJ. (C. Bigwood). Open 8.30-5.00. CL: Sat. *STOCK: Victorian furniture including extending tables.* TEL: 01892 863840. SER: Restorations (furniture); upholstery.

Linden Park Antiques
7 Union Sq., The Pantiles. TN4 8HE. (H.A. La Trobe and C. Bigwood). Est. 1993. Open 10-5.30, Sun. by appointment. SIZE: Medium. *STOCK: Victorian dining room furniture, £300-£5,000; other occasional furniture, £100-£2,000; prints, watercolours, copper and brass, pottery and porcelain, £10-£500.* PARK: Easy. TEL: 01892 538615. SER: Restorations; French polishing and re-leathering.

Howard Neville Antiques
21 The Pantiles. (H.C.C. Neville). Est. 1967. Open 9-6. SIZE: Medium. *STOCK: General antiques, furniture, sculpture and works of art, 16th-18th C.* PARK: Easy. TEL: 01892 511461; home - 01435 882409. SER: Valuations; restorations. VAT: Spec.

The Pantiles Antiques
31 The Pantiles. (Mrs E.M. Blackburn). Est. 1979. Open 10-5. SIZE: Medium. *STOCK: Georgian, Victorian and Edwardian furniture; 19th C porcelain, barometers, Jobling glass, silver.* PARK: Easy. TEL: 01892 531291.

Pantiles Spa Antiques
4/5/6 Union House, The Pantiles. TN4 8HE. (J.A. Cowpland). Est. 1985. Open 9.30-5, Sat. 9.30-5.30. SIZE: Large. *STOCK: Furniture, especially dining tables and chairs, £200-£10,000; pictures, £50-£3,000; clocks, £100-£5,000; porcelain, £50-£2,000; jewellery, £50-£200; silver, £50-£1,000; all 17th-19th C; dolls, bears and toys.* PARK: Nearby. TEL: 01892 541377; fax - 01435 865660. SER: Restorations (furniture). VAT: Spec.

Phoenix Antiques
48 and 51 St. John's Rd. TN4 9TP. (P. Janes, Miss J. Stott and R. Pilbeam). Est. 1982. Open 10-5.30 or by appointment. SIZE: Medium. *STOCK: Country and mahogany furniture, 18th-19th C, £50-£1,000; decorative furnishings, 18th-19th C, £5-£500.* LOC: On A26 from A21 into town, by St. John's church. PARK: Easy. TEL: 01892 549099. FAIRS: Brocante, Kensington Town Hall.

nbridge Wells continued

n Relf Antiques
2/134 Camden Rd. Open 9.30-1.30 and 2.30-30. *STOCK: Mainly furniture.* TEL: 01892 3362.

hn Thompson
The Pantiles. TN2 5TD. (J. Macdonald and N. ompson). Est. 1982. Open 9.30-1 and 2-5. ZE: Medium. *STOCK: Furniture, late 17th to rly 19th C; paintings 17th-20th C; decorative ms.* Not Stocked: Jewellery, silver and militaria. RK: Linden Road or Warwick Park. TEL: 392 547215. VAT: Spec.

nbridge Wells Antique Centre
Union Sq., The Pantiles. TN4 8HE. (N.J. rding). Est. 1980. Open 9.30-5. SIZE: Large. *OCK: Antiques and collectables including vellery, silver, Georgian and Victorian fur- ure, arms and militaria, Victorian Staffordshire ures, clocks and watches, Tunbridgeware, iques related books, fountain pens, £2-£4,000.* RK: Nearby. TEL: 01892 533708. SER: Valu- ons; shipping. VAT: Stan/Spec.

Country
e Corn Stores, 68 St. Johns Rd. TN4 9PE. (G.J. ce and C.M. Springett). Est. 1988. Open 9-5.30. ZE: Large. *STOCK: British and European intry furniture, £50-£5,000; associated decor- ve and interesting items, £5-£500; all 18th-19th* LOC: On main London Rd. to Southborough A21 trunk road which joins M25 and M26 at venoaks intersection. PARK: Own at rear. TEL: 392 523341. VAT: Stan.

EST MALLING

e Old Clock Shop
High St. ME19 6NA. (S.L. Luck). Est. 1970. en 9-5. SIZE: Large. *STOCK: Grandfather cks, 17th-19th C; carriage, bracket and wall cks.* LOC: Half a mile from M20. PARK: Easy. L: 01732 843246. VAT: Spec.

West Malling continued

Victoria Pataky Antiques and Reproductions
3 The Colonnade, West St. ME19 6QX. CL: Wed. *STOCK: General antiques, Victoriana.* TEL: 01732 843646.

Andrew Smith Antiques
89 High St. ME19 6NA. Est. 1978. Open 9.30-5.30, Sun. by appointment. SIZE: Medium. *STOCK: Jewellery, silver, porcelain and clocks; £50-£2,000.* LOC: Off M20, junction 4, A228. PARK: Easy. TEL: 01732 843087; home - same. VAT: Stan/Spec.

WESTERHAM

Apollo Galleries — LAPADA
19 -21 Market Sq. TN16 1AN. Open 9.30-5.30. SIZE: Large. *STOCK: Oil and watercolour paintings, bronzes, 19th to early 20th C; English and Continental furniture, clocks, 18th-19th C; porcelain, glass, silver.* TEL: 01959 562200. VAT: Spec.

Aquarius Antiques
Market Square. TN16 1AY. (G.W. Barr). Open 9.30-5.30. *STOCK: Mainly pictures, bronzes and small furniture.* TEL: 01959 561792; mobile - 0802 689253/0585 883441.

Brazil Antiques — LAPADA
2 The Green. TN16 1AS. *STOCK: Furniture, 18th-20th C.* TEL: 01959 563048; fax - 01959 563020. VAT: Stan/Spec.

Castle Antiques Centre
1 London Rd. TN16 1BB. (Stewart Ward Properties). Est. 1974. Open 10-5. SIZE: Small - 8 dealers. *STOCK: General antiques including tools, lace and linen, £5-£500.* LOC: Just off town centre. PARK: Easy - nearby. TEL: 01959 562492. SER: Valuations; clock repair; props for stage productions.

Anthony J. Hook
3 The Green. TN16 1AT. Est. 1948. Open 9-5.30, Sat. 10.30-4.30. SIZE: Medium. *STOCK: English furniture, 18th-19th C.* LOC: A25. TEL: 01959 562161. VAT: Stan/Spec.

Westerham continued

London House Antiques

4 Market Sq. TN16 1AW. Est. 1977. Open 10-5, Sun. 12-4. SIZE: Medium. *STOCK: Furniture, 18th-19th C, £500-£1,000; paintings, prints and engravings, 19th-20th C, £100-£2,000; English and German teddy bears and dolls, 19th-20th C, £100-£3,000; clocks and bronzes, 19th C, £300-£5,000; silver and porcelain, 19th-20th C, £50-£1,500.* LOC: Off M25, junction 6 on A25 to Westerham. PARK: Easy. TEL: 01959 564479.

Marks Antiques

5 The Green. TN16 1AS. (Alan and Michael Marks). Est. 1954. Open 9.30-5. SIZE: Medium. *STOCK: Furniture, £500-£30,000; clocks, barometers, porcelain, bronzes and pictures, £200-£3,000: all 18th-19th C.* LOC: A25. PARK: Easy. TEL: 01959 562017; home - 01268 542621. SER: Valuations; restorations (furniture, including upholstery); buys at auction (furniture). VAT: Stan/Spec.

Regal Antiques

2 Market Square. TN16 1AW. (E. Lawrence). Open 10-5. CL: Mon. and Tues. *STOCK: Vintage watches, portrait miniatures, porcelain and jewellery.* TEL: 01959 561778.

Denys Sargeant

21 The Green. TN16 1AX. Est. 1949. Open 9.30-5.30. *STOCK: Glass, especially chandeliers and candelabras, decanters and lustres.* TEL: 01959 562130. SER: Restorations (chandeliers); cleaning (chandeliers). VAT: Stan/Spec.

Taylor-Smith LAPADA

4 The Grange, High St. TN16 1AH. Open 10-5. CL: Wed. *STOCK: Fine 18th and 19th C furniture; paintings, porcelain, glass and decorative items.* TEL: 01959 563100; fax - 01959 561561.

Taylor-Smith LAPADA

2 High St. TN16 1RF. Open 10-5, Sun. 2.30-5. CL: Mon. and Tues. *STOCK: Books and Sir Winston Churchill items.* TEL: 01959 561561; fax - 01959 561561.

Westerham House Antiques

The Green. TN16 1AY. (W.R. Barr). Open 9.30-5.30. *STOCK: Victorian and period furniture, pictures and bronzes.* TEL: 01959 561622; mobile - 0802 689253/0585 883441.

WHITSTABLE

Laurens Antiques

2 Harbour St. CT5 1AG. (G. A. Laurens). Est. 1965. Open 9.30-5.30. SIZE: Medium. *STOCK: Furniture, 18th-19th C, £300-£500+.* LOC: Turn off Thanet Way at Longreach roundabout, straight down to one-way system in High St. PARK: Easy. TEL: 01227 261940; home - same. SER: Valuations; restorations (cabinet work); buys at auction.

Whitstable continued

Tankerton Antiques

136 Tankerton Rd. CT5 2AN. (Mrs. F. Hollan Est. 1985. Open 10-5, Tues. 10-4, Wed. 10-1. C Mon. SIZE: Medium. *STOCK: Furniture, Rege to 1930's, £50-£1,500; china, from 18th C, £1,500; glass, Regency to 1930's, to £4 postcards and other collectables.* LOC: Fr A299 Thanet Way take A290/B2205 turn off Whitstable. Through town and into Tankert Shop on right just past roundabout. TEL: 012 266490. SER: Valuations.

WINGHAM, Nr. Canterbury

Bridge Antiques

97 High St. CT3 1DE. (A. and C. Cripp Resident. Est. 1968. Open Thurs., Fri. and Sat. 9 or by appointment any time. SIZE: Lar *STOCK: English and Continental furnitu clocks, dolls and toys, books, shipping goo bric-a-brac.* TEL: 01227 720445.

Silvesters LAPA

33 High St. CT3 1AB. (S.N. Hartley and and Mrs G.M.A. Wallis). Est. 1953. Open 9. 5 by appointment. *STOCK: Furnitu Georgian and Victorian; decorative items, sil porcelain, glass.* LOC: At main junction town. TEL: 01227 720278 and 01843 841524.

WITTERSHAM

Old Corner House Antiques

6 Poplar Rd. TN30 7PG. (G. and F. Shephe Open 10-5. CL: Fri. *STOCK: General antiq country furniture, samplers; 18th-19th C Eng pottery including blue and white and creamwa watercolours, 19th to early 20th C.* PARK: Ea TEL: 01797 270236.

WOODCHURCH, Nr. Ashford

Richard Moate Antiques

Garth House, Redbrook St. Est. 1987. Open appointment seven days. *STOCK: Unstrip pine furniture, £10-£2,000.* LOC: 2 miles fr A28. PARK: Easy. TEL: 01233 860400; mobi 0831 655414. VAT: Stan. *Trade Only.*

Treasures of Woodchurch

1-3 The Green. TN26 3PE. (Mrs S. Cottre Open 10-5.30. CL: Thurs. SIZE: Medi *STOCK: Continental and English pine, some d wood; china, linen, domestic collectables, £800.* LOC: At top of green close to church. T 01233 860249.

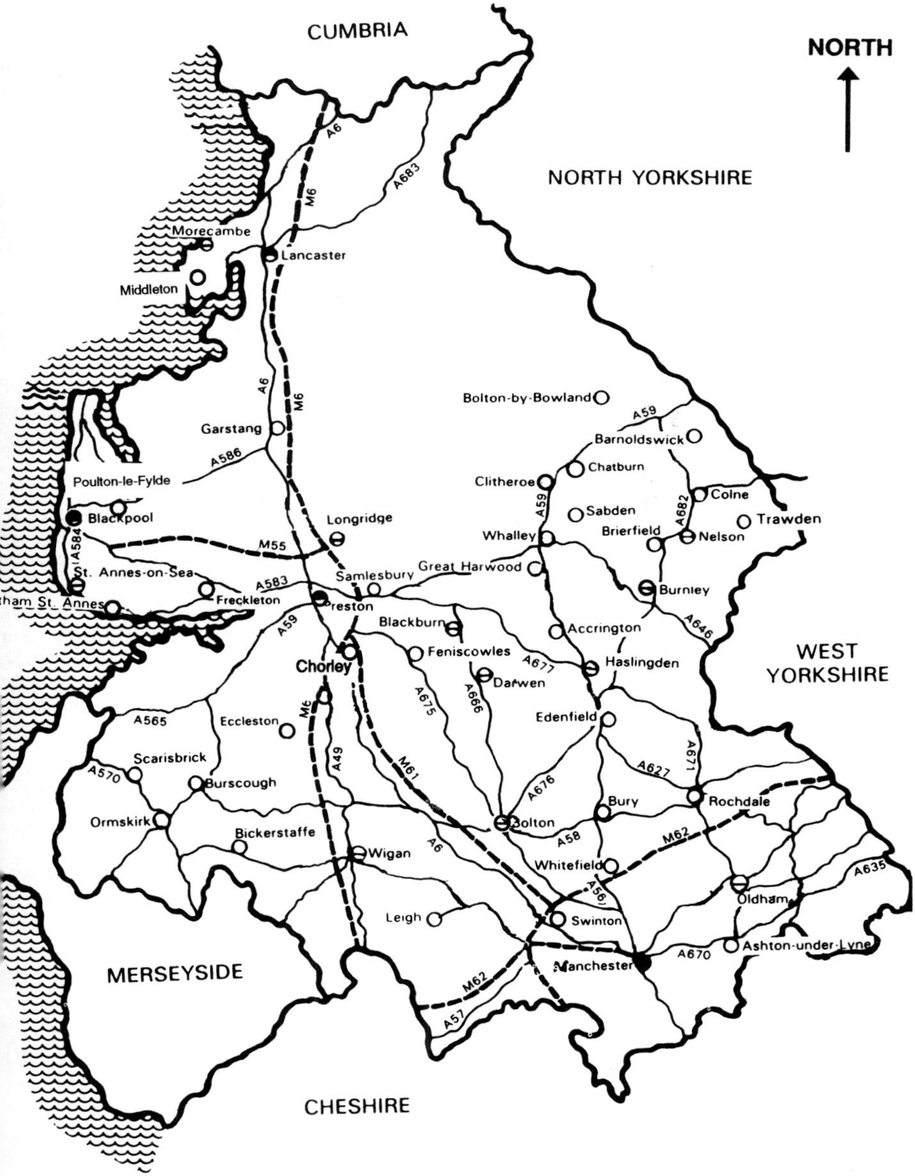

○ 1-2
⊖ 3-5
6-12
● 13+

Key to number of shops in this area.

e note this is only a rough map
ned to show dealers the number of
in the various towns, and is not
sarily totally accurate.

ACCRINGTON

The Coin and Jewellery Shop
129a Blackburn Rd. BB5 0AA. Est. 1977. Open 10-5.30. CL: Wed. *STOCK: Coins, medals and jewellery.* TEL: 01254 384757.

ASHTON-UNDER-LYNE

Kenworthys Ltd BADA
226 Stamford St. OL6 7LW. (C.J. and M. Collings). Est. 1880. Open by appointment only. *STOCK: Silver and jewellery, all periods, £1-£5,000.* PARK: 50yds. away behind shop. TEL: 0161 330 3043 (2 lines). SER: Valuations; restorations; buys at auction. FAIRS: Harrogate (NADF); Chester; Buxton; Olympia (June and Autumn). VAT: Stan/Spec.

BARNOLDSWICK, Nr. Colne

Roy W. Bunn LAPADA
34/36 Church St. BB8 5UT. Est. 1986. Open by appointment only. *STOCK: Staffordshire figures, 18th-19th C, £45-£2,000.* LOC: Main road. PARK: Easy. TEL: 01282 813703; fax - same; home - same. SER: Valuations; restorations (ceramics); buys at auction. VAT: Spec.

BICKERSTAFFE, Nr. Ormskirk

E.W. Webster
Wash Farm, Rainford Rd. L39 0HG. Est. 1975. Open anytime by appointment. SIZE: Medium. *STOCK: Furniture, early metal, needlework, treen, decorative items, 1650-1850.* Not Stocked: Bric-a-brac. LOC: Exit 3, M58 on to A570, turn left 100yds. PARK: Easy. TEL: 01695 724326. VAT: Spec.

BLACKBURN

Ancient and Modern
17 New Market St. BB1 7DR. Est. 1943. Open 9-5.30. *STOCK: Jewellery, Victorian to date, up to £25,000; clocks, watches, paintings, militaria, antique and modern silver, objets de vertu.* LOC: Town centre, opposite side entrance of Marks & Spencer. PARK: Easy. TEL: 01254 677866. SER: Valuations; repairs; restorations.

Mitchell's (Lock Antiques)
76 Bolton Rd. BB2 3PZ. (S. Mitchell). Open 9-5. *STOCK: General antiques, gold and silver jewellery, wrist watches.* TEL: 01254 664663.

Anthony Walmsley
93 Montague St. BB2 1EH. Est. 1968. Open 10-6. CL: Sun. except by appointment. SIZE: Medium. *STOCK: General furniture, clocks.* Not Stocked: Guns or weapons. LOC: 2 minutes from town centre. Montague St. links Preston New Rd.

Blackburn continued

and Preston Old Rd. PARK: Easy. TEL: 012 698755 any time. SER: Valuations; restoratio buys at auction; shipping and packing; courier.

BLACKPOOL

Chard Coins
521 Lytham Rd. FY4 1RJ. Est. 1965. Open 9 CL: Sat. SIZE: Large. *STOCK: Paintings a furniture, English and ancient coins, gold bull coins, jewellery and silver, £50-£20,000+.* LC Lytham Rd. runs from Central Promenade so to Blackpool Airport main gates. Shop is 1/4 m from airport. PARK: Easy. TEL: 01253 3430 SER: Valuations. VAT: Stan/Spec.

Ann and Peter Christian
400/402 Waterloo Rd., Marton. FY4 4BL. O 10-5.30. *STOCK: Decorative arts and p furniture.* TEL: 01253 763268.

Peter Ireland Ltd
31 Clifton St. FY1 1JQ. Open 9-5. *STOC Coins, banknotes, war medals and militar general antiques, jewellery, pottery, porcela commemorative ware, silver.* TEL: 01253 2158

R.H. Latham Antiques
45 Whitegate Drive. FY3 9DG. Resident. E 1958. Open 10-5.30. SIZE: Large. *STOC Stripped pine, brass, copper and porcelain.* TE 01253 393950; home - same. SER: Shipping a courier.

Nostalgia
95 Coronation St. FY1 4QE. (P. Jackson). E 1978. Open 10-4, including Sun. in summ SIZE: Small. *STOCK: Royal commemorativ 19th-20th C, £3-£500; also antiquarian a modern prints.* LOC: Town centre, near Wir Gardens. PARK: Easy. TEL: 01253 293251.

BOLTON

Bolton Antique Centre
Central St. Open 9.30-5, Sun. 11-4. SIZE: dealers. *STOCK: General antiques.* LOC: To centre behind McDonalds. PARK: Opposite. TE 01204 362694.

Drop Dial Antiques
Last Drop Village, Hospital Rd., Bromley Cr BL7 9PZ. (I.W. and I.E. Roberts). Est. 19 Open every afternoon including Sun. SIZ Small. *STOCK: Clocks, mainly English a French, 18th-20th C, £100-£4,000; merc barometers, 19th-20th C, £100-£500; paintin silver and general antiques, £20-£500.* N Stocked: Stamps and armour. PARK: Easy. TE 01204 307186; home - 01257 480995. SE Valuations; restorations (clocks and baromete VAT: Stan/Spec.

lton continued

. Oakes and Son

0-162 Blackburn Rd. BL1 8DR. Est. 1958. en 9-5. *STOCK: Furniture and bric-a-brac.* L: 01204 526587; e-mail - 100410.3406@ mpuserve.can. SER: Shipping and packing; ys at auction. VAT: Stan.

rk Galleries Antiques, Fine Art d Decor

7 Mayor St. BL1 4SJ. (Mrs S. Hunt). Est. 1964. en Thurs., Fri. and Sat. 11-4 or by appoint- nt. SIZE: Medium. *STOCK: English and ntinental furniture, 17th to early 20th C; glish and Continental pottery and porcelain, niatures, glass, brass, silver, copper; paintings, th C; decorative and collectable items.* Not cked: Weapons, coins, medals, stamps. LOC: B6202. PARK: Side and rear. TEL: 01204 9827; home - 0161 764 5853. SER: Valuations; torations (furniture; metalwork replating, tery and porcelain, paintings; frames regilded; ck movements).

OLTON-BY-BOWLAND, Nr. Clitheroe

rmhouse Antiques

Main St. BB7 4NY. (M. Howard). Est. 1980. en Sat., Sun. and Bank Holidays 12-4.30, or by ointment. SIZE: Small. *STOCK: Textiles, linen d quilts, from 1830; beads and jewellery, toriana, china, kitchenalia and brasses.* LOC: A59, past Clitheroe, through Sawley to village. RK: Easy. TEL: 01200 441457/447294.

rrop Fold Clocks (F. Robinson)

rop Fold, Lane Ends. BB7 4PJ. Est. 1974. en by appointment. SIZE: Medium. *STOCK: tish clocks, barometers, 18th-19th C, £1,000- 000.* LOC: Through Clitheroe to Chatburn and ndleton. Take Slaidburn road, turn left after 3 es. PARK: Own. TEL: 01200 447665; home - e. SER: Valuations; restorations (clocks).

IERFIELD, Nr. Nelson

I. Blakey and Sons Ltd (Est. 1905)

nley Rd. BB9 5AD. *STOCK: Furniture, brass, per, pewter, clocks, curios.* TEL: 01282 593. SER: Restorations. VAT: Stan.

RNLEY

un Lea Antiques

Standish St. BB11 1AP. Open 9.30-5.30. CL: s. *STOCK: General antiques and shipping ds.* TEL: 01282 413513.

un Lea Antiques (J. Waite Ltd)

t 1, Rear Elm Street Mill,Travis Street. BB10 Z. Open 8.30-5.30, Fri. and Sat. 9-4. SIZE: rehouse. *STOCK: Georgian furniture to 0's shipping goods.* TEL: 01282 413513.

Burnley continued

King's Mill Antique Centre

Unit 2 King's Mill, Queen St., Harle Syke. (Michael and Linda Heller). Open 10-5, Thurs. 10-8, Sun. 11-4. SIZE: Large. *STOCK: Furniture and bric-a-brac, Edwardian and Victorian, £5-£1,000.* LOC: From General Hospital, follow brown tourist signs for Queen's Mill. PARK: Easy. TEL: 01282 431953; home - 01282 702216. SER: Restorations (furniture).

BURSCOUGH, Nr. Ormskirk

West Lancs. Antique Exports LAPADA

Victoria Mill, Victoria St. L40 0SN. (W. and B. Griffiths). Est. 1959. Open 9-5.30, Sat. and Sun.10-5. SIZE: Large. *STOCK: Shipping furniture.* TEL: 01704 894634/896036; fax - 01704 894486. SER: Courier; packing and shipping. VAT: Stan.

BURY

Newtons

151 The Rock. BL9 0ND. (Newtons of Bury). Est. 1931. Open 9-5. SIZE: Small. *STOCK: General antiques, 18th-19th C, £5-£500.* Not Stocked: Continental furniture. LOC: From Manchester through Bury town centre, shop is on left 200yds. before Fire Station. PARK: 50yds. behind shop. TEL: 0161 764 1863. SER: Valuations; restorations (furniture). VAT: Stan.

CHATBURN, Nr. Clitheroe

T. Brindle Antiques LAPADA

6 and 8 Sawley Rd. BB7 4AS. Open 9.30-5.00, Sat. and other times by appointment. *STOCK: Antique and decorative items.* TEL: 01200 440025; fax - 01200 440090.

CHORLEY

Antiques and Crafts Centre

Botany Bay Villages Ltd., Canal Mill, Botany Brow. PR6 8AX. Open daily including Sun. SIZE: Large - 5 floors. *STOCK: Dateline room with porcelain, china and jewellery; antique furniture, memorabilia and curios, wide range of crafts.* LOC: Opposite J8 of the M61. PARK: Easy. TEL: 01257 261220. VAT: Stan.

CLITHEROE

Folly Antiques

22 Moor Lane. BB7 1BE. (N.P. Medd). Est. 1967. Open 9-6, Wed. and Sun. by appointment. SIZE: Medium. *STOCK: Decorative and upholstered items, furniture, £100-£2,000; pictures, brass and objects, £5-£2,000; all 19th-20th C; garden furniture, small architectural items, 18th-20th C, £20-£2,000.* LOC: 15 miles from junction 31, M6, via A59. PARK: Opposite. TEL: 01200 29461. VAT: Stan/Spec.

Clitheroe continued

Lee's Antiques
59 Whalley Rd. BB7 1EE. (P.A. Lee). *STOCK: General antiques.* TEL: 01200 424921; home - 01200 425441.

COLNE

Enloc Antiques
Birchenlee Mill, Lenches Rd. BB8 8ET. Est. 1978. Open 9-5, Sat. 9-1 or by appointment. SIZE: Warehouse. *STOCK: Pine, 18th-19th C, £5-£1,000; kitchen chairs, 19th C, £25-£45.* TEL: 01282 867101. SER: Restorations (hot stripping, polishing and joinery). VAT: Stan.

DARWEN

Cottage Antiques
135 Blackburn Rd. SIZE: Small. *STOCK: Fine porcelain including Crown Derby, Worcester and Doulton, £100-£2,000; 19th C furniture, £100-£5,000.* LOC: A666 towards Blackburn, opposite St Cuthbert's Church. PARK: Opposite. TEL: 01254 775891 or 01254 676840 (24 hour).

Darwen Antiques
Percival St. BB3 1HG. Est. 1971. Open 9.30-5, Sun 11-5. *STOCK: Pottery, glass, pictures and furniture, £1-£5,000.* PARK: Easy. TEL: 01254 760565; home - 01254 776644/776551. SER: Valuations; buys at auction. VAT: Stan/Spec.

K.C. Antiques
538 Bolton Rd. BB3 2JR. (K. and J. Anderton). Resident. Open 9-6, Sun. 12-5. *STOCK: Georgian, Victorian and Edwardian furniture and decorative items.* LOC: A666. PARK: Easy. TEL: 01254 772252. SER: Buys at auction. VAT: Stan/Spec.

ECCLESTON

3 L's Antiques
Units 3 & 4, Grove Development Centre. PR7 5PD. (L. and L.C. Frost). Est. 1989. Open 12-3.30, Sun. 11-5. SIZE: Small. *STOCK: Furniture, 1850-1940, £50-£700; gramophones, £50-£500; pottery, porcelain and brassware.* LOC: Junction 27, M6, village is 4 miles north via Mossy Lea Rd. Shop situated at Bygone Times Centre. PARK: Easy. TEL: 01257 450290.

Bygone Times Ltd
Grove Mill, The Green. PR7 5PD. (S. Higham). Open 8-6 including Sun. SIZE: 150 dealers. *STOCK: General antiques including architectural and North American artifacts.* TEL: 01257 453780.

EDENFIELD, Nr. Bury

The Antique Shop
17 Market St. BL0 0JA. (J. and J.C. Salisbury).

Edenfield continued

Est. 1964. Open 10-4. SIZE: Large. *STOC[K]: General antiques, shipping goods, £1-£10,0[00].* LOC: On A56. PARK: Easy. TEL: 0170 6[...] 3107/2351. SER: Valuations. VAT: Stan/Spec.

FENISCOWLES, Nr. Blackburn

Old Smithy
726 Preston Old Rd. BB2 5EP. (R.C. Lynch). E[st.] 1967. Open 9.30-5. SIZE: Large. *STOCK: Per[iod] and Victorian fireplaces, pub and architectu[ral] items, violins and musical instruments, brass be[ds,] lamps, furniture, shipping items, jewellery, bra[ss,] copper, Victorian lace and linen.* LOC: Oppos[ite] Fieldens Arms. PARK: Own or nearby. TE[L:] 01254 209943/580874. SER: Valuations; rest[or]ations (wooden items); buys at auction. FAI[RS:] Park Hall, Charnock Richard, Newark, Lincs.

FRECKLETON, Nr. Preston

L. Booth Antiques and Reproductio[ns]
Freckleton Boat Yard, Poolside. PR4 1HB. O[pen] 10-5 including Sun. *STOCK: Victorian a[nd] Edwardian furniture.* TEL: 01772 632439. SE[R:] Restorations.

GARSTANG

Clare's Antiques and Auction Galleries
Wheatsheaf Buildings, Park Hill. PR3 1EL. (M[r] C.A.L. Campbell-Cameron and Mrs C.L. Alle[n]). Est. 1960. Open Thurs., Fri. and Sat. 10-4. SIZ[E:] Large. *STOCK: Royal Worcester porcelain, ea[rly] 20th C, £150-£4,000; Rudelstadt, Meiss[en,] Dresden figures, 19th C, £500-£2,000; silv[er,] jewellery, small furniture.* LOC: Off A6. PAR[K:] Easy. TEL: 01995 605702; home - same. SE[R:] Valuations; restorations (porcelain, jeweller[y]); buys at auction.

GREAT HARWOOD, Nr. Blackburn

Benny Charlesworth's Snuff Box
51 Blackburn Rd. BB6 7DF. (N. Walsh). E[st.] 1984. Open 10-5. SIZE: Small. *STOCK: F[ur]niture, china, linen, costume jewellery, tedd[y bears].* LOC: 200yds. from town centre, off A6[...]. PARK: Next to shop. TEL: 01254 8885[...]. FAIRS: Local.

HASLINGDEN

P.J. Brown Antiques
8 Church St. BB4 5QU. Open 10-5, Sat. and S[un.] by appointment. SIZE: Large and wareho[use]. *STOCK: General antiques and shipping goo[ds].* LOC: Town centre, off Bury Road and Regent [St.] close to A680, M65-M66. PARK: Easy. T[EL:] 01706 224888. VAT: Stan.

ıslingden continued

eldings Antiques

6, 178 and 180 Blackburn Rd. BB1 2LG. Est. 56. Open 9-4.30, Fri. 9-4. CL: Thurs. SIZE: ırge. *STOCK: Longcase clocks, £30-£2,000; ıll clocks, sets of chairs, pine, period oak, ench furniture, glass, shipping goods, toys, am engines, veteran cars, vintage and veteran ıtor cycles.* PARK: Easy. TEL: 01706 214254; ıbile - 0973 698961; home - 01254 263358.

W. Norgrove - Antique Clocks

Bury Rd. BB4 5LR. Normally open 9-5.30, t. 10-5, but prior 'phone call advisable. *'OCK: Longcase, wall, bracket and mantel ıcks.* TEL: 01706 211995.

ıNCASTER

he Assembly Rooms Market

ng St. Open Thurs., Fri. and Sat. 10-4.30. ZE: Several dealers. *STOCK: General tiques, jewellery, collectables, model railways, riod costume/clothing, books, records and lectors' comics.* TEL: Market Superintendent - 524 66627.

.B. Antiques Ltd

ncaster Leisure Park, Wyresdale Rd. LA1 A. (Mrs G. Blackburn). Open 10-5 including n. SIZE: Large. 100+ dealers. *STOCK: rcelain, glass and silver, late 19th to early th C; small furniture, Victorian to early 20th C.*)C: Off M6, junction 33 or 34. PARK: Easy. L: 01524 844734; fax - 01524 844735; home - 772 861593. SER: Valuations; buys at auction. ıT: Stan/Spec.

ıncaster Leisure Park Antiques ıntre

/resdale Rd. (on site of former Hornsea Pottery ınt). LA1 5LA. Open every day 10-5. SIZE: 0 dealers. *STOCK: Wide range of general tiques.* LOC: Off M6, junction 33. TEL: 01524 4734.

ıncastrian Antiques & Co

/72 Penny St. LA1 1XN. (S.P. and H.S. ılkinson). Open 10-4. CL: Wed. *STOCK: rniture, lighting, period beds, bric-a-brac.* L: 01524 847004.

.B. McCormack

nd 6a Rosemary Lane. LA1 1NR. Open 10-5. .: Wed. *STOCK: Rare and secondhand books; ps and prints.* TEL: 01524 36405.

ıcary Antiques

ı Brock St. LA1 1VV. Est. 1974. Open 10-5. .: Wed. SIZE: Small. *STOCK: Paintings, nts, art pottery, works of art, 1850-1950; arts l crafts, furniture, quilts.* TEL: 01524 843322.

LEIGH

Leigh Jewellery

3 Queens St. (R. Bibby). Open 9.30-5.30, Wed. 9.30-12.30. *STOCK: Jewellery.* TEL: 01942 607947.

LONGRIDGE, Nr. Preston

The Attic Centre

29-33 Berry Lane. (Mrs T. Harber). Est. 1986. Open 10.30-4.30, Sat. and Sun. 10-4, prior telephone call advisable. CL: Mon. SIZE: Large - 20 units. *STOCK: Wide variety of general antiques, Victorian to 1950's, £5-£1,000.* LOC: Main road, top floor of old Co-op Building. PARK: Easy and nearby. TEL: 01772 786366; home - 01254 813868. SER: Valuations; restorations; buys at auction. FAIRS: Newark, Ardingly, Kempton, Parkhall (Lancs).

Charnley Fine Arts

Charnley House, Preston Rd. PR3 3BD. (R. and J. Crosbie). Est. 1989. Open by appointment. SIZE: Medium. *STOCK: Paintings, 19th-20th C, £100-£10,000.* LOC: Off M55/M6, north of Preston on B6243. PARK: Easy. TEL: 01772 782800; home - same. SER: Restorations; cleaning.

Longridge continued

Joys
83 Berry Lane. PR3 3WH. (Mrs J. Roberts). Est. 1986. Open 9-5. CL: Wed. SIZE: Small. *STOCK: Pine and oak furniture, Art Deco china, jewellery, mirrors, lamps, rugs.* LOC: 6 miles from exit 31, M6. PARK: Easy. TEL: 01772 782083.

Kitchenalia
'The Old Bakery', 36 Inglewhite Rd. PR3 3JS. (J. Chilton). *STOCK: Kitchenalia, brass, copper ware, pottery, pine and oak country furniture, butchers' blocks, Victorian church pews.* TEL: 01772 785411. VAT: Stan/Spec.

LYTHAM ST. ANNES

All Our Yesterdays of Lytham
3 Station Rd. FY8 5DH. (S. Brickwood and P. Harrison). Open 11-5. CL: Mon. and Wed. *STOCK: General antiques.* TEL: 01253 734748.

Snuff Box
5 Market Buildings, Hastings Pl. FY8 5LW. (Mrs J.C. Rimmer). Open 10-5. CL: Wed. *STOCK: Silver and plate, jewellery, watches and linen.* TEL: 01253 738656.

MANCHESTER

A.S. Antique Galleries
26 Broad St, Salford. M6 5BY. (A. Sternshine). Est. 1975. Open 10-5.30. CL: Tues. SIZE: Large. *STOCK: Art Nouveau and Art Deco bronzes, bronze and ivory figures, silver, glass, furniture, jewellery, lighting and general antiques.* Not Stocked: Weapons. LOC: On A6, one mile north of Manchester city centre, next to Salford University College. PARK: Easy. TEL: 0161 737 5938; mobile - 0836 368230; fax - 0161 737 6626. SER: Valuations; restorations; commission purchasing.

Antique Fireplaces
1090 Stockport Rd, Levenshulme. M19 2SU. (J. McMullan & Son). Open 9-6, Sun. 11-5. *STOCK: Fireplaces and architectural items.* TEL: 0161 431 8075.

Antiques Village
The Old Town Hall, 965 Stockport Rd., Levenshulme. M19 3NP. Est. 1978. Open 10.15-5, Sun. 12-4.45. SIZE: 40+ dealers. *STOCK: Furniture, fireplaces, collectables.* LOC: A6 between Manchester and Stockport. PARK: Own. TEL: 0161 256 4644. SER: Valuations; pine stripping; picture framing. FAIRS: Newark; G MEX. VAT: Stan/Spec.

Authentiques
(S.G. Rubenstein). Est. 1978. Open by appointment only. *STOCK: Decorative items - silver, plate, porcelain, glass, boxes, Staffordshire,*

Manchester continued

watercolours and prints, small furnitu miniatures, brass, curios, early 19th C to 19 £50-£500. LOC: 1/2 mile from junction 17, M on A56. PARK: Easy. TEL: 0161 773 9601; fa same. SER: Valuations; restorations (silver); b at auction (pictures, silver, furniture). FAI British International, Birmingham.

The Baron Antiques
1-11 Church Lane, Prestwich. M25 5AN. Brunsveld). Open 9.30-6. SIZE: Large. *STOC 18th C mahogany and early oak furnitu Victorian walnut, clocks, porcelain, objets d' shipping goods.* TEL: 0161 773 9929; fax - 01 758101. SER: Valuations; restorations.

Boodle and Dunthorne Ltd
1 King St. M2 6AW. Est. 1798. Open 9-5. SIZE: Large. *STOCK: 18th-19th C silv Victorian jewellery, £100-£30,000; clocks clock sets, mid-19th C, £100-£1,000.* Not Stock Furniture. TEL: 0161 833 9000. VAT: Stan/Sp

Bulldog Antiques
393 Bury New Rd., Prestwich. M25 1AW. Wordsworth). Est. 1971. Open 10.30-6. CL: S except by appointment. SIZE: Large. *STOC Georgian, Victorian and Edwardian furnitu clocks especially longcase and wall clock s 18th-19th C; militaria, swords, guns, pist shotguns, war medals, pottery, prints, pictu general antiques and shipping goods.* LOC: 17, M62. PARK: At rear. TEL: 0161 798 9 home - 0161 790 7153. SER: Restorati (furniture); French polishing, watch and cl repairs.

Bus Stop Curios
1 Beech Rd., Chorlton-cum-Hardy. M21 8 (John and Jean Higginbotham). Resident. 1989. Open Thurs. 11-5.30, Fri. 11.15-5.45, 10.30-4.30. SIZE: Medium. *STOCK: Milita WW1 & WW2, £1-£100; Victorian and Art D pottery and glass and smalls, £1-£100.* PA Easy. TEL: 0161 860 6232.

Cathedral Jewellers
4 Todd St. M3 1WU. Open 9.30-5. *STOC Jewellery.* TEL: 0161 832 3042.

Didsbury Antiques (Chorlton)
21 Range Rd., Whalley Range. M16 8FS. Karczewski-Slowikowski). Est. 1973. Open appointment. *STOCK: Furniture, pictu ceramics, 18th-19th C, from £250.* PARK: E TEL: 0161 227 9979; home - same. SER: V ations; buys at auction (furniture, paintin VAT: Stan.

Family Antiques
405/407 Bury New Rd., Prestwich. (J. an Ditondo). Open daily. *STOCK: General antiq* TEL: 0161 798 0036.

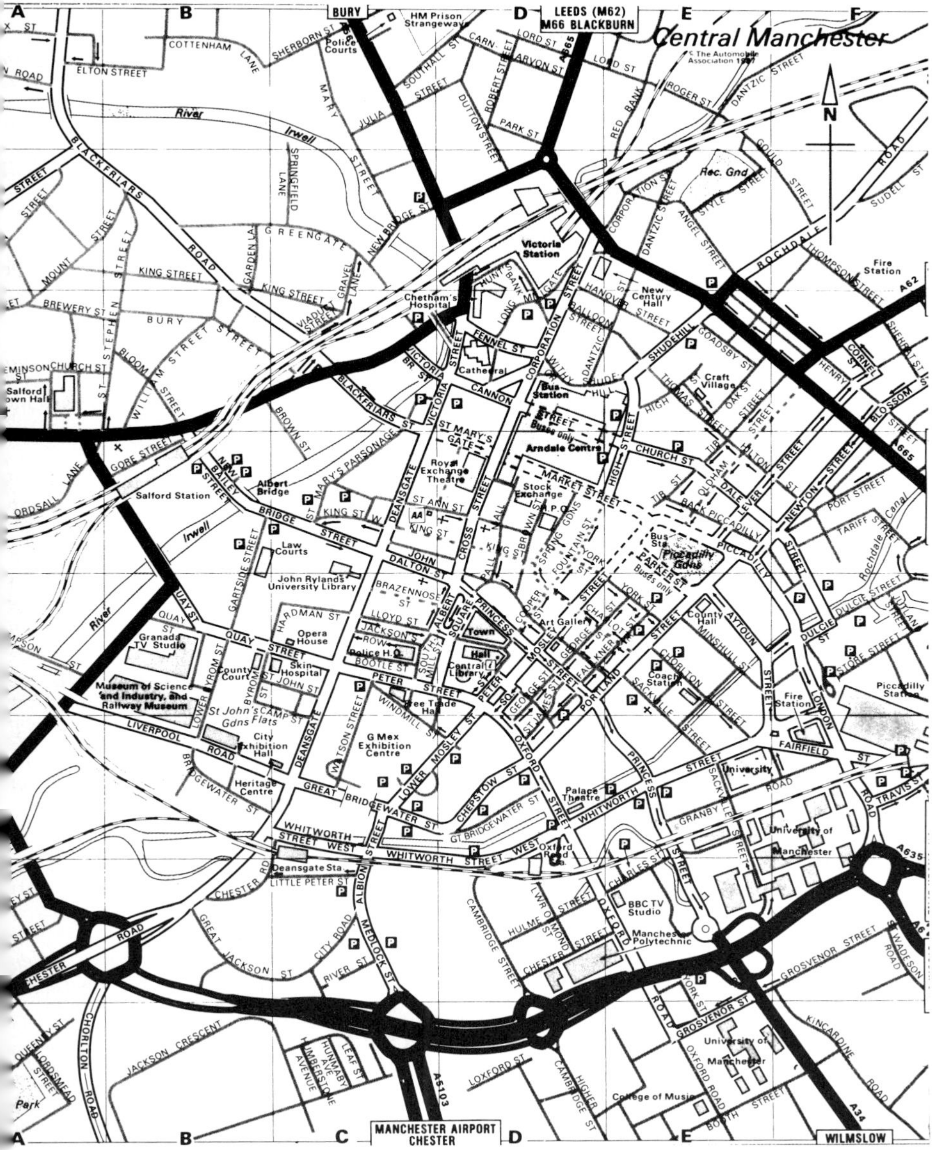

Key to Town Plan

AA Recommended roads		Car Parks	P
Other roads		Parks and open spaces	
Restricted roads		AA Service Centre	AA
Buildings of interest			

Manchester continued

Fernlea Antiques
Failsworth Antique Centre, Failsworth Mill, Ashton Rd West, Failsworth. (A.J. and Mrs B. McLaughlin). Open 10-5. *STOCK: General antiques and shipping goods.* TEL: 0161 682 0589.

Forest Books of Cheshire
in The Ginnel, 18-22 Lloyd St. M2 5WA. (Mrs E. Mann). Open 9.30-5.30. *STOCK: Antiquarian, art, collecting, drama and humanities books and prints.* TEL: 0161 834 0747; 0161 833 9037 (The Ginnel).

Fulda Gallery Ltd
19 Vine St., Salford. M7 3PG. (M.J. Fulda). Est. 1969. Open by appointment only. *STOCK: Oil paintings, 1500-1950, £500-£30,000; water-colours, 1800-1930, £350-£10,000.* LOC: Near Salford Police Station off Bury New Rd. TEL: 0161 792 1962; mobile - 0836 518313. SER: Valuations; restorations; buys at auction.

Gibb's Bookshop Ltd
10 Charlotte St. M1 4FL. Est. 1926. *STOCK: Books.* TEL: 0161 236 7179.

The Ginnell Gallery Antique Centre
18-22 Lloyd St. M2 5WA. (Mr and Mrs J.K. Mottershead). Est. 1973. Open 9.30-5.30. *STOCK: Art Deco and Art Nouveau,1950's pottery, furniture, glass, fishing tackle, antiquarian and other books.* LOC: Opposite Town Hall. TEL: 0161 833 9037.

In-Situ Architectural Antiques
607 Stretford Rd., Old Trafford. M16 0QT. (Laurence Green and Stan Newsham). Est. 1983. Open 9-5.30, Sun. 10-4. SIZE: Large. *STOCK: Architectural items including fireplaces, doors, panelling, sanitary ware, radiators, flooring, glass, gardenware, staircasing.* LOC: Trafford Bar, on main Chester Rd. PARK: Easy. TEL: 0161 848 7454. SER: Valuations; restorations (architectural items). VAT: Stan.

Irving Antique Toys
c/o Ginnel Gallery, 18-22 Lloyd St. M2 5WA. SIZE: Large. *STOCK: Dinkies, teddies and dolls.* LOC: Off Albert Square. TEL: 0161 833 9037.

Manchester Antique Company
Ballbrook Ave.,West Didsbury. M20 0UT. (J. Long). Est. 1964. Open 9.30-5.30. SIZE: Large. *STOCK: Mainly marquetry walnut and mahogany, some period furniture, silver, and pianos.* LOC: 3 miles from airport on M56 towards city. PARK: Easy. TEL: 0161 434 7752. SER: Valuations; buys at auction (clocks). VAT: Stan.

Eric J. Morten
Warburton St., Didsbury. M20 6WA. Est. 1959. Open 10-6. SIZE: Large. *STOCK: Antiquarian books, 16th-20th C, £5-£5,000.* LOC: Off Wilmslow Rd., near traffic lights in Didsbury village. A34. PARK: Easy. TEL: 0161 445 76 and 01265 277959. SER: Valuations; buys auction (antiquarian books).

Manchester continued

R.J. O'Brien and Son Antiques
Failsworth Mill,Ashton Rd. West, Failswor M35 0FD. Est. 1970. Open 9-5. CL: Sat. SIZ Large. *STOCK: Furniture, Victorian, Edwardi and 1930's; shipping goods, general antiques a pianos.* PARK: Own. TEL: 0161 688 441 mobile - 0850 485201. SER: Container a courier service.

Premiere Antiques
373 Bury New Rd., Prestwich. M25 5AW. Harris). GADAR. *STOCK: Furniture, mai Victorian and Edwardian inlaid.* TEL: 0161 7 0500; fax - 0161 792 0232. SER: Restoratic (furniture).

Prestwich Antiques Ltd
371-373 Bury New Rd., Prestwich. (T. Finn a Y. Gray). Est. 1973. Open 10.30-6, Sun. 11.30 SIZE: Large. *STOCK: Victorian furniture, dec ative lighting, to £1,000.* LOC: Off junction M62. PARK: Own at rear. TEL: 0161 798 09 home - 01282 618270. SER: Valuations; rest ations (upholstery, polishing and repairs). VA Stan/Spec.

Paul Quentin
626 Manchester Rd., Bury. BL9 9SU. (D. and Eccleston). Est. 1965. Open 10-6. SIZE: Lar *STOCK: General antiques, weapons, copp brass, pewter, 1650-1920.* Not Stocked: F porcelain. LOC: On A56, 2 miles north junction 17, M62; 1 mile west of junction 3, M PARK: Easy. TEL: 0161 766 6673.

Secondhand and Rare Books
Corner Church St/High St. M4 1PW. Open 12 *STOCK: Books.* TEL: 0161 834 5964 or 01 861608.

St. James Antiques
41 South King St. M2 6DE. *STOCK: Jewelle silver and paintings.* LOC: Off Deansgate, town centre. TEL: 0161 834 9632.

Village Antiques
416 Bury New Rd., Prestwich. M25 1BD. Weidenbaum). Est. 1981. Open 10-5, Wed. 1 SIZE: Medium. *STOCK: 19th C pottery porcelain, £5-£300; 18th C glass; small furnit Art Deco clocks, figurines and lamps; Nouveau figurines.* LOC: Village centre, 2 m from M62. PARK: Easy - side and opposite. T 0161 773 3612.

MIDDLETON VILLAGE, Nr. Morecam

G.G. Exports
Newfield House, Middleton Rd. LA3 3JS. Goulding). Est. 1970. Always available but p telephone call essential. SIZE: Large. *STO Shipping goods, £30-£500; Victoriana, £3,0*

Iiddleton Village continued

ɜneral antiques and pine. LOC: On main road ɜtween Morecambe promenade and Middleton ʲllage. PARK: Easy. TEL: 01524 850757; fax - 1524 851565. SER: Courier; packing; 40ft con- ɿiners weekly worldwide. VAT: Stan. *Trade Only.*

ɪORECAMBE

'he Magpies Nest

'nit 1 Plaza Arcade and 48 Pedder St. LA4 5YJ. ȝ. Byrne). Open 10-5. CL: Wed. *STOCK: Bric- -brac, cutlery, china, glass, militaria.* TEL: 1524 423328.

'yson's Antiques

lark St. (George, Andrew and Shirley Tyson). st. 1952. Open Sat. 9-12, other times by appoint- ɪent. SIZE: Large. *STOCK: Georgian, Victorian ɪd Edwardian furniture.* LOC: Opposite fire .ation. PARK: Easy. TEL: 01524 416763/ 25235/420098; home - 01524 416763. VAT: :an/Spec. *Trade Only.*

,uigino Vescovi

and 3 Back Avondale Rd. East. LA3 1JX. Est. 970. Open by appointment every day. SIZE: 'arehouse. *STOCK: Georgian, Victorian and dwardian items, £50-£5,000.* PARK: Easy. TEL: 1524 416732; mobile - 0860 784856. VAT: :an/Spec.

IELSON

'olin Blakey Fireplaces

5 Manchester Rd. BB10 2LS. Est. 1906. Open 30-5.30, Sat. 9.30-5. *STOCK: Fireplaces and ɜarth furniture, French clock sets, paintings and ɪints.* LOC: Exit 12, M65. PARK: Opposite. EL: 01282 614941. SER: Manufacturers and ɪppliers of hand-carved marble fireplaces and ɪrdwood mantels. VAT: Stan.

rittons Jewellers and Antiques

Scotland Rd. BB9 7UU. Est. 1970. CL: Tues. *TOCK: Jewellery, collectors' watches and ɜneral small antiques.* PARK: Opposite. TEL: 282 697659; fax - 01282 618867.

Nelson continued

Brooks Antiques

7 Russell St. BB9 7NL. (D. and S.A. Brooks). Est. 1979. Open 9-5.30, Sun. and Tues. by appointment. SIZE: Medium. *STOCK: Furniture, £50-£2,000; smalls, £5-£500; both 1750-1930; postcards, ephemera, early 20th C, to £20.* LOC: Town centre, 2 mins. from junction 13, M65. PARK: Easy. TEL: 01282 698148; home - 01282 866234. SER: Valuations.

Margaret's Antique Shop

79a Scotland Rd. BB9 7UY. (S. Rhodes). Est. 1948. Open 10-6. CL: Tues. SIZE: Small. LOC: Town centre. PARK: Easy.

OLDHAM

Heritage Antiques

123 Milnrow Rd., Shaw. OL2 7TN. Est. 1986. Open 2-8, Sat. and Sun. 12-6. *STOCK: General antiques and shipping goods.* LOC: 3 miles from Oldham on A663. PARK: Easy. TEL: 01706 842385.

Charles Howell Jeweller

2 Lord St. OL1 3EY. (N.G. Howell). NAG. Est. 1870. Open 9.15-5.15. SIZE: Small. *STOCK: Edwardian and Victorian jewellery, £25-£2,000; silver, early to mid 20th C, £40-£1,500; watches, Victorian to mid 20th C, £50-£800.* LOC: Town centre, off High St. PARK: Limited or by arrangement. TEL: 0161 624 1479. SER: Valuations; restorations (jewellery and watches); buys at auction (jewellery and watches). VAT: Stan/Spec.

H.C. Simpson and Sons Jewellers (Oldham)Ltd

37 High St. OL3 5AW. Open 9-5.30. *STOCK: Clocks, jewellery, watches.* TEL: 0161 624 7187. SER: Restorations (clocks).

Valley Antiques

Soho St. OL4 2AD. (J. Chadwick). Est. 1973. Open 10-6. SIZE: Warehouse. *STOCK: General antiques including stripped pine, oak furniture, 19th C, £25-£600.* PARK: Easy. TEL: 0161 624 5030. SER: Valuations; restorations (pine stripping, upholstery, clocks).

Oldham continued

Waterloo Antiques
16 Waterloo St. OL1 1SG. (B.J. and S. Marks). Est. 1969. Open 9.30-5. SIZE: Medium. *STOCK: General antiques, furniture, jewellery.* LOC: Town centre. TEL: 0161 624 5975; fax - same. SER: Valuations.

ORMSKIRK

Alan Grice Antiques
106 Aughton St. L39 3BS. Open 10-6. *STOCK: Period furniture.* PARK: Easy. TEL: 01695 572007.

POULTON-LE-FYLDE

Ray Wade Antiques
P O Box 39. FY6 9GA. Est. 1978. Open by appointment. *STOCK: Decorative items, sculpture, European and Oriental works of art, paintings.* TEL: 01253 700715; fax - 01253 702342; mobile - 0836 291336. VAT: Stan/Spec.

PRESTON

The Antique Centre
56 Garstang Rd. PR1 1NA. (Paul Allison). Open 9-5.30, Sat. 9.30-5.30, Sun. 10.30-5.30. SIZE: 35 dealers. *STOCK: Georgian to Edwardian furniture and pine, porcelain, bric-a-brac and pictures.* TEL: 01772 882078; fax - 01772 252842. SER: Worldwide shipping; containers.

Duckworth's Antiques
45 New Hall Lane. PR1 5NX. (V.K. and M. Duckworth). Est. 1960. Open 9.30-4. SIZE: Small. *STOCK: Shipping goods, kitchenalia.* Not Stocked: Arms, armour, coins, medals. LOC: Main road leading from M6 motorway. PARK: Easy. TEL: 01772 794336; home - 01772 742720.

Hackler's Jewellers
6b Lune St. (N.E. Oldfield). FBHI. *STOCK: Antique clocks.* TEL: 01772 258465. VAT: Stan.

Halewood and Sons
37 Friargate. PR1 2AT. Est. 1867. CL: Thurs. pm. *STOCK: Antiquarian books and maps.* TEL: 01772 252603.

Nelson's Antiques
113 New Hall Lane. PR1 5PB. (W. and L. Nelson). Open 9.30-5.30 or by appointment. CL: Sat. *STOCK: General antiques and collectors' items, dolls.* LOC: Half mile from J31, M6. PARK: Easy. TEL: 01772 792950/862066. SER: Valuations.

The Odd Chair Company
70-72 Blackbull Lane, Fulwood. PR2 3JX. (Sue and James Cook). Est. 1969. Open daily by appointment, evenings and weekends by arrangement.SIZE: Large. *STOCK: Upholstered 19th*

Preston continued

chairs and sofas, including Knole. LOC: 1.3 mil from M6, junction 32. Follow signs towar Preston until 2nd set of traffic lights, then tu right into Blackbull Lane, premises 800 yards c left. PARK: Own. TEL: 01772 787990; fax 01772 787950. SER: Valuations; restoration a re-upholstery using traditional methods ar materials (horsehair, coarfibre, wool wadding a feathers); complementary curtains and loo covers made; buys at auction.

Preston Antique Centre
The Mill, New Hall Lane. PR1 5UH. Open 8.3 5.30, Sat.10-4, Sun. 9-4. SIZE: Large - 4C dealers. *STOCK: General antiques, Georgia Victorian and Edwardian; shipping furnitur* TEL: 01772 794498/654531; fax - 01772 6516 SER: Container packing.

Preston Book Co
68 Friargate. PR1 2ED. Est. 1950. Open 9.3 5.30. *STOCK: Antiquarian books.* TEL: 017 252613. SER: Buys at auction.

Swag
24 Leyland Rd., Penwortham. PR1 9XS. (M Fletcher). Est. 1967. Open 9-6. CL: Thurs. p SIZE: Small. *STOCK: Dolls, especially 183 1920, £5-£250; pottery, porcelain, furnitur* LOC: 3 miles from exit 29, M6, following S Anne's signs. PARK: Easy. TEL: 01772 7449 SER: Restorations (dolls).

Frederick Treasure Ltd LAPAD
The Antique Centre, 56 Garstang Rd. PR 1NA. (J.F. Treasure). Est. 1908. Open 9-6, Su 10-4. SIZE: Large. *STOCK: Furniture, 165 1900, £20-£10,000.* PARK: Easy. TEL: 017 882078; office - 01253 736801. SER: Val ations. VAT: Stan/Spec.

ROCHDALE

S.C. Falk LAPAL
OL12 6LE. Open by appointment onl *STOCK: Fine English period furniture.* TE 01706 44946. VAT: Stan/Spec.

Owen Antiques
191 Oldham Rd. OL16 5QZ. (J.G.T. Owen). E 1891. Open 11.30-7, Sun. 2-6. *STOCK: Cloc and paintings, 17th-19th C, £100-£5,000; ea oak and walnut, spinning wheels, silver, pewte pistols, phonographs, wireless sets, coins, mo ships, orreries and gothic clocks, nautical iten violins, antiquarian books, early ciné equipme* LOC: A627 from town centre up hill (Oldha road) for 1/2 mile. Next block to high lev pavement on left hand side past railway brid PARK: Nearby. TEL: 01706 48138; hom 01706 353270. SER: Valuations; restoratio (clocks and furniture).

·ABDEN, Nr. Blackburn

Valter Aspinall Antiques

endle Antiques Centre, Union Mill, Watt St. B7 9ED. Est. 1964. Open 9-5, Sat. and Sun. 11-4, r by appointment. SIZE: Large. *STOCK: urniture and bric-a-brac.* LOC: On Pendle Hill etween Clitheroe and Padiham. TEL: 01282 78642; fax - 01282 778643. SER: Export; acking; courier; containers.

AMLESBURY, Nr. Preston

amlesbury Hall

)ating from 1325). Preston New Rd. PR5 0UP. amlesbury Hall Trust). Est. 1969. Open 11-4.30. dmission - adults £2.50, children £1. CL: Mon. IZE: Large. *STOCK: General collectable ntiques.* LOC: Exit 31, M6 on A677 between reston and Blackburn. PARK: Easy. TEL: 01254 12010/2229.

CARISBRICK

arrcross Gallery

25 Southport Rd. (G.D. Fairclough). Est. 1985. pen Sat. 10-5 and Sun. 12-5. SIZE: Medium. *TOCK: Victorian fireplaces, £50-£1,000.* PARK: asy. TEL: 01704 880638. SER: Valuations; storations (cast-iron, brass).

T. ANNES-ON-SEA

he Antique Shop

Wood St. FY8 1QS. (June Spargo). Est. 1990. pen 10.30-5. SIZE: Small. *STOCK: Dis-ntinued Royal Doulton, 1900-1990, £30-£300; ina and pottery, 1850-1950, £25-£250; rniture, late Victorian to early 20th C, £50-,000; brass, copper and silver, mainly 20th C, -£100.* LOC: Parallel with main shopping area - he Square. PARK: Easy. TEL: 01253 714957. ER: Buys at auction (Royal Doulton figures, aracter jugs, seriesware). FAIRS: Harrogate, ork, Charnock Richard, Stafford.

ine Antiques

-61 St. Andrew Rd. South. FY8 1PZ. (R. and G. aw). Open 9-5.30. *STOCK: Pine furniture, 19th £150-£2,500; cast-iron fireplaces, 1890-1930, 00-£500.* PARK: Easy. TEL: 01253 720492. ER: Restorations (pine stripping).

he Victorian Shop

Alexandria Drive. FY8 1JF. (G.O. Freeman). pen 10-5. *STOCK: General antiques.* TEL: 253 725700.

SWINTON

Ambassador House

273 Chorley Rd. M27 2AZ. (G. White). Open 2-6, prior telephone call advisable. *STOCK: General antiques including clocks, silver, paintings, furniture, pottery and porcelain, 17th-18th C.* TEL: 0161 794 3806. SER: Valuations.

TRAWDEN, Nr. Colne

Jack Moore Antiques and Stained Glass

The Old Rock, Keighley Rd. BB8 8RW. Open Mon.-Fri. 9-5, or by appointment. SIZE: Large. *STOCK: Furniture and stained glass.* PARK: Easy. TEL: 01282 869478; home - same; fax - 01282 865193; mobile - 0831 145325. SER: Restoration and manufacture of stained glass; container packing; courier. VAT: Stan.

WHALLEY, Nr. Blackburn

Davies Antiques

32 King St. BB7 9SL. (G.E. and P. Davies). Est. 1960. Open 10-5. SIZE: Medium (Trade warehouse). *STOCK: Oak and country furniture and longcase clocks, to £10,000; jewellery to £500.* Not Stocked: Coins and weapons. LOC: A59 (11 miles from M6). PARK: Easy. TEL: 01254 823764. VAT: Stan/Spec.

WHITEFIELD, Nr. Manchester

Henry Donn Gallery

138/142 Bury New Rd. M45 6AD. Est. 1954. Open 9.30-5.30. *STOCK: Paintings, 19th-20th C, £20-£20,000.* LOC: Off M62, junction 17 towards Bury. TEL: 0161 766 8819. SER: Valuations; framing; restorations (pictures). VAT: Stan/Spec.

WIGAN

Colin de Rouffignac

57 Wigan Lane. WN1 2LF. Open 10-5. CL: Wed. *STOCK: Furniture, jewellery, oils and water-colours.* TEL: 01942 237927.

John Robinson Antiques

172-176 Manchester Rd., Higher Ince. WN2 2EA. Est. 1965. Open any time. SIZE: Large. *STOCK: General antiques.* LOC: A577 near Ince Bar. PARK: Easy. TEL: 01942 247773/241671. SER: Export packing. VAT: Stan. *Export and Trade Only.*

John Roby Antiques

12 Lord St. WN1 2BN. Open 10-5. CL: Sat. and Wed. *STOCK: Furniture, to 1940; bric-a-brac.* TEL: 01942 230887.

NORTH

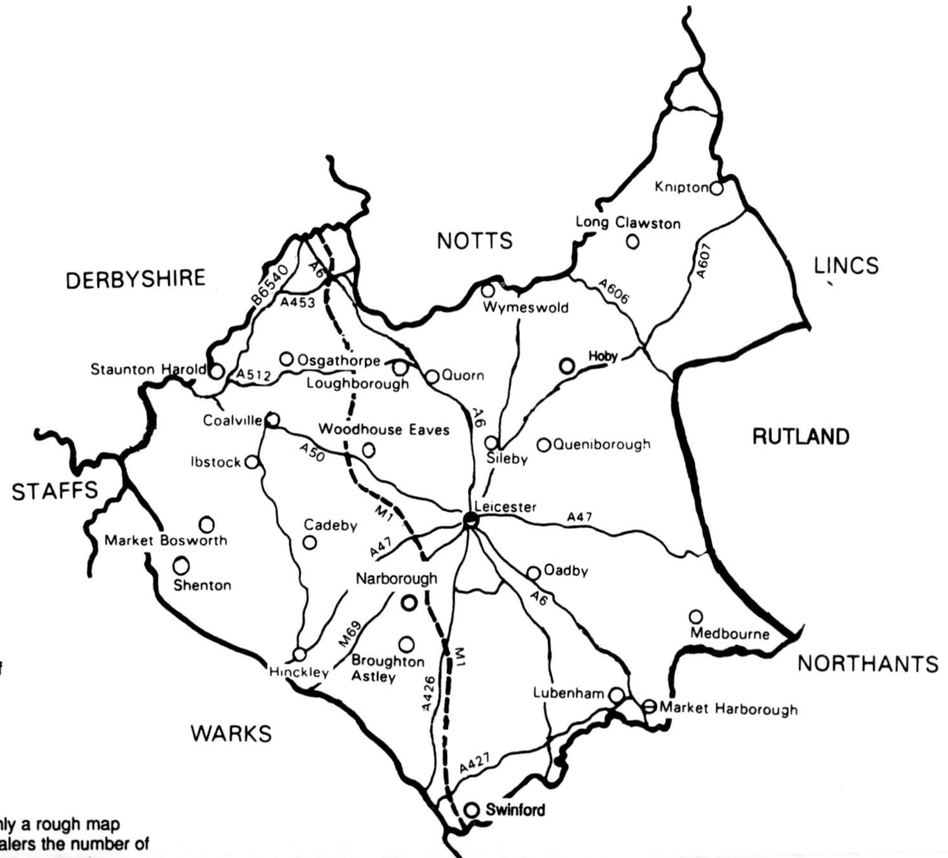

○ 1-2
⊖ 3-5
◒ 6-12
● 13+

Key to number of shops in this area.

Please note this is only a rough map designed to show dealers the number of

See also Rutland for Empingham, Manton, Oakham, Rutland Water, Uppingham and Wing

ROUGHTON ASTLEY, Nr. Leicester

ld Bakehouse Antiques and Gallery
Green Rd. LE9 6RA. (S.R. Needham). Open urs.-Sat. 10-6, Sun. 2-5. *STOCK: Period furture.* PARK: Easy. TEL: 01455 282276.

ADEBY, Nr. Nuneaton

. Stanworth (Fine Arts)
he Grange. CV13 0AX. (Mr and Mrs G. anworth). Resident. Est. 1965. Open by appointent. SIZE: Medium. *STOCK: Oil paintings, 18th early 20th C, £100-£8,000.* LOC: Just off 447. PARK: Easy. TEL: 01455 291023. VAT: ec.

OALVILLE

eystone Antiques LAPADA
Ashby Rd. LE67 3LF. (I. and H. McPherson). GA. Est. 1979. Open 10-5, Sat. 10-4. CL: ed. SIZE: Medium. *STOCK: Jewellery, ctorian and Georgian, £25-£1,500; silver, 00-1920, £20-£500; small collectable items, th-19th C, £15-£300; furniture, cranberry, edlework tools, Victorian and Georgian table ass.* LOC: A50, town centre. PARK: At rear. EL: 01530 835966. SER: NAG registered luer; gem testing. VAT: Stan/Spec.

assey's Antiques
Hotel St. LE67 2EP. (Mr and Mrs C.A. Irons). t. 1969. Open 9-5. CL: Wed. SIZE: Small. *OCK: Bric-a-brac and bygones, small furture, 1890-1960.* PARK: Rear. TEL: 01530 2374; home - 01530 832448.

NCKLEY

ouse Things Antiques
inity Lane, 44 Mansion St. LE10 0AU. (P.W. bertson). Est. 1976. Open 10-6. SIZE: Small. *OCK: Stripped pine, satinwood, oak and lnut, mainly Victorian and Edwardian, £50-00; small collectors' items, 1860-1930s, £5-00; cast iron fireplaces, brass and iron beds, 90-1920's, £50-£1,000.* LOC: On inner ring d 200yds. from Leisure Centre. PARK: Easy. L: 01455 618518; home - 01455 212797.

OBY, Nr. Melton Mowbray

ithers of Leicester
e Old Rutland, Church Lane. LE14 3DU. (S.

Hoby continued

Frings). Est. 1860. Open 9-5.30. CL: Thurs. pm. and Sat. SIZE: Medium. *STOCK: Furniture, 17th-19th C, £50-£3,000; china, 18th-19th C, £10-£300; oil paintings, 19th C, £5-£500.* Not Stocked: Jewellery and coins. PARK: Easy. TEL: 01664 434803. SER: Valuations; restorations (furniture). VAT: Stan/Spec.

IBSTOCK, Nr. Leicester

Mandrake Stevenson Antiques
99 and 101 High St. LE67 6LJ. Est. 1979. Open 10-5, Sat. 10-2.30. SIZE: Small. *STOCK: Furniture, pre 1930's.* PARK: Easy. TEL: 01530 260898. SER: Valuations; restorations (furniture).

KNIPTON, Nr. Grantham

Anthony W. Laywood
NG32 1RF. ABA. Est. 1967. Open by appointment. SIZE: Medium. *STOCK: Antiquarian books, pre-1850, £20-£2,000.* LOC: 1.5 miles off the Grantham-Melton Mowbray road. PARK: Easy. TEL: 01476 870224; fax - 01476 870198. SER: Valuations; buys at auction.

LEICESTER

Betty's
9 Knighton Fields Rd. West. LE2 6LH. (A. Smith). Est. 1968. Open 9.30-5. SIZE: Small. *STOCK: Satinwood and pine items, brass and copper, pictures.* LOC: Off Saffron Lane. PARK: Easy. TEL: 0116 2839048. SER: Valuations; buys at auction.

Boulevard Antique and Shipping Centre
Bow Bridge Dye House, Richard III Rd. LE3 5PT. Open 9-6, Sun. 10-5 or by appointment. SIZE: 10 dealers. *STOCK: Furniture including oak, mahogany, pine and shipping; general antiques and collectables, jewellery, silver and smalls.* LOC: 15 minutes junction 21, M1 on to A46. PARK: Own. TEL: 0116 233 8828/287 8500; fax - 0116 233 8829. VAT: Stan/Spec.

Britain's Heritage
Shaftesbury Hall, 3 Holy Bones. (Mr and Mrs J. Dennis). Est. 1980. Open daily, Sun. 2-5. SIZE: Large. *STOCK: Fireplaces, 18th-20th C, £100-£12,000.* LOC: Off Vaughan Way, 70 yards from Holiday Inn. PARK: Easy. TEL: 0116 2519592. SER: Valuations; restorations (antique fireplaces). VAT: Stan/Spec.

Leicester continued

Corry's LAPADA
24/26 Francis St., Stoneygate. LE2 2BD. (Mrs E.I. Corry). Est. 1962. Open 10-5. CL: Wed. SIZE: Medium. *STOCK: Furniture, 18th-19th C, £500-£10,000; paintings, 19th C, £100-£8,000; silver, porcelain and jewellery, 19th-20th C, £5-£5,000.* TEL: 0116 270 3794; mobile - 0860 195376. SER: Restorations. FAIRS: NEC (Jan., April, Aug.); LAPADA London; Robert Baileys'; Dorchester; Claridges; Park Lane. VAT: Spec.

Letty's Antiques
6 Rutland St. LE1 1RA. Est. 1952. *STOCK: Silver, jewellery, china and brass.* TEL: 0116 2626435.

Walter Moores and Son LAPADA
89 Wellington St. LE1 6HJ. (P. Moores). Est. 1925. Open 8.30-5.30, Sat. 8.30-12.30. CL: Mon. except by appointment. *STOCK: Mainly furniture, 1680-1880, £10-£10,000.* LOC: From London Rd. railway station go up Waterloo Way, first right into South Albion St., left at T-junction. PARK: Easy. TEL: 0116 2551402; mobile - 04100 19045. VAT: Spec.

Oxford Street Antique Centre
16-26 Oxford St. LE1 5XU. Open 10-5.30, Sun. 2-5, or by appointment. SIZE: Large trade warehouse. *STOCK: Period furniture, shipping goods, pine, bric-a-brac and general antiques, 18th to mid-20th C, 50p-£5,000.* LOC: Main ring road. PARK: Own. TEL: 0116 2553006; fax - 0116 2555863. SER: Container loading facilities. VAT: Stan/Spec.

The Rug Gallery
50 Montague Rd., Clarendon Park. LE2 1TH. (Dr. Roy Short). Est. 1987. Open Fri. and Sat. 10-4 or by appointment. SIZE: Medium. *STOCK: Oriental rugs and kilims, early 19th to 20th C, £100-£2,000; Swat and Afghan furniture, 18th-19th C, £50-£1,000; tribal embroidery and jewellery, 19th-20th C, £10-£1,000.* LOC: From London Rd. A6, take Victoria Park Rd., to Queen's Rd., then Montague Rd. PARK: Easy. TEL: 0116 2700085; home - 0116 2700113.

Hammond Smith (Fine Art)
31 Dukes Drive. LE2 1TP. Est. 1981. Open by appointment. Also available by appt. in London W1. SIZE: Small. *STOCK: British watercolours, 1750-1950, £300-£10,000; British etchings, 19th-20th C, £100-£500.* TEL: 0116 270 9020; fax - same; mobile - 0973 483231. SER: Valuations; restorations (watercolours and prints cleaned, mounted and framed); buys at auction (watercolours). VAT: Spec.

LONG CAWSTON, Nr. Melton Mowbray

Victoriana Architectural
Old Hall Farm, Hose Lane. LE14 4NG. Op 8.30-5.30. *STOCK: Pine, French antiques, g (electric) wall lights and shades, architectu items.* TEL: 01949 860274; fax - 01949 8612 SER: Restorations (oak, mahogany, architectu items, pine stripping); sash windows and ledg doors made from reclaimed pine.

LOUGHBOROUGH

Lowe of Loughborough
37-40 Church Gate. LE11 1UE. Est. 1846. C Sat. SIZE: Large and warehouse. *STOCK: Fu niture and period upholstery from early oak, 16 to Edwardian; mahogany, walnut, oak, £2 £8,000; clocks, bracket and longcase, £9 £2,500; porcelain, maps, copper and brass.* N Stocked: Jewellery. LOC: Opposite parish chur PARK: Own. TEL: 01509 212554/217876. SE Upholstery; restorations; interior design. VA Stan/Spec.

LUBENHAM, Nr. Market Harboroug

Leicestershire Sporting Gallery and Brown Jack Bookshop
The Old Granary, 62 Main St. LE1 9DG. (R Leete). Est. 1958. Prior 'phone call advisab SIZE: Large. *STOCK: Oil paintings, pri including Vanity Fair and sporting; engravin maps, furniture, including pine, mahogany a oak; antiquarian books, horse brass martingales, swingers.* LOC: Centre of villa PARK: Rear of village green opposite. TE 01858 465787.

Stevens and Son
61 Main Street. LE16 9TF. (M.J. Steven Resident. Est. 1977. Open 10-5. *STOCK: Gene antiques, mainly furniture.* LOC: A427 junction 20 M1. TEL: 01858 463521. SE Restorations (furniture).

MARKET BOSWORTH

Corner Cottage Antiques
7 Market Place, The Square. CV13 0LF. (J. a B. Roberts). Est. 1969. Open 10-5 or by appoi ment. *STOCK: 18th-20th C furniture, silv paintings; clocks, porcelain, glass, brass a copper, general antiques.* PARK: Easy. TE 01455 290344; home - 01455 282583. VA Global/Stan/Spec.

Country Pine Antiques
4 Main St. CV13 0JW. (M. and A. Boylan). E 1980. Open 10-5.30. CL: Tues. SIZE: Mediu *STOCK: Stripped pine.* LOC: Off A447 in Mar Place. PARK: Easy. TEL: 01455 291303; hom same.

ıARKET HARBOROUGH

ıbbey Antiques
7 Abbey St. LE16 9AA. (M. and M.A. Muckle). st. 1977. Open 10.30-5. SIZE: Medium. *STOCK: urniture, 18th-19th C, £50-£2,000; decorative ems, bric-a-brac, £1-£250; pine.* LOC: 100yds. ff town centre. PARK: Easy. TEL: 01858 52282; home - 01858 464085. SER: Valuations. 'AT: Global/Stan/Spec.

raftons of Market Harborough
2 St Mary's Rd. LE16 7DX. (F. Ingall). Est. 967. Open Mon., Tues., Fri. and Sat. 10-5.30, ther times by appointment. *STOCK: Oils, atercolours, etchings and engravings, 18th-19th* . TEL: 01858 433557.

ichard Kimbell Ltd
ockingham Rd. Est. 1966. Open 9-6, Sun. 10.30-.30; Riverside trade warehouse - open by ppointment. SIZE: Large + trade warehouse. *TOCK: Pine, 19th to early 20th C and repro-uction, £20-£3,000; home accessories.* LOC: eft turn off A427, past railway station towards orby. TEL: 01858 433444; fax - 01858 461301; iverside trade warehouse - 01858 461800; fax - 1858 467627. SER: Shipping and packing; anufacturer. VAT: Stan.

. Stamp and Sons
ne Chestnuts, 15 Kettering Rd. LE16 8AN. (M. amp). Resident. Est. 1947. Open 8-5.30, Sat. 9-2.30 or by appointment. SIZE: Medium. *TOCK: Mahogany and oak furniture, 18th-19th , £500-£5,000; Victorian furniture, £250-2,500; Edwardian furniture, £100-£1,000.* LOC: n A6. PARK: Easy. TEL: 01858 462524; fax - 858 465643. SER: Valuations (furniture); storations (furniture). VAT: Stan/Spec.

EDBOURNE

. and C. Royall Antiques
Waterfall Way. LE16 8EE. Open 9-5. *STOCK: rniture, pictures, silver, porcelain, glassware, ories and Oriental bronzes.* TEL: 01858 5744; home - same. SER: Restorations (bronzes, ories, brassware, metalware, including brass lay work, woodcarving, upholstery, French lishing).

ARBOROUGH

en Smith Antiques Ltd
5-217 Leicester Rd. (K.W. Sansom). Est. 1888. pen 9.30-5, Sun. 10-4. SIZE: Large. *STOCK: rniture, mainly 1880-1930, £100-£5,000; ocks, smalls and paintings.* TEL: 0116 286 41; fax - 0116 275 3151. VAT: Stan/Spec.

OADBY

John Hardy Antiques
91 London Rd. LE2 5DP. Open every day. *STOCK: General antiques.* TEL: 0116 2712862. VAT: Stan/Spec.

OSGATHORPE, Nr. Loughborough

David E. Burrows LAPADA
Manor House Farm. LE12 9SY. Est. 1973. *STOCK: Pine, oak, mahogany and walnut furniture, clocks, smalls, £50-£20,000.* LOC: Exit 23, M1, turn right off Ashby road, farm next to church. TEL: 01530 222218; mobile - 0836 598664; fax - 01530 223139. VAT: Stan/Spec.

QUENIBOROUGH, Nr. Leicester

J. Green and Son
1 Coppice Lane. LE7 3DR. (R. Green). Resident. Est. 1932. Appointment advisable. SIZE: Medium. *STOCK: 18th-19th C English and Continental furniture.* LOC: Off A607 Leicester-Melton Mowbray Rd. PARK: Easy. TEL: 0116 2606682. SER: Valuations; buys at auction. VAT: Stan/Spec.

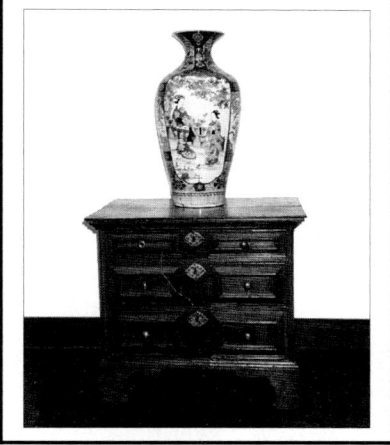

QUORN

Mill on the Soar Antiques Ltd

1/3 High St. LE12 8DS. (T.O. and J. York). CL: Sun. and Mon. except by appointment. *STOCK: 17th-19th C furniture and associated articles.* LOC: In centre of village, on old A6. PARK: Easy. TEL: 01509 414218.

Quorn Pine and Decoratives

The New Mills, Leicester Rd. LE12 8ES. (S. Yates and S. Parker). Open 9-6, Sat. 9.30-5.30. *STOCK: Pine and country furniture.* TEL: 01509 416031. SER: Stripping and restorations (pine). VAT: Stan/Spec.

SHENTON, Nr. Market Bosworth

Whitemoors Antiques and Fine Art

CV13 6BZ. Est. 1987. Open 11-5, Sun. and Ban Holidays (except Christmas) 10-6. SIZE: Large 20+ unitholders. *STOCK: Furniture, £25-£2,000 smalls, £5-£200; prints and pictures, Victoria and early 20th C, £40-£400.* LOC: A5 onto A44 towards Burton-on-Trent, first right then secon left. PARK: Easy. TEL: 01455 212250; home 01455 212981.

SILEBY, Nr. Loughborough

R. A. James Antiques

Ammonite Gallery, 15a High St. LE12 7RX *STOCK: Mainly stripped pine, general antique* TEL: 01509 812169.

STAUNTON HAROLD

Ropers Hill Antiques

Ropers Hill Farm. LE65 1SE. (S. and F Southworth). Est. 1974. Open by appointmen SIZE: Small. *STOCK: General antiques, silve and metalware.* LOC: On A453. PARK: Eas TEL: 01530 413919. SER: Valuations.

SWINFORD, Nr. Lutterworth

Old Timers

Holmwood, High St. LE17 6BL. (M. S. Harris Est. 1993. Open every day but appointme preferred. SIZE: Small. *STOCK: 18th-19th clocks - longcase, £1,000-£5,000; wall, £15 £1,500; bracket and mantle, £150-£3,000; som brass and copper.* LOC: Village centre, half mile from M1, junction 19. PARK: Nearby. TE 01788 860311; home - same. SER: Valuation restorations (clocks).

WOODHOUSE EAVES, Nr. Leicester

Paddock Antiques

The Old Smithy, Brand Hill. LE12 8SS. (M C.A. and T.M. Bray). Open Thurs. - Sat. 10-5.3 other times by appointment. *STOCK: Furnitur 1750-1910, to £3,000; porcelain, 1750-1930's, £2,000; prints, glass, copper and brass.* PARK Outside shop.

WYMESWOLD, Nr. Loughborough

N. Bryan-Peach Antiques

28 Far St. LE12 6TZ. Resident. Open 10-6, Su by appointment. SIZE: Medium. *STOCK: Clock barometers, watches; 18th-19th C furniture, £5 £5,000.* PARK: Easy. TEL: 01509 880425. SE Valuations; restorations; buys at auction. VA Spec.

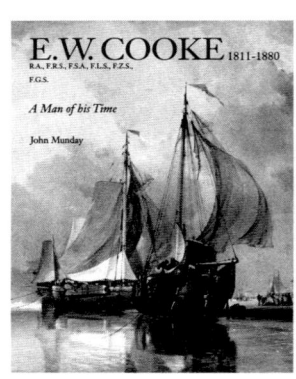

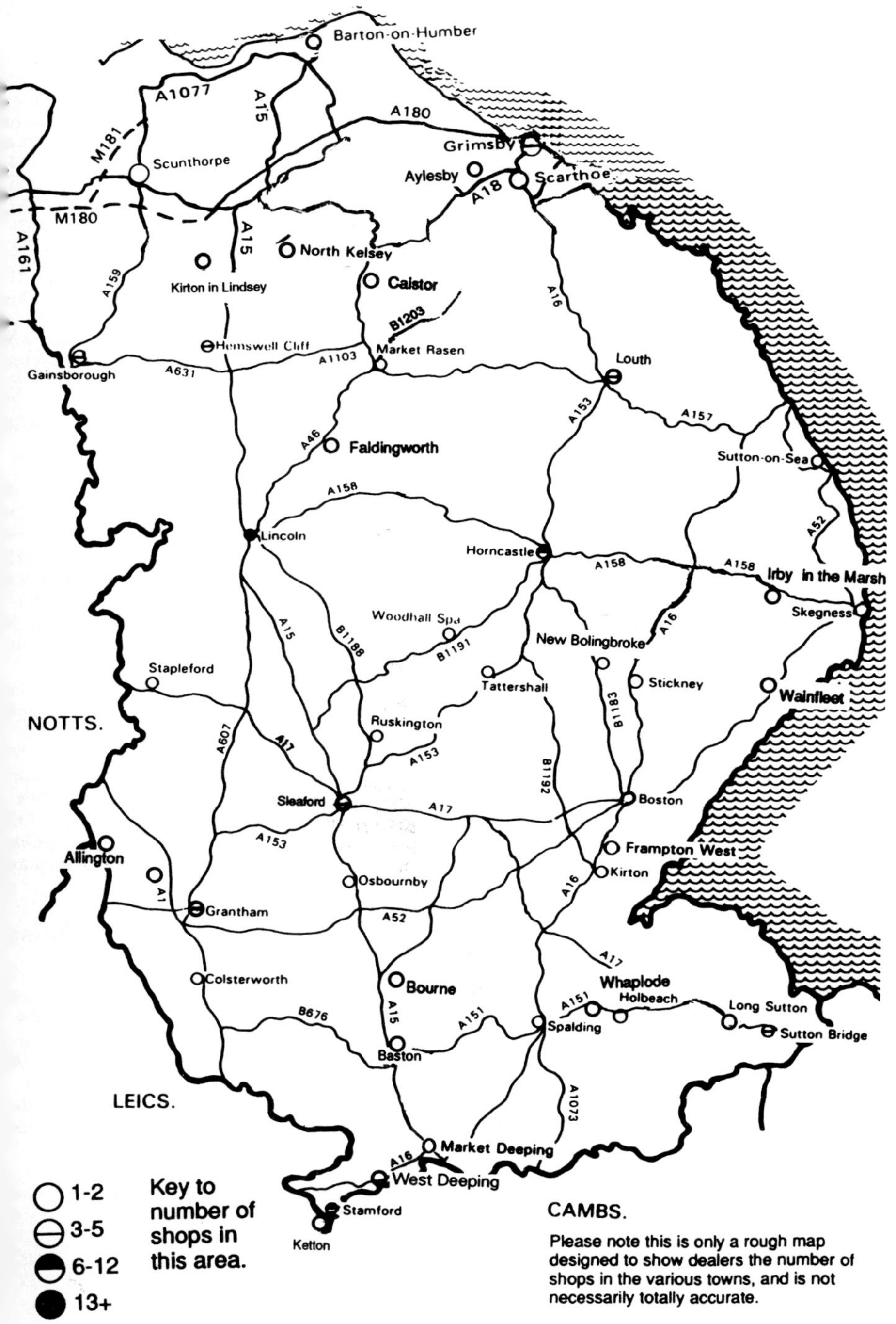

Please note this is only a rough map designed to show dealers the number of shops in the various towns, and is not necessarily totally accurate.

ALLINGTON, Nr. Grantham

Garth Vincent Antique Arms and Armour LAPADA

The Old Manor House. NG32 2DH. Est. 1979. Open by appointment. SIZE: Medium. *STOCK: Militaria including firearms, swords, rapiers and daggers; armour, 16th-19th C, £50-£15,000.* LOC: Opposite church. PARK: Easy. TEL: 01400 281358; home - same; fax - 01400 282658. SER: Valuations; restorations; buys at auction. FAIRS: London and major city Arms; Period Homes and Gardens, NEC Aug. VAT: Spec.

AYLESBY, Nr. Grimsby

Robin Fowler (Period Clocks)

Washing Dales, Washing Dales Lane. DN37 7LH. Open by appointment. SIZE: Large. *STOCK: Clocks and barometers, 17th-18th C.* TEL: 01472 751335. SER: Restorations (clocks, barometers).

BARTON-ON-HUMBER

Streetwalker Antiques

35 High St. (J.N. Chapman). Open 9.30-1 and 2-5. CL: Thurs. SIZE: Small. *STOCK: General antiques, 18th-19th C.* LOC: South bank of Humber Bridge, first exit. PARK: Easy. TEL: 01652 633960/660050. SER: Valuations. VAT: Stan.

Streetwalker Antiques Warehouse

The Old Leisure Centre, Brigg Rd. DN18 5DH. (J.N. Chapman). Open 9-5.30. SIZE: Large. *STOCK: General antiques and shipping furniture, oak and mahogany.* TEL: 01652 660050/633960; fax - 01652 633472. *Trade Only.*

BASTON, Nr. Peterborough

The Complete Automobilist

Dept. GD, 35 Main St. PE6 9NX. Est. 1967. Open 9-5. CL: Sat. *STOCK: Hard-to-get parts for older vehicles.* LOC: On A15, east of Stamford. PARK: Easy. TEL: 01778 560312; fax - 01778 560738. SER: Catalogue available £1.

BOSTON

Tony Coda Antiques

121 High St. PE21 8TS. Est. 1967. Open 9.30-12.30 and 1.30-5.30. SIZE: Medium. *STOCK: Furniture, 17th-19th C, from £100; paintings, 19th C, to £500; china, silver and clocks, to £200.* LOC: From A16 turn right at roundabout in to London Rd. and then to High St. PARK: Easy. TEL: 01205 352754; home - 01205 722104. SER: Valuations. FAIRS: International Antique and Collectors.

Boston continued

Portobello Row Antique & Collectors' Centre

93-95 High St. Open 10-4. SIZE: 9 dealer[s]. *STOCK: Shipping furniture, kitchenalia, blue a[nd] white china, 1940's-60's clothing, bric-a-bra[c].* TEL: 01205 368692.

BOURNE

Antique and Secondhand Traders

39 West St. (C.A. and A.L. Thompson). E[st.] 1962. Open Mon., Thurs., Fri. and Sat. 9-5, Tu[es.] and Wed. by appointment. SIZE: Warehous[e]. *STOCK: Furniture, antique shipping oak, pi[ne,] modern and smalls, £5-£5,000.* LOC: On A15, [..] miles from Stamford A1. PARK: Own. TE[L:] 01778 394700; mobiles - Alan - 0585 6942[..]; Clyde - 0860 734742. SER: Valuations. FAIR[S:] Newark; Ardingly. VAT: Spec/Global.

CAISTOR

Caistor Antiques

12 High St. (Susan Rutter). Est. 1982. Open [..] appointment day or night. *STOCK: Potte[ry,] furniture, jewellery, dolls, linen, 18th-20th [C.]* LOC: Off A46 between Grimsby and Mark[et] Rasen. PARK: Own. TEL: 01472 851975; hom[e -] same. SER: Valuations.

COLSTERWORTH

Clive Underwood Antiques

46 High St. NG33 5NF. Est. 1970. Open 9.30-5.[..] *STOCK: Furniture, oak, mahogany, 17th-19th [C,] £45-£10,000; some pictures, glass, porcelain.* LO[C:] ½ mile off A1 between Stamford and Grantha[m.] TEL: 01476 860689. SER: Valuations; restoratio[ns;] rushing; caning. VAT: Stan/Spec.

FALDINGWORTH, Nr. Market Rasen

Brownlow Antiques Centre

Lincoln Rd. LN8 3SF. (Sylvia and Al[..] Stephens). Est. 1994. Open 10-6 including S[un.] and by appointment. CL: Mon. SIZE: Lar[ge.] *STOCK: Furniture, mainly 19th C to pre 19[..] £100-£1,000; bric-a-brac, collectables, from [..]* LOC: A46 towards Grimsby, 10 miles north [of] Lincoln. PARK: Own. TEL: 01673 885367; ho[me] - same. FAIRS: Local.

FRAMPTON WEST, Nr. Boston

Robert J. Kent Antiques

Pinewood, Ralphs Lane. PE20 1QZ. *STOC[K:] Pine furniture.* LOC: B1391. TEL: 01205 7237[..] VAT: Stan.

;AINSBOROUGH

. Carrick's Antiques and Shipping
30 Trinity St. DN21 5PD. Open 8.30-5. *STOCK: eneral antiques and shipping furniture.* TEL: 1427 611393/810409.

tanley Hunt Jewellers
2 Church St. (S. and R.S. Hunt). Est. 1952. Open -5. CL: Wed. SIZE: Medium. *STOCK: Jewel- ry, 19th C, £50-£500+.* LOC: Main street from larket Place. PARK: Easy. TEL: 01427 613051; ome - same. SER: Valuations; restorations (gold, lver, clocks).

ilgrims Antiques Centre
5 Church St. DN21 2JR. Est. 1986. CL: Mon. id Wed. SIZE: Large. *STOCK: Jewellery and lver, £5-£1,000; pictures, ceramics and textiles, 5-£1,000; pine and furniture, £50-£1,000.* LOC: ear Old Hall. PARK: Easy. TEL: 01427 810897. ER: Valuations. FAIRS: Newark; Birmingham.

RANTHAM

rantham Clocks
) Lodge Way. NG31 8DD. (R. Conder). esident. Open by appointment. *STOCK: Clocks.* ARK: Easy. TEL: 01476 561784. SER: Restor- ions.

rantham Furniture Emporium
6 Wharf Rd. NG31 6BA. (K. and J.E. amilton). Est. 1970. Open 10-4.30, Sun. 11-4. .: Mon. and Wed. SIZE: Large. *STOCK: Vict- ian, Edwardian and shipping furniture, £5- ,000.* LOC: Town centre, near Post Office. ARK: Own at rear. TEL: 01476 562967.

otions
Market Place. NG31 6LQ. (Mrs S. Checkley). t. 1982. Open 10-5, Sat. 9.30-5, Sun. 1-4. SIZE: edium. *STOCK: China, collectables and decor- ve accessories, £1-£500; furniture, £30-£800, th-20th C.* LOC: Opposite Angel and Royal otel. PARK: Easy. TEL: 01476 563603. SER: pairs; re-upholstery; French polishing. FAIRS: wark; Ardingly; Stoneleigh; Peterborough.

illiam Redmile Antiques
Elmer St. North. NG31 6RE. (J.W. Redmile). t. 1936. Open 9-6. *STOCK: General antiques.*)C: From London turn right at Angel Hotel. L: 01476 564074.

ilkinson's
e Tyme House, 1 Blue Court. NG31 6NJ. (M. l P. Wilkinson). Est. 1935. Open 10-1 and 2-4. .: Wed. SIZE: Small. *STOCK: Jewellery, tches and silver, 19th C, £50-£1,000.* PARK: arby. TEL: 01476 560400 and 01529 413149. R: Valuations; restorations (including clock l watch movements); buys at auction (rings and tches). VAT: Spec.

GRIMSBY

Bell Antiques
68 Harold St. DN32 7NQ. (V. Hawkey). Est. 1964. Open by appointment, telephone previous evening. SIZE: Large. *STOCK: Antique pine and grandfather clocks.* Not Stocked: Reproduction. PARK: Easy. TEL: 01472 695110; home - same.

Simon Antiques
7 Saunders St. (S.N. Goodman). Open by appoint- ment only. *STOCK: Jewellery, smalls, 1950's glass lamps, bric-a-brac, 19th-20th C, £5-£50.* TEL: Mobile - 0802 382237. SER: Valuations (jewellery); buys at auction. FAIRS: Linc's Showground and local. *Trade Only.*

HEMSWELL CLIFF, Nr. Gainsborough

Astra House Antiques Centre
RAF Hemswell. DN21 5TL. (M. Frith). Open daily including Sun. 10-5. SIZE: 50 dealers. *STOCK: Wide variety of general antiques and shipping goods, including Victorian, Edwardian and Continental furniture and smalls.* LOC: Near Caenby Corner Roundabout A15/A631. TEL: 01427 668312.

Hemswell Antiques Centre
Caenby Corner Estate. DN21 5TJ. (P.J. and A.R. Miller). Est. 1986. Open 10-5 including Sun. SIZE: 270+ dealers. *STOCK: Period furniture, 17th-19th C; watercolours and oils, 19th C; silver and plate, clocks, porcelain, china, jewellery, dolls, toys, books, prints, clothes.* LOC: A15 from Lincoln then A631 towards Gainsborough, 1 mile from roundabout, follow signs. PARK: Easy. TEL: 01427 668389; fax - 01427 668935. SER: Valuations; restorations (oak, mahogany and pine; upholstery); container packing.

Kate
Kate House, Caenby Corner Estate. DN21 5TJ. (Mr Shamsa). Open 9-4.30, Sat. 10-1. *STOCK: Pine including reproduction.* TEL: 01427 668724/668904; fax - 01427 668905.

Second Time Around
Hemswell Antique Centre, Caenby Corner Estate. DN21 5TJ. (G.L. Powis). Open 10-5 including Sun. *STOCK: Longcase and bracket clocks, pre 1830, £1,450-£20,000.* LOC: A15 from Lincoln to Caenby Corner roundabout, left towards Gainsborough for 1 mile. (A631). PARK: Easy. TEL: 01427 668389; home - 01522 543167. SER: Restorations (clocks).

HOLBEACH, Nr. Spalding

P.J. Cassidy (Books)
1 Boston Rd. PE12 7LR. Est. 1974. Open 10-6. SIZE: Medium. *STOCK: Books, 19th-20th C, £2- £300; maps, prints and engravings, 17th-19th C, £10-£500.* LOC: 1/4 mile from A17. PARK: Nearby. TEL: 01406 426322; fax - same; e-mail - bookscass@aol.com. SER: Valuations; framing and mount cutting. VAT: Stan.

HORNCASTLE

Clare Boam
22-38 North St. LN9 5DX. Est. 1977. Open 9-5, Sun 2-4.30. SIZE: Large. *STOCK: Furniture and bric-a-brac, 19th-20th C, to £1,000.* LOC: Louth/Grimsby road out of town. PARK: Easy. TEL: 01507 522381; home - same. VAT: Stan.

Great Expectations
39-41 East St. (Clare Boam). Est. 1977. Open 9-5, Sun. and Bank Holidays 1-4.30. SIZE: Large. *STOCK: Wide variety of general antiques including pine, oak, mahogany, kitchenalia, luggage, books, china, glass, collectables, 50p to £1,000.* LOC: A158, 100 yards from traffic lights. PARK: At rear or in street opposite. TEL: 01507 524202; home - 01507 522381. SER: Restorations (china, glass and furniture).

Robert Kitching
9-11 West St. LN9 5JE. Open 9.30-5. *STOCK: Clocks and general antiques.* TEL: 01507 522120.

The Lincolnshire Antiques Centre
Bridge St. LN9 5HZ. (Karen White). Open 9-5, including Sun. SIZE: 30+ dealers. *STOCK: General antiques, £5-£5,000.* PARK: Own. TEL: 01507 527794; fax - 01507 526670. SER: Weekly auction. VAT: Stan/Spec.

Alan Read Period Furniture
60 & 62 West St. LN9 5AD. Open 10-4. CL: Mon. and Wed. *STOCK: 17th-18th C furniture; decorative items, Eastern rugs.* TEL: 01507 524324. SER: Bespoke copies.

Seaview Antiques
Stanhope Rd. LN9 6AA. (M. Chalk and Tracey Collins). Open 9-5. SIZE: Large + warehouse. *STOCK: Victorian, Edwardian and decorative furniture; smalls, brassware, silver, silver plate, lamps, boxes.* LOC: A158. PARK: Easy. TEL: 01507 524524; home - 01507 523287.

Laurence Shaw Antiques
77 East St. LN9 6AA. Open 8.30-5. SIZE: Medium. *STOCK: Furniture, china, glass, metalware, books, collectables, general antiques, 17th-20th C.* LOC: Opposite Tourist Information Centre. TEL: 01507 527638. SER: Consultant; valuations. VAT: Stan/Spec.

Staines Antiques
25 Bridge St. LN9 5HZ. (Mrs M.E. Staines). Est. 1991. Open 10-5. CL: Mon. SIZE: Large. *STOCK: Furniture, pictures and clocks, £50-£5,000; ceramics, £25-£1,000; all 18th-20th C.* LOC: A158 Lincoln to Skegness road, turn off by-pass towards town centre. Shop 200 yards on right, opposite Antiques Centre. PARK: Easy and nearby. TEL: 01507 527976; home - same. SER: Valuations.

IRBY-IN-THE-MARSH, Nr. Skegness

Irby Antiques Centre
Pinfold Lane. (P. and K. Hines). Resident. Es 1975. Open 10.30-5 including Sun. CL: We SIZE: Medium. *STOCK: Porcelain, bras pictures and collectables, 19th and 20th C, £ £500.* LOC: B1195 Wainfleet to Spilsby roa PARK: Own. TEL: 01754 810943. FAIRS: Loca

KETTON, Nr. Stamford

Robin Cox Antiques
Manor Farmhouse, High St. PE9 3TA. Est. 196 Open strictly by appointment. *STOCK: Engli and Continental furniture, and works of a including early oak, mahogany and decorate wood carvings and sculpture, architectur fittings, garden items, £50-£10,000.* TEL: 017 720240. VAT: Stan/Spec.

KIRTON

Kirton Antiques LAPAI
3 High St. PE20 1DR. (A.R. Marshall). E 1973. Open 8.30-5, Sat. 8.30-12, or by appoi ment. SIZE: Large - warehouse. *STOC Furniture, all periods; painted pine, chai decorative items, glass, metal, pottery, chin picture frames.* TEL: 01205 722595; evening 01205 722134; fax - 01205 722895. VAT: Stan

KIRTON IN LINDSEY

Mr Van Hefflin
12 High St., DN21 4LU. Est. 1820. Open 10 *STOCK: Jewellery, curios, silver, paintin* PARK: Easy. TEL: 01652 648044. SER: Guide

LINCOLN

20th Century Frocks
65 Steep Hill. LN1 1YN. (Patricia Rowberr Est. 1986. Open 11-5. SIZE: Small. *STOC Ladies clothes, hats and accessories, jewell including costume, mainly '20's and '30's, 1970, £5-£150; textiles including Canton a paisley shawls, curtains and chenille cloths, £300.* LOC: Opposite the Jews House, bottom Steep Hill. PARK: Danes Terrace. TEL: 015 545916; home - 01507 533638. SER: Valuatio FAIRS: Newark.

Annette Antiques
77 Bailgate. LN1 3AR. (Mrs A. Bhalla). E 1972. Open Mon. 11-5, Tues.-Sat. 12-6. SI Small. *STOCK: Porcelain, glass and small sil 19th-20th C; clocks, silver flatware, watercolo prints and drawings, 18th-20th C; all £10-£5* LOC: 2 minutes from castle and cathedral. PAF Nearby. TEL: 01522 546838; home - 01 260219. SER: Restorations (furniture, cloc FAIRS: Alexandra Palace.

incoln continued

Iichael Brewer

Iorthgate Lodge, Northgate. LN2 1QS. (M.N. Brewer). Est. 1954. Open by appointment. SIZE: Medium. *STOCK: Furniture, oil paintings, silver, orcelain, bronzes, works of art.* Not Stocked: Coins. LOC: Close to Cathedral. PARK: 20yds. EL: 01522 545854. SER: Valuations; buys at uction. VAT: Stan/Spec. *Trade Only.*

. and K.E. Dring

11 High St. LN5 7PY. Open 10-5.30. CL: Wed. *TOCK: Victorian and Edwardian inlaid urniture; shipping goods, porcelain, clocks, tin-lated toys, trains and Dinkys.* TEL: 01522 40733/792794.

Golden Goose Books

0 and 21 Steep Hill. LN2 1LT. (R. West-Skinn nd Mrs A. Cockram). Est. 1983. Open 10-5.30. *TOCK: Antiquarian books, maps and prints, £5-10,000.* TEL: 01522 522589; home - 01673 78622.

David J. Hansord and Son BADA

2 Steep Hill. LN2 1LU. Est. 1972. Open 9.30-1 nd 2-5.30. SIZE: Medium. *STOCK: English nd Continental furniture, 17th to early 19th C, 100-£10,000; clocks, barometers and scientific nstruments, mainly 18th C, from £50.* Not tocked: Later items. LOC: Few yards from athedral. PARK: Easy. TEL: 01522 530044; ome - 01522 526983. SER: Valuations; buys at uction. VAT: Stan/Spec.

Harlequin Gallery

2 Steep Hill. LN2 1LT. (R. West-Skinn). Est. 962. Open 10-5.30. *STOCK: Antiquarian books, rints, maps, 50p-£15,000.* TEL: 01522 522589; ome - 01673 858294.

Dorrian Lambert Antiques

4 Steep Hill. LN1 1YN. (R. Lambert). Est. 1981. pen 10-5, Wed. and Sun. by appointment. SIZE: edium. *STOCK: Small furniture, clocks, chairs, ottery, porcelain, jewellery, books, sporting ntiques, books and collectables, 18th to early 9th C.* PARK: Loading only or nearby. TEL: 522 545916; home - 01427 848686. SER: Valuations; restorations (clocks). FAIRS: Newark howground.

Lincoln Fine Art

ernstall House, 33 The Strait. LN2 1JD. (Mrs D. en-Doepel). Est. 1973. Open 10-1 and 2-5.30. *TOCK: Oil paintings including decorative ortraits, landscapes, marine, watercolours, bstracts (Dorothy Lee Roberts), miniatures, Old aster paintings, drawings, porcelain and objets art, 17th-20th C, £80-£10,000.* LOC: Top of gh St., opposite Stadz Café. PARK: Nearby. EL: 01522 533029. SER: Valuations.

Lincoln continued

Mansions

5a Eastgate. LN2 1QA. Open 10-5. *STOCK: General antiques, decorative items, period lighting.* TEL: 01522 513631/560271.

J. and R. Ratcliffe

46 Steep Hill. LN2 1LU. Est. 1954. CL: Wed. *STOCK: English and Continental furniture, pottery, porcelain, 1600-1830.* LOC: Near cathedral. PARK: Easy. TEL: 01522 537438.

Roundabout Antique and Craft Centre

187 Burton Rd. (A. Buchanan). Open 10-5.30 including Sun. SIZE: 30 dealers. *STOCK: Wide range of general antiques and crafts.* TEL: 01522 541920; home - 01522 535078.

Rowletts of Lincoln

338 High St. LN5 7DQ. (A.H. Rowlett). Open 9-5. *STOCK: Coins and jewellery.* TEL: 01522 524139.

The Strait Antiques

5 The Strait. LN2 1JD. (Q.G. Quinn). Est. 1970. Open 10-5. SIZE: Medium. *STOCK: Early porcelain, Victorian Doulton ladies.* LOC: At the start of the ascent to the Cathedral from the top of the High St. PARK: Easy, behind shop. TEL: 01522 523130.

James Usher and Son Ltd

6 Silver St. LN2 1DY. Open 9-5.30. *STOCK: Silver, jewellery.* TEL: 01522 527547.

LONG SUTTON

J.W. Talton

15-19 Market St. PE12 9DD. (J., W. and J.J. Talton). Resident. Est. 1952. Open 9-5, Wed. 9-12. SIZE: Small. *STOCK: General antiques.* LOC: On old A17. PARK: Easy. TEL: 01406 362147; home - same. SER: Restorations (furniture and cabinet making).

Trade Antiques

7 Market St. PE12 9EF. (P.E. Poole). Est. 1961. CL: Sat. SIZE: Medium. *STOCK: General shipping goods, clocks and watches.* LOC: Old A17. PARK: Easy. TEL: 01406 363758. VAT: Stan. *Trade Only.*

LOUTH

A Barn Full of Brass Beds

Abbey House, Eastfield Rd. LN11 7HJ. (J.J. Tebbs). Est. 1985. Open by appointment. SIZE: Large. *STOCK: Brass and iron beds, 1860-1910, £250-£1,000.* LOC: 1/4 mile from Louth on right, off Eastfield Rd. PARK: Easy. TEL: 01507 603173; home - same. SER: Valuations; restorations. FAIRS: Lincolnshire Show. VAT: Stan.

Louth continued

Haydn Earl Restorations

119A Eastgate. LN11 9QE. Est. 1990. Open 10-6. SIZE: Medium + large workshop at Unit 4 Church View Business Centre, Louth Rd., Binbrook. *STOCK: Furniture, late 18th to mid 19th C, £200-£1,000; pictures, 19th C, £100-£500.* TEL: 01507 609906. SER: Valuations; restorations (French polishing, re-veneering, re-leathering, metal, re-upholstery); interior furnishing and decoration. FAIRS: Newark, Ardingly and NEC. VAT: Stan/Spec.

The Louth Antique Centre

Aswell St. (D. Jackman). Est. 1982. Open 10-4. SIZE: Large. *STOCK: Victorian, Edwardian and secondhand furniture.* LOC: 2 minutes walk from town centre. PARK: Easy. TEL: 01507 600366; home - 01507 343354. SER: Valuations; restorations; pine stripping.

MARKET DEEPING

Portland House Antiques

23 Church St. PE6 8AN. (G.W. Cree and V.E. Bass). Est. 1987. Open Mon.-Sat. or by appointment. SIZE: Medium. *STOCK: Porcelain, glass, furniture, 18th-19th C, £100-£10,000.* PARK: Easy. TEL: 01778 347129; home - same. SER: Buys at auction. FAIRS: Kings College. VAT: Stan/Spec.

MARKET RASEN

Harwood Tate

Church Mill, Caistor Rd. LN8 3HX. (J. Harwood Tate). Open 9.30-5.30, Sat. 10-1. SIZE: Large. *STOCK: Furniture, mahogany, rosewood, oak; clocks, 18th to early 19th C; ornamental items including pictures and prints, 18th-19th C.* Not Stocked: Shipping goods. LOC: Take A46 from Lincoln, Church Mill is off town centre, north of church. PARK: Easy. TEL: 01673 843579. VAT: Stan/Spec.

NEW BOLINGBROKE, Nr. Boston

Junktion

The Old Railway Station. (J. Rundle). Est. 1981. Open Wed., Thurs. and Sat. SIZE: Large. *STOCK: Early advertising, decorative and architectural items; toys, automobilia, mechanical antiques and bygones; early slot machines, wireless, telephones, 20th C collectables.* Not Stocked: Porcelain and jewellery. LOC: B1183 Boston to Horncastle. PARK: Easy. TEL: 01205 480087/480068.

NORTH KELSEY MOOR, Nr. Caistor

Moor Pine

New Warehouse, Station Yard. LN7 6HD. SIZI Large. *STOCK: English and Continental pine an French furniture; old pine reproduction furnitur* PARK: Own. TEL: 01652 678036. SEI Containers. VAT: Stan.

OSBOURNBY, Nr. Sleaford

Audley House LAPAD

35 High St. NG34 0DN. (R. and S. Galloway Est. 1948. Open by appointment only. *STOC 17th-18th C oak and country furniture, textil and treen.* PARK: Easy. TEL: 01529 45547 mobile - 0850 876752.

RUSKINGTON

Pinfold Antiques LAPAD

3 Pinfold Lane. NG34 9EU. (J. and G.I Ballinger). Est. 1981. Open by appointmen SIZE: Medium. *STOCK: Longcase clock £1,500-£15,000; period English furniture, £20 £10,000; also wall, bracket and mantel clock* PARK: Easy. TEL: 01526 832057; fax - 015 834550. SER: Valuations; restorations (lon case and bracket clocks, period furniture buys at auction. FAIRS: Olympia, Robe Bailey, NEC.

SCARTHOE, Nr. Grimsby

Scarthoe Gifts and Antiques

38 Louth Rd. DN33 2EP. (P. Bridges). Est. 197 Open 10-5. CL: Mon. and Thurs. SIZE: Mediu *STOCK: Jewellery, silver, porcelain, collector items, maps, prints, linen.* LOC: A16. PAR Easy. TEL: 01472 877394.

SCUNTHORPE

Guns and Tackle

Rear of 251A Ashby High St. DN16 2SQ. (J. Bowden). Open 9-5.30. CL: Wed. *STOCK: Gu and militaria.* TEL: 01724 865445. SE Restorations and repairs (guns).

SKEGNESS

G & J Crowson

50 High St. PE25 3NW. Open daily 10- *STOCK: General antiques and reproductio* TEL: 01754 764360. *Mainly Trade.*

Romantiques

93 Roman Bank. PE25 2SW. Open 9.30-5. *STOCK: Clocks, furniture, smalls, jewelle (shipping stock).* PARK: Easy. TEL: 017 610660. SER: Restorations (furniture includi French polishing); clock and watch repairs.

SLEAFORD

Mill Antiques
19A Northgate. NG34 7BH. (John Noble and A. Crabtree). Est. 1988. Open 9-5. SIZE: Medium. *STOCK: General antiques including furniture, porcelain and pictures, 18th-20th C, £5-£1,500.* LOC: 100 yds. from Market Square. PARK: Loading only. TEL: 01529 413342; home - 01529 415101. SER: Valuations; restorations (furniture and porcelain).

Victoriana
1 Jermyn St. (Mrs P.C. Pywell). Est. 1970. Open Mon. and Fri. 10.30-5 and usually Sat. 11-5. SIZE: Small. *STOCK: General small antiques, 1820's to 1940's, £5-£250.* LOC: A17. PARK: Nearby. TEL: Home - 01205 722785.

Wilkinson's
The Little Tyme House, 13 Southgate. NG34 7SU. (M. and P. Wilkinson). Est. 1935. Open 10- and 2-4. CL: Thurs. SIZE: Small. *STOCK: Jewellery, watches and silver, £50-£1,000.* PARK: Nearby. TEL: 01529 413149 and 01476 0400. SER: Valuations; restorations (including clock and watch movements); buys at auction (rings and watches). VAT: Stan.

SPALDING

Dean's Antiques
"The Walnuts", Weston St. Mary's. PE12 6JB. (Mrs B. Dean). Est. 1969. Open daily. SIZE: Medium. *STOCK: General antiques, farm and country bygones, £2-£200.* LOC: On Spalding to Holbeach main road A151. PARK: Easy. TEL: 1406 370429.

STAMFORD

Dawson of Stamford
Red Lion Sq. PE9 2AJ. (J Dawson). Open 9-.30. SIZE: Medium. *STOCK: Jewellery, silver and Georgian furniture.* LOC: Town centre between St. John's church and All Saint's church. TEL: 01780 54166. VAT: Stan/Spec.

Claire Langley Antiques
a St. Mary's Hill. PE9 2DP. Open 9.30-5.30. CL: Thurs. SIZE: Medium. *STOCK: Period mahogany and oak furniture, clocks, barometers and unusual decorative items.* LOC: Just over town bridge, on the left. PARK: George Hotel. TEL: 01780 30544. SER: Restorations (furniture, clocks and barometers). VAT: Stan/Spec.

Graham Pickett Antiques
) Water St. PE9 2NJ. (G.R. Pickett). Est. 1990. Open 10-5, Sun. and Thurs. by appointment. SIZE: Medium. *STOCK: Furniture - country, 650-1900, French provincial, 1700-1900, both 50-£2,000; French and English beds, 1750-900, £350-£2,000.* LOC: From A1 north into

Stamford continued

town, at first lights, turn right into Water St. PARK: Easy. TEL: 01780 481064; home - 01780 64502. SER: Valuations; buys at auction. FAIRS: Newark IACF. VAT: Stan/Spec.

Sinclair's
11/12 St. Mary's St. (J.S. Sinclair). Est. 1970. Open 9-5.30. SIZE: Large. *STOCK: Oak country furniture, 18th C, £200-£3,000; Victorian mahogany furniture, £100-£1,000; Edwardian furniture.* LOC: Near A1. PARK: George Hotel. . TEL: 01780 65421. VAT: Stan/Spec.

St. George's Antiques
1 St. George's Sq. PE9 2BN. (G.H. Burns). Est. 1974. Open 9-1 and 2-4.30. CL: Sat. SIZE: Small and trade only warehouse. *STOCK: Period and Victorian furniture, some small items.* TEL: 01780 54117; home - 01780 460456. VAT: Stan/Spec.

St. Martins Antiques Centre
23a High St., St. Martin's. PE9 2LF. (P. B. Light). Open 10-5, Sat., Sun. 10.30-5. SIZE: 40 dealers. *STOCK: Period, Art Nouveau and Art Deco furniture, porcelain, ceramics, pictures, prints, clocks, watches, silver, jewellery, books, toys, military books, textiles, clothes, dolls, glass and all sorts of collectables.* TEL: 01780 481158. SER: Shipping arranged.

St. Mary's Galleries
5 St. Mary's Hill. PE9 2DP. (David E. Clark and Mrs O.M. and R.D. Cox). Est. 1955. Open 9-5. SIZE: Medium. *STOCK: Furniture, 18th-19th C, £50-£10,000; Victorian and Georgian jewellery, £5-£1,000; unusual items, textiles, oil paintings.* LOC: Nr. Stamford river bridge. PARK: At rear of shop. TEL: 01780 64159; mobile - 0860 340358.

Stamford Antiques Centre
The Exchange Hall, Broad St. PE1 9PX. Open 10-5, Sun. 11.30-5.30. SIZE: 35 dealers. *STOCK: General antiques (with dateline); collectables; specialising in Art Nouveau.* LOC: Town centre. PARK: Easy. TEL: 01780 62605.

Staniland (Booksellers)
4/5 St. George's St. PE9 2BJ. (M.G. Staniland and B.J. Valentine-Ketchum). Est. 1973. Open 10-5. SIZE: Large. *STOCK: Books, mainly 19th-20th C, 50p-£500.* LOC: High St. PARK: St. Leonard's St. TEL: 01780 55800.

Andrew Thomas
Old Granary, 10 North St. PE9 2YN. Est. 1970. Open 9-6. SIZE: Large. *STOCK: Pine and country furniture in original paint; ironware.* LOC: From south take old A1 through Stamford. Turn right at second set of traffic lights, warehouse on right. PARK: Opposite. TEL: 01780 62236; home - 01780 410627. VAT: Stan.

STAPLEFORD

Allens Antiques - Pine Furniture
Moor Farm. LN6 9LE. Open 9-5, Sat. 9-1. *STOCK: Pine.* LOC: Off A17 Sleaford Rd. TEL: 01522 788392.

STICKNEY

B and B Antiques
Main Rd. PE22 8AD. (B.J. Whittaker and J. Shooter). Open by appointment. *STOCK: General antiques.* PARK: Easy. TEL: 01205 480 204.

SUTTON BRIDGE

The Antique Shop
100 Bridge Rd. PE12 9SA. (G. and R. Gittins). Est. 1973. Open 9-5.30, Sun. 11-5. SIZE: Large - 10 showrooms + Trade warehouse. *STOCK: Victorian furniture, glass, china, oil lamps and clocks.* Not Stocked: Pine. LOC: On old A17. PARK: Easy. TEL: 01406 350535; home - same. VAT: Spec.

Bridge Antiques
30-32 Bridge Rd. PE12 9UA. Open 8-5. CL: Sat. SIZE: Large. *STOCK: Shipping furniture - barleytwist, linenfold, pineapple, Jacobean styles.* LOC: Old A17. PARK: Easy. TEL: 01406 350704/351669.

Old Barn Antiques Warehouse
220 New Rd. PE12 9QE. (S. and Mrs T.J. Jackson). Open 9-5.30, or by appointment. SIZE: Large. *STOCK: 19th and 20th C furniture - shipping oak, carved, pineapple, Jacobean, barley twist, etc; also mahogany, walnut and pine original and reclaimed timber copies.* LOC: 1 mile out of village turn by Barclays Bank. PARK: Own. TEL: 01406 350435; fax - same; mobile - 0468 744050. SER: Container facilities. *Trade & Export Only.*

SUTTON-ON-SEA

Knicks Knacks
41 High St. LN12 2EY. (Mr and Mrs R.A Nicholson). Est. 1983. Open 10-1 and 2-5, including Sun. CL: Mon. SIZE: Medium + small warehouse. *STOCK: Victorian gas lights, brass and iron beds, cast-iron fireplaces, bygones, curios, tools, collectables, pottery, porcelain, Art Deco, Art Nouveau, advertising items, furniture and shipping goods, £1-£1,000.* LOC: A52. PARK: Easy. TEL: 01507 441916; home - 01507 441657.

TATTERSHALL

Wayside Antiques
Market Place. LN4 4LQ. (G. Ball). Est. 1969.

Tattershall continued

Open 10-5.30. *STOCK: General antiques.* LOC A158. PARK: Easy. TEL: 01526 342436. VAT Stan/Spec.

WAINFLEET, Nr. Skegness

Haven Antiques
Bank House, 36 High St. PE24 4BJ. (Colin an Julie Crowson). Est. 1980. Open daily excep Thurs., Sun. by appointment. SIZE: Small *STOCK: General antiques, mainly jeweller porcelain and small furniture.* LOC: A52. PARK Easy and opposite. TEL: 01754 880661; home same. SER: Valuations; restorations (pottery) buys at auction.

WEST DEEPING

Quality Antiques
The Barn, 43a King St. PE6 9HP. (Barry an Lindy Vaughan). Est. 1993. Open seven days SIZE: Large. *STOCK: Furniture and smalls.* TEL 01778 342053.

WHAPLODE, Nr. Spalding

Francis Bowers Chess Suppliers
34 Middle Rd. PE12 6TW. Resident. Est. 199 Open 9-9, Fri. 9-6, Sat. and Sun. by appointmen SIZE: Small. *STOCK: Chess sets, boards, clock and tables, 18th-20th C, £20-£1,000; books o chess and others, 18th-20th C, £1-£1,000; garde chess sets, computers, 19th-20th C, £50-£1,50* LOC: From north - A1, A17, A151, 4th turning o left, near Texaco garage. From south - A1, A1 A1073, A151, 5th turning on right. PARK: Eas TEL: 01406 370166; fax - same; mobile - 08 408992. SER: Valuations; restorations (min repairs, book binding); buys at auction (che related items). FAIRS: Spalding, King's Lyn Peterborough, Skegness, Grantham Che Congress.

WOODHALL SPA

Underwoodhall Antiques
The Broadway. LN10 6ST. Open 10-5. CL: We SIZE: Medium. *STOCK: Furniture, £10-£1,00 porcelain and china, £5-£500; general antique £1-£500; pictures, £5-£500, all 1750 to dat* LOC: B1191. PARK: Easy. TEL: 01526 353815.

V.O.C. Antiques LAPAD
27 Witham Rd. LN10 6RW. (D.J. and C Leyland). Resident. Est. 1970. Open 9.30-5.3 Sun. 2-5. SIZE: Medium. *STOCK: 17th-19th furniture, to £5,000; period brass and coppe pottery, porcelain and pictures.* LOC: B119 PARK: Easy. TEL: 01526 352753; fax - sam home - same. SER: Valuations.

'lease note this is only a rough map lesigned to show dealers the number of hops in the various towns, and is not ecessarily totally accurate.

1-2	Key to number of shops in this area.
3-5	
6-12	
13+	

NORTH

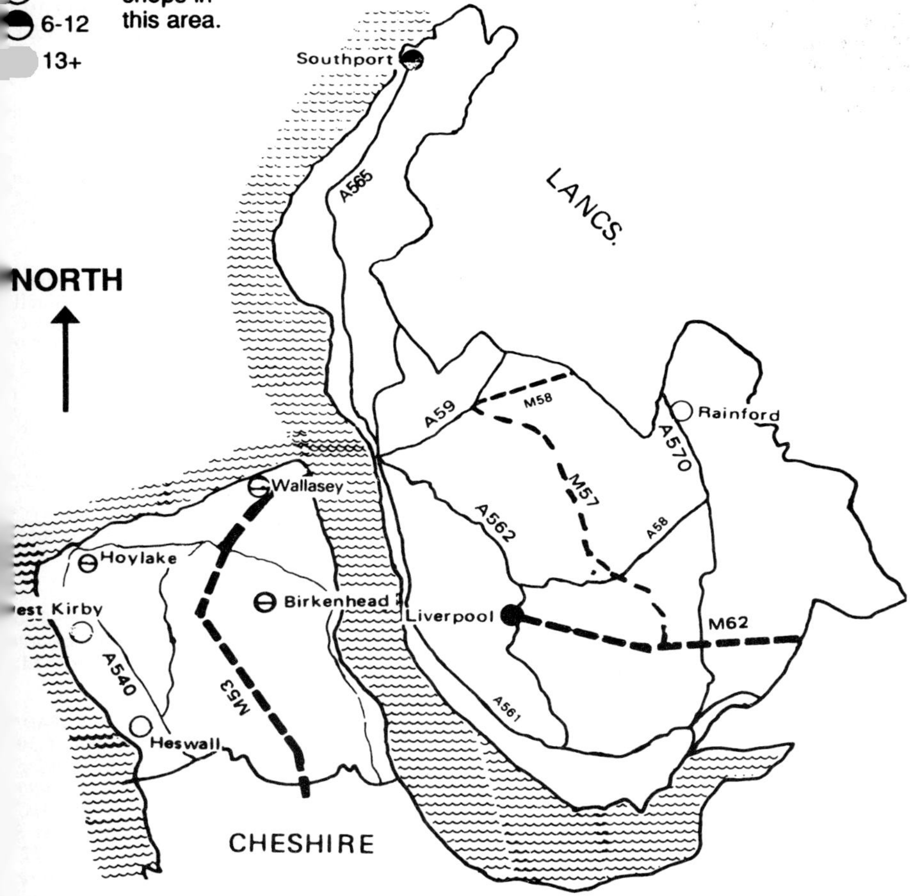

BIRKENHEAD

David Allan Antiques

281 Woodchurch Rd., Prenton. L42 9LE. Est. 1975. Open 10-6. SIZE: Medium. *STOCK: 19th C fireplaces, paintings, flintlock pistols.* LOC: Main road. PARK: Easy. TEL: 0151 608 7118; home - same. SER: Valuations; restorations (fireplaces).

Bodhouse Antiques

379 New Chester Rd., Rock Ferry. (G. and F.M. Antonini). Open 9-5, Sat. and Sun. by appointment. SIZE: Large. *STOCK: Furniture, 19th C; ceramics, from 19th C; silver plate, 18th-20th C; all £5-£1,000+; prints and pictures, 19th C, £25-£1,000+.* LOC: 1/2 mile from Birkenhead Tunnel, A41 towards Chester. PARK: Easy. TEL: 0151 644 9494; home - 0151 327 6233. SER: Packing; courier; regular containers to Italy and Spain. VAT: Stan/Spec.

Rose Mount

2 Rose Mount. (A.J. Bampton). Open 10-5. *STOCK: General antiques.* TEL: 0151 653 9060.

HESWALL

C. Rosenberg

The Antique Shop, 120-122 Telegraph Rd. L60 0AQ. Est. 1960. Open 10-5. CL: Wed. pm. *STOCK: Jewellery, silver, porcelain, objets d'art.* TEL: 0151 342 1053. VAT: Stan.

HOYLAKE

M. Fearn Antiques

124A Market St. L47 3BH. (Marion Fearn). Est. 1994. Open 10-5, Wed. 10-1, Sat. 10-2. SIZE: Small. *STOCK: Furniture, china, glass and silver, from £10.* PARK: At rear. TEL: 0151 632 0892.

Hoylake Antique Centre

128-130 Market St. L47 3BH. Open 9.15-5.30. CL: Wed. *STOCK: Furniture, pine, silver, pictures, porcelain, glass and decorative arts.* LOC: A540, in town centre. PARK: At rear. TEL: 0151 632 4231.

Market Antiques

80 Market St. L47 3BB. (W. Bateman). Est. 1969. Open Thurs. and Fri. 10-1 and 2.15-5, Sat. 10-5, other times by appointment. SIZE: Medium. *STOCK: Furniture, £10-£1,000; trade and shipping goods, silver, glass, china, £2-£250; paintings, prints, £5-£500.* Not Stocked: Weapons, medals, coins. LOC: On main street in town centre A563 or A540. PARK: From Ship Inn forecourt, cars drive in, vans at rear. TEL: 0151 632 4059 (24 hr).

Kevin Whay's Clock Shop and Antiques

The Quadrant. L47 2EE. Est. 1969. Open Thurs. and Fri. 10-4.30, Sat. 10-2 and by appointment. *STOCK: Clocks, barometers and jewellery.*

Hoylake continued

PARK: Easy. TEL: 0151 631 1888; fax - 0151 236 1070; e-mail - 100665.765@compuserve.con. SER: Restorations (clocks, barometers, dials and cases).

LIVERPOOL

Antique Fireplaces

43a Crosby Road North, Waterloo. (J. Toole). Est. 1978. Open 10-5, Sat. 10-5.30. SIZE: Medium. *STOCK: Fireplaces, 18th-19th C, £100-£1,000+; doors, 19th C, from £35.* PARK: Easy. TEL: 0151 949 0819. SER: Valuations; restorations. VAT: Stan.

Boodle and Dunthorne Ltd

Boodles House, Lord St. L2 9SQ. Est. 1798. Open 9-5.30. SIZE: Large. *STOCK: Silver, 18th-19th C, £100-£5,000; clocks and clock-sets, mid-19th C, £200-£4,000; jewellery, Victorian and Georgian, £100-£30,000.* Not Stocked: Furniture. PARK: Paradise St. TEL: 0151 227 2525. VAT: Stan/Spec.

Edward's Jewellers

45a Whitechapel. (R.A. Lewis). FGA. Est. 1967. Open by appointment. CL: Sat. SIZE: Small. *STOCK: Jewellery, silver and plate, 19th-20th C, £50-£600.* LOC: City centre. TEL: 0151 236 2909. SER: Valuations. VAT: Stan/Spec.

Kensington Tower Antiques Ltd

Christ Church, 170 Kensington. L7 2RJ. (R Swainbank). Est. 1960. Open 9-5, Sat. and Sun by appointment. CL: Mon. SIZE: Large. *STOCK: Shipping goods, general antiques.* LOC: A57 PARK: Easy. TEL: 0151 260 9466; fax - 0151 260 9130; home - 0151 924 6538. VAT: Stan *Trade Only.*

Liverpool Militaria

48 Manchester St. (Bill Tagg). Open 10.30-5.30. CL: Wed. *STOCK: Militaria especially Japanese swords.* LOC: Next to old tunnel entrance. TEL: 0151 236 4404.

Lyver & Boydell Galleries LAPADA

15 Castle St. L2 4SX. Est. 1861. Open 10.30-5.30. CL: Sat. SIZE: Medium. *STOCK: Paintings and watercolours, 18th-20th C, £50-£10,000; maps and prints, 16th-19th C, £1-£1,500.* LOC: City centre, opposite Town Hall. PARK: Pay & Display. TEL: 0151 236 3256; fax - 0151 227 3293. SER: Valuations; cleaning; framing; restorations; buys at auction. FAIRS: National. VAT: Stan/Spec.

Maggs Antiques Ltd

26-28 Fleet St. L1 4AR. (G. Webster). Est. 1965. Open daily. *STOCK: General antiques, period and shipping smalls, £1-£1,000.* LOC: In town centre by Central station. PARK: Meters. TEL: 0151 708 0221; evenings - 01928 564958. SER: Restorations; container packing, courier.

Liverpool continued

The Original British American Antiques
Halsall Hall, 2 Carrmoss Lane, Halsall. L39 8RS. (John Nolan). Est. 1970. Open by appointment including Sun. and evenings. SIZE: Large. *STOCK: Export items, especially for US decorator market.* LOC: On A5147. TEL: 01704 841065; mobile - 0802 604007. SER: Courier; packing and shipping. VAT: Stan/Spec. *Trade Only*

E. Pryor and Son
110 London Rd. L3 5NL. (Mr Wilding). Est. 1876. CL: Wed. *STOCK: General antiques, jewellery, Georgian and Victorian silver, pottery, porcelain, coins and medals, clocks, paintings, ivory and carvings.* TEL: 0151 709 1361. VAT: Stan.

Ryan-Wood Antiques
102 Seel St. L1 4BT. Est. 1972. Open 9.30-5. *STOCK: Furniture, paintings, china, silver, curios, bric-a-brac, Victoriana, Edwardiana, Art Deco.* TEL: 0151 709 7776; home/fax - 0151 709 3203. SER: Restorations; valuations. VAT: Stan/Spec.

Stefani Antiques
497 Smithdown Rd. L15 5AE. (T. Stefani). Est. 1969. Open 10-5. SIZE: Medium. *STOCK: Furniture, to 1910, £200-£2,000; jewellery, £25-£2,000; pottery, silver, old Sheffield plate, porcelain, bronzes.* LOC: On main road, near Penny Lane. PARK: Easy. TEL: 0151 734 1933; home - 0151 737 1360. SER: Valuations; restorations.

Swainbanks Ltd
Christchurch, 170 Kensington. L7 2RJ. Open 9-5 or by appointment. CL: Sat. SIZE: Large. *STOCK: Shipping goods and general antiques.* TEL: 0151 260 9466/924 6538; fax - 0151 260 9130. SER: Containers. VAT: Stan.

Theta Gallery
29-33 Parliament St. (J. Matson). Open by appointment. SIZE: Warehouse. *STOCK: General antiques, especially furniture and clocks.* TEL: 0151 709 1217. *Trade Only.*

RAINFORD, Nr. St. Helens

Colin Stock BADA
Mossborough Rd. WA11 8QN. Est. 1895. Open by appointment. *STOCK: Furniture, 18th-19th C.* TEL: 0174 488 2246.

SOUTHPORT

C.K. Broadhurst and Co Ltd
5-7 Market St. PR8 1HD. Est. 1926. Open 9-5.30. *STOCK: Rare books, first editions, art and architecture, collecting.* TEL: 01704 532064/534110; fax - 01704 542009.

Southport continued

Decor Galleries
52 Lord St. PR8 1QB. (F.D. Glover). CL: Tues. *STOCK: Decorative items, furniture, 18th-19th C.* TEL: 01704 535134. VAT: Stan/Spec.

King Street Antiques
27 King St. PR8 1LH. (John Nolan). Open 10-5. *STOCK: General antiques.* TEL: 01704 540808.

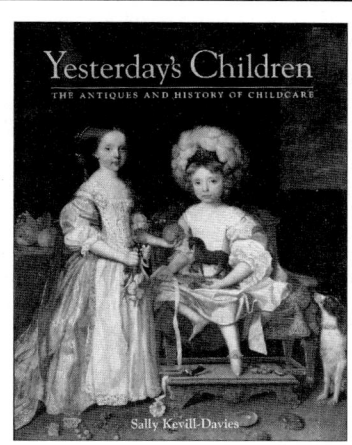

Southport continued

Molloy's Furnishers Ltd
6-8 St. James St. PR8 5AE. (P. Molloy). Est. 1955. Open daily. SIZE: Large. *STOCK: Mahogany and oak, shipping and Edwardian furniture.* LOC: On A570, Scarisbrick new road. PARK: Easy. TEL: 01704 535204; fax - 01704 548101. VAT: Stan.

John Nolan Antiques Ltd
29 King St. PR8 1LH. Open Mon.-Sat. *STOCK: Furniture and decorative items.* TEL: 01704 540808; mobile - 0802 604007; home - 01704 841065. SER: Courier; packing and shipping.

Osiris Antiques
104 Shakespeare St. (C. and P. Wood). Est. 1983. Open 10.45-4.45, Sat. 11-5.15, Sun. by appointment. CL: Tues. SIZE: Small. *STOCK: Art Nouveau and Art Deco, £10-£1,000; period clothing and accessories, 1850-1950, £5-£200; jewellery, 1880-1960, to £150.* LOC: Just out of town, off main road leading to motorway. PARK: Easy. TEL: 01704 500991; mobile - 0802 818500; home - 01704 560418. SER: Valuations; buys at auction (Art Nouveau, Art Deco); lectures given on Decorative Arts 1895-1930.

The Southport Antiques Centre
27/29 King St. PR8 1LH. (J. Nolan). Open 10-5. TEL: 01704 540808; mobile - 0802 604007. Below are listed the dealers at this centre.

British-American Antiques
Shipping goods.

Halsall Hall Antiques
Country furniture.

King St. Antiques
General antiques.

John Nolan
Period furniture.

Pine Antiques
Country pine furniture.

The Spinning Wheel
1 Liverpool Rd., Birkdale. PR8 4AR. (R. Bell). Est. 1966. Open 10-5. CL: Tues. SIZE: Small. *STOCK: General antiques, old golf items, £5-£1,000+.* TEL: 01704 568245; home - 01704 567613.

Tony and Anne Sutcliffe Antiques
130 Cemetery Rd. and warehouse - 37A Linaker St. Est. 1969. Open 8.30-5 including Sun. or by appointment. SIZE: Large. *STOCK: Shipping goods, Victorian and period furniture.* LOC: Town centre. TEL: 01704 537068; home - 01704 533465. SER: Containers; courier. VAT: Stan/Spec.

Southport continued

H.S. Walne
183 Lord St. PR8 1PF. Open 10-5. *STOCK: Diamonds, gold, silver, jewellery.* TEL: 01704 532469.

Weldons Jewellery and Antiques
567 Lord St. PR9 0BB. (H.W. and N.C. Weldon). Est. 1914. Open 9.30-5.30. SIZE: Medium. *STOCK: Furniture, clocks, watches, jewellery, silver, coins.* Not Stocked: Militaria. PARK: Easy. TEL: 01704 532191; fax - 01704 500091. SER: Valuations; restorations. VAT: Stan.

WALLASEY

Arbiter
10 Atherton St., New Brighton. L45 2NY. (W.D.L. Scobie and P.D. Ferrett). Resident. Est. 1983. Open Tues.-Sat. 1-5, or by appointment. *STOCK: Arts and Crafts movement and decorative arts, £20-£2,000; Oriental, ethnographic and antiquities, £40-£1,500; original prints and drawings, £80-£500.* LOC: Opposite New Brighton station. PARK: Easy. TEL: 0151 639 1159. SER: Valuations; buys at auction; consultant.

Decade Antiques
62 Grove Rd. L45 3HW. (A.M. Duffy). Open 10-5. SIZE: Large. *STOCK: General antiques, textiles, decorative items, Continental furniture.* LOC: J1 M53, take A554 to Wallasey/New Brighton, turn right along Harrison Drive into Grove Rd. TEL: 0151 638 0433; 0151 639 6905/8728.

Victoria Antiques/City Strippers
155-157 Brighton St. L44 8DU. (J.M. Colyer). Open 9.30-5.30. *STOCK: Pre-1930 furniture.* TEL: 0151 639 0080.

Yarnall Antiques
244A Wallasey Village. L45 0JT. (Richard and Joy Yarnall). Est. 1970. Open 10.30-1 and 2-5, Wed. by appointment, Sat. 11-5. SIZE: Large. *STOCK: Furniture, 18th-19th C, £100-£3,000; collectables, 18th-20th C, £5-£500; curios, £1-£1,000.* LOC: Main road, 5 minutes from end of M53. PARK: Easy. TEL: 0151 638 2286; home 0151 639 5204. SER: Valuations. FAIRS: Newark, Stafford, Ardingly, Bluith Wells, G-Mex. VAT: Stan/Spec.

WEST KIRBY

Helen Horswill Antiques and Decorative Arts
62 Grange Rd. L48 4EG. Open 10-5 or by appointment. SIZE: Medium. *STOCK: Furniture, 17th-19th C; decorative items.* LOC: A540. PARK: Easy. TEL: 0151 625 8660/625 2803.

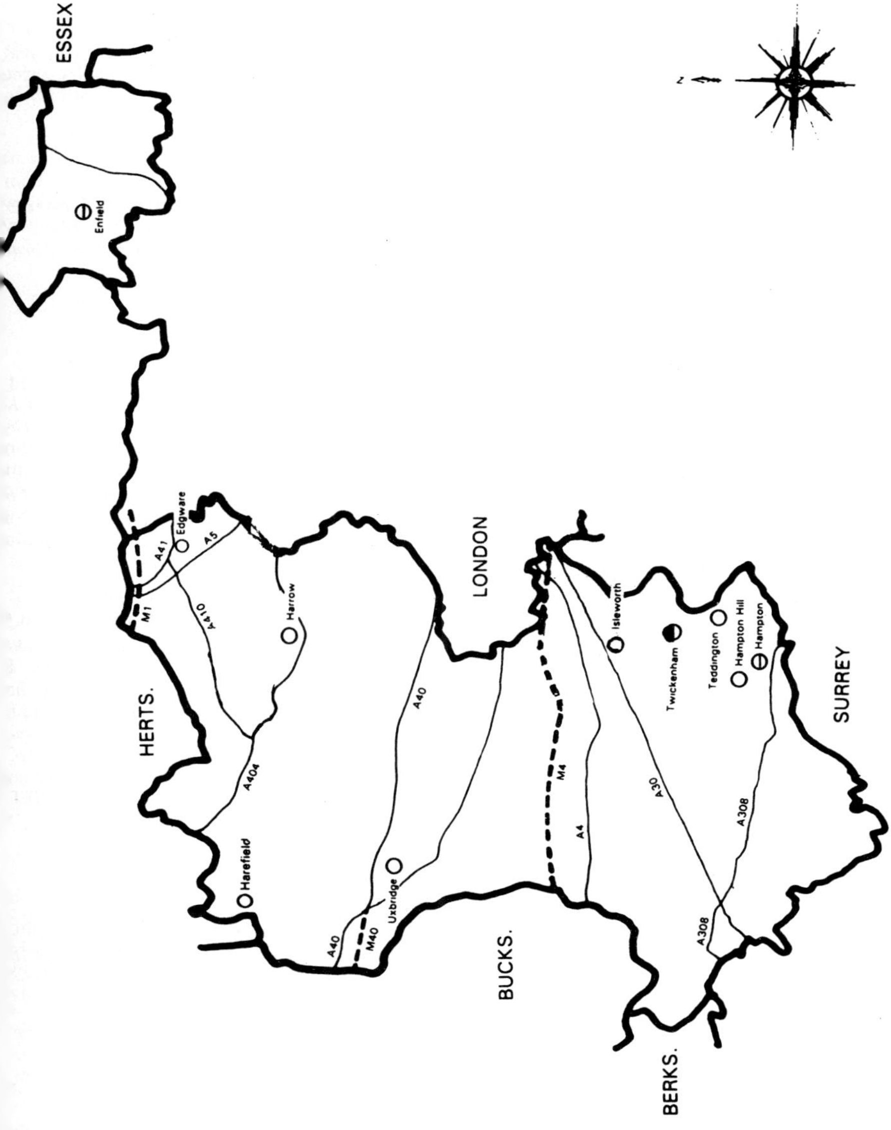

1–2
3–5
6–12
13+

Key to number of shops in this area.

Please note this is only a rough map designed to show dealers the number of shops in the various towns, and is not necessarily totally accurate.

EDGWARE

Edgware Antiques

19 Whitchurch Lane. HA8 7JZ. (E. Schloss). Est. 1972. Open Thurs.- Sat. 10-5 or by appointment. SIZE: Medium. *STOCK: Furniture, pictures, silver and plate, brass and copper, clocks, bric-a-brac, porcelain and shipping goods.* PARK: Easy. TEL: 0181 952 1606; home - 0181 952 5924.

ENFIELD

Richard Kimbell

Country World, Cattlegate Rd., Crews Hill. Est. 1966. Open 9-6 including Sun. SIZE: Large. *STOCK: Pine, 19th C, £50-£1,000.* LOC: Off junction 24, M25 via A1005 to Enfield, then left into East Lodge Lane. PARK: Easy. TEL: 0181 364 6661. VAT: Stan.

La Trouvaille

1A Windmill Hill. EN2 6SE. (Mrs C.M. Waring). Est. 1982. Open 9.30-5.30. CL: Wed. SIZE: Medium. *STOCK: Small general antiques, collectors' items, furniture and prints, 1800-1930.* Not Stocked: Weapons. LOC: West of town. PARK: Easy. TEL: 0181 367 1080.

Cynthia Morgan Interiors

Unit 41, 26-28 The Queensway, Ponders End. EN3 4SA. Open by appointment. SIZE: Medium. *STOCK: 18th-19th C furniture.* LOC: Off Hertford road, off A10. PARK: At rear. TEL: 0181 805 0353; fax - 0181 372 9946.

HAMPTON

Peco

72 Station Rd. TW12 2BT. (C.D. and E.S. Taylor). Est. 1969. Open 9-5.15. SIZE: Large. *STOCK: Doors, 18th-20th C, £75-£250; fireplaces including French and marble, 18th-19th C, £350-£3,500; stoves; French beds.* LOC: 1.5 miles from Hampton Court. Turning off Hampton Court/Sunbury Rd. PARK: Own. TEL: 0181 979 8310. SER: Restorations (stained glass, cast iron fireplaces, doors); stained glass made to order. VAT: Stan.

Ian Sheridan's Bookshop Hampton

Thames Villa, 34 Thames St. TW12 2DX. Est. 1960. Open 10.30-6 (7 in summer) including Sun. SIZE: Large. *STOCK: Antiquarian and second-hand books.* LOC: 1 mile from Hampton Court Palace. TEL: 0181 979 1704.

Valtone Pine

78-80 Station Rd. TW12 2RX. (A.P. Frost). Open 9-6. *STOCK: Pine and darkwoods.* TEL: 0181 979 4060.

HAMPTON HILL

The Hampton Hill Gallery

203 and 205 High St. TW12 1NP. *STOCK:*

Hampton Hill continued

Watercolours, drawings, prints, 18th-20th C TEL: 0181 977 1379; fax - 0181 977 3876. SER Restorations and cleaning (watercolours, prints and paintings); mounting; framing. VAT: Stan Spec.

HAREFIELD

The Jay's Middlesex Antique Centre

25/29 High St. Open 10-6, Sun. 11-5. SIZE: 1 dealers. *STOCK: General antiques, bric-a-brac gold and silver.* TEL: 01895 824738.

HARROW

Kathleen Mann - The Other Shop

49 High St. HA1 3HT. Est. 1973. Open Wed. Thurs. and Fri. 9.30-5. SIZE: Medium. *STOCK Furniture, 19th-20th C, £25-£3,000; decorativ items, £5-£1,000.* LOC: Follow Harrow road, o take A40 turning at Greenford roundabout PARK: Easy. TEL: 0181 422 1892. SER: Buys a auction; cat museum.

ISLEWORTH

Crowther of Syon Lodge Ltd

Busch Corner, London Rd. TW7 5BH. Open 9-5 Sat. and Sun. 11-4.30. SIZE: Large. *STOCK: Perio panelled rooms, in pine and oak; chimney-pieces i marble, stone and wood; life-sized classical bronz and marble statues; wrought iron entrance gate garden temples, vases, wellheads, tanks, anima figures, seats, fountains and other statues.* LOC Just off the A4, half-way between the West End an London Airport. TEL: 0181 560 7978. SER Bespoke summerhouses. VAT: Stan/Spec.

TEDDINGTON

Parade Antiques

107 High St. TW11 8HG. (D. Rogers). Est. 199 Open Wed.-Sat. 11-5.30. SIZE: Small. *STOCK Ceramics, lighting, glass and furniture, 190 1940, £5-£500.* PARK: Nearby. TEL: 0181 97 3295; home - 01628 25763.

TWICKENHAM

Ailsa Gallery

32 Crown Rd. (C.A. Wiltshire). Open Thurs., Fr and Sat. 10-5, other times by appointment. SIZE Small. *STOCK: Paintings, 19th-20th C, £20 £3,000; bronze, decorative arts, small furnitur silver and glass.* LOC: Off St. Margarets Rd., ne station. PARK: Easy. TEL: 0181 891 2345; hom - 0181 892 0188.

Alberts Cigarette Card Specialists

113 London Rd. TW1 1EE. (J.A. Wooster). Op 10-6, Sat. 10-4. CL: Mon. *STOCK: Origin cigarette cards; accessories.* TEL: 0181 8

wickenham continued

067; fax - 0181 744 3133. SER: Mail order; ıipping; framing; catalogue; Guide to Cigarette ard Collecting; postal auctions - worldwide ervice.

;olden Oldies

13 London Rd. TW1 1EE. (Janet S. Wooster). pen 10-6, Sat. 10-4. CL: Mon. *STOCK: Film emorabilia - stills, photos, posters, postcards, ints, statues, models, film magazines, books.* EL: 0181 891 3067; fax - 0181 744 3133. SER: egular catalogues/stock lists available; worldwide ailing.

thony C. Hall

) Staines Rd. TW2 5AH. Est. 1966. Open 9-30. CL: Wed. pm. and Sat. SIZE: Medium. *TOCK: Antiquarian books.* PARK: Easy. TEL: 181 898 2638; fax - same.

ohn Ives Bookseller

Normanhurst Drive, St. Margarets. TW1 1NA. esident. Est. 1977. Open by appointment at any ne. SIZE: Medium. *STOCK: Scarce and out of int books on antiques and collecting, £1-£500.* OC: Off St. Margarets Rd. near its junction with hertsey Rd. PARK: Easy. TEL: 0181 892 6265; x - 0181 744 3944. SER: Valuations (as stock).

obias Jellinek Antiques BADA

) Broadway Avenue, St Margarets. TW1 IR. (Mrs D.L. and T.P. Jellinek). Est. 1963. y appointment only. SIZE: Small. *STOCK: ine early furniture and objects, 16th-17th C or ırlier, £500-£1,000+.* LOC: Near Richmond ridge. PARK: Easy. TEL: 0181 892 6892; ome - same; fax - 0181 744 9298. SER: aluations; restorations; buys at auction (as ock). VAT: Stan/Spec.

larble Hill Gallery

)/72 Richmond Rd. TW1 3BE. (D. and L. ewson). Est. 1974. Open 10-5.30. *STOCK: ictorian watercolours and fireside furniture, rench marble, pine and white Adam style antels.* PARK: Easy. TEL: 0181 892 1488. AT: Stan/Spec.

avid Morley Antiques

'1 Richmond Rd. TW1 2EF. Est. 1968. Open)-5. CL: Wed. SIZE: Medium. *STOCK: General ıtiques, collectors' items, old toys.* Not Stocked: ırge furniture. LOC: Approx. 200yds. from chmond Bridge. PARK: In side road (adjacent shop). TEL: 0181 892 2986.

helps Antiques LAPADA

3-135 St. Margarets Rd. TW1 1RG. (R.C. ıelps). Est. 1870. Open 9-5.30, Sat. 9.30-5.30, ın. 12-4. SIZE: Large - several dealers. *TOCK: Furniture, 1800-1920's.* LOC: ljacent St. Margaret's station. PARK: Easy, rear of shop. TEL: 0181 892 1778/7129; fax - 81 892 3661. SER: Restorations. VAT: an/Spec.

Twickenham continued

Rita Shenton

142 Percy Rd. TW2 6JG. Est. 1973. Open by appointment only. SIZE: Medium. *STOCK: Clocks, watches, barometers, sundials, scientific instruments, automata and ornamental turning books, £1-£1,000.* LOC: Continuation of Whitton High St. PARK: Easy. TEL: 0181 894 6888; fax - 0181 893 8766. SER: Valuations; buys at auction (horological books, clocks); catalogues available. *International postal service.*

Neil Willcox

113 Strawberry Vale. TW1 4SJ. Open by appointment. *STOCK: Wine, apothecary, medical and other bottles, British and Continental, 17th to mid 19th C.* TEL: 0181 892 5858 (24 hrs). SER: Valuations; mail order, photos supplied; prop hire.

UXBRIDGE

Antiques Warehouse (Uxbridge)

34-36 Rockingham Rd. UB8 2TZ. Est. 1966. Open 10-6. SIZE: Large. *STOCK: General antiques, shipping items, £1-£4,000.* PARK: Easy. TEL: 01895 256963/271012. VAT: Stan.

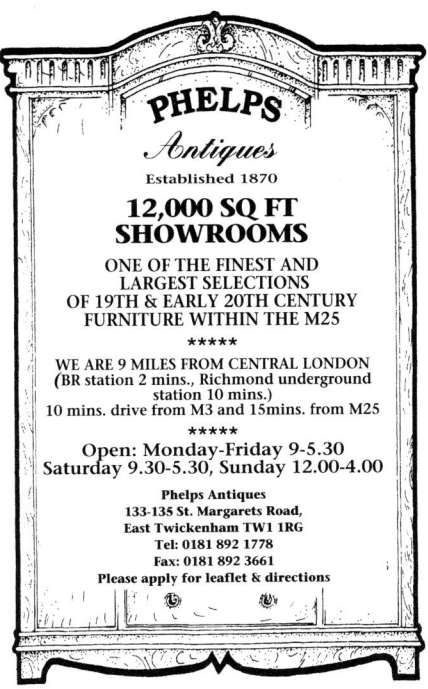

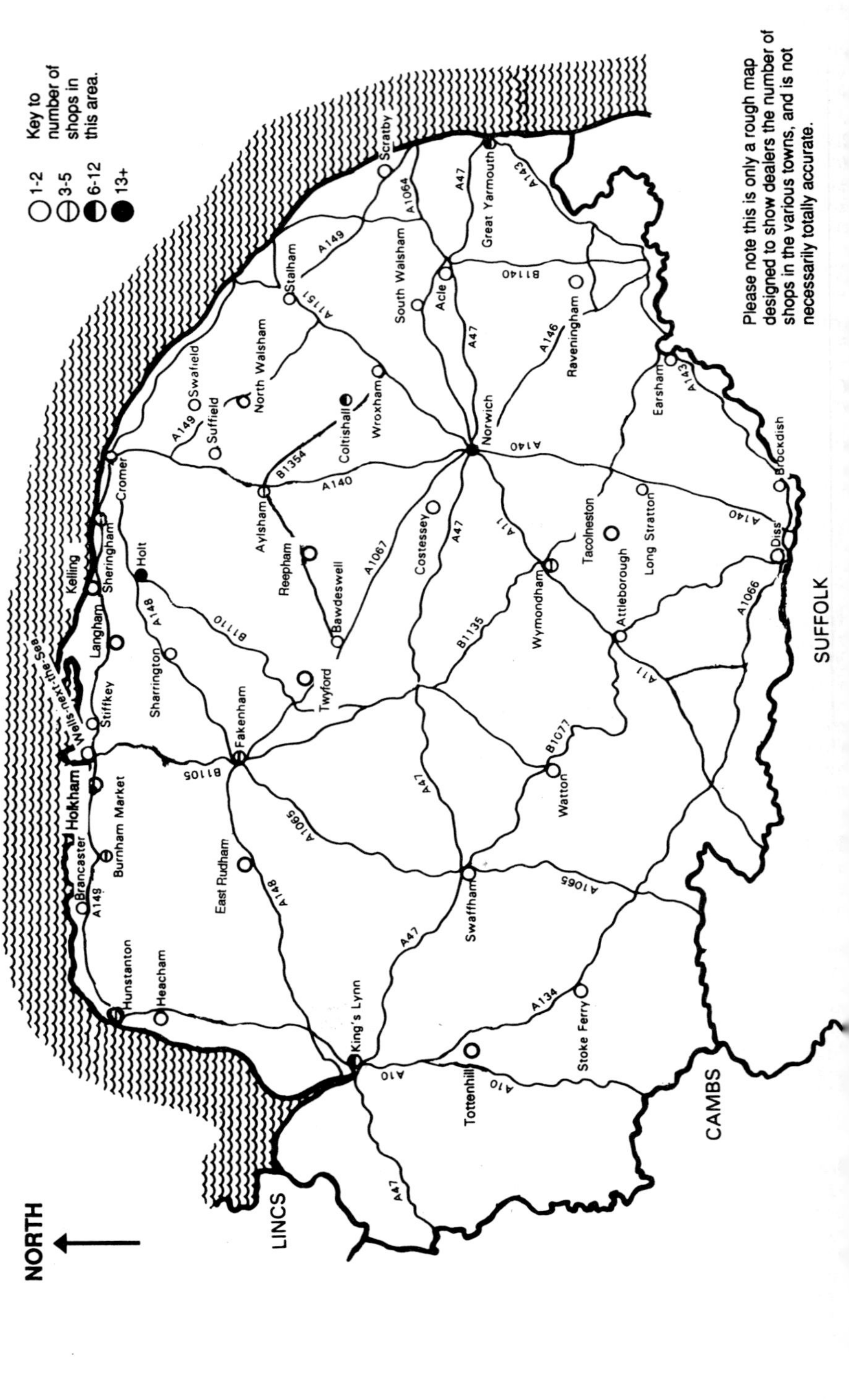

Please note this is only a rough map designed to show dealers the number of shops in the various towns, and is not necessarily totally accurate.

CLE, Nr. Norwich

vy House Antiques
y House, The Street. NR13 3BH. (N. Pratt). Est. 70. Open 9-5. SIZE: Small. *STOCK: Furniture, rcelain, pottery, glass, metalware, 18th-20th C, 25-£2,000; pictures, 19th C; garden furniture, th-20th C, both £50-£500.* LOC: Village centre. ARK: Easy. TEL: 01493 750682; home - same. ER: Valuations. FAIRS: Norwich. VAT: Stan/ pec.

TTLEBOROUGH

.E. Bush and Partners
ineyards Antiques Gallery, Leys Lane. NR17 NE. (A.G., M.S. and J.A. Becker). Est. 1940. pen 9-1 and 2-5.30. SIZE: Large. *STOCK: alnut and mahogany, 18th-19th C.* LOC: Town tskirts. PARK: Easy. TEL: 01953 454239/ 2175. SER: Restorations; wholesale antiques d export; storage; buys at auction. VAT: an/Spec.

YLSHAM

s Time Goes By - Antique and xterior Clocks
ofields Loke, Off Red Lion St. NR11 6ES. (S. illips). MBHI. Est. 1981. Open 9.30-5, Sat. 30-1. CL: Wed. SIZE: Small. *STOCK: Clocks, 50-£8,000.* LOC: Off A140 between Cromer d Norwich. PARK: Easy. TEL: 01263 731069; me - 01603 278080; fax - same; mobile - 0836 3869. SER: Valuations; restorations (clocks). AT: Stan/Spec.

heila Hart and John Giles LAPADA
R11 7QQ. Open by appointment. *STOCK: urniture, 18th-19th C, £200-£5,000; objects, 0-£1,000.* PARK: Easy. TEL: 01263 768216; x - same. SER: Courier. *Trade Only.*

earse Lukies
e Old Vicarage. Open preferably by appoint- ent. *STOCK: Period oak, sculpture, objects, th C furniture.* TEL: 01263 734137. *Trade nly.*

AWDESWELL, Nr. East Dereham

orfolk Polyphon Centre
ood Farm. NR20 4RX. (N.B. Vince). Open ekends, week days preferably by appointment. *OCK: Mechanical music - polyphons, cylinder usical boxes, organs, orchestrions, automata.* OC: On B1145, 1 mile east of Bawdeswell llage and junction with A1067. TEL: 01362 8230. VAT: Stan/Spec.

BRANCASTER STAITHE, Nr. King's Lynn

Brancaster Staithe Antiques
Coast Rd. PE31 8BJ. (M.J. Wilson). Open every day including Sun. *STOCK: Victorian tables, chairs; oak, unusual pine, bookpresses, Art Deco.* TEL: 01485 210600.

BROCKDISH, Nr. Diss

Brockdish Antiques
Commerce House. IP21 4JL. (M. and L.E. Palfrey). Est. 1975. Open 9-5.30. CL: Wed. *STOCK: Mainly 19th C furniture and upholstery.* LOC: A143. TEL: 01379 668498. SER: Restorations; re-upholstery.

BURNHAM MARKET

M. and A. Cringle
The Old Black Horse. PE31 8HD. Est. 1965. Open 10-1 and 2-5. CL: Wed. SIZE: Medium. *STOCK: 18th to early 19th C furniture, £50-£2,000; china, glass, pottery, prints, maps, £10-£500.* Not Stocked: Large furniture. LOC: In village centre. PARK: Easy. TEL: 01328 738456. VAT: Spec.

Anne Hamilton Antiques
North St. PE31 8HG. (A. Hudson). Open 10-1 and 2-5. SIZE: Medium. *STOCK: Georgian furniture; porcelain, decorative items.* LOC: 20yds. from village green towards coast. PARK: Easy. TEL: 01328 738187. VAT: Stan/Spec.

Market House BADA
PE31 8HF. (D.H. and J. Maufe). Resident. Est. 1978. Open 10-6 or by appointment. SIZE: Medium. *STOCK: English furniture - walnut, mahogany, rosewood and some oak, late 17th to mid-19th C, £25-£20,000; works of art, mirrors, small decorative items, some porcelain.* Not Stocked: Silver, jewellery. LOC: B1355, large Queen Anne house on green in village centre. PARK: Easy. TEL: 01328 738475. SER: Valuations; buys at auction. VAT: Spec.

COLTISHALL

Liz Allport-Lomax
NR12 7EF. Open by appointment only. *STOCK: Objets de vertu, collectors' items, porcelain, pottery and silver, 18th-19th C; glass, watercolours and oils, all £5-£1,000; copper, brass and furniture, 19th C, £5-£2,000.* TEL: 01603 737631. FAIRS: Langley Park Spring, East Anglian Antique Dealers, Norwich Fine Art & Antiques (organiser).

Coltishall continued

Eric Bates and Sons
30 High St. NR12 7AA. Est. 1973. Open 9-5. SIZE: Large. *STOCK: General antiques, Georgian, Victorian, Edwardian and shipping furniture.* TEL: 01603 738716; fax - 01603 738966. SER: Restorations (furniture); upholstery; container packing. VAT: Stan/Spec.

Roger Bradbury Antiques
Church St. NR12 7DJ. Est. 1967. Open by appointment. *STOCK: Period furniture, Nanking cargo, Diana cargo, objets d'art.* PARK: Easy. TEL: 01603 737444. VAT: Stan.

Coltishall Antiques Centre
High St. NR3 7AA. (I. Ford). Est. 1980. Open 10-5. SIZE: Several specialists. *STOCK: A wide variety of items including porcelain and pottery, silver, jewellery, collectors' items, militaria, glass, Oriental porcelain, plated cutlery, clocks.* LOC: B1150 on corner of main street. PARK: Easy. TEL: 01603 738306. SER: Valuations; restorations (pottery and porcelain, furniture, objets de vertu).

Gwendoline Golder
Point House, 5 High St. NR12 7AA. Est. 1974. Open 11-5. CL: Sun. except by appointment. *STOCK: General antiques and collectors' items.* PARK: Easy. TEL: 01603 738099.

Isabel Neal Cabinet Antiques
Bank House, 20 High St. NR12 7DH. Est. 1968. Open 10-5. SIZE: Small. *STOCK: Porcelain, pottery, including Delft, 17th-20th C; small furniture, pictures, collectors' items.* LOC: B1150 towards North Walsham, shop - blue door on right. PARK: Easy. TEL: 01603 737379.

Village Clocks
High St. Open Tues.-Sat. *STOCK: Clocks - 18th-19th C longcase and bracket, 19th C regulators, wood and marble mantel clocks.* LOC: Main North Walsham road. PARK: Easy. TEL: 01603 736047. SER: Valuations; restorations (cases and movements).

COSTESSEY, Nr. Norwich

The Coach House
Townhouse Rd., Old Costessey. NR8 5BX. (J. Hines). Resident. Open by appointment. *STOCK: Modern British paintings; drawings, Victorian watercolours and post-war artists; original prints, etchings, engravings; Baxter and Le Blond.* TEL: 01603 742977. SER: Cleaning prints and water-colours; framing.

CROMER

Bond Street Antiques (inc. Jas. J. Briggs Est. 1820)
6 Bond St. and 38 Church St. NR27 9DA. (M.R.T. and J.A. Jones). NAG, FGA. Est. 1958. Open 9-1 and 2.15-5.30, Sat. 9-6, Sun. by appoint-

Cromer continued

ment. SIZE: Medium. *STOCK: Jewellery, silv porcelain, china, glass, small furniture, 18th-2 C, £50-£5,000.* LOC: From Church St. bear ri to Post Office, shop on opposite side on str further along. PARK: Easy. TEL: 01263 5131 home - same. SER: Valuations; restoratio (watches and jewellery); gem testing and analy VAT: Stan.

A.E. Seago
15 Church St. NR27 9ES. (D.C. Seago). E 1937. Open 9-1 and 2-5.15. CL: Sun. and W October to April. SIZE: Small. *STOCK: Fu niture, 1790-1910, £25-£2,500.* Not Stock Silver, garden furniture, oil paintings. LOC: Fr Sheringham take main coast road, then New into High St. PARK: Easy. 50 yds away arou church. TEL: 01263 512733. SER: Valuations.

DISS

Diss Antiques **LAPA**
2 & 3 Market Place. Open 9-1 and 2-5, or appointment. SIZE: Large. *STOCK: Furnitu barometers, clocks, porcelain, copper, bra* PARK: Nearby. TEL: 01379 642213; hom 01379 651369. SER: Restorations; restorati materials; export facilities. VAT: Stan/Spec.

EARSHAM, Nr. Bungay

Earsham Hall Pine
Earsham Hall. NR35 2AN. (R. Derham). E 1966. Open 8-5, Sat. and Sun. 10-4. SIZE: Lar *STOCK: Pine furniture.* LOC: On Earsham Hedenham Rd. PARK: Easy. TEL: 019 893423; fax - 01986 895656. SER: Containers.

EAST RUDHAM

Anne Hamilton Antiques
Mulberry Tree House, The Green. PE31 8RD. (Hudson). Open by appointment. SIZE: Mediu *STOCK: Georgian furniture; longcase cloc porcelain, decorative items.* LOC: On A1 PARK: Easy, on village green. TEL: 014 528387. VAT: Stan/Spec.

FAKENHAM

Fakenham Antique Centre
Old Congregational Chapel, 14 Norwich F NR21 8AZ. (Mrs Quainton Allen). Est. 19 Open 10-4.30, until 5 in summer (Eas onwards), Thurs. 9-4.30. SIZE: 15 dealers. LC Turn off A148 at roundabout to town, turn righ traffic lights, to town centre, turn left, cen 50yds. on right. PARK: Easy. TEL: 013 862941; home - 01328 738131. SER: Restoratio (furniture and china); polishing; replacem handles.

kenham continued

larket Place Antiques
Upper Market Place. (Jean and Donna nnent). Open 10-4.30, Wed. 10-1. *STOCK: ctorian jewellery, silver, collectors' items and neral antiques.* TEL: 01328 862962.

e Rivett Antiques and Bygones
Norwich Rd. (Mrs S. Rivett). Est. 1969. Open -1. *STOCK: General antiques and bygones.*)C: On Norwich Rd. into Fakenham. TEL: 328 862924; home - 01263 860462.

T. YARMOUTH

rry's Antiques
King St. NR30 2PN. Open 9-5.30. SIZE: rge. *STOCK: Jewellery, porcelain, clocks, iss, pictures.* LOC: In main shopping street. RK: Opposite. TEL: 01493 842713. VAT: n/Spec.

vid Ferrow
Howard St. South. NR30 1LN. ABA, PBFA. . 1940. Open 9.30-5.30. CL: Thurs. SIZE: rge. *STOCK: Books, some antiquarian maps, al prints, manuscripts.* LOC: From London, n before river bridge to The Docks, keep to rside, turn left and then right to car park. RK: Easy. TEL: 01493 843800; home - 01493 2247. SER: Valuations; restorations (books and nts). VAT: Stan.

e Ferrow Family Antiques LAPADA
nd 7 Hall Quay and 1 George St. NR30 X. Est. 1957. Open 9-5. CL: Thurs. pm. *OCK: General antiques, £50-£5,000.* Not cked: Guns, medals, coins, jewellery. LOC: ar Haven Bridge, off A12. TEL: 01493 5391; home - 01493 663605. SER: Valu- ons; restorations; buys at auction; hire. T: Stan/Spec.

lkes Antiques and Jewellers
Victoria Arcade. NR30 2NU. (Mrs J. Baldry). . 1946. Open 10-4. *STOCK: General antiques ecially jewellery and collectables.* LOC: From 7 into town centre, shop on right. PARK: Easy. L: 01493 851354. SER: Valuations. FAIRS: al collectors.

ld and Silver Exchange
atre Plain. NR30 2BE. (C. Birch). Open 9.30- 5. *STOCK: Coins, medals and secondhand ellery.* TEL: 01493 859430.

e Haven Gallery LAPADA
Hall Quay. NR30 1HX. (M. and J. Ferrow). en 9-5. CL: Thurs. pm. *STOCK: Water- urs, drawings, prints, oil paintings, 19th C, -£6,000.* LOC: Near Haven Bridge, off A12. L: 01493 855391; home - 01493 663605. R: Valuations; restorations (framing, ections). VAT: Stan/Spec.

Gt. Yarmouth continued

Peter Howkins
39, 40, 41 and 135 King St. NR30 2PQ. Est. 1946. Open 9-5. SIZE: Large. *STOCK: At 135 King St. - jewellery, Victorian to present day, £5-£5,000; silver, George III to present day, £1-£2,000; at 39 and 40 King St. - furniture, upholstery, Georgian to Victorian, £5-£5,000; at 41 King St. - investment antiques.* LOC: From Norwich through town one-way system to road signposted Lowestoft which intersects King St. PARK: Easy. TEL: 01493 844639. SER: Valuations; restorations (jewellery, silver, gold, furniture).

Wheatleys
16 Northgate St., White Horse Plain and Fullers Hill. NR30 1BA. Est. 1971. Open 9.30-5, Thurs. 9.30-1. SIZE: Large. *STOCK: Jewellery and general antiques.* LOC: 2 minutes walk from Market Place. PARK: Easy. TEL: 01493 857219. VAT: Stan.

HEACHAM, Nr. King's Lynn

Peter Robinson
Pear Tree House, 7 Lynn Rd. PE31 7HU. Est. 1880. Open 9-5. Appointment advisable Mon. and Sat. SIZE: Medium. *STOCK: Furniture, 1600-1900, £10-£5,000; china, 1750-1900, metalwork, 1700-1870; both £2-£1,000.* LOC: Shop on left on entry to village. PARK: Easy. TEL: 01485 570228. SER: Valuations; buys at auction. VAT: Stan/Spec.

HOLKHAM, Nr. Wells-next-the-Sea

The Potting Shed
Main Rd. (Bill Jellings). Est. 1993. Open Sat. afternoons, Trade mid-week by appointment. SIZE: Medium. *STOCK: Antique flowerpots.* LOC: On north Norfolk coast road (A149) by entrance to Holkam Hall. PARK: Easy. TEL: 01692 402424; home - same.

HOLT

Baron Art
9 Chapel Yard, Albert St. NR25 6HG. (Anthony R. Baron and Michael J. Bellis). Est. 1992. Open 9.30-5.30, Sun. by appointment. SIZE: Medium. *STOCK: Paintings, 19th-20th C, £50-£5,000; prints and lithographs, 19th-20th C, £5-£500; collectables, 1830-1940, £5-£500.* PARK: Easy. TEL: 01263 713906; home - 01263 588435. SER: Valuations; buys at auction (paintings). VAT: Stan/Spec.

Collectors Cabin
7 Cromer Rd. NR25 6HA. (J.M.E. Codling). Est. 1983. Open 10-1 and 2-4.30. CL: Thurs. pm. SIZE: Small. *STOCK: Bric-a-brac, bygones, toys, 19th C, £5-£25.* LOC: Near Post Office. PARK: Bull St. TEL: 01263 712241.

Holt continued

Simon Gough Books
5 Fish Hill. NR25 6BD. Est. 1976. Open 9.30-5. *STOCK: Antiquarian and secondhand books; bindings.* TEL: 01263 712650.

Heathfield Antiques
15 Chapel Yard, Albert St. NR25 6HQ. (J.E., H.B. and S.M. Heathfield). Est. 1990. Open 11-5. CL: Thurs. SIZE: Medium. *STOCK: Stripped pine, 19th-20th C, £20-£800; bric-a-brac, £1-£100.* PARK: Easy. TEL: 01263 711122; home - 01263 711531. VAT: Stan/Global.

Heathfield Country Pine
The Warehouse, 39 Hempstead Rd. (J.E., H.B. and S.M. Heathfield). Est. 1994. Open 9-5. SIZE: Large. *STOCK: Pine furniture, £50-£1,000.* LOC: Follow signs to Hempstead. PARK: Own. TEL: 01263 711609; home - 01263 711531. VAT: Stan/Global.

Maura Henry Antiques and Interiors
17 Chapel Yard, Albert St. NR25 6HG. (Mrs M.E. Henry). Est. 1974. CL: Thurs. SIZE: Medium. *STOCK: Furniture, 18th-19th C; mirrors, objects, £10-£3,000.* PARK: Easy. TEL: 01263 711240; home - 01362 668796. SER: Valuations.

Judy Hines - Prints and Paintings
3 Fish Hill. NR25 6BD. *STOCK: 20th C prints and paintings.* TEL: 01263 713000; fax - same. SER: Framing.

Holt Antique Centre
Albert Hall, Albert St. (David Attfield). Est. 1980. Open 10-5, Sat. 10-5.30 (Sun. Easter-October) SIZE: Large. *STOCK: Pine and country furniture, china, glass, lighting, silver plate and kitchenalia, jewellery, clothes, soft furnishings, 18th-20th C, £1-£1,500.* LOC: Turn right from Chapel Yard car park, 100 yards. PARK: Easy. TEL: 01263 712097; home - 01263 860347.

In the Picture (The Golf Collection)
16 Chapel Yard. NR25 6HG. (T.R. Groves). Open 10-4. SIZE: Medium. *STOCK: Decorative prints, limited editions, maps, sporting (especially golf), £5-£500.* PARK: Easy. TEL: 01263 713720/822265/824728; fax - 01263 822097. SER: Framing. VAT: Stan.

Past Caring
6 Chapel Yard. NR25 6HG. (L. Mossman). Est. 1988. Open 11-5. CL: Thurs. SIZE: Medium. *STOCK: Period clothes, linen and textiles, Victorian to 1950, £5-£100; jewellery and accessories, Victorian to 1960, £2-£75.* PARK: Easy. TEL: 01263 713771; home - 01362 683363. SER: Valuations; restorations (christening gowns and some beadwork). FAIRS: Alexandra Palace, Stand W60.

Holt continued

Pretty Things
10/11 Chapel Yard, Albert St. (Mr J.A. Tucke Est. 1982. Open 10.30-5, Sun. by appointme SIZE: Medium. *STOCK: Collectables, furnitu bric-a-brac and books, to £1,000.* PARK: Ea TEL: 01263 711012.

Richard Scott Antiques
30 High St. NR25 6BH. Est. 1967. Open 11 Tues. late night. CL: Thurs. SIZE: Large. *STOC Pottery, porcelain, period furniture, oil lamps a spares, general antiques.* LOC: On A148. PAR Easy. TEL: 01263 712479. SER: Valuations; co servation advice. VAT: Stan.

HUNSTANTON

Delawood Antiques
10 Westgate. PE36 5AL. (R.C. Woodhous Resident. Est. 1975. Open 10-5 Wed., Fri., S and most Sun., other times by chance or appoi ment. SIZE: Small. *STOCK: General antiqu furniture, jewellery, collectors' items, books, £1,000.* LOC: Near town centre and bus stati PARK: Easy. TEL: 01485 532903; home - san SER: Valuations: restorations (porcelain a china); items sold on commission.

Le Strange Old Barns Antiques, Ar & Craft Centre
Golf Course Rd., Old Hunstanton. PE36 6J (R.M. Weller). TEL: 01485 533402.

R.C. Woodhouse (Antiquarian Horologist)
10 Westgate. PE36 5AL. MBHI and BWC Resident. Est. 1975. Open Wed., Fri, Sat., usua Sun. Other days or eves. by chance or appoi ment. SIZE: Small. *STOCK: Georgian, Victor and Edwardian longcase, dial, wall and ma clocks; some watches and barometers.* LOC: N town centre and bus station. PARK: Easy. T 01485 532903; home - same. SER: Valuatio restorations (longcase, bracket, chiming, carria French, wall clocks, dials, barometers); sm locks repaired and lost keys made - postal serv if required.

KELLING, Nr. Holt

Baron Art
The Old Reading Room. NR25 7EL. (Anthony Baron and Michael J. Bellis). Est. 1994. Open 5.30 including Sun. Easter to Oct. SIZE: La *STOCK: Paintings and prints, 19th-20th C, £5,000; modern, first editions, poetry, art children's books, £1-£500; furniture collectables, 1830-1940, £5-£2,000.* LOC: A coast road between Weybourne and Cley, at

elling continued

emorial in village. PARK: Easy. TEL: 01263 ;8227; home - 01263 588435. SER: Valuations; ıys at auction (paintings and books). VAT: an/Spec.

ING'S LYNN

im Clayton Jewellery

Chapel St. PE30 1EG. Open 9-5. *STOCK: wellery, clocks, watches, furniture and pictures.* EL: 01553 772329; fax - same. SER: Restor- ons (silver); bespoke jewellery made to order.

orfolk Galleries

ilway Rd. PE30 1PF. (B. Houchen and G.R. ımbley). Open 8.30-5.30, Sat. 8.30-12.30. *'OCK: Victorian and Edwardian furniture.* ARK: Nearby. TEL: 01553 765060.

ld Curiosity Shop

St. James St. PE30 5DA. (Mrs R.S. Wright). t. 1980. Open 10.30-5, Sat. 9.30-6. SIZE: nall. *STOCK: General collectable smalls, glass, othing, linen, jewellery, lighting, Art Deco and t Nouveau, furniture, prints, stripped pine and intings, pre 1930, £1-£500.* LOC: Off Saturday arket place towards London Rd. PARK: At rear nearby. TEL: 01553 766591. FAIRS: Alexandra lace, Newark and local.

he Old Granary Antiques and ollectors Centre

ng Staithe Lane, Off Queens St. PE30 1LZ. en 10-5. *STOCK: China, glass, books, silver, vellery, brass, copper, postcards, linen, some niture, and general antiques.* PARK: Easy. EL: 01553 775509.

ne and Things

Tower St. Open 9-5.30. CL: Wed. SIZE: 8 alers. *STOCK: General antiques including all items, pine, mahogany and oak furniture, gones, ornate plasterwork, ceiling roses and 'am style fireplaces.* TEL: 01553 766532.

lverton Antiques

Chapel St. PE30 1EG. (Mrs S. Clayton). Open 5. *STOCK: Glass, porcelain, clocks, baro- ters, furniture and paintings, pre-1900.* TEL: 553 772329; fax - same. SER: Restorations ocks, barometers and jewellery).

NGHAM, Nr. Holt

e Miller Antiques and Collectables

Courtyard, Langham Glass. Est. 1993. Open -1.30 and 2-5 including Sun. SIZE: Small. *OCK: Glass - table, decorative and unusual, h-20th C, £1-£1,000; porcelain and pottery, inly 19th to early 20th C, £10-£500; furniture, luding early country oak, walnut and hogany, 17th-19th C, £500-£2,500.* LOC: Turn A148 Cromer/Fakenham road at Bale and low Langham signs. PARK: Own. TEL: 01328 511. SER: Valuations.

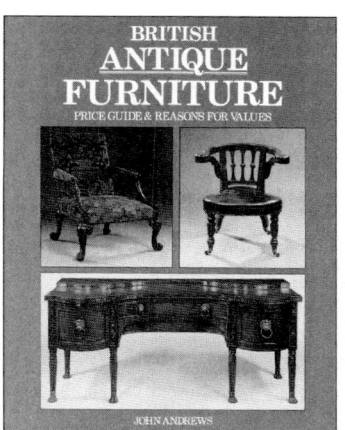

LONG STRATTON

Old Coach House

Ipswich Rd. NR15 2TA. Est. 1976. Open 10-1 and 2-5. CL: Mon. *STOCK: General antiques, pine, Victorian and Edwardian export furniture, paintings, copper, brass, china.* TEL: 01508 530942.

NORTH WALSHAM

Eric Bates and Sons

Melbourne House, Bacton Rd. NR28 0RA. Est. 1973. Open 8-5. SIZE: Large. *STOCK: Victorian and Edwardian furniture.* TEL: 01692 403221; fax - 01692 404388. SER: Restorations (furniture); upholstery; shipping and container packing. VAT: Stan/Spec.

NORWICH

Albrow and Sons Family Jewellers

10 All Saints Green. NR1 3NA. (R. Albrow). NAG Registered Valuer. Est. 1868. Open 9.30-4.30. SIZE: Medium. *STOCK: Jewellery, silver, plate, china, glass, furniture.* LOC: Opposite Bond's store. PARK: Behind Bond's store. TEL: 01603 622569. SER: Valuations; repairs.

Norwich continued

The Bank House Gallery LAPAD

71 Newmarket Rd. NR2 2HW. (R.S. Mitche Resident. Est. 1979. Open by appointme *STOCK: English oil paintings especia Norwich and Suffolk schools, 19th C, £1,00 £50,000.* LOC: On A11 between city centre a ring road. PARK: Own. TEL: 01603 6333 fax - 01603 633387. SER: Valuations; rest ations. VAT: Stan/Spec.

Arthur Brett and Sons Ltd BA

42 St. Giles St. NR2 1LW. Est. 1870. Op 9.30-1 and 2-5. CL: Sat. except by appoi ment. SIZE: Large. *STOCK: Antique furnitu mahogany, walnut and oak; sculpture a metalwork.* LOC: Near City Hall. PARK: Ea TEL: 01603 628171; fax - 01603 6302 FAIRS: Olympia. VAT: Stan/Spec.

J & D Clarke Book and Print Deale

St Michael at Plea Church, Redwell St. NR2 4S Est. 1988. Open 9.30-5. SIZE: Medium. *STOC Books and prints, £1-£1,000.* LOC: Twixt E Hill and city centre. PARK: Limited. TEL: 01 617700/619226. SER: Book repairs; print colour and mounting.

Cloisters Antiques Fair

St. Andrew's and Blackfriars Hall, St. Andre Plain. NR3 1AU. (Norwich City Council). E 1976. Open Wed. only 9.30-3.30. SIZE: dealers. *STOCK: Wide variety of gene antiques.* PARK: Easy. TEL: 01603 628477; fa 01603 762182; bookings - 01603 425158.

Country and Eastern

8 Redwell St. (J. Millward). Est. 1978. Op daily. *STOCK: Oriental rugs, kelims and texti late 19th C to early 20th C, £50-£500; primit and country furniture, 18th-19th C, £25-£5 woolwork pictures, 17th-19th C, £10-£2 bygones, 18th-19th C, £2-£75.* LOC: Top of E Hill. PARK: Nearby. TEL: 01603 623107. V Stan/Spec.

Crome Gallery and Frame Shop

34 Elm Hill. NR3 1HG. (J. Willis). Est. 19 Open 9.30-5. SIZE: Medium. *STOCK: Mai 20th C watercolours, oils and prints; some 1 C.* LOC: Near cathedral. PARK: Easy. TE 01603 622827. SER: Crome Gallery Conservat (oils, watercolours, prints, frames, furnitu porcelain).

Peter Crowe, Antiquarian Book Selle

75-77 Upper St. Giles St. NR1 2AB. Open 9 *STOCK: Antiquarian books, 17th-18th C, c 19th C, cloth and fine bindings, trav topography and Norfolk; maps and prints.* T 01603 624800.

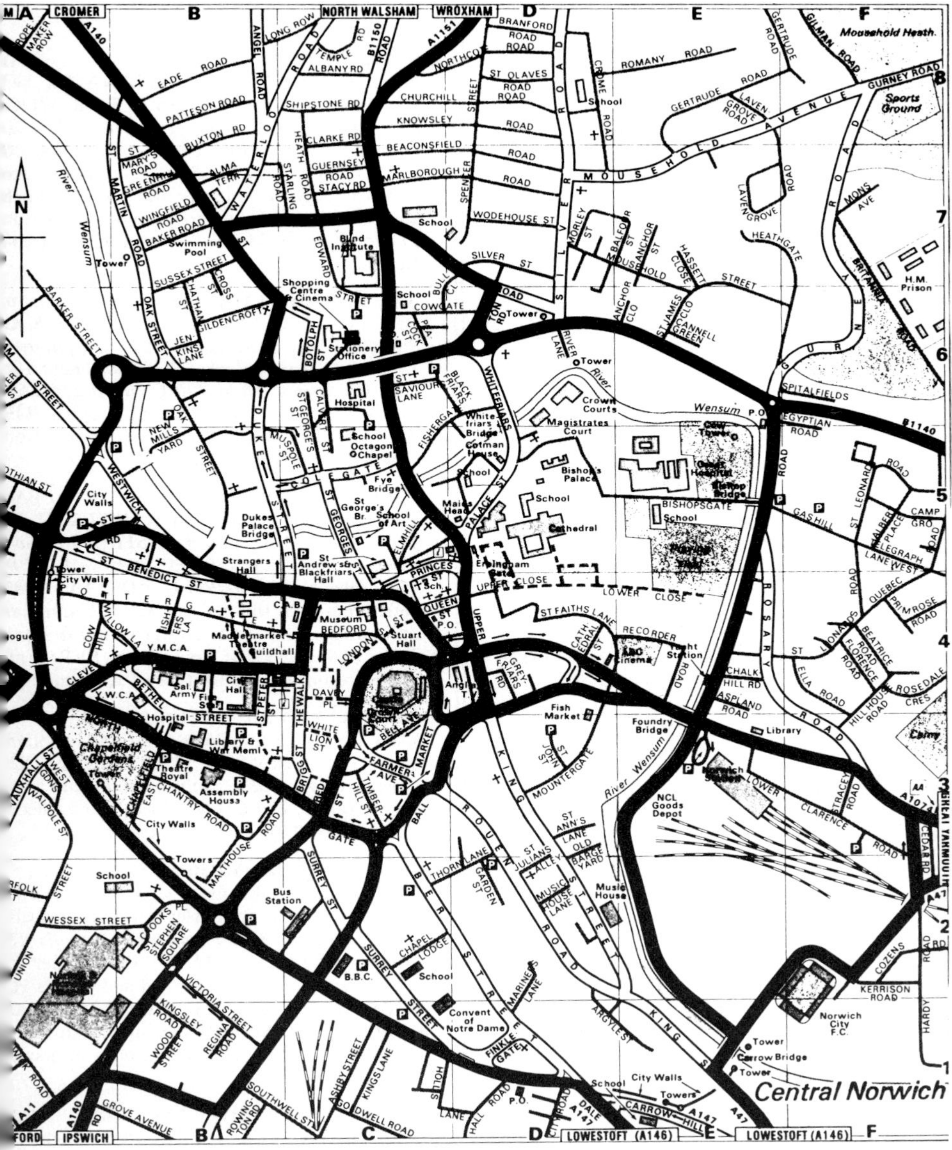

Key to Town Plan

AA Recommended roads		Car Parks	P
Other roads		Parks and open spaces	
Restricted roads		AA Service Centre	AA
Buildings of interest			

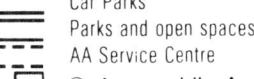

Norwich continued

Clive Dennett Coins
66 St. Benedicts St. NR2 4AR. BNTA. Est. 197 CL: Thurs. and lunchtime. SIZE: Small. *STOC Coins and medals, ancient Greek to date, £ £5,000; jewellery, 19th-20th C; banknotes, 20 C; both £5-£1,000.* PARK: Easy. TEL: 016 624315. SER: Valuations; buys at auction (stock). FAIRS: All Simmons; Cumberland Hot London; Coinex; Marriott Hotel, London; Tiena Belgium.

The Fairhurst Gallery
Bedford St. NR2 1AS. Est. 1951. Open 9-5. C Sat. pm. SIZE: Medium. *STOCK: Oil painting £5-£5,000; watercolours, £5-£2,000, both 19t 20th C; frames, 18th-20th C; furniture, £50 £10,000.* LOC: Behind Travel Centre. TE 01603 614214. SER: Valuations; restoration cleaning; framemakers. VAT: Spec.

Nicholas Fowle Antiques BAD
Websdale Court, Bedford St. NR2 1AR. Es 1965. Open 9-5, Sat. 9-1. SIZE: Mediu *STOCK: Furniture, £500-£10,000; works of a £5-£1,000; both 17th-19th C.* LOC: City cent pedestrian area (limited access for loading a unloading). PARK: St Andrews multi-store TEL: 01603 219964; fax - same. SER: Va ations; restorations (furniture). VAT: Stan/Spe

Michael Hallam Antiques
Black Horse Gallery, Wensum St. (M.J. Hallan Est. 1969. Open 9.30-5. SIZE: Small. *STOC Furniture, porcelain, pictures and small iten mainly 19th C, £10-£2,000.* LOC: Near Cathedr TEL: 01603 413692. SER: Valuations.

John Howkins Antiques
1 Dereham Rd. NR2 4HX. (J.G. Howkins). E 1973. Open 10-5, prior telephone call advisab SIZE: Large. *STOCK: Furniture and smalls, 18 to early 20th C, £25-£15,000.* LOC: Inner ri road, junction of Dereham Road and Grapes H PARK: Own at rear. TEL: 01603 627832; fa 01603 666626. SER: Valuations; restoratio (furniture, clocks, upholstery); buys at auctic VAT: Stan/Spec.

Leona Levine Silver Specialist BA
35 St. Giles St. NR2 1JN. Est. 1865. Open 9.3 5. CL: Thurs. *STOCK: Silver and Sheffie plate.* TEL: 01603 628709. SER: Valuatio engraving; restorations. VAT: Stan/Spec.

Maddermarket Antiques
18c Lower Goat Lane. NR2 1EL. Est. 1955. Op 9.30-4.30. *STOCK: Jewellery, silverware.* TE 01603 620610. SER: Part exchange.

lorwich continued

1andell's Gallery BADA
lm Hill. NR3 1HN. Est. 1964. Open 9-5.30. IZE: Large. *STOCK: Oils and watercolours, specially English and Continental works and 'orwich and Suffolk painters, 19th-20th C.* OC: Near shopping centre, close to cathedral. ARK: Easy. TEL: 01603 626892/629180; fax - 1603 767471. SER: Conservation; framing. AT: Spec.

'he Movie Shop
ntiquarian and Nostalgia Centre, 11 St. regory's Alley. NR2 1ER. Open 10-5. SIZE: arge. *STOCK: Books, magazines and movie phemera; telephones, pre-1940 clothes and xtiles, collectables and general antiques.* TEL: 1603 615239.

'orwich Antiques Centre
ugustine Steward House, 14 Tombland. NR3 HF. (MrsBetty Godsafe). Est. 1974. Open 10-5. IZE: Large. *STOCK: Furniture, 19th to early)th C, £50-£1,000; china and porcelain, 1850- 950, £20-£200; collectables, 1850-1950, £5-£50.* OC: City centre, opposite cathedral. PARK: Elm ill. TEL: 01603 619129. SER: Valuations; storations (furniture, caning).

'he Scientific Anglian (Bookshop)
)-30a St. Benedict St. NR2 4AQ. (N.B. Peake). st. 1965. Open 10-5.30. CL: Mon. am. and hurs. am. SIZE: Large. *STOCK: Secondhand ooks, old and modern, 30p-£200; antiquarian ems, 1500-1900, from £1.* Not Stocked: Maps or ints. LOC: 3 minutes walk from City Hall raight down Upper Goat Lane, turn left into St. enedict's. PARK: Limited nearby or multi- orey St. Andrew's St. TEL: 01603 624079. ER: Valuations; buys at auction. VAT: Stan.

swald Sebley
) Lower Goat Lane. NR2 1EL. (P.H. Knights). st. 1895. Open 9-5.15. CL: Thurs. SIZE: Small. *TOCK: Silver, 18th-20th C, £15-£2,000; wellery, Victorian, £10-£4,000.* LOC: 150yds. to ght of City Hall, down paved street. PARK: earby. TEL: 01603 626504. SER: Valuations; storations (silver and gold jewellery). VAT: an/Spec.

t Mary's Antique Centre
Mary's Church, St Mary's Plain, Duke St. NR3 AF. (I. Ford). Est. 1982. Open 10-4.30. SIZE: arge - 30 dealers. *STOCK: Wide range of neral antiques including furniture, porcelain, ys and teddies, trains and dolls, jewellery, ilitaria, paintings and prints, plated ware, art, riod clothes, watches, clocks and collectables.* OC: Near HMSO. PARK: 200 yds. TEL: 01603 2582. SER: Valuations.

Norwich continued

St. Michael at Plea Antiques Centre
Bank Plain. NR2 4SN. (Manager - K.J. Burton). Est. 1984. Open 9.30-5. SIZE: Medium - 30 dealers. *STOCK: General antiques, pre-1940, £1-£2,500.* LOC: Near top of Elm Hill. PARK: 30 minutes roadside, multi-storey nearby. TEL: 01603 618989. SER: Restorations and repair (clocks, china); French polishing; re-caning.

James and Ann Tillett LAPADA
12 and 13 Tombland. NR3 1HF. Est. 1972. Open 9-6, Sat. 9-1.30. *STOCK: English domestic silver, flatware and jewellery, from 17th C; mustard pots, collectors' items, barometers, barographs, from 18th C.* LOC: Opposite Erpingham Gate, Norwich Cathedral and Maid's Head Hotel. TEL: 01603 624914; fax - 01603 764310. SER: Valuations; restorations (silver); export facilities. VAT: Stan/Spec.

Thomas Tillett & Co
17 St. Giles St. NR2 1JL. Open daily. SIZE: Medium. *STOCK: Diamond jewellery, 19th-20th C, £50-£2,000; silver, 18th-19th C, £20-£1,000.* PARK: Easy. TEL: 01603 625922. SER: Valuations; restorations (jewellery, silver). VAT: Stan/Spec.

The Tombland Bookshop
8 Tombland. NR3 1HF. (J.G. and A.H. Freeman). Open 9.30-5. *STOCK: Antiquarian and secondhand books.* TEL: 01603 760610; fax - 01603 611631.

Malcolm Turner
15 St. Giles St. NR2 1JL. Open 9-5. CL: Thurs. SIZE: Small. *STOCK: Bronzeware, Oriental ceramics, silver, Staffordshire, Imari, mostly 19th C, £50-£1,000.* PARK: Nearby. TEL: 01603 627007. SER: Valuations. VAT: Stan/Spec.

RAVENINGHAM

M.D. Cannell Antiques
Castell Farm, Beccles Rd. NR14 6NU. Resident. Open 10-6 including Sun. SIZE: Large. *STOCK: Oriental rugs and carpets, Eastern furniture, pine, metalwork.* LOC: On B1140. PARK: Easy. TEL: 01508 548441. VAT: Stan/Spec.

REEPHAM

Echo Antiques
Church Hill. NR10 4JL. (Ms M. Stiefel and N. Bundock). Est. 1986. Open 10-5. CL: Thurs. SIZE: Medium. *STOCK: Furniture, 1650-1900, £10-£2,000; pine, 1800-1900, £50-£1,000; small items and telescopes, 1650-1900, £10-£1,000.* Not Stocked: Jewellery. PARK: Market Sq. TEL: 01603 873291; home - 01603 872068. SER: Valuations; restorations (furniture); buys at auction.

SCRATBY, Nr. Gt. Yarmouth

Keith Lawson Antique Clocks

Scratby Garden Centre, Beach Rd. NR29 3AJ. LBHI. Est. 1979. Open seven days 9-6. SIZE: Large. *STOCK: Clocks and barometers.* LOC: B1159. PARK: Easy. TEL: 01493 730950. SER: Valuations; restorations. VAT: Stan/Spec.

SHARRINGTON, Nr. Holt

Sharrington Antiques

NR24 2PQ. (P. Coke). Est. 1944. Open by chance 9.30-5.00, or by appointment. CL: Jan.-Mar. SIZE: Medium. *STOCK: Small and interesting items, £5-£1,500; china, pictures, embroideries, treen, papier mâché.* LOC: 3 miles west of Holt. PARK: Easy. TEL: 01263 861411; home - 01263 860719.

SHERINGHAM

R.L. Cook

12 Sycamore Grove. NR26 8PG. Est. 1950. Open by appointment. *STOCK: Antiquarian books.* TEL: 01263 822050.

Sheringham continued

Dorothy's Antiques

23 Waterbank Rd. NR26 8RB. (Mrs D.E Collier). Est. 1975. *STOCK: Glass, especiall cranberry; Royal Worcester, Meissen, Sitzendor porcelain, commemoratives, Goss china, bras copper, small furniture, clocks, cased birds ribbon plates, porcelain shoes, collectors' item* TEL: 01263 822319; home - 01263 823018.

Parriss

20 Station Rd. NR26 8RE. (J.H. Parriss). Es 1947. Open 9-5.30. CL: Wed. SIZE: Mediun *STOCK: Jewellery, £30-£2,500; silver, £40 £2,000; clocks, £100-£3,000.* LOC: A1082, i main street. PARK: Within 150yds. TEL: 0126 822661. SER: Valuations; restorations (jeweller silver, clocks). VAT: Stan.

The Westcliffe Gallery

2-8 Augusta St. NR26 8LA. (Parks & Vinsen Resident. Est. 1979. Open 9.30-1 and 2-5.30, Sa 9.30-5.30, Sun. 10-4. SIZE: Medium. *STOCK Oils, watercolours and drawings, 19th-20th C £100-£15,000; furniture.* LOC: Town centre PARK: Easy. TEL: 01263 824320. SER: Valu ations; restorations (oils, watercolours, prints gilding. VAT: Stan/Spec.

;OUTH WALSHAM

.eo Pratt and Son LAPADA

)ld Curiosity Shop. NR13 6EA. (R. and E.D. 'ratt). Est. 1890. Open 9-1 and 2-5.30. SIZE: .arge. *STOCK: Furniture, from 1700; por-elain, glass, pottery, 1830; shipping furniture, ıetalware.* PARK: Easy. TEL: 01603 270204. ER: Restorations (furniture); buys at auction. 'AIRS: Norwich; Snape; Bury St Edmunds. 'AT: Stan/Spec.

TALHAM

·talham Antique Gallery LAPADA

ligh St. NR12 9AH. (M.B. Hicks). Est. 1970.)pen 9-1 and 2-5. SIZE: Medium. *STOCK: 'urniture, 17th C to 19th C; pictures, china, lass, brass.* Not Stocked: Reproductions. ARK: Easy. TEL: 01692 580636. SER: Valu-tions; restorations. VAT: Spec.

TIFFKEY

·tiffkey Antiques

he Old Methodist Chapel. NR23 1AJ. Open by rrangement with Stiffkey Lamp Shop. *STOCK: ictorian and Edwardian bathroom fittings; fire ons, door furniture, bric-a-brac, Japanese and her tinplate toys (many boxed and mint).* PARK: asy. TEL: 01328 830460; fax - 01328 830005.

'he Stiffkey Lamp Shop

ownshend Arms. NR23 1AJ. (R. Belsten and D. lann). Est. 1976. Open 10-5 including Sun. IZE: Medium. *STOCK: Lamps, gas, electric and l, 1800-1920, £25-£2,000; rare lamp fittings.* OC: Coast road near Wells-on-Sea. PARK: asy. TEL: 01328 830460; fax - 01328 830005. ER: Restorations (lamp fittings). VAT: Stan.

TOKE FERRY, Nr. King's Lynn

armhouse Antiques

'hite's Farmhouse, Barker's Drove. PE33 9TA. . Philpot). Resident. Est. 1969. Open by pointment. *STOCK: General antiques.* TEL: 366 500588. SER: Restorations; furniture made order in old timber.

UFFIELD, Nr. Aylsham

. and E. Brière

eeper's Cottage. NR11 7ER. Resident. Est. 66. Open by appointment only. SIZE: Medium. *'OCK: Small period furniture, mirrors, oil intings.* LOC: First fork left past the garage on 145 Aylsham-North Walsham Rd. TEL: 01263 2651. SER: Restoration and cleaning (oil intings).

SWAFFHAM

Cranglegate Antiques

Market Place. PE37 7LE. (Mrs R.D. Buckie). Resident. Est. 1965. Open Tues., Thurs. and Sat. 10-1 and 2-5.30. SIZE: Small. *STOCK: General antiques and collectors' items, 17th-20th C, £5-£1,000.* LOC: A47. PARK: In square opposite or in passage at rear. TEL: Home - 01760 721052. FAIRS: Local.

Swaffham Antiques Supplies

The Old Cold Store Buildings, 7 Cley Rd. PE37. (M. and R. Cross). Est. 1959. Open by appointment only. SIZE: Large. *STOCK: General antiques, 18th-19th C; shipping furniture, £100-£5,000.* LOC: Off Market Place. PARK: Easy. TEL: 01760 721697/337666; home - 01760 721697.

SWAFIELD, Nr. North Walsham

Staithe Lodge Gallery

Staithe Lodge. NR28 0RQ. (M.C.A. Foster). Resident. Est. 1976. Open 9-5, Sun. by appointment. CL: Wed. pm. SIZE: Medium. *STOCK: Watercolours, paintings and prints, 1800-1950, £50-£500.* LOC: On B1145 at the Mundesley end of the North Walsham by-pass. PARK: Easy. TEL: 01692 402669. SER: Restorations; framing; buys at auction (mainly watercolours).

TACOLNESTON, Nr. Norwich

Freya Antiques

St. Mary's Farm, Cheneys Lane. NR16 1DB. Usually open but appointment advisable; evenings by appointment. SIZE: Large. *STOCK: General antiques, especially pine and country furniture; upholstery.* TEL: 01508 489252; mobile - 0831 651898. SER: Valuations; restorations; re-upholstery.

TOTTENHILL, Nr. King's Lynn

Jubilee Antiques

Coach House, Whin Common Rd. PE33 0RS. (Mr and Mrs A.J. Lee). Est. 1953. Open daily including Sun. SIZE: Medium. *STOCK: Furniture especially Victorian chairs, £50-£4,000; post boxes, interesting items.* LOC: Between King's Lynn and Downham Market, adjacent to A10. PARK: Easy. TEL: 01553 810681; home - same. SER: Valuations; restorations (furniture); buys at auction (furniture).

TWYFORD, Nr. Fakenham

Norton Antiques

(T. and N. Hepburn). Est. 1966. Open by appointment only. *STOCK: Furniture 1680-1900, £25-£3,500; oils and watercolours, 19th to early 20th C, £25-£2,500; clocks, 18th-19th C, £40-£3,500; woodworking and craftsman's hand tools.* TEL: 01362 683331. SER: Valuations.

WATTON

Clermont Antiques
Clermont Hall. IP25 6LY. (P. Jones). Residen Est. 1983. Open daily. SIZE: Large. *STOCK Furniture, decorative items, 18th to early 19th C* LOC: Down farm track, off B1108. PARK: Easy TEL: 01953 882189. VAT: Spec.

WELLS-NEXT-THE-SEA

Church Street Antiques
2 Church St. NR23 1JA. (Paula Ford and Lesle Ann Irons). Open 10-4 including Sun., Mon. b appointment. SIZE: Small. *STOCK: Textile lace, costume jewellery, hat pins, kitchenali ephemera, collectables, £1-£500.* LOC: A14 main coast road, opposite church. PARK: Eas TEL: 01328 711698.

Wells Antique Centre
The Old Mill, Maryland. NR23 1LX. Open 10- including Sun. SIZE: 12 dealers. *STOCK General antiques and collectables.* PARK: Eas TEL: 01328 711433.

WROXHAM

T.C.S. Brooke BAD
The Grange. NR12 8RX. (S.T. Brooke). Es 1952. Open 9.30-1 and 2.15-5.30. CL: Mo *STOCK: English porcelain, 18th C; furnitur mainly Georgian; silver, glass, works of a Oriental rugs.* PARK: Easy. TEL: 016(782644. SER: Valuations. VAT: Spec.

WYMONDHAM

King
Market Place. NR18 0AX. (M. King). Est. 196 Open 9-4. CL: Mon. and Wed., except b appointment. *STOCK: General antique furniture, copper, brass, silver, jeweller porcelain.* PARK: Easy. TEL: 01953 60475 evenings - 01953 602427.

M.E. and J.E. Standley
"Acorns", 23 Norwich Rd. and warehouses Chandlers Hill. NR18 0NT. Open Sat. or appointment. *STOCK: Furniture, 17th-19th and Victorian.* TEL: 01953 602566.

Turret House
27 Middleton St. NR18 0AB. (Dr and Mrs D. Morgan). PBFA. Resident. Est. 1972. SIZ Small. *STOCK: Antiquarian books, especia science and medical; scientific instruments.* LO Corner of Vicar St., adjacent to War Memori TEL: 01953 603462. SER: Buys at auctic FAIRS: London and major provincial PBF VAT: Stan/Spec.

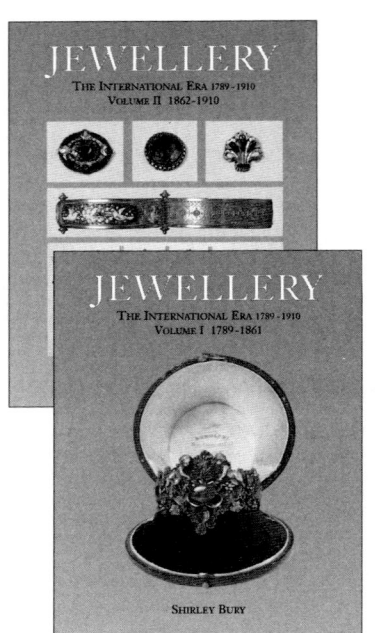

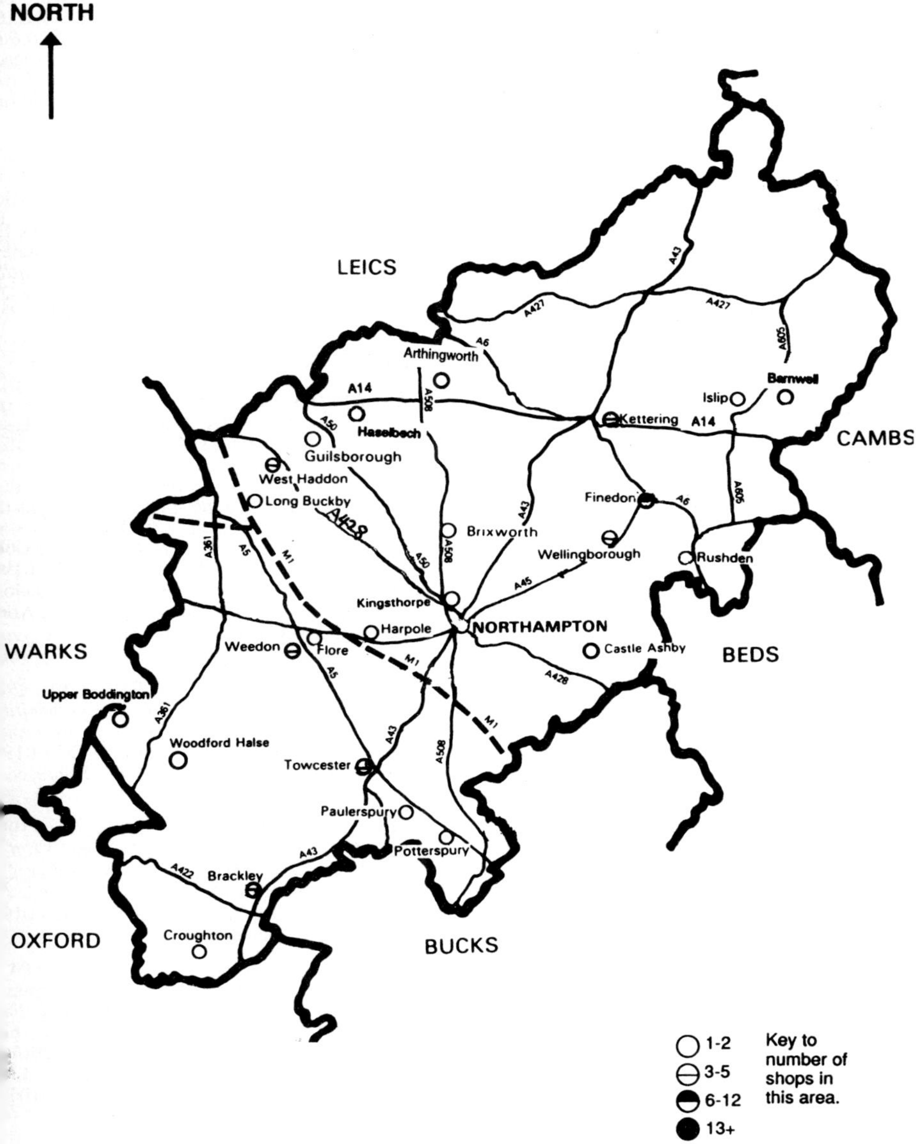

Please note this is only a rough map designed to show dealers the number of shops in the various towns, and is not necessarily totally accurate.

ARTHINGWORTH
Nr. Market Harborough (Leics)

Coughton Galleries Ltd
The Old Manor. LE16 8JT. (Lady Isabel Throckmorton). Est. 1968. Open Wed., Thurs., Sat. and Sun. 10.30-5, or by appointment. SIZE: Medium. *STOCK: Modern British and Irish oil paintings and watercolours.* TEL: 01858 525436. VAT: Spec.

BARNWELL, Nr. Oundle

Berengar Antiques
Barnwell Manor. (Paul R.M. Howell). Est. 1995. Open 10-5, Sun. by appointment. SIZE: Large. *STOCK: Furniture, 17th-19th C, £500-£50,000; paintings, 17th-20th C, £100-£20,000.* LOC: 5 miles north of A14 (Junc.13) on the A605. PARK: Own. TEL: 01832 274070; home - same; fax - 01832 272726. VAT: Spec.

BRACKLEY

Brackley Antiques
69 High St. NN13 7BW. (Mrs B.H. Nutting). Est. 1977. Open 10-6, Wed. 10-12, Sun. by appointment. SIZE: Medium. *STOCK: Furniture, especially traditionally upholstered, 19th C, £50-£2,000; ceramics, 18th-20th C, £2-£400; interesting and unusual items.* LOC: A43. PARK: Easy. TEL: 01280 703362; home - same. SER: Restorations (furniture and upholstery).

Peter Jackson Antiques
3 Market Place. NN13 7AB. Open 10.30-1 and 2-5. *STOCK: English and Continental porcelain and pottery, 18th-19th C; furniture, paintings, silver, jewellery, glass, watercolours and prints.* TEL: 01280 703259; mobile - 04022 30074. SER: Valuations; restorations.

Juno Antiques
4 Bridge St. NN13 7EP. Open 10-1 and 2-5. CL: Wed. *STOCK: General antiques.* LOC: Northampton/Oxford road. TEL: 01280 700639.

The Old Hall Bookshop
32 Market Place. NN13 7DP. (J. and Lady Juliet Townsend). Est. 1977. Open 9.30-1 and 2-5.30. SIZE: Large. *STOCK: Antiquarian, secondhand and new books.* LOC: Town centre on east side of Market Place. PARK: Easy. TEL: 01280 704146. VAT: Stan.

Right Angle
24 Manor Rd. NN13 6AJ. Open 9.30-5.30, Wed. 9.30-1. *STOCK: Watercolours, oils, prints and maps.* TEL: 01280 702462. SER: Restorations (frames); gilding and framing.

BRIXWORTH, Nr. Northampton

B.R. Gunnett
128 Northampton Rd. NN6 9BU. Open by appointment. *STOCK: Furniture.* TEL: 01604 880057.

CASTLE ASHBY

Castle Ashby Gallery
The Old Farmyard. NN7 1LF. (G.S. Wright - Fi Paintings). Open 10.30-5. CL: Mon. *STOCK: (paintings - British, 1850-1950, £200-£20,00 significant Contemporary artists.* LOC: Adjace to Castle Ashby House. PARK: Easy. TEL: 016 696787; fax - 01604 415055. SER: Valuatior restorations (oils). VAT: Spec.

CROUGHTON, Nr. Brackley

Croughton Antiques
29 High St. NN13 5LT. (L.T. and N. Cross). E 1971. Open Wed.-Sun. 10-6 or by appointme SIZE: Medium. *STOCK: General antique decorators' items and shipping goods.* LO B4031. PARK: Easy. TEL: 01869 810203.

FINEDON

Aspidistra Antiques
51 High St. NN9 5JN. (Pat and Geoff Mos Resident. Est. 1993. Open 9-5.30, Sun. 11-5. SIZ Large. *STOCK: Art Nouveau and Art Deco met ceramics, plaster and furniture, £25-£1,00 general antiques, £1-£500.* LOC: Off A14 juncti 10 - turn right just before roundabout in villa centre. From junction 11, turn right at roundab and immediate left. PARK: Easy. TEL: 019 680196; mobile - 0468 071948. SER: Valuatio restorations (furniture); buys at auction. FAIR IACF; Alexander Palace, Sandown, NEC.

Simon Banks Antiques
28 Church St. NN9 5NA. (S. Banks). Est. 19 SIZE: Medium. *STOCK: 17th-20th C furnitu £30-£3,000; glass, silver, ceramics, prints, copp decorative and collectable items.* TEL: 019 680371; mobile - 0374 740508. VAT: Stan/Spec.

C B Antiques
13 High St. NN9 5JN. (R. Cheney). Est. 19 Open 9-5.30, Sun. 11-5. SIZE: Medium. *STOC 18th C furniture, £500-£1,000; 19th C china, £ £100; 20th C collectables, £5-£25.* LOC: PARK: Easy. TEL: 01933 681048; home - 019 680085. SER: Valuations.

M.C. Chapman LAPA
11-25 Bell Hill. NN9 5ND. Est. 1967. Open 5.30, Sun. 11-5. SIZE: Large. *STOCK: F niture, 18th-19th C; clocks, 18th-20th C; b £100-£3,000; decorative items, 19th-20th* LOC: 400 yds. off A510. PARK: Easy. TE 01933 681260. SER: Container faciliti FAIRS: Newark. VAT: Stan/Spec.

E.K. Antiques
37 High St. NN9 5NB. Est. 1967. Open 9.30-5. Sun. 11-5. SIZE: Medium- several deale *STOCK: Furniture, china, silver, glass, pictu needlework and decorative items, 1780-1950,* £3,500. PARK: Easy. TEL: 01933 681882; hc - 01933 410245. SER: Restorations (furnitu French polishing; period interiors; valuations.

inedon continued

'inedon Antiques (Antiques Centre)
1-25 Bell Hill. NN9 5ND. (M.C. Chapman). Est. 973. Open 9-5.30, Sun. 11-5. SIZE: Large - 30 ealers. *STOCK: Furniture, ceramics, glass, aintings, prints and clocks, silver and plate, ainly 18th to early 20th C.* LOC: From roundbout at junction of A6 and A510 take A510 wards Wellingborough, turn right after half a ile, premises 400yds. on right. PARK: Easy. EL: 01933 681260. SER: Export facilities. VAT: tan/Spec.

LORE, Nr. Weedon

Iuntershield Antiques
he Huntershields. NN7 4LZ. (Mrs. C. Madeira). st. 1968. Open 9-7, Sun. by appointment. SIZE: arge. *STOCK: Furniture, 17th-19th C, £50-5,000; decorative items, 19th C, £50-£2,000; etalware, 18th-19th C, £10-£1,000.* LOC: Off M1, nction 16, into Flore, last turning on left, premises right. PARK: Easy. TEL: 01327 340718; home - me; fax - 01327 349263. VAT: Stan/Spec.

'hristopher Jones at Flore House
ore House, The Avenue. NN2 4LZ. Est. 1977. pen 10-5, Sat. 11-4.30, Sun. by appointment. ZE: Large. *STOCK: Period and decorative furture, lighting, porcelain, glass and objects, 18th-)th C.* PARK: Easy. TEL: 01327 342165. SER: terior decor advice. FAIRS: Olympia. VAT: Spec.

UILSBOROUGH

ick Goodwin Exports
e Firs, Nortoft Rd. NN6 8QB. Open every day appointment. SIZE: Warehouse. *STOCK: Oak, ahogany, walnut, stripped and painted pine, alls.* TEL: 01280 813115; 01604 740234; fax - me. SER: Restorations; pine stripping, export, ipping and packing; courier.

ARPOLE

glenook Antiques
High St. NN7 4DH. (T. and P. Havard). Est. '71. Open 9-7. CL: Wed. SIZE: Small. *STOCK: neral antiques, £1-£500.* LOC: In main street. RK: Easy. TEL: 01604 830007.

ASELBECH, Nr. Northampton

vage Fine Art LAPADA
S.J. Savage & Son, The Gate House. NN6 Q. (Michael Savage). Est. 1905. Open by pointment only. *STOCK: Oils and waterlours, 19th and 20th C; local antiquarian maps d prints, mirrors, work by local artists past and esent.* TEL: 01604 686232; fax - 01604 686378. R: Valuations; restorations (paintings and mes); framing. FAIRS: LAPADA; World of awings & Watercolours, Park Lane; NEC; xton; Snape; Olympia.

ISLIP, Nr. Thrapston

John Roe Antiques
The Furnace Site, Kettering Rd. NN14 3JW. Est. 1968. Open 9-5.30, Sat. 10-4. *STOCK: General antiques; Continental and American shipping goods; jewellery.* TEL: 01832 732937. VAT: Stan.

KETTERING

Alexis Brook
74 Lower St. NN16 8DL. (Mrs A. Brook). Est. 1959. Open from 11.30, appointment advisable. CL: Sun. am. SIZE: Medium. *STOCK: General small antiques, £1-£1,500.* LOC: On A6 from Market Harborough. House halfway up hill on left before main shopping centre. PARK: At Collingwood Motors, adjacent. TEL: 01536 513854.

Dragon Antiques
85 Rockingham Rd. NN16 8LA. Open 10-4. CL: Thurs. *STOCK: Watercolours and oils; Oriental items and general antiques.* TEL: 01536 517017. SER: Framing.

C.W. Ward Antiques
Deene House, 40 Lower St. NN16 8DJ. (Mrs J. Wilson). Est. 1912. Open by appointment only. SIZE: Medium. *STOCK: General antiques, furniture, pottery, porcelain, pewter, glass and pictures.* LOC: 25yds. from GPO on A6. PARK: Opposite. TEL: 01536 513537. SER: Valuations; upholstery and curtain making. VAT: Stan.

KINGSTHORPE, Nr. Northampton

Laila Gray Antiques
25 Welford Rd. NN2 8AQ. Open 9-5.30. *STOCK: Pine.* TEL: 01604 715277. SER: Waxing; stripping.

The Old Brigade
10a Harborough Rd. NN2 7AZ. (S.C. Wilson). Est. 1978. Open by appointment. SIZE: Small. *STOCK: Military items, 1850's to 1945, £5-£5,000.* LOC: Junction 15, M1. PARK: Easy. TEL: 01604 719389; fax - 01604 712489. SER: Valuations; illus. catalogue (£4 + SAE). VAT: Stan/Spec.

LONG BUCKBY

Antique Coffee Pot
15 High St. NN6 7RE. Open 8-5, Sun. 11-2. *STOCK: Furniture and bric-a-brac.* TEL: 01327 843849.

R.E. Thompson
17 Church St. NN6 7QH. Est. 1968. Open 8-5. SIZE: Large. *STOCK: Shipping goods, furniture, 19th-20th C; stripped pine, clocks, £1-£1,000.* PARK: Easy. TEL: 01327 842242/843487. VAT: Stan.

NORTHAMPTON

Buley Antiques
164 Kettering Rd. NN1 4BE. Est. 1966. Open 10.30-4.45, Thurs. by appointment. SIZE: Medium. *STOCK: Victoriana, £5-£200.* PARK: Nearby. TEL: 01604 31588; home - 01604 491577. SER: Valuations.

F. and C.H. Cave
111 Kettering Rd. NN1 4BA. Est. 1879. Open 9-5.30. CL: Thurs. SIZE: Large. *STOCK: Furniture - Georgian, Victorian and decorative; general antiques.* LOC: Near town centre, quarter mile outside pedestrianised area. PARK: Adjoining side streets. TEL: 01604 38278. VAT: Spec.

Michael Jones Jeweller
1 Gold St. NN1 1SA. Est. 1919. *STOCK: Silver, gold and gem jewellery, French and carriage clocks.* TEL: 01604 32548. VAT: Stan/Spec.

Occultique
73 Kettering Rd. NN1 4AW. (M.J. Lovett). Est. 1973. Open 10-5. SIZE: Small. *STOCK: Books, 50p-£500.* PARK: Nearby. TEL: 01604 27727; fax - 01604 603860. VAT: Stan.

Penny's Antiques
83 Kettering Rd. NN1 4AW. (Mrs P. Mawby). Est. 1976. Open 11-4, Sat. 10-5. CL: Thurs. SIZE: Small. *STOCK: Shipping goods, kitchen chairs,*

Northampton continued

pictures, army badges, furniture, china, smal glass and brass, Victorian to 1940, £5-£10 LOC: On A43 near town centre. PARK: Eas TEL: 01604 32429.

PAULERSPURY, Nr. Towcester

The Antique Galleries BAI
Watling St. NN12 6LQ. (M. Cameron). E 1948. Open 10-5.30. SIZE: Large. *STOC English furniture, 1650-1830; barometers, 178 1830.* LOC: 3 miles south of Towcester on A PARK: Own. TEL: 01327 811238. VAT: Spe

POTTERSPURY, Nr. Towcester

Reindeer Antiques Ltd BADA LAPAI
43 Watling St. NN12 7QD. (J.W. Butterwort Est. 1959. Open 9-6. SIZE: Large. *STOC Period English furniture, paintings, met clocks, garden furniture and statuary.* LOC: A TEL: 01908 542407/542200; fax - 019 542121. VAT: Stan/Spec.

RUSHDEN

D.W. Sherwood Antiques Ltd
59 Little St. NN10 0LS. Est. 1960. *STOC General antiques.* TEL: 01933 53265.

TOWCESTER

Clark Galleries
215 Watling St. NN12 6BX. (A. Clark). FABI Est. 1964. Open 8.30-5.30, Sat. 9.30-4. SIZ Medium. *STOCK: Landscape paintings, 18th £500-£15,000; portraits, 17th-18th C, £5(£5,000.* LOC: M1, junction 15, on A5. PAR Easy and at rear. TEL: 01327 352957. SE Valuations; restorations and re-lining (paintings). VAT: Stan/Spec.

Ron Green
227-239 Watling St. West. NN12 7BX. Est. 19 Open 9-6 or by appointment. SIZE: Lar *STOCK: English and Continental furniture, £ £30,000; oil paintings, £100-£10,000; decora items.* TEL: 01327 350387/350615.

R. and M. Nicholas
161 Watling St. NN12 6BX. Open 9.30-5. SI Small. *STOCK: 18th-19th C porcelain, silver glass.* TEL: 01327 350639.

Shelron Collectors Shop
9½ Brackley Rd. NN12 6DH. (R. Grosvenor). P Resident. Est. 1973. Open Tues.-Fri. 10-4, Sat. 1 SIZE: Medium. *STOCK: Postcards, from 1890; arette and trade cards, from 1880; ephemera, b a-brac, books, prints, models, £1-£100.* LOC: Le M1, junction 15A, 100yds. from A5 traffic li going west. PARK: Easy. TEL: 01327 3502 SER: Valuations (postcards and cigarette cards).

JPPER BODDINGTON

)oric Antiques LAPADA

:herry Tree House, Warwick Rd. NN11 6DH. Keith and Jane Riley). Est. 1975. SIZE: ledium. *STOCK: English oak, 17th-19th C, £50-'5,000; associated items and pottery.* LOC: lidway between Banbury and Daventry. 'ARK: Easy. TEL: 01327 263125; home - same. ER: Buys at auction (country furniture). AIRS: NEC; ICAF. VAT: Stan/Spec.

VEEDON

rchitectural Heritage of Northants

'he Woodyard. NN7 4LB. Open Tues.-Sat. 10-5, un. 11-5. *STOCK: Architectural antiques.* LOC: .5, 2 miles north of Weedon. TEL: 01327 349249; ax - 01327 349397.

3all & Claw Ltd

uilding 14, Royal Ordnance Depot. NN7 4PS. Mrs. J.M. Saunders). Open 8-5.30, Sat. 8-12, other mes by appointment, telephone call advisable. IZE: Large. *STOCK: French decorative and nglish furniture, mostly light woods, some ahogany; pine and mahogany reproductions; anelled rooms, architectural items, stained glass, ainted furniture.* TEL: 01327 340766; fax - 01327 40808. SER: Furniture made to order.

lelios & Co (Antiques)

5/27 High St. NN7 4QD. (J. Skiba and B. Walters). pen 9-6 including Sun. SIZE: Large. *STOCK: nglish and Continental furniture especially dining bles; decorative accessories.* PARK: Easy. TEL: 1327 340264; fax - 01327 342235; evenings - 1525 270247. SER: Suppliers and restorers to H. . Govt. VAT: Spec.

ococo Antiques and Interiors

New St., Lower Weedon. NN7 4QS. (N.K. riffiths). Resident. Usually available. *STOCK: onwork, brass and iron beds, fireplaces, pine rniture, sanitary ware - toilets, sinks, taps.* LOC: 3 iles junction 16, M1, quarter mile off A5. PARK: asy. TEL: 01327 341288. VAT: Stan/Spec.

he Village Antique Market

High St. NN7 4QD. (E.A. and J.M. Saunders). t. 1967. Open 9.30-5.30, Sun. 10.30-5.30. SIZE: rge - 40 dealers. *STOCK: General antiques and teresting items.* LOC: On A45, just off A5. ARK: At side of market. TEL: 01327 342015.

VELLINGBOROUGH

ntiques and Bric-a-Brac Market

arket Sq. NN8 1BN. Open Tues. 9-4. SIZE: 135 lls. *STOCK: General antiques and collectables.*)C: Town Centre.

Wellingborough continued

Park Book Shop

12 Park Rd. NN8 4PG. (J.A. Foster). Est. 1979. Open 10-5. CL: Thurs. SIZE: Medium. *STOCK: Books, 19th C maps and prints, £1-£250; postcards, 20th C, 10p-£5.* PARK: Easy. TEL: 01933 222592. SER: Valuations.

Park Gallery

16 Cannon St. NN8 5DJ. (Mrs J. Foster). Est. 1988. Open 10-5. CL: Thurs. SIZE: Medium. *STOCK: Prints, maps, 18th-19th C, £2-£200.* LOC: Continuation of A510 into town. PARK: Easy. TEL: 01933 222592.

Bryan Perkins Antiques

Finedon Rd. NN8 4DJ. (J., B.H. and S.C. Perkins). Est. 1971. Open 9-5. CL: Sat. pm. SIZE: Large. *STOCK: Furniture and paintings, 19th C, £200-£2,000; small items.* PARK: Easy. TEL: 01933 228812; home - 01536 790259. SER: Valuations; restorations (furniture). VAT: Spec. *Trade Only.*

WEST HADDON

Antiques

9 West End. NN6 7AY. Est. 1978. Open Wed.-Sat. 10-5.30. SIZE: Medium. *STOCK: Country furniture, period metalwork, brass and copper, treen and other domestic items.* LOC: A428. PARK: Easy. TEL: 01788 510772. VAT: Spec.

The Country Pine Shop

The Romney Building, Northampton Rd. NN6 7AS. (Ryan and Dodd). Est. 1985. Open 8-5. SIZE: Large. *STOCK: English and Continental stripped pine, £30-£1,200.* LOC: A428. TEL: 01788 510430.

Paul Hopwell Antiques BADA LAPADA

30 High St. NN6 7AP. Est. 1974. Open 9-6. CL: Sun. except by appointment. SIZE: Large. *STOCK: 17th-18th C oak and walnut country furniture, longcase clocks, metalware: oil paintings and prints mainly sporting and country pursuits.* LOC: A428. PARK: Easy. TEL: 01788 510636; fax - 01788 510044. SER: Valuations; restorations (furniture and metalware); buys at auction. VAT: Spec.

WOODFORD HALSE, Nr. Daventry

The Corner Cupboard

14 & 18 Station Rd. NN11 6RB. (T.R. and Mrs H.M. Stuart). Est. 1980. Open 9-7 six days a week. CL: Tues. SIZE: Medium. *STOCK: English and Continental stripped pine, Victorian and Edwardian, £50-£1,000; iron and brass beds, Victorian, £175-£650; sofas, chairs, chesterfields, Victorian, £50-£450.* LOC: Off A361 towards village. After 1 mile turn right up Phipps Rd. to village centre, shops in parade at top of hill. PARK: Easy. TEL: 01327 260725; home - same.

Northumberland

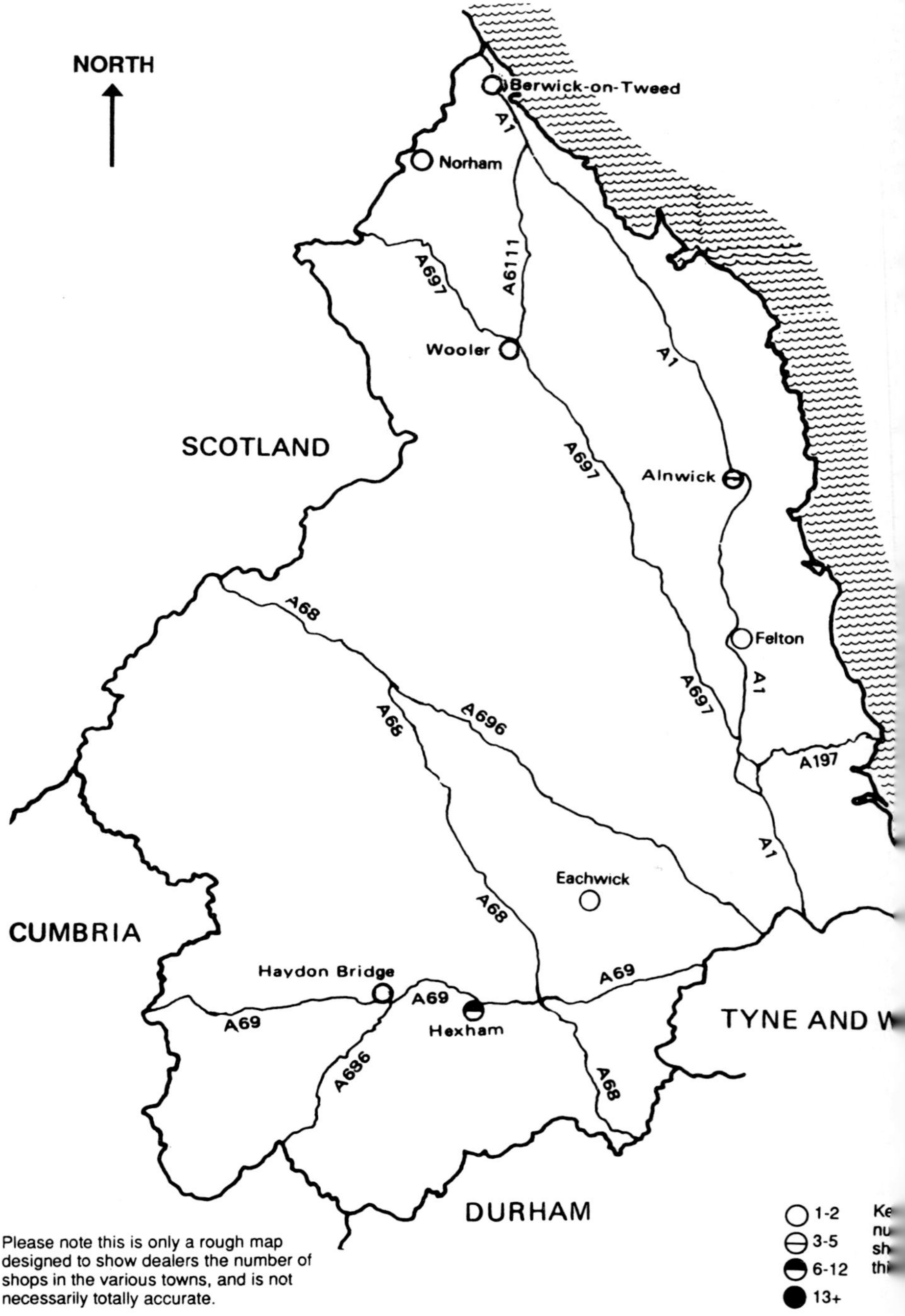

Please note this is only a rough map designed to show dealers the number of shops in the various towns, and is not necessarily totally accurate.

ALNWICK

G.M. Athey
Castle Corner, Narrowgate. NE66 0NP. *STOCK: English oak, mahogany furniture, glass, china and brass, 18th-19th C.* TEL: 01665 604229.

Bailiffgate Antique Pine
22 Bailiffgate. NE66 1LX. (S. Aston). Est. 1994. Open 10-4.30. CL: Mon. and Wed. SIZE: Large. *STOCK: Country pine furniture.* LOC: Opposite the castle. PARK: Easy. TEL: 01665 603616. SER: Valuations; restorations; buys at auction.

Pottergate Antiques
Doxford Farm, Chathill. NE67 5DY. (Mrs L. Shell). Open 10-5 every day in summer. CL: Mon. in winter. SIZE: Medium. *STOCK: General antiques, £3-£3,000; jewellery, to £2,000.* LOC: 2 miles off A1 at Charlton Mires on B6347 Seahouses Road. TEL: 01665 510034; home - 01665 830855. VAT: Stan/Spec.

Tamblyn
12 Bondgate Without. NE66 1PP. (Mrs S.M. Hirst). Est. 1981. Open 10-4.30. SIZE: Medium. *STOCK: General antiques including country furniture, pottery, pictures; antiquities, glass, to 20th C, £5-£1,500.* LOC: Diagonally opposite war memorial at southern entrance to town. PARK: Easy. TEL: 01665 603024; home - same. SER: Valuations.

BERWICK-ON-TWEED

Treasure Chest
3 Bridge St. TD15 2DX. (Y. Scott). Est. 1988. Open 10.30-4. SIZE: Medium. *STOCK: China, jewellery, glass, silver plate and small furniture, from 1860, £5-£150.* LOC: Approximately 1 mile from A1. PARK: Easy. TEL: Home - 01289 307736. SER: Restorations (china). FAIRS: Local.

... ACHWICK

Hazel Cottage Clocks
Hazel Cottage. NE18 0BE. (E. and M. Charlton). Open 9.30-5.30. SIZE: Medium. *STOCK: Clocks, £300-£8,000.* LOC: Just off Darras Hall to Stamfordham road, opposite Wylam turn-off. PARK: Easy. TEL: 01661 852415. SER: Restorations and repairs (clocks). VAT: Spec.

... ELTON, Nr. Morpeth

... elton Park Antiques
...elton Park. NE65 9HN. (D. and A. Burton). Resident. Est. 1973. By appointment only. *STOCK: Pottery and porcelain, 1795-1935.* PARK: Easy. TEL: 01670 787319. SER: Valuations; restorations; polishing.

HAYDON BRIDGE, Nr. Hexham

Haydon Bridge Antiques
3 Shaftoe St. NE47 6BQ. (J. and J. Smith). Est. 1974. Open 10.30-5 and by appointment. CL: Mon. and Thurs. SIZE: Large. *STOCK: Stripped pine, £5-£500; Victorian and Edwardian oak and mahogany, shipping goods, Victorian oils and watercolours.* PARK: Easy. TEL: 01434 684200; home - 01434 684461. VAT: Stan.

Haydon Gallery
3 Shaftoe St. NE47 6BQ. (J. Smith). Est. 1975. Open 10.30-5.30, Sun., Mon. and Thurs. by appointment. SIZE: Small. *STOCK: Oils and watercolours by North Eastern artists and others, mainly 19th C; some bronzes.* TEL: 01434 684200; home - 01434 684461. SER: Valuations; restorations (oil paintings).

HEXHAM

Boadens Antiques
29 and 30 Market Place. NE46 3PB. (R.J. Boaden). Est. 1948. Open 9-5. SIZE: Large. *STOCK: Small furniture, antique and Victorian, £100-£3,000; Victorian bric-a-brac, £10-£500; paintings, 19th-20th C, £50-£1,000; Victorian jewellery, from £30.* LOC: Opposite Hexham Abbey, off A69. PARK: Nearby. TEL: 01434 603187. SER: Valuations; jewellery repairs. VAT: Stan/Spec.

Gordon Caris
16 Market Place. NE46 1XQ. Est. 1972. Open 9-5. CL: Thurs. *STOCK: Clocks and watches.* TEL: 01434 602106. SER: Restorations (clocks and watches).

Hallstile Antiques
17 Hallstile Bank. NE46 3PG. (Mrs P. Neumann). Est. 1982. Open 10-5. CL: Thurs. SIZE: Large. *STOCK: Furniture, 18th to early 20th C, 50-£5,000; paintings and prints, £15-£400; clocks, silver plate, china, porcelain and glass.* LOC: Town centre, just off Market Place. PARK: Nearby. TEL: 01434 602239. SER: Buys at auction.

Hedley's of Hexham
3 St. Mary's Chare. NE46 1NQ. (P. Torday). Est. 1819. Open 9-5. CL: Thurs. pm. SIZE: Medium. *STOCK: Furniture, 17th C to Victorian; porcelain, silver and glass, 18th-20th C.* LOC: Off Battle Hill (A69). PARK: 200 yds. TEL: 01434 602317. SER: Valuations; restorations. VAT: Stan/Spec.

Hexham continued

Hexham Antiques (Inc. Hotspur Antiques)
6 Rear Battle Hill. NE46 1BB. (J. and D. Latham). Est. 1977. Open 10.30-4, Sat. 9.30-4. CL: Wed. and Thurs. SIZE: Large. *STOCK: Furniture, clocks, pictures, glass, china, boxes and collectors' items, to Art Deco.* LOC: Main shopping street, opposite NatWest Bank. PARK: 400 metres. TEL: 01434 603851; home - 01434 604813. SER: Valuations; buys at auction.

The Violin Shop
27 Hencotes. NE46 2EQ. (N. Cain and D. Mann). Est. 1970. Open 10-5 or by appointment. *STOCK: Violins, violas, cellos, basses and bows.* TEL: 01434 607897.

MINISTERACRES

Ministeracres Pine & Oak
Ivy Cottage. DH8 9RR. Est. 1984. Open by appointment. SIZE: Medium. *STOCK: Stripped pine including wardrobes, dressers, etc; also pine furniture made to order in reclaimed wood, oak furniture to order.* LOC: Turn into Ministeracres monastry off A68. PARK: Easy. TEL: 01434 682601; home - same; workshop - 01434 673075.

NORHAM, Nr. Berwick-on-Tweed

J. and D. Stewart
6 and 8 West St. TD15 2LB. Resident. Est. 196 SIZE: Medium. *STOCK: China, glass, collector items, mainly Victorian.* LOC: 7 miles north c Berwick-on-Tweed. PARK: Easy. TEL: 0128 382376.

WOOLER

Hamish Dunn Antiques
17 High St. NE71 6BU. Est. 1986. Open 9.30-1 and 1-4.30, Thurs. 9.30-12. SIZE: Mediun *STOCK: Curios and collectables, 19th-20th C £5-£500; antiquarian and secondhand book 18th-20th C, £1-£200; small furniture, 19th-20 C, £15-£1,000.* LOC: Off A697. PARK: Eas TEL: 01668 281341; home - 01668 28201 VAT: Stan/Spec.

James Miller Antiques LAPAD
1-5 Church St. NE71 6BZ. Est. 1947. Ope Mon.-Fri. 9.30-5. SIZE: Large, and war houses. *STOCK: Georgian, Regency an Victorian furniture.* LOC: A697. PARK Nearby. TEL: 01668 281500; fax - 0166 282383; home - 01668 217281VAT: Stan/Spec.

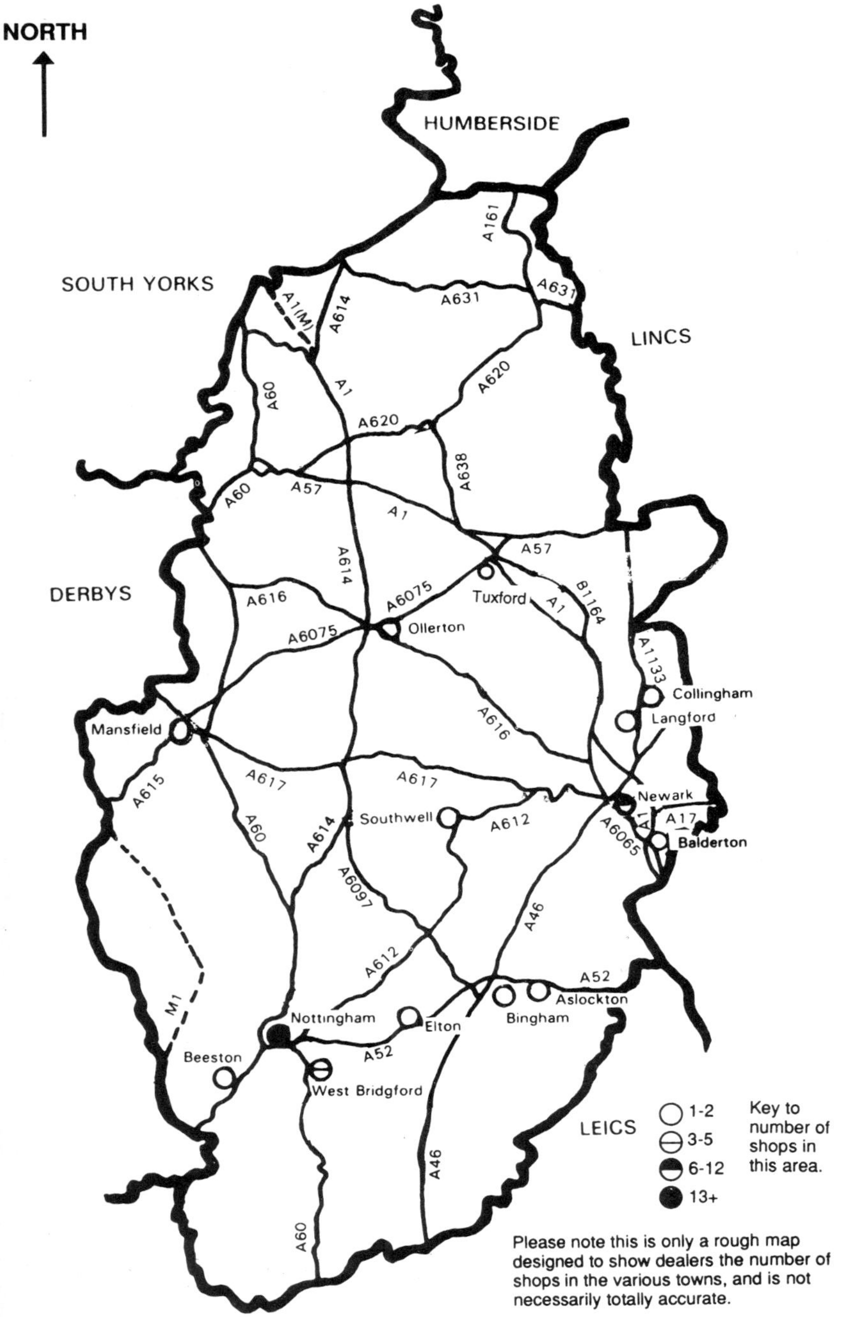

Please note this is only a rough map designed to show dealers the number of shops in the various towns, and is not necessarily totally accurate.

ASLOCKTON, Nr. Nottingham

Jane Neville Gallery

Elm House, Abbey Lane. NG13 9AE. (F Repetto-Wright and J. Neville). Resident. Es 1979. Open 10-4. SIZE: Medium. *STOCK Paintings and prints including sporting, 19th-20 C, £50-£5,000.* LOC: A52. PARK: Easy. TE 01949 850220. SER: Valuations; restoration framing; research; print publishers; buys auction (sporting paintings). VAT: Stan/Spec.

BALDERTON

Blacksmiths Forge

74 Main St. NG24 3NP. (K. and J. Sheppard). E 1982. Open 9-6, Sun. by appointment. SIZ Medium. *STOCK: Original pine furniture, so oak, Georgian to 1920, £20-£450; kitchenalia a pictures, £5-£100; fireplaces, cast iron and pi surrounds, Georgian to 1920, £20-£400.* LO Off A1, follow signs to village, turn right at traf lights, shop on right next to church. PARK: Eas TEL: 01636 700008; home - same. SER: Val ations; restorations; stripping; polishing; buys auction (furniture).

BEESTON

Elizabeth Bailey

33 Chilwell Rd. NG9 1EH. Est. 1966. Open 10 and 2-5.30. CL: Mon. and Thurs. SIZE: Sma *STOCK: Furniture, 18th C to shipping; sma and decorative items, lamps and light fittin some pine.* TEL: 0115 9255685; home - 01 9259259.

BINGHAM

E.M. Cheshire BADA LAPA

Banks House, The Banks. NG13 8BT. appointment only. *STOCK: Furniture, 17th oak; 18th-19th C mahogany, early metalwa* TEL: 01949 838861/838455. FAIRS: A premier. VAT: Stan/Spec.

COLLINGHAM, Nr. Newark

The Barn

NG23 7NL. (J. Richardson). Open by appoi ment. *STOCK: 18th-19th C furniture a furnishings, treen, textiles, linen and lace, Bax prints and licencees, Stevengraphs.* TEL: 016 892884.

ELTON, Nr. Bingham

Rectory Bungalow Workshop

Main Rd. NG13 9LF. (E.M. and Mrs M. Mackie). Est. 1981. Open Sat. 9.30-4.30 summer, 10-12 and 2-3 in winter, other times appointment. SIZE: Small. *STOCK: Furnitu*

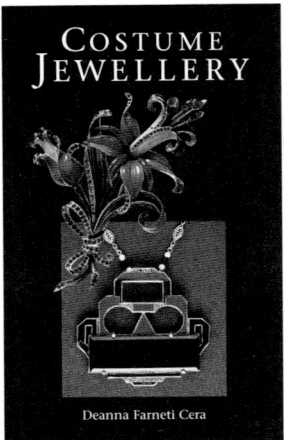

lton continued

8th-20th C; hand-painted, decorative items. OC: A52 between Nottingham and Grantham, ear Granby/Orston crossroads. PARK: Easy. EL: 01949 850330/850878; home - same. SER: estorations (cane and rush seating).

ANGFORD, Nr. Newark

. Baker

angford House Farm. NG23 7RR. Est. 1966. CL: un. except by appointment and Sat. SIZE: ledium. *STOCK: Victoriana, period furniture id oak.* LOC: A1133. PARK: Own. TEL: 01636)4026. *Trade Only.*

IANSFIELD

he Book Shelf

\ Albert St. NG18 1EA. (S. Payton). Open 9.30- CL: Wed. SIZE: Medium. *STOCK: Antiquarian id secondhand books.* LOC: Town centre. TEL: .623 648231; home - 01623 640601. SER: Book arch.

air Deal Antiques

38 Chesterfield Rd. North. NG19 7JD. (D.)we). Est. 1972. Open 9.30-5.30. CL: Sat. pm. d Sun. except by appointment. SIZE: Large. *'OCK: Shipping goods, £50-£100; furniture, ainly mahogany, Victorian, £100-£1,000; period rniture, metalware and small items.* PARK: sy. TEL: 01623 653768/512419. VAT: Stan. *ade Only.*

EWARK

astle Gate Antiques Centre

Castle Gate. NG24 1BE. Est. 1985. Open 9.30- SIZE: Large. LOC: A46 through town, 250yds. m castle. PARK: Easy. TEL: 01636 700076. R: Restorations. Below are listed the dealers at s centre.

& Barrington
Fine antique and modern silver. TEL: 0850 577724.

N. Bryan-Peach Antiques
18th-19th C furniture, clocks and barometers, metalware, £50-£3,000. TEL: Home - 01509 880425. VAT: Stan/Spec.

Evelyn Buckle Antiques
Oak and mahogany furniture, 18th-19th C; decorative items. TEL: Home - 01476 870796. VAT: Stan/Spec.

Mrs E.M. Cheshire BADA LAPADA
***18th and 19th C furniture and related items.* TEL: 01949 838455.**

Sylvia Cozens
Victorian and Edwardian mahogany furniture.

Newark continued

John Dench Antiques
17th-19th C oak, mahogany and walnut furniture; early English pottery. VAT: Stan/Spec.

Leasingham Antiques
18th-19th C mahogany and porcelain.

Parkside Antiques
Georgian and Victorian furniture, £100-£3,500. TEL: Home - 0115 920 9734. VAT: Stan/Spec.

Margaret M. Thompson Antiques LAPADA
***19th C oak and mahogany furniture, pictures and decorative items.* TEL: Home - 01949 850204. SER: Valuations. VAT: Stan/Spec.**

John Winterbotham
Oak and country furniture, 17th and 18th C.

R.R. Limb Antiques

31-35 Northgate. NG24 1HD. Open 9-6. *STOCK: General antiques and pianos.* TEL: 01636 74546.

Newark Antiques Centre

Regent House, Lombard St. NG24 1XP. (Marks Tinsley). Open 9.30-5, Sun. 11-4. SIZE: 55 units and 30 cabinets. *STOCK: Georgian, Victorian and period furniture, pottery, porcelain, glass, textiles, militaria, clocks, pictures, books, silver, antiquities, jewellery, paintings, coins, Oriental, pine, oil lamps.* TEL: 01636 605504.

Newark Antiques Warehouse

Old Kelham Rd. NG24 1BX. Open 8.30-5.30, Sat. 10-4. LOC: Just off A1. PARK: Easy. TEL: 01636 74869; fax - 01636 612933. Below are listed the dealers at this warehouse. *Trade Only.*

A. & J. Antiques
17th-19th C country furniture. VAT: Stan/Spec.

A. M. Antiques
17th-19th C furniture. VAT: Stan/Spec.

Atkinson Antiques
17th-19th C furniture and architectural items. VAT: Stan/Spec.

Chris Baylis
Windsor chairs and country furniture.

B. Benson
Furniture, clocks and decorative items.

John Dench Antiques
17th-19th C furniture, English pottery, decorative items, longcase clocks. VAT: Stan/Spec.

Dukeries Antiques
(J. and J. Coupe). *17th-19th C furniture; vintage and classic cars.* VAT: Stan/Spec.

D.J. Green Antiques
Furniture and decorative items. VAT: Stan/Spec.

Newark continued

R. Harrison
17th-19th C furniture.

C. Hicks
19th C furniture.

Highfield Antiques
19th C mahogany, walnut and shipping furniture. VAT: Stan/Spec.

R. Leverton
19th C and shipping furniture.

Mansfield Antiques
18th-19th C furniture and decorative items. VAT: Stan/Spec.

E. Snodgrass
18th-19th C furniture.

St. Georges Antiques
17th-19th C furniture. VAT: Stan/Spec.

Thompson Antiques
18th-19th C furniture. VAT: Stan/Spec.

Wickersley Antiques
Mainly Victorian and Edwardian furniture. VAT: Stan/Spec.

Portland Antiques
20 Portland St. NG24 4XG. Est. 1968. Open 9.30-5. CL: Mon.-Thurs. SIZE: Medium. *STOCK: General antiques and smalls, shipping items, £5-£1,000.* LOC: A46, 2 mins. from town centre. PARK: At rear. TEL: 01636 701478. SER: Valuations.

Portland Street Antiques Centre
Portland St. NG24 4XF. (Barbara Conlon). Est. 1972. Open 10-5. SIZE: 100 dealers. *STOCK: Furniture, Art Deco, clocks including longcase, silver, glass, ceramics, militaria, toys, dolls and taxidermy, mainly 18th-19th C, £1-£5,000.* LOC: A46 200 yards from traffic lights in town centre. PARK: Own at rear. TEL: 01636 74397; home - 01636 702836.

Jack Spratt Antiques
Unit 5, George St. NG24 1LU. Open 8-5.30, Sat. 8-4, Sun. 10.30-3.30. SIZE: Warehouse. *STOCK: Pine and oak.* PARK: Easy. TEL: 01636 707714/74853; fax - 01636 640595. VAT: Stan.

Tudor Rose Antiques Centre
12-13 Market Place. NG24 1DU. Open 10-5. SIZE: 25 cabinets + 10 stands. *STOCK: Furniture including oak and country, pine, mahogany and fine; metalware, copper, brass and silver, militaria, clocks, English, Continental and Oriental porcelain, pottery, glass, decorative items and soft furnishings, treen, toys, pictures and linen, dateline 1940.* PARK: Nearby. TEL: 01636 610311. VAT: Stan/Spec.

NOTTINGHAM

Antiques and General Trading Co
145 Lower Parliament St. NG1 1EE. (C. and M Drummond-Hoy). Est. 1965. Open 10-5. Cl Thurs. SIZE: Large. *STOCK: Furniture, fro 17th C oak to decorative furniture and objec £50-£5,000.* LOC: A52. PARK: At side. TE 0115 9585971; home - 01664 62184. SER: Val ations; restorations (furniture). VAT: Stan/Spec.

N.J. Doris - 'Dorisbooks'
Cathedral Antiques, 66-68 Derby Rd. NG1 5F Open 9.30-5. *STOCK: Books, antiquarian a secondhand; music, maps and prints.* TEL: 01 947 3913; fax - same.

The Golden Cage
99 Derby Rd., Canning Circus. NG5 4FE. (Pearson and J. Paradise). Open 10-5. *STOC Formal wear to buy or hire.* TEL: 01 9411600/9476478. SER: Hire (including 20' 40's and period costume); clothes copied to orde

Granny's Attic
308 Carlton Hill, Carlton. NG4 1GD. (Mrs Pembleton). Open Tues., Thur., Fri. and Sat. 9 *STOCK: Dolls, miniatures, general antiques a furniture.* TEL: 0115 9265204.

Harlequin Antiques
79 Mansfield Rd., Daybrook. (P.R. Hinchley a J.W. Attenborough). Est. 1992. Open daily, S by appointment. SIZE: Medium. *STOCK: 18 19th C pine furniture, £300-£1,200; oak a mahogany, 18th to early 19th C, £300-£1,0* LOC: A60 Mansfield road, north from Nottingha PARK: Easy. TEL: 01159 674590; home - 011 654197/569117. SER: Valuations; restoratic (oak and mahogany). FAIRS: Newark. VA Stan/Spec.

Hockley Coins
170 Derby Rd. NG7 1LR. (D.T. Peake). Open 4. CL: Thurs. *STOCK: Coins, medals, badg postcards, cigarette cards, toys, silver, colle ables.* TEL: 0115 9790667.

Melville Kemp Ltd LAPA
79-81 Derby Rd. NG1 5BA. Est. 1900. Open 5.30. CL: Thurs. SIZE: Small. *STOCK: Jew lery, Victorian; silver, Georgian and Victori both £5-£10,000; ornate English and Co nental porcelain, Sheffield plate.* LOC: Fr Nottingham on main Derby Rd. PARK: Ea TEL: 0115 9417055; fax - 0115 9417055. SE Valuations; restorations (silver, china, jew lery); buys at auction. VAT: Stan/Spec.

Michael D. Long - Trident Arms
96-98 Derby Rd. NG1 5FB. Est. 1970. Open 9. 5, Sat. 10-4. SIZE: Large. *STOCK: Arms armour of all ages and nations.* LOC: From centre take main Derby Rd., shop on right. PA Easy. TEL: 0115 9474137; fax - 0115 9414 SER: Valuations. VAT: Stan/Spec.

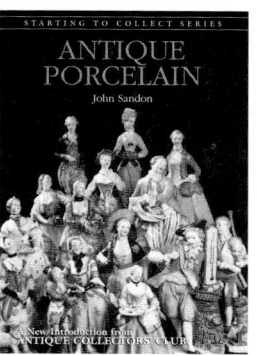

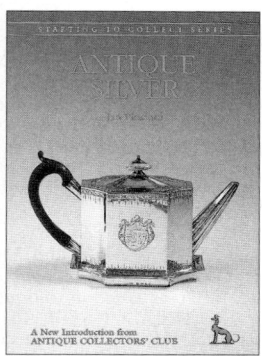

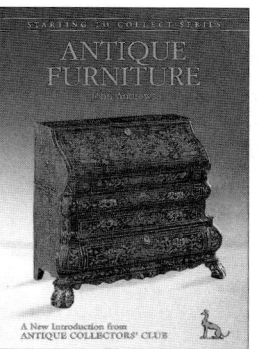

Nottingham continued

Meadow Lane Antiques
Meadow Lane. NG2 3HG. (Dave Buckley). Open 8-6, Sat. 7.30-2.30 and Sun. prior to Newark Antiques Fair. SIZE: Large warehouse. *STOCK: Period, Victorian, Edwardian and reproduction furniture (including pine) and shipping goods, smalls and bric-a-brac for US, European and Japanese markets; brass and iron beds.* LOC: Opposite Arthur Johnson's Auction Rooms, near Trent bridge. 30 minutes from Newark Showground. TEL: 0115 9867374; fax - 0115 9867375; e-mail - 106213.2444@compuserve.com. SER: Container packing; export facilities.

Anthony Mitchell Fine Paintings
Sunnymede House, 11 Albemarle Rd., Woodthorpe. NG5 4FE. (M. Mitchell). Est. 1965. Open by appointment. *STOCK: Oil paintings, £2,000-£100,000; watercolours, £500-£30,000.* LOC: North on Nottingham ring road to junction with Mansfield road, turn right, then 3rd left. PARK: Easy. TEL: 0115 9623865; fax - same. SER: Valuations; restorations. VAT: Spec.

Pegasus Antiques
62 Derby Rd. NG1 5FD. (P. and J. Clewer). Open 9.30-5. *STOCK: Fine 18th-19th C furniture, paintings, silver, jewellery, metalware.* TEL: 0115 9474220.

S. Pembleton
306 Carlton Hill, Carlton. Open Tues., Thur. and Fri. 9-5, Sat. 10-5. *STOCK: General antiques.* TEL: 0115 9265204.

David and Carole Potter Antiques
LAPADA
76 Derby Rd. NG1 5FD. Est. 1966. Open 10-4. CL: Mon. SIZE: Medium. *STOCK: Clocks, 18th-19th C, £50-£5,000; period furniture, 17th-19th C; pottery, porcelain and glass, 18th-19th C, £20-£7,000; trade and shipping goods.* LOC: From Nottingham centre, take main Derby Rd., shop on right. PARK: Easy. TEL: 0115 9417911; mobile - 0973 689962. VAT: Stan/Spec.

Val Smith Coins and Antiques
170 Derby Rd. NG7 1LR. Open 10-4.30. CL: Thurs. *STOCK: Coins, medals, badges, postcards, cigarette cards, toys, jewellery, small collectables.* TEL: 0115 9781194.

Top Hat Antiques Centre
70-72 Derby Rd. NG1 3EN. (Top Hat Exhibitions Ltd). Est. 1978. Open 9.30-5. SIZE: Large. *STOCK: Furniture, Georgian to Edwardian; small porcelain and metal items, to Art Deco; oils, watercolours and prints, 19th-20th C, £30-£1,000.* LOC: A52 town centre. PARK: Easy. TEL: 0115 9419143; home - 0115 9258769. VAT: Stan/Spec.

Nottingham continued

Vintage Wireless Shop
The Hewarths, Sandiacre. NG10 5NQ. (Mr Yates). *STOCK: Early wireless and pre-war televisions, crystal sets, horn speakers, valves, books and magazines.* TEL: 0115 9393139; fax - 0115 9490180; mobile - 0860 362655.

OLLERTON

Hamlyn Lodge
Station Rd. NG22 9BN. (N., J.S. and M.J Barrows). Open 10-5, Sat. and Sun. by appointment. SIZE: Small. *STOCK: General antiques 18th-19th C, £100-£3,000.* LOC: Off A614. PARK: Easy. TEL: 01623 823600. SER: Restorations (furniture).

SOUTHWELL

Strouds (of Southwell Antiques)
3-7 Church St. NG25 0HQ. (V.N. and J. Stroud). Est. 1972. Open 9.30-5, or by appointment. SIZE: Large. *STOCK: Furniture, clocks, metalware and decorative items, 17th-19th C, £10-£50,000.* LOC: Town centre. PARK: Easy. TEL: 0163 815001. VAT: Stan/Spec.

TUXFORD

Sally Mitchell's Gallery
9 Eldon St. NG22 0LB. FATG. Est. 1966. Open 10-5, Sun. by appointment. SIZE: Medium. *STOCK: Contemporary sporting and animal paintings, £200-£5,000; limited edition sporting and animal prints, 20th C, £20-£350; sporting paintings.* LOC: 1 minute from A1, 14 miles north of Newark. PARK: Easy. TEL: 01777 83 234/655. FAIRS: CLA Game and Burghley Horse Trials. VAT: Stan/Spec.

WEST BRIDGFORD

Bridgford Antiques
2A Rushworth Ave. NG2 7LF. Open 10-5, Sat. 10-1. SIZE: Small. *STOCK: Furniture and general antiques, pictures, books and postcards.* LOC: Opposite County Hall. TEL: 011 9821835; home - 0115 9817161.

Joan Cotton (Antiques)
5 Davies Rd. NG2 5JE. Est. 1969. Open 9-4.3 CL: Wed. *STOCK: General antiques, Victorian jewellery, silver, china, glass and bygones.* LOC: 1/2 mile along Bridgford Rd. from Trent Bridge in town centre. PARK: On forecourt. TEL: 01 9813043.

Moulton's Antiques
5 Portland Rd. NG2 6DN. (J. Moulton). Open 1 5. CL: Mon. *STOCK: General antiques; fabric* TEL: 0115 9814354; home - 0115 9815973. SER: Restorations (furniture); stripping (pine); pi furniture made to order.

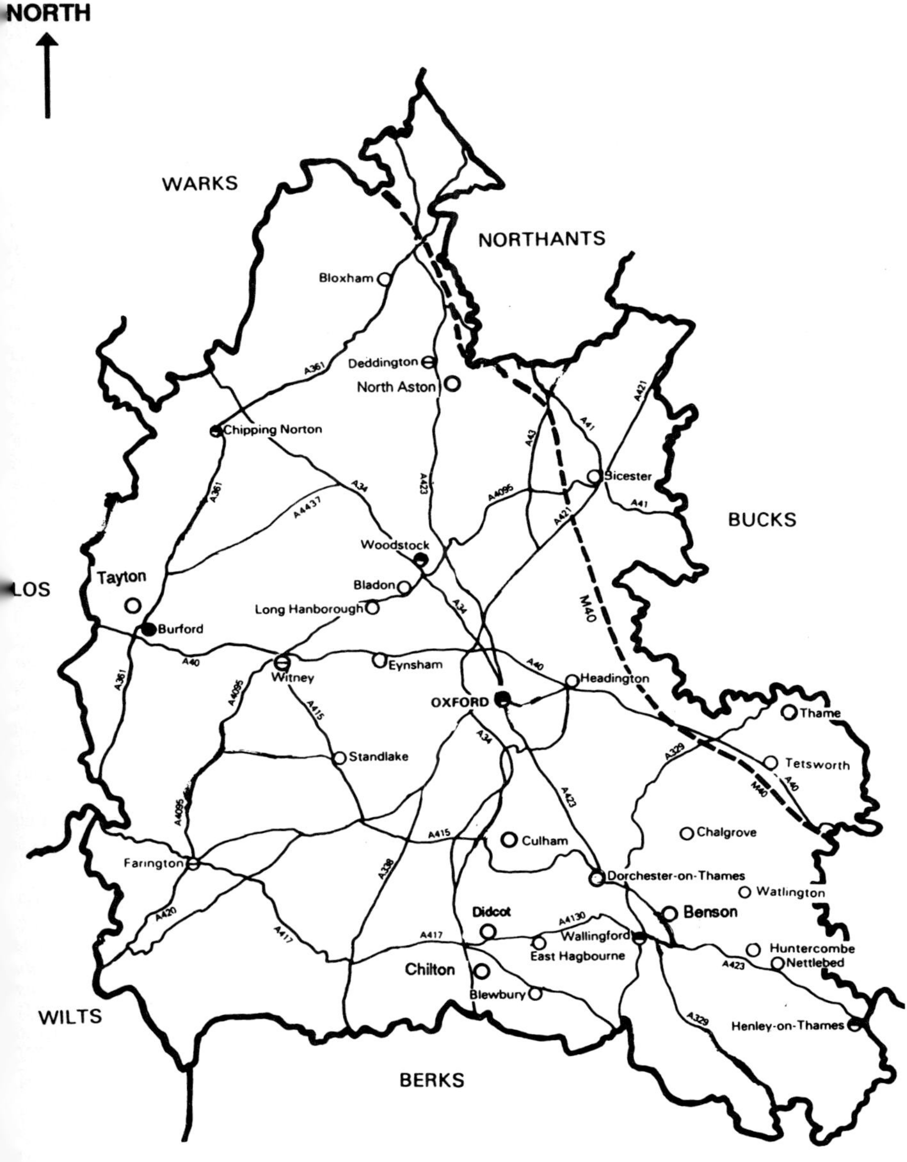

1-2
3-5
6-12
13+

Key to number of shops in this area.

Please note this is only a rough map designed to show dealers the number of shops in the various towns, and is not necessarily totally accurate.

ASTON TIRROLD, Nr. Didcot

John Harrison Fine Art

Skirmers, Aston St. OX11 9DQ. (J.M.C. Harrison). TVADA. Open strictly by appointment. *STOCK: Drawings and watercolours, 18th-19th C.* TEL: 01235 850260. SER: Commissions undertaken.

BENSON, Nr. Wallingford

Benson Antiques and Gallery

The Old Bakehouse, Castle Sq. OX10 6SD. (Dane Clouston). TVADA. Est. 1978. Open 10-5, Sun. 2-5. CL: Mon. SIZE: Medium. *STOCK: Furniture, 17th to early 20th C, £100-£5,000; ceramics, glass, silver, 18th to early 20th C, £5-£1,000; bronze, pewter, oils and watercolours, 19th-20th C, £25-£5,000.* LOC: Village centre. PARK: Easy. TEL: 01491 832525. SER: Valuations. FAIRS: TVADA.

BICESTER

Lisseter of Bicester

3 Kings End. OX6 7DR. (D. Lisseter). Est. 1945. Open 9-5. *STOCK: Furniture, all periods; Victoriana.* PARK: Easy, opposite. TEL: 01869 252402. VAT: Stan/Spec.

BLADON, Nr. Woodstock

Park House Tearoom & Antiques

26 Park St. OX7 0BY. (H.R. and T. Thomas). Resident. Open daily. *STOCK: Small furniture and decorative smalls.* PARK: Own. TEL: 01993 812817; fax - 01993 812912. SER: Valuations; restorations.

BLEWBURY

Blewbury Antiques

London Rd. OX11 9NX. (S. and E. Richardson). Est. 1973. Open 10-6 including weekends. CL: Tues. *STOCK: General antiques, books, bric-a-brac, country and garden items, oil lamps and oil lamp parts.* PARK: Easy. TEL: 01235 850366.

BLOXHAM, Nr. Banbury

H.C. Dickins

High St. OX15 4LT. (P. and H.R. Dickins). Open 10-5.30, Sat. 10-1. *STOCK: 19th-20th C British sporting and landscape paintings, watercolours, drawings and prints.* TEL: 01295 721949.

BURFORD

Ashton Gower Antiques LAPADA

Cheltenham Rd., Burford Roundabout. OX18 4JA. (C. Gower and B. Ashton). Est. 1987. Open 10-5.30 and Sun. pm. *STOCK: English and*

Burford continued

***Continental furniture, mirrors and decorati accessories, 18th-20th C, £25-£5,000.* LOC: O roundabout (A40) Oxford/Cheltenham roac PARK: Easy. TEL: 01993 822450; fax - sam SER: Valuations; restorations; buys at auctio VAT: Stan/Spec.**

Burford Antique Centre

Cheltenham Rd., At the Roundabout. (C Viventi). Est. 1979. Open 10-6 including Su SIZE: Large. *STOCK: Furniture, 18th-19th C £100-£5,000; china and pictures.* LOC: A4 PARK: Easy. TEL: 01993 823227. SE Restorations (furniture including re-leathering).

The Burford Gallery

Classica House, High St. OX18 4QA. (I Etheridge). Est. 1976. Open 9.30-5.30. SIZ Medium. *STOCK: British and Continental wate colours, 18th-20th C, £40-£6,000.* LOC: 400yd from A40 roundabout. PARK: Easy. TEL: 019 822305; home - same. SER: Valuations; framir and mounting; buys at auction (watercolours VAT: Spec.

Denver House Antiques and Collectables

Denver House, Witney St. OX8 4RU. (T. and Radman). Resident. Est. 1976. Open 10-5.3 Sun. by appointment. SIZE: Medium. *STOC Coins and medals, B.C. to date; orders, meda badges, decorations, military books, police a fire brigade memorabilia, stamps and pap money, 1560 to date; maps, books.* PARK: Ea and nearby. TEL: 01993 822040 (24 hours); fa 01993 822769. SER: Valuations; restoratio (maps and bank notes); buys at auction (coir stamps, medals, sovereign and stamp cases, ma covers and tokens). VAT: Stan.

Jonathan Fyson Antiques

50 High St. OX18 4QF. (J.R. Fyson). CAD Est. 1970. Open 9.30-1 and 2-5.30. SIZ Medium. *STOCK: English and Continent furniture, decorative brass and steel includi lighting and fireplace accessories; papier mâc tôle, treen, porcelain, glass, jewellery.* LOC: junction of A40/A361 between Oxford a Cheltenham. PARK: Easy. TEL: 01993 8232 fax - same; home - 01367 860223. SE Valuations. VAT: Spec.

Gateway Antiques

Cheltenham Rd., Burford Roundabout. OX8 4J (M.C. Ford and P. Brown). CADA. Est. 19 Open 10-5.30 and Sun. pm. SIZE: Lar *STOCK: English and Continental furniture, 18 19th C; decorative accessories.* LOC: roundabout (A40) Oxford/Cheltenham ro PARK: Easy. TEL: 01993 823678. SE Valuations. VAT: Stan/Spec.

urford continued

Iorseshoe Antiques and Gallery
7 High St. OX18 4QA. (B. Evans). Open 9-5.30, un. by appointment only. SIZE: Medium. *TOCK: Clocks including longcase (all fully 'stored); early oak and country furniture; oil aintings and watercolours; copper and brass, orse brasses.* LOC: East side of High St. PARK: asy. TEL: 01993 823244; home - 01993 822429. AT: Spec.

Iubert's Antiques LAPADA
urford Roundabout, Cheltenham Rd. OX18 IA. (Michael R. Hinds). Est. 1987. Open 10-30. SIZE: Large. *STOCK: Furniture, £150-10,000; oils, £50-£5,000; clocks, £250-£5,000; l 17th-19th C.* LOC: A40 half way between xford and Cheltenham. TEL: 01993 822151; x - same.

nthony Nielsen Antiques
) High St. OX18 4QF. Est. 1977. Open 9.30-1 d 2-5.30. SIZE: Large. *STOCK: Furniture, ahogany, walnut, rosewood, oak, William and ary to Edwardian, £200-£20,000; copper, brass, 20-£500.* PARK: Easy. TEL: 01993 822014; fax ame; after hours - 01451 821710.

Burford continued

Old George Inn Antique Galleries
104 High St. (E. Lyle-Cameron). Est. 1992. Open 10-5, Sun. 12-5. SIZE: Large. *STOCK: General antiques including oak, mahogany, china and treen, early 18th C to 1930's.* LOC: Main road. PARK: Around corner. TEL: 01993 823319.

David Pickup BADA
115 High St. OX18 4RG. CADA. Est. 1977. Open 9.30-1 and 2-5.30, Sat. 10-1 and 2-4. SIZE: Medium. *STOCK: Fine furniture, from £1,000+; works of art, £500-£10,000; decorative objects, from £100+; all late 17th-19th C.* PARK: Easy. TEL: 01993 822555. FAIRS: New York International; BADA. VAT: Spec.

Richard Purdon BADA
158 High St. OX18 4QY. CADA. Open 9.30-5.30. SIZE: Medium. *STOCK: Antique Eastern and European carpets, village and tribal rugs, needlework, textiles and related items.* TEL: 01993 823777; fax - 01993 823719. SER: Valuations; restorations. VAT: Stan/Spec.

Manfred Schotten Antiques
109 High St. OX18 4RH. CADA. Est. 1974. Open 9-5.30 or by appointment. *STOCK: Sporting antiques and library furniture.* TEL: 01993 822302; fax - 01993 822055. SER: Restorations.

Burford continued

The Stone Gallery
93 High St. OX18 4QA. (Mrs Phyllis M. and Simon Marshall). Est. 1918. Open 9.15-6. SIZE: Medium. *STOCK: Pre-Raphaelite and modern British pictures, 1840-1980, £120-£30,000; paperweights, from 1845, £50-£15,000; enamel boxes, from 1760, £50-£1,000.* LOC: Halfway down High St. PARK: Easy. TEL: 01993 823302; fax/home - same. SER: Valuations (paperweights); buys at auction (pictures and paperweights). VAT: Stan/Spec.

Swan Gallery LAPADA
High St. OX18 4RE. (D. Pratt). CADA. Est. 1966. Open 9.30-5.30. SIZE: Large. *STOCK: Country furniture in oak, yew, walnut and fruitwood, 17th-19th C, £300-£9,000; oil paintings; Staffordshire figures and small decorative items, 18th-20th C, £50-£800.* PARK: Easy. TEL: 01993 822244. VAT: Mainly Spec.

Zene Walker, Burford
The Bull House, High St. OX8 3RG. (A.E. Walker). Est. 1954. Open 9-5. SIZE: Large. *STOCK: 18th-19th C English furniture.* TEL: 01993 823284. VAT: Stan/Spec.

Wren Gallery
4 Bear Court, High St. OX18 4RR. (S. Hall and G. Mitchell). Est. 1986. Open 10-5.30. SIZE: Medium. *STOCK: 19th-20th C watercolours and drawings.* TEL: 01993 823495. SER: Valuations; restorations (watercolours); buys at auction (watercolours). VAT: Spec.

CHALGROVE, Nr. Oxford

Rupert Hitchcox Antiques
Warpsgrove Lane. OX44 7RW. (P. and R. Hitchcox). Est. 1957. Open 10-5, Sun. 2-5 or by appointment. SIZE: Large - 6 barns. *STOCK: Georgian, Victorian, Edwardian and 1920's furniture.* LOC: Halfway between Oxford and Henley, just off the B480, 6 miles from junction 6 M40. TEL: 01865 890241; fax - same. VAT: Stan/Spec.

CHILTON, Nr. Oxford

Country Markets Antiques and Collectables
at Country Gardens Garden Centre, Newbury Rd. OX11 0QN. Est. 1991. Open 10-5.30, Mon. 10.30-5.30, Sun. 10.30-4.30. SIZE: Large - 30 dealers. *STOCK: Wide variety of general antiques including furniture, books, jewellery and porcelain, £5-£5,000.* LOC: Off A34 near Harwell, 10 mins. from junction 13, M4, 20 mins. from Oxford. PARK: Easy. TEL: 01235 835125; fax - 01235 831266. SER: Restorations (furniture and ceramics).

CHIPPING NORTON

Bugle Antiques LAPAD
9 Horsefair. OX7 5AL. (M. and D. Hardin Hill). CADA. Est. 1971. Open 9.30-6. *STOC Windsor chairs, including sets; English count furniture in oak, elm and fruitwood; dresser bureaux and large tables.* TEL: 01608 64332 fax - same. VAT: Stan/Spec.

Chipping Norton Antique Centre
Ivy House, 1 Middle Row and 21/44 West St. OX 5NH. (G. Wissinger). Open 10-5.30 including Su SIZE: 20 dealers. *STOCK: A wide variety of sma and furniture.* PARK: Own. TEL: 01608 644212.

The Emporium
26 High St. OX7 5AD. Open 10-1 and 2-5.3 Collectors Room open 2-5, Sat. 10-1 and 2-5. C Mon. *STOCK: Bric-a-brac, china, glass, pos cards and prints.* TEL: 01608 643103.

Georgian House Antiques LAPAI
21 West St. OX7 5EU. Open 9-6. *STOCK: 17t 19th C furniture and paintings.* TEL: 016 641369.

Jonathan Howard
21 Market Place. OX7 5NA. (J.G. Howard). E 1979. Open by appointment or ring bell. SIZ Small. *STOCK: Clocks - longcase, wall a carriage, 18th-19th C.* PARK: Easy. TEL: 016 643065. SER: Valuations; restorations (moveme dials and cases).

Key Antiques BA
11 Horse Fair. OX7 5AL. (D. and Robinson). CADA. Resident. Open 9.30-5.30 by appointment. SIZE: Medium. *STOC Period oak and country furniture, domes metalware including lighting and downhear equipment, early carvings, firemarks, ke* LOC: On main road. PARK: Easy. TE 01608 643777. VAT: Spec.

Station Mill Antiques
Station Mill, Station Rd. OX7. (R. Stewart). E 1994. Open 10-5 including Sun. SIZE: Lar *STOCK: Furniture, fine art, bric-a-brac a collectables, 17th-20th C, £2-£2,000.* LOC: Just of town off A44 towards Moreton in Marsh. PAR Easy. TEL: 01608 644563; fax - same; hom 01608 641828. SER: Valuations; restorations.

TRADA
21 High St. OX7 5AD. Open 9-5.30. CL: Thu *STOCK: Antiquarian prints, maps and engravin 1600-1900.* TEL: 01608 644325. SER: Pr renovation and colouring; picture frame making

Peter Wiggins
Raffles Farm, Southcombe. OX7 5QH. Est. 19 Usually available. *STOCK: Barometers.* LOC mile from Chipping Norton on A34. TEL: 01 642652; home - same. SER: Valuations; rest ations (barometers, clocks, automata); cl repairs; buys at auction.

CULHAM, Nr. Abingdon

Rob Dixon Fine Engravings
Warren Farmhouse, Thame Lane. OX14 3DT. By appointment only. *STOCK: Fine and decorative English and French prints, to 18th C; portraits including fine mezzotints, 16th-19th C; period frames.* LOC: Behind European School. TEL: 01235 524676.

DEDDINGTON

Castle Antiques Ltd LAPADA
Manor Farm, Clifton. OX15 0PA. (J. and J. Vaughan). Est. 1968. Open 10-5. SIZE: Large. *STOCK: Furniture, £25-£3,000; silver, metalware, £10-£1,000; pottery, porcelain, £10-£200; kitchenalia.* LOC: B4031 (Aynho Road), 6 miles from junction 10, M40. PARK: Easy. TEL: 01869 338688; evenings - 01869 338294. VAT: Stan/Spec.

Deddington Antiques Centre
Laurel House, Bull Ring, Market Sq. OX15 0TT. (Mrs. B.J. Haller). TVADA. Est. 1972. Open 10-5. SIZE: Medium -16 dealers. *STOCK: Furniture, Georgian to Edwardian, £30-1,000; porcelain, silver, pictures, 1800-1930, £10-£400; collectables, £10-£200.* LOC: Off A4260 Oxford-Banbury road at Deddington traffic lights. PARK: Easy, free. TEL: 01869 338968; fax - 01869 338916. SER: Valuations. FAIRS: NEC.

Deddington continued

Tuckers Country Store and Art Gallery
Market Place. OX15 0SA. (R. Gregory). Ope daily and Sun. SIZE: Medium. *STOCK: Furnitu including country pine, collectors' items, 18th 19th C, £25-£500; oils and watercolours, main 19th C, £50-£1,000; clocks, wall and mante Victorian linen and costume.* PARK: Outside TEL: 01869 338215; home - 01295 812266. SER Valuations; restorations; cleaning (oil paintings VAT: Stan./Spec.

DIDCOT

Didcot Antiques Centre
220 The Broadway. (Dr. A. Vetta). TVADA. Es 1995. Open 10-5, Sun. 11-4. CL: Mon. SIZE Large. *STOCK: Furniture, £50-£1,000; silver an plate, books and ephemera, all 19th-20th C* PARK: Own. TEL: 01235 510819; fax - 0123 512178. SER: Valuations; buys at auction.

DORCHESTER-ON-THAMES

Dorchester Antiques LAPAD
(formerly The Shambles) The Barn, 3 High S OX10 7HH. (J. and S. Hearnden). TVADA Est. 1992. Open Tues.-Sun. 10-5. SIZE Medium. *STOCK: Chairs and decorativ country pieces, 18th-19th C.* LOC: Opposit Abbey. PARK: Easy. TEL: 01865 34137 SER: Restorations; upholstery; finder.

Dorchester-on-Thames continued

Hallidays (Fine Antiques) Ltd LAPADA
The Old College, High St. OX10 7HL. TVADA. Est. 1950. Open 9-5, Sat. 10-1 and 2-4. SIZE: Large. *STOCK: Furniture, 17th-19th C, £100-£40,000; paintings, 18th-19th C, £100-£20,000; decorative and small items, pine and marble mantelpieces, firegrates, fenders, 18th-20th C; room panelling.* PARK: At rear. TEL: 01865 340028; fax - 01865 341149. FAIRS: Olympia. VAT: Stan/Spec.

EAST HAGBOURNE

Craig Barfoot
Tudor House. OX11 9LR. (I.C. Barfoot). Est. 1993. Open any time by appointment. SIZE: Medium. *STOCK: Longcase clocks, £1,500-£8,500; wall clocks, £250-£1,000; all 1700-1900; lantern clocks.* LOC: Just off A34 halfway between Oxford and Newbury. PARK: Easy. TEL: 01235 818968; home - same. SER: Restorations (clocks); buys at auction (clocks, English oak furniture). VAT: Stan/Spec.

E.M. Lawson and Co
Kingsholm. OX11 9LN. (W.J. and K.M. Lawson). Est. 1921. Usually open 10-5 but appointment preferred. CL: Sat. *STOCK: Antiquarian and rare books, 1500-1900.* PARK: Easy. TEL: 01235 812033. VAT: Stan.

EYNSHAM, Nr. Oxford

John Wilson (Autographs) Ltd
50 Acre End St. OX8 1PD. ABA. Est. 1967. Open 9-6, Sat. by appointment. SIZE: Large. *STOCK: Autograph letters, historical documents, manuscripts, £10-£50,000.* LOC: From Oxford, off the A40 towards Cheltenham. PARK: Easy. TEL: 01865 880883. SER: Valuations; commissions. FAIRS: ABA London. VAT: Stan/Spec/Global.

FARINGDON

Aston Pine Antiques
16-18 London St. SN7 7AA. (P. O'Gara). Est. 1982. Open Thurs.-Sat. 9-5. *STOCK: Victorian and Continental pine; Victorian fireplaces, doors and bathrooms.* TEL: 01367 243840.

The Faringdon Antique Centre
35 Marlborough St. SN7 7JL. Open 10-5 including Sun. CL: Mon. except Bank Holidays. SIZE: Large. *STOCK: Mahogany, oak, walnut and pine furniture, Georgian to Edwardian, £500-£1,000+.* LOC: Off A420 at Faringdon roundabout, signposted A417 Lechlade, opposite Peugeot garage. PARK: Easy. TEL: 01367 243650. SER: Valuations; restorations (furniture, clocks, porcelain and china).

La Chaise Antique LAPADA
30 London St. SN7 7AA. (Roger Clark). Est. 1968. Open 10-6. CL: Sun. except by appointment. SIZE: Large. *STOCK: Chairs, pre-1860; furniture, 18th-19th C; general antiques, decorators' items.* Not Stocked: Silver, porcelain and glass. LOC: A420. PARK: At rear. TEL: 01367 240427; mobile - 0831 205002; fax - 01367 241001. SER: Valuations; restorations; upholstery (leather and fabrics); table top liners. FAIRS: NEC (April and Aug); LAPADA NEC (Jan.). VAT: Spec.

HEADINGTON, Nr. Oxford

Barclay Antiques
107 Windmill Rd. OX3 7BT. (C. Barclay). Est. 1979. Open 10-5.30. CL: Wed. SIZE: Small. *STOCK: Porcelain, silver and jewellery, 18th-19th C, £50-£100; period lamps, 20th C, £50-£500.* PARK: Easy. TEL: 01865 69551. SER: Valuations. FAIRS: Oxford.

HENLEY-ON-THAMES

Friday Street Antique Centre

4 Friday St. RG9 4QL. Open 9.30-5.30, Sun. 12-5. SIZE: 10 dealers. *STOCK: Furniture, china, silver, engravings and prints.* LOC: First left after Henley bridge, then first right, business on left. PARK: Nearby. TEL: 01491 574104. SER: Valuations; buys at auction.

Henley Antique Centre

Rotherfield Arcade, 2-4 Reading Rd. RG9 1AG. Open 9.30-6, Sun. 12-6 including Bank Holidays. SIZE: Large. *STOCK: General antiques, curios and fine arts.* TEL: 01491 411468.

The Barry M. Keene Gallery

12 Thameside. RG9 1BH. (B.M. and J.S. Keene). TVADA, FATG. Est. 1971. Open 9.30-5.30, Sun. 11-5.30, and by appointment. *STOCK: Watercolours, drawings, paintings, etchings, prints, 18th to early 20th C, contemporary works and sculpture.* LOC: Junction 8/9 M4, over bridge, immediate left, 5th building on right. TEL: 01491 577119. SER: Restorations; framing, cleaning, relining, gilding, export. VAT: Stan/Spec.

Richard J. Kingston BADA

95 Bell St. RG9 2BD. TVADA. Open 9.30-5 or by appointment. SIZE: Medium. *STOCK: Furniture, 17th to early 19th C; silver, porcelain, glass, paintings, antiquarian and secondhand books.* PARK: Easy. TEL: 01491 574535; home - 01491 573133. SER: Restorations. FAIRS: Surrey, Buxton, Snape. VAT: Stan/Spec.

Market Lane Antiques

20 Market Place. RG9 2AH. (David Potter). Open 10.15-5.15, Sun. 11-4. SIZE: 4 dealers. *STOCK: General antiques.* TEL: 01491 411162/576365.

Thames Gallery

Thameside. RG9 2LJ. (S. Came). TVADA. Open 10-5. *STOCK: Georgian and Victorian silver; paintings, 19th C.* TEL: 01491 572449; fax - 01491 410273.

Thames Oriental Rug Co

Thames Carpet Cleaners Ltd, 48/56 Reading Rd. RG9 1AG. (D. Benardout and C. Aigin). Resident. Est. 1955. Open 9-12.30 and 1.30-5, Sat. 9-12.30. SIZE: Medium. *STOCK: Oriental rugs, mid-19th C to modern.* PARK: Easy. TEL: 01491 574676. SER: Valuations; restorations and cleaning (carpets). VAT: Stan.

HUNTERCOMBE

The Country Seat LAPADA

Huntercombe Manor Barn. RG9 5RY. (W. Clegg and H. Ferry). TVADA. Est. 1965. Open 9-5.30, Sun. by appointment. SIZE: Large. *STOCK: Furniture - English, 1660-1830, signed*

Huntercombe continued

***and designed, 1830-1900, Chinese, 19th C; ar pottery and metalwork, garden statuary and fur niture; panelled rooms, lighting and upholstere furniture.* LOC: 200 yds down right-hand tur off A4130 Nettlebed-Wallingford. PARK: Eas TEL: 01491 641349; fax - 01491 641533. SER Restorations; buys at auction. VAT: Spec.**

LONG HANBOROUGH

David A. Hallett Antiques (Hanborough Antiques)

125 and 127 Main Rd. OX7 2JX. Open 10.3(4.30 (Sun. 2-4.30 from Easter through summer CL: Mon. SIZE: Medium. *STOCK: Furnitur country and period; pottery, porcelain, Vi toriana, rural and domestic bygones, brass an copper, collectors' items.* LOC: Going north fro Oxford on A34 turn left before Woodstock on t A4095 near Witney. PARK: Easy. TEL: 0199 882767.

NETTLEBED, Nr. Henley-on-Thames

Willow Antiques and The Nettlebed Antique Merchants

The Barns, 1 High St. RG9 5AA. (Willo Bicknell and Michael Plummer). TVADA. Ope Tues.-Sat 9-5.30, Sun. 11-4, other times b appointment. SIZE: Large. *STOCK: Decorativ fine and unusual furniture, objects and deco ations, including architectural items.* LOC Between Wallingford and Henley on A407 PARK: Easy. TEL: 01491 642062; mobile - 037 152353. SER: Cottage Upholstery - fabric upholstery.

NORTH ASTON

Elizabeth Harvey-Lee

1 West Cottages, Middle Aston Lane. OX6 3Q TVADA. Est. 1986. Open by appointmen *STOCK: Original prints, 15th-20th C; artist etchings, engravings, lithographs, £100-£6,00* LOC: 6 miles from junction 10, M40, 15 mil north of Oxford. TEL: 01869 347164. SE Illustrated catalogue available twice yearly (£ p.a.). FAIRS: London Original Print, Roy Academy. VAT: Spec.

Gerald E. Marsh (Antique Clocks) BAD

Jericho House. OX6 4HX. Open by appoin ment only. *STOCK: Clocks, watches, bar meters; some furniture, mid-18th C an Regency.* TEL: 01869 340087; fax - same.

ↄXFORD

ℨlackwell's Rare Books
8 Holywell St. OX1 3SW. Est. 1879. Open 9-6, 'ues. 9.30-6. *STOCK: Antiquarian and rare ıodern books.* TEL: 01865 792792; fax - 01865 48833; internet - http://www.blackwell.co.uk/ ookshops/rarebooks/; e-mail - rarebooks@ ·lackwell.co.uk. SER: Buys at auction. VAT: 'tan/Spec.

The Corner Shop
Valton St. (P. Hitchcox and D. Florey). Est. 1978.)pen 10-5. *STOCK: Pictures, china, glass, silver, mall furniture and general items.* LOC: Central .orth Oxford. TEL: 01865 553364.

Reginald Davis Ltd BADA
4 High St. OX1 4AN. Est. 1941. Open 9-5. CL: 'hurs. *STOCK: Silver, English and Continental, 7th to early 19th C; jewellery, Sheffield plate, ieorgian and Victorian.* Not Stocked: Glass, hina, pewter. LOC: On A40. PARK: Easy. EL: 01865 248347. SER: Valuations; restor-tions (silver, jewellery). VAT: Stan/Spec.

eremy's (Oxford Stamp Centre)
8 Cowley Rd. OX4 1JE. Open 10-12.30 and 2-5. *TOCK: Stamps, postcards and cigarette cards.* 'EL: 01865 241011.

Christopher Legge Oriental Carpets
5 Oakthorpe Rd., Summertown. OX2 7BD. (C.T. .egge). Est. 1970. SIZE: Medium. *STOCK: Rugs, arious sizes, 19th-early 20th C, £100-£6,000.* .OC: Near shopping parade. PARK: Easy. TEL: 1865 57572; fax - 01865 54877. SER: Valu-tions; restorations; re-weaving; handcleaning. 'AT: Stan.

.aurie Leigh Antiques LAPADA
6 High St. OX1 4AN. (L. and D. Leigh). Est. 963. Open 10.30-5.30. CL: Thurs. *STOCK: ilass, keyboard musical instruments, clocks.* 'EL: 01865 244197. VAT: Stan/Spec.

Magna Gallery
1 High St. OX1 4AP. (Martin J. Blant). TVADA. st. 1969. Open 10-5.30. SIZE: Medium. *STOCK: Maps especially Oxfordshire, general topography, rints including botanical, caricatures, 1550-895.* TEL: 01865 245805. SER: Valuations; aming. VAT: Stan.

The Oxford Antique Trading Co
0/41 Park End St. OX1 1JD. (D.A. Jones and .S.J. Howse). Open 10-6. SIZE: Large. *STOCK: 'eneral antiques, from 18th C to 1930s, £50-5,000.* LOC: 150yds. from railway station. ARK: Easy. TEL: 01865 793927. SER: Valu-tions; restorations (furniture, upholstery). VAT: tan/Spec.

Oxford continued

Payne and Son (Goldsmiths) Ltd BADA
131 High St. OX1 4DH. (E.P., G.N. and J.D. Payne, P.J. Coppock, A. Salmon, D. Thornton). Est. 1790. Open weekdays 9-5. SIZE: Medium. *STOCK: British silver, antique, modern and secondhand; jewellery, all £50-£10,000+.* LOC: Town centre near Carfax traffic lights. PARK: 800yds. TEL: 01865 243787; fax - 01865 793241. SER: Restorations (English silver). VAT: Stan/Spec.

Sanders of Oxford Ltd
104 High St. OX1 4BW. Open 10-6 , Sun. 11-4. SIZE: Large. *STOCK: Prints, especially Oxford; maps and Japanese woodcuts.* TEL: 01865 242590; fax - 01865 721748. VAT: Stan/Spec.

A.J. Saywell Ltd. (The Oxford Stamp Shop)
15 Hollybush Row. OX1 1JH. (I.H. and H.J. Saywell). Est. 1943. Open 10-5.30, Thurs. 10-1. SIZE: Small. *STOCK: Stamps, accessories, coins and some medals.* LOC: Off Park End St. near railway station. PARK: Easy. TEL: 01865 248889. SER: Valuations. VAT: Stan.

Thorntons of Oxford Ltd
11 Broad St. OX1 3AR. Open 9-6. SIZE: Large. *STOCK: Antiquarian books.* TEL: 01865 242939; fax - 01865 204021; e-mail - Thorntons@book news.demon.co.uk

Titles - Old and Rare Books
15 Turl St. OX1 3DQ. Est. 1972. Open 9.30-5.30. *STOCK: Antiquarian and secondhand books, general subjects, especially literature, natural history, travel, history of science, bindings, illustrated.* TEL: 01865 727928; fax - same.

Waterfield's
36 Park End St. OX1 1HJ. Open 9.30-5.30, Sat. 9.30-6. *STOCK: Antiquarian and secondhand books, all subjects, especially academic in the humanities; literature, history, philosophy, 17th-18th C English books.* TEL: 01865 721809.

STANDLAKE, Nr. Witney

Manor Farm Antiques
Manor Farm. OX8 7RL. (C.W. Leveson-Gower). Est. 1964. Open daily, Sun. by appointment. SIZE: Large. *STOCK: Victorian brass and iron beds.* PARK: Easy, in farmyard. TEL: 01865 300303.

TAYNTON, Nr. Burford

Wychwood Antiques
Upper Farm Cottage. Open by appointment only. *STOCK: English country furniture and decorative items.* TEL: 01993 822860.

TETSWORTH, Nr. Thame

The Swan at Tetsworth
High St. OX9 7AB. TVADA. Est. 1995. Open every day including Sun. LOC: A40, 5 minutes from junctions 6 and 8, M40. PARK: Own large. TEL: 01844 281777; fax - 01844 281770. SER: Valuations; restorations (clocks, cabinet work and gilding). Below are listed the dealers at this centre.

Deborah Abbot
Jewellery and objet d'art.

Jason Abbot
Antique and sporting guns.

S.J. Allison
Decorative ceramics, small furniture and silver.

Ariol Antiques
Country furniture, paintings and smalls.

Denis Ashworth
Jewellery and ceramics.

Barn Antiques
Jewellery and smalls.

Suzanne Barton
Country items and kitchenalia.

Beagle Antiques
Fine porcelain.

David Binns
Books and paperweights.

Peter Bond
Prints, watercolours. SER: Gilding.

G. Buckle
Clocks and Oriental items.

Hugh Carter
Victorian furniture, paintings and ceramics.

John Chaffer
Framed antiquarian prints and maps.

Elsa Chamberlain
Linen, china and kitchenalia.

Clavic Lee Antiques
Silverware.

Audrey Cooper
Kitchenalia and country items.

Jenny Corkhill-Callin
Antique textiles including cushions, curtains, braid and quilts.

Country Cottage Antiques
Victorian furniture.

Andrew Crawforth
Metalware and smalls.

Tetsworth continued

Richard Deryn Antiques
Porcelain, furniture and framed prints.

Carolyn Dines
Antique rugs, carpets and textiles.

Diane Dyson Antiques
Georgian/Victorian furniture, ceramics.

Maureen Elder
Period furniture and smalls.

Bridget Farwagi
Ceramics, furniture and objet d'art.

Mavis Foster-Abbott
Jewellery, glass and ceramics.

Framed Antiques
Collectable cigarette cards.

John Freeman
Antique Indian furniture and smalls.

Joanna Glyn
18th C fine porcelain.

Gillian Gould
Maritime Antiques.

Chris Gransbury
Sporting antiques.

Grove Antiques Limited
Decorative and Continental furniture and lighting.

Gill Hedge
Silver, glassware, ceramics and paintings.

John Hedge
Antiquarian books.

Martin Isenberg
Period/decorative furniture, treen and ceramics.

Esther Jones
19th C furniture, boxes and porcelain.

Sandra Lawless
Antique needle and sewing related items.

Gerald and Elisabeth Ledger
18th and 19th C furniture and ceramics.

David Litt
French country furniture.

Manzaroli
Fine antique paintings.

Marlborough Book Shop & Sporting Gallery
Sporting prints and engravings.

Nicholas Mitchell
Unusual period furniture and smalls.

Tetsworth continued

George Morris
Jewellery.

W.B. Otter
Period furniture, boxes and writing slopes.

Penningtons
Pine and kitchenalia.

Sandra Prudhoe
Georgian/Victorian furniture.

Quail Collectables
Fine antique glassware.

Janet Raisey
Silverware.

T.H.A. & F.M. Sharland
Frames, prints and watercolours.

J. MacNaughton Smith
Salon furniture.

Carole Solway
China, prints and smalls.

Sovereign Art
Collectors' silver items.

Steeple Antiques
Large period furniture and chandeliers.

Jackie Stent
Silverware, and small decorative items.

Peter Stevens
Ceramics.

Celia Thompson
Objet d'art.

J.D. Tye
Furniture, porcelain and oil paintings.

Andrew & Vicky Warburton
Period country furniture and smalls.

Allan Wardle
Period clocks and watches.

Carol Wardle
Furniture, clocks and watches.

Susan Wilson
Pine and kitchenalia.

Russell Wood Antiques
Victorian/country furniture.

Nigel Worboys
Useful antique household furniture.

Wright Associates
Jewellery, glass and boxes.

Tetsworth continued

Tetsworth Antiques
High St. OX9 7DU. (M. and D. Vine). Open 11-5 including Sun., Sat. 10-5. CL: Mon. and Wed. SIZE: Medium. *STOCK: Furniture, china, glass, pine, clocks, £1-£4,000.* LOC: A40 between exits 6 and 7, M40. PARK: Easy. TEL: 01844 281636. SER: Valuations; restorations. VAT: Stan/Spec.

THAME

Rosemary and Time
42 Park St. OX9 3HR. Open 9-6. *STOCK: Clocks, watches, barometers.* TEL: 01844 216923. SER: Valuations; restorations; old spare parts. VAT: Stan/Spec.

WALLINGFORD

Michael and Jane de Albuquerque
12 High St. OX10 0BP. Open 10-5. *STOCK: Furniture and decorative items, 18th-19th C.* PARK: At rear. TEL: 01491 832322. SER: Restorations (pictures); framing. VAT: Spec.

John Charles Antiques and Fine Art
20 High St. OX10 0BP. (John and Mary Ostroumoff). Est. 1984. Open 9.30-5.30, Sun. by appointment. SIZE: Medium. *STOCK: Furniture and paintings, to 1920, £50-£5,000; clocks, silver, glass, pewter, copper and brass.* LOC: From A423, over bridge into High St. PARK: Nearby. TEL: 01491 825200; fax - 01491 825544. SER: Valuations; restorations (furniture); upholstery; buys at auction (furniture and pictures). FAIRS: Eton; Henley-on-Thames. VAT: Stan/Spec.

The Lamb Arcade
83 High St. OX10 0BX. TVADA. Open 10-5, Sat. 10-5.30. TEL: 01491 835166. SER: Restorations (furniture). Below are listed some of the dealers at this centre.

Alicia Antiques
(A. Collins). *China, silver and collectors' items.* TEL: 01491 33737.

Wallingford continued

Anne Brewer Antiques
TVADA. *Furniture, china, jewellery and obje d'art.* TEL: 01491 38486.

Great Expectations
(N. McKie). *Victorian brass bedsteads, linens an bedroom furnishings.* TEL: 01491 39909.

Griffon Antiques
Antique furniture and decorative items.

Pat Hayward
Antiques and decorative furnishings.

Old Cottage Antiques
Boxes, 18th-19th C furniture and metalware.

Phoenix Antiques
Victorian furniture, Continental and English pin lighting.

Margaret Richmond
Small 17th-19th C oak country furniture, acces ories, decorative items and kitchenalia. TEL: 0149 35166.

Simply Antiques
General antiques and collectables. TEL: 0149 824854.

Gretel Stone
Small furniture, porcelain, silver, pictures an objets d'art.

Julie Strachey
Pine. TEL: 01491 35166.

Tags
(T. and A. Green). *Collectors' items, curios, doll house furniture, jewellery, militaria, scientif instruments and furniture.* TEL: 01491 35048; hon - 01491 872962.

Waters Violins
Old violins, violas and cellos. TEL: 01491 2561 SER: Valuations; restorations.

Vallingford continued

1GJ Jewellers Ltd.

A St. Martins St. OX10 0AQ. (Mrs M. Jane). st. 1971. Open 10-4.30, Sat. 10-5. SIZE: Small. *TOCK: Jewellery, Victorian and secondhand, 100-£2,500.* LOC: Town centre. PARK: Nearby. EL: 01491 834336. VAT: Stan/Spec.

:hris and Lin O'Donnell Antiques

5 High St. OX10 0BU. Open 9.30-1 and 2-5. IZE: Medium. *STOCK: Furniture, 18th C to dwardian, to £2,000; rugs, to £500; small ollectables, especially Oriental items; maps.* OC: Into town over Wallingford Bridge, 50yds. along High St. on left-hand side. PARK: hames St. TEL: 01491 839332.

1ike Ottrey Antiques

5 High St. (M.J. Ottrey). Est. 1955. Open 9-5.30. L: Sat. SIZE: Large. *STOCK: Furniture, 17th-th C; oil paintings, copper and brass, decorative d unusual items.* LOC: A429. PARK: At rear. EL: 01491 836429. VAT: Stan/Spec.

ummers Davis Antiques Ltd BADA LAPADA

alleva House, 6 High St. OX10 0BP. Graham Wells). CINOA, TVADA. Est. 1917. pen 8.30-5.30, Sat. 9-5, Sun. 11-5. SIZE: arge. *STOCK: English and Continental rniture, decorative items and objects.* Not tocked: Silver, shipping goods. LOC: From

Wallingford continued

London, shop is on left, 50yds. from Thames Bridge. PARK: Opposite, behind castellated gates. TEL: 01491 836284; fax - 01491 833443. VAT: Spec.

WATLINGTON, Nr. Oxford

F.E.A. Briggs Ltd

The Antiques Warehouse, Shirburn Road. OX9 5BZ. *STOCK: Furniture and textiles, Victorian, Edwardian and Georgian.* TEL: 0171 727 0909/ 221 4950. SER: Valuations. VAT: Stan/Spec.

Cross Antiques

37 High St. OX9 5PZ. (R.A. and I.D. Crawley). TVADA. Est. 1986. Open 10-6, Sun. and Wed. by appointment. SIZE: Small. *STOCK: Furniture, £100-£5,000; decorative smalls, clocks and garden items, £50-£2,000; all 1600-1900.* LOC: Off B4009 in village centre. PARK: Easy and at rear. TEL: 01491 612324; home - same.

Stephen Orton Antiques

The Antiques Warehouse, Shirburn Rd. OX9 5BZ. TVADA. Open Mon.-Fri. 9-5, other times by appointment. SIZE: Warehouse. *STOCK: 18th-19th C furniture, some decorative items.* LOC: 2 mins. from exit 6, M40. TEL: 01491 613752; fax - 01491 613875. SER: Valuations; restorations; buying agent. VAT: Stan/Spec.

Watlington continued

Mark Shanks BADA
The Royal Oak, High St. OX9 5QB. TVADA. Est. 1960. Open 10-5 or by appointment. *STOCK: Furniture, £100-£20,000; barometers, £100-£10,000; both mainly 18th-19th C. Decorative items, £50-£5,000.* Not Stocked: Silver, jewellery, coins. LOC: 3 miles from junction 6, M40. Turn right into High St. (one-way). PARK: Own. TEL: 01491 613317; fax - 01491 613318.

WITNEY

Colin Greenway Antiques
90 Corn St. OX8 7BU. Resident. Est. 1975. Ope 9.30-6 or by appointment. SIZE: Large. *STOC Furniture, 17th-20th C; metalware, decorati and unusual items.* LOC: Along High St. to tov centre, turn right, shop 400yds. on right. PAR Easy. TEL: 01993 705026. VAT: Stan/Spec.

W.R. Harvey & Co (Antiques) Ltd BAD
86 Corn St. OX8 7BU. CADA. GMC. Open 9.3 5.30, and by appointment. SIZE: Large. *STOC Fine English furniture, £500-£50,000; clock mirrors, objets d'art, £250-£20,000; all 1680-183* LOC: 100 yds. from Market Place. TEL: 019 706501; fax - 01993 706601. SER: Valuation restorations; consultancy. FAIRS: BAD Chelsea (March & Sept.) VAT: Stan/Spec.

Joan Wilkins Antiques
158 Corn St. OX8 7BY. (Mrs J. Wilkins). E 1973. Open 10-5. CL: Tues. *STOCK: Furnitu 18th-19th C, £150-£3,500; 19th C glass, met ware, £10-£1,500.* LOC: Town centre. PAR Easy. TEL: 01993 704749. VAT: Spec.

Windrush Antiques
107 High St. OX8 6HG. (B. Tollett). Reside Est. 1978. Open 10-5. SIZE: Large. *STOC Furniture, especially 17th-18th C oak and coun chairs; Georgian mahogany, some metalware a porcelain.* LOC: A40, corner of Mill St. and Hi St. PARK: Private at rear. TEL: 01993 772536.

Witney Antiques BADA LAPA
96/100 Corn St. OX8 7BU. (L.S.A. and C Jarrett and R.R. Jarrett-Scott). CADA. E 1962. Open 10-5. SIZE: Large. *STOC English furniture, 17th-18th C; bracket a longcase clocks, mahogany, oak and waln metalware, needleworks and works of art.* LO From Oxford on old A40 through Witney High St., turn right at T-junction, 400yds. right. PARK: Easy. TEL: 01993 7039 703887; fax - 01993 779852. SER: Restoratio FAIRS: BADA; Grosvenor House. VAT: Sp

'OODSTOCK

hris Baylis Country Chairs

instrel House, 60 Oxford St. OX20 1TT. 'ADA. Open 10.30-5.30, Sun. 11-5. *STOCK: ıglish country chairs, from 1780; Windsors, lder and spindlebacks, kitchen chairs; good untry furniture and reproductions including m tables and chairs.* TEL: 01993 813887; fax - 993 812379.

Woodstock continued

Bees Antiques

30 High St. OX20 1TG. (Jo and Jim Bateman). TVADA. Est. 1991. Open 10-1 and 1.30-5, Sun. 11-5. CL: Tues. SIZE: Small. *STOCK: Pottery, porcelain and glass, 18th-20th C, £30-£1,500; small furniture, 19th to early 20th C, £50-£2,000; metalware, 19th C, £30-£200; jewellery, 19th-20th C, £30-£1,000.* LOC: Just off A3440 Oxford/ Stratford-on-Avon road, in town centre. PARK: Opposite. TEL: 01993 811062; home - 01993 771593. SER: Valuations; buys at auction (as stock). FAIRS: Wakefield Ceramics; TVADA.

Myles Birkett Foster (1825-1899), 'At Sandhills, Surrey', signed with monogram, watercolour heightened with white, 10in. x 14in. Sold for £8,280 in March 1995. Foster's talent as a landscape artist is often overlooked. His technique and eye for a good composition can rarely be faulted. Small vignettes start at about £700.

From an article entitled "English Landscape Watercolours" by Richard Kay of Phillips which appeared in the October 1996 issue of **Antique Collecting**

Woodstock continued

Le Print Antique Centre

16 High St. OX20 1TF. Est. 1973. Open 10-5, Sun. 11-5. SIZE: 20+ dealers. *STOCK: General antiques and collectables including porcelain, pottery, glass, brass, copper, silver and plate, books, woodworking tools, furniture.* PARK: Easy. TEL: 01993 813900; home (Manager) - 01865 66181. SER: Valuations; restorations (ceramics and furniture repairs including re-covering); picture framing. FAIRS: Various specialist.

Robin Sanders and Sons LAPADA

11 Market Street. OX20 1SU. CINOA. *STOCK: English and some French furniture, 17th-19th C; Staffordshire and Masons ironstone pottery, brass, treen and English glass pictures.* TEL: 01993 813930.

Span Antiques

6 Market Place. OX20 1TA. TVADA. Est. 1978. Open 10-1 and 2-5, Sun 1-5. SIZE: Medium. LOC: Near Town Hall. PARK: Easy. Below are listed some of the dealers selling from these premises. TEL: 01993 811332.

Irene Cain
Porcelain and decorative items.

Woodstock continued

Doreen Caudwell
Table linen and textiles.

Diana Clark
Old and interesting books.

Mike and Kate Cowdy
Silver.

Andrew Crawforth
Iron, copper, brass, kitchen bygones, corkscrews.

Maureen Gough
Period furniture and engravings.

Lis Hall-Bakker
Art Nouveau and Deco.

Jasper Antiques
Silver and decorative items.

Alan Stuart-Mobey
Furniture and glass.

Thistle House Antiques

14 Market Place. OX7 1TA. Open 10-6. *STOCK 18th-19th C furniture, porcelain, pictures.* TEL 01993 811736. SER: Restorations.

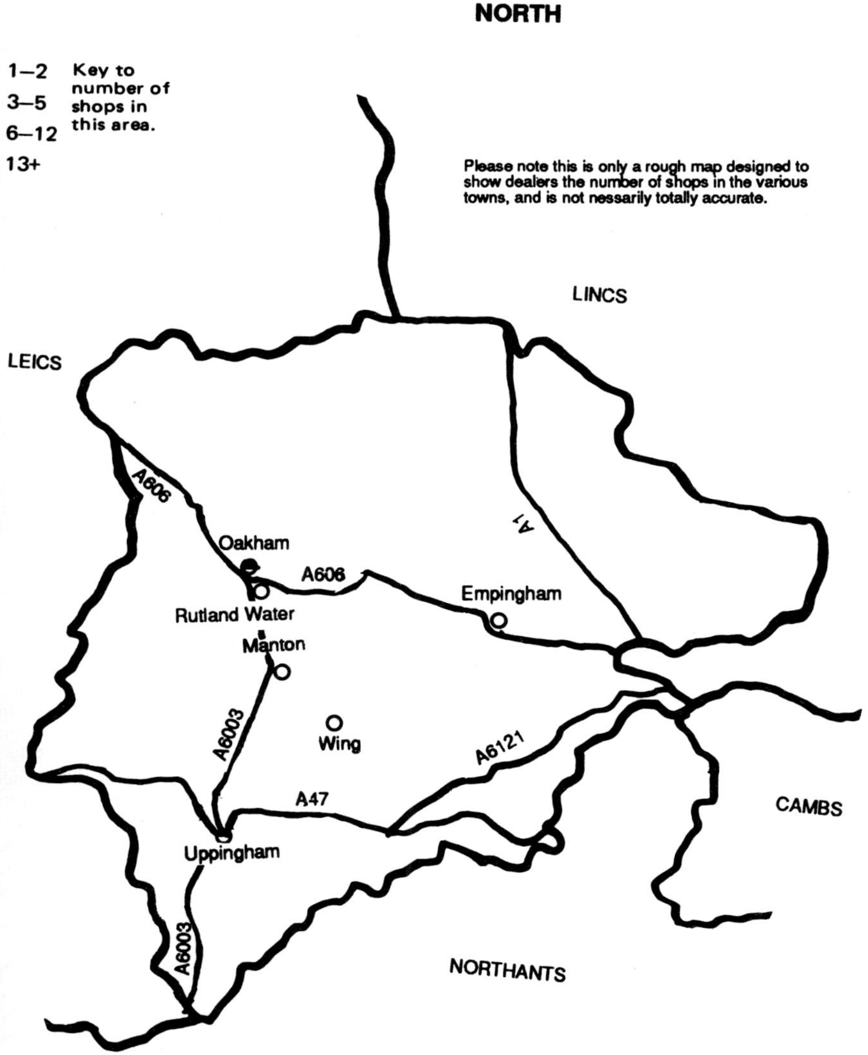
NORTH
1–2
3–5
6–12
13+
Key to number of shops in this area.
Please note this is only a rough map designed to show dealers the number of shops in the various towns, and is not nessarily totally accurate.
LINCS
LEICS
A606
A1
Oakham
A606
Empingham
Rutland Water
Manton
A6003
Wing
A6121
A47
CAMBS
Uppingham
A6003
NORTHANTS

EMPINGHAM, Nr. Oakham

Churchgate Antiques
13 Church St. LE15 8PN. (R. Wheatley). Open Wed., Fri., Sat. and Sun. 12-6, other times by appointment. SIZE: Medium. *STOCK: Furniture, mainly 18th-19th C, £50-£4,000; paintings and prints, £25-£1,000; silver and plate, 19th-20th C, £5-£1,000.* LOC: Opposite church, off A606. PARK: Easy. TEL: 01780 460528.

Old Bakery Antiques
Church St. LE15 8PN. (Mr and Mrs P.B. Margerison). Open 10.30-5.30, Sun. 10.30-4.30. CL: Thurs. SIZE: Medium. *STOCK: Furniture, 17th C to 1920, £50-£6,000; china, 1830-1920, £5-£500; copper and brass, 19th C.* Not Stocked: Jewellery. LOC: 4 miles off A1 on A606 towards Oakham. PARK: Easy. TEL: 01780 460243; home - same. SER: Restorations (furniture). VAT: Stan/Spec.

MANTON

David Smith Antiques
Old Cottage, 20 St. Mary's Rd. LE15 8SU. Est. 1953. Open 9-5. CL: Sun., except by appointment. *STOCK: Furniture, glass, silver.* PARK: Easy. TEL: 01572 737244/737473.

OAKHAM

Fine Art of Oakham BADA LAPADA
4 High St. LE15 6AL. (Dr A.J. Smith). Open 10-5. CL: Mon. *STOCK: Continental oils and watercolours, Victorian and 19th C.* TEL: 01572 755221; fax - 01572 770047.

Gallery Antiques LAPADA
17 Mill St. LE15 6EA. (P.W. Jones). Open 9.30-5.30, Sun. 2-5.30. *STOCK: English furniture, 18th-19th C, £100-£12,000; French beds.* TEL: 01572 755094; home - 01572 812199. SER: Valuations; restorations (furniture). VAT: Stan/Spec.

The Old House Gallery
13-15 Market Place. LE15 6DT. (R.A. Clarke). Est. 1979. Open 9.30-5, Sat. 9.30-4. CL: Thurs. SIZE: Medium. *STOCK: Oil paintings, £50-£3,500; art studio pottery, 1850-1990, £5-£500; watercolours, £25-£2,000; prints and objets d'art, £5-£500; antiquarian county maps, £15-£250.* PARK: Easy. TEL: 01572 755538. SER: Valuations; restorations (oils, watercolours, prints, frames); framing.

Rutland Antique Clock Gallery
37 Trent Rd. LE15 6HE. (K.G. Neale). Est. 1986. Open by appointment only. SIZE: Small. *STOCK: 17th C clocks, £45-£2,000.* LOC: A606, Oakham High St., Mill St., Brooke Rd., corner plot between Trent Rd. and Spey Rd. PARK: Easy. TEL: 01572 723375; home - same. SER: Valuations; restorations.

Oakham continued

Rutland Antiques
16 Melton Rd. (Mrs J. Freeman). Open 10-3 or [illegible] appointment. CL: Tues. and Thurs. *STOC[illegible] Brass, glass, small furniture, postcards, lam[illegible] pictures, prints, silver.* TEL: 01664 474571.

Swans LAPA[illegible]
27 Mill St. LE15 6EA. (P.W. Jones). Est. 19[illegible] Open 9.30-5.30, Sun. 2-5.30. SIZE: Large - pa[illegible] of Gallery Antiques. *STOCK: French a[illegible] English beds and bedroom furniture, £20[illegible] £2,000; upholstered furniture, £150-£2,0[illegible] mirrors, pictures and side tables.* LOC: 150y[illegible] from High St. PARK: Easy. TEL: 01572 7243[illegible] home - 01572 812199. SER: Valuations; rest[illegible] ations. VAT: Stan/Spec.

RUTLAND WATER

Barnsdale Antiques Centre
Barnsdale Lodge Hotel, The Avenue. LE15 8A[illegible] (Cecilia Gray Smith). Est. 1974. Open 10-6, S[illegible] 12-6. SIZE: Large. *STOCK: A wide variety [illegible] general antiques, pre 1940, £5-£20,000.* LO[illegible] A606 between Stafford and Oakham. PAR[illegible] Own large. TEL: 01572 722322; fax - same. SE[illegible] Valuations; restorations. VAT: Spec.

UPPINGHAM

Clutter
14 Orange St. LE15 9SQ. (M.C. Sumner). E[illegible] 1982. Open 10-5. *STOCK: Victorian linen a[illegible] lace; textiles including Durham quilts, chenill[illegible] interesting silver, porcelain, glass, sm[illegible] furniture, kitchenalia, 10p-£1,000.* LOC: Take [illegible] A47 from by-pass, shop 25yds. from traffic ligh[illegible] PARK: Nearby. TEL: 01572 823745; hom[illegible] 01572 717243. SER: Valuations; restoratio[illegible] (furniture, brass, copper, silver, bronze, ivo[illegible] lacquer, shibayama and associated materia[illegible] ceramics); hire (christening gowns and Victor[illegible] wedding dress and accessories).

John Garner
51-53 High St. East. LE15 9PY. Est. 1966. O[illegible] 9-5.30, Sun. by appointment. SIZE: Large + wa[illegible] house. *STOCK: Oil paintings, furniture includ[illegible] pine, 18th-19th C; clocks, bronzes, handcolou[illegible] sporting, coaching, marine and genre engravi[illegible] and etchings; decorative pieces; mirrors; fram[illegible] Warehouse - old wood pine; garden statua[illegible]* LOC: Just off A47, close to market place. PAR[illegible] Easy. TEL: 01572 823607; fax - 01572 821[illegible] SER: Valuations; restorations (furnitu[illegible] paintings, prints); framing; courier; export. V[illegible] Stan/Spec.

Gilberts of Uppingham
Ayston Rd. (M. Gilbert). Open Wed., Fri. [illegible] Sat. 9.30-5, Mon. and Tues. 9.30-1 and 2[illegible] *STOCK: General antiques.* TEL: 01572 82348[illegible]

Ippingham continued

;oldmark Books

4 Orange St. LE15 9SQ. (M.M. Goldmark).)pen 9.30-5.30 and Sunday afternoons. *STOCK: ntiquarian and secondhand books.* LOC: ;etween Market Sq. and traffic lights. PARK: Iearby. TEL: 01572 822694.

Iarc Oxley Fine Art

0 Orange St. LE15 9SQ. Resident. Est. 1981.)pen 9.30-5.30, Sat. 10-6, Sun. 2.30-5.30. SIZE: mall. *STOCK: Original watercolours and rawings, 1700-1950, £5-£850; prints, mainly 9th C, £5-£50; maps, 17th-19th C, £10-£375.* OC: From A47 on main road into town, just efore Market Sq. PARK: Market Sq. TEL: 01572 22334; home - same. SER: Valuations; restorions (watercolours, drawings and prints); buys at uction (watercolours and drawings).

'.J. Roberts

9/41 High St. East. LE15 9PY. Resident. Open .30-5.30. *STOCK: Furniture, 18th-19th C; orcelain, pottery, English, Chinese, European, 8th-19th C; Staffordshire figures, paintings.* ARK: Easy. TEL: 01572 821493.

Uppingham continued

E. and C. Royall Antiques

Printers Yard, High St. East. LE15 1XX. Open 10-4.30. CL: Thurs. *STOCK: Furniture, pictures, silver, porcelain, glassware, ivories and Oriental bronzes.* TEL: 01858 565744.

Tattersall's

14b Orange St. LE15 9SQ. (J. Tattersall). Est. 1985. Open 9.30-5. CL: Thurs. SIZE: Small. *STOCK: Persian rugs, mirrors, sofas, 19th-20th C.* PARK: Easy, 200yds. TEL: 01572 821171. SER: Restorations (rugs, carpets, tapestries); upholstery.

WING, Nr. Oakham

Robert Bingley Antiques

Home Farm, Church St. LE15 8RS. Open 9-5, Sun. 11-4. SIZE: Large. *STOCK: Furniture, 17th-19th C, £50-£5,000; glass, clocks, silver and plate, pictures and porcelain.* LOC: Next to church. PARK: Own. TEL: 01572 737725; home - 01572 737314. SER: Valuations; restorations. VAT: Spec.

Shropshire

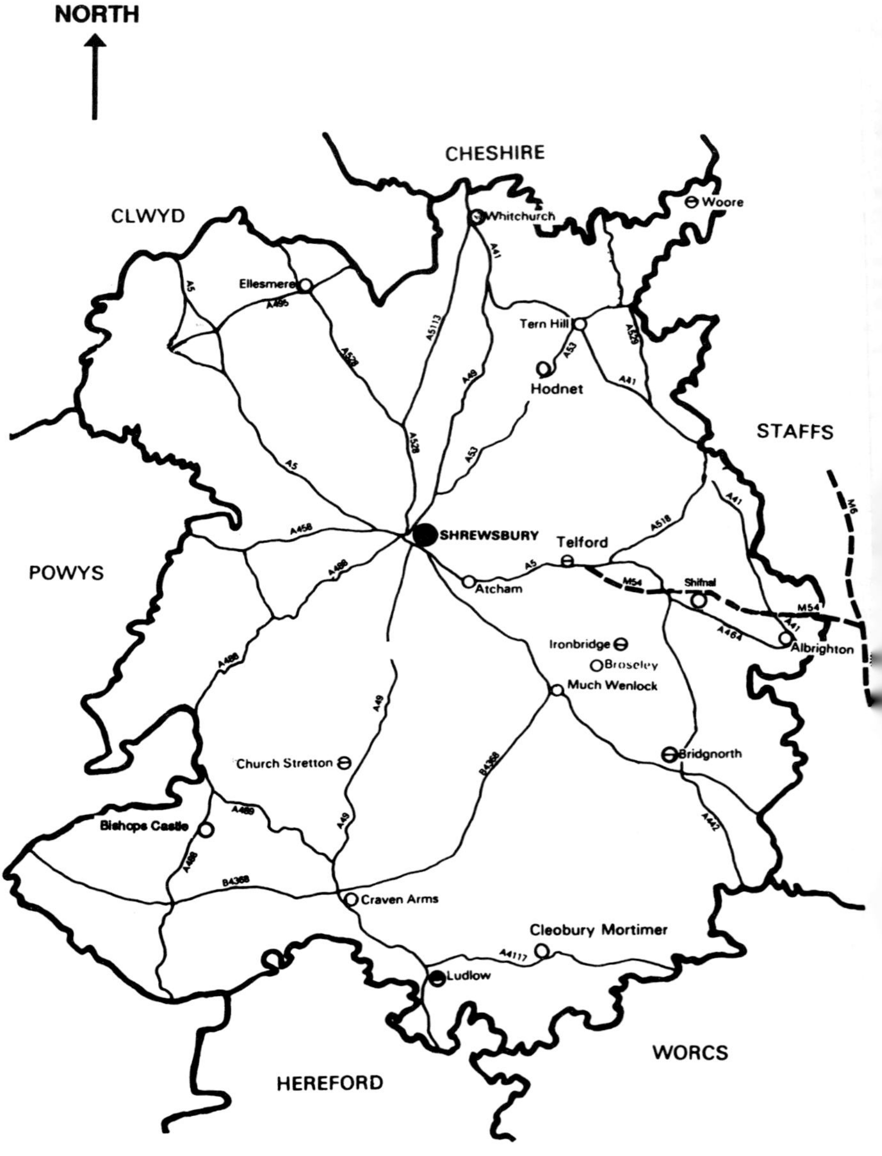

○ 1-2
⊖ 3-5
◒ 6-12
● 13+

Key to number of shops in this area.

Please note this is only a rough map designed to show dealers the number of shops in the various towns, and is not necessarily totally accurate.

ᴧLBRIGHTON (NEACHLEY)

)overidge House of Neachley BADA LAPADA

.ong Lane (alongside RAF Cosford). TF11 8PJ. Cdr and Mrs H.E.R. Bain). CINOA. Est. 1967. pen 9-5 seven days a week and/or by ppointment. SIZE: Large. *STOCK: 17th-19th C 'nglish and Continental furniture, fine art, locks, decorative artifacts.* LOC: From London 11 or M40 to M6. Junction 10A via M54 for orth and Mid Wales. Leave at Junction 3 (A41) Wolverhampton/Cosford direction. Half a ile see Neachley signpost, turn immediately ight into Long Lane, 4th entrance (Lodge ates). From the North, M6 Junction 11, A460 wards Wolverhampton. Join M54 at Junction then as Junction 3 above. PARK: Easy. TEL: 1902 373131. SER: Valuations; restorations urniture and oils); interior design; export.

TCHAM, Nr. Shrewsbury

Iytton Antiques

orton Cross Roads. SY4 4UM. (M.A., E.A. and M. Nares and Manager - Hugh Norton). Est. 1972. pen 9.30-5 .30 or by appointment. SIZE: Medium. *TOCK: General antiques, furniture, 1700-1900, 50-£3,000; clocks, all types, £35-£2,000; smalls, '5-£1,000.* LOC: On B5061 (the old A5) between rewsbury and Wellington. PARK: Own. TEL: .952 740229(24hrs.); fax - 01952 461154; internet http://www.enta.net/mytton. SER: Buys at .ction; suppliers of reference books and restor-ion materials. VAT: Stan/Spec.

BISHOP'S CASTLE

Ark Antiques

9 Market Square. (Jill Thomas). Est. 1974. Open 10.30-4.30 and Bank Holidays. CL: Mon. and Wed. SIZE: Small. *STOCK: Oak and pine country furniture, 18th-19th C; country and rural tools, brass and iron beds.* PARK: Easy. TEL: Home - 01588 638608. SER: Valuations; restorations (metal and wood); buys at auction (cottage furniture and artifacts).

BRIDGNORTH

English Heritage

2 Whitburn St., High Town. WV16 4QN. (P.J. Wainwright). Open 9.30-5, Mon. 10-5.SIZE: Medium. *STOCK: Jewellery, silverware and general antiques, militaria.* LOC: Just off High St. PARK: High St. TEL: 01746 762097. SER: Framing. VAT: Stan/Spec.

Micawber Antiques

64 St. Mary's St. WV16 4DR. (M. and N. Berthoud). Open 10-5, other days by appointment. CL: Mon. and Thurs. SIZE: Medium. *STOCK: English porcelain and pottery, decorative items, £5-£500; small furniture, £100-£1,000.* LOC: 100yds. west of town hall in High St. PARK: Easy. TEL: 01746 763254; home - same. SER: Buys at auction (English porcelain).

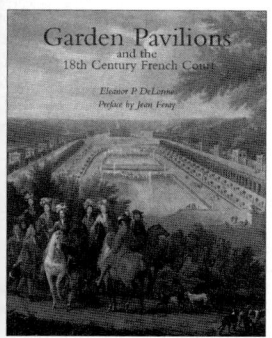

Bridgnorth continued

Old Mill Antique Centre
Mill St. WV15 5AG. (D.A. and J.R. Ridgeway). Est. 1996. Open 10-6 including Sun. SIZE: Large - 70 dealers. *STOCK: Wide range of general antiques including period furniture, porcelain and silver, jewellery, prints and watercolours, collectables.* LOC: Main road. PARK: Own. TEL: 01746 768778; fax - 01746 762248. SER: Valuations; restorations. VAT: Stan.

BROSELEY

Gallery 6
6 Church St. TF12 5DG. (J.A. Boulton). Resident. Est. 1983. Open 9-5, Sun. 2-5. SIZE: Medium. *STOCK: Oils, watercolours and prints, late 19th C to contemporary, £100-£2,500.* LOC: Junction 4, M54, take A442. PARK: Easy. TEL: 01952 882860. FAIRS: Buxton; NEC Birmingham; Shrewsbury; Edinburgh.

CHURCH STRETTON

Antiques on the Square
2 Sandford Court, Sandford Ave. SY6 6DA. (Chris Radford). Est. 1985. Open 9.30-5, Sun. by appointment. SIZE: Medium. *STOCK: Art Deco ceramics, Clarice Cliff, furniture, glass, 1880-1930, £5-£3,000; collectors items, TV's, radios, £5-£500; decorative items, £5-£1,000; both pre-1939.* Not Stocked: Armour, stamps, period furniture. LOC: Off A49. PARK: Easy. TEL: 01694 724111; home - 01694 723072; mobile - 0831 336052. SER: Valuations; restorations (furniture, glass, tapestry, metalware, paintings and ceramics); buys at auction (English furniture pre-1830); research; Clarice Cliff exhibition annually. FAIRS: Chester (Art Deco); Loughborough; Warwick (Art Deco). VAT: Stan/Spec.

Cardingmill Antiques
1 Burway Rd. SY6 6DL. (Mrs P. A. Benton). Est. 1976. Open Thurs., Fri. and Sat. 10.30-5, Mon., Tues. and Wed. by appointment. *STOCK: Wall clocks and furniture, 18th-19th C, £250-£1,250; Measham teapots, 19th-20th C, £100-£450; ribbon place plates, 19th-20th C, £10-£40; horse brasses (NHBS), 19th-20th C, £10-£250.* LOC: A49. PARK: Valuations; restorations (longcase and wall clocks). TEL: 01694 724555; home - 01584 877880.

Longmynd Antiques
Crossways. SY6 6PG. (David Coomber). Est. 1994. Open 10.30-5, Sun. 11-5. CL: Wed. SIZE: Large. *STOCK: Furniture, 17th C to Edwardian, £100-£10,000; collectables, 19th-20th C, £5-£500.* LOC: A49. Premises immediately south of traffic lights. PARK: Own. TEL: 01694 724474; fax - same. SER: Buys at auction. VAT: Spec.

Stretton Antiques Market
36 Sandford Ave. SY6 6BH. (T. and L. Elvins). Est. 1986. Open 9.30-5.30, Sun. and Bank Holidays

Church Stretton continued

10.30-4.30. SIZE: Large - 55 dealers. *STOC[K: General antiques, shipping items and collectabl[e*[s]. LOC: Town centre. PARK: Easy. TEL: 016[9]4 723718. SER: Valuations; buys at auction.

CLEOBURY MORTIMER Nr. Kidderminster

Cleobury Mortimer Antique Centre
Childe Rd. DY14 8PA. Open 10-5 including Su[n]. SIZE: Large. *STOCK: Georgian, Victoria[n], Edwardian and old pine furniture, period be[ds], bric-a-brac and architectural items.* PARK: Ow[n]. TEL: 01299 270513.

CRAVEN ARMS

I. and S. Antiques
Stokesay, Ludlow Rd. SY7 9QL. (J. Brisco[e]). Open 9-5, Sun. 10.30-4.30 in summer. *STOC[K]: Unstripped pine, shipping goods, treen, coun[try] items, bric-a-brac, books, 19th to early 20th* [C]. TEL: 01588 672263; home - 01588 640374.

ELLESMERE

Lynne Davies Antiques
14 High St. SY12 0EP. Open 9.30-5.30. SI[ZE]: Medium. *STOCK: Furniture, glass, china, sil[ver], jewellery.* TEL: 01691 623835.

HODNET, Nr. Market Drayton

Hodnet Antiques
13a and 19a Shrewsbury St. TF9 3NP. (Mr Scott). Est. 1976. Open Tues. and Thurs. 2-5, o[ther] times by appointment. SIZE: Small. *STO[CK]: General antiques - china, glass, silver, jewell[ery], pictures, brass and copper, collectables, £5-£1,0[00]; Victorian and Edwardian furniture, £50-£3,0[00].* LOC: A53. PARK: Outside shop. TEL: Ho[me] 01630 638591. SER: Valuations.

IRONBRIDGE

Ironbridge Antique Centre
Dale End. TF8 7DS. (F.G. Cooke). Est. 1[9..]. Open 10-5, Sun. 2-5. SIZE: Large. *STO[CK]: Porcelain, 1800-1950, £1-£3,000; furnit[ure], pictures, jewellery, general antiques and bri[c-a-]brac, 1700-1930, 50p-£1,000.* PARK: Easy. T[EL]: 01952 433784. SER: Valuations; restorat[ions] (cabinet making); buys at auction.

Tudor House Antiques (Bill Dickenson)
11 Tontine Hill. TF8 7AL. Open 10-5, Sun. [...] CL: Mon. *STOCK: General antiques, espec[ially] porcelain including Caughley and Coalport.* L[OC]: Opposite bridge. TEL: 01952 433783.

UDLOW

ntique Corner
2 Old St. SY8 1NP. (J. Clegg). Resident. Est. 960. Open 8.30-5. *STOCK: Country and other riod furniture, metalware and decorative items.* EL: 01584 873176.

rchitectural Antiques and Interiors
40 Corve St. SY8 2PG. (R.G. and J. Dickinson). pen 9.30-1 and 2-5. *STOCK: Bathrooms, fire-aces, lighting, doors and other architectural ntiques.* TEL: 01584 876207.

.W. and A.B. Bayliss
Old St. SY8 1NP. Resident. *STOCK: Furniture, th-19th C; silver, decorative items.* TEL: 01584 3634. SER: Valuations.

.G. Cave and Sons Ltd BADA LAPADA
Broad St. SY8 1NG. Resident. Est. 1962. pen 9.30-5.30. *STOCK: Furniture, 1630-1830; ocks, barometers, metalwork, fine art and llectors' items.* PARK: Easy. TEL: 01584 3568. SER: Valuations. VAT: Spec.

he Curiosity Shop
7 Old St. SY8 1NU. (J. Luffman). Resident. en 9.30-5 or by appointment. *STOCK: Longcase, acket and mantel clocks, music boxes, country rniture, paintings and militaria, £5-£20,000.* L: 01584 875927; mobile - 0836 592898. SER: luations; buys at auction (militaria, paintings). AT: Spec.

Ludlow continued

G. & D. Ginger Antiques
5 Corve St. SY8 1DA. Resident. Open 9-5. SIZE: Large. *STOCK: Oak dressers and farmhouse tables, Welsh cupboards and presses, country and mahogany furniture; decorative and associated items.* TEL: 01584 876939; mobile - 0468 350618.

Mitre House Antiques
Corve Bridge. SY8 1DY. (L. Jones). Open 9-5.30. SIZE: Shop + trade warehouse. *STOCK: Clocks, pine and general antiques. Warehouse - unstripped pine and shipping goods.* TEL: 01584 872138.

Pepper Lane Antiques
Pepper Lane. SY8 1PX. (D. Nicholas and C. Reid). Est. 1985. Open 10-5. SIZE: Large. *STOCK: Furniture, porcelain, silver and plate.* LOC: Just off King St. PARK: Easy. TEL: 01584 876494. SER: Re-upholstery.

M. and R. Taylor (Antiques)
53 Broad St. SY8 1NH. (M. Taylor). Est. 1977. Open from 9 am. including evenings. SIZE: Medium. *STOCK: Furniture, mahogany, oak and walnut, Persian rugs, brass and copper, 17th-19th C.* PARK: Nearby. TEL: 01584 874169; home - same. VAT: Stan/Spec.

Ludlow continued

Teme Valley Antiques
1 The Bull Ring. SY8 1AD. (C.S. Harvey). E 1979. Usually open 10-5.30, Sun. by appointme SIZE: Medium. *STOCK: English and Continen porcelain, 18th to early 20th C, £25-£2,5(furniture, oil and watercolour paintings, £ £2,500; jewellery, silver, plate, metalware a glass, £10-£3,500; both 17th to early 20th C.* N Stocked: Militaria, coins and carpets. LOC: To centre opposite Lunn Poly. PARK: Easy. TE 01584 874686. SER: Valuations; buys at auct (porcelain). VAT: Stan/Spec.

Valentyne Dawes Gallery
Dawes Mansion, Church St. SY8 1AP. (B McCreddie). Open 10-5.30, Sun. in summer Bank Holidays. SIZE: Medium. *STOC Paintings, 19th to early 20th C, £200-£40,0 furniture, 17th-19th C, £50-£4,000; porcel 19th C, £5-£500.* LOC: Town centre n Buttercross. PARK: Nearby. TEL: 01584 8741 SER: Valuations; restorations (oil paintin watercolours, furniture). VAT: Spec.

MUCH WENLOCK

Cruck House Antiques
23 Barrow St. TF13 6EN. (B. Roderick Smi Est. 1985. Open 9.30-5.30. CL: Wed. SI

'uch Wenlock continued

mall. *STOCK: Silver and watercolours, 19th-0th C, £25-£300; furniture, 19th C, £50-£500; eneral antiques.* Not Stocked: Weapons and old. LOC: Near Square. PARK: Easy. TEL: 1952 727165.

Venlock Fine Art
The Square. TF13 6LX. (P. Cotterill). Est. 990. Open Wed.-Sat. 10-5. SIZE: Medium. *TOCK: Modern British paintings, mainly 20th , some late 19th C, £100-£6,000.* PARK: 'earby. TEL: 01952 728232; home - 01952 52376. SER: Valuations; restorations (cleaning); ounting; framing; buys at auction (as stock). 'AT: Spec.

HIFNAL

ntiques of Shifnal
Church St. TF11 9AA. (C. Weaver). Open 10-.30. CL: Mon. and Thurs. SIZE: Medium. *TOCK: Furniture, 18th-19th C, £200-£1,000; ramics, silver and prints, 19th C, £25-£500; orks of art, £25-£100.* LOC: Town centre, under ilway bridge, follow road round then 1st right to one-way street (Church St). PARK: 100 yards right of shop on left. TEL: 01952 462986. SER: ane and rush seating; picture framing.

HREWSBURY

andle Lane Books
-29 Princess St. SY1 1LW. (J. Thornhill). pen 9.30-5. *STOCK: Antiquarian and condhand books.* TEL: 01743 365301.

liet Chilton Antiques and Interiors
Wyle Cop. SY1 1UX. Open 9.30-6. SIZE: rge. *STOCK: Furniture and smalls, mainly 700's-1920's and some reproduction.* TEL: 743 358699/366553; fax - 01743 366563. SER: ipping and packing.

ollectors' Gallery
7 Castle Gates. SY1 2AE. Open 9-5.30. SIZE: rge. *STOCK: Coins and medals; stamps and stcards; related books and accessories.* TEL: 743 272140; fax - 01743 366041.

xpressions
Princess St. SY1 1LP. Open 10.30-4.30. CL: urs. *STOCK: Art Deco originals, ceramics, rniture, jewellery, lighting, mirrors, prints.* L: 01743 351731.

utton Antiques
Princess St. SY1 1LP. (Mrs P.I. Hutton). Est. 78. Open 10-1 and 2.15-4. CL: Thurs. SIZE: dium. *STOCK: Silver, porcelain and glass, th-19th C, £50-£500; small furniture, £50-300; Victorian jewellery.* LOC: Off square, ar Music Hall. PARK: Easy. TEL: 01743 5810. SER: Valuations.

Shrewsbury continued

The Little Gem
18 St. Mary's St. SY1 1ED. (M.A. Bowdler). Est. 1969. Open 9-5.30. CL: Thurs. (except Dec.). SIZE: Medium. *STOCK: Georgian and Victorian jewellery; unusual gem stones, watches.* Not Stocked: Weapons, coins, medals, furniture. LOC: Opposite St. Mary's Church along from G.P.O. PARK: In side road (St. Mary's Place) opposite shop. TEL: 01743 352085. SER: Watch repairs.

F.C. Manser and Son Ltd LAPADA
53/54 Wyle Cop. SY1 1XJ. Est. 1944. Open 9-5.30. CL: Thurs. pm. SIZE: Large. *STOCK: Furniture, 17th-20th C, £150-£12,000; Oriental items, 15th-20th C, £5-£3,000; silver, plate, copper, 18th-20th C, £5-£6,000; oils and watercolours, £100-£20,000; jewellery, 19th-20th C, £50-£6,000.* Not Stocked: Coins, books. LOC: 150yds. town side of English bridge. PARK: Own. TEL: 01743 351120/245730; fax - 01743 271047. SER: Valuations; restorations. VAT: Stan/Spec.

Princess Antique Centre
14a The Square. (J. Langford). Open 9.30-5.30. SIZE: 35 dealers. *STOCK: General antiques and collectables.* TEL: 01743 343701.

Raleigh Antiques
23 Belle Vue Rd. SY5 7LN. (R. and E. Handbury-Madin). GADAR. Est. 1968. Open 10-5. *STOCK: Furniture, pottery, porcelain, glass, jewellery, silver.* PARK: Easy. TEL: 01743 359552. SER: Valuations; restorations (furniture, clocks).

Roushill Antiques Warehouse
The Old Maltings, Roushill. (Jean and Chris Winter). Open 10-5. CL: Mon. & Thurs. SIZE: Large. *STOCK: Victorian and Edwardian furniture, especially dining tables and sets of chairs, desks, bookcases, beds, wardrobes.* LOC: Town centre, off Smithfield Rd. next to C.R. Birch. PARK: Nearby. TEL: 01743 360490; workshop - 01948 665838; home - 01948 830363. SER: Restorations (furniture); countrywide delivery.

Shrewsbury Antique Centre
15 Princess House, The Square. SY1 1JZ. (J. Langford). Est. 1978. Open 9.30-5.30. SIZE: Large - 50 dealers. *STOCK: General antiques and collectables.* LOC: Town centre just off the Square. PARK: Nearby. TEL: 01743 247704.

Shrewsbury Antique Market
Frankwell Quay Warehouse. SY3 8LG. (J. Langford). Open 9.30-5. SIZE: Large - 45 units. *STOCK: General antiques and collectors' items, £1-£2,000.* LOC: Alongside Frankwell Quay car park. PARK: Easy. TEL: 01743 350916.

Shrewsbury continued

Tiffany Antiques
Shrewsbury Antique Centre, 15 Princess House, The Square. SY1 1JZ. (A. Wilcox). Est. 1988. Open 9.30-5.30. *STOCK: Metalware, collectables, curios, china and glass.* LOC: Town centre. PARK: Multi-storey. TEL: Home - 01270 257425; mobile - 0370 380261. SER: Buys at auction.

Welsh Bridge Antique Centre
135 Frankwell. SY3 8JX. (Peter Connor). Resident. Est. 1994. Open 9.30-5.30, Sun. 1-5. SIZE: Medium. *STOCK: General antiques and collectables, 19th-20th C, £1-£1,000.* LOC: Just before Frankwell car park. PARK: Easy. TEL: 01743 248822.

STANTON, Nr. Shrewsbury

Marcus Moore Antiques
Booley House, Booley. SY4 4LY. (M.G.J. and M.P. Moore). Est. 1980. Usually open but prior telephone call advisable. SIZE: Medium. *STOCK: Oak and country furniture, late 17th to 18th C; Georgian mahogany furniture, 18th to early 19th C; all £50-£7,000; some Victorian furniture; associated items.* LOC: Half a mile north of Stanton on right. PARK: Easy. TEL: 01939 200333. SER: Restorations (furniture); polishing; search; shipping. VAT: Stan/Spec.

TELFORD

Haygate Gallery
40 Haygate Rd., Wellington. TF1 1QT. (Mrs M. Kuznierz). Open 9-5, Sat. 9-1. CL: Wed. *STOCK: Watercolours, oils and general antiques.* LOC: One mile from junction 7, M54. PARK: Easy. TEL: 01952 248553. SER: Framing.

Brian James Antiques
Old Maltings, The Lawns, Wellington. TF1 3AF. Est. 1985. Open 9-6, Sat. 9.30-12.30, Sun. by appointment. SIZE: Large. *STOCK: Chests of drawers, Georgian to Victorian, £50-£1,500.* LOC: Off M54, junction 6. Follow signs for Telford Hospital then Wellington Centre, turn right at Red Lion. PARK: Easy. TEL: 01952 256592/243906. SER: Restorations and conversions; linen presses and chests made to order. VAT: Stan. *Trade Only.*

Bernie Pugh Antiques
120 High St., Wellington. TF1 1JU. Resident. Open by appointment only. *STOCK: General antiques.* TEL: 01952 256184 (answerphone).

St. George's Antiques
The Chapel, Church St., St George's. (McNulty Wholesalers). Est. 1983. Open 11-5, Sun. 1-5. CL: Mon. SIZE: Large. *STOCK: Painted pine,*

Telford continued

mahogany; small interesting items. LOC: minutes from town centre. PARK: Easy. TEL 01952 616613. FAIRS: Newark. VAT: Stan.

TERN HILL, Nr. Market Drayton

L. Onions - White Cottage Antiques
White Cottage, 8 Tern Hill. TF9 3PR. Est. 196 Open 9.30-5.30. SIZE: Medium. *STOCK: Furniture, oak and some walnut, brass, 16th-18th* LOC: On A41, 200yds. from roundabout at Tern Hill cross roads. PARK: Easy. TEL: 0163 638222. VAT: Stan/Spec.

WHITCHURCH

Dodington Antiques
15 Dodington and The Old Music Hall. SY 1EA. (G. MacGillivray). Resident. Est. 1978. appointment. SIZE: Large. *STOCK: Oak, fruitwood, walnut country and 18th to early 19th mahogany furniture, longcase clocks, barometers £10-£6,000.* LOC: On fringe of town centre. PARK: Easy. TEL: 01948 663399. SER: Buys auction. VAT: Stan/Spec.

WOORE, Nr. Crewe

The Mount
12 Nantwich Rd. CW3 9SA. Est. 1978. Op most afternoons and weekends (prior telepho call advisable). *STOCK: Watercolours, oils a drawings, Victorian to early 20th C; county ma prints, engravings and topographical items, fr 17th C; all £2-£500.* LOC: Junction of A51 a A525. PARK: Easy. TEL: 01630 647274; hom same. SER: Framing; finder (maps and topograph

No. 7 Antiques
7 Nantwich Rd. CW3 9SA. (D. and J. Belche Est. 1983. Open daily, Sun. by appointment. Mon. SIZE: Medium. *STOCK: Kitchenalia a fine country furniture, £25-£5,000; fine ceram £5-£500; garden furniture, £50-£500; small ite £50-£200; all 18th to early 20th C.* LOC: Junct A51 and A525. PARK: Easy. TEL: 016 647118. FAIRS: NEC. VAT: Spec.

Peter Wain BA
7 Nantwich Rd. CW3 9SA. Open 10-5, Sun. appointment. CL: Mon. SIZE: Mediu *STOCK: European and Oriental ceramics works of art, 16th-20th C, £50-£5,000.* LC A51, opposite church. PARK: Easy. TE 01630 647118. SER: Valuations; buys auction. VAT: Spec.

Somerset

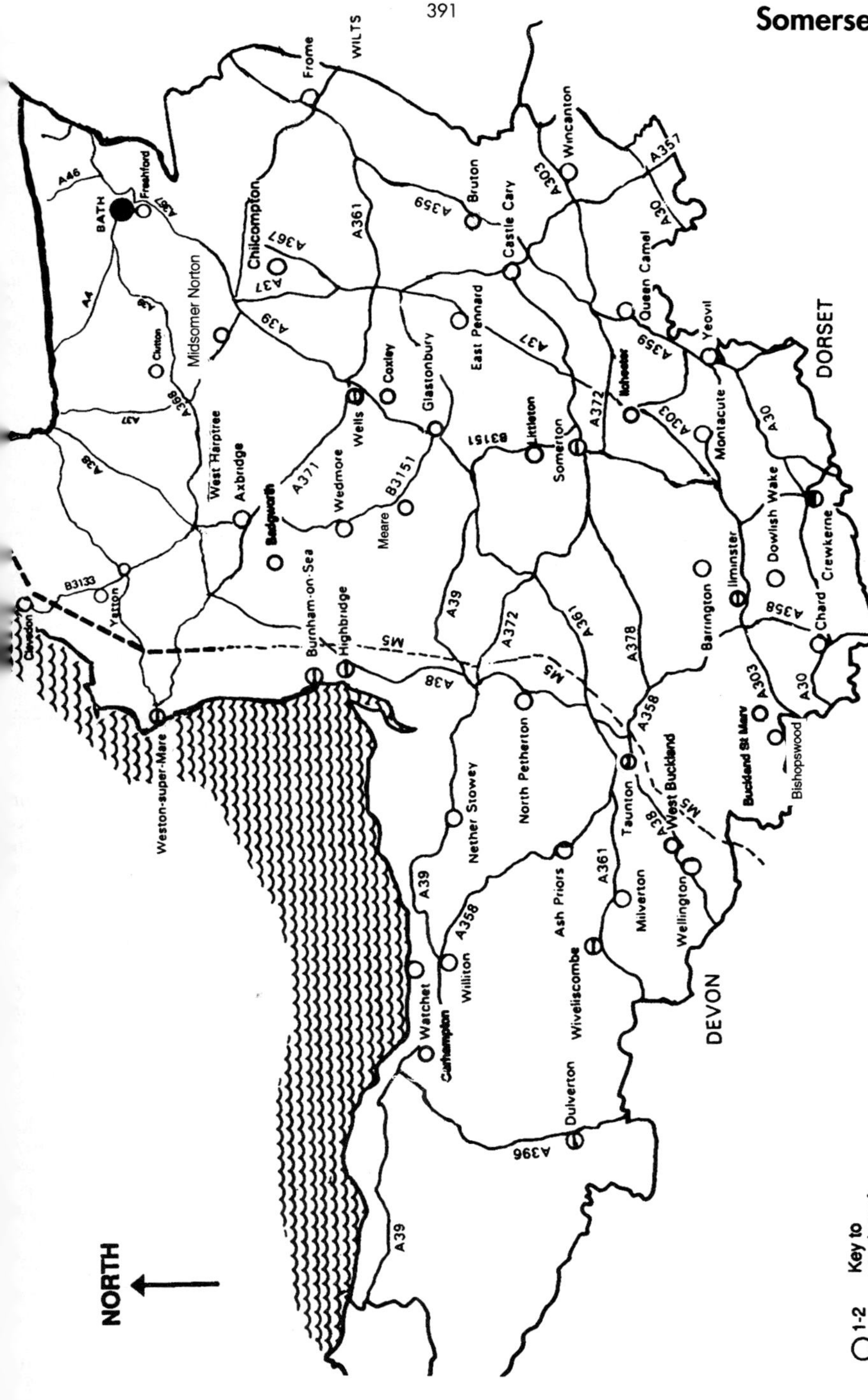

Please note this is only a rough map designed to show dealers the number of shops in the various towns, and is not necessarily totally accurate

○ 1-2 ⊖ 3-5 ◓ 6-12 ● 13+ Key to number of shops in this area.

ABBOTS LEIGH, Nr. Bristol

David and Sally March Antiques

LAPADA

Oak Wood Lodge, Stoke Leigh Woods. BS8 3QB. (D. and S. March). Est. 1981. Open by appointment. *STOCK: 18th to early 19th C English porcelain especially figures and Bristol.* PARK: Easy. TEL: 01275 372422; mobile - 0374 838376; fax - 01275 371032. SER: Valuations; buys at auction (as stock). FAIRS: LAPADA; Chelsea; NEC; Cumberland Ceramic. VAT: Spec.

ASH PRIORS, Nr. Taunton

The Granary Galleries

Court House. TA4 3NQ. (R. Hall). Est. 1969. Open 8.30-5.30. SIZE: Large. *STOCK: Period items, general antiques, 18th-19th C furniture, some shipping goods.* PARK: Easy. TEL: 01823 432402; home - (after 6.30) 01823 432816. VAT: Stan/Spec.

Hall's Antiques

Court House. TA4 3NQ. (A.R. and J.M. Hall). Est. 1945. Open 8.30-5.30. CL: Sun. except by appointment. SIZE: Large. *STOCK: English and Continental furniture, 18th-19th C; oil paintings,*

Ash Priors continued

watercolours, 17th-19th C; all £25-£10,00(shipping goods. LOC: On A358. PARK: Eas TEL: 01823 432402; home - same. SER: Val ations; buys at auction. VAT: Stan/Spec.

AXBRIDGE

The Old Post House

Weare, Bridgewater Rd. BS26 2JF. (Ray ar Mollie Seaman). *STOCK: General antiques ar country furniture.* TEL: 01934 732372.

BADGWORTH, Nr. Axbridge

John Hawley (MBHI) Antique Clock

Court Barn, Church Lane. BS26 2QP. Est. 197 Open by appointment. *STOCK: Clocks especia longcase, bracket, wall and carriage.* TE 01934 733444. SER: Valuations; restoratior repairs.

BARRINGTON, Nr. Ilminster

Stuart Interiors (Antiques) Ltd

LAPA

Barrington Court. TA19 0NG. Open 9-5, S 10-5. SIZE: Large. *STOCK: Oak furnitu*

3arrington continued

£100-£10,000; accessories, £50-£2,500; both pre-1720. Not Stocked: 18th C mahogany. LOC: Between A303 and M5, 5 miles north-east of Ilminster. House is National Trust property, ignposted in area. PARK: Easy. TEL: 01460 240349. SER: Valuations; buys at auction early oak furniture and accessories, interior lesign and architectural items including oak anelling). VAT: Spec.

3ATH

'27A" "27B"

.7a 27b Belvedere, Lansdown. BA1 5HR. (Paul Aichael Farnham and Associates). Est. 1970.)pen 10-6. SIZE: Large. *STOCK: Interesting urniture and objects from all periods.* PARK: :asy. TEL: 01225 428256; fax - same; internet - ttp://www.all-about-antiques.co.uk/ arnham.html.

Miles Buildings - Nick Kuhn

Miles Buildings, Off George St. BA1 2QS. Est. 992. Always open Sat. 10-5, other times by hance or appointment. SIZE: Small. *STOCK: 'ritish fine art, £30-£1,500; popular art - naive rt, unusual furniture, hooked rugs, country ottery, £10-£500; all 19th-20th C.* LOC: City entre, near Bartlett Street Antiques Centres. ARK: Nearby. TEL: 01225 425486. FAIRS: ath & Bradford-on-Avon Antique Dealers.

\bbey Galleries

Abbey Churchyard. BA1 1LY. (R. Dickson). st. 1930. Open 10.30-5.30. *STOCK: Jewellery, 50; Oriental, £100; both 18th-19th C; silver, 8th C, £100.* Not Stocked: Furniture. TEL: 1225 460565. SER: Valuations; restorations ewellery and clocks); buys at auction. VAT: tan.

.dam Gallery

3 John St. BA1 2JL. (P. and P. Dye). Open 9.30-30 or by appointment. *STOCK: Late Victorian ad Modern British oil paintings and water-lours, especially figurative and landscape, and lasgow and Newlyn Schools, £200-£20,000.* EL: 01225 480406; fax - same. SER: Contemp-ary exhibitions.

lderson BADA

3 Brock St. BA1 2LW. (C.J.R. Alderson). ABADA. Est. 1975. Open 9.30-1 and 2-5.30. *TOCK: Furniture, 17th-18th C; period etalwork, glass, silver.* LOC: Between the ircus and Royal Crescent. PARK: Easy. EL: 01225 421652. SER: Valuations. VAT: pec.

ntique Linens and Lace

Pulteney Bridge. BA2 4AY. (Mrs R. Mellor). ABADA. Est. 1971. Open 10-5.30 including

Bath continued

Sun. SIZE: Small. *STOCK: Quality linens and lace, bedspreads, sheets, tablecloths, pillow cases, christening gowns, baby bonnets, collars, veils and shawls, 1850-1920, £10-£600.* LOC: City centre. PARK: Great Pulteney St.- 100 yards. TEL: 01225 465782; fax - 01225 754067. VAT: Stan/Spec.

The Antiques Warehouse

57 Walcot St. BA1 5BN. BABADA. Open 10.30-5.30. SIZE: Medium. *STOCK: 19th C mahogany furniture, £300-£2,000 and decorative objects, £20-£200.* LOC: From junction 18 M4 along A46 then A4, at first mini-roundabout veer left into Walcot St. Shop 300yds on right. PARK: Easy. TEL: 01225 444201; mobile - 0836 338131. VAT: Stan/Spec.

Arkea Antiques

10A Monmouth Place. (G. Harmandian). Est. 1972. *STOCK: Furniture and china.* TEL: 01225 429413/835382. SER: Repairs (antiques); traditional French polishing.

G.A. Baines of Bath

BA2 4BT. (G. and J. Baines). By appointment only. *STOCK: Early oak country and French provincial furniture.* TEL: 01225 332566. VAT: Spec.

Bartlett Street Antique Centre

5-10 Bartlett St. BA1 2QZ. BABADA. Open 9.30-5, Wed. 8-5. SIZE: 100+ dealers. *STOCK: Wide range of general antiques.* TEL: 01225 466689; stallholders - 01225 310457/446322; fax - 01225 444146.

Bath Antiques Market

Guinea Lane, Off Lansdown Rd. BA1 5NB. BABADA. Est. 1968. Open Wed. only 6.30-2.30. SIZE: 60 dealers. *STOCK: General antiques and collectables.* LOC: From London A4 across two sets of traffic lights after entering Bath. Right at third set (Lansdown Rd.) and first right again. PARK: Nearby. TEL: 01225 337638; enquiries - 0171 351 5353; fax - 01225 422510. SER: Valuations.

Bath Galleries

33 Broad St. BA1 5LP. (J. Griffiths). Open 9.30-5. SIZE: Medium. *STOCK: Always 50 clocks in stock, furniture, paintings, porcelain, jewellery, barometers, silver.* LOC: 50yds. from Central Post Office. PARK: Walcot St. multi-park, 30yds. TEL: 01225 462946. SER: Valuations; restorations; buys at auction. VAT: Stan/Spec.

Bath Saturday Antiques Market

Walcot St. (J. Whittingham). Est. 1978. Open Sat. 7-5. SIZE: 100 stalls. *STOCK: Wide variety of general antiques, £1-£500.* LOC: Close to Hilton Hotel. PARK: Multi-storey. TEL: 01225 317154.

Bath continued

Bath Stamp and Coin Shop
Pulteney Bridge. BA2 4AY. (H. and A. Swindells). Est. 1946. Open 9.30-5.30. *STOCK: Coins - Roman, hammered, early milled, G.B. gold, silver and copper, some foreign; literature and accessories; banknotes, medals, stamps and postal history.* PARK: Laura Place; Walcott multi-storey. SER: Valuations. VAT: Stan.

George Bayntun
Manvers St. BA1 1JW. (H.H. Bayntun-Coward). BABADA. Est. 1829. Open 9-1 and 2-5.30, Sat. 9.30-1. SIZE: Large. *STOCK: Rare books. First or fine editions of English literature, standard sets, illustrated and sporting books, poetry, biography and travel, mainly in new leather bindings; also large stock of antiquarian books in original bindings.* LOC: By railway and bus stations. PARK: 50 yds. by station. TEL: 01225 466000; fax - 01225 482122. SER: Restorations (rare books). VAT: Stan.

Beau Nash Antiques
1st Floor, Beau Nash House, Union Passage. BA1 1RD. BABADA. Est. 1973. Open 10-5. SIZE: Large. *STOCK: English furniture, 1700-1840, £1,000-£25,000; oil paintings, 1800-1890, £750-£10,000; decorative objects, 1760-1890, £150-£1,500.* LOC: 75 yds. from Guildhall in lanes opposite. PARK: Waitrose public. TEL: 01225 447806; fax - same. VAT: Spec.

Bladud House Antiques
8 Bladud Buildings. BA1 5LS. (Mrs E. Radosenska). Open 9.30-1 and 2-4.30. CL: Mon. and Thurs. *STOCK: Jewellery and small items.* Not Stocked: Furniture. TEL: 01225 462929.

Blyth Antiques
28 Sydney Buildings. BA2 6BZ. (B. Blyth). Resident. Est. 1971. Open by appointment. *STOCK: Small furniture, samplers, brass and unusual decorative items.* LOC: Off Bathwick Hill. PARK: Easy. TEL: 01225 469766.

Lawrence Brass
PO Box 1942. BA1 3SD. BAFRA: UKIC. Est. 1973. Open by appointment. SIZE: Small. *STOCK: Furniture, 16th-19th C, £50-£5,000.* Not Stocked: Ceramics, silver, glass. LOC: Main road into town centre. PARK: Easy. TEL: 01225 852222. SER: Restorations (furniture, clocks and barometers). VAT: Stan/Spec.

Geoffrey Breeze LAPADA
6 George St. BA1 2EH. BABADA. Open 10-5. *STOCK: Furniture, 18th-20th C.* TEL: 01225 466499.

David Bridgwater
Heather Cottage, Lansdown. BA1 9BL. Open by appointment. *STOCK: Traditional garden architecture, sculpture, pots, watering cans, implements and decorative items for the period garden and conservatory.* TEL: 01225 463435.

Bath continued

Bruton Gallery
35 Gay St., Queen Sq. BA1 2NT. (Mrs S. L Marchant). Est. 1975. Open 10-1 and 2-5.30 SIZE: Medium. *STOCK: European sculpture 19th-20th C; contemporary paintings an sculpture.* PARK: Nearby. TEL: 01225 466292 fax - 01225 461294. FAIRS: Art '96. VAT Stan/Spec.

Bryers Antiques
Entrance to the Guildhall Market, High St. BA 1JQ. (S. Bryers). Est. 1940. *STOCK: Furniture decorative items, porcelain, glass, silver an Victorian plate.* TEL: 01225 466352/46053 VAT: Stan/Spec.

Sheila Cooper t/a Sheila Smith Antiques
Stand 61, Bartlett St. Antique Centre, 5-1 Bartlett St. BA2. (S.M. Cooper). Est. 1967. Ope 9.30-5. *STOCK: Fans, needlework tools an accessories, collectors' items.* LOC: A4 into cit At 3rd set of traffic lights, turn right int Lansdown then 2nd left into Alfred St. TEL 01225 442730.

Corridor Stamp Shop
7a The Corridor. BA1 5AP. (G.H. and S.M Organ). Est. 1970. Open 9.30-5.30. CL: Mo SIZE: Small. *STOCK: Stamp and postal histor 1700 to date, 5p-£500; albums, reference book picture postcards, cigarette cards, 1895-194* LOC: Within 200yds. of Abbey. PARK: Walc St. TEL: 01225 463368; home - 01225 31644 SER: Valuations.

Brian and Caroline Craik Ltd
8 Margaret's Buildings. BA1 2LP. *STOCK: Decorative items, mainly 19th C; metalwor treen, glass and pewter.* TEL: 01225 337161.

John Croft Antiques LAPADA
3 George St. BA1 2EH. BABADA. Open 10-5.3 CL: Mon. SIZE: Medium. *STOCK: Furnitur 17th to early 19th C; decorative objec paintings.* LOC: A4, turn left at top of Milso St., opposite 'Hole in the Wall' restaura PARK: Broad St. 100yds. TEL: 01225 4662 VAT: Spec.

Mary Cruz LAPADA
15 Broad St. BA1 5LJ. (Mary Cruz-Agat BABADA. CINOA. Est. 1974. Open 10-6. Sun. by appointment. SIZE: Medium. *STOCK: 17th-19th C furniture and decorative item 19th-20th C paintings and bronzes.* PAR Easy. TEL: 01225 334174; home - 012 858000. SER: Valuations; restorations. VA Stan/Spec.

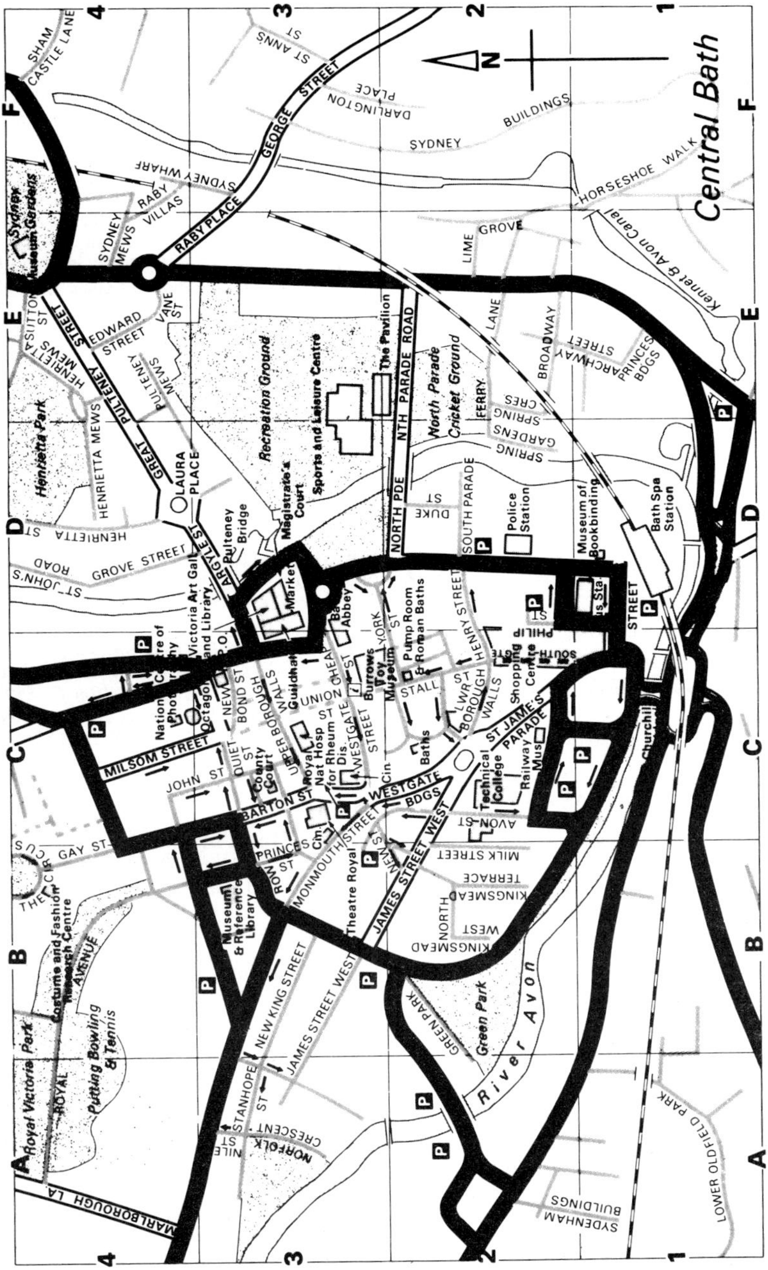

Key to Town Plan

AA Recommended roads		Car Parks	P
Other roads		Parks and open spaces	
Restricted roads		AA Service Centre	AA
Buildings of interest			

Bath continued

Andrew Dando BADA

4 Wood St., Queen Sq. BA1 2JQ. (A.P. and J.M. Dando). Est. 1915. Open 9.30-5.30, Sat. 10-1. SIZE: Large. *STOCK: English, Continental, Oriental porcelain and pottery, 17th to mid-19th C; furniture, 18th to mid-19th C.* LOC: 200yds. from bottom of Milsom St. towards Queen Sq. TEL: 01225 422702. SER: Valuations. VAT: Stan/Spec.

D. and B. Dickinson BADA

22 New Bond St. BA1 1BA. (S.G., D. and N.W. Dickinson and Mrs E.M. Dickinson). BABADA. Est. 1917. Open 9.30-1 and 2-5. CL: Sat. pm. SIZE: Small. *STOCK: Jewellery, 1770-1900, £20-£2,000; silver, 1750-1900, £25-£3,000; Sheffield plate, 1770-1845, £50-£1,000.* LOC: Next to Post Office. PARK: 100yds. at bottom of street, turn left then right for multi-storey. TEL: 01225 466502. VAT: Stan/Spec.

Frank Dux Antiques

33 Belvedere, Lansdown Rd. BA1 5HR. (F. Dux and M. Hopkins). Resident. BABADA. Open 10-6. SIZE: Medium. *STOCK: Georgian and earlier furniture (mainly oak), £250-£5,000; 18th C and later glass, £10-£1,000; unusual decorative items - pottery, pewter, pictures, rugs.* LOC: From Broad St. up Lansdown Hill, on right 100yds.

Bath continued

past Guinea Lane. PARK: Easy. TEL: 01225 312367; fax - same. SER: Restorations (furniture); replicas made to order; search service. VAT: Spec.

The Galleon

33 Monmouth St. BA1 2AN. (D.L. Gwilliam and M.J. Wren). Est. 1972. Open Tues.-Sat. 10-5.30 or by appointment. SIZE: Medium. *STOCK: Furniture, jewellery, silver, china, copper, brass, general collectables and antiques, Georgian to Art Deco, £5-£1,500.* LOC: Near rear of Theatre Royal. PARK: Easy. TEL: 01225 312330. VAT: Stan/Spec.

George Gregory

Manvers St. BA1 1JW. (H.H. Bayntun-Coward). Est. 1845. Open 9-1 and 2-5.30, Sat. 9.30-1. SIZE: Large. *STOCK: Books, 1600 to date; engravings.* LOC: By rail station. PARK: By rail station. TEL: 01225 466055. SER: Restorations (fine books). VAT: Stan.

Haliden Oriental Rug Shop

98 Walcot St. BA1 5BG. (B.W. Dennis). Est 1963. Open 10-5. SIZE: Medium. *STOCK: Caucasian, Turkish, Persian, Chinese, Afghan Turcoman and tribal rugs and carpets, 19th C £50-£3,000; some Oriental textiles - coats embroideries, wall hangings, 19th C, £50-£750* LOC: Off main London road, into town by Walcot Reclamation. PARK: Walcot St. or multi storey. TEL: 01225 469240. SER: Valuations cleaning; restorations (as stock); buys at auction (as stock).

Helena Hood and Co

3 Margarets Buildings, Brock St. BA1 2LP. (Mr L.M. Hood). BABADA. Est. 1973. Open 9.30- and 2.15-5.30, Sat. 10.30-1. CL: Mon. SIZE Medium. *STOCK: Decorative items - furniture prints, paintings and porcelain, 18th-19th C, £50 £2,500.* LOC: Pedestrian walkway running nort from Brock St. PARK: Easy. TEL: 0122 424438. SER: Restorations. VAT: Stan/Spec.

Jadis Ltd

The Old Bank, 17 Walcot Buildings, London Rd BA1 6AD. (S.H. Creese-Parsons and N.A Mackay). BABADA. Est. 1970. Open 9.30-6 Sun. by appointment. SIZE: Medium. *STOCK: Furniture, English and European, 18th-19th C decorative items.* LOC: On left hand side of A London Rd., entering Bath. PARK: At rear. TEL 01225 338797; fax - same; mobile - 046 232133. VAT: Stan/Spec.

Orlando Jones

10b Monmouth Place, Upper Bristol Rd. BA 2AX. Open 9.30-5.30. *STOCK: Victorian an Edwardian brass bedsteads.* TEL: 01225 42275

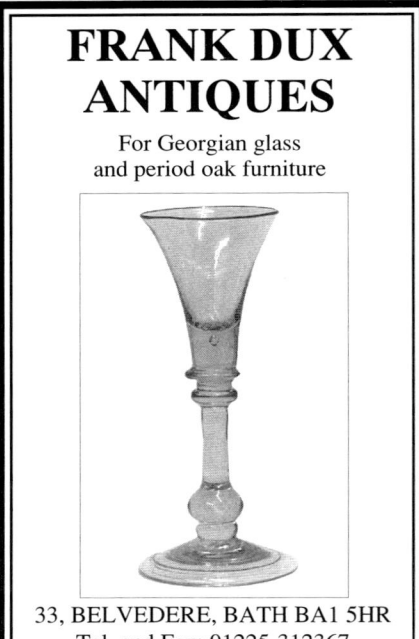

Bath continued

K & D Antique Clocks
Bartlett Street Antique Centre, 5 Bartlett Street. BA1 2QZ. (E. Kembery). Est. 1993. Open 10-5. *STOCK: Longcase, bracket, mantel, wall and carriage clocks and barometers, 18th-19th C, £200-£10,000.* TEL: 0117 956 5281. SER: Valuations; restorations. VAT: Spec.

Ann King
38 Belvedere, Lansdown Rd. BA1 5HR. Est. 1977. Open 10-5. SIZE: Small. *STOCK: Period clothes, 19th C to 1960; baby clothes, shawls, bead dresses, linen, lace, curtains, cushions, quilts and textiles.* LOC: Around corner from Guinea Lane Antique Market. PARK: Easy. TEL: 01225 336245.

Kingsley Gallery
16 Margarets Buildings, Brock St. BA1 2LP. BABADA. Open 10.30-5.30 including Sun., or by appointment. SIZE: Medium. *STOCK: 19th-20th C furniture, paintings, silver and decorative items.* LOC: Off Brock St. between The Circus and Royal Crescent. PARK: Nearby. TEL: 01225 448432.

Lansdown Antiques
23 Belvedere, Lansdown Rd. BA1 5ED. (Chris and Ann Kemp). BABADA. Open 9.30-6, Sat. 9.30-5.30, Sun. by appointment. *STOCK: Painted pine and country furniture, 17th-19th C; metalware, unusual and decorative items.* LOC: From A4/A46 junction across 1st set of traffic lights, right at mini roundabout, right at next traffic lights, shop 350yds. on left. PARK: Easy. TEL: 01225 313417; home - same. VAT: Stan/Spec.

Looking Glass of Bath
96 Walcot St. BA1 5BG. (Anthony Reed). Est. 1972. Open 9-6. SIZE: Small. *STOCK: Large mirrors and picture frames, 18th-19th C, £50-£5,000; decorative prints, 18th-20th C.* PARK: Easy. TEL: 01225 461969; home - 01275 333595. SER: Valuations; restorations (re-gilding, gesso and compo work, re-silvering and bevelling glass); manufactures arched top overmantel, pier, convex and triptych mirrors; old mirror plates supplied; buys at auction (mirrors and pictures). VAT: Stan/Spec.

E.P. Mallory and Son Ltd — BADA
1-4 Bridge St. and 5 Old Bond St. BA2 4AP. BABADA. Est. 1856. Open 10-5. *STOCK: Period silver and Sheffield plate, jewellery, objets de vertu, £50-£5,000.* TEL: 01225 465885; fax - 01225 442210. VAT: Stan/Spec.

Moderne
4 Whitcombe Parade, Claverton St. BA2 4JT. (P. Marshall and T. de Kyme). Est. 1969. Open Tues.-Sat. 10.30-5.30. SIZE: Small. *STOCK: Art Deco, 50's and 60's.* TEL: 01225 465000.

Bath continued

Montague Antiques
16 Walcot Buildings, London Rd. BA1 6AD. (A. R. Schlesinger and D.K. Moore). BABADA. Resident. Est. 1986. Open 10-6, Sun.11-4. CL: Thurs. SIZE: Medium. *STOCK: Furniture, 17th C to 1920, £50-£1,000; collectables, Oriental rugs, ceramics, glass, £1-£500; glass light shades and fittings, to 1939, £5-£1,500.* Not Stocked: Weapons and jewellery. LOC: A4. Shop near pedestrian crossing past bus depot. PARK: Own at rear, via Bedford St. TEL: 01225 469282; home - same. SER: Valuations.

Francis O'Dwyer Antiques
16a High St., Rode. BA3 6NZ. (Francis and Dominic O'Dwyer). Open Mon.-Fri. 9-6, or by appointment. *STOCK: Period antiques and country furniture.* TEL: 01373 830531; fax - 01373 830792. *Trade and Export.*

Paragon Antiques and Collectors Market
3 Bladud Buildings, The Paragon. BA1 5LS. (T.J. Clifford and Son Ltd). Est. 1978. Open Wed. 6.30-3.30. SIZE: Large. LOC: Milsom St./Broad St. PARK: 50yds. TEL: 01225 463715.

Patterson Liddle
10 Margaret's Buildings, Brock St. BA1 2LP. ABA, PBFA. Open 10-5.30. *STOCK: Antiquarian books and prints especially art and architecture, illustrated and transport history, travel, English literature, maps.* PARK: Nearby. TEL: 01225 426722; fax - same. SER: Catalogues issued.

Pennard House Antiques — LAPADA
3/4 Piccadilly, London Rd. BA1 6PL. (M. and S. Dearden). BABADA. Est. 1966. Open 9.30-5.30. SIZE: Large. *STOCK: Pine, 18th-19th C, £100-£2,000; French provincial furniture, 17th-19th C; £500-£2,500; decorative items, 19th C, £30-£350.* LOC: On A4 from east when entering city. PARK: Easy and at rear. TEL: 01225 313791; fax - 01225 448196; home - 01749 860266. SER: Valuations; restorations (furniture). VAT: Stan/Spec. The following dealers are also trading from these premises.

Robin and Jan Coleman Antiques
Interesting and decorative items. VAT: Stan/Spec.

John Davies
18th-19th C furniture especially country and Gothic oak, and decorative smalls. TEL: Home - 01225 852103.

Gene and Sally Foster (Antiques)
Decorative and unusal items, 17th-19th C; Continental and English painted furniture, paintings, needlework, prints and metalware, £25-£2,500. VAT: Stan/Spec.

Bath continued

John Holden
Furniture and decorative accessories, 18th -19th C.

Mike Holt
19th C decorative metalware.

Denny Leroy
Country furniture, primitive and naïve artefacts, samplers and quilts.

Quiet Street Antiques
3 Quiet St. and 14/15 John St. BA1 2JS. (K. Hastings-Spital). BABADA. Est. 1985. Open 10-6. SIZE: Large - 8 showrooms. *STOCK: Furniture, 1750-1870, £250-£6,000; objects including bronzes, caddies, boxes, mirrors, £50-£2,000; Royal Worcester porcelain, £30-£2,000; clocks including longcase, wall, bracket and carriage, 1750-1900, £150-£5,000.* LOC: 25yds. from Milsom St. PARK: Nearby. TEL: 01225 315727. SER: Buys at auction (furniture and clocks); upholstery; free delivery service 100 mile radius of Bath.

P.R. Rainsford
23a Manvers St. BA1 1JW. Est. 1967. *STOCK: Architecture, fine and applied art.* TEL: 01225 445107; fax - 01225 482122. VAT: Stan.

T.E. Robinson BADA
3 and 4 Bartlett St. BA1 2QZ. Est. 1957. *STOCK: Period furniture, unusual and rare items.* TEL: 01225 463982; fax - same; home - 01225 832307. VAT: Spec.

Michael and Jo Saffell
3 Walcot Buildings, London Rd. BA1 6AD. Est. 1975. Open 9.30-5, Sat. by appointment. SIZE: Small. *STOCK: British tins and other advertising material including showcards and enamels, 1870-1939; decorative items; all £5-£500.* LOC: A4 - main road into city from M4. PARK: Side streets opposite. TEL: 01225 315857; home - same.

Susannah
142/144 Walcot St. BA1 5BC. (Susan M. Holley). Open 10-5. *STOCK: Decorative antiques and textiles.* TEL: 01225 445069.

Bruce Tozer Rugs & Antiques
4 Cleveland Terrace, London St. BA1 5DF. (Bruce and Jan Tozer). BABADA. Open 10-5.30, or by appointment. SIZE: Small. *STOCK: Tribal rugs, room size carpets, kilims, textile fragments, saddle bags and trappings; tables, cupboards, chests, sofas covered in carpet, from £20.* LOC: On A4 into Bath, 5 mins. from city centre. PARK: Easy. TEL: 01225 420875; home - same. SER: Valuations; cleaning; restoration. FAIRS: BABADA.

Bath continued

Trimbridge Galleries
2 Trimbridge. BA1 1HD. (Mr and Mrs A Anderson). Est. 1973. SIZE: Medium. *STOCK: Watercolours and drawings, £50-£3,000; prints and oil paintings; all 18th to early 20th C.* LOC: Just off lower end of Milsom St. PARK: Easy. TEL: 01225 466390.

Walcot Reclamation
108 Walcot St. BA1 5BG. BABADA. Est. 197- Open 8.30-5.30, Sat. 9-5. SIZE: Large. *STOCK: Architectural items - chimney pieces, ironwork doors, fireplaces, garden statuary, period bath and fittings and traditional building materials.* PARK: Own and multi-storey nearby. TEL: 01225 444404/335532. SER: Valuations; restorations; brochure available. VAT: Stan.

BISHOPSWOOD, Nr. Chard

M. Wood
Est. 1980. Open by appointment. SIZE: Medium. *STOCK: 18th-19th C pottery, porcelain and glass.* LOC: 1 mile off A303 and 1 mile off B317- PARK: Easy. TEL: 01460 234639.

BRUTON

Michael Lewis Gallery
17 High St. BA10 0AB. Open 9.30-5.30, or by appointment. CL: Thurs. pm. SIZE: Large. *STOCK: Maps, 17th-19th C; prints, mostly 18th-19th C.* LOC: A359. PARK: High St. TEL: 017- 813557; home - same. SER: Picture framing.

M.G.R. Exports
Station Rd. BA10 0EH. Open 8.30-5.30 or by appointment. SIZE: Large. *STOCK: Georgian, Victorian, Edwardian and shipping items, barley twist oak, Lloyd loom and smalls.* PARK: Easy. TEL: 01749 812460; fax - 01749 812882. SER: Packing and shipping by Camion 01749 81372-

BUCKLAND ST. MARY, Nr. Chard

Combesbury Antiques
Comesbury Farm. TA20 3ST. (Susan and Trev- Micklem). Est. 1962. Appointment preferred. *STOCK: Fine early furniture, antiques and works of art.* TEL: 01460 234323; home - same.

BURNHAM-ON-SEA

Adam Antiques
30 Adam St. TA8 1PQ. (R. Coombes). Open 9- SIZE: Large. *STOCK: Furniture, clocks, brass, porcelain and shipping goods.* PARK: Easy. TEL: 01278 783193.

Burnham-on-Sea continued

Castle Antiques
Victoria Court, Victoria St. TA8 1AL. (T.C. Germain). Open daily except Wed. *STOCK: Jewellery, silver, 18th-19th C furniture, porcelain, clocks.* TEL: 01278 785031.

Heape's Antiques
39 Victoria St. TA8 1AN. (Mrs M.M. Heap). FATG. Open 10-1 and 2.30-4.30. *STOCK: Small furniture, fine arts, porcelain, glass, memorabilia.* TEL: 01278 782131.

CARHAMPTON

J.C. Giddings
Open 11-5.30 including Sun. SIZE: Large warehouses. *STOCK: Mostly 18th-19th C furniture, iron-work and general building reclamation materials.* LOC: A39 coast road. TEL: 01643 821873.

CASTLE CARY

Cary Antiques Ltd
High St. (Mrs. J.A. Oldham). Est. 1977. Open 10.30-5. CL: Mon. and Wed. SIZE: Small. *STOCK: Furniture, Victorian and Edwardian, £30-£500; china, brass and copper, glass, bric-a-brac, pictures, 18th-19th C, £5-£150.* LOC: Town centre, B3152. PARK: Easy. TEL: 01963 350437. SER: Valuations; picture framing; caning and rushing; repairs (china).

CHARD

Guildhall Antique Market
The Guildhall. TA20 1PH. Open Thurs. 9-3. SIZE: 26 dealers. *STOCK: General antiques and collectables.*

CHILCOMPTON, Nr. Bath

Billiard Room Antiques
The Old School, Church Lane. BA3 4HP. (Mrs J. McKeivor). Est. 1992. Open by appointment. SIZE: Small. *STOCK: Billiard, snooker and pool tables and accessories, 19th C, £100-£10,000.* PARK: Easy. TEL: 01761 232839; home and fax same. SER: Valuations; restorations; buys at auction; search.

CLEVEDON

Beach Antiques
Adelaide House, 13 The Beach. BS21 7QU. (D.A. Coles). Open 2-5, Sat. and Sun. 11-5. CL: Mon. and Fri. *STOCK: Jewellery, silver frames, china, brass, glass, mainly small items.* PARK: Easy. TEL: 01275 876881.

CLUTTON

Ian McCarthy
Arcadian Cottage, 112 Station Rd. BS18 4RA. Resident. Est. 1958. Open by appointment. SIZE: Medium. *STOCK: Lamps - oil, gas, electric for domestic, industrial, shipping and transport usage; unusual candle lamps; copper and brassware, 17th C to 1920, £5-£2,000.* PARK: Easy and opposite. TEL: 01761 453188. SER: Valuations; restorations (metalware); cleaning; spares and lamp-shades. *Trade Only.*

COXLEY, Nr. Wells

Wells Reclamation Company
The Old Cider Farm. BA5 1RQ. (H. Davies). Est. 1984. Open 9-5.30. SIZE: Large. *STOCK: Architectural items, 18th-19th C.* LOC: A39 towards Glastonbury from Wells. PARK: Easy. TEL: 01749 677087; home - 01749 677484. SER: Valuations. VAT: Stan.

CREWKERNE

Antique and Country Pine
14 East St. TA18 7AG. (R.W.H. and M.J. Wheeler). Open Tues.-Sat. 10-5 or by appointment. *STOCK: Country pine.* TEL: 01460 75623.

Julian Armytage
Open by appointment only. *STOCK: Fine sporting, marine and decorative prints, 18th-19th C.* TEL: 01460 73449; fax - same.

Crewkerne Furniture Emporium
Viney Bridge, South St. TA18 8AE. (A.P. and J.F. Bucke). Est. 1974. Open 8.30-5.30, Sun. 11-5. *STOCK: Furniture, shipping goods, collectors' items, agricultural bygones.* TEL: 01460 75319.

David Gibson BADA LAPADA
5 Church St. TA18 7HR. Est. 1975. Open 2-5, Sat. 10-2. SIZE: Medium. *STOCK: Longcase clocks, £3,000-£28,000; barometers.* PARK: Easy. TEL: 01460 76667. SER: Valuations; restorations. FAIRS: Olympia, NEC, and Northern (Harrogate). VAT: Spec.

Hennessy LAPADA
42 East St. TA18 7AG. (Carl Hennessy). Est. 1977. Open Tues., Wed., Fri. and Sat. 10-5, other times by appointment. SIZE: Large. *STOCK: Furniture - pine, country, painted and French provincial; related decorative items.* LOC: A30 from Yeovil. PARK: Easy. TEL: 01460 78060; fax - 01460 78600. VAT: Stan/Spec.

Crewkerne continued

Octopus Antique Centre
16 Market St. TA18 7LA. (W. Minton). Est. 198 Open 10-5. CL: Mon. SIZE: Medium. *STOC Furniture, £25-£1,000; collectables, £5-£20 pictures, £10-£200; all 19th-20th C.* LOC: A3 westward. A359 to Crewkerne, Chard ro through town. PARK: Easy. TEL: 01460 7711 SER: Valuations; restorations (French polishi and repairs); buys at auction. FAIRS: Ardingl Newark, Shepton Mallet. VAT: Stan.

Oscars Antiques
13-15 Market Sq. and North St. TA18 7LE. (B and H.M. Hall). Est. 1966. Open 10-5. SIZE: Lar *STOCK: Victoriana, shipping goods, china a books.* LOC: Centre of the square on A30. PAR Easy. TEL: 01460 72718. VAT: Stan/Spec.

DOWLISH WAKE, Nr. Ilminster

Dowlish Wake Antiques
TA19 0NY. (Mrs G. Estling). Est. 1973. Open 1 and 2.30-5.30. SIZE: Medium. *STOCK: Ceram only - English porcelain and pottery, late 18th C early 20th C.* LOC: Take Ilminster/Crewkerne r and turn off at Kingstone corner, downhill village. PARK: Easy. TEL: 01460 52784; fa same. VAT: Stan/Spec.

)ULVERTON

\corn Antiques
·9 High St. TA22 9DW. (P. Hounslow). Est. 988. Open 9.30-5.30. SIZE: Medium. *STOCK: :ountry furniture, 18th-19th C; fine art, textiles, vorks of art, £5-£5,000.* LOC: Town centre. 'ARK: Nearby. TEL: 01398 323286; home - ame. SER: Interior design.

;uy Dennler Antiques
'he White Hart, 23 High St. TA22 9HB. Open 0-5. *STOCK: English furniture, decorative bjects, papier mâché, pictures, porcelain and amps, 18th-19th C.* TEL: 01398 324300; fax - ·1398 324301.

'aded Elegance
9 High St. TA22 9DW. (M. Delbridge). Open .30-5.30. *STOCK: 18th-19th C decorative ntiques, textiles, upholstery.* TEL: 01398 323286.

₹othwell and Dunworth
Bridge St. TA22 9HJ. (Mrs C. Rothwell and M.)unworth). ABA. Est. 1975. Open 10.30-1 and .15-5. SIZE: Medium. *STOCK: Antiquarian and econdhand books especially on hunting and orses.* LOC: 1st shop in village over River Barle. 'ARK: 100yds. TEL: 01398 323169; fax - 01398 31161. SER: Valuations.

:AST PENNARD, Nr. Shepton Mallet

'ennard House
;A4 6TP. (M. and S. Dearden). Resident. Est. 979. Open by appointment. SIZE: Large. *TOCK: Pine furniture, 18th-19th C, £100-2,000; French provincial tables, armoires, uffets, £300-£3,000.* LOC: From Shepton Mallet, miles south off A37. PARK: Easy. TEL: 01749 60266; home - same. SER: Valuations; restortions (pine and country furniture). VAT: tan/Spec. *Trade Only.*

'RESHFORD, Nr. Bath

anet Clarke
Woodside Cottages. BA3 6EJ. Open by appointnent. *STOCK: Antiquarian books on gastronomy, ookery and wine.* TEL: 01225 723186. SER: 'atalogue issued.

ROME

\ntiques & Country Living
3-44 Vallis Way, Badcox. BA11 3BA. (Mrs ·.M. Williams). Est. 1994. Open 9.30-5.30 ncluding Sun. SIZE: Medium. *STOCK: Furniture ncluding country, 19th-20th C, £15-£1,000; orcelain, 18th-19th C, £5-£500.* LOC: A362 rome to Radstock road. PARK: Free opposite. EL: 01373 463015. SER: Valuations.

Frome continued

Sutton and Sons
15 and 33 Vicarage St. BA11 1PX. *STOCK: Furniture, 18th-19th C; clocks, pictures, decorative pieces.* TEL: 01373 462062/462526. SER: Restorations and upholstery. VAT: Stan/Spec.

GLASTONBURY

Abbey Antiques
51 High St. BA6 9DS. (G.E. Browning and Son). Est. 1952. Open 8-5. CL: Sat. SIZE: Small. *STOCK: Glass and furniture.* TEL: 01458 831694. VAT: Stan.

HIGHBRIDGE

C.W.E. and R.I. Dyte Antiques
LAPADA

The Old Bacon Factory, Huntspill Rd. TA9 3DE. Open 8-5.30 or by appointment. SIZE: Large. *STOCK: Mahogany, oak, walnut, 18th-20th C, shipping goods.* PARK: Easy. TEL: 01278 788590/788603; home - 01278 683761. SER: Packing; transport; documentation.

T.M. Dyte Antiques
1 Huntspill Rd. Open 8.30-5.30. CL: Sat. *STOCK: Shipping goods.* TEL: 01278 786495.

Terence Kelly Antiques
Huntspill Court, West Huntspill. TA9 3QZ. Open by appointment. *STOCK: Furniture, decorative and collectors' items.* TEL: 01278 785052.

The Treasure Chest
The Jays, 19 Alstone Lane. TA9 3DS. (R.J. and V. Rumble). Est. 1964. CL: Sun., except by appointment. SIZE: Medium. *STOCK: General antiques including furniture, 17th-20th C; smalls especially silver plate, glass, clocks and musical boxes.* LOC: Off A38 down lane by Royal Artillery public house, 200yds. on left. PARK: Easy. TEL: 01278 787267. SER: Valuations; restorations (pictures); buys at auction. VAT: Stan/Spec. *Trade Only.*

ILCHESTER

Gilbert & Dale
The Old Chapel, Church St. Est. 1965. Open 9-5.30 or by appointment. SIZE: Large. *STOCK: English and French country furniture and accessories.* LOC: Centre of village on A37. PARK: Easy. TEL: 01935 840464; fax - 01935 841599; home - 01458 250193.

ILMINSTER

County Antiques Centre

17 Court Barton. TA19 0DU. (Mrs J.P. Barnard). Resident. Est. 1981. Open Mon., Thurs., Fri. and Sat. 10.30-5.30, or by appointment. SIZE: Medium - 12 dealers. *STOCK: 18th-19th C pottery, porcelain, metalwork, furniture and decorative antiques.* LOC: PARK: TEL: 01460 54151; home - 01460 52269; mobile - 0378 371967.SER: Upholstery.

James Hutchison

5 West St. TA19 9AA. *STOCK: Pictures, frames, china and glass, collectables, furniture.*

West End House Antiques

34-36 West St. TA19 9AB. (T.H. Sabine). Est. 1964. Open 9.30-5. SIZE: Large. *STOCK: Furniture, 18th to early 20th C, £50-£700; Art Deco china including Clarice Cliff, £5-£1,000; pictures, 19th-20th C, £10-£500.* LOC: Old A303. PARK: Easy. TEL: 01460 52793; home - 01404 42140. SER: Valuations; buys at auction.

LITTLETON, Nr. Somerton

Westville House Antiques

TA11 6NP. (D. and M. Stacey). Est. 1986. Open daily, Sun. by appointment. SIZE: Large. *STOCK: 18th-19th C pine furniture, £100-£5,000, country*

Littleton continued

antiques. LOC: B3151 approximately 1.5 mil north of Somerton. PARK: Own. TEL: 0145 273376; fax - same. SER: Valuations; buys auction. VAT: Stan/Spec.

MEARE, Nr. Glastonbury

Borough Antiques

St. Mary's Rd. BA6 9SP. (R.C. and L. Tincknel Resident. Open 10-6 or by appointment. *STOCK Town and country furniture, decorative acces ories and 19th C brass.* LOC: B3151 betwee Glastonbury and Wedmore. TEL: 01458 860701.

MIDSOMER NORTON

Somervale Antiques BADA LAPAD

6 Radstock Rd. BA3 2AJ. (Wing Cdr. R. Thomas). BABADA. CINOA. Resident. Ope by appointment only. *STOCK: English drinkin glasses, decanters, cut and coloured; "Bristo and "Nailsea"glass; bijouterie; glass sce bottles, 18th to early 19th C.* LOC: On A362 o Radstock side of town. PARK: Easy. TEI 01761 412686 (24hrs); fax - same; mobile - 05 088022. SER: Valuations; buys at auctio trains to Bath met by arrangement. VA Stan/Spec.

MILVERTON, Nr. Taunton

Milverton Antiques

Fore St. TA4 1JU. (A. Waymouth). Est. 1972. Resident, open any time. SIZE: Medium. *STOCK: Pine and oak country furniture, longcase clocks, interesting china, copper, brass and treen.* LOC: 3 miles from Taunton on B3227 Barnstaple road. PARK: 50yds. TEL: 01823 400597. VAT: Stan/Spec.

J.C. White

The Granary, Fitzhead. TA4 3JT. Est. 1960. *STOCK: Country furniture and clocks.* TEL: 01823 400427.

MONTACUTE, Nr. Yeovil

Montacute Antiques

April Cottage, 12 South St. TA15 6XD. (E.M. and J.K. Warrick). Open 9-6 including Sun. *STOCK: Small furniture, porcelain, glass, pictures, metalware, decorative and interesting items.* PARK: Easy. TEL: 01935 824786.

NETHER STOWEY, Nr. Bridgwater

The Court Gallery

2 Lime St. TA5 1NG. (John Wilcox). Est. 1990. Open Tues.- Sat. 10-1 and 2-5, or by appointment. SIZE: Medium. *STOCK: British paintings, 1880-1939, especially Newlyn, St Ives and London Group, £50-£15,000.* LOC: Bridgwater turn off M5, then A39 towards Minehead. PARK: Easy. TEL: 01278 732539; home - same. SER: Valuations; restorations; buys at auction. VAT: Spec.

House of Antiquity

St. Mary St. TA5 1LJ. (M.S. Todd). Est. 1967. Open 10-5 or by appointment. SIZE: Medium. *STOCK: Philatelic literature, world topographical, maps, handbooks, postcards, ephemera, postal history.* LOC: A39. PARK: Easy. TEL: 01278 732426; fax - same. SER: Valuations; buys at auction. VAT: Stan.

NORTH PETHERTON, Nr. Taunton

Harrison House Antiques

40 Fore St. TA6 6QA. (J.B. Yarrow). Open by appointment. SIZE: Medium. *STOCK: Wooden bowls and buckets, primitive slipware, country furniture and carpets.* LOC: A38. PARK: Easy. TEL: 01278 662535. *Trade Only.*

QUEEN CAMEL, Nr. Yeovil

Steven Ferdinando

The Old Vicarage. BA22 7NG. Open by appointment. *STOCK: Antiquarian and secondhand books.* TEL: 01935 850210.

SOMERTON

John Gardiner Antiques

Monteclefe House. TA11 7NL. Appointment advisable. *STOCK: General antiques; decorative Edwardian, Georgian and quality old reproduction furnishings.* LOC: A303, close to M5. TEL: 01458 272238; fax/answerphone - 01458 274329; mobile - 0831 274427.

The London Cigarette Card Co. Ltd

West St. TA11 6NB. (I.A. and E.K. Laker, F.C. Doggett and Y. Berktay). Est. 1927. Open daily. SIZE: Medium. *STOCK: Cigarette and trade cards, 1885 to date; sets from £1.50; other cards, from 15p; frames for mounting cards and special albums.* PARK: Easy. TEL: 01458 273452. SER: Publishers of catalogues, reference books and monthly magazine; mail order.

Times Past

(Above Rocking Horse Children's Shop), Market Place. TA11 7NB. (D. and G. Rogers). *STOCK: Linen, lace, samplers, quilts, textiles, watercolours, metalware, treen, period oak and country furniture.* LOC: 1.5 miles off A303 at Podimore. 10 minutes from Clark's Village, Street. PARK: Easy. TEL: 01458 274393.

TAUNTON

East Reach Antiques

38 East Reach. TA1 3ES. (R.E. and C.S. Salmon). Open 9-5. SIZE: Medium. *STOCK: Furniture, 19th to early 20th C, £50-£1,000; porcelain and glass, 19th C, £25-£500; watercolours and etchings, £50-£1,000; silver, £20-£250; marine and scientific instruments, £10-£1,500.* LOC: From junction 25, M5 into town centre. PARK: Easy. TEL: 01823 322432; fax - same. SER: Valuations. FAIRS: ICAF.

Richard Joslin Galleries

38-40 Bridge St. TA1 1UD. Est. 1922. Open 9-5.30. SIZE: Large. *STOCK: Prints, limited edition, 19th C and contemporary, £5-£500; contemporary oil paintings and watercolours, £250-£10,000; European oils and watercolours, 19th C, £750-£25,000.* LOC: Continuation of Fore St., off High St. PARK: Public opposite shop. TEL: 01823 272234; fax - 01823 353103. SER: Valuations; framing; restorations (as stock); buys at auction. VAT: Stan/Spec.

Selwoods

Queen Anne Cottage, Mary St. TA1 3PE. Est. 1927. Open 9.30-5. SIZE: Large. *STOCK: Furniture, including Victorian and Edwardian.* TEL: 01823 272780.

Taunton continued

Staplegrove Lodge Antiques
Staplegrove Lodge. (T. Atkins). Est. 1958. Open by appointment only. SIZE: Medium. *STOCK: General antiques, furniture, silver, porcelain, pot-lids.* LOC: Pink house just off A358 Taunton/ Barnstaple road up No Through Road just before the Cross Keys inn. PARK: Own. TEL: 01823 331153; home - same.

Taunton Antiques Market - Silver Street
27/29 Silver St. TA1 3DH. (Bath Antiques Market Ltd.). Est. 1978. Open Mon. 9-4 including Bank Holidays. SIZE: 100+ dealers. *STOCK: General antiques and collectables, including specialists in most fields.* LOC: 2 miles from M5 Junc. 25, to town centre, 100yds. from Sainsburys car park across lights. PARK: Easy - Sainsburys (town centre branch). TEL: 01823 289327; fax - same; enquiries - 0171 351 5353. SER: Valuations.

WATCHET

Clarence House Antiques
41 Swain St. TA23 0AE. Est. 1970. Open 10-6.30. CL: Sun. in winter. SIZE: Medium. *STOCK: General antiques, pine, brass, copper, bric-a-brac, upholstered furniture.* TEL: 01984 631389. VAT: Stan.

Nick Cotton Fine Art
Beachstone House, 46/47 Swain St. TA23 0AG. Est. 1970. Open by appointment only. SIZE: Large. *STOCK: Paintings, 1800-1970; some period furniture.* TEL: 01984 631814. SER: Restorations; conservation; research. VAT: Spec.

WEDMORE

Coach House Gallery
Church St. BS28 4AA. (Mrs V. Davies). Est. 1976. Open 9-6 or by appointment. SIZE: Small. *STOCK: English watercolours, 19th to early 20th C; small furniture, English porcelain; glass and silver, 18th C.* LOC: Opposite St. Mary's Church. TEL: 01934 712718; home - same.

WELLINGTON

Michael and Amanda Lewis Oriental Carpets and Rugs LAPADA
8 North St. TA21 8LT. UKIC. Est. 1982. Open 10-1 and 2-5.30, Mon. and weekends by appointment. SIZE: Medium. *STOCK: Oriental carpets and rugs, mainly 19th-20th C, £25-£25,000.* PARK: 100yds. TEL: 01823 667430. SER: Valuations; restorations; repairs and cleaning; courses.

WELLS

Courtyard Antiques
Palace Courtyard, Priory Rd. BA5 2SY. (Mr ar Mrs M.J. Mitchell). Est. 1985. Open 9-5, Sun b appointment. SIZE: Medium. *STOCK: Furnitur £100-£300; smalls, £10-£50; both 19th-20th C* LOC: Just off High St., towards Glastonbur PARK: Easy. TEL: 01749 679533; home - 0174 675028. SER: Valuations; restorations (upholster cane and rush work, china and furniture). FAIR: Bath and West Showground, Shepton Malle Newark, Ardingly.

Bernard G. House
Market Place. BA5 2RF. Est. 1963. Open 9.3 5.30. SIZE: Medium. *STOCK: Barometers ar scientific instruments, barographs, telescope tripod and hand held; furniture includin miniatures and apprentice pieces, 18th-19th C longcase and bracket clocks, metalwar decorative and architectural items.* PARK Opposite shop. TEL: 01749 672607. SER Repairs; restorations. VAT: Stan/Spec.

Edward A. Nowell BAD
12 Market Place. BA5 2RB. Est. 1952. Ope 9.15-5. SIZE: Large. *STOCK: Furniture, clock barometers, 17th to early 19th C; jeweller silver, porcelain, English and Continental, a prices.* Not Stocked: Victoriana, bric-a-bra curios, weapons, books. LOC: From an direction, turn left into Market Place (one-wa system). PARK: 20yds. facing shop. TE 01749 672415; fax - 01749 673519. SER Valuations; restorations (furniture, silve clocks and jewellery); re-upholstery. VAT Stan/Spec.

Sadler Street Gallery,
7a Sadler St. BA5 2RR. Open 10-5.30. CL: Mo *STOCK: 19th-20th C watercolours and oils; o prints.* SER: Framing.

WEST BUCKLAND, Nr. Taunton

Tim Everett
Pitminster Studio, Budleigh. Open by appoin ment. *STOCK: 19th and 20th C paintings ar sculpture, £200-£10,000.* PARK: Easy. TE 01823 421710. SER: Restorations; conservatic (paintings and frames). VAT: Stan/Spec.

WEST HARPTREE, Nr. Bristol

Tilly Manor Antiques
Tilly Manor. BS18 6EB. (J.D. Scott). Est. 197 Open Thurs.-Sat. 10-5, other times by appoin ment. SIZE: Large. *STOCK: Town and count furniture, 18th-19th C, £100-£5,000; bras copper and metalware, 17th-19th C, decorati collectors items, 18th-19th C; all £5-£500.* LO Next to church on A368. PARK: Own. TE 01761 221888; home - same. SER: Restorations.

VESTON-SUPER-MARE

Bay Tree House Antiques
tevens Lane, Lympsham. BS24 0BY. (N.W. and .M. Adams). Est. 1982. Open 10-5.30 including un. SIZE: Warehouse. *STOCK: Stripped pine, atin walnut and mahogany furniture, some nalls, £25-£2,000.* LOC: Off A370 - turn left nmediately after first Jeff Brown garage, remises about 3/4 mile on right. PARK: Easy. EL: 01934 750367; home - same. VAT: tan/Spec.

D.M. Restorations
Laburnum Rd. (D. Pike). Open 9-5. *STOCK: mall mahogany furniture.* PARK: Easy. TEL: 1934 811120.

Sterling Books
3A Locking Rd. BS23 3DG. Est. 1966. Open 9-6. *TOCK: Books, antiquarian and secondhand, ome new; ephemera and prints.* TEL: 01934 25056. SER: Bookbinding and picture framing.

Toby's Antiques
7 Upper Church Rd. BS23 2DY. (D. White). pen 9-5, Tues., Thurs. and Sun. by appointment. *TOCK: Furniture and general antiques.* TEL: 1934 623555.

Winter's Antiques LAPADA
2 Severn Rd. BS23 1DT. (R.N. and E.P. Vinters). Open 9-12 and 2-3.30. CL: Sat. pm. nd Thurs. SIZE: Large. *STOCK: Furniture, locks, smalls and fine art, all periods.* Not tocked: Coins, stamps. LOC: Off sea front. ARK: Easy. TEL: 01934 620118/81460.

WILLITON

Edward Venn
nit 3, 52 Long St. TA4 4QU. Est. 1979. Open 0-5. *STOCK: Furniture, clocks.* TEL: 01984 32631; fax - same. SER: Restorations (furniture, arometers and clocks).

WINCANTON

Green Dragon Antiques Centre
and 1A South St. BA9 9DH. (Mrs Sally enning). Est. 1986. Open 9-5.15, Sun. 1.30-5. IZE: 46 dealers. *STOCK: Wide variety of eneral antiques and collectables, £1-£1,000.* OC: Off A303. PARK: Free nearby. TEL: 01963 4111. SER: Valuations.

Harry M. Sainsbury
7 High St. BA9 9JT. Est. 1958. *STOCK: Oak nd mahogany furniture, china, glass, pictures, ecorative items.* TEL: 01963 32289. SER: estorations; cabinet makers. VAT: Stan/Spec.

WIVELISCOMBE

J.C. Giddings
TA4 2SN. Open by appointment only. SIZE: Large warehouses. *STOCK: Mostly 18th-19th C furniture, iron-work and general building reclamation materials.* TEL: 01984 623703. VAT: Stan. *Mainly Trade.*

Heads 'n' Tails
Bournes House, 41 Church St. TA4 2LT. (D. McKinley). Resident. Open by appointment. *STOCK: Taxidermy including Victorian cased and uncased birds, mammals and fish, £5-£2,000; decorative items, glass domes.* LOC: Opposite church. PARK: Easy. TEL: 01984 623097; fax - 01984 624445. SER: Taxidermy; restorations; commissions; hire. VAT: Spec.

Peter Lee Antiques
1 Silver St. TA4 2PA. (P. and A. Lee). Open 9-5. CL: Sat. pm. *STOCK: Furniture, china, general antiques, fine arts and unsual items.* LOC: B3227, town centre. PARK: Nearby. TEL: 01984 624055.

YATTON, Nr. Bristol

Glenville Antiques LAPADA
120 High St. BS19 4DH. (Mrs S.E.M. Burgan). Est. 1969. Open 10.30-5. CL: Sun. except by appointment. SIZE: Small. *STOCK: Glass, £5-£750; small furniture, £25-£2,500; pottery and porcelain, £5-£1,500, all mainly 19th C; collectors' items, sewing items.* Not Stocked: Pewter, guns, antique foreign curios, coins, stamps. LOC: On B3133. PARK: Easy. TEL: 01934 832284. VAT: Stan/Spec.

YEOVIL

John Hamblin
Unit 6, 15 Oxford Rd., Penn Mill Trading Estate. BA21 5HR. (J. and M. A. Hamblin). Est. 1980. Open 8.30-5. CL: Sat. SIZE: Small. *STOCK: Furniture, 1750-1900, £300-£3,000.* PARK: Easy. TEL: 01935 71154; home - 01935 76673. SER: Restorations (furniture); cabinet work. VAT: Stan.

The Somerset and Dorset Antique Centre
Main Hall, Main St, Mudford. BA21 5TE. (Michael Shortall). Open 10-5, Sun. 1-4. *STOCK: General antiques including furniture, ceramics, silver, jewellery and collectors' items.* TEL: 01935 851511.

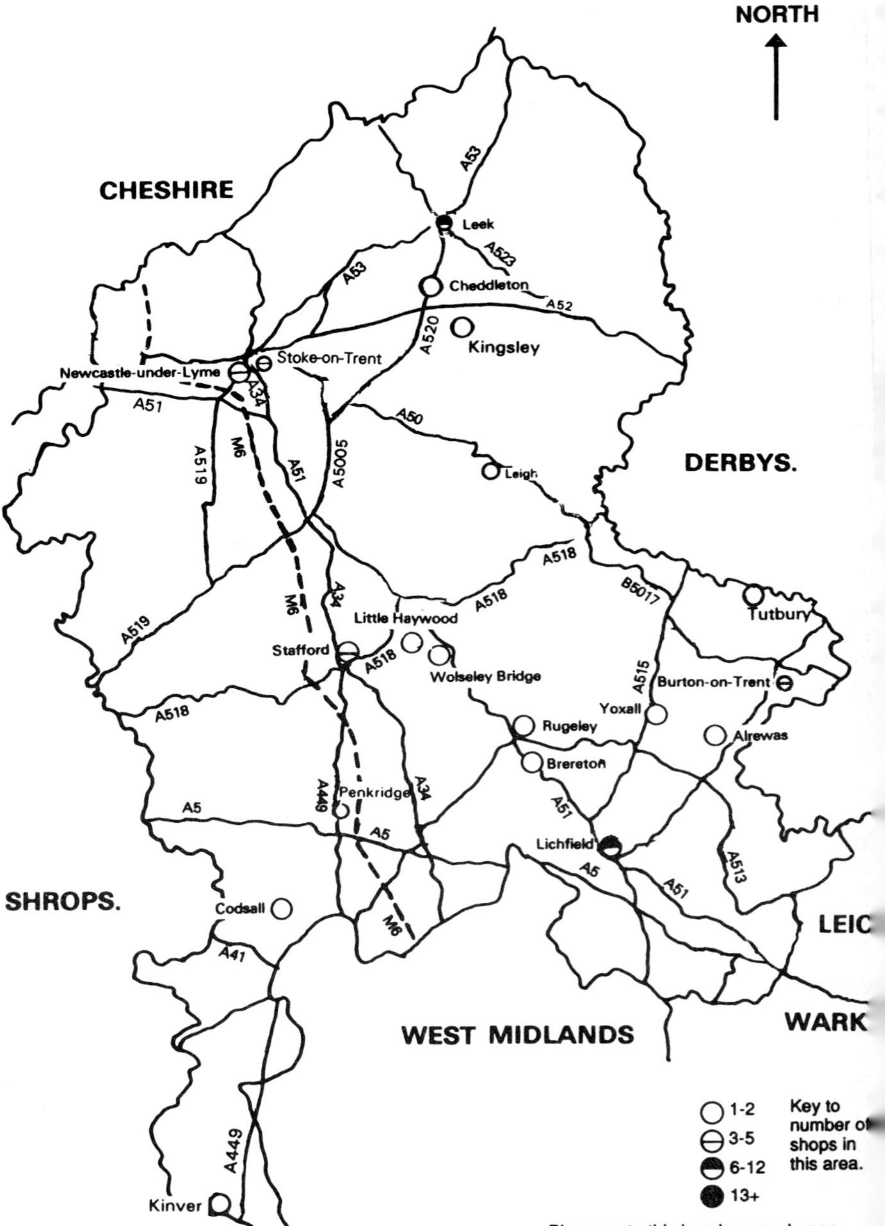

Please note this is only a rough map designed to show dealers the number of shops in the various towns, and is not necessarily totally accurate.

ALREWAS, Nr. Burton-on-Trent

Poley Antiques
Main St. DE13 7AA. (D.T. and A.G. Poley). st. 1977. Open Thurs., Fri. and Sat. 10-5, other imes by arrangement. SIZE: Small. *STOCK: eneral antiques, furniture, silver, china, glass, opper, brass.* Not Stocked: Stamps, coins and ilitaria. LOC: 20yds. from A38, between ichfield and Burton. PARK: Own. TEL: 01283 91151; home - same; fax - same.

RERETON, Nr. Rugeley

Rugeley Antique Centre
61/3 Main Rd. WS15 1DX. Open 9-5, Sun. 12-.30. SIZE: Large - 28 units. *STOCK: China, lass, pottery, pictures, furniture, pine, treen, nen and shipping goods.* LOC: A51, one mile outh of Rugeley town, opposite Cedar Tree otel. PARK: Own. TEL: 01889 577166. VAT: tan/Spec.

URTON-ON-TRENT

Burton Antiques
and 2 Horninglow Rd. (C.H. Armett). Est. 1977. pen 10-5 every day. SIZE: Large. *STOCK: hipping and pine furniture.* LOC: A50. PARK: earby. TEL: 01283 542331. SER: Valuations; ine stripping; buys at auction.

ustin Pinewood Ltd
he Maltings, Wharf Rd. DE14 1PZ. (S. ilvester). Open 9-5.30, including Sun. *STOCK: tripped pine furniture and decorative ccessories.* TEL: 01283 510860.

. and R. Scattergood LAPADA
32 Branston Rd. DE14 3DQ. Open 9-6. *TOCK: Fine English and Continental glass.* EL: 01283 546695.

HEDDLETON, Nr. Leek

ewel Antiques
Whitegates', 63 Basford Bridge Lane. ST13 EQ. (B. and D.J. Smith). Est. 1967. Open by ppointment. *STOCK: Paintings, prints, wellery, oil lamps, small furniture and clocks, 8th-19th C, £25-£2,000.* PARK: Easy. TEL: 1538 360744/361247.

ODSALL

am Mill Antiques
irches Rd. WV8 2JR. (H. Bassett). Est. 1977. pen 10-1 and 2.30-5.30. CL: Tues. and Thurs. ZE: Small. *STOCK: General antiques, small rniture, china, glass, copper, brass, silver and wellery.* PARK: Easy. TEL: 01902 843780.

KINGSLEY, Nr. Leek

Country Cottage Interiors
Newhall Farmhouse, Hazels Crossroads. ST10 2AY. (L. Salmon). Resident. Est. 1972. Open 10-5. SIZE: Medium. *STOCK: Pine, £5-£500; kitchenalia, 25p-£100.* LOC: Off A52. PARK: Own. TEL: 01538 754762.

KINVER

The Antique Centre
128 High St. DY7 6HQ. (R. Williams). Open 10-5.30. SIZE: Several dealers. *STOCK: Furniture, brass and copper, china, mechanical/musical, unusual collectables, bric-a-brac.* TEL: 01384 277918. SER: Restorations (furniture).

LEEK

Antiques and Objets d'Art of Leek
70 St. Edwards St. ST13 5DL. Est. 1955. Open 10-6. CL: Thurs. *STOCK: English and Continental furniture; porcelain, silver, glass, oil paintings.* TEL: 01538 382587. FAIRS: Buxton. VAT: Spec.

Anvil Antiques Ltd
Cross Mills, Cross St. ST13 6BL. (J.S. Spooner and N.M. Sullivan). Est. 1975. Open 9-6. SIZE: Large. *STOCK: Stripped pine, architectural and oak, mahogany, bric-a-brac, decorative items and painted furniture, prints and art.* LOC: Ashbourne Rd., from town centre roundabout, turn first left, Victorian mill on right. PARK: Easy. TEL: 01538 371657. VAT: Stan.

Sylvia Chapman Antiques
56 St. Edward St. ST13 5DL. Est. 1983. Open 10-5.30. CL: Thurs. SIZE: Medium. *STOCK: Small oak, mahogany and country furniture; general antiques and collector's items, especially 19th to early 20th C pottery and porcelain, Staffordshire jugs, Victorian coloured glass, copper, brass and kitchenalia.* PARK: Outside. TEL: 01538 399116.

England's Gallery
Ball Haye House, 1 Ball Haye Terr. ST13 6AP. (F.J. and S. England). Est. 1968. Open 10-5.30. CL: Mon. SIZE: Large. *STOCK: Oils and watercolours, 18th-19th C, £500-£10,000; etchings, engravings, lithographs, mezzotints, £50-£4,000.* LOC: Towards Ball Haye Green from A523 turn at lights. PARK: Nearby. TEL: 01538 373451; home - 01538 386352. SER: Valuations; restorations (cleaning, relining, regilding); framing, mount cutting; buys at auction (paintings). VAT: Stan.

Leek continued

Gemini Trading
Limes Mill, Abbotts Rd. ST13 6EY. (T.J. Lancaster and Mrs Y.A. Goldstraw). Est. 1981. Open Mon.-Fri. 9-5, other times by appointment. SIZE: Large. *STOCK: Pine, £25-£850; kitchenalia, £5-£35; both 19th C.* LOC: Turn off A53 along Abbotts Rd. before town centre. PARK: Easy. TEL: 01538 387834; fax - 01538 399819. VAT: Stan.

Leek continued

Gilligans Antiques
59 St. Edward St. ST13 5DN. (M.T. Gilligan Est. 1977. *STOCK: Victorian and Edwardia furniture.* TEL: 01538 384174.

Grosvenor Clocks
Overton Bank House. ST13 5ES. Open 9-4.3 *STOCK: Clocks, watches and barometers; som furniture.* TEL: 01538 385669.

Roger Haynes - Antiques Finder
31 Compton. ST13 5NJ. Open by appointmen *STOCK: Pine, smalls and decorative items.* TE 01538 385161.

Johnson's
120 Mill Street. ST13 8HA. Est. 1976. Open 5.30. SIZE: Large. *STOCK: 18th and 19th English, Irish and French country furniture, £5 £2,000; decorative accessories, £10-£500.* PAR Own. TEL: 01538 386745; fax - same.

The Leek Antiques Centre
4-6 Brook St. ST13 5JE. Est. 1977. Open 10- Sun. by appointment. *STOCK: Furnitu including sets of chairs and extending dini tables; pottery, oils, watercolours, prints; pin* TEL: 01538 398475; home - 01782 394383. SE Valuations; restorations (furniture). FAIR Bowman's - Staffordshire Showground and NE VAT: Stan/Spec.

Molland Antique Mirrors
40 Compton. ST13 5NH. (John and Kar Molland). Est. 1980. Open 7.30-6. SIZE: Mediu *STOCK: Mirrors - gilt, painted and wooden, 19th £100-£2,000.* LOC: From Stoke-on-Trent, right 1st traffic lights, shop 200 yards on right. PAR Easy. TEL: 01538 372553. SER: Export packin FAIRS: NEC (Aug). VAT: Stan/Spec.

Odeon Antiques
76-78 St. Edward St. ST13 5PA. (Steve For Open 10-5. *STOCK: Lighting, beds, pine a general antiques.* TEL: 01538 387188; fax - sam SER: Restorations (lighting).

LEIGH, Nr. Stoke-on-Trent

John Nicholls
Open by appointment only. *STOCK: O furniture and related items, 17th-18th C.* LOC: miles from Uttoxeter, just off A50 towards Stok on-Trent. TEL: 01889 502351; mobile - 08 244024.

LICHFIELD

Mike Abrahams Books
9 Burton Old Rd.,Streethay. WS13 8LJ. Est. 197 Open by appointment. SIZE: Large. *STOCK: Boo and ephemera especially Midlands topograp sport, transport, childrens, illustrated, militarya antiquarian, 17th C to date, £2-£1,000.* LOC: L

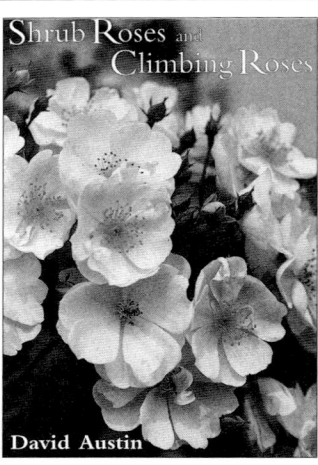

ichfield continued

ut one R/H turn A5127 Lichfield to Burton-on-'rent before road joins A38 by-pass, house on left ear corner. PARK: Easy.TEL: 01543 256200; ome - same. SER: Valuations. FAIRS: Stafford, ingley Hall and Pavillion; Midland Antiquarian ook (organiser).

'he Antique Shop
1 Tamworth St. WS13 6JP. (Mrs P.M. ackham). Open 9.30-1.30 and 2.30-5.30. SIZE: Iedium. *STOCK: Furniture, pottery, porcelain, ilver, prints, paintings, copper and brass, wellery, glass, £5-£1,000.* PARK: Easy. TEL: 1543 268324.

'he Bournemouth Gallery Ltd
'.O Box 23. WS14 ODQ. *STOCK: Limited dition prints.* TEL: 01543 481880. SER: Mail rder.

'ordelia and Perdy's Antique Junk hop
3 Tamworth St. WS13 6JW. (C.R.J. and P.J. Iellor). *STOCK: General antiques and trade hipping goods.* TEL: 01543 263223.

mages - Peter Stockham
: The Staffs Bookshop, 4 & 6 Dam St. WS13 AA. Open 9.30-5.30. *STOCK: Early children's ooks, art and illustrated books, printed phemera; antique toys, mainly wooden; games nd associated items; fine printing; prints and 'ood engravings.* TEL: 01543 264093.

ames A. Jordan
The Corn Exchange. CMBHI. Open 9-5.30. *TOCK: Clock, especially longcase; watches and arometers.* TEL: 01543 416221; fax 0121 522 004. SER: Valuations; restorations (clocks and hronometers).

Iilestone Antiques LAPADA
Main St., Whittington. WS14 9JU. (H. and E. 'rawshaw). Resident. Est. 1988. Open Thurs.-at. 10-6, Sun. 11-3, other times by ppointment. *STOCK: Furniture, porcelain, ottery, pictures, brass and copper, 18th-19th C.* .OC: A51 Lichfield/Tamworth road, turn orth at Whittington Barracks, shop 50yds. ast crossroads in village. PARK: Outside. 'EL: 01543 432248. VAT: Stan/Spec.

. Royden Smith
hurch View, Farewell Lane, Burntwood. WS7 DP. Est. 1972. Open Wed. and Sat. 10.30-5 or by ppointment. *STOCK: Antiquarian books, general ntiques, bric-a-brac, shipping goods.* TEL: 1543 682217.

'he Staffs Bookshop
& 6 Dam St. WS13 6AA. Open 9.30-5.30. *TOCK: Rare, secondhand, antiquarian and ollectors books, especially 18th-19th C.* TEL: 1543 264093.

Lichfield continued

Tudor of Lichfield Antique Centre
Bore St. WS13 6LL. (Miss S. Burns-Mace). Est. 1992. Open 10-5. SIZE: 5 rooms. *STOCK: Furniture, clocks, jewellery, china, collectables, 50p-£2,500.* LOC: Above tea rooms. TEL: 01543 263951. SER: Buys at auction.

LITTLE HAYWOOD, Nr. Stafford

Jalna Antiques
Coley Lane. ST18 0UP. Resident. Est. 1974. Open most times. *STOCK: Furniture, pre-1900.* Not Stocked: Shipping goods. LOC: 1/2 mile off A51, 12 miles north of Lichfield. TEL: 01889 881381. SER: Restorations; re-upholstery. VAT: Spec.

NEWCASTLE-UNDER-LYME

Antique Market
The Stones. ST5 2AG. (Antique Forum Ltd). Every Tues. 9-4. SIZE: 70 dealers. *STOCK: General antiques.* TEL: 01782 595805; mobile - 0836 322343.

Errington Antiques
63 George St. ST5 1JT. (G.K. Errington). Open 10-12.30 and 1.30-4.30 CL: Thurs. *STOCK: Oriental items, English furniture, general antiques, lamps.* LOC: Corner of George and Albert St. TEL: 01782 632822.

NEWCASTLE-UNDER-LYME

Richard Midwinter Antiques
31 Bridge St. ST5 2RY. (Mr and Mrs R. Midwinter). Est. 1987. Open 10-5, Thurs. by appointment. SIZE: Medium. *STOCK: Furniture, oak, walnut, mahogany, 17th-19th C, £50-£10,000; textiles, samplers and embroideries; longcase, mantel and wall clocks, £150-£4,000; paintings, £35-£3,000, both 18th-19th C; ceramics and watercolours, 19th C, £15-£1,500.* Not Stocked: Pine and ephemera. LOC: Close to Sainsburys and the Magistrates Courts. TEL: 01782 712483; home - 01630 672289. SER: Valuations; restorations (framing, clock repair). VAT: Spec.

PENKRIDGE, Nr. Stafford

Golden Oldies
1 and 5 Crown Bridge. ST19 5AA. (W.A. and M.A. Knowles). Open 10-5.30, Mon. 10-2. *STOCK: Victorian, Edwardian and later furniture; paintings, decorative items.* PARK: Easy. TEL: 01785 714722. VAT: Stan/Spec.

RUGELEY

Eveline Winter
1 Wolseley Rd. WS15 2QH. (Mrs E. Winter). Est. 1962. Open 10.30-5. CL: Tues. and Wed. except by appointment. SIZE: Small. *STOCK: Staffordshire figures, pre-Victorian, from £90; Victorian, £30-£500; copper, brass, glass and general antiques.* Not Stocked: Coins and weapons. LOC: Coming from Lichfield or Stafford stay on A51 and avoid town by-pass. PARK: Easy and at side of shop. TEL: 01889 583259.

STAFFORD

The Antique Restoration Studio
1 Newport Rd. ST18 9JH. (P. Albright). GADAR. Est. 1989. Open 9-5. *STOCK: General antiques.* LOC: Main road. TEL: 01785 780424. SER: Valuations; repair and restoration (furniture, ceramics, glassware and paintings). VAT: Stan.

Browse
127 Lichfield Rd. ST17 4LF. (H. Barnes). Est. 1981. Open 9.30-5. SIZE: Large. *STOCK: Furniture, 1860-1940 and reproduction.* LOC: Outskirts of town. PARK: Easy. TEL: 01785 241097; home - 01785 660336. SER: Valuations; restorations.

Windmill Antiques
9 Castle Hill, Broadeye. ST16 2QB. Open 10-5. SIZE: Medium - several dealers. *STOCK: General antiques and decorative items.* PARK: Easy. TEL: 01785 228505.

STOKE-ON-TRENT

Ann's Antiques
24/26 Leek Rd., Stockton Brook. ST9 9MN. Open 10-5. CL: Thurs. *STOCK: Victorian furniture, brass, copper, jewellery, paintings, pottery and unusual items.* TEL: 01782 503991. VAT: Stan.

Five Towns Antiques
17 Broad St., Hanley. ST1 4HS. (B. and B. Arkinstall). Open 10-5.30. CL: Thurs. SIZE: Small. *STOCK: 1930's pottery and porcelain, general antiques.* PARK: Nearby. TEL: 01782 272930.

Manor Court Antiques
4 Manor Court St., Penkhull.(R. Broad). Est. 1995. Open 10-5. SIZE: Medium. *STOCK: Edwardian and Victorian furniture, Art Deco, clocks, pottery.*LOC: Opp. church, next door to Greyhound pub. PARK: Outside. TEL: 01782 410140.

The Potteries Antique Centre
271 Waterloo Rd., Cobridge. ST6 3HR. (W. Buckley). Est. 1972. Open 9-6 including Sun. SIZE: Large+ Trade and export warehouse.

Stoke-on-Trent continued

STOCK: Furniture including pine and shippin[g] 18th-20th C; pottery and porcelain includin[g] Doulton, Moorcroft, Beswick, Wedgwoo[d] Coalport, Shelley, 19th-20th C; collectors' item[s] silver plate, clocks, brass, jewellery, picture[s] 18th-20th C; all £1-£5,000. LOC: Off M[6] junction 15 or 16 on to A500, follow signs f[or] Festival Park or Potteries Shopping Centr[e]. PARK: Easy. TEL: 01782 201455; fax - 017[82] 201518. SER: Valuations; export facilities supply and packing; buys at auction (pottery a[nd] collectors' items). VAT: Stan/Spec.

Top of the Hill - Ceramic Search
14/14a Nile St., Burslem. (A. Phillips and E. Butterton). Est. 1995. Open 9.30-5, Sun. b[y] appointment. SIZE: Medium. *STOCK: Staffor[d]shire ceramics especially Doulton and Beswic[k] £5-£500; furniture, £30-£1,000; architectur[al] items, £10-£1,000; all 19th-20th C.* LOC: Follo[w] Doulton signs from A500, premises opposi[te] factory shop. PARK: Easy. TEL: 01782 83450[.] SER: Valuations; buys at auction (Staffordshi[re] pottery). FAIRS: Bingley, Stafford.

TUTBURY, Nr. Burton-on-Trent

Old Chapel Antique & Collectables Centre
High St. (P. Tuckley). Open 9-5, incl. Su[n]. *STOCK: China, glass, furniture.* PARK: Eas[y]. TEL: 01283 815255.

WOLSELEY BRIDGE, Nr. Rugeley

Jalna Antiques
The Old Barn. ST18 0UP. (G. and D. Hanco[x]). Open 10-5. *STOCK: Furniture and smalls.* LO[C]: Junction A51/A513. TEL: 01889 881381.

YOXALL, Nr. Burton-on-Trent

Armson's of Yoxall Antiques LAPA[DA]
The Hollies. DE13 8NH. (F.R.B. and P.[M]. Armson). Est. 1955. Open Mon.-Fri. 9-5, Sat. 12, other times by appointment. SIZE: Larg[e]. *STOCK: Period furniture and shipping goo[ds].* LOC: On A515. TEL: 01543 472352; fa[x] same. VAT: Stan/Spec.

H.W. Heron and Son Ltd LAPA[DA]
The Antique Shop, 1 King St. DE13 8N[] (H.N.M. and J. Heron). Est. 1949. Open 9[-] Sat. 10.30-5.30, Sun. 2-6. SIZE: Mediu[m]. *STOCK: Furniture, porcelain, glass, pictures, [all] prices.* LOC: On A515 in centre of villag[e] opposite church. PARK: Easy. TEL: 015[43] 472266; home - same. SER: Valuations. VA[T]: Stan/Spec.

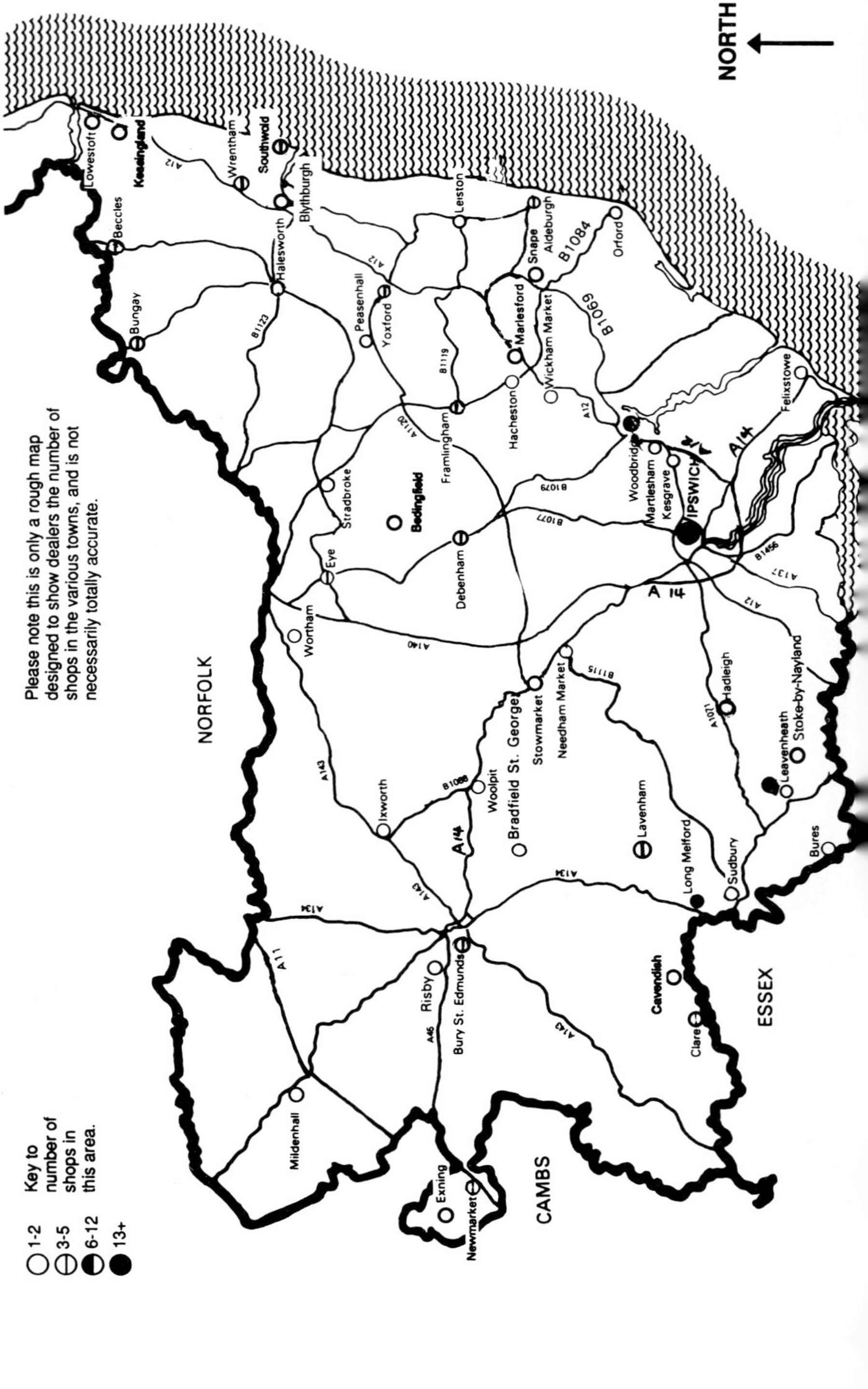
NORTH
Please note this is only a rough map designed to show dealers the number of shops in the various towns, and is not necessarily totally accurate.
Key to number of shops in this area.
1-2
3-5
6-12
13+
NORFOLK
ESSEX
CAMBS
Lowestoft
Kessingland
Wrentham
Southwold
Blythburgh
Beccles
Halesworth
Bungay
Peasenhall
Yoxford
Leiston
Aldeburgh
Snape
Orford
Marlesford
Wickham Market
Hacheston
Framlingham
Woodbridge
Martlesham
Kesgrave
Felixstowe
IPSWICH
Stradbroke
Bedingfield
Debenham
Eye
Wortham
Stowmarket
Needham Market
Bradfield St. George
Woolpit
Ixworth
Hadleigh
Stoke-by-Nayland
Leavenheath
Bures
Lavenham
Long Melford
Sudbury
Cavendish
Clare
Bury St. Edmunds
Risby
Mildenhall
Exning
Newmarket
A12
A14
A11
A45
A134
A143
A140
A1120
A1071
A137
B1084
B1069
B1119
B1123
B1079
B1077
B1088
B1115
B1456

ALDEBURGH

Aldeburgh Galleries
132 High St. IP15 5AQ. (Mr and Mrs W. Dandy and Mr and Mrs S. Haslam). Open 10-5. *STOCK: Jewellery, silver, glass, studio pottery, books, Steiff bears, furniture, pictures, collectables and general antiques.* TEL: 01728 453963.

Guillemot
134/136 High St. IP15 5AQ. (L. Weaver). Est. 1973. Open 10-1 and 2-5, Sat. 10-1 and 2-6, Wed. pm. and Sun. by appointment. SIZE: Medium. *STOCK: Pine, elm, oak and fruitwood country furniture, dressers, tables and treen.* LOC: Town centre. PARK: Easy. TEL: 01728 453933. VAT: Stan.

Mole Hall Antiques
102 High St. IP15 5AB. (Peter Weaver). Est. 1976. Open 10-5, Sun. by appointment. SIZE: Small. *STOCK: Country furniture, kitchenalia and decorative items.* PARK: Easy. TEL: 01728 452361; home - same.

Thompson's Gallery
175 High St. IP15 5AN. (J. and S. Thompson). Open 10-5 or by appointment. SIZE: Medium. *STOCK: Oils and watercolours, 18th-19th C; furniture, 18th to early 20th C; both £300-£10,000.* PARK: Easy. TEL: 01728 453743. SER: Valuations; restorations; framing; buys at auction. VAT: Spec.

BECCLES

Besleys Books
4 Blyburgate. NR34 9TA. (P.A. and P.F. Besley). Est. 1978. Open 9.30-1 and 2-5. CL: Wed. SIZE: Medium. *STOCK: Books, 50p-£1,000; prints, £7-£50; maps, £3-£100; all 17th-20th C.* LOC: Town centre. PARK: Nearby. TEL: 01502 715762; home - 01502 675649. SER: Valuations; restorations (book binding); buys at auction (books). FAIRS: Various PBFA.

Saltgate Antiques
11 Saltgate. NR34 9AN. (A.M. Ratcliffe). Resident. Est. 1971. Open 10-5. CL: Wed. pm. SIZE: Medium. *STOCK: Furniture, 17th-19th C, £100-£4,500; clocks, collectors' items, brass, copper, Staffordshire figures, paintings and prints, 19th C bric-a-brac, £5-£300.* LOC: Town centre opposite bus station. PARK: Easy. TEL: 01502 712776.

Waveney Antiques Centre
Peddars Lane. Open 10-5.30. SIZE: Several dealers. *STOCK: General antiques, books, furniture, jewellery, silver, clocks and collectors' items.* PARK: Easy. TEL: 01502 716147.

BEDINGFIELD, Nr. Eye

The Olde Red Lion
The Street. IP23 7LQ. Est. 1973. Open by appointment. *STOCK: Furniture and general antiques.* LOC: 3 miles from Eye, 2 miles from Debenham. TEL: 01728 628491. SER: Restorations (furniture, oil paintings, ceramics, snuff boxes, wood carvings).

BLYTHBURGH, Nr. Halesworth

E.T. Webster
Westwood Lodge. IP19 9NB. Open by appointment. *STOCK: Ancient oak beams, oak ceilings, panelling, quality reproduction oak furniture, doors, mullioned windows.* TEL: 01502 478539.

BRADFIELD ST. GEORGE, Nr. Bury St. Edmunds

Denzil Grant Antiques BADA LAPADA
Hubbards Corner. IP30 0AQ. Est. 1979. Open anytime by appointment. *STOCK: Furniture, 16th to early 19th C; tapestry, metalware.* LOC: Off A14 between Bury St. Edmunds and Ipswich. PARK: Easy. TEL: 01449 736576; fax - 01449 737679.

BUNGAY

Black Dog Antiques
51 Earsham St. NR35 2PB. (K. Button). Est. 1986. Open seven days a week. *STOCK: General antiques including oak, mahogany and pine, china, linen and collectables, antiquities, Saxon and Roman, £1-£1000.* LOC: Opposite Post Office. PARK: Easy. TEL: 01986 895554; home - 01986 894489. SER: Valuations.

Broadly Antiques
30A Broad St. NR35 1EE. (Patricia Walker and Joan Gibson). Est. 1971. Open 10.30-5. CL: Wed. SIZE: Medium. *STOCK: General antiques including furniture, ceramics, pictures, costume jewellery.* LOC: A143. PARK: Easy.TEL: 01986 894692. SER: Valuations.

Cork Brick Antiques
6 Earsham St. NR35 1AG. (G. and K. Skipper). Open 10.30-5.30. CL: Mon. *STOCK: Country and decorative antiques; architectural decorative.* PARK: Easy. TEL: 01986 894873; home - 015 712646.

Country House Antiques
30 Earsham St. Est. 1979. CL: Wed., and Sat. pm except by appointment. SIZE: Medium and trade warehouse. *STOCK: Mahogany, inlaid, oak and walnut furniture, 18th-19th C; 19th C porcelain and collectables, £1-£5,000.* LOC: Near Post Office. PARK: Easy. TEL: 01986 892875; home and warehouse - 01508 558144.

·URES

·oord Antiques and Restoration

:O8 5EW. (C.G. and E.S. Foord). Open by ppointment. *STOCK: Furniture, boxes, treen, ıetalware, decorative items.* TEL: 01787 227268; ·obile - 0836 533655. SER: Restorations; ·aluations.

·URY ST. EDMUNDS

·orner Shop Antiques

Guildhall St. IP33 1PR. Open 10-5. CL: Thurs. *'TOCK: Victoriana, porcelain, jewellery, silver, ·lass and collectors' items.* LOC: Corner of ·bbeygate St., opposite Corn Exchange. TEL: ·1284 701007.

·he Enchanted Aviary

·apwings, Rushbrooke Lane. IP33 2RS. (C.C. ·rost). Est. 1970. Open by appointment only. *'TOCK: Cased and uncased mounted birds, ·nimals and fish, mostly late Victorian, £15-£800.* ·ARK: Easy. TEL: 01284 725430.

·uildhall Street Antiques

·7 Guildhall St. IP33 1QD. (Mrs T. Cutting). Est. 965. Open 9.30-5.30. CL: Mon. am. and Thurs. IZE: Medium. *STOCK: General antiques, bric- -brac, £25-£2,500.* LOC: From town centre ·own Guildhall St. to below Churchgate St. ·unction. PARK: Easy. TEL: 01284 703060/ 35278.

·eppers Period Pieces

3 Churchgate St. IP33 1RG. (M.E. Pepper). Est. 975. Open 10-5. *STOCK: Furniture, oak, elm, ·ew, fruitwood, mahogany, 16th-19th C; English ·omestic implements in brass, copper, lead, tin, ·on, pewter and treen, 16th to early 20th C; some ·ottery and porcelain, bygones and collectables, ·ate 19th to early 20th C.* Not Stocked: ·eproductions. PARK: Easy. TEL: 01284 68786; home - 01359 250606. SER: Valuations; ·epairs and polishing.

·Vinston Mac (Silversmith)

5 St. John's St. IP33 1SJ. (E.W. McKnight). Est. ·978. Open 9-5. CL: Sun. except by appointment ·nd Sat. SIZE: Small. *STOCK: Silver tea services, ·reamers, salts.* PARK: Easy. TEL: 01284 67910. SER: Restorations (silver and plating). ·AT: Stan/Spec.

·AVENDISH

·avendish Rose Antiques

·igh St. and Lower St. (T. Patterson). Est. 1972. ·pen afternoons (except Thurs.) and all day Sat. ·r by appointment. SIZE: Large. *STOCK: Fur- ·iture, 18th-19th C, £500-£2,500.* PARK: Easy. ·EL: 01787 280332; home - same. SER: Restor- ·tions. VAT: Spec.

CLARE, Nr. Sudbury

Clare Antique Warehouse

The Mill, Malting Lane. CO10 8NW. (D. Edwards and J. Tanner). Est. 1989. Open 9.30-5.30, Sun. 1-5. SIZE: Large - over 40 dealers. *STOCK: 17th-20th C furniture, textiles, pictures, porcelain, glass, silver, decorative items.* LOC: 100yds. from High St. Follow signs for Clare Castle, Country Park. PARK: Easy. TEL: 01787 278449. SER: Valuations; restorations. VAT: Stan/Spec.

J. de Haan & Son BADA

Market Hill. CO10 8NN. Est. 1905. Open Mon.-Wed. by appointment, Thurs. and Fri. 10-5, Sat., 10-1. SIZE: Medium. *STOCK: English furniture, barometers, gilt mirrors and fine tea caddies, all 18th-19th C.* LOC: Corner of Market Hill. PARK: Easy. TEL: 01787 278870; home - 01787 277304. VAT: Stan/Spec.

Granny's Attic

22 High St. CO10 8NY. (M. Sadler-Chapman). Est. 1972. Open Sat. only 10.30-5. *STOCK: Victorian to 1940's cottage bygones, linens, collectors' items, fashions/accessories.* LOC: Off main road, opposite church tower doorway. PARK: Easy.

F.D. Salter Antiques

1-2 Church St. CO10 8NN. Est. 1959. Open 9-5. CL: Wed. pm. SIZE: Medium. *STOCK: 18th to early 19th C English furniture, porcelain and glass.* LOC: A1092. PARK: Easy. TEL: 01787 277693. SER: Valuations; restorations (furniture). FAIRS: Harrogate (Feb.); Barbican. VAT: Stan/Spec.

Trinders' Fine Tools

Malting Lane. CO10 8NW. (P. and R. Trinder). Est. 1975. Open Sat. 10-1 and 2-5, Sun. 2-5, weekdays telephone or ring the doorbell. SIZE: Medium. *STOCK: Woodworking and metal-working books, some art and antiques reference books; hand tools for craftsmen and collectors.* PARK: Nearby. TEL: 01787 277130; home - same.

DEBENHAM

C. & A.C. Bigden Antiques

No. 1 High St. IP14 6QL. Est. 1969. Open 10-5. SIZE: Large. *STOCK: 17th-19th C furniture and paintings, £50-£10,000.* PARK: Easy. TEL: 01728 860707; fax - 01728 860333. VAT: Stan/Spec.

Ian Collins Antiques

48 High St. IP14 6QW. Open 10-5.30, Sun. 12-5. *STOCK: Furniture, mainly mahogany and oak, 17th-18th C; decorative works of art.* TEL: 01728 861450; fax - 01728 861297; mobile - 0802 492153. SER: Buys at auction. VAT: Stan/Spec.

Debenham continued

Debenham Antique Centre - Gil Adams Antiques

Foresters Hall, High St. IP14 6QW. Open 10-5 and by appointment. SIZE: Large - 2 floors. *STOCK: 18th-20th C English and Continental furniture and decorative pieces.* PARK: Opposite. TEL: 01728 860777; fax - 01728 860142. SER: Restorations (furniture). VAT: Stan/Spec.

N.A.J. Lanchester

21 High St. IP14 6QL. Open every day. *STOCK: General antiques, 18th-19th C shipping goods and smalls.* TEL: 01728 860756.

Quercus

4 High St. IP14 6QH. (Peter Horsman and Bill Bristow-Jones). Resident. Est. 1972. Open by appointment. SIZE: Medium. *STOCK: Oak furniture, 17th-18th C, £1,000-£5,000.* PARK: Easy. TEL: 01728 860262; home - same. SER: Valuations; restorations (17th C oak furniture). VAT: Spec.

EXNING, Nr. Newmarket

Derby Cottage Collectables

Fordham Rd. CB8 7LG. (V. Cole). Open 9-6 including Sun. SIZE: Medium. *STOCK: Furniture and ceramics especially Derby porcelain, 19th to early 20th C, £5-£1,500; bygones and collectors' items, £1-£300.* LOC: Just off A14 Newmarket by-pass on A142 to Ely. PARK: Easy. TEL: 01638 578422; home - same. VAT: Stan/Spec.

EYE

Allsorts

3 Castle St. IP23 7AN. (David and Joy Fielding-Gooderham). Est. 1993. Open Wed.-Sat. 11-6, Tues. by appointment. SIZE: Small. *STOCK: Memorabilia, 19th C; collectibles and bric-a-brac, 19th-20th C, £5-£50.* PARK: Nearby. SER: Valuations.

Bramley Antiques LAPADA

4 Broad St. (C. Grater). Open Wed.-Sat. 10-1 and 2-5, other times by appointment. SIZE: Medium. ***STOCK: Furniture, £20-£5,000; glass, £5-£500; boxes, pictures, general antiques, all 18th-early 20th C.*** **PARK: Fairly easy. TEL: 01379 871386. SER: Valuations; restorations.**

English and Continental Antiques

1 Broad St. IP23. (Roger Ford). Est. 1977. Open 9-5.30. CL: Mon. SIZE: Large. *STOCK: Furniture, 17th-19th C, £50-£4,000.* PARK: Easy. TEL: 01379 871199. *Trade Only.*

Laburnum Cottage Antiques LAPADA

Laburnum Cottage, 2 Broad St. (S. Grater). Resident. Est. 1978. Open Wed.-Sun. 10-1 and 2-5, other times by appointment. SIZE: Small.

Eye continued

STOCK: Porcelain and glass, £5-£250; furnitur £30-£2,500; linen, silver, jewellery, brass, £2.5 £500; all 18th to early 20th C. **PARK: Fair easy. TEL: 01379 871386. SER: Valuation restorations. VAT: Stan/Spec.**

Raymond Norman Antiques/ George Norman Antiques/Jenny Norman

Home Farm, South Green. IP23 7NN. Resider Open by appointment. *STOCK: Clocks especial longcase, dolls, mechanical music.* LOC: Fro A140 take B1117 to Eye, then towards Stradbro for 2 miles, turn left to Hoxne, after half mi South Green is on right, Home Farm at very e of lane. PARK: Easy. TEL: 01379 87004 mobile - 0374 887045. SER: Valuations; resto ations (furniture, clocks and musical boxes finder (specialist pieces of period and Victori furniture). VAT: Stan/Spec.

FELIXSTOWE

George Eliot Antique and Country Things

10 Orwell Rd. IP11 7HN. (George Eliot a Partners). Est. 1994. Open 10-5. CL: Mon. SIZ Small. *STOCK: General antiques, collectab and country things, 19th-20th C, £25-£100.* LO Down Hamilton Rd. towards sea, turn left crossroads (Lloyds Bank and church). PAR Nearby. TEL: 01394 275577. SER: Buys auction. FAIRS: IACF, Tradex and R & S.

John McCulloch Antiques

1a Hamilton Rd. IP11 7HN. Open 9.30-5, We 9.30-1. *STOCK: Furniture, copper, bras pictures, clocks and bric-a-brac.* LOC: Ma street, sea front end at top of Bent Hill. PAR Around corner. TEL: 01394 283126; home 01394 272179.

FRAMLINGHAM

Antiques Warehouse

The Old Station. IP13 9EE. (Bed Bazaar a Richard Goodbrey). Est. 1992. Open 10-5, Sun. 5. *STOCK: Decorative furniture and Victori brass and iron bedsteads.* PARK: Easy. TE 01728 723756; fax - 01728 724626. SER: Rest ations (beds); mattresses and bases made-t measure.

Dix-Sept

17 Station Rd. IP13. (S. Goodbrey and Cluzan). Est. 1996. Open Sat. 10-1 and 2-5, ot times by appointment. *STOCK: French coun furniture and decoration, pottery, gard furniture, mirrors.* LOC: On approach road fr A12. PARK: Easy. TEL: 01728 621505. VA Global.

ramlingham continued

;oodbreys
9 Double St. IP13 9BN. (R. and M. Goodbrey). st. 1965. Open Sat. 9-5.30, other times by ppointment. SIZE: Large. *STOCK: Decorative ems including sleighbeds, upholstery, iedermeier, simulated bamboo, painted cup-oards, garden furniture, country pieces; pottery, lass, textiles, mirrors, bric-a-brac.* LOC: Up hurch St. towards Framlingham Castle. Opposite nurch gates turn right into Double St. PARK: asy. TEL: 01728 621191; fax - 01728 724626. AT: Mainly Spec. *Mainly Trade.*

ACHESTON, Nr. Wickham Market

oyce Hardy Pine and Country urniture
'13 0DS. Resident. Open 9.30-5.30, Sun. 9.30-2. *STOCK: Pine - dressers, corner cupboards, utcher's blocks, farmhouse tables.* LOC: B1116, ramlingham Rd. PARK: Easy. TEL: 01728 46485. SER: Hand-made furniture from old pine.

ADLEIGH, Nr. Ipswich

andolph BADA
7 and 99 High St. IP7 5EJ. (B.F. and H.M. arston). Est. 1921. Open 9.30-5.30, appoint-ent advisable. Sun. by appointment only. ZE: Medium. *STOCK: Furniture, 1600-1830, 0-£25,000; brass, copper, porcelain, delftware, een.* Not Stocked: Silver. PARK: Easy. TEL: 473 823789; fax - 01473 823867. SER: Valu-ions; restorations (furniture). FAIRS: ADA. VAT: Spec.

ara's Hall
ictoria House, Market Place. IP7 5DL. (B. 'Keefe). Est. 1977. Open 10-5. CL: Wed. SIZE: edium. *STOCK: Textiles and linen, jewellery, t Nouveau and Art Deco, small items.* PARK: sy. TEL: 01473 824031. SER: Valuations; buys auction (jewellery, Art Nouveau objects).

ALESWORTH

alesworth Antiques Market
Bridge St. IP19 8AB. (Tony Hull and Miles irhurst). Est. 1994. Open 10-5, Thurs. 10-1. ZE: Medium. *STOCK: Victorian furniture, £50-,500; Victorian china, £5-£150; general small tiques, 20th C, £5-£1,000.* PARK: Easy. TEL: 379 852420; home - same.

SWICH

. Abbott Antiques
7 Woodbridge Rd. IP4 4NE. (C. Lillistone). t. 1965. Open 10.30-5. CL: Wed. SIZE: edium. *STOCK: Small items, especially clocks and jewellery; Victorian, Edwardian and shipping furniture, £5-£1,000.* PARK: Easy. TEL: 01473 728900; fax - same; mobile - 0802 813848.

Ipswich continued

Tony Adams Wireless & Bygones Shop
175 Spring Rd. IP4 5NG. Open 10-5. CL: Wed. and Thurs. *STOCK: Bygones, especially wireless sets; toy trains, cameras.*

Ashley Antiques
20A Fore St. IP4 1JU. (A.M. Warren). Open 9-1 and 2-5, Sat. 10-1. SIZE: Medium. *STOCK: Furniture, 18th-19th C, £200-£4,000; 19th C barometers, £300-£1,000; Victorian coloured glass, £30-£200.* Not Stocked: Silver and jewellery. LOC: Off Star Lane. PARK: Easy. TEL: 01473 251696; fax - 01473 233974; mobile - 0802 823745. SER: Restorations (furniture). FAIRS: NEC (Aug.).

Atfield and Daughter
17 St. Stephen's Lane. IP1 1DP. (D.A. and Miss S.F. Atfield). Est. 1920. Open 9.30-5.30. SIZE: Medium. *STOCK: Furniture, clocks, metal, pottery, china, £5-£500; pistols, swords, guns, militaria, £25-£1,000; books on collecting, local history, military history and all kinds of transport, £5-£75.* LOC: Opposite bus station, Old Cattle Market. PARK: Very nearby. TEL: 01473 251158. SER: Restorations (cabinet work). VAT: Stan.

Paul Bruce Antiques
Frobisher Rd. IP3 0HR. Est. 1972. Open by appointment. SIZE: Warehouse. *STOCK: Oak, walnut and mahogany, paintings, general antiques, £20-£6,500.* TEL: 01473 255400/ 233671; fax - 01473 233656. VAT: Stan/Spec.

Claude Cox at College Gateway Bookshop
3 Silent St. IP1 1TF. Open 10-5. CL: Wed. SIZE: Medium. *STOCK: Books, from 1470; some local maps and prints.* LOC: Leave inner ring road at Novotel double roundabout, turn into St. Peters St. PARK: Cromwell Square and Buttermarket Centre. TEL: 01473 254776; fax - same. SER: Valuations; restorations (rebinding); buys at auction; catalogue available.

The Edwardian Shop
556 Spring Rd. IP4 4NT. Est. 1979. Open 9-5. *STOCK: Victorian, Edwardian and 1920's shipping goods, £10-£400.* LOC: Half-mile from hospital. PARK: Own. TEL: 01473 716576.

The Fortescue Gallery
27 St. Peter's St. IP1 1XF. (L. Fortescue). Open Tues.-Fri. 10-4. *STOCK: 19th C pictures.* PARK: Easy. TEL: 01473 251342.

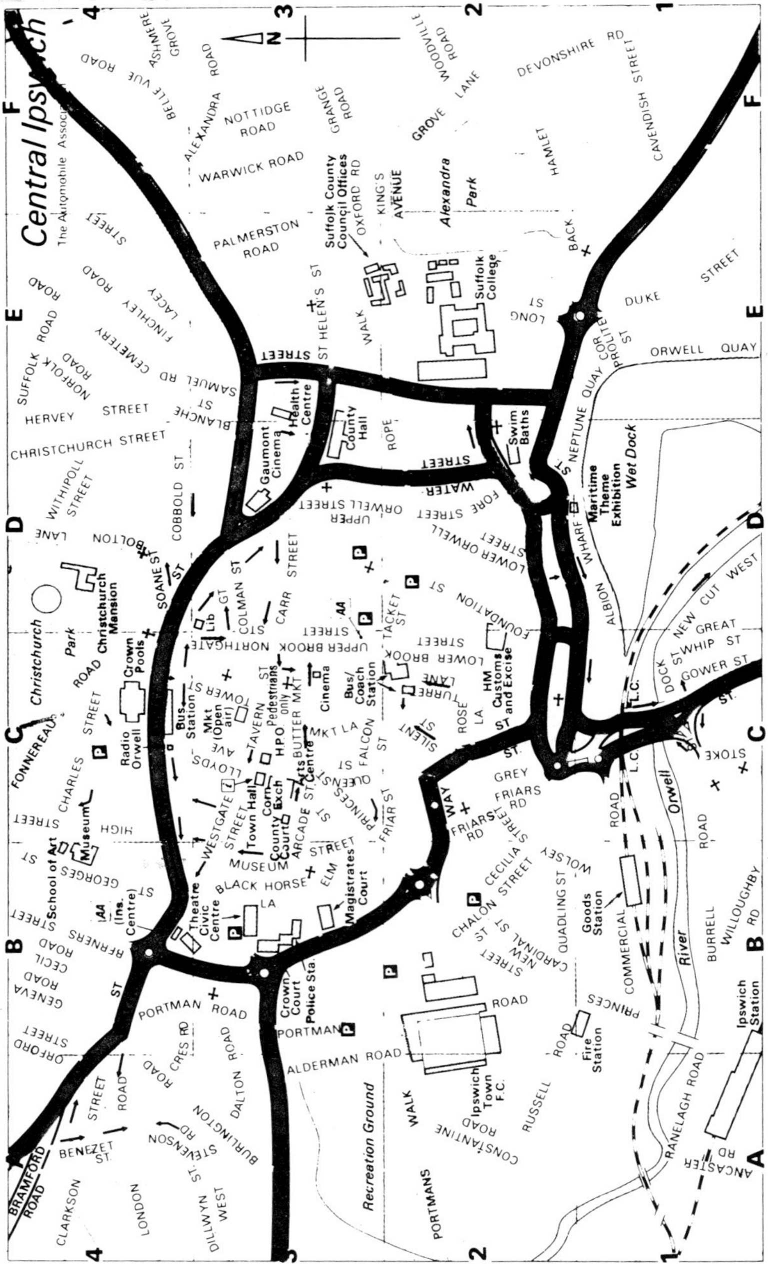

Key to Town Plan

AA Recommended roads		Car Parks	P
Other roads		Parks and open spaces	
Restricted roads		AA Service Centre	AA
Buildings of interest			

pswich continued

Iubbard Antiques
6-18 St. Margarets Green. IP4 2BS. Est. 1964.)pen 9-6 and by appointment. SIZE: Large. *TOCK: Furniture and decorative items, 18th-9th C.* PARK: Easy. TEL: 01473 226033/33034; fax - 01473 212726. SER: Valuations; estorations. VAT: Stan/Spec. *Trade & Export.*

Iyland House Antiques
5 Felixstowe Rd. IP3 8DX. (J. Burton). Open .30-5. CL: Wed. and Thurs. SIZE: Large. *TOCK: Pre-war furniture and bric-a-brac.* TEL: 1473 210055/712536.

)rwell Pine Co Ltd
alifax Mill, 427 Wherstead Rd. IP2 8LH. (M. Veiner). Open 8.30-5.30, Sat. 8.30-4. *STOCK: ine.* TEL: 01473 680091. SER: Restorations; tripping; pine furniture and kitchens made to rder from old wood.

'om Smith Antiques
3A St. Peter's St. IP1 1XF. Est. 1959. *STOCK: eriod furniture, shipping goods, pine and gifts, 2-£1,000.* TEL: 01473 210172.

'hompson's
18 Norwich Rd. IP1 5DX. (D. and Mrs S. hompson). Est. 1978. Open 9-5. CL: Sun. except y appointment. SIZE: Medium. *STOCK: urniture, mainly late Victorian and shipping,*

Ipswich continued

1870 to date, £10-£1,000. LOC: 1 mile from town centre, on corner at traffic lights next to railway bridge. PARK: Own, at side of premises. TEL: 01473 747793; fax - same. SER: Valuations; buys at auction (shipping items). VAT: Stan/Spec.

IXWORTH, Nr. Bury St. Edmunds

E.W. Cousins and Son LAPADA
27 High St. and The Old School. IP31 2HJ. CL: Sat. pm. SIZE: Large and warehouse. *STOCK: General antiques, 18th-19th C, £50-£6,000; shipping items.* LOC: A143. PARK: Easy. TEL: 01359 230254; fax - 01359 232370. SER: Valuations; restorations. VAT: Stan/Spec.

Ixworth Antiques
17 High St. IP31 2HH. (M. Ginders). Open 10-5, Sat. 10-1. *STOCK: Victorian and Edwardian furniture, brass and silver plate.* PARK: Easy. TEL: 01359 231691. SER: Polishing (brass); plating (silver).

KESGRAVE

Mainline Furniture
83 Main Rd. IP5 7AF. (Mr and Mrs R.S. Rust). Est. 1977. Open 9.30-5. CL: Mon., Wed. and Sat. *STOCK: Furniture, Victorian to 1950's; china and collectables, clocks.* TEL: 01473 623092.

KESSINGLAND

Kessingland Antiques

36A High St. NR33 7QQ. Est. 1976. Open 10-5.30. SIZE: Large. *STOCK: Edwardian, Victorian furniture, general antiques and collectables, watches, clocks, jewellery, shipping goods.* LOC: On A12, 3 miles south of Lowestoft. PARK: On forecourt and own. TEL: 01502 740562.

LAVENHAM, Nr. Sudbury

R.G. Archer

7 Water St. CO10 9RW. Est. 1970. Open 9-5, Sun. 10-5. *STOCK: Antiquarian and secondhand books.* TEL: 01787 247229.

J. and J. Baker

12-14 Water St. and 3a High St. CO10 9RW. (C.J. and Mrs B.A.J. Baker). Est. 1960. Open 9-1 and 2-5.30. SIZE: Medium. *STOCK: Oak and mahogany furniture, 1600-1870, £100-£10,000; oils and watercolours, 19th C, £150-£5,000; English porcelain and metalware, 18th-19th C, £20-£1,000; collectors' items, £20-£1,000.* LOC: Below Swan Hotel at T junction of A1141 and B1071. PARK: Easy. TEL: 01787 247610. VAT: Stan/Spec.

One Bell

46 High St. CO10 9PY. (J.F. and M.A. Tinworth). Open 11-4.30, Sat. 10.30-5, Sun. 11-5. CL: Wed. and Thurs. SIZE: Small. *STOCK: Militaria and collectables.* LOC: A134. PARK: Easy. TEL: 01787 248206; home - same.

Tom Smith Antiques

36 Market Place. Est. 1959. SIZE: Large and warehouse. *STOCK: Furniture, early Staffordshire figures, rugs, early maps and decorative prints.* TEL: 01787 247463. SER: Valuations; restorations. VAT: Stan/Spec.

LEAVENHEATH

Clock House

Locks Lane. CO6 4PF. (A.G. Smeeth). Est. 1983. Open by appointment. SIZE: Small. *STOCK: English clocks, 17th to early 19th C, £1,500-£6,000; French and English clocks, Victorian and Edwardian, £300-£2,000.* PARK: Easy. TEL: 01206 262187; home - same. SER: Valuations; restorations (clocks and furniture); buys at auction (clocks and furniture).

The Persian Carpet Studio

Harrow St. CO6 4PN. (Sara Barber). Est. 1990. Open 9-5, Sun. morning by appointment. SIZE: Medium. *STOCK: Antique and decorative Oriental carpets and rugs, from 1860, from £50.* LOC: .75 mile off A134. PARK: Easy. TEL: 01787 210034; fax - same. SER: Valuations; repairs and hand-cleaning (Oriental rugs); buys at auction (Oriental carpets, rugs and textiles). Exhibitions held. FAIRS: Snape. VAT: Stan/Spec.

LEISTON

Leiston Trading Post

13a High St. IP16 4EL. (A.E. Moore). Est. 196 Open 10-1 and 2-5, other times by appointmer CL: Wed. pm. *STOCK: Bric-a-brac, Victorian Victorian and Edwardian furniture.* PARK: Eas TEL: 01728 830081; home - 01728 83028 VAT: Stan.

Warrens Antiques Warehouse

High St. IP16 4EL. (J.R. Warren). Est. 1980. C Wed. and Sat. pm. except by appointment. SIZ Medium. *STOCK: Furniture, Georgian, Victoria Edwardian and shipping oak, £20-£2,000.* LO Off High St., driveway beside Geaters Floris PARK: Easy. TEL: 01728 831414; home - sam mobile - 0385 564905. SER: Valuations; resto ations (furniture). VAT: Stan/Spec.

LONG MELFORD

Antique Clocks by Simon Charles

Little St. Mary's Court, Hall St. CO10 9LQ. E 1970. Open 10.30-5.30, Sun. by appointme only. SIZE: Medium. *STOCK: Clocks - especia longcase, lantern and early bracket, 17th-19th £150-£10,000; barometers, 18th-19th C, £15 £1,000.* LOC: Opposite fire station on main ro PARK: Easy. TEL: 01787 880040; home - 017 375931. SER: Valuations; restorations (clo movements and cases); buys at auction (clock FAIRS: Snape and Bury St. Edmunds. VA Stan/Spec.

Ashley Gallery

Belmont House, Hall St. CO10 9JF. Est. 19 Open 9.30-5.30 or by appointment. SIZ Medium. *STOCK: Paintings, watercolo drawings, furniture, porcelain.* LOC: A1 opposite Crown Hotel. PARK: Easy. TEL: 017 375434.

Roger Carling and Tess Sinclair

LAPA

Coconut House, Hall St. CO10 9JQ. Reside Usually open 10-1 and 2-5, other times appointment. *STOCK: Furniture, mahoga and oak, 18th-19th C; general antiqu metalware, clocks, barometers, textiles, mirr decorative items.* TEL: 01787 312012.

Charles Antiques

Little St. Marys. (Meg Charles). Est. 1992. O 10-5, Thurs. 10.30-5, Sat. 10-5.30. SIZ Medium. *STOCK: Georgian furniture includ bureaux, dining tables and chairs, to £5,0 period pieces, £85-£1,000; marine oils, £2. £1,000; both Georgian and Victorian.* LC Sudbury end of village, opposite fire stati PARK: Easy. TEL: 01787 880040; home - 01 375931. SER: Restorations (period furniture).

ong Melford continued

andy Cooke Antiques

all St. CO10 9JQ. Est. 1982. Open Mon., Fri. nd Sat. 10-1 and 2-5. SIZE: Large. *STOCK: urniture, 17th to early 19th C, £100-£40,000.* ot Stocked: Silver and glass. LOC: A134. ARK: Easy. TEL: 01787 378265; fax - 01284 30935. SER: Valuations; restorations; buys at uction (furniture). VAT: Stan/Spec.

ountry Antiques

Westgate St. CO10 9DS. (Mrs E. Pink). Est. 984. Open 11-5. CL: Mon. and Thurs. SIZE: mall. *STOCK: Objects and jewellery, 18th-20th , £50-£500; small furniture, 18th-20th C, £50- ,000; toys and unusual objects, 19th-20th C, 25-£500.* LOC: Outskirts of village, on Clare oad. PARK: Easy. TEL: 01787 310617.

he Court Antiques

ittle St. Mary's Court. CO10 9LQ. (Tinka eigham and Karen Bryan). Est. 1975. Open 10- Sat. 10-5.30. SIZE: Medium. *STOCK: Decor- ive and unusual furniture, 18th-19th C, £200- ,000; prints, paintings and mirrors, 19th C, 0-£500; objects of vertu, 19th to early 20th C, 0-£400.* PARK: Easy. TEL: 01787 312613. ER: Valuations. VAT: Spec.

Long Melford continued

Long Melford Antique Centre

Chapel Maltings and the adjacent White Hart Annexe. CO10 9HX. (Baroness V. von Dahlen). Est. 1984. Open 9.30-5.30 or by appointment. SIZE: Large - 42 dealers. *STOCK: Furniture - oak, Georgian, Edwardian and Victorian; silver, china, glass, clocks and decorators' items.* LOC: A134, Sudbury end of village. PARK: Ample, behind White Hart. TEL: 01787 379287/310316. SER: Packing and shipping. VAT: Stan/Spec.

Alexander Lyall Antiques

Belmont House, Hall St. CO10 9JF. (A.J. Lyall). Est. 1977. Open 9.30-5.30. SIZE: Medium. *STOCK: Furniture, 18th-19th C.* LOC: A134 opposite Crown Hotel. PARK: Easy. TEL: 01787 375434; home - same. SER: Restorations (furniture); buys at auction (English furniture). VAT: Stan/Spec.

Magpie Antiques

Hall St. CO10 9JT. (Mrs P. Coll). Est. 1985. Open 10.30-1 and 2.15-5, Sat. 10.30-5. CL: Mon. and Wed. SIZE: Small. *STOCK: Smalls including hand-painted china; furniture, Victorian and stripped pine.* LOC: Main street. PARK: Easy. TEL: 01787 310581; home - same.

Long Melford continued

Patrick Marney

The Gate House, Melford Hall. CO10 9AA. Est. 1964. Open by appointment. SIZE: Small. *STOCK: Fine barometers, 18th-19th C, £1,000-£5,000; pocket aneroids, 19th C, £150-£1,000; scientific instruments, 18th-19th C, £250-£2,000; all fully restored.* LOC: A134. PARK: Easy. TEL: 01787 880533. SER: Valuations; restorations (mercury barometers). VAT: Stan.

Melford Antique Warehouse

Hall St. (D. Edwards and J. Tanner). Open 9.30-5.30. SIZE: 90 dealers on four floors. *STOCK: General antiques, 17th-20th C.* TEL: 01787 379638; fax - 01787 311788; home - same.

Noel Mercer Antiques

Aurora House, Hall St. CO10 9RJ. Est. 1990. Open 10-5. SIZE: Large. *STOCK: Early oak, walnut and country furniture and works of art, £500-£20,000.* LOC: Centre of Hall St. PARK: Easy. TEL: 01787 311882.

Seabrook Antiques

Hall St. CO10 9JG. (J. Tanner). Est. 1965. Open 9.30-5.30, Sun. 1-5. SIZE: Large - 10 showroms. *STOCK: Furniture, £500-£15,000; objects, £100-£2,000; both 17th-18th C.* LOC: A134 near Bull Hotel. TEL: 01787 375787; fax - same; home - 01787 311788. SER: Valuations; restorations (17th-18th C furniture); buys at auction (17th-18th C furniture). FAIRS: International.

Oswald Simpson BADA

Hall St. CO10 9JL. Est. 1971. Open 10-5.30, other times by appointment. *STOCK: Early oak and country furniture, £25-£10,000; brass, copper, pewter and country items, £10-£500; all 17th-19th C; samplers and needlework, 17th-20th C, £25-£1,000; Staffordshire figures, £100-£1,000.* PARK: Easy. TEL: 01787 377523; home - 01449 740030. SER: Valuations; restorations. VAT: Spec.

Suthburgh Antiques

Red House, Hall St. CO10 9JQ. (R.P. Alston). Est. 1977. Open by appointment. SIZE: Medium. *STOCK: Furniture, 17th C oak, 18th C walnut and mahogany, £500-£5,000; portraits, 17th-19th C, £2,000-£10,000; Georgian barometers and clocks, £400-£15,000; small collectors' items, boxes, glass, brass, copper, oak carvings and panels, £50-£600; English county maps and prints, £40-£500.* Not Stocked: Victorian furniture and later items. LOC: Opposite Bull Hotel, A134. PARK: Easy. TEL: 01787 374818; fax - same; home - same. SER: Valuations; restorations (furniture, barometers); buys at auction. VAT: Stan/Spec.

Long Melford continued

Trident Antiques LAPAD

2 Foundry House, Hall St. CO10 9JR. (Thoma McGlynn). Est. 1989. Open 10-5.30, Sat. 10- Sun. by appointment. SIZE: Medium. *STOCK: Oak furniture, 17th C, £250-£10,000; baro meters, 19th C, £450-£2,500; paintings, 17th 18th C, £2,000-£6,000; objects including bottle spoons and carvings, 17th-18th C, £100-£60* LOC: Next to Cock and Bell Inn. PARK: Eas TEL: 01787 883388; home - 01787 37186 SER: Valuations; restorations (early Englis oak); buys at auction (oak furniture). FAIR LAPADA (NEC); Kenilworth (Mar. and Oct City of London. VAT: Spec.

Tudor Antiques

Little St. Marys. CO10 9HY. (A.H. Denton-Ford Est. 1974. Open 9.30-5.30. SIZE: Large + war house. *STOCK: General antiques, £5-£5,00 curios, silver, objets d'art, furniture, bygones, boo on antiques.* LOC: Sudbury end of Long Melfor shop with yellow blind. PARK: Easy. TEL: 017 375950; mobile - 0585 768739. SER: Valuation metal polishing; repairs (metal, clocks, barometers mail-order catalogue. VAT: Stan/Spec.

Village Clocks

Little St. Mary's. CO10 9LQ. (J.C. Massey). E 1975. Open 10-5, Sat. 9.30-5. CL: Wed. SIZ Small. *STOCK: Clocks - longcase, bracket, w and mantle, 18th-19th C, £500-£5,000; carria 19th C, £500-£1,000.* PARK: Easy. TEL: 017 375896. SER: Valuations; restorations (as stoc buys at auction (clocks). FAIRS: Uxbrid Horological, Brunel University.

LOWESTOFT

Carlton Road Antiques

1 Carlton Rd. NR34 7PF. (A. and I. Murray). E 1983. Open 9.30-5, Sat. 9.30-5.30. SIZE: Lar *STOCK: Stripped pine, £25-£1,000; Victori furniture, £100-£2,000; china, paintings, mirro silver and collectables, £25-£100; all 18th-2 C.* LOC: From A12 into Lowestoft, approximat 2 miles from Bloodmoor Lane roundabout, tu left into Carlton Road. PARK: Easy. TEL: 015 512946; home - 01502 713896.

North End Antiques

56-57 High St. NR32 1JA. (Mr and Mrs Fletche Open 9-5.30. *STOCK: Victorian furniture a collectables.* TEL: 01502 568535.

MARLESFORD

Antique Warehouse

Main Rd. IP13 0AQ. Open 9-4. SIZE: Lar *STOCK: Furniture, general antiques and shipp goods.* LOC: A12. PARK: Easy. TEL: 017 747438; fax - 01728 747627. SER: Manufactu of country furniture.

MARTLESHAM, Nr. Woodbridge

Martlesham Antiques

The Thatched Roadhouse. IP12 4RJ. (R.F. Frost). Est. 1973. Open daily, Sun. by appointment. SIZE: Large. *STOCK: Furniture and decorative items, 17th-20th C, £25-£3,000.* LOC: A1214 opposite Red Lion public house. PARK: Own. TEL: 01394 386732; fax - 01394 382959.

Martlesham continued

John Read

29 Lark Rise, Martlesham Heath. IP5 7SA. Est. 1992. By appointment. *STOCK: Pre. 1840 Staffordshire figures, animals and English pottery, including coloured glaze, underglaze (Pratt) and enamel decoration, 1750-1840, £100-£4,000.* LOC: A12 Ipswich bypass, opposite B.T. tower. PARK: Easy. TEL: 01473 624897; home - same. SER: Valuations; restorations (as stock).

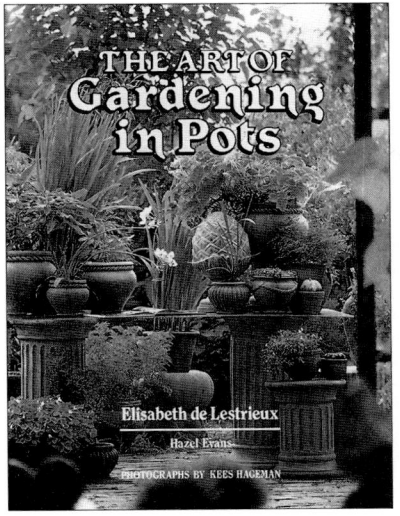

MILDENHALL

Mildenhall Antiques

10 North Terrace. IP28 7AA. Open 10-5. *STOCK: Pine, Victorian, Edwardian and 1920's shipping goods.* TEL: 01638 718025.

NEEDHAM MARKET

Roy Arnold

77 High St. IP6 8AN. Est. 1974. Open 9.30-5.30 appointment advisable, Sun. by appointment. SIZE: Medium. *STOCK: Woodworkers' and craftsmen's tools; scientific instruments; books - new, secondhand and antiquarian - on tools; all £10-£5,000.* LOC: A14, centre of High St. PARK: Easy. TEL: 01449 720110; fax - 01449 722498; e-mail - Roy.Arnold@btinternet.com. VAT: Stan/Spec.

The Old Town Hall Antique Centre

High St. IP6 8AL. (S. and R. Abbott). Open 10-5. SIZE: Several dealers. *STOCK: General antiques.* TEL: 01449 720773. SER: Repairs (jewellery).

NEWMARKET

Equus Art Gallery

Sun Lane. CB8 8EW. (Mr and Mrs M. Minahan). Est. 1989. Open 9.30-5.30. CL: Wed. pm. SIZE: Medium. *STOCK: Equine oils, watercolours and sculpture, 19th-20th C, £300-£1,000; equine prints, 18th-20th C, £50-£2,000.* LOC: Off High St. PARK: Nearby. TEL: 01638 560445; home - 01638 666637. VAT: Stan.

Jemima Godfrey

5 Rous Rd. CB8 8DH. (Miss A. Lanham). Est. 1968. Open Thurs. and Fri. 10-1 and 2-4.30. SIZE: Small. *STOCK: Small antiques, jewellery and linen, 19th C.* LOC: Just off High St., near clock tower. PARK: Easy. TEL: 01638 663584.

R.E. and G.B. Way

Brettons, Burrough Green. CB8 9NA. Open 8.30-5 appointment advisable. *STOCK: Antiquarian and secondhand books on shooting, fishing, horses, racing and hunting and small general section.* TEL: 01638 507217; fax - 01638 508058.

ORFORD

Castle Antiques

Market Sq. IP12 2LH. (S. Simpkin). Est. 1969. Open daily including Sun. 11-4.30. SIZE: Medium. *STOCK: Furniture, general small antiques, bric-a-brac, glass, china, clocks.* TEL: 01394 450100.

PEASENHALL, Nr. Saxmundham

Peasenhall Art and Antiques Gallery

The Street. IP17 2HJ. (A. and M. Wickins) Resident. Est. 1972. Open every day. *STOCK: 19th C watercolours and oils; country furniture all woods; walking sticks.* TEL: 01728 660224 home - same. SER: Restorations (oils, watercolours, furniture).

RISBY, Nr. Bury St. Edmunds

The Risby Barn

IP28 6QU. (R. and S. Martin). Open 9-5.30, Sun and Bank Holidays 10-5. SIZE: 24 dealers. *STOCK: Furniture, porcelain, metalware, tools, pine, Art Deco.* LOC: Just off A14 west of Bury St. Edmunds. TEL: 01284 811126; fax - 01284 810783.

SNAPE

Snape Antiques and Collectors Centre

Snape Maltings. IP17 1SR. Est. 1992. Open days 10-6 or until dusk in winter. SIZE: 3[illegible] dealers. *STOCK: Antiques and collectables especially smalls - sewing, silver, jewellery ceramics from 18th C-Doulton-Deco-Studio glass, maps, prints, paintings, textiles, country decorative and useful furniture, stamps, coins, a[illegible] and music books, costume jewellery.* LOC: Next to the Concert Hall. PARK: Easy. TEL: 0172[illegible] 688038.

SOUTHWOLD

The Emporium Antiques and Collectors Centre

70 High St. IP18 6DN. (Michael Brown). Est. 1992. Open 10-5.30, Sun. 12-5. SIZE: Over 4[illegible] dealers. *STOCK: Wide range of general antiques and collectables.* PARK: Nearby. TEL: 015[illegible] 723909.

T. Schotte Antiques

The Old Bakehouse, Black Mill Rd. IP18 6A[illegible] (T. and J. Schotte). Open 10-1 and 2-4. CL: We[illegible] SIZE: Small. *STOCK: Small furniture, £25-£50[illegible] decorative objects, £5-£250; both 18th-19th [illegible] Unusual collectables, £5-£100.* LOC: Turn rig[illegible] at the King's Head, then first left. TEL: 015[illegible] 722083. FAIRS: Snape Summer; Long Melfo[illegible] monthly; Adams, Horticultural Hall, London.

S. J. Webster-Speakman BAD[illegible]

Open by appointment only. *STOCK: Englis[illegible] furniture, clocks, Staffordshire pottery, gener[illegible] antiques.* TEL: 01502 722252. SER: Valuation[illegible] restorations (clocks, furniture, ceramics[illegible] FAIRS: Various.

ƚTOKE BY NAYLAND, Nr. Colchester

ƚuffolk Antique Connection LAPADA

ƚcotland Place, Scotland St. CO6 4QG. 'Matthew Pike and Julia Pike). ***STOCK: 17th- 9th C country furniture, especially English and 'rench farmhouse and refectory tables.*** **TEL: 1206 262098; fax - 01206 263339; mobile - ·802 644420. FAIRS: London; Boston USA.**

·TOWMARKET

'rench Puzzles

'hree Cow Green, Bacton. IP14 4HJ. *STOCK: ·ntique, old jigsaw and mechanical puzzles.* TEL: 1449 781178. *Mail Order Only.*

·TRADBROKE, Nr. Eye

·lary Palmer Antiques

he Cottage Farm, New St. IP21 5JG. (Mrs M. almer Stones). Resident. Est. 1980. Open 9-9, un. by appointment. SIZE: Small. *STOCK: nglish glass, 1750-1850; furniture, 1700-1900.* OC: B1117. PARK: Easy. TEL: 01379 388100. ER: Valuations; restorations (furniture).

tubcroft Period Furnishings and ≀estorations

he Cottage Farm, New St. IP21 5JG. (G.G. ːones). Est. 1984. Open 9-9 and Sun. pm. SIZE: mall. *STOCK: London and country period ·rniture.* LOC: B1117. PARK: Easy. TEL: 01379 ·8100.

·UDBURY

ntique Clocks by Simon Charles

ıe Limes, 72 Melford Rd. CO10 6LT. Est. 1970. pen by appointment only. *STOCK: Interesting ɔcks, especially English longcase, lantern and ·usual skeleton clocks, 17th-19th C.* TEL: 01787 '5931. SER: Valuations; free estimates; storations; repairs.

apier House Antiques

ıurch St. CO10 6BJ. Open 10-4.30, or by ·pointment anytime. SIZE: Large. *STOCK: ɜorgian and Victorian dining tables, linen ·esses, bureaux, chests of drawers, wardrobes.* ·RK: Easy. TEL: 01787 375280; fax - 01787 8757.

·ICKHAM MARKET

·rafers Antiques

·e Hill. IP13 0QS. (Mrs Elizabeth Davies). Est. 70. Open Tues.-Sat. 10-5. CL: Lunchtimes ·es. and Thurs. only and Fri. afternoons. *'OCK: 18th-19th C porcelain and pottery, glass, ·ver, jewellery, small furniture and collectors' ·ms.* LOC: Corner of Square, opposite church. ·RK: Easy. TEL: 01728 747347.

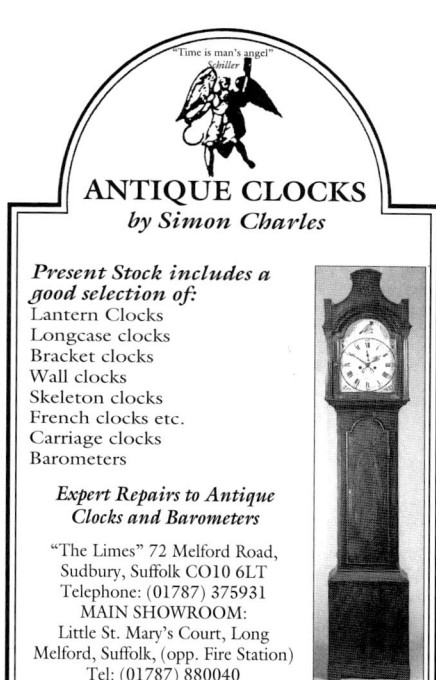

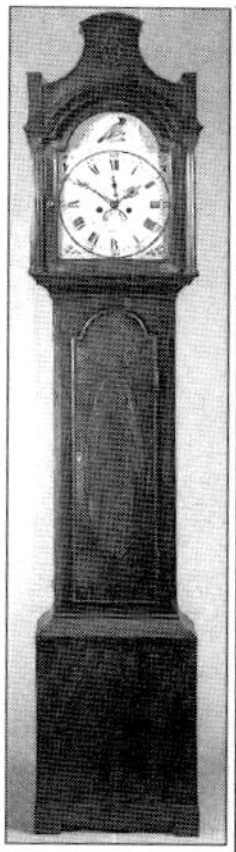

Wickham Market continued

Roy Webb

179 & 181 High St. Open Mon., Thurs. and Sat. 10-6 or by appointment. *STOCK: Furniture, 18th-19th C; clocks.* TEL: 01728 746077; home - 01394 382697. VAT: Stan.

WOODBRIDGE

Antique Furniture Warehouse

Old Maltings, Crown Pl. IP12 1BU. (H.T. and R.E. Ferguson). Est. 1976. Usually open 9-5, but prior 'phone call advisable. CL: Sat. and Sun. except by appointment. SIZE: Medium. *STOCK: Furniture, 17th to early 20th C, £200-£10,000; small items.* LOC: In centre of town, off Quay St. First warehouse in Crown Place. TEL: 01394 387222; fax - 01394 383832. VAT: Stan/Spec. *Trade and Export Only.*

Bagatelle

40 Market Hill. IP12 4LU. (N. Lambert). Est. 1990. Open 10.30-5, Wed. 10.30-1. CL: Thurs. SIZE: Medium. *STOCK: Orientalia, water-colours, oils and engravings, furniture, china, glass and collectables, 18th-20th C, £10-£2,000.* PARK: Nearby. TEL: 01394 380204.

EDWARD MANSON
Antiquarian Horology

8 Market Hill, Woodbridge,
Suffolk IP12 4LU.
Tel: 01394 380235

**I specialise in
Longcase Clocks and have
probably the largest stock of
quality clocks in the
East of England**

The stock usually consists of
about 24 Longcases mostly
30hrs and 8 day clocks, both
Brass and Painted Faces. I try to
stock attractive clocks at prices
mainly between £1,500 and
£3,000. I am happy to take
"trade ins". I am particularly
anxious to buy
East Anglian Clocks.

For 25 years I have restored
antique clocks from
local 30hrs to Knibbs

Woodbridge continued

Simon Carter Gallery
23 Market Hill. IP12 4LX. Est. 1960. Open 9.15-5.30. SIZE: Large. *STOCK: English and Continental oil paintings, 17th-20th C; English watercolours and drawings, 18th-20th C; furniture, oak and mahogany, 17th-19th C; decorative objects, Art Deco, studio pottery, some porcelain and prints.* Not Stocked: Clocks, silver. PARK: 60yds. behind gallery in Theatre St. TEL: 01394 382242; fax - 01394 388146; home - 01394 411894. SER: Six exhibitions held annually - catalogues available; restorations; valuations. VAT: Spec.

David Gibbins Antiques BADA
21 Market Hill. IP12 4LX. Est. 1964. Open 9.30-5.30, Wed. 9.30-1. *STOCK: English furniture, late 16th to early 19th C, £300-£15,000; English pottery and porcelain, metalwork.* PARK: Own in Theatre St. TEL: 01394 383531; fax - same; home - 01394 382685. SER: Valuations; buys at auction. VAT: Spec.

Hamilton Antiques LAPADA
5 Church St. IP12 1DH. (H.T. and R.E. Ferguson). Est. 1976. Open 10-5. *STOCK: Furniture - mahogany, walnut, oak, fruitwood, 17th-20th C, £200-£10,000.* TEL: 01394 387222; fax - 01394 383832. VAT: Stan/Spec.

Woodbridge continued

Anthony Hurst Antiques LAPAD.
13 Church St. IP12 1DS. (C.G.B. Hurst). Es▪ 1957. Open 9.30-1 and 2-5.30. CL: Wed. an▪ Sat. pm. SIZE: Large. *STOCK: English fur niture, oak, walnut and mahogany, 1600-190(£100-£5,000.* PARK: Easy. TEL: 0139▪ 382500. SER: Valuations; restoration▪ (furniture); buys at auction. VAT: Stan/Spec.

Lambert's Barn
24A Church St. Open 9.30-1 and 2-5. CL: We▪ pm. SIZE: Large. *STOCK: Mainly Victorian an▪ 20th C furniture, miscellaneous items.* PARK Easy. TEL: 01394 382380.

Edward Manson (Clocks)
8 Market Hill. IP12 4LU. Open 10-5.30, We▪ 10-1. *STOCK: Clocks.* TEL: 01394 380235. SE▪ Restorations (clocks).

Melton Antiques
Kingdom Hall, Melton Rd., Melton. (A. Harve▪ Jones). Est. 1975. Open 9.30-5. SIZE: Sma▪ *STOCK: Silver, collector's items, £5-£50▪ decorative items and furniture, £15-£500; bo▪ 18th-19th C; Victoriana and general antique 19th C, £5-£500.* LOC: On right hand-si▪ coming from Woodbridge. PARK: Easy. TE▪ 01394 386232.

Woodbridge continued

Sarah Meysey-Thompson Antiques
10 Church St. IP12 1DH. Est. 1962. Open 10-5., Sun. by appointment. SIZE: Medium. *STOCK: Small furniture, late 18th to early 19th C; china, glass, decorative items, 19th C; textiles and curtains.* PARK: Easy. TEL: 01394 382144. VAT: Spec.

Isobel Rhodes
10-12 Market Hill. *STOCK: Furniture, oak, country, mahogany; brassware.* PARK: Easy. TEL: 01394 382763. VAT: Spec.

A.G. Voss
24 Market Hill. IP12 4LU. Est. 1965. Open 10-1 and 2.15-5. CL: Wed. *STOCK: Furniture, glass, late 17th-early 20th C.* PARK: Nearby. TEL: 01394 385830. SER: Valuations; restorations.

WOOLPIT, Nr. Bury St. Edmunds

J.C. Heather
The Old Crown. IP30 9SA. Est. 1946. Open every day 9-8. SIZE: Large. *STOCK: Furniture, 18th-19th C, £20-£1,000.* Not Stocked: China. LOC: Near centre of village on right. PARK: Easy. TEL: 01359 240297. VAT: Stan/Spec.

WORTHAM, Nr Eye

The Falcon Gallery
Honeypot Farm. IP22 1PW. (N. Smith). Est. 1974. Open by appointment seven days. SIZE: Medium. *STOCK: Watercolours and oils, 19th C.* LOC: South side of A143 in village centre, overlooking village green, 4 miles west of Diss. PARK: Easy. TEL: 01379 783312; fax - 01379 783293; e-mail - smith@macserious.source.co.uk.SER: Valuations; restorations (oils, watercolours); framing. VAT: Stan/Spec.

WRENTHAM, Nr. Beccles

Wren House Antiques
1 High St. NR34 7HD. (Valerie and Tony Kemp). Open Thurs.-Sun. 10.30-5. *STOCK: Furniture, china, glass, jewellery and collectables.* TEL: 01502 675276.

Wrentham continued

Wrentham Antiques
40-44 High St. NR34 7HB. (B. Spearing). Alway open. SIZE: Large. *STOCK: Victorian, Georgia Edwardian and decorative furniture.* LOC: A1 PARK: Easy. TEL: 01502 675583; fax - 015C 675707; home - 01502 513633. SER: Buys auction. VAT: Stan/Spec.

Wrentham Antiques Centre
The Old Reading Rooms, 7 High St. Open 10- Sun. 11-4. CL: Wed. *STOCK: Furniture, chin glass, jewellery, pictures, prints and bric-a-bra* TEL: 01502 675376.

YOXFORD

Red House Antiques
The Red House, Old High Rd. IP17 3HW. (J. ar Mrs M. Trotter). Est. 1987. Open by appointme only. *STOCK: 18th and early 19th C ceramic £20-£1,000.* Not Stocked: Stamps, arms, silve pictures, furniture and clocks. LOC: Off eith A1120 or A12, opposite churchyard. PARI Easy. TEL: 01728 668615.

Joan Stevens, Bookseller
Rosslyn House, High St. IP17 3EP. By appoir ment only. *STOCK: Books on literature, poetr art and women's history.* TEL: 01728 66836 SER: Catalogues issued.

Suffolk House Antiques BAD
High St. IP17 3EP. (A. Singleton). Open 10 and 2.15-5.15. CL: Wed. SIZE: Large. *STOC 17th-18th C oak and country furniture, works art, paintings, clocks, delftware and metalwar* LOC: A1120, just off A12. PARK: Easy. TE 01728 668122; fax - same; mobile - 08 521583.

Susan Wells Antiques
Haven House, High St. IP17 3EP. Est. 1984. Op 10-1 and 2-4, Sat. 10-1 and 2-5. CL: Wed. SIZ Medium. *STOCK: Furniture, 18th-19th C, £3C £3,000; Wemyss, £100-£1,000; mirrors, 18th-2C C, £50-£1,000.* LOC: Opposite Post Office main street. PARK: Easy. TEL: 01728 66848 SER: Buys at auction (furniture).

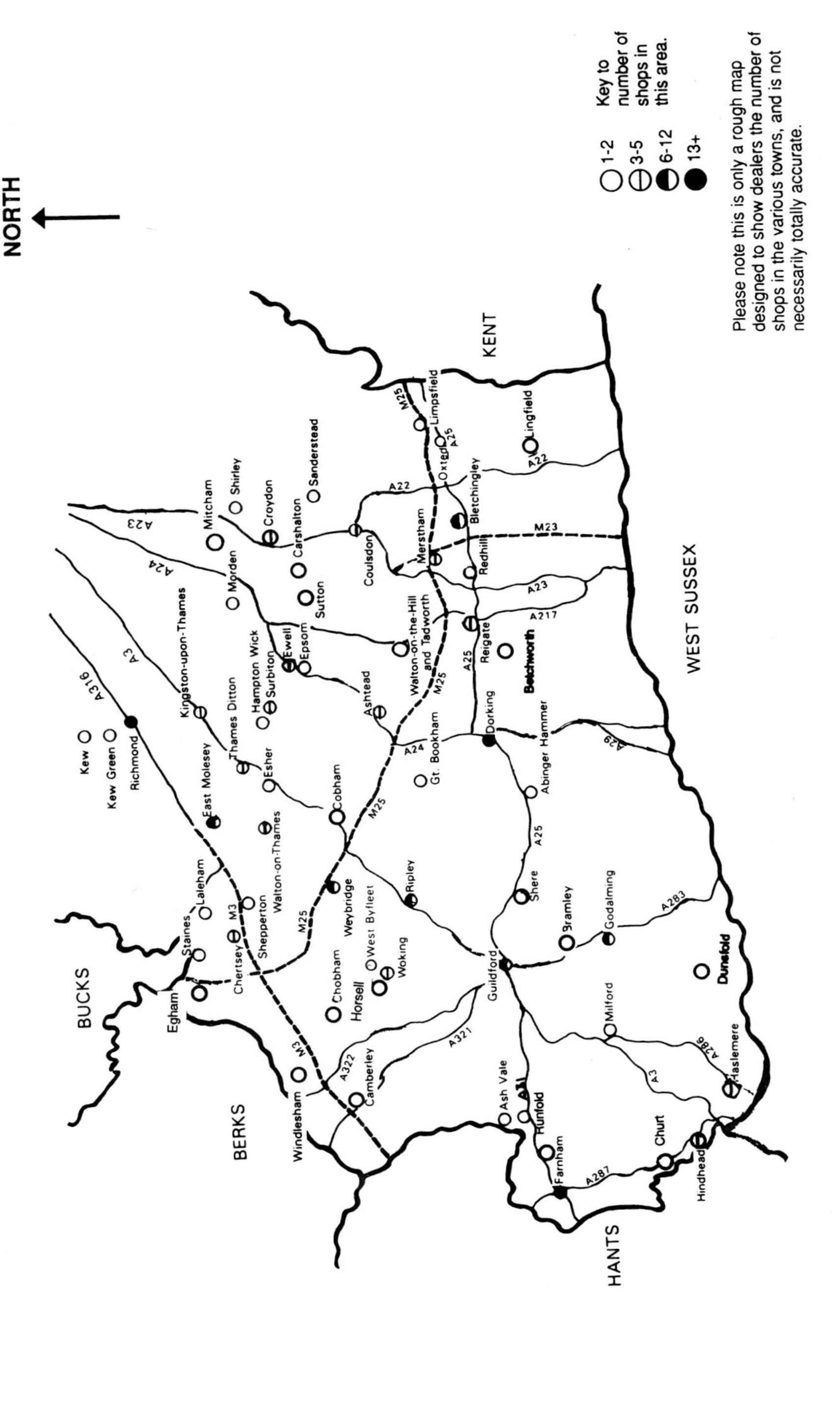
NORTH
1-2
3-5
6-12
13+
Key to number of shops in this area.
Please note this is only a rough map designed to show dealers the number of shops in the various towns, and is not necessarily totally accurate.
BUCKS
BERKS
HANTS
KENT
WEST SUSSEX
Kew
Kew Green
Richmond
East Molesey
Kingston-upon-Thames
Thames Ditton
Hampton Wick
Surbiton
Esher
Walton-on-Thames
Shepperton
Laleham
Staines
Chertsey
Egham
Windlesham
Camberley
Chobham
Horsell
Woking
West Byfleet
Weybridge
Cobham
Ripley
Guildford
Ash Vale
Runfold
Farnham
Churt
Hindhead
Haslemere
Milford
Dunsfold
Bramley
Godalming
Shere
Abinger Hammer
Dorking
Gt. Bookham
Ashtead
Epsom
Ewell
Walton-on-the-Hill and Tadworth
Betchworth
Reigate
Redhill
Merstham
Bletchingley
Oxted
Limpsfield
Lingfield
Coulsdon
Sutton
Carshalton
Morden
Mitcham
Croydon
Shirley
Sanderstead
A3
A23
A24
A25
A22
A217
A29
A283
A286
A287
A31
A321
A322
A316
M3
M23
M25

ABINGER HAMMER

Abinger Bazaar

Guildford Rd. RH5 6SA. (C. and G. Field). Est. 1978. Open Thurs., Sat. and Sun. 11.30-5. SIZE: Medium. *STOCK: Porcelain, glass, metal, fireplaces; Victorian, Edwardian, 30's and 50's, £1-£300; books, to £50.* LOC: A25 next to Frog Island Restaurant. PARK: Nearby. TEL: 01306 730756.

Stirling Antiques

Aberdeen House. RH5 6RY. (V.S. Burrell). Est. 1968. Open 9.30-6.30. CL: Thurs. *STOCK: Stained glass, furniture, copper, brass, jewellery, silver, curios, dolls.* PARK: Easy. TEL: 01306 730706. VAT: Stan.

ASH VALE, Nr. Aldershot (Hants)

House of Christian

5-7 Vale Rd. GU12 5HH. (A. Bail). Est. 1978. Open 10-5.30, Sat. 10-5. SIZE: Medium. *STOCK: Pine, 19th-20th C, £30-£1,500; some mahogany, oak, 19th-20th C.* LOC: On A321 between Ash and Mytchett. From Ash Wharf over canal bridge, shop (bright green) on left on hill. PARK: Easy - opposite. TEL: 01252 314478. SER: Valuations; restorations (including stripping, waxing, staining). FAIRS: Restorations; valuations; stockists of Briwax and Uberon products.

ASHTEAD

Bumbles

90 The Street. KT21 1AW. (Bob and Barbara Kay). Open 9.30-5.30. *STOCK: Furniture, lighting, clocks and barometers, oil lamps and parts.* PARK: Easy. TEL: 01372 276219. SER: Restoration and repair (furniture, clocks and barometers, oil lamps); gilding; brass polishing; silver plating; French polishing; leathering.

Memory Lane Antiques

102 The Street. KT21 1AW. (J. Westwood). Est. 1984. Open 10-5. CL: Wed. *STOCK: Toys and general antiques, pre-1920, £5-£1,000.* PARK: Easy. TEL: 01372 273436.

Temptations

88 The Street. KT21 1AW. (Pauline Watson). FGA, NAG. Open 10-5. *STOCK: Jewellery and silver.* LOC: Main street. PARK: Easy. TEL: 01372 277713. SER: NAG registered valuer; security photography; lecturer. VAT: Stan/Spec.

BETCHWORTH, Nr. Dorking

Stoneycroft Farm

Reigate Rd. RH3 7EY. (J.G. Elias). Open Mon.-Fri. 8-5.30, evenings and weekends by appointment. *STOCK: Large oak and country furniture, library bookcases, dining tables and chairs, special writing furniture.* TEL: 01737 845215.

BLETCHINGLEY

Castle Antiques

Castle Corner, Castle Sq. RH1 4LB. (C. A Porter). Open Tues.-Sat. 10-5. SIZE: Small *STOCK: Furniture, works of art, accessories an objects of vertu, 18th-19th C.* LOC: A25. PARK Easy. TEL: 01883 744100; fax - 01883 74446 VAT: Spec.

Cider House Galleries Ltd

Norfolk House, 80 High St. RH1 4PA. (T Roberts). Est. 1967. Open 9.30-5.30. CL: Sat. pm and Sun. except by appointment. SIZE: Large *STOCK: Paintings, 17th-20th C, from £20* LOC: A25, behind F.G. Lawrence Auctioneer PARK: Own. TEL: 01883 742198; fax - 0188 744014. SER: Valuations. VAT: Stan/Spec.

John Anthony Antiques

71 High St. RH1 4LJ. (J.A. and N. Hart Resident. Open by appointment only. *STOCK 18th to early 19th C furniture.* TEL: 0188 743197; fax - 01883 742108.

Simon Marsh

The Old Butchers Shop, High St. RH1 4P BAFRA. Est. 1970. Open by appointmen *STOCK: Grandfather clocks; 18th-19th furniture.* PARK: Easy. TEL: 01883 743350; fax 01883 744844. SER: Restorations (furniture an clocks).

Post House Antiques

32 High St. RH1 4PE. (P. and V. Bradley). Op daily, Sun. by appointment. *STOCK: Antiqu lighting; general antiques including mirror fenders, decorative items.* LOC: A25. PAR Easy. TEL: 01883 743317. VAT: Stan/Spec.

Quill Antiques

86 High St. RH1 4PA. (Mrs J. Davies). Est. 197 Open 10-1 and 2-5.30, other times by appoin ment. CL: Wed. pm. *STOCK: General antiqu including copper, brass, china, farming bygon kitchenalia, linen and lace, 50p-£500.* LOC: A2 PARK: Easy. TEL: 01883 743755; home - same

BRAMLEY, Nr. Guildford

Drummonds of Bramley Architectural Antiques Ltd

Birtley Farm. GU5 0LA. Est. 1988. Open 9 including Sun. SIZE: Very large. *STOCK: Arc tectural and decorative antiques, garden statu and furniture, salvaged building materia especially period bathroom equipment, 180 1950, £30-£30,000.* LOC: 1 mile south Bramley on A281, on left. PARK: Easy. TE 01483 898766; fax - 01483 894393. SER: Rest ations (stonework and gates); vitreous r enamelling of baths. VAT: Stan/Spec.

Bramley continued

Memories
High St. GU5 0HB. (P. Kelsey). Est. 1984. Open 10-5. SIZE: Small - 7 dealers. *STOCK: Victorian and Edwardian furniture, china and glass, silver, linen and lace, collectables and bygones, kitchenalia, stripped pine furniture, Art Deco.* LOC: South of Guildford on A281. PARK: Easy. TEL: 01483 892205.

CAMBERLEY

235 Antiques
235 London Rd. GU17 9ED. (R.G. and P.T. Ellis). Est. 1977. Open 10-1 and 2-4. CL: Mon. and Wed. SIZE: Small. *STOCK: Furniture, clocks and silver, 19th-20th C, from £20.* LOC: A30. PARK: Easy. TEL: 01276 24071/32123. SER: Restorations (furniture and clocks).

CARSHALTON

Carshalton Antique Galleries
High St. SM5 3AP. (B.A. Gough). Est. 1968. Open 9-5. CL: Wed. SIZE: Large. *STOCK: General antiques, furniture, clocks, glass, china, pictures.* Not Stocked: Silver, jewellery, bronze, firearms. PARK: Nearby. TEL: 0181 647 5664; home - 01306 887187. VAT: Stan/Spec.

Cherub Antiques
12 Carshalton Rd. SM5 3QB. (M. Wisdom). Open 10.30-5.30. CL: Wed. *STOCK: Pine and general antiques.* TEL: 0181 643 0028.

CHERTSEY

Chertsey Antiques
0 Windsor St. KT16 8AS. (Leandro Ulisse). Open 10-5. SIZE: 8 dealers. *STOCK: Furniture, jewellery, glass, pottery and porcelain, silver, pictures, kitchenalia, memorabilia, books, linen, lace and Wedgwood specialists.* TEL: 01932 63313; fax - 0153 682082.

Mister Sun Antiques
6 Guildford St. KT16 9AD. (R. Lee). Open 10-.30. *STOCK: General antiques and pine furniture.* TEL: 01932 566323.

CHOBHAM

Greengrass Antiques LAPADA
Hookstone Farm, Hookstone Lane, West End. GU24 9QP. (D. Greengrass). Open by appointment only. *STOCK: Decorative items; furniture, 19th C; works of art; shipping goods.* TEL: 01276 857582; fax - 01276 855289.

CHURT, Nr. Farnham

Churt Curiosity Shop
Crossways. GU10 2JE. (Mrs G. Gregory). Est. 1996. Open Tues., Thurs., Fri. and Sat. 10-4. SIZE: Small. *STOCK: Pottery, porcelain and collectables, Victorian and Edwardian furniture.* LOC: A287 Farnham to Hindhead road. PARK: Easy. TEL: 01428 714096.

COBHAM

Cobham Galleries LAPADA
65 Portsmouth Rd. KT11 1JQ. (Mrs Jerry Burkard). Open Mon. by appointment, Tues.-Sat. 10-5, Sun. 11-5. SIZE: Medium. *STOCK: Period and country furniture, 19th to early 20th C oils and watercolours.* LOC: South off A3, on second roundabout. 5 minutes from M25. PARK: Driveway beside shop or Vermont Exchange Restaurant. TEL: 01932 867909; mobile - 0850 651743; home - 01932 845360. SER: Buys at auction; searches.

COULSDON

Decodream
233 Chipstead Valley Rd. CR5 3BY. Open by appointment only. *STOCK: Pottery - Clarice Cliff, Shorter, Shelley, Foley, F. and C. Rhead and Carlton ware.* PARK: Free. TEL: 0181 668 5534.

D. Potashnick Antiques
7 Stoats Nest Parade, 73 Stoats Nest Rd. CR5 2JJ. Open 9-5.30, Sat. 9-12 or by appointment. *STOCK: General antiques.* TEL: 0181 660 8403. SER: Restorations (furniture).

Victoria Antiques
147 Brighton Rd. CR5 2NJ. (Mrs S.M. Davidson). Est. 1993. Open 9.30-5.30, Sun. and Bank Holidays 11-5. SIZE: 12 dealers. *STOCK: Lighting, small furniture, silver, pictures, china, copper and brass, tools and collectables, £5-£500.* LOC: A23 corner Victoria Rd. in town centre. PARK: Nearby. TEL: 0181 763 9650.

CROYDON

Oscar Dahling Antiques
87 Cherry Orchard Rd. CR0 6BE. (Oscar Dahling and Liz Lancaster). Est. 1988. Open Mon.-Sat. 10.30-6, Sun. and other times by appointment only. SIZE: Medium. *STOCK: Furniture, £100-£500; ceramics, £10-£250; jewellery and costume, £10-£500; all 18th-20th C.* LOC: Ist left after leaving East Croydon B.R. station. shop 300 yards, near Grouse and Claret public house. PARK: Easy. TEL: 0181 681 8090; home - same. SER: Valuations.

Croydon continued

G.E. Griffin

43a Brighton Rd., South Croydon. CR2 6EB. (E.J.H. Robinson). Est. 1896. Open 8-5.30, Sat. 10-4.30. SIZE: Large. *STOCK: General antiques.* TEL: 0181 688 3130. SER: Restorations; upholstery.

Trengove

46 South End. CR0 1DP. Est. 1890. SIZE: Large. *STOCK: General antiques, Victoriana; oils, watercolours, 18th-19th C.* LOC: On main road through Croydon. TEL: 0181 688 2155. SER: Valuations. VAT: Stan/Spec.

The Whitgift Galleries

77 South End. CR0 1BF. FATG. Est. 1945. *STOCK: Paintings, 19th-20th C.* TEL: 0181 688 0990. SER: Restorations; conservation, framing. VAT: Spec.

DORKING

Howard Blay Antiques

56 West St. RH4 1BS. Open 10-5. SIZE: Medium. *STOCK: English walnut, oak and mahogany furniture, pre 1800, £500-£10,000.* TEL: 01306 743398.

T. M. Collins

70 High St. RH4 1AY. Est. 1963. SIZE: Medium. *STOCK: Jewellery, 1800-1900, £25-£3,000.* LOC: Opposite Boots chemist. PARK: Behind shop. TEL: 01306 880790. SER: Valuations; restorations (jewellery). VAT: Stan.

J. and M. Coombes

44 West St. RH4 1BU. Est. 1965. Open 9-5, Sun. 11-4. *STOCK: General antiques.* TEL: 01306 885479. VAT: Stan.

Dolphin Square Antiques

42 West St. RH4 1BU. (Mr and Mrs N. James). Est. 1991. Open 10-5.30. SIZE: Medium. *STOCK: Furniture, £500-£5,000; china and glass, £50-£2,000; all 18th-19th C.* LOC: Western end of High St. PARK: Nearby. TEL: 01306 887901. SER: Valuations; buys at auction.

Dorking Antique Centre

17/18 West St. RH4 1BS. (Mrs G.D. Emburey). Est. 1989. Open 10-5. SIZE: 30 dealers. *STOCK: Period and pine furniture, silver, porcelain, jewellery, copper and brass, pictures and prints, decorative and collectors' items.* LOC: Continuation of High St. into one-way system. PARK: Opposite. TEL: 01306 740915. SER: Restorations.

Dorking Desk Shop LAPADA

41 West St. RH4 1BU. (J.G. Elias). Est. 1969. Open 8-1 and 2-5.30, Sat. 10.30-1 and 2-5. SIZE: Large. *STOCK: Desks, especially partners, cylinder bureaux, davenports, kneehole*

Dorking continued

and pedestal, 18th to mid-20th C, £100-£10,00 **PARK: Nearby. TEL: 01306 883327; evenings 01306 880535; fax - 01306 875363. VAT: Sta Spec.**

Dorking Emporium Antiques Centre

1A West St. RH4 1BL. (Mrs S.M. Kenny). Es 1982. Open 10-5. SIZE: Medium. *STOCK Furniture, mainly mahogany, 18th-19th C; Britis and Continental ceramics, country bygones, boo and collectables; Art Deco ceramics, includin Clarice Cliff, Shelley, Susie Cooper, £5-£5,00* LOC: A25. PARK: Nearby. TEL: 01306 87664 home - 01883 627270.

Hampshires of Dorking LAPAD

50-52 West St. RH4 1BU. Open 9.30-1 an 2.15-5.30. SIZE: Large. *STOCK: Fine Englis walnut, mahogany, rosewood and satinwoo furniture, 18th-19th C, £500-£70,000.* PAR Own. TEL: 01306 887076; fax/ansaphone 01306 881029. VAT: Spec.

Harman's Antiques

19 West St. RH4 1QH. (Paul and Nick Harma Est. 1953. Open 10-5. SIZE: Large. *STOC Furniture including tables, linen presse sideboards, bookcases, 18th-19th C, £1,50 £10,000.* PARK: Nearby. TEL: 01306 74333 home - same; fax - 01306 742593. SER: Resto ations (polishing and repairs). VAT: Stan/Spec.

Harvey's Period Decor

5 West St. RH4 1BC. (Neil C. Harvey). Est. 196 Open 10-1 and 2-5. SIZE: Medium. *STOC Furniture, £50-£1,000+; copper and brass, gla and china, £5-£500; all 18th-19th C.* LOC: To centre. PARK: Nearby. TEL: 01306 87776 home - 01903 506656.

Hebeco

47 West St. RH4 1BU. Est. 1982. Open 10.30- SIZE: Small. *STOCK: Silver and plate, antiq and 20th C, £5-£1,000; glass, 18th-20th C, £ £300; pewter, 17th-19th C; blue and whi porcelain, 18th-19th C.* LOC: Off High St. PAR Nearby. TEL: 01306 875396 (answerphone). SE Valuations. FAIRS: Country Houses. VAT: Stan.

E. Hollander BA

The Dutch House, Horsham Road, Holmwoo RH5 4NF. CINOA. Strictly by appointme *STOCK: Longcase and bracket clocks, 167 1860; silver, Sheffield plate, English baromete 18th-19th C.* TEL: 01306 888921; fax - 013 887392. SER: Restorations (clock mechanis and cases, barometers). FAIRS: Olymp VAT: Stan/Spec.

Holmwood Antiques

Norfolk Rd., South Holmwood. RH5 4LA. (Dewdney). Open 9-6.30, evenings and weeke by appointment. *STOCK: Georgian and Victor furniture.* TEL: 01306 888174/888468.

Dorking continued

King's Court Galleries
54 West St. RH4 1BS. (Mrs J. Joel). Open 9.30-5.30. *STOCK: Antique maps, engravings, decorative and sporting prints.* TEL: 01306 881757. SER: Framing.

Mayfair Antiques
43 West St. (R.G. Dewdney). Est. 1963. Open 9-1 and 2-5. SIZE: Large. *STOCK: Furniture, mainly 18th-19th C, to £500+.* LOC: Opposite Junction Rd. PARK: Nearby. TEL: 01306 885007. VAT: Spec.

Norfolk House Galleries
48 West St. RH4 1BU. Open 10-5. *STOCK: Georgian and Regency furniture, especially dining tables and chairs; period antique clocks, longcase always in stock.* TEL: 01306 881028.

Pilgrims Antique Centre
7 West St. RH4 1BL. (Jo F. Pritchard). Resident. Est. 1974. Open 10-5.30. SIZE: 10 dealers. *STOCK: Furniture, 18th to early 20th C, £65-£2,000; paintings, 18th-20th C, £50-£1,200; smalls, 17th-20th C, £5-£1,000.* LOC: A25 through town, just off High St. PARK: Opposite. TEL: 01306 875028. SER: Valuations; restorations (furniture); buys at auction.

Elaine Saunderson Antiques BADA.
18/18a Church St. RH4 1DW. (Mrs E.C. Saunderson). Est. 1988. Open 10-1 and 2-5.30, Sat. 9.30-6, other times by appointment. SIZE: Medium. *STOCK: Furniture, late 18th to early 19th C, £50-£10,000; decorative items.* Not Stocked: Silver and jewellery. LOC: Turn left into North St. at end of West St. one-way. 100yds. up North St., opposite junction with Church St. PARK: Easy. TEL: 01306 881231/886082; home - same; mobile - 0836 597485. SER: Valuations; restorations (furniture). VAT: Spec.

Michael Schryver Antiques Ltd
The Granary, 10 North St. RH4 1DN. Est. 1964. Open 8.30-1 and 2-5.30, Sat. 8-12. *STOCK: Furniture.* LOC: Turn left at top of West St., business at end on right. PARK: Own. TEL: 01306 881110. SER: Valuations; restorations (cabinet work, polishing and upholstery). VAT: Stan/Spec.

Surrey Antiques
1 West St. RH4 1BL. (J. L. Rolls). Est. 1971. Open 10-5.30, Sun. 11-4. SIZE: Large. *STOCK: Furniture, Georgian and early Victorian, from £500; smalls including clocks and pictures, 17th-19th C.* PARK: Opposite. TEL: 01306 881777; fax - same; mobile - 0860 896171. SER: Valuations; restorations; buys at auction. VAT: Stan/Spec.

Thorpe and Foster Ltd LAPADA
1 West St. RH4 1BU. Open 9.30-1 and 2.15-5.30. SIZE: Large. *STOCK: Fine English walnut, mahogany, rosewood and satinwood furniture, 18th-19th C, £500-£70,000.* LOC: On A24. PARK: Own. TEL: 01306 887076; fax - 01306 881029. VAT: Spec.

Victoria and Edward Antiques Centre
61 West St. RH4 1BS. Est. 1972. Open 9.30-5.30. SIZE: Medium - 28 dealers. *STOCK: General antiques.* PARK: Nearby. TEL: 01306 889645.

Pauline Watson
Old King's Head Court. RH5 1AR. FGA, NAG. Est. 1960. Open 9.30-5. SIZE: Small. *STOCK: Jewellery and silver especially Victorian.* LOC: In the High Street at the top of West Street. PARK: Behind shop in North St. TEL: 01306 885452. SER: NAG registered valuer; lecturer. VAT: Stan/Spec.

West Street Antiques
63 West St. RH4 1BS. (J.G. Spooner, R.A. Ratner and P.J. Spooner). Est. 1980. Open 9.30-1 and 2.15-5.30. SIZE: Medium. *STOCK: Furniture, 17th to early 20th C, £100-£10,000; arms and armour, 17th-19th C, £100-£20,000; brass and copper, ceramics, paintings and collectors' items.* Not Stocked: Jewellery and carpets. LOC: A25, one-way system. PARK: Nearby. TEL: 01306 883487; fax - same; home - 01306 730182 or 01372 452877. VAT: Spec.

DUNSFOLD, Nr. Godalming

Antique Buildings Ltd
GU8 4NP. (Peter Barker). Resident. Est. 1975. Open daily, Sat. and Sun. by appoint. SIZE: Large. *STOCK: Oak timbers, 17th C, £25-£1,000; architectural items, 15th-18th C, £25-£500; barn frames, 17th C, £2,000-£50,000.* LOC: From Sun public house 500 yards down Alford road, row of white posts, premises up tarmac drive between last two. PARK: Easy. TEL: 01483 200477; fax - 01483 200752. SER: Valuations; restorations (ancient oak framed buildings); buys at auction (buildings and architectural items). VAT: Stan.

EAST MOLESEY

Abbott Antiques
75 Bridge Rd. KT8 9HH. Est. 1970. *STOCK: Clocks.* TEL: 0181 941 6398.

The Antiques Arcade
77 Bridge Rd. KT8 9HN. (J.L. Abbott). Open 10-5. SIZE: 14 dealers. *STOCK: General antiques.* TEL: 0181 979 7954.

B.S. Antiques
39 Bridge Rd. KT8 9ER. (S. Anderman). Est. 1983. Open 10-5. CL: Wed. SIZE: Medium. *STOCK: Clocks, barometers, prints, some furniture.* LOC: Near Hampton Court. PARK: Easy. TEL: 0181 941 1812. SER: Valuations; restorations and repairs (clocks and barometers). VAT: Spec.

East Molesey continued

The Court Gallery
16 Bridge Rd. KT8 9HA. (J. Clark). Est. 1980. Open 8.30-4.30. CL: Mon. *STOCK: Oils, watercolours, drawings and engravings, 18th-20th C, £35-£2,000.* LOC: From Scilly Isles roundabout turn into Hampton Court Way, Bridge Rd. is on left by Hampton Court Bridge. PARK: Easy. TEL: 0181 941 2212. SER: Valuations; restorations (oils and watercolours); framing.

The Gooday Shop and Studio
48-50 Bridge Rd., Hampton Court. KT8 9EU. (R. Gooday). Open Sat. afternoon. *STOCK: Arts and crafts, 1950's and 1960's.* TEL: 0181 979 9971.

Hampton Court Antiques
75 Bridge Rd., Hampton Court. KT8 9HH. (H. Abbott). Open 10-5. *STOCK: General antiques including clocks, furniture, lamps and decorative objects.* TEL: 0181 941 6398.

Hampton Court Emporium
52-54 Bridge Rd., Hampton Court. KT8 9HA. Open 9.30-5.30, Sun 10-5. SIZE: Medium. *STOCK: Furniture, paintings, silver, jewellery, mirrors, books, clocks, brass and copper, objets d'art, lamps, china and porcelain, collector's cameras, Art Deco.* PARK: Palace Rd. station. TEL: 0181 941 8876. SER: Valuations; restorations. VAT: Stan/Spec.

Howard Hope Phonographs and Gramophones
21 Bridge Rd. KT8 9EU. Open Fri. and Sat. 10-5 and by appointment. *STOCK: Mechanical and musical items.* LOC: Close by Hampton Court Palace. TEL: 0181 941 2472; 0181 398 7130. SER: Spare parts.

Nicholas Antiques
31 Bridge Rd. KT8 9ER. Open 9.30-5. *STOCK: Furniture, general antiques and decorative items.* TEL: 0181 979 0354. VAT: Stan/Spec.

The Sovereign Antique Centre
53B Bridge Rd. KT8 9ER. SIZE: 11 dealers. *STOCK: Furniture, cigarette cards, silver, jewellery, glass, pictures and collectables.* LOC: Near Hampton Court. TEL: 0181 783 0595.

EGHAM

The Pine Warehouse
195 High St. (A. and C. Perry). Open 10-5.30. CL: Mon. *STOCK: Old and new pine.* TEL: 01784 472621.

EPSOM

Vandeleur Antiquarian Books
6 Seaforth Gdns. KT19 0NR. (E.H. Bryant). By appointment only. *STOCK: Antiquarian and secondhand books on all subjects; prin including rowing, and maps.* TEL: 0181 393 775 (24 hrs). SER: Valuations; catalogues issue searches undertaken. VAT: Stan.

ESHER

Jenny Asplund Fine Art
KT10 9NB. Open by appointment only. *STOC Fine watercolours and selected oils, 19th to ear 20th C.* TEL: 01372 464960.

EWELL

A. E. Booth & Son
9 High St. KT17 1SG. (David J. and Mrs An Booth). BAFRA, Assn. Master Upholsterers. Es 1934. Open 9-5. SIZE: Large. *STOCK: Furnitur 1700-1900, £200-£2,000; porcelain, from 180 £20-£200.* LOC: A24 to Ewell village. PARK Own - through gates beside shop. TEL: 0181 39 5245; fax - same; home - 0181 391 0705. SE Restorations (furniture including polishin repairs and upholstery). VAT: Stan/Spec.

J.W. McKenzie
12 Stoneleigh Park Rd. KT19 0QT. Est. 197 Appointment advisable. *STOCK: Old and ne books on cricket.* TEL: 0181 393 7700.

Token House Antiques
7 Market Parade, High St. KT17 1SL. (Mrs I Walker). Est. 1966. Open 11-5. CL: Wed. *STOC Furniture, 18th-19th C; porcelain, decorati items, metalware and general antiques.* LO Opposite post office. PARK: At rear. TEL: 018 393 9654. VAT: Stan/Spec.

FARNHAM

Annie's Antiques
1 Ridgway Parade, Frensham Rd. GU9 8UZ. Es 1982. Open 9.30-5.30, Fri. 10.30-5.30, Sun. b appointment. SIZE: Medium. *STOCK: Furnitu bric-a-brac, jewellery, 19th to early 20th C, £ £1,000; general antiques.* LOC: 1 mile out Farnham on A287 towards Hindhead. PAR Easy. TEL: 01252 713447; home - 01252 72321

The Antiques Warehouse
Badshot Farm, St George's Rd., Badshot Le GU19 9HY. (Hilary Burroughs). Est. 1995. Op 10-5.30, including Sun. SIZE: Large - 2 bar *STOCK: Furniture, 19th C to 1930's, £75-£1,00 china, pictures and interesting collectables, 19 C to 1940's, £5-£200.* LOC: A31 from Farnha towards Guildford, 1st exit (signed Runfold), le at end of slip road towards Badshot Lea, premis 200 yds on left. PARK: Easy. TEL: 012 317590; fax - 01252 879750. SER: Restoratio (woodwork including dipping, veneering, caning

arnham continued

3its and Pieces
:2 West St. GU9 7EN. (Mrs C.J. Wickins). CL: Ved. pm. *STOCK: Victoriana, furniture, Art Jouveau, Art Deco.* TEL: 01252 722355/715043. ;ER: Costume hire.

3ourne Mill Antiques
·9-43 Guildford Rd. GU9 9PY. Est. 1960. Open 0-5.30 every day. SIZE: Large - 83 dealers. *TOCK: Antique and reproduction furniture in ·ak, walnut, mahogany, yew and pine; china, ·lass, pictures, jewellery, fireplaces, beds, itchenalia, bespoke furniture, collectors' items, ·ooks, bric-a-brac; garden ornaments, furniture nd buildings.* PARK: Own. TEL: 01252 716663.

Casque and Gauntlet Militaria
5/59 Badshot Lea Rd., Badshot Lea. GU9 9LP. R. Colt). Est. 1957. SIZE: Large. *STOCK: Ailitaria, arms, armour.* LOC: On Aldershot to 'arnham road. PARK: Easy. TEL: 01252 20745, xt. 2. SER: Restorations (metals); re-gilding.

Childhood Memories
7a South St. GU9 7QU. (Miss M.A. Stanford). *TOCK: Teddy bears, dolls, Dinky and Britains ·oys, games and childhood collectables.* TEL: 1252 724475.

Christopher's Antiques
;andford Lodge, 39a West St. GU9 7DX. (Mr and Ars C.M. Booth). Resident. Est. 1972. Open 8-1 nd 2-5.30, weekends by appointment. SIZE: ,arge. *STOCK: Fruitwood country and mahogany urniture, 18th-19th C; walnut furniture, 17th-8th C.* LOC: From Guildford on the A31, turn ight at second roundabout. PARK: Easy. TEL: 1252 713794. SER: Valuations; restorations furniture). VAT: Stan/Spec.

Farnham Antique Centre
7 South St. GU9 7QU. (Miss M.A. Stanford). 'st. 1976. Open 9.30-5. SIZE: 6 dealers. *STOCK: Jeneral antiques including silver, jewellery, orcelain, brass and copper, clocks, small urniture and collectors' items.* LOC: On the one-·ay system into Farnham, large corner site. ARK: At rear. TEL: 01252 724475.

Ieytesbury Antiques BADA LAPADA
'.O. Box 222. GU10 5HN. (I. and S. Ingall). ;st. 1974. Open by appointment only. SIZE: Aedium. *STOCK: Pre-1830 mahogany, walnut nd rosewood furniture, and 19th C decorative urniture, textiles and associated items, £200-12,000; paintings and bronzes, 19th C, £100-2,000.* TEL: 01252 850893; mobile - 0836 75727; fax - 01252 850828. FAIRS: West ,ondon, Olympia, Kensington, Decorators and thers. VAT: Mainly Spec.

Farnham continued

Maltings Monthly Market
Bridge Sq. GU9 7QR. Est. 1969. First Sat. monthly. SIZE: 190+ stalls. *STOCK: 60% of the dealers sell a wide variety of antiques, bric-a-brac, postcards and collectables.* LOC: Follow signs to Wagon Yard car park, Maltings over footbridge. TEL: 01252 717434; fax - 01252 718177.

Karel Weijand Fine Oriental Carpets
LAPADA

Lion and Lamb Courtyard. GU9 7LL. Est. 1975. Open 9.30-5.30. SIZE: Large. *STOCK: Fine antique and contemporary Oriental rugs and carpets, from £150.* LOC: Off West St. PARK: Easy. TEL: 01252 726215. SER: Valuations; restorations; cleaning. VAT: Stan/Spec.

GODALMING

Church Street Antiques
10 Church St. GU7 1EH. (L. Bambridge). Est. 1985. Open 10-5, Wed. 10-1. SIZE: Medium. *STOCK: British ceramics, 1800-1930, £5-£1,000; glass, 1800-1930, £5-£200; silver, 1750-1930, £20-£500.* LOC: Off A3. PARK: Easy and behind shop. TEL: 01483 860894. SER: Valuations; commission buying. VAT: Stan/Spec.

Cry for the Moon
31 High St. GU7 1AU. (J.L. Ackroyd). Est. 1977. Open 9.30-5.30. SIZE: Medium. *STOCK: Mainly jewellery, £50-£10,000; silver and objets d'art.* TEL: 01483 426201; fax - 01483 860117. SER: Valuations; repairs (jewellery); jewellery commissions undertaken. VAT: Stan/Spec.

Heath-Bullocks BADA
8 Meadrow. GU7 3HN. (R.J. and M.E. Heath-Bullock). Est. 1926. Open 10-5. SIZE: Large. *STOCK: English and Continental furniture, upholstered seat furniture, works of art, fine art.* LOC: A3100. From Guildford on the left side approaching Godalming. PARK: Own. TEL: 01483 422562; fax - 01483 426077. SER: Valuations; restorations; upholstery. FAIRS: Exhibitors at and Organisers of Buxton and Surrey.

The Olde Curiosity Shoppe
99 High St. GU7 1AQ. *STOCK: Silver, brass, copper, china, collectables and jewellery.* TEL: 01483 415889.

Priory Antiques
29 Church St. (P. Rotchell). Open 10-4. CL: Wed. *STOCK: General antiques.* TEL: 01483 421804.

Barbara Rubenstein Fine Art
at Heath-Bullocks, 8 Meadrow. GU7 3HN. Open 10-5. *STOCK: Watercolours and some oils, 19th-20th C, £250-£10,000.* TEL: 01483 422562.

GREAT BOOKHAM, Nr. Leatherhead

Bookham Galleries
Leatherhead Rd. KT23 4RQ. (J. Rowe). Est. 1969. Open by appointment only. SIZE: Large. *STOCK: Furniture, 18th-19th C.* LOC: A246. PARK: Easy. TEL: 01372 452668. VAT: Stan/Spec.

Roger A. Davis Antiquarian Horologist
19 Dorking Rd. KT23 4PU. Est. 1971. Open 9.30-12.30 and 2-5.30. CL: Mon. and Wed., Fri. pm. and Sun. am. except by appointment. SIZE: Small. *STOCK: Clocks, 18th-19th C, £100-£4,000.* LOC: From Leatherhead A246 to centre of village, turn left at sign for Polesden Lacey, shop ¼ mile along Dorking Rd. PARK: Easy. TEL: 01372 457655; home - 01372 453167. SER: Valuations; restorations (mechanical and case work); buys at auction (antique clocks).

GUILDFORD

The Antiques Centre
22 Haydon Place, Corner of Martyr Rd. GU1 4LL. (Mrs J. Carter). Est. 1969. Open 10-4. CL: Mon. and Wed. *STOCK: Wide range of general antiques.* LOC: Close to Surrey Advertiser. PARK: 100yds. on left from North St. Below are listed the dealers at this centre. TEL: 01483 567817.

Jennifer Carter
China, collectables, bygones.

Joan Goggin
China, collectables, bygones.

Jony's
Pictures, linens, costume and small furniture.

Sylvia Pullen
Silver, jewellery, Devon ware.

Denning Antiques
1 Chapel St. GU1 3UA. Open 10-5. *STOCK: Silver, jewellery, lace, linen, and collectors' items.* LOC: Off High St. PARK: Nearby. TEL: 01483 539595.

Horological Workshops BADA
204 Worplesdon Rd. GU2 6UY. (M.D. Tooke). Est. 1968. Open 8.30-5.30, Sat. 9-12.30 or by appointment. *STOCK: Clocks, watches, barometers.* TEL: 01483 576496.

Manor House
96 Stoke Rd. Est. 1952. *STOCK: Furniture, 18th C; copper and brass, 18th-19th C; clocks, prints - mainly sporting and military; china and glass.* TEL: 01483 574740. VAT: Stan/Spec

Guildford continued

Thomas Thorp Bookseller
170 High St. GU1 3HP. Est. 1883. Open 9-5, 5.3[0] on Sat. SIZE: Large. *STOCK: Books includin[g] antiquarian and out-of-print.* LOC: At traffi[c] lights at top of High St. PARK: Road runnin[g] parallel High St. 200yds. away. TEL: 0148[3] 562770. SER: Valuations; buys at auction (ant[i]quarian books). Private collections bought.

Tramp Jewellers
14 Swan Lane. GU1 4EQ. (Mrs N. Harper). Es[t.] 1968. Open daily 10-5.30. *STOCK: Jeweller[y].* TEL: 01483 504138. VAT: Stan.

Charles W. Traylen
Castle House, 49/50 Quarry St. GU1 3UA. Es[t.] 1945. Open 9-1 and 2-5. CL: Mon. SIZE: Larg[e]. *STOCK: Fine books and manuscripts, 13th C [to] date.* PARK: 200yds. TEL: 01483 572424; fax 01483 450048. SER: Valuations; restoratio[ns] (bindings); catalogues issued. VAT: Stan.

HAMPTON WICK

Hampton Wick Antiques
48 High St. KT1 4DB. Est. 1957. Open 11-[6]. *STOCK: Furniture including pine; religious item[s] and statues.* TEL: 0181 977 3178.

HASLEMERE

Allen Avery Interiors
1 High St. Est. 1971. Open 9-1 and 2.15-5. C[L:] Sat. pm. and Wed. *STOCK: English furnitur[e].* TEL: 01428 643883.

Bow Antiques Ltd
(R.C. Blandford). Est. 1992. Open by appointme[nt] only. *STOCK: Furniture, 18th-19th C.* TEL: Mobi[le] - 0374 467684. SER: Restorations (furnitu[re] including French polishing). VAT: Stan/Spec.

Haslemere Antique Market
1A Causewayside, High St. GU10 2LJ. Est. 199[.] Open 9.30-5. SIZE: Large. *STOCK: Wide varie[ty] of general antiques.* LOC: Off High St. (A286[)]. PARK: Easy. TEL: 01428 643959. SER: Val[u]ations; restorations; buys at auction.

Surrey Clock Centre
3 Lower St. GU27 2NY. (J.P. Ingrams and [S.] Haw). Est. 1962. Open 9-1 and 2-5. SIZE: Larg[e]. *STOCK: Clocks and barometers.* PARK: Eas[y]. TEL: 01428 651313. SER: Restorations; han[d] made parts; shipping orders; clocks made to orde[r]. VAT: Stan/Spec.

Wood's Wharf Antiques Bazaar
56 High St. GU27 2LA. SIZE: 12 dealer[s]. *STOCK: A wide selection of antiques.* LO[C:] Opposite The Georgian Hotel. TEL: 0142[8] 642125; fax - same.

ꟷINDHEAD

ꟷlbany Antiques Ltd
-10 London Rd. GU26 6AF. (T. Winstanley). ꞉st. 1965. Open 9-6. CL: Sun. except by appointꟷent. *STOCK: Furniture, 17th-18th C, £20-£400; ꟷhina including Chinese, £5-£400; metalware, £7-50; both 18th-19th C.* Not Stocked: Silver. LOC: ꟷ3. PARK: Easy. TEL: 01428 605528. VAT: tan/Spec.

ꟷI. J. Bowdery BADA
2 London Rd. GU26 6AF. Est. 1970. Always vailable, prior telephone call advisable. *TOCK: Furniture, 18th-19th C.* TEL: 01428 ꟷ06376; mobile - 0374 821444. VAT: Stan/Spec.

)riel Antiques
Royal Parade, Tilford Rd. GU26 6TD. (J. Gear). ꟷst. 1974. Open 9-5. CL: Wed. pm. *STOCK: Furꟷiture and pictures, 18th-19th C.* TEL: 01428 ꟷ06281.

Second Hand Rose"
ortsmouth Rd., Bramshott Chase. GU26 6DB. ꟷ.J. Ridout). Est. 1980. Open 10-5.30 and by ꟷppointment. SIZE: Large. *STOCK: Furniture, ꟷaintings, bric-a-brac, 18th-20th C.* LOC: On A3, mile S.W. of Hindhead. PARK: Easy. TEL: ꟷ1428 604880; home - same. VAT: Stan/Spec.

ꟷVhat Not Antiques
ꟷrossways Rd., Grayshot. (Mrs M. Wylie). Open -5.30. *STOCK: General antiques and pine.* TEL: ꟷ1428 604871.

ꟷIORSELL, Nr. Woking

ꟷIorsell Antiques
7 High St. GU21 4UA. (Philip Gilbert). Est. ꟷ974. Open 10-5. SIZE: Small. *STOCK: Brown ꟷrniture, 18th-19th C, £100-£3,000; pictures and ꟷina, 18th-20th C, £5-£600; small collectables, ꟷ9th-20th C, £5-£50.* LOC: From A322 along ꟷnaphill High St. At roundabout turn right into ꟷorsell High St. PARK: High St. TEL: 01483 ꟷ56807. SER: Restorations (French polishing, ꟷabinet work, upholstery); buys at auction ꟷurniture). VAT: Spec.

ꟷEW

ꟷloyds of Kew
Mortlake Terrace. TW9 3DT. (S. Cobley). Open ꟷues.-Sat. 10-6. *STOCK: Out-of-print books on ꟷardening, botany and some general.* LOC: ꟷnction of Kew and Mortlake Roads, 10 mins ꟷalk from Kew Gardens Station (District line). ꟷARK: Easy. TEL: 0181 940 2512. SER: Annual ꟷatalogues (Oct.).

ꟷennis Woodman Oriental Carpets
ꟷ5 North Rd. TW9 4HJ. Est. 1991. Open Wed.-ꟷın. 10-6. SIZE: Medium. *STOCK: Islamic ꟷrpets, rugs, kilims, embroideries and weavings.*

Kew continued

LOC: At Kew Gardens station. PARK: Easy. TEL: 0181 878 8182. SER: Valuations; restorations; buys at auction. VAT: Stan/Spec.

KEW GREEN

Andrew Davis
6 Mortlake Terrace. TW9 3DT. Resident. Est. 1969. *STOCK: Decorative and functional items of all periods, including furniture, ceramics, glass, pictures, clocks, garden and architectural items.* TEL: 0181 948 4911. SER: Valuations; restorations.

KINGSTON-UPON-THAMES

Glencorse Antiques LAPADA
321 Richmond Rd., Ham Parade, Ham Common. KT2 5QU. (M. Igel and B.S. Prydal). Open 10-5.30. *STOCK: 18th-19th C furniture; 19th C oils and modern British watercolours.* PARK: Own. TEL: 0181 541 0871.

Glydon and Guess Ltd
14 Apple Market. KT1 1JE. Est. 1940. Open 9.30-5. CL: Wed. *STOCK: Jewellery, small silver, £100-£5,000.* LOC: Town centre. TEL: 0181 546 3758. SER: Valuations; restorations.

Kingston Antiques Centre
The Kingston Exchange, 29-31 London Rd. KT2 6ND. (Reflections Ltd). Est. 1995. Open daily including Sun. SIZE: 80 dealers. *STOCK: Antique and period furniture, Art Deco, Art Nouveau, exotic, glass, fabrics, jewellery, objets d'art, pine, clocks, militaria, books.* LOC: Off Clarence St. PARK: Easy. TEL: 0181 549 2004. SER: Valuations; restorations; buys at auction.

LALEHAM, Nr. Staines

Laleham Antiques
23 Shepperton Rd. TW18 1SE. (E. Potter). Est. 1970. Open 10.30-5. SIZE: Medium. *STOCK: Furniture, porcelain, mirrors, pine, antique lighting, silver, general and trade antiques.* LOC: B376. PARK: Easy. TEL: 01784 450353; mobile - 0589 951652.

LIMPSFIELD

Limpsfield Watercolours
High St. RH8 0DT. (Mrs C. Reason). FATG. Est. 1985. Open Tues.-Fri. 10.30-4, Sat. 10-5. SIZE: Small. *STOCK: Watercolours, £15-£5,000; prints and etchings, £5-£200; all 1850-1940 and contemporary.* Not Stocked: Oils. LOC: From junction 6, M25 on B269. PARK: Easy. TEL: 01883 717010. SER: Valuations; restoration and cleaning of watercolours, prints and oils; framing including conservation. VAT: Spec.

LINGFIELD

I.O.U. (Interesting, Old & Unusual)
Paris House, 52/56 High St. RH7 6AA. (Keith Wheeler and Emma Tingley). Est. 1979. Open 9.30-5, Mon. 9.30-4.30. SIZE: Large. *STOCK: Victorian, Edwardian and traditional furniture; collectors' items, ephemera, china.* LOC: Southbound A22 turn east to Lingfield, follow signs for racecourse - 4th to last shop out of village at corner of Talbot Rd. PARK: Easy. TEL: 01342 836565; home - 01732 865651. SER: Valuations; commission sales.

MERSTHAM

Elm House Antiques
3 High St. RH1 3BA. (Robert Black). Est. 1983. Open 10.30-5.30. SIZE: Medium. *STOCK: Georgian to Edwardian town and country furniture, mahogany, oak and decorative items, £50-£5,000; country furniture, pine, kitchenalia, decorative items, textiles, £5-£500; brass and copper, £5-£100; period cabinet fittings.* LOC: A23 just past beginning of M23. PARK: Own. TEL: 01737 643983. SER: Valuations; restorations (textiles, boxes, inlay, gesso work, furniture including French polishing).

MILFORD, Nr. Godalming

Michael Andrews Antiques
Portsmouth Rd. GU8 5AU. Est. 1974. Open daily, Thurs. and Sun. by appointment. SIZE: Medium. *STOCK: Furniture, 18th-19th C.* LOC: Corner of Cherry Tree Rd. (on traffic lights, from A3 slip road to Petworth). PARK: Own. TEL: 01483 420765; home - same. VAT: Stan/Spec.

E. Bailey
Portsmouth Rd. GU8 5DR. (Eric Bailey). Est. 1979. Open 9-5. CL: Thurs. SIZE: Small. *STOCK: Furniture and tools, from Victorian, £5-£100; china, £5-£25.* LOC: Main road. PARK: Easy. TEL: 01483 422943.

MITCHAM

Cherub Antiques
177 Streatham Rd. CR4 2AG. (M. Wisdom). Open 10.30-5.30. *STOCK: Pine and general antiques.* TEL: 0181 640 7179.

MORDEN

A. Burton-Garbett
35 The Green. SM4 4HJ. Est. 1959. By appointment only. Prospective clients met (at either Morden or Wimbledon tube station) by car. *STOCK: Books on travel, the arts, antiquities of South and Central America, Mexico and the Caribbean, 16th-20th C, £5-£5,000.* TEL: 018 540 2367. SER: Buys at auction (books, picture fine arts, ethnographica). VAT: Stan.

OXTED

Antiques Centre
80-84 Station Rd. East. RH8 0PG. (D. Quigle and Mrs J. Wagstaff). Est. 1992. Open 9.45-5.3 SIZE: Large. *STOCK: Furniture, Georgia Victorian, Edwardian and 30's, £50-£3,50 clocks, barometers and watches, 19th C, £5 £3,000; metalware, fire accessories, china an porcelain, £1-£1,000; silver and jewellery, £2 £1,000; second-hand books.* LOC: 3 miles sou junction 6, M25; off A25. Almost opposi railway station. PARK: Easy and at rear. TEL 01883 712806; restorations - 01474 872307. SE Restorations (upholstery).

REDHILL

F.G. Lawrence and Sons
89 Brighton Rd. RH1 6PS. Est. 1891. Open 9- Sat. 9-1. SIZE: Large. *STOCK: Edwardia Victorian and Georgian furniture.* LOC: On A2 PARK: Own. TEL: 01737 764196. SER: Val ations. VAT: Stan.

REIGATE

Bourne Gallery Ltd LAPAD
31/33 Lesbourne Rd. RH2 7JS. (J. Robertson Est. 1970. Open 10-1 and 2-5. CL: Mon. SIZ Large. *STOCK: 19th-20th C oils and wate colours, £250-£25,000.* PARK: Easy. TEL: 017 241614. SER: Restorations (oil paintings). VA Spec.

The Gallery
3/5 Church St. RH2 0AA. (Jeffrey S. Cohen Open 10-6. SIZE: Medium. *STOCK: 19th-20th oil paintings and watercolours, especially Mode British artists post 1850, £250-£15,000; 18th-19 C furniture and mirrors, especially sma decorative pieces, £500-£10,000.* LOC: Tov centre, PARK: Easy and opposite. TEL: 017 242813; fax - 01737 362819. SER: Valuation restorations (paintings and furniture); buys auction (Modern British artists). VAT: Stan/Spe

Bertram Noller (Reigate)
14a London Rd. RH2 9HY. (A.M. Noller). E 1970. Open 9.30-1 and 2-5.30. CL: Tues. a Wed. SIZE: Small. *STOCK: Collectors' item furniture, grates, fenders, mantels, copper, bra glass, pewter, £1-£500.* LOC: West side of on way traffic system. Opposite Upper West St. c park. PARK: Opposite. TEL: 01737 24254 SER: Valuations; restorations (furniture, clock bronzes, brass and copper, marble).

eigate continued

eigate Galleries Ltd
5a Bell St. RH2 7AQ. (J.S. Morrish). Est. 1958. pen 9-5.30, Wed. 9-1. SIZE: Large. *STOCK: ld prints, engravings, antiquarian books.* ARK: Opposite. TEL: 01737 246055. SER: icture framing. VAT: Stan.

ICHMOND

ntique Mart
2-74 Hill Rise. TW10 6UB. (G. and Y. Katz). pen 10-5, Sun. 2-6. CL: Wed. SIZE: Large. *TOCK: Furniture, 18th-19th C.* TEL: 0181 940 942. SER: Buys at auction. VAT: Stan/Spec.

ntiques Arcadia
2 Richmond Hill. TW10 6QX. Est. 1984. Open aturdays, otherwise by appointment. SIZE: mall. *STOCK: English porcelain, Staffordshire gures, historical commemoratives, especially elsonia.* TEL: 0181 940 2035; fax - same; nternet - http:www.all-about-antiques.co.uk. anec.hlml. SER: Masterclass lectures.

he Chair Set - Antiques
4 Hill Rise. TW10 6UB. (Allan James). Est. 1982. pen 10-5.30, Mon. 11-5, Sat. 10-5. CL: Wed. IZE: Medium. *STOCK: Sets of chairs, £1,000-8,000; single and pairs of chairs, £200-£3,000; ining tables and accessories, £800-£5,000; all arly 18th to late 19th C.* LOC: 2 minutes walk om Richmond Bridge. PARK: Meters nearby. EL: 0181 332 6454; fax - same. SER: Valuations; storations (woodwork and upholstery); buys at uction (sets of chairs). VAT: Spec.

ourt Antiques (Richmond)
2/14 Brewers Lane. (A. and L. Coombs). Est. 958. Open 9.30-5.30. SIZE: Small. *STOCK: eneral antiques, jewellery, furniture, silver.* Not tocked: Coins and stamps. LOC: From Richmond ation turn left along the Quadrant into George t., Brewers Lane is on the right. PARK: 30yds. rn left. TEL: 0181 940 0515. VAT: Stan.

ollie Evans
2 Hill Rise. TW10 6UB. Est. 1965. Open Thurs. nd Sat. 10.30-5.30, Sun. 2.30-5.30 other times by ppointment. SIZE: Medium. *STOCK: Early untry and painted furniture, interesting bygones, nusual bold decorative items, original works of t, bronzes and sculpture, £50-£5,000.* LOC: From entre of Richmond, take A307 towards Kingston etersham Rd.). Fork left up hill immediately after assing Richmond Bridge on right. PARK: Meters. EL: 0181 948 0182; fax/answerphone - same; e-ail - antiques.info@ all-about-antiques.co.uk. ER: Buys at auction. VAT: Spec.

he Gooday Gallery
) Richmond Hill. TW10 6QX. (Debbie Gooday). st. 1971. Open Thurs.-Sat. 11-5. SIZE: Medium. *TOCK: Decorative and applied design, 1980,*

Richmond continued

Arts & Crafts, Art Nouveau - especially Liberty pewter, Art Deco, 1940-1970 furniture, pictures, ceramics, metalwork, jewellery; African and oceanic tribal artefacts; all £20-£5,000. LOC: 100yds. from Richmond Bridge. PARK: Easy. TEL: 0181 940 8652. SER: Buys at auction.

Roland Goslett Gallery
139 Kew Rd. TW9 2PN. Est. 1974. Open Thurs. and Fri. 10-6, Sat. 10-2 or by appointment. SIZE: Small. *STOCK: English watercolours and oil paintings, 19th to early 20th C, £100-£5,000.* PARK: Easy. TEL: 0181 940 4009. SER: Valuations; restorations (oils, watercolours and frames); framing. VAT: Spec.

Hill Rise Antiques LAPADA
26 Hill Rise. TW10 6UA. (P. Hinde and D. Milewski). Est. 1978. Open 10.30-5.30, Sun. 2.30-5.30. CL: Wed. SIZE: Large. *STOCK: 18th-19th C walnut and mahogany furniture and longcase clocks, £100-£10,000; silver and plate, mirrors, boxes and glassware.* LOC: 1 mile from A316 (M3). PARK: At rear by arrangement. TEL: 0181 332 2941; home - same. FAIRS: Olympia (June). VAT: Stan/Spec.

Horton's LAPADA
2 Paved Court, The Green. TW9 1LZ. (D. and R. Horton). FGA. *STOCK: Jewellery and silver, 18th-20th C, £500-£2,000.* TEL: 0181 332 1775.

Lionel Jacobs
16 Brewers Lane. TW9 1HH. Open 9-5. *STOCK: Silver and jewellery.* TEL: 0181 940 8069.

Robin Kennedy
P.O Box 265. TW9 1UB. Open by appointment. *STOCK: Japanese prints, £50-£5,000.* TEL: 0181 940 5346; fax - same; e-mail - 106025.2327@ compuserve.com.

F. and T. Lawson Antiques
13 Hill Rise. TW10 6UQ. Resident. Est. 1965. Open 10-5.30, Sat. 10-5. CL: Wed. and Sun. am. SIZE: Medium. *STOCK: Furniture, 1680-1870; paintings and watercolours; both £30-£1,500; clocks, 1650-1930, £50-£2,000; bric-a-brac, £5-£300.* LOC: Near Richmond Bridge at bottom of Hill Rise on the river side, overlooking river. PARK: Limited and further up Hill Rise. TEL: 0181 940 0461. SER: Valuations; buys at auction.

Marryat LAPADA
88 Sheen Rd. TW9 1AJ. (Marryat (Richmond) Ltd.). Est. 1990. Open 10-5.30. SIZE: Large. *STOCK: English and Continental furniture, watercolours and oils, £100-£8,000; ceramics, glass, silver and objets, £5-£500; all 18th-19th C.* LOC: Follow M3/A316 towards Richmond, first left into Church Rd. then left again. PARK: Easy. TEL: 0181 332 0262. SER: Valuations; restorations. VAT: Stan/Spec.

Richmond continued

Palmer Galleries

10 Paved Court. TW9 1LZ. (C.D. and V.J. Palmer). Est. 1984. Open 10-5. SIZE: Medium. *STOCK: Prints, watercolours and engravings, 19th-20th C, £50-£1,000.* PARK: Richmond Green. TEL: 0181 948 2668. VAT: Stan/Spec.

Piano Nobile Fine Paintings

26 Richmond Hill. TW10 6QX. (Dr. Robert A. Travers). Est. 1986. Open Tues.-Sat. 10-5.30. SIZE: Medium. *STOCK: Fine 19th C Impressionist and 20th C Post-Impressionist and Modernist British and Continental oil paintings and sculpture, especially Les Petit Maitres of the Paris Schools, £500-£50,000.* PARK: Easy. TEL: 0181 940 2435; fax - same. SER: Valuations; restorations (paintings and sculpture); framing; buys at auction (19th-20th C oil paintings). FAIRS: Grosvenor; 20th C British Art & London Contemporary. VAT: Stan/Spec.

Richmond Antiques

28, 30/32 Hill Rise. Open 10.30-5.30, Sun. 2-5. CL: Wed. SIZE: 20 dealers. *STOCK: General antiques.* TEL: 0181 948 4638.

Roderic Antiques

6/8 Richmond Hill. (R. Arnoldi and E. Gunawardena). Est. 1971. Open 10-5.30, Sun. 2-5.30. CL: Wed. SIZE: Large. *STOCK: Furniture including colonial, and decorative items, 18th-19th*

Richmond continued

C, £200-£10,000. PARK: Nearby. TEL: 0181 33 6766; mobile - 0831 385634. FAIRS: Olymp (June); City of London. VAT: Stan/Spec.

RIPLEY

Cedar House Gallery LAPAD

High St. GU23 6AE. Resident. Est. 198 *STOCK: Watercolours and oils, 19th to ear 20th C, £500-£10,000.* LOC: ½ mile M25/A junction. PARK: Easy. TEL: 01483 21122 SER: Restorations.

J. Hartley Antiques Ltd LAPAD

186 High St. GU23 6BB. Est. 1949. Open 8.4 5.45, Sat. 9.45-4.45. *STOCK: Queen Ann Georgian and Edwardian furniture.* TEL: 014 224318. VAT: Stan.

Ripley Antiques LAPAD

67 High St. GU23 6AN. (H. Denham). Es 1960. Open 9.30-5.30, Sun. by appointmen SIZE: Large. *STOCK: Furniture, English ar French, 18th-19th C; decorative items - mirr and chandeliers.* LOC: 2 mins. from junctio 10 at M25/A3 interchange. Between Heathro and Gatwick Airports. PARK: Easy. TE 01483 224981; fax - 01483 224333. SER: Val ations; restorations. VAT: Stan/Spec.

ipley continued

age Antiques and Interiors LAPADA
ligh St. GU23 6BB. (H. and C. Sage). GMC. st. 1971. Open 9.30-5.30. SIZE: Large. ***TOCK: Furniture, mahogany, oak, walnut, 600-1900, £150-£8,000; oil paintings, £100-5,000; watercolours, £50-£1,000, china, £2-500, all 18th-19th C; silver, Sheffield plate, rass, pewter, decorative items, 18th-19th C, 50-£1,000.*** **LOC: Village centre, on main oad. PARK: Easy. TEL: 01483 224396; fax - 1483 211996. SER: Restorations (furniture, ictures); interior furnishing. VAT: Stan.**

weerts de Landas BADA
unsborough Park, Newark Lane. GU23 6AL. A.J.H. and A.C. Sweerts de Landas). Est. 979. Open by appointment only. SIZE: arge. ***STOCK: Garden ornaments and tatuary, 17th-20th C, £250-£150,000.*** **LOC: rom High St. turn into Newark Lane etween estate agent and Suzuki garage), ontinue 400 yds, go through archway on ght, follow drive to end. PARK: Easy. TEL: 1483 225366; home - same. SER: Valuations; estorations (stone, lead, cast iron, marble); uys at auction (as stock). FAIRS: Olympia, laastricht, Basle. VAT: Stan/Spec.**

Ripley continued

Anthony Welling Antiques BADA
Broadway Barn, High St. GU23 6AQ. Est. 1970. Open 9-1 and 2-5.30. Sun. and evenings by appointment. SIZE: Large. ***STOCK: English oak, 17th-18th C, £250-£8,000; country furniture, 18th C, £200-£6,000; brass, copper, pewter, 18th C, £100-£750.*** **Not Stocked: Glass, china, silver. LOC: Turn off A3 at Ripley, shop in village centre on service road. PARK: Easy. TEL: 01483 225384; fax - same. VAT: Spec.**

RUNFOLD, Nr. Farnham

The Packhouse
Hewetts Kilns, Tongham Rd. GU10 1PQ. (Mr and Mrs P. Hewett). Est. 1991. Open 10.30-5.30 including Sun. SIZE: Large. *STOCK: Furniture, including period, 1930's, country pine; garden statuary, architectural items.* LOC: Off A31 (Hogs Back). PARK: Easy. TEL: 01252 783863; fax - 01252 783876.

SANDERSTEAD

Raymond Slack FRSA & Shirley Warren

STOCK: Reference books on antique collecting, emphasis on glass. TEL: 0181 657 1751. SER: Catalogue. FAIRS: London and Birmingham Glass Fairs. *Mail Order.*

SHEPPERTON

Rickett & Co. Antiques

Church Sq. TW17 9JY. (A.L. Spencer). Est. 1968. Open 10-5, Wed. 10-1, prior telephone call advisable. *STOCK: Brass and copper, 18th-19th C, £100-£300; fenders and fire tools, oil lamps, inkwells, chandeliers, grandfather clocks.* LOC: 10 mins. from London airport. PARK: Easy. TEL: 01932 243571; home - 01932 222508. SER: Restorations (metal repairs and polishing). VAT: Spec.

SHERE, Nr. Guildford

Shere Antiques Centre

Middle St. GU5 9HL. (Jean Watson). Est. 198 Open 10-5, Sun. 11-5. SIZE: Large. *STOC Victorian and Edwardian items, £5-£500.* LO A25 - between Dorking and Guildford. PAR Easy. TEL: 01483 202846. VAT: Stan/Spec.

Yesterdays Pine

Parklands Farm, Hound House Rd. GU5. (J. a V. Stuart). Est. 1985. Open 10-5. CL: Mo *STOCK: Victorian and Continental pine.* LO Midway between Guildford and Dorking off A2 PARK: Easy. TEL: 01483 203198.

SHIRLEY

Norman Witham

217 Wickham Rd. Est. 1959. Open Fri. and S *STOCK: Porcelain, glass, small furniture, mai Victorian, £5-£500.* TEL: 0181 655 444 evenings - 0181 650 4651. SER: Valuations.

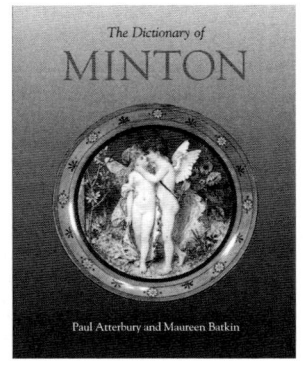

TAINES

..W. Dunster Antiques
3 Church St. TW18 4EN. Open 9.30-5.30. CL: hurs. SIZE: Medium. *STOCK: Clocks, furniture, eneral antiques, interior decor, jewellery, autical items.* TEL: 01784 453297; home - 1784 483146. VAT: Stan/Spec.

Iargaret Melville Watercolours
LAPADA

1 Colnebridge, Market Sq. TW18 4RZ. 'VADA. Est. 1980. Open by appointment only. *TOCK: English watercolours, 1850-1950, £75-7,000.* TEL: 01784 455395. SER: Valuations; ommissions. FAIRS: Eton College (Easter); xford (Oct); Bellhouse Hotel, Beaconsfield nd. Sun. each month; LAPADA; NEC (Jan.); enman Fairs ('phone for tickets). VAT: Spec.

URBITON

;ockrell Antiques
78 Ewell Rd. KT6 7AG. (Sheila and Peter ockrell). Resident. Est. 1982. Open Thurs., Fri. nd Sat. 9-6, other days by appointment. SIZE: Iedium. *STOCK: Furniture including Art Deco, om 18th C, £50-£3,000+; decorative items, £50-500.* LOC: Off A3 at Tolworth Tower on A240. ARK: Easy. TEL: 0181 390 8290; home - same; -mail - antiques@cockrell.co.uk; internet - ttp://www.cockrell.co.uk. FAIRS: IACF and empton Park. VAT: Stan/Spec.

Iouse of Mallett
7 Brighton Rd. KT6 5NF. (K. Mallett). Est. 974. Open Mon., Fri. and Sat. 10-5, Sun. (trade nly) 10-1. SIZE: Large. *STOCK: Mahogany rniture, general antiques and art pottery, arts nd crafts.* PARK: Easy. TEL: 0181 390 5973.

. M. and E. Newlove
39-141 Ewell Rd. KT6 6AL. Est. 1958. Open 30-5.30, Sat. by appointment. CL: Wed. SIZE: Iedium and store. *STOCK: Furniture especially rly oak and Georgian mahogany, 17th-19th C, 200-£5,000; china, 18th-19th C, £75-£200; aintings, all periods, £50-£2,000; longcase ocks, Georgian barometers.* Not Stocked: Potds, fairings. LOC: Down Kingston by-pass at olworth underpass, turn right into Tolworth roadway, then into Ewell Rd. Shop one mile on. ARK: Easy. TEL: 0181 399 8857. VAT: tan/Spec.

.aurence Tauber Antiques
31 Ewell Rd. KT6 6AL. Open 10-5. CL: Wed. n. *STOCK: General antiques, especially for rade.* PARK: Easy. TEL: 0181 390 0020. VAT: tan/Spec.

SUTTON

Euro-Pine
Spring House, Benhill Road. SM1 3RN. (M.A. Wisdom). Est. 1993. Open 9-5.30. SIZE: Large. *STOCK: Continental and English painted, stripped and restored pine, £10-£1,000.* PARK: Easy. TEL: 0181 661 7427; home - 0181 643 0028. SER: Restorations (stripping, polishing and repairs). FAIRS: Ardingly. VAT: Stan/Spec. *Trade Only.*

S. Warrender and Co
4 and 6 Cheam Rd. (F.R. Warrender). Est. 1953. Open 9-5.30. CL: Wed. SIZE: Medium. *STOCK: Jewellery, 1790 to date, £10-£1,500; silver, 1762 to date, £10-£1,000; carriage clocks, 1860-1900, £115-£800.* TEL: 0181 643 4381. SER: Valuations; restorations (jewellery, silver, quality clocks). VAT: Stan.

THAMES DITTON

Clifford and Roger Dade
LAPADA

Boldre House, Weston Green. KT7 0JP. Resident. Est. 1937. Open 9.30-6. SIZE: Large. *STOCK: Mahogany furniture, 18th to early 19th C, £500-£5,000.* LOC: A309 between Esher and Hampton Court, near Sandown Park Racecourse. PARK: Outside shop. TEL: 0181 398 6293; fax - same. VAT: Spec.

Fern Cottage Antiques
28/30 High St. KT7 0RY. Est. 1960. Open 10-5.30. CL: Wed. SIZE: Large. *STOCK: General antiques, 18th-19th C furniture, prints, porcelain, Art Deco, Clarice Cliff, Shelley, Susie Cooper, and silver.* TEL: 0181 398 2281.

Elizabeth Gant
52 High St. KT7 0SA. ABA. PBFA. Est. 1981. CL: Wed. SIZE: Small. *STOCK: Antiquarian, secondhand and illustrated books, especially childrens; ephemera, 10p-£1,000.* PARK: Nearby. TEL: 0181 398 0962; 0181 398 5107; fax - 0181 398 5107. SER: Valuations; buys at auction (books). FAIRS: PBFA (London); ABA (Chelsea); Grosvenor House.

WALTON-ON-THAMES

Susan Becker
LAPADA

P O Box 160. KT12 3HJ. (S. Becker Fleming). Est. 1959. Open by appointment only. *STOCK: English (especially Royal Worcester), and Continental porcelain, 18th-20th C, £200-£25,000; glass and fine objects.* LOC: 10 minutes A3, M25, M4. PARK: Easy. TEL: 01932 227820. SER: Valuations. VAT: Spec.

Boathouse Gallery
The Towpath, Manor Rd. KT12 2PG. (B.E. Clark). CL: Mon. *STOCK: Oil paintings, watercolours, engravings.* TEL: 01932 242718. SER: Picture framing, mounting and restorations. VAT: Stan.

Walton-on-Thames continued

Chancellor's Church Furnishings

Green Door Warehouse, The Farm, Sunnyside. KT12 2ET. (L. Skilling and S. Williams). Est. 1989. Open strictly by appointment at any time. SIZE: Large. *STOCK: Church chairs and pews, £10-£750; altar tables and screens, pulpits, lecterns, reredos, pine and architectural items, £20-£2,000; all late 19th C to early 20th C.* LOC: Between A3050 and River Thames. PARK: Easy. TEL: 0171 385 7480; fax - same; warehouse - 01932 252736; fax - same. SER: Valuations; buys at auction (church fixtures and furnishings, stained glass). FAIRS: Newark. VAT: Stan/Spec.

WALTON-ON-THE-HILL AND TADWORTH

Ian Caldwell LAPADA

9a Tadworth Green, Dorking Rd. KT20 5SQ. Est. 1978. Open 10-5. CL: Wed. SIZE: Medium. *STOCK: Oak, walnut and mahogany furniture especially Georgian.* LOC: 2 miles from M25, ¼ mile from A217 on B2032 in Dorking direction. PARK: Easy. TEL: 01737 813969. SER: Valuations; restorations. VAT: Stan/Spec.

WEST BYFLEET

Academy Billiard Company

5 Camphill Industrial Estate. KT14 6EW. (R.W. Donnachie). Est. 1975. Open anytime by appointment. SIZE: Large warehouse and showroom. *STOCK: Period and antique billiard/snooker tables, all sizes, 1830-1920; combined billiard/dining tables, period accessories including lighting.* LOC: On A245, 2 miles from M25/A3 junction. PARK: Easy. TEL: 01932 352067; mobile - 0860 523757; fax - 01932 353904. SER: Valuations; restorations; removals; structural advice. VAT: Stan/Spec.

WEYBRIDGE

Brocante

120 Oatlands Drive, Oatlands Village. (Barry Dean and Ray Gwilliams). Est. 1988. Open 10-5.30, Sun. 10-5. CL: Mon. and Wed. SIZE: Small. *STOCK: Furniture, 19th C, £300-£1,500; porcelain, 19th C, £10-£250; Sheffield plate, 18th-19th C, £10-£300.* PARK: Easy. TEL: 01932 857807; home - 01932 345524. SER: Valuations. FAIRS: Oatlands Park Hotel; Seven Hills Hilton, Cobham.

Church House Antiques LAPADA

42 Church St. KT13 8DP. (M.I. Foster). Est. 1886. Open Thurs., Fri., Sat. 10-5.30. SIZE: Medium. *STOCK: Furniture, 18th-19th C, £95-£7,000; jewellery, 18th-19th C, some modern,*

Weybridge continued

***£30-£5,000; pictures, silver, plate, decorati[ve] items.* Not Stocked: Coins and stamps. PAR[K]: Behind library. TEL: 01932 842190. VA[T]: Stan/Spec.**

The Clock Shop Weybridge

64 Church St. KT13 8DL. Est. 1970. Open 10-[...] SIZE: Medium. *STOCK: Clocks, 1685-1900, fro[m] £500; French carriage clocks, from £300.* LO[C]: Opposite Midland Bank on corner. PARK: Eas[y]. TEL: 01932 840407/855503. SER: Valuation[s]; restorations (clocks). VAT: Stan/Spec.

Edward Cross - Fine Paintings

128 Oatlands Drive. KT13 9HL. Est. 1973. Op[en] Fri. 10-12.30 and 2-4, Sat. 10-12.30. SIZ[E]: Medium. *STOCK: Fine paintings and bronze[s], 19th-20th C, £500-£30,000.* LOC: A3050. PAR[K]: Opposite. TEL: 01932 851093. SER: Valuation[s]; restorations (watercolours and oil paintings); bu[ys] at auction (pictures). VAT: Spec.

Not Just Silver

16 York Rd. KT13 9DT. (Mrs S. Hughes). E[st]. 1969. Open 9.30-5.30, Sun. by appointmen[t]. *STOCK: Silver, Georgian to Modern.* LO[C]: Opposite car park, just off Queens Rd. TE[L]: 01932 842468; fax - 01932 830054; mobile[e] 0374 298151; home - 01932 829088. SE[R]: Valuations.

Olde Forge Antiques

37 St Mary's Rd., Oatlands Village. KT13 9P[...] (Ian and Joan Porter). Est. 1976. Open Tues.-S[at]. 11-4.30, or any time by prior appointment. SIZ[E]: Small. *STOCK: Edwardian, Victorian and la[te] furniture, £500-£1,500; motoring and sporti[ng] memorabilia, £25-£50; old radios and gram[o]phones.* LOC: Off Oatlands Drive. PARK: Ea[sy]. TEL: 01932 828789; fax - 01932 253686. SE[R]: Valuations; restorations (furniture includi[ng] French polishing and upholstery).

R. Saunders

71 Queen's Rd. KT13 9UQ. (J.B. Tonkinso[n]). Est. 1878. Open 9.30-1 and 2.30-5. CL: We[d]. SIZE: Medium. *STOCK: English mahogany, o[ak] and walnut furniture, wheel and stick baromete[rs], 1650-1830, £50-£5,000; glass, porcelain, silv[er], watercolours, pewter and brass.* Not Stocke[d]: Reproductions. PARK: 150yds. in York Rd. TE[L]: 01932 842601. SER: Valuations; restoratic[ns] (furniture). VAT: Spec.

Village Antiques

39 St Mary's Rd., Oatlands Village. KT13 9[...] (B. Mulvany). Est. 1976. Open 10-4.30. CL: W[...] SIZE: Small. *STOCK: Furniture, small silver a[nd] china, 19th-20th C, £50-£100.* LOC: Off Oatla[nds] Drive. PARK: Easy. TEL: 01932 846554. SE[R]: Valuations; restorations (French polishing, sm[all] furniture repairs). FAIRS: Ardingly.

'Veybridge continued

eybridge Antiques
3 Church St., The Quadrant. KT13 8XD. (P. 'ocock). Est. 1974. Open 10-5.30. SIZE: Large. *TOCK: Furniture, 18th-19th C; paintings, bjects.* LOC: From M25 into town, Church St. is rst right. PARK: Opposite in Mayfield Road. EL: 01932 852503. SER: Restorations (oil aintings, porcelain, furniture, leathering). VAT: pec.

Villow Gallery LAPADA
5 Queens Rd. KT13 9UQ. (Andrew and Jean tevens). Est. 1987. Open Tues.-Sat. 11-6, Sun. nd Mon. by appointment. SIZE: Medium. *TOCK: British and European oil paintings, 9th C, £1,000-£40,000; furniture, 1750-1900, 500-£5,000.* LOC: Near town centre. PARK: asy and nearby. TEL: 01932 846095/6; fax nd home - 01932 846095. SER: Valuations; estorations; conservation; framing; catalogue vailable. FAIRS: LAPADA, City of London, lympia, Royal College of Art and NEC. 'AT: Spec.

VINDLESHAM

Country Antiques
'ountry Gardens Garden Centre, London Rd. 'U20 6LL. (S. Sommers and C. Martin). Est. 990. Open 10-5 including Sun. SIZE: Large. *TOCK: Victorian and Edwardian, some 'eorgian, furniture, £50-£2,000; china and lass, collectables including lace and prints, ictorian to 1930's, £2-£100.* LOC: A30, etween Sunningdale and Bagshot; off M3, inction 3. PARK: Easy. TEL: 01344 873404.

Richard Kimbell Antiques
ountry Gardens Garden Centre, London Rd. U20 6LL. Open 9-6. *STOCK: Antique pine.* OC: A30 between Sunningdale and Bagshot; off 13, junction 3. PARK: Easy. TEL: 01344 75168; fax - 01344 875172.

VOKING

lan's Antique Restorations
O Box 355. GU22 9QE. (A.V. Wellstead). pen by appointment. *STOCK: General antiques, ine.* TEL: 01483 724666; fax - 01483 750366; obile - 0860 851956. SER: Valuations; storations (furniture, clocks and pictures); icture framing; caning and re-rushing; oodturning.

Keith Baker
2 Arnold Rd. GU21 5JU. (K.R. Baker). *STOCK: eneral antiques.* TEL: 01483 767425.

Woking continued

Chattels Antiques
156 High St., Old Woking. GU22 9JH. (John Kendall). Open by appointment only. SIZE: Small. *STOCK: Clocks, barometers, some small furniture.* LOC: Two miles off A3 at Ripley. PARK: Own. TEL: 01483 771310. SER: Restorations (English clocks, furniture).

The Venture
High St., Old Woking. GU22 9ER. (D. Wilkins and D. Law). Resident. Est. 1946. Always open. *STOCK: General antiques especially pine, pre-1920.* TEL: 01483 772103.

Wych House Antiques
Aberdeen House, Wych Hill. GU22 0EU. (A. and C. Perry). Est. 1965. Open Tues., Thurs. and Sat. 10-5. SIZE: Large warehouses. *STOCK: Continental and English furniture, pine, decorative items, paintings, kitchenalia.* TEL: 01483 764636. SER: Interior design. VAT: Stan.

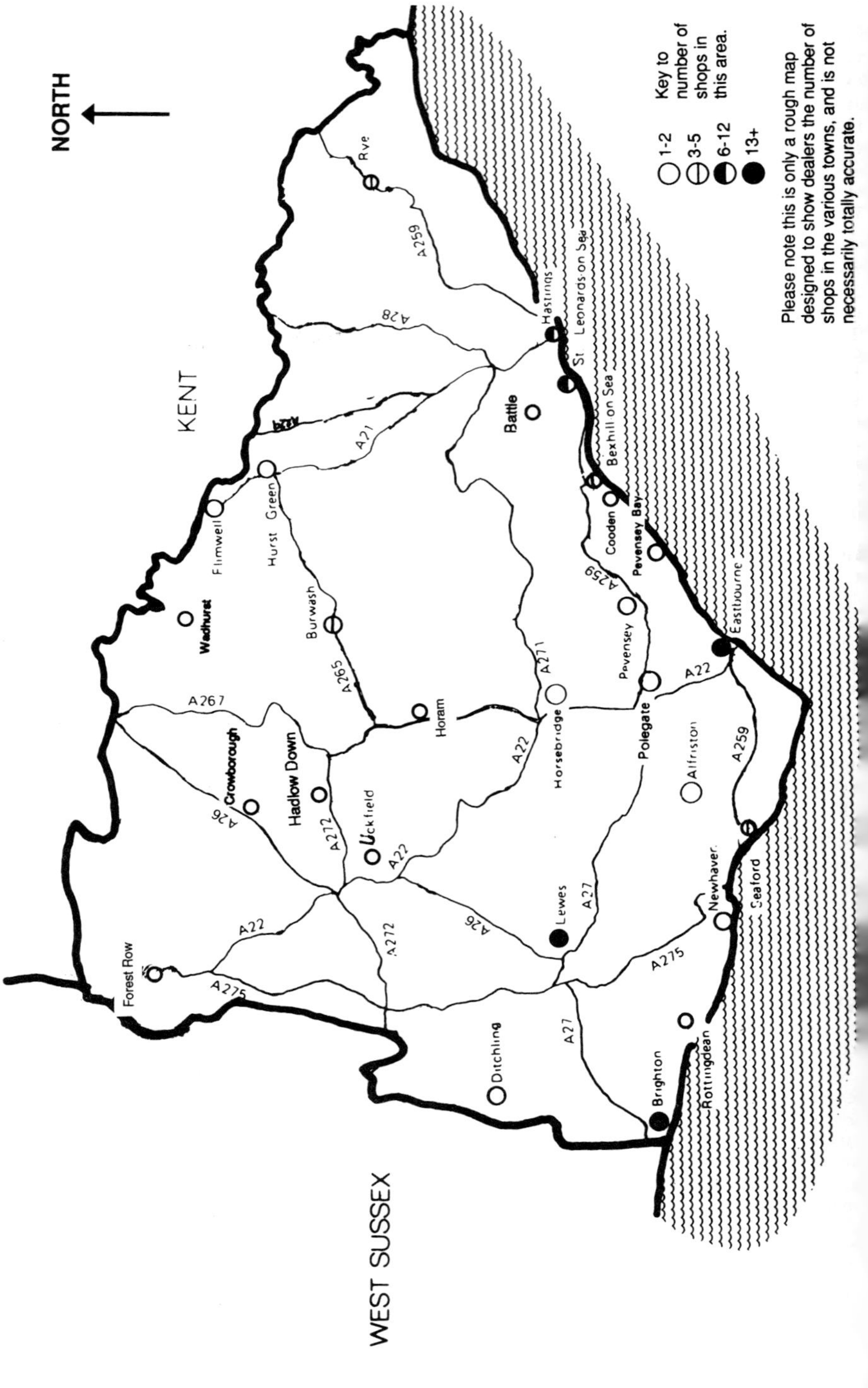

NORTH
KENT
WEST SUSSEX
Rye
A259
Hastings
St Leonards-on Sea
Battle
Bexhill-on Sea
Cooden
Pevensey Bay
Pevensey
Eastbourne
A22
Polegate
Alfriston
A259
Seaford
Newhaven
A275
Rottingdean
Brighton
Ditchling
A27
Lewes
A26
A272
Uckfield
Hadlow Down
Crowborough
A267
Wadhurst
Flimwell
Hurst Green
Burwash
A265
Horam
Horsebridge
A271
A21
A28
Forest Row
Key to number of shops in this area.
1-2
3-5
6-12
13+
Please note this is only a rough map designed to show dealers the number of shops in the various towns, and is not necessarily totally accurate.

ALFRISTON, Nr. Polegate

Alfriston Antiques
'he Square. BN26 5UD. (J. Tourell). Est. 1967.)pen 10.30-1 and 2-5.30, appointment advisable uring winter months. CL: Mon. and Tues. SIZE: mall. *STOCK: Collectors' items, vinaigrettes, nuff boxes, caddy spoons, silver, plate, carriage nd other clocks, jewellery, paintings, pot-lids, opper, brass, books.* PARK: Easy. TEL: 01323 70498; fax - same. VAT: Stan/Spec.

ATTLE

'ymes Past Antiques
6 High St. (Mrs S. Fasey). Open 10-5, Sun. by ppointment. SIZE: Medium. *STOCK: Mainly 8th and 19th C furniture, some Edwardian ılaid; general antiques - clocks, boxes, treen, ramophones, porcelain, glass, silver, games, ommemorative ware and linen.* LOC: Near the oundabout. PARK: Nearby. TEL: 01424 774404.

BEXHILL-ON-SEA

Bexhill Antique Exporters LAPADA
6 Turkey Rd. and Quakers Mill, Old Town. N40 2HA. (H. and K. Abbott). Open 8-5.30, un. by appointment. SIZE: Warehouse. *TOCK: Antique and shipping furniture.* TEL: 1424 225103/210182; fax - 01424 731430. ER: Container packing.

'he Old Mint House LAPADA
5 Turkey Rd. TN39 5HB. (J.C. and A.J. icholson). Est. 1960. Open 9-5.30. CL: Sat. IZE: Large. *STOCK: Furniture - Victorian, dwardian and shipping, some period; clocks, arometers and porcelain, 18th-19th C, £20-10,000.* PARK: Easy. TEL: 01424 216056; 1323 762337; fax - 01323 762337. SER: Buys t auction; worldwide container packing. VAT: tan.

Recollections
7 St. Leonards Rd. TN40 1JA. (A.R. Harmer). st. 1993. Open 10-1 and 2-5. CL: Mon. SIZE: Iedium. *STOCK: Decorative objects, £5-£300; ld and new pine, all hand finished, £10-£500; estored Victorian and Edwardian baths, taps and ccessories; architectural salvage items.* LOC: own centre, near station. TEL: 01424 730650; ome - 01424 892357. FAIRS: Newark; Ardingly. 'AT: Spec.

BRIGHTON

Alexandria Antiques
Hanover Place, Lewes Rd. BN2 2SD. (A.H. hmed). Open 9.30-6, Sat. morning by appointent. *STOCK: Georgian and Victorian furniture; Oriental and European porcelain; oil and watercolour paintings; Oriental carpets, objets d'art.* TEL: 01273 688793.

Brighton continued

Art Deco Etc.
73 Upper Gloucester Rd. BN1 3LQ. (John Clark). Est. 1979. Open 12-5.30, Sun. and other times by appointment. SIZE: Medium. *STOCK: Pottery, especially Poole; glass, furniture, lighting, mirrors, pictures and collectors' items, Art Deco, Art Nouveau, Arts and Crafts, 1950's, £5-£2,000.* LOC: From Brighton station down Queens Rd., first on right. PARK: Easy. TEL: 01273 329268; home - 01273 202937. SER: Valuations. FAIRS: Decorative Arts, Kensington; Art Deco, Battersea; Alexandra Palace; Ardingly and Newark.

Ashton's Antiques
1-3 Clyde Rd., Preston Circus. BN1 4NN. (R. Ashton). Open 9.30-5.30, Wed. 9.30-1. SIZE: 4 showrooms. *STOCK: Victorian and Edwardian furniture, upholstery and decorative items.* TEL: 01273 605253; fax - same. VAT: Stan/Spec.

Attic Antiques
23 Ship St. BN1 1AD. (F.B. and M.J. Moorhead). Est. 1965. Open 11-1 and 2.15-5, Sat. 12-1, prior telephone call advisable. *STOCK: General antiques, 1720-1920, £15-£1,500; English and Continental paintings, mainly Victorian and Georgian; clocks, barometers, Oriental antiques, bronzes, English and continental china, tantalus, Victorian oil lamps, copper, brass, pewter; Imari, Canton, Satsuma and Worcester china; Georgian, Victorian, Edwardian and Continental furniture.* TEL: 01273 326378. VAT: Stan. *Mainly Trade.*

H. Balchin and Son
18-19 Castle St. BN1 2HD. (E.E. Balchin). Resident. Est. 1930. Open 9.30-1 and 2.30-5.30. CL: Thurs. and Sat. pm. SIZE: Large. *STOCK: General antiques, 18th-19th C.* LOC: From Western Rd., down Preston St., Castle St. is second turning on left. PARK: Loading only. SER: Valuations.

Bears and Friends
41 Meeting House Lane, The Lanes. BN1 1HB. (P. Goble). Est. 1989. Open 9-5.30, Sat. 9-6, Sun. 10-6 or by appointment. *STOCK: Teddy bears and bear related items; antique dolls and miniatures.* TEL: 01273 208940; fax - 01273 202736. SER: Valuations; export; mail order; museum of childhood. FAIRS: Major London Hugglets Teddy Bear fairs; TBT Brighton (Dec.). VAT: Stan/Spec.

Brighton Antique Wholesalers
39 Upper Gardner St. SIZE: Several dealers. *STOCK: 18th-19th C furniture, £50-£5,000.* LOC: Off North Rd. PARK: Easy. TEL: 01273 695457.

Brighton continued

Brighton Architectural Salvage
33-34 Gloucester Rd. BN1 4AQ. (L. F. Moore). Open 9.30-5, Sat. 10-4.30. *STOCK: Restored architectural items including pine furniture; fireplaces and surrounds - marble, pine, mahogany, cast-iron Victorian tiled and cast inserts and over-mantels; doors, stained glass, panelling; cast-iron balcony and street railings, spiral staircases; stonework, lamp posts and light fittings; garden seats and ornaments.* TEL: 01273 681656.

Brighton Flea Market
31A Upper St. James's St. BN2 1JN. (A. Wilkinson). Est. 1990. Open seven days. SIZE: Large. *STOCK: Bric-a-brac, furniture and collectables, 19th-20th C, £5-£1,000.* LOC: 50 yards from coast road, Kemp Town. TEL: 01273 624006.

Mary Brown
42 Surrey St. BN1 3PB. Open 11-5.30. *STOCK: Period clothes, linen and lace, costume jewellery.* LOC: Near station and CAB office. TEL: 01273 721160.

David Burkinshaw
17a Farm Road, Hove. BN3 1FB. Open by appointment. *STOCK: Pedestal and partner desks, 1760-1880.* TEL: 01273 738400.

C.A.R.S. (Classic Automobilia & Regalia Specialists)
4-4a Chapel Terrace Mews, Kemp Town. BN2 1HU. (G.G. Weiner). *STOCK: Collectors' car badges, mascots and associated automobilia and related motoring memorabilia; children's pedal cars, electric cars, collectors' veteran and vintage pedal cars, 1930's-1970's.* TEL: 01273 601960; fax - same. SER: Catalogue/price list on receipt of SAE.

P. Carmichael
33 Upper North St. BN1 3FG. (H. Mileham). Est. 1946. Open 9.30-5.30. CL: Sat. pm. *STOCK: Furniture, 18th-19th C.* TEL: 01273 328072; fax - same. VAT: Stan/Spec.

Sheila Cashin Antiques
40 Upper North St. BN1 3FH. Est. 1982. Open 10-5, Sat. and Sun. by appointment. SIZE: Small. *STOCK: Restored decorative Victorian bamboo and lacquer furniture, £50-£1,000; painted and faux-bamboo furniture and decorative items, especially mirrors.* PARK: Voucher parking nearby. TEL: 01273 326619.

Connoisseur Antique Gallery
113 Church Rd., Hove. BN3 2AF. *STOCK: General antiques.* TEL: 01273 777398.

Harry Diamond and Son
9 Union St., The Lanes. BN1 1HA. (R. and H. Diamond). Est. 1937. Open 9-5. *STOCK: Diamond*

Brighton continued

jewellery, antique silver, £50-£20,000. N Stocked: Coins, furniture. TEL: 01273 32969 VAT: Stan.

James Doyle Antiques
10 Union St., The Lanes. BN1 1HA. (J.R. Doyle Est. 1975. Open 9.30-6. *STOCK: Jeweller silver.* TEL: 01273 323694; fax - 01273 324330.

D.H. Edmonds Ltd
28 Meeting House Lane, The Lanes. BN1 1H Est. 1965. Open 10-5.30. SIZE: Large. *STOC Jewellery, silver, objets d'art, watches, £5 £20,000.* TEL: 01273 327713/328871. VAT: Sta

Faques Gallery
32 Upper St James's St., BN2 1JN. Est. 196 Open 10-5.30. SIZE: Large. *STOCK: Repr duction oil paintings.* LOC: Kemp Town are PARK: Side roads. TEL: 01273 624432; fax 01273 683692. VAT: Stan.

Alan Fitchett Antiques
5-5A Upper Gardner St. BN1 4AN. Est. 196 Open 9-5.30. CL: Sat. SIZE: Large. *STOC Furniture, 18th-20th C, £50-£10,000; works art.* LOC: North Laines (Station area). PAR Easy. TEL: 01273 600894; fax - same. SE Valuations; restorations. VAT: Stan.

Paul Goble
44 Meeting House Lane, The Lanes. BN1 1H Est. 1965. Open 9-5.30, Sun. 10-5.30 or appointment. *STOCK: Jewellery, watches, silv pictures and prints, teddy bears and dolls.* TE 01273 202801; fax - 01273 202736. SE Trade/export valuation. VAT: Stan/Spec.

The Gold and Silversmiths of Hove
3 Planet House, 1 The Drive, Hove. BN3 3J Open 8.45-5. *STOCK: Jewellery and silver.* TE 01273 738489.

Douglas Hall Ltd
23 Meeting House Lane. BN1 1HB. (A. Longthorne). Est. 1968. Open 9.30-5. *STOC Silver, jewellery.* TEL: 01273 325323. VAT: Sta

Hallmarks
4 Union St., The Lanes. BN1 1HA. (J. Hersheso Est. 1966. Open 9-5. SIZE: Small. *STOCK: Sil and plate, jewellery and clocks, collectables.* TE 01273 725477. VAT: Stan/Spec.

Mark and David Hawkins
The Lanes Armoury, 27 Meeting House La The Lanes. BN1 1HB. Open 9-5.30, Sun. appointment. *STOCK: General antiques, milita arms and armour, £10-£7,500.* TEL: 012 321357.

Holleyman and Treacher Ltd
21a and 22 Duke St. BN1 1AH. Est. 1937. Op 9-5. CL: Mon. *STOCK: Books including an quarian, music.* TEL: 01273 328007.

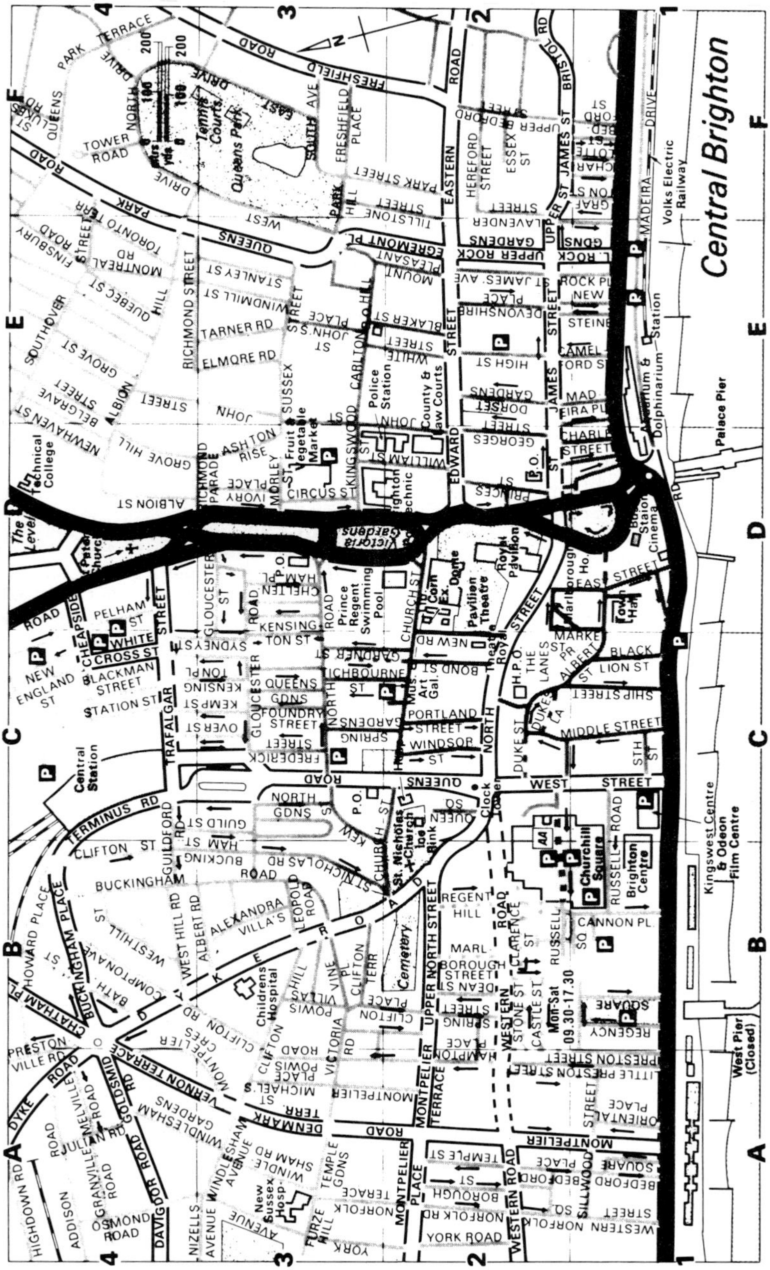

Key to Town Plan

AA Recommended roads	══════	Car Parks	**P**
Other roads	──────	Parks and open spaces	
Restricted roads	─ ─ ─	AA Service Centre	**AA**
Buildings of interest	☐	© Automobile Association 1988.

Brighton continued

The House of Antiques LAPADA
17 Prince Albert St. BN1 1HF. (A. Margiotta). Open 10-5.30. *STOCK: Jewellery and silver.* TEL: 01273 327680/324961. VAT: Stan.

Hove Antique Clocks
68 Western Rd., Hove. BN3 2JQ. (D.E. Humphrey). Est. 1990. Open 9-5. SIZE: Medium. *STOCK: Clocks - longcase, mantel, bracket, boulle, regulators, wall, skeleton and carriage, 18th-19th C, £50-£2,000.* LOC: Near Floral Clock. PARK: Easy. TEL: 01273 722123; home - 01273 557552/561484. SER: Restorations and repairs.

Dudley Hume
46 Upper North St. BN1 3FH. Est. 1973. CL: Sat. pm. and Sun., except by appointment. SIZE: Medium. *STOCK: Period and Victorian furniture, metal, light fittings, decorative items.* LOC: Parallel to the Western Rd., one block to the north. TEL: 01273 323461; fax - same. VAT: Stan/Spec.

Hyndford Antiques
143 Edward St. BN2 2JG. (Mrs M.C. Skelson). Est. 1968. Open Thurs.-Sat. 10.30-4 or by appointment. SIZE: Small. *STOCK: Bygones, china, collectables, Oriental carvings, £1-£150; prints, ephemera, postcards, 50p-£75; small furniture, £10-£250; all 19th-20th C.* LOC: Edward St. east at right angles to Brighton Pavilion. PARK: Vouchers, near shop. TEL: 01273 679936/602220. FAIRS: Ardingly and Brighton Centre.

Leoframes
70 North Rd. BN1 1YD. (H. and Mrs A. Schofield and S. Round). Open 9-5.30. *STOCK: Prints and maps.* TEL: 01273 695862. SER: Restorations; framing.

Harry Mason
P O Box 687, Hove. BN3 6JY. Est. 1954. Open by appointment. *STOCK: Silver and plate, 18th-20th C; jewellery, 19th-20th C.* TEL: 01273 500330; fax - 01273 553300; e-mail - mason@fastnet.co.uk. SER: Valuations; restorations (silver and jewellery); buys at auction (as stock); buyers of scrap silver and gold. FAIRS: Sunday London Hotel. VAT: Stan/Spec.

Patrick Moorhead Antiques
22B Ship St. and 15B Prince Albert St. BN1 1AD. Open 10-5.30 or by appointment. CL: Sat. SIZE: Shop and large trade showroom. *STOCK: 19th C furniture, Oriental and English porcelain, clocks, bronzes, paintings for the overseas market.* TEL: 01273 326062; fax - 01273 774227; mobile - 0385 725202.

Michael Norman Antiques Ltd BADA
Palmeira House, 82 Western Road, Hove. BN3 1JB. Est. 1965. Open 9-1 and 2-5.30, other times by appointment. *STOCK: English furniture.* TEL: 01273 329253 or 01273 326712; fax - 01273 206556. VAT: Stan/Spec.

Brighton continued

Oasis Antiques
39 Kensington Gdns. BN1 4AL. (I. and A. Stevenson). Est. 1970. Open 10-5, Mon. 11-5, Sat. 8-5. SIZE: Medium. *STOCK: Lighting and furniture, to 1930, £1-£5,000; European and Oriental items including bronzes, art glass, period clothes, linen and lace, gramophones, Art Nouveau, Art Deco.* LOC: Off North Road from railway station, centre of North Laines. PARK: Nearby. TEL: 01273 683885. SER: Restoration (furniture, metals and ceramics); polishing.

Colin Page Antiquarian Books
36 Duke St. BN1 1AG. (C.G. Page). Est. 197[illegible] Open 9-5.30. *STOCK: Antiquarian and secondhand books, especially topography, travel, natural history, illustrated and leather bindings, 16th-20th C, £1-£5,000.* LOC: Town centre. PARK: Multi-storey nearby. TEL: 01273 32595[illegible] fax - 01273 746246; e-mail - cpage@pavilion.co.uk.

Brian Page Antiques
18 Regent Arcade, East St. BN1 1HR. Open 1[illegible]-5.30. *STOCK: Chinese and Japanese antiques and works of art, 200 BC-20th C; antiquarian and rare books.* LOC: Adjacent to Town Hall. TEL: 01273 723956; fax - 01273 746246.

Dermot and Jill Palmer Antiques
7-8 Union St., The Lanes. BN1 1HA. Resident. Est. 1968. Open 9-6, Sun. by appointment. *STOCK: French and English furniture, objects, pictures, mirrors, screens, garden furniture and ornamental pieces, textiles, £50-£5,000.* TEL: 01273 328669 (2 lines); fax - 01273 77764[illegible] FAIRS: Olympia; Decorative Antique & Textile Fair. VAT: Stan/Spec.

Sue Pearson
13 1/2 Prince Albert St. BN1 1HE. Open 10[illegible] SIZE: Small. *STOCK: Antique dolls, teddy bears, dolls' house miniatures.* LOC: Lanes area. PARK: NCP. TEL: 01273 329247. SER: Valuations; restorations; buys at auction (dolls and bears). FAIRS: Major London Doll and Bear. VAT: Stan/Spec.

Ben Ponting Antiques
53 Upper North St. Open 9.30-5.30, Sat. 10[illegible] *STOCK: Furniture, 18th-19th C.* TEL: 012[illegible] 329409.

Recollections
1a Sydney St. BN1 4EN. (B. Bagley). Est. 19[illegible] Open Tues., Thurs., Fri. and Sat. 10.30-4. SIZE: Small. *STOCK: Small collectable items, 19th-20th C, £5-£250; brass and copper, especially fireplace furniture; Victorian oil lamps.* LOC: From railway station down Trafalgar [illegible] last turning on right. PARK: Opposite in Belm[illegible] St. TEL: 01273 681517. SER: Valuations; restorations (metal, china, oil lamps).

Brighton continued

Ruddy Antiques

39 Upper North St. (Paula Ruddy). Est. 1994. Open 9.30-5.30, Sat. 10-1. SIZE: Medium. STOCK: *Interesting decorative English and Continental furniture, 18th-19th C, £100-£2,000; nirrors and decorative objects, £100-£500.* LOC: Parallel to Western Rd., north side. PARK: Easy. TEL: 01273 772060.

Rutland Antiques

48 Upper North St. BN1 3FH. Open 10.30-5.30. SIZE: Small. *STOCK: Porcelain, china, textiles, clocks and watches and general antiques.* LOC: North of and parallel to Western Rd. PARK: Reasonable. TEL: 01273 329991.

Savery Antiques

257 Ditchling Rd., (Fiveways). BN1 1JH. (J. and I. Savery). Resident. Est. 1968. Open 9-5. CL: Wed. SIZE: Small. *STOCK: Glass and china, £5-500; copper and brass, £20-£200; all 19th-20th* C. LOC: Near Midland Bank. TEL: 01273 64899. FAIRS: Ardingly; Sandown Park.

S.L. Simmons

Meeting House Lane, The Lanes. BN1 1HB. MAG. Est. 1948. Open 9.30-5.30. *STOCK: ewellery and silver, 19th C.* TEL: 01273 327949. VAT: Stan.

Sleeping Beauty Antique Beds

12 Church Rd., Hove. BN3 2DT. (Mr and Mrs oberts). Est. 1975. Open 10-5 including Sun. IZE: Medium. *STOCK: Brass, iron and French ooden beds, 19th C, £500-£1,000.* LOC: Continuation of Western Rd. PARK: Nearby. TEL: 1273 205115; home - same. SER: Valuations; estorations; buys at auction (beds).

Tapsell Antiques LAPADA

9 and 59a Middle St. and 10 Ship St. Gdns. N1 1AL. Est. 1948. Open 9-5.30, other times y appointment. SIZE: Large. *STOCK: English nd Continental furniture, clocks, bronzes, eneral antiques; Oriental ceramics, lacquer, urniture and bronzes.* TEL: 01273 328341; 1273 775245. VAT: Stan/Spec.

Michael Tidey Antiques

7 St. Georges Rd., Kemp Town. BN2 1EE. esident. *STOCK: English furniture.* TEL: 01273 02389.

imewarp

Sydney St. BN1 4EN. (Miss J. Whiskin). Est. 982. Open 10.30-5.45, Sat. 9-6, Sun. by ppointment. SIZE: Large. *STOCK: Lamps and ades, Art Deco to 1960's, £15-£55; Victorian l lamps and spare parts, to £250; bakelite, rniture, 1930-1940, £2-£300.* LOC: 5 minutes om station, turn right off Trafalgar St. TEL: 273 607527. SER: Restorations (oil lamps).

Brighton continued

Graham Webb

59A Ship St. BN1 1AE. Est. 1961. Open 10-5. CL: Mon. SIZE: Small. *STOCK: Cylinder and disc musical boxes, all mechanical musical instruments, £650-£45,000.* LOC: Close to the Lanes. PARK: Middle St. TEL: 01273 321803; fax - same; home - 01273 772154. VAT: Stan/Spec.

Stephen Welbourne

20 Bond St. BN1 1RD. Resident. Est. 1977. Open 11-5. SIZE: Medium. *STOCK: 19th C oil paintings, watercolours and prints; decorative antiques and light fittings.* LOC: Off Church St. PARK: Easy. TEL: 01273 694464; fax - 01273 620021. SER: Valuations; buys at auction. VAT: Spec.

E. and B. White

43-47 Upper North St. and warehouse at 36 Robertson Rd. BN1 3FH. Est. 1962. Open 9.30-5. CL: Sat. pm. SIZE: Medium. *STOCK: Oak furniture, £50-£2,000.* LOC: Upper North St. runs parallel to and north of Western Rd. (the main shopping street). TEL: 01273 328706. VAT: Spec.

Wilkinsons

11 Church St. Est. 1985. Open Mon.-Sat. SIZE: Small. *STOCK: Furniture and collectables, 18th-20th C, £50-£2,000.* LOC: 200 m. north of Brighton Pavilion. TEL: 01273 328665.

The Witch Ball

48 Meeting House Lane. BN1 1HB. (Mrs Gina Daniels). Est. 1967. Open 10.30-6. *STOCK: 18th-19th C topographical and decorative engravings; 16th-19th C maps.* TEL: 01273 326618. VAT: Stan/Spec.

Witney & Airault

at Prinny's,3 Meeting House Lane. BN1 1HB. Open 9.30-5. *STOCK: Art Deco including Clarice Cliff, Susie Cooper.* TEL: 01273 735479.

Yellow Lantern Antiques Ltd LAPADA

34 Holland Rd., Hove. BN3 1JL. (B.R. and E.A. Higgins). Est. 1950. Open 10-1, Sat. 10-4. SIZE: Medium. *STOCK: Mainly English furniture, £50-£3,000; French and English clocks; both to 1850; bronzes, 19th C, £100-£1,500; Continental porcelain, 1820-1860, £50-£1,000.* Not Stocked: Pottery, oak, 18th C porcelain. LOC: From Brighton seafront to Hove, turn right at Hotel Alexander, shop 100yds. on left past traffic lights, opposite Michael Norman Antiques. PARK: Easy. TEL: 01273 771572; mobile - 0860 342976; home - 01273 455476. SER: Valuations; restorations; buys at auction. FAIRS: Buxton; Harrogate; NEC; Guildford; Bath; Kensington. VAT: Spec.

BURWASH, Nr. Etchingham

Chateaubriand Antiques Centre
High St. TN19 7ES. Open 10-5, Sun. 12-5.30. SIZE: 15 dealers. *STOCK: Lace, linen, furniture, country oak, glass, bronzes, paintings, smalls.* LOC: A265. PARK: Nearby. TEL: 01435 882535. SER: Shipping.

Chaunt House
High St. TN19 7ES. (M. Walsh). Est. 1976. Open Thurs.-Sat. SIZE: Small. *STOCK: Clocks, 19th C, £50-£1,000; watches and barometers.* LOC: A265. PARK: Easy. TEL: 01435 882221; home - same. SER: Valuations; restorations; buys at auction (as stock). VAT: Stan/Spec.

COODEN

Annies
4 Bixlea Parade, Little Common Rd. TN39 4SD. (P.A. Rose). Est. 1990. Open 10-5, Wed. and Sun. by appointment. SIZE: Small. *STOCK: China, glass, porcelain and linen, 1800-1930, £5-£500; furniture, from 1880, £50-£750; silver plate, kitchenalia, copper, brass and clocks, from 1800, £5-£150.* LOC: A259 between Bexhill and Eastbourne by Little Common roundabout. PARK: Easy. TEL: 01424 846966. SER: Valuations; buys at auction. FAIRS: De La Warr, Bexhill. VAT: Stan/Spec.

CROWBOROUGH

Broadway Hall Antiques
The Broadway. (B. Ross). Open 10-4. SIZE: 8+ dealers. *STOCK: General antiques, books.* LOC: Top of Crowborough Hill, opposite the Town Hall. PARK: Easy - nearby. TEL: 01892 664225.

DITCHLING

Dycheling Antiques
34 High St. BN6 8TA. (E.A. Hudson). Est. 1977. Open 10.30-5.30. CL: Wed. SIZE: Large. *STOCK: Georgian, Victorian and Edwardian furniture, especially dining chairs, £25-£4,000.* LOC: Off A23 on A273-B2112 north of Brighton. PARK: Easy. TEL: 01273 842929; home - same; mobile - 0585 456341. VAT: Spec.

Jonathan Holley Antiques
8 West St. BN6 8TS. Est. 1983. SIZE: Medium. *STOCK: Furniture, copper and brass, glass and decorative items.* TEL: 01273 843290. VAT: Stan/Spec.

EASTBOURNE

Bell Antiques
47 South St. BN21 4UT. (Mrs M.J. Everett). Open 10-1 and 2-4.30. SIZE: Small. *STOCK: Porcelain*

Eastbourne continued

and small bijou items, 18th-19th C, £10-£300; furniture, Victorian and Edwardian, £50-£400; paintings and prints, to 1930, £10-£150. LOC Road opposite Town Hall. PARK: Easy. TEL 01323 641339. SER: Valuations.

Wm. Bruford and Son Ltd
11/13 Cornfield Rd. BN21 3NA. Est. 1883. Ope 9.30-5.15. SIZE: Medium. *STOCK: Jewellery Victorian, late Georgian; some silver, clock (bracket, carriage).* Not Stocked: China, glas brass, pewter, furniture. TEL: 01323 72545 SER: Valuations; restorations (clocks and silver VAT: Stan/Spec.

Camilla's Bookshop
57 Grove Rd. BN21 4TX. (C. Francombe and Broad). Est. 1976. Open 10-6. *STOCK: Book including antiquarian and on art, antiques an collectables, and especially naval, militar aviation, technical, needlework, broadcastin* LOC: Next to police station. TEL: 01323 73600 SER: Valuations; book search; postal servic own book tokens.

John Cowderoy Antiques LAPAD
42 South St. BN21 4XB. (R., D.J. and R. Cowderoy). GMC. Est. 1973. Open 9.30-5. C Wed. pm. and Sat. pm. SIZE: Large. *STOC Clocks, musical boxes, furniture, porcelai silver and plate, jewellery, copper, bras paintings.* LOC: 150yds. from Town Ha PARK: Easy. TEL: 01323 720058. SE Restorations (clocks, barometers, music box and furniture). VAT: Stan/Spec.

Crest Collectables
54 Grove Rd. BN21 4UD. (C. Powell). Open 6. *STOCK: General antiques and collectabl* TEL: 01323 721185.

John Day of Eastbourne Fine Art
9 Meads St. BN20 7QY. Est. 1964. Open 9.3 and 2-5 (prior 'phone call advisable). CL: W and Sat. pm. SIZE: Medium. *STOCK: Englis especially East Anglian, and Continent paintings and watercolours, 19th C.* LOC: Mea village, west end of Eastbourne. PARK: Ea TEL: 01323 725634; mobile - 0860 466197. SE Restorations; framing (oils and watercolours).

Roderick Dew
10 Furness Rd. BN21 4EZ. Est. 1971. *STOC Antiquarian books, especially on art and antiqu* TEL: 01323 720239. *Postal Only.*

Eastbourne Antiques Market
80 Seaside. BN22 7QP. Est. 1969. Open 10-5. Sat. 10-5. SIZE: Large - 30+ stalls. *STOCK: wide selection of general antiques and colle ables.* PARK: Easy. TEL: 01323 642233.

Eastbourne continued

Elliott and Scholz Antiques
12 Willingdon Rd. BN21 1TH. (C.R. Elliott and K.V. Scholz). Est. 1981. Open 9.30-4.30, Wed. and Sat. 9.30-1. SIZE: Small. *STOCK: Small furniture, £100-£500; clocks, £20-£300; bric-a-brac, £10-£100; all 19th-20 C.* LOC: A22. PARK: Easy. TEL: 01323 732200. SER: Valuations.

Enterprise Collectors Market
The Enterprise Centre, Station Parade. Est. 1989. Open 9.30-5. SIZE: Medium. *STOCK: Wide range of general antiques and collectables.* LOC: Next to railway station. PARK: Easy. TEL: 01323 732690. SER: Valuations.

A. & T. Gibbard
(formerly Raymond Smith). 30 South St. BN21 4XB. Open 9-5.30. SIZE: Large. *STOCK: Secondhand and antiquarian books, 16th-20th C, £1-£1,000; publishers' remainders, 75p-£30; maps and prints, 17th-20th C, 50p-£350.* LOC: 100yds. east of Town Hall. PARK: Easy. TEL: 01323 734128. SER: Valuations. VAT: Stan.

The Old Town Antiques Centre
52 Ocklynge Rd. BN21 1PR. (V. Franklin). Est. 1990. Open 9.30-5. SIZE: Medium. *STOCK: General antiques.* LOC: East Dean coast road. PARK: Easy. TEL: 01323 416016. FAIRS: Ardingly.

Timothy Partridge Antiques
46 Ocklynge Rd. Open 10-1. *STOCK: Victorian, Edwardian and 1920's furniture.* LOC: In old town, near St. Mary's Church. PARK: Easy. TEL: 01323 638731.

Pharoahs Antiques Centre
28 South St. BN21 4UJ. (W. and J. Pharoah). Est. 1973. Open 10-5. SIZE: Medium. 14 stallholders. *STOCK: A wide range of antiques including jewellery, pine, kitchenalia, china, curios, lace, linen, Victorian furniture, original light fittings and lamps.* LOC: Near Town Hall. PARK: Easy. TEL: 01323 738655. FAIRS: Ardingly.

Ernest Pickering
4 South St. BN21 4XB. Est. 1946. Open 9-5. CL: Wed. pm. and Sat. pm. *STOCK: Furniture, porcelain, grandfather clocks.* TEL: 01323 730483. VAT: Stan/Spec.

Premier Gallery
4 South St. BN21 4XB. (D. Mazzoli). Est. 1983. Open 10-5.30, Sun. by appointment. SIZE: Large. *STOCK: Antiquarian and second-hand books, antiquarian prints, watercolours, modern British paintings (John Bratby RA).* LOC: Near station. PARK: Easy. TEL: 01323 736023. SER: Valuations; restorations (oil paintings, watercolours and prints). VAT: Stan.

Stewart Gallery
Grove Rd. BN21 4TT. (Gallery Laraine Ltd.). Est. 1970. Open 9-5.30. SIZE: Large. *STOCK: Paintings and ceramics, 19th-20th C, £5-£25,000.* LOC: Next to library, 150yds. from station.

Eastbourne continued

PARK: Easy. TEL: 01323 729588; fax - 01323 412900. SER: Valuations; restorations (paintings and frames). VAT: Stan/Spec.

Terminus Antiques Emporium
40 Terminus Rd. BN21 3LP. (E. Warner). Est. 1951. Open 9.30-5. SIZE: Large. *STOCK: Furniture, jewellery and porcelain, from 18th C, £5-£6,000.* LOC: Opposite railway station. PARK: 50 yards. TEL: 01323 638999. SER: Valuations; buys at auction (furniture and jewellery).

Wellers Restoration Centre
12 North St. BN21 3HG. (D. Ricketts). Est. 1892. Open 9.15-4.45. *STOCK: Trophies, silver, pewter, brass.* TEL: 01323 723592. SER: Restorations; polishing; silver plating; engraving; repairs; plaques, hardwood bases, etc.

Lloyd Williams - Antique Anglo Am Warehouse
2a Beach Rd. BN22 7EX. Est. 1976. Open 9.30-5, Sat. and Sun. by appointment. SIZE: Large. *STOCK: Shipping furniture, 1850-1920, £50-£3,000; period furniture, pre 1850, £500+; general antiques.* LOC: Off Seaside Rd. PARK: Easy. TEL: 01323 648661; fax - 01323 648658; home - 01892 536627. SER: Restorations; containers. VAT: Stan. *Trade Only.*

FLIMWELL

Graham Lower
Stonecrouch Farmhouse. TN5 7QB. Open by appointment. *STOCK: English and Continental 17th-18th C oak furniture.* LOC: A21. TEL: 01580 879535. SER: Valuations. VAT: Spec.

FOREST ROW

Aspidistra Antiques
16 Hartfield Rd. RH18 5ND. (Trudy and Jeroen Markies). Est. 1980. Open 10-5, Wed. 10-1, Sat. 9.30-5. *STOCK: Furniture, 18th-19th C, £1,000-£3,500; silver, Oriental and European ceramics, linen, 19th-20th C, £20-£500.* LOC: 3 miles south of East Grinstead, 100 yards down Hartfield Rd. PARK: Behind shop. TEL: 01342 824980; fax - 01342 823677. SER: Valuations; restorations (furniture and silver); buys at auction. VAT: Spec.

HADLOW DOWN, Nr. Uckfield

Hadlow Down Antiques
Hastingford Farm, School Lane. TN22 4DY. (Adrian Butler). Est. 1989. Open 10-5 including Sun., Wed. by appointment. SIZE: Large. *STOCK: Country and mahogany furniture, 18th-19th C, £15-£1,500; stripped pine, 19th C, £15-£900; decorative accessories, 19th C, £5-£500.* LOC: 2 mins. down School Lane from A272 in village. PARK: Easy. TEL: 01825 830707; home - same. SER: Valuations; restorations (furniture).

HASTINGS

Coach House Antiques
48 George St. TN34 3EG. (R.J. Luck). Est. 1972. Open 10-5 including Sun. SIZE: Medium. *STOCK: Longcase clocks, 18th-19th C, £1,000+; furniture, 19th C, £100+; collectables including Dinky toys, trains, dolls houses.* PARK: Nearby. TEL: 01424 461849. SER: Valuations; restorations (clocks and furniture); buys at auction (clocks and furniture). VAT: Spec.

George Street Antiques Centre
47 George St. TN34 3EA. (F. Stanley and P. Heuduk). Est. 1969. Open 9-5, Sun. 11-4. SIZE: Medium - 20 dealers. *STOCK: Small items, 19th-20th C, £5-£500.* LOC: In old town, parallel to seafront. PARK: Seafront. TEL: 01424 429339; home - 01424 813526/713300.

Howes Bookshop
Trinity Hall, Braybrooke Terrace. TN34 1HQ. ABA. Est. 1920. Open 9.30-1 and 2.15-5. CL: Sat. pm. *STOCK: Antiquarian and academic books in literature, history, arts, bibliography.* TEL: 01424 423437; fax - 01424 460620. FAIRS: ABA.

Nakota Curios
12 Courthouse St. TN35 3AU. (D.E. Taylor). Est. 1964. Open 10.30-1 and 2.30-5. CL: Wed. and Fri. SIZE: Medium. *STOCK: General trade items, decorative china, furniture, Victoriana, jewellery.* Not Stocked: Coins, medals. PARK: Easy. TEL: 01424 438900.

J. Radcliffe
40 Cambridge Rd. TN34 1DT. Open 10-1 and 2-5. CL: Wed. pm. *STOCK: General antiques, trade goods.* TEL: 01424 426361.

Spice
Samphire House, 75 High St., Old Town. TN34 3EL. (S. Dix). Open by appointment. *STOCK: Early furniture and decorative items.* TEL: Mobile - 0410 209556.

HORAM, Nr. Heathfield

John Botting Antiques
Winstan House, High St. TN21 0ER. Open 9-5.30 or by appointment. SIZE: Medium. *STOCK: Victorian, Edwardian and some Georgian furniture, mahogany, oak and pine; French furniture; bric-a-brac.* PARK: Easy, on forecourt. TEL: 01435 813553.

HORSEBRIDGE, Nr. Hailsham

Horsebridge Antiques Centre
1 North St. BN27 4DJ. (R. Lane). Resident. Est. 1978. Open 10-1 and 1.30-5. SIZE: Large. *STOCK: General antiques including furniture, silver, glass, pottery, brass and copper.* LOC: A271. PARK: Easy. TEL: 01323 844414; fax - 01323 844000; e-mail - lenny@enterprise.net. SER: Valuations.

HURST GREEN

Delmas
Little Bernhurst. TN19 7PN. (P.D. Stimpson). Est 1973. Open 10-6.30. CL: Wed. *STOCK: English and Continental furniture and paintings.* TEL: 01580 860345. VAT: Stan/Spec.

Libra Antiques
81 London Rd. TN19 7PN. (Janice Hebert). Resident. Est. 1976. Open 9.30-6, Sun. and Mon by appointment. SIZE: Medium. *STOCK: Lighting 19th to early 20th C, £100-£400; pine furniture £50-£500; decorative items, £10-£200; both 18th-19th C.* LOC: A21. PARK: Easy. TEL: 0158 860569; home - same.

LEWES

John Bird Antiques
Norton House, Iford. BN7 3EJ. Est. 1970. Ope anytime by appointment. *STOCK: Furniture country, pine, oak, fruitwood, mahogany, painte architectural, garden and upholstery.* TEL: 0127 483366; mobiles - 0973 421070/0802 803440.

Bow Windows Book Shop
175 High St. BN7 1YE. (A. and J. Shelley). Ope 9.30-5. SIZE: Large. *STOCK: Books includin natural history, English literature, trave topography.* LOC: Off A27. TEL: 01273 48078 fax - 01273 486686. FAIRS: Antiquarian Book.

Castle Antiques
163a High St. (C. J. Harris). Est. 1984. Open 1 5, Sun. 2-5. SIZE: Medium. *STOCK: Pi furniture, late 19th C, £80-£120; kitchenalia, la 19th C, £5-£25; bric-a-brac, late 19th to ear 20th C, £5-£25.* LOC: Top part of High St., dow a twitten, opposite Lloyds Bank. TEL: 012 475176.

Lennox Cato
BADA LAPAD

Coombe House Antiques, 121 Malling St. B 2RJ. (Mr and Mrs Cato). Resident. Est. 197 Open 9.30-6, weekend by appointment. SIZ Medium. *STOCK: 18th C English and Con nental furniture and related items, gard furniture.* LOC: Opposite Esso petrol stati on A26. PARK: Own forecourt. TEL: 012 473862; mobile - 0836 233473. SER: Val ations; restorations. FAIRS: Major Lond fairs. VAT: Stan/Spec.

Church Hill Antiques Centre
6 Station St. BN7 2DA. (S. Miller and S. Ramn Est. 1970. Open 9.30-1 and 2-5. CL: Sat. a Wed. afternoons. SIZE: 60 stalls and cabine *STOCK: Antiques of all periods, furniture, gla china, silver.* LOC: From railway station, in to centre. PARK: Easy, own. TEL: 01273 4748 VAT: Stan.

Lewes continued

Cliffe Antiques Centre
47 Cliffe High St. BN7 2AN. (M. Nash). Est. 1984. Open 9.30-5. SIZE: Medium - 16 dealers. *STOCK: General antiques, £5-£1,000.* LOC: Follow town centre signs, turning left 200 yds. past Safeways. PARK: Easy. TEL: 01273 473266.

Cliffe Gallery Antiques
39 Cliffe High St. BN7 2AN. (Grimes & Hayward). Open 9.30-5. *STOCK: 18th-20th C furniture and objects, including pine, mahogany, oak, china and lighting.* TEL: 01273 471877.

A.J. Cumming
34 High St. BN7 1XN. Est. 1976. Open 10-5, Sat. 10-5.30. *STOCK: Antiquarian and out of print books.* TEL: 01273 472319. SER: Buys at auction.

The Drawing Room
53 High St. BN7 1XE. Open 9.30-5.30. SIZE: Medium. *STOCK: Furniture, pictures, objets d'art.* TEL: 01273 478560.

The Emporium Antique Centre
42 Cliffe High St. (Doyle and Madigan). Open 9.30-5 (Sun. - Dec. only). SIZE: 48 dealers. *STOCK: General antiques and collectables - vintage and collector's toys, books, militaria (including western arms, weaponary), Clarice Cliffe, Moorcroft, Carlton, Royal Winton.* TEL: 01273 486866.

Felix Gallery
Corner of Sun St. and Lancaster St. BN7 2QB. (W.S.H. and Mrs M.M. Whitehead). Est. 1981. Open 10-6, Sun. 12-6. SIZE: Small. *STOCK: Cats only - pottery, porcelain, bronze and silver, pictures, general objets d'art, English and Continental.* LOC: 2 mins. from town centre. PARK: Nearby. TEL: 01273 472668; home - same.

Fifteenth Century Bookshop
99 High St. BN7 1XH. (S. Mirabaud). Est. 1938. Open 10-5.30. *STOCK: Antiquarian and general secondhand books, especially children's and illustrated; prints and teddies.* TEL: 01273 474160.

Renée and Roy Green BADA
Ashcombe House, Lewes Rd. BN7 3JR. Prior telephone call advisable. *STOCK: Furniture and objects, 17th to early 19th C.* LOC: From Brighton A27, entrance on left-hand side 400yds. before Lewes (A275) turn-off. TEL: 01273 474794; fax - 01273 705959; mobile - 0860 720731.

Bob Hoare Pine Antiques
Unit Q, Phoenix Place, North St. BN7 2DQ. Open 9-6, Sat. 9-2. *STOCK: Pine.* TEL: 01273 480557; fax - 01273 471298.

Lewes continued

Lewes Antique Centre
20 Cliffe High St. BN7 2AH. (C. Keen). Est. 1968. Open 9.30-5. SIZE: Large - 42 stallholders. *STOCK: Furniture, china, copper and metalware, glass, clocks.* LOC: A27 from Brighton, 2nd roundabout into Lewes, end of tunnel turn left, then next left, next right into Phoenix car park. 100m. walk to Cliffe High Street. PARK: Easy. TEL: 01273 476148. SER: Shipping.

Lewes Flea Market
14a Market St. Est. 1995. Open daily including Sun. SIZE: Large. *STOCK: Bric-a-brac, furniture, collectables, 18th-20th C, £5-£1,000.* LOC: 50 metres north of monument. TEL: 01273 480328.

Pastorale Antiques
15 Malling St. and 33 Cliffe High St. BN7 2RA. (O. Soucek). Open 9.30-6 or by appointment. SIZE: Large. *STOCK: Pine and European country furniture, Georgian and Victorian mahogany and decorative items and garden items.* TEL: 01273 473259; home - 01435 863044; fax - 01273 473259.

Southdown Antiques
48 Cliffe High St. BN7 2AN. (Miss P.I. and K.A. Foster). Est. 1969. Open by appointment. SIZE: Medium. *STOCK: Small antiques, especially 18th-19th C English, Continental and Oriental porcelain, objets d'art, works of art, glass, papier mâché trays, silver plate, £50-£350,000; reproduction and interior decor items.* LOC: A27. One-way street north. PARK: Easy. TEL: 01273 472439. VAT: Stan/Spec.

NEWHAVEN

Newhaven Flea Market
28 South Way. BN9 9LA. (R. Mayne and A. Wilkinson). Est. 1971. Open every day 10-5.30 except 25th Dec. *STOCK: Victoriana, Edwardian, bric-a-brac.* TEL: 01273 517207/516065.

Leonard Russell
21 Kings Ave., Mount Pleasant. BN9 0NB. Resident. Est. 1981. Open by appointment. SIZE: Small. *STOCK: English pottery figures, groups, animals, Toby jugs, 1750-1830.* LOC: 500 yards from A259 South Coast Rd., ¾ mile from town centre. PARK: Easy. TEL: 01273 515153. SER: Valuations; buys at auction (pottery).

PEVENSEY

The Old Mint House LAPADA

High St. BN24 5LF. (J.C. and A.J. Nicholson). Est. 1901. Open 9-5.30, Sat. by appointment. SIZE: Large + export warehouse. *STOCK: Furniture, Period, Victorian, Edwardian and shipping; porcelain, clocks, barometers, 18th-19th C, £20-£10,000.* LOC: A259 coast road, 1 mile from Eastbourne. PARK: Easy. TEL: 01323 762337; fax - 01323 762337. SER: Worldwide container packing; Victoria trains met at Polegate station. VAT: Stan/Spec.

PEVENSEY BAY

Murray Brown

The Studio, Silverbeach, Norman Rd. BN2 6JE. (G. Murray-Brown). Open by appointment only. *STOCK: Paintings and prints.* TEL: 01323 764298. SER: Valuations; restorations; cleaning; publishing.

POLEGATE

Graham Price Antiques Ltd

4 Chaucer Industrial Estate, Dittons Rd. BN26 6JD. Open 9-6. SIZE: Large. *STOCK: Mainly furniture - pine, country, decorative, French, Irish, European, period and Victorian oak, mahogany and walnut; bric-a-brac and kitchenalia.* LOC: Between Hastings and Brighton on A27. TEL: 01323 487167; fax - 01323 483904. SER: Export, packing, shipping and courier; restorations.

Polegate continued

E. Stacy-Marks Limited BADA

"The Flint Rooms", P O Box 808. BN26 5ST. Est. 1889. SIZE: Large. *STOCK: Paintings English, Dutch and Continental schools, 18th-20th C.* TEL: 01323 482156; fax - 01323 482513. VAT: Stan.

ROTTINGDEAN

Trade Wind

Little Crescent. BN2 7GF. (R. Morley Smith). Est. 1974. Open by appointment only. *STOCK: Caddy and sifter spoons, wine labels and other interesting items, including coloured glass, Bristol blue, green and amethyst; small furniture, George III to Victoria.* TEL: 01273 301177.

RYE

Bragge and Sons

Landgate House. TN31 7LH. (N.H. and J.R. Bragge). Est. 1840. Open 9-5. CL: Tues. pm. *STOCK: 18th C furniture and works of art.* LOC: Entrance to town - Landgate. TEL: 0179 223358. SER: Valuations; restorations. VAT: Spec.

ye continued

Ierbert Gordon Gasson
ıe Lion Galleries, Lion St. TN31 7LB. (T.J. ooth). Est. 1909. Open 9-1 and 2-5.30. CL: ıes. pm. SIZE: Large. *STOCK: 17th-18th C oak ıd walnut; Staffordshire and Chinese porcelain.* ot Stocked: Silver and glass. PARK: Easy. TEL: ı797 222208. SER: Restorations. VAT: an/Spec.

andgate Antiques
Landgate. TN31 7LH. (J. Jones). Resident. ıt. 1974. Open 10-5.30. *STOCK: Furniture, corative items, clocks, desks.* TEL: 01797 :4746.

nn Lingard - Rope Walk Antiques
LAPADA

-22 Rope Walk. TN31 7NA. Est. 1972. SIZE: rge. *STOCK: English antique pine furniture d accessories; kitchen shop.* Not Stocked: wellery, silver and plate. PARK: Own, and blic next door. TEL: 01797 223486; fax - 797 224700. VAT: Stan.

ye Antiques
High St. TN31 7JN. (Mrs D. Turner). Est. 1966. en 9.30-5.30. CL: Sun. except by appointment. ZE: Small. *STOCK: Small oak, walnut and hogany furniture, 17th-19th C, £50-£1,000; talware, jewellery, silver and plate, 18th-19th C, £1,000.* Not Stocked: Coins, bric-a-brac. PARK: sy. TEL: 01797 222259.

AFORD

olly Alexander
ɔuch House, Crouch Lane. BN25 1PX. Est. 57. *STOCK: Paintings, watercolours and iquities.* LOC: Opposite new Constitutional b. PARK: Opposite. TEL: 01323 896577.

ıe Courtyard Antiques Market
High St. BN25 1PD. (Mrs S.E. Barrett). Open , Wed. 9-1. SIZE: Medium - 13 dealers. *ɔCK: General antiques and collectables; cks.* TEL: 01323 892091. SER: Clock oration and repair.

Seaford continued

John Cowderoy Antiques
59-63 Broad Street (North) BN25 1NR. (R., D.J. and R.A. Cowderoy). GMC. Est. 1973. Open 9.30-5. CL: Wed. pm. and Sat. pm. *STOCK: Clocks, musical boxes, furniture, porcelain, silver and plate, jewellery, copper, brass, paintings.* SER: Restorations (clocks, barometers, music boxes and furniture). VAT: Stan/Spec.

The Old House
15/17 High St. BN25 1PD. (S.M. Barrett). Est. 1928. Open 9-5, Wed. 9-1. SIZE: Large. *STOCK: 18th-20th C furniture, china and glass, £5-£5,000.* LOC: Near railway station. PARK: Opposite in Pelham Yard. TEL: 01323 892091/893795. SER: Valuations; restorations (furniture); shippers. VAT: Stan/Spec.

Seaford's "Barn Collectors' Market" and Studio Bookshop
The Barn, Church Lane. BN25 1HL. Est. 1967. Open 9.30-5. SIZE: Several dealers. *STOCK: Collectables, ephemera, books, post and cigarette cards.* LOC: Off High St. TEL: 01323 890010.

ST. LEONARDS-ON-SEA

Aarquebus Antiques
37 & 46 Norman Rd. TN38 0EJ. (Mr and Mrs G. Jukes). Resident. Est. 1957. Open 9.30-5, Sat. 9.30-1. SIZE: Medium. *STOCK: Furniture, 18th C, £500-£1,000; shipping goods, Victorian to 1930, £5-£500; glass, gold and silver, 18th-19th C, £5-£1,000.* LOC: Take A2100 to St. Leonards-on-Sea, turn right after main P.O. PARK: Easy. TEL: 01424 433267. SER: Valuations.

Banner Antiques
56 Norman Rd. TN38 3EJ. (G.M. Schofield). Est. 1972. Open 10-1 and 2.15-5.30. CL: Wed. SIZE: Large. *STOCK: Furniture, porcelain, pottery, copper, brass, watercolours.* Not Stocked: Jewellery, silver, weapons. PARK: Easy. TEL: 01424 420050.

The Book Jungle
24 North St. TN38 0EX. (M. Gowen). Est. 1988. Open 10-5. CL: Wed. SIZE: Medium. *STOCK: Secondhand books.* LOC: Just off seafront. PARK: Nearby. TEL: 01424 421187.

St. Leonards-on-Sea continued

Chapel Antiques
1 London Rd. TN37 6AE. (Mrs. Gordana). Est. 1946. Open 10-5. *STOCK: Furniture, paintings, militaria, decorative items, 18th-19th C, £20-£10,000.* PARK: Easy. TEL: 01424 440025. SER: Valuations; restorations (furniture).

Nicholas Cole Antiques
7 Grand Parade. TN38 0DA. Est. 1973. Open 9-6, Sat. 9-1 or by appointment, Sun. by appointment. SIZE: Medium. *STOCK: Victorian, Edwardian and 1920's oak and mahogany furniture, £50-£500.* LOC: A259 junction with A21. PARK: Easy. TEL: 01424 420671; home - 01424 461031. SER: Valuations; restorations. VAT: Stan.

Gensing Antiques
70 Norman Rd.TN38 0EJ. (Peter Cawson). Open normal shop hours and by appointment. *STOCK: General antiques especially early Chinese furniture and other Oriental items.* TEL: 01424 424145/714981.

The Hastings Antique Centre
59-61 Norman Rd. TN38 0EG. (R.J. Amstad). Open 10-5.30, Sun. by appointment. TEL: 01424 428561. Below are listed some of the dealers at this centre.

R. J. Amstad
Furniture.

Harry Bolden
Metal work and clocks.

Sarah Brixton
Lace and linen, jewellery.

Clive Brown
Pictures, prints, decorative furniture.

I. Copeland/S. Longmead
Furniture.

Terry Cuthbert
Furniture.

S. Dahms
Clocks.

Dee's Antiques
Decorative items.

Brenda Fox and Bridget Howett
Decorative items.

K. Gumbrell
Decorative items.

Tony Mathews
Tribal art.

G. Mennis
Sporting, leather goods.

Steven Owen
Period furniture.

Robert Paul Antiques
Furniture and shipping goods.

St. Leonards-on-Sea continued

V. Russell
Gold and silver.

Ken and Iris Saunders
Clocks, silver and collectables.

Pat Shawl
Smalls, collectables.

Tiffany Antiques
Furniture.

Helgato
121 Bohemia Rd. TN37 6RL. (Helga E. and R Nicholls). Est. 1961. Open by appointment onl SIZE: Medium. *STOCK: Porcelain, glass, objec of vertu and art, books, prints and maps, 165 1890, £2-£500.* LOC: A21. TEL: 01424 423049.

Monarch Antiques
5, 6, 9 and 19 Grand Parade. TN38 0DD. (J. King). Est. 1983. Open Mon.-Fri. 9-5, or a other time by appointment. SIZE: Large. *STOC General furniture, especially 1930's oak furnitu for the European and Japanese markets.* LO A259. PARK: Easy. TEL: Home - 01424 2141 460010; mobiles - 0802 217842/213081; page 01425 253204. SER: Restorations.

K. Nunn
at Chapel Antiques, Chapel House, 1 London R TN37 6RN. Open 9.30-5.30. *STOCK: Gene antiques, weapons, ship and aero models, to and unusual items.* TEL: 01424 431093. SE Buys at auction. VAT: Stan/Spec.

John H. Yorke Antiques
Filsham Farmhouse, 111 Harley Shute Rd. TN 8BY. (J.H. Yorke). Open 9-5.30. *STOCK: F niture for trade, export and shipping.* TEL: 01 433109. VAT: Stan.

UCKFIELD

Ivan R. Deverall
Duval House, The Glen, Cambridge Way. TN 2AB. *STOCK: Maps.* TEL: 01825 762474. S Catalogue available; colouring.

Ringles Cross Antiques
Ringles Cross. TN22 1HF. (C. and J. Dunfo Resident. Est. 1965. Open 9.30-6 or by appo ment. *STOCK: English furniture, 17th-18th C accessories; Oriental items.* LOC: 1 mile nort Uckfield. PARK: Own. TEL: 01825 762909.

WADHURST

Park View Antiques
High St., Durgates. TN5 6DE. (B. Ross). 1985. Open 10-5. CL: Wed. SIZE: Medi *STOCK: Pine, oak and country furniture, 1 19th C, £100-£1,500; decorative items, 193 £25-£150; iron and metalware, 17th-19th C, £250.* LOC: On B2099 Frant-Hurst Green r PARK: Easy. TEL: 01892 783630; home - 01 740264. SER: Valuations; restorations (furnitu

Sussex West

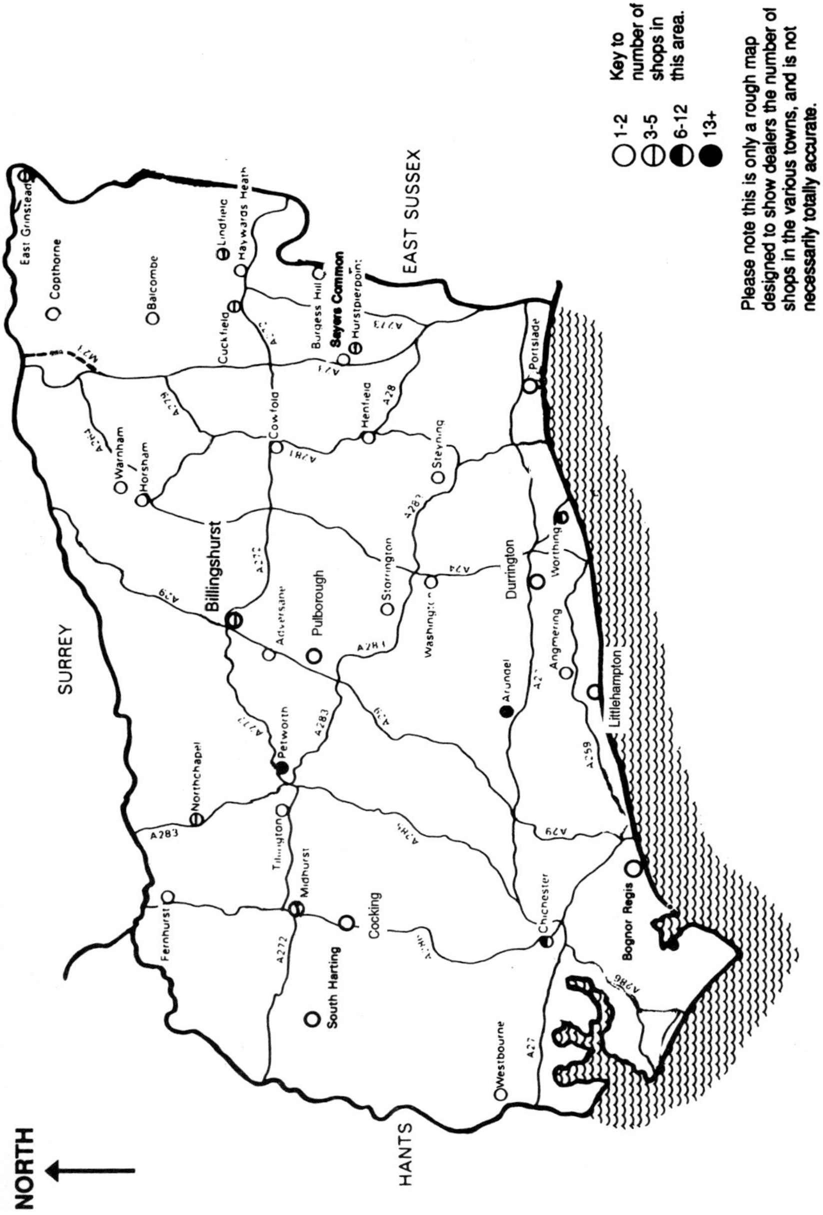

Key to number of shops in this area.
1-2
3-5
6-12
13+
Please note this is only a rough map designed to show dealers the number of shops in the various towns, and is not necessarily totally accurate.
NORTH
SURREY
HANTS
EAST SUSSEX
East Grinstead
Copthorne
Balcombe
Lindfield
Haywards Heath
Cuckfield
Burgess Hill
Sayers Common
Hurstpierpoint
Portslade
Henfield
Cowfold
Warnham
Horsham
Steyning
Billingshurst
Storrington
Durrington
Worthing
Washington
Adversane
Pulborough
Angmering
Arundel
Littlehampton
Petworth
Northchapel
Tillington
Midhurst
Cocking
Fernhurst
Chichester
Bognor Regis
South Harting
Westbourne
A283
A272
A29
A24
A281
A23
A273
A27
A259
A286
M23

ADVERSANE, Nr. Billingshurst

Old House Antique Centre
Old House. RH14 9TT. Open daily including Sun. SIZE: 30+ stallholders. *STOCK: General antiques and collectors' items.* PARK: Easy. TEL: 01403 783594/782186.

ANGMERING

Bygones
The Square. BN16 4EQ. (R.A. and Mrs L.R. Whittaker). Est. 1965. Open Tues. and Thurs. 10-1 and 2.15-5, Sat. 10-12. SIZE: Medium. *STOCK: Furniture, £50-£2,500; china, £5-£750; silver, £10-£250; linen, £5-£75; all 1790-1940.* LOC: A280. PARK: Easy. TEL: 01903 786152; home - same. SER: Valuations; buys at auction (furniture).

ARUNDEL

Antiquities
5 Tarrant St. BN16 3ER. (Ian and Christina Fenwick). Est. 1990. Open 10-5, or by appointment. SIZE: Medium + warehouse. *STOCK: English and Irish pine and country furniture, 19th C; unusual, decorative and painted items; majolica, French mirrors, pond yachts, luggage, some mahogany and fruitwood.* LOC: Just off town square. PARK: Nearby. TEL: 01903 884355; fax - same. SER: Shipping. VAT: Stan/Spec.

Arundel Clocks
Lasseters Corner, High St. BN18 9AB. (F.M. Henderson). Open 9.30-1 and 2-5. SIZE: Small. *STOCK: Longcase clocks, £1,500-£6,000; dial clocks, £300-£4,000.* LOC: Corner of High St. and Mill Lane. PARK: Easy. TEL: 01903 884525; fax - same. SER: Valuations; restorations (clocks including dials). VAT: Spec.

Baynton-Williams
37A High St. BN18 9AG. (R.H. and S.C. Baynton-Williams). Est. 1946. Open 10-6. *STOCK: Maps, views, sporting, marine and decorative prints.* TEL: 01903 883588; fax - same. SER: Valuations; cataloguing. VAT: Stan/Spec.

Richard Davidson Antiques
Romsey House, 51 Maltravers St. BN18 9BQ. Open by appointment only. *STOCK: Fine furniture, decorative accessories.* TEL: 01903 883141; fax - 01903 883914. SER: Interior decoration; valuations; restorations. VAT: Spec.

Faringdon Gallery
27 Tarrant St. BN18 9DG. (Mr and Mrs G.E. Lott). Est. 1970. Open 10-5, Sun. and Mon. by appointment. SIZE: Small. *STOCK: Watercolours and etchings, late 19th C to contemporary, £100-£3,000.* LOC: From A27, first right down High St. hill. PARK: 100 yards at rear. TEL: 01903 882047; home - 01243 554572. SER: Valuations; restorations; buys at auction (watercolours and etchings).

Arundel continued

Peter Francis Antiques
9 Tarrant St. BN18 9DG. (P. R. Francis). Est 1992. Open 9.30-5, Sat. 9-5, Sun. by appointmen SIZE: Medium. *STOCK: Furniture, 1810-1920's £50-£2,000; ceramics, Doulton and Beswick, £20 £1,000; paintings, 1860-1920's, £50-£3,000* TEL: 01903 884641; home - 01903 892481; fax same. SER: Valuations; buys at auction.

Pat Golding
6 Castle Mews, Tarrant St. BN18 9DG. Open 10- and 2-5. *STOCK: Ceramics and glass, 18th-20th C*

Phyllis Gordon
BN18 9DW. Est. 1972. Open by appointmer only. *STOCK: Georgian and Victorian furniture button back chairs, porcelain, silver, glass an clocks.* TEL: 01903 885064.

Tom Littlefair Antiques
5 River Rd. BN18 9DG. Open 11-5, Sat. 9- *STOCK: Furniture, decorative fine art.* PARK Easy. TEL: 01903 884774.

Mamie's Antiques Centre
5 River Rd. BN18 9DH. (Mrs M. Eyers). Es 1965. PARK: Easy. TEL: 01903 882012. Th following dealers trade from this address.

Tom Littlefair Antiques
(N. Spencer). *Antiques and decorative fine art.* TE 01903 884474/884774; mobile - 0831 106420.

Mamie's Shop
General antiques. TEL: 01903 882012.

Sussex Fine Art
7 Castle Mews, Tarrant St. BN18 9DG. (G.C. a P.A. Miller). Est. 1987. Open Fri. and Sat. 10.3 5.30, Sun. 12-5, other days by appointment. SIZ Small. *STOCK: English watercolours, 1760-193 from £200.* LOC: Off High St. PARK: 50yd TEL: 01903 884055. SER: Framing; buys auction. VAT: Spec.

Spencer Swaffer LAPAD
30 High St. BN18 9AB. Est. 1974. Open Mo Fri. 9-6, other times by appointment. SIZ Large. *STOCK: Unusual decorative and tra itional items, brass, blue and white, Staffor shire, dinner services, pine, oak dressers, mar tables, bamboo, shop fittings, candlestic majolica, French, English, painted and gard furniture.* PARK: Easy. TEL: 01903 8821 fax - 01903 884564. VAT: Stan/Spec.

Tarrant Street Antique Centre
Nineveh House, Tarrant St. BN18 9DG. (Miss Millar). Open 10-5, Sun. 11-5. SIZE: Large - dealers. *STOCK: Wide range of general antiq including Edwardian and Victorian, country a pine furniture, jewellery and silver, paintings a prints, china and glass, luggage and Oriental ru* LOC: Off A27 and A29 into town then second off High St. PARK: Own forecourt. TEL: 01 884307. SER: Valuations; restorations.

Arundel continued

Treasure House Antiques and Collectors Market

31b High St. and Crown Yard Car Park. BN18 9AG. Est. 1972. Open 9-5; Crown Yard Sat. 9-5 only. CL: Wed. *STOCK: Victoriana, domestic bygones, porcelain, Goss and crested china models, toys, Royal commemoratives, lace, lamps, curios, metalware, small furniture.* PARK: Easy. TEL: 01903 507446/883101/882908.

The Walking Stick Shop

Stuart Thompson (Fine Canes) 39 Tarrant St. BN18 9DG. Est. 1981. Open 8.30-5.30, Wed. .30-1, Sun. pm. by appointment. SIZE: Medium. *STOCK: Walking sticks and canes, 1620 to date, 10-£2,000.* LOC: Off High St. PARK: Easy. TEL: 01903 883796; home - 01903 882713; fax - 1903 884491. SER: Valuations; buys at auction canes). VAT: Stan.

Whitehouse Antique Interiors

Tarrant Square, Tarrant St. BN18 9DE. (G.G. Cross). Open 10-5. *STOCK: Furniture, porcelain, ecorative items.* TEL: 01903 882443.

BALCOMBE

English Interiors

Haywards Heath Rd. RH17 6PE. (J.M. Nelson nd G. Lindsay-Stewart). Est. 1977. CL: Sun. IZE: Medium. *STOCK: Small furniture, sofas nd chairs, mirrors and pictures.* LOC: B2036. ARK: Easy. TEL: 01444 811700. SER: Interior esign service; kitchen and bedroom furniture nade to order. VAT: Stan.

Woodall and Emery Ltd

Haywards Heath Rd. RH17 6PG. Est. 1884. TEL: 1444 811608. VAT: Stan.

BILLINGSHURST

Susan and Robert Botting LAPADA

reat Grooms Antiques Centre, Great rooms, Parbrook. RH14 9EU. Est. 1979. pen every day. SIZE: Medium. *STOCK: Oil aintings and watercolours, 19th and 20th C, 100-£25,000.* LOC: Half-mile south of illingshurst on A29. TEL: 01243 584515; ome - same. SER: Valuations; restorations. AIRS: NEC; LAPADA; Claridges; Petworth.

Great Grooms Antique Centre

reat Grooms, Parbrook. RH14 9EU. Est. 1983. pen Mon.-Sat. 9.30-5.30, Sun. 10-6. SIZE: 25+ ealers. *STOCK: Wide variety of specialist ealers in 18th-19th C English and Continental wn and country furniture, pottery and porcelain, lver and plate, works of art, metalware, glass, ocks, Oriental, oils and watercolours, prints, ms and armour, books, clocks and watches, ientific instruments.* LOC: A29 south of llingshurst. PARK: Easy. TEL: 01403 786202; x - 01403 786224. SER: Valuations; restorations rniture, pictures, silver and jewellery); buys at ction. VAT: Spec.

Billingshurst continued

Lannards Gallery

Okehurst Lane. RH14 9HR. (Mr and Mrs Derek Sims). Open by appointment; open every day during exhibitions. *STOCK: Watercolours, oils and furniture, from 1850.* TEL: 01403 782692. SER: Exhibitions held, please telephone for details.

Michael Wakelin and Helen Linfield

BADA LAPADA

P.O Box 48. RH14 0YZ. Est. 1968. Open any time by appointment only. *STOCK: Fine English and Continental formal and country furniture - walnut, fruitwoods, faded mahogany and other exotic woods; early brass, bronze, iron and steel; wood carvings, treen, needlework, naïve pictures and lighting.* TEL: 01403 700004; fax - same. VAT: Stan/Spec.

Jeremy Wood Fine Art

95 High St. RH14 9QX. Est. 1974. Open 10-1 and 2-5. CL: Mon. *STOCK: Oils and watercolours, 1850-1950, £5-£1,500; art reference books, illustrated art and travel books, motoring/motor racing art and books, £1-£50.* TEL: 01403 783633; fax - 01403 784258. VAT: Spec.

BOGNOR REGIS

Gough Bros. Art Shop and Gallery

71 High St. PO21 1RZ. (S. Neal). Est. 1916. CL: Wed. pm. SIZE: Medium. *STOCK: Watercolours, £50-£1,000; oils, £100-£1,500; miniatures, £150-£400; all 19th-20th C.* LOC: Off High St., behind Unicorn public house. PARK: Nearby. TEL: 01243 823773. SER: Valuations; restorations (oils and watercolours, frames and gilding). VAT: Stan/Spec.

BURGESS HILL

British Antique Replicas LAPADA

School Close, Queen Elizabeth Ave. RH15 9RX. Est. 1962. Open 9-5.30. SIZE: Large. *STOCK: Furniture, £100-£20,000.* LOC: 3 miles west A23. PARK: Easy. TEL: 01444 245577. SER: Bespoke furniture. VAT: Stan.

CHICHESTER

Almshouses Arcade

19 The Hornet. Est. 1983. Open 9.30-4.30. LOC: 200yds. from Cattle Market at eastern end of city. On one-way system (A286) just before traffic lights at Market Ave. PARK: Easy. Below are listed the dealers at these premises.

West Antics

(P. German). *General antiques and collectables.* TEL: 01243 786327.

R. K. Barnett

Antiques and collectables, furniture. TEL: 01243 528089.

Helter Skelter

Records, tapes, CDs. TEL: 01243 771744.

Chichester continued

Overlord
(D. Rowe). *Militaria, toys and general antiques, £5-£100.* TEL: 01243 774613.

Panormo Antiques
(M. Panormo) *General antiques and collectables.*

Squirrel Antiques
(L. Hampshire) *Small antiques, toys, collectables.*

Yesteryears
(J.A. Cook) *Lighting (oil), general antiques and collectables.* TEL: 01243 771994.

Antique Shop
Frensham House, Hunston. PO20 6NX. (J. and M. Riley). Est. 1966. Open 9-6. *STOCK: English furniture, 1700-1830, £500-£5,000; clocks, paintings, copper.* LOC: One mile south of Chichester by-pass on B2145. PARK: Easy. TEL: 01243 782660.

Chichester Antiques Centre
46-48 The Hornet. PO10 4JG. (Andrew Davies). Est. 1994. Open 10-5, Sun. 11-5. SIZE: 50 stalls. *STOCK: General antiques and collectables, 50p to £10,000.* LOC: M27 onto A27 to town. PARK: Loading only and nearby. TEL: 01243 530100. SER: Clock restoration on premises.

County Place Antiques
9 South St. PO19 1EH. (G. Hawkins). Est. 1991. Open 9.30-5. SIZE: Large. *STOCK: Furniture and porcelain, 18th-19th C, £500-£2,000; Victorian furniture and fine art, 19th C, £100-£2,000.* LOC: 50 yards from Market Cross, near cathedral. PARK: South St. TEL: 01243 537699. SER: Valuations; restorations (furniture and porcelain); buys at auction.

The Delightful Muddle
82 Fishbourne Rd. West. PO19 3JL. Open Wed. 1-5, Thurs.-Sat. 10-5. *STOCK: China, glass, objets d'art, Victorian and Edwardian, £1-£100; lace £1-£50; linen, general antiques and bric-a-brac, £3-£65.* LOC: 1 mile west of Chichester on A259, opposite Fishbourne P.O & Stores. PARK: Easy.

Gems Antiques
39 West St. PO19 1RP. (M.L. Hancock). Open 10.30-1 and 2.30-5.30. *STOCK: Period furniture, Staffordshire and porcelain figures, glass and pictures.* TEL: 01243 786173.

Peter Hancock Antiques
40-41 West St. PO19 1RP. Articles on coins. Est. 1950. Open 10.30-1 and 2.30-5.30. SIZE: Medium. *STOCK: Silver, jewellery, porcelain, furniture, £20-£2,000; pictures, glass, clocks, books, £20-£1,500; all 18th-19th C; enthnographica, Art Nouveau, Art Deco, 19th-20th C, £5-£500.* LOC: From Chichester Cross, 17 doors past Cathedral. PARK: Easy. TEL: 01243 786173. SER: Valuations. VAT: Stan/Spec.

Heritage Antiques
77D, 83 and 84 St. Pancras. PO19 4LS. (D.R. and D.A. Grover). Open 9.30-5.30. *STOCK: Furnitur and decorative items.* TEL: 01243 783796 783470.

Chichester continued

St. Pancras Antiques
150 St. Pancras. PO19 1SH. (R.F. and M. Willatt Est. 1980. Open 9.30-1 and 2-5. CL: Thurs. pm SIZE: Small. *STOCK: Arms and armour militaria, medals, documents, uniforms and map 1600-1914, £5-£3,000; china, pottery an ceramics, 1800-1930, £2-£500; small furnitur 17th-19th C, £20-£1,000; coins, ancient to dat* Not Stocked: Silver and carpets. TEL: 0124 787645. SER: Valuations; restorations (arms an armour); buys at auction (militaria).

COCKING, Nr. Midhurst

The Victorian Brass Bedstead Company
Hoe Copse. GU29 0HL. (David Woolley Resident. Est. 1970. Open by appointment. SIZ Large. *STOCK: Victorian and Edwardian bra and iron bedsteads, bases and mattresses, 19t 20th C, £300-£3,5000.* LOC: Right behind villa Post Office, 3/4 mile left turning to Hoe Cops PARK: Easy. TEL: 01730 812287. SER: Val ations; restorations (brass and iron bedstead VAT: Stan.

COPTHORNE, Nr. Crawley

Copthorne Antiques
Copthorne Bank. RH10 3QZ. (Mrs M. Pealling). Open 10-5. *STOCK: Pine, oa mahogany furniture; china, brass, collectabl pictures.* LOC: 10 minutes from Gatwick. C M23, junction 10. TEL: 01342 712802. SE Restorations (furniture); re-upholstery.

COWFOLD

Squire's Pantry Pine and Antiques
Station Rd. RH13 8DA. (L.M. Lasham). Open 1 1 and 2-5. *STOCK: Pine.* TEL: 01403 864869; f - 01403 865283. VAT: Stan/Spec.

CUCKFIELD

David Foord-Brown Antiques LAPA
High St. RH17 5QL. Est. 1988. Open 10-5. SIZE: Medium. *STOCK: Furniture, 1780-18 £300-£5,000; porcelain, 1800-1850, £20-£1,5* Not Stocked: Country furniture. LOC: A2 PARK: Easy. TEL: 01444 414418. SE Valuations. VAT: Stan/Spec.

Richard Usher Antiques
23 South St. RH17 5LB. Est. 1978. Open 10-5. CL: Wed. pm. and Sat. pm. SIZE: Mediu *STOCK: Furniture, 17th-19th C, £50-£3,0 decorative items.* LOC: A272. PARK: Easy. T 01444 451699. SER: Valuations; restorations.

)URRINGTON

lary Gregory's
Manor Parade, Farthington Rd. BN13 2JP. Est. 990. Open 10-4, Sat. 9-3. CL: Wed. *STOCK: urniture, Royal Doulton.* TEL: 01903 264922.

:AST GRINSTEAD

The Antique Atlas
1A High St. RH19 3AF. View by appointment. *TOCK: Maps, charts, plans and views world-vide.* LOC: Entrance Cantelupe Rd. TEL: 01342 15813.

The Antique Print Shop
1 Middle Row. RH19 3AX. (A.A.W. Daszewski nd Mrs A.C. Keddie). Est. 1988. Open 9.30-6. IZE: Small. *STOCK: Prints, pre-1880, £10-£200; aps especially British county, 1500-1870, £20-1,000; English watercolours and drawings, 1700-880, £100-£1,000.* LOC: On island in middle High t., opposite St. Swithins church. PARK: Lewes Rd. EL: 01342 410501; fax - 01342 410795. SER: estorations; framing. FAIRS: Park Lane Hotel, ondon (Sundays); NEC. VAT: Stan.

Keith Atkinson Antiques
loorhawes, Sandhawes Hill. RH19 3NR. Open y appointment. *STOCK: 19th C furniture.* LOC: 264, close to Dormans Park. PARK: Easy. TEL: 1342 870765; fax - 01342 870767; mobile - 860 323387 and 0836 640041. VAT: Stan/Spec.

ERNHURST, Nr. Haslemere

heelagh Hamilton
o Midhurst Rd. GU27 3EE. Open 9-5, Sat. 9-1, un. by appointment. *STOCK: Period furniture, ictures.* LOC: A286 village centre. TEL: 01428 53253.

IAYWARDS HEATH

ulian Ramm
3 Sussex Rd. RH16 4DZ. Open 9-5.30. *STOCK: urniture.* TEL: 01444 453067.

IENFIELD

lexander Antiques
ost House, Small Dole. BN5 9XE. (Mrs J.A. oodinge). Est. 1971. CL: Sun. except by ppointment. SIZE: Medium. *STOCK: Country rniture, brass, copper, pewter, samplers, small ollectors' and decorative items, treen.* LOC: 2037. PARK: Easy. TEL: 01273 493121; home same. VAT: Stan/Spec.

ORSHAM

.E. Lampard and Sons
-25 Springfield Rd. RH12 2PG. Est. 1920. pen 8-1 and 2-5. SIZE: Medium. *STOCK: ahogany and oak furniture, firebacks, grates.* EL: 01403 254012. VAT: Stan/Spec.

HURSTPIERPOINT

Julian Antiques
124 High St. BN6 9DX. Est. 1964. Open 9-6. CL: Sat. *STOCK: French 19th C clocks, bronzes, Art Deco, fireplaces, mirrors, furniture.* TEL: 01273 832145.

Michael Miller
The Lamb, 8 Cuckfield Rd. BN6 9RU. (M. and V. Miller). Est. 1880. Open Sat. 9.30-5, other times appointment advisable. *STOCK: Arms and armour, post-1460, from £5; general antiques.* TEL: 01273 834567. SER: Buys at auction; exporters.

Samuel Orr Antique Clocks LAPADA
34-36 High St. Open 9-6, or by appointment. CL: Sat. *STOCK: 18th and 19th longcase and table clocks.* TEL: 01273 832145. SER: Restorations (clocks and furniture).

LINDFIELD

Alma Antiques
79 High St. RH16 2HN. Est. 1976. Open 10.30-5. CL: Wed. *STOCK: Small collectable items, porcelain, glass, silver, copper, brass, furniture, watercolours and prints.*

Hinsdale Antiques
75 High St. RH16 2HN. Open 10-5. SIZE: Medium. *STOCK: Furniture, 18th to early 20th C; dolls and related items, late 19th to early 20th C; silver; small items.* TEL: 01444 483200; fax - 01444 484736.

Lindfield Galleries - David Adam BADA
62 High St. RH16 2HL. Est. 1972. Open 9.30-5.30. *STOCK: Oriental carpets.* TEL: 01444 483817. VAT: Stan/Spec.

LITTLEHAMPTON

The Round Pond
Faux Cottage, 4a Selborne Rd. BN17 5NN. (John Haynes and Kay Meader). Est. 1962. Open by appointment. SIZE: Small. *STOCK: Vintage model boats especially yachts, 19th C to 1950's, £50-£2,000.* PARK: Easy. TEL: 01903 714261; home - same. SER: Valuations.

MIDHURST

Churchill Clocks
Rumbolds Hill. GU29 9BZ. (W.P. and Dr. E. Tyrrell). Open 9-5, Wed. 9-1. *STOCK: Clocks and furniture.* LOC: Main street. TEL: 01730 813891; fax - same. SER: Clock restoration.

Curfew Antiques Centre
Knockhundred Row. GU29 9DQ. (D.M. Brindle-Wood-Williams). Est. 1974. Open 9.30-5. TEL: 01730 814231.

Eagle House Antiques Market
Market Sq. GU29 9NJ. (J.H. Brown). Open daily. SIZE: Medium - 15 dealers. *STOCK: General antiques, furniture, silver, porcelain, pictures and glass, £5-£1,000.* PARK: Easy. TEL: 01730 812718.

Midhurst continued

West Street Antiques & Presents
West St. (Janet Lintott and Angela Campbell). Est. 1984. Open 9.30-1 and 2-4.30. SIZE: Medium. *STOCK: Decorative and country furniture, brass, pottery and porcelain; quilts, rugs, £5-£1,000.* PARK: Easy. TEL: 01730 815232. SER: Buys at auction.

NORTHCHAPEL, Nr. Petworth

D. and A. Callingham Antiques
GU28 9HL. Est. 1966. CL: Wed. *STOCK: English furniture.* LOC: On A283. TEL: 01428 707379.

N. and S. Callingham Antiques
GU28 9HL. Est. 1979. Open 9-5.30. CL: Wed. SIZE: Medium. *STOCK: Furniture, 1700-1900, £10-£10,000.* LOC: London Road 5 miles north of Petworth. PARK: Easy. TEL: 01428 707379; home - 01903 724233. SER: Valuations; restorations. VAT: Stan/Spec.

PETWORTH

Majid Amini - Persian Carpet Gallery
Church St. GU28 0AD. Open 9.30-5. *STOCK: Old and new Oriental rugs and carpets.* LOC: A272. PARK: Nearby. TEL: 01798 343344; fax - 01798 342673. SER: Valuations; restorations; hand cleaning.

Angel Antiques
Church St. GU28 0AD. (Nick and Barbara Swanson). Open 10-5.30, Sun. by appointment. SIZE: Medium. *STOCK: Country furniture and associated items, 17th-19th C, £100-£6,000.* LOC: Opposite Petworth House and church. TEL: 01798 343306; fax - 01798 342665. VAT: Spec.

Bacchus Gallery
Lombard St. GU28 0AG. (R. and A. Gillett). Est. 1988. Open 10-1 and 2.30-5. SIZE: Small. *STOCK: Wine related items.* LOC: Cobbled street leading off town square. PARK: Town square. TEL: 01798 342844; fax - 01798 342634. SER: Buys at auction (as stock). VAT: Stan/Spec.

Baskerville Antiques BADA
Saddlers House, Saddlers Row. GU28 0AN. (A. and B. Baskerville). Est. 1978. Open 9.30-6, Sun. by appointment. SIZE: Medium. *STOCK: English clocks, barometers and furniture, £1,000-£20,000; decorative items and instruments, £500-£5,000; all 18th-19th C.* LOC: Town centre. PARK: Public, adjoining shop. TEL: 01798 342067; home - same; fax - 01798 343956. VAT: Spec.

Lesley Bragge Antiques LAPADA
Fairfield House, High St. GU28 0AU. Est. 1974. Open 10-1 and 2-5.30. SIZE: Medium. *STOCK: Decorative furniture, 18th-19th C; silver and plate, porcelain, textiles, ormolu, brass, copper, objets d'art, garden furniture.* LOC: Off Golden Square. PARK: Nearby. TEL: 01798 342324. SER: Valuations; restorations; upholstery. VAT: Stan/Spec.

Petworth continued

The Canon Gallery BADA LAPADA
New St. (Jeremy Green and James Fergusson Open 10-5.30. SIZE: Medium. *STOCK: Oi and watercolours, 18th-20th C, £500-£25,00* LOC: Main road. PARK: Easy. TEL: 017 344422. SER: Valuations; restoration. FAIR World of Watercolours; NEC; Harrogate; Ne York; Hong Kong; BADA. VAT: Spec.

J. Du Cros Antiques
1 Pound St. GU28 0DX. (J. and P. Du Cros). E 1982. Open 10-5.30. CL: Wed. pm. SIZ Medium. *STOCK: English furniture, 1660-190 £100-£5,000; treen, metalware, Staffordshi figures, some glass.* LOC: Corner of Sadlers Ro PARK: Nearby. TEL: 01798 342071. VA Stan/Spec.

Richard Gardner Antiques
Millhouse, Market Sq. GU28 0AN. (R. and J. Gardner). Resident. Est. 1992. Open 10-5. including Sun. *STOCK: Fine period furniture a works of art, up to £20,000.* PARK: 50 yar TEL: 01798 343411.VAT: Spec.

George House Gallery
George House, East St. GU28 0AB. (Jo Morgan). Est. 1993. Open 10-6, Sun. by appoi ment. CL: Some Mon. SIZE: Small. *STOC Prints and engravings, 18th-20th C, £5-£50; o and watercolours, £50-£1,000; cartoons country, sporting and fishing, to £50.* LO Opposite Petworth House and church. PAR Easy. TEL: 01798 342312; fax/home - sam SER: Restorations; buys at auction.

Granville Antiques BA
High St. GU28 0AU. (I.E.G. Miller). Est. 19 Open 10-5.30, Wed. 10-2.30 or by appointme SIZE: Medium. *STOCK: Period furniture, p 1840, £50-£15,000; accessories and pictures.* N Stocked: Militaria and jewellery. LOC: 100y from market square. PARK: Nearby. TE 01798 343250; home - 01243 542293. SE Valuations (furniture); restorations (furnitur buys at auction. FAIRS: West London. VA Spec.

William Hockley Antiques LAPA
East St. GU28 0AB. (D. and V. Thrower). E 1974. *STOCK: Fine 18th to early 19th furniture and decorative items; early Engli pottery.* TEL: 01798 343172.

The Madison Gallery
Swan House, Market Sq. GU28 0AH. (L. Long). Open 10-5.30 including Sun. SIZE: Lar *STOCK: Furniture including decorative; pictur accessories.* PARK: Easy. TEL: 01798 3436 SER: Restorations; upholstery. VAT: Stan/Spec

Petworth Antique Market
East St. GU28 0AB. (D.M. Rayment). Est. 19 Open 10-5.30. SIZE: Large - 36 dealers. *STOC General antiques, books, furniture, brass, cop pictures, textiles.* LOC: Near church. PAR Adjoining. TEL: 01798 342073. VAT: Stan/Sp

Petworth continued

Red Lion Antiques

New St. GU28 0AS. (R. Wilson and D. Swanson). Est. 1981. Open 10-5.30. SIZE: Large. *STOCK: Antiques for the country home, oak, walnut and pine furniture, 17th-19th C, £100-£10,000.* LOC: Town centre. PARK: Easy. TEL: 01798 344485; fax - 01798 342367; e-mail - redlion@tangent.demon.col.uk; Web - http://.demon.co.uk/Tangent/redlion. VAT: Spec.

Stewart Antiques

High St. GU28 0AU. (John and Sandra Moore). Est. 1984. Open 10-5.30, Sun. by appointment. SIZE: Medium. *STOCK: Stripped pine, Victorian, £25-£2,000; kitchenalia, Victorian, £5-£100; collectables, 19th-20th C, £1-£50.* LOC: Town centre. PARK: Easy. TEL: 01798 342136. SER: Valuations. VAT: Spec.

J.C. Tutt Antiques

Angel St. GU28 0BQ. Open 10-5. CL: Some Mon. SIZE: Large. *STOCK: Mahogany and country furniture and accessories.* PARK: Nearby. TEL: 01798 343221.

T.G. Wilkinson Antiques Ltd BADA

Lombard St. GU28 0AG. (T. and S. Wilkinson). Est. 1979. Open 10-5.30. SIZE: Medium. *STOCK: English and Continental furniture, paintings and works of art, 17th-19th C, £500-£15,000.* PARK: Town centre. TEL: 01798 344443. VAT: Stan/Spec.

PORTSLADE

J. Powell (Hove) Ltd LAPADA

20 Wellington Rd. BN4 1DN. Est. 1949. Open 7.30-5.30. CL: Sun. and Sat. pm. except by appointment. SIZE: Large. *STOCK: Bookcases, display cabinets, £110-£1,500; writing tables and desks, £120-£1,200; longcase and bracket clocks, £50-£2,000; general furniture, shipping goods, 18th-20th C, £5-£1,500.* Not Stocked: Porcelain, jewellery, silver. LOC: 150yds. west of Boundary Rd., on seafront. PARK: Easy. TEL: 01273 411599; fax - 01273 421591; home - 01273 593274. SER: Restorations (furniture). VAT: Stan.

PULBOROUGH

Thakeham Furniture

Marehill Rd. RH20 2DY. (T.J.G. Chavasse). Est. 1988. Open Fri. and Sat. 9-5. SIZE: Medium. *STOCK: Furniture and clocks, 1750-1880, £100-£5,000.* LOC: 1 mile east of Pulborough. PARK: Easy. TEL: 01798 872006. SER: Restorations (furniture); buys at auction (furniture). VAT: Stan/Spec.

SAYERS COMMON

Recollect Studios

The Old School, London Rd. BN6 9HX. (P. Jago) Est. 1970. Open 10-5. CL: Mon. and Sat. *STOCK: Dolls, dolls house miniatures, doll restoration materials.* LOC: B2118. PARK: Own. TEL: 01273 833314. SER: Restorations (dolls); catalogues available (£2 cash/stamps).

SOUTH HARTING, Nr. Petersfield (Hants.)

Julia Holmes Antique Maps and Prints

South Gardens Cottage. GU31 5QJ. By appointment only. SIZE: Medium. *STOCK: Maps 1600-1850, £10-£1,000; prints, especially sporting, all periods, to £500.* LOC: End of main street, on the Chichester road. PARK: Opposite. TEL: 01730 825040. SER: Valuations; restorations (cleaning and colouring maps and prints); framing; buys at auction; catalogues. FAIRS: Local and major sporting events. VAT: Stan.

STEYNING

David R. Fileman

Squirrels, Bayards. BN44 3AA. Open daily. *STOCK: Table glass, £20-£1,000; chandeliers, candelabra, £500-£20,000; all 18th-19th C. Collectors' items, 17th-19th C, £25-£2,000; paperweights, 19th C, £50-£5,000.* LOC: A283 to north of Steyning village. TEL: 01903 813229. SER: Valuations; restorations (chandeliers and candelabra). VAT: Stan/Spec.

STORRINGTON

Stable Antiques

46 West St. RH20 4EE. (Ian J. Wadey). Est. 199[illegible] Open 10-6 including Sun. SIZE: Large. *STOCK: General antiques, furniture and bric-a-brac, £1-£1,000.* LOC: A283 west of A24 towards Pulborough, just before Amberley turn. PARK: Easy. TEL: 01903 740555; home - 01903 740441.

TILLINGTON, Nr. Petworth

Loewenthal Antiques

Tillington Cottage. GU28 0RA. CL: Wed. *STOCK: 18th C furniture and objets d'art.* LOC: A272, 1 mile west of Petworth. TEL: 0179[illegible] 342969.

WARNHAM, Nr Horsham

Sayer Antiques

Bailing Hill Farmhouse. Est. 1971. Open by appointment, including Sun. *STOCK: 19th-20th C French furniture and decorative antiques.* PARK: Easy. TEL: 01403 257546; fax - 01403 269880; mobile - 0585 191652. SER: Containers. VAT: Margin. *Trade Only.*

WASHINGTON

Chanctonbury Antiques

Clematis Cottage. RH20 4AP. (G. D. Troche). Est. 1961. Open by appointment only. SIZE: Small. *STOCK: Pottery, porcelain, needlework, small furniture and collectables.* LOC: Just off A24. PARK: Easy. TEL: 01903 892233.

Early 19th century painting of a horse in a storm. (Above) During restoration showing removal of discoloured varnish, and (top) the painting after completion of restoration by Plowden & Smith of London.

From an article entitled "Restoration of Oil Paintings" by Julie Targett which appeared in the June 1997 issue of **Antique Collecting.**

WESTBOURNE, Nr. Emsworth

Westbourne Antiques

3 Lamb Buildings, The Square. PO10 8SH. (H.. and V.J. Lain). Est. 1951. Open Thurs., Fri. an Sat. 9-5. SIZE: Large. *STOCK: Silver, jeweller collectors' items.* PARK: Nearby. TEL: 0124 373711. SER: Valuations; repairs (jewellery an watches).

WORTHING

A. Biscoe

122 Montague St. BN11 3HG. (R. Byskou). Ope 10-6. *STOCK: Furniture, silver, porcelain, 18th 19th C; jewellery, clocks and objets d'art.* TEL 01903 202489; home - 01903 782723.

Chloe Antiques

61 Brighton Rd. BN11 3EE. (Mrs D. Peters). Es 1960. Open 10-12.30 and 1.30-4.30. CL: Wed SIZE: Small. *STOCK: General antiques, furniture jewellery, china, glass, bric-a-brac.* LOC: Fron Brighton, on main rd. just past Beach House Par on corner. PARK: Opposite. TEL: 01903 202697

Rathbone Law Antiques

7-9 The Arcade. BN11 3AY. (R. Law). Open 10- CL: Some Wed. *STOCK: Victorian an Edwardian fine jewellery, silver, objets d'ar porcelain dolls.* TEL: 01903 200274.

Rococo Antiques

21 Warwick Rd. BN11 3ET. (K.P. Jakes). Ope 11-5. CL: Fri. *STOCK: General antiques.* TEL 01903 235896.

Steyne Antique Gallery

29 Brighton Rd. BN11 3EF. (H.W. and V. Melling). Open 9.30-5.30. CL: Mon. *STOCK Furniture, porcelain, clocks and general antique* TEL: 01903 200079.

Robert Warner and Son Ltd

1-13 South Farm Rd. BN14 7AB. Est. 1940. CL Wed. pm. SIZE: Large. *STOCK: Furniture, bric a-brac.* TEL: 01903 232710; fax - 01903 21751 VAT: Stan.

Wilsons Antiques LAPAD

57/59 Broadwater Rd. BN14 8AH. (F. Wilson Est. 1936. Open 10-5. SIZE: Large. *STOCK Period furniture, 18th-19th C, £100-£10,000 Edwardian furniture, £50-£4,000; decorativ items, 19th C, £10-£750; watercolours and o paintings, 19th-20th C.* Not Stocked: Pine PARK: At rear. TEL: 01903 202059; fax 01903 202059; mobile - 0378 813395. SER Valuations; restorations (furniture). FAIRS Olympia (June); Goodwood House. VAT Stan/Spec.

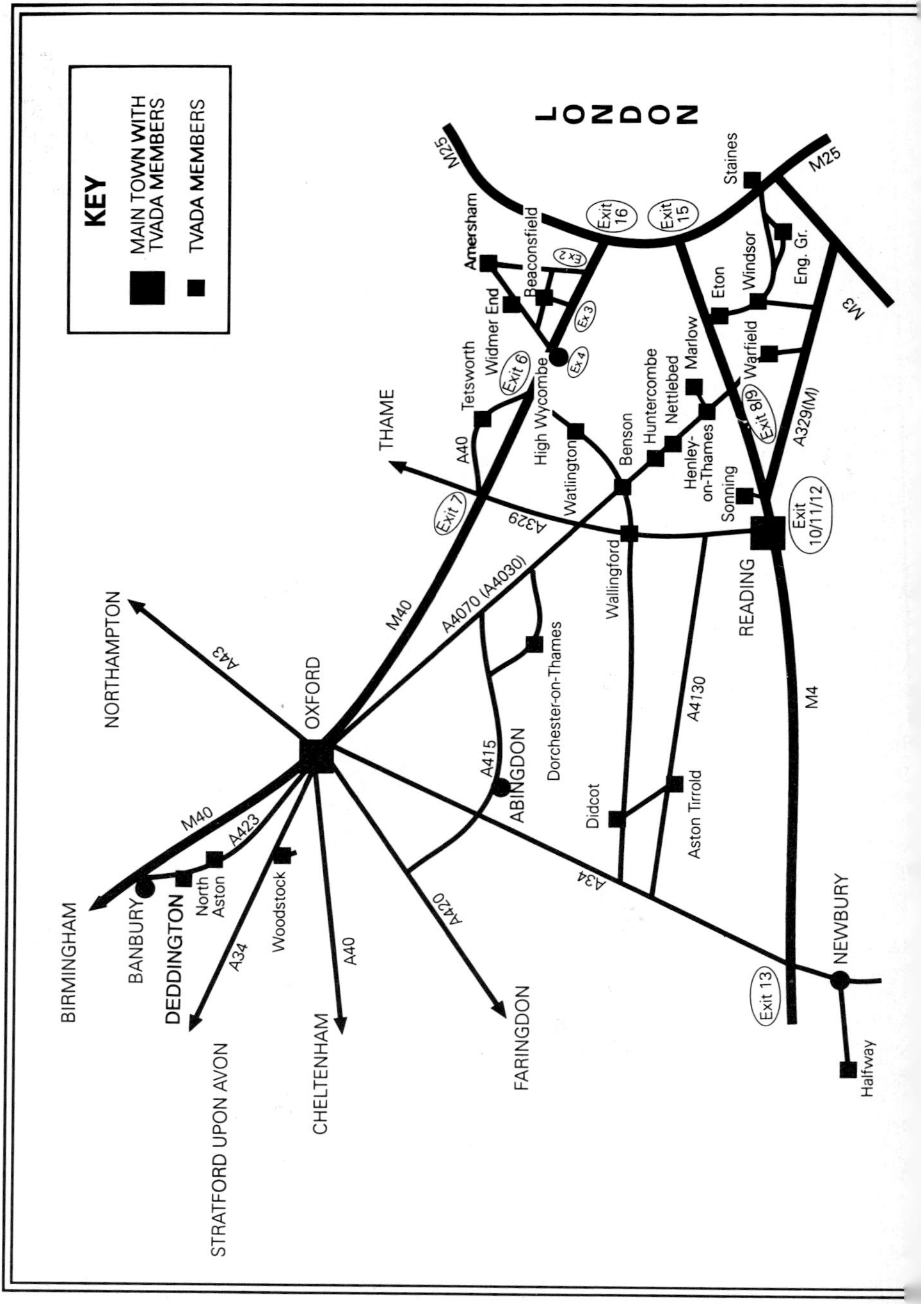
KEY
MAIN TOWN WITH TVADA MEMBERS
TVADA MEMBERS
LONDON
M25
Amersham
Beaconsfield
Ex 2
Exit 16
Exit 15
Staines
M25
Widmer End
Ex 3
Ex 4
Tetsworth
Exit 6
High Wycombe
THAME
A40
Watlington
Benson
Huntercombe
Nettlebed
Marlow
Henley-on-Thames
Eton
Windsor
Eng. Gr.
M3
Warfield
Exit 8/9
A329(M)
Sonning
Exit 10/11/12
READING
Exit 7
A329
Wallingford
A4070 (A4030)
M40
NORTHAMPTON
A43
OXFORD
Dorchester-on-Thames
A415
ABINGDON
A4130
M4
Didcot
Aston Tirrold
M40
A423
BANBURY
DEDDINGTON
North Aston
Woodstock
A34
A40
A420
A34
NEWBURY
Exit 13
Halfway
BIRMINGHAM
STRATFORD UPON AVON
CHELTENHAM
FARINGDON

THAMES VALLEY ANTIQUE DEALERS' ASSOCIATION

T.V.A.D.A.

The Thames Valley Antique Dealers Association has over 40 members offering a vast range of antiques and services to all its customers. The area covered by T.V.A.D.A. stretches from **Windsor** to **Woodstock.** The eastern end of the area is conveniently close to London (less than 20 minutes drive from Heathrow Airport) and is served by the major routes of the M4, M25 and M40.

The Thames Valley area is one of outstanding natural beauty. From the magnificent castle at **Windsor,** following the river you travel through many historic and picturesque towns and villages along the way - past **Eton College,** through Marlow and **Henley,** then the busy town of **Reading,** on to Pangbourne, through Goring Gap, where the river cuts through the Chiltern Hills to **Wallingford,** where the Norman invaders crossed the river on their way to London in 1066, and on again to the pretty village of **Dorchester-on-Thames.** Here the river goes into a big sweeping bend and you can follow this bend through the picturesque village of Clifton Hampden to **Culham** and the market town of Abingdon, then turning northwards, approach the dreaming spires of **Oxford.** From here it is just a short step to the pretty **Woodstock** and Blenheim Palace, with a visit to Churchill's burial place at **Bladon** to round off your visit.

Throughout the area you will find our members - see the gold and black T.V.A.D.A. sign in the windows of their shops, showing our Logo (as above), Old Father Thames (Tamesis), taken from the stone sculpture to be found on Henley Bridge.

You will be welcomed by T.V.A.D.A. members and will find them anxious to give help in finding whatever antique pieces you seek. If the shop in question does not have exactly what you require they will look for it amongst other members of the group. A courier service is available by contacting our office (details below).

The route has a wide variety of antique shops offering an infinite choice of antiques from paintings to furniture, silver to porcelain, collectables and decorative objects for inside and out. For collectors, exporters, trade and tourists alike this is an Aladdin's cave where simple small items or whole consignments can be purchased with ease.

So come and spend some time in the land of 'Three Men in a Boat' and see for yourselves the countryside described by Jerome K Jerome. Sit in a riverside pub or go to a friendly local hotel and browse amongst the treasures this area holds.

For further details please contact the Secretary, T.V.A.D.A., The Old College, Queen Street, Dorchester-on-Thames, Oxon OX10 7HL. Tel/Fax: 01865 341639

AMERSHAM

The Cupboard Antiques LAPADA
80 High St., Old Amersham. HP7 0DS. (N. Lucas). TVADA. Open 10-5. CL: Fri. SIZE: 4 showrooms. *STOCK: Georgian, Regency and early Victorian furniture and decorative items.* PARK: Easy. TEL: 01494 722882.

ASTON TIRROLD, Nr. Didcot

John Harrison Fine Art
Skirmers, Aston St. OX11 9DQ. (J.M.C. Harrison). TVADA. Strictly by appointment. *STOCK: Drawings and watercolours, 18th-19th C.* TEL: 01235 850260. SER: Commissions undertaken.

BEACONSFIELD

Period Furniture Showrooms
49 London End. HP9 2HW. (R.E.W. Hearne and N.J. Hearne). TVADA. Est. 1965. Open 9-5.30. SIZE: Large. *STOCK: Furniture, 1700-1900, £50-£3,000.* LOC: A40 Beaconsfield Old Town. PARK: Own. TEL: 01494 674112; fax - 01494 681046. SER: Restorations (furniture). VAT: Stan/Spec.

BENSON, Nr. Wallingford

Benson Antiques and Gallery
The Old Bakehouse, Castle Sq. OX10 6SD. (Dane Clouston). TVADA. Est. 1978. Open 10-5, Sun. 2-5. CL: Mon. SIZE: Medium. *STOCK: Furniture, 17th to early 20th C, £100-£5,000; ceramics, glass, silver, 18th to early 20th C, £5-£1,000; bronze, pewter, oils and watercolours, 19th-20th C, £25-£5,000.* LOC: Village centre. PARK: Easy. TEL: 01491 832525. SER: Valuations. FAIRS: TVADA.

CAVERSHAM, Nr. Reading

The Clock Workshop LAPADA
17 Prospect St. RG4 8JB. (J. M. Yealland). FBHI, TVADA. Est. 1980. Open 9.30-5.30, Sat. 10-1. SIZE: Small. *STOCK: Clocks, late 17th to late 19th C, £350-£60,000; barometers, 18th-19th C, £500-£8,000.* LOC: Prospect St. is the beginning of main Reading to Henley road. PARK: North St. TEL: 0118 9470741. SER: Valuations; restorations (clocks and barometers); buys at auction. FAIRS: TVADA; LAPADA. VAT: Stan/Spec.

DEDDINGTON

Deddington Antiques Centre
Laurel House, Bull Ring, Market Sq. OX15 0TT (Mrs B. J. Haller). TVADA. Est. 1972. Open 10-5. SIZE: Medium -16 dealers. *STOCK: Furniture, Georgian to Edwardian, £30-1,000; porcelain, silver, pictures, 1800-1930, £10-£400; collectables, £10-£200.* LOC: Off A4260 Oxford-Banbury road at Deddington traffic lights. PARK: Easy, free. TEL: 01869 338968. SER: Valuations. FAIRS: NEC.

DIDCOT

Didcot Antiques Centre
220 The Broadway. (Dr. A. Vetta). TVADA. Est. 1995. Open 10-5, Sun. 11-4. CL: Mon. SIZE: Large. *STOCK: Furniture, £50-£1,000; silver and plate, books and ephemera, all 19th-20th C.* PARK: Own. TEL: 01235 510819; fax - 01235 512178. SER: Valuations; buys at auction.

DORCHESTER-ON-THAMES

Dorchester Antiques (formerly The Shambles) LAPADA
The Barn, 3 High St. OX10 7HH. (J. and S. Hearnden). TVADA. Est. 1992. Open Tues.-Sun. 10-5. SIZE: Medium. *STOCK: Chairs and decorative country pieces, 18th-19th C.* LOC: Opposite Abbey. PARK: Easy. TEL: 01865 341373. SER: Restorations; upholstery; finder.

Hallidays (Fine Antiques) Ltd LAPADA
The Old College, High St. OX10 7HL. TVADA. Est. 1950. Open 9-5, Sat. 10-1 and 2-4. SIZE: Large. *STOCK: Furniture, 17th-19th C, £100-£40,000; paintings, 18th-19th C, £100-£20,000; decorative and small items, pine and marble mantelpieces, firegrates, fenders, 18th-20th C; room panelling.* PARK: At rear. TEL: 01865 340028; fax - 01865 341149. FAIRS: Olympia. VAT: Stan/Spec.

HALFWAY, Nr. Newbury

Walker and Walker BADA
Halfway Manor. RG20 8NR. (Alan and Kyn Walker). TVADA. Open by appointment. *STOCK: Fine barometers and weather instruments.* TEL: 01488 658693; mobile - 0831 147480. SER: Restorations.

'ENLEY-ON-THAMES

he Barry M. Keene Gallery

' Thameside. RG9 1BH. (B.M. and J.S. Keene). VADA, FATG. Est. 1971. Open 9.30-5.30, Sun. l-5.30, and by appointment. *STOCK: Water-olours, drawings, paintings, etchings, prints, 8th to early 20th C, contemporary works and ulpture.* LOC: Junction 8/9 M4, over bridge, mediate left, 5th building on right. TEL: 01491 77119. SER: Restorations; framing, cleaning, lining, gilding, export. VAT: Stan/Spec.

ichard J. Kingston BADA

5 Bell St. RG9 2BD. TVADA. Open 9.30-5 or y appointment. SIZE: Medium. *STOCK: urniture, 17th to early 19th C; silver, porcelain, ass, paintings, antiquarian and secondhand oks.* PARK: Easy. TEL: 01491 574535; home 01491 573133. SER: Restorations. FAIRS: urrey, Buxton, Snape. VAT: Stan/Spec.

hames Gallery

ameside. RG9 2LJ. (S. Came). TVADA. Open)-5. *STOCK: Georgian and Victorian silver; aintings, 19th C.* TEL: 01491 572449; fax - 491 410273.

IGH WYCOMBE

'indmill Fine Art

idmer End. (Ray and Carol White). TVADA. y appointment only. *STOCK: Fine Victorian and rly 20th C watercolours.* TEL: 01494 713757; x - same; mobile - 0585 370408. SER: aluations; commissions search. FAIRS: Most ajor.

UNTERCOMBE

he Country Seat LAPADA

untercombe Manor Barn. RG9 5RY. (W. egg and H. Ferry). TVADA. Est. 1965. Open 5.30, Sun. by appointment. SIZE: Large. *'OCK: Furniture - English, 1660-1830, signed d designed, 1830-1900, Chinese, 19th C; art ttery and metalwork, garden statuary and rniture; panelled rooms, lighting and holstered furniture.* LOC: 200 yds down ght-hand turn off A4130 Nettlebed-allingford. PARK: Easy. TEL: 01491 1349; fax - 01491 641533. SER: Restorations; ys at auction. VAT: Spec.

MARLOW

Glade Antiques

(Sonia Garry). TVADA. By appointment only. *STOCK: Fine Oriental ceramics, bronzes and jades; Chinese items from Han, Tang, Song, Ming and Quing periods; Japanese items - mainly Kakiemon, Nabeshima, Kutani, Satsuma and Imari; also Korean Koryo, Yi and Choson periods.* TEL: 01628 487255; fax - 01628 476601; mobile - 0976 159669.

Marlow Antiques Centre

35 Station Rd. SL7 1NW. (Kay Darby and Keith Hill). TVADA. SIZE: 30+ dealers. *STOCK: Wide range and general antiques and collectables including Georgian, Victorian and Edwardian furniture, country pine, silver, glass, china, bedsteads, clocks, old tools and garden items, cameras books, jewellery.* TEL: 01628 473223; fax - 01628 778834.

NETTLEBED, Nr. Henley-on-Thames

Willow Antiques and The Nettlebed Antique Merchants

The Barns, 1 High St. RG9 5AA. (Willow Bicknell and Michael Plummer). TVADA. Open Tues.-Sat 9-5.30, Sun. 11-4, other times by appointment. SIZE: Large. *STOCK: Decorative, fine and unusual furniture, objects and decorations, including architectural items.* LOC: Between Wallingford and Henley on A4074. PARK: Easy. TEL: 01491 642062; mobile - 0378 152353. SER: Cottage Upholstery - fabrics; upholstery.

NORTH ASTON

Elizabeth Harvey-Lee

1 West Cottages, Middle Aston Lane. OX6 3QB. TVADA. Est. 1986. Open by appointment. *STOCK: Original prints, 15th-20th C; artists' etchings, engravings, lithographs, £100-£6,000.* LOC: 6 miles from junction 10, M40, 15 miles north of Oxford. TEL: 01869 347164. SER: Illustrated catalogue available twice yearly (£12 p.a.). FAIRS: London Original Print, Royal Academy. VAT: Spec.

OXFORD

Magna Gallery

41 High St. OX1 4AP. (Martin J. Blant). TVADA. Est. 1969. Open 10-5.30. SIZE: Medium. *STOCK: Maps especially Oxfordshire, general topography, prints including botanical, caricatures, 1550-1895.* TEL: 01865 245805. SER: Valuations; framing. VAT: Stan.

READING

P.D. Leatherland Antiques

68 London St. RG1 4SQ. TVADA. Est. 1970. Open 9-5. *STOCK: Furniture, 18th C to 1920's; decorative china, clocks, metalware, mirrors and pictures, £5-£4,000.* PARK: Easy. TEL: 0118 9581960. VAT: Stan/Spec.

SONNING-ON-THAMES

Cavendish Fine Arts - Janet Middlemiss LAPADA

The Dower House. RG4 6UL. TVADA. Open by appointment only. *STOCK: Fine Queen Anne and English Georgian furniture, glass and porcelain.* TEL: 01189 691904; mobile - 0831 295575. VAT: Stan/Spec.

STAINES

Margaret Melville Watercolours LAPADA

11 Colnebridge, Market Sq. TW18 4RZ. TVADA. Est. 1980. Open by appointment only. *STOCK: English watercolours, 1850-1950, £75-£7,000.* TEL: 01784 455395. SER: Valuations; commissions. FAIRS: Eton College (Easter); Oxford (Oct); Bellhouse Hotel, Beaconsfield 2nd. Sun. each month; LAPADA; NEC (Jan.); Penman Fairs ('phone for tickets). VAT: Spec.

TETSWORTH, Nr. Thame

The Swan at Tetsworth

High St. OX9 7AB. TVADA. Est. 1995. Open every day including Sun. LOC: A40, 5 minutes from junctions 6 and 8, M40. PARK: Own large. TEL: 01844 281777; fax - 01844 281770. SER: Valuations; restorations (clocks, cabinet work and gilding).

WALLINGFORD

The Lamb Arcade

83 High St. OX10 0BX. TVADA. Open 10-5, Sat. 10-5.30. TEL: 01491 835166. SER: Restorations (furniture).

Wallingford continued

Summers Davis Antiques Ltd BAD LAPAD

Calleva House, 6 High St. OX10 0BP. (Graha Wells). CINOA, TVADA. Est. 1917. Open 8.3 5.30, Sat. 9-5, Sun. 11-5. SIZE: Large. *STOC English and Continental furniture, decorati items and objects.* Not Stocked: Silver, shippi goods. LOC: From London, shop is on le 50yds. from Thames Bridge. PARK: Opposit behind castellated gates. TEL: 01491 83628 fax - 01491 833443. VAT: Spec.

WARFIELD

Moss End Antique Centre

Moss End Garden Centre. RG12 6EJ. TVAD Open 10.30-5. CL: Mon. SIZE: Large - dealers. *STOCK: General antiques a collectables.* LOC: A3095. PARK: Own. TE 01344 861942.

WATLINGTON, Nr. Oxford

Cross Antiques

37 High St. OX9 5PZ. (R.A. and I.D. Crawle TVADA. Est. 1986. Open 10-6, Sun. and Wed. appointment. SIZE: Small. *STOCK: Furnitu £100-£5,000; decorative smalls, clocks a garden items, £50-£2,000; all 1600-1900.* LO Off B4009 in village centre. PARK: Easy and rear. TEL: 01491 612324; home - same.

Stephen Orton Antiques

The Antiques Warehouse, Shirburn Rd. O 5BZ. TVADA. Open Mon.-Fri. 9-5, other tin by appointment. SIZE: Warehouse. *STOCK: 18 19th C furniture, some decorative items.* LOC mins. from exit 6, M40. TEL: 01491 613752; - 01491 613875. SER: Valuations; restoratio buying agent. VAT: Stan/Spec.

Mark Shanks BA

The Royal Oak, High St. OX9 5QB. TVAD Est. 1960. Open 10-5 or by appointme *STOCK: Furniture, £100-£20,000; baromete £100-£10,000; both mainly 18th-19th Decorative items, £50-£5,000.* Not Stocke Silver, jewellery, coins. LOC: 3 miles fr junction 6, M40. Turn right into High St. (o way). PARK: Own. TEL: 01491 613317; fa 01491 613318.

VINDSOR AND ETON

'ountry Furniture
) St. Leonards Rd., Windsor. SL4 3BZ. (Jan -ks and Austin Maude). TVADA. Open 9.30-.30. *STOCK: French provincial furniture and nusual decorative items.* TEL: 01753 830154; ıx - same.

hirley Hayden Antiques
) High St., Eton. SL4 6AF. TVADA. Est. 1980. pen 10-5.30, Sun. 11.30-5. SIZE: Small. *TOCK: English mahogany furniture, 18th-19th , £350-£4,500; decorative items - pictures, irrors, lamps and porcelain.* LOC: First ntiques shop on left over the bridge from Vindsor. PARK: Meadow Lane. TEL: 01753 33085; home - 01753 540203. FAIRS: TVADA. AT: Spec.

eter J. Martin
) High St., Eton. SL4 6BD. TVADA. Est. 1963. pen 9-1 and 2-5. CL: Sun. SIZE: Large and arehouse. *STOCK: Period, Victorian and corative furniture and furnishings, £50-£5,000; etalware, £10-£500, all from 1800.* PARK:)yds. opposite. TEL: 01753 864901; home - 1753 863987. SER: Restorations; shipping ranged; buys at auction. VAT: Stan/Spec.

lorgan Stobbs
7 High St., Eton. SL4 6AX. (Glenn Morgan). VADA. Open 10.30-5.30, Sun. 1-5. *STOCK: rts & Crafts, Art Deco furniture and objects, 380-1940.* TEL: 01753 840631.

riental Rug Gallery Ltd
15-116 High St., Eton. SL4 6AQ. (Richard Iathias and Julian Blair). TVADA, BORDA. pen 10-5.30. *STOCK: Russian, Afghan, Turkish nd Persian carpets, rugs and kelims; Oriental bjets d'art.* PARK: Behind showroom. TEL: 753 623000; fax - same.

VOODSTOCK

hris Baylis Country Chairs
linstrel House, 60 Oxford St. OX20 1TT. VADA. Open 10.30-5, Sun. 11-5. *STOCK: nglish country chairs, from 1780; Windsors, dder and spindlebacks, kitchen chairs; good untry furniture and reproductions including rm tables and chairs.* TEL: 01993 813887; fax - 993 812379.

ees Antiques
) High St. OX20 1TG. (Jo and Jim Bateman). VADA. Est. 1991. Open 10-1 and 1.30-5, Sun. -5. CL: Tues. SIZE: Small. *STOCK: Pottery, rcelain and glass, 18th-20th C, £30-£1,500; nall furniture, 19th to early 20th C, £50-£2,000;*

Woodstock continued

metalware, 19th C, £30-£200; jewellery, 19th-20th C, £30-£1,000. LOC: Just off A3440 Oxford/Stratford-on-Avon road, in town centre. PARK: Opposite. TEL: 01993 811062; home - 01993 771593. SER: Valuations; buys at auction (as stock). FAIRS: Wakefield Ceramics; TVADA.

Span Antiques
6 Market Place. OX20 1TA. TVADA. Est. 1978. Open 10-1 and 2-5, Sun 1-5. SIZE: Medium. LOC: Near Town Hall. PARK: Easy. TEL: 01993 811332.

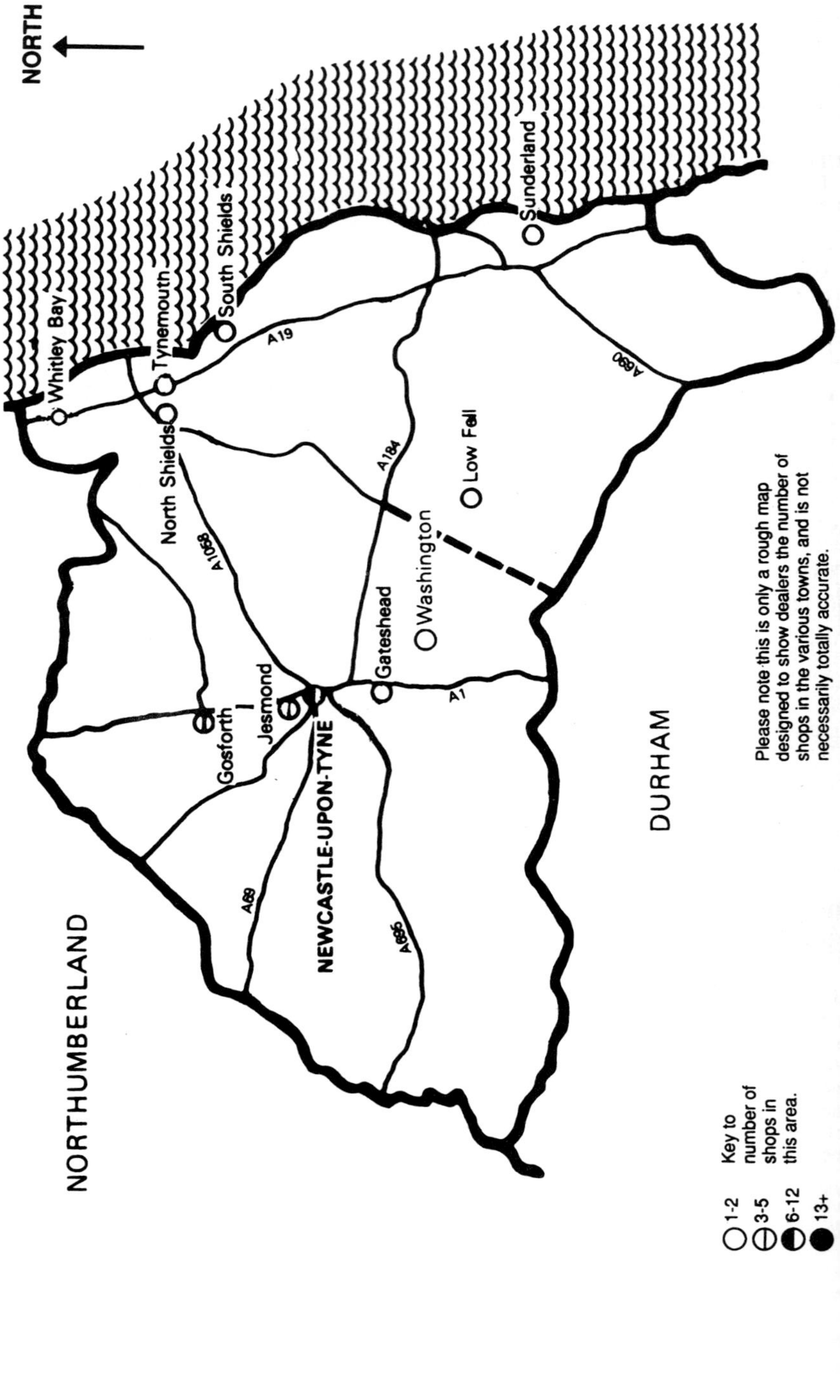
NORTH
Whitley Bay
Tynemouth
South Shields
Sunderland
North Shields
A19
A690
A184
Low Fell
Washington
A1058
Gateshead
Gosforth
Jesmond
NEWCASTLE-UPON-TYNE
A1
A69
A695
NORTHUMBERLAND
DURHAM
Please note this is only a rough map designed to show dealers the number of shops in the various towns, and is not necessarily totally accurate.
Key to number of shops in this area.
1-2
3-5
6-12
13+

;ATESHEAD

·overeign Antiques
5 The Boulevard, Antique Village, Metrocentre. ·E11 9YN. Open Mon.-Wed. 10-8, Thurs. 10-9, ·at. 9-6. *STOCK: Fine antique and modern ·wellery, diamonds, silver, original prints and ·aps.* TEL: 0191 460 9604; fax - 0191 460 7600.

;OSFORTH, Nr. Newcastle-upon-Tyne

·ntiques
· H. & S. Collectables, 149 Salters Rd. NE3 DU. (H. and Mrs S. Shorrick). Est. 1989. Open)-5, Sun. by appointment. SIZE: Small. *STOCK: 'eneral antiques, china, clocks and collectable ·ems, 1800-1930, £5-£900.* LOC: Off High St, ·rner of Linden Road. PARK: Easy. TEL: 0191 84 6626; home - 0191 286 3498.

;ausey Antique Shop
ausey St. NE3 4DL. *STOCK: Silver, Victoriana ·nd collectors' items.*

·nna Harrison Antiques Centre
LAPADA

·range Park, Great North Rd. NE3 2DQ. Est. ·976. Open 10-5, Sat. 10.30-5. SIZE: Large. *TOCK: Furniture and porcelain, 18th-20th C, 20-£2,000; paintings and prints, 19th-20th C, 50-£2,000.*LOC: Old A1 through Gosforth. ARK: Easy. TEL: 0191 284 3202. SER: Valu- ·tions; restorations (upholstery, French ·olishing, cabinet making, china). VAT: ·tan/Spec.

·nna Harrison Fine Antiques LAPADA
·range Park, Great North Rd. NE3 2DQ. Est. ·976. Open 9-5. SIZE: Large. *STOCK: English ·rniture, porcelain, oils and watercolours.* LOC: ·6125, 3 miles north of city centre, near Regent ·entre. PARK: Forecourt. TEL: 0191 284 3202. ·ER: Valuations; restorations. VAT: Stan/Spec.

lacDonald Fine Art
Ashburton Rd. NE3 4JB. (T. and C. MacDonald). ·st. 1976. Open 10-1 and 2.30-5.30. CL: Wed. ·ZE: Medium. *STOCK: Watercolours and oils, ·ainly north-eastern artists, English and Scottish, ·8th-20th C.* LOC: 1 mile west of A1. PARK: ·asy. TEL: 0191 284 4214; home - 0191 285 6188. ·ER: Valuations; restorations (watercolours and ·ls); framing; buys at auction (watercolours and ·ls). VAT: Spec.

·ESMOND, Nr. Newcastle-upon-Tyne

·eoffrey Hugall
· Clayton Rd. NE2 4RP. Est. 1970. Open 10-5 or · appointment. SIZE: Medium. *STOCK: General ·ntiques, furniture, china, silver, period and ·corative items.* Not Stocked: Weapons, musical ·struments, books. PARK: Easy. TEL: 0191 281 ·08. SER: Valuations. VAT: Stan/Spec.

Jesmond continued

Owen Humble LAPADA
11-12 Clayton Rd. NE2 4RP. Est. 1958. Open 6 days. SIZE: Large and warehouse. *STOCK: Furniture, general antiques.* PARK: Easy. TEL: 0191 281 4602; fax - 0191 281 9076. SER: Restorations. VAT: Stan/Spec.

Osborne Art and Antiques
18c Osborne Rd. NE2 2AD. (F.T. and J. Jackman). Est. 1974. Open 10-5.15. *STOCK: Victorian oil paintings and watercolours, drawings, topographical engravings and antiquarian maps, etchings, marine etchings, 19th-20th C.* TEL: 0191 281 6380. SER: Restorations (pictures); bespoke picture-framing. VAT: Stan/Spec.

LOW FELL, Nr. Gateshead

N. Jewett
639/643 Durham Rd. NE9 5HA. Est. 1948. SIZE: Large. *STOCK: Antique and reproduction furniture, glass, china, £5-£5,000.* LOC: On A6127, 3 miles south of Newcastle-upon-Tyne. PARK: Easy. TEL: 0191 487 7636. SER: Valuations. VAT: Stan/Spec.

NEWCASTLE-UPON-TYNE

Antiques Centre
8-10 St. Mary's Place East. NE1 7PN. (B. and G. Punton). Est. 1985. Open 10-5. CL: Mon. SIZE: 18 dealers. *STOCK: General antiques and collectables.* LOC: Opposite Civic Centre. PARK: Nearby. TEL: 0191 232 3821/232 9832. SER: Valuations; restorations (furniture); metal polishing; repairs (watch/clock, jewellery). FAIRS: York, Leeds, Glasgow. VAT: Stan.

Davidson's The Jewellers Ltd
94 and 96 Grey St. NE1 6AG. Open 9-5. *STOCK: Jewellery, silver.* TEL: 0191 232 2551/232 2895.

The Dean Gallery Ltd
42 Dean St. NE1 1PG. Est. 1970. Open 10-5. CL: Sat. pm. SIZE: Large. *STOCK: Oils, watercolours, local and national, 18th to early 20th C, £500-£10,000.* LOC: Going north over Tyne Bridge, turn left, and left again. PARK: Easy. TEL: 0191 232 1208. SER: Valuations; restorations; framing. VAT: Stan/Spec.

Intercoin
103 Clayton St. NE1 5PZ. Open 9-4.30. *STOCK: Coins and items of numismatic interest; jewellery, silver.* LOC: City centre. TEL: 0191 232 2064.

Steve Johnson Medals & Militaria
P O Box 1SP. NE99 1SP. *STOCK: Medals and militaria.* TEL: Fax - 01207 545073. Mail Order Only

Newcastle-upon-Tyne continued

Owen's Jewellers

14 Shields Rd., Byker. NE6 1DR. (D.W. Robertson). Est. 1968. Open 9-5. *STOCK: Jewellery.* TEL: 0191 265 4332.

Shiners Architectural Reclamation

123 Jesmond Rd. NE2 1JY. (B. and A. Lawson). Open 9-5. SIZE: Large. *STOCK: Architectural items including Victorian and Edwardian fireplaces.* LOC: On main road. PARK: Easy. TEL: 0191 281 6474. SER: Valuations; metal polishing.

R.D. Steedman

9 Grey St. NE1 6EE. Est. 1907. CL: Sat. pm. *STOCK: Rare books.* TEL: 0191 232 6561.

NORTH SHIELDS

Maggie May's

(Incorporating Tynemouth Fine Art) 49 Kirton Park Terrace. NE29 0LJ. (Miss M.L. Hayes). Est. 1960. Open Thurs.-Sat. 11-5.30. SIZE: Medium. *STOCK: General antiques and collectors' items, Art Deco, Victorian and Edwardian furniture, china, glass; paintings and watercolours, especially Northumbrian artists, 1800-1950; Continental furniture, glassware, porcelain, decorative items, gramophones.* LOC: Opposite The Gunner Inn. TEL: 0191 237 6933. SER: Valuations; restorations; framing; French polishing; buys at auction.

SOUTH SHIELDS

The Curiosity Shop

16 Frederick St. NE33 5EA. Est. 1969. CL: Wed. *STOCK: General antiques, paintings, jewellery, furniture, Royal Doulton.* TEL: 0191 456 5560.

SUNDERLAND

Peter Smith Antiques LAPADA

12-14 Borough Rd. SR1 1EP. Est. 1968. Open 9.30-4.30, Sat. 10-1, other times by appointment. SIZE: Warehouse. *STOCK: Georgian, Victorian, Edwardian longcase clocks, shipping goods, £5-£15,000.* LOC: 10 miles from A1(M); towards docks/Hendon from town centre. PARK: Easy. TEL: 0191 567 3537/567 7842; fax - 0191 514 2286; home - 0191 514 0008. SER: Valuations; restorations; some shipping; containers packed; buys at auction. VAT: Stan/Spec.

TYNEMOUTH

Renaissance Antiques

11 Front St. NE30 4RG. (E. and N. Moore). E 1977. Open Mon., Tues. and Sat. 10.30-1 and 2- SIZE: Medium and trade goods store. *STOC Furniture, Victorian to Art Deco, £50-£1,00 china and porcelain, silver, brass and copper, £ £100; shipping goods.* LOC: Main coast ro from Newcastle. PARK: Easy. TEL: 0191 2 5555; home - 0191 257 4073. SER: Valuations.

Ian Sharp Antiques

23 Front St. NE30 4DX. Open 10-5.30 or appointment. *STOCK: Furniture, 18th to ea 20th C; British oil paintings and watercolou British pottery including northern especia Sunderland and Tyneside lustreware, 18th early 20th C.* TEL: 0191 296 0656.

WASHINGTON

Harold J. Carr Antiques LAPA

Field House, Rickleton. NE38 9HQ. Open appointment. *STOCK: General antiques a furniture.* TEL: 0191 388 6442. SER: Shipper

Grate Expectations (Fireplaces)

Unit 6, Lee Close, Pattinson North Industr Estate. NE38 8QA. (Geoffrey Moore). Est. 19 Open 9-5. SIZE: Large. *STOCK: Fireplaces, £ £550; fireplace accessories, £10-£125; both 1 C.* LOC: Close to A1 and A19. PARK: Easy. TE 0191 416 0609. SER: Restorations (cast-ir refurbishment, repair and welding). VAT: Stan.

WHITLEY BAY

Northumbria Pine

54 Whitley Rd. NE26 2NF. (C. and V. Dowlan Est. 1979. Open 9-5.30. SIZE: Medium. *STOC Stripped pine and reproduction items.* LO Cullercoats end of Whitley Rd., behind sea fro PARK: Easy. TEL: 0191 252 4550. VAT: Stan.

Treasure Chest

2 and 4 Norham Rd. Est. 1974. Open 10.30-1 a 2-4. CL: Wed. and Thurs. SIZE: Small. *STOC General antiques.* LOC: Just off main shoppi area of Park View, leading to Monkseat Railway Station. PARK: Easy. TEL: 0191 2 2052.

NORTH

LEICS

Coleshill

Bulkington

Stretton-under-Fosse

WEST MIDLANDS

Brinklow

WORCS

Kenilworth

Hatton

Henley-in-Arden

Leamington Spa

Warwick

Dunchurch

NORTHANTS

Alcester

Gaydon

Bidford-on-Avon

Stratford-upon-Avon

Atherstone

Stretton on Fosse

Shipston-on-Stour

OXFORD

GLOS

| Key to |
| number of |
| ○ 1-2 | shops in |
| ⊖ 3-5 | this area. |
| ◓ 6-12 |
| ● 13+ |

Please note this is only a rough map
designed to show dealers the number of
shops in the various towns, and is not
necessarily totally accurate.

ALCESTER

High St. Antiques

11A High St. B49 5AE. (B.J. Payne). Est. 1979. Open Tues. 11-1 and 2.30-4.30, Fri. 11-1, Sat. 11-1 and 2.30-5. SIZE: Small. *STOCK: Glass and china, 18th-20th C, £5-£200; brass, copper and silver, 19th-20th C, £5-£100+; postcards and Art Deco china.* LOC: On left-hand side near church coming from Stratford-on-Avon road. PARK: Rear of High St. TEL: 01789 764009; home - same. SER: Valuations.

Malthouse Antiques Centre

Market Place. B49 5AE. (J. and P. Allcock). Est. 1982. Open 10-5, Sun. 2-5. SIZE: Large. *STOCK: Furniture, china, silver, collectables and objets d'art, 18th-20th C, £1-£2,000.* LOC: Adjacent to free town car park. TEL: 01789 764032. SER: Restorations.

ATHERSTONE

Down Memory Lane

18-20 Church St. (Mrs Lynne Robinson). Est. 1989. Open 9-5, Thurs. 9-1, Sun. 10-3. SIZE: Large. *STOCK: Oak and country furniture, 17th-18th C, £50-£1,000; Victorian and Edwardian furniture, £50-£500; clocks, 1720's to 1930's, £30-£1,500; smalls including china.* LOC: Off A5, shop on market square. PARK: Easy, at rear. TEL: 01827 7133335. SER: Valuations; buys at auction.

BIDFORD-ON-AVON

Bidford Antiques Centre

High St. Est. 1983. Open 10-5, Tues. until 7, Sun. 2-5. SIZE: 12 dealers. *STOCK: Furniture, china, glass, jewellery, pictures, books, records, linen, collectables.* PARK: Easy. TEL: 01789 773680.

BRINKLOW, Nr. Rugby

Cottage Pine Antiques

19 Broad St. CV23 0LS. (Chris and Jill Peters). Est. 1987. Open 10-5.30, Sun. by appointment. SIZE: Medium. *STOCK: Pine furniture including wardrobes, armoires, dressers, chests of drawers, 18th-19th C, £250-£2,000.* LOC: B4455 Fosseway; 15 minutes M40, M1, M6. PARK: Easy. TEL: 01788 832673; home - 01926 632517. SER: Valuations; restorations (pine stripping and repairs); buys at auction (period oak and pine). VAT: Stan/Spec.

BULKINGTON, Nr. Nuneaton

Sport and Country Gallery LAPADA

Northwood House. CV12 9RX. (R. and S. Hill). Open any time by appointment. *STOCK: 19th-20th C oils and watercolours; bronzes and small furniture.* TEL: 01203 314335. VAT: Spec.

COLESHILL

Coleshill Antiques and Interiors Ltd

12 and 14 High St. B46 1AZ. (A.J. Webster). E 1958. Open Tues.-Sat. 9.30-5, or by appointme SIZE: Large. *STOCK: Porcelain, furniture, jew lery and silver, £100-£10,000.* LOC: 1 mile fro NEC. PARK: Easy. TEL: 01675 462931; 016 467416. SER: Valuations; restorations; repai VAT: Stan/Spec.

DUNCHURCH, Nr. Rugby

Dunchurch Antique Centre

16/16a Daventry Rd. CV22 6NS. (M. and Mrs Vandervelden). Est. 1981. Open 10-5 includi Sun. SIZE: Medium - 18 dealers. *STOCK: Mai pre-1930 house furnishings and fitmen collectors' items, toys, antiquities, fireplac clocks, shipping goods and pine.* LOC: Oppos Guy Fawkes cottage. PARK: Easy. TEL: 017 817147. VAT: Stan/Spec.

GAYDON

MPA Warwick Ltd LAPA

(Martin Payne). Est. 1971. Open by appoi ment only. *STOCK: Silver especially cutl including canteens, 18th-19th C.* TEL: 019 641109; mobile - 0850 494948. SER: Va ations; restorations. FAIRS: Most maj VAT: Spec.

HATTON, Nr. Warwick

The Stables Antique Centre

Hatton Country World, Dark Lane. CV35 7L (John and Margaret Colledge). Est. 1990. Op 10-5 including Sun. SIZE: Large - 25 uni *STOCK: Furniture, 18-19th C, £50-£3,000; chi 19th-20th C, £5-£200; clocks, 18th-19th C, £2 £4,000; linen, glass,brass and copper, painti and prints, kitchenalia and jewellery.* LOC: J off A4177 Solihull-Warwick road, 5 minutes fr junction 15, M40. PARK: Own. TEL: 019 842405; home - 01926 499731. SER: Valuation

Summersons

The Stables Antique Centre, Hatton Coun World. CV35 8XA. (Peter Lightfoot). CMB Open 10-5 including Sun. *STOCK: Clocks a barometers.* TEL: 01926 843443. SER: Rest ations; horological and barometer materi supplied.

HENLEY-IN-ARDEN

Arden Gallery

B95 5AN. (G.B. Horton). Est. 1963. Open 1 CL: Sat. SIZE: Medium. *STOCK: Oil paintin Victorian, £20-£1,000; watercolours, all peric to £1,500; portrait miniatures.* LOC: A34 PARK: Easy. TEL: 01564 792520. VAT: Spec.

Ienley-in-Arden continued

Colmore Galleries Ltd LAPADA
'2 High St. B95 5AN. Open 11-5.30, Sat. 11-.30. *STOCK: Pictures, 19th-20th C.* TEL: 1564 792938; fax - same. SER: Valuations; estorations; framing.

KENILWORTH

Janice Paull Antiques BADA LAPADA
Beehive House, 125 Warwick Rd. CV8 1HY. Est. 1965. Open by appointment. SIZE: Medium. *STOCK: Mason's Ironstone, 1813-880; pottery.* LOC: Main st. PARK: At rear. EL: 01926 855253; fax - 01926 863384; mobile - 0831 691254. FAIRS: Olympia June/Nov); Kenilworth (March/Oct). VAT: Spec.

LEAMINGTON SPA

Hague Antiques
Regent St. (J. Hague). Est. 1967. Open 10-2.30. SIZE: Medium. *STOCK: Pine including oors, fireplaces and cupboard fronts.* LOC: One f the main roads which cross the Parade. PARK: asy. TEL: 01926 337236. VAT: Stan/Spec.

David Hooper Antiques
) Regent St. CV32 5HQ. Open 10-6. *STOCK: eneral antiques, fairground, circus and unusual ms.* TEL: 01926 429679.

The Incandescent Lighting Company
5 Regent St. CV32 5EG. (Mrs Patricia unningham). Est. 1988. Open 9.30-5.30, Sat. 9-SIZE: Medium. *STOCK: Lighting and pecially glass shades, 19th to early 20th C, £25-2,500; reproduction period-style lighting, shades d components, £2-£1,000.* LOC: Town centre. ARK: Easy. TEL: 01926 422421. SER: Valuions. VAT: Stan.

King's Cottage Antiques LAPADA
Windsor St. CV32 5EB. (G. and A. Jackson). pen 9.30-5. *STOCK: Early oak and country rniture, 16th-18th C.* TEL: 01926 422927.

Leamington Pine and Antique Centre
Regent St. CV32 5HQ. Open 10-6. SIZE: 12 alers. *STOCK: General antiques.* TEL: 01926 9679.

Trading Post
Chandos St. (B. Morris). Est. 1949. Open 10-and 2-4. CL: Thurs. pm. *STOCK: Small neral antiques, Victorian jewellery.* TEL: 01926 1857.

Yesterdays
Portland St. CV32 5EY. (D. and Mrs K. rbury). Est. 1986. Open Tues.-Sat. 10-5. SIZE: edium. *STOCK: Furniture, George III to*

Leamington Spa continued

Edwardian, £75-£3,500; china, prints, 1850-1910, £10-£200. Not Stocked: Pine. LOC: Parallel to The Parade. PARK: Easy. TEL: 01926 450238.

SHIPSTON-ON-STOUR

Fine-Lines (Fine Art) LAPADA
The Old Bake House Gallery, at The Old Rectory Lodge, West St. CV36 4HD. (L.W. and R.M. Guthrie). Est. 1975. Open seven days by appointment only. SIZE: Medium. *STOCK: British and European watercolours, pastels, drawings and selected oils, from 1850, £300-£20,000.* PARK: Easy and nearby. TEL: 01608 662323 (answerphone). SER: Valuations; restorations, cleaning and framing; buys at auction (paintings, watercolours and drawings). VAT: Spec.

The Grandfather Clock Shop
2 Bondgate House, West St., Granville Court. CV36 4AL. (M.S. Chambers). Est. 1978. Open 9.30-5. CL: Mon. and Thurs. pm. SIZE: Medium. *STOCK: Clocks - longcase, pre-1800, £1,000-£4,000; wall, £250-£1,000; mantle and bracket, 1790-1890, £200-£2,000; barometers, 1790-1860, £350-£1,000; furniture including oak, 17th-18th C.* PARK: Easy. TEL: 01608 662144; home - 01926 57487.

Pine and Things
Portobello Farm, Campden Rd. CV36 4PY. (John Hudson). Est. 1991. Open 9-5. SIZE: Large. *STOCK: Pine, 18th-19th C, £50-£1,000.* LOC: A429. PARK: Easy. TEL: 01608 663849; home - same. VAT: Stan/Spec.

'Time in Hand'
11 Church St. CV36 4AP. (F.R. Bennett). Open 9-1 and 2-5.30 or by appointment. SIZE: Large. *STOCK: Longcase, carriage and wall clocks, barometers.* PARK: Town centre. TEL: 01608 662578. SER: Restorations (clocks, watches, barometers and mechanical instruments).

STRATFORD-UPON-AVON

Abode
Shrieve's House, 40 Sheep St. CV37 6EE. (Mrs A. and Miss J. Bannister). Est. 1975. Open 9-5.30. SIZE: Large. *STOCK: Furniture, pine, interior design items.* LOC: Town centre. TEL: 01789 268755. SER: Buys at auction (furniture). VAT: Stan/Spec.

Arbour Antiques Ltd
Poet's Arbour, Sheep St. CV37 6EF. (R.J. Wigington). Est. 1952. Open 9-5, Sat. by appointment. *STOCK: Arms, armour.* LOC: From town centre towards Theatre and River, behind Lamb's Café through archway at right. PARK: Easy. TEL: 01789 293453. VAT: Spec.

Stratford-upon-Avon continued

Art Deco Ceramics

Unit 1 The Courtyard, Stratford Antique Centre, Ely St. CV37 6LN. (Howard and Pat Watson). SIZE: Medium. *STOCK: Art Deco pottery, figurines, face masks and lamps.* Not Stocked: Militaria, coins and stamps. LOC: Town centre. PARK: Nearby. TEL: 01789 204351; home - 01789 299524. SER: Finder. FAIRS: Warwick Midland Art Deco; Alexander Palace; Classic Art Deco, Coventry.

Jean A. Bateman LAPADA

41 Sheep St. CV37 6EE. NAG. Open 9.30-5. *STOCK: Victorian and Georgian jewellery, objets d'art et vertu, including scent bottles.* TEL: 01789 298494. SER: Valuations. VAT: Stan/Spec.

Bow Cottage Antiques

30 Henley St. CV37. (R. Harvey-Morgan). Open 10-5.30. *STOCK: English porcelain, glass, silver, paintings, engravings, maps, books; general antiques, all 18th-20th C, £5-£150+.* TEL: 01789 205883. FAIRS: Classic.

Burman Antiques

34 College St. CV37 6DD. (J. and J. Burman Holtom). Est. 1973. Open by appointment only. *STOCK: Ruskin ware, pot-lids, fishing tackle.* TEL: 01789 295164. SER: Restorations (clocks).

Tim Harrison Wholesale Exports

Hatton Rock. CV37 0NU. Est. 1971. Open by appointment only. SIZE: Warehouse. *STOCK: Shipping goods and large Victorian and Edwardian furniture.* LOC: Off M40, junction 15. PARK: Easy. TEL: Mobile - 0831 299993. *Trade Only.*

Howards Jewellers

44a Wood St. CV37 6JG. (Howards of Stratford Ltd). Est. 1985. Open 9.30-5.30. *STOCK: Jewellery, silver, objets d'art, 19th C.* LOC: Town centre. PARK: Nearby. TEL: 01789 205404. SER: Valuations; restorations (as stock); buys at auction (as stock). VAT: Stan/Spec.

The Loquens Gallery

The Minories, Rother St. CV37 6NE. (S. and J. Loquens). Est. 1975. Open 9.15-5, Sun. by appointment. SIZE: Medium. *STOCK: English watercolours, some oil paintings, late 18th to early 20th C, to £5,000.* LOC: From island in town centre, follow Wood St. to Rother St. junction, entrance to Minories is on right. PARK: Easy. TEL: 01789 297706; home - 01789 750469. SER: Valuations; restorations (cleaning watercolours, relining oils); framing. VAT: Stan/Spec.

Meer Street Antiques Arcade

10A/11 Meer St. (Roy Griffiths). *STOCK: Wide range of general antiques.* LOC: Close to Shakespeare's birthplace. TEL: 01789 297249.

Stratford-upon-Avon continued

Stratford Antique Centre

Ely St. CV37 6LN. (N. Sims). Open 10-5.30 every day. SIZE: 60 dealers. *STOCK: General antiques.* TEL: 01789 204180.

The Stratford Antiques and Interiors Centre Ltd

Dodwell Industrial Park, Evesham Rd. CV37 9ST. (Andrew and Suszanna Kerr). Est. 1980. Open 10-5 including Sun., evenings by appointment. SIZE: 25+ dealers. *STOCK: Georgian, Victorian, Edwardian and shipping furniture, £100-£2,000; china and smalls, 19th-20th C, £5-£300; reclaimed pine, £50-£2,000.* LOC: B439. PARK: Easy. TEL: 01789 297729; fax - 01789 29771[illegible]; home - 01386 765122. SER: Valuations; restorations; buys at auction. FAIRS: Newark and Ardingly.

The Stratford Bookshop

45A Rother St. CV37 6LY. (J. and S. Hill). Est. 1993. Open 10-6. SIZE: Medium. *STOCK: Secondhand and out-of-print books.* LOC: From island in town centre follow Wood St., shop opposite police station. PARK: Easy. TEL: 0178[illegible] 298362.

Robert Vaughan

20 Chapel St. CV37 6EP. (C.M. Vaughan). ABA. Est. 1953. Open 9.30-5.30. SIZE: Medium. *STOCK: Antiquarian and out-of-print books, maps and prints.* LOC: Town centre. PARK: Easy. TEL: 01789 205312. SER: Valuations; buys at auction (books). VAT: Stan.

James Wigington Arms and Armour

'Winchester 73', 276 Alcester Rd. CV37 9Q[illegible]. Open by appointment. *STOCK: General antique arms and armour, cannons, early fishing tackle.* TEL: 01789 261418; fax - 01789 261600.

Windsor Place Antiques Centre

Windsor St. Open 10-5.30, Sun. 11-5. SIZE: Large. *STOCK: Wide variety of general antiques and collectables, 16th-20th C, £20-£20,000.* LOC: 100 yards from Shakespeare's birthplace, Henley St. PARK: Multi-storey opposite. TEL: 017[illegible] 297770; fax - 01789 269722. VAT: Stan/Spec.

STRETTON-ON-FOSSE, Nr. Moreton-in-Marsh

Astley House - Fine Art LAPADA

The Old School. GL56 9SA. (D. and N. Glaisyer). CADA. Est. 1974. Open by appointment. SIZE: Large. *STOCK: Large decorative oil paintings, 19th-20th C.* LOC: Village centre. PARK: Easy. TEL: 01608 650601; fax - 01608 651777. SER: Restorations; framing; exhibitions; mailing list. VAT: Spec.

STRETTON-UNDER-FOSSE, Nr. Rugby

The Old Forge

29 Main St. CV23. (C.J. Hall). Est. 1991. Open 10-1 and 2-5, Sat. and Sun. 11-1 and 2-4.30. CL: Thurs. SIZE: Large. *STOCK: Hardwood furniture, £50-£5,000; pine, £50-£1,000; ceramics, £5-£300; glass, £5-£100.* LOC: Half mile from Fosse Way, 2 miles north of Brinklow and 8 miles north east of Coventry. PARK: Easy. TEL: 01788 832191/833161. SER: Buys at auction (furniture).

WARWICK

Duncan M. Allsop

26 Smith St. CV34 4HS. ABA. Est. 1965. Open 9.30-5.30. SIZE: Medium. *STOCK: Antiquarian and modern books.* LOC: 50yds. east of Eastgate. PARK: Nearby. TEL: 01926 493266.

Apollo Antiques Ltd LAPADA

The Saltisford, Birmingham Rd. CV34 4TD. (R.H. Mynott). Est. 1968. Open 9-6, Sat. 9.30-12.30. SIZE: Large. *STOCK: Period, decorative English and Continental furniture, sculpture, paintings, decorative objects; Victorian, Arts & Crafts and unrestored furniture.* PARK: Easy. TEL: 01926 494746; fax - 01926 401477. VAT: Stan/Spec

Eastgate Fine Arts

Smith St. CV34 4HH. (K. Pittaway). Open 10-.30. *STOCK: Original maps, prints, paintings.* TEL: 01926 499777.

Fynewood Antiques

7 Jury St. CV34 4EH. (R. and C. Haynes). Est. 1976. Open 10-5. SIZE: Medium. *STOCK: Furniture, 18th-19th C, Edwardian, inlaid, £100-5,000.* LOC: Adjoining High St. PARK: Easy. TEL: 01926 49122; home - same. SER: Valuations; buys at auction (furniture). FAIRS: Newark, NEC. VAT: Stan/Spec.

John Goodwin and Sons

3 West St., Westgate. CV34 6AN. Open 8.30-.30, Sat. 10-4 or by appointment. *STOCK: Victorian and Edwardian furniture, paintings, pottery and porcelain, books and collectables.* TEL: 01926 491191; fax - same. SER: Restorations (furniture).

Russell Lane Antiques

4 High St. CV34 4AP. (R.G.H. Lane). Open 10-. *STOCK: Fine jewellery and silver.* TEL: 01926 494494.

Warwick continued

Patrick and Gillian Morley Antiques

LAPADA

62 West St. CV34 6AW. Est. 1968. Open 9-5.30, Sat. and Sun. by appointment. SIZE: Large. *STOCK: Furniture, 17th to late 19th C; unusual and decorative items, sculpture, carvings and textiles; all £50-£20,000.* LOC: Almost opposite Warwick Castle 2nd car park. PARK: Easy. TEL: 01926 494464; home - 01926 54191; mobile - 0468 835040; fax - 01926 400531. SER: Valuations; buys at auction. VAT: Mainly Spec.

Warwick continued

The Old Cornmarket Antiques Centre

70 Market Place. CV34 4SO. (Jonathan Lysaght) Est. 1993. Open 10-5, Sat. 9.30-5.30. LOC: Tow centre. TEL: 01926 419119. Below are listed th dealers at this Centre:

Cliffe Antiques
Est. 1973. *Antique jewellery, silver and porcelain.*

J & S Antiques
(J.Lysaght). *Clocks, from carriage to bracket.*

Midland Goss and Commemoratives
Est. 1978. *Ceramics especially Goss and crested ware.*

Richmond Antiques
(Terry Hare-Walker). Est. 1981. *Period jewellery, wooden boxes, barometers and porcelain.*

James Reeve

at Quinneys of Warwick, 9 Church St. CV 4AB. Est. 1865. Open 9.30-5.30. CL: Sat. pı *STOCK: Furniture, mahogany, oak, and ros wood, 17th-18th C, £80-£8,000; furniture, 19th £50-£3,500; glass, copper, brass, pewter, chin* TEL: 01926 498113. VAT: Stan/Spec.

Smith St. Antiques Centre

7 Smith St. CV34 4JA. (E. Brook and V Mechilli). Est. 1971. Open 10-5.30. SIZE: Larg LOC: Corner position, Smith St. is an extensi of High St. PARK: Easy and at rear. TEL: 019 497864; home - 01926 882060. VAT: Stan/Spe Below are listed the dealers at this centre.

Simon Bowler
Oriental porcelain, silver and furniture.

Erol Brook
Silver and plate, decanters, curios, taxidermy, barometers.

Gary Eames
Furniture, clocks, silver, porcelain, jewellery.

Warwick continued

Eleanor Antiques
(Mrs E. W. E. Creed). *Porcelain, 18th to early 20th C, £5-£500; glass, 18th to early 20th C, £2-£75; needlework tools, 19th-20th C, £2-£25.* TEL: 01926 400554.

Farfalla
Sporting and natural history antiques.

Mick Howe
Cigarette cards. SER: Framing.

Chris James
Military medals, swords, guns.

Walter Mechilli
Silver, plate, porcelain, hickory shafted golf clubs.

Jean Stapley
Silver, porcelain, Doulton figures, jewellery.

Turtons Antiques
Jewellery, silver, gold, pocket watches.

Don Spencer Antiques
36a Market Place. CV34 4SH. Est. 1963. Open daily. SIZE: Large. *STOCK: Desks, 1850-1920, £500-£5,000; dining furniture and bookcases, 1800-1920, £500-£3,000.* PARK: Easy. TEL: 01926 499857/407989; home - 01564 775470. VAT: Stan/Spec.

Vintage Antiques Centre
36 Market Place. CV34 4SH. (Peter Sellors). Est. 1977. Open 10-5.30, Sun. 11-4. SIZE: 15 dealers - cabinets. *STOCK: Ceramics, glass, collectables and small furniture, 19th-20th C.* PARK: Easy. TEL: 01926 491527.

The Warwick Antique Centre
20-22 High St. CV34 4AP. Est. 1973. Open 10-5. SIZE: 25 dealers. *STOCK: Porcelain, silver and plate, jewellery, coins, militaria, books, furniture, stamps, metalware, toys, collectables, postcards, glass.* TEL: 01926 491382/495704..

Warwick Antiques
16-18 High St. CV34 4AP. (M. Morrison). Est. 1969. Open 9-5, Sat. 10-5. SIZE: Large and warehouses. *STOCK: Furniture, mahogany, oak, Chinese; metalware, copper, brass, pewter, glass, china, bygones, curios, statuary, garden furniture, shipping goods.* LOC: Midway between E. and W. Gate clock towers. PARK: At rear. TEL: 01926 492482; fax - 01926 493867. SER: Restorations (furniture). VAT: Stan/Spec.

Westgate Antiques LAPADA
18 West St. CV34 6AN. (D.M. Cunningham). Open 10-5.30, Sat. 10-1. *STOCK: Silver - Sheffield and plate; canteens, mahogany furniture, glass, decorative items and boxes, all*

Warwick continued

***18th-19th C.* LOC: Near town centre, beyond the West Gate. PARK: Easy. TEL: 01926 494106. SER: Valuations; restorations (silver including re-plating, and furniture). VAT: Stan/Spec.**

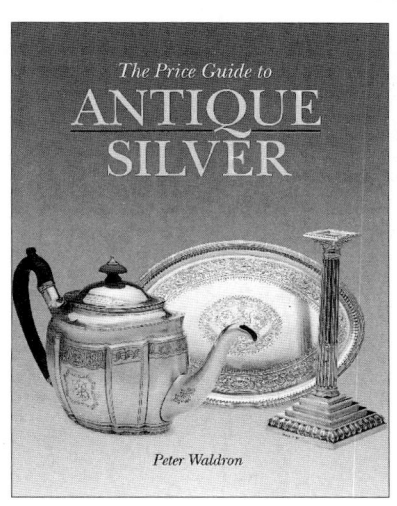

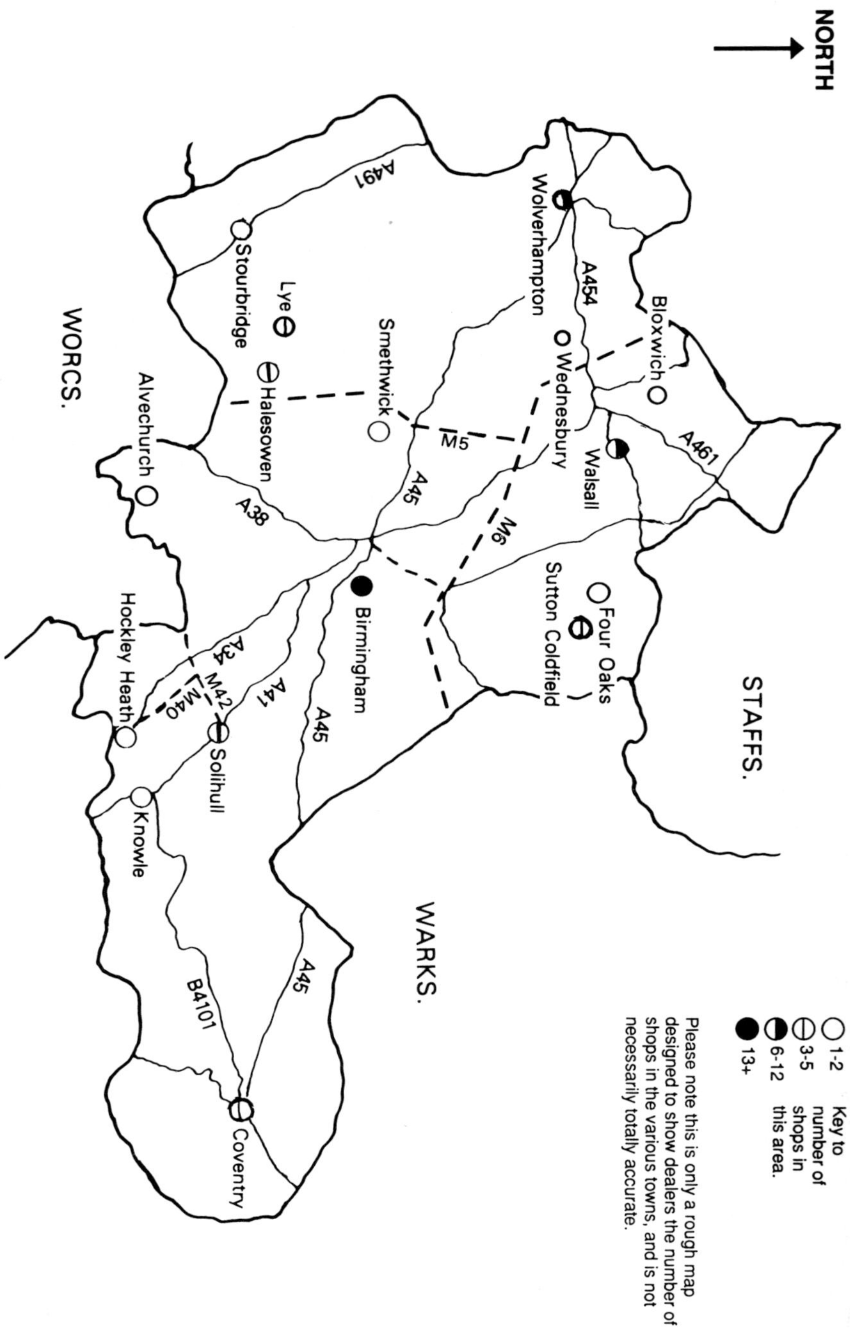
NORTH
STAFFS.
WORCS.
WARKS.
Wolverhampton
A491
A454
Bloxwich
Stourbridge
Lye
Smethwick
Wednesbury
Walsall
A461
Halesowen
M5
A45
Alvechurch
A38
M6
Sutton Coldfield
Four Oaks
Birmingham
Hockley Heath
A34
M42
M40
A41
A45
Solihull
Knowle
A45
B4101
Coventry
1-2
3-5
6-12
13+
Key to number of shops in this area.
Please note this is only a rough map designed to show dealers the number of shops in the various towns, and is not necessarily totally accurate.

ALVECHURCH

Woodland Fine Art

16 The Square. B48 7LA. (C. Haynes). Est. 1971. Open 10-6, Sun. by appointment. SIZE: Medium. *STOCK: Oil paintings, fine watercolours and decorative prints, 19th to early 20th C, £20-£5,000; general antiques.* LOC: 1.5 miles from exit 2, M42. PARK: Easy. TEL: 0121 445 5886. SER: Valuations; restorations; framing. FAIRS: NEC Birmingham. VAT: Stan/Spec.

BIRMINGHAM

Always Antiques

285 Vicarage Rd., Kings Heath. B14 7NE. (R. and D. Messenger). Open Thurs.-Sat. 9-6, other times by appointment. *STOCK: Victorian and Edwardian furniture, dolls, linen, lace and curios.* TEL: 0121 444 8701.

Architectural Antiques of Moseley

23A St. Mary's Row, Moseley. B13 8HW. (R. Stevenson). Open Tues.-Sat. 10-6, Sun. 10-3. SIZE: Large. *STOCK: Antique fireplaces, interesting architectural fixtures and fittings, stained glass, doors, garden statuary, tiles, pine furniture, 1800-1930's.* PARK: Own. TEL: 0121 442 4546; fax - same.

Archives

496 Bristol Rd., Selly Oak. B29 6BD. (S.D. and J. Healey). Open 9.30-5.30. *STOCK: Victorian and Edwardian furniture; clocks and upholstery, to 1930.* TEL: 0121 472 4026.

Peter Asbury Antiques

Greenfield House Farm, 6 Hales Lane, Smethwick, Warley. B67 6RS. Open 9.30-5. *STOCK: General antiques.* TEL: 0121 558 0579. SER: Doll repairs.

Ashleigh House Antiques LAPADA

Ashleigh House, 5 Westbourne Rd. B15 3TH. (P. and R. Hodgson). Est. 1974. Open by appointment. SIZE: Large. *STOCK: Furniture, oils and watercolours, £200-£5,000; clocks, £300-£2,000; objets d'art, £75-£2,000; all 1700-1880.* LOC: From Five Ways Edgbaston take Calthorpe Rd. and bear right into Westbourne Rd., premises 150 yards on left. PARK: Easy. TEL: 0121 454 6283; home - same. SER: Valuations; restorations (furniture and paintings); buys at auction. FAIRS: Most Dateline, Midlands area. VAT: Stan/Spec.

Paul Baxter

Open by appointment only. *STOCK: Oriental ceramics and general antiques.* TEL: 01564 824920.

The Birmingham Antique Centre Ltd (formerly "Treasure Chest")

1407 Pershore Rd., Stirchley. B30 2JR. Est. 1960.

Birmingham continued

Open 9-5.30, Sun. 10-5. *STOCK: General antiques; trade display cabinets.* TEL: 0121 459 4587/689 6565.

Birmingham Piano Warehouse

Unit L, 68 Wyrley Rd., Witton. B6 7BN. (Gavin Burrell). Open Mon.-Thurs. 10-2, Fri. and Sat. 9-4. SIZE: Warehouse. *STOCK: Upright and grand pianos.* LOC: 3 minutes from Spaghetti junction (M6, junction 6). PARK: Easy. TEL: 0121 327 2701/449 6869; mobile - 0831 560518.

Carleton Gallery

91 Vivian Rd., Harborne. B17 0DR. (D. Dunnett). Open 9-5.30, Wed. 9-1. *STOCK: Maps and prints.* TEL: 0121 427 2487.

Chesterfield Antiques

181 Gravelly Lane. B23 5SG. (Mara Cirjanic and Tom McIntosh). Est. 1977. Open 9.30-5.30. *STOCK: General antiques and fine art.* TEL: 0121 373 3876.

Peter Clark Antiques LAPADA

36 St. Mary's Row, Moseley. B13 8JG. Open 9-5.30. SIZE: Medium. *STOCK: Furniture, mid-17th C to early 20th C, £175-£2,500; silver, early 19th C to early 20th C, £100-£500.* LOC: Centre of Moseley. PARK: At rear. TEL: 0121 449 8245. SER: Valuations; restorations (furniture). VAT: Stan/Spec.

R. Collyer

185 New Rd., Rubery. B45 9JP. Open 9-5.30. *STOCK: Clocks including longcase; watches, barometers, secondhand jewellery.* LOC: 1 mile from Lydiate Ash roundabout. TEL: 0121 453 2332. SER: Valuations; restorations.

Dolly Mixtures

Open by appointment. *STOCK: Dolls and teddies.* TEL: 0121 422 6959. SER: Restorations.

Maurice Fellows

21 Vyse St., Hockley. B18 6LE. *STOCK: Objets d'art, jewellery.* TEL: 0121 554 0211. SER: Valuations; restorations.

Format of Birmingham Ltd

18 Bennetts Hill. B2 5QJ. (G. Charman and D. Vice). Open 9.30-5. CL: Sat. *STOCK: Coins, medals.* PARK: New St. station. VAT: Stan/Spec.

Garratt Antiques

22 Great Western Arcade. Est. 1958. *STOCK: Jewellery, clocks, brass, silver, copper, pewter, silver plate, china, crystal, dolls and bric-a-brac.* TEL: 0121 212 1248; fax - 0121 236 0848. SER: Valuations; restorations. VAT: Stan/Spec.

Bob Harris and Sons, Antiques LAPADA

2071 Coventry Rd., Sheldon. B26 3DY. (R.E. Harris). Resident. Est. 1953. Open 9-6. CL: Sun. except by appointment. *STOCK: 18th-19th C furniture and general antiques.* TEL: 0121 743 2259. VAT: Stan/Spec.

Birmingham continued

A.W. Hone and Son Oriental Carpets
1486 Stratford Rd., Hall Green. B28 9ET. (Ian Hone). Est. 1949. Open 9.30-5.30, Sun. by appointment. SIZE: Medium. *STOCK: Persian rugs and carpets, late 19th C to date.* LOC: A34 south of city on Robin Hood Island. PARK: Own forecourt. TEL: 0121 744 1001; fax - same. SER: Valuations; restorations; finder service.VAT: Stan.

John Hubbard Antiques and Fine Art
LAPADA

224-226 Court Oak Rd., Harborne. B32 2EG. Est. 1968. Open 9-6. SIZE: Large. *STOCK: Furniture, 18th-19th C; paintings and watercolours, all £50-£15,000; lighting, silver, plate and decorative items.* LOC: 3 miles from city centre. PARK: Outside. TEL: 0121 426 1694. SER: Valuations; restorations; leather linings. VAT: Stan/Spec.

James Antiques
29 Abbots Rd., King's Heath. B14 7QD. (P. and D. James). Est. 1969. Open by appointment only. SIZE: Small. *STOCK: Decorative antiques, small furniture, stained glass, tiles, painted goods, folk art, general, some 18th, mainly 19th C, to £500; architectural items.* TEL: 0121 444 4628. SER: Valuations; restorations; stained glass repairs; buys at auction.

Rex Johnson and Sons
8 Corporation St. B2 4RN. (D. Johnson). Open 9.15-5.15. *STOCK: Gold, silver, jewellery, porcelain and glass.* TEL: 0121 643 9674.

Kestrel House Antiques and Auction Salerooms
72 Gravelly Hill North, Erdington. B23 6BB. (E.C. Jones). Est. 1895. Open 10.30-7. SIZE: Large. *STOCK: 19th C oil paintings and watercolours.* TEL: 0121 373 2375. SER: Fortnightly auctions; restorations; framing; paintings re-lined and cleaned; canvases repaired. VAT: Stan.

March Medals
113 Gravelly Hill North, Erdington. B23 6BJ. (M.A. March). Est. 1975. Open 10-5, Sat. 10-2. *STOCK: Orders, decorations, campaign medals, militaria and military books.* TEL: 0121 384 4901. SER: Catalogues issued. VAT: Stan/Spec.

F. Meeks & Co
197 Warstone Lane, Hockley. B18. (M.L. and S.R. Durham). Open 9-5, Sat. 9-12. *STOCK: Clocks especially longcase, mantle and wall; vintage wrist watches and antique pocket watches; all £100-£10,000.* TEL: 0121 236 9058. SER: Valuations; restorations (clocks); clock and watch parts supplied. VAT: Stan/Spec.

Birmingham continued

The Old Bakehouse
71 Station Rd., Harborne. B17 9LR. (Andrew Brooker-Carey). Est. 1989. Open Tues.-Sat. 11 5.30. SIZE: Medium. *STOCK: Pine furniture fireplaces and mirrors, Georgian-Victorian, £50 £1,000; lighting, Victorian to 1920's, £50-£500 garden furniture, from Victorian, £10-£500 Victorian beds, £200-£600; furniture, Georgian t 1920's, £50-£800.* LOC: Parallel to High St PARK: Easy. TEL: 0121 428 1928. SER Valuations; restorations (wood and meta including polishing and painting). VAT Stan/Spec.

The Original Choice Ltd
1340 Stratford Rd. Hall Green. B28 9EH. (. Ellis). Open 10-6. *STOCK: Fireplaces, tiles stained glass windows.* TEL: 0121 7783821.

Piccadilly Jewellers
105 New St. B2 4HD. (R. and R. Johnson). Ope 10-5. *STOCK: Jewellery, silver and objects.* TEI 0121 643 5791.

Alan Richards Brocante
168 Gravelly Lane, Erdington. B23 5SN. Ope 10-5.30. *STOCK: French 19th-20th C furnitur Art Deco and books.* TEL: Mobile - 0410 20290 fax - 0121 384 6831.

S.R. Furnishing and Antiques
18 Stanley Rd., Oldbury. B68 0DY. (S. Willder Est. 1975. *STOCK: General antiques an shipping furniture.* TEL: 0121 422 9788.

David Temperley Fine and Antiquarian Books
19 Rotton Park Rd., Edgbaston. B16 9JH. (D. an R.A. Temperley). Resident. Est. 1967. Open 9.3 5.30 by prior appointment. SIZE: Small. *STOC Fine antiquarian and rare books especially fi bindings, illustrated and press; fine colour pla books - natural history, costume, trave topography and atlases, 16th-20th C; early a rare English and European playing cards.* LO 150 yards off Hagley Rd. (A456) and under miles from city centre. 4 miles junction 3, M PARK: Easy. TEL: 0121 454 0135; fax - 01 454 1124. SER: Valuations; restorations (bo binding and paper); buys at auction (antiquari books).

Warley Antique Centre
146 Pottery Rd., Warley Woods. B68 9HD. (A. Hamilton). Open seven days. SIZE: 50+ cabin and 4 furniture showrooms. *STOCK: Gener antiques and furniture, mainly 19th-20th including Worcester, Doulton, clocks, dolls a shipping.* LOC: Off the A4123, J2/3 M5. PAR Easy. TEL: 0121 434 3813; home - 0121 5 1525.

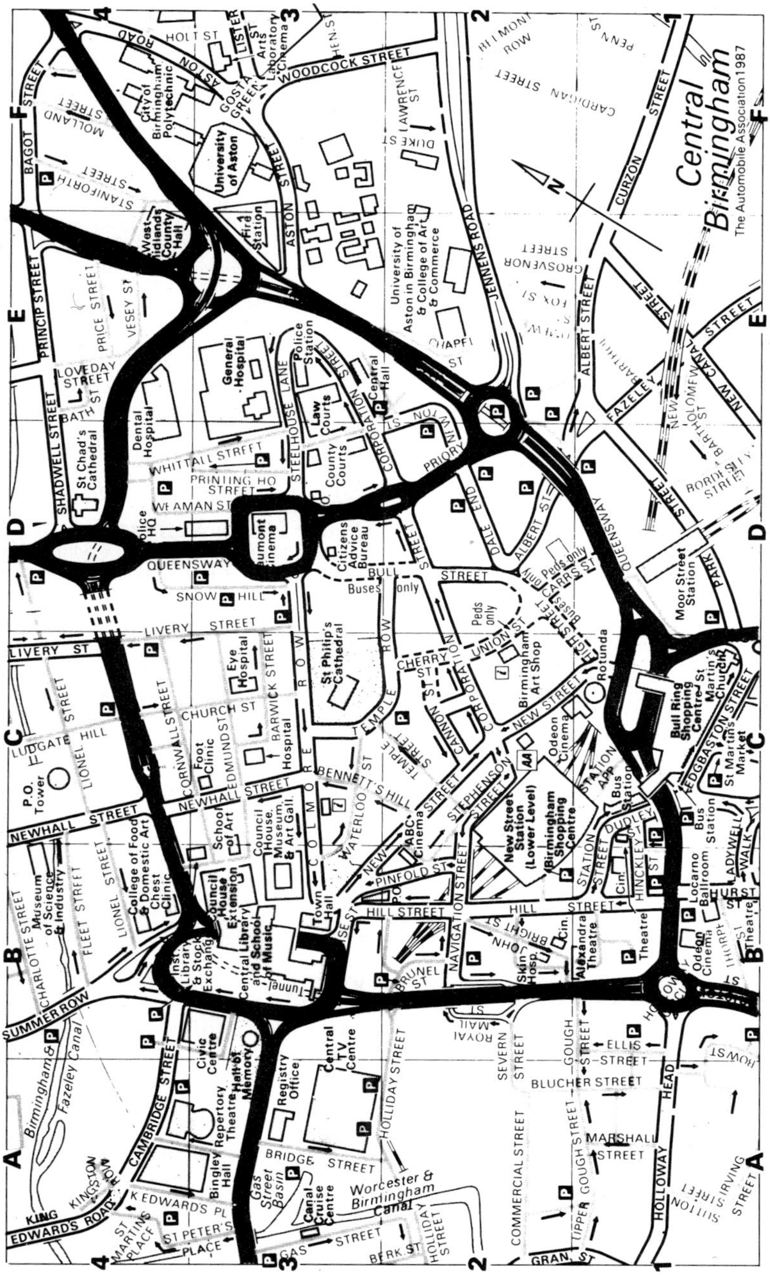

Key to Town Plan

AA Recommended roads	Car Parks
Other roads	Parks and open spaces
Restricted roads	AA Service Centre
Buildings of interest	

Birmingham continued

The Windmill Gallery
6 Ernest St., Holloway Head. B1 1NS. (M. and C. Ashton). Est. 1985. Open 9-5.30, Sat. and Sun. by appointment. SIZE: Medium. *STOCK: Watercolours and drawings, 18th-20th C, £100-£3,000+.* LOC: City centre. PARK: Easy. TEL: 0121 622 3986; fax - 0121 666 6630. SER: Valuations; restorations; mounting, framing. VAT: Spec.

BLOXWICH, Nr. Walsall

Cobwebs
639d Bloxwich Rd., Leamore. WS3 2BQ. (Mrs M. Hannaway). Open 10.30-4.30. CL: Mon. and Thurs. *STOCK: Bric-a-brac.* PARK: Easy. TEL: 01922 493670.

COVENTRY

The Antique Shop
107 Spon End. CV1 3HF. (J. Branagh). Open 9-5.30. *STOCK: General antiques.* TEL: 01203 525915.

Nicholas Green's Antiques
The Antique Warehouse, Rugby Rd., Binley Woods. Est. 1964. Open 9-5, Sun. 12-4. SIZE: Large. *STOCK: Furniture, 18th-20th C, £30-£3,000.* LOC: 2 minutes from M6 and A45 on A46 Coventry by-pass. PARK: Easy. TEL: 01203 453878. SER: Buys at auction. FAIRS: Newark. VAT: Stan.

Memories Antiques
400A Stoney Stanton Rd. CV6 5DH. (R.D. Seymour). Est. 1964. Open 10-2.30. CL: Wed. *STOCK: General antiques, Victorian and Edwardian furniture, shipping goods, stripped pine, china, gold, silver, paintings and collectors' items; Royal Doulton.* TEL: 01203 687994.

FOUR OAKS, Nr. Sutton Coldfield

M. Allen Watch and Clockmaker
76A Walsall Rd. B74 4QY. (M.A. Allen). Est. 1969. Open 9-5.30, Sun. by appointment. SIZE: Small. *STOCK: Vintage wristwatches - Omega, Longines, Girard, Perregaux and Jaeger le Coultre; clocks - Vienna regulators, 1820-1880, mantle and wall clocks.* LOC: By Sutton Park, close to television mast. PARK: Easy. TEL: 0121 308 6117; home - 0121 308 8134. SER: Valuations; restorations (clocks and watches). VAT: Stan/Spec.

Robert Taylor
Windy Ridge, Worcester Lane. B75 5QS. Est. 1983. Open 9-6.30 by appointment only, including Sun. *STOCK: Old collectable toys, including Dinky, Corgi, clockwork, tinplate,*

Four Oaks continued

£1,000. PARK: Easy. TEL: 0121 308 4209; fax 0121 323 3473. SER: Valuations; buys at auction FAIRS: NEC; Donnington; Windsor.

HALESOWEN, Nr. Birmingham

Martyn Brown Antiques
130 Hagley Rd., Hayley Green. B63 1DY. Ope 10-1. CL: Wed. *STOCK: Furniture, clocks paintings and collectables.* TEL: 0121 585 5758.

Clent Books
52 Summer Hill. B63 3BU. (Ivor Simpson). Es 1977. Open 10-4, Tues. 10-1. SIZE: Smal *STOCK: History, local history, topography, natura history, antiquarian books, art, autobiograph bindings, cinema/films, national history, poetr theatre, war, Francis Brett Young, £4-£200.* LOC Town centre. PARK: Opposite. TEL: 0121 55 0309; home - 01299 401090. SER: Valuation FAIRS: Waverley Antique and Book (Organiser).

Tudor House Antiques
68 Long Lane. B62 9LS. (D. Taylor). Open 9.3 5.30. *STOCK: Doors, fireplaces, pine includin kitchens and furniture.* TEL: 0121 561 5563.

Robert Withers Paintings
242 Hagley Rd., Hasbury. B63 4QQ. Open 9.3 6. *STOCK: 18th and 19th C oils, watercolour portraits, landscapes, still life, prints.* PARK: rear of gallery. TEL: 0121 585 0513; home - 01 550 9033.

HOCKLEY HEATH, Nr. Solihull

Magpie House
2212 Stratford Rd. B94 6NU. (D.P. Fair). E 1958. CL: Sat. except by appointment. SIZ Medium. *STOCK: Oak and mahogany.* LO A3400 - 1 mile from J4 M42 and from J1 M4 PARK: Easy. TEL: 01564 782005. *Trade Only.*

KNOWLE

Chadwick Antiques
Chadwick End. B93 0BP. (Mrs P. Tibenha Resident. Est. 1973. Open 10-5, also some S SIZE: Medium. *STOCK: Furniture, 18th-19th collectors' items, general antiques.* Not Stock Oil paintings. LOC: A41. PARK: Easy. TE 01564 782096. SER: Valuations.

LYE, Nr. Stourbridge

The Lye Curios, inc. Lye Antique Furnishings
181 High St. DY9 8LH. (Mr and Mrs P. Smit Est. 1979. Open 9-5. SIZE: Medium. *STOC Furniture, china, glass, metalware.* PARK: Ea TEL: 01384 897513; mobile - 0378 421137. SE Valuations.

'.ye continued

Retro Products
Antique Warehouse, The Yard, Star St. DY9 8TU. M. McHugo). Est. 1980. Open 10-5. CL: Sat. ;IZE: Large. *STOCK: Furniture - Victorian, Edwardian, garden and shipping, £5-£1,000; cast ron metalwork; architectural items.* LOC: Off Stourbridge to Birmingham Rd. PARK: Easy. TEL: 01384 894042; home - 01384 373332. FAIRS: Ardingly and Newark. VAT: Stan.

Smithfield Antiques
'0 Stourbridge Rd. DY9 7DL. (R. Harling). Open -5.30, other times by appointment. *STOCK: General antiques and shipping goods.* TEL: 01384 897821.

SMETHWICK, Nr. Warley

Grannies Attic Antiques
37 Bearwood Rd. B66 4DH. (B.A. Seymour). Est. 1965. Open 10-6 or by appointment to trade. IZE: Medium. *STOCK: Dolls, oak, mahogany nd walnut furniture, curios, Art Deco, Victorian nd Edwardian clothes, porcelain, books, ictures, fans, toys, records, stuffed animals, rass, copper, jewellery, tools, mirrors, smalls nd shipping items, pre-1930, £5-£1,000.* LOC: ff Hagley Rd. PARK: Easy. TEL: 0121 429 180; home - 0121 454 7507. SER: Valuations; uys at auction. *Mainly Trade.*

OLIHULL

Geoffrey Hassall Antiques
) New Rd. B91 3DP. Est. 1972. Open 9.30-1 and -5.30. CL: Mon. SIZE: Small. *STOCK: urniture, 18th-19th C.* PARK: Easy. TEL: 0121)5 0068. SER: Restorations (furniture).

Renaissance
3 Marshall Lake Rd., Shirley. B90 4PL. (S.K. acrow). MGMC. Est. 1981. Open 9-5. SIZE: mall. *STOCK: General antiques.* LOC: Near tratford Rd. TEL: 0121 745 5140. SER: estorations (repairs, re-upholstery and olishing).

illeys Antiques LAPADA
.A. Alpren). Open by appointment only. *TOCK: British glass, Oriental pottery, rcelain, shipping goods; silver, 19th C; orcester.* TEL: 0121 704 1813. SER: aluations; restorations (jewellery, silver); pairs (clock, watch).

TOURBRIDGE

alcon Antiques Centre
0 Hagley Rd., Pedmore. DY8 2JU. (Eileen D. nes). Est. 1976. Open 10-5. CL: Thurs. SIZE: edium. *STOCK: Furniture, £50-£1,000; china*

Stourbridge continued

and porcelain, lace and collectibles, £1-£250; all 19th-20th C. LOC: A491 Hagley road. PARK: Easy. TEL: 01384 371603.

Oldswinford Gallery
106 Hagley Rd., Oldswinford. DY8 1QU. (A.R. Harris). Open 9.30-5. *STOCK: 18th-20th C oil paintings, watercolours and prints.* TEL: 01384 395577. SER: Restorations; framing.

Regency Antique Trading Centre
116 Stourbridge Rd. DY9 7BU. (D. Bevan). Open 9.30-5. SIZE: Several dealers. *STOCK: General antiques and collectables, fireplaces and pine.* TEL: 01384 868778.

SUTTON COLDFIELD

Thomas Coulborn and Sons BADA
Vesey Manor, 64 Birmingham Rd. B72 1QP. (P. Coulborn). Est. 1939. Open 9-5.30. SIZE: Medium. *STOCK: General antiques, 1600-1830; fine English furniture, 17th-18th C; paintings and clocks.* LOC: 3 miles from Spaghetti Junction. From Birmingham A5127 through Erdington, premises on main road opposite cinema. PARK: Easy. TEL: 0121 354 3974; fax - 0121 354 4614. SER: Valuations; restorations (furniture and paintings); buys at auction. FAIRS: British International, Birmingham (Spring). VAT: Spec.

Driffold Gallery
78 Birmingham Rd. B72 1QR. (David Gilbert). Open 10.30-5.30. CL: Thurs. *STOCK: Oil paintings and watercolours, 19th-20th C.* TEL: 0121 355 5433.

Kelford Antiques
14a Birmingham Rd. B72 1QG. (E.S. Kelsall). Est. 1968. Open 9-5. CL: Thurs. *STOCK: General antiques, Georgian and Victorian furniture, silver, porcelain, Staffordshire figures, pot-lids, jewellery.* TEL: 0121 354 6607. VAT: Stan/Spec.

Osborne Antiques
91 Chester Rd., New Oscott. B73 5BA. (C. Osborne). Est. 1976. Open 9-5, Sat. 9.15-12.15. CL: Mon. *STOCK: Barometers and clocks.* TEL: 0121 355 6667. SER: Restorations; spares (clocks, barometers); glass-blowers (barometers).

H. and R.L. Parry Ltd
23 Maney Corner. B72 1QL. (H. Parry). Est. 1925. Open 9.30-5.30. CL: Wed. SIZE: Medium. *STOCK: Porcelain, silver and jewellery, all periods; metalware, paintings.* LOC: A38 from Birmingham road into Sutton. Cinema on right, on corner of service road in which premises are situated. TEL: 0121 354 1178. SER: Valuations. VAT: Stan/Spec.

WALSALL

Hardwick Antiques
317B Chester Rd., Aldridge. WS9 0PH. (P. Chatfield). Open 11-6. CL: Wed. am. *STOCK: Jewellery, silver, porcelain, furniture.* LOC: Opposite Ruby Rest. TEL: 0121 353 1489.

Jomarc Pianos Ltd.
The Piano Craft Centre, Mill Green Farm, Chester Rd., Aldridge. WS9 0LR. (P. Hoskinson). Open 9.30-5.30, Sat. 9.30-4. *STOCK: Pianos.* TEL: 01922 743292; 01922 743826.

L.P. Antiques (Mids) Ltd
The Old Brewery, Short Acre St. WS2 8HW. (Pierre Farouz). Est. 1982. Open daily, Sun. by appointment. SIZE: Warehouse. *STOCK: French and Continental beds and decorative furniture, period armoires, farm and rustic furniture, parquet tables, rush chairs, early pots, Spanish country.* LOC: Junction 10, M6, take A34 towards Cannock. PARK: Easy. TEL: 01922 746764; mobile - 0860 249097. SER: Packing, shipping. VAT: Stan.

Nicholls Jewellers and Antiques
57 George St. WS1 3RS. (R. Nicholls). Open 9-5. *STOCK: Jewellery; dolls by Gotz, Zapf, Alberon and Fair Lady.* TEL: 01922 641081. SER: Repairs.

Past and Present
66 George St. WS1 1RS. (G. Ellis). Open 9.30-5. *STOCK: Satin, walnut, mahogany and oak furniture, curios, collectables, linen, ceramics, pottery, porcelain.* LOC: Opposite Sainsbury's car park. TEL: 01922 611151.

Jon and Kate Rutter
The Doghouse, 309 Bloxwich Rd. WS2 7BD. Open 9-5.30, Sun. by appointment. SIZE: Large. *STOCK: General antiques.* TEL: 01922 30829/ 24263. VAT: Stan.

WEDNESBURY

Brett Wilkins Antiques
81 Holyhead Rd. WS10 7PS. Est. 1983. Open Fri. and Sat., other days (including Sun.) by appointment. SIZE: Medium. *STOCK: Shipping items, 1900-1940, £5-£250; Victorian mahogany, 19th C, £100-£500; some pine, 19th-20th C, £100-£500.* LOC: 2 miles off M6, junction 9 on A41. PARK: Easy. TEL: 0121 502 0720; mobile - 0860 541260. FAIRS: All major. VAT: Stan.

WOLVERHAMPTON

Antiquities
75-76 Dudley Rd. Est. 1968. Open 10-6. *STOCK: General antiques.* TEL: 01902 459800.

Alan M. France
Open by appointment only. *STOCK: Clocks, wrist and pocket watches.* TEL: 01902 731167.

Wolverhampton continued

Ghiberti Antiques and Fine Art
297 Tettenhall Rd., Newbridge. WV6 0LB. (Mis M. Horvath-Toldi). Est. 1986. Open 10-5, Sun. by appointment. SIZE: Small. *STOCK: French furniture, 19th C, £500-£10,000; objets d'art 19th C, £50-£3,000; English furniture, 18th C £500-£3,000.* LOC: 8 miles from junction 10, M6 6 miles from junction 3, M54. PARK: At rear TEL: 01902 750519. SER: Valuations; restorations (furniture including upholstery); buys at auction (furniture and objets d'art). FAIRS: NEC.

Golden Oldies
5 St. Georges Parade. WV2 1AZ. (W.A. and M.A Knowles). Open 10-5.30. CL: Mon. *STOCK Victorian, Edwardian and later furniture, £25 £2,000; paintings, decorative items.* PARK: Easy TEL: 01902 22397. VAT: Stan/Spec.

Kimber & Son
at Martin Taylor Antiques, 140b Tettenhall Rd *STOCK: 18th-20th C antiques for the English Continental and American markets.* PARK: Easy TEL: 01902 751166; home - 01684 57200(VAT: Stan/Spec.

Martin-Quick Antiques LAPAD
323 Tettenhall Rd. WV6 0JZ. Est. 1965. Open 9-6, Sat. 9.30-4. SIZE: Large. *STOCK: 18th 19th C furniture including French an upholstered, shipping goods, stripped pin* LOC: One mile from town centre on A4 PARK: Easy. TEL: 01902 754703; home 01902 752908; fax - 01902 756889. SER Packing and shipping. VAT: Stan/Spec.

Pendeford House Antiques
1 Pendeford Ave., Claregate, Tettenhall. WV 9EG. (Mrs B. Tonks). Est. 1980. Open 10.30- CL: Thurs. SIZE: Medium. *STOCK: China and porcelain, £5-£500; furniture and clocks, £5 £1,500; oil paintings and watercolours, £5 £500; all 19th-20th C; glass, linen, brass and copper, jewellery and silver.* LOC: From main Tettenhall Rd., turn at traffic lights towards Codsall. At first small traffic island, take 3rd ex shop next to Jet Garage. PARK: Easy. TEL 01902 756175; home - 01902 752650.

The Red Shop
7 Hollybush Lane, Penn. (B. Savage). Open 9.3 5.30. *STOCK: Furniture including pine.* TE 01902 342915.

Martin Taylor Antiques LAPAD
140b Tettenhall Rd. WV6 0BQ. Est. 196 Open 8.30-5.30, Sat. 9.30-1.30. SIZE: Larg *STOCK: Furniture, mainly 1800-1930 especia for USA, Australian, South African a European markets, £50-£10,000.* LOC: O mile from town centre on A41. PARK: Ea TEL: 01902 751166; fax - 01902 74650 mobile - 0836 636524; home - 01785 2845 VAT: Stan/Spec

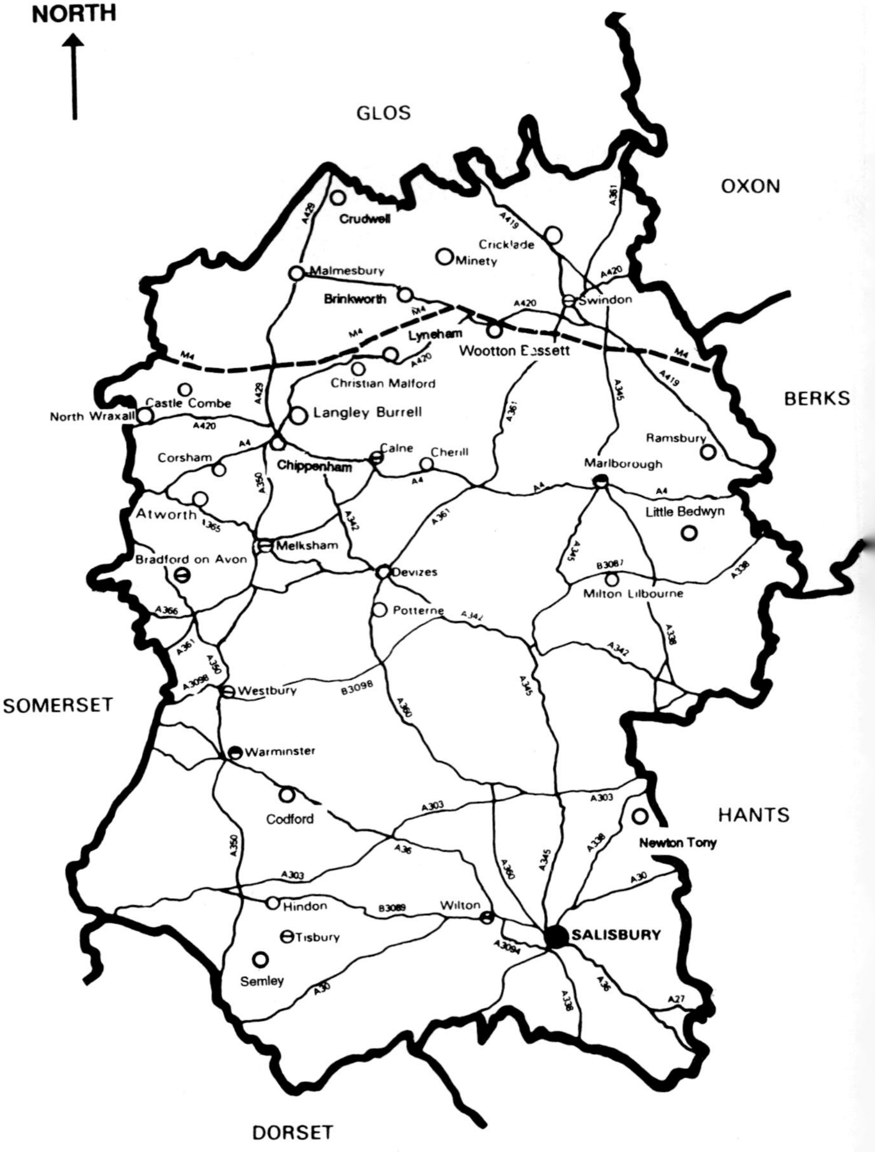

1-2
3-5
6-12
13+

Key to number of shops in this area.

Please note this is only a rough map designed to show dealers the number of shops in the various towns, and is not necessarily totally accurate.

ATWORTH, Nr. Melksham

Peter Campbell Antiques

59 Bath Rd. SN12 8JY. (P.R. Campbell). Est 1976. Open 10-5, Sun. and Thurs. by appoint-ment. SIZE: Medium. *STOCK: General antique and decorative items, 18th-19th C.* Not Stocked Silver and jewellery. LOC: Between Bath an Melksham on A350. PARK: Easy. TEL: 0122 709742; home - same. VAT: Stan/Spec.

BRADFORD-ON-AVON

Avon Antiques BAD

25, 26 and 27 Market St. BA15 1LL. (V. and A Jenkins BA). BABADA. Est. 1963. Open 9.45 5.30, Sun. by appointment. SIZE: Large *STOCK: English and some Continental furniture 1600-1880; metalwork, treen, clocks, barometers some textiles, painted and lacquer furniture* LOC: A363, main street of town. PARK: Ask a shop for key to private parking opposite. TEL 01225 862052. FAIRS: Grosvenor House. VAT Spec.

Mac Humble Antiques BAD

7-9 Woolley St. BA15 1AD. (W. Mc. A. and B. Humble). BABADA. Open 9-6. SIZE: Medium *STOCK: 17th-19th C oak, mahogany, fruitwoods metalware, treen, samplers, silkwork picture decorative objects.* TEL: 01225 866329. SER Valuations; restorations. VAT: Stan/Spec.

Moxhams Antiques LAPAD

17, 23 and 24 Silver St. BA15 1JZ. (R. and Bichard). BABADA. Est. 1966. Open 9-5.30 c by appointment. SIZE: Large. *STOCK: Englis and Continental furniture, clocks, 1650-183 £200-£15,000; European and Oriental potte and porcelain, 1700-1830, £10-£3,000; metal treen, decorative items, 1600-1900, £5-£5,00* PARK: Own, at rear. TEL: 01225 862789; fax 01225 867844; home - 01380 828677. SE Valuations. VAT: Stan/Spec.

Paul Nash Antiques LAPAD

11 Silver St. BA15 1JY. Est. 1961. Open Mor Sat., otherwise by appointment. *STOC Period furniture.* TEL: 01225 866561; mobile 0385 570701; fax - 01225 867455. VAT: Spec.

Town and Country Antiques

34 Market St. BA15 1LL. (Rosemary Drewett a Michael Hughes). BABADA. Open 10.15-5, oth times by appointment. *STOCK: Fine peri furniture, metalware, caddies, boxes and peri decorative items.* PARK: Nearby. TEL: 012 867877; fax - same. VAT: Spec.

BRINKWORTH, Nr. Malmesbury

North Wilts Exporters

Farm Hill House. SN15 5AJ. (M. Thornbury). Est. 1972. Open Mon.-Sat. or by appointment. *STOCK: Imported Continental pine, 18th-19th C; shipping goods.* LOC: Off M4, junction 16 Malmesbury road. TEL: 01666 510876; mobile - 0836 260730. SER: Valuations; shipping; import and export. VAT: Stan.

CALNE

Calne Antiques

London Rd. SN11 0AB. (M. Blackford). Open 9-5 including Sun. *STOCK: Victorian and Edwardian furniture including pine; shipping goods and smalls.* LOC: Next to White Hart Hotel. TEL: 01249 816311.

Clive Farahar and Sophie Dupré - Rare Books, Autographs and Manuscripts

Horsebrook House, 15 The Green. SN11 8DQ. Open by appointment. SIZE: Medium. *STOCK: Rare books on voyages and travels, autograph letters and manuscripts, 15th-20th C, £5-£5,000.* LOC: Off A4 in town centre. PARK: Easy. TEL: 01249 821121; fax - 01249 821202. SER: Valuations; buys at auction (as stock). FAIRS: ABA; Universal Autograph Collectors' Club. VAT: Stan.

Calne continued

Hilmarton Manor Press

Hilmarton Manor. SN11 8SB. (H. Baile de Laperriere). Est. 1967. Open 9-6. SIZE: Medium. *STOCK: New and out-of-print art and photography reference books, some antiquarian.* LOC: 3 miles from Calne on A3102 towards Swindon. PARK: Easy. TEL: 0124 976 208. SER: Buys at auction.

CASTLE COMBE, Nr. Chippenham

Combe Cottage Antiques

SN14 7HU. (B. and A. Bishop). Est. 1960. Open 10-1 and 2-6, prior telephone call advisable. SIZE: Medium. *STOCK: Country furniture, £20-£5,000; metalware, £10-£2,000; both 17th to early 19th C; treen, pottery, 18th-19th C, £5-£500; early lighting devices.* Not Stocked: Mahogany furniture, glass, silver, Victoriana. LOC: A420 from Chippenham towards Bristol. After 3 miles bear right on B4039. PARK: 20yds. TEL: 01249 782250; fax - 01249 782250. SER: Valuations; specialists in cottage furnishings. VAT: Spec.

CHERHILL, Nr. Calne

P.A. Oxley Antique Clocks and Barometers LAPADA

The Old Rectory, Main Rd. SN11 8UX. Est. 1971. Open 9.30-5, other times by appointment. CL: Wed. SIZE: Large. *STOCK: Longcase, bracket, carriage clocks and barometers, 17th-19th C, £500-£30,000.* LOC: A4, not in village. PARK: Easy. TEL: 01249 816227; fax - 01249 821285. VAT: Spec.

CHIPPENHAM

Lucy Cope Designs

Foxhill House, Allington. SN14 6LL. (G.E. and L. Cope). Resident. Est. 1986. Open 7 days 9-6 by appointment. SIZE: Medium. *STOCK: Lamps, small decorative accessories and paintings.* LOC: Off A420 towards Bath, 2 miles from Chippenham. PARK: Easy. TEL: 01249 650446; fax - 01249 444936. SER: Restorations (period lampshades); lampshade makers. *Trade Only.*

CHRISTIAN MALFORD Nr. Chippenham

Harley Antiques

The Comedy. SN15 4BS. (G.J. Harley). Est. 1959. Open 9-6 including Sun., or later by appointment. SIZE: Large. *STOCK: Furniture, 18th-19th C, £150-£3,000; decorative objects, £30-£1,000.* LOC: B4069, 4 miles off M4, junction 17. PARK: Own. TEL: 01249 720112; home - same; fax - 01249 720553. SER: Colour brochure available (export only). VAT: Stan. *Trade Only.*

CODFORD, Nr. Warminster

Tina's Antiques

75 High St. BA12 0ND. (T.A. Alder). Open 9-6, Sat. 9-1. *STOCK: General antiques.* TEL: 01985 850828.

CORSHAM

Matthew Eden

Pickwick End. SN13 0JB. Resident. Est. 195 SIZE: Large. *STOCK: Country house furnitu and garden items, 17th-19th C.* TEL: 0124 713335; fax - 01249 713644. VAT: Spec.

CRICKLADE, Nr. Swindon

Edred A.F. Gwilliam

Candletree House, Bath Rd. SN6 6AX. Est. 197 Open by appointment. SIZE: Medium. *STOCK Arms and armour, swords, pistols, long gun £50-£20,000+.* PARK: Easy. TEL: 0179 750241; fax - 01793 750359. SER: Valuation buys at auction. FAIRS: Major arms. VA Stan/Spec.

Robin Shield Antiques BADA LAPAD

23 High St. SN6 6AP. Est. 1974. Open 9.30-5.3 but appointment advisable. SIZE: Mediun *STOCK: Furniture and paintings, £200-£20,00 works of art, £100-£5,000; all 17th-19th C* PARK: Easy. TEL: 01793 750205; mobile - 086 520391. SER: Valuations; buys at auction. VA Stan/Spec.

CRUDWELL

Crudwell Furniture

Odd Penny Farm. SN16 9SJ. (Philip A Ruttleigh). Est. 1990. Open 9.30-5.30 and b appointment. CL: Sat. SIZE: Small. *STOCK Furniture including pine in the paint, an decorative items, £10-£2,000.* LOC: Next to RA Kemble on A429, 5 minutes from Cirencester, 1 mins from junction 17, M4. TEL: 01285 77097 SER: Restorations including paint stripping ar upholstery.

DEVIZES

Cross Keys Jewellers

The Ginnel, Market Pl. SN10 1HN. (D. and D. Pullen). Est. 1967. Open 9.30-5.30. *STOCK: Jewellery, silver.* LOC: Alley adjacent Nationwide Building Society. PARK: Easy. TEL: 01380 726293. VAT: Stan.

HINDON, Nr. Salisbury

Monkton Galleries

High St. SP3 6DR. (J. and B. Dempsey). Resident. Est. 1967. CL: Wed. SIZE: Medium. *STOCK: Early oak and country furniture; metalware, longcase clocks.* PARK: Easy. TEL: 01747 820235. SER: Valuations; restorations (metalware, prints and pictures). FAIRS: Buxton; Surrey. VAT: Spec.

LANGLEY BURRELL Nr. Chippenham

Harriet Fairfax Fireplaces and General Antiques

Langley Green. Open by appointment only. *STOCK: China, glass, dolls, furniture, fabrics and needlework; architectural items and fittings, brass and iron knobs, knockers; fireplaces, pine and iron, 1780-1950.* TEL: 01249 652030. SER: Polishing; welding; design consultancy.

LITTLE BEDWYN, Nr. Marlborough

Turpin's Antiques BADA LAPADA

Old Manor Cottage. SN8 3JG. (Jane Sumner). Open by appointment. SIZE: Large. *STOCK: 17th-18th C walnut, oak and mahogany, metalware.* TEL: 01672 870727. SER: Restorations. VAT: Spec.

LYNEHAM, Nr. Chippenham

Pillars Antiques

10 The Banks. (K. Clifford). Resident. Est. 1986. Open 10-5, including Sun. CL: Thurs. SIZE: Medium. *STOCK: Victorian and Edwardian pine, £5-£1,000; shipping oak, 1900-1940's, from £15.* LOC: B4069 Chippenham road, 1 mile from village. PARK: Easy. TEL: 01249 890632; home - same.

MALMESBURY

Antiques - Rene Nicholls

56 High St. SN16 9AT. (Mrs. R. Nicholls). Est. 1980. Open 10-5.30, Sun. by appointment. SIZE: Small. *STOCK: English pottery and porcelain, 18th to early 19th C, £50-£900; small furniture.* PARK: Opposite. TEL: 01666 823089; home - same.

Malmesbury continued

Andrew Britten Antiques

48 High St. SN16 9AT. (T.M. Tyler and T.A Freeman). Est. 1975. Open 9.30-6, Sun. b appointment. SIZE: Medium. *STOCK: Furnitur 1700-1900, £100-£1,500; decorative brass, woo glass and porcelain items, £15-£500.* PARK Opposite. TEL: 01666 823376. VAT: Spec.

Cross Hayes Antiques LAPAD

The Antique and Furniture Warehouse, 1 Bristol St. SN16 0AY. (D. Brooks). Est. 197 Open 9-5 or by appointment. SIZE: Ware house. *STOCK: Shipping oak, plus Victoria and Edwardian mahogany and walnut, Frenc furniture, 1850-1920's; bric-a-brac.* TEL: 0166 824260; home - 01666 822062; fax - 0166 823020. SER: Valuations. VAT: Stan/Spec.

J.P. Kadwell

Silver St. SN16 0BX. Est. 1981. Open 8.15-5.3 including Sun. SIZE: Medium. *STOCK: Gener antiques, £5-£500.* PARK: Easy. TEL: 0166 823589; home - same. SER: Restorations (wood buys at auction.

MARLBOROUGH

The Antique and Book Collector

Katharine House, The Parade. SN8 1NE. (C.C Gange). Est. 1983. Open 9.45-5.30. SIZE Medium. *STOCK: Furniture, 17th-19th C, £20 £2,000; decorative items, £100-£1,000; glas silver, brass, china, 18th-19th C, £20-£50 paintings and prints, £10-£1,000; books, £5-£50* PARK: Easy. TEL: 01672 514040; home - sam FAIRS: PBFA monthly; Oxfam annually. VA Stan/Spec.

Cook of Marlborough Fine Art Ltd LAPAD

High Trees House, Savernake Forest. SN 4NE. (W.J. Cook). BAFRA. Est. 1963. Ope 10-5, Sat. and Sun. by appointment. SIZE Medium. *STOCK: Furniture, 18th to early 19 C; objets d'art, 18th-19th C; pictures, 19th-20 C.* LOC: 1.5 miles from Marlborough on A34 towards Burbage. PARK: Easy. TEL: 0167 513017; fax - 01672 514455. SER: Valuation restorations (furniture including polishing an gilding); buys at auction (furniture). FAIR Café Royal; Olympia; Barbican; Harrogat VAT: Stan/Spec.

Cross Keys Jewellers

21a High St. SN8 1LW. (D. and D. Pullen). Es 1967. Open 9.30-5.30. *STOCK: Jewellery, silve* LOC: Entrance to Waitrose car park. TEL: 0167 516260. VAT: Stan.

Robert Kime Antiques

Upper Farm, Fosbury. SN8 3NJ. Est. 1968. Ope by appointment only. *STOCK: Decorative, peric furniture.* TEL: 01264 731268. VAT: Spec.

1arlborough continued

'he Marlborough Parade Antique :entre

'he Parade. SN8 1NE. (T. Page and N. Cannon). :st. 1985. Open 10-5 including Sun. SIZE: 57 ealers. *STOCK: Good quality furniture, paintings, ilver, porcelain, glass, clocks, jewellery, copper, rass and pewter, £5-£5,000.* LOC: Adjacent A4 in own centre. PARK: Easy. TEL: 01672 515331. 'ER: Valuations; restorations (furniture, porcelain, opper, brass). VAT: Spec.

'he Military Parade Bookshop

'he Parade. SN8 1NE. (G. and P. Kent). *STOCK: 1ilitary history books especially regimental istories and the World Wars.* LOC: Next to The ,amb. TEL: 01672 515470; fax - 01980 630150.

'rincipia Arts and Sciences

London Rd. SN8 1PH. (M.D.C. Forrer). Open -6, Sun. 10-5. *STOCK: Collectors' items, cientific instruments, country furniture, treen, ictures, clocks, china, porcelain and books.* TEL: 1672 512072; fax - 01672 511551.

›tuart Gallery

London Rd. SN8 1PH. (A.B. Loncraine). Est. 968. Open Thurs., Fri. and Sat. 9-6.30. *STOCK: ;eneral antiques especially small collectables,*

Marlborough continued

watercolours, oils and prints, china, glass, interior design pieces, books, garden items. PARK: Easy. TEL: 01672 513593.

Annmarie Turner Antiques

22 Salisbury Rd. SN8 4AD. Resident. Est. 1960. Open 10-6, Sun. by appointment. SIZE: Small. *STOCK: Country and Welsh primitive furniture, £50-£1,500; English treen, kitchen and architectural items, £10-£300; paintings and decorative items, £20-£500; all 17th-19th C.* Not Stocked: Mahogany, jewellery, silver and weapons. LOC: Left side of first roundabout approaching town centre from Hungerford on A4. PARK: Easy and at rear. TEL: 01672 515396; home - same. SER: Valuations. VAT: Spec.

MELKSHAM

Dann Antiques Ltd

Unit 1, Avonside Enterprise Park, New Broughton Rd. SN12 8BS. BABADA. Open 9-5.30, Sat. 9-1. SIZE: Large. *STOCK: 18th-19th C mahogany and walnut furniture and accessories including majolica, Masons and Staffordshire.* TEL: 01225 707329; fax - 01225 790120; home - 01380 812228.

Melksham continued

Alan Jaffray
16 Market Place. SN12 6EX. BABADA. Est 1956. Open 10-1 and 2-5, Sat. by appointment SIZE: Large. *STOCK: Furniture and smalls, 18th 19th C, £50-£2,000.* LOC: Main Bath to Devize Rd. PARK: On premises. TEL: 01225 702269 fax - 01225 790413. VAT: Stan/Spec.

King Street Curios
8 King St. SN12 6HD. Est. 1991. SIZE: 20 units *STOCK: China, glass, jewellery, Art Deco kitchenalia, furniture.* LOC: A350. PARK: Ow at rear. TEL: 01225 790623. FAIRS: Oasis Swindon; Neeld Hall, Chippenham; Templemead (Brunel), Bristol.

MILTON LILBOURNE, Nr. Pewsey

Rupert Gentle Antiques BADA
The Manor House. SN9 5LQ. Est. 1954. Open 9.15-6. SIZE: Medium. *STOCK: English and Continental domestic metalwork, 1650-1850 furniture, needlework and domestic accessories.* LOC: From Hungerford on A4 take A338 for Pewsey. PARK: Easy. TEL: 01672 563344; fax - 01672 564136. SER: Valuations; buys at auction. VAT: Stan/Spec.

MINETY, Nr. Malmesbury

Sambourne House Antiques
Sambourne House. SN16 9RQ. (T. Cove). Est 1984. Open daily, Sun. by appointment. SIZE Large. *STOCK: Pine, 19th C, £75-£1,000 furniture, 20th C, £20-£1,000; containers from Eastern Europe.* LOC: 10 mins. from M4 junction 16. PARK: Easy. TEL: 01666 860288 home - 01666 822271. SER: Valuations; restorations (pine, renovating, stripping and finishing) furniture made from reclaimed pine; export arranged. VAT: Stan.

NEWTON TONY, Nr Salisbury

Ray Best Antiques LAPADA
Owl Cottage SP4 0HF. Est. 1964. Open by appointment. *STOCK: Period furniture and decorative objects.* TEL: 01980 629528; mobile 0831 766340. *Trade Only.*

NORTH WRAXALL, Nr. Chippenham

Delomosne and Son Ltd BADA
Court Close. SN14 7AD. (T.N.M. Osborne and M.C.F. Mortimer). BABADA. Articles on chandeliers, glass and porcelain. Est. 1905. Open 9.30-5.30; Sat. 9.30-1 (except Bank Holiday weekends). SIZE: Large. *STOCK: English and*

North Wraxall continued

rish glass, pre-1830, £20-£20,000; glass, chan-'eliers, English and European porcelain, needle-vork, papier mâché and treen. LOC: Off A420 ›etween Bath and Chippenham. PARK: Easy. 'EL: 01225 891505; fax - 01225 891907. SER: 'aluations; buys at auction. FAIRS: Inter-›ational Ceramic. VAT: Spec.

'OTTERNE, Nr. Devizes

Victoria C - The Antique Gallery Potterne)

7 High St. SN10 5NA. (V. Cross). Open Tues. 2-, Thurs., Fri. and Sat 10-5, other times by ppointment. SIZE: Small. *STOCK: Furniture, 8th-19th C, £15-£1,000; giltwood frames and nirrors, architectural and decorative items.* LOC: ›360 near George and Dragon. PARK: Easy. 'EL: 01380 728007; home - same.

RAMSBURY, Nr. Marlborough

Heraldry Today

'arliament Piece. SN8 2QH. Est. 1954. Open .30-4.30. CL: Sat. *STOCK: Heraldic and enealogical books and manuscripts, £3-£6,000.* 'EL: 01672 520617; fax - 01672 520183; e-mail - eraldry@cccp.net.; internet - http://www. eraldrytoday.co.uk.

nglenook Antiques

9 High St. SN8 2QN. (D. White). Est. 1969.)pen 10-5. CL: Mon. and Wed. except by ppointment. *STOCK: Oil lamps, clocks, barom-ters and spare parts, some furniture.* LOC: Off ›4. TEL: 01672 520261. SER: Restorations longcase clock movements and barometers).

SALISBURY

Antique and Collectors Market

7 Catherine St. SP1 2DH. Open 9-5. SIZE: arge. *STOCK: Silver, plate, china, glass, toys, ooks, taxidermy, postcards, pens and furniture.* 'EL: 01722 326033.

The Avonbridge Antiques and Collectors Market

Jnited Reformed Church Hall, Fisherton St. Open 'ues. 9-3.30. SIZE: 15 dealers. *STOCK: General ntiques.*

The Barn Book Supply

8 Crane St. SP1 2QD. (J. and J. Head). Est. 958. Open 9.30-5. CL: Sat. *STOCK: Antiquarian ooks on angling, shooting, horses, deerstalking.* 'EL: 01722 327767; fax - 01722 339888.

).M. Beach

2 High St. SP1 2PG. (A. Beach). Est. 1930.)pen 9-5.30. SIZE: Large. *STOCK: Antiquarian*

Salisbury continued

books, 1500 to date, 5p-£1,000; maps, prints, oils and watercolours, to £1,500. LOC: From Bournemouth into city, take first possible turn left. Shop is on next corner. PARK: 120yds. down Crane St. TEL: 01722 333801: fax - 01722 333720. SER: Valuations; restorations (leather bindings); buys at auction.

Derek Boston Antiques

223 Wilton Rd. and warehouse at Wilton. SP2 7JY. Est. 1964. Open 9.30-5. *STOCK: 18th-19th C furniture.* TEL: 01722 322682; home - 01722 324426. VAT: Stan/Spec.

Robert Bradley

71 Brown St. SP1 2BA. Est. 1970. Open 9.30-5.30. CL: Sat. *STOCK: Furniture, 17th-18th C; decorative items.* TEL: 01722 333677; fax - 01722 339922. VAT: Spec.

Ronald Carr

6 St. Francis Rd. SP1 3QS. (R.G. Carr). Est. 1983. Open by appointment. SIZE: Small. *STOCK: Modern British etchings, wood engravings and colour wood cuts, £5-£1,000.* LOC: 1 mile north of city on A345. PARK: Easy. TEL: 01722 328892; home - same. SER: Buys at auction.

Castle Galleries

81 Castle St. SP1 3SP. (John C. Lodge). Est. 1971. Open 9-5, Sat. 9-1. CL: Mon. and Wed. *STOCK: General antiques, coins and medals.* PARK: Easy. TEL: 01722 333734.

Jonathan Green Antiques

87 Castle St. SP1 3SP. Est. 1975. Open 9.30-4.30, Sat. 9.30-12.30. CL: Mon. SIZE: Small. *STOCK: Silver and plate, Georgian to modern, £5-£5,000.* PARK: Easy. TEL: 01722 332635. SER: Valuations; restorations (silver including re-plating). VAT: Stan/Spec.

Edward Hurst Antiques

The Garden Room, Netherhampton. SP2 8PU. Est. 1983. Open 9.30-5.30, Sat. by appointment. SIZE: Medium. *STOCK: English furniture and associated works of art, 1650-1820.* LOC: Just west of Salisbury. PARK: Easy. TEL: 01722 743042. VAT: Spec.

The Jerram Gallery LAPADA

7 St John St. SP1 2SB. (Mark Jerram). Open Tues.-Fri. 9.30-5.30, Sat. 10-4. SIZE: Large. *STOCK: British oil paintings and watercolours, 1850-1950; 20th C etchings, contemporary pictures and sculptures, £100-£15,000.* LOC: St John St. is an extension of Exeter St., opposite Queen Anne's Gate. PARK: Loading and unloading, or nearby. TEL: 01722 412310; fax - 01722 323577. SER: Valuations; restorations; framing; finder; buys at auction.

Salisbury continued

Micawber's
53 Fisherton St. SP2 7SU. (Mr. and Mrs. E.M. Johnson and others). Est. 1981. Open 9.30-5. CL: Wed. SIZE: 10 stalls. *STOCK: General antiques including jewellery, silver, furniture, clocks, books, military prints, porcelain, pine, bottles, glass, lace, linen and clothes.* LOC: 350yds. from railway station towards town centre. PARK: Opposite, behind shops. TEL: 01722 337822. SER: Valuations; picture framing; repairs (watches and jewellery). FAIRS: Local.

Salisbury Antiques Warehouse LAPADA
94 Wilton Rd. SP2 7JJ. (Chris Watts). Est. 1964. Open 9.30-5.30, Sat. and Sun. by appointment. SIZE: Large. *STOCK: Furniture, clocks and shipping goods, 18th-19th C, £50-£3,000; paintings, 19th C, £100-£2,000.* LOC: A36 Warminster-Southampton road. PARK: Easy. TEL: 01722 410634; mobile - 0802 635055. VAT: Stan/Spec.

William Sheppee
Old Sarum Airfield. SP4 6BJ. (W. Hiley and A. Cox). Est. 1989. Open Mon.-Fri. 9-5.30 by appointment only. SIZE: Large. *STOCK: Anglo-Indian and Indian furniture, 19th C, £500-£6,000; treen, £50-£250.* TEL: 01722 334454; fax - 01722 337754. SER: Valuations; export. VAT: Stan.

Chris Wadge Clocks
83 Fisherton St. SP2 7ST. Open 9-5. CL: Mon. *STOCK: Clocks, movements and spare parts.* TEL: 01722 334467. SER: 400 day specialist.

SEMLEY, Nr. Shaftesbury

May and May Ltd
Whitebridge. SP7 9QP. Est. 1963. Open by appointment. *STOCK: Antiquarian music and music literature.* TEL: 01747 830034; fax - 01747 830035. SER: Buys at auction.

SWINDON

Antiques and All Pine
11 Newport St., Old Town. SN1 3DX. (J. and M. Brown). Open 10-5.30. CL: Wed. SIZE: Medium. *STOCK: Pine, traditional brass and iron beds, china, lace, linen and costume jewellery.* LOC: From M4, junction 15 or 16 follow signs to Old Town. PARK: 100yds. TEL: 01793 520259. VAT: Stan/Spec.

Savernake Antiques Arcade
Victoria Centre, 138/9 Victoria Rd., Old Town. SN1 3BU. (Peter and Carol Dent). Est. 1977. Open 10-5, Sun. 11-4. SIZE: Large. *STOCK: Furniture, £350-£650; china and porcelain, £20-£100; jewellery and silver, £10-£300.* LOC: On left on hill between Old Town and college. PARK: Prospect Place. TEL: 01793 536668; fax - 01488 684004; home - 01488 686800. SER: Restorations (furniture); buys at auction. VAT: Stan.

Swindon continued

Allan Smith Antique Clocks
162 Beechcroft Rd., Upper Stratton. SN2 6QE. Est. 1988. Open by appointment. SIZE: Medium. *STOCK: 40+ longcase clocks, including automata, moonphase, painted dial, brass dial, 30 hour, 8 day, London and Provincial, £1,350-£8,950; stick and banjo barometers, mantel, wall, bracket, Vienna and lantern clocks.* LOC: Near Bakers Arms Inn. PARK: Own. TEL: 01793 822977; mobile - 0378 834342. VAT: Spec.

Victoria Bookshop
30 Wood St., Old Town. SN1 4AB. (S. Austin). Est. 1965. Open 9-5.30. SIZE: Large. *STOCK: Books, most subjects, old postcards.* LOC: Middle of Old Town shopping area. PARK: Nearby. TEL: 01793 527364.

TISBURY

Edward Marnier Antiques
17 High St. SP3 6HF. (E.F. Marnier). Resident. Est. 1989. Open 10-6, Sun. and Wed. by appointment. *STOCK: English and Continental furniture, pictures, rugs, carpets and interesting decorative objects, 17th-20th C, £5-£5,000.* PARK: Easy. TEL: 01747 870213; fax - same. SER: Valuations; buys at auction. VAT: Spec.

WARMINSTER

Bishopstrow Antiques
55 East St. BA12 9BZ. (J.M. Stewart Cox). Est. 1974. Open 10-1 and 2-5.30. SIZE: Medium. *STOCK: 18th-19th C mahogany, oak and painted furniture; pottery and porcelain, boxes, small silver and decorative items.* LOC: On left of old A36 leaving Warminster on Salisbury road, opposite Esso garage. PARK: Easy. TEL: 0198[5] 212683; home - 01985 840877. VAT: Spec.

Choice Antiques
4 Silver St. BA12 8PS. (Avril Bailey). Open 10-1 and 2-5.30. SIZE: Medium. *STOCK: General antiques and decorative items, 18th-19th C, £2-£2,000.* PARK: Easy. TEL: 01985 218924. VAT: Stan/Spec.

Emma Hurley Antiques and Textiles
3 Silver St. BA12 8PS. (Emma and John Hurley). Est. 1970. Usually open 10-5. SIZE: Medium. *STOCK: Decorative furnishings, 19th C; textiles 18th-19th C; both £25-£1,000.* LOC: From Bath or Frome road, 200 yards past obelisk monument on right. PARK: Nearby. TEL: 01985 21972[illegible] home - 01985 847021. FAIRS: Shepton Mallet, Sandown Park.

Warminster continued

Isabella Antiques
11 Silver St. BA12 8PS. (B.W. Semke). Est. 1990. Open 10-5.30. SIZE: Medium. *STOCK: Furniture, late 18th C to late 19th C, £100-£5,000; boxes and mirrors, 19th C, £50-£500.* LOC: Main road. PARK: Easy. TEL: 01985 218933. SER: Buys at auction (furniture). VAT: Spec.

Obelisk Antiques LAPADA
2 Silver St. BA12 8PS. (P. Tanswell). Open 10-1 and 2-5.30. SIZE: Large. *STOCK: English and Continental furniture, 18th-19th C; decorative items, objets d'art.* TEL: 01985 846646; fax - 01985 219901.

K. and A. Welch
1A Church St. BA12 8PG. Est. 1967. Open 8-6, Sat. 9-1. SIZE: Large. *STOCK: Shipping furniture, 18th-19th C, £10-£2,000.* LOC: A36 west end of town. PARK: Own. TEL: 01985 214687; home - 01985 213433. VAT: Stan/Spec.

WEST YATTON, Nr. Chippenham

Heirloom & Howard Limited
Manor Farm. SN14 7EU. (D.S. Howard BABADA. Est. 1972. Open 9.30-5.30, Sat. 11 or by appointment. SIZE: Medium. *STOCK Porcelain mainly Chinese armorial and expo 18th C, £100-£5,000; heraldic items, 18th-19th £10-£1,000; portrait engravings, 17th-19th £10-£50.* LOC: 10 miles from Bath, 1/4 mile c A420 Chippenham/Bristol road. Transport fro Chippenham station (4 miles) if required. PAR Own. TEL: 01249 783038; fax - 01249 78303 SER: Valuations; buys at auction (Chine porcelain). VAT: Spec.

WESTBURY

Ray Coggins Antiques
1 Fore St. BA13 3AU. Open 9-5.30. *STOC Antique and decorative furniture and arch tectural fittings.* TEL: 01373 826574.

WILTON, Nr. Salisbury

Ian J. Brook, Antiques and Picture Gallery
26 North St. SP2 0HJ. Resident. Est. 1962. Op after hours to trade by appointment. CL: We pm. *STOCK: Furniture, oil paintings and wate colours, £5-£5,000.* TEL: 01722 743392. VA Stan/Spec.

Hingstons of Wilton
36 North St. SP2 0HJ. Open 9-5, Sat. 10-4. SIZ Large. *STOCK: Mainly furniture, Victoria 1930's.* TEL: 01722 742263; home - 017 812143.

Pamela Lynch
18 West St. SP2 0DF. Resident. Open Tue Wed. and Thurs. 10-5, other times by appoi ment. *STOCK: Small furniture, needlewo pictures, decorative items, objets de vertu.* TE 01722 744113.

A.J. Romain and Sons
The Old House, 11 and 13 North St. SP2 0H *STOCK: Furniture, mainly 17th-18th C; ea oak, walnut and marquetry; clocks, copper, br and miscellanea.* TEL: 01722 743350. VA Stan/Spec.

WOOTTON BASSETT, Nr. Swindon

Tubbjoys Antique Market
118 High St. SN4 7AU. (Charles and Brid Tubb). Est. 1992. Open 10-5. SIZE: 15 uni *STOCK: General antiques, 1880-1980, £5-£5* LOC: 2 miles off M4, junction 16. PARK: E and at rear. TEL: 01793 849499; home - sa fax - 01793 849689.

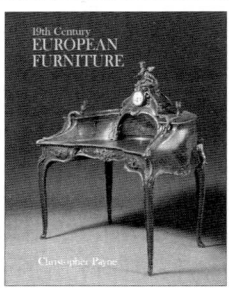

Worcestershire

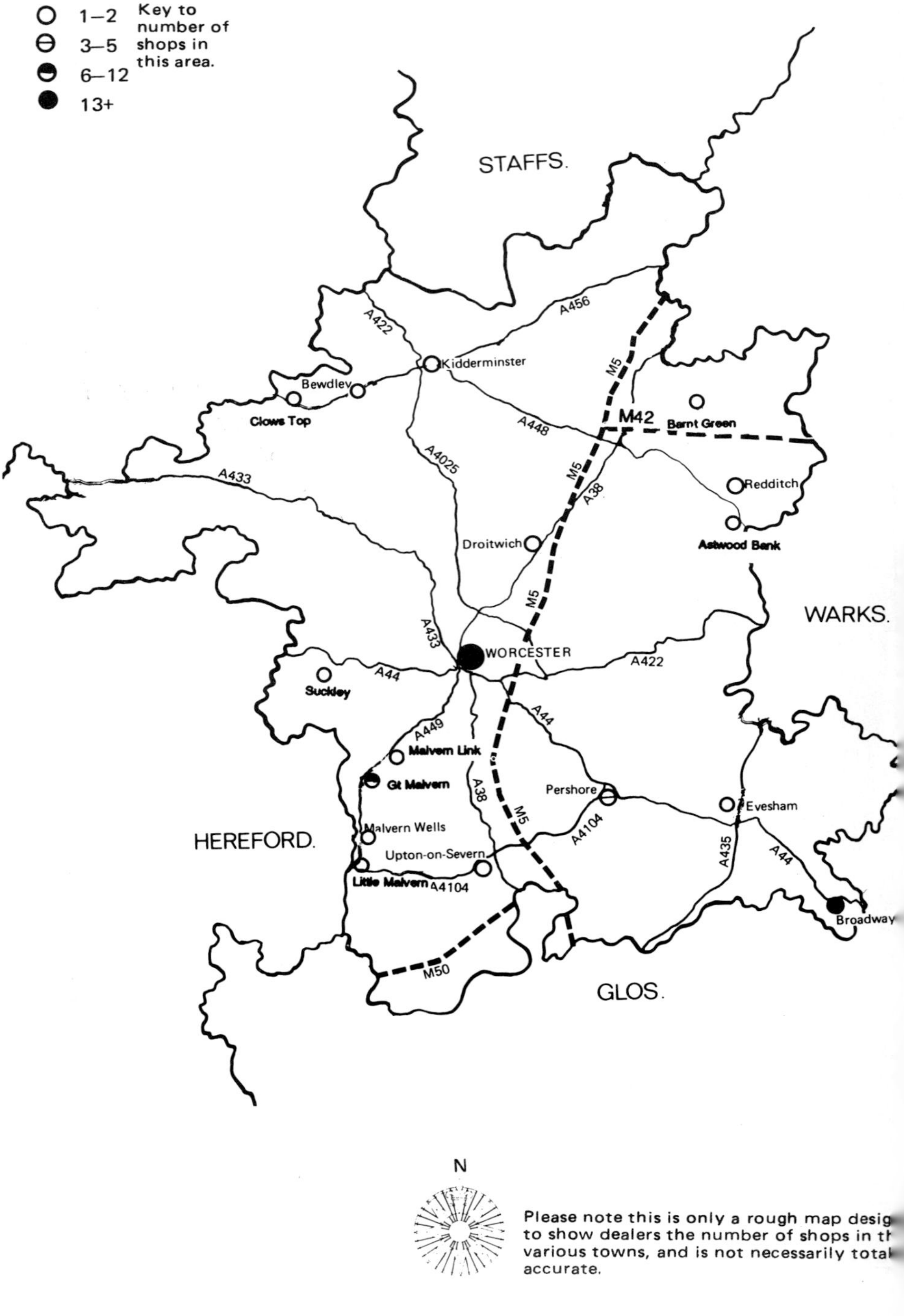

Please note this is only a rough map designed to show dealers the number of shops in the various towns, and is not necessarily totally accurate.

ASTWOOD BANK, Nr. Redditch

Bracebridge Gallery
'Robindale', 49 The Ridgeway. B96 6LU. Est. 1987. Open by appointment only. *STOCK: 18th-20th C oil paintings, and rare signed limited edition prints.* TEL: 01527 893444.

BARNT GREEN, Nr. Birmingham

Barnt Green Antiques
93 Hewell Rd. B45 8NL. (N. Slater). BAFRA. Est. 1965. Open 9-5.30. SIZE: Medium. *STOCK: Furniture, 17th-19th C, £100-£5,000.* PARK: Easy. TEL: 0121 445 4942. SER: Restorations (furniture, gilt frames, clocks, oils). VAT: Stan/Spec.

BEWDLEY

Clent Books
Rose Cottage, Habberley Rd. DY12 1JA. (Ivor Simpson). Open by appointment. *STOCK: Midlands topography and history, antiquarian, military, fine and rare, £20-£200.* TEL: 01299 401090. SER: Valuations. FAIRS: Waverley Antique and Book (Organiser).

BROADWAY

'Broadway Bears & Dolls'
76 High St. WR12 7AJ. (Janice Longhi). Open 9-6. *STOCK: Antique and modern artist's dolls and teddy bears.* TEL: 01386 858323. SER: Teddy bear museum.

Broadway Clocks
Kennel Lane, High St. WR12 7DP. (R.J. Kemp). FBHI. Est. 1992. Open 10-1 and 2.15-5. CL: Thurs. *STOCK: Longcase clocks, 17th-19th C, £1,500-£6,000; also bracket, French mantel, carriage and wall clocks.* LOC: 30 yds up lane next to Lloyds Bank. TEL: 01386 852458. SER: Clock restoration and repairs. VAT: Stan/Spec.

Broadway Old Books (formerly Stratford Trevers)
The Long Room, 45 High St. WR12 7DP. (Mary Jane Grant-Zeid). Open 9.30-1 and 2-5.30, Sun. 11 -1 and 2.30-5.30. SIZE: Large. *STOCK: Antiquarian books, maps and prints.* TEL: 01386 853668. SER: Valuations; restorations; framing; book-binding. VAT: Stan.

Fenwick and Fenwick Antiques
88-90 High St. WR12 7AJ. CADA. Est. 1980. Open 10-6, and by appointment. SIZE: Large. *STOCK: Furniture, oak, mahogany and walnut, 17th to early 19th C; samplers, boxes, treen, Tunbridgeware, Delft, decorative items and corkscrews.* TEL: 01386 853227; after hours - 01386 858502; fax - 01386 858504.

Broadway continued

Richard Hagen
Yew Tree House. WR12 7DT. Open 9.30-5.3 Sun. by appointment. *STOCK: 20th C oil watercolours and bronzes.* TEL: 01386 85362 858561; fax - 01386 852172. SER: Valuation restorations; framing. VAT: Spec.

Hay Loft Gallery
Berry Wormington. WR12 7NH. (Mrs J.R. Pitt a Miss S.A. Pitt). Resident. Est. 1984. Open 10.3 5.30 or by appointment. SIZE: Medium. *STOC Victorian paintings, £250-£15,000; Victori watercolours, £250-£3,000.* LOC: From Broadwa 4 miles on B4632 towards Cheltenham, farm right hand side. PARK: Easy. TEL: 01242 6212 511324. SER: Restorations. VAT: Spec.

Haynes Fine Art of Broadway BAI LAPAI
The Bindery Galleries, 69 High St. WR12 7D Est. 1971. Open 9-6. SIZE: Large. *STOC 16th-20th C paintings.* LOC: From Moreto 50yds. past the Stratford turn off on the le PARK: Easy. TEL: 01386 852649; fax - 013 858187. SER: Valuations; restorations; framin catalogue. VAT: Spec.

Haynes Fine Art of Broadway BAI
Picton House Galleries LAPAI
42 High St. Open 9.30-6. SIZE: Large. *STOC 19th-20th C watercolours and 20th C paintin* LOC: From Lygon Arms, 100 yds up High on left. PARK: Easy. TEL: 01386 858889; fa 01386 858882. SER: Valuations; restoratio framing; catalogue available (£4). VAT: Spec

Howards of Broadway
27a High St. WR12 7DP. Open 9.30-5.30. SIZ Small. *STOCK: Jewellery, 1750 to modern, £2 £5,000; silver, 1700 to modern, £20-£5,00 objects of vertu, 1700-1900, £50-£500.* PAR Easy and nearby. TEL: 01386 858924. SE Valuations; restorations. VAT: Stan/Spec.

H.W. Keil Ltd BAI
Tudor House. WR12 7DP. (V.M. Keil). CAD Est. 1925. Open 9-5.30. CL: Thurs. pm. SIZ Large. *STOCK: Walnut, oak, mahogany a rosewood furniture; early pewter, brass a copper, tapestry, glass and works of art, 17t 18th C.* LOC: By village clock. TEL: 013 852408; fax - 01386 852069. VAT: Spec.

John Noott Galleries BADA LAPAI
14 Cotswold Court, The Green and at T Lygon Arms, High St. WR12 7AA. CADA. E 1972. Open 9.30-1 and 2-5, also by appoir ment only at The Manor House, West En Broadway. SIZE: Large. *STOCK: Paintin and watercolours, 19th C to Contempora* PARK: Easy. TEL: 01386 852787/858969; fa 01386 858348. SER: Valuations; restoratio framing. VAT: Stan/Spec.

roadway continued

)live Branch Antiques

0 High St. WR12 7AJ. (P. and S. Riley). esident. Est. 1977. Open 9-5.30 including Sun. IZE: Small. *STOCK: Furniture, to 1900, from 100; clocks, £90-£800; pottery, £5-£150.* LOC: op end of High St. PARK: Easy and at rear. EL: 01386 853831. SER: Silver repairs; silver ating. VAT: Stan/Spec.

ROITWICH

;rant Fine Art

he Coach House, New Road, Cutnall Green. VR9 0PQ. Est. 1976. Open 9-5 or by appoint-ent. CL: Sat. SIZE: Small. *STOCK: Golfiana, ooks, prints, pictures, clubs, £5-£1,000.* TEL: 1299 851588; fax - 01299 851446.

Iigh Park Antiques Ltd

) High St. Est. 1973. Open Tues., Fri. and Sat.)-5. *STOCK: Furniture, early 19th C; silver, hina, porcelain, paintings.* TEL: 01905 796989; ome - 01905 772163.

VESHAM

Iagpie Jewellers and Antiques and Iagpie Arms & Armour LAPADA

Port St. and 61 High St. (R.J. and E.R. unn). Est. 1975. Open 9-5.30. SIZE: Large. *TOCK: Silver, jewellery, furniture, general ntiques, arms and armour, books, stamps and oins.* TEL: 01386 41631.

REAT MALVERN

'arlton Antiques

3 Worcester Rd. WR14 4RB. (Dave Roberts). pen 10-5. *STOCK: Edwardian postcards and garette cards; Victorian and Edwardian rniture, stripped pine; oil paintings, water-lours and prints.* TEL: 01684 573092. SER: aluations.

oan Coates of Malvern

St. Ann's Rd. WR14 4RG. Resident. Est. 1969. pen Thurs. and Fri. 10-1 and 2.30-5.30, Sat. 10-1. ZE: Small. *STOCK: Silver, £10-£250; small rniture, £50-£800; both 18th-20th C; small ms.* LOC: From Worcester take A449, in town oley Arms Hotel on left-hand side, take first ght. PARK: Easy. TEL: 01684 575509.

oley Furniture

oley Bank. (Dave Roberts). *STOCK: Furniture - ipping, modern and old; postcards, cigarette rds.* TEL: 01684 891255.

Ialvern Arts

3 Worcester Rd. WR14 4RB. (S.A. Conein-eber). Est. 1988. Open 10-5. SIZE: Small. *TOCK: Watercolours, Victorian and Edwardian,*

Great Malvern continued

£50-£500; oil paintings, 19th-20th C; £80-£1,000+. LOC: Town centre. PARK: Easy. TEL: 01684 575889. SER: Valuations; restorations (pictures).

Malvern Bookshop

7 Abbey Rd. WR14 3ES. (J.P. and A.M. Gibbs). Open 9.15-5.30 (Nov.-Feb. 9.15-5). *STOCK: Antiquarian, secondhand books and remainders.* LOC: Near GPO by Priory steps. PARK: Short stay on road above. TEL: 01684 575915.

Malvern Studios

56 Cowleigh Rd. WR14 1QD. (L.M. Hall). BAFRA. Open 9-5.15, Fri. and Sat. 9-4.45. CL: Wed. *STOCK: Period, Edwardian painted and inlaid furniture, general furnishings.* TEL: 01684 574913; fax - 01684 569475. SER: Restorations; woodcarving; polishing; interior design. VAT: Stan/Spec.

Miscellany Antiques

20 Cowleigh Rd. WR14 1QD. (Ray and Liz Hunaban). Resident. Est. 1974. SIZE: Medium showroom + large trade warehouse. *STOCK: Victorian, Edwardian and Georgian furniture, including shipping goods, £300-£20,000; some porcelain, silver, bronzes and jewellery.* LOC: B4219 to Bromyard. PARK: Own. TEL: 01684 566671; fax - 01684 560562; mobile - 0836 507954. SER: Valuations. VAT: Stan/Spec.

Promenade Antiques

41 Worcester Rd. WR14 4RB. (Mark Sylvester).

Whitmore

Teynham Lodge, Chase Rd., Upper Colwall. WR13 6DT. *STOCK: British and foreign coins, 1700-1950, £1-£500; trade tokens, 1650-1900, £1-£200; commemorative medallions, 1600-1950, £1-£200.* TEL: 01684 540651. *Postal Only.*

KIDDERMINSTER

B.B.M. Jewellery and Antiques

8 and 9 Lion St. DY10 1PT. (W.V. and A. Crook). Est. 1977. Open 10-5. CL: Tues. SIZE: Medium. *STOCK: Jewellery, 19th C, £50-£3,000; coins, £5-£1,000; general antiques, £5-£500.* LOC: Adjacent Youth Centre, off ring road. PARK: Easy. TEL: 01562 744118. SER: Valuations; restorations (jewellery, porcelain, silver). VAT: Stan/Spec/Global.

LITTLE MALVERN

St. James Antiques

De Lys Wells Rd. WR14 4JL. (H. Van Wyngaarden). Open 10-5 or by appointment. *STOCK: Continental pine furniture.* PARK: Easy. TEL: 01684 563404. SER: Restorations. VAT: Stan.

MALVERN LINK

Kimber & Son
6 Lower Howsell Rd. WR14 1EF. Est. 1956. Open 9-6, Sat. 9-1. *STOCK: 18th-20th C, antiques for the English, Continental and American markets.* TEL: 01684 574339; home - 01684 572000. VAT: Stan/Spec.

MALVERN WELLS

Gandolfi House
211-213 Wells Rd. WR14 4HF. (P. and R. Weller). Open 10-5.30 or by appointment. CL: Mon. *STOCK: Paintings, watercolours, prints, 19th-20th C; country furniture and smalls.* TEL: 01684 569747.

PERSHORE

Hansen Chard Antiques
126 High St. WR10 1EA. (P.W. Ridler, LBHI). Est. 1984. Open 10-5, Thurs. 10-12 but appointment advisable. CL: Mon. SIZE: Large. *STOCK: Clocks, pre-1940; longcase clocks, pre-1850, £10-£3,000; barometers £50-£1,500.* LOC: On A44. PARK: Easy. TEL: 01386 553423; home - same. SER: Valuations; restorations (as stock); buys at auction (as stock). VAT: Spec.

Penoyre Antiques
9 and 11 Bridge St. WR10 1AJ. Est. 1969. Open 10-5, other times by appointment. CL: Thurs. SIZE: Medium. *STOCK: 18th-19th C mahogany, rosewood and satinwood furniture, especially dining; giltwood mirrors, framed prints and engravings, £20-£20,000.* PARK: Easy (in main square or opposite). TEL: 01386 553522; fax - 01905 754129; home - 01386 710214. SER: Valuations. VAT: Stan/Spec.

S.W. Antiques
Abbey Showrooms, Newlands. WR10 1BP. (R.J. Whiteside). Est. 1978. Open 9-5, Sun. 10.30-4. SIZE: Large. *STOCK: 19th-20th C furniture including beds and bedroom furniture, to £4,000.* Not Stocked: Jewellery, small items. LOC: 2 mins. from Abbey. PARK: Own. TEL: 01386 555580; fax - 01386 556205. VAT: Stan/Spec.

REDDITCH

Lower House Fine Antiques
Lower House, Far Moor Lane, Winyates Green. B98 0QX. (Mrs J.B. Hudson). Est. 1987. Usually open but prior appointment advisable. SIZE: Small. *STOCK: Furniture, 17th to early 20th C, £100-£4,000; silver and plate, 18th to early 20th C, £10-£1,000; oil lamps, 19th C, £50-£500.* Not Stocked: Pine furniture. LOC: 3 miles due east

Redditch continued

Redditch town centre and half a mile fro Coventry Highway island, close to A435. PARK Own. TEL: 01527 525117; home - same. SER Valuations; restorations (including porcelain).

SUCKLEY

Holloways
Lower Court. WR6 5DE. (Edward and Dia Holloway). SIZE: Large. *STOCK: Garden statuar £50-£3,000; garden salvage, £20-£300; arch tectural antiques, £20-£3,000; all 18th-20th C* LOC: A44 from Worcester towards Leominster, le to village, premises next to church. PARK: Eas TEL: 01886 884665; home - same. SER: Val ations; restorations; buys at auction. VA Stan/Spec.

UPTON-UPON-SEVERN

The Highway Gallery
40 Old St. WR8 0HW. (J. Daniell). Est. 196 Open 10.30-5, but appointment advisable. C Thurs. and Mon. SIZE: Small. *STOCK: Oil watercolours, 19th-20th C, £100-£10,000.* N Stocked: Prints. LOC: 100yds. from crossroa towards Malvern. PARK: Easy. TEL: 016 592645; home - 01684 592909. SER: Valuation restorations (reline and clean); buys at auctic (pictures).

WORCESTER

Antique Map and Print Gallery
61 Sidbury. WR1 2HU. (M. Nichols). Open 9-5.3 *STOCK: Antiquarian maps, prints and book Baxter and Le Blond prints.* TEL: 01905 61292 SER: Framing.

Antique Warehouse
Rear of 74 Droitwich Rd, Barbourne. WR3 8B (D. Venn). Open 9-5, Sat. 10-4.30. *STOC General antiques, shipping, restored pine a satin walnut, also door furniture.* PARK: Eas TEL: 01905 27493. SER: Stripping pine, waln and metal.

Antiques and Curios
50 Upper Tything. WR1 1JZ. Open 9.30-5.3 SIZE: Large - 6 dealers on three floors. *STOC 18th to early 20th C furniture, oak, mahogan walnut, especially Victorian and Edwardi desks, dining and bedroom, decorative a upholstered, furnishings, mirrors, pictures, cloc curios, treen, objects d'art.* LOC: Fro Birmingham A38 into Worcester on right-ha side. PARK: Easy. TEL: 01905 25412/76454 SER: Restorations; re-polishing; upholster valuations.

Worcester continued

Antiques and Interiors
37 Upper Tything. WR1 1JT. (D. Twinberrow). Est. 1970. Open 9-5.30. *STOCK: Furniture especially dining tables, desks and Victorian mahogany; jewellery, silver, china, pictures and mirrors.* LOC: A38, extension of Foregate St. TEL: 01905 616606. SER: Restorations (furniture).

Antiques and Pine
47b Upper Tything. (D. Twinberrow). Open 9.30-5.30. *STOCK: Antique pine.* TEL: 01905 29014.

Andrew Boyle (Booksellers) Ltd
21 Friar St. WR1 2NA. Est. 1928. Appointments advisable. CL: Thurs. and Sat. *STOCK: Antiquarian and secondhand books.* TEL: 01905 611700. SER: Buys at auction.

Bygones by the Cathedral LAPADA
Cathedral Sq. (Gabrielle Doherty Bullock). FGA DGA. Est. 1946. Open 9.30-5.30, Sat. 9.30-1 and 2-5.30. *STOCK: Furniture, 17th-19th C; silver, Sheffield plate, jewellery, paintings, glass; English and Continental pottery and porcelain especially Royal Worcester.* LOC: Adjacent main entrance to Cathedral. TEL: 01905 25388.

Bygones (Worcester) LAPADA
55 Sidbury. WR1 2HU. (Gabrielle Bullock). FGA. Est. 1946. Open 9.30-1 and 2-5.30. *STOCK: Furniture, 17th-19th C; silver, Sheffield plate, jewellery, paintings, glass; English and Continental porcelain and pottery especially Royal Worcester.* LOC: Opposite the public car park in Sidbury and adjacent to the City Walls road junction. TEL: 01905 23132. VAT: Stan/Spec.

John Edwards Antiques
Worcester Antiques Centre, 15 Reindeer Court, Mealcheapen St. WR1 4DF. *STOCK: English majolica and porcelain, Royal Worcester and Doulton.* TEL: 01905 610680; home - 01905 353840; mobile - 0589 468934; fax - 01905 764370.

Gray's Antiques of Worcester
49 and 50a Upper Tything. (D. and M. Gray). Open 8.30-5.30. *STOCK: General antiques and soft furnishings.* TEL: 01905 724456; fax - same.

Gray's Antiques of Worcester
28 Lowesmoor. (D. and M. Gray). Open 8.30-5.30. *STOCK: Antiques and shipping goods.* TEL: 01905 616868.

Heirlooms
46 Upper Tything. WR1 1JZ. (W. MacMillan, D. Tarran and L. Rumford). Open 9.30-4.30. *STOCK: General antiques, objets d'art, Royal Worcester porcelain and prints.* TEL: 01905 23332.

Worcester continued

Sarah Hodge
Peachley Manor, Hallow Lane, Lower Broadheath. WR2 6QL. Resident. Est. 1985. Open daily including Sun. SIZE: Large. *STOCK: General antiques, country bygones, pine and kitchenalia.* LOC: Off B4204, 3 miles N.W. Worcester. PARK: Easy. TEL: 01905 640255.

M. Lees and Sons LAPADA
Tower House, Severn St. WR1 2NB. Resident. Est. 1955. Open 9.15-5.15, Sat. by appointment. CL: Thurs. pm. SIZE: Medium. *STOCK: Furniture, 1780-1880; porcelain, 1750-1920.* LOC: At southern end of Worcester Cathedral adjacent to Edgar Tower; near Royal Worcester Porcelain Museum and factory. PARK: Easy. TEL: 01905 26620; home - 01905 427142. VAT: Stan/Spec.

Round the Bend
1 Deansway. (Gabrielle Doherty Bullock). FGA DGA. Open 10-5.30. *STOCK: Eccentricities, brocante-type goods and jolly junk.* TEL: 01905 616516.

St. Georges Antiques
31B Barbourne Rd. WR1 1SA. Open 10-5.30. TEL: 01905 25915. The following dealers trade from this address.

Collectors World
Coins, militaria, cameras and Royal Worcester porcelain.

Yestertime Antiques
Clocks, barometers, furniture and small boxes.
SER: Restorations.

Long Tran Antiques LAPADA
WR9 9EW. (L. Tran). Open by appointment only. *STOCK: Fine porcelain and pottery, English and Continental.* TEL: 01905 776685; mobile - 0831 400685.

The Tything Antique Centre
39 The Tything. WR1 1KX. Open 10-5. SIZE: Medium - 30 units. *STOCK: Wide variety of general antiques.* PARK: Easy. TEL: 01905 610597.

Worcester Antiques Centre
15 Reindeer Court, Mealcheapen St. WR1 4DF. (Stephen Zacaroli). Est. 1992. Open 10-5. SIZE: Large. *STOCK: Pottery and porcelain, 1750-1940, £10-£2,000; silver, 1750-1940, £10-£3,000; jewellery, 1800-1940, £5-£2,000; furniture, 1650-1930, £50-£5,000.* PARK: Loading only or 50 yards. TEL: 01905 610680/1; fax (after 5 p.m.) - 01905 610681. SER: Valuations; restorations. FAIRS: NEC (April and Aug); East Berkshire (May and Oct). VAT: Stan/Spec.

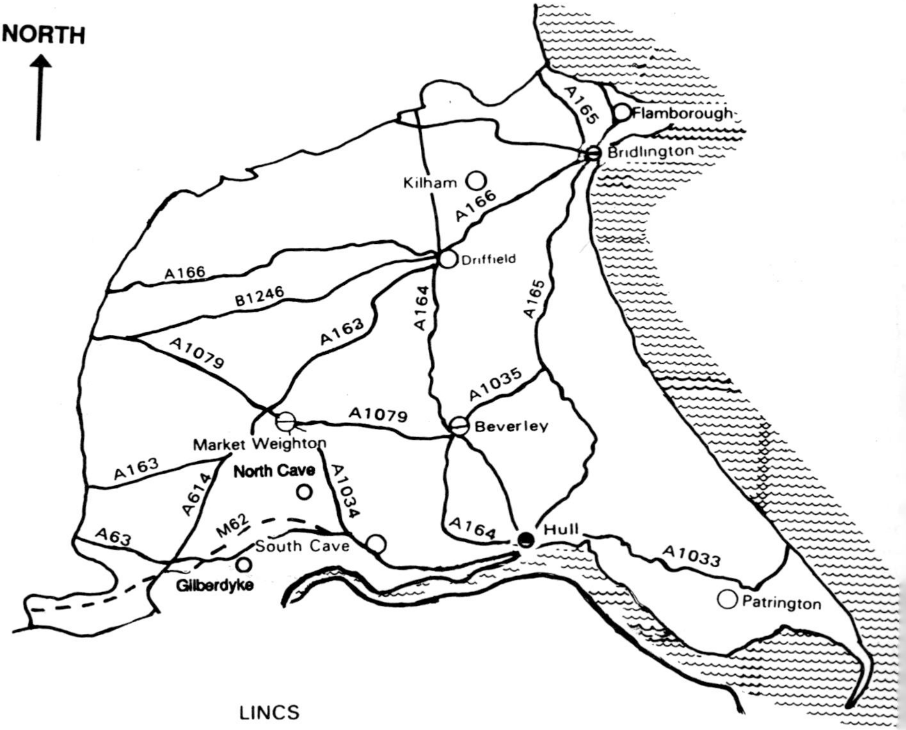

○	1-2	Key to number of shops in this area.
⊖	3-5	
◓	6-12	
●	13+	

Please note this is only a rough map designed to show dealers the number of shops in the various towns, and is not necessarily totally accurate.

BEVERLEY

Bridge House Antiques (formerly Avenue Antiques of Hull)

Hull Bridge, Tickton. HU17 9RY. (Peter White and Adele Wilkinson). Resident. Est. 1988. Open 10-5. CL: Mon. SIZE: Medium. *STOCK: Art Deco ceramics and collectables, general furniture, paintings and costume jewellery, £5-£500.* LOC: 2 miles east of Beverley on A1035. Turn right at 2nd sign for Hull Bridge - shop opposite Crown & Anchor. PARK: Own. TEL: 01964 542355. SER: Valuations. FAIRS: Hessle Foreshore and Grange Park, Willerby.

Hawley Antiques LAPADA

5 North Bar Within. HU17 8AP. Open 9.30-4, Sat. 9.30-5. *STOCK: General antiques, furniture, pottery, porcelain, glass, oil paintings, watercolours, silver.* TEL: 01482 868193. SER: Restorations (fine furniture). VAT: Stan/Spec.

James H. Starkey Galleries

49 Highgate. HU17 0DN. Est. 1968. Open 10-5, Sat. 10-1 or by appointment. SIZE: Medium. *STOCK: Oil paintings, 16th-19th C; drawings and watercolours, 17th-19th C.* LOC: Opposite minster. PARK: Easy. TEL: 01482 881179; fax - 01482 861644. SER: Valuations; restorations (paintings); buys at auction. VAT: Stan/Spec.

Time and Motion

1 Beckside. HU17 0PB. (Peter A. Lancaster). BHI. Est. 1977. Open 10-5, Thurs. and Sun. by appointment. SIZE: Medium. *STOCK: English longcase clocks, 18th-19th C, £1,500-£8,000; English, German and French mantel and wall clocks, 19th C, £300-£3,500; aneroid and mercurial barometers, 18th-19th C, £150-£3,000.* LOC: .25 mile from town centre and minster, 300 yards from Army Museum of Transport. PARK: Easy. TEL: 01482 881574; home - same. SER: Valuations; restorations (clocks and barometers). VAT: Stan/Spec.

BRIDLINGTON

C.J. and A.J. Dixon Ltd

1st Floor, 23 Prospect St. YO15 2AE. Est. 1969. Open 10-4.30. SIZE: Large. *STOCK: War medals and decorations, British and foreign.* LOC: Town centre. PARK: Easy. TEL: 01262 676877/603348; fax - 01262 606600. SER: Valuations; renovations. VAT: Stan/Spec.

Priory Antiques

47-49 High St. YO16 4PR. (P.R. Rogerson). Est. 1979. Open 10-5. CL: Thurs. *STOCK: Georgian and Victorian furniture.* TEL: 01262 601365.

Bridlington continued

Sedman Antiques

Carnaby Court, Off Moor Lane, Carnaby. YO15 3QQ. (R.H.S. and M.A. Sedman). Est. 1971. Open 10-5.30, Sun. by appointment. *STOCK: General antiques, period and shipping furniture, Oriental porcelain, Victorian collectors' items.* LOC: Off A165. TEL: 01262 674039.

Sweet's Antiques

24 West St. YO15 3DX. (John Sweet). Est. 1950. Open 10-6. *STOCK: General antiques, porcelain, glass.* TEL: 01262 677396.

G. M. Wheeler Antiques: Style & Design

53 Flamborough Rd. YO16 2JH. Est. 1989. Open 1.30-5.30. CL: Thurs. SIZE: Small. *STOCK: Furniture including stripped pine, country oak, period and decorative pieces; curios, pictures, collectables.* PARK: Easy. TEL: 01262 604308. SER: Valuations; restoration.

DRIFFIELD

The Antique Pine & Country Furniture Shop

58A Middle St. North. YO25 7SU. (D. A. Smith and A.E. Gravells). Est. 1977. Open 9.30-5.30, Sat. 9.30-5, Sun. by appointment. SIZE: Medium + warehouse. *STOCK: Furniture including pine and country, 18th to early 20th C, £50-£2,000; furniture designed and made to order, from £50+.* LOC: Main street. PARK: Easy. TEL: 01377 256321; home - same; e-mail - antique@ssdesign.demon.co.uk. SER: Restorations.

The Crested China Co

Station House. YO25 7PY. (D. Taylor). Est. 1978. Open by appointment or by chance. *STOCK: Goss and crested china.* PARK: Easy. TEL: 01377 257042 (24 hr.). SER: Sales catalogues.

FLAMBOROUGH, Nr. Bridlington

Lesley Berry Antiques

The Manor House. YO15 1PD. (Mrs L. Berry). Resident. Est. 1972. Open 9.30-5.30, other times

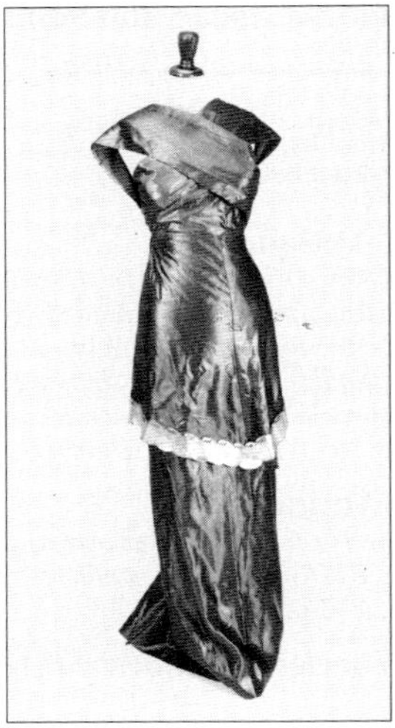

Estimated at £500-£700, this Schiaparelli 1930s petrol blue ciré silk evening gown soared to £6,800.

From an article entitled "Auction Report: Costume and Textiles at Sotheby's, 13th March" by Tom Flynn which appeared in the June 1997 issue of **Antique Collecting**

Flamborough continued

by appointment. SIZE: Small. *STOCK: Furniture, silver, jewellery, amber, Whitby jet, oils, watercolours, prints, copper, brass, textiles, fountain pens.* Not Stocked: Shipping goods. LOC: On corner of Tower St. and Lighthouse Rd. PARK: Easy. TEL: 01262 850943. SER: Buys at auction.

GILBERDYKE, Nr. Howden

Lewis E. Hickson FBHI

Antiquarian Horologist, Sober Hill Farm. HU1: 2TB. Est. 1965. Open by appointment only. SIZE Small. *STOCK: Longcase, bracket clocks, barometers and instruments..* TEL: 01430 449113. SER Restorations; repairs.

HULL

De Grey Antiques

96 De Grey St., Beverley Rd. HU5 2SB. (G Dick). Est. 1962. Open 10.30-1 and 2-5.45. SIZE Medium. *STOCK: Furniture, clocks, paintings and watercolours, Victorian; glass, china, pewter brass, copper and oil lamps.* LOC: Off main Beverley Rd., near overhead railway bridge PARK: Easy. TEL: 01482 442184. SER: Valuations; buys at auction.

Steven Dews Fine Art

66-70 Princes Ave. HU5 3QJ. Open 9-6. CL: Sa SIZE: Medium. *STOCK: Paintings, 19th-20th C* TEL: 01482 345345; fax - 01482 447928. SER Valuations; restorations; framing. VAT: Spec.

Grannie's Parlour

33 Anlaby Rd. HU1 2PG. (Mrs N. Pye). Open 11- *STOCK: General antiques, ephemera, Victoriana dolls, toys, kitchenalia.* TEL: 01482 22825 home - 01482 341020.

Grannie's Treasures

1st Floor, 33 Anlaby Rd. HU1 2PG. (Mrs N. Pye Open 11-5. SIZE: 2 dealers. *STOCK: Advertising items, postcards, tins, bottles, small furniture and pre-1940s clothing.* TEL: 01482 228258; home 01482 341020.

David K. Hakeney Antiques LAPAD

Albion House, Albion St. HU1 3TE. Est. 197 Open 10.30-6. SIZE: Medium plus warehous *STOCK: Georgian, Victorian, Edwardian furniture, smalls, shipping goods.* LOC: Ci centre. PARK: Easy. TEL: 01482 22819 mobile - 0860 507774. VAT: Stan/Spec.

Imperial Antiques

397 Hessle Rd. HU3 4EH. (M. Langton). E 1982. Open 9-5.30. *STOCK: British stripped pi furniture, antique, old and reproduction.* TE 01482 327439; fax - same. FAIRS: Newar VAT: Stan.

Hull continued

Lesley's Antiques
329 Hessle Rd. HU3 4BL. Est. 1967. Open 10-5.30. SIZE: Medium. *STOCK: General antiques, shipping goods; collectors' items, mostly under £25.* LOC: On main Hull to Hessle Rd. PARK: Easy. TEL: 01482 323986; home - 01482 646280. SER: Restorations; hire.

Kevin Marshall's Antiques Warehouse
17-20a Wilton St. (Off Dansom Lane South), Holderness Rd. HU8 7LG. Est. 1981. Open 10-5, Sun. by appointment. SIZE: Large. *STOCK: Bathroom ware, architectural items, fires, lighting, furniture and reproductions, 19th C, £5-£5,000.* LOC: 1st right off Dansom Lane South. PARK: Easy. TEL: 01482 326559; fax - same. SER: Valuations; restorations; boardroom tables made to order. VAT: Stan/Spec.

Geoffrey Mole/Antique Exports
400 Wincolmlee. HU2 0QL. Est. 1974. Open 9-5, Sat. 9-1. SIZE: Large. *STOCK: Shipping furniture, 1850-1920, £50-£2,000; general antiques, 19th C.* LOC: Half mile east off main Beverley Rd. PARK: Easy. TEL: 01482 327858; fax - 01482 218173. SER: Packing, shipping. VAT: Stan.

Pearson Antiques
The Warehouse, 6 Dalton St. HU17 0RR. (W.B.T. Grozier). Est. 1972. Open 10-5, Sat. by appointment. SIZE: Large. *STOCK: Furniture, pottery, brass, silver and plate, stuffed birds, stone figures, late 17th C to Edwardian, £50-£1,000.* LOC: Off Cleaveland St. PARK: Easy. TEL: 01482 329647; home - 01482 862927. SER: Valuations. VAT: Spec. *Trade Only.*

Sandringham Antiques
54a Beverley Rd. HU5 1NE. (P. and P. Allison). Est. 1968. *STOCK: General antiques.* TEL: 01482 347653/320874.

KILHAM, Nr. Driffield

The Old Ropery Antique Clocks
East St. YO25 0SG. *STOCK: Clocks - longcase, bracket, carriage and French, Vienna regulator, fusee and wall.* LOC: Village centre, near PO. PARK: Easy. TEL: 01262 420233. SER: Valuations; restorations (furniture and clocks); spares.

MARKET WEIGHTON, Nr. York

Garforth Gallery
57 Market Place. YO4 3AJ. Est. 1956. Open 9-5, Sat. 9-4. SIZE: Small. *STOCK: Paintings, prints, maps, clocks, jewellery, silver, £20-£600.* Not Stocked: Porcelain. LOC: On main road in town centre. TEL: 01430 872391. SER: Valuations; restorations.

Market Weighton continued

Houghton Hall Antiques
Cliffe/North Cave Rd. YO4 3RE. (M.E. Watson). Est. 1965. Open daily 8-4, Sun. 11-4. SIZE: Large. *STOCK: Furniture, 17th-19th C, £5-£8,000; china, 19th C, £1-£600; paintings and prints, £20-£1,000; objets d'art.* Not Stocked: Coins, guns. LOC: Turn right on new by-pass from York (left coming from Beverley), 3/4 mile, signposted North Cave - sign on entrance. PARK: Easy. TEL: 01430 873234. SER: Valuations; restorations (furniture); buys at auction. FAIRS: New York (USA). VAT: Stan/Spec.

Pieter Plantenga
49 Holme Rd. YO4 3EW. Open 9-4.30. *STOCK: Stripped pine, general furniture.* TEL: 01430 872473.

NORTH CAVE

Penny Farthing Antiques
Albion House, 18 Westgate. (C.E. Dennett). Est. 1987. Open 9.30-6. SIZE: Medium. *STOCK: Furniture, 19th-20th C, Victorian brass and iron bedsteads, £25-£2,000; linen, textiles and samplers, 18th-20th C, £5-£500; general collectables, china and glass, 19th-20th C, £5-£500.* LOC: Main road (B1230). PARK: Easy. TEL: 01430 422958. SER: Valuations; buys at auction. FAIRS: Newark.

PATRINGTON

Clyde Antiques
12 Market Place. HU12 0RB. (S. M. Nettleton). Est. 1978. Open 10-5. CL: Sun., Mon. and Wed. except by appointment. SIZE: Medium. *STOCK: General antiques.* PARK: Easy. TEL: 01964 630650; home - 01964 612471. SER: Valuations. VAT: Stan.

SOUTH CAVE

The Old Copper Shop and Post House Antiques
69 and 75 Market Place. HU15 2AS. (Mrs E.A. Featherstone). Est. 1986. Open 9.30-4.30. SIZE: Medium. *STOCK: Furniture, 19th-20th C; linen, general antiques and collectors' items.* Not Stocked: Militaria, coins. LOC: A1034. PARK: Easy. TEL: 01430 423988; home - 01482 631110. SER: Valuations.

Yorkshire North

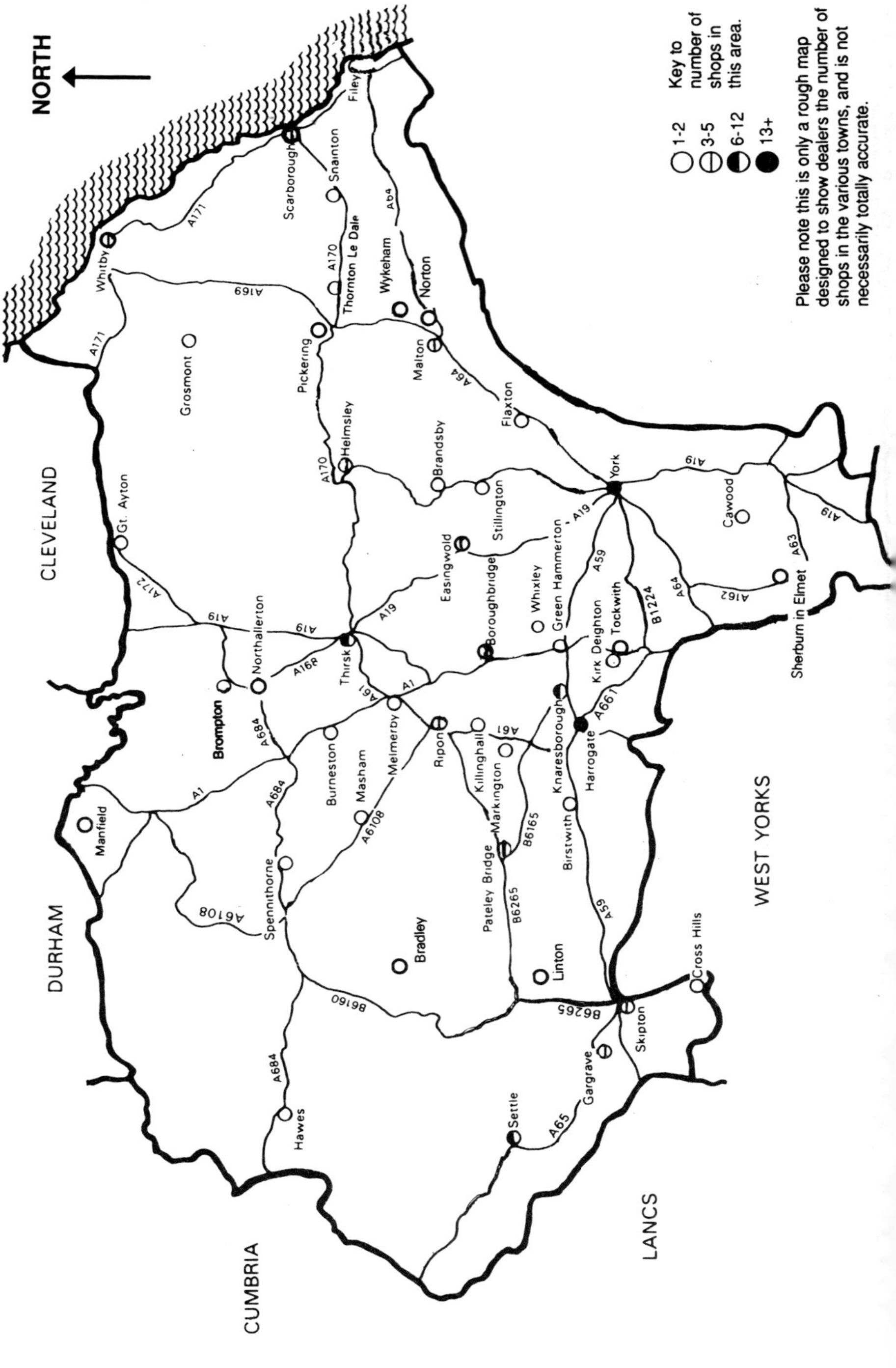

BIRSTWITH, Nr. Harrogate

John Pearson Antique Clock Restoration

Church Cottage. HG3 2NG. Est. 1978. Open by appointment. *STOCK: Longcase, bracket and wall clocks, 18th C.* LOC: Off A59. PARK: Easy. TEL: 01423 770828; home - same. SER: Restorations (clocks, cases, movements and especially dials).

BOROUGHBRIDGE

Country Antiques

38 High St. YO5 9AW. (P.W. Raine). Resident. Est. 1969. Open 10-4, prior telephone call advisable if travelling from a distance. CL: Thurs. and Fri. SIZE: Small. *STOCK: Silver, 17th-20th C, £25-£500; metalware, small furniture, 18th-19th C, and objet d'art.* PARK: Easy. TEL: 01423 324017. SER: Buys at auction (silver).

Galloway Antiques

High St. YO5 9AW. (Mr and Mrs J.E. Gay). Est. 1977. Open 9.30-5.30. SIZE: Large. *STOCK: Furniture, 18th-20th C, £50-£3,000; paintings, 19th-20th C, £75-£2,000; decorative items.* Not Stocked: Arms and medals. LOC: 1 mile off A1. PARK: Easy. TEL: 01423 324602; home - 01423 506719. SER: Valuations. FAIRS: Organiser - Galloway Antiques Fairs.

Anthony Graham Antiques

Aberure, Bridge St. YO5 9LA. Resident. Est. 1985. Open Sat. 10-5, or by appointment. SIZE: Medium. *STOCK: Furniture, 18th-19th C, £50-£2,500; pictures, 19th-20th C, £50-£2,000; general antiques, 18th-19th C, from £5.* LOC: Off A1. PARK: Easy. TEL: 01423 323952; fax - same. SER: Valuations.

St. James House Antiques LAPADA

St. James Sq. YO5 9AR. (J.D. Wilson). Est. 1989. Open 9-5.30, Thurs. and Sun. by appointment. SIZE: Medium. *STOCK: Period and later furniture, brass, copper and china.* LOC: Town centre. PARK: Own. TEL: 01423 322508; home - same. SER: Valuations; restorations ; upholstery. FAIRS: Galloways. VAT: Stan/Spec.

R.S. Wilson and Sons

4 Hall Square. YO5 9AN. Est. 1917. Open 9-5.30, Thurs. 9-12.30. *STOCK: 17th-19th C furniture and accessories.* TEL: 01423 322417; fax - same. VAT: Stan/Spec.

BRADLEY

Ryefield House Antiques

Ryefield House, Skipton Rd. BD20 9EF. (Mr and Mrs I.C. Roberts). Est. 1976. Open Mon., Thurs. and Fri. 8.30-5, other times by appointment. SIZE: Small. *STOCK: Pottery and porcelain, 18th-20th C,*

Bradley continued

£5-£10,000; bronzes, spelter and metalware, 19th C, £5-£500; small furniture, 19th C to Edwardian, £50-£2,500. LOC: Village 2 to 3 miles south of Skipton, off A629. From village centre, turn left, premises on right, lions on gateposts. PARK: Easy. TEL: 01535 633192; home - same. SER: Valuations; restorations (furniture); buys at auction (pottery and porcelain).

BRANDSBY

L.L. Ward and Son

Bar House. YO6 4RQ. (R. Ward). Est. 1970. Open 8.30-5. *STOCK: Antique pine.* TEL: 01347 888651

BROMPTON, Nr. Northallerton

Country Pine Antiques

Unit 45, The Old Mill. DL6 2UP. (C. Tindle). Open 9-5, Sat. by appointment. *STOCK: Victorian pine.* TEL: 01609 774322.

BURNESTON, Nr. Bedale

Simon Greenwood Antiques

DL8 2JD. (S. and C. Greenwood). Est. 1976. Open by appointment. *STOCK: Furniture, including upholstered items, 17th-20th C, £5-£1,000; decorative items and textiles.* LOC: 1/4 mile from A1. PARK: Easy. TEL: Home - 01677 422554. SER: Valuations; buys at auction. VAT: Stan/Spec.

W. Greenwood (Fine Art)

Oak Dene, Church Wynd. DL8 2JE. Est. 1978. Open by appointment. *STOCK: Paintings and watercolours, 19th-20th C, £100-£5,000; frames, £20-£500; mirrors.* LOC: Take B6285 left off A1 northbound, house 1/4 mile on right. PARK: Easy. TEL: 01677 424830; home - 01677 423217. SER: Valuations; restorations (paintings and frames); framing.

CAWOOD, Nr. Selby

Cawood Antiques

Sherburn St. YO8 0SS. (J.E. Gilham). Open 9-6 including Sun. *STOCK: General antiques, shipping, furniture, copper, brass, porcelain, pictures, collectors' items.* PARK: Easy. TEL: 01757 268533.

CROSS HILLS, Nr. Keighley

Heathcote Antiques

1 Aire St. BD20 7RT. (M. Webster). Resident. Est. 1979. Open 10-5.30, Sun. 12.30-4. CL: Mon. and Tues. SIZE: Warehouse. *STOCK: Furniture, including pine especially unstripped; smalls.* PARK: Easy. TEL: 01535 635250.

EASINGWOLD

Fox's Antique Pine
108 Long St. YO6 3HY. (M.J. Fox). Est. 1958. Open 10-5.30. *STOCK: Pine furniture.* PARK: Easy. TEL: 01347 822977. SER: Stripping (pine and metals).

Milestone Antiques
Farnley House, 101 Long St. (A.B. and S.J. Streetley). Open daily, Sun. by appointment. SIZE: Medium. *STOCK: Mahogany and oak furniture, £100-£2,000; longcase and wall clocks, upholstered and pine furniture, pictures, prints. oils and watercolours, £100-£800; all 18th to early 20th C.* LOC: A19, village centre. PARK: Easy. TEL: 01347 821608; home - same. SER: Valuations. VAT: Stan/Spec.

Old Flames
30 Long St. YO6 3HT. (P. Lynas and J.J. Thompson). Est. 1988. Open 10-5. SIZE: Medium. *STOCK: Fireplaces, 18th-19th C, £100-£1,000; lighting, 19th C, £25-£250; architectural items, 18th-19th C, £50-£500.* PARK: Easy. TEL: 01347 821188. SER: Valuations. FAIRS: Newark. VAT: Stan/Spec.

Mrs B.A.S. Reynolds
42 Long St. *STOCK: General antiques, Victorian.* TEL: 01347 821078.

White House Farm Antiques
Thirsk Rd. YO6 3NF. (G. Hood). Resident. Est. 1960. Usually open but prior 'phone call advisable. *STOCK: Rural and domestic bygones, stone troughs, architectural reclamation and garden ornaments.* LOC: 1 mile north of Easingwold, 200 yds from northern junction of bypass (A19). PARK: Easy. TEL: 01347 821479.

FILEY

Cairncross and Sons
31 Bellevue St. YO14 9HU. (G. Cairncross). Open 9.30-12.45 and 2-4.30. CL: Wed. (Oct.-March). *STOCK: Medals, uniforms, insignia, cap badges.* Not Stocked: Weapons. TEL: 01723 513287.

Filey Antiques
1 Belle Vue St. YO14 9HU. Est. 1970. Open daily 11-4.30; Thurs. to Sat. 11-4 in winter. SIZE: Small. *STOCK: Small furniture, prints, china, bric-a-brac, jewellery.* Not Stocked: Coins, militaria. LOC: Town centre, at corner of Belle Vue St. and West Ave. PARK: Easy. TEL: 01723 513440.

FLAXTON, Nr. York

Elm Tree Antiques
YO6 7RJ. (R. and J. Jackson). Est. 1975. Open 9-5, Sun. 10-5. SIZE: Large. *STOCK: Furniture, 17th*

Flaxton continued

C to Edwardian; small items, £5-£5,000, Staffordshire figures. LOC: 1 mile off A64. PARK: Easy. TEL: 01904 468462; home - same; fax - 01904 468728. SER: Valuations; restorations (cabinet making, polishing and upholstery).

GARGRAVE, Nr. Skipton

Antiques at Forge Cottage
22A High St. BD23 3RB. Est. 1979. Open Tues., Thurs., Sat. 11-4.30, or by appointment. *STOCK: Porcelain, small silver, glass, collectables, brass.* LOC: A65. PARK: Easy. TEL: 01756 748272.

Bernard Dickinson
Estate Yard, West St. BD23 0RD. (H.H. and A.E. Mardall). Resident. Est. 1958. Open 9-5.30 or by appointment. *STOCK: Early English furniture.* LOC: Just off A65 Skipton-Settle road. PARK: Easy. TEL: 01756 748257. VAT: Spec.

Gargrave Gallery
48 High St. BD23 3RB. (B. Herrington). Appointment advisable. *STOCK: General antiques.* PARK: Easy. TEL: 01756 749641.

R.N. Myers and Son BADA
Endsleigh House, High St. BD23 3LX. Est. 1890. Open 9-5.30 or by appointment. SIZE: Medium. *STOCK: Furniture, oak, mahogany 17th to early 19th C; pottery, porcelain and metalware.* Not Stocked: Victoriana, weapons, coins, jewellery. LOC: A65. Skipton-Settle road. PARK: Behind shop and opposite. TEL: 01756 749587. SER: Valuations. VAT: Spec.

GREAT AYTON

The Great Ayton Bookshop
47 & 53 High St. TS9 6NH. (M.S. Jones). Est. 1978. Open 10-5.30, Wed. 10-2, Sun. 2-5.30. CL: Mon. SIZE: Medium. *STOCK: Books, rare and secondhand, 50p-£100; postcards, pre-1930, 10p-£20; prints, 10p-£50.* LOC: 7 miles south of Middlesbrough off Stokesley road. PARK: Easy. TEL: 01642 723358. SER: Valuations. FAIRS: PBFA. VAT: Stan.

GREEN HAMMERTON, Nr. York

The Main Pine Co
Grangewood, The Green. YO5 8DB. (C. and K.M. Main). Est. 1976. Open 9-5, Sun. 11-4. SIZE: Large. *STOCK: Pine furniture, 18th-19th C, £100-£1,500; reproductions from old pine.* LOC: Just off A59. PARK: Easy. TEL: 01423 330451; home - 01423 331078; fax - 01423 331278; e-mail - mainpine@onyxnet.co.uk. SER: Export; containers packed. VAT: Stan.

ɜROSMONT, Nr. Whitby

ːountry Connections (Esk House Arts)
ʻront St. Workshop and Framing Dept., Esk Iouse, Grosmont. YO22 5PF. (J.M. Stonehouse).)pen 11-5 including Sun. *STOCK: Fine art, ʻrints especially sporting, steam engine and andscapes, some originals by local artists; china nd pottery by local craftsmen.* LOC: First floor, bove the Co-op. TEL: 01947 895319; fax - ame; home - 01947 895469.

ꞁARROGATE

ʌnn-tiquities
2 Cheltenham Parade. (Mrs A. Wilkinson). ʻpen 12-4. CL: Wed. *STOCK: Antique linen and ʻnall collectables.* TEL: 01423 503567.

ʌrmstrong BADA LAPADA
0-11 Montpellier Parade. HG1 2TJ. (M.A. rmstrong). Est. 1976. Open 10-5.30. SIZE: Iedium. *STOCK: Fine English furniture, 18th ʻ early 19th C; glasses and works of art, 18th C.* ARK: Easy. TEL: 01423 506843. FAIRS: ʻlympia (Feb., June, Nov.); BADA; Chelsea. ʼAT: Spec.

ʒill Bentley
ʼ5 Montpellier Parade. HG1 2TG. Open 9.30-.30 or by appointment. SIZE: Large. *STOCK: ʻak furniture, 1600-1800; country furniture, 700-1800; period metalwork and treen.* PARK: asy. TEL: 01423 564084; home - 01423 ʖ4564. VAT: Spec.

ryan Bowden
akleigh, 1 Spacey View, Leeds Rd., Pannal. G3 1LQ. Est. 1969. By appointment only. IZE: Small. *STOCK: English pottery and ʻrcelain, 1750-1850; small Georgian furniture.* OC: 2.5 miles south of Harrogate on Leeds ʻad. PARK: Easy. TEL: 01423 870007; home - me. SER: Valuations; restorations (pottery and ʻrcelain); buys at auction (English pottery and ʻrcelain). FAIRS: Northern; Buxton; Wakefield ɛramic. VAT: Spec.

Harrogate continued

Derbyshire Antiques Ltd
27 Montpellier Parade. HG1 2TG. (R.C. and M.T. Derbyshire). Est. 1960. Open 10-5.30. SIZE: Medium. *STOCK: Early oak and walnut, 16th-18th C; Georgian furniture to 1820; decorative items.* TEL: 01423 503115/564242. VAT: Spec.

Dragon Antiques
10 Dragon Rd. HG1 5DF. (P.F. Broadbelt). Resident. Est. 1954. Open 11-6. Always available. SIZE: Small. *STOCK: Victorian art glass, £30-£300; art pottery, postcards, G.B. and foreign.* LOC: 5 mins. from town centre, opposite Dragon Road car park. PARK: Easy. TEL: 01423 562037.

Garth Antiques LAPADA
2 Montpellier Mews. HG1 2TQ. (I. Chapman). Open 10-5.30. SIZE: Medium. *STOCK: Furniture, 18th-19th C, £50-£3,000; brass and copper, 19th C, £1-£500; oils and watercolours, £5-£3,000.* LOC: Turn left from Montpellier Parade at Montpellier public house. TEL: 01423 530573. VAT: Stan/Spec.

The Ginnel
Harrogate Antique Centre, The Ginnel. HG1 2RB. (P. Stephenson). Open 9.30-5.30. *STOCK: All date-lined and vetted - see individual entries.* LOC: Off Parliament St. opposite Debenhams. PARK: Nearby. TEL: 01423 508857. SER: Courier. Below are listed the specialist dealers at this centre.

Anglo-Scandinavian
Cutlery, silver plate, inkwells, collectors' and decorative items.

Appleton Antiques
Art pottery - Moorcroft, Carlton ware specialist. TEL: Home - 01642 316417. SER: Valuations.

Fiona Aston
Objets d'art including porcelain and miniatures.

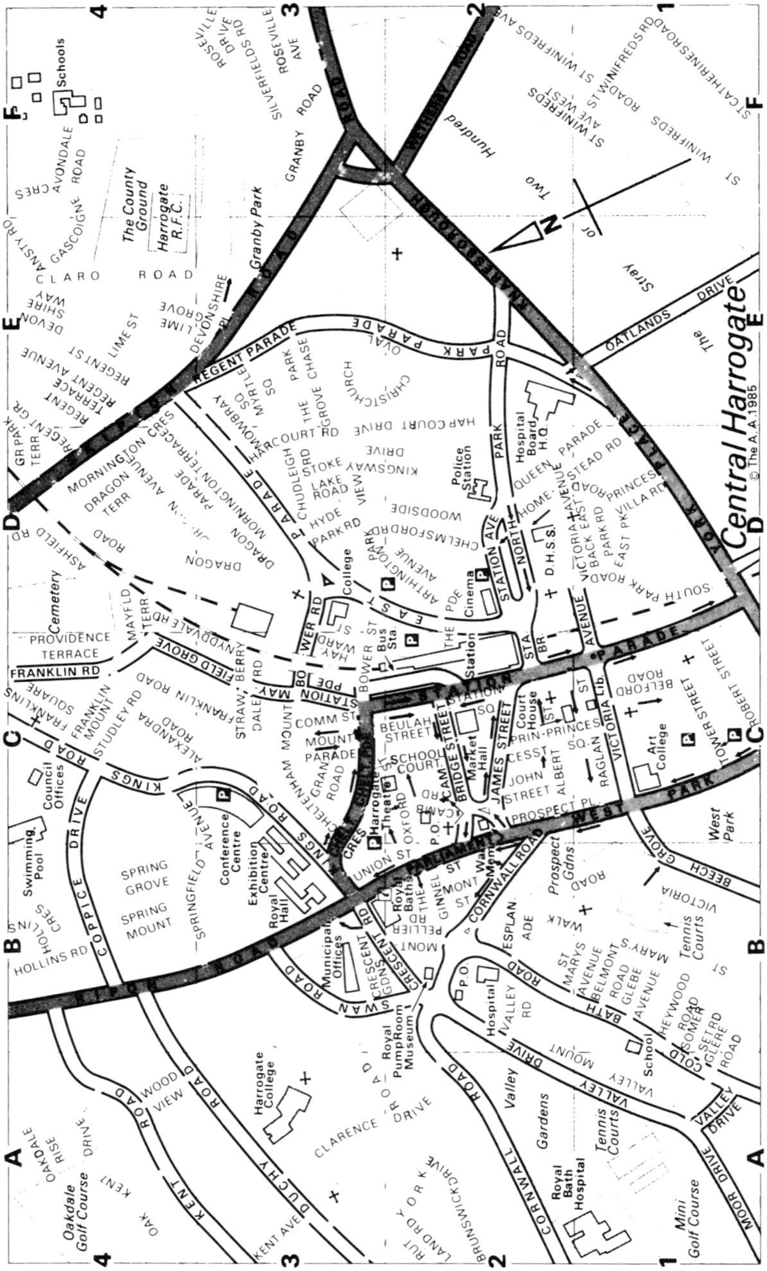

Key to Town Plan

AA Recommended roads
Other roads
Restricted roads
Buildings of interest
Car Parks
Parks and open spaces
AA Service Centre

Harrogate continued

J. Bottomley
Victorian jewellery and silver items.

Brackmore Antiques
Silver, porcelain and objets d'art.

Bygones
Objets d'art including dolls, small silver, porcelain and jewellery.

Mary Cooper
Antique costumes and textiles to 1929, including lace, fans, shawls, linen, quilts, samplers, woolwork and beadwork. TEL: 01423 567182.

A. & A. Cox
Period pottery and porcelain.

Dale Antiques
Silver and objet d'art.

P. Danby
19th and early 20th C jewellery.

Richard Freeman
British, Oriental and Continental ceramics, 18th to early 19th C. TEL: Mobile - 0421 645788.

Georgian House
Victorian and Edwardian furniture.

R. Gillingham
Small 19th C furnishings and general works of art.

Jeffrey and Pauline Glass
Porcelain and glass, objets d'art, 19th to early 20th C.

V. Jones
Victorian and Edwardian jewellery.

B. & R. Jordan
Paintings, specialising in Yorkshire artists.

Ian Leggard
18th and 19th C silver and works of art.

Libra Antiques
Georgian, Victorian and Edwardian furniture and decorative items, including cranberry glass.

Brian Loomes
Longcase clocks, small period furniture.

Catherine Lough
Small 19th C furniture and furnishings, French influence.

MBA
Fine antique and later silver. TEL: Mobile - 0860 710001.

Harrogate continued

Milestone Antiques
Porcelain and pottery.

Brian Naylor
Pottery including Mason's and Staffordshire figures; boxes; all 18th-19th C.

Parker Gallery
19th to early 20th C oils and watercolours, £100-£3,000.

Past Reflections
Victorian and Edwardian furniture, porcelain and silver.

Jane Robson
Collectables.

Ian Sharp
Early 19th C furniture and quality porcelain.

Beverley Shaw
Fine period silver and cutlery.

J. Steele
Victorian and Edwardian silver.

Stella-Mar
Fine quality 19th C furniture and furnishings, wide variety of object d'art.

Ann Wilkinson
Silver and porcelain.

Wycliffe Antiques
19th C pottery and porcelain.

Michael Green Traditional Interiors
Library House, Regent Parade. HG1 5AN. Est. 1976. Open 8.30-5.30, Sat. 8.45-4, Sun. by appointment. SIZE: Medium. *STOCK: Pine furniture, Georgian, Victorian, Edwardian, £5-£2,000; treen, kitchenalia and collectors' items.* LOC: Overlooking the Stray. PARK: Easy. TEL: 01423 560452. SER: Valuations; restorations; stripping. VAT: Stan/Spec.

Grove Collectors Centre
Grove Rd. HG1 5EW. Open 10-4. CL: Fri. SIZE: 8 dealers. *STOCK: General antiques including silver, porcelain, cigarette cards, collectables and furniture.* TEL: 01423 561680.

Havelocks
15-17 Westmoreland St. HG1 5AY. (Philip Adam). Est. 1989. Open 10-5, Wed. 10-1. SIZE: Large. *STOCK: Original pine, oak, general antique furniture.* LOC: A59 towards Skipton, turn left into Westmoreland St. TEL: 01423 506721. SER: Valuations; restorations; stripping and finishing; buys at auction.

Harrogate continued

Haworth Antiques

26 Cold Bath Rd. HG2 0NA. (G. and J. White). Open 10-5 or by appointment. CL: Mon. SIZE: Medium. *STOCK: Clocks, 18th-19th C, £100-£3,000; small furniture, Georgian and Victorian, £50-£1,000.* LOC: 300yds. from Crown Hotel. PARK: Easy. TEL: 01423 521401; mobile - 0831 692263. SER: Restorations (clocks, dials, re-painted and re-silvered). VAT: Stan/Spec.

London House Oriental Rugs and Carpets

9 Montpellier Parade. HG1 2TJ. Est. 1981. Open 10-5.30. SIZE: Medium. *STOCK: Persian, Turkish, Indian, Tibetan, Nepalese, Afghan, Chinese and Rumanian rugs and carpets, 19th-20th C, £25-£5,000; kelims and camel bags, 19th-20th C, £25-£2,000.* LOC: Town centre on The Stray. PARK: Easy. TEL: 01423 567167; home - 01937 845123. SER: Valuations; restorations (handmade rugs). VAT: Stan.

David Love BADA

10 Royal Parade. HG1 2SZ. Est. 1969. Open 9-1 and 2-5.30. SIZE: Large. ***STOCK: Furniture, English, 17th-19th C; pottery and porcelain, English and Continental; decorative items, all periods.*** **LOC: Opposite Pump Room Museum. PARK: Easy. TEL: 01423 565797. SER: Valuations; buys at auction. VAT: Stan/Spec.**

Harrogate continued

Charles Lumb and Sons Ltd BADA

2 Montpellier Gardens. HG1 2TF. (F. and A.R. Lumb). Est. 1920. Open 9-1 and 2-6. SIZE: Medium. ***STOCK: Furniture, 17th to early 19th C; metalware, period accessories.*** **PARK: 20yds immediately opposite. TEL: 01423 503776; home - 01423 863281; fax - 01423 530074. VAT: Spec.**

D. Mason & Son

7/9 Westmoreland St. HG1 5AY. FGA, NAG. Open 9-5. *STOCK: Victorian, Edwardian and secondhand jewellery; clocks.* TEL: 0142 567305. SER: Repairs (clocks and jewellery).

McTague of Harrogate

17/19 Cheltenham Mount. HG1 1DW. (P. McTague). Open 9.30-1 and 2-5.30. SIZE: Medium. *STOCK: Prints, watercolours, some oil paintings, mostly 18th to early 20th C.* LOC: From Conference Centre on Kings Rd., go up Cheltenham Parade and turn first left. PARK: Easy. TEL: 01423 567086. VAT: Stan/Spec.

Montpellier Mews Antique Market

Montpellier St. HG1 2TG. Open 10-5. SIZE: Various dealers. *STOCK: General antiques, porcelain, jewellery, furniture, paintings, interior decor, linen, glass and silver.* LOC: Behind Weatherells. TEL: 01423 530484.

Ogden of Harrogate Ltd BADA

38 James St. HG1 1RQ. Est. 1893. Open 9.15-5. SIZE: Large. ***STOCK: Jewellery, English silver and plate.*** **TEL: 01423 504123; fax - 0142 522283. VAT: Stan/Spec.**

Omar (Harrogate) Ltd

The Smithy, Haggs Farm, Haggs Rd., Follifoot. Est. 1946. Open by appointment. SIZE: Medium. *STOCK: Persian, Turkish, Caucasian rugs and carpets.* PARK: Easy. TEL: 01423 873796/86319. SER: Cleaning and restoration. VAT: Stan.

Paraphernalia

38A Cold Bath Rd. HG2 0NA. (P.F. Hacker). Open 10-5. *STOCK: Postcards, crested china and commemoratives, collectors' items, bric-a-brac, small furniture.* TEL: Evenings - 01423 567968.

Paul M. Peters Antiques LAPADA

15a Bower Rd. HG1 1BE. Est. 1967. Open 10-. CL: Sat. SIZE: Medium. ***STOCK: Chinese and Japanese ceramics and works of art, 17th-19th C; European ceramics and glass, 18th-19th C; European metalware, scientific instruments and unusual objects.*** **LOC: Town centre, at bottom of Station Parade. PARK: Easy. TEL: 0142 560118. SER: Valuations. VAT: Stan/Spec.**

Elaine Phillips Antiques Ltd BADA

1 and 2 Royal Parade. HG1 2SZ. Open 9.30-5.30, other times by appointment. SIZE: Large. ***STOCK: Oak furniture, 1600-1800; country furniture, 1700-1840; some mahogany, 18th***

Harrogate continued

early 19th C; period metalwork and decoration. LOC: Opposite Crown Hotel. TEL: 01423 569745. VAT: Spec.

Smith's (The Rink) Ltd

Dragon Rd. HG1 5DR. Est. 1906. Open 9-5.30. SIZE: Large. *STOCK: General antiques, 1750-1820, £150; Victoriana, 1830-1900, £50.* LOC: From Leeds, right at Prince of Wales crossing, left at Skipton Rd. and left before railway bridge. PARK: Easy. TEL: 01423 567890. VAT: Stan/Spec.

Sutcliffe Galleries BADA

5 Royal Parade. HG1 2SZ. Est. 1947. Open 10-5. CL: Mon. *STOCK: Paintings, 19th C.* LOC: Opposite Crown Hotel. TEL: 01423 562976; fax - 01423 528729. SER: Valuations; restorations; framing.

Thorntons of Harrogate LAPADA

1 Montpellier Gdns. HG1 2TF. Open 9.30-5.30. *STOCK: 17th-19th C furniture, metalware, clocks, paintings, porcelain, arms and armour, scientific instruments.* TEL: 01423 504118; fax - 01423 528400. VAT: Spec.

Walker Galleries Ltd BADA LAPADA

6 Montpellier Gdns. HG1 2TF. Est. 1972. Open 9.30-1 and 2-5.30. SIZE: Medium. *STOCK: Oil paintings and watercolours, 18th C furniture.* TEL: 01423 567933. SER: Valuations; restorations; framing. FAIRS: Chelsea, Harrogate, Olympia. VAT: Spec.

Christopher Warner BADA

15 Princes St. HG1 1NG. (C.C. Warner and G.S.M. Brown). Est. 1770. Open 9.30-5. SIZE: Small. *STOCK: Jewellery, 1740-1890; silver, 1720-1840; both £50-£12,000.* PARK: Easy. TEL: 01423 503617. SER: Valuations; restorations (silver and jewellery); buys at auction. FAIRS: Harrogate and NEC. VAT: Stan/Spec.

Weatherell's of Harrogate Antiques and Fine Arts LAPADA

29 Montpellier Parade. HG1 2TG. Open 9-5.30. SIZE: Large. *STOCK: Period and fine decorative furniture.* TEL: 01423 507810/525004; fax - 01423 520005.

Chris Wilde Antiques LAPADA

The Courtyard, Mowbray Sq., Westmoreland St. HG1 5AU. (C.B. Wilde). Est. 1996. Open Mon.-Fri. 10-4, or by appointment. SIZE: Large. *STOCK: Furniture, 1730-1920, £300-3,000; longcase clocks, 1750-1920, £250-2,500.* LOC: North side of town. PARK: Easy. TEL: Mobile - 0831 543268; fax - 01423 506030. SER: Valuations. VAT: Stan/Spec.

Windmill Antiques

Montpellier Mews, Montpellier St. HG1 2TJ. (B. and J. Tildesley). Est. 1980. Open 10-5.30. SIZE: Small. *STOCK: Furniture, £250-£5,000; copper and brass, £20-£500; boxes, inkstands, rocking horses and children's chairs, £50-£5,000;*

Harrogate continued

all 18th-19th C. LOC: Behind Montpellier Parade. PARK: Nearby. TEL: 01423 530502; home - 01845 501330.

HAWES

Sturman's Antiques LAPADA

Main St. DL8 3QW. Open 10-5 including Sun. *STOCK: Georgian and Victorian furniture; porcelain, silver plate, paintings; longcase, wall and mantel clocks.* TEL: 01969 667742.

HELMSLEY

Rievaulx Books

18 High St. YO6 5AG. (C. Howard). Est. 1986. Open 10.30-5. CL: Mon. SIZE: Medium. *STOCK: Antiquarian books especially on natural history, field sports, Yorkshire, art and antiques.* LOC: From Market Sq., past church, shop 100 yards past Feversham Arms inn. PARK: Easy. TEL: 01439 770912; home - same.

Westway Pine

28 Bond Gate and Carlton Lane. YO6 5DE. (J. and J. Dzierzek). Est. 1986. Open 9-5, Sat. 10-5, other times by appointment. SIZE: Medium. *STOCK: Pine furniture, 19th C, £20-£2,000.* LOC: From A170 from Scarborough, first right into town, first left, then left again 100m. PARK: Easy. TEL: 01439 771399; home - 01439 770172. SER: Valuations; restorations (pine).

York Cottage Antiques LAPADA

7 Church St. YO6 5AD. (G. and E.M. Thornley). Est. 1976. Open May-Oct. Thurs., Fri. and Sat.; Nov.-April Fri. and Sat. 10-4 or by appointment. *STOCK: Early oak and country furniture; 18th-19th C metalware; drinking glasses, pottery and porcelain especially Ironstone, Staffordshire figures, lustre and blue and white; cranberry glass.* LOC: Opposite church. PARK: Adjacent. TEL: 01439 770833; home - same.

KILLINGHALL, Nr. Harrogate

Norwood House Antiques

88 Ripon Rd. HG3 2DH. (R.M. Mallaby). Resident. Est. 1981. Open 10-4. CL: Wed. *STOCK: English and Continental furniture, 19th C; porcelain, clocks, silver, decorative items.* PARK: Easy. TEL: 01423 506468.

KIRK DEIGHTON, Nr. Wetherby

Elden Antiques

23 Ashdale View. LS22 4DS. (E. and D. Broadley). Est. 1970. Open 9-6, Sat. 12-5.30. SIZE: Medium. *STOCK: General antiques including furniture.* LOC: Main road between Wetherby and Knaresborough. PARK: Easy. TEL: 01937 584770; home - same.

KNARESBOROUGH

Robert Aagaard & Co
Frogmire House, Stockwell Rd. HG5 0JP. Est. 1961. Open 9-5, Sat. 10-4. SIZE: Medium. *STOCK: Chimney pieces, marble fire surrounds and interiors.* LOC: Town centre. PARK: Own. TEL: 01423 864805. VAT: Stan.

Bowkett
9 Abbey Rd. HG5 8HY. (E.S. Starkie). Resident. Est. 1919. Open 9-6. SIZE: Medium. *STOCK: Chairs, small furniture, brass, copper, pot-lids, Goss, books.* LOC: By the river at the lower road bridge. PARK: Easy. TEL: 01423 866112. SER: Restorations (upholstery and small furniture).

Cheapside Antiques
4 Cheapside. (Mrs M.E. Hanson). Open 10.30-5. CL: Mon. and Thurs. *STOCK: Furniture, porcelain, metalware and small collectors' items, 1750-1900.* TEL: 01423 867779. VAT: Spec.

The Emporium
Market Flat Lane, Lingerfield. HG5 9JA. (N. Wadley). Open by appointment. SIZE: Medium and warehouse. *STOCK: Pine and general antiques.* PARK: Easy. TEL: 01423 868539. SER: Packing; shipping; courier. VAT: Stan.

Milton J. Holgate BADA
36 Gracious St. HG5 8DS. Est. 1972. Open 9-5.30 or by appointment. CL: Thurs. *STOCK: 17th-19th C furniture and associated items.* PARK: Easy. TEL: 01423 865219. VAT: Mainly Spec.

The Gordon Reece Gallery
24 Finkle St. HG5 8AA. Open 10.30-5, Sun. 2-5. CL: Thurs. SIZE: Large. *STOCK: Flat woven rugs and nomadic carpets, tribal sculpture, jewellery, furniture, decorative and non-European folk art especially ethnic and Oriental ceramics.* TEL: 01423 866219; fax - 01423 868165. SER: Restorations.

Reflections
23 Waterside. HG5 8DE. (J. and M.V. McNamara). Resident. Est. 1977. Open Tues.-Sun. 9.30-6, other times by appointment. SIZE: Small. *STOCK: Furniture, 19th C; paintings, 19th to early 20th C, both £50-£1,000; bric-a-brac and brassware.* LOC: Turn off A59 at World's End Inn. PARK: Easy. TEL: 01423 862005.

John Thompson Antiques LAPADA
Swadforth House, Gracious St. HG5 8DT. Est. 1968. *STOCK: 18th-19th C furniture and related decorative objects.* TEL: 01423 864698. VAT: Spec.

LINTON, Nr. Skipton

Ings House Antiques
Thorpe Lane. BD23 5HL. (Miss Sonia P. Barnes). Est. 1988. Open if signs displayed, otherwise by appointment. SIZE: Medium. *STOCK: Furniture,*

Linton continued

18th-19th C, £100-£1,000; pottery and porcelain, general interesting objects, brass, copper and glass, 18th-20th C, £10-£500. LOC: Between Cracoe and Thorpe, signposted at junction of B6265 Skipton-Grassington road. PARK: Easy. TEL: 0175 730301; home - same. SER: Restorations (furniture, pottery); buys at auction (as stock).

LONG PRESTON

Gary K. Blissett
3 Station Rd. BD23 4NH. Open by appointmen only. *STOCK: 19th-20th C paintings and watercolours.* TEL: 01729 840384.

MALTON

Crambe Antiques
10 The Shambles. (Mrs L. M. Cole). Open Tues. Fri. and Sat. 10-4. SIZE: Small. *STOCK: Countr furniture, 18th-19th C; blue and white, Stafford shire, brass, textiles and decorative items.* LOC Off Market Place. PARK: Market Place. TEL 01653 618667. FAIRS: Harrogate; Newark Alexandra Palace.

Malton Antique Market
2 Old Maltongate. YO17 0EG. (Mrs M.A Cleverly). Est. 1970. Open 9.30-12.30 and 2-5 CL: Thurs. SIZE: Medium. *STOCK: Furniture Georgian to Victorian, to £1,500; glass, bric-a brac, porcelain, pottery, copper and brass.* LOC From York take A64, shop is at main traffic ligh junction in Malton. PARK: 20yds. further. TEL 01653 692732. SER: Commission sales.

Talents Fine Arts Ltd
7 Market Place. YO17 0LP. (J. Burrows). Es 1986. Open daily. SIZE: Medium. *STOCK: Oils watercolours and prints, 19th C, £500-£3,000 contemporary local artists.* LOC: A64 nea church. PARK: Easy. TEL: 01653 600020. SER Restorations; framing.

MANFIELD, Nr. Darlington

Trade Antiques - D.D. White
Lucy Cross Cottage. DL2 2RJ. Est. 197 *STOCK: Georgian, Victorian and expor furniture.* LOC: B6275, Scotch Corner t Piercebridge road, on left 3 miles after leavin A1. PARK: Easy. TEL: 01325 374303; 0183 638329. VAT: Stan/Spec.

MARKINGTON, Nr. Harrogate

Daleside Antiques
Hinks Hall Lane. HG3 3NU. Est. 1978. Open 8- Sat. and Sun. by appointment. *STOCK: Pin furniture, decorative items, architectural feature and fittings, 18th-19th C, £50-£3,500; Georgia mahogany furniture; Victorian shop fittings.* TE 01765 677888; fax - 01765 677886. SEF Containers; courier; restorations. VAT: Stan.

MASHAM, Nr. Ripon

Aura Antiques
1-3 Silver St. HG4 4DX. (R. and R. Sutcliffe). Est. 1985. Open 9.30-5, Sun. by appointment. SIZE: Medium. *STOCK: Furniture especially period mahogany dining furniture, 18th to mid-19th C, £50-£5,000; metalware - brass and copper, fenders, £5-£250; china, glass, silver and decorative objects, £5-£1,000; all 18th-19th C.* LOC: Corner of Market Sq. PARK: Easy. TEL: 01765 689315; home - 01765 658192. SER: Valuations; delivery throughout UK. VAT: Spec.

MELMERBY, Nr. Ripon

Kindon Antiques Ltd
Unit 23 Melmerby Industrial Estate, Green Lane. Open 9.30-5, other times by appointment. CL: Sat. *STOCK: Large and unusual pine.* TEL: 01765 640522. SER: Containers. *Trade Only.*

NORTHALLERTON

The Antique and Art
7 Central Arcade. DL7 8PY. (Mrs J. Willoughby). Open 10-4. CL: Thurs. *STOCK: Porcelain, pottery, silver, jewellery, glass, prints and paintings.* TEL: 01609 772051; home - 01609 774157.

Collectors Corner
145/6 High St. DL7 8SL. (J. Wetherill). Est. 1972. Open 10-4, Sat. 10-5, or by appointment. CL:Thurs. *STOCK: General antiques, collectors' items.* LOC: Opposite GPO. TEL: 01609 777623; home - 01609 775199.

NORTON, Nr. Malton

Northern Antiques Company
2 Parliament St., Scarborough Rd. YO17 9HE. (Sara Ashby-Arnold). Est. 1991. Open 9-1 and 2-5, Sat. 9.30-12.30, Sun. and evenings by appointment. SIZE: Medium. *STOCK: Country oak furniture, from 17th C, £200-£2,000; pine, Georgian to Victorian, to £1,000; upholstered sofas and chairs, cast-iron beds, decorative items and prints, from 19th C, to £800; some contemporary interior design items.* LOC: From Malton town centre on old Scarborough Rd., through Norton, shop on right above Aga shop. PARK: Easy. TEL: 01653 697520; home - 01423 340398.

PATELEY BRIDGE

Cat in the Window Antiques
22 High St. HG3 5JU. (Mrs S. Morgan). Est. 1976. Open 2.30-5 and by appointment. CL: Mon. and Wed. *STOCK: Small furniture, metalware, glass, ceramics, Art Nouveau, Art Deco, amber, coral, jet, pictures, sewing items, linen, lace and collectors' items.* PARK: Easy. TEL: 01423 711343.

Pateley Bridge continued

Brian Loomes
Calf Haugh Farm. HG3 5HW. (Author of clock reference books). Est. 1966. Open 9-5 by appointment. SIZE: Medium. *STOCK: British clocks, especially longcase, wall, bracket and lantern, pre-1840, £500-£10,000.* Not Stocked: Foreign clocks. LOC: From Pateley Bridge, first private lane on left on Grassington Rd. (B6265). PARK: Own. TEL: 01423 711163; home and fax - same. VAT: Spec.

Pateley Bridge Antiques
The Apothecary's House, 35 High St. HG3 5QG. (A.D. Gora and Ms C. Simmons). Est. 1977. Open Wed.-Sat. 1.30-5, other times by appointment (including Sun.). SIZE: Medium. *STOCK: Oak and country furniture, 17th-18th C, £100-£3,000; longcase clocks and Windsor chairs, 18th-19th C, £250-£2,000; metalware including copper and pewter, 17th-19th C, £30-£300; small antiquities, from 3000 BC, £10-£200.* LOC: Ripon-Grassington road. PARK: Almost opposite. TEL: 01423 711004; home - 01423 711517. SER: Valuations.

PICKERING

Country Collector
11-12 Birdgate. Y018 7AL. (G. and M. Berney). Est. 1991. Open 10-5. CL: Wed. SIZE: Small. *STOCK: Ceramics, including blue and white and Art Deco pottery, and collectables, 1800-1940, £5-£500.* LOC: Top of the Market Place, at crossroads of A169 and A170. PARK: Eastgate. TEL: 01751 477481. SER: Valuations; buys at auction (ceramics). VAT: Stan.

Eastgate Antiques
30 Eastgate. YO13 9QP. (J.D. and C. Vance). Est. 1988. Open 10.30-5. CL: Wed. SIZE: Small. *STOCK: Metalware, 19th C, £50-£200.* LOC: A170. PARK: Easy. TEL: 01751 472954; home - same. SER: Restorations (metalware).

C.H. Reynolds
122 Eastgate. YO18 7DW. Open 9.30-5.30, Sun. by appointment. *STOCK: General antiques.* TEL: 01751 472785.

RIPON

Balmain Antiques
13 High Skellgate. HG4 1BA. Open 10-4. *STOCK: Fine furniture, paintings, silver and porcelain.* TEL: 01765 601294.

Rose Fine Art and Antiques
13 Kirkgate. HG4 1PA. (Mr and Mrs S. Rose). Est. 1984. Open daily, Sun. by appointment. CL: Wed. SIZE: Medium. *STOCK: Pictures, 18th to early 20th C, £5-£2,000; furniture, £50-£1,000; porcelain and glass, £5-£500; both 19th to early 20th C.* LOC: Between Market Place and cathedral. PARK: Nearby. TEL: 01765 690118; home - same. SER: Valuations; restorations (pictures); buys at auction (pictures and prints); framing. VAT: Stan.

Sigma Antiques and Fine Art
Water Skellgate. HG4 1BQ. (D. Thomson). Est. 1963. Open 10.30-5, other times by appointment. *STOCK: 17th-20th C furniture, furnishing items, pottery, porcelain, objets d'art, paintings, jewellery and collectors' items.* PARK: Nearby. TEL: 01765 603163; fax - 01765 690933.

Skellgate Curios
2 Low Skellgate. HG4 1BE. (J.I. Wain and P.S. Gyte). Est. 1974. Open 11-5. CL: Wed. *STOCK: General antiques, silver, jewellery and curios.* TEL: 01765 601290; home - 01765 635336/01748 812140.

SCARBOROUGH

Browns Antiques
6 Seamer Rd. Corner. YO12 5BA. (Miss L. Brown). Est. 1973. Open 10-5. SIZE: Medium. *STOCK: Furniture, pictures, porcelain, pottery, objets d'art, Victorian, Georgian, £5-£4,500; Art Deco, Art Nouveau.* LOC: At junction of Seamer Rd. and Falsgrave Rd. PARK: Nearby. TEL: 01723 377112/891812.

Scarborough continued

Hanover Antiques
10 Hanover Rd. YO11 1LS. Est. 1976. Open 10-4 CL: Wed. *STOCK: Militaria, medals, badges and general small items, Dinky toys, 50p-£500* PARK: Easy. TEL: 01723 374175.

Shuttleworths
7 Victoria Rd. YO11 1SB. (L.R. Shuttleworth) Open 10-4. CL: Wed. *STOCK: General antiques* TEL: 01723 366278.

SCARTHINGWELL, Nr. Tadcaster

Scarthingwell Arcades
Scarthingwell Centre, Scarthingwell Farm. LS2 9PG. (Mrs G. Brier). Est. 1990. Open 10- including Sun. SIZE: Large. *STOCK: General antiques - bric-a-brac, pine, small period furniture, from £5.* LOC: Off A162 between Sherburn-in-Elmet and Tadcaster. PARK: Easy TEL: 01937 557877. SER: Valuations; restorations (furniture); buys at auction.

SETTLE

Benita - Antique Textiles and Interiors
King William House, High St. BD24 9EX. Est. 1987. Open 9-5.30. CL: Wed. SIZE: Large *STOCK: Period textiles, cushions, curtains needlework pictures and tapestries, 17th-20th C Old Master drawings, French decorative objects some period furniture and smalls.* LOC: Opposite Post Office, on old High St. PARK: Easy. TEL 01729 822085; fax - 01729 824179. SER: Full interior design; suppliers of National Trust paint and quality modern fabrics and wallpapers. VAT Stan/Spec.

Mary Milnthorpe and Daughters Antique Shop
Market Place. BD24 9DX. Est. 1958. Open 9.30 5. CL: Wed. SIZE: Small. *STOCK: Antique and 19th C jewellery and English silver.* LOC Opposite Town Hall. PARK: Easy. TEL: 0172 822331. VAT: Stan/Spec.

Nanbooks
Roundabout, 41 Duke St. BD24 9AJ. (J.L. and N.M. Midgley). Resident. Est. 1955. Open Tues Fri. and Sat. 11-12.30 and 2-5.30. CL: Jan., Feb and Mar. SIZE: Small. *STOCK: English pottery porcelain including Oriental, glass, general small antiques, 17th-19th C, to £250.* Not Stocked Jewellery. LOC: A65. PARK: Easy. TEL: 0172 823324; home - 01729 823856.

Roy Precious
King William House, High St. BD24 9EX Resident. Est. 1972. Open 10-5.30 or by appointment. CL: Wed. SIZE: Large. *STOCK: Oak walnut, mahogany and country furniture, 17th-19th C, £30-£6,000; oil paintings, main portraits, 17th-19th C, £300-£10,000; som*

Settle continued

pottery and prints; textiles, needlework pictures and tapestries, 17th-19th C. LOC: Opposite Post Office, on the old High St. PARK: Easy. TEL: 01729 823946; fax - 01729 824179. SER: Valuations. VAT: Stan/Spec.

Settle Antiques Agency
3 Kirkgate. BD24 9DX. (Ann Gent). Resident. Est. 1994. Open 10-5.30, Sat. 10.30-5.30, Wed. and Sun. by appointment only. SIZE: Small. *STOCK: Country furniture, 17th-19th C; pine, mainly 19th C, all £50-£1,000; railwayana, £10-£500.* LOC: Near the Market Place. PARK: Ashfield. TEL: 01729 822355; home - same. SER: Restorations (furniture); polishing; pine-stripping; trade warehouse by appointment.

Anderson Slater Antiques
6 Duke St. BD24 7DW. (K.C. Slater). Est. 1962. Open 10-1 and 2-5. CL: Wed. SIZE: Medium. *STOCK: Furniture, 18th-19th C, £200-£2,000; porcelain, 18th-19th C, £25-£500; pictures, 19th-20th C, £200-£1,500.* LOC: Main street out of Market Place. PARK: Nearby. TEL: 01729 822051. SER: Valuations; restorations (furniture and porcelain); buys at auction. VAT: Stan/Spec.

E. Thistlethwaite
The Antique Shop, Market Sq. BD24 9EF. Est. 1972. Open 9-5. CL: Wed. SIZE: Medium. *STOCK: Country furniture and metalware, 18th-19th C.* LOC: Town centre, A65. PARK: Forecourt. TEL: 01729 822460. VAT: Stan/Spec.

SHERBURN IN ELMET

Drey Antique Centre
56 Low St. LS25 6BA. (Valerie L. Keates). Est. 1979. Usually 10-5 including Sun. CL: Wed. SIZE: Medium. *STOCK: Country furniture, 18th-19th C, £150-£1,000; collectables and Doulton figures, £2-£200; paintings and prints, £5-£1,000; books on Yorkshire.* LOC: 3 miles east A1 between Leeds and Selby. PARK: Easy. TEL: 01977 681404. SER: Valuations; restorations (furniture, clocks, pictures including framing); buys at auction. FAIRS: Local and Newark.

SKIPTON

Adamson Armoury
Otley Rd. BD23 1ET. (J.K. Adamson). Est. 1975. Open Tues.-Sat. 10-4.15, Mon. 10-12. SIZE: Medium. *STOCK: Weapons, 17th-19th C, £10-£1,000.* LOC: A65, 200yds. from town centre. PARK: Rear. TEL: 01756 791355. SER: Valuations. FAIRS: London.

Corn Mill Antiques
High Corn Mill, Chapel Hill. BD23 1NL. (Mrs M. Hawkridge). Est. 1984. Open 10-4. CL: Tues. and Wed. SIZE: Medium. *STOCK: Oak, mahogany and walnut furniture, £100-£2,000; porcelain, silver plate, prints, pictures, brass and copper, £5-£500; all Georgian to 1920's.* Not Stocked: Jewellery, gold and silver. LOC: From town

Skipton continued

centre take Grassington Road, Chapel Hill is first right. PARK: Easy. TEL: 01756 792440; home - 01729 830489. SER: Valuations. VAT: Spec.

Craven Books
23 Newmarket St. BD23 2JE. (Miss K. Farey and Miss M.G. Fluck). Open 10.30-12.30 and 1.30-5, Sat. until 4. CL: Tues. and first and last Mon. every month. *STOCK: General items.* TEL: 01756 792677. SER: Finder (books).

Old Co-op
Off Main Street, Hellifield. (Graham Coles). Est. 1988. Usually open daily but prior 'phone call advisable. SIZE: Large. *STOCK: 17th-19th C furniture and railwayana.* TEL: 01729 850573. SER: Restorations (furniture); polishing.

SNAINTON, Nr. Scarborough

Cottage Antiques
19 High St. YO13 9AE. (Mrs E.A. Shackleton). Resident. Est. 1984. CL: Sat. pm. SIZE: Small. *STOCK: Georgian furniture especially longcase clocks; china, glass, Victorian rocking horses, pictures, unusual cottage items, £1-£3,500.* Not Stocked: Weapons and stamps. LOC: A170, equidistant Scarborough and Pickering. PARK: Easy. TEL: 01723 859577. SER: Valuations; restorations (cabinet work, rocking horses).

SPENNITHORNE, Nr. Leyburn

N.J. and C.S. Dodsworth
Thorney Hall. DL8 5PW. Est. 1973. Open by appointment. SIZE: Medium. *STOCK: Furniture, clocks and small items, 17th-19th C.* LOC: Off A684. TEL: 01969 622277. VAT: Margin.

STILLINGTON

Pond Cottage Antiques
Brandsby Rd. YO6 1NY. (C.M. and D. Thurstans). Resident. Est. 1972. *STOCK: Pine, kitchenalia, country furniture, treen, metalware, brass, copper.* TEL: 01347 810796.

THIRSK

Richard Bennett
18 Kirkgate. Est. 1979. Open by appointment. SIZE: Small. *STOCK: Oil paintings, £50-£2,000; watercolours, £50-£500; both 19th to mid-20th C.* LOC: Joins Market Place. PARK: Nearby. TEL: 01845 524085; home - same. SER: Restorations (oil paintings); buys at auction; framing.

Cottage Antiques and Curios
1 Market Place. YO7 1HQ. (Mrs E.H. and S.R. Ballard). Est. 1970. Open 9-5. CL: Wed. *STOCK: Victorian porcelain and glass, £5-£500; paintings, £20-£1,000, furniture, from 1750, £20-£1,000; brass, copper, silver and plated ware, £5-£500.* PARK: Easy. TEL: 01845 522536/523212; home - 01845 577461.

Thirsk continued

Barry Alexander Ogleby (Jnr) Antiques
St James' House & rear of 39 The Green, St James' Green. YO7 1AQ. Open every day 10-5 and by appointment. SIZE: Medium - shop and workshop. *STOCK: Mainly period oak and country furniture, also Georgian and Victorian mahogany.* LOC: A1, A168 to Thirsk. TEL: 01845 526565/524120. SER: Restorations (furniture).

B. Ogleby - St James' House Antiques
35-37 St James' Green. YO7 1AQ. Est. 1966. Open 10-5 and by appointment. SIZE: Large. *STOCK: Mahogany, oak, walnut, rosewood and pine furniture, 17th-20th C.* LOC: A1, A168 to Thirsk 6 minutes. TEL: 01845 526565; fax - same; mobile - 0410 353534. SER: Packing; shipping. VAT: Stan/Spec.

Potterton Books
The Old Rectory, Sessay. YO7 3LZ. (Clare Jameson). Open 9-5. SIZE: Large. *STOCK: Classic reference works on art, architecture, interior design, antiques and collecting.* TEL: 01845 501218; fax - 01845 501439. SER: Book search; catalogues. FAIRS: London; Frankfurt; Paris; New York; Milan; Dubai.

Eileen Quigley
The Warehouse, Rear of 39 St James' Green. YO7 1AQ. Est. 1980. Open 10-5 and by appointment. SIZE: Large. *STOCK: 17th-20th C furniture.* TEL: 01845 526565; fax - same; mobile - 0850 187692. SER: Packing and shipping; export. VAT: Stan/Spec.

THORNTON LE DALE, Nr. Pickering

Stable Antiques
4 Pickering Rd. YO18 7LG. (Mrs S. Kitching Walker). Open 2-5 (later in summer), mornings by appointment. CL: Mon. SIZE: Medium. *STOCK: Porcelain, £5-£500; furniture, £20-£700; silver, glass, brass, plate, copper, collectors' items, £5-£150, all 19th C to 1930's.* LOC: A170. PARK: Easy. TEL: 01751 474332; home - 01751 474435. SER: Valuations.

TOCKWITH, Nr. York

Tomlinson (Antiques) Ltd. & Period Furniture Ltd
LAPADA

Moorside. YO5 8QG. Est. 1971. Open 8-5, Sat. 9-4.30 or by appointment. SIZE: Large. *STOCK: Furniture, £5-£8,000; clocks, £10-£3,000.* LOC: A1 Wetherby take B1224 towards York. After 3 miles turn left on to Rudgate. At end of this road turn left, business 200m on left. PARK: Easy. TEL: 01423 358833; fax - 01423 358188. SER: Export; restorations; container packing. VAT: Stan/Spec. *Trade Only (Mon-Fri.).*

WHITBY

Aird-Gordon Antiques
15 Baxtergate. Open Mon.-Sat. *STOCK: Glass, jewellery, jet, china, small furniture.* TEL: 0194 601515.

The Bazaar
7 Skinner St. YO21 3AH. (F.A. Doyle). Est. 1970. Open 10.30-5.30. *STOCK: Jewellery, furniture, general antiques, 19th C.* TEL: 01947 602281.

'Bobbins' Wool, Crafts, Antiques
Wesley Hall, Church St. YO22 4DE. (D. and P. Hoyle). Open 10.30-5 every day. SIZE: Small. *STOCK: General antiques especially oil lamps, bric-a-brac, kitchenalia, 19th-20th C.* LOC: Between Market Place and steps to Abbey on cobbled East Side. PARK: Nearby (part of Church St. is pedestrianised). TEL: 01947 60058 (answerphone). SER: Repairs and spares (oil lamps). VAT: Stan.

Caedmon House
14 Station Sq. YO21 1DU. (E.M. Stanforth). Est. 1977. Open 10-5. SIZE: Medium. *STOCK: General, mainly small, antiques including jewellery, dolls, Disney and china, especially Dresden, to £1,200.* PARK: Easy. TEL: 01947 602120; home - 0194 603930. SER: Valuations; restorations (china); repairs (jewellery). VAT: Stan/Spec.

Coach House Antiques
75 Coach Rd., Sleights. YO22 5BT. (C.J. Rea). Resident. Est. 1973. Open 10-5 (winter months 10.30-4.30). CL: Sun. and Thurs. except by appointment. SIZE: Small. *STOCK: Furniture, especially oak and country; glass, jewellery, linen, metalware, paintings, porcelain, pottery, silver, unusual and decorative items.* LOC: On A169, 3 miles south west of Whitby. PARK: Easy, opposite. TEL: 01947 810313.

WHIXLEY

Garth Antiques
The Old School, Franks Lane. YO5 8AP. (Chapman). Est. 1978. Open Tues-Sat. 10-5. SIZE: Medium. *STOCK: Furniture, 18th-19th C, £50-£3,000; brass and copper, 19th C, £1-£500; oil and watercolours, £5-£3,000.* LOC: A59, turn towards Whixley at the Cattle/Whixley junction then left opposite The Anchor into old village next to Village Hall. PARK: Easy. TEL: 0142 331055. VAT: Stan/Spec.

WYKEHAM, Nr. Scarborough

Village Farm Antiques
30 The Village. YO13 9QP. (J.D. and C. Vance). Est. 1996. Open 10.30-5, Sun. 12-5. CL: Tues. and Wed. SIZE: Small. *STOCK: Victorian brass and iron beds; French wooden beds, 1900's.* LOC: Off A170, turn opposite Downe Arms Hotel in village. PARK: Easy. TEL: 01723 86542 home - same. SER: Restorations (metalware).

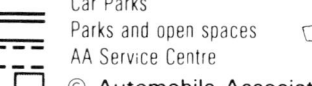

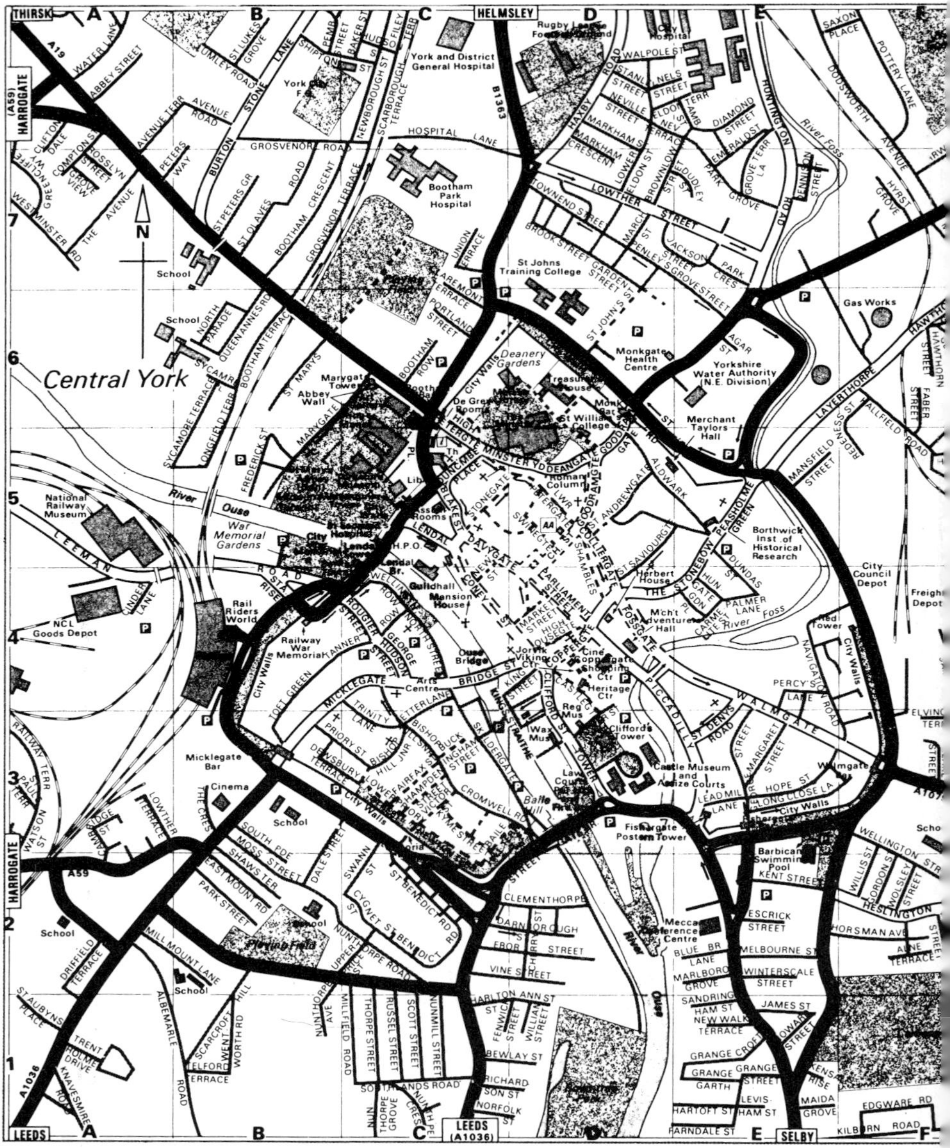

Key to Town Plan

AA Recommended roads
Other roads
Restricted roads
Buildings of interest
Car Parks
Parks and open spaces
AA Service Centre

YORK

Barbican Bookshop
24 Fossgate. YO1 2TA. Est. 1961. Open 9.15-5.30. *STOCK: Antiquarian books.* TEL: 01904 653643; fax - 01904 653643. VAT: Stan.

Barker Court Antiques and Bygones
44 Gillygate. YO3 7EQ. (Mrs D. Yates). Est. 1970. Open 10.30-5.30. SIZE: Small. *STOCK: Pottery and porcelain, glass, flatware, jewellery, Victorian to 1970, £3-£100.* LOC: 3 mins. walk from Minster. PARK: Nearby. TEL: 01904 622611.

Bishopsgate Antiques
23/24 Bishopsgate St. YO2 1JH. (R. Wetherill). Open 9.15-6. *STOCK: General antiques.* TEL: 01904 623893; fax - 01904 626511.

Barbara Cattle BADA
45 Stonegate. YO1 2AW. Open 9-5.30. *STOCK: Jewellery and silver, Georgian to date.* TEL: 01904 623862.

Coulter Galleries
YO2 2LX. Open by appointment only. *STOCK: Watercolours and oils, pre-1900; frames.* TEL: 01904 702101.

The Emporium
77 Walmgate. YO1 2TZ. Open 10-5. CL: Tues. *STOCK: General antiques, including furniture and fireplaces, and collectables.* PARK: Nearby. TEL: 01904 634124.

Fettes Fine Art
YO2 1QB. (T. and G. Thornton). Open by appointment only. SIZE: Medium. *STOCK: Parian statuary, bronzes, alabaster and marble figureens, and Victorian paintings.* TEL: 01904 641344.

Ruth Ford Antiques
39 Fossgate. Est. 1976. Open 11.30-4.30. CL: Mon. and Wed. SIZE: Small. *STOCK: 18th-19th C country furniture, pine, treen and collectables, £5-£1,000.* LOC: Near Merchant Adventurers Hall. PARK: Nearby. TEL: Home - 01904 632864.

Golden Memories of York
4 Newgate. YO1 2LA. (M.S. and D.J. Smith). NAG. Est. 1991. Open 9-5.30. SIZE: Small. *STOCK: Antique and secondhand jewellery and silver, £5-£3,000.* LOC: Adjacent York market, off Parliament St. PARK: Multi-storey. TEL: 01904 655883. VAT: Stan/Spec.

Robert M. Himsworth
28 The Shambles. YO1 2LX. Est. 1949. Open 9-5. SIZE: Small. *STOCK: Antique jewellery.* TEL: 01904 625089. VAT: Stan/Spec.

Holgate Antiques
Holgate Rd. YO2 4AB. (E.J.W. Mellors and A.C.R. Kent). Est. 1980. Open 10-5. *STOCK: Furniture and general antiques.* TEL: 01904 630005.

York continued

Minster Antiques
24 Goodramgate. YO1 2LG. (M. Tanner and K. Nevens). Est. 1982. Open daily. SIZE: Small. *STOCK: Brass and copper, silver, scientific instruments, 19th C, £5-£500.* LOC: 2 minutes from Minster, past St. William's College towards Monk Bar. PARK: Loading only. TEL: 01904 655481. SER: Valuations.

Minster Gate Bookshop
8 Minster Gates. YO1 2HL. (N. Wallace). Est. 1970. Open 9.30-5.30. SIZE: Large. *STOCK: Antiquarian and secondhand books; old maps and prints.* LOC: Opposite south door of Minster. PARK: Nearby. TEL: 01904 621812. SER: Valuations; restorations; book finding.

Robert Morrison and Son BADA
Trentholme House, 131 The Mount. YO2 2DA. (C. Morrison). Est. 1890. Open 9.30-5. SIZE: Large. *STOCK: English furniture, 1700-1900; porcelain and clocks.* LOC: Near racecourse, one mile from city centre on Leeds Rd. From A1, take A64 to outskirts of York, then take A1036 York west road. PARK: Easy. TEL: 01904 655394. VAT: Stan/Spec.

O'Flynn Antiquarian Booksellers
35 Micklegate. YO1 1JH. Open 9-6. *STOCK: Prints and maps, many hand coloured; antiquarian and secondhand books on history, travel, natural history, sciences, poetry, biographies, literary criticism, general fiction and Scotland.* TEL: 01904 641404.

Ken Spelman
70 Micklegate. YO1 1LF. (P. Miller and A. Fothergill). ABA. Est. 1948. SIZE: Large. *STOCK: Secondhand and antiquarian books especially fine arts and literature, 50p-£10,000; early English watercolours.* PARK: Easy. TEL: 01904 624414; fax - 01904 626276; e-mail - spelman.@dial.pipex.com.; internet (rare books viewable on-line) - http://dspace.dial,pipex.com/spelman/. SER: Valuations; buys at auction (books); catalogues issued. FAIRS: Bath, Oxford, York, Harrogate, Cambridge and London PBFA and ABA. VAT: Spec.

St. John Antiques
26 Lord Mayor's Walk. YO3 7HA. (R. and N. Bell). Open 10-5. CL: Mon. *STOCK: Victorian stripped pine, curios, blue and white pottery.* PARK: At rear. TEL: 01904 644263.

York Antiques Centre
2 Lendal. YO1 2AA. Open 9.30-5.30, winter 10-5. SIZE: 20 dealers. *STOCK: Antiques and collectable items, 18th-20th C.* LOC: Opposite the museum gardens. PARK: Easy. TEL: 01904 641445/641582.

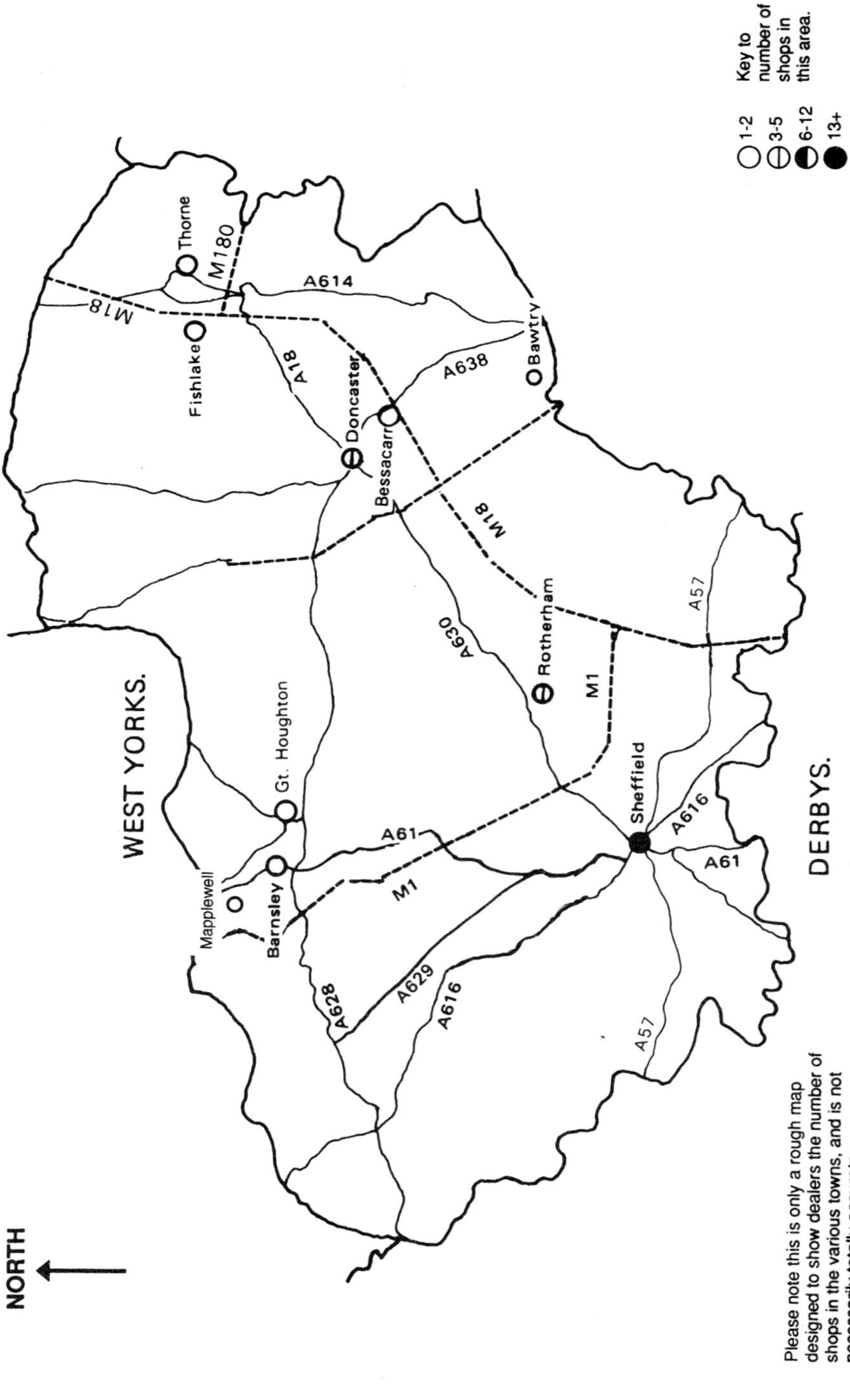

Please note this is only a rough map designed to show dealers the number of shops in the various towns, and is not necessarily totally accurate.

BARNSLEY

Charisma Antiques Trade Warehouse
St. Paul's former Methodist Chapel, Market St., Hoyland. S74 9QR. (J.C. Simmons). Est. 1980. Open 10-5. SIZE: Large. *STOCK: Furniture, shipping goods, pictures.* LOC: 1.5 miles off M1, exit 36. PARK: Easy. TEL: 01226 747599; home - 01226 790482.

Christine Simmons Antiques
St. Paul's Former Methodist Chapel, Market St., Hoyland. S74 9QR. Est. 1976. Open 10-4. SIZE: Medium. *STOCK: Smalls and pictures.* LOC: 1.5 miles from exit 36, M1. PARK: Easy. TEL: 01226 747599/790482.

BAWTRY, Nr. Doncaster

Swan Antiques
2 Swan St. DN10 6JQ. Open 10-5 including Sun. SIZE: Large. *STOCK: Furniture, silver, ceramics, collectables, costume jewellery.* PARK: Easy. TEL: 01302 710301.

Treasure House Antiques Centre
4-10 Swan St. DN10 6JR. Est. 1982. Open 10-5 including Sun. CL: Wed. SIZE: Large - various dealers. *STOCK: Silver, porcelain, furniture, carnival glass, postcards, toy trains and general antiques.* PARK: Easy. TEL: 01302 710621.

BESSACARR, Nr. Doncaster

Keith Stones Grandfather Clocks
5 Ellers Drive. DN4 7DL. Est. 1988. Open by appointment. SIZE: Small. *STOCK: Grandfather clocks especially painted dial with 30 hour and 8 day movements, Georgian to early 19th C, £750-£2,000.* LOC: Take A638 Bawtry road off racecourse roundabout, through traffic lights after 3/4 mile, take second right into Ellers Rd. then second left. PARK: Easy. TEL: 01302 535258; home - same. SER: Valuations.

DONCASTER

Doncaster Sales and Exchange
20 Copley Rd. DN1 2PF. Open 9.30-5. CL: Thurs. *STOCK: General small antiques.* TEL: 01302 344857. VAT: Stan.

FISHLAKE

Fishlake Antiques
Pinfold Lane. DN7 5LA. Resident. Est. 1972. Open Sat. 1-5, and by appointment. SIZE: Medium. *STOCK: Rural furniture especially stripped pine; clocks including longcase and wall clocks, Victorian to mid-19th C, £30-£1,000; smalls, £3-£70.* LOC: Off A63. PARK: Own. TEL: 01302 841411.

GREAT HOUGHTON, Nr. Barnsley

Farmhouse Antiques
7 High St. S72 0AA. Open 10-12 and 1-5. CL: Wed. and Fri. *STOCK: Antique and later furniture, stripped pine, satin walnut; porcelain, ceramics, especially Susie Cooper; linen, pictures, jewellery, collectables.* TEL: 01226 754057; home - 01226 751917; mobile - 0836 362309.

MAPPLEWELL, Nr. Barnsley

A Maze of Pine and Roses
1 Blacker Rd. S75 6BW. (Mrs Gioia L. Padgett). Est. 1983. Open Mon. and Fri. 10-5, Tues. and Thurs. 10-4, Sun. 2-4. SIZE: Small. *STOCK: Pine, walnut and mahogany furniture and doors.* LOC: Off M1, exit 38, head back towards Barnsley, turn into Darton at the church, carry on to Mapplewell, premises on crossroads. PARK: Easy. TEL: 01226 388014; fax and ansaphone - 01226 282992. SER: Valuations; curtains, loose covers, bedspreads made to order from designer fabrics.

ROTHERHAM

Roger Appleyard Ltd LAPADA
Fitzwilliam Rd., Eastwood Trading Estate. S65 1SL. Open 8-5, Sat. 8-12. SIZE: Large. *STOCK: General antiques, £5-£1,500.* LOC: A630. PARK: Easy. TEL: 01709 367670/377770; fax - 01709 829395. SER: Packing and shipping. VAT: Stan/Spec. *Trade Only.*

Foster's Antique Centre
Foster's Garden Centre, Doncaster Rd., Thrybergh. S65 4BE. (The Foster Family). Est. 1996. Open 10-4.30, Sun. 11-5. SIZE: 20 dealers. *STOCK: Wide range of general antiques and collectables including furniture, jewellery, Clarice Cliff and Rockingham china.* LOC: A630 between Rotherham and Doncaster. PARK: Large own. TEL: 01709 850337; fax - 01709 851905.

John Mason Jewellers Ltd
36 High St. S60 1PP. Open 9-5.30. *STOCK: Silver, jewellery.* TEL: 01709 382311. SER: Valuations; repairs. VAT: Spec.

South Yorkshire Antiques
88-94 Broad St. S62 6DZ. (A. Swindells). Est. 1955. Open 9.30-4.30. *STOCK: General antiques and shipping furniture.* PARK: Easy. TEL: 01709 526514/582688 (ansaphone); mobile - 0378 46154. SER: Valuations; restorations.

Philip Turnor Antiques
94a Broad St., Parkgate. Open 9-5, Sat. 10-4. *STOCK: Shipping furniture including oak, 1880-1940.* PARK: Easy. TEL: 01709 524640. SER: Export.

SHEFFIELD

A. and C. Antiques
239 Abbeydale Rd. S7 1FJ. (C.E. Maltby). Est. 1984. Open 10.30-5. SIZE: Medium. *STOCK: General antiques, smalls, jewellery, £30-£500.* LOC: Main road south of city centre, towards Chesterfield. PARK: Easy. TEL: 0114 2589161.

Anita's Holme Antiques
144 Holme Lane, Hillsborough. S6 4JW. (A.L. Spalton). Est. 1986. Open 9-5. SIZE: Medium. *STOCK: General antiques, 19th C, £50-£100.* LOC: A61, turn left at traffic lights opposite Owlerton Sports Stadium, shop 1.5 miles on right. PARK: Easy. TEL: 0114 2336698.

Chimney Piece Antique Fires
262 South Rd., Walkley. S6 3TB. (J. Young). Open 9.30-5. CL: Wed. *STOCK: Fireplaces.* TEL: 0114 2346085.

Court House Antique Centre
2-6 Town End Rd., Ecclesfield. S30 3YY. (P.A. and S.P. Owram). Open 10.30-5, Sun. 11.30-5. SIZE: Large. *STOCK: Furniture, from Georgian, £20-£2,500; ceramics, books, militaria, paintings and bric-a-brac, from Victorian, £1-£750.* LOC: 2 miles from M1, junction 35. Down hill, bear left into Nether Lane, through lights to church, turn left 250 yards on right. PARK: Easy. TEL: 0114 257 0641.

Sheffield continued

Dronfield Antiques
375-377 Abbeydale Rd. S7 1FS. (H.J. Greaves) Est. 1968. Open 10.30-5.30. CL: Thurs. and Sat except by appointment. SIZE: Large + warehouses. *STOCK: Trade and shipping goods, Victoriana, glass, china.* LOC: A621, 1 mile south of city centre. PARK: Easy. TEL: 0114 2550172/2581821; home and fax - 0114 2556024. VAT: Stan.

Ellis's
144 Whitham Rd. S10 2SR. Est. 1943. Open 10-6. *STOCK: Oriental carpets and rugs.* TEL: 0114 2662920. VAT: Stan.

F S Antiques
Court House Antiques Centre, 2-6 Town End Rd., Ecclesfield. 10.30-5, Sun. 11.30-4.30. SIZE: Small. *STOCK: Longcase, wall and mantel clocks and barometers, 1790-1920, £60-£2,500.* LOC: 2 miles from M1, junction 35. PARK: Easy. TEL: 0114 257 0641; home - 01226 382805. SER: Restorations.

Fulwood Antiques and The Basement Gallery
7 Brooklands Ave. S10 4GA. (Mrs H.J. Wills). Est. 1977. Open Wed. and Fri. 10-5, Sat. 10-1. SIZE: Medium. *STOCK: Fine furniture, clocks, barometers, oil paintings and watercolours, 19th to early 20th C, £50-£5,000.* LOC: From city centre towards Broomhill, Fulwood Rd., Nethergreen and straight on for Fulwood. PARK: Easy. TEL: 0114 2307387; home - 0114 2301346. SER: Valuations; restorations (furniture, pictures and clocks).

Fun Antiques
72 Abbeydale Rd. S7 1FD. (B. Harrap). Est. 197[illegible] Open by appointment. SIZE: Medium. *STOCK: Unusual and collectable items including sporting items, toys, advertising, Christmas, arcade and fairground items, 20th C, £5-£1,000.* PARK: Easy. TEL: 0114 2553424. SER: Valuations; installations. FAIRS: Harrow, Ardingly, Newark, Stoneleigh. VAT: Stan. *Trade Only.*

Gilbert and Sons
8-16 Abbeydale Rd. S7 2JE. (B. and C. Gilbert). Open 9.30-5. *STOCK: Shipping items.* TEL: 011[illegible] 2552043.

Julie Goddard Antiques
Court House Antiques Centre, Town End Rd., Ecclesfield. S30 3YY. Est. 1982. Open 10.30-5, Sun. 11.30-4.30. SIZE: Small. *STOCK: Furniture, Georgian-Edwardian, oak and mahogany.* LOC: [illegible] mins from J36 M1, next to St. Mary's Church. PARK: Easy. TEL: 0114 257 0641; mobile - 041[illegible] 098748. SER: Buys at auction. VAT: Spec.

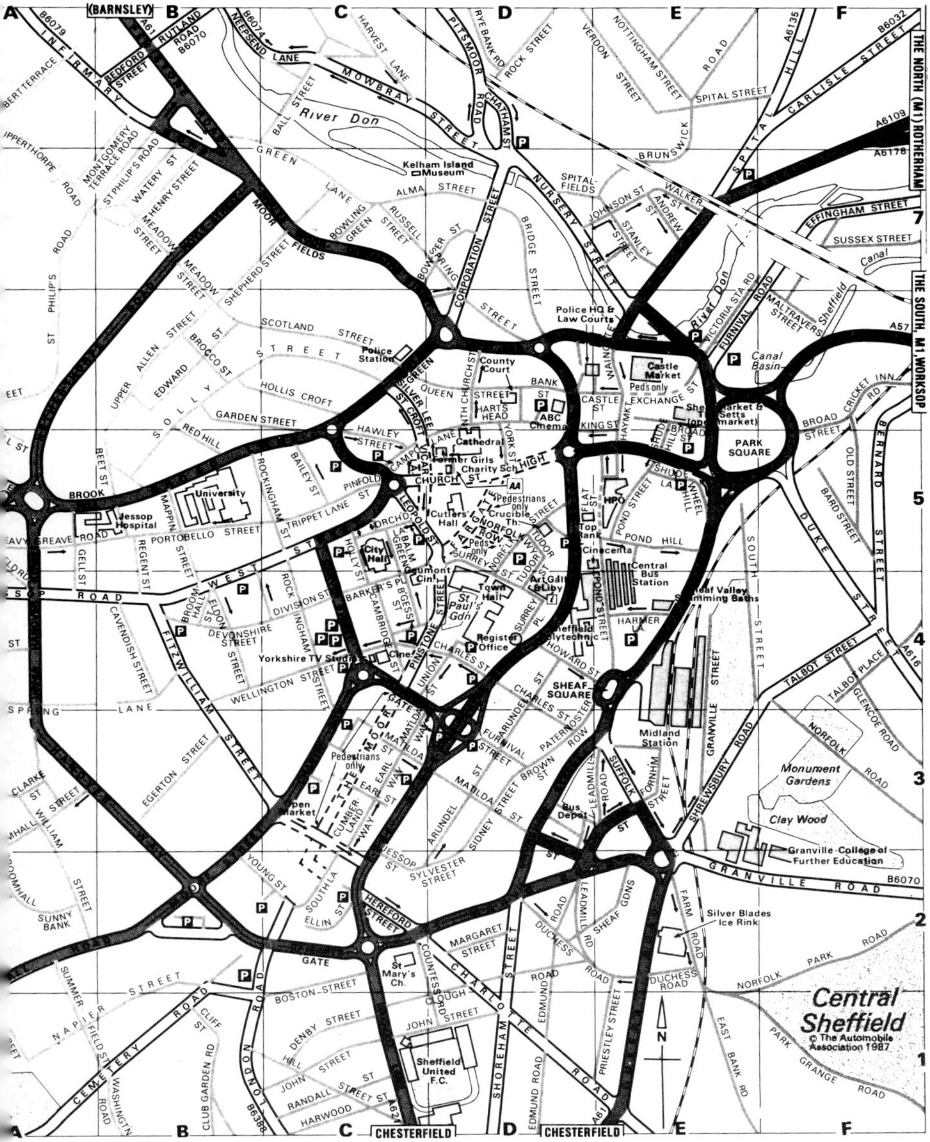

Key to Town Plan

AA Recommended roads

Other roads

Restricted roads

Buildings of interest

Car Parks

Parks and open spaces

AA Service Centre

Sheffield continued

Hibbert Brothers Ltd
117 Norfolk St. S1 2JE. (Paul Hibbert-Greaves). Est. 1834. Open 9-5. SIZE: Large. *STOCK: 19th-20th C paintings, £500-£10,000.* LOC: City centre, next to town hall. PARK: Easy. TEL: 0114 2722038. SER: Restorations; framing. FAIRS: NEC. VAT: Stan/Spec.

Alan Hill Books, Sheffield
261 Glossop Rd. S10 2GZ. Est. 1980. Open 10.30-5.30. *STOCK: Antiquarian books, maps and prints.* TEL: 0114 2780594.

Peter James Antiques
336 Abbeydale Rd. S7 1FN. (P.J. Conboy). Est. 1980. Open 9.30-4.30. SIZE: Medium. *STOCK: Mahogany, walnut, pine, oak and satin walnut, watercolours, 1800-1920.* PARK: Easy. TEL: 0114 2551554. SER: Restorations. VAT: Stan.

A.E. Jameson and Co LAPADA
257 Glossop Rd. S10 2GZ. (P. Jameson). Est. 1883. Open 9-5.45. SIZE: Large. *STOCK: Furniture, pre-1820, £20-£15,000; glass, china, weapons.* LOC: A57. TEL: 0114 2723846; home - 0114 2726189. SER: Valuations; restorations (furniture); buys at auction. VAT: Stan/Spec.

Langsett Road Antiques & Pine Centre
314-318 Langsett Rd. (B. Findley). Est. 1973. Open 9.30-5.30, Sun. by appointment. SIZE: 3 dealers. *STOCK: General antiques and pine, architectural items.* LOC: 1 mile from city centre on A616. PARK: Easy. TEL: 0700 344444. SER: Door stripping. VAT: Stan.

The Oriental Rug Shop
763 Abbeydale Rd. S7 2BG. (Kian A. Hezaveh). Open 10-5. *STOCK: Handmade rugs and carpets.* TEL: 0114 2552240/2589821; fax - 0114 2509088.

Sheffield continued

Paraphernalia
66/68 Abbeydale Rd. Est. 1972. *STOCK: Gener[al] antiques, stripped pine, lighting, brass and ir[on] beds.* TEL: 0114 2550203. VAT: Stan.

Renishaw Antiques
32 Main Rd., Renishaw. S31 9UT. (B. Findley). Open by appointment. *STOCK: Architectur[al] antiques, old doors.* TEL: 01246 435521. SE[R]: Door stripping.

N.P. and A. Salt Antiques LAPAD[A]
Unit 2, Barmouth Rd. S7 2DH. Open 9.30-4.3[0] CL: Sat. SIZE: Large. *STOCK: Victorian fu[r]niture, shipping goods, smalls and toys.* TE[L] 0114 2582672. SER: Valuations; packin[g] shipping; courier. *Trade Only.*

Sheffield Antiques Emporium
15 Clyde Rd., (Off Broadfield Rd.), Heeley. a[nd] The Chapel, 19 Broadfield Rd. S8 0XQ Open 1[0]-5, Sun. 11-5. SIZE: 60+ dealers. *STOC[K] Furniture, collectables, jewellery, linens, gla[ss] china, books, £1-£5,000.* LOC: Clyde Rd 1st rig[ht] off Broadfield Rd., which is opposite Broadfie[ld] public house on Abbeydale Rd. PARK: Eas[y]. TEL: 0114 258 4863/255 0881. SER: Valuatio[ns]; restorations (furniture and pottery).

Sheffield Pine Centre (inc. Canterbury Place Antiques)
356/358 South Rd. Warehouse - Unit E, Lowfie[ld] Cutlery Forge, Guernsey Rd. S6 3TE. (Coldwell). Open 9-5.30. SIZE: Large. *STOC[K]: Stripped pine and general antiques.* TEL: 01[14] 2336103/2587458.

Tilley's Vintage Magazine Shop
281 Shoreham St. (A.G.J. and A.A.J.C. Tille[y]) Est. 1979. Open 9-5, other times by appointme[nt]. SIZE: Large. *STOCK: Magazines, comics, new[s]papers, books, postcards, programmes, poste[rs], cigarette cards, prints, ephemera.* LOC: Oppos[ite] Sheffield United F.C. PARK: Easy. TEL: 01[14] 2752442; fax - same. SER: Mail order; valuatio[ns].

Paul Ward Antiques
Owl House, 8 Burnell Rd., Owlerton. S6 2A[...] Resident. Est. 1976. Open by appointment. SIZ[E]: Large. *STOCK: Matched sets of Victorian din[ing] and kitchen chairs, country chairs, gene[ral] antiques.* LOC: 2 miles north of city on A6[...]. TEL: 0114 2335980. VAT: Stan/Spec.

THORNE, Nr. Doncaster

Canterbury House
24 Finkle St. DN8 5DE. Est. 1977. Open 9[...] *STOCK: Jewellery and watches.* TEL: 014[...] 812102.

Yorkshire West

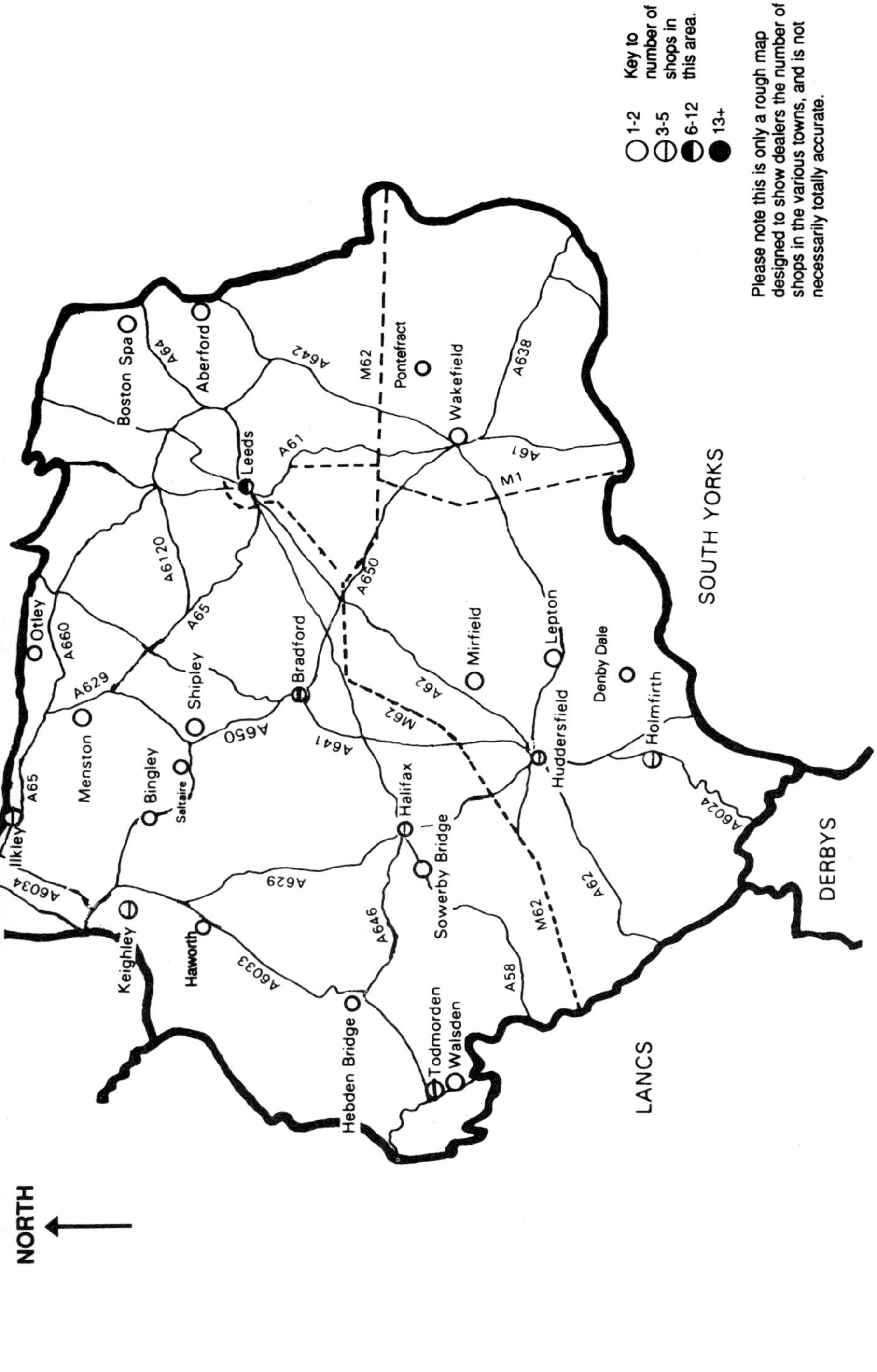

ABERFORD

Aberford Antiques Ltd
Hicklam House. LS25 3DP. (J.W.H. Long and C.A. Robinson). Est. 1973. Open 9-5.30, Sundays 10-5.30. SIZE: Large. *STOCK: Stripped pine, oak and mahogany, Victorian and period, £10-£1,500; Victoriana, collectables and memorabilia, £5-£1,000; local prints and maps.* LOC: Opposite Almshouses at southern end of village. PARK: Easy. TEL: 0113 2813209; fax - 0113 2813121. SER: Fitted pine kitchens. VAT: Stan/Spec.

ADDINGHAM, Nr. Ilkley

Manor Barn
Burnside Mill, Main St. LS29 0PJ. (Whiteley Wright Ltd). Est. 1972. Open 8-5.30. SIZE: Warehouse. *STOCK: Pine, 17th-19th C and reproduction; oak and shipping goods.* PARK: Easy. TEL: 01943 830176. VAT: Stan/Spec.

BINGLEY

E. Carrol
5 Ryshworth Hall, Keighley Rd., Crossflatts. BD16 2EL. Est. 1970. Open by appointment. SIZE: Small. *STOCK: Oil paintings, watercolours.* LOC: A650. PARK: Easy. TEL: 01274 568800. VAT: Stan.

BOSTON SPA, By Wetherby

London House Oriental Rugs and Carpets
London House, High St. LS23 6AD. (M.A. and Mrs I.T.H. Ries). Open 10-5.30 including Sun. CL: Mon. SIZE: Large. *STOCK: Caucasian, Turkish, Afghan and Persian rugs, runners and carpets, £50-£10,000; kelims, tapestries and textiles.* LOC: Off A1, south of Wetherby. PARK: Easy. TEL: 01937 845123; home - same. SER: Valuations; restorations (Oriental carpets and rugs); buys at auction (Oriental carpets and rugs). VAT: Stan.

BRADFORD

The Corner Shop
89 Oak Lane. BD9 4QU. (Miss Badland). Est. 1961. Open Tues., Thurs. and Fri. 2-5.30, Sat. 11-5.30. *STOCK: Pottery, small furniture, clocks and general items.*

Cottingley Antiques
286 Keighley Rd., Frizinghall. (Peter and Barbara Nobbs). Est. 1981. Open 9-5. SIZE: Medium. *STOCK: Victorian stripped and restored pine, £100-£500.* LOC: Right hand side of A650 from Keighley. PARK: Easy. TEL: 01274 545829; home - 01274 569091. SER: Restorations (furniture).

Bradford continued

Heaton Antiques
1 Hammond Place, Emm Lane, Heaton. BD9 4A (T. Steward). Est. 1991. Open 10-5. CL: Mo SIZE: Medium. *STOCK: Furniture, silver plate a bric-a-brac, pre 1930, £10-£1,000.* LOC: Ne A650. PARK: Easy. TEL: 01274 480630. SE Valuations. FAIRS: NEC; Yorkshire Showgroun Harrogate; Newark.

Langley's (Jewellers) Ltd
59 Godwin St. BD1 2SH. TEL: 01274 72228 VAT: Stan.

DENBY DALE, Nr. Huddersfield

Joan's Antiques
1A Denby Dale Industrial Park, Wakefield R (Mrs J.M. Hirst). Est. 1988. Open 10-4.30, Su 1-4. SIZE: Medium. *STOCK: Victorian a Edwardian furniture, to £2,500.* LOC: Off M PARK: Easy. TEL: 01484 864209; home - sam SER: Restorations; waxing and stripping; Fren polishing. FAIRS: Wentworth Village Ha Rockingham.

HALIFAX

Collectors Old Toy Shop and Antique
89 Northgate. HX1 1XF. (S. Haley). Open 10.3 4.30. *STOCK: Collectors toys, clocks a antiques.* TEL: 01422 360434/822148.

Halifax Antiques Centre
Queens Rd. HX1 4LR. Est. 1981. Open Tues.-S 10-5. SIZE: Large - 30 dealers. *STOCK: A Deco, jewellery, porcelain, linen, costume, mec anical music, pine, oak, mahogany, kitchenal decorative collectables.* LOC: Follow A58 King Cross, turn at Trafalgar Inn into Queens R corner, 3rd set of lights. PARK: Own. TE 01422 366657.

Muir Hewitt Art Deco Originals
Halifax Antiques Centre, Queens Rd. Open 10 CL: Mon. *STOCK: Pottery including Clari Cliff, Susie Cooper, Charlotte Rhead; Shell ceramics; furniture, lighting and mirrors.* LOC mile west of town centre on the A58 (A646), tu right into Queens Rd. at Trafalgar Inn traf lights, centre is at next traffic lights, oppos Lloyds Bank. PARK: Easy. TEL: 01422 3473 fax - same; home - 01274 882051. VAT: Stan.

North Bridge Antiques
5 North Bridge. (S. Lester). Open 9-5, Thurs. 9 *STOCK: Shipping goods.* TEL: 01422 358474.

Halifax continued

Andy Thornton Architectural Antiques Ltd
Victoria Mills, Stainland Rd., Greetland. HX4 8AD. Est. 1973. Open 8-5.30, Sat. 9-5, Sun. 11-5. SIZE: Large. *STOCK: Architectural antiques - doors, stained glass, fireplaces, panelling, garden furniture, light fittings, pews and decor items.* PARK: Easy. TEL: 01422 377314; fax - 01422 310372. VAT: Stan.

HAWORTH, Nr. Keighley

Bingley Antiques
Springfield Farm Estate, Flappit. BD21 5PT. (J.B. and J. Poole). Est. 1965. Open 8.30-5. SIZE: Large. *STOCK: Furniture, 18th-19th C; shipping goods, porcelain, architectural antiques.* LOC: Near Haworth. PARK: Easy. TEL: 01535 646666. SER: Valuations. VAT: Stan/Spec.

HEBDEN BRIDGE, Nr. Halifax

Cornucopia Antiques
West End. HX7 8JP. (C. Nassor). Open Thurs., Fri. and Sun. 1-5, Sat. 11-5. *STOCK: Stoves, 1920-1940s; furniture, pottery, lamps, lighting, bric-a-brac.* LOC: Town centre behind Pennine Information Centre. PARK: Easy. TEL: 01422 844497.

HOLMFIRTH, Nr. Huddersfield

Andrew Spencer Bottomley
The Coach House, Huddersfield Rd. HD7 2TT. Open by appointment. *STOCK: Arms and armour including pistols, swords, daggers, helmets and suits of armour.* TEL: 01484 685234; fax - 01484 681551. SER: Valuations; catalogues available. *Mail order only.*

Chapel House Fireplaces
Netherfield House, St. Georges Rd., Scholes. HD7 1UH. Open strictly by appointment Tues. 9-7, Wed.-Sat. 9-5. SIZE: Large. *STOCK: Georgian, Victorian and Edwardian grates and mantels; French chimneypieces.* TEL: 01484 682275.

The Toll House Bookshop
32/34 Huddersfield Rd. (E.V. Beardsell). Est. 1978. Open 10-5. *STOCK: Books including antiquarian.* TEL: 01484 686541.

Upperbridge Antiques
Huddersfield Rd. HD7 1JR. (Mrs M. Coop and Ridings). Open 1-5, Sun. 2-5. CL: Tues. SIZE: Small. *STOCK: Pottery, linen, metalware,*

Holmfirth continued

interesting items, Victorian to Art Deco, £5-£150. Not Stocked: Jewellery. LOC: A635. PARK: Nearby. TEL: 01484 687200.

HUDDERSFIELD

Beau Monde Antiques
343a Bradford Rd., Fartown. HD2 2QF. (R.M. Schofield). Est. 1963. Open 9.30-6, Sat. 9.30-5. CL: Wed. pm. SIZE: Medium. *STOCK: Furniture, general antiques, bric-a-brac, £5-£500.* LOC: On A641, 1 mile from town centre. PARK: Easy. TEL: 01484 427565.

Peter Berry Antiques
119 Wakefield Rd., Moldgreen. HD5 9AN. Open 9.30-5.30, Sat. 9.30-4 and by appointment. *STOCK: Georgian and Victorian furniture; 18th and early 19th C pottery figures, cream ware, Leeds Pottery and watercolours.* TEL: 01484 544229 (answerphone); fax - 01484 544229. SER: Valuations; restorations.

D.W. Dyson (Antique Weapons)
Wood Lea, Shepley. HD8 8ES. Est. 1974. Open by appointment only. *STOCK: Antique weapons including cased duelling pistols, armour, miniature arms, rare and unusual items.* LOC: Off A629. PARK: Easy. TEL: 01484 607331; home - same. SER: Valuations; buys at auction (antique weapons); special presentation items made to order in precious metals; advice on restoration; interior design; finder (film props). FAIRS: Dorchester Hotel, London; Dortmund, Stuttgart and other major foreign. VAT: Spec.

Huddersfield Antiques
170 Wakefield Rd., Moldgreen. HD5 9AW. Est. 1971. Open 10.30-4.30 or by appointment. SIZE: Medium. *STOCK: Victoriana, bric-a-brac, collectors' items, postcards; warehouse of trade and shipping goods.* PARK: Easy. TEL: 01484 539747. SER: Valuations; buys at auction.

Geoff Neary (incorporating Fillans Antiques Ltd)
2 Market Walk. HD1 2QA. NAG, FGA. Est. 1852. Open 9.30-5.15. SIZE: Small. *STOCK: English silver, 1700-1980; Sheffield plate, 1760-1840, £10-£500; jewellery, £50-£10,000.* Not Stocked: Other than above. PARK: Town centre multi-storey. TEL: 01484 531609. SER: Valuations; restorations; buys at auction (English silver and jewellery). VAT: Stan/Spec.

ILKLEY

Coopers of Ilkley LAPADA
46-50 Leeds Rd. LS29 8EQ. Est. 1910. Open 9-1 and 2-5.30. SIZE: Large. *STOCK: English furniture, pre-1830, £100-£10,000; porcelain and silver, pictures.* LOC: A65. PARK: Own. TEL: 01943 608020. SER: Valuations; restorations (furniture); buys at auction. VAT: Stan/Spec.

The Grove Bookshop
10 The Grove. LS29 9EG. (Andrew and Janet Sharpe). PBFA. Open 9-5.30. SIZE: Medium. *STOCK: Antiquarian books and maps; topographical and sporting prints.* LOC: 200 yards from A65. PARK: Easy. TEL: 01943 609335. SER: Valuations; restorations (book-binding and framing); buys at auction (as stock).

Keith Richardson Antiques
26 Leeds Rd. LS29 8DS. Est. 1974. Open 9-5. CL: Wed. SIZE: Medium. *STOCK: Jewellery, dolls, glass, furniture, Victoriana, commemorative ware.* PARK: Adjacent street. TEL: 01943 600045.

Jack Shaw and Co
The Old Grammar School, Skipton Rd. LS29 9EJ. Est. 1945. Open 9.30-12.45 and 2-5.30, Thurs.-Sat. *STOCK: Silver especially cutlery and 18th C domestic; furniture.* TEL: 01943 609467. VAT: Spec.

KEIGHLEY

Barleycote Hall Antiques
2 Janet St., Crossroads. BD22 9ET. (R. Hoskins Resident. Est. 1968. Open most days 11- *STOCK: Georgian and Victorian furniture, porcelain, metalwork, paintings, jewellery, Victoria and Edwardian clothing, clocks of all types.* LOC A629, turn right towards Haworth, 600yds. o right. TEL: 01535 644776. VAT: Stan/Spec.

Keighleys of Keighley
153 East Parade. BD21 5HX. (B. Keighley an Son). Est. 1939. Open 9-5. CL: Tues. *STOCK Furniture, jewellery, gold and silver, china.* LOC Next to the Victoria Hotel. PARK: Easy. TEL 01535 663439; home - 01535 607180. VAT: Sta

Real Macoy
2 Janet St. BD22 9ET. (D. Seal). Open most da 11-5. *STOCK: Quilts, textiles, period clothin* TEL: 01535 644776.

D. Richardson Antiques
72 Haworth Rd., Crossroads. Open 9-5. CL: Sa *STOCK: General antiques and shipping good* PARK: Easy at rear. TEL: 01535 644982.

EEDS

laddin's Cave
9 Queens Arcade. LS1 6LF. (P. D. and S. saacs). Est. 1954. CL: Mon. SIZE: Small. *TOCK: Jewellery, £15-£250; collectors' items; ll 19th-20th C.* LOC: Town centre. PARK: 100 ards. TEL: 0113 2457903; 0113 2842425. SER: 'aluations. VAT: Stan.

'he Antique Exchange
00 Kirkstall Rd. LS4 2JX. (S. Wood). Est. 1976. pen 10.30-3. CL: Tues. and Wed. *STOCK: Furiture including satin walnut and ash, 19th-20th ', £195-£3,000.* LOC: Kirkstall Rd. is ½ mile 'est of Yorkshire Television Studios. PARK: asy. TEL: 0113 2743513. VAT: Stan/Spec.

ishop House Antiques
69 Town St., Rodley. LS13 1HW. (Mrs J.M. ishop). Est. 1977. Open by appointment only. *TOCK: General antiques, porcelain and glass.* EL: 0113 2563071.

'oins International and Antiques nternational
and 2 Melbourne St. LS2 7PS. (J.M. Harrison). pen 9-5. CL: Sat. *STOCK: Coins, banknotes, edals, silver, gold, general antiques, jewellery, ested china, cigarette cards.* PARK: Easy. TEL: 113 2434230; fax - 0113 2345544.

eary Antiques
14 Richardshaw Lane, Stanningley, Pudsey. LS28 BN. (J.A. Geary). Est. 1933. Open 10-5.30, Sun. 2-4. SIZE: Warehouse. *STOCK: Furniture, eorgian, Victorian and Edwardian; copper and rass.* LOC: 500 yds. from West Leeds Ring Rd. ARK: Easy. TEL: 0113 2564122. SER: Restorions (furniture). VAT: Stan/Spec.

. Howorth Antiques/Swiss Cottage 'urniture
5 Westfield Crescent, Burley. LS3 1DJ. Est. 986. Open Fri. and Sat. 9-6, Sun. 12.30-6. SIZE: 'arehouse. *STOCK: Collectables, furniture, rchitectural items, £5-£3,000.* LOC: Town hall Burley Rd., road opposite YTV. PARK: Easy. EL: 0113 2306268/2429994. FAIRS: Newark. 'AT: Stan/Spec.

eeds Antiques Centre
5 Globe Rd. LS11 5QG. Open 10-5. CL: Mon. IZE: 40 dealers. *STOCK: General antiques.* OC: On the Canal Basin, M1 to Leeds Hilton, rn left, 170 mtrs on right. TEL: 0113 2423194.

akwood Gallery
3 Roundhay Rd., Oakwood. Open 9-6. *STOCK: ine paintings and prints.* PARK: Easy. TEL: 113 2401348. SER: Framing; restorations; nservation.

Leeds continued

The Piano Shop
39 Holbeck Lane. LS11 9XE. (B. Seals). Open 9-5. *STOCK: Pianos, especially decorated cased grand.* TEL: 0113 2443685. SER: Restorations; French polishing; hire.

Swiss Cottage Antiques
182 Cardigan Rd., Burley. LS6 1QL. (John Howorth). Est. 1986. Open 9.30-6, Sun. 12.30-5.30. SIZE: Warehouse. *STOCK: Furniture and architectural items.* LOC: Kirkstall Rd. from town centre, turn right at traffic lights towards Headingley cricket ground. PARK: Easy. TEL: 0113 2429994/2306268. FAIRS: Newark. VAT: Stan/Spec.

Thirkills Antiques
107 West End Lane, Horsforth. LS18 5ES. Est. 1963. *STOCK: Paintings, musical, violins, 18th C pottery, porcelain, furniture, smalls.* LOC: 5 mins. south of Leeds-Bradford Airport. TEL: 0113 2589160.

Windsor House Antiques (Leeds) Ltd.
LAPADA

18-20 Benson St. LS7 1BL. (D.K. Smith). Est. 1959. Open 9-5. CL: Sat. SIZE: Large. *STOCK: English furniture, 18th-19th C; paintings, objects.* PARK: Easy. TEL: 0113 2444666; fax - 0113 2426394. VAT: Stan/Spec.

Year Dot
15 Market St. Arcade. LS1 6EN. (P. Davis). Open 9.30-5. *STOCK: Oriental pottery and porcelain, paintings, clocks, barometers, glass, copper, brass, bric-a-brac, jewellery, watches.* TEL: 0113 2460860.

LEPTON, Nr. Huddersfield

K.L.M. & Co. Antiques
The Antique Shop, Wakefield Rd. HD8 0EL. (K.L. & J. Millington). Est. 1980. Open 10.30-5, other times by appointment. SIZE: 8 showrooms and warehouse. *STOCK: Furniture including stripped pine, satin walnut, to 1940's; pianos, all £25-£1,500.* LOC: A642 Wakefield road from Huddersfield, shop opposite village church. PARK: Easy and at rear. TEL: 01484 607763; home - 01484 607548. SER: Valuations. VAT: Stan.

MENSTON

Antiques
101 Bradford Rd. (W. and J. Hanlon). Est. 1974. Open 2.30-5. CL: Tues. and Wed. *STOCK: Handworked linen, textiles, pottery, porcelain, Art Nouveau, Art Deco, silver, plate, jewellery, small furniture, collectors items, barometers.* PARK: Forecourt. TEL: 01943 877634; home - 01943 463693.

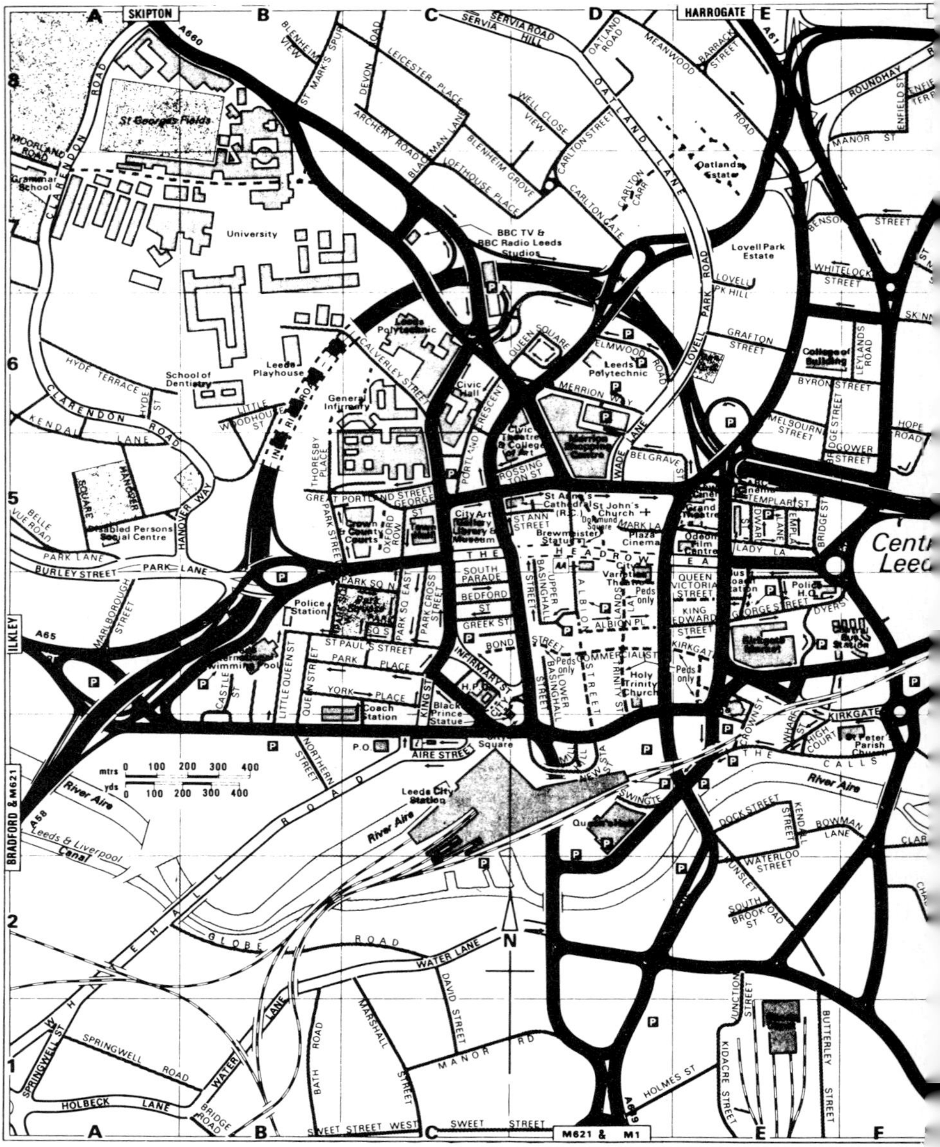

Key to Town Plan

AA Recommended roads		Car Parks	P
Other roads		Parks and open spaces	
Restricted roads		AA Service Centre	AA
Buildings of interest			

Menston continued

Park Antiques
2 North View, Main St. LS29 6JU. Resident. Est. 1975. Open 10-6.30, Sun. 10-5.30. CL: Mon. and Tues. SIZE: Medium. *STOCK: Furniture, Georgian to Edwardian, £500-£5,000; decorative items, £100-£1,000, soft furnishings, £500-£2,000.* Not Stocked: Pine, silver. LOC: Opposite the park. PARK: Easy. TEL: 01943 872392. VAT: Stan/Spec.

MIRFIELD

Lawn and Lace
5 Knowl Rd. WF14 9NQ. (G.D. Hurst and Mrs N. Gunson). Est. 1988. Open Wed.-Sat. 9.30-5.30. SIZE: Small. *STOCK: Textiles including linen and lace, 17th-20th C, £5-£250; dolls and ceramics, £5-£300; small furniture, £15-£500; both 19th-20th C.* LOC: 2 miles east of junction 25, M62. Just off main Huddersfield to Dewsbury road. PARK: Easy. TEL: 01924 491083. SER: Valuations; restorations (textiles and dolls). FAIRS: Newark.

OTLEY, Nr. Leeds

Martin-Clifton Antiques
18 Westgate. LS21 3AS. (A.S. Ambler). Est. 1972. Open 10-5.30. CL: Wed. and Thurs. SIZE: Medium. *STOCK: Furniture, china, copper and brass, barometers, mirrors.* LOC: A650. PARK: Easy. TEL: 01943 851117. SER: Restorations and repairs (furniture); polishing.

PONTEFRACT

Cottage Antiques
Ropergate End. (Sheila Whittaker). Est. 1987. Open 12-4. CL: Thurs. SIZE: 3 rooms. *STOCK: Pine and antique furniture, 19th C, £150-£450; Victorian pottery, £50-£150; linen and kitchenalia, 19th-20th C, £20-£100.* LOC: Town centre. PARK: Easy. TEL: 01977 611146. SER: Restorations (furniture). FAIRS: Newark (Stand F32).

D. Turner Antiques
The Old Coach House, Bondgate. (Dennise Turner). Est. 1988. Open 11-5. CL: Thurs. SIZE: Medium. *STOCK: Furniture, £30-£300; pottery, £20-£100, both late 19th to early 20th C; collectables, £5-£25.* LOC: Just off A1 towards town. PARK: Easy. TEL: 01977 798818; home - 01226 751802. SER: Valuations; buys at auction (furniture). FAIRS: Newark, Harrogate and Ardingly.

SALTAIRE, Nr Shipley

The Victoria Centre
3-4 Victoria Rd. BD18 3LA. (Margaret and Malcolm Gray). Est. 1989. Open 10-5.30. CL: Mon. and Tues. SIZE: Large - 36 units. *STOCK: Wide range of general antiques including fine furniture, paintings, silver, clocks, porcelain, pine and collectables, £5-£10,000.* PARK: Nearby. TEL: 01274 530611. SER: Valuations. VAT: Stan/Spec.

SHIPLEY

Price-Less Antiques
2 Gaisby Lane. BD18 1AZ. (Mrs P. Lee). Open 11-6. *STOCK: China, bric-a-brac, general antiques.* TEL: 01274 581760.

The Titus Gallery
1 Daisy Place, Saltaire Rd. BD18 4NA. (C.A. Grice). Est. 1975. Open 10-5.30, Sun. 11-5.30 or by appointment. SIZE: Medium. *STOCK: Oil paintings and watercolours, 18th-20th C, £100-£35,000; occasional furniture, 18th-19th C, £400-£5,000; objets d'art, 18th-20th C, £50-£2,000.* LOC: Near roundabout, at junction of A650 and A657. PARK: Own. TEL: 01274 581894; home - same. SER: Valuations; restorations (oil paintings, watercolours and frames). VAT: Stan/Spec.

SOWERBY BRIDGE, Nr. Halifax

Memory Lane
69 Wakefield Rd. HX6 2UX. (L. Robinson). Open 10.30-5. SIZE: Warehouse. *STOCK: Pine, oak, dolls and teddies.* TEL: 01422 833223.

Talking Point Antiques
66 West St. HX6 3AP. (P. and L. Austwick). Open Thurs., Fri., Sat. 10.30-5.30, other days by appointment. *STOCK: Restored gramophones and phonographs, 78rpm records, gramophone accessories and related items; small furniture; pottery, porcelain and curios.* TEL: 01422 834126.

TODMORDEN

Echoes
650a Halifax Rd., Eastwood. OL14 6DW. (P. Oldman). Est. 1980. CL: Tues. SIZE: Medium. *STOCK: Costume, textiles, linen and lace, £5-£500; jewellery, £5-£150; all 19th-20th C.* LOC: A646. PARK: Easy. TEL: 01706 817505; home - same. SER: Valuations; restorations (costume); buys at auction (as stock).

Todmorden continued

Fagin & Co.

54-56 Burnley Rd. OL14 5EY. (J. Ratcliff). Est. 1982. Open 10-5, Sun. by appointment. SIZE: Medium + warehouse. *STOCK: Country, antique and quality furniture, £50-£2,000; small architectural items and curiosities.* LOC: A646 Burnley road. PARK: Easy. TEL: 01706 819499; home - 01706 814773. SER: Valuations.

Todmorden Antiques Centre

Sutcliffe House, Halifax Rd. OL14 5DG. (Mr and Mrs Hoogeveen). Open 10-5, Sat. 11-5, Sun. 1-5. CL: Tues. SIZE: 14 dealers. *STOCK: General antiques, furniture and jewellery.* TEL: 01706 818040.

Todmorden Fine Art

27 Water St. OL14 5AB. (Mr Gunning and Mr Middleton). Est. 1981. Usually open 7 days but prior telephone call advisable. SIZE: Small. *STOCK: Contemporary collectable oil paintings, £100-£1,000.* LOC: Off M62, Junction 20. PARK: Hall St. opposite. TEL: 01706 814723; home - same. SER: Valuations; restorations; framing. VAT: Spec.

WAKEFIELD

Robin Taylor Fine Arts

36 Carter St. WF1 1XJ. Open 9.30-5.30. *STOCK: Oils and watercolours.* TEL: 01924 381809.

WALSDEN, Nr. Todmorden

Cottage Antiques (1984) Ltd

788 Rochdale Rd. OL14 7UA. (G. Slater). Resident. Est. 1978. Open Tues.-Sun. SIZE: Medium. *STOCK: Pine furniture, kitchenalia 19th C, £5-£1,000; general antiques.* PARK: EasyTEL: 0170 681 3612. SER: Restorations pine stripping; import and export of Continental pine.

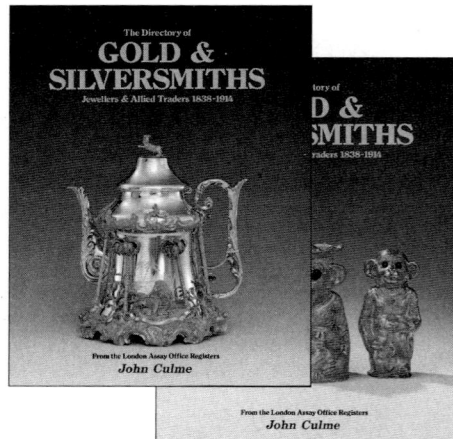

Guernsey

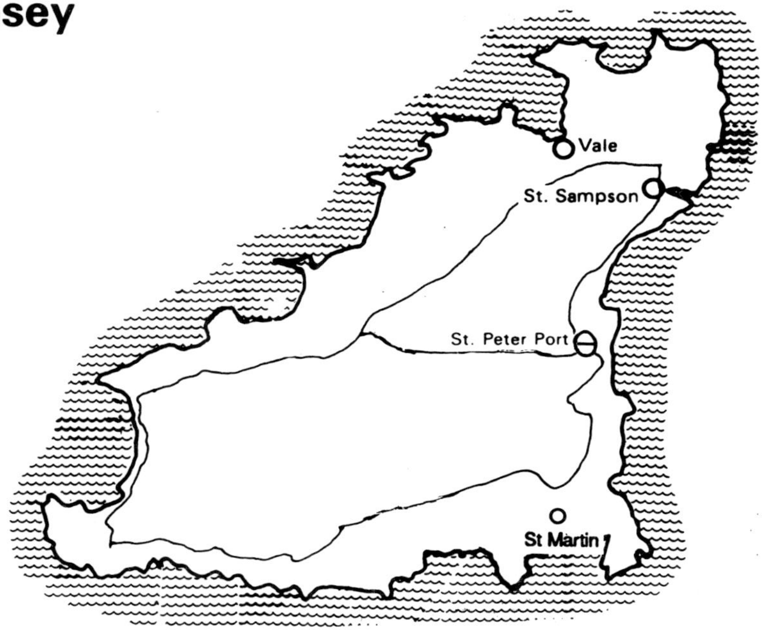

NORTH

Jersey

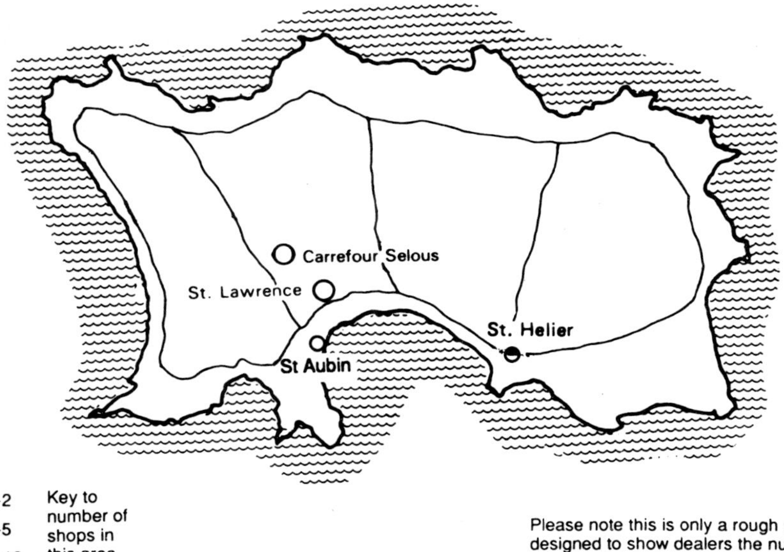

1-2
3-5
6-12
13+

Key to number of shops in this area.

Please note this is only a rough map designed to show dealers the number of shops in the various towns, and is not necessarily totally accurate.

Alderney

Beverley J. Pyke - Fine British Watercolours
22 Victoria St. Open by appointment only. *STOCK: 20th C watercolours, £150-£2,000.* TEL: 01481 824092

Victoria Antiques
St. Catherine's, Victoria St. (P.A. Nightingale). Open 10-12.30 and 2.30-4.30. *STOCK: Period and Victorian furniture, glass, silver, china, jewellery, small objets d'art.* TEL: 01481 823260. SER: Valuations.

Guernsey

ST. MARTIN

Mark Blower Antiques
Les Chenes, Rue de Putron. Est. 1978. Open by appointment only. SIZE: Small. *STOCK: Furniture, 18th C, £1,000-£10,000; pictures, 18th-19th C, £500-£5,000.* PARK: Easy. TEL: 01481 39098. SER: Valuations; restorations (furniture and pictures); fine art packing and shipping; buys at auction.

ST. PETER PORT

The Antique Centre
12 Mansell St. Est. 1973. Open 10-1 and 2-5. CL: Thurs. pm. SIZE: 5 dealers. *STOCK: Period, Victorian and Edwardian furniture, clocks, nautical items, oils, watercolours, silver and plate, items of local interest.* PARK: Nearby. TEL: 01481 726808; home - 01481 46025.

Channel Islands Galleries Ltd
Trinity Sq. Centre, Trinity Sq. GY1 1LX. (G.P. and Mrs C. Gavey). Est. 1967. Open 10-12.30 and 2-5, or by appointment. CL: Thurs. pm. *STOCK: Antique maps, sea charts and prints of the Channel Islands; oil paintings, watercolours, Channel Islands' books, illustrated, historical, social, geographical and natural history.* Not Stocked: General antiques. TEL: 01481 723247; home - 01481 47337.

Grange Antiques
7/8 The Grange. GY1 2PX. (Mrs K.M. Carré). Est. 1968. Open 9.30-5. CL: Sat. pm., Thurs. and Sun. except by appointment. SIZE: Medium. *STOCK: Objets d'art, and small furniture, 18th-19th C, £25-£1,000; pottery and porcelain, 18th C to Art Deco, £5-£500; jewellery, antique and secondhand, £1-£500; linens, silver and plate.* LOC: One of main roads from harbour going inland, shop opposite the Elizabeth College. PARK: 50yds. on right. TEL: 01481 721480. SER: Valuations; buys at auction.

St. Peter Port continued

The Pine Collection
17 Mansell St. (P. Head). Est. 1986. Open 9.30 5.30. *STOCK: Pine.* TEL: 01481 726891.

St. James's Gallery Ltd
18-20 Smith St and 18-20 The Bordage. GY 2JQ. (C.O. Whittam). Est. 1945. CL: Lunch times SIZE: Large. *STOCK: Furniture, £100-£20,000 porcelain, both 18th-19th C; paintings, 18th-20th C.* TEL: 01481 720070; home - 01481 723999 SER: Valuations; restorations (furniture).

ST. SAMPSON

The Old Curiosity Shop
Commercial Rd. GY2 4QP. Est. 1978. CL: Mon and Thurs. *STOCK: Old and antiquarian books prints, postcards, coins, ephemera, paintings small furniture, china, glass, silver, brass, £1 £5,000.* TEL: 01481 45324. FAIRS: Organiser.

VALE

Geoffrey P. Gavey
Les Clospains, Rue de L'Ecole. GY3 5LL. Es 1967. Open by appointment. *STOCK: Maps, se charts and prints of the Channel Islands; oil an watercolour paintings; Channel Islands books illustrated, historical, social, geographic an natural history.* Not Stocked: General antiques TEL: 01481 47337.

Jersey

CARREFOUR SELOUS, St Lawrence

David Hick Antiques
Alexandra House. Est. 1977. Open Wed., Fri. an Sat. 9.30-5. SIZE: Large and warehouse. *STOCK Furniture and small items.* TEL: 01534 865965 fax - 01534 865448.

ST AUBIN

Boulevard Antiques
Charing Cross House. (Veronica Mileti). Es 1996. Open 10-5.30 (late night opening i summer). SIZE: Small. *STOCK: French an Italian gilt small furniture; interesting an unusual items from Europe.* PARK: Town Hal TEL: 01534 45753.

ST. HELIER

John Blench & Son
50 Don St. JE2 4TR. *STOCK: Fine book bindings, local maps and prints.* TEL: 0153 25281.

St. Helier continued

John Cooper Antiques
16 The Market. *STOCK: General antiques.* TEL: 01534 23600.

Grange Gallery and Fine Arts Ltd
39 New St. JE2 3RA. (G.J. Morris). Est. 1974. Open 9-5.30. CL: Sun., Tues. and Thurs. except by appointment. SIZE: Medium. *STOCK: Oil paintings, 18th-19th C, local prints, 19th C; all £100-£9,000.* LOC: Antique area of St. Helier. PARK: Multi-storey 100yds. TEL: 01534 616810; fax - 01534 880460. SER: Valuations; restorations (pictures); buys at auction; framing.

David Hick Antiques
45 Halkett Place. JE2 4WG. Open 10-5, Thurs. 10-1. *STOCK: Furniture and smalls.* TEL: 01534 21162; fax - same.

Jeremiah's Antiques
14 1/2 Queen St. (K.J. O'Keeffe). Est. 1981. Open 10-5. CL: Mon. SIZE: Small. *STOCK: Fine wrist and pocket watches, clocks; silver, porcelain, bronzes, jewellery, small furniture.* LOC: Main shopping area. PARK: Nearby. TEL: 01534 23153. SER: Valuations; restorations (clocks and watches); buys at auction (clocks and watches). FAIRS: Miami, Munich, London. *Trade Only.*

Rae Antiques
Savile St. JE2 3XF. Est. 1946. Open daily. SIZE: Large. *STOCK: General antiques, furniture, pictures, clocks and silver.* TEL: 01534 32171

Sheila Rae Antiques
Clare St. and Savile St. JE2 3XF. *STOCK: Clocks, paintings, silver, porcelain and furniture.* TEL: 01534 58071/32171.

The Selective Eye Gallery
50 Don St. JE2 4TR. (J. and P. Blench). Est. 1958. Open 9-5. CL: Thurs. and Sat. pm. SIZE: Medium. *STOCK: Oil paintings, 19th-20th C; maps, prints and antiquarian books, 16th-20th C.* Not Stocked: General antiques. LOC: Town centre. PARK: Multi-storey 100yds. TEL: 01534 25281. SER: Valuations; restorations (pictures). FAIRS: Jersey.

Thesaurus (Jersey) Ltd
3 Burrard St. JE2 4WS. (I. Creaton). Est. 1973. Open 8.30-6. SIZE: Large. *STOCK: Antiquarian and out of print books, £1-£2,000; maps and prints.* Not Stocked: General antiques. LOC: Town centre. PARK: 100yds. TEL: 01534 37045. SER: Buys at auction. VAT: Spec.

Joan Thomson Antiques
2 Burrard St. Est. 1967. Open 10-4. CL: Mon. and Thurs. SIZE: Medium. *STOCK: Smalls, £10-500, jewellery, linen, collectors' items, Oriental.* PARK: Nearby. TEL: 01534 37206; home - 01534 854156.

St. Helier continued

Thomson's
4 Wharf St. JE2 3NR. Est. 1967. Open 10-5. CL: Thurs. SIZE: Large. *STOCK: General antiques especially furniture.* LOC: Rear of Pomme d'Or Hotel. PARK: Easy and Pier Road. TEL: 01534 23673/601081. SER: Valuations.

Union Street Antique Market
8 Union St. (A.L. Thomson). Est. 1965. Open 10-5. SIZE: Large - several dealers. *STOCK: General antiques.* PARK: 150yds. TEL: 01534 873805; home - 01534 22475. SER: Buys at auction.

ST. LAWRENCE

I.G.A. Old Masters Ltd
5 Kimberley Grove, Rue de Haut. (I.G. and Mrs C.B.V. Appleby). Est. 1953. Open by appointment. *STOCK: Old Master and 19th C paintings.* LOC: Near glass church. PARK: Easy. TEL: 01534 24226; home - same.

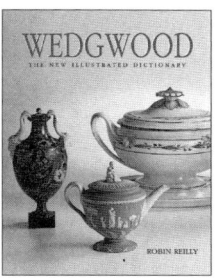

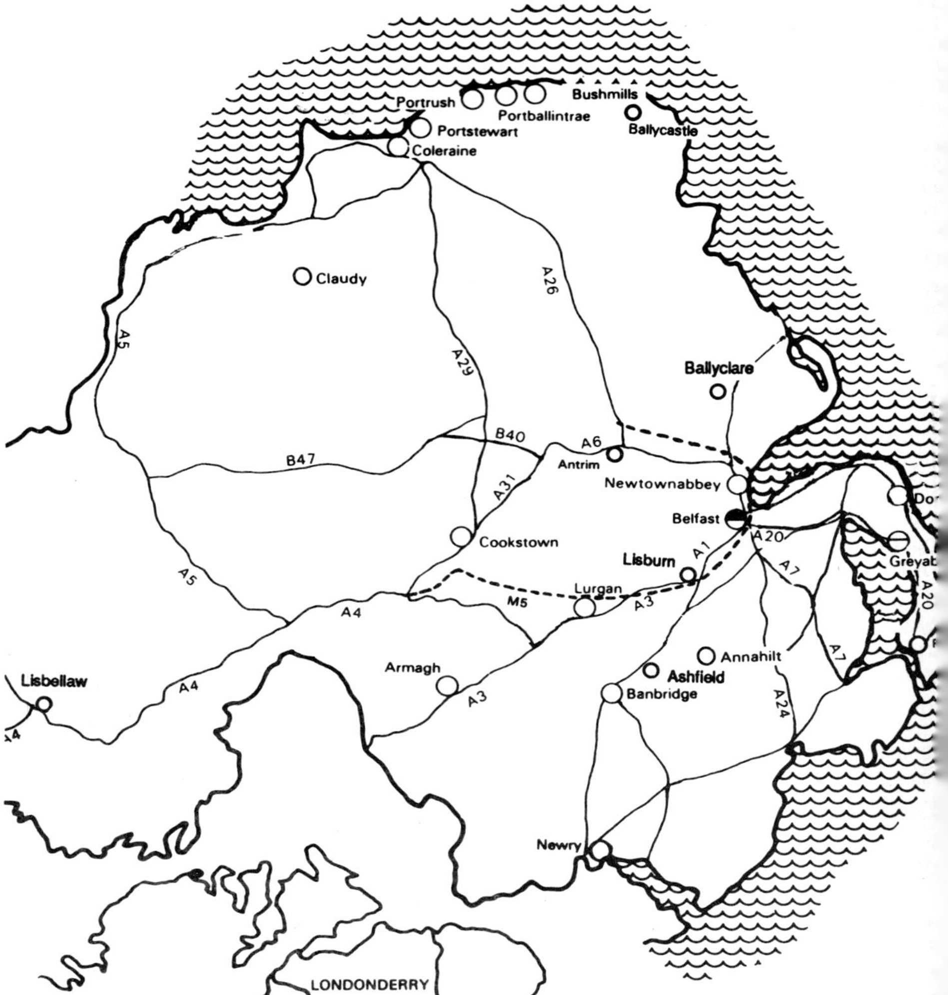

1-2
3-5
6-12
13+

Key to numb
shops
this ar

Please note this is only a rough map designed to show dealers the numb shops in the various towns, and is n necessarily totally accurate.

BELFAST

The Bell Gallery
13 Adelaide Park. BT9 6FX. (J.N. Bell). Est. 1964. Open 10-6. SIZE: Medium. *STOCK: British and Irish art, 19th-20th C.* LOC: Off Malone Rd. TEL: 01232 662998. SER: Valuations; restorations (paintings); buys at auction. VAT: Stan/Spec.

Emerald Isle Books
539 Antrim Rd. BT15 3BU. Est. 1966. Open by appointment. *STOCK: Travel, Ireland, theology.* TEL: 01232 370798; fax - 01232 777288. SER: Catalogues available.

Hearth and Home
29 Howard St. BT6 1ND. (C. Heath and M.P.W. Smith). Open 9.30-5.30, Thurs. until 9. *STOCK: Pine furniture and decorative items.* LOC: City centre. PARK: Easy. TEL: 01232 322355. SER: Pine decorative items made to size.

T.H. Kearney & Sons
Treasure House, 123 University St. BT7 1HP. Resident. *STOCK: Small antiques.* TEL: 01232 231055. SER: Restorations and upholstery. VAT: Stan.

Charlotte and John Lambe
41 Shore Rd. BT15 3PG. Open 10-5. CL: Sat. *STOCK: English and French furniture, 19th C; pictures and works of art.* TEL: 01232 370761.

Mews Antique and Reproduction Fireplaces & Architectural Salvage
The Gate Lodge, 260 Antrim Rd. BT15 2AT. (P. O'Flaherty). Open 10.30-5. CL: Mon. *STOCK: Restored Victorian fireplaces, wood flooring and miscellaneous items.* TEL: 01232 751319.

Sinclair's Antique Gallery
19 Arthur St. BT1 4GA. Est. 1900. Open 9-5.30. CL: Sat. SIZE: Small. *STOCK: Victorian jewellery, china, glass, £10-£1,000; silver, coins.* LOC: 100yds. from city centre. TEL: 01232 322335. VAT: Stan.

Co. Antrim

ANTRIM

The Country Antiques LAPADA
219B Lisnevenagh Rd. BT41 2JT. (David Wolfenden). Open 10-6. SIZE: Large. *STOCK: Furniture, £200-£5,000; jewellery and porcelain, £100-£3,000; all 19th C.* LOC: Main Antrim-Ballymena line. PARK: Easy. TEL: 01849 429498. SER: Valuations; restorations. VAT: Stan/Spec.

BALLYCASTLE

Antiques and Gallery
8 Quay Rd. BT54 6BH. (E. McCarroll). Resident. Est. 1993. Open 11-6.30, Sun. 2.30-6.30, or any time by appointment. SIZE: Large.

Ballycastle continued

STOCK: Pictures and prints, pottery and glass, bric-a-brac, 1880 to date, to £5,000. PARK: Easy. TEL: 012657 63078.

BALLYCLARE

Robert Christie Antiques
20 Calhame Rd., Straid. IADA. Est. 1976. Usually open, prior telephone call appreciated. SIZE: Medium. *STOCK: Furniture, 1750-1900, £200-£3,000; clocks, 1750-1900, £500-£2,000; decorative objects, 1800-1900, £50-£500.* LOC: 1/4 mile off A8 Belfast-Larne road. PARK: Easy. TEL: 01960 341149; home - same. SER: Valuations; buys at auction. FAIRS: Newcastle: Culloden Hotel, Holywood.

BUSHMILLS

Dunluce Antiques
33 Ballytober Rd. BT57 8UU. (Mrs C. Ross). Est. 1978. Open 2-6 or by appointment. CL: Fri. SIZE: Small. *STOCK: Furniture, £50-£1,000; porcelain and glass, £1-£1,000; silver, £5-£5000; all Georgian to 1930's; paintings, mainly Irish, £50-£10,000.* LOC: 1.5 miles off Antrim coast rd. at Dunluce Castle. PARK: Easy. TEL: 012657 31140. SER: Restorations (porcelain).

LISBURN

Parvis Sigaroudinia
Mountainview House, 40 Sandy Lane, Ballyskeagh. BT27 5TL. IADA. Est. 1974. Open by appointment at any time. *STOCK: Oriental carpets, 19th-20th C, £500-£1,000; furniture, 18th-19th C, £1,000-£10,000; stools upholstered in antique carpets and kelims, from £250+.* LOC: Take Malone Road from Belfast, then Upper Malone Road towards Lisburn, cross Ballyskeagh bridge over M1, 1st left into Sandy Lane. PARK: Easy. TEL: 01232 621824; home - same. SER: Valuations; buys at auction (mainly Oriental carpets, tapestries, antique furniture); Quarterly exhibitions held in Belfast, Enniskillen and Antrim. FAIRS: Culloden, Belfast; IADA in RDS Dublin. VAT: Stan.

NEWTOWNABBEY

MacHenry Antiques
Caragh Lodge, Glen Rd., Jordanstown. BT37 0RY. (A. MacHenry). IADA. Est. 1964. Open 2-7, or by appointment. SIZE: Medium. *STOCK: Georgian and Victorian furniture and objects.* LOC: 6 miles from Belfast to Whiteabbey village, left at traffic lights at Woody's, then left into Old Manse Rd. and continue into Glen Rd. PARK: Easy. TEL: 01232 862036; fax - 01232 853281. SER: Valuations. FAIRS: Dublin, Belfast and Irish. VAT: Stan/Spec.

PORTBALLINTRAE, Nr. Bushmills

Brian R. Bolt Antiques

88 Ballaghmore Rd. BT57 8RL. IADA. Open 11-5.30, and by appointment. CL: Wed. and Fri. *STOCK: Silver - small and unusual items, objects of vertu, snuff boxes, vesta cases, table, Scottish and Irish provincial; treen; English and Continental glass, antique and 20th C; art and studio glass and ceramics; Arts and Crafts, Art Nouveau and Art Deco jewellery and metalwork; vintage fountain pens.* TEL: 012657 31129. SER: Search; illustrated catalogues available; world-wide postal service; valuations.

PORTRUSH

Alexander Antiques

108 Dunluce Rd. BT56 8NB. (Mrs M. and D. Alexander). Est. 1974. Open 10-6. CL: Sun. except by appointment. SIZE: Large. *STOCK: Furniture, silver, porcelain, fine art, 18th-20th C; oils and watercolours, 19th-20th C.* Not Stocked: Militaria, jewellery, coins. LOC: 1 mile from Portrush on A2 to Bushmills. PARK: Easy. TEL: 01265 822783. SER: Valuations; buys at auction. VAT: Stan/Spec.

Co. Armagh

ARMAGH

The Hole-in-the-Wall

Market St. BT61 7BW. (I. Emerson). Est. 1953. *STOCK: General antiques.* LOC: City centre. VAT: Stan/Spec.

LURGAN

Charles Gardiner Antiques

48 High St. BT66 8AU. Est. 1968. Open 9-1 and 2-6. CL: Wed. *STOCK: Clocks, furniture and general antiques.* PARK: Own. TEL: 01762 323934.

PORTADOWN

Moyallon Antiques

54 Moyallon Rd. Est. 1975. Usually open. SIZE: Medium. *STOCK: Furniture, 19th C, £50-£1,000; pine and country furniture, 18th-19th C, £50-£500; ceramics and bric-a-brac, £5-£100.* LOC: Portadown - Gilford Rd., 1 mile from Gilford on right-hand side. PARK: Easy. TEL: 01762 831615.

Co. Down

ANNAHILT

Period Architectural Features and Antiques

263 Ballynahich Rd. BT26 6BP. (J. Cousans). Open 9.30-5.30. SIZE: Large. *STOCK: Marble chimney pieces, early 18th to late 19th C, £5-£1,000; period panelling and pine pews, stained*

Annahilt continued

glass, Victorian bathrooms, decorative architectural items. TEL: 01846 638091. SER: Valuations; restorations (marble); pine stripping; French polishing; buys at auction. VAT: Stan.

ASHFIELD, Nr. Dromore

Clifford J. Auld Antiques (Old Cross Antiques) LAPADA

54 Killysorrell Rd. IADA. Est. 1966. Open by appointment. SIZE: Small. *STOCK: Furniture, 1750-1940 and silver, 1700-1940, £50-£3,000, unusual and interesting objets d'art; 18th-19th C pottery and porcelain.* Not Stocked: Books, coins, medals, etc. LOC: 1.5 miles off main A1, turn off past Thompson's Motors, Rowantree Rd. PARK: Easy. TEL: 01846 692670; mobile - 0850 183947.

BANBRIDGE

Cameo Antiques

41 Bridge St. BT32 3LY. (D. and J. Bell). Est. 1966. TEL: 0182 06 23241.

DONAGHADEE

Furney Antiques and Interiors

3-4 Shore St. BT21 0DG. (The Furney Family). Est. 1976. Open Fri. and Sat. 11-1 and 2-5.30, or by appointment. *STOCK: Period furniture and decorative items.* TEL: 01247 888721/883826; fax - 01247 888729.

GREYABBEY, Nr. Newtownards

Phyllis Arnold Gallery Antiques

Hoops Courtyard. BT22 2NE. Est. 1968. Open Wed., Fri. and Sat. 11-5. *STOCK: General antiques, jewellery, small furniture, 19th-20th C; watercolours, portrait miniatures, maps and prints of Ireland.* TEL: 012477 88199; home - 01247 853322; fax - same. SER: Restoration (maps, prints, watercolours, portrait miniatures); conservation framing. FAIRS: Culloden.

Marjorie McAuley - The Antique Shop

9 Main St. BT22 2NE. Est. 1968. *STOCK: General antiques.* TEL: Home - 012477 38333.

Old Priory Antiques LAPADA

3-5 Main St. BT22 2NE. (Patty Loane). Est. 1983. Open 11.30-5.30, other times by appointment. CL: Tues. *STOCK: Jewellery, 1780-1930, silver and furniture, 1750-1930.* Not Stocked: Books, stamps, coins, medals. LOC: Village centre. PARK: Easy. TEL: 012477 88346.

Timecraft

18 Main St. BT22 2NE. Est. 1976. Open 11-5.30. CL: Sun. and Thurs. except by appointment. SIZE: Small. *STOCK: Clocks and watches, 19th C, £100-£2,000; jewellery, 19th-20th C*

Greyabbey continued

£500. PARK: Easy. TEL: 012477 88416/88252; fax - 012477 88250. SER: Valuations; restorations; buys at auction (clocks and watches).

HOLYWOOD

Herbert Gould and Co.
21-23 Church Rd. BT18 9BU. (Stephen Gould). Est. 1897. Open 9.15-5.30. SIZE: Medium.. *STOCK: Pine, 19th C, £75-£200; collectables, architectural antiques, 19th-20th C, £10-£100.* LOC: 20 yards from maypole in town centre. PARK: Opposite. TEL: 01232 427916. SER: Valuations; pine stripping; buys at auction (as stock). VAT: Stan.

NEWRY

Downshire House Antiques
52 Downshire Rd. (H. and R. McCabe). Open 9-5.30. *STOCK: General antiques including furniture and porcelain, 18th-19th C, £50-£10,000.* TEL: 01693 66689/69199. SER: Valuations; restorations (furniture); deliveries.

McCabe's Antique Galleries
62 Downshire Rd. (R. McCabe). Est. 1910. Open 9-5.30, Wed., Sun. and evenings by appointment. SIZE: Large and warehouse. *STOCK: General antiques including furniture and porcelain, 18th-19th C.* PARK: Own. TEL: 01693 62695/66689/69199. SER: Valuations; restorations (furniture). FAIRS: Conway Hotel, Lisburn; Drumkeen Hotel, Belfast. VAT: Stan.

PORTAFERRY

Time & Tide Antiques
Ferry St. BT22 1PB. (D. Dunlop). Open Wed., Fri., Sat. and Sun. 12-5.30, or by appointment. SIZE: Medium. *STOCK: Clocks, barometers, marine instruments, pictures and nautical memorabilia and small furniture, £50-£2,500.* LOC: A20 from Newtownards through Greyabbey. PARK: Easy. TEL: 012477 28935; home - same. SER: Valuations; restorations and repairs.

WARRENPOINT

Antiques and Fine Art Gallery
Charlotte St. BT34 3LF. (B. Woods). Est. 1991. Open 10.30-1 and 2.30-5.30. CL: Mon. and Wed. SIZE: Medium. *STOCK: Furniture, Georgian to Edwardian, £50-£5,000; paintings especially Irish, 20th C, £50-£10,000.* LOC: Turn off main road at Newry. PARK: Easy. TEL: 016937 52905. SER: Valuations.

Co. Fermanagh

LISBELLAW

Forge Antiques
Brooke St. (Mrs I. Burton and K. Johnston). Est. 1989. Open 2-5.30, Sat. 9.30-5.30. SIZE: Medium. *STOCK: Georgian, Victorian and Edwardian furniture, £50-£3,000; porcelain and ceramics including Belleek, pictures and glass.* LOC: 5 miles from Enniskillen, off A4 Belfast road. PARK: Easy. TEL: 01365 387777; home - 01365 387774. SER: Valuations. FAIRS: Major Northern Ireland.

Co. Londonderry

CLAUDY

K.O. Hagan
'Bensara', 162 Foreglen Rd. BT47 4ED. *STOCK: Georgian, Victorian and Edwardian furniture, especially pine.* TEL: 01504 338506.

COLERAINE

The Forge Antiques
24 Long Commons. BT52 1LH. (M.W. Walker). Est. 1977. Open 10-5.30. CL: Thurs. *STOCK: General antiques, silver, clocks, jewellery, porcelain, paintings.* TEL: 01265 51339. VAT: Stan.

Homes, Pubs and Clubs
1-5 Portrush Rd. (McNulty Wholesalers). Resident. Est. 1983. Open 9-6, Sun. 2.30-6. SIZE: Large. *STOCK: Pine and mahogany, small interesting items.* LOC: Main Portrush road, near traffic lights. PARK: At rear of premises. TEL: 01265 55733. SER: Valuations; restorations. FAIRS: Newark. VAT: Stan.

PORTSTEWART

The Smithy
Cappagh, 182 Coleraine Rd. BT55 7PL. (Mrs Bea Macafee). Est. 1967. Open 2-5. SIZE: Medium. *STOCK: Porcelain, jewellery, furniture, silver, bric-a-brac.* LOC: Main road between Coleraine and Portstewart. PARK: Easy. TEL: 01265 832209; home - 01265 52153.

Co. Tyrone

COOKSTOWN

Cookstown Antiques
16 Oldtown St. BT80 8EF. (T.H. Jebb). Est. 1976. Open Thurs. and Fri. 2-5.30, Sat. 10.30-5.30. SIZE: Small. *STOCK: Jewellery, silver, £10-£2,000; coins, £25-£200; pictures, ceramics and militaria, £5-£1,000; general antiques, all 19th-20th C.* Not Stocked: Large furniture. LOC: Going north, through both sets of traffic lights, on left at rear of estate agency. PARK: Easy. TEL: 016487 65279; fax - 016487 62946; home - 016487 62926. SER: Valuations; buys at auction.

The Saddle Room Antiques
4 Coagh St. BT80 8NG. (C.J. Leitch). Est. 1968. Open 10-5.30. CL: Mon. and Wed. *STOCK: China, silver, furniture, glass, jewellery.* TEL: 016487 64045.

SCOTLAND NORTH

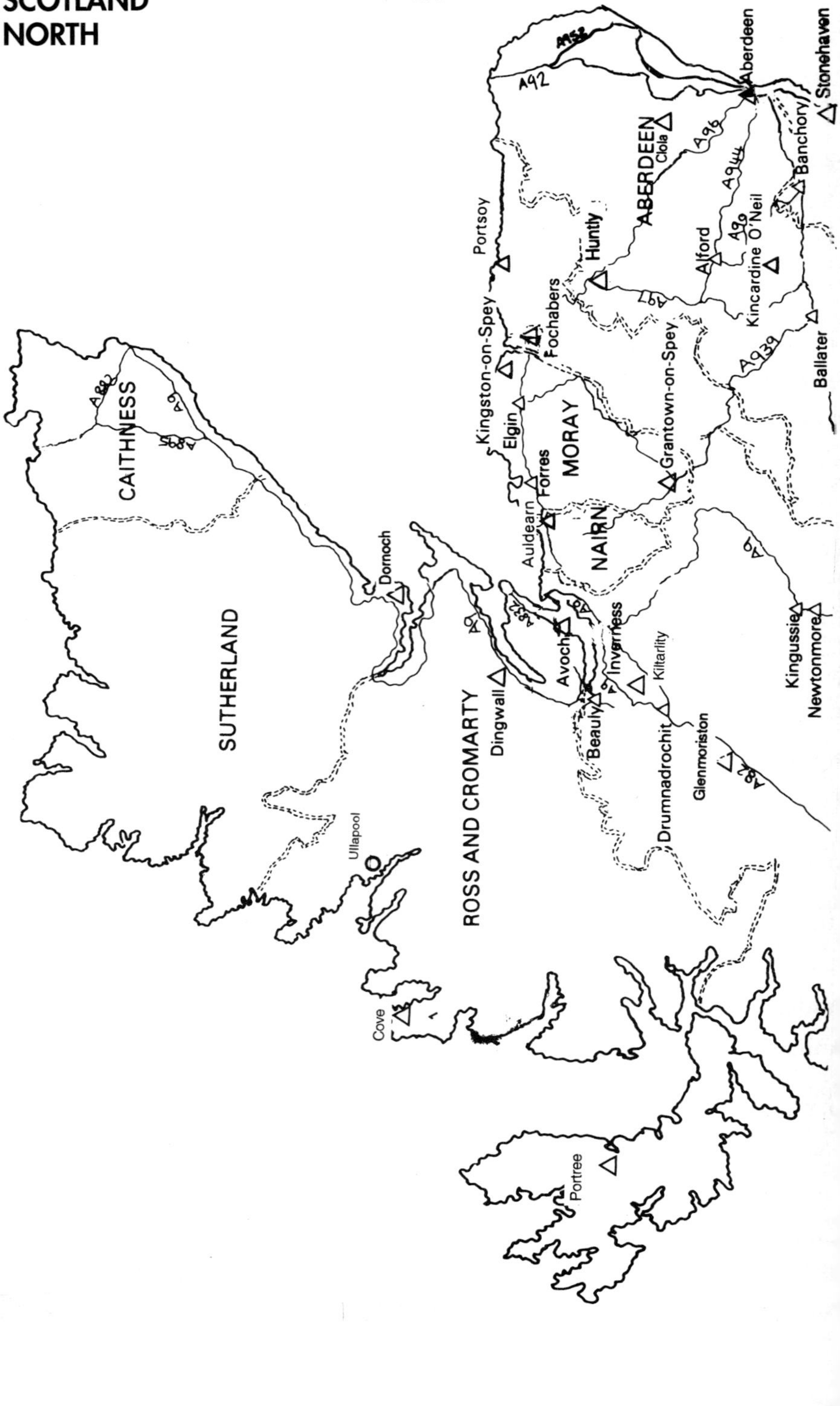

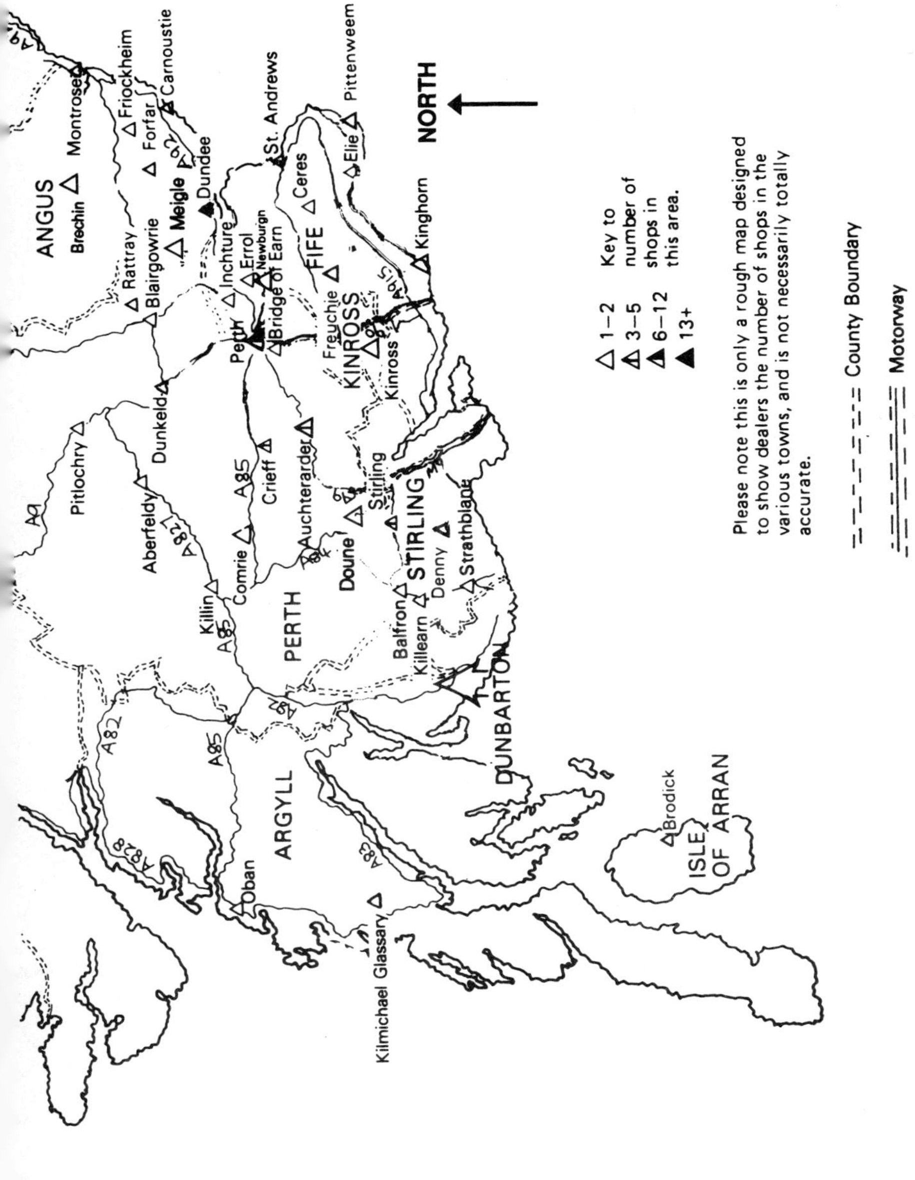
NORTH
Key to number of shops in this area.
1–2
3–5
6–12
13+
Please note this is only a rough map designed to show dealers the number of shops in the various towns, and is not necessarily totally accurate.
County Boundary
Motorway
ANGUS
Brechin
Montrose
Friockheim
Forfar
Carnoustie
Dundee
Meigle
Rattray
Blairgowrie
Inchture
Errol
Newburgh
St. Andrews
Ceres
Elie
Pittenweem
FIFE
Kinghorn
Bridge of Earn
Perth
Freuchie
KINROSS
Kinross
Dunkeld
Pitlochry
Aberfeldy
Crieff
Auchterarder
Stirling
STIRLING
Strathblane
Denny
Doune
Comrie
Killin
PERTH
Balfron
Killearn
DUNBARTON
ARGYLL
Oban
Kilmichael Glassary
Brodick
ISLE OF ARRAN
A9
A92
A85
A827
A84
A82
A828
A83
A91
A915

SCOTLAND SOUTH

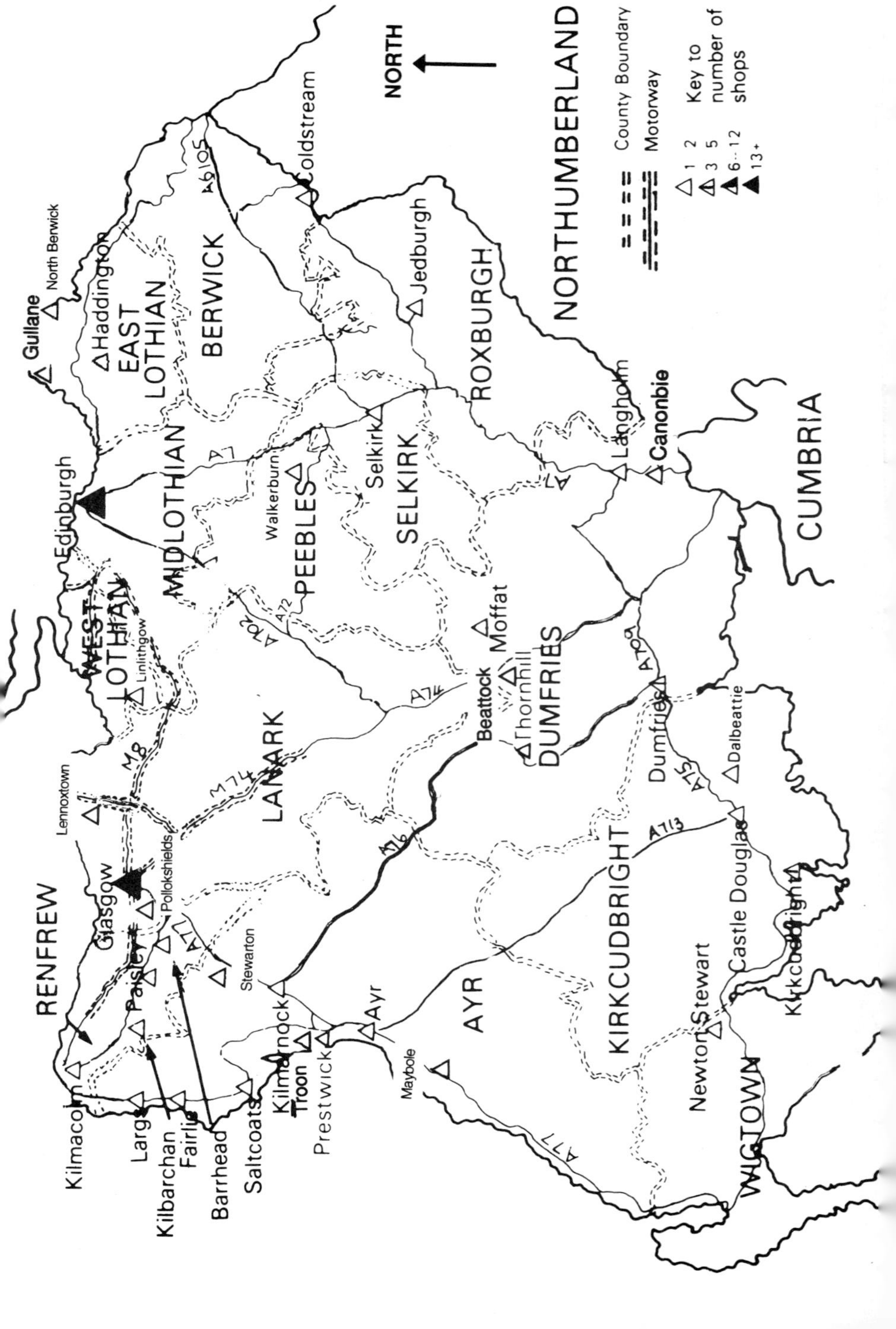
NORTH
NORTHUMBERLAND
County Boundary
Motorway
Key to number of shops
1 2
3 5
6-12
13+
CUMBRIA
RENFREW
WEST LOTHIAN
MIDLOTHIAN
EAST LOTHIAN
BERWICK
ROXBURGH
PEEBLES
SELKIRK
LANARK
DUMFRIES
AYR
KIRKCUDBRIGHT
WIGTOWN
Gullane
North Berwick
Haddington
Edinburgh
Linlithgow
Coldstream
Jedburgh
Selkirk
Walkerburn
Langholm
Canonbie
Moffat
Beattock
Thornhill
Dumfries
Dalbeattie
Castle Douglas
Kirkcudbright
Newton Stewart
Lennoxtown
Glasgow
Pollokshields
Paisley
Stewarton
Kilmarnock
Troon
Prestwick
Ayr
Maybole
Kilmacolm
Largs
Kilbarchan
Fairlie
Barrhead
Saltcoats
A6105
A7
A72
A702
A74
A709
A75
A713
A76
A77
M8
M74

SCOTTISH COUNTY BOUNDARIES

ABERDEEN (Aberdeenshire)

Atholl Antiques
322 Great Western Rd. AB1 6PL. Open 10.30-1 and 2.30-6 or by appointment. *STOCK: Scottish paintings and furniture.* TEL: 01224 593547. VAT: Stan/Spec.

Burning Embers
165-167 King St. AB2 3AE. (J. Bruce). Open 10-5. *STOCK: Fireplaces, bric-a-brac and pine.* TEL: 01224 624664.

Gallery
239 George St. (M. Gray). Est. 1981. Open 9-5.30. SIZE: Large. *STOCK: Jewellery, post 1850; curios and Victoriana, paintings and prints, post 1800.* TEL: 01224 632522. SER: Valuations; repairs (jewellery and clocks).

McCalls (Aberdeen)
90 King St. AB1 2JH. (B. McCall). Est. 1948. Open 10-5.30. *STOCK: Jewellery.* PARK: Nearby. TEL: 01224 641916.

McCalls Limited
11 Bridge St. AB1 2JL. Open 9.30-5.30, Thurs. 9.30-8. *STOCK: Jewellery.* TEL: 01224 584577.

The Rendezvous Gallery
100 Forest Ave. AB15 6TL. Est. 1973. Open 10-1 and 2.30-6. CL: Fri. SIZE: Medium. *STOCK: Art Nouveau, Art Deco, glass, jewellery, bronzes,*

Aberdeen continued

furniture, £100-£5,000; paintings, watercolours, Scottish School, £200-£5,000. LOC: Just off Grea Western Rd. to Braemar. PARK: Easy. TEL: 01224 323247. VAT: Stan/Spec.

Mr Reynolds
162/164 Skene St. AB1 1TP. Resident. *STOCK: General antiques.* SER: Restorations.

Thistle Antiques LAPADA
28 Esslemont Ave. AB2 4SN. Est. 1967. TEL: 01224 634692. VAT: Spec.

Elizabeth Watt
69 Thistle St. AB1 1UY. Est. 1976. Open 10-5, Sat 10-1. SIZE: Small. *STOCK: General antiques* LOC: Off the west end of Union St. PARK Nearby. TEL: 01224 647232. SER: Restoration (china, glass).

The Waverley Gallery
18 Victoria St. AB3 1XA. (G. Wood). Open 9.30 6. *STOCK: Oil paintings and watercolours, £50 £6,000; prints, £20-£2,000; etchings, £40-£400 all 18th-20th C.* LOC: Corner of Waverley Place TEL: 01224 640633. SER: Valuations; restorations; framing.

Colin Wood (Antiques) Ltd
25 Rose St. AB1 1TX. Est. 1968. Open 9.15-5 Wed., Thurs., Sat. 10-1 and 2-5. SIZE: Medium *STOCK: Furniture, 17th-19th C; works of art Scottish paintings and silver.* PARK: Multi-store in Chapel St. TEL: 01224 644786 (answerphone) fax - same. VAT: Stan/Spec.

William Young Antiques & Fine Art
1 Gaelic Lane, off Belmont St. AB1 1JF. Est 1887. Open 9.30-5.30, Sat. 10-4. *STOCK: 17th 19th C furniture, paintings and silver.* TEL 01224 644757; fax - same.

ABERFELDY (Perthshire)

Sonia Cooper
19 Bridgend. PH15 2DF. Est. 1983. Open Fri. an Sat. 11-5, Thurs. 11-4; Mon. 11-5 in summer SIZE: Medium. *STOCK: China and glass, woo and metal, from 18th C, £1-£100.* LOC: 10 mile from A9. PARK: Easy. TEL: 01887 82026 SER: Buys at auction.

ABERNYTE (Perthshire)

Fine Antique Glass
Smithy Cottage. PH14 9ST. (S.D. Hole). Open b appointment. SIZE: Small. *STOCK: Decante and bowls, £40-£1,500; drinking glasses, £2 £1,000; candelabra and chandeliers, £200+; c 1750-1900.* LOC: A90 from Perth, then north c B953. Cottage has stone pillars and is opposi duck pond. TEL: 01828 686350.

ALFORD (Aberdeenshire)

R.S. Gordon Antiques
Main St. AB33 8AA. (R. and J. Gordon). Est. 1959. Open 9-5.30. *STOCK: Furniture, clocks, Victoriana, bric-a-brac.* LOC: A944 between Aberdeen and Huntly. TEL: 01975 562404. VAT: Stan/Spec.

AUCHTERARDER (Perthshire)

Paul Hayes Gallery
71 High St. PH3 1BN. PADA. Est. 1962. Open 10-1 and 2-5 or by appointment. CL: Wed. *STOCK: Fine paintings, especially Scottish landscapes, marine and Scottish post-impressionist, 18th-20th C.* TEL: 01764 662320/663442; fax - 01764 662320. VAT: Spec.

Old Abbey Antiques
4 High St. PH3 1DF. (Gordon M. Cockain). Est. 1982. Open 10.30-5.30. SIZE: 4 rooms. *STOCK: Furniture, £25-£750; silver and plate, Victorian to 1960's, £10-£250; collectables - glass, ceramics, bric-a-brac.* LOC: Off Stirling-Perth road, 1.5 miles from Gleneagles Hotel. PARK: Easy. TEL: 01764 664073; home - 01259 742441. VAT: Stan/Spec.

Times Past Antiques
Broadfold Farm. PH3 1DR. (J.M. Brown). Est. 1970. Open 8-5, weekends and holidays 10-4. SIZE: Large. *STOCK: Stripped pine, 19th-20th C, from £50; shipping goods, £5-£500.* LOC: From town centre take Abbey Rd. to flyover A9 at T junction. Turn left, 1st farm on left. PARK: Easy. TEL: 01764 663166; home - same. SER: Restorations (pine); courier; container-packing. VAT: Stan.

John Whitelaw and Sons Antiques
LAPADA
120 High St. PH3 1AD. Open 9-5, Sat. 9-2. *STOCK: General antiques; furniture, 17th-19th C.* PARK: Easy. TEL: 01764 662482. VAT: Stan/Spec.

AULDEARN, Nr. Nairn (Nairnshire)

Auldearn Antiques
Dalmore Manse, Lethen Rd. IV12 5HZ. Est. 1980. Open 10-6 including Sun. SIZE: Medium. *STOCK: Victorian linen and lace, kitchenalia, china, furniture, architectural items.* LOC: 1 mile from village. TEL: 01667 453087; home - same.

AVOCH (Ross-shire)

Highland Antiques
The Old Post Office. IV9 8RQ. (J. and H. Hesling). HADA. Est. 1962. Open 10.30-5. CL: Thurs. and Mon. (winter). *STOCK: Furniture, £100-£1,000; paintings, £50-£1,000; both 19th C; general antiques, 18th-19th C, £20-£1,000; antiquarian books especially of Scottish interest.* LOC: Village centre. PARK: Easy. TEL: 01381 621000; home - 01463 772250. SER: Valuations; buys at auction.

Avoch continued

AYR (Ayrshire)

Antiques
39 New Rd. KA7 2PL. (T. Rafferty). Est. 1970. Open 10-5. *STOCK: General antiques.* TEL: 01292 265346.

Mansfield Antiques
27-29 Crown St. KA8 8AG. (J. Kelly). Est. 1987. Open 9-5, Sat. 9-3. SIZE: Medium. *STOCK: Furniture, smalls, paintings, £10-£2,000.* LOC: Cross 'Auld Brig' leaving Ayr for Prestwick, 1st left after traffic lights. PARK: Easy. TEL: 01292 266284. SER: Valuations; restorations; French polishing.

BALFRON (Stirlingshire)

Amphora Galleries
16-18 Buchanan St. G63 0TT. (L. Ruglen). Resident. Est. 1961. Open 10-5.30 and by appointment. SIZE: Large. *STOCK: General antiques, furniture, decorative items.* LOC: On A81. TEL: 01360 440329.

BALLATER (Aberdeenshire)

The McEwan Gallery LAPADA

Bridge of Gairn. AB35 5UB. (D., P. and R. McEwan). Est. 1968. Open 10-5, Sun. 2-5, prior telephone call advisable during winter. SIZE: Medium. *STOCK: 18th-20th C British and European paintings, specialising in Scottish; rare and elusive Scottish, sporting and natural history books.* LOC: First house on the east side of A939 after its junction with A93 outside Ballater. PARK: Easy. TEL: 013397 55429; fax - 013397 55995. SER: Valuations; restorations (framing); buys at auction (paintings, watercolours, books); golf catalogues. VAT: Spec.

BANCHORY (Kincardineshire)

Bygones

6 Dee St. AB31 3ST. (V. Watt). Est. 1983. Open 10-1 and 2-5, Sat. 10-5. SIZE: Medium. *STOCK: Victoriana, bric-a-brac, small furniture, to £500.* LOC: Town centre. PARK: Easy. TEL: 01330 823095. SER: Valuations. VAT: Global.

BARRHEAD, Nr. Glasgow (Renfrewshire)

C.P.R. Antiques and Services

96 Main St. G78 1SE. (Mr and Mrs Porterfield). Est. 1965. Open 10-1 and 1.30-5. CL: Tues. SIZE: Medium. *STOCK: Brass, furniture and curios, 19th-20th C, to £5,000.* PARK: Easy. TEL: 0141 881 5379.

BEATTOCK (Dumfriesshire)

T.W. Beaty

Lochhouse Farm. DG10 9SG. Open 9.30-5; trade any time by appointment. SIZE: Large and warehouse. *STOCK: Furniture, china, glass, brass, pictures, 18th-20th C.* TEL: 01683 300451. VAT: Stan/Spec.

BEAULY (Inverness-shire)

Iain Marr Antiques

3 Mid St. IV4 7DP. (I. and A. Marr). HADA. Est. 1975. Open 10.30-1 and 2-5.30. CL: Thurs. *STOCK: Silver, jewellery, clocks, porcelain, scientific instruments, arms, oils, watercolours, small furniture.* LOC: Off Square, on left going north, next to Gael's Coffee Shop. TEL: 01463 782372. VAT: Stan/Spec/Global.

BLAIRGOWRIE (Perthshire)

Roy Sim Antiques

The Granary Warehouse, Lower Mill St. PH10 6AQ. Est. 1977. Open 9-5.30, Sun. 12-5. SIZE: Large. *STOCK: Furniture, clocks, silver and plate, collectables.* TEL: 01250 873860.

BRECHIN (Angus)

Harper-James

40 High St. (D.R. James). *STOCK: Furniture, clocks, silver and jewellery, 1690-1910, £5-£6,000; ceramics and pottery, 1800-1945, £10-650+; general antiques and curios, £2-£750.* PARK: Easy. TEL: 01356 626300. SER: Valuations; restorations (furniture, upholstery); French polishing; export.

BRIDGE OF EARN (Perthshire)

Imrie Antiques LAPADA

Back St. PH2 9AE. (Mr and Mrs I. Imrie). Est. 1969. Open 10-1 and 2-5.30. SIZE: Large. *STOCK: Victorian and 18th C shipping goods.* PARK: Easy. TEL: 01738 812784. VAT: Stan.

BRODICK AND WHITING BAY (Isle of Arran)

Kames Antiques & Jewellery and Kames Antiques & Furnishings

Kames Cottage, Shore Rd. KA27 8AS. (C.J. and J.M. Fieldhouse). Open 10-5. SIZE: 2 shops. *STOCK: Furniture, porcelain, paintings, jewellery, collectables, objets d'art, silver and artists' materials.* TEL: 01770 302213/700201.

CANONBIE (Dumfreisshire)

John Mann Antique Clocks

The Clock Showroom. DG14 0RY. (John R. Mann). MBHI. Est. 1987. Open by appointment. SIZE: Large. *STOCK: Clocks - over 70 longcase, 17th-19th C, £2,000-£20,000; bracket, 17th-19th C, £500-£4,000; wall, 19th C, £500-£2,000.* LOC: Leave M6, junction 44, A7 north through Longtown, follow sign to village, premises next to Cross Keys Hotel. PARK: Easy. TEL: 013873 71337/71827; mobile - 0850 606147. SER: Valuations; restorations (clock movements, cases and dials); buys at auction (clocks).

CASTLE DOUGLAS (Kirkcudbrightshire)

Bendalls Antiques LAPADA

221-223 King St. DG7 1DT. (R.A. Mitchell). Est. 1949. Open 9.30-12.30 and 1.30-5. CL: Thurs. pm. and Sat. pm. TEL: 01556 502113. VAT: Stan/Spec.

CERES (Fife)

Ceres Antiques

1 High St. (Mrs E. Norrie). SIZE: Medium *STOCK: General antiques, china.* PARK: Easy TEL: 01334 828384.

Ceres continued

Steeple Antiques

38 Main St. KY15 5NH. (Mrs Elizabeth Hart). Est. 1980. Open 2-5 including Sun., mornings by appointment. CL: Wed. pm. SIZE: Medium. *STOCK: Porcelain including some Wemyss, 1800-1950, £5-£500; cutlery, silver and plate, £5-£200+; Victorian linen, some furniture, £50-£400.* LOC: 3 miles from Cupar. PARK: Easy. TEL: Home - 01334 828553. SER: Valuations; buys at auction (silver, china and furniture).

CLOLA BY MINTLAW Nr. Peterhead (Aberdeenshire)

Clola Antiques Centre

Shannas School House. AB42 8AE. (Joan and David Blackburn). Est. 1985. Open 10-5, Sun. 11-4.30 or by appointment. SIZE: Large - 10 dealers. *STOCK: Victorian and Edwardian furniture, antique and modern jewellery, collectables, china and militaria.* LOC: 3 miles south of Mintlaw and 25 miles north of Aberdeen on A92. PARK: Own. TEL: 01771 624584; fax - same. SER: Valuations. FAIRS: Various - Aberdeen

COLDSTREAM (Berwickshire)

Coldstream Antiques

44 High St. TD12 4AS. (Mr and Mrs J. Trinder). Resident. Open daily. SIZE: Large. *STOCK: Furniture, 17th-20th C; general antiques, clocks, silver and shipping goods, 17th-19th C.* LOC: A697. TEL: 01890 882552. VAT: Stan/Spec.

Fraser Antiques

65 High St. TD12 4DL. Est. 1968. Open Tues.-Fri. 10-5, other times by appointment. SIZE: Medium. *STOCK: Porcelain, glass, pictures, silver, small furniture, general antiques.* TEL: 01890 882450. SER: Restorations.

COLLESSIE By Cupar (Fife)

Collessie Antiques

The Glebe. KY7 7RQ. (Mary Malocco). Est. 1989. Open Fri., Sat. and Sun 2-5, other times by appointment. SIZE: Small. *STOCK: Porcelain, small furniture, 19th C, £5-£500; Paisley shawls and rugs, 19th C, £100-£600.* LOC: Just off A91. PARK: Easy. TEL: 01337 810338; home - same. SER: Restorations (porcelain and furniture). FAIRS: Aberdeen, Edinburgh.

COVE (Dunbartonshire)

Cove Curios

Shore Road. G84 0NY. (K.J. Young). Open at weekends and by appointment. *STOCK: General antiques.* TEL: 01436 850261.

CRIEFF (Perthshire)

Antiques and Fine Art

11 Comrie St. PH7 4AX. (Mrs S. Drysdale). Open 10-1 and 2-5. CL: Wed. pm. SIZE: Medium. *STOCK: Furniture, paintings, silver, general antiques, French paperweights.* LOC: A85. PARK: Easy. TEL: 01764 654496; home - 01764 652653. VAT: Spec.

DALBEATTIE (Kirkcudbrightshire)

Wildman's Antiques

3 Maxwell St. DG5 4AH. (P. Wildman). Est. 1960. Open 10-12.30 and 1.30-5. SIZE: Medium. *STOCK: Jewellery, £50-£500; furniture, £100-£1,500; silver and plate, £50-£1,500; all 19th-20th C.* LOC: A711. PARK: Easy. TEL: 01556 610260. SER: Valuations. VAT: Stan/Spec.

DENNY (Stirlingshire)

Ian Burton

Viewfield, 74 Glasgow Rd. FK6 5DN. Open by appointment only anytime. *STOCK: Mainly clocks.* LOC: From M80, junction 4 or junction 9, M9, on main road through village, corner house opposite fire station. PARK: Easy. TEL: 01324 823333; fax - 01324 825207; mobile - 0385 114800. VAT: Stan/Spec.

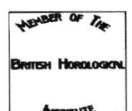

DINGWALL (Ross-shire)

Mercat Antiques
6 Church St. IV15 9SB. (Hazel Macmillan). Est. 1988. Open 10-5. SIZE: Medium. *STOCK: Books, secondhand; china and glass, linen, £1-£200.* PARK: Easy. TEL: 01349 865593. VAT: Stan.

DORNOCH (Sutherland)

Castle Close Antiques
Castle Close. IV25 3SN. (Mrs J. Maclean). Est. 1982. Open 10-1 and 2-5, Thurs. 10-1. SIZE: Medium. *STOCK: General antiques including, furniture, stripped pine, porcelain, jewellery and silver, paintings.* PARK: Easy. TEL: 01862 810405; home - 01862 81057. VAT: Spec.

DRUMNADROCHIT (Inverness-shire)

Joan Frere Antiques
Drumbuie House. (Mrs J. Frere). Open daily 9-8 May-October, other times by appointment. SIZE: Medium. *STOCK: Furniture especially English oak, pre-1800.* Not Stocked: Victoriana, reproductions. LOC: On Loch Ness just before Drumnadrochit village, on A82. PARK: Easy. TEL: 01456 450210; home - same.

DUMFRIES (Dumfriesshire)

The Antiquarian
71 Queensberry St. DG1 1BH. (H. Mulholland). Est. 1988. Open 10-5. SIZE: Large. *STOCK: Furniture, Georgian to Edwardian, £250-£5,000; silver, plate and brass, china and glass, paintings and prints, clocks, £25-£2,500.* LOC: Town centre. PARK: Easy. TEL: 01387 259970; 01698 264077; mobile - 0831 892091.

Cairnyard Antiques
Cairnyard House, Beeswing. DG2 8JE. (B. Farnell). Est. 1971. Open daily or by appointment. SIZE: Medium. *STOCK: General antiques, furniture and clocks.* LOC: A711, 5 miles S.W. of Dumfries (follow Dalbeattie signs). PARK: Easy. TEL: 01387 730218; home - same.

Dix Antiques
100 English St. DG1 2BY. (B. and M. Hughes). Est. 1965. Open 10-4.30. CL: Thurs. SIZE: Small and store. *STOCK: General antiques, £5-£1,000.* LOC: Near cinema. TEL: 01387 264234; home - 01387 265259.

Vennel Antiques
15 Friars Vennel. (Mr and Mrs T.L. Burford). Est. 1987. Open 10-4.30. SIZE: Small. *STOCK: General antiques, furniture and collectors' items, 18th-20th C.* PARK: Easy. TEL: 01387 247929. SER: Buys at auction; restoration (furniture); upholstery.

DUNDEE (Angus)

Angus Antiques
4 St. Andrews St. DD1 2BY. Est. 1964. Open 10-4 CL: Sat. *STOCK: Militaria, badges, medals swords, jewellery, silver, gold, collectors items, Ar Nouveau, Art Deco, advertising and decorativ items, tins, toys, teddy bears.* TEL: 01382 322128.

Neil Livingstone LAPADA
Unit 9 South Grove Works, Lower Pleasance, Brewery Lane. Open any time by appointment SIZE: Large. *STOCK: Furniture and decorative items, 18th-20th C.* TEL: 01382 667454/221618 221751; fax - 01382 566332. SER: Packing and shipping.

McLaren's Antiques
4 Johnston's Lane, Westport. DD1 5ET. (Jea McLaren). Est. 1994. Open 10-4.30 or by appointment. SIZE: Small. *STOCK: Jewellery, pottery ceramics, bric-a-brac and furniture, 19th-20th C £1-£500.* LOC: Small lane off Westport. PARK Easy. TEL: 01382 206888; fax - 01382 566332 home - 01382 450032. SER: Valuations; restorations; buys at auction.

Westport Fine Art
3 Old Hawkhill. Est. 1975. Open 9-5.30. SIZE Medium. *STOCK: 18th-19th C furniture paintings and works of art.* LOC: Near Westport TEL: 01382 322033. SER: Valuations; restorations. VAT: Stan/Spec

Westport Gallery
48 Westport. DD1 5ER. Est. 1976. Open 9-5. SIZE Medium. *STOCK: Decorative items including paintings.* LOC: At city centre end of Perth Road turn into Tay St. and bear left, shop on the right PARK: Easy. TEL: 01382 221751. SER: Valuations; restorations (furniture, ceramics, paintings) buys at auction (paintings). VAT: Stan/Spec.

DUNKELD (Perthshire)

Dunkeld Antiques LAPADA
Tay Terrace. PH8 0AQ. (D. Dytch). Est. 1986 Open 10-5.30, Sun. 12-5.30. SIZE: Large *STOCK: General antiques especially boxes office and library furniture, good books, 19th 20th C, £10-£10,000.* LOC: Overlooking River Tay, premises are a converted church. PARK Easy. TEL: 01350 728832; home - same mobile - 0860 852480. SER: Valuations; buys at auction. VAT: Stan/Spec.

Dunkeld Interiors
14 Bridge St. PH8 0AH. (Mrs B. Cowe). Est 1984. Open 10-5. CL: Thurs. *STOCK: Furniture 18th-19th C, £500-£6,000; decorative items, 19th 20th C.* LOC: 2 mins. off A9, Perth to Inverness road. PARK: Easy. TEL: 01350 727582; home same. SER: Finder. VAT: Stan/Spec.

EDINBURGH (Midlothian)

Another World
25 Candlemaker Row. EH1 2QG. (D. Harrison). Est. 1974. Open Wed., Fri. and Sat. 12-4.30 or by appointment. *STOCK: Netsuke and Oriental art.* TEL: 0131 225 1988. VAT: Spec.

Antiques
48 Thistle St. EH2 1EN. (E. Humphrey). Est. 1946. Open 10-4, Sat. 10-12.30 or by appointment. *STOCK: Paintings, glass, china, curios, postcards.* TEL: 0131 226 3625.

Paddy Barrass
15 The Grassmarket. EH1 2HS. Est. 1974. Open 12-6, Sat. 10.30-5.30, Sun. in Aug. 2-7. SIZE: Small. *STOCK: Period clothing and household linen, 19th-20th C, £5-£100.* LOC: South side of High St., directly below castle. PARK: Easy. TEL: 0131 226 3087. SER: Valuations.

Berland's of Edinburgh
143 Gilmore Place. EH3 9PW. (R. Melvin). Open 9-5. *STOCK: Restored antique light fittings.* TEL: 0131 228 6760.

Laurance Black Ltd BADA
60 Thistle St. EH2 1EN. Est. 1967. Open 10.15-5, Sat. 10.15-3. SIZE: Small. *STOCK: Scottish furniture and decorative items, £50-£5,000; pottery and porcelain, £5-£1,000; paintings and prints, £50-£20,000; all 18th-19th C.* TEL: 0131 220 3387. VAT: Spec.

Joseph Bonnar, Jewellers
72 Thistle St. EH2 1EN. Open 10.30-5 or by appointment. SIZE: Medium. *STOCK: Antique and period jewellery.* LOC: Parallel with Princes St. TEL: 0131 226 2811; fax - 0131 225 9438. VAT: Stan/Spec.

Bourne Fine Art Ltd
6 Dundas St. EH3 6HZ. (P. Bourne). Est. 1978. Open 10-6, Sat. 10-1. SIZE: Medium. *STOCK: British paintings, 1700-1950.* PARK: Easy. TEL: 0131 557 4050. SER: Valuations; restorations; buys at auction; framing. VAT: Stan/Spec.

Bruntsfield Antiques
1 Viewforth Gardens. EH10 4ET. (Robert Sinclair). Est. 1986. Open 10-6. SIZE: Small. *STOCK: British and Oriental ceramics, 16th-20th C, £50-£1,000; furniture, 18th-19th C, £150-£1,500; musical instruments, 18th-20th C, £150-£750.* LOC: Just off Bruntsfield Place, uphill from Bruntsfield Hotel. PARK: Easy. TEL: 0131 229 3180. SER: Valuations; buys at auction.

Calton Gallery BADA.
10 Royal Terr. EH7 5AB. (A. and S. Whitfield). Est. 1979. Open 10-6, Sat. 10-1. SIZE: Large. *STOCK: Paintings, especially Scottish marine and watercolours, £100-£100,000; prints, £10-£1,000; sculpture, to £20,000; all 19th to early 20th C.* PARK: Easy. TEL: 0131 556 1010; home - same; fax - 0131 558 1150. SER: Valuations; restorations (oils, watercolours, prints); buys at auction (paintings). VAT: Stan/Spec.

The Carson Clark Gallery. Scotia Maps - Mapsellers
173 Canongate, The Royal Mile. EH8 8BN. (A.Carson Clark). FRGS. Est. 1971. Open 10.30-5.30. *STOCK: Maps and sea charts.* TEL: 0131 556 4710; fax - same. SER: Valuations.

Collector Centre
127 Gilmore Place. EH3 9PP. (Mrs Katharine M. Chalmers). Est. 1983. Open 10-6. CL: Wed. SIZE: Small. *STOCK: General antiques and collectors' items including silver spoons, glass, pottery and porcelain, jewellery, militaria and kitchenalia, from late 17th C, £1-£1,000.* LOC: From King's Theatre to Gilmore Place, on left about 50 yds before traffic lights. PARK: Meters in Viewforth (except Sat.). TEL: 0131 229 1059. SER: Valuations; advice; research.

The Collectors Shop
49 Cockburn St. EH1 1BS. (D. Cavanagh). Est. 1960. Open 11-5. *STOCK: Coins, medals, militaria, cigarette and postcards, small collectors' items, jewellery, silver and plate.* Not Stocked: Postage stamps. TEL: 0131 226 3391. SER: Buys at auction.

Craiglea Clocks
88 Comiston Rd. EH10 5QJ. (R.J. Rafter). Est. 1978. Open 10-5. CL: Wed. SIZE: Small. *STOCK: Antique clocks and barometers.* LOC: On Biggar road from Morningside. PARK: Adjacent streets. TEL: 0131 452 8568. SER: Restorations (clocks and barometers).

Alan Day Antiques LAPADA
12 Marchhall Crescent. EH16 5HL. By appointment only. *STOCK: Furniture, 19th C; general antiques.* TEL: 0131 667 7120.

A.F. Drysdale Ltd
20 and 35 North West Circus Place. EH3 6JW. Est. 1974. Open 10-1 and 2-5, Sat. 10-1. *STOCK: Quality Continental reproduction lamps, decorative furniture; antique prints.* TEL: 0131 225 4686/220 1903. VAT: Stan.

George Duff Antiques
254 Leith Walk. Open by appointment. *STOCK: Shipping goods, pre-1940.* TEL: 0131 554 8164; home - 0131 337 1422. VAT: Stan. *Export Only.*

Dunedin Antiques Ltd
4 North West Circus Place. EH3 6ST. (D. Ingram and Theresa Ingram). Est. 1973. Open 10.30-1 and 2.30-5. SIZE: Large. *STOCK: Furniture, period items, chimney pieces, architectural fittings, 18th-19th C, £100-£15,000.* LOC: From Princes St. down Frederick St. PARK: Easy. TEL: 0131 220 1574; fax - 0131 556 4423; home - 0131 556 8140. SER: Valuations; buys at auction (furniture, weapons). VAT: Stan/Spec.

Edinburgh continued

EASY - Edinburgh & Glasgow Architectural Salvage Yards
Unit 6, Couper St., Leith. EH6 6HH. Est. 1985. Open 9-5, Sat. 12-5. SIZE: Large. *STOCK: Fireplaces, doors, radiators, baths.* TEL: 0131 554 7077.

Edinburgh Coin Shop
Box No 14082. EH10 4YH. (T.D. Brown). Open 10-5. CL: Sun. *STOCK: Coins, medals, badges, militaria, postcards, cigarette cards, stamps, jewellery, clocks and watches, general antiques, bullion dealers.* TEL: 0131 229 3007/229 2915. VAT: Stan.

Eklektikos Antiques Centre
Corner Grange Rd. and Causewayside. (Hugo Laughton). Open 10-6, including Sun. *STOCK: Light fittings, 1820-1930; large furniture.* TEL: 0131 667 2328.

Donald Ellis incorporating Bruntsfield Clocks
7 Bruntsfield Place. (D.G. and C.M. Ellis). Est. 1970. Open 9.30-5.30. CL: Wed. pm. *STOCK: Clocks.* LOC: Opposite Links Garage at Bruntsfield Links. PARK: Nearby. TEL: 0131 229 4720. SER: Clock repairs.

Tom Fidelo
49 Cumberland St. EH3 6RA. Open 2-6, Sat. 12-6. *STOCK: Paintings, works of art, 18th-20th C.* LOC: Left at corner of Dundas St. and Cumberland St. PARK: Easy. TEL: 0131 557 2444.

Pamela George Antiques
37 Thistle St. EH2 1DY. Est. 1986. Open 11-3, Sat. 10-3. SIZE: Small. *STOCK: Blue and white ceramics, Scottish pottery, horse harness and brasses, collectables, clocks, Staffordshire figures and small furniture, all 19th C.* LOC: 400 metres north of Princes St. PARK: Easy. TEL: 0131 225 6350; home - 0131 225 2159. SER: Valuations. FAIRS: Mammoth. VAT: Spec.

Georgian Antiques LAPADA
10 Pattison St., Leith Links. EH6 7HF. Est. 1976. Open 8.30-5.30, Sat. 10-2. SIZE: Large - 2 warehouses. *STOCK: Furniture, Georgian, Victorian, inlaid, Edwardian; shipping goods, smalls, £10-£10,000.* LOC: Off Leith Links. PARK: Easy. TEL: 0131 553 7286 (24 hrs.); fax - 0131 553 6299. SER: Valuations; restorations; buys at auction; packing; shipping; courier. VAT: Stan/Spec.

Gladrags
17 Henderson Row. EH3 5DH. (Kate Cameron). Est. 1977. Open Tues.-Sat. 10.30-6. *STOCK: Period clothes, linen, lace, beadwork, silk and paisley shawls, costume jewellery, silks and satins, cashmeres and accessories.* TEL: 0131 557 1916.

Edinburgh continued

Goodwin's Antiques Ltd
15-16 Queensferry St., 106A-108A Rose St. an at The Sheraton Grand, 1 Festival Square. EH 4QW. Est. 1952. Open 9.30-5.30, Sat. 9.30-1 *STOCK: Jewellery, silver.* LOC: Off Princes St. West end. TEL: 0131 225 4717/229 9131 Ext 5808. VAT: Stan/Spec.

Hand in Hand
3 North West Circus Place. EH3 6ST. (Mr an Mrs O. Hand). Est. 1969. Open 10-5.30. CL Mon. *STOCK: Victorian linen, embroidery furnishings, lace, Paisley shawls; period costum and accessories including jewellery.* TEL: 013 226 3598; fax - same. VAT: Stan/Spec.

Tim Hardie Antiques
30 Bruntsfield Place. Est. 1991. Open 10-1 and 2 5.30. SIZE: Small. *STOCK: Victorian an upholstered furniture, also country home pieces* LOC: 300 yards from Tollcross, near King' Theatre. PARK: Nearby. TEL: 0131 229 1819 VAT: Spec.

Malcolm Innes Gallery
4 Dundas St. EH3 6HZ. Est. 1981. Open 9.30-6 Sat. 10-1. *STOCK: Scottish landscape, sportin and military pictures.* TEL: 0131 558 9544/5; fa - 0131 558 9525. SER: Valuations; restorations buys at auction; framing. VAT: Spec.

Kaimes Smithy Antiques
79 Howdenhall Rd. EH14 2LQ. (J. Lynch). Es 1972. Open 1.30-5.30. SIZE: Medium. *STOCK Furniture, clocks, porcelain, glass, painting curios, 18th-20th C, £10-£3,000.* LOC: From Cit bypass take A701 (at Straiton junction) into cit centre, located at 1st set of traffic lights. PARK Easy. TEL: 0131 441 2076/664 0124. SER Valuations; restorations.

London Road Antiques
15 Earlston Place, London Rd. EH7 5SU. (R. an C. Forrest). Open Thurs.-Sat. 11-5, Sun. 1-5, othe times by appointment. SIZE: Large + trade stor *STOCK: Georgian, Victorian and stripped pin furniture.* TEL: 0131 652 2790.

John Mathieson and Co
48 Frederick St. EH2 1EX. Open 9-5.30, Sat. 9 4.30. *STOCK: Paintings, watercolours, print* TEL: 0131 225 6798. SER: Restorations (framin gilding). VAT: Stan/Spec.

McNaughtan's Bookshop
3a and 4a Haddington Place. EH7 4AE. Est. 195 Open 9.30-5.30. CL: Mon. *STOCK: Antiquaria books.* TEL: 0131 556 5897; fax - 0131 556 822

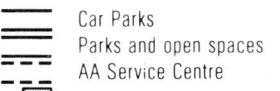

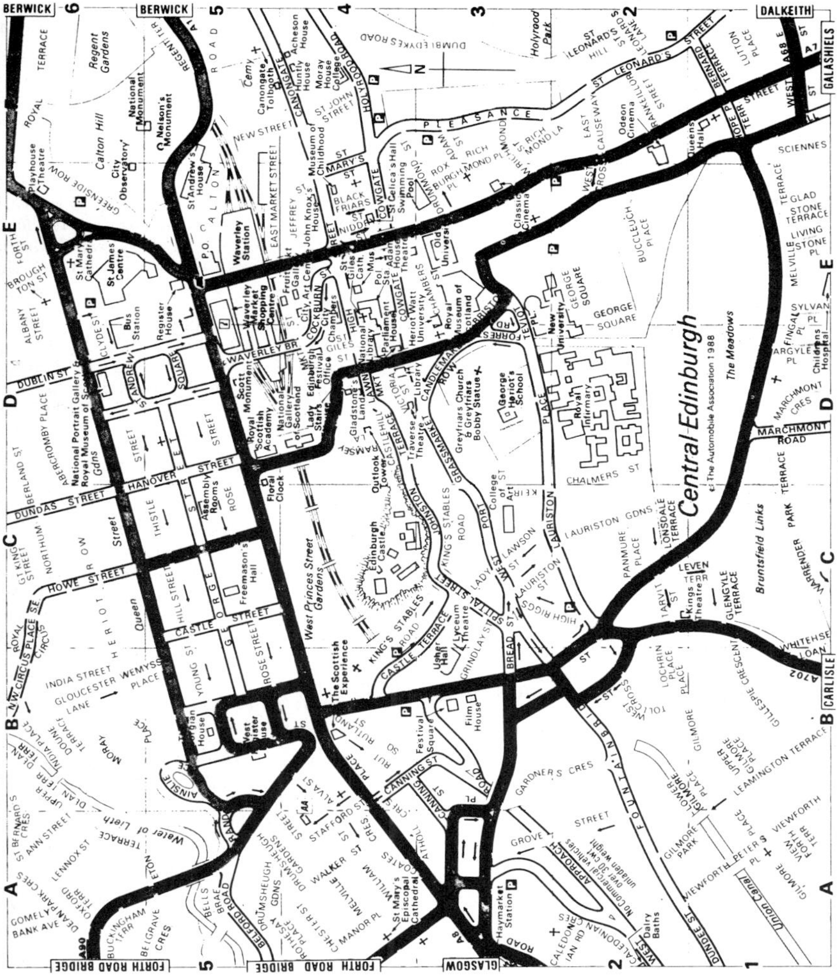

Key to Town Plan

- AA Recommended roads
- Other roads
- Restricted roads
- Buildings of interest
- Car Parks
- Parks and open spaces
- AA Service Centre

Edinburgh continued

Montresor

35 St. Stephen St. EH3 5AH. (Pierre De Fresne and Gareth Jones). Est. 1989. Open 10.30-1 and 2-6. SIZE: Small. *STOCK: Costume and designer jewellery, 1850-1950, £50-£200; Art Deco and Art Nouveau lighting, china and glass, £50-£1,000.* LOC: North from Princes St. to Stockbridge. PARK: Easy. TEL: 0131 220 6877. SER: Valuations; restorations (paste jewellery). VAT: Stan.

T. and J. W. Neilson Ltd

76 Coburg St., Leith. EH6 6HJ. (J. and A. Neilson). Est. 1932. Open 9.30-5. SIZE: Large. *STOCK: Fireplaces, 18th-20th C, £100-£20,000; interiors, stoves, fenders, fire irons; marble (including French), wood and stone chimney pieces.* LOC: Continuation of Ferry Rd. PARK: Own. TEL: 0131 554 4704; fax - 0131 555 2071. SER: Installations (fireplaces). VAT: Stan.

Now and Then (Toy Centre)

7 and 9 West Crosscauseway. EH8 9JW. Open 11-6, Sat. 10-6. *STOCK: Telephones, tin and die-cast toys, clockwork and electric model trains, collectable mechanical ephemera, automobilia, juvenalia, clocks, gold and silver watches, small furniture, old advertisements, bric-a-brac.* LOC: City centre off A68. PARK: Nearby. TEL: 0131 668 2927; 0131 226 2867 (answerphone). SER: Valuations; buys at auction.

Open Eye Gallery Ltd

75/79 Cumberland St. EH3 6RD. (T. and P. Wilson). Est. 1976. Open 10-6, Sat. 10-4. SIZE: Medium. *STOCK: Early 20th C etchings, contemporary paintings, ceramics and jewellery.* LOC: From Princes St. go east, left into Frederick St. right at bottom of hill. PARK: Easy. TEL: 0131 557 1020. SER: Valuations; restorations (paintings and ceramics); buys at auction. VAT: Mainly Spec.

H. Parry

Castle Antiques, 330 Lawnmarket. EH1 2PN. *STOCK: Silver, porcelain, English and Continental furniture, clocks.* TEL: 0131 225 7615.

Present Bygones

61 Thistle St. EH2 1DY. (Pat and Simon McIntyre). Est. 1982. Open 10-5, other times by appointment. SIZE: Small. *STOCK: Ceramics, 18th-20th C, £25-£1,000; samplers, fans and sewn work, 18th-19th C, £100-£1,000; small period and later furniture, £100-£2,000; silver, 18th-20th C, £10-£1,000.* LOC: City centre, between George St. and Queen St. PARK: Meters. TEL: 0131 226 7646. SER: Buys at auction. VAT: Stan/Margin.

Alan Rankin

72 Dundas St. EH3 6QZ. Est. 1964. Open by appointment. SIZE: Small. *STOCK: Antiquarian books, £5-£500; out-of-print scholarly books from 1850, £1-£40; prints, maps from earliest times to 1860, £1-£200.* LOC: From Princes St., dowr Hanover St. to first block on left past Gt. King St PARK: Easy. TEL: 0131 556 3705; home - same SER: Valuations; buys at auction.

Royal Mile Curios

363 High St. EH1 1PW. (L. Bosi and R. Eprile) Open 10.30-5. *STOCK: Jewellery and silver* TEL: 0131 226 4050.

James Scott

43 Dundas St. EH3 6JN. Est. 1964. Open 11.30-1 and 2-5.30. CL: Thurs. pm. *STOCK: Curiosities unusual items, silver, jewellery, small furniture* TEL: 0131 556 8260; home - 0131 332 0617 VAT: Stan.

The Scottish Gallery

16 Dundas St. EH3 6HZ. (Aitken Dott Ltd.). Est 1842. Open 10-6, Sat. 10-4. *STOCK: 20th C an contemporary Scottish paintings and con temporary crafts.* LOC: New Town. TEL: 013 558 1200. VAT: Stan/Spec.

Stockbridge Antiques and Fine Art

8 Deanhaugh St., Stockbridge. EH4 1LY. Est 1988. Open 2-5.30. CL: Mon. SIZE: Small *STOCK: Fine French and German dolls, 19th t early 20th C; small furniture and paintings, tedd bears, from 1900; juvenilia, tinplate toys clockwork trains; costume Victorian whitewor including christening robes, dolls clothes Oriental items, ceramic and glass.* Not Stocked Silver, jewellery and militaria. LOC: 1/2 mil north of Princes St. PARK: Easy. TEL: 0131 33 1366. SER: Restorations (doll and teddy repai and re-costuming).

James Thin (Booksellers)

53-59 South Bridge. EH1 1YS. Est. 1848. Ope seven days, weekdays until 10pm (Antiquaria Section not available evenings/Sundays). *STOCK Antiquarian and secondhand books.* TEL: 013 556 6743. SER: Buys at auction.

This and That Antiques and Bric-a-Brac

22 Argyle Place. EH9 1JJ. Open Tues., Thurs Fri., Sat. 2.30-5. *STOCK: Porcelain, silver, sma furniture, Scottish pottery, bric-a-brac.* TEL 0131 229 6069; home - 0131 447 1309.

The Thrie Estaits

49 Dundas St. EH3 6RS. Est. 1970. Open Tues Sat. *STOCK: Pottery, porcelain, glass, painting and prints, unusual and decorative items, som furniture.* TEL: 0131 556 7084.

The Thursday Shop

5 Clermiston Rd., Corstorphine. (Mrs I. Robertson). Est. 1982. Open 10.30-5, Sat. 10- CL: Mon. and Wed. SIZE: Small. *STOCK: Gener antiques and bric-a-brac especially unusual item £5-£500.* LOC: Near St. John's Rd. PARK: Nearb TEL: 0131 334 3696. SER: Valuations. FAIR Scotfairs, Edinburgh, Ingliston.

Edinburgh continued

Unicorn Antiques
65 Dundas St. EH3 6RS. (N. Duncan). Est. 1967. Usually open 11-6. SIZE: Medium. *STOCK: Architectural and domestic brassware, lights, mirrors, glass, china, cutlery and bric-a-brac.* Not Stocked: Weapons, coins, jewellery. LOC: From Princes St. turn into Hanover St. Dundas St. is a continuation of Hanover St. TEL: 0131 556 7176; home - 0131 332 9135.

John Whyte
116b Rose St. EH2 3JF. Est. 1928. Open 9.30-5.15, Sat. 9.30-5. *STOCK: Jewellery, watches, clocks and silver.* TEL: 0131 225 2140. VAT: Stan.

Whytock and Reid
Sunbury House, Belford Mews. EH4 3DN. (D.C. Reid). Est. 1807. Open 9-5.30. CL: Sat. pm. SIZE: Large. *STOCK: Furniture, English and Continental, 18th-19th C, £50-£20,000; Eastern rugs, carpets, £50-£10,000.* LOC: ½ mile from West End, off Belford Rd. PARK: Own. TEL: 0131 226 4911; fax - 0131 226 4595. SER: Restorations (furniture, rugs); buys at auction; interiors. VAT: Stan/Spec.

Wild Rose Antiques
15 Henderson Row. EH3 5DH. (K. and E. Cameron). Est. 1975. Open Tues.-Sat. 10.30-6. *STOCK: General antiques - silver, jewellery, glass, pottery, porcelain, small furniture, objects, Paisley shawls, brassware.* TEL: 0131 557 1916.

Aldric Young
49 Thistle St. *STOCK: General antiques; English and Continental furniture, paintings, 18th-19th C.* TEL: 0131 226 4101/01506 882121. VAT: Spec.

Young Antiques
185 Bruntsfield Place. EH10 4DG. (T.C. Young). Est. 1979. Open 10.30-1.30 and from 2.30. CL: Wed. pm. SIZE: Medium. *STOCK: Victorian and Edwardian furniture, £50-£1,000; ceramics, £20-£2,000; Persian rugs, oils and watercolours, £50-£1,500.* LOC: Bruntsfield. PARK: Easy. TEL: 0131 229 1361. SER: Valuations; buys at auction (Persian rugs, art pottery).

ELGIN (Morayshire)

Antiques and Interior Design
1 Mayne Rd. IV30 1PF. (B. Alexander-Forsyth). Open by appointment only. *STOCK: Furniture and paintings.* TEL: 01343 549313.

West End Antiques
5 High St. IV30 1EE. (F. Stewart). HADA. Est. 1969. Open daily 9-5.30, Wed. 9-1. *STOCK: Silver, clocks and watches, Victorian jewellery, bric-a-brac.* TEL: 01343 547531; home - 01343 13019. VAT: Stan/Spec.

ELIE (Fife)

Malcolm Antiques
5 Bank St. KY9 1BW. Est. 1965. *STOCK: Victoriana, collectors' items, curios, clocks.* TEL: 01333 330116.

ERROL (Perthshire)

Greycroft Antiques
Greycroft, Station Rd. PH2 7SN. (D. and Mrs. J. Pickett). Est. 1981. Open 10-5.30 or by appointment. SIZE: Medium. *STOCK: Furniture including desks, bureaux and sofas, to mid-19th C, £500-£8,000; tables, chairs, Oriental porcelain, £50-£1,000; porcelain, brass, copper and bronze, £15-£150.* LOC: A85 between Perth and Dundee. PARK: Easy. TEL: 01821 642221; home - same. SER: Restorations (furniture); buys at auction (furniture). VAT: Stan/Spec.

FAIRLIE (Ayrshire)

Fairlie Antique Shop
86 Main Rd. KA29 0AD. (Mrs. Alvarino). Est. 1976. Open 11-5. CL: Mon. SIZE: Small. *STOCK: Ornaments, £10-£500; small furniture, clocks and silver, £10-£500; jewellery; all Victorian or Edwardian.* LOC: A78. PARK: 25yds. TEL: 01475 568613. SER: Valuations.

FOCHABERS (Morayshire)

Antiques (Fochabers)
22 The Square. (J. and M.L. Holstead). Est. 1983. Open 10-1 and 2-5. SIZE: Medium. *STOCK: General collectables, Oriental, clocks including longcase, from 18th C oak to 1930's.* PARK: Easy. TEL: 01343 820838; home - 01343 820572. FAIRS: Tree Tops.

Pringle Antiques
High St. IV32 7EP. (G. A. Christie). Est. 1983. Open 9.30-1 and 2-6 (5 in winter) every day. SIZE: Medium. *STOCK: Furniture, Victorian, £20-£5,000; general antiques, pictures, brass, pottery, silver and jewellery.* Not Stocked: Books and clothing. LOC: A96, premises are a converted church. PARK: Easy. TEL: 01343 821204; home - 01343 820599. VAT: Stan/Spec.

Marianne Simpson
61/63 High St. IV32 7DU. (M.R. Simpson). Est. 1990. Open Easter-Oct: Mon.-Sat. 10-1 and 2-4; Oct.-Easter: Tues., Thurs., Sat. 10-1 and 2-4, or by appointment. SIZE: Small. *STOCK: Books, 19th-20th C, prints, 19th C; ephemera, 19th-20th C; all £1-£100.* LOC: A96. PARK: Easy. TEL: 01343 821192; home - same.

FORFAR (Angus)

Gow Antiques

Pitscandly Farm. DD8 3NZ. (Jeremy Gow). Est. 1986. Open all hours (prior telephone call advisable). SIZE: Small. *STOCK: 17th-18th C furniture, £50-£5,000.* LOC: Take B9134 out of Forfar, through Lunenhead, then first right marked Myreside, premises next left, 3 miles off A90. PARK: Easy. TEL: 01307 465342; mobile - 0410 018229; home - 01307 465342. SER: Valuations; restorations (17th-18th C furniture especially marquetry); buys at auction (furniture). FAIRS: Scone Game.

FORRES (Morayshire)

Michael Low Antiques

45 High St. IV36 0PB. Est. 1967. TEL: 01309 673696. VAT: Stan.

FREUCHIE (Fife)

Freuchie Antiques

Oxley House, Main St. KY15 7EY. (C.P. Wakefield). Est. 1980. Sometimes open, prior telephone call advisable. CL: Mainly Fri., Sat. and Sun. and Mon. SIZE: Medium. *STOCK: Mainly small collectables and postcards, £5-£100.* PARK: Easy. TEL: 01337 857348.

FRIOCKHEIM, Nr. Arbroath (Angus)

M.J. and D. Barclay

29 Gardyne St. DD11 4SQ. Est. 1965. Open 11-1 and 2-5.30. CL: Thurs. *STOCK: General antiques including furniture, jewellery, silver, porcelain and clocks.* Not Stocked: Stamps, books, coins. PARK: Easy. TEL: 01241 828265. VAT: Stan.

GLASGOW (Lanarkshire)

Albany Antiques LAPADA

1347 Argyle St. G3 8AD. (P.J. O'Loughlin). Est. 1969. Open 9.30-5.30 or by appointment. CL: Sat. *STOCK: Chinese and Japanese porcelain, Georgian, Victorian and Edwardian furniture, shipping goods.* TEL: 0141 339 4267. VAT: Stan/Spec.

All Our Yesterdays

6 Park Rd., Kelvinbridge. G4. (Susie Robinson). Est. 1989. Open 11.30-5.30. SIZE: Small. *STOCK: Kitchenalia, mainly 1850-1949, £5-£500; smalls, especially decorative arts, advertising related items, books, etchings and postcards, mechanical items and oddities, to £500.* LOC: Near junction of Gt. Western Rd. and Park Rd. and university. PARK: Easy. TEL: 0141 334 7788; fax - 0141 339 8994. SER: Valuations; buys at auction; search and hire.

Glasgow continued

Bath Street Antiques Galleries

203 Bath St. G2 4HZ. (A.E. Alvarino). Open 10-5 Sat.10-1. SIZE: Large. PARK: Easy. TEL: 0141 221 1888. SER: Valuations; restorations (clocks); buys at auction. VAT: Stan/Spec. Below are listed the dealers at this market.

E. A. Alvarino Antiques

Edwardian, Victorian and Georgian furniture and accessories; general antiques, silver, clocks instruments and paintings. TEL: 0141 221 1888.

Brown's Clocks Ltd

(J. Wilson). FBHI. *Longcase, wall and mantel clocks and barometers.* TEL: 0141 248 6760. SER: Valuations; restorations; buys at auction. VAT: Stan/Spec.

Cooper Hay Rare Books

Antiquarian books and prints. TEL: 0141 226 3074; fax - same.

John Green Fine Art

19th-20th C British and Continental oils, watercolours and etchings. TEL: 0141 221 6025. SER: Restorations; framing.

Barclay Lennie Fine Art Ltd

Oil paintings, watercolours and sculpture, mainly Scottish, 19th-20th C. TEL: 0141 226 5413.

The Roger Billcliffe Fine Art

134 Blythswood St. G2 4EL. Est. 1876. Open 9.30-5.30, Sat. 10-1. SIZE: Large. *STOCK: British paintings, watercolours, drawings, sculpture, especially Scottish, from 1850; jewellery, metalwork, glass and woodwork.* TEL: 0141 332 4027; fax - 0141 332 6573. VAT: Spec.

Butler's Furniture Galleries Ltd

24-26 Millbrae Rd., Langside. G42 9TU. (L. Butler). Open 9.30-5.30 or by appointment. CL: Sat. *STOCK: Furniture, Georgian, Victorian, Edwardian; small decorative items.* TEL: 0141 632 9853/639 3396. SER: Valuations.

The Den of Antiquity

Langside Lane, 539 Victoria Rd., Queenspark. G42 8BH. Est. 1960. Open 9.30-5.30, Sun. 12-5. *STOCK: General antiques.* TEL: 0141 423 7122; evenings - 0141 644 5860. VAT: Stan/Spec.

EASY - Edinburgh and Glasgow Architectural Salvage Yards

85/87 Colvend St. G40 4DU. (Neil Barrass). Open 9-5, Sat. 12-5. *STOCK: Fireplaces, doors, radiators, baths.* TEL: 0141 556 7772. VAT: Stan.

James Forrest and Co (Jewellers) Ltd

53 West Nile St. G1 2QB. Est. 1957. CL: Sat. pm. *STOCK: Silver, jewellery, clocks.* LOC: City centre. TEL: 0141 221 0494. VAT: Stan.

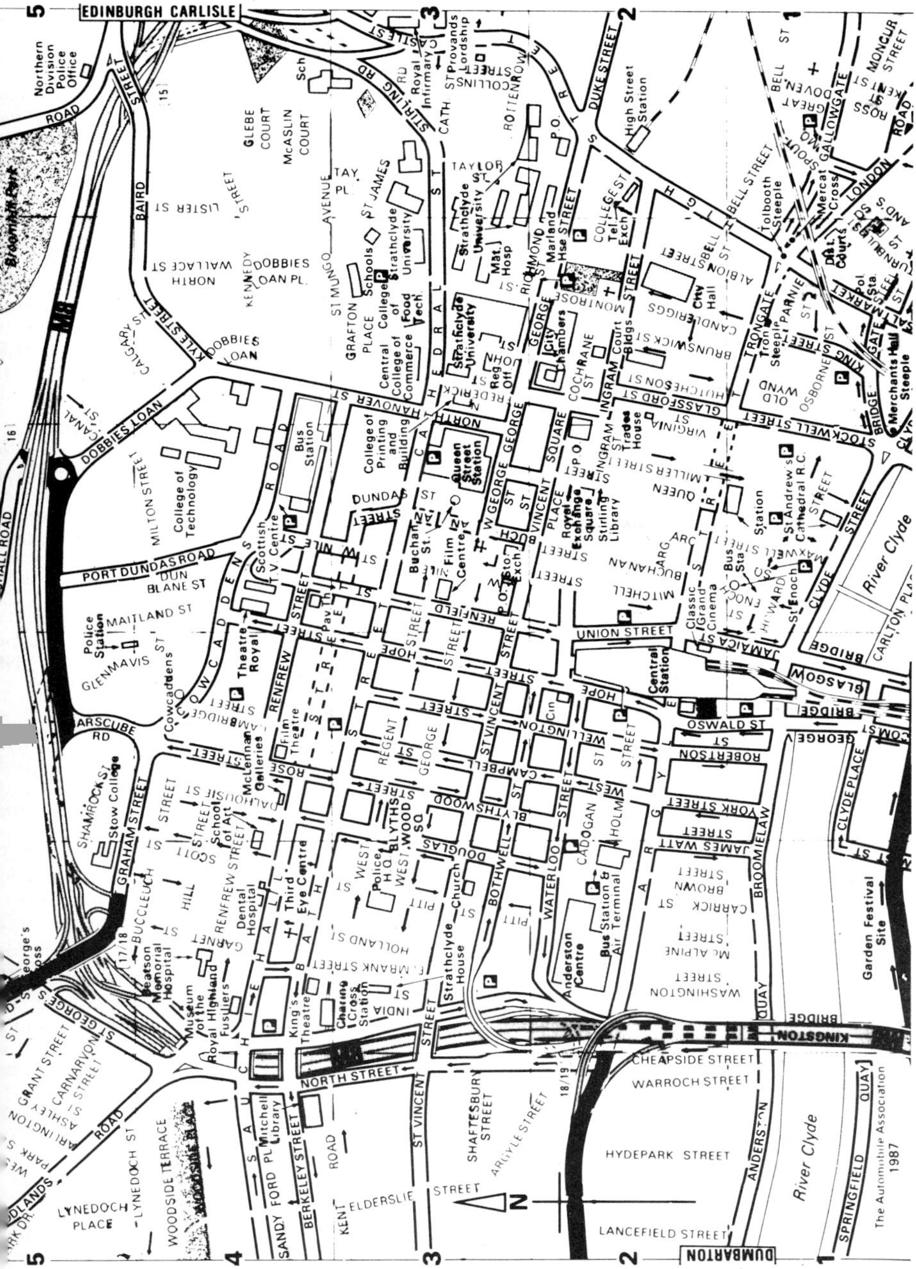

Key to Town Plan

AA Recommended roads		Car Parks	P
Other roads		Parks and open spaces	
Restricted roads		AA Service Centre	AA
Buildings of interest			

Glasgow continued

A.D. Hamilton and Co
7 St. Vincent Place. G1 2DW. (Jeffrey Lee Fineman). Est. 1890. Open 9-5.15. SIZE: Small. *STOCK: Jewellery and silver, 19th to early 20th C, £100-£3,000; British coins, medals and banknotes, £10-£1,000.* LOC: City centre, next to George Square. PARK: Meters. TEL: 0141 221 5423; fax - 0141 248 6019. SER: Valuations. VAT: Stan/Spec.

Heritage House Antiques
Unit 3b, Yorkhill Quay. G3 3QE. (P. Mangan). Open 9-5, Sat. 10-5, Sun. 12-5. SIZE: 19 dealers. *STOCK: Antique pine, Oriental rugs and carpets, general antiques, furnishings, smalls and fine arts.* TEL: 0141 334 4924. SER: Import and export worldwide.

King's Court Antique Centre
Units 1-4, King's Court, King St. (King's Court Traders Assn). Open 10-5 including Sun. CL: Mon. SIZE: 6 dealers. *STOCK: Furniture, silver and general antiques, pre-1940.* LOC: Opposite King St. car park, behind St. Enoch shopping centre. PARK: Easy. TEL: 0141 552 7854/7856. SER: Valuations; buys at auction.

Jean Megahy
481 Great Western Rd. (F.G. Halliday). Open 10-5. CL: Sat. pm. *STOCK: Furniture, brass, silver, Oriental items.* TEL: 0141 334 1315. VAT: Stan/Spec.

Mercat-Hughes Antiques
85 Queen St., 1 Royal Exchange Court. G2 4QY. (P. Hughes and C. Forrester). Open 10-5.30 or by appointment. CL: Sat. *STOCK: Small furniture, brass, ceramics, clocks, watches, E.P. and silver, jewellery and trade items.* TEL: 0141 204 0851; home - 0141 770 4572.

Muirhead Moffat and Co
182 West Regent St. G2 4RU. (D.J. Brewster and J.D. Hay). Est. 1896. Open 10-12.30 and 1.30-5. CL: Sat. and Sun. except by appointment. SIZE: Medium. *STOCK: Period furniture, barometers and jewellery; clocks, silver, weapons, porcelain, tapestries and pictures.* LOC: Off Blythswood Sq. PARK: Easy. TEL: 0141 226 4683/226 3406. SER: Valuations; restorations (furniture, clocks, barometers and jewellery); buys at auction. VAT: Stan/Spec.

Ewan Mundy Fine Art Ltd
Lower Ground Floor, 211 West George St. G2 2LW. Est. 1981. Open daily. SIZE: Medium. *STOCK: Fine Scottish, English and French oils and watercolours, 19th-20th C, from £250; Scottish and English etchings and lithographs, 19th-20th C, from £100; Scottish contemporary paintings, from £50.* LOC: City centre. PARK: Nearby. TEL: 0141 248 9755. SER: Valuations; restorations arranged; buys at auction (pictures). FAIRS: New York. VAT: Stan/Spec.

Glasgow continued

Nice Things Old and New
1010 Pollokshaws Rd. G41 2HG. (J. and E. Lake) Est. 1962. Open 12-6. *STOCK: Interesting and unusual pieces.* LOC: Facing Langside Halls and Marlborough House (Shawlands). TEL: 0141 64 3826. FAIRS: Organiser.

Pastimes Vintage Toys
126 Maryhill Rd. G20 7QS. (Gordon and Ann Brown). Est. 1980. Open 10-5. SIZE: Medium *STOCK: Vintage toys, die-cast, railways and dolls' houses, from 1910, £1-£300.* LOC: From west off junction 17, M8; from east junction 16 M8. PARK: Easy. TEL: 0141 331 1008. SER Valuations. FAIRS: Toy & Collectors auctions - annually. VAT: Stan.

The Renaissance Furniture Store
103 Niddrie Rd., Queens Park. G42 8PR (Caroline Kerr). Open 10.30-5, Sat. and Sun 12.30-5. CL: Mon. *STOCK: General antiques Arts & Crafts and Art Nouveau furniture; fir inserts and surrounds.* PARK: Easy. TEL: 014 423 0022. SER: Buys at auction.

R.L. Rose and Co
Unit 3b, Yorkhill Quay. G2 8EQ. Open 9-4 *STOCK: Oriental and decorative carpets and rugs.* TEL: 0141 339 7290; fax - 0141 334 149 SER: Restorations (as stock); repair; cleaning.

Scottish Art Heritage
Burlington House, 183 Bath St. G2 4HU. (J. McIlroy and A. Murray). Est. 1984. Open 10- Sat. 10-3. SIZE: Medium. *STOCK: Oil painting 17th to early 20th C, £300-£5,000; watercolour 19th-20th C, £200-£2,000.* LOC: Town centr corner of Blythswood St. PARK: Easy. TEL 0141 221 4004. SER: Valuations; buys at auctic (as stock). FAIRS: HADA; Houston, Texa Washington DC; New York Armoury. VAT Spec.

Jeremy Sniders Antiques
158 Bath St. G2 4TB. Est. 1983. Open 9-5, Sa 10-4. SIZE: Medium. *STOCK: British decorati arts including furniture, 1850-1960, £30-£1,00 Scandinavian decorative arts including furnitur 1900 to date, £30-£5,000; silver, mainly 19th-20 C, £30-£3,000.* LOC: Next door to Christie PARK: Nearby - Sauchiehall St. Centre. TEL 0141 332 4033; fax - 0141 332 5505. SER: Val ations; restorations (silver and jewellery); buys auction (as stock). VAT: Spec.

Stenlake and McCourt - Kollectables
51 Parnie St. G1 5LU. Est. 1984. Open 10- SIZE: Small. *STOCK: Edwardian postcard cigarette cards, stamps.* LOC: Directly behi Tron Theatre. PARK: Meters. TEL: 0141 5 2208. SER: Valuations (as stock). FAIR Scottish Philatelic Congress and others.

Glasgow continued

Victoria Antiques Ltd
100 Torrisdale St. G42 8PH. Est. 1963. CL: Sat. SIZE: Large. *STOCK: General antiques, Victoriana, shipping goods.* LOC: Adjacent Queen's Park railway station. TEL: 0141 423 7216; fax - 0141 423 6497; home - 0141 423 6567/632 4372. SER: Valuations; buys at auction. VAT: Stan/Spec.

The Victorian Village
57 West Regent St. G2. Open 10-5, Sat. 10-4. LOC: Near Renfield St. PARK: Meters. TEL: 0141 332 0808. VAT: Stan/Spec. Below are listed the dealers at these premises.

Anne's Antiques
Jewellery, china, silver.

"Golden Oldies"
Jewellery. SER: Repairs; commissions.

Marjory Kerr
Jewellery, silver, clocks.

Iona & Isla McKinnon
Fine china and small furniture.

Cathy McLay "Saratoga Trunk"
Textiles, lace, jewellery. TEL: 0141 331 2707.

Putting-on-the-Ritz
Art Deco, china, jewellery, 1920's curios. TEL: 0141 332 9808.

Rosamond Rutherford
Victorian jewellery, Scottish agate, silver, Sheffield plate. TEL: 0141 332 9808.

Virginia Antique Galleries
31/35 Virginia St., (Off Argyle St). G1 1DT. (M. Robinson). Open 10-5, Sun. 12-5. SIZE: 20 dealers. *STOCK: Furniture, glass, jewellery, silver, porcelain and brass.* TEL: 0141 552 2573/8640; office - 0141 552 5840.

West of Scotland Antique Centre Ltd
Langside Lane, 539 Victoria Rd., Queen's Park. G42 8BH. (Wosac Ltd). Est. 1969, Open 9.30-5.30, Sun. 12-5. SIZE: Large - 8 dealers. *STOCK: Pine, Georgian to Edwardian, £50-£3,000.* PARK: Easy. TEL: 0141 423 7122. VAT: Stan/Spec.

Tim Wright Antiques LAPADA
147 Bath St. (T. and J. Wright). Est. 1971. Open 9.45-5, Sat. 10.30-2. SIZE: 6 showrooms. *STOCK: Furniture; European and Oriental ceramics and glass, decorative items, silver and plate, brass and copper, mirrors and prints, all £50-£6,000.* LOC: On opposite corner to Christie's. PARK: Multi-storey opposite and meters. TEL: 0141 221 0364. VAT: Mainly Spec.

Glasgow continued

Yesteryear
14 Kildrostan St., Pollokshields. G41 4LY. (Ian Taylor). Open 9.30-5.30, prior telephone call advisable. *STOCK: General antiques, silver, jewellery.* TEL: 0141 423 0099; fax and ansaphone - 0141 339 8994.

GRANTOWN-ON-SPEY (Morayshire)

Strathspey Gallery LAPADA
40 High St. PH26 3EH. (Franfam Ltd). HADA. Resident. Est. 1971. Open 10-1 and 2-5 (1-2 by appointment), Thurs. 10-1. SIZE: Medium. *STOCK: Furniture including early oak; collectors' ceramics and metalware; pictures including wildlife and sporting.* LOC: Town centre. PARK: Easy and behind shop. TEL: 01479 873290; home - same. SER: Valuations. VAT: Mainly Spec.

GULLANE (East Lothian)

Gullane Antiques
5 Rosebery Place. EH31 2BQ. (E.A. Lindsey). Est. 1981. Open 10.30-1 and 2.30-5. CL: Wed. SIZE: Medium. *STOCK: China and glass, 1850-1930, £5-£100; prints and watercolours, early 20th C, £25-£100; metalwork, 1900's, £5-£50.* LOC: 6 miles north of Haddington, off A1. PARK: Easy. TEL: 01620 842326.

HADDINGTON (East Lothian)

Elm House Antiques
The Sands, Church St. EH41 3EX. (Mrs I. MacDonald). Est. 1972. Open daily, appointment advisable, and Sat. 10-1 and 2-5. SIZE: Small. *STOCK: English porcelain and pottery, 18th and 19th C, £20-£600; blue and white earthenware, Scottish pottery, £20-£900; boxes, furniture, £25-£800.* LOC: Off A1, end of High St. PARK: Easy. TEL: 0162 082 3413; home - same.

Leslie and Leslie
EH41 3JJ. Open 9-1 and 2-5. CL: Sat. *STOCK: General antiques.* TEL: 01620 822241; fax - same. VAT: Stan.

HUNTLY (Aberdeenshire)

Huntly Antiques
43 Duke St. (Mrs J. Barker). Open Mon. and Sat. 10-1 and 2-5, Thurs. 10-1, other times by appointment. SIZE: Small. *STOCK: Jewellery, china, glass and furniture, 19th-20th C, £5-£250.* LOC: Off Aberdeen/Inverness road. PARK: Easy. TEL: 01466 793307; home - 01466 792638. FAIRS: Assembly Rooms, Edinburgh, Scotfairs.

INCHTURE (Perthshire)

C.S. Moreton (Antiques)

Inchmartine House. PH14 9QQ. (P.M. and Mrs M. Stephens). Est. 1922. Open 9-5.30. *STOCK: Furniture, £50-£10,000; carpets and rugs, £50-£3,000; ceramics, metalware; all 16th C to 1860; old cabinet makers' tools.* LOC: Take A90 Perth/Dundee road, entrance on left at Lodge. PARK: Easy. TEL: 01828 686412; home - same; fax - 01828 686096; mobile - 0402 190128. SER: Valuations; cabinet making and repairs. FAIRS: Buxton, Tatton Park, Northern at Harrogate, Hocker Hall. VAT: Mainly Spec.

INVERNESS (Inverness-shire)

The Attic

Riverside, 17 Huntly St. IV1 5PR. (P. Gratton). HADA. Est. 1976. Open 10.30-1 and 2-5. CL: Wed. Jan.-Mar. Mon. and Wed. SIZE: Small. *STOCK: Art Deco china, jewellery, linen, textiles, period clothes, Victorian to 1940's, from £5.* PARK: The Riverside. TEL: 01463 243117/240224. SER: Valuations. FAIRS: Aberdeen.

Gallery Persia

Upper Myrtlefield, Nairnside. IV1 2BX. (G. MacDonald). Open by appointment only. *STOCK: Persian, Turkoman, Afghanistan, Caucasus, Anatolian rugs and carpets, late 19th C to 1940, £500-£2,000+; quality contemporary pieces, £100+.* LOC: From A9 1st left after flyover, 1st left at roundabout, then 2.25 miles on B9006, then 1st right, 1st left. PARK: Easy. TEL: 01463 792198; home - same. SER: Valuations; restorations (cleaning and repair). FAIRS: Treetops Hotel, Aberdeen (monthly); Inverness (July); Game, Scone Palace, Perth (July).

JEDBURGH (Roxburghshire)

Mainhill Gallery

Ancrum. TD8 6XA. (B. and D. Bruce). Est. 1981. Open 10.30-5.30, prior telephone call advisable, or by appointment. SIZE: Medium. *STOCK: Oil paintings, watercolours, etchings and sculpture,*

Jedburgh continued

19th-20th C, some prints, £35-£7,000. LOC: Ju off A68, 3 miles north of Jedburgh, centre c Ancrum. PARK: Easy. TEL: 01835 830518. SEF Valuations; buys at auction. VAT: Spec.

R. and M. Turner (Antiques Ltd)

LAPAD

34-36 High St. TD8 6AG. Est. 1965. Open 9.3 5.30, Sat. 10-5. SIZE: Large. *STOCK: Furnitur clocks, porcelain, paintings, silver, jewellery, 17t 20th C and fine reproductions.* LOC: On A68 t Edinburgh. PARK: Own. TEL: 01835 86344 fax - 01835 863349. SER: Valuations; packin shipping; interior design. VAT: Stan/Spec.

KILBARCHAN (Renfrewshire)

Gardner's The Antique Shop LAPAD

Wardend House, Kibblestone Rd. PA10 2P (G.D. and R.K.F. Gardner). Est. 1950. Open Trade 7 days, retail 9-6, Sat. 10-1. SIZ Large. *STOCK: General antiques.* LOC: 1 miles from Glasgow, at far end of Tandlehi Rd. 10 mins. from Glasgow Airport. TEI 01505 702292.

KILLEARN, Nr. Glasgow (Stirlingshir

Country Antiques

G63 9AJ. (Lady J. Edmonstone). Est. 1975. Op Mon.-Sat. *STOCK: Small antiques and decorati items.* Not Stocked: Reproduction. LOC: A81. main street. PARK: Easy. TEL: Home - 013 770215.

KILLIN (Perthshire)

Maureen H. Gauld

Cameron Buildings, Main St. FK21 8TE. Est. 197 Open March-Oct. 10-5, Nov.-Feb. Thurs., Fri., S SIZE: Medium. *STOCK: General antiques, fu niture, silver and paintings, £5-£3,500.* PAR Easy. TEL: 01567 820475; home - 01567 820605.

LARGE STOCK OF FURNITURE, PORCELAIN ETC.

GARDNER'S

THE ANTIQUE SHOP

WARDEND HOUSE, KIBBLESTON ROAD
KILBARCHAN PA10 2PN

20 MINUTES FROM GLASGOW CENTRE
10 MINUTES FROM GLASGOW AIRPORT

LAPADA MEMBER

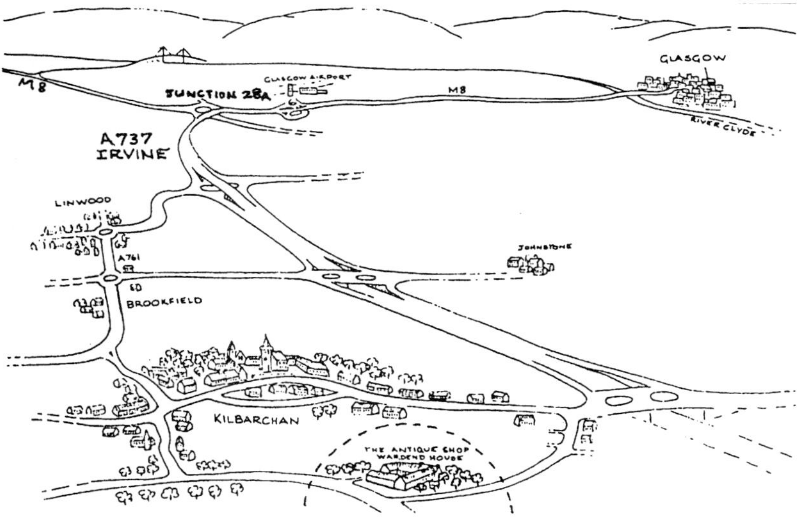

TELEPHONE KILBARCHAN 01505 702292

ESTABLISHED 1950

KILMACOLM (Renfrewshire)

Kilmacolm Antiques Ltd
Stewart Place. PA13 4AF. (H. Maclean). Est. 1973. Open 10-1 and 2.30-5.30. CL: Sun. except by appointment. SIZE: Medium. *STOCK: Furniture, 18th-19th C, £100-£8,000; objets d'art, 19th C; jewellery, £5-£5,000; paintings, £100-£5,000.* LOC: First shop on right when travelling from Bridge of Weir. PARK: Easy. TEL: 01505 873149. SER: Restorations (furniture, silver, jewellery, porcelain). FAIRS: Hopetown, Roxburghe, Edinburgh, Inverness. VAT: Stan/Spec.

KILMARNOCK (Ayrshire)

MacInnes Antiques
5c David Orr St., Bonnington. KA1 2KQ. (Mrs M. MacInnes). Est. 1973. Open by appointment. *STOCK: General antiques.* TEL: 01563 526739.

QS Antiques and Cabinetmakers
Moorfield Industrial Estate. KA2 0DP. (J.R. Cunningham and D.A. Johnson). Est. 1980. Open 9-5.30, Sat. 9-5. SIZE: Large. *STOCK: Furniture including stripped pine, 18th-19th C; shipping goods, architectural and collectors' items.* PARK: Easy. TEL: 01563 571071. SER: Restorations (upholstery, stripping); custom-built kitchens and furniture. VAT: Stan.

KILMICHAEL GLASSARY By Lochgilphead (Argyllshire)

Rhudle Mill
PA31 8QE. (D. Murray). Est. 1979. Open daily, weekends by appointment. SIZE: Medium. *STOCK: Furniture, 18th C to Art Deco, £30-£3,000; small items and bric-a-brac, £5-£500.* LOC: Signposted 3 miles south of Kilmartin on A816 Oban to Lochgilphead road. PARK: Easy. TEL: 01546 605284; home - same. SER: Restorations (furniture); French polishing; buys at auction.

KILTARLITY By Beauly (Inverness-shire)

Old Pine Furniture and Jouet
Fuaranbuie, 8 Kinerras. IV4 7JL. (J. and A. Jeorrett). Open by appointment. *STOCK: Restored pine including Victorian, £25-£600+.* TEL: 01463 741261.

KINCARDINE O'NEIL, Nr. Aboyne (Aberdeenshire)

Amber Antiques
Stranduff Croft. AB34 5AA. (V. Watson). Est. 1982. Open by appointment only. SIZE: Small. *STOCK: Jewellery especially amber, Victorian*

Kincardine O'Neil continued

and Edwardian, £25-£500; silver, Georgian Edwardian, £10-£500; Oriental objets d'art, £5 £1,000; pictures, 16th-20th C, £25-£500 antiquarian books. LOC: On North Deeside Rd PARK: Easy. TEL: 01339 884338. SER: Valuations; buys at auction. FAIRS: Aberdeen Inverness, Banchory, Newark.

KINGHORN (Fife)

The Pend Antiques
53 High St. KY3 9UW. Est. 1990. Open 11- (afternoons only in winter), Sat. 10.30-5. CL Tues. SIZE: Large. *STOCK: Pre-1930's furniture prints, china, glass, textiles and general collectables, £1-£750.* PARK: Easy. TEL: 0159 890207; home - 01592 890140. SER: Valuations restorations; stripping, waxing, small repairs.

KINGSTON-ON-SPEY (Morayshire)

Collectables
Lein Rd. IV32 7NW. (J. Penman and B. Taylor) Est. 1987. Open daily and last Sun. of month prior telephone call required. SIZE: Small *STOCK: Militaria and jewellery, lap desks, china collectables, small furniture, £5-£200.* LOC: O B9105. PARK: Easy. TEL: 01343 870462. SER Valuations. FAIRS: Inverness and Aberdeen.

KINGUSSIE (Inverness-shire)

Mostly Pine
High Street. PH21 1HR. Est. 1980. Open 10-5.3 (also store in Spey Street - open Sat. 10-5.30 an by appointment). *STOCK: Furniture and collectibles.* LOC: A9. TEL: 01540 661838. SER Restorations (pine). VAT: Stan/Spec.

KINROSS (Kinross)

Miles Antiques LAPAD
Mill St. KY13 7DR. (K. and S. Miles). Est. 197 Open 9-5, weekends by appointment. SIZE Large. *STOCK: Furniture including decorative Georgian, Victorian and Edwardian, £100-£5,00 china and pottery, £50-£500.* LOC: Off M9 junction 6. Take right at High St. then secon left. PARK: Easy. TEL: 01577 864858; home 01577 863881. SER: Restorations (upholster polishing, small repairs). VAT: Stan/Spec.

Portcullis Antiques
76 High St. KY13 7AJ. (Charles Cranston). Es 1982. Open 2-5.30, Sat. 11-4.30, Sun. 1-4.30. Cl Mon. and Thurs. SIZE: Small. *STOCK: Chin and porcelain, 19th-20th C, £10-£600; sma furniture, 20th C, £50-£500; brass, silver ar plate, 19th-20th C, £5-£700.* LOC: Just off M9 PARK: Opposite in Avenue Rd. TEL: 0157 862276; home - same.

KIRKCUDBRIGHT (Kirkcudbrightshire)

The Antique Shop
59 St Mary St. DG6 4DU. Open 10-5. SIZE: 3 dealers. *STOCK: General antiques, collectors' items, linen and lace, kichenalia, furniture and bric-a-brac, 18th-20th C, to £1,500.*

Chapel Antiques
Chapel Farm. DG6 4NG. (A. Bradley). Est. 1981. Open 2-5 and by appointment. SIZE: Small. *STOCK: China, small and shipping furniture, silver, brass and copper, 18th-20th C, £5-£1,000.* LOC: 200yds. off A75 between Ringford and Twynholm by-passes on A762, 2.5 miles from Kirkcudbright. PARK: Easy. TEL: 01557 820281.

Osborne
41 Castle St. DG6 4JD. (R.A. Mitchell). Est. 1948. Open 9-12.30 and 1.30-5. CL: Wed. pm and Sat. pm. TEL: 01557 330441; fax - 01557 331791. VAT: Stan/Spec.

LANGHOLM (Dumfriesshire)

The Antique Shop
High St. DG13 0DH. (R. and V. Baird). Est. 1970. Open 10.30-5. CL: Wed. pm. SIZE: Small. *STOCK: China, glass, pictures, 18th-20th C; jewellery, rugs, 19th-20th C; also Trade Warehouse of furniture, shipping goods and antiquarian books.* LOC: 20 miles north of Carlisle on A7. PARK: 100yds. TEL: 0138 73 80238.

LARGS (Ayrshire)

Narducci Antiques
1 Waterside St. KA30 9LN. (G. Narducci). Open Tues., Thurs. and Sat., 2.30-5.30 or by appointment - Trade anytime. SIZE: Warehouse. *STOCK: General antiques and shipping goods.* TEL: 01475 672612; 01294 461687/467137. SER: Packing and shipping; road haulage (Europe). *Mainly Trade and Export.*

LENNOXTOWN (Lanarkshire)

Campsie Antiques
Service St. (Mrs May Knox). Open 10-5, Sun. 12-5, Mon. 10-1. SIZE: Small. *STOCK: Furniture, paintings, Art Nouveau, Art Deco, ceramics, memorabilia, 19th-20th C, £5-£1,000.* LOC: A891. PARK: Easy. TEL: 01360 311100.

LINLITHGOW (West Lothian)

Heritage Antiques
22 High St. EH49 7ES. (Ann J. R. Davidson). Est. 1980. Open 10-1 and 2-5. CL: Wed. *STOCK: Jewellery, china, glass, silver, small furniture and objects.* PARK: Nearby. TEL: 01506 847460. SER: Valuations; repairs (jewellery).

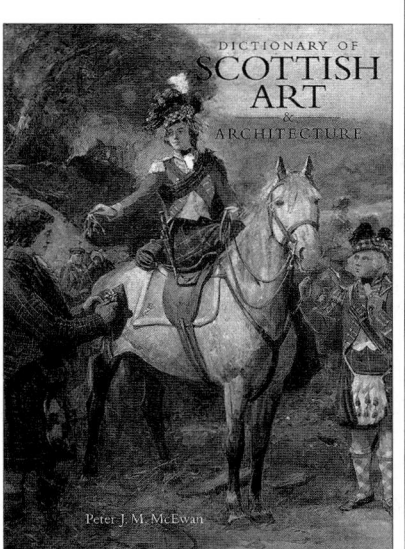

Linlithgow continued

Mir Russki

28 Beechwood. (Ian Bateman). Est. 1994. Open by appointment only. *STOCK: Russian silver, 18th C to 1917; Norwegian and Danish silver, 19th to early 20th C.* TEL: 01506 843973. SER: Buys at auction (Russian silver); mail order stocklist available. FAIRS: NEC and other major.

MAYBOLE (Ayrshire)

The Wee Glass Works

The Nest Factory Unit, Drumellan St. KA19 7RN. (Mr and Mrs B. Dickson). Est. 1986. Open 9.30-5.30: Fri.-Sun. by appointment. SIZE: Small. *STOCK: Stained glass panels and windows, £10-£200.* LOC: From centre of Maybole take St Cuthberts Rd., turn second on right, shop/studio first building on left through gates. PARK: Easy. TEL: 01655 883379. SER: Restorations; commission work (stained glass).

MEIGLE (Perthshire)

Henderson Antiques

Meigle Antiques Centre. Est. 1984. *STOCK: Furniture and clocks.* TEL: 01828 640617. VAT: Stan.

Herrald of Edinburgh

Kings of Kinloch. PH12 8QX. Est. 1882. Open 9.30-1 and 2-5, Sun. by appointment. SIZE: Large. *STOCK: Furniture, Persian rugs, Continental and Eastern china, brass, copper and crystal.* TEL: 01828 640273; fax - same. SER: Restorations; custom build. VAT: Stan/Spec.

MOFFAT (Dumfriesshire)

Alton House Antiques

Moffat Antiques Centre, Well Street. DG10 9LB. (Terry Hull). Resident. Est. 1995. Open 9.30-5. SIZE: Medium + store. *STOCK: Stripped pine, 18th-20th C, £3-£1,000; other stripped woods, 19th-20th C, £5-£500; hand-made reproduction pine, £15-£500.* PARK: Easy. TEL: 01683 220903; mobile - 0850 129105. SER: Restorations (stripping and repairs); buys at auction.

T.W. Beaty

22 Well St. *STOCK: Furniture, china, glass, brass, pictures, 18th-20th C.* TEL: 01683 220380.

MONTROSE (Angus)

Harper-James LAPADA

25-27 Baltic St. DD10 8EX. (D.R. James). Resident. Est. 1991. Open 9-5, other times by appointment. SIZE: Large. *STOCK: Furniture, clocks, silver and jewellery, 1690-1910, £50-£6,000; ceramics and pottery, 1800-1945,*

Montrose continued

£650+; general antiques and curios, £2-£750 **LOC: From south turn right at Peel statue then first left. PARK: Easy. TEL: 01674 671307; home - same. SER: Valuations; restorations (furniture, upholstery); French polishing; export. FAIRS: Major U.K. VAT: Stan/Spec.**

NEWBURGH (Fife)

Newburgh Antiques

222 High St. KY14 6DZ. (Miss D.J. Fraser). Est. 1991. Open 10.30-12 and 1.30-5. CL: Mon. SIZE: Small. *STOCK: Wemyss ware, 1882-1930, £100-£2,000; Scottish watercolours and oil paintings, 1800-1950's, £100-£1,500; furniture, 1750-1900, £200-£2,000.* LOC: A913. PARK: Easy. TEL: 01337 841026; home - 01337 840725. SER: Valuations.

NEWTONMORE (Inverness-shire)

The Antique Shop

Main St. PH20 1DD. (J. Harrison). Est. 196- Open 9.30-5.30. SIZE: Medium. *STOCK: Furniture, £20-£1,000; glass, china, silver, plate, copper, brass, secondhand books, vintage fishing tackle.* LOC: On A86 opposite Mains Hotel. PARK: Easy. TEL: 01540 673272.

NORTH BERWICK (East Lothian)

Fraser Antiques

129 High St. EH39 4HB. Est. 1968. Open Sat. only 9.30-12.30 or by appointment. *STOCK: Porcelain, glass, pictures, silver, furniture and general antiques.* TEL: 01620 892722. SER: Restorations.

Kirk Ports Gallery

49A Kirk Ports. (Alan Lindsey). Open 10-5.30 and Sun. in summer 11-4.30. CL: Thurs. in winter. SIZE: Medium. *STOCK: Oil paintings, £100-£500; watercolours, £50-£300; etchings and prints, £30-£100; all 19th C to 1940.* LOC: Behind main street. PARK: Easy. TEL: 0162- 894114. SER: Valuations.

Lindsey Antiques

49a Kirk Ports. (Stephen Lindsey). Est. 199- Open 10-1 and 2-5, Sun. 12-3. CL: Thurs. SIZE: Medium. *STOCK: Ceramics and glass, 1800-1935, £50-£150; furniture, 1800-1910, £150-£400.* LOC: Behind main street. PARK: Easy. TEL: 01620 894114. SER: Valuations; buys at auction. FAIRS: Inglston, Meadowbank Stadium and The Assembly Rooms, all Edinburgh.

OBAN (Argyllshire)

The Fitzroy Gallery (formerly The McIan Gallery)
10 Argyll Sq. PA34 4AZ. Est. 1973. Open 10-5. *STOCK: Russian sculpture; contemporary paintings.* TEL: 01631 566755. SER: Restorations; framing; regular exhibitions.

Oban Antiques
35 Stevenson St. PA34 5NA. (P. and P. Baker). Est. 1970. Open 10-5.30. SIZE: Medium. *STOCK: Furniture and general antiques, mainly 19th C; books, collectables, some Art Deco, £5-£1,500.* LOC: Off George (main) St. PARK: Easy. TEL: 01631 566203.

PAISLEY (Renfrewshire)

Corrigan Antiques
Woodlands, High Calside. Open by appointment only. SIZE: Small. *STOCK: Furniture and accessories.* LOC: 5 minutes from Glasgow Airport. TEL: 0141 887 7542; fax - same; mobile - 0860 382285.

Paisley Fine Books
17 Corsebar Crescent. PA2 9QA. (Mr and Mrs B. Merrifield). Est. 1985. Open by appointment. SIZE: Small. *STOCK: Books on architecture, art, antiques and collecting.* TEL: 0141 884 2661; fax - same. SER: Free book search; catalogues issued.

PERTH (Perthshire)

Ainslie's Antique Warehouse
Unit 3, Gray St. PH2 0JH. (T.S. and A. Ainslie). Open 9-5, by appointment at weekends. SIZE: Large. *STOCK: General antiques.* TEL: 01738 636825.

A.S. Deuchar and Son
10-12 South St. PH2 8PG. (A.S. and A.W.N. Deuchar). Open 10-1 and 2-5. CL: Sat. SIZE: Large. *STOCK: Victorian shipping goods, furniture, 19th C paintings, china, brass, silver and plate.* LOC: Glasgow to Aberdeen Rd., near Queen's Bridge. PARK: Easy. TEL: 01738 626297; home - 07138 551452. VAT: Stan/Spec.

Forsyth Antiques
2 St. Paul's Sq. PH1 5QW. (A. McDonald Forsyth). Est. 1961. Open 10-5. SIZE: Medium. *STOCK: Silver, 18th-19th C, £5-£1,000; jewellery, 19th-20th C, £5-£750; Monart glass, 20th C, £5-£500.* LOC: Behind St. Paul's Church, junction of High St. and Methven St. PARK: Easy. TEL: 01738 624877. SER: Valuations; buys at auction (silver). VAT: Stan/Spec.

Gallery One
1/2 St. Paul's Sq. PH1 5QW. (A. McDonald Forsyth). Est. 1990. Open 10-5. *STOCK: Scottish*

Perth continued

pictures, Monart glass, silver, jewellery, furniture. LOC: Junction of High St. and Methven St. PARK: Easy. TEL: 01738 624877. SER: Valuations.

The George Street Gallery
38 George St. PH1 5JL. (S. Hardie). Open 10-1 and 2-5. CL: Wed. and Sat. pm. *STOCK: 20th C oil paintings, watercolours, etchings and prints by Scottish artists.* TEL: 01738 638953.

Hardie Antiques
25 St. John St. PH1 5SH. (T.G. Hardie). PADA. Est. 1980. Open 9.30-5, Sat. 10-4.30. SIZE: Medium. *STOCK: Jewellery and silver, 18th-20th C, £5-£5,000.* PARK: Nearby. TEL: 01738 633127; fax - 01738 552025; home - 01738 551764. SER: Valuations. VAT: Stan/Spec.

Henderson
5 North Methven St. PH1 5PN. (J.G. Henderson). Est. 1935. Open 9-5.30. CL: Wed. pm. SIZE: Small. *STOCK: Porcelain, glass, 1720-1950, £5-£500; silver, jewellery, 1800-1900, £2-£1,000; coins, medals and stamps, £1-£500.* Not Stocked: Furniture. LOC: On A9. PARK: Easy. TEL: 01738 624836; home - 01738 621923. SER: Valuations. VAT: Stan.

Ian Murray Antique Warehouse
21 Glasgow Rd. PH2 0NZ. Open 9-5, Sat. 10-1. SIZE: Large - 8 dealers. *STOCK: General antiques, Victorian, Edwardian and shipping items.* PARK: Easy. TEL: 01738 637222. VAT: Stan/Spec.

Nigel Stacy-Marks Ltd
23 George St. PH1 5JY. (Nigel and Ginny Stacy-Marks). Open 9-5.30. SIZE: Medium. *STOCK: Oils and watercolours, 19th-20th C, £250-£25,000; British etchings, late 19th C to mid 20th C, £100-£1,000; Oriental rugs, 20th C, £150-£5,000.* LOC: Town centre, just south of museum, behind Tay St. PARK: Nearby. TEL: 01738 626300; fax - 01738 620460. SER: Valuations; restorations; framing; regular exhibitions (catalogues on request). VAT: Stan/Spec.

Tay Street Gallery
70 Tay St. PH2 8NN. (I.C. Ingram). Est. 1972. Open Tues., Thurs. and Fri. 10-1 and 2-3.30 or by appointment. SIZE: Small. *STOCK: Furniture and related items, pictures and prints, 17th-19th C.* LOC: Overlooking River Tay. PARK: Easy. TEL: 01738 620604. VAT: Stan/Spec.

PITLOCHRY (Perthshire)

Blair Antiques
14 Bonnethill Rd. PH16 5BS. (Duncan Huie). Est. 1976. Open 9-5. CL: Thurs. pm. *STOCK: Period furniture, Scottish oil paintings, silver - some provincial, curios, clocks, pottery and porcelain.* LOC: Beside Scotlands Hotel, off A9 to Inverness. TEL: 01796 472624; fax - 01796 474202. SER: Valuations; buys at auction. VAT: Stan/Spec.

PITTENWEEM (Fife)

The Little Gallery
20 High St. KY10 2LA. (Dr. Ursula Ditchburn-Bosch). Est. 1988. Open 10-5, Sun. 2-5. CL: Mon. and Tues. (and Wed. in winter). SIZE: Small. *STOCK: China, 18th C to 1930's, £5-£100; small furniture, mainly Victorian, £30-£300; rustica, £5-£150; contemporary paintings, £40-£700.* LOC: From Market Sq. towards church, on right. PARK: Easy. TEL: 01333 311227; home - same. SER: Valuations.

POLLOKSHIELDS, Nr. Glasgow

Strachan Antiques
40 Darnley St. G41 2SE. (Alex and Lorna Strachan). Est. 1990. Open 10-5, Sun. 12-5. CL: Wed. SIZE: Warehouse. *STOCK: Furniture, Arts and Crafts, Art Nouveau, Victorian and Edwardian, £50-£1,500.* LOC: Off M8, junction 20. PARK: Easy. TEL: 0141 429 4411. VAT: Stan/Spec.

PORTREE (Isle of Skye)

Croft Comforts Antiques
2 Wentworth St. IV51 9EJ. (Ms Fiona Middleton). Est. 1984. Open daily. CL: Tues. and Wed. Oct. to April. SIZE: Small. *STOCK: China, porcelain, curios and stoneware, 19th-20th C; furniture, 19th C and Edwardian.* PARK: Nearby. TEL: 01478 613762; fax - same. SER: Buys at auction.

PORTSOY (Banff)

Other Times Antiques
13-15 Seafield St. AB45 2QT. (D. McLean and T. Matheson). Est. 1986. Open 10-5 including Sun. CL: Wed. *STOCK: General antiques, 1700-1950.* TEL: 01261 842866. VAT: Stan/Spec.

PRESTWICK (Ayrshire)

Crossroads Antiques
7 The Cross. KA9 1AJ. (Timothy Okeeffe). Est. 1989. Open 9-5. SIZE: Medium. *STOCK: Furniture, 18th-20th C, £5-£1,000+; china and silver, 19th-20th C, £5-£500+.* PARK: Nearby. TEL: 01292 474004. SER: Valuations; buys at auction.

RAIT (Perthshire)

Rait Village Antiques Centre
PH2 7RT. LOC: Midway between Perth and Dundee, 1 mile north of A90. PARK: Easy. Below are listed the dealers at this centre:

Fair Finds
(Lynda Templeman). *Antique and early 20th C country house furnishings, pictures, rugs, silver and clocks, £50-£10,000.* TEL: 01821 670379.

Rait continued

Guiscard Miniatures
Fine miniature furniture and collectables dolls, juvenilia. TEL: 01821 670392; fax - same. SER: Miniature furniture made to order.

Gordon Loraine Antiques
(Liane and Gordon Loraine). *Georgian, Victorian and Edwardian furniture, decorative items and collectables.* TEL: 01821 670760.

J. and L. Newton
Upholstered furniture, antique pine, decorative accessories, textiles and cushions. TEL: 0182[illegible] 670205

Rait Antiques
Period and decorative furniture, woodworkin[illegible] tools. TEL: 01821 670318.

Templemans
Period and decorative furniture, £200-£20,000 TEL: 01821 670344; home - 01821 670278. SER Valuations; museum acquisitions. VAT: Spec.

Whimsical Wemyss
(Lynda Templeman). *Wemyssware, £50-£3,00[illegible]* TEL: 01821 67039.

SALTCOATS (Ayrshire)

Narducci Antiques
57 Raise St. KA21 5JZ. (G. Narducci). Est. 197[illegible] Open 10-1 and 2.30-5.30 or by appointmen[illegible] *STOCK: General antiques and shipping good[illegible]* TEL: 01294 461687/01475 672612; mobiles 0831 100152/0374 102748. SER: Packing, expor[illegible] shipping and European haulage. *Mainly Trad[illegible] and Export.*

SELKIRK (Selkirkshire)

Heatherlie Antiques
6/8 Heatherlie Terrace. TD7 5AH. (A.F.D. Scott[illegible] Est. 1979. Open 9-12.30 and 2-5. CL: Sat. p[illegible] SIZE: Medium. *STOCK: Furniture, £50-£5,00[illegible] pottery and porcelain, general antiques, bras[illegible] bric-a-brac and copper, £5-£250; all 19th-20th* [illegible] LOC: Leave A7 at Selkirk market place and ta[illegible] Moffat/Peebles road for ½ mile. PARK: Eas[illegible] TEL: 01750 20114.

ST. ANDREWS (Fife)

Bygones
68 South St. KY16 9JT. (Mrs J. Guest). Open 1[illegible] 4.30, Sun. 2-4.30. CL: Thurs. *STOCK: Furnitu[illegible] smalls, silver, bric-a-brac.* LOC: Near town ha[illegible] PARK: Easy. TEL: 01334 475849.

St. Andrews continued

A. and F. McIlreavy Rare and Interesting Books
57 South St. KY16 9QR. (Alan and Fiona McIlreavy). ABA. Est. 1977. Open 9.30-5. SIZE: Medium. *STOCK: Books, 17th-20th C; antiquarian maps and prints.* PARK: Easy. TEL: 01334 472487; home - 01334 870982. SER: Valuations. FAIRS: ABA Edinburgh and Chelsea.

Old St. Andrews Gallery
9 Albany Place. KY16 9HH. (Mr and Mrs D.R. Brown). Est. 1973. CL: 1-2 daily. SIZE: Medium. *STOCK: Golf memorabilia, 19th C, £100-£20,000; silver, jewellery especially Scottish 19th-20th C, £100-£10,000; general antiques, from 18th C, £50-£5,000.* LOC: Main street. PARK: Easy. TEL: 01334 477840. SER: Valuations; restorations (jewellery, silver); buys at auction (golf memorabilia). VAT: Stan.

St. Andrews Fine Art
34a Market St. KY16 9PA. Open 10-1 and 2-5. *STOCK: Scottish oils, watercolours and drawings, 19th-20th C.* TEL: 01334 474080.

STEWARTON (Ayrshire)

Woolfsons of James Street Ltd t/a Past & Present
3 Lainshaw St. KA3 5BY. Est. 1983. Open 9.30-5.30, Sun. 12-5.30. SIZE: Medium. *STOCK: Furniture, £100-£500; porcelain, £25-£500; bric-a-brac, £5-£50; all from 1800.* LOC: Stewarton Cross. PARK: Easy. TEL: 01560 484113. SER: Valuations; restorations (French polishing, upholstery, wood). VAT: Stan/Spec.

STIRLING (Stirlingshire)

Abbey Antiques
5 Friars St. FK8 1HA. (S. Campbell). Resident. Est. 1980. Open 10-5. SIZE: Small. *STOCK: Jewellery, £10-£5,000; silver, £5-£1,000; furniture including pine, £20-£1,000; paintings, £50-£1,000; bric-a-brac, £1-£100; coins and medals, £1-£1,000; all 18th-20th C.* LOC: Off Murray Place, part of main thoroughfare. PARK: Nearby. TEL: 01786 447840; home - 01786 470595. SER: Valuations; restorations (china, furniture, jewellery); buys at auction (paintings, furniture, jewellery).

STONEHAVEN (Kincardineshire)

Bygones & Contemporaries
6 Evan St. (L. Watt). Open 10-5.30. SIZE: Medium. *STOCK: Victoriana, collectables, small furniture, to £1,000.* LOC: Town centre. PARK: Easy. TEL: 01569 767484.

STRATHBLANE (Stirlingshire)

Whatnots
16 Milngavie Rd. G63 9EH. (F. Bruce). Est. 1965. *STOCK: Furniture, paintings, jewellery, silver and plate, clocks, small items, shipping goods, horse drawn and old vehicles.* LOC: 25 miles from Stirling and 10 miles from Glasgow. PARK: Easy. TEL: 01360 770310. VAT: Stan/Spec.

THORNHILL, Nr. Dumfries (Dumfries-shire)

Thornhill Gallery
47-48 Drumlanrig St. DG3 5LJ. (A.S.B. Crawford). Est. 1984. Open 9-5.30 or by appointment. SIZE: Small. *STOCK: Fine art, glass, ceramics.* LOC: A76 in village centre. PARK: Easy. TEL: 01848 330566; home - same.

TROON (Ayrshire)

Old Troon Sporting Antiques
49 Ayr St. KA10 6EB. (R.S. Pringle). Est. 1984. CL: Wed. pm. and Sat. pm. SIZE: Medium. *STOCK: Golf items, 19th C, to £500+.* LOC: 5 minutes from A77. PARK: Easy. TEL: 01292 311822; home - 01292 313744; fax - 01292 313111. SER: Valuations; buys at auction (golf items). VAT: Stan.

ULLAPOOL (Wester Ross)

Wishing Well Antiques
Garve Rd. (Simon and Eileen Calder). Est. 1988. Open 9-6, including Sun., 9-9 June-Sept, other times by appointment. SIZE: Medium. *STOCK: Furniture, £10-£2,000; country artefacts, treen, Scottish pottery, all 18th-20th C.* LOC: 500 metres before entering Ullapool. PARK: Easy. TEL: 01854 613188. SER: Valuations; restorations; buys at auction (furniture). FAIRS: Robert Soper Hopetown, Newark; Ann Young Aberdeen, Drumossie, Inverness.

UPPER LARGO (Fife)

Waverley Antiques
13 Main St. KY8 6EL. (D.V. and C.A. St. Clair). Est. 1962. Open 10.30-5.30, Sun. by appointment. SIZE: Medium. *STOCK: Pictures, furniture, china, pottery, glass and works of art.* LOC: Coast road from Leven to St. Andrews. PARK: Easy. TEL: 01333 360437; home - same. SER: Valuations. VAT: Spec.

WALKERBURN (Peebleshire)

Townhouse Antiques
EH43 6AY. (B. Brett and J. Juett). Open 10.30-4.30. CL: Wed. *STOCK: Textiles, collectables, china, furniture.* LOC: On A72, 7 miles east of Peebles. TEL: 01896 870694/870371.

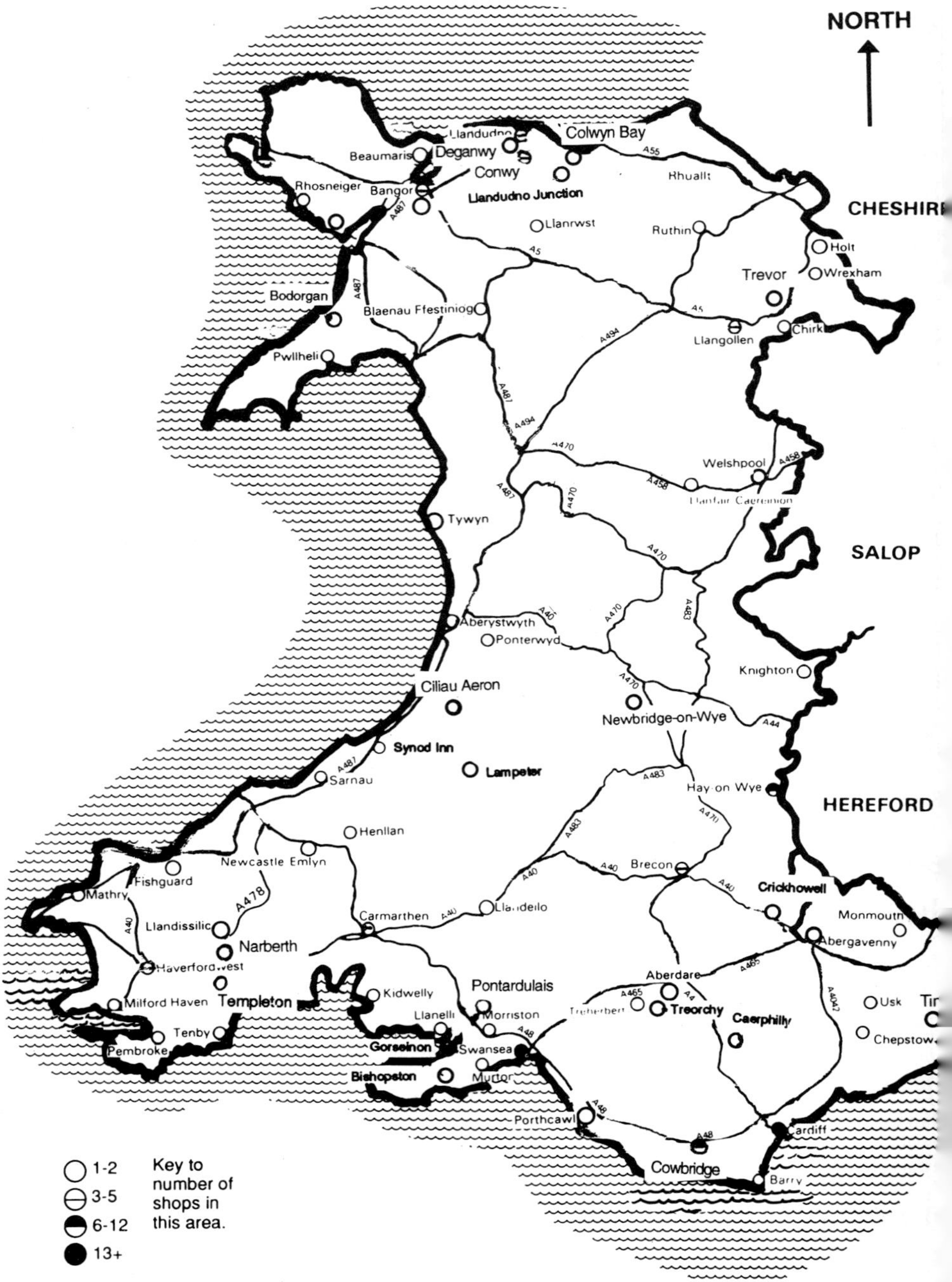

Key to number of shops in this area.

- 1-2
- 3-5
- 6-12
- 13+

Please note this is only a rough map designed to show dealers the number of shops in the various towns, and is not necessarily totally accurate.

ABERDARE

Market Antiques
Aberdare Market. (J.A. Toms). Open 9-5.30. *STOCK: General antiques.* LOC: Town centre. TEL: 01685 870242.

ABERGAVENNY

Henry H. Close
36 Cross St. NP3 3AY. (Mr and Mrs H. Close). Est. 1968. Open 9-5 and by appointment. *STOCK: 18th-19th C furniture, porcelain, pottery, glass, brass, copper, silver, prints.* TEL: 01873 853583. VAT: Stan.

H.K. Lockyer
22 Monk St. NP7 5NP. Open 9.30-5.30. *STOCK: Antiquarian maps, prints and books.* PARK: Opposite. TEL: 01873 855825. VAT: Stan/Spec.

ABERYSTWYTH

The Furniture Cave
33 Cambrian St. SY23 1NZ. (P. David). Est. 1975. Open 9-5, Wed. 9-3, Sat. 10-4. *STOCK: Pine, 1700-1930, from £100; general antiques, Victorian and Edwardian, £30-£3,000; small items, 19th C, £10-£500.* LOC: First right off Terrace Rd., at railway station end. PARK: Nearby. TEL: 01970 611234. SER: Restorations.

Howards of Aberystwyth BADA LAPADA
10 Alexandra Rd. SY23 1LE. Open by appointment only. *STOCK: Welsh pottery including Gaudy, copper lustre, Staffordshire pottery animal and decorative figures, early pottery.* TEL: 01970 624973; fax - same; mobile - 0831 850544.

BANGOR

Jones and Dyson, Ann Evans LAPADA
10 Wellfield Arcade. (E.C.P. Dyson, K. Jones and A. Evans). Est. 1994. Open Thurs. Fri. and Sat. 10-4.30. SIZE: Small. *STOCK: Late Victorian and Edwardian jewellery, £50-£3,500; furniture and porcelain.* LOC: Near High St. PARK: Easy. TEL: 01248 370898. SER: Valuations; restorations. FAIRS: NEC, Country House Events, Towy. VAT: Spec.

Wellfield Antique Centre
Wellfield Court. LL71 8EA. (T. Andrew). Open Thurs.-Sat. 10-5. SIZE: 20 stands. TEL: 01248 361360.

David Windsor Gallery
201 High St. LL57 1NU. Est. 1970. Open 10-5. CL: Wed. *STOCK: Oils and watercolours, 18th-20th C; maps, engravings, lithographs.* TEL: 01248 364639. SER: Restorations; framing; mounting. VAT: Stan/Spec.

BARRY

Flame 'n' Grate
99-100 High St. CF6 8DS. (A. Galsworthy). Open 9-5.30. *STOCK: Antique and reproduction fireplaces and surrounds.* TEL: 01446 744788.

BEAUMARIS

Castle Antiques
13 Church St. LL58 8AB. (J. and S. Jones). Open 9-5.30, including Sun. in summer. *STOCK: Oak, mahogany and upholstered furniture; pictures, silver and decorative items.* LOC: Opposite Post Office. TEL: 01248 810474.

Museum of Childhood
1 Castle St. LL58 8AP. *STOCK: Children's toys and memorabilia collectables.* TEL: 01248 712498.

BISHOPSTON, Nr. Swansea

Maybery Antiques
1 Brandy Cove Rd. SA3 3HB. (W. Maybery). Est. 1969. Open 11 -5. CL: Mon. and Tues. *STOCK: Furniture, 18th-19th C; porcelain and pottery, 18th-20th C; paintings, general antiques, 19th-20th C.* LOC: .75 of a mile from Murton P.O. PARK: Easy. TEL: 01792 232550. SER: Valuations.

BLAENAU FFESTINIOG

The Antique Shop
Bryn Marian. LL41 3HD. (Mrs R. Roberts). Est. 1971. *STOCK: Victoriana, furniture, brass and copper, oil lamps, clocks and watches.* TEL: 01766 830629/830041.

BODORGAN, (Anglesey)

Michael Webb Fine Art LAPADA
Open by appointment only. *STOCK: Victorian and 20th C oil paintings and watercolours.* TEL: 01407 840336. SER: Valuations; restorations; framing. VAT: Spec.

BRECON

Hazel of Brecon
6 The Bulwark. LD3 7LB. (H. Hillman). Est. 1969. Open 10-5.30. CL: Wed. SIZE: Medium. *STOCK: Jewellery, 19th-20th C, £50-£4,000.* LOC: Main square, town centre. PARK: Easy. TEL: 01874 625274 (24 hr. answering service). SER: Valuations; repairs.

Maps, Prints and Books
7 The Struet. LD3 7LL. (Mr and Mrs D.G. Evans). Est. 1961. Open 9-1 and 2-5. CL: Wed. SIZE: Large. *STOCK: Books, maps, prints, 17th C, £5-£500.* LOC: A438, opposite Kwik Save. PARK: Opposite. TEL: 01874 622714. VAT: Stan.

Brecon continued

Ship Street Galleries
14 Ship St. LD3 9AD. (Toni and Christine Constantinescu). Est. 1974. Open by appointment only. *STOCK: Continental and English period furniture, pine, shipping goods, 18th-19th C; Continental and English glass and porcelain.* TEL: 01874 623926.

Silvertime
6 The Bulwark. LD3 7LB. (L. Hillman). Open 10-5.30. CL: Wed. SIZE: Small. *STOCK: Silver and gold watches; antique and collectors' clocks; 19th-20th C silver and plate.* LOC: Town centre, on main square. PARK: Easy. TEL: 01874 625274 (24 hr. answering service). SER: Valuations; repairs.

CAERPHILLY

G.J. Gittins and Son
10 Clive St. Open 9-5, Sat. 10-5. CL: Wed. *STOCK: General antiques, jewellery and shipping goods.* TEL: 01222 868835.

CARDIFF

Alexander Antiques
312 Whitchurch Rd. (J.R. Bradley). Open 10-5.30. *STOCK: Jewellery, clocks and furniture.* TEL: 01222 621824.

Back to the Wood
Old Post Office Sorting Office, West Canal Wharf. CF1 5DB. (I. Cooling). Open 9-5. *STOCK: Pine and fireplaces.* LOC: Next door to Jacobs Antique Centre. TEL: 01222 390939. SER: Restorations (fireplaces); pine stripping.

Charlotte's Wholesale Antiques
129 Woodville Rd., Cathays. CF2 4DZ. (P.G. Cason). Open 9.30-4. SIZE: Large and warehouse. *STOCK: Shipping goods, general antiques, period furniture.* TEL: 01222 759809/224632.

Cronin Antiques
12 Mackintosh Place, Roath. CF2 4RQ. (J. Cronin). Open 9.30-4.30. *STOCK: General antiques, silver and jewellery.* TEL: 01222 498929.

Heritage Antiques and Stripped Pine
Rear of 1a Mortimer Rd., Pontcanna. (D. Lloyd). Est. 1974. Open 9-6. SIZE: Medium. *STOCK: Pine and general antiques, 19th C, £50-£500.* PARK: Easy. TEL: 01222 390097; mobile - 0585 095940. SER: Restorations (mainly pine). FAIRS: Sophia Gardens, Cardiff. VAT: Stan.

Jacobs Antique Centre
West Canal Wharf. C51 5DB. Open Wed.-Sat. 9.30-5. SIZE: Large - 80 dealers. *STOCK: General antiques, stripped pine and furniture.*

Cardiff continued

LOC: 2 mins. from main railway and bus stations. PARK: 100yds. TEL: Thurs. and Sat. only 01222 390939. SER: Valuations; restorations; buys at auction.

Kings Fireplaces, Antiques and Interiors
The Old Church, Adamsdown Sq., Adamsdown. (B. Quinn). Est. 1984. SIZE: Medium. *STOCK: Period fireplaces including French marble; Victorian and Edwardian furniture.* TEL: 01222 492439. SER: Restorations (furniture and fireplaces); fireplace installations. VAT: Stan.

Llanishen Antiques
26 Crwys Rd., Cathays. CF2 4NL. (Mrs J. Boalch). Open 10.30-4.30. CL: Wed. except by appointment. *STOCK: Furniture, silver, china, glass, bric-a-brac.* TEL: 01222 397244.

Manor House Fine Arts
73 Pontcanna St., Pontcanna. CF1 9HS. (S.K. Denley-Hill). Est. 1976. Open Thurs.-Sat. 10.30-5.30, other times by appointment. SIZE: Medium. *STOCK: Watercolours, oil paintings and prints, £50-£2,000; general antiques and smalls, £10-£1,000; all 1800-1960.* LOC: Pontcanna St. is at north end of Cathedral Rd. PARK: Easy. TEL: 01222 227787. SER: Valuations; restorations; framing and mounting; buys at auction. VAT: Stan/Spec.

Past and Present
242 Whitchurch Rd., Heath. CF4 3ND. (C. and J. Rowles). Est. 1970. Open 10-5.30. Open to trade all week at rear of shop. SIZE: Medium. *STOCK: Clocks, 19th C, £50-£3,000+; furniture, 18th-19th C, £5-£1,000+; china and bric-a-brac, £5-£500.* LOC: From M4 along eastern avenue by-pass, city turn-off by University Hospital, 1st left into Whitchurch Rd. PARK: Nearby. TEL: 01222 621443/759529. SER: Valuations; buys at auction.

Rowles Fine Antiques
The Royal Arcade, St Mary St. (C. and J. Rowles). Open 10-5.30. *STOCK: Clocks, 19th C, £50-£3,000+; furniture, 18th-19th C, £5-£1,000+; china and bric-a-brac, £5-£500.* LOC: Town centre. TEL: 01222 621443/759529; mobile - 0850 963454.

San Domenico Stringed Instruments
175 Kings Rd., Pontcanna. CF1 9DF. (H.W. Morgan). Open 10-4, Sat. 10-1. SIZE: Small. *STOCK: Fine violins, violas, cellos and bows, mainly 18th-19th C, £300-£20,000.* LOC: Off Cathedral Rd. or Cowbridge Rd. PARK: Easy. TEL: 01222 235881; home - 01222 777156; fax 01222 344510. SER: Valuations; restorations; buys at auction. VAT: Stan/Spec.

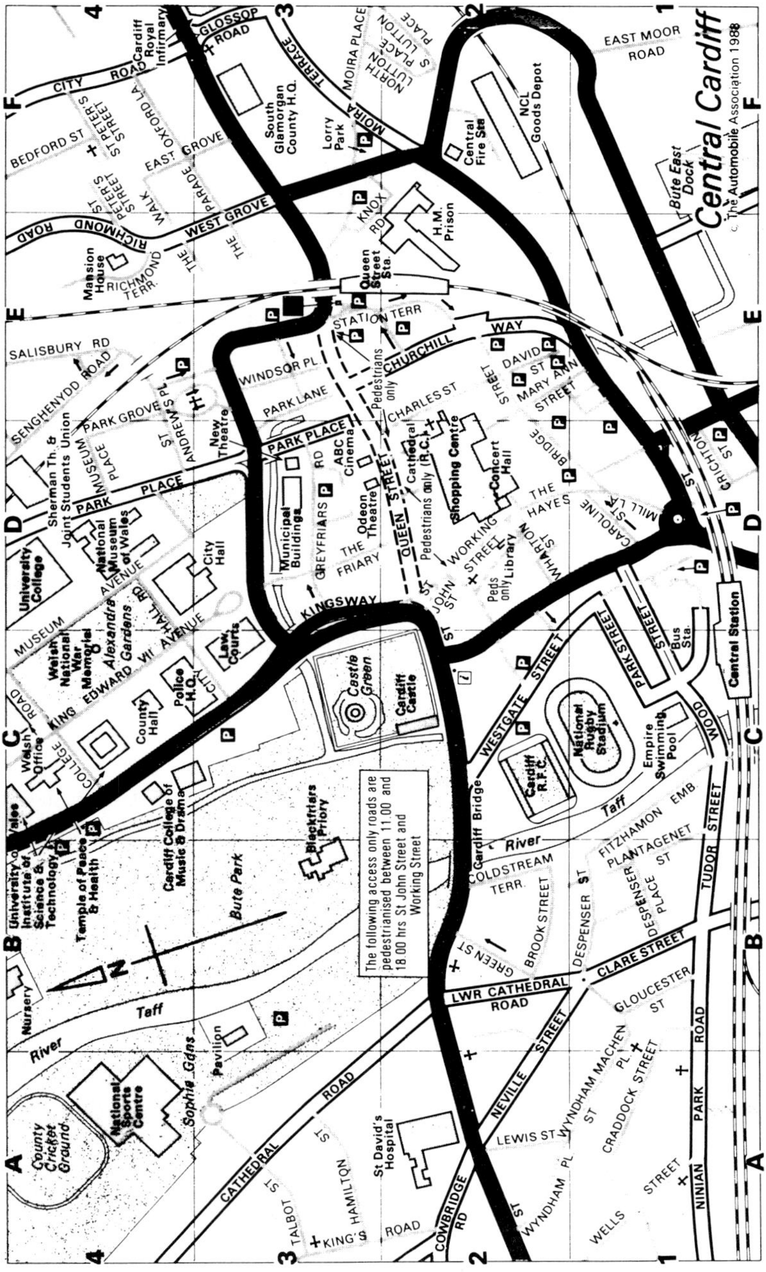

Key to Town Plan

AA Recommended roads		Car Parks	P
Other roads		Parks and open spaces	
Restricted roads		AA Service Centre	AA
Buildings of interest			

CARMARTHEN

Cwmgwili Mill
Bronwydd Arms. SA33 6HX. (M.J. Sandell). Est. 1950. Open 9-1 and 2-6, Sat. 9-1 and 2-6, Sun. by appointment. SIZE: Large. *STOCK: Furniture, oak, mahogany, pine, 18th-20th C.* PARK: Easy. TEL: 01267 231500; home - 01267 237215. VAT: Spec.

Merlins Antiques
Market Precinct. SA31 1QY. (Mrs J.R. Perry). Open 10-4.30. CL: Mon. *STOCK: Small items - porcelain, pottery, glass, silver and plate, postcards.* TEL: 01267 237728.

The Pot Board
30 King St. (Nigel and Gill Batten). Est. 1987. Open 9.30-5.30. SIZE: 5 showrooms. *STOCK: Pine furniture, mainly Victorian, £100-£1,000; chairs, mainly reproduction, £50-£300.* LOC: Town centre, near St Peter's church. PARK: Loading only and 50 yards. TEL: 01267 236623; fax - 01834 842788; home - 01834 842699. SER: Restorations (furniture, including stripping); buys at auction (pine). VAT: Spec.

CHEPSTOW

Foxgloves
St. Mary Street. (Leslie Brain). Open Tues.-Sat. 10ish-5. *STOCK: Period and antique furniture; pictures, china and objet d'art.*

Glance Back Bookshop
17 Upper Church St. NP6 5EX. Open 10ish-5.30 daily, Bank Holidays and Sun. (Easter to Oct.) - lunchtime to 5.30. SIZE: 8 rooms. *STOCK: Books including antiquarian; stamps, coins, tokens, medals, postcards pre-1930, banknotes, pens, military cap badges, antiquarian maps and prints.* LOC: Town centre. PARK: Easy. SER: Restorations (works of art on paper, canvas or board); framing and colouring.

Glance Gallery
17a Upper Church St. NP6 5EX. Open 10ish-5.30, Sun. in summer 1-5.30. SIZE: Large. *STOCK: Antiquarian prints and maps.* LOC: Town centre. PARK: Easy. SER: Valuations; restorations (canvas, board or paper); framing; hand-colouring.

Jones Centre
23 St. Mary St. Open 10-5. SIZE: 2 floors - several dealers. *STOCK: General antiques, furniture, china, bric-a-brac.*

Plough House Interiors
Upper Church St. NP6 5HU. (Mr and Mrs P. Jones). Est. 1972. Open 10-5, Sat. 10-4.30, Sun. by appointment. CL: Wed. SIZE: Large. *STOCK: Victorian and Edwardian furniture and shipping goods.* LOC: 2 miles from Severn Bridge and M4. PARK: Easy. TEL: 01291 625200; home - same. SER: Valuations; restorations; buys at auction. VAT: Stan/Spec.

CHIRK

Seventh Heaven
Chirk Mill. LL14 5BU. (Mr and Mrs J.J. Butler). Est. 1971. Open every day. SIZE: Large. *STOCK: Brass, iron and wooden beds including half-tester, four-poster and canopied, mainly 19th C.* LOC: B5070, below village, off A5 bypass. PARK: Easy. TEL: 01691 777622/773563; fax - 01691 777313. VAT: Stan.

CILIAU AERON, Nr. Lampeter

K.W. Finlay Antiques
The Forge, Neuaddlwyd. SA48 8DQ. Est. 1969. Usually open but prior telephone call advisable. SIZE: Medium. *STOCK: Furniture, 18th-20th C, £50-£3,000; smalls.* Not Stocked: Militaria, jewellery. LOC: A482. PARK: Easy. TEL: 01545 570536; home - same. VAT: Stan/Spec.

COLWYN BAY

North Wales Antiques - Colwyn Bay
58 Abergele Rd. LL29 7PP. (F. Robinson). Est 1971. Open 9-5. SIZE: Large warehouse. *STOCK: Shipping items, Victorian, early oak, mahogany and pine.* LOC: On A55. PARK: Easy. TEL: 01492 530521; evenings - 01352 720253. VAT: Stan.

CONWY

Conwy Antiques
17 Bangor Rd. LL32 8NG. (E. Calligan). Open 10-5. *STOCK: General antiques and collectables.* TEL: 01492 592461.

Paul Gibbs Antiques and Decorative Arts
25 Castle St. LL32 8AY. Open 10-5. *STOCK: Antiques and decorative arts, 1880-1940's; art pottery, especially major factories.* TEL: 0149[illegible] 593429.

Teapot Museum and Shop
25 Castle St. LL32 8AY. Open every day Easter to end Oct. *STOCK: Traditional and novelty teapots and tea-related items. Also permanent display of 1,000+ antique, rare and novelty teapots from 1730.* TEL: 01492 593429; fax - same.

COWBRIDGE

The Antiques Centre
Ebenezer Chapel, 48A Eastgate. SIZE: 10 stands and Sat. fleamarket. *STOCK: General antiques.* TEL: 01446 771100. SER: Valuations; restorations; buys at auction.

Cowbridge continued

Bulmer's

42 Eastgate. (Hugh and Louise Bulmer). Est. 1992. Open 10-1 and 2-5.30 (by appointment 1-2), Sat.10-5.30. CL: Mon. SIZE: Small. *STOCK: Furniture, 18th C, £1,000-£2,000; ceramics, 19th C, £50-£200.* PARK: Easy. TEL: 01446 775744; home - 01656 890721. SER: Valuations; buys at auction. VAT: Stan/Spec.

Cowbridge Antique Centre

75 Eastgate. (T.C. Monaghan). Est. 1974. Open 10-5.30. SIZE: Medium. *STOCK: Furniture, 18th-19th C, £50-£1,000+; ceramics, 18th-20th C, £10-£750; collectables, 19th-20th C, £10-£500.* PARK: Easy. TEL: 01446 775841; home - same. SER: Valuations; restorations; upholstery.

Eastgate Antiques

6 High St. (Liz Herbert). Est. 1984. Open 10-1 and 2-5.30. CL: Mon. SIZE: Medium. *STOCK: Furniture, silver, jewellery, oils and watercolours, 18th C to Edwardian.* LOC: Off A48. PARK: Nearby. TEL: 01446 775111; home - 01446 773505. SER: Buys at auction (furniture). VAT: Stan/Spec.

Havard and Havard LAPADA

9 Eastgate. CF71 7EL. (Philip and Christine Havard). Est. 1992. Open 10-1 and 2-5.30, Sat. 10-5.30. CL: Wed. and Mon. SIZE: Small. *STOCK: Oak, mahogany and walnut furniture especially provincial, £100-£5,000; metalware and samplers, £25-£1,000; all 18th-19th C.* LOC: Main street, 500 yards after lights on right. PARK: Easy. TEL: 01446 775021. SER: Valuations. FAIRS: Margam. VAT: Stan/Spec.

Renaissance Antiques

The Antiques Centre, Ebenezer Chapel, 48A Eastgate. (R.W. and J.A. Barnicott). Est. 1984. Open 10-5, Sun. 2-4. SIZE: Small. *STOCK: Small furniture, Georgian, Victorian and Edwardian, £100-£3,000; brass, copper, plate, decorative ceramics, Staffordshire figures, objets d'art, 18th to 20th C, £5-£500.* Not Stocked: Coins, militaria, reproductions. LOC: Main street. SER: Caning.

CRICKHOWELL

Gallop and Rivers Architectural Antiques

Ty'r Ash, Brecon Rd. NP8 1SF. (G. P. Gallop and A. Rivers). Open 9.30-5. *STOCK: Architectural items, pine and country furniture.* TEL: 01873 811084. VAT: Stan.

DEGANWY

Acorn Antiques

Castle Buildings. LL31 9EJ. (K.S. Bowers-Jones). Open 10-5. *STOCK: Ceramics, glass, furniture, pictures, brass and copper, 19th C.* TEL: 01492 584083.

FISHGUARD

Hermitage Antiquities

10 West St. SA65 9AE. (J.B. Thomas). Est. 1976. Open 10-12.30 and 2-5. CL: Wed. and Sat. pm. SIZE: Small. *STOCK: Arms, armour and militaria - full suits of armour, 16th-17th C; military long-guns, pistols, swords; cased pistol sets, military headgear, ethnographica, 16th-19th C, £50-£5,000; antiquities, jewellery, objets d'art.* LOC: 50yds. on right after leaving Square on Harbour road (West St.). PARK: 300yds. TEL: 01348 873037; home - 01348 872322. SER: Valuations; restorations (arms and armour, inlay work on wheel locks, flintlock parts re-built, woodwork repairs); buys at auction (arms and armour). VAT: Spec.

Manor House Antiques

Main St. SA65 9HG. (R.E. Davies). Open 9.15-5.30. *STOCK: General antiques especially porcelain and pottery.* TEL: 01348 873260.

GORSEINON, Nr. Swansea

Gold and Silver Shop

1 Cross St. SA1 1BA. (D. Paine). Open 10-1 and 2-4. *STOCK: Gold and silver, general antiques.* TEL: 01792 891874.

HAVERFORDWEST

Kent House Antiques

Kent House, Market St. SA61 1NF. (G. Fanstone and P. Thorpe). Est. 1987. Open 10-5, Sun. by appointment. SIZE: Medium. *STOCK: Victoriana, decorative items, hand-made rugs, £5-£500+.* LOC: Town centre. PARK: Easy. TEL: 01437 768175; home - same. SER: Valuations; restorations (furniture, some china); buys at auction (china and furniture).

Gerald Oliver Antiques

14 Albany Terrace, St. Thomas Green. SA61 1RH. Est. 1957. Open 9.30-1 and 2-5. CL: Thurs. pm. SIZE: Small. *STOCK: Furniture, pre-1890, £20-£6,000; ceramics, treen, metalwork, small silver, from £20; unusual, decorative and local interest items.* LOC: Via by-pass and up Merlins Hill to St. Thomas Green. PARK: Easy. TEL: 01437 762794. SER: Valuations. VAT: Spec.

Pine Corner Antiques

19 Bridgend Sq. SA61 2ND. (B. and J. Palmer). Open 10-5, Fri. 10-4, Sat. 10-2. *STOCK: Pine.* TEL: 01437 765676.

Prendergast Antiques

162-164 Prendergast. SA61 2PQ. Est. 1982. Open 10-5. CL: Thurs. SIZE: Medium. *STOCK: Furniture, pine, oak, mahogany; china and decorative items, £5-£1,000.* LOC: From Haverfordwest take A40 Fishguard Rd, turn on to B4329 Cardigan Rd, after Withybush roundabout premises 2 mins, next to Jensons. PARK: Easy. TEL: 01437 765695. SER: Valuations; restorations (furniture). FAIRS: Newark.

HAY-ON-WYE

Antique Market
6 Market St. HR3 5AD. Open 10-5, Sun. 11-5. SIZE: 17 dealers. *STOCK: General antiques and collectables.* LOC: By the Butter Market. TEL: 01497 820175.

Richard Booth's Bookshop Ltd
44 Lion St. and Hay Castle. HR3 5AA. Est. 1974. Open 7 days 9-5.30, later at weekends and during summer. SIZE: Very large. *STOCK: Books, magazines, photographs, records, postcards, leather bindings.* LOC: Town centre. TEL: 01497 820322; fax - 01497 821150; Hay Castle - 01497 820503; fax - 01497 821314.

Hebbards of Hay
7 Market St. HR3 5AF. (P.E. Hebbard). Est. 1958. Open 10-5. SIZE: Small. *STOCK: Pottery and porcelain.* LOC: A438, opposite the Post Office. PARK: Own. TEL: 01497 820413.

Tamara Le Bailly Antiques
5 Market St. HR3 5AF. Open 10-5.30, but appointment advisable. CL: Tues. SIZE: Shop + Trade barn. *STOCK: Decorative antiques, furniture, lighting.* PARK: Nearby. TEL: 01497 821157/820656; mobile - 0831 630883.

Lion Fine Arts
21 Lion St. HR3 5AD. (Charles and Sylvia Spencer). Est. 1986. Open May-Dec. 10-1 and 2-5, Tues, and Fri. 10-1; Jan.-April by appointment. SIZE: Small. *STOCK: Pottery, porcelain and glass, 18th to early 19th C, £50-£100; early oak, 17th-18th C, £500-£1,000; antiquarian books.* LOC: Turn right from Oxford Rd. car park, then second turning left. PARK: Limited. TEL: 01497 821726; home - same.

Mark Westwood Antiquarian Books
High Town. HR3 5AE. ABA. PBFA. Est. 1976. Open 10.30-5.30, including Sundays in summer. *STOCK: Antiquarian and secondhand books on most subjects, £2-£1,000.* TEL: 01497 820068. SER: Valuations; buys at auction (antiquarian books). VAT: Stan.

HENLLAN, Nr. Newcastle Emlyn

Michael Lloyd
Dolhaidd Mansion. SA44 5TG. Est. 1987. Open by appointment. SIZE: Large. *STOCK: Country furniture, pine, general antiques.* LOC: On A484, 2 miles Newcastle Emlyn. TEL: 01559 370582. VAT: Stan/Spec. *Trade Only.*

Tortoiseshell Antiques
Trebedw House. SA44 5TN. (Mrs P. Taylor). Est. 1972. Open by appointment only. SIZE: Small. *STOCK: Carved European ivories, £45-£4,000; jewellery and objects, £35-£1,000; textiles,*

Henllan continued

samplers, needlework tools, £40-£1,000; all 17th to early 19th C. LOC: Off Carmarthen/Cardigan Rd. PARK: Easy. TEL: 01559 370943; home - same. SER: Valuations; restorations (jewellery). FAIRS: Olympia, NEC, West London, Buxton, Kensington, Snape, Tatten Park, Bath, Wilton House and major provincial. VAT: Spec.

HOLT, Nr. Wrexham

Furn Davies Partnership
Rock Cottage, Bridge St. LL13 9JG. Open Thurs., Fri. and Sat. 10-5, other times by appointment. *STOCK: Furniture, 18th-19th C and decorative items.* TEL: 01829 270210. SER: Valuations; restorations.

KIDWELLY

Country Antiques (Wales) BADA LAPADA
Old Castle Mill. SA17 4UU. (R. and L. Bebb). Open 10-5. CL: Mon. SIZE: Large. *STOCK: Welsh furniture and folk art; Welsh clocks, pottery.* LOC: Leave bypass (A484), into centre of village, turn by Boot and Shoe public house. PARK: Easy. TEL: 01554 890534. SER: Valuations; lectures. VAT: Stan/Spec.

Kidwelly Antiques LAPADA
31 Bridge St. SA17 4UU. (R. and L. Bebb). Open 10-5. CL: Mon. SIZE: Large. *STOCK: Georgian and Victorian furniture and accessories; collectables.* LOC: Leave bypass (A484), into centre of village. PARK: Opposite shop. TEL: 01554 890328. VAT: Stan/Spec.

KNIGHTON

Offa's Dyke Antique Centre
4 High St. LD7 1AT. (Mrs. H. Hood and Watkins). Est. 1985. Open 10-1 and 2-5. SIZE: Medium - 16 dealers. *STOCK: Pottery, bijouterie, 18th-19th C furniture, £5-£1,000.* LOC: Near town clock. PARK: Easy. TEL: 01547 528635; evenings - 01547 528940/560272.

Islwyn Watkins
1 High St. LD7 1AT. Est. 1978. Open 10-1 and 2.30-5, prior telephone call advisable, Mon. and Wed. by appointment. SIZE: Small. *STOCK: Pottery including studio, 18th-20th C, £25-£350; country and domestic bygones, treen, 18th-20th C, £5-£100; small country furniture, 18th-19th C, £20-£400.* Not Stocked: Jewellery, silver, militaria. LOC: By town clock. PARK: Easy. TEL: 01547 520145; home - 01547 528940. SER: Valuations.

AMPETER

ʾarn Antiques

Market St. SA48 7DR. (N. Megicks). Est. 1980. ›pen 9-5.30, Wed. 9-1. SIZE: Medium. *STOCK: ʾine, oak, mahogany, mainly 19th C, £50-£1,000; ɛproduction pine and oak.* LOC: Pedestrianised ːreet just off town centre. PARK: Easy. TEL: 1570 423526. SER: Valuations; restorations (re-ɛneering, inlay work, French polishing, pine ːripping and finishing). VAT: Stan.

LANDEILO

ïm and Pat Ash

ne Warehouse, 5 Station Rd. SA19 6NG. Est. 977. Open 9.30-5. SIZE: Large. *STOCK: ïctorian and antique furniture, Welsh country, ık, pine, mahogany, walnut.* LOC: 50yds. off 40. PARK: Easy. TEL: 01558 823726. SER: aluations; shipping. VAT: Stan/Margin/Export.

ANDISSILIO, Nr. Clynderwen

eremiah Antiques

ne Old Saddlery. SA66 7TF. (S. and S. remiah). Est. 1980. Open Tues.-Sat. 9.30-5 or appointment. SIZE: Small. *STOCK: Mahogany rniture, 19th C, £50-£3,500.* LOC: Halfway

Llandissilio continued

through village on A478. PARK: Easy. TEL: 01437 563848; home - same. SER: Restorations (furniture, excluding pine); buys at auction.

LLANDUDNO

The Antique Shop

24 Vaughan St. LL30 1AH. (C.G. Lee). Est. 1938. Open 9-5.30. SIZE: Medium. *STOCK: Jewellery, silver, porcelain, glass, ivories, metal goods, from 1700; period furniture, shipping goods.* LOC: Near promenade. PARK: Easy. TEL: 01492 875575.

LLANDUDNO JUNCTION

Collinge Antiques

Old Fyffes Warehouse, Conwy Rd. LL31 9LU. (Nicky Collinge). Est. 1978. Open seven days. SIZE: Large. *STOCK: General antiques including Welsh dressers, dining, drawing and bedroom furniture, clocks, porcelain and pottery, silver, copper and brass, paintings, prints, glass and collectables, mainly Victorian and Edwardian.* LOC: Just off A55, Conwy exit. PARK: Easy. TEL: 01492 580022; fax - same. SER: Valuations; restorations including French polishing; buys at auction. VAT: Stan/Spec.

Llandudno Junction continued

The Country Seat
35 Conwy Rd. LL31 9LU. (Steve and Helen Roberts). Open 10-4.30, Mon 10-1, Tues. 12-4 or by appointment. CL: Wed. SIZE: Small. *STOCK: Old and interesting items including paintings, pottery and porcelain, jewellery, furniture, linen, ephemera and bric-a-brac; decorative arts, 19th-20th C.* LOC: Just off A55. PARK: Easy. TEL: 01492 573256.

LLANELLI

Alice's Antiques
24 Upper Park St. SA15 3YN. (Mrs A. Davies). Est. 1940 Open 10-1 and 2-6. CL: Tues. pm. SIZE: Small. *STOCK: General antiques, 1850-1950, £5-£50; paintings, silver, Georgian and Victorian, china, metalware.* LOC: On main road in town centre. PARK: At rear. TEL: 01554 773045. SER: Valuations; buys at auction. VAT: Stan.

John Carpenter
Resident. Est. 1973. Open by appointment. *STOCK: Musical instruments, furniture, general antiques.* LOC: 5 minutes from Cross Hands. TEL: 01269 831094.

LLANFAIR CAEREINION Nr. Welshpool

Heritage Restorations
Maes y Glydfa. SY21 0HD. (Jo and Fran Gluck). Est. 1970. Open 9-5. SIZE: Large. *STOCK: Pine and country furniture, £50-£2,000; some oak and architectural items, all 18th-19th C.* LOC: A458 from Welshpool. Past village, after 2 miles take first left after river bridge and caravan park, then follow signs. PARK: Easy. TEL: 01938 810384; home - same. SER: Restorations (furniture including pine stripping). VAT: Stan/Spec.

LLANGOLLEN

Deco on the Dee
Castle Courtyard, Castle St. (James and Claire Davies). Est. 1993. Open 12-5, Sat. 10-5 (prior telephone call advisable) and by appointment. SIZE: Small. *STOCK: Ceramics including Clarice Cliff, Charlotte Rhead, Susie Cooper, Shelley, Crown Devon, Carlton, Poole, Burleigh and Myott, and decorative items, 1920-1940, £25-£500.* LOC: Off main street, down alley to arcade behind Barclays Bank. PARK: Easy. TEL: 01978 860372; fax - same; home - 01978 810159. SER: Valuations; buys at auction. FAIRS: Chester, Loughborough, Stratford-upon-Avon, Coventry, Art Deco Fairs.

Llangollen continued

J. and R. Langford
12 Bridge St. LL20 8HA. (P. and M. Silverston) Est. 1960. CL: Thurs. pm. and 1-2 daily. SIZE: Medium. *STOCK: Furniture, £100-£7,000 pottery and porcelain, £50-£2,000; silver, general antiques, clocks, paintings, £20-£4,000; all 18th-20th C.* LOC: Turn right at Royal Hotel, shop on right. PARK: Easy. TEL: 01978 860182; home 01978 860493. SER: Valuations.

Passers Buy (Marie Evans)
Oak St/Chapel St. LL20 8NR. (Mrs M. Evans) Est. 1970. Open 11-5 - always on Tues., Fri. and Sat, often on Mon., Wed. and Thurs. - prior 'phone call advisable, Sun. by appointment. SIZE: Medium. *STOCK: Furniture, Staffordshire figures, Gaudy Welsh, fairings and general antiques.* LOC: Just off A5. Junction of Chapel St and Oak St. PARK: Easy. TEL: 01978 86086[illegible] 757385. FAIRS: Portmeirion (Autumn).

LLANRWST

Snowdonia Antiques
LL26 0EP. (J. Collins). Est. 1961. Open 9-5.30 Sun. by appointment. SIZE: Medium. *STOCK: Period furniture especially longcase clocks.* LOC: Turn off A5 just before Betws-y-Coed on to A49[illegible] for 4 miles. PARK: Easy. TEL: 01492 64078[illegible] SER: Restorations (furniture); repairs (grandfather clocks).

MATHRY

Cartrefle Antiques
SA62 5AD. (M. Hughes and Y. Chesters). Open in summer 10-5.30; in winter Wed.-Sat. 10.30- evenings by appointment. *STOCK: General antiques especially jewellery.* PARK: Easy. TEL: 01348 831591.

MILFORD HAVEN

Milford Haven Antiques
Robert St. SA73 2HS. Est. 1968. Open 10- *STOCK: General antiques.* TEL: 01646 692152.

MONMOUTH

Carol Freeman Antiques
The Gallery, Nailers Lane. NP5 3SE. Open 10- *STOCK: General antiques and secondhand items.* TEL: 01600 772252; home - 01600 712658.

MORRISTON, Nr. Swansea

Richard Davies Antiques
66 Martin St. SA6 7BJ. Est. 1971. Open 10 *STOCK: Furniture, longcase clocks, shipping goods.* TEL: 01792 773271. VAT: Stan.

MURTON, Nr. Swansea

West Wales Antiques LAPADA

18 Manselfield Rd. SA3 3AR. (W.H. Davies). Est. 1956. Open 10-1 and 2-5. *STOCK: Porcelain, 18th C, £20-£800; Welsh porcelain, 1814-1820, £20-£1,000; dolls, 1880-1920; 18th-19th C furniture, silver, pottery, glass, jewellery and collectors' items.* LOC: M4-A4067-B4436, entrance to Gower Peninsula. TEL: 01792 234318. VAT: Stan/Spec.

NARBERTH

Peter Thomas Antiques

32 High St. SA67 7AS. Est. 1987. Open 10-4.30, Sun., Mon. and Tues. by appointment. SIZE: Medium. *STOCK: Oak and fruitwood furniture, metalwork and paintings, 16th to late 18th C, £500-£15,000.* LOC: Town centre. PARK: Easy. TEL: 01834 860671; home - same. SER: Valuations; restorations; buys at auction. VAT: Spec.

NEWBRIDGE-ON-WYE Nr. Llandrindod Wells

Allam Antiques

Old Village Hall LD1 6HL. (Paul Allam). Est. 1985. Open 11-6, Sun. by appointment. SIZE: Medium. *STOCK: Furniture, 1700-1930, £50-£1,000; reproduction furniture, £50-£500; smalls, 19th-20th C, £1-£100.* LOC: A470. PARK: Easy. TEL: 01597 860654; home - 01597 860455. SER: Valuations; restorations; commission reproduction.

NEWCASTLE EMLYN

Castle Antiques

Market Sq. SA38 9AE. (Mr and Mrs B.G. ouser). Est. 1986. Open 9.30-5.30. SIZE: Small. *STOCK: Furniture, 1700 to 1920s, £500-£2,000; china and glass, 18th-19th C, £50-£200.* LOC: Town centre by clock tower. PARK: Castle St. TEL: 01239 710420; home - same.

Emlyn Antiques

Sycamore St. SA38 9AJ. (John and Norma irkby). Est. 1962. Open 10.30-5.30, Sun. by appointment. CL: Wed. SIZE: Medium. *STOCK: Mahogany furniture, 18th-19th C, £500-£1,000+; oils and watercolours, 19th C, £100-£500; mechanical music, 18th-20th C, £1,000-£5,000.* LOC: Main street. PARK: Nearby. TEL: 01239 [illegible]1235; home and fax - 01559 362758.

John Latter Antiques

Market Sq. SA38 9AQ. Est. 1959. Open 10-1 and 2-5, Sun. by appointment. SIZE: Small. *STOCK: Decorative furniture, 18th-20th C, £100-[illegible]00; fabrics, 19th-20th C, £100-£200; objets de vertu, 18th-20th C, £50-£100.* LOC: Town centre by clock tower. PARK: Easy. TEL: 01239 [illegible]1117; home - 01239 711500. SER: Valuations.

Newcastle Emlyn continued

Water Street Antiques

London Stores, Water St. SA38 9BH. (M. Bain). Est. 1981. Open 10-5. CL: Wed. SIZE: Medium. *STOCK: Mahogany, rosewood, walnut and satinwood furniture, 17th-19th C, £500-£10,000; decorative items and prints, 19th C, £100-£500.* LOC: M4 junction 49, A48 to Carmarthen, then A484. PARK: Rear of shop and 100 yards. TEL: 01239 711453. SER: Restorations (furniture). FAIRS: NEC. VAT: Spec.

PEMBROKE

Pembroke Antiques Centre

Wesleyan Chapel, Main St. Open 10-5. SIZE: Large. *STOCK: Pine, oak, mahogany and shipping furniture; china, rugs, paintings.* TEL: 01646 687017.

PONTARDDULAIS, Nr. Swansea

The Emporium

112 St Teilo St. SA4 1SS. (Laura Jeremy). Est. 1992. Open 10.30-6. SIZE: Medium. *STOCK: Furniture, 1900-1950, £5-£500; Victorian metalware, collectables, bric-a-brac.* LOC: Off M4, junction 48. PARK: Easy. TEL: 01792 885185. SER: Restorations. FAIRS: Local.

PONTERWYD, Nr. Aberystwyth

Doggie Hubbard's Bookshop

Ffynnon Cadno. (C.L.B. Hubbard). ABA. Est. 1946. Open 10-5, Sun. by appointment. SIZE: Medium. *STOCK: Rare books on dogs, 16th-19th C, £50-£500; scarce books on dogs, 19th-20th C, £25-£100; other books on dogs, 20th C, £5-£25.* LOC: 1/2 mile from Ponterwyd westwards on A44. PARK: Easy. TEL: 01970 890224; home - same. SER: Valuations; buys at auction (rare dog books).

PORTHCAWL

Harlequin Antiques

Dock St. CF36 3BL. (Ann and John Ball). Est. 1974. Open 9-5. *STOCK: General antiques; textiles; early 19th to 20th C books.* TEL: 01656 785910.

Number Eight

Dock St. CF36 3BL. (Ann Ball). Open 10-5. *STOCK: Decorative arts, antiques, textiles.* TEL: 01656 786033.

PWLLHELI

Rodney Adams Antiques

Hall Place, 10 Penlan St. LL53 5DH. Resident. Est. 1965. CL: Sun. except by appointment. *STOCK: Longcase clocks and period furniture.* TEL: 01758 613173; evenings - 01758 614337. VAT: Stan/Spec.

Pwllheli continued

Penlan Pine
7 Penlan St. *STOCK: Period pine and furnishings.* TEL: Mobile - 0370 592603.

RHOSNEIGR

Fan-Fayre Antiques
High St. LL64 5UQ. (S. Richards). Resident. Est. 1976. Open summer only, by appointment. SIZE: Small. *STOCK: Jewellery, porcelain, silver, collectable items, 19th C, £25-£500.* LOC: 5 miles off A5 from the Holyhead Rd., on Anglesey Island. PARK: Easy. TEL: 01407 810580 (anwerphone). SER: Valuations. FAIRS: St. Martins, Birmingham; Newark and Nottinghamshire Showground.

RHUALLT, Nr. St. Asaph

Barbara Trefor Antiques
Rhuallt Hall. LL17 0TR. Est. 1967. Open by appointment any time. SIZE: Medium. *STOCK: General antiques and country furniture, £5-£5,000.* Not Stocked: Jewellery, cards and medals. LOC: On A55 take Rhuallt turning, B5429, grey stone farmhouse at end of village, close to Smithy Arms. PARK: Easy. TEL: 01745 583604.

RUTHIN

R. and S. M. Percival Antiques
Porth-y-Dwr, 65 Clwyd St. LL15 1HN. Est. 1979 Open daily, Sun. and Mon. by appointment. SIZE Medium. *STOCK: Pine, mahogany and oa furniture and decorative smalls, 18th-19th C £100-£1,000+.* PARK: Behind shop. TEL: 0182 704454; home - 01978 790370. SER: Valuations buys at auction (furniture). FAIRS: Newark.

SARNAU

Ffynnon Las
SA44 6QT. (P. and G. Palmer). Est. 1971. Open a any time. SIZE: Small. *STOCK: Decorate furniture in American and European styles, 19t to early 20th C; stripped pine.* LOC: Off A487 miles north of Cardigan, down track. PARK Easy. TEL: 01239 654648; home - same.

SWANSEA

James Allan
22 Park St. SA1 3DJ. (S.J. Allan). Est. 1929. Ope 9.30-4.30. SIZE: Small. *STOCK: Jewellery, 1850 date, £50-£5,000.* LOC: Off Kingsway, roun corner from Mothercare. PARK: Nearby. TEI 01792 652176. SER: Valuations. VAT: Stan.

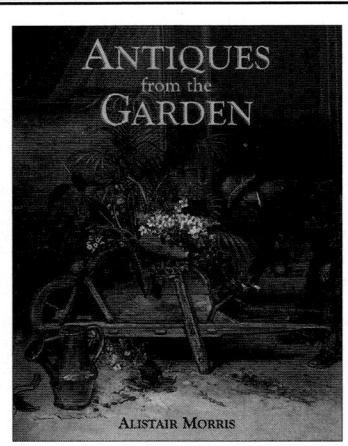

Swansea continued

The Antique Emporium
76 St. Helens Rd. SA1 4BG. Est. 1977. Open 10-2 and 3-5. SIZE: 7 dealers. *STOCK: Wide range of general antiques.* TEL: 01792 654697.

Bygone Antiques
37-39 St. Helens Rd. (C.A. Oliver). Open 9.30-5. *STOCK: China, furniture, linen and collectors' items.* TEL: 01792 468248.

Keith Chugg Antiques
Gwydr Lane, Uplands. Open 9-5.30, Sat. 9-1. *STOCK: Pianos and general antiques including furniture.* TEL: 01792 472477.

Clydach Antiques
33 High St., Clydach. SA6 5LJ. (R.T. Pulman). Open 10-5, Sat. 10-1. *STOCK: General antiques.* TEL: 01792 843209.

Philip Davies Fine Art LAPADA
130 Overland Rd., Mumbles. SA3 4EU. Open 10-5 (prior telephone call advisable). *STOCK: British oils, watercolours and prints, 1850-1950, £25-£10,000.* TEL: 01792 361766; fax - same. SER: Valuations; restorations (paintings and frames); commission sales.

Dylan's Bookshop
Salubrious Passage. SA1 3RT. (J.M. Towns). Open 10-5. *STOCK: Antiquarian books on Welsh history and topography, Anglo/Welsh literature and general books.* TEL: 01792 655255; fax - same.

Eynon Hughes Antiques
Henrietta St. (rear of 21 Walters Rd.) (E. and M. Hughes). Est. 1984. Open 10.30-5.30. *STOCK: Longcase clocks, £500-£3,000; furniture, 18th-20th C, £50-£1,500; china and collectables, £5-£500.* PARK: Easy. TEL: 01792 651446; home - 01994 427253.

Anne and Colin Hulbert (Antiques and Firearms)
17 Approach Rd., Manselton. SA5 8PD. Est. 1962. CL: Sun. pm. SIZE: Small. *STOCK: Shipping goods and general antiques.* PARK: Easy. TEL: 01792 653818; home - same. SER: Valuations; buys at auction (furniture). *Trade Only.*

Magpie Antiques
57 St. Helens Rd. SA1 4BH. (H. Hallesy). Est. 1984. Usually open 10-5. CL: Thurs. *STOCK: Ceramics including Swansea, Llanelly and other Welsh potteries; oak and country furniture.* PARK: Opposite. TEL: 01792 648722. SER: Valuations; restorations (furniture).

Kim Scurlock
5 Russell St. SA1 4HR. (B.D. and E.A. Leigh). Est. 1982. Open 9.30-5, Sat. 9.30-1. SIZE: Medium. *STOCK: Victorian pine and country furniture, £25-£1,000; general antiques, china, glass and collectables; reproduction pine.* LOC: Between Walters Rd. and St. Helens Rd. PARK: Easy. TEL: 01792 643085. SER: Restorations. VAT: Stan.

Swansea Antique Centre
21 Oxford St. SA1 3AQ. Open 10-5 although dealers' times vary. TEL: 01792 466854. Below are listed some of the dealers at this centre.

Aladdin's Cave
General antiques. TEL: 01792 459576.

Bric-a-Brac Antiques

City Antiques
Jewellery. SER: Repairs.

Mair's Antiques
Jewellery, glass, china, brass, gold and silver.

Number Ten
Toys.

Past Times
(G. Williams). *Porcelain, Doulton, militaria and postcards.*

Purdy and Lloyd Antiques
Porcelain, pottery, glass, collectables and bric-a-brac. TEL: 01792 648883; home - 01792 799906.

Allan Treharne
Jewellery. SER: Repairs.

Winkies
Pre-1950's clothes.

Thicke Galleries LAPADA
(T.G. Thicke). Est. 1981. Open by appointment only. SIZE: Medium. *STOCK: Oils and watercolours, 19th C to early 20th C, to £8,000.* LOC: Coast road to West Swansea. PARK: Easy. TEL: 01792 207515. SER: Valuations; restorations (oils and watercolours). FAIRS: Robert Soper exhibitions; Alan Lewis; Towy; Cardiff Fine Art; Craig-y-nos. VAT: Spec.

SYNOD INN, Nr. Llandysul

Norman Williams
Trewyddel Forge, Gwenlli. SA44 6JJ. Open 10-4 (longer in summer), by appointment almost any time. SIZE: Medium. *STOCK: General antiques, furniture and decorative items, some Welsh quilts and blankets, 19th-20th C.* LOC: Between Aberaeron and Cardigan on the A487. PARK: Easy. TEL: 01545 580707; home - 01239 810330.

TEMPLETON, Nr. Narberth

Barn Court Antiques

Barn Court. SA67 7AR. (D., A. and M. Evans). Est. 1989. Open 10-7, including Sun. SIZE: Medium. *STOCK: Mahogany, walnut, rosewood and oak furniture, Georgian to late Victorian, £100-£3,000; oils and watercolours, £100-£2,000; china and glass, mainly Victorian, £10-£500.* LOC: Off A40 on A478 Narberth to Tenby road. PARK: Easy. TEL: 01834 861224.

TENBY

Audrey Bull

15 Upper Frog St. SA70 7DJ. Open 9.30-5. *STOCK: Period and Welsh country furniture, general antiques, especially jewellery and silver.* TEL: 01834 843114; workshop - 01834 871873; home - 01834 813425. VAT: Spec.

Clareston Antiques

Warren St. SA70 7JS. (K. and Mrs M.J.A. Hunt). Est. 1964. Open 10-5 or by appointment. CL: Wed. SIZE: Small. *STOCK: Georgian and Victorian furniture; English and Welsh porcelain and pottery; silver and models.* LOC: Town centre, near police station. PARK: Easy. TEL: 01834 843350; home - same. SER: Valuations.

TINTERN

Tintern Antiques

The Old Bakehouse. NP6 6SE. (Dawn Floyd). Open 9.30-5.30. *STOCK: Antique jewellery and general antiques.* TEL: 01291 689705.

TREHERBERT

All Old Exports Ltd.

The Warehouse, Abertonllwyd St. CF42 6AH. (S.D. Evans). Est. 1981. Open by appointment. SIZE: Warehouse. *STOCK: Large furniture - Victorian mahogany, Edwardian inlaid, American shipping, £5-£5,000.* LOC: Junction 34, M4, then A4119. PARK: Own. TEL: 01443 776410/777045; mobile - 0385 308567. SER: Valuations; restorations; North American specialists; container packing and shipping. VAT: Stan.

TREORCHY

Steven Evans Antiques

Regent St. CF42 6PR. Open 9-5, Sun. by appointment. SIZE: Warehouse. *STOCK: Victorian mahogany, Edwardian inlaid, American shipping, £5-£5,000.* LOC: Junction 34, M4, then A4119. PARK: Own. TEL: 01443 776410/777045/431756; mobile - 0385 308567. SER: Valuations; restorations; North American specialists; container packing and shipping. VAT: Stan.

TREVOR, Nr. Llangollen

Romantiques

Bryn Seion Chapel, Station Rd. LL20 7TP . (Miss S.E. Atkin). Est. 1994. Open 10-4 including Sun. SIZE: Large. *STOCK: Furniture, £100-£3,500, smalls, £1-£1,000.* LOC: Off A5 and A539 Llangollen road. PARK: Easy. TEL: Mobile - 0378 279614; home - 01978 752140. SER: Valuations; restorations (furniture, upholstery, clocks); buys at auction.

TYWYN

Welsh Art

(Miles Wynn Cato). Open by appointment only (also in London). *STOCK: Welsh paintings, 1550-1950; Welsh portraits of all periods and historical Welsh material.* TEL: 0171 259 0306 and 01654 711715.

USK

Castle Antiques

41 Old Market St. NP5 1AL. (S. Lockyer). Open 12-5 or by appointment. *STOCK: General antiques especially English and Welsh pottery, porcelain, blue and white transfer ware.* TEL: 01291 672424; home - 01495 785286.

WELSHPOOL

F.E. Anderson and Son LAPADA

5-6 High St. SY21 7JF. (D. and I. Anderson). Open daily. *STOCK: Furniture, 17th-18th C, English and Chinese ceramics, glass, silver, paintings, early metalware.* TEL: 01938 553340; home - 01938 590509/553324.

WREXHAM

Granny Midge's Emporium

Watery Rd. LL13 7NW. (Midge, Richard and Heugo Heard). Est. 1979. Open 10-5.30, Sun. by appointment. SIZE: Large. *STOCK: Pine painted, unpainted and stripped, to 1890's, £100-£2,000; decorative, garden, architectural and country items.* LOC: 5 minutes off Wrexham bypass, leave at Ruthin turning. PARK: Own. TEL: 01978 365463. SER: Valuations; restorations (pine stripping, finishing and small repairs); buys at auction (as stock). FAIRS: Decorative and Textile, King's College, Chelsea; Chester Racecourse. VAT: Stan/Spec.

Index of Packers and Shippers: Exporters of Antiques (Containers)

LONDON

Anglo Pacific International plc LAPADA
Bush Industrial Estate, Standard Rd., NW10 6DF. Tel: 0181 965 0667; fax - 0181 965 4954. ***Specialist antique and fine art packers serving worldwide destinations by land, sea or air. Free estimates and advice.***

AR. GS International Transport Ltd
North London Freight Centre, York Way, Kings Cross, N1 0BB. Tel: 0171 833 3955; fax - 0171 837 8672. *Fine art and antiques removals by road transport, Europe especially Italy, door-to-door service. Documentation.*

B B F Fine Art Services Ltd
Copenhagen House, Copenhagen Place, E14 7DE. Tel: 0171 515 7005; fax - 0171 515 6001. *Fine art packers, worldwide shippers by sea, air and road.*

Robert Boys Shipping
175D Bermondsey St., Newhams Row, SE1 3UW. Tel: 0171 357 7168; fax - 0171 357 7179. *Worldwide shipping. Air and sea cargo. Specialists in fine art and furniture to Japan and part load containers to Japan (all ports) on a weekly basis. Japanese speaking staff.*

Bullens Ltd.
East Wing, The Granary, York Way. N1 0PF. Tel: 0181 347 9135. *Specialist comprehensive removal service.*

London continued

Davies Turner Worldwide Movers Ltd.
London Headquarters : 49 Wates Way, Mitcham, CR4 4HR. Tel: 0171 622 4393; fax - 0171 720 3897; telex - 8956479. *Fine art and antiques packers and shippers. Courier and finder service. Full container L.C.L. and groupage service worldwide.*

Featherstons
7 Ingate Place, SW8 3NS. Tel: 0171 720 0422; fax - 0171 720 6330. *Antiques and fine art packed and shipped or airfreighted worldwide. Security storage.*

Gander and White Shipping Ltd.
LAPADA
Head Office, 21 Lillie Rd., SW6 1UE. Tel: 0171 381 0571; fax - 0171 381 5428. ***Specialist packers and shippers of antiques and works of art.***

Gander and White Shipping Ltd.
LAPADA
14 Mason's Yard, Duke St., St. James's, SW1Y 6BU. Tel: 0171 930 5383; fax - 0171 930 4145; cables - Gandite.

London continued

Hedleys Humpers Ltd LAPADA
Units 3 and 4, 97 Victoria Rd., North Acton, NW10 6ND. Tel: 0181 965 8733 (10 lines); fax - 0181 965 0249. ***Weekly door to door services to Europe, plus part load shipments by air and sea worldwide. Offices in London, Paris and New York.***

Interdean Ltd.
3/5 Cumberland Ave., NW10 7RU. Tel: 0181 961 4141; telex - 922119; fax - 0181 965 4484. *Antiques and fine art packed, shipped and airfreighted worldwide. Storage and international removals. Full container L.C.L. and groupage service worldwide.*

Interpack Worldwide plc
3 Standard Road, North Acton. NW10 6EX. Tel: 0181 965 5550; fax - 0181 453 0544. *Worldwide shipping, packing, insurance.*

Kuwahara Ltd. LAPADA
6 McNicol Drive, NW10 7AW. Tel: 0181 963 1100; fax - 0181 963 0100. ***Specialist packers and shippers of antiques and works of art. Regular groupage service to Japan.***

London continued

Lockson Services Ltd LAPADA
29 Broomfield St., Limehouse, E14 6BX. Tel: 0171 515 8600 (6 lines); fax - 0171 515 4043; mobile (weekends) - 0831 621428. ***Specialist packers and shippers of fine art and antiques by air, sea and road to the USA, Japan, Thailand, Far East, Canada and many more worldwide destinations. A complete personalised service. At all Olympia, Newark and Ardingly fairs.***

Masterpack Ltd - Fine Art Packers & Shippers
Nationwide Building, Stanley Gardens, The Vale, W3 7SZ. Tel: 0171 262 8274; fax - 0171 262 5334. *Fine art packers and shippers. Personal service guaranteed.*

Momart plc
199-205 Richmond Rd., E8 3NJ. Tel: 0181 986 3624; fax - 0181 533 0122. *Fine art handling including transportation, case making and packing: import/export services, exhibition installation and storage.*

'Old King Cole' tile panel by William Rowe from the Seymour Ward at St. Thomas's Hospital. It cost the hospital £8,000 to buy back.

From an article entitled "Doulton Lambeth Wares" by Mark Oliver of Phillips which appeared in the June 1997 issue of **Antique Collecting.**

London continued

Stephen Morris Shipping plc
Barpart House, Kings Cross Freight Depot, York Way, N1 0UZ. Tel: 0171 713 0080; fax - 0171 713 0151. *Specialist packers and shippers of antiques and fine art worldwide. Weekly European service.*

Nelson Shipping
Unit C3, Six Bridges Trading Estate, Marlborough Grove, SE1 5JT. Tel: 0171 394 7770; fax - 0171 394 7707. *Expert export and packing service.*

London continued

Nippon Express (UK) Ltd
Unit A, Six Bridges Trading Estate, Marlborough Grove, SE1 5JT. Tel: 0171 237 8293; fax - 0171 231 4463. *Mainly Japanese imports/exports, both commercial and removals. Also import/export all other Far East countries.*

The Packing Shop
Plaza G13, 535 Kings Rd., SW10 0SZ. Tel: 0171 352 2021; fax - 0171 351 7576. *Fine art and general antiques shipped worldwide, especially United States and Europe.*

The Packing Shop
Unit L, London Stone Business Estate, Broughton St., SW8 3QR. Tel: 0171 498 3255. *Specialised service to overseas antique fairs and exhibitions. USA, Australasia and Europe regularly serviced.*

Pitt and Scott Ltd
Regeneration House, York Way, N1 0PT. Tel: 0171 278 5585; fax - 0171 278 5592. *Packers and shippers of antiques and fine art. Shipping, forwarding and airfreight agents. Comprehensive service provided for visiting antique dealers. Insurance arranged.*

L.J. Roberton Ltd LAPADA
Marlborough House, Cooks Rd., Stratford, E15 2PW. Tel: 0181 519 2020; fax - 0181 519 8571.

London continued

Robinsons International LAPADA
The Gateway, Staples Corner. NW2 7AJ Tel: 0181 208 8484; fax - 0181 208 8488. ***Specialist packers and shippers of antiques and fine art worldwide. Established over 100 years.***

T. Rogers and Co. Ltd
PO Box No. 8, 1A Broughton St., SW8 3QJ. Tel: 0171 622 9151; fax - 0171 627 3318. *Specialists in storage, packing, removal, shipping and forwarding antiques and works of art. Insurance.*

London continued

Trans-Euro Fine Art Division LAPADA
Drury Way, Brent Park, NW10 0JN. Tel: 0181 784 0100; fax - 0181 459 3376. ***Specialist packing and worldwide shipping services by air, sea and road. Single items, part loads or full containers. Courier and buyer services.***

Charles Walter Simpson (1885-1971), 'Skinning Fish, St Ives'. Signed. Canvas, 23½in. x 29½in.

From an article entitled "His School and his Gospel - Collecting Artists of the Herkomer Art School" by Laura Wortley which appeared in the June 1997 issue of **Antique Collecting.**

London continued

Wingate and Johnston Ltd LAPADA
134 Queens Road, Peckham, SE15 2HR. Tel: 0171 732 8123; fax - 0171 732 2631. ***Specialists in the international movement of antiques and fine art for over a hundred and fifty years - services incorporate all requirements from case making to documentation and insurance. Freight groupage specialists.***

BUCKINGHAMSHIRE

Paget Shipping Ltd
Spaceregal Centre, Coln Industrial Estate, Old Bath Rd., Colnbrook, SL3 0NJ. Tel: 01753 682426; fax - 01753 686367. *Packing and shipping of antiques and works of art worldwide especially South America and Bermuda.*

CHESHIRE

The Rocking Chair Antiques
Unit 3, St. Peters Way, Warrington, WA27 7BL. Tel: 01925 652409; fax - same. *Exporters and packers.*

DEVON

Bishop's Blatchpack
Kestrel Way, Sowton Industrial Estate, Exeter EX2 7PA. Tel: 01392 420404; fax - 01392 423851 *International fine art packers and shippers.*

DORSET

Alan Franklin Transport LAPADA
26 Blackmoor Rd., Ebblake Industrial Estate Verwood, BH31 6BB. Tel: 01202 826539; fax 01202 827337. ***Container packing and shipping Weekly door to door European service. Paris Office - 2 Rue Etienne Dolet, 93400 St. Ouen Paris. Tel: 00 33140 115000; fax - 00 33140 114821. Belgian office - De Klerckstraat 41 B8300, Knokke. Tel: 00 3250 623579; fax - same.***

ESSEX

Geo. Copsey and Co. Ltd
Danes Rd., Romford. Tel: 01708 740714 or 018 592 1003. *Worldwide packers and shippers.*

Crown Worldwide Movers
Security House, Abbey Wharf Industrial Estate Kingsbridge Rd., Barking, IG11 0BD. Tel: 018 591 3388; fax - 0181 594 4571. *Packers an shippers - 12 offices throughout U.K.*

:ssex continued

›panpak Export Services
nternational House, Horsecroft Rd., The ›innacles, Harlow CM19 5SX. Tel: 01279 ‹56645; 01279 427473. *Antiques and fine art :xport, packers and shippers worldwide. Fully omprehensive service with all types of packing :nd casing undertaken by our experienced team. ;hipments to all destinations by sea, land and air. ;pecialised Spanish service.*

;LOUCESTERSHIRE

The Removal Company - Loveday & .oveday
: Wilkinson Rd., Cirencester, GL7 1YT. Tel: 1285 651505. *Shipping and packing.*

\.J. Williams (Shipping) LAPADA
07 Sixth Ave., Central Business Park, Iengrove, Bristol, BS14 9BZ. Tel: 01275 92166; fax - 01275 891333.

IAMPSHIRE

:antay International LAPADA
'elford Rd., Basingstoke, RG21 6YU. Tel: 1256 465533; fax - 01256 858930. ***Specialist***

Hampshire continued

packers and shippers of antiques and fine art worldwide. A member of the Robinsons Group.

Robinsons International LAPADA
Guildford St., Southampton, SO14 5AS Tel: 01703 220069; fax - 01703 331274. ***Specialist packers and shippers of antiques and fine art worldwide. Established over 100 years.***

KENT

Sutton Valence Antiques LAPADA
Unit 4, Haslemere Parkwood Estate, Sutton Rd., Maidstone, ME15 9NL. Tel: 01622 675332; fax - 01622 692593. ***Antique and shipping furniture. Container packing and shipping. Facilities for 20ft and 40ft containers, all documentation. Worldwide service.***

LANCASHIRE

A.M. Blackburn
14 Rainhall Crescent, Barnoldswick. Tel: 01282 815419. *Export, packers, shippers, courier service.*

Alan Butterworth (Horwich)
7 Ardley Rd., Horwich, Bolton, BL6 7EG. Tel: 01204 468094. *Dealers, export packers and shippers; courier service - UK and Continent.*

Lancashire continued

Robinsons International LAPADA
Whitefield, Manchester, M45 8FH. Tel: 0161 766 8414; fax - 0161 767 9057. ***Specialist packers and shippers of antiques and fine art worldwide. Established over 100 years.***

Anthony Walmsley Antiques
93 Montague St., Blackburn, BB2 1EH. Tel: 01254 698755.

LEICESTERSHIRE

Richard Kimbell Ltd
The Old Bus Station, Harborough Road, Desborough. NN14 2QX. Tel: 01536 762093; fax - 01536 763263. *Container packers and shippers. Speedy despatch - competitive rates.*

MERSEYSIDE

John Mason International Ltd LAPADA
35 Wilson Rd., Huyton, Liverpool, L36 6AE. Tel: 0151 449 3938. ***Specialist packer, full and part container loads, groupage service worldwide, courier and finder service.***

MIDDLESEX

Air-Sea Packing Group Ltd
Air-Sea House, Third Cross Rd., Twickenham, TW2 5EB. Tel: 0181 893 3303; fax - 0181 893 3068. *Specialist packers and shippers.*

Ferrari International Freight Forwarding
Unit 3 Blackburn Trading Estate, Northumberland Close, Stanwell, TW19 7LN. Tel: 01784 258664; fax - 01784 248457. *Specialised importers and exporters of valuable cargo.*

Sovereign International Freight Ltd
Sovereign House, 8-10 St. Dunstans Rd., Feltham, TW13 4JU. Tel: 0181 751 3131; fax - 0181 751 4517. *Heathrow Airport based shippers and packers registered to BS 5750 quality. Holders of the Queen's Award for Export and National Training Award. Specialist in antiques and the fine art trades.*

Vulcan International Services Ltd
LAPADA

Units 13/14, Ascot Rd., Clockhouse Lane, Feltham, TW14 8QF. Tel: 01784 244152; 01784 248183. ***Fine art packers and shippers worldwide.***

OXFORDSHIRE

Cantay International LAPADA
Nuffield Way, Abingdon, OX14 1TN. Tel: 01235 552255; fax - 01235 553573. ***Specialist packers and shippers of antiques and fine art worldwide. A member of the Robinsons Group.***

Cotswold Carriers
Unit 9, Worcester Rd. Industrial Estate, Chipping Norton, OX7 5XW. Tel: 01608 642856; fax 01608 642856. *Removals, storage, shipping door-to-door Continental deliveries.*

Robinsons International LAPADA
Nuffield Way, Abingdon, OX14 1TN. Tel: 01235 552255; fax - 01235 553573. ***Specialist packers and shippers of antiques and fine art worldwide. Established over 100 years.***

SOMERSET

Robinsons International LAPADA
Ashmead Rd., Keynsham, BS18 1SX. Tel: 011 986 6266; fax - 0117 986 2723. ***Specialist packers and shippers of antiques and fine art worldwide. Established over 100 years.***

SURREY

W. Ede & Co
The Edes Business Park, Restmor Way, Wallington, SM2 5AA. Tel: 0181 773 9388/993; fax - 0181 773 9011. *Worldwide packing and shipping, complete documentation and removal service, container packing.*

J.B. International Ltd LAPADA
06 Beta Way, Thorpe Industrial Park, Crabtree Road, Egham, TW20 8RE. Tel: 0178 470000; fax - 01784 436252. ***Fine art packing, freight forwarding. USA - 21-41 45th Road, Long Island City, New York 11101. Tel: (718) 392 9770; fax - (718) 392 2470.***

SUSSEX EAST

Furniture Finders Ltd
Module A1 West, Enterprise point, Melbourne St., Brighton, BN2 3LH. Tel: 01273 705004; fax 01273 705005. *Export packers and shippers, in house couriers.*

Global Services
West St., Lewes, BN7 2NJ. Tel: 01273 47590 *Packers and shippers of antiques, arms, armour and fine works of art.*

SUSSEX WEST

Gander and White Shipping Ltd

LAPADA

Newpound, Wisborough Green, Billingshurst, RH14 0AY. Tel: 01403 700044; fax - 01403 700814. ***Specialist packers and shippers of fine art and antiques.***

Martells International

32 London Rd., East Grinstead, RH19 4DW. Tel: 01342 321303; fax - 01342 317522. *International removers, export packers and shippers.*

TYNE AND WEAR

Owen Humble (Packing and Shipping) Ltd

Clayton House, Walbottle Rd., Lemington, Newcastle-upon-Tyne, NE15 9RU. Tel: 0191 267 7220. *Worldwide service.*

WARWICKSHIRE

Crown Worldwide

Unit 9 Ratcliffe Road Industrial Estate, Ratcliffe Rd., Atherstone, CV9 1JA. Tel: 01827 714631.

WEST MIDLANDS

Thomas Blakemore Ltd - Shipping U.S.A.

Atlas Works, Sandwell Street, Walsall, WS1 3DR. Tel: 01922 25951/613230; fax - 01922 611330; telex - 338212 G Chacom Blkmr. (USA - 910 882 5343/910 889 5158; fax - 910 889 3226) *Weekly container from Birmingham to High Point, North Carolina, USA. Pick-up and pack, no minimums.*

Robinsons International LAPADA

585 Moseley Rd., Birmingham, B12 9BJ. Tel: 0121 449 4731; fax - 0121 449 9942. ***Specialist packers and shippers of antiques and fine art worldwide. Established over 100 years.***

WORCESTERSHIRE

Simon Hall Freight

Units 5 and 6, Willersey Industrial Estate, Willersey, Nr. Broadway, WR12 7PR. Tel: 01386 858555; fax - 01386 858501. *Specialist packers and shippers for fine art and antiques world wide. UK collections and deliveries. Humidity controlled containerised and conventional storage.*

YORKSHIRE EAST

Peter Smith t/a Boothferry Antiques

188 Wincolmlee, Hull, HU2 0QL. Tel: 01482 225220/666033. *Single items or container loads. Couriers covering north of England. Full documentation.*

SCOTLAND

Crown Worldwide

Containerbase, Gartsherrie Rd., Coatbridge, Lanarkshire. ML5 2EL. Tel: 01236 449666; fax - 01236 449888. *Packers and shippers.*

Kuwahara Ltd LAPADA

33 Royal Park Terrace, Edinburgh, EH8 8JA. Tel: 0131 652 2131; fax - same. ***Specialist packers and shippers of antiques and works of art. Regular groupage service to Japan.***

WALES

Kuwahara Ltd LAPADA

54 Cathedral Rd., Cardiff, CF1 9LL. Tel: 01222 224537; fax - 01222 229747. ***Specialist packers and shippers of antiques and works of art. Regular groupage service to Japan.***

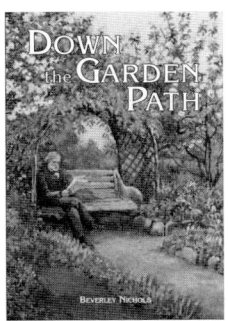

Index of Auctioneers

LONDON

Academy Auctioneers and Valuers
Northcote House, Northcote Avenue, Ealing, W5 3UR. Tel: 0181 579 7466. *Monthly sales of antiques, collectables, works of art, furniture, paintings, ceramics, jewellery and silver. Regular general sales. Open 9-5. Valuations.*

Bloomsbury Book Auctions
3 and 4 Hardwick St., EC1R 4RY. Tel: 0171 833 2636/7 and 0171 636 1945. *Twenty-four sales per year of books, manuscripts and maps and especially disposal of academic libraries. Occasional sales of prints, posters and drawings. Sellers commission 15 % (trade 12.5%); buyers premium 15%.*

Bonhams Chelsea
65-69 Lots Rd., Chelsea, SW10 0RN. Tel: 0171 393 3900; fax - 0171 393 3906. *Regular sales of British, European and Russian Pictures including watercolours, oils, prints and frames; silver & objects of vertu; jewellery & clocks; ceramics including Art Nouveau & Art Deco; furniture, carpets & objects of art; architectural including light fittings, fireplaces and garden statuary; collectors items such as toys, dolls & teddies, textiles, cameras & scientific instruments, rock & pop, rare records & entertainment sales. Viewing Mon.-Fri. 9-4.30, Sun. 11-4.*

Bonhams Knightsbridge
Montpelier St., Knightsbridge, SW7 1HH. Tel: 0171 393 3900; fax - 0171 393 3905. *Regular auctions of watercolours, Old Masters, European and modern pictures, portrait miniatures, prints, carved frames, furniture, clocks and watches, Lalique, commercial scent bottles, Oriental, European and contemporary ceramics, Art Deco, Art Nouveau, objects of art, tribal art and antiquities, silver, jewellery, objects of vertu, books and manuscripts, antique and modern guns, musical instruments, Oriental carpets and rugs. Annual theme sales to coincide with Cowes Week, The Boat Show and Crufts - pictures, sculptures and related works of art. Viewing Mon.-Fri. 9-4.30, Sun. 11-4.*

Christie's
8 King St., St.James's, SW1Y 6QT. Tel: 0171 839 9060; fax - 0171 839 1611. *Porcelain, pottery, objets d'art and miniatures, pictures including Old Masters, English, Victorian, Continental,*

London continued

Impressionist, Contemporary, prints, drawings watercolours, Art Deco, Art Nouveau; Japanes and Chinese, Islamic and Persian works of art glass, silver, jewellery, books, modern guns furniture, carpets, tapestries, clocks and watches garden statuary, photographs, Russian works o art, sculpture, wine, house sales (contents only).

Christie's South Kensington Ltd
85 Old Brompton Rd., SW7 3LD. Tel: 0171 58 7611; fax - 0171 321 3321; telex - 922061. *Sale of jewellery, silver, pictures, watercolours drawings and prints; furniture and carpets ceramics and works of art, printed books costume, textiles and embroidery; toys and games dolls, wines, Art Nouveau, Art Deco, cameras Periodic sales of automata, mechanical music an vintage machines, motoring and aeronautica items including car mascots; Staffordshir portrait figures, pot-lids and Goss; miniatures antiquities and cigarette and postcards.*

Forrest and Co Ltd
17-31 Gibbins Rd. Stratford, E15 2HU. Tel: 018 534 2931. *Fortnightly general sales (Thurs) including antiques and household furniture china, glassware, carpets, rugs, pictures, prints etc.*

Stanley Gibbons Auctions
399 Strand, WC2R 0LX. Tel: 0171 836 8444; fa - 0171 836 7342. *2-3 sales annually of philateli material in London with Gt. Britian, Britis Empire and overseas stamps and postal history Postal and telephone bidding available. Pleas send for a free copy of our Auction Informatio Pack and a sample catalogue.*

Glendining and Co
101 New Bond St., W1Y 0AS. Tel: 0171 49 2445. *Specialist auctioneers of coins and medals Quarterly sales of coins; three sales annually o orders, decorations and medals.*

Harmers of London Stamp Auctioneers Ltd.
91 New Bond St., W1A 4EH. Tel: 0171 629 0218 fax - 0171 495 0260. *Auctions of Great Britain British Commonwealth, Foreign countries, Airma stamps, also postal history and literature, month (Sept.-July). Fully illustrated catalogues. Valu ations for sale, probate or insurance.*

London continued

Hornsey Auctions Ltd
54-56 High St., Hornsey, N8 7NX. Tel: 0181 340 5334; fax - same. *Sales weekly on Wed. at 6.30. Viewing Tues. 5-8 and Wed. from 10. Open Thurs, Fri. and Mon. 9.30-5.30 and Sat. 11-4 to take in for next auction.*

Lloyds International Auction Galleries Ltd
118 Putney Bridge Rd., Putney, SW15 2NQ. Tel: 0181 788 7777. *Fortnightly sales of antique and modern furniture, china, glassware, pictures and collectables.*

Lots Road Galleries
71 Lots Rd., Chelsea, SW10 0RN. Tel: 0171 351 7771 (24 hours); fax - 0171 376 8349. *Auction sales every Mon. at 2 pm and 6 pm, approximately 600 lots of antique, traditional and decorative furniture, Oriental carpets, curtains, paintings, prints, ceramics, clocks, glass, silver, objets d'art. On view Thurs. 5-7, Fri., Sat. and Sun. 10-4 and all day Mon. Items accepted Mon.-Fri. (Settlement 7 days after sale). Catalogue details and auction results by fax, phone, or live auction line. Valuers, consultants and carriers. VAT registered.*

Thomas Moore Auctioneers Ltd.
217-219 High Rd., Greenwich, SE10 8NB. Tel: 0181 858 7848. *Weekly sales of porcelain, glass, silver, prints and furniture etc., mainly antique items. Periodic sales throughout the year of period antiques and objects - details on application. All sales on Thurs. at 10. Viewing Wed. 2-8 and Thurs. 9-10.*

Phillips
101 New Bond St., W1Y 0AS. Tel: 0171 629 6602; fax - 0171 629 8876; Internet - http://www.phillips-auctions.com/ *Regular sales of fine furniture, paintings, ceramics, jewellery, silver, clocks, watches, Oriental works of art, textiles, books, musical instruments, works of art, stamps, medals and decorative arts.*

Phillips Bayswater
10 Salem Rd., W2 4DL. Tel: 0171 229 9090. *Sales of furniture, porcelain and works of art each Mon. with the exception of four pre-arranged dates reserved for pianos. Sales of pictures/paintings alternate with those of collectors' items each Tues. Viewing Thurs. 5.15-7.30pm, Fri. 9-5, Sat. 9-12.30, Sun. 2-5, morning of sale. Buyers premium 15% plus VAT.*

Rippon Boswell and Co.
The Arcade, South Kensington Station, SW7 2NA. Tel: 0171 589 4242. *International specialist auctioneers of old and antique Oriental carpets. Approximately two auctions annually in London. Also in Germany, Switzerland, USA and Far East.*

London continued

Rosebery Fine Art Ltd.
The Old Railway Station, Crystal Palace Station Road, SE19 2AZ. Tel: 0181 778 4024. *Sales of antique furniture, ceramics, glass, works of art, pictures, silver, jewellery, books, toys, musical instruments, held twice a month on Tues. and Wed.*

Sotheby's
34-35 New Bond St., W1A 2AA. Tel: 0171 493 8080. *Open for free valuations Mon.-Fri. 9-4.30. Daily sales of paintings, drawings, watercolours, prints, books and manuscripts, European sculpture and works of art, antiquities, silver, ceramics, glass, jewellery, Oriental works of art, furniture, musical instruments, clocks and watches, vintage cars, wine, postage stamps, coins, medals, toys and dolls and other collectors' items.*

Southgate Auction Rooms
55 High St., Southgate, N14 6LD. Tel: 0181 886 7888. *Weekly Mon. sales at 6.30 pm of jewellery, silver, china, porcelain, paintings, furniture. Viewing Sat. 9-12 noon and from 9 on day of sale.*

AVON - See Gloucestershire & Somerset

BEDFORDSHIRE

Downer Ross (Auctioneers)
The Old Town Hall, Woburn, MK17 9PZ. Tel: 01525 290502. *Sales every four weeks on a Thurs.*

Wilson Peacock
The Auction Centre, 26 Newnham St., Bedford, MK40 3JR. Tel: 01234 266366. *Antiques sale first Fri. monthly. Viewing Thurs. prior 9-6. General sales every Sat. at 9.30.*

BERKSHIRE

Dreweatt Neate
Donnington Priory, Donnington, Nr. Newbury, RG14 2JE. Tel: 01635 31234; fax - 01635 522639. *Sales on the premises mainly on a weekly basis. General furnishings - fortnightly on Tues. Antique furniture - six annually. Paintings, books, prints, silver and jewellery, ceramics - three of each annually. Buyers' premium 11.75% inc. VAT.*

Edwards & Elliott
32 High St., Ascot, SL5 7HG. Tel: 01344 872588. *Regular sales of antique furniture, porcelain and glass; silver, plate and jewellery; oil paintings, watercolours and prints; rugs and assorted collectables at the Silver Ring Grandstand, Ascot Racecourse.*

Berkshire continued

Martin and Pole Nicholas
The Auction House, Milton Road, Wokingham, RG40 1DB. Tel: 0118 979 0460; fax - 0118 977 6166. *Sale of antiques and collectables held usually on 3rd Wed. every month at above address.*

Shiplake Fine Art Sales
(Thimbleby & Shorland and Duncan Vincent) 31 Great Knollys Street, Reading, RG1 7HU. Tel: 0118 950 8611. *About six collective sales annually of antique, Victorian and all good quality modern furniture and effects, approximately 700 lots at Memorial Hall, Shiplake, Nr. Henley-on-Thames.*

Thimbleby & Shorland
31 Great Knollys St., Reading, RG1 7HU. Tel: 01734 508611. *Collective sales of antique and modern furniture and effects held monthly on Sat. at Reading Cattle Market. Also four specialist sales of horse-drawn vehicles, harness, horse brasses, driving sundries, whips and lamps, etc.*

BUCKINGHAMSHIRE

Amersham Auction Rooms
125 Station Rd., Amersham, HP7 0AH. Tel: 01494 729292. *Weekly general and monthly selected antique sales held on Thurs. at 10.30.*

CAMBRIDGESHIRE

Cheffins, Grain and Comins
The Cambridge Saleroom, 2 Clifton Rd., Cambridge, CB1 4BW. Tel: 01223 213343 (10 lines). *Regular weekly and other specialist sales of furniture, clocks, porcelain, silver, pictures, sporting items, wine, rural and domestic bygones.*

Grounds and Co.
2 Nene Quay, Wisbech, PE13 1AG. Tel: 01945 585041/2. *Three specialist sales annually, each approximately 600 lots.*

Phillips
The Golden Rose, 17 Emmanuel Rd., Cambridge, CB1 1JW. Tel: 01223 66523. *Regular sales of good furniture, pictures, silver, jewellery, ceramics and Victoriana, enquiries to David Fletcher.*

Wilson Peacock
The Auction Centre, 75 New Street, St Neots PE19 1AN. Tel: 01480 474550. *General sale every Thurs. at 11. Viewing Wed. prior, 9-8.*

CHESHIRE

Andrew, Hilditch and Son Ltd.
Hanover House, 1A The Square, Sandbach, CW1 0AP. Tel: 01270 767246/762048. *Quarterly sale of fine pictures and period furnishings. Genera and Edwardian furniture sales held weekly.*

Cheyne's
38 Hale Rd., Altrincham, WA14 2EX. Tel: 016 941 4879. *Bi-monthly sales held at All Saint Church Hall, Hale Barns. Viewing day prior 2.30 4.30 and 6-8 and sale morning 9-10.30.*

Frank R. Marshall and Co.
Marshall House, Church Hill, Knutsford, WA1 6DH. Tel: 01565 653284. *Regular sales o antique furniture, objets d'art, silver, pewter glass, porcelain, pictures, brass and copper Fortnightly household collective sales includin bric-a-brac. Specialised sales in The Knutsfor Auction Salerooms.*

Phillips North West
New House, 150 Christleton Rd., Chester, CH 5TD. Tel: 01244 313936; fax - 01244 340028. *2 salerooms countrywide including Chester.*

Peter Wilson Fine Art Auctioneers
Victoria Gallery, Market St., Nantwich, CW 5DG. Tel: 01270 623878; fax - 01270 610508. *Bi monthly sale on Wed. and Thurs. of fine art an antiques, Victorian and Edwardian items; viewin Sun. 2-4, Mon. and Tues. 10-4. Sales of late furnishings and household effects weekly o Thurs. at 11, viewing Wed. 10-4.*

Wright Manley
Beeston Sales Centre, Beeston Castle Smithfiel Tarporley, CW6 0DR. Tel: 01829 26031 *Fortnightly general sales and bi-monthly fine a and furniture sales.*

CORNWALL

Jefferys
The Auction Rooms, 5 Fore St., Lostwithiel, PL2 0BP. Tel: 01208 872245; fax - 01208 87326 *Sales of antique furniture, ceramics, glas jewellery, silver and plate, pictures and prints an collectors items held in February, April, Jul September and November.*

Lambrays incorporating R.J. Hamm
Polmorla Walk, Wadebridge, PL27 7AE. Te 0120 881 3593. *Fortnightly sales of antiques ar objets d'art. Illustrated catalogues issued.*

W.H. Lane & Son
Fine Art Auctioneers, 65 Morrab Rd., Penzanc TR18 2QT. Tel: 01736 61447; fax - 01736 5009 *Twelve sales annually of antiques and obje d'art. Two specialist book sales annually. S picture sales annually (specialists in the Newl and St. Ives Schools). Two specialist toy sal annually. Frequent house sales.*

Cornwall continued

David Lay FSVA
The Penzance Auction House, Alverton, Penzance, TR18 4RE. Tel: 01736 61414; fax - 01736 60035. *Regular sales of fine art, antiques, collectors' items, books and studio pottery. Three-weekly general household sales.*

Phillips Cornwall
Cornubia Hall, Par, PL24 2AQ. Tel: 01726 814047. *Monthly sales of antiques, Victorian and later furnishings, silver, jewellery, pictures and collectors' items.*

Pooley & Pearce
Regent Auction Rooms, Abbey St., Penzance. Salerooms - 01736 68814; office - 01736 63816. *Bi-monthly sales of antique furniture, objets d'art, silver and jewellery.*

Martyn Rowe Auctioneers and Valuers
Truro Auction Centre, Calenick St., Truro, TR1 2SG. Tel: 01872 2160020; fax - 01872 261794. *Weekly on Thurs. at 10 am - Victorian, Edwardian and general sales. Viewing morning of sale and previous Wed 2-6 pm. Antique and picture sales - every 6-8 weeks. Collectors and sporting sales - every 6-8 weeks. Quarterly sales of vintage and classic motorcycles, cars and automobilia. House, commercial, industrial and receivership sales on site or at auction centre.*

CUMBRIA

Cumbria Auction Rooms
2 Lowther St., Carlisle, CA3 8DA. Tel: 01228 5259. *Weekly sales of Victorian and later furniture and effects. Quarterly catalogue sales of antiques and works of art. Valuations.*

Mitchell's Auction Co.
The Furniture Hall, 47 Station Rd., Cockermouth, CA13 9PZ. Tel: 01900 827800; fax - 01900 26780. *Weekly (Thurs.) sales of antique, reproduction and modern furniture and effects, approximately 800 lots, starting at 9.30 am. Viewing Wed. 2.30-4.30 and throughout sale. Five fine art sales per annum, viewing Wed. previous 2-7 and prior to sale.*

James Thompson
4 Main St., Kirkby Lonsdale, LA6 2AJ. Tel: 15242 71555; fax - 015242 72939. *Monthly two day sales of silver, ceramics, general antiques. Picture sales six times a year.*

Thomson, Roddick and Laurie Ltd.
9 Crosby St., Carlisle, CA1 1DQ. Tel: 01228 8939/39636. *Bi-monthly catalogue sales of antiques and collectors' items and regular specialist sales particularly antiquarian books, sporting guns, silver and pictures at Dumfries and Carlisle. Monthly general furniture sales at Wigton and Annan (Dumfriesshire).*

DERBYSHIRE

Neales
Becket Street, Derby DE1 3HW Tel: 01332 203601. *Fortnightly sales (Tues) of general antique and other furniture and effects, silver and metalwork, ceramics and glass, pictures and decorative goods. Quarterly Fine Art and Antiques sales covering most fields of applied arts with particular emphasis on the ceramics and artists of Derbyshire.*

Noel Wheatcroft
Matlock Auction Gallery, Old English Rd., Off Dale Rd., Matlock, DE4 3LX. Tel: 01629 55770. *Monthly sales of antiques and general items.*

DEVON

Bearne's
St Edmund's Court, Okehampton St. Exeter EX4 1DU. Tel: 01392 422800. *Regular sales of antique furniture, works of art, silver, jewellery, collectors' items, books, clocks and watches, paintings, ceramics and glass, carpets and rugs.*

Bonhams - West Country
Dowell St., Honiton, EX14 8LX. Tel: 01404 41872; fax - 01404 43137. *Regular monthly auctions of furniture, works of art, ceramics, pictures, silver and jewellery, and collectors' items.*

Kingsbridge Auction Sales (J.A.S. Hawkins) inc. Charles Head and Son
113 Fore St., Kingsbridge, TQ7 1BG. Tel: 01548 856829. *Regular sales of antique and general household furniture and effects.*

Phillips
Alphin Brook Rd., Alphington, Exeter, EX2 8TH. Tel: 01392 439025; fax - 01392 410361. *Thurs. sales of antique and reproduction furniture and furnishings; oil paintings, watercolours and quality prints; silver and plate, jewellery, porcelain, glass, Victoriana and objets d'art. Book sales held twice a year.*

Potbury and Sons
The Auction Rooms, Temple St., Sidmouth, EX10 8LN. Tel: 01395 515555; fax - 01395 512608. *Fortnightly sales; fine arts every two months.*

Rendells
Stone Park, Ashburton, TQ13 7RH. Tel: 01364 653017: fax - 01364 654251. *Sales every four weeks (Thurs. and Fri.) of antique and reproduction furniture, ceramics, silver, jewellery, pictures, clocks and barometers, copper and brass and miscellanea. No buyers premium.*

Taylor's
Honiton Galleries, 205 High St., Honiton, EX14 8LF. Tel: 01404 42404. *Sales of paintings and prints, antiques, silver, books and porcelain every seven weeks.*

Devon continued

Ward and Chowen
Tavistock Auction Rooms, Market Rd., Tavistock, PL19 0BW. Tel: 01822 612603; fax - 01822 617311.

Whitton and Laing
32 Okehampton St., Exeter, EX4 1DY. Tel: 01392 52621; fax - 01392 496607. *Monthly auctions of antiques, silver and jewellery. Book auctions two or three times a year. General auctions weekly.*

DORSET

Cottees
The Market, East St., Wareham, BH20 4NR. Tel: 01929 552826; fax - 01929 554916. *Furniture and effects every two weeks.*

Hy. Duke and Son
Fine Art Salerooms, Weymouth Avenue, Dorchester, DT1 1QS. Tel: 01305 265080; fax - 01305 260101. *Regular six weekly sales including specialist sections of silver and jewellery, Oriental and English porcelain, English and Continental furniture, pictures, books and Oriental rugs. Complete valuation and advisory service, including insurance, probate and forward tax planning.*

House and Son
Lansdowne House, Christchurch Rd., Bournemouth, BH1 3JW. Tel: 01202 298044. *Fortnightly sales of selected furniture, pictures, books, silver, porcelain and glass. Catalogues £2.50 including postage.*

Wm. Morey and Sons
Salerooms, St. Michaels Lane, Bridport, DT6 3RB. Tel: 01308 422078. *Antique and general sales held every three to four weeks.*

Phillips Auctioneers
Gild House, 70 Norwich Ave. West, Bournemouth, BH2 6AW and Long Street Salerooms, Sherborne. Tel: 01202 769352/01935 815271.

Riddetts of Bournemouth
Richmond Hill, Bournemouth Square, Bournemouth, BH2 6EJ. Tel: 01202 555686; fax - 01202 311004. *Fortnightly sales which include fine antiques, jewellery, silver, plate, pictures. Illustrated sale programme free. Catalogue subscription £40 p.a.*

Southern Counties Auctioneers
The Livestock Market, Christys Lane, Shaftesbury, SP7 8PH. Tel: 01747 851735. *Monthly sales of antique furniture and effects.*

DURHAM

Denis Edkins
Auckland Auction Rooms, 58 Kingsway, Bishop Auckland, DL14 7JF. Tel: 01388 603095 *General and antique sales from time to time.*

G. Tarn Bainbridge and Son
Northern Rock House, High Row, Darlington, DL3 7QN. Tel: 01325 462633/462553. *Three to fou collective sales annually and country house sales.*

Thomas Watson and Son
Northumberland St., Darlington, DL3 7HJ. Tel 01325 462559. *Regular sales of antiques an good quality house contents.*

ESSEX

Black Horse Agencies - Ambrose
149 High Rd., Loughton, IG10 4LZ. Tel: 018 502 3951; fax - 0181 508 9516. *Sales held on las Thurs. and Fri. monthly.*

Cooper Hirst Auctions
The Granary Salerooms, Victoria Rd., Chelmsford CM2 6LH. Tel: 01245 260535. *Regular sales c antiques every 8/9 weeks and weekly Tues. sale of Victoriana, bric-a-brac etc. Catalogu subscription service available.*

Reeman Dansie Howe & Son
Head Gate Auction Rooms, 12 Head Gate Colchester, CO3 3BT. Tel: 01206 574271. *Sale held every Wed. Viewing 9-7 Tues. prior. B. monthly Fine Art sales.*

Simon H. Rowland
Chelmsford Auction Rooms, 42 Mildmay Rd Chelmsford, CM2 0DZ. Tel: 01245 35425 *Regular sales by order of the Sheriff of Essex an private vendors.*

Saffron Walden Auctions
1 Market St., Saffron Walden, CB10 1JB. Te 01799 513281. *Sales of antique and fine furnitur antique effects and objets d'art held every month*

John Stacey & Sons (Leigh-on-Sea) Lt
Leigh Auction Rooms, 86-90 Pall Mall, Leigh-o Sea, SS9 1RG. Tel: 01702 77051. *Monthly sal of period and other furniture, works of art ar collectors' items. Catalogue subscription £40.*

Stanfords
11-14 East Hill, Colchester, CO1 2QX. Te 01206 868070. *Weekly Tuesday sales of antiq and modern furniture, china, glass, silver ar decorative items at 10 am Extra specialist sal last Monday each month at 1 pm*

G.E. Sworder and Sons
14 Cambridge Road, Stansted Mountfitchet CM 8BZ. Tel: 01279 817778; fax - 01279 81777 *Monthly auctions of antique furniture, ceramic silver, pictures, decorative items. Viewing Sa prior 9-12 and Mon. prior 9-5. Weekly Thurs.*

Essex continued

11 auction of Victorian, Edwardian and later furniture and collectables. Viewing morning of sale and Wed. 2-5.

Trembath Welch (incorporating J.M. Welch & Son)

Old Town Hall, Great Dunmow, CM6 1AU. Tel: 01371 873014; fax - 01371 875936. *At the Salerooms, Chequers Lane - selected antique furniture and effects sales quarterly. Sales of collectables, household furniture and antiques every three weeks. Catalogue subscription service available.*

GLOUCESTERSHIRE

Auction Centres - Bristol

Prewett St., Redcliffe, Bristol, BS1 6PB. Tel: 0117 926 5996; fax - same. *Weekly sales, fine art and antiques monthly, Victoriana and general sales. Sales in country houses, cottages, etc. throughout the West Country. Catalogues by post. Valuations. Storage and delivery.*

Bristol Auction Rooms Ltd

St. John's Place, Apsley Rd., Clifton, Bristol, BS8 2ST. Tel: 0117 973 7201; fax - 0117 973 5671. *Six-weekly auctions of antique furniture, clocks, rugs, textiles, paintings and prints, glass, pottery, porcelain, books and ephemera, silver, objects of vertu, toys and collectables. View Sat. prior 9.30-1; day prior from 9.30-7, and on day from 9 to sale at 10.30. Fortnightly auctions of Victorian and modern household furniture and effects. View day prior to sale from 12-6 and on day from 9 until sale at 10.30. Specialist auctions and house sales held throughout the year. Catalogue subscription service. Buyers' premium.*

Bruton, Knowles

Albion Chambers, 111 Eastgate St., Gloucester, GL1 1PZ. Tel: 01452 521267. *Fine art auctioneers and valuers. House and collective sales held throughout the year. Valuations and inventories prepared.*

Corinium Galleries

25 Gloucester St., Cirencester, GL7 2DJ. Tel: 01285 659057. *Mon. auctions of postcards and small collectables every six weeks.*

Fraser Glennie and Partners

The Old Rectory, Siddington, Cirencester, GL7 6HL. Tel: 01285 659677; fax - 01285 642256. *Monthly sales of antiques, other furniture, collectors' items and musical instruments at the Bingham Hall, Cirencester.*

Mallams Fine Art Auctioneers and Valuers

26 Grosvenor St., Cheltenham, GL52 2SG. Est. 1788. Tel: 01242 235712; fax - 01242 241943.

Gloucestershire continued

Regular sales of furniture, ceramics, paintings, textiles, rugs and works of art, sporting, toy and collectors items.

Moore, Allen and Innocent

33 Castle St., Cirencester, GL7 1QD. Tel: 01285 651831. *Monthly collective sales of over 1,000 lots of antique and other furniture and effects. Bi-annual specialist picture sales and sporting sales. Fri. at 10. Viewing day prior 10.30-8. 10% buyers premium.*

Short Graham and Co

City Chambers, 4/6 Clarence St., Gloucester, GL1 1DX. Tel: 01452 521177. *Sales of Georgian, Victorian, Edwardian and later furniture, ceramics, glass, metalwork, silver, plate, jewellery, miscellanea, collectors' items, books, pictures and outside effects every four to six weeks.*

Wotton Auction Rooms Ltd

(formerly Sandoe Luce Panes) Tabernacle Rd., Wotton-under-Edge, GL12 7EB. Tel: 01453 844733; fax - 01453 845448. *Large monthly catalogued two-day sales of 1,200-1,500 lots - all categories. House contents sales as instructed.*

HAMPSHIRE

Basingstoke Auction Rooms

82-84 Sarum Hill, Basingstoke, RG21 1ST. Tel: 01256 840707. *Regular sales of antiques and fine art and fortnightly general sales. Occasional specialist sales. Catalogues available. Buyers' premium 10%.*

Hants. & Berks. Auctions

82-84 Sarum Hill, Basingstoke. Tel: 01256 840707. *Monthly sales at Heckfield Village Hall on Sat. 10.30. Viewing previous day 11-9. Sales include antiques, reproduction and household furniture, clocks, porcelain, glass, silver and pictures. Occasional specialist sales. Catalogues available.*

Jacobs and Hunt

Lavant St., Petersfield, GU32 3EF. Tel: 01730 262744. *General antique sales every six to eight weeks on Fri.*

George Kidner

The Old School, The Square, Pennington, Lymington, SO41 8GN. Tel: 01590 670070; fax - 01590 675167. Emsworth Rd. - 01590 679487. *Monthly specialist sales - furniture, works of art, silver and jewellery, modern and antique guns and related items, collectors' items, oils, prints and watercolours, European ceramics and Oriental works of art. Viewing - Sat. previous 9.30-1, Mon. 9.30-4.30, Tues. 9.30-7. Also saleroom at Emsworth Rd., Lymington - Victorian, Edwardian and later furniture and effects. Viewing - day previous 9.30-7.*

Hampshire continued

May and Son
18 Bridge St., Andover, SP10 1BH. Tel: 01264 323417/363331; fax - 01264 338841. *Monthly sales of antique furniture and effects at Penton Mewsey Village Hall (Lots from private sources only). Private house contents sales.*

D.M. Nesbit and Co.
7 Clarendon Rd., Southsea, Portsmouth, PO5 2ED. Tel: 01705 864321; fax - 01705 295522. *Monthly sales of antique furniture, silver, porcelain and pictures.*

Phillips Auctioneers
54 Southampton Rd., Ringwood, BH24 1JD. Tel: 01425 473333.

Phillips Auctioneers
The Red House, Hyde St., Winchester, SO23 7DX. Tel: 01962 862515; fax - 01962 865166. *Sales of fine furniture, pictures, silver, jewellery, ceramics, metalware, clocks, rugs and works of art.*

Romsey Auction Rooms
86 The Hundred, Romsey, SO51 8BX. Tel: 01794 513331; fax - 01794 511770. *Monthly sales of antique and period furniture and effects and bi-monthly sales of silver, jewellery and plated items; regular toy sales.*

HEREFORDSHIRE

Russell, Baldwin and Bright
The Fine Art Saleroom, Ryelands Rd., Leominster, HR6 8NZ. Tel: 01568 611122; fax - 01568 610519. *Monthly 2-day sales of antiques and collectors' items (approx. 1,000 lots per sale). Two or three sales per month of antique and household effects.*

HERTFORDSHIRE

Brown and Merry - Tring Market Auctions
Brook Street, Tring, HP23 5EF. Tel: 0144282 6446.

Hertfordshire continued

Fortnightly Sat. sales of antiques and collectables held at The Market Premises, Brook St., Tring. Fine art sales held on last Fri. of month.

ISLE OF WIGHT

Shanklin Auction Rooms
79 Regent St., Shanklin, PO37 7AP. Tel: 0198[illegible] 863441. *Monthly auctions of antiques and fine arts.*

Ways
The Auction House, Garfield Rd., Ryde, PO3[illegible] 2PT. Tel: 01983 562255. *Five-weekly sales of antique and modern furniture, silver, copper and brass, oils, watercolours and prints, jewellery china, clocks.*

KENT

Albert Andrews Auctions and Sales
Maiden Lane, Crayford, Dartford, DA1 4LX. Tel 01322 528868. *Weekly auctions including antiques, Victorian and Edwardian furniture bric-a-brac, paintings and clocks, on Wed. at 1[illegible] Viewing Tues. 4.30-8.30.*

Bracketts
Fine Art Auctioneers, Auction Hall, Pantiles Tunbridge Wells, TN2 5QL. Tel: 01892 54450[illegible] *Fortnightly sales of antique and later furnitur[illegible] and effects and specialist antique sales.*

The Canterbury Auction Galleries
40 Station Rd. West, Canterbury, CT2 8AN. Tel 01227 763337; fax - 01227 456770. *Bi-monthl[illegible] auctions of Fine Art and Antiques held on Tues. a[illegible] 10.30, viewing Mon. prior 10-7. Auctions o[illegible] Victorian and later furniture held on the first Sa[illegible] of the month at 10, viewing Fri. prior 3-[illegible] Valuations.*

Halifax Property Services formerly John Hogbin & Son
53 High St., Tenterden, TN30 6BG. Tel: 015[illegible] 763200. *Antique and other furniture and effec[illegible] on Wednesdays, 18 sales per year.*

Kent continued

Hobbs Parker
Romney House, Ashford Market, Ashford, TN23 1PG. Tel: 01233 622222; fax - 01233 646642. *Monthly sales of antiques and household furniture.*

Hogben Auctioneers & Valuers
St. John St., Off Dover Rd., Folkestone, CT21 3JU. Tel: 01303 240808/246810; fax - 01303 240809. *Regular antique and collectables sales.*

Hogben Auctioneers & Valuers
Unit C Highfield Industrial Estate, Off Warren Rd., Folkestone. Tel: 01303 240808/246810; fax - 01303 240809. *Fine art saleroom - monthly sales.*

Ibbett, Mosely
125 High St., Sevenoaks, TN13 1UT. Tel: 01732 456731. *Antiques and objets d'art.*

Lambert and Foster Auction Sale Rooms
102 High St., Tenterden, TN30 6HU. Tel: 01580 762083. *Three offices in Kent. Monthly general sales of good quality antique furniture and effects.*

B.J. Norris
The Quest, West St., Harrietsham. ME17 1JD. Tel: 01622 859515. *Regular sales at The Agricultural Hall, Maidstone at 10. Viewing from 8 on morning of sale.*

Phillips
11 Bayle Parade, Folkestone, CT20 1SQ. Tel: 01303 245555; fax - 01303 259178. *Seventeen fine art and Victoriana sales each year.*

Phillips International Auctioneers & Valuers
49 London Rd., Sevenoaks, TN13 1AR. Tel: 01732 740310. *Alternating sales of antiques, collectors' items and Victoriana, 14 per year.*

LANCASHIRE

Acorn Auctions
PO Box 152, Salford, Manchester, M17 1BP. Tel: 0161 877 8818. *Tues. sales, approximately every 5 weeks, held at Unit 6, Block C, Astra Business Centre, Guiness Rd., Trafford Park, Manchester. 10 per year all specialising in paper collectables - postage stamps and history, manuscripts, autographs, picture and cigarette cards, books, prints, drawings and watercolours. Sales commence at 2 pm., viewing Mon. previous 10.30-6.30, and sale morning 9-1.15.*

Capes Dunn & Co Fine Art Auctioneers & Valuers
The Auction Galleries, 38 Charles St., Manchester, M1 7DB. Est. 1826. Tel: 0161 273 1911; fax - 0161 273 3474. *Catalogues of weekly specialist sales available on request. Regional offices in Rochdale and Lytham.*

Lancashire continued

Entwistle Green (Black Horse Agencies)
The Galleries, Kingsway, Ansdell, Lytham St. Annes, FY8 1AB. Tel: 01253 735442. *Sales of antique, reproduction and modern furnishings and appointments held fortnightly on Tues. Approximately 400-600 lots commencing 9.30. Viewing Fri. 2-4, Mon. 9-7 and prior to sale. Buyers' premium 10%.*

Tony & Sons Ltd
2-8 Lynwood Rd., Blackburn, BB2 6HP. Tel: 01254 691748. *Monthly sales of antique, second-hand and modern jewellery. Valuations.*

Warren & Wignall Ltd
The Mill, Earnshaw Bridge, Leyland PR5 3PH. Tel: 01772 451430; fax - 01772 454516. *Sales of general antiques every three weeks. All sales Wed. at 10, viewing Tues. 9-7.*

LEICESTERSHIRE

Freckeltons
1 Leicester Rd., Loughborough, LE11 2AE. Tel: 01509 214564; fax - 01509 236114. *Monthly sales of general antiques.*

Gilding's Auctioneers and Valuers
Roman Way, Market Harborough, LE16 7PQ. Tel: 01858 410414. *Regular antique and Victoriana sales, with weekly general household sales.*

Heathcote Ball & Co
Castle Auction Rooms, 78 St. Nicholas Circle, Leicester, LE1 5NW. Tel: 0116 2536789; fax - 0116 2538517. *Auctions every four to six weeks.*

LINCOLNSHIRE

Dickinson, Davy and Markham
DDM Auction Rooms, Old Courts Road, Brigg, DN20 8JJ. Tel: 01652 650172; fax - 01652 650085. *Fine art and antique auctions held every six to eight weeks, also Victorian and household effects every two weeks. Catalogue subscription service available.*

Dowse
Foresters' Galleries, Falkland Way, Barton-upon-Humber, DN18 5RL. Tel: 01652 632335. *Monthly sales of general antiques and collectors' items.*

Eleys Auctioneers
1 Main Ridge West, Boston, PE21 6QQ. Tel: 01205 361687. *Regular antique and collectors sales.*

Escritt and Barrell
Saleroom - Dysart Rd. Office - 24 St Peter's Hill, Grantham, NG31 6QF. Tel: 01476 566991. *Three-weekly general shipping and antique sales, quarterley antique sales.*

Lincolnshire continued

Thomas Mawer and Son
63 Monks Rd., Lincoln, LN2 5HP. Tel: 01522 524984. *General sales fortnighly. Catalogued antique sales quarterly.*

Richardsons
Bourne Auction Rooms, Spalding Rd., Bourne, PE10 9LE. Tel: 01778 422686. *Antiques sales every month. Antique and modern sales every other Sat. Various specific sales periodically, eg silver, clocks, bygones, transport.*

Marilyn Swain
The Old Barracks, Sandon Rd., Grantham, NG31 9AS. Tel: 01476 568861; fax - 01476 576100. *Quarterly antiques and fine art sales. Fortnightly sales of Victorian and later general household furniture and effects.*

MERSEYSIDE

J. Kent (Auctioneers) Ltd.
2/6 Valkyrie Rd., Wallasey, L45 4RQ. Tel: 0151 638 3107; fax - same. *Weekly general sale; antiques, fine art and collectors' items on first Wed. of each month at 10. Viewing Tues. 9-6.30.*

Kingsley and Co. Auctioneers
3/4 The Quadrant, Hoylake, Wirral, L47 2EE. Tel: 0151 632 5821; fax - 0151 632 5823. *Sales every Tues. at 10, of antiques, fine arts, general chattels. Viewing Sat. 9-12.30, Mon. 9-5 and Tues. 9-10.*

Outhwaite and Litherland
Kingsway Galleries, Fontenoy St., Liverpool, L3 2BE. Tel: 0151 236 6561; fax - 0151 236 1070. *Victorian, Edwardian and modern furnishings - weekly Tues. General antiques and fine quality reproductions - monthly Tues. Fine art sales, including all works illustrative of the fine arts - monthly Wed. Specialist sales of books, wines, stamps etc. periodically. Members of SOFAA.*

NORFOLK

Hugh Beck Auctions
The Cornhall, Cattle Market St., Fakenham, NR21 9AW. Tel: 01328 851557. *Weekly sales of antique and other furniture every Thurs. at 11. Country house sales as instructed.*

Clowes Nash Auctions
Norwich Livestock & Commercial Centre, Hall Rd., Norwich, NR4 6EQ. Tel: 01603 504488. *Antiques and general furniture weekly sales.*

Ewings
Market Place, Reepham, Norwich, NR10 4JJ. Tel: 01603 870473. *Periodic sales of antiques and modern furniture and effects.*

Norfolk continued

Thos. Wm. Gaze and Son
Diss Auction Rooms, Roydon Rd., Diss, IP22 3LN. Tel: 01379 650306. *Weekly catalogue sales of antiques and cottage furniture on Fri. at 11am. Periodic specialist sales including Fine Antiques, rural bygones, architectural, horse tack and carriages, automobilia, toys and scientific etc.*

G.A. Key - Aylsham Salerooms
Incorporated Auctioneers, 8 Market Place, Aylsham, NR11 6EH. Tel: 01263 733195. *Three weekly sales of period, antique and Victorian furniture, silver, porcelain etc. Bi-monthly picture sales - oils, watercolours and prints etc. Six book and collectors sales annually. Weekly sales of shipping and secondhand furniture.*

NORTHAMPTONSHIRE

Goldsmiths
15 Market Place, Oundle, PE8 4BA. Tel: 01832 272349. *Sales approximately bi-monthly.*

Heathcote Ball & Co
The Northampton Auction Galleries, Commercial St., Northampton, NN1 1PJ. Tel: 01604 22735 (office); 01604 37263 (auction). *Regular fine art and antique sales, fortnightly general sales, specialist sales. Mailing subscription £30 p.a; general sales details faxed fortnightly, £5 p.a. subscription.*

Southams
Corn Exchange, Thrapston, NN14 4JJ. Est. 1900. Tel: 01832 734486. *First Thurs. each month, viewing Wed. 9.30-8 sales of antiques and superior furniture, silver, plate, copper and brass, fine china, glass, Oriental rugs, oil paintings, watercolours and prints. 10% buyer's premium. Catalogues £2 including postage. Annual subscription £18.*

H. Wilford Ltd.
Midland Rd., Wellingborough, NN8 1NB. Tel: 01933 222760/222762. *Weekly sales of antique and modern furniture, shipping goods, jewellery etc. every Thurs. (over 1200 lots).*

NOTTINGHAMSHIRE

Arthur Johnson and Sons (Auctioneers)
The Nottingham Auction Centre, Meadow Lane Nottingham, NG2 3GY. Tel: 0115 986 9128; fax 0115 986 2139. *Approximately 1,000 lots weekly on Sat. at 10 am of antique and shipping furniture silver, gold, porcelain, metalware and collectables.*

Mellors & Kirk
Gregory St., Lenton Lane, Nottingham. Tel: 0115 979 0000. *Fortnightly auctions of antique and shipping goods. Fine antiques and pictures every two months.*

Nottinghamshire continued

Neales

192-194 Mansfield Rd., Nottingham, NG1 3HU. Tel: 0115 962 4141. *Bi-monthly specialist sales of paintings, drawings, prints and books; silver, jewellery, bijouterie and watches; European and Oriental ceramics and works of art, glass; furniture and decoration; metalwork, fabrics, needlework, carpets and rugs; collectors' toys and dolls; stamps, coins and medals, post and cigarette cards; autographs and collectors' items. Weekly collective sales (Mon.) of general antique and later furnishings, shipping goods and reproduction furnishings. Period and later ceramics, glass and decorative effects. Sales on the premises of the contents of town and country properties.*

Phillips Inc. Henry Spencer and Sons - Fine Art Auctioneers

20 The Square, Retford, DN22 6XE. Tel: 01777 708633; fax - 01777 706724. *Specialist sales of furniture, carpets, ornamental items, works of art; paintings, drawings and prints; porcelain and glass, silver, jewellery and bijouterie. Non-specialist sales of furniture and effects held twice a month. Sales on the premises at town and country houses. Regular fine sales at Kelham Hall, Nr Newark.*

Richard Watkinson and Partners

17 Northgate, Newark, NG24 1EX. Tel: 01636 77154. *Monthly sales of antique and Victorian furniture, oil paintings, silver etc. Weekly sales of early 20th C and general household furniture.*

OXFORDSHIRE

Dreweatt Neate Holloways

49 Parsons St., Banbury, OX16 8PF. Tel: 01295 253197; fax - 01295 252642. *General or specialist sales on the premises every other week. Buyers' premium 11.75% inc. VAT.*

Mallams

Fine Art Auctioneers, Bocardo House, 24A St. Michael's St., Oxford, OX1 2EB. Tel: 01865 241358. *Frequent sales of furniture, silver, paintings and works of art. House sales arranged on the premises.*

Messengers

Messengers Auction Centre, 27 Sheep St., Bicester, OX6 7JF. Tel: 01869 252901; fax - same. *Victorian and general household sales, monthly. Antique auctions every 6-8 weeks. Bi-annual specialist sales of woodworking and other tools.*

Oxfordshire continued

Phillips International Fine Art Auctioneers

39 Park End St., Oxford, OX1 1JD. Tel: 01865 723524; fax - 01865 791064; internet - http://www.phillips-auctions.com. *Fortnightly sales of Victoriana and general effects. Specialist sales of fine furniture, rugs, works of art, silver, jewellery, ceramics, collectors' items and paintings throughout the year.*

Simmons and Sons

32 Bell St., Henley-on-Thames, RG9 2BH. Tel: 01491 571111; fax - 01491 579833. *Eight antique sales and eight general sales per year held at the saleroom Watcombe Manor, Ingham Lane, Watlington, Oxon. Sales start 10.30, viewing Sat. previous 9.30-12.30, previous day 10-8 and morning of sale.*

SHROPSHIRE

Halls Fine Art

Welsh Bridge Salerooms, Shrewsbury, SY3 8LA. Tel: 01743 231212; fax - 01743 271014. *Weekly household and Victoriana sales (Fri.). Monthly catalogued antique sales.*

Ludlow Antique Auctions Ltd

29 Corve St., Ludlow, SY8 1DA. Tel: 01584 875157/873496; fax - 01584 876491. *Regular specialist fine art and antique auctions (Tues.) on the premises.*

Perry and Phillips

Auction Rooms, Old Mill Antique Centre, Mill St., Bridgnorth, WV15 5AQ. Tel: 01746 762248. *Weekly (Tues.) sales of good quality household furniture and effects. Monthly sales of antique furniture, Victoriana, china, porcelain, pictures etc. Regular specialist and house contents sales.*

SOMERSET

Aldridges of Bath

The Auction Galleries, 130-132 Walcot St., Bath, BA1 5BG. Tel: 01225 462830; fax - 01225 311319. *Weekly (Tues.) sales, broken down into specialist categories - antique furniture to include clocks and Oriental carpets; silver and porcelain, glass and metalware; paintings and prints; Victorian and general furniture. Viewing Sat. mornings and Mon. Catalogues available upon annual subscription. Large car park.*

Auction Centres - Mudford

Main Hall, Main Street, Mudford, Yeovil, BA21 5TE. Tel: 01935 851511. *Weekly sales, fine art and antiques monthly, Victoriana and general sales, country house sales. Catalogues by post. Valuations. Storage and delivery.*

Somerset continued

Auction Centres - Yeovil

Central Hall, South St., Yeovil. Tel: 01935 413111; fax - same. *Weekly sales, fine art and antiques. Monthly, Victorian and general sales. Sales in country houses, cottages, etc. througout the West Country. Catalogues by post. Valuations, storage and delivery.*

Clevedon Salerooms

Herbert Rd., Clevedon, BS21 7ND. Tel: 01275 876699; fax - 01275 343765. *Bi-monthly auctions of antique furniture, fine art and collectors' items. Fortnightly sales of Victorian, Edwardian and general furniture and effects. Occasional specialist sales and sales held on vendors' property. Valuations.*

Cooper & Tanner Rural Surveyors

Frome Market, Standerwick, Frome, BA11 2QB. Tel: 01373 831010. *Weekly sales of antiques and general household chattels 11.15 Wednesdays. Viewing morning of sale. Haulage service.*

Gardiner Houlgate

The Old Malthouse, Comfortable Place, Upper Bristol Rd., Bath, BA1 3AJ. Tel: 01225 447933. *Regular sales of antique furniture and works of art. Frequent sales of Victorian and later furnishings. Fortnightly jewellery sales, quarterly musical instrument sales, specialist clocks and watches sales. Valuations.*

Greenslade Hunt Fine Art

Magdalene House, Church Square, Taunton, TA1 1SB. Tel: 01823 332525; fax - 01823 323923. *Weekly Wed. sales of Victorian and later furniture and household effects. Monthly, last Thurs., sales of antique furniture, metalwork, ceramics, glass, paintings and prints. Quarterly sales of silver, plate, jewellery and objects of vertu. Viewing 2 days prior 10-4.*

Lawrence Fine Art Auctioneers Ltd.

South St., Crewkerne, TA18 8AB. Tel: 01460 73041; fax - 01460 74627. *Specialist auctioneers and valuers. Regular sales of antiques and fine art. General sales every Wednesday except first Wednesday of each month.*

Lawrence Fine Art Auctioneers Ltd.

The Corfield Hall, Magdalene St., Taunton, TA1 1SG. Tel: 01823 330567; fax - 01823 330596. *Twice-monthly sales, on the first and third Tuesdays.*

The London Cigarette Card Co. Ltd

Sutton Rd., Somerton, TA11 6QP. Tel: 01458 273452. *Suppliers of thousands of different series of cigarette and trade cards and special albums. Publishers of catalogues, reference books and monthly magazine. Regular auctions in London and Somerset. S.A.E. for details. Showroom in West St. open Mon-Sat. or mail order.*

Somerset continued

Mart Road Salerooms

Office - 13 The Parade, Minehead, TA24 5NL. Tel: Office - 01643 702281; saleroom - 01643 703646. *Regular sales every three weeks of antique and other furniture and effects at Mart Road Salerooms, Minehead. Occasional house clearances.*

Phillips Auctioneers - Bath

1 Old King St., Bath, BA1 2JT. Tel: 01225 310609. *Member of the Phillips Auction Group. Regular sales of antique furniture and Victoriana, silver and jewellery, pictures, books and fine wine, ceramics and glass.*

Richards

The Town Hall, Axbridge, BS26 2AR. Tel: 01934 732969. *Bi-monthly sales of privately entered fine art and selected antiques of all categories and all types of collectable items. Valuations; inventories prepared.*

Tamlyn and Son

56 High St., Bridgwater, TA6 3BN. Tel: 01278 458241/2; saleroom - 01278 445251.

Wellington Salerooms

Mantle St., Wellington, TA21 8AR. Tel: 01823 664815. *Six-weekly sales of general antiques. Fortnightly sales of Victorian, Edwardian and shipping goods.*

Woodspring Auctions

Churchill Rd., Weston-super-Mare, BS23 3HD. Tel: 01934 628419. *Fortnightly sales of Edwardian and general furniture, brass, copper, glass, china and bric-a-brac.*

STAFFORDSHIRE

Armstrong Auctions

Midland Rd., Swadlincote, Burton-on-Trent, DE11 0AH. Tel: 01283 217772. *Weekly general sales and periodic antique sales held in Swadlincote Auction Rooms.*

Bagshaws

The Estate Saleroom, High St., Uttoxeter, ST14 7HP. Tel: 01889 562811, fax - 01889 563795. *Monthly sales of Victorian and general household furniture and effects.*

John German

1 Lichfield St., Burton-on-Trent, DE14 3QZ. Tel: 01283 512244; fax - 01283 517896. *Occasional sales of major house contents; specialist fine art valuation department.*

Hall and Lloyd, Auctioneers

South St., Stafford, ST16 2DZ. Est. 1882. Tel: 01785 58176; fax - 01785 228224. *Regular fortnightly sales of antique and general household furniture and effects, 1,000 or more lots every other Thurs. Special catalogued sales of antiques held regularly.*

Staffordshire continued

Louis Taylor Fine Art Auctioneers
Britannia House, 10 Town Rd., Hanley, Stoke-on-Trent. ST1 2QG. Tel: 01782 214111. *Quarterly fine art sales including furniture, pictures, pottery, porcelain, silver and works of art. Specialist Royal Doulton and Beswick auctions. General Victoriana auctions held every two weeks.*

Wintertons
Lichfield Auction Centre, Fradley Park, Fradley, Lichfield, WS13 8NF. Tel: 01543 263256. *Bi-monthly sales of antiques and fine art and sales of Victorian and general furniture every 2-3 weeks.*

SUFFOLK

Abbotts Auction Rooms
Campsea Ashe, Nr. Woodbridge, IP13 0PS. Tel: 01728 746323; fax - 01728 746880. *Monthly sales of antique furniture & effects held on Wednesdays. Viewing two days prior. Sales calendar and catalogues available. Weekly sales of Victoriana & household furniture held on Mondays to coincide with livestock market. Viewing Sat. 9-11 am.*

H.A. Adnams
The Auction Room, St. Edmunds Rd. Office - 98 High St., Southwold, IP18 6DP. Tel: 01502 723292/724794.

Boardman - Fine Art Auctioneers
Station Road Corner, Haverhill, CB9 0EY. Tel: 01440 730414. *Large sales held quarterly specialising in selected fine furniture (particularly oak), clocks and paintings.*

Diamond Mills and Co. Fine Art Auctioneers
117 Hamilton Rd., Felixstowe, IP11 7BL. Tel: 01394 282281 (3 lines). Ipswich office - 01473 218600. *Periodic fine art sales. Monthly general sales. Auctions at The Orwell Hall, Orwell Rd., Felixstowe.*

Durrant's
10 New Market, Beccles, NR34 9HA. Tel: 01502 712122. *Antique and general furniture auctions every Fri. at Gresham Rd., Beccles.*

Lacy Scott Fine Art & Furniture
10 Risbygate St., Bury St. Edmunds, IP33 3AA. Tel: 01284 763531; fax - 01284 704713. *Quarterly sales of fine art including antique and decorative furniture, silver, pictures, ceramics etc. on behalf of executors and private vendors. Regular (every three weeks) sales of Victoriana and general household contents. Also 3 annual sales of diecast and tinplate toys (2 of which include working steam scale models) and annual fine wine sales.*

Suffolk continued

Neal Sons and Fletcher
26 Church St., Woodbridge, IP12 1DP. Tel: 01394 382263. *Two special mixed antiques sales annually. Individual specialised sales and complete house contents sales as required. Household furniture sales on Wed. of each month.*

Olivers
The Saleroom, Burkitts Lane, Sudbury, CO10 6HB. Tel: 01787 880305. *Fortnightly sales of Victorian and later furniture and household effects. Regular sales of antiques and works of art. Enquiries to James Fletcher FRICS.*

Phillips East Anglia
32 Boss Hall Rd., Ipswich, IP1 5DJ. Tel: 01473 740494. *Four two-day specialist sales annually at Bury St. Edmunds. Twelve mixed sales in Ipswich.*

Suffolk Sales
The Saleroom, Church St., Clare, CO10 8PD. Tel: 01787 277993. *Sales of antiques and chattles held every three weeks on Sat. at 11 a.m., viewing Fri. 5-9 p.m, Sat. from 9 a.m.*

SURREY

Chancellors Auctions
74 London Rd., Kingston, KT2 6PX. Tel: 0181 541 4139. *Weekly sales on Thurs. One fine art and antiques sale each month. Viewing previous Tues. 2-8 and Wed. 9-5. Three general sales each month, viewing Wed. 2-8 and Thurs. 9-10.30. All sales start at 10.30.*

Clarke Gammon Fine Art Auctioneers
The Guildford Auction Rooms, Bedford Rd., Guildford, GU1 4SJ. Tel: 01483 566458; fax - 01483 563555.

Croydon Auction Rooms (Rosan and Co.) (incorporating E. Reeves Auctions)
144/150 London Rd., Croydon, CR0 2TD. Tel: 0181 688 1123/4/5. *Fortnightly collective sales - 10 am Sat., viewing Fri. prior.*

Ewbank Auctioneers
Burnt Common Auction Rooms, London Rd., Send, Woking, GU23 7LN. Tel: 01483 223101; fax - 01483 222171. *Monthly general and fine art sales on a Thurs., viewing Wed. 10am-9pm.*

Hamptons
93 High St., Godalming, GU7 1AL. Tel: 01483 423567; fax - 01483 426392. *Regular fine art sales at 93 High Street, specialising in selected fine furniture, rugs, paintings and watercolours, porcelain, glass, jewellery, silver, objets d'art and books. Held on a Wednesday and Thursday. Two sales each month of general and Victorian furniture, shipping goods and household effects, held on first and third Sat. House sales conducted on the premises when instructed. Valuations.*

Surrey continued

Lawrences' - Auctioneers
Norfolk House, 80 High St., Bletchingley, RH1 4PA. Tel: 01883 743323; fax - 01883 744578. *Six-weekly antique and reproduction furniture and effects.*

Parkins
18 Malden Rd., Cheam, SM3 8SD. Tel: 0181 644 6633. *Weekly sales of general household furniture and effects on Mon. at 10. Viewing Fri. 2-4 and Sat. 10-4 Special antique and collectors sales first Mon. monthly. Small antiques and collectors sales one Fri. evening monthly at 7 pm.*

Richmond and Surrey Auctions
The Old Railway Parcels Depot, Kew Road, Richmond, TW9 2NA. Est. 1992. Tel: 0181 948 6677; fax - 0181 948 2021. *Auctioneers, valuers and consultants. Sales every Thurs. 6pm.*

Wentworth Auction Galleries
21 Station Approach, Virginia Water, GU25 4DW. Tel: 01344 843711. *Antique and general sales every four to six weeks.*

P.F. Windibank Fine Art Auctioneers & Valuers
Dorking Halls, Reigate Rd., Dorking, RH4 1SG. Tel: 01306 884556/876280; fax - 01306 884669. *Antique auctions held every four to five weeks throughout the year.*

SUSSEX EAST

Burstow and Hewett
Abbey Auction Galleries and Granary Sale Rooms, Battle, TN33 0AT. Tel: 01424 772374. *Monthly sales of antique furniture, silver, jewellery, porcelain, brass, rugs etc. at the Abbey Auction Galleries. Also monthly evening sales of fine oil paintings, watercolours, prints, and engravings. At the Granary Sale Rooms - monthly sales of furniture, china, silver, brass, etc.*

Gorringe's Auction Galleries
Terminus Rd., Bexhill-on-Sea, TN39 3LR. Tel: 01424 212994; fax - 01424 224035. *Monthly sales of antique and modern furniture, metalware, European, Oriental, ceramics and glass, silver plate, plated goods, jewellery, bijouterie, objet d'art, pictures, libraries of books, etc.*

Gorringe's Auction Galleries
15 North St., Lewes, BN7 2PD. Tel: 01273 472503. *Sales approximately every six weeks of period furniture, Oriental carpets and rugs, oil paintings, watercolour drawings and prints, decorative china, glass, silver plate, jewellery etc.*

Sussex East continued

Graves, Son and Pilcher Fine Arts
Hove Street, Hove, BN3 2GL. Tel: 01273 735266; fax - 01273 723813. *Monthly sales of fine art including antique furniture, pictures, silver, Oriental carpets and rugs and ornamental items. Specialised sales of primitive art, coins, books and jewellery.*

Edgar Horn's Fine Art Auctioneers
46/50 South St., Eastbourne, BN21 4XB. Tel 01323 410419. *Fortnightly antique and later furniture and effects sales (Tues). Six specialist antique furniture, silver and jewellery, ceramics and glass, oil paintings and watercolours and works of art sales (Wed).*

Raymond P. Inman
The Auction Galleries, 35 and 40 Temple St. Brighton, BN1 3BH. Tel: 01273 774777; fax 01273 735660. *Monthly sales of antiques furniture, china, brass, pictures, silver, jewellery collectables, etc.*

Lewes Auction Rooms (Julian Dawson)
56 High St., Lewes, BN7 1XE. Tel: 01273 478221. *Antique furniture and effects every six weeks. General furniture and effects every Mon. (Salerooms - Garden Street).*

Wallis and Wallis
West Street Auction Galleries, West St., Lewes BN7 2NJ. Est. 1928. Tel: 01273 480208. *Nine annual sales of arms and armour, militaria, coins and medals. Specimen catalogue £4.50. Current combined catalogues £7. Die-cast and tin plate toys and models - catalogues £3.25. Commission bids (without charge) accepted. Valuations.*

SUSSEX WEST

John Bellman Ltd
New Pound, Wisborough Green, Billingshurst RH14 0AY. Tel: 01403 700858; fax - 01403 700059. *Two day sale once a month - Thurs. am ceramics and Oriental; Thurs. pm - silver, jewellery, clocks; Fri. am - furniture, Fri. pm collectables, works of art, paintings. Viewing Mon. 10-4, Tues. 10-8, Wed. 10-4. Book sales quarterly.*

Denham's
Horsham Auction Galleries, Warnham, RH12 3RZ Tel: 01403 255699; fax - 01403 253837. *Antique sales held monthly - good furniture of all periods silver, jewellery, European and Oriental ceramics and collectors' items, paintings, drawings, prints and bronzes, metalware and Oriental carpets and rugs. Also monthly sales of general antique modern and shipping furniture. Periodic sales of books, stamps, coins and medals, arms and armour and specialist collections as advertised.*

Sussex West continued

R.H. Ellis and Sons
44/46 High St., Worthing, BN11 1LL. Tel: 01903 238999. *Monthly specialist auctions of antique, Victorian and Edwardian furniture and porcelain. Quarterly auctions of silver, watercolours, paintings, Oriental carpets and rugs.*

King & Chasemore
Midhurst Auction Rooms, West St., Midhurst, GU29 9NG. Tel: 01730 812456; fax - 01730 814514. *General sales of antique and modern furniture and effects every six weeks.*

Phillips Fine Art Salerooms
Baffins Hall, Baffins Lane, Chichester, PO19 1UA. Tel: 01243 787548. *Sales monthly on Wed. at 10 am of antique and reproduction furniture, clocks, silver, porcelain, paintings, Persian and other carpets. Viewing day prior and Sat morning prior.*

Sotheby's Sussex
Summers Place, Billingshurst, RH14 9AD. Tel: 01403 783933; fax - 01403 785153. *Regular sales of paintings, furniture, carpets, clocks, ceramics, glass, silver, jewellery, vertu, sporting guns, medals, militaria, armour, toys, dolls, Oriental items and garden statuary.*

Stride and Son
Southdown House, St. John's St., Chichester, PO19 1XQ. Tel: 01243 780207; fax - 01243 786713. *Sales last Fri. monthly - antiques and general; periodic book and document sales.*

Sussex Auction Galleries
59 Perrymount Rd., Haywards Heath, RH16 3DR. Tel: 01444 414935. *Auctions of antiques and reproduction furniture and effects including ceramics, silver and jewellery, clocks, Persian rugs and Victoriana. Also regular sales of lost/found property from Sussex Police Authority and handling agents from Gatwick Airport. Annual catalogue subscription £22.*

Worthing Auction Galleries
Fleet House, Teville Gate, Worthing, BN11 1UA. Tel: 01903 205565. *Fortnightly sales alternating between antique, general, reproduction and modern furniture and china, glass, silver, plate, jewellery, objet d'art, pictures and clocks. Viewing Sat. prior 9-12 and Mon. 9-1 and 2-4 prior to sale on Tues. or Wed. commencing at 10 am.*

TYNE AND WEAR

Anderson and Garland
Fine Art Salerooms, Marlborough House, Marlborough Crescent, Newcastle-upon-Tyne, NE1 4EE. Tel: 0191 232 6278; fax - 0191 261 8665. *Regular sales of paintings, prints, antique furniture, silver and collectors' items.*

Tyne and Wear continued

Anderson and Garland
Kepier Chare, Crawcrook, Ryton, NE40 4TS. Tel: 0191 413 8348. *Fortnightly sales of Victorian and later furnishings.*

Boldon Auction Galleries
24a Front St., East Boldon, NE36 0SJ. Tel: 0191 537 2630. *Quarterly antique auctions.*

Thomas N. Miller Auctioneers
Algernon Rd., Byker, Newcastle-upon-Tyne, NE6 2UN. Tel: 0191 265 8080; fax - 0191 265 5050. *Antique auctions every Tuesday and Wednesday.*

WARWICKSHIRE

Bigwood Auctioneers Ltd
The Old School, Tiddington, Stratford-upon-Avon, CV37 7AW. Tel: 01789 269415. *Monthly Victoriana sales. Monthly sales of fine furniture and works of art. Quarterly sales of wines, sporting goods and other specialist sales. Catalogues and calendars on request. Valuations for all purposes.*

Black Horse Agencies - Locke and England
18 Guy St., Leamington Spa, CV32 4RT. Tel: 01926 889100; fax - 01926 470608. *Antique furniture, porcelain, pictures, silver each month at The Salerooms Walton House, 11 The Parade, Leamington Spa. Shipping goods, Victorian and Edwardian furniture, household effects and collectables weekly. House contents sales. All sales held Thurs. 11 am. Telephone for further details or catalogues.*

John Briggs and Parsley
17 Market Street, Atherstone, CV9 1ET. Tel: 01827 718912. *Auctions on clients' instructions.*

Henley-in-Arden Auction Sales Ltd
The Estate Office, Warwick Rd., Henley-in-Arden, B95 5BH. Tel: 01564 792154. *Sales of antique and modern furniture and effects, second Sat. each month.*

Warwick and Warwick Ltd
Pageant House, Jury St., Warwick, CV34 4EW. Tel: 01926 499031; fax - 01926 491906. *Philatelic auctioneers and private treaty specialists. Stamp auctions held monthly. Postcards, cigarette cards, autographs, ephemera, medals and militaria and other collectables sold by auction periodically.*

WEST MIDLANDS

Biddle & Webb
Ladywood Middleway, Birmingham, B16 0PP. Tel: 0121 455 8042. *Fine art sales first Fri. monthly; antique sales on second Fri. monthly; silver, jewellery, medals, coins and watches on*

West Midlands continued

fourth Fri. monthly; toys, dolls, model railways and juvenalia sales and musical instrument sales, violins, pianos, guitars, etc., both on Fri. alternate months all sales at 11. Weekly Tues. sales of Victoriana and collectables at 10.30.

Fellows and Sons
Augusta House, 19 Augusta St., Hockley, Birmingham, B18 6JA. Tel: 0121 212 2131; fax - 0121 212 1249. *Auctioneers and valuers of jewels, silver, fine art.*

James and Lister Lea
1741 Warwick Rd., Knowle, B93 0LX. Est. 1846. Tel: 01564 779187. *Three sales annually of contents of country and town houses as required. All sale items are from private sources with an emphasis on the more unusual collectors' items. Buyer's premium 10% plus VAT.*

Old Hill Antiques & Auction Rooms
220 Halesowen Rd., Old Hill, Cradley Heath, B64 6HN. Tel: 01384 411121. *Auctioneers and valuers.*

Phillips Midlands
The Old House, Station Rd., Knowle, Solihull, B93 0HT. Tel: 01564 776151. *Specialised weekly sales of fine furniture and works of art; silver and jewellery; Victoriana; paintings; collectors' items; ceramics and 19th-20th C decorative arts; books. Free sales programme and subscription on request.*

Walker Barnett and Hill
Waterloo Road Salerooms, Clarence St., Wolverhampton, WV1 4JE. Tel: 01902 773531; fax - 01902 712940. *Monthly sales of fine reproduction furniture and effects on second Sat of each month at 10.30. Bailiffs/County Court auctions. Fine art and antique sales every 6/8 weeks.*

Weller and Dufty Ltd
141 Bromsgrove St., Birmingham, B5 6RQ. Tel: 0121 692 1414; fax - 0121 622 5605. *Ten sales annually, approximately every five weeks, of antique and modern firearms, edged weapons, militaria etc. Periodic sales of specialist items - military vehicles and associated military equipment. Postal bids accepted. Illustrated catalogue available.*

WILTSHIRE

Hamptons Auctioneers & Valuers
20 High St., Marlborough, SN8 1AA. Tel: 01672 516161; fax - 01672 515882. *Antique and selected quality furniture and effects sales first Wed. bi-monthly. General household sales first Wed. bi-monthly and every third Wed. monthly.*

Swindon Auction Rooms
The Planks, Old Town, Swindon, SN3 1QP. Tel: 01793 615915. *General sales every Saturday at 10am. Antique section on first Saturday in the month.*

Wiltshire continued

Woolley and Wallis
Salisbury Salerooms, Castle St., Salisbury, SP1 3SU. Tel: 01722 411422; fax - 01722 422192. *Monthly sales of antique furniture. Special sales of porcelain and pottery, glass and metalwork, Eastern carpets and rugs, books and maps, paintings, watercolours and prints, textiles, fans, lace, toys and dolls, musical instruments, collectables, Oriental furniture and ceramics, works of art. Quarterly sales of silver and plate, jewellery, watches, objects of art and wines. Fortnightly sales of household furniture.*

WORCESTERSHIRE

R.A. Bennett & Partners t/a Broadway Auction Rooms
41-43 High St., Broadway, WR12 7DP. Tel 01386 852456. *Periodic collective antique an modern furniture sales.*

Griffiths and Co.
57 Foregate St., Worcester, WR1 1DZ. Tel: 0190 26464.

Philip Laney FRICS - Fine Art
The Portland Room, Portland Rd., Malvern WR14 2TA. Tel: 01684 893933. *Monthly sales o antiques and collectors' items.*

Phipps and Pritchard
Bank Buildings, Kidderminster, DY10 1BU. Te 01562 822244 and 822187. *Regular monthly sale of antique furniture, watercolours and o paintings, copper, brass, glass, china and por celain, stamps and coins, weapons. Private hous sales also conducted.*

Philip Serrell - Auctioneers & Valuers
The Malvern Salerooms, Barnards Green Rd. Malvern. Tel: 01684 892314. *Bi-monthly cata logued antique and fine art auctions. Fortnight general sales. Specialist on the premises sales. Fre sales estimates.*

YORKSHIRE EAST

Gilbert Baitson
The Edwardian Auction Galleries, Wiltshire R Hull, HU4 6PG. Tel: 01482 500500; after hours 01482 645241; fax - 01482 500501. *Sales antique and modern furnishings every Wed. 10.30. Viewing day prior until 8 pm.*

Dee Atkinson & Harrison - Agricultural and Fine Arts
The Exchange Saleroom, Driffield, YO25 7L Tel: 01377 253151; fax - 01377 241041. *Regul bi-monthly sales of antiques, Victorian, Edwardia and quality furnishings, paintings, silve jewellery etc. Viewing two days prior. Fortnight household sales. Biennial collectors' toys a sporting sales.*

Yorkshire East continued

H. Evans and Sons
1 St. James's St., Hessle Rd., Hull, HU3 2DH. Tel: 01482 323033; fax - 01482 211954. *Five antiques sales annually, fortnightly general furniture and effects.*

Spencers Auctioneers and Estate Agents
The Imperial and Repository Salerooms, 18 Quay Rd., Bridlington, YO15 2AP. Tel: 01262 676724. *General auctions every Thurs. Regular sales of antiques and fine arts.*

YORKSHIRE NORTH

Bairstow Eves Fine Art
27 Flowergate, Whitby, YO21 3AX. Tel: 01947 603433. *Monthly antiques sales. 10% buyers premium. VAT: Stan.*

Boulton and Cooper Ltd
St. Michaels House, Market Place, Malton, YO17 0LR. Tel: 01653 696151. *Members of SOFAA. Alternating monthly antique sales at Malton and York. Fortnightly general sales at Pickering.*

H.C. Chapman and Son Ltd
The Auction Mart, North St., Scarborough, YO11 1DL. Tel: 01723 372424; fax - 01723 500697. *Members of SOFAA. Monthly special sales of antiques and fine art held on Tues., viewing Fri. 4-7, Sat. 10-4, Mon. 9-12 . Annual catalogue subscription £35. Weekly Mon. sales of Edwardian and later shipping furniture, bric-a-brac and modern furnishings. Viewing Sat. 10-4 and Mon. from 9.*

Hutchinson-Scott
The Grange, Marton-le-Moor, Ripon, HG4 5AT. Tel: 01423 324264. *Periodic general sales plus two or three catalogue sales annually. Specialist in fine antiques and works of art.*

James Johnston
The Square, Boroughbridge, YO5 9AS. Tel: 01423 322382. *Monthly collective auction sales of antique and later furniture and effects at The Village Hall, Whixley, Nr. York and occasional private dispersal sales.*

Morphets of Harrogate
6 Albert St., Harrogate, HG1 1JL. Tel: 01423 530030. *Sales of antiques and works of art, interspersed with regular sales of general furniture and effects. Catalogue subscription scheme.*

Scarthingwell Auction Centre
Scarthingwell, Nr. Tadcaster, LS24 9PG. Tel: 01937 557955. *Evening antique and general sales held twice-monthly on Mon. and Tues. evenings, approx 900 lots. Viewing on prior Sun. 12-5 and from 4 on sale days.*

Yorkshire North continued

Stephenson and Son
20 Castlegate, York, YO1 1RT. Tel: 01904 625533. *Six sales annually of antique and Victorian furniture, silver and paintings.*

Summersgill Auctioneers
8 Front St., Acomb, York, YO2 3BZ. Tel: 01904 791131. *Auctions of antiques and household effects and collectors' items.*

Summersgill Auctioneers
Market Place, Easingwold, YO6 3BJ. Tel: 01347 821366. *Auctions of antiques and household effects and collectors' items.*

Tennants
The Auction Centre, Leyburn, DL8 5SG. Tel: 01969 623780. *Three Saturday sales a month - antiques and modern residual house contents, approximately 1,000 lots. No catalogues. View Fri. On-site parking.*

YORKSHIRE SOUTH

A.E. Dowse and Son Sheffield
Cornwall Galleries, Scotland St., Sheffield, S3 7DE. Tel: 0114 2725858; fax - 0114 2490550. *Monthly Sat. sales of antiques. Quarterly sales of diecast, tin plate and collectors' toys. Monthly sales of modern furniture and shipping goods.*

YORKSHIRE WEST

De Rome
12 New John St., Westgate, Bradford, BD1 2QY. Tel: 01274 734116/9. *Regular sales.*

Andrew Hartley Fine Arts
Victoria Hall Salerooms, Little Lane, Ilkley, LS29 8EA. Tel: 01943 816363. *Fifty sales annually including six good antique and fine art and other specialist sales.*

Phillips at Hepper House
17a East Parade, Leeds, LS1 2BH. Tel: 0113 2448011; fax - 0113 2429875. *Monthly sales of antique furniture and objets d'art and regular speciality sales of pictures, ceramics, silver and jewellery, etc.*

John H. Raby
Salem Auction Rooms, 21 St. Mary's Rd., Bradford, BD8 7QL. Tel: 01274 491121. *Sales of antique furniture and pictures every four to six weeks, shipping goods and collectables every week.*

CHANNEL ISLANDS

Bonhams & Langlois Auctioneers
Westaway Chambers, Don St., St. Helier, Jersey, JE2 4TR. Tel: 01534 22441; fax - 01534 59354. *Regular antique and specialised auctions, weekly general sales (Wed).*

SCOTLAND

Christie's Scotland
164-166 Bath St., Glasgow, Lanarkshire, G2 4TB. Tel: 0141 332 8134; fax - 0141 332 5759. *Regular specialist sales of jewellery, silver, furniture, paintings, together with sales of particular Scottish interest, including golfing and football memorabilia, whisky, Wemyss Ware.*

Frasers (Auctioneers)
8a Harbour Rd.,Inverness, Inverness-shire, IV1 1SY. Tel: 01463 232395; fax - 01463 233634. *Weekly sales on Wed. at 6 pm.*

Leslie and Leslie
Haddington, East Lothian, EH41 3JJ. Tel: 01620 822241; fax - same. *General auctions every three months.*

Loves Auction Rooms
52-54 Canal St., Perth, Perthshire, PH2 8LF. Tel: 01738 633337; fax - 01738 629830. *Regular sales of antique and decorative furniture, jewellery, silver and plate, ceramics, works of art, metalware, glass, pictures, clocks, mirrors, pianos, Eastern carpets and rugs, garden furniture, architectural items. Weekly Fri. sales of Victoriana and household effects at 10.30. Specialist sales of books and collectors' items. Valuations.*

Lyon and Turnbull Ltd
51 George St., Edinburgh, Midlothian, EH2 2HT. Tel: 0131 225 4627.

Macdougalls Auctioneers & Valuers
Lower Breakish, Breakish, Isle of Skye, IV42 8QA Tel: 01471 822053; fax - same. *Sales held every eight weeks of antiques and general furniture. Sales held Sat. at 2pm in Broadford Hall (10 mins. from the Skye bridge).*

McTear's
Clydeway Business Centre, 8 Elliot Place, Glasgow, Lanarkshire, G3 8EP. Tel: 0141 221 4456; fax - 0141 641 5035. *Weekly Fri. sales at 10.30 of antique, reproduction and shipping furniture, jewellery, silver, porcelain and paintings. Viewing prior Thurs. 10-5.*

John Milne
9 North Silver St., Aberdeen, Aberdeenshire, AB1 1RJ. Tel: 01224 639336. *Weekly general sales, regular catalogue sales of antiques, silver, paintings, books, jewellery and collectors' items.*

Robert Paterson & Son
8 Orchard St., Paisley, Glasgow, PA1 1UZ. Tel: 0141 889 2435. *Fortnightly Tuesday sales.*

Phillips Scotland
207 Bath St., Glasgow, G2 4HD. Tel: 0141 221 8377. *Monthly general sales of Victorian and Edwardian items; specialist sales of jewellery,*

Scotland continued

silver, ceramics, furniture, works of art, books, carpets, 20th C decorative arts and Scottish contemporary art and oil paintings, throughout the year.

Phillips Scotland
65 George St., Edinburgh, Midlothian, EH2 2JL. Tel: 0131 225 2266. *Regular specialist sales of oil paintings and watercolours; furniture, Oriental carpets, clocks and works of art; silver and jewellery; books, Oriental and European ceramics and glass. Bi-annual sales of decorative arts; dolls and textiles. Fortnightly sales of Victoriana.*

L.S. Smellie and Sons Ltd.
The Furniture Market, Lower Auchingramont Rd., Hamilton, Lanarkshire, ML10 6BE. Tel: 01698 282007. *Fine antiques auctions - third Thurs. in Feb., May, Aug. and Nov. Weekly sales every Mon. at 10 am. (600 lots) household furniture, porcelain and jewellery.*

Taylor's Auction Rooms
11 Panmure Row, Montrose, Angus, DD10 8HH Tel: 01674 672775. *Antiques sales held every second Sat.*

Thomson, Roddick & Laurie Ltd.
60 Whitesands, Dumfries, Dumfriesshire, DG1 2RS. Tel: 01387 255366. *Quarterly catalogued antique and collectors sales, sporting sales, silver and jewellery sales. Monthly sales of household furnishing and effects in Annan.*

WALES

Dodds Property World
Victoria Auction Galleries, Mold, CH7 1EB. Tel: 01352 752552. *Weekly Wed. auctions of general furniture and shipping goods at 10.30am. Bi-monthly auctions of antique furniture, silver, porcelain and pictures etc. at 10.30am on Sat. Catalogues available.*

Peter Francis
Curiosity Salerooms, King St., Carmarthen, SA3 1BH. Tel: 01267 233456/7. *Antiques sales held every six weeks. Household sales at regular intervals.*

Harry Ray and Co.
Lloyds Bank Chambers, Welshpool, SY21 7RR Tel: 01938 552555. *Fortnightly country sales.*

Rennies
87 Monnow St., Monmouth, NP5 3EW. Tel: 01600 712916. *Periodic sales of antique furniture and effects, usually on Thurs.*

Fairs Calendar

Because this list is compiled in advance, alterations or cancellations to the fairs listed can occur. We strongly advise anyone wishing to attend a Fair, especially if they have to travel any distance, to telephone the organiser to confirm the details given here.

LONDON

Sunday 1st June
Antique & Collectors' Fair, The Dartmouth House, 37 Charles Street, (Off Berkeley Square), Mayfair, W.1. *(Adams Antiques Fairs - 0171 254 4054)*
Antiques Fair, The Rembrandt Hotel, Thurloe Place, S.W. 7.
(Heritage Antiques Fairs - 0171 624 5173)
Antique & Collectors' Fair, The Lee Valley Leisure Centre, Picketts-Lock Lane, Off Meridian Way, Edmonton, N.9. *(Jax Fairs - 01444 400570)*

Thursday 5th/Sunday 15th June
The Olympia Fine Art & Antiques Fair, Olympia, Hammersmith Road, W.14. *(P & O Events - 0171 370 8234)*

Sunday 8th June
The ADA Antiquities Fair, The Britannia Hotel, Grosvenor Square, W.1. *(ADA Fairs - 0181 979 1585)*
The London International Antique Dolls, Toys, Miniatures & Teddy Bears Fair, The Kensington Town Hall, Exhibition & Conference Centre, Hornton Street, W.8. *(Granny's Goodies - 0181 693 5432)*
Antiques Fair, The London Marriott Hotel, Grosvenor Square, W.1. *(Heritage Antiques Fairs - 0171 624 5173)*
Antique & Collectors' Fair, The Assembly Hall, The Green, Station Road (Town Centre), Chingford, E.4. *(Oakleigh Fairs - 01279 871110)*

Thursday 12th/Saturday 21st June
The Grosvenor House Art & Antiques Fair, Under the Patronage of Her Majesty Queen Elizabeth The Queen Mother, The Great Room, Grosvenor House, Park Lane, W.1. *(Alison Vaissiere - 0171 495 8743/499 6363)*

Friday 13th/Monday 16th June
The International Ceramics Fair & Seminar, The Park Lane Hotel, Piccadilly, W.1. *(Brian & Anna Haughton - 0171 734 5491)*

Saturday 14th June
Antique & Collectors' Fair, The Chelsea Town Hall, King's Road, S.W.3. *(Adams Antiques Fairs - 0171 254 4054)*
Antique & Collectors' Fair, The Muswell Hill Centre, Entrance Summerland Gardens, Muswell Hill Road, N.10. *(M & S Enterprises - 0181 440 2330)*

London continued

Sunday 15th June
The Kensington Brocante Antiques Fair, The Kensington Town Hall, Hornton Street, Kensington, W.8. *(Adams Antiques Fairs - 0171 254 4054)*
Antiques Fair, The Kensington Palace Hotel, De Vere Gardens, Kensington High Street, W.8. *(Heritage Antiques Fairs - 0171 624 5173)*

Sunday 15th June
Antiques Fair, The Chelsea Town Hall, King's Road, S.W.3. *(Mainwarings Antique Fairs - 01225 723 094)*

Saturday 21st/Sunday 22nd June
Antiquarian Map & Print Fair, The Bonnington Hotel, Southampton Row, W.C.1. *(David Bannister - 01242 514287)*

Sunday 22nd June
Antique & Collectors' Fair, The Royal Horticultural Hall, Vincent Square, Victoria, S.W.1. *(Adams Antiques Fairs - 0171 254 4054)*
Antiques Fair, The London Hilton on Park Lane, 22 Park Lane, W.1. *(Heritage Antiques Fairs - 0171 624 5173)*
Antiques Fair, Atkinson Morley's Hall, Copse Hill, Wimbledon, S.W.20. *(P & A Antiques - 0181 543 5075)*

Sunday 23rd June
The Largest International Map Fair, The Forte Crest Bloomsbury, Coram Street, W.C.1. *(International Map Collectors' Society - 0181 349 207)*

Thursday 26th/Sunday 29th June
The 38th Antiquarian Book Fair, Grosvenor House, Park Lane, W.1. *(Antiquarian Booksellers Association - 0171 439 3118)*

Saturday 28th June
Antique & Collectors' Fair, St. Mark's Church Hall, Compton Road, Wimbledon, S.W.19. *(P & J Hobbs - 0181 542 4675)*

Sunday 29th June
Antiques Fair, The London Marriott Hotel, Grosvenor Square, W.1. *(Heritage Antiques Fairs - 0171 624 5173)*

Saturday 5th July
Antique & Collectors' Fair, The Chiswick Town Hall, Chiswick, W.4. *(Albion Fairs - 0181 987 8827)*

Sunday 6th July
Antique & Collectors' Fair, The Dartmouth House, 37 Charles Street, (Off Berkeley Square), Mayfair, W.1. *(Adams Antiques Fairs - 0171 254 4054)*
Antiques Fair, The London Hilton on Park Lane, 22 Park Lane, W.1. *(Heritage Antiques Fairs - 0171 624 5173)*

London continued

Saturday 12th July
Antique & Collectors' Fair, The Chelsea Town Hall, King's Road, S.W.3. *(Adams Antiques Fairs - 0171 254 4054)*

Sunday 13th July
Antique & Collectors' Fair, The Royal Horticultural Hall, Vincent Square, Victoria, S.W.1. *(Adams Antiques Fairs - 0171 254 4054)*
Antiques Fair, The Hotel Inter-Continental London, 1 Hamilton Place, Hyde Park Corner, W.1. *(Heritage Antiques Fairs - 0171 624 5173)*
Antiques Fair, The Chelsea Town Hall, King's Road, S.W.3. *(Mainwarings Antique Fairs - 01225 723 094)*

Monday 14th July
Antiquarian Map & Print Fair, The Bonnington Hotel, Southampton Row, W.C.1. *(David Bannister - 01242 514287)*

Sunday 20th July
Antique & Collectors' Fair, The Kensington Town Hall, Hornton Street, Kensington, W.8. *(Adams Antiques Fairs - 0171 254 4054)*
Antiques Fair, The London Marriott Hotel, Grosvenor Square, W.1. *(Heritage Antiques Fairs - 0171 624 5173)*

Saturday 26th July
Antique & Collectors' Fair, St. Mark's Church Hall, Compton Road, Wimbledon, S.W.19. *(P & J Hobbs - 0181 542 4675)*

Saturday 2nd August
Antique & Collectors' Fair, The Chiswick Town Hall, Chiswick, W.4. *(Albion Fairs - 0181 987 8827)*

Monday 11th August
Antiquarian Map & Print Fair, The Bonnington Hotel, Southampton Row, W.C.1. *(David Bannister - 01242 514287)*

Thursday 14th/Sunday 17th August
The Great Antiques Fair, Earls Court 2, Earls Court Exhibition Centre, S.W.5. *(P & O Events, Linda Colban - 0121 782 2899)*
The Kensington Arts Fair, Kensington Town Hall, Hornton Street, W.8 *(Penman Antiques Fairs - 01444 482514)*

Sunday 24th August
Antique & Collectors' Fair, The Royal Horticultural Hall, Vincent Square, Victoria, S.W.1. *(Adams Antiques Fairs - 0171 254 4054)*

Monday 25th August
Antique & Collectors' Fair, The Wembley Exhibition Centre - Hall 3, Empire Way, Wembley. *(Jax Fairs - 01444 400570.)*

Saturday 30th August
Antique & Collectors' Fair, The Chelsea Town Hall, King's Road, S.W.3. *(Adams Antiques Fairs - 0171 254 4054)*
Antique & Collectors' Fair, St. Mark's Church Hall, Compton Road, Wimbledon, S.W.19. *(P & J Hobbs - 0181 542 4675)*

London continued

Sunday 31st August
Antique & Collectors' Fair, The Kensington Town Hall, Hornton Street, Kensington, W.8. *(Adams Antiques Fairs - 0171 254 4054)*
Antiques Fair, The Chelsea Town Hall, King's Road, S.W.3. *(Mainwarings Antique Fairs - 01225 723 094)*

Sunday 7th September
Antique & Collectors' Fair, The Dartmouth House, 37 Charles Street, (Off Berkeley Square), Mayfair, W.1. *(Adams Antiques Fairs - 0171 254 4054)*
Antiques Fair, The London Hilton on Park Lane, 22 Park Lane, W.1. *(Heritage Antiques Fairs - 0171 624 5173)*
Antique & Collectors' Fair, The Lee Valley Leisure Centre, Picketts-Lock Lane, Off Meridian Way, Edmonton, N.9. *(Jax Fairs - 01444 400570)*

Thursday 11th/Saturday 20th September
The 85th Chelsea Antiques Fair, Chelsea Old Town Hall, King's Road, Chelsea, S.W.3. *(Penman Antiques Fairs - 01444 482514)*

Sunday 14th September
The London International Antique Dolls, Toys, Miniatures & Teddy Bears Fair, The Kensington Town Hall, Exhibition & Conference Centre, Hornton Street, W.8. (*Granny's Goodies - 0181 69[illegible] 5432)*
Antiques Fair, The London Marriott Hotel, Grosvenor Square, W.1. *(Heritage Antiques Fairs - 0171 624 5173)*

Monday 15th September
Antiquarian Map & Print Fair, The Bonnington Hotel, Southampton Row, W.C.1. *(David Bannister - 01242 514287)*

Saturday 20th September
The Decorative Arts & Vintage Fashion Fair, The Kensington Town Hall, Hornton Street, Kensington, W.8 *(Arabella Collins - 01985 850008)*
Antique & Collectors' Fair, The Muswell Hill Centre, Entrance Summerland Gardens, Muswell Hill Road, N.10. *(M & S Enterprises - 0181 44[illegible] 2330)*

Sunday 21st September
The Kensington Brocante Antiques Fair, The Kensington Town Hall, Hornton Street, Kensington, W.8. *(Adams Antiques Fairs - 0171 254 4054)*
The London Collectables Fair, The BAC, Battersea Old Town Hall, 176 Lavender Hill, S.W.11. *(Keith Gretton - 0171 228 0741)*
Antiques Fair, The Hotel Inter-Continental London, Hamilton Place, Hyde Park Corner, W.1. *(Heritage Antiques Fairs - 0171 624 5173)*

Tuesday 23rd/Sunday 28th September
The Decorative Antique and Textiles Fair, The Marquee, The Riverside Terraces, Battersea Park by the Pagoda. *(Heritage Antiques Fairs - 0171 62[illegible] 5173)*

STYLE & QUALITY & AUTHENTICITY

1997

July 25 - 27	*SUSSEX Art & Country Antiques Fair*
August 14 - 17	*KENSINGTON Art Fair*
September 11 - 21	*The 85th CHELSEA Antiques Fair*
October 16 - 19	*The City of LONDON Art Fair*
Oct 30 - Nov 2	*KENSINGTON Antiques & Fine Art Fair*

1998

January 22 - 25	*WEST LONDON Antiques & Fine Art Fair (p)*
February 12 - 15	*CHESTER Antiques & Fine Art Show*
March 19 - 29	*The 86th CHELSEA Antiques Fair (p)*
April 23 - 26	*The CHELSEA Art Fair*
July 24 -26	*SUSSEX Art & Antiques Fair (p)*

Provisional Date: (p)

All fairs offer a wide selection of Authenticated Antiques & Art for Sale from Dealers of Integrity

PENMAN ART Fairs 1997/8

Trade admitted Free

Illustrated colour brochures available from
Penman Fairs
P.O. Box 114, Haywards Heath,
W.Sussex. RH16 2YU.

01444 482514. Fax: 01444 483412

Penman Antiques Fairs

London continued

Saturday 27th September

Antique & Collectors' Fair, The Chelsea Town Hall, King's Road, S.W.3. *(Adams Antiques Fairs - 0171 254 4054)*

Antique & Collectors' Fair, The Chiswick Town Hall, Chiswick, W.4. *(Albion Fairs - 0181 987 8827)*

Antique & Collectors' Fair, St. Mark's Church Hall, Compton Road, Wimbledon, S.W.19. *(P & J Hobbs - 0181 542 4675)*

Sunday 28th September

Antique & Collectors' Fair, The Royal Horticultural Hall,Vincent Square, Victoria, S.W.1. *(Adams Antiques Fairs - 0171 254 4054)*

Antiques Fair, The Rembrandt Hotel, Thurloe Place, S.W. 7.
(Heritage Antiques Fairs - 0171 624 5173)

Antiques Fair, The Chelsea Town Hall, King's Road, S.W.3. *(Mainwarings Antique Fairs - 01225 723 094)*

The Alexandra Palace Antique & Collectors' Fair, The Great Hall, Alexandra Palace, Wood Green, N.22. *(Pig & Whistle Promotions - 0181 883 7061)*

Sunday 5th October

Antique & Collectors' Fair, The Dartmouth House, 37 Charles Street, (Off Berkeley Square), Mayfair, W.1. *(Adams Antiques Fairs - 0171 254 4054)*

Antiques Fair, The London Marriott Hotel, Grosvenor Square, W.1. *(Heritage Antiques Fairs - 0171 624 5173)*

Antique & Collectors' Fair, The Lee Valley Leisure Centre, Picketts-Lock Lane, Off Meridian Way, Edmonton, N.9. *(Jax Fairs - 01444 400570)*

Sunday 12th October

Antique & Collectors' Fair, The Royal Horticultural Hall,Vincent Square, Victoria, S.W.1. *(Adams Antiques Fairs - 0171 254 4054)*

Antiques Fair, The London Hilton on Park Lane, 22 Park Lane, W.1. *(Heritage Antiques Fairs - 0171 624 5173)*

Antique & Collectors' Fair, The Assembly Hall, The Green, Station Road (Town Centre), Chingford, E.4. *(Oakleigh Fairs - 01279 871110)*

The London Glass & Ceramics Fair, The Commonwealth Institute, Kensington High Street, W.8. *(P & A Antiques - 0181 543 5075)*

Monday 13th October

Antiquarian Map & Print Fair, The Bonnington Hotel, Southampton Row, W.C.1. *(David Bannister - 01242 514287)*

Thursday 16th/Sunday 19th October

The 2nd London Art Fair, Armoury House, Honourable Artillery Company's HQ, City Road, E.C.1 *(Penman Antiques Fairs - 01444 482514)*

Saturday 18th October

Antique & Collectors' Fair, The Muswell Hill Centre, Entrance Summerland Gardens, Muswell Hill Road, N.10. *(M & S Enterprises - 0181 440 2330)*

London continued

Sunday 19th October

Antique & Collectors' Fair, The Kensington Town Hall, Hornton Street, Kensington, W.8. *(Adams Antiques Fairs - 0171 254 4054)*

Antiques Fair, The Hotel Inter-Continental London, 1 Hamilton Place, Hyde Park Corner, W.1. *(Heritage Antiques Fairs - 0171 624 5173)*

Saturday 25th October

Antique & Collectors' Fair, St. Mark's Church Hall, Compton Road, Wimbledon, S.W.19. *(P & J Hobbs - 0181 542 4675)*

Saturday 25th/Sunday 26th October

The Battersea Contemporary Arts Fair, The BAC, Battersea Old Town Hall, 176 Lavender Hill, S.W.11. *(Keith Gretton - 0171 228 0741)*

Sunday 26th October

The 23rd International Antique Scientific & Medical Instrument Fair, The Radisson SAS Portman Hotel, Portman Square, W.1. *(Peter Delehar - 0181 866 8659)*

Antiques Fair, The London Marriott Hotel, Grosvenor Square, W.1. *(Heritage Antiques Fairs - 0171 624 5173)*

Thursday 30th October/Sunday 2nd November

The Kensington Antiques & Fine Art Fair, Kensington Town Hall, Hornton Street, W.8 . *(Penman Antiques Fairs - 01444 482514)*

Saturday 1st November

Antique & Collectors' Fair, The Chelsea Town Hall, King's Road, S.W.3. *(Adams Antiques Fairs - 0171 254 4054)*

Antiques & Collectors' Fair, The Chiswick Town Hall, Chiswick, W.4. *(Albion Fairs - 0181 987 8827)*

Sunday 2nd November

Antique & Collectors' Fair, The Dartmouth House, 37 Charles Street, (Off Berkeley Square), Mayfair, W.1. *(Adams Antiques Fairs - 0171 254 4054)*

Antiques Fair, The London Marriott Hotel, Grosvenor Square, W.1. *(Heritage Antiques Fairs - 0171 624 5173)*

Antique & Collectors' Fair, The Lee Valley Leisure Centre, Picketts-Lock Lane, Off Meridian Way, Edmonton, N.9. *(Jax Fairs - 01444 400570)*

Antiques Fair, The Chelsea Town Hall, King's Road, S.W.3. *(Mainwarings Antique Fairs - 01225 723 094)*

Friday 7th/Saturday 8th November

The 7th Chelsea Book Fair, The Chelsea Town Hall, King's Road, S.W.3. *(Antiquarian Booksellers Association - 0171 439 3118)*

Sunday 9th November

Antiques Fair, The Rembrandt Hotel, Thurloe Place, S.W. 7.
(Heritage Antiques Fairs - 0171 624 5173)

Antiques & Collectors' Fair, The Assembly Hall, The Green, Station Road (Town Centre), Chingford, E.4. *(Oakleigh Fairs - 01279 871110)*

Monday 10th November

Antiquarian Map & Print Fair, The Bonnington Hotel, Southampton Row, W.C.1. *(David Bannister - 01242 514287)*

London continued

Saturday 15th November
Antique & Collectors' Fair, The Chelsea Town Hall, King's Road, S.W.2. *(Adams Antiques Fairs - 0171 254 4054)*
The Decorative Arts & Vintage Fashion Fair, The Kensington Town Hall, Hornton Street, Kensington, W.8 *(Arabella Collins - 01985 850008)*
Antique & Collectors' Fair, The Muswell Hill Centre, Entrance Summerland Gardens, Muswell Hill Road, N.10. *(M & S Enterprises - 0181 440 2330)*
Sunday 16th November
Antique & Collectors' Fair, The Royal Horticultural Hall,Vincent Square, Victoria, S.W.1. *(Adams Antiques Fairs - 0171 254 4054)*
Antiques Fair, The London Hilton on Park Lane, 22 Park Lane, W.1. *(Heritage Antiques Fairs - 0171 624 5173)*
Antiques Fair, The Chelsea Town Hall, King's Road, S.W.3. *(Mainwarings Antique Fairs - 01225 723 094)*
The Alexandra Palace Antique & Collectors' Fair, The Great Hall, Alexandra Palace, Wood Green, N.22. *(Pig & Whistle Promotions - 0181 883 7061)*
Tuesday 18th/Sunday 23rd November
The Winter Fine Art & Antiques Fair, The National Hall, Olympia, Hammersmith Road, W.14. *(P & O Events - 0171 370 8234)*
Saturday 22nd/Sunday 23rd November
The Studio Art Fair, The Showcase for Living Artists, The Commonwealth Institute, Kensington High Street, W.8. *(P & A Antiques - 0181 543 5075)*
Sunday 23rd November
The Kensington Brocante Antiques Fair, The Kensington Town Hall, Hornton Street, Kensington, W.8. *(Adams Antiques Fairs - 0171 254 4054)*
Antiques Fair, The Hotel Inter-Continental London, 1 Hamilton Place, Hyde Park Corner, W.1. *(Heritage Antiques Fairs - 0171 624 5173)*
Saturday 29th November
Antique & Collectors' Fair, St. Mark's Church Hall, Compton Road, Wimbledon, S.W.19. *(P & J Hobbs - 0181 542 4675)*
Antique & Collectors' Fair, The Muswell Hill Centre, Entrance Summerland Gardens, Muswell Hill Road, N.10. *(M & S Enterprises - 0181 440 2330)*
Sunday 30th November
Antiques Fair, The London Marriott Hotel, Grosvenor Square, W.1. *(Heritage Antiques Fairs - 0171 624 5173)*
Saturday 6th December
Antique & Collectors' Fair, The Chelsea Town Hall, King's Road, S.W.3. *(Adams Antiques Fairs - 0171 254 4054)*
Sunday 7th December
Antique & Collectors' Fair, The Dartmouth House, 37 Charles Street, (Off Berkeley Square), Mayfair, W.1. *(Adams Antiques Fairs - 0171 254 4054)*
Antiques Fair, The London Hilton on Park Lane, 22 Park Lane, W.1. *(Heritage Antiques Fairs - 0171 624 5173)*
Antique & Collectors' Fair, The Lee Valley Leisure Centre, Picketts-Lock Lane, Off Meridian Way, Edmonton, N.9. *(Jax Fairs - 01444 400570)*
Antiques Fair, The Chelsea Town Hall, King's Road, S.W.3. *(Mainwarings Antique Fairs - 01225 723 094)*

London continued

Saturday 13th December
Antique & Collectors' Fair, St. Mark's Church Hall, Compton Road, Wimbledon, S.W.19. *(P & J Hobbs - 0181 542 4675)*
Sunday 14th December
Antique & Collectors' Fair, The Royal Horticultural Hall,Vincent Square, Victoria, S.W.1. *(Adams Antiques Fairs - 0171 254 4054)*
Antiques Fair, The London Marriott Hotel, Grosvenor Square, W.1. *(Heritage Antiques Fairs - 0171 624 5173)*
Antiques & Collectors' Fair, The Assembly Hall, The Green, Station Road (Town Centre), Chingford, E.4. *(Oakleigh Fairs - 01279 871110)*
Monday 15th December
Antiquarian Map & Print Fair, The Bonnington Hotel, Southampton Row, W.C.1. *(David Bannister - 01242 514287)*
Saturday 20th December
Antique & Collectors' Fair, The Chiswick Town Hall, Chiswick, W.4. *(Albion Fairs - 0181 987 8827)*
Antique & Collectors' Fair, The Muswell Hill Centre, Entrance Summerland Gardens, Muswell Hill Road, N.10. *(M & S Enterprises - 0181 440 2330)*
Saturday 27th December
Antique & Collectors' Fair, The Wembley Exhibition Centre - Hall 3, Empire Way, Wembley. *(Jax Fairs - 01444 400570.)*

REGIONS

Sunday 1st June
Antiques Fair, The Centre for Epilepsy, Chalfont St Peter, Bucks. *(Chiltern Fairs - 01753 890301)*
The Malvern Antique & Collectors' Fair, The Three Counties Showground, Malvern, Worcestershire. *(County Antiques Fairs - 01278 784912)*
Antiques Fair, The Village Hall, Lewes Road, Ditchling, W. Sussex. *(Mr G Deakin - 01273 845141)*
The Midlands Clock & Watch Fair, The National Motorcycle Museum, Solihull, Near Birmingham, West Midlands. *(Mr P Dungate - 01895 834694)*
Glass Collectors' Fair, The Derngate, Northampton, Northants. *(E W Services - 01933 225674)*
Antiques Fair, The Balmer Lawn Hotel, Brockenhurst, Hants. *(Forest Fairs - 01202 875167)*
Antique & Collectors' Fair, The Fourways Inn, Chester Road, Delamere, Near Northwich, Cheshire. *(Pine Promotions - 01565 652092)*
Specialist Clock, Watch, Barometer & Scientific Instrument Fair, The Grove Leisure Centre, Newark, Notts. *(Right Time Clock Fairs - 01933 225674)*
Antique & Collectors' Fair, The Royal Enclosure, The Racecourse, Ascot, Berks. *(Silhouette Fairs - 01635 44338)*
Antique & Collectors' Fair, The Exhibition Halls, Park Hall, Charnock Richard, Lancs. *(Unicorn Fairs Ltd - 0161 773 7001)*
The Sandown Park Antiques Fair, Sandown Exhibition Centre, Sandown Park Racecourse, Esher, Surrey. *(Wonder Whistle Enterprises - 0171 249 4050)*

Regions continued

Tuesday 3rd June
The International Antique & Collectors' Fair, The Newark & Nottinghamshire Showground, Newark, Notts. *(IACF Fairs - 01636 702326)*
Wednesday 4th June
Antiques Fair, The Village Hall, Long Melford, Suffolk. *(Caring for the Past - 01473 658224)*
Thursday 5th/Saturday 7th June
The Petersfield Antiques Fair, The Town Hall, Petersfield, Hants. *(Gamlin Exhibition Services - 01452 862557)*
Friday 6th/Sunday 8th June
The Thoresby Park Antiques & Fine Art Fair, The Thoresby Park Exhibition Centre, Off the A614, Near Ollerton, Notts. *(Whittington Exhibitions - 0181 644 9327)*
Saturday 7th June
Antiques Fair, The Chorleywood Memorial Hall, Common Road, Chorleywood, Herts. *(Chiltern Fairs - 01753 890301)*
Antique & Collectors' Fair, The Salisbury Leisure Centre, The Butts, Hulse Road, Salisbury, Wilts. *(Devon County Antiques Fairs - 01363 82571)*
Antiques & Collectors' Fair, The Winter Gardens, (Seafront), Weston-Super-Mare, Avon. *(Melba Fairs - 01934 624854)*
Saturday 7th/Sunday 8th June
Antique & Collectors' Fair, The Royal Welsh Showground, Builth Wells, Powys, Wales. *(County Antiques Fairs - 01278 784912)*
Sunday 8th June
Antiques Fair, The Old Swan Hotel, Harrogate, N.Yorks. *(Abbey Antiques Fairs - 01482 445785)*
The Dorking Dolls House & MIniatures Fair, The Dorking Halls, Surrey. *(Dolls House World Masazine - 01403 711511)*
Antique & Collectors' Fair, The Allendale Centre, Wimborne, Dorset. *(Forest Fairs - 01202 875167)*
Antiques & Collectors' Fair, The Kesgrave War Memorial Hall, Twelve Acre App. off Bell Lane, Kesgrave, Ipswich, Suffolk. *(Josef's Fairs - 01473 212423/685692)*
Antique & Collectors' Fair, The Memorial Hall, West Parley, Dorset.*(Renaissance Fairs - 01202 319914)*
Specialist Clock, Watch, Barometer & Scientific Instrument Fair, The Salisbury Leisure Centre, Salisbury, Wilts. *(Right Time Clock Fairs - 01933 225674)*
Antiques Fair, The Park Royal International Hotel, Stretton Road, Stretton, Warrington, Cheshire. *(Georgina Stevens - 01625 536926)*
Antique & Collectors' Fair, The Exhibition Halls, Park Hall, Charnock Richard, Lancs. *(Unicorn Fairs Ltd - 0161 773 7001)*
Wednesday 11th June
Antiques & Collectors' Fair & Drive-In, The Racecourse, Newton Abbot, Devon. *(Melba Fairs - 01934 624854)*

Regions continued

Friday 13th/Sunday 15th June
Antique & Collectors' Fair, The Bingley Hall County Showground, Stafford, Staffs. *(Bowman Antiques Fairs - 0113 284 3333)*
The Cheshire County Antiques Fair, Arley Hall, Near Knutsford, Cheshire. *(Cooper Antiques Fair - 01249 661111)*
The Duncombe Park Antiques Fair, Near Helmsley, N. Yorks. *(Galloway Antiques Fairs - 01423 324602)*
Saturday 14th/Sunday 15th June
Art Nouveau & Art Deco Fair, The Kettering Leisure Village, Kettering, Northants. *(E W Services - 01933 225674)*
Antique & Collectors' Fair, The Pavilion Gardens, Buxton, Derbys. *(Unicorn Fairs Ltd - 0161 773 7001)*
Sunday 15th June
Antiques Fair, The Coach House Inn, Tricketts Cross, Ferndown, Dorset. *(Forest Fairs - 01202 875167)*
Antique & Collectors' Fair, The The Hatfield Red Lion, Great North Road, Near Town Centre, Hatfield, Herts. *(Oakleigh Fairs - 01279 871110)*
Antique & Collectors' Fair, The Bowdon Rooms, The Firs, Bowdon, Near Altrincham, Cheshire. *(Pine Promotions - 01565 652092)*
Antique & Collectors' Fair, The Abbey Hall, Abingdon, Oxon. *(Silhouette Fairs - 01635 44338)*
Antique & Collectors' Fair, The Exhibition Halls, Park Hall, Charnock Richard, Lancs. *(Unicorn Fairs Ltd - 0161 773 7001)*
Tuesday 17th June
Antique & Collectors' Fair, The Suffolk Showground, Bucklesham Road, Ipswich, Suffolk. *(IACF Fairs - 01636 702326)*
Friday 20th/Sunday 22nd June
The Avington Park Antiques Fair, Winchester, Hants. *(Galloway Antiques Fairs - 01423 324602)*
Saturday 21st/Sunday 22nd June
Antiques Fair, The Westpoint Exhibition Centre, Clyst St Mary, Exeter, Devon. *(Devon County Antiques Fairs - 01363 82571)*
Sunday 22nd June
Antiques Fair, The Old Swan Hotel, Harrogate, N.Yorks. *(Abbey Antiques Fairs - 01482 445785)*
Antiques Fair, The Racecourse, Windsor, Bucks. *(Chiltern Fairs - 01753 890301)*
Antiques Fair, The Burton Latimer Community Centre, Burton Latimer, Northants. *(E W Services - 01933 225674)*
Antiques Fair, The King's Arms Hotel, Christchurch, Dorset. *(Forest Fairs - 01202 875167)*
Antique & Collectors' Fair, The Newmarket Racecourse, Newmarket, Suffolk. *(IACF Fairs - 01636 702326)*
Antique & Collectors' Fair, The Plumley Village Hall, near Knutsford, Cheshire. *(N & B Fairs - 01565 722144)*
Antiques Fair, The Town Hall, Hungerford, Berks. *(Silhouette Fairs - 01635 44338)*
Antique & Collectors' Fair, The Exhibition Halls, Park Hall, Charnock Richard, Lancs. *(Unicorn Fairs Ltd - 0161 773 7001)*

Regions continued

Tuesday 24th June
Antiques Fair, The Public Hall, Southdown Road, Harpenden, Herts. *(Chiltern Fairs - 01753 890301)*
Wednesday 25th June
Antique & Collectors' Fair, The Corn Exchange, High Street, Dorchester, Dorset. *(Forest Fairs - 01202 875167)*
Sunday 29th June
Antique & Collectors' Fair, The Willerby Manor Hotel, Hull, E. Yorks. *(Abbey Antiques Fairs - 01482 445785)*
Antiques Fair, The Mount Vernon Hospital, Northwood, Middlesex. *(Chiltern Fairs - 01753 890301)*
The Brunel Clock & Watch Fair, Brunel University, Kingston Lane, Uxbridge, Middlesex. *(Mr P Dungate - 01895 834694*
Antique & Collectors' Fair, The Guildhall, Salisbury, Wilts. *(Forest Fairs - 01202 875167)*
Antique & Collectors' Fair, The Harrow Leisure Centre, Christchurch Avenue, Harrow, Middlesex. *(Garden City Promotions - 0181 368 1902)*
Antiques Fair, The Haberdashers Askes School, Aldenham Road, Elstree, Herts. *(Harlequin Fairs - 01462 671688)*
Antique & Collectors' Fair, The Racecourse, Cheltenham, Glos. *(Melba Fairs - 01934 624854)*
Antique & Collectors' Fair, The Village Hall, Bashley, Hants. *(Renaissance Fairs - 01202 319914)*
Antiques Fair, The Wilmslow Moat House Hotel, Altrincham, Near Wilmslow, Cheshire. *(Georgina Stevens - 01625 536926)*
Antique & Collectors' Fair, The Exhibition Halls, Park Hall, Charnock Richard, Lancs. *(Unicorn Fairs Ltd - 0161 773 7001)*
Tuesday 1st July
The Sandown Park Antiques Fair, Sandown Exhibition Centre, Sandown Park Racecourse, Esher, Surrey. *(Wonder Whistle Enterprises - 0171 249 4050)*
Wednesday 2nd July
Antiques Fair, The Village Hall, Long Melford, Suffolk. *(Caring for the Past - 01473 658224)*
Thursday 3rd July
Antique & Collectors' Fair, The Bingley Hall County Showground, Stafford, Staffs. *(Bowman Antiques Fairs - 0113 284 3333)*
Saturday 5th July
Antiques Fair, The Chorleywood Memorial Hall, Common Road, Chorleywood, Herts. *(Chiltern Fairs - 01753 890301)*
Saturday 5th/Sunday 6th July
Antique & Collectors' Fair, The Pavilion Gardens, Buxton, Derbys. *(Unicorn Fairs Ltd - 0161 773 7001)*
Sunday 6th July
Antiques Fair, The Centre for Epilepsy, Chalfont St Peter, Bucks. *(Chiltern Fairs - 01753 890301)*
Antiques Fair, The Balmer Lawn Hotel, Brockenhurst, Hants. *(Forest Fairs - 01202 875167)*
Antiques & Collectors' Fair, The Kesgrave War Memorial Hall, Twelve Acre App. off Bell Lane, Kesgrave, Ipswich, Suffolk. *(Josef's Fairs - 01473 212423/685692)*

Regions continued

Antique & Collectors' Fair, The Fourways Inn, Chester Road, Delamere, Near Northwich, Cheshire. *(Pine Promotions - 01565 652092)*
Antique & Collectors' Fair, The Village Hall, Corfe Castle, Dorset. *(Renaissance Fairs - 01202 319914)*
Specialist Clock, Watch, Barometer & Scientific Instrument Fair, Kettering Leisure Village, Kettering, Northants. *(Right Time Clock Fairs - 01933 225674)*
Antique & Collectors' Fair, The Friendly Hotel, Tongwynlais, Cardiff, Wales. *(David Robinson Fairs - 01222 620520)*
Antique & Collectors' Fair, The Royal Enclosure, The Racecourse, Ascot, Berks. *(Silhouette Fairs - 01635 44338)*
Antique & Collectors' Fair, The Pembrokeshire Showground, Haverfordwest, Dyfed, Wales. *(Towy Antiques Fairs - 01225 314713)*
Antique & Collectors' Fair, The Exhibition Halls, Park Hall, Charnock Richard, Lancs. *(Unicorn Fairs Ltd - 0161 773 7001)*
Wednesday 9th July
Antiques & Collectors' Fair & Drive-In, The Racecourse, Newton Abbot, Devon. *(Melba Fairs - 01934 624854)*
Friday 11th/Sunday 13th July
The Tatton Park Decorative Antiques Fair, Tatton Park, Knutsford, Cheshire.
(Bailey Fairs - 01277 214677)
The 26th Annual Edinburgh Antiques Fair, The Roxburghe Hotel, Charlotte Square, Edinburgh, Scotland. *(Galloway Antiques Fairs - 01423 324602)*
Saturday 12th July
Antiques & Collectors' Fair, The Winter Gardens, (Seafront), Weston-Super-Mare, Avon. *(Melba Fairs - 01934 624854)*
Saturday 12th/Sunday 13th July
The Summer Little Easton Manor Antiques Fair, Little Easton, Near Great Dunmow, Essex. *(Caring for the Past - 01473 658224)*
The Shepton Mallet Antique & Collectors' Fair, The Royal Bath & West Showground, Shepton Mallet, Somerset. *(County Antiques Fairs - 01278 784912)*
Sunday 13th July
Antique & Collectors' Fair, The Allendale Centre, Wimborne, Dorset. *(Forest Fairs - 01202 875167)*
Antique & Collectors' Fair, The Potters Heron Hotel, Ampfield, Hants. *(Grandma's Attic Antique Fairs - 01590 677687)*
Antiques Fair, The Park Royal International Hotel, Stretton Road, Stretton, Warrington, Cheshire. *(Georgina Stevens - 01625 536926)*
Antique & Collectors' Fair, The Exhibition Halls, Park Hall, Charnock Richard, Lancs. *(Unicorn Fairs Ltd - 0161 773 7001)*
Thursday 17th/Sunday 20th July
The 31st Annual Snape Antiques Fair, The Pavilion on the Hepworth Lawn, Snape Maltings, Snape, Suffolk. *(Mr Donald Newby - 01986 875180)*
Saturday 19th July
Antique & Collectors' Fair, The Masonic Hall, High Street, Lymington, Hants. *(Grandma's Attic Antique Fairs - 01590 677687)*

Regions continued

Saturday 19th/Sunday 20th July

The North Cotswolds Antiques Fair, Stanway House, Near Winchcombe, Glos. *(Cooper Antiques Fair - 01249 661111)*

Sunday 20th July

The Malvern Antique & Collectors' Fair, The Three Counties Showground, Malvern, Worcestershire. *(County Antiques Fairs - 01278 784912)*

Antiques Fair, The Coach House Inn, Tricketts Cross, Ferndown, Dorset. *(Forest Fairs - 01202 875167)*

Antique & Collectors' Fair, The Village Hall, (Off Sway Road), New Forest, Brockenhurst, Hants. *(Grandma's Attic Antique Fairs - 01590 677687)*

Antiques Fair, The Haberdashers Askes School, Aldenham Road, Elstree, Herts. *(Harlequin Fairs - 01462 671688)*

Antique & Collectors' Fair, The The Hatfield Red Lion, Great North Road, Near Town Centre, Hatfield, Herts. *(Oakleigh Fairs - 01279 871110)*

Antique & Collectors' Fair, The Bowdon Rooms, The Firs, Bowdon, Near Altrincham, Cheshire. *(Pine Promotions - 01565 652092)*

Antique & Collectors' Fair, The Memorial Hall, West Parley, Dorset.*(Renaissance Fairs - 01202 319914)*

Specialist Clock, Watch, Barometer & Scientific Instrument Fair, The Federation Brewery, Newcastle. *(Right Time Clock Fairs - 01933 225674)*

Antique & Collectors' Fair, The Abbey Hall, Abingdon, Oxon. *(Silhouette Fairs - 01635 44338)*

Antique & Collectors' Fair, The Exhibition Halls, Park Hall, Charnock Richard, Lancs. *(Unicorn Fairs Ltd - 0161 773 7001)*

Tuesday 22nd July

Antiques Fair, The Public Hall, Southdown Road, Harpenden, Herts. *(Chiltern Fairs - 01753 890301)*

Wednesday 23rd July

Antique & Collectors' Fair, The Corn Exchange, High Street, Dorchester, Dorset. *(Forest Fairs - 01202 875167)*

The International Antique & Collectors' Fair, The South of England Showground, Ardingley, Sussex. *(IACF Ltd - 01636 702326)*

Friday 25th/Sunday 27th July

The Annual Lakes School Antiques Fair, Lakes School, Troutbeck Bridge, Windermere, Cumbria . *(Bailey Fairs - 01277 214677)*

Antique & Collectors' Fair, The Bingley Hall County Showground, Stafford, Staffs. *(Bowman Antiques Fairs - 0113 284 3333)*

The Ripley Castle Antiques Fair, Ripley, Near Harrogate, N. Yorks. *(Galloway Antiques Fairs - 01423 324602)*

The Great Northern International Antique & Collectors' Fair, The Yorkshire Showground, Harrogate, N. Yorks. *(Great Northern Antique Fairs - 01325 380077)*

The Welsh Borders Antiques Fair, Christ College, Brecon, Wales. *(Allen Lewis Fairs - 01202 604306)*

Regions continued

Saturday 26th July

Antique & Collectors' Fair, The St. Thomas' Church Hall, top of High Street, Lymington, Hants. *(Grandma's Attic Antique Fairs - 01590 677687)*

Saturday 26th/Sunday 27th July

The Morecambe Bay Deco Fair, The Midland Grand Hotel, Morecambe, Lancs. *(E W Services - 01933 225674)*

Sunday 27th July

Antiques Fair, The Racecourse, Windsor, Bucks. *(Chiltern Fairs - 01753 890301)*

Antique & Collectors' Fair, The Guildhall, Salisbury, Wilts. *(Forest Fairs - 01202 875167)*

Antique & Collectors' Fair, The Lyndhurst Park Hotel, High Street, Lyndhurst, Hants. *(Grandma's Attic Antique Fairs - 01590 677687)*

Antique & Collectors' Fair, The Racecourse, Cheltenham, Glos. *(Melba Fairs - 01934 624854)*

Antique & Collectors' Fair, The Plumley Village Hall, near Knutsford, Cheshire. *(N & B Fairs - 01565 722144)*

Antique & Collectors' Fair, The Village Hall, Bashley, Hants. *(Renaissance Fairs - 01202 319914)*

Antiques Fair, The Town Hall, Hungerford, Berks. *(Silhouette Fairs - 01635 44338)*

Antiques Fair, The Wilmslow Moat House Hotel, Altrincham, Near Wilmslow, Cheshire. *(Georgina Stevens - 01625 536926)*

Antique & Collectors' Fair, The Exhibition Halls, Park Hall, Charnock Richard, Lancs. *(Unicorn Fairs Ltd - 0161 773 7001)*

Tuesday 29th/Thursday 31st July

Antique & Collectors' Fair, The New Forest & Hants County Show, Brockenhurst, Hants.*(Forest Fairs - 01202 875167)*

Saturday 2nd August

Antiques Fair, The Chorleywood Memorial Hall, Common Road, Chorleywood, Herts. *(Chiltern Fairs - 01753 890301)*

Antique & Collectors' Fair, The Exeter Livestock Centre, Matford Park Road, Marsh Barton, Exeter, Devon. *(Devon County Antiques Fairs - 01363 82571)*

Antique & Collectors' Fair, The Masonic Hall, High Street, Lymington, Hants. *(Grandma's Attic Antique Fairs - 01590 677687)*

Sunday 3rd August

Antiques Fair, The Centre for Epilepsy, Chalfont St Peter, Bucks. *(Chiltern Fairs - 01753 890301)*

Antiques Fair, The Village Hall, Lewes Road, Ditchling, W. Sussex. *(Mr G Deakin - 01273 845141)*

Antique & Collectors' Fair, The Winchester Guildhall, The Broadway, Winchester, Hants. *(Grandma's Attic Antique Fairs - 01590 677687)*

Antique & Collectors' Fair, The Fourways Inn, Chester Road, Delamere, Near Northwich, Cheshire. *(Pine Promotions - 01565 652092)*

Antique & Collectors' Fair, The Village Hall, Corfe Castle, Dorset. *(Renaissance Fairs - 01202 319914)*

Antique & Collectors' Fair, The Copthorne Hotel, Culverhouse Cross, Cardiff, Wales. *(David Robinson Fairs - 01222 620520)*

Regions continued

Antique & Collectors' Fair, The Exhibition Halls, Park Hall, Charnock Richard, Lancs. *(Unicorn Fairs Ltd - 0161 773 7001)*

Tuesday 5th August

The Malvern Antique & Collectors' Fair, The Three Counties Showground, Malvern, Worcestershire. *(County Antiques Fairs - 01278 784912)*

Wednesday 6th August

Antiques Fair, The Village Hall, Long Melford, Suffolk. *(Caring for the Past - 01473 658224)*

Thursday 7th/Sunday 10th August

The N.E.C. Antiques Fair, 'Antiques for Everyone', Hall 5, National Exhibition Centre, Birmingham, West Midlands. *(Mrs Louise Goodwin - Centre Exhibitions - 0121 767 2760)*

Friday 8th/Sunday 10th August

The Fulbeck Hall Antiques Fair, Near Grantham, Lincs. *(Galloway Antiques Fair - 01423 324602)*

Sunday 10th August

Antiques & Collectors' Fair, The Kesgrave War Memorial Hall, Twelve Acre App. off Bell Lane, Kesgrave, Ipswich, Suffolk. *(Josef's Fairs - 01473 212423/685692)*

Antique & Collectors' Fair, The Memorial Hall, West Parley, Dorset. *(Renaissance Fairs - 01202 319914)*

Specialist Clock, Watch, Barometer & Scientific Instrument Fair, The Grove Leisure Centre, Newark, Notts. *(Right Time Clock Fairs - 01933 225674)*

Antiques Fair, The Park Royal International Hotel, Stretton Road, Stretton, Warrington, Cheshire. *(Georgina Stevens - 01625 536926)*

Antique & Collectors' Fair, The Exhibition Halls, Park Hall, Charnock Richard, Lancs. *(Unicorn Fairs Ltd - 0161 773 7001)*

Tuesday 12th August

The International Antique & Collectors' Fair, The Newark & Nottinghamshire Showground, Newark, Notts. *(IACF Fairs - 01636 702326)*

Friday 15th/Sunday 17th August

The Summer Chester Racecourse Antiques Fair, The Racecourse, Chester, Cheshire. *(Bailey Fairs - 01277 214677)*

The South Cotswolds Antiques Fair, The Westonbirt School, Tetbury, Glos. *(Cooper Antiques Fairs - 01249 661111)*

The Pendley Manor Antiques Fair, Tring, Herts. *(Galloway Antiques Fairs - 01423 324602*

Saturday 16th August

Antiques & Collectors' Fair, The Winter Gardens, (Seafront), Weston-Super-Mare, Avon. *(Melba Fairs - 01934 624854)*

Saturday 16th/Sunday 17th August

Antiques Fair, The Village Hall, Long Melford, Suffolk. *(Caring for the Past - 01473 658224)*

Sunday 17th August

The Malvern Antique & Collectors' Fair, The Three Counties Showground, Malvern, Worcestershire. *(County Antiques Fairs - 01278 784912)*

The Midlands Clock & Watch Fair, The National Motorcycle Museum, Solihull, Near Birmingham, West Midlands. *(Mr P Dungate - 01895 834694)*

Regions continued

The 20th Century Decorative Arts Fair, The Clifton Leisure Centre, Nottingham, Notts. *(E W Services - 01933 225674)*

Antiques Fair, The Balmer Lawn Hotel, Brockenhurst, Hants. *(Forest Fairs - 01202 875167)*

Antique & Collectors' Fair, The Kingston Maurward House (The Dorset College of Agriculture & Horticulture), Dorchester , Dorset. *(Grandma's Attic Antiques Fairs - 01590 677687)*

Antique & Collectors' Fair, The Newmarket Racecourse, Newmarket, Suffolk. *(IACF Fairs - 01636 702326)*

Antique & Collectors' Fair, The The Hatfield Red Lion, Great North Road, Near Town Centre, Hatfield, Herts. *(Oakleigh Fairs - 01279 871110)*

Antique & Collectors' Fair, The Bowdon Rooms, The Firs, Bowdon, Near Altrincham, Cheshire. *(Pine Promotions - 01565 652092)*

Antique & Collectors' Fair, The Abbey Hall, Abingdon, Oxon. *(Silhouette Fairs - 01635 44338)*

Antique & Collectors' Fair, The Exhibition Halls, Park Hall, Charnock Richard, Lancs. *(Unicorn Fairs Ltd - 0161 773 7001)*

Tuesday 19th August

Antique & Collectors' Fair & Drive-In, The Racecourse, Cheltenham, Glos. *(Melba Fairs - 01934 624854)*

Wednesday 20th August

Antiques & Collectors' Fair & Drive-In, The Racecourse, Newton Abbot, Devon. *(Melba Fairs - 01934 624854)*

Friday 22nd/Sunday 24th August

The Wiltshire Antiques Fair, The Marlborough College, Malborough, Wilts. *(Cooper Antiques Fairs - 01249 661111)*

Friday 22nd/Monday 25th August

The Annual Ilkley Antiques Fair, The Kings Hall and Wintergarden, Station Road, Ilkley, W. Yorks. *(Bailey Fairs - 01277 214677)*

The Naworth Castle Antiques Fair, Brampton, Carlisle, Cumbria. *(Galloway Antiques Fairs - 01423 324602)*

Saturday 23rd August

Antique & Collectors' Fair, The Masonic Hall, High Street, Lymington, Hants. *(Grandma's Attic Antique Fairs - 01590 677687)*

Saturday 23rd/Monday 25th August

Antique & Collectors' Fair, The Pavilion Gardens, Buxton, Derbys. *(Unicorn Fairs Ltd - 0161 773 7001)*

Sunday 24th August

Antiques Fair, The Racecourse, Windsor, Bucks. *(Chiltern Fairs - 01753 890301)*

Antique & Collectors' Fair, The Harrow Leisure Centre, Christchurch Avenue, Harrow, Middlesex. *(Garden Citty Promotions - 0181 368 1902)*

Antique & Collectors' Fair, The Village Hall, (Off Sway Road), New Forest, Brockenhurst, Hants. *(Grandma's Attic Antique Fairs - 01590 677687)*

Antiques Fair, The Town Hall, Hungerford, Berks. *(Silhouette Fairs - 01635 44338)*

Regions continued

Antique & Collectors' Fair, The Pembrokeshire Showground, Haverfordwest, Dyfed, Wales. *(Towy Antiques Fairs - 01225 314713)*

Antique & Collectors' Fair, The Exhibition Halls, Park Hall, Charnock Richard, Lancs. *(Unicorn Fairs Ltd - 0161 773 7001)*

Sunday 24th/Monday 25th August

Antique & Collectors' Fair, The Friendly Hotel, Tongwynlais, Cardiff, Wales. *(David Robinson Fairs - 01222 620520)*

Monday 25th August

Antiques Fair, The Mount Vernon Hospital, Northwood, Middlesex. *(Chiltern Fairs - 01753 890301)*

Antiques Fair, The King's Arms Hotel, Christchurch, Dorset. *(Forest Fairs - 01202 875167)*

Antique & Collectors' Fair, The Allendale Centre, Wimborne, Dorset. *(Grandma's Attic Antique Fairs - 01590 677687)*

Antique & Collectors' Fair, The Community Hall, Station Road, Woodbridge, Suffolk. *(Kyson Fairs - 01473 735528)*

Wednesday 27th August

Antique & Collectors' Fair, The Corn Exchange, High Street, Dorchester, Dorset. *(Forest Fairs - 01202 875167)*

Friday 29th/Sunday 31st August

The Hatfield House Antiques Fair, Hatfield House, Herts. *(Bailey Fairs - 01277 214677)*

Saturday 30th August

Antique & Collectors' Fair, The St. Thomas' Church Hall, top of High Street, Lymington, Hants. *(Grandma's Attic Antique Fairs - 01590 677687)*

Saturday 30th/Sunday 31st August

Antiques Fair, The Westpoint Exhibition Centre, Clyst St Mary, Exeter, Devon. *(Devon County Antiques Fairs - 01363 82571)*

Sunday 31st August

Glass Collectors' Fair, The Derngate, Northampton, Northants. *(E W Services - 01933 225674)*

Antique & Collectors' Fair, The Guildhall, Salisbury, Wilts. *(Forest Fairs - 01202 875167)*

Antique & Collectors' Fair, The Lyndhurst Park Hotel, High Street, Lyndhurst, Hants. *(Grandma's Attic Antique Fairs - 01590 677687)*

The International Antique & Collectors' Fair, The South of England Showground, Ardingley, Sussex. *(IACF Ltd - 01636 702326)*

Antique & Collectors' Fair, The Racecourse, Cheltenham, Glos. *(Melba Fairs - 01934 624854)*

Antique & Collectors' Fair, The Plumley Village Hall, near Knutsford, Cheshire. *(N & B Fairs - 01565 722144)*

Antique & Collectors' Fair, The Village Hall, Bashley, Hants. *(Renaissance Fairs - 01202 319914)*

Antiques Fair, The Wilmslow Moat House Hotel, Altrincham, Near Wilmslow, Cheshire. *(Georgina Stevens - 01625 536926)*

Antique & Collectors' Fair, The Exhibition Halls, Park Hall, Charnock Richard, Lancs. *(Unicorn Fairs Ltd - 0161 773 7001)*

Regions continued

Tuesday 2nd September

Antique & Collectors' Fair, The Suffolk Showground, Bucklesham Road, Ipswich, Suffolk. *(IACF Fairs - 01636 702326)*

Wednesday 3rd September

Antiques Fair, The Village Hall, Long Melford, Suffolk. *(Caring for the Past - 01473 658224)*

Thursday 4th/Saturday 6th September

The Petersfield Antiques Fair, The Town Hall, Petersfield, Hants. *(Gamlin Exhibition Services - 01452 862557)*

Thursday 4th/Sunday 7th September

Antiques & Fine Arts Fair, The Caerleon Campus of the University of Wales College, Newport, Wales. *(Caerleon Antiques & Fine Art - 01594 564001)*

Friday 5th/Sunday 7th September

The Great Northern International Antique & Collectors' Fair, The Yorkshire Showground, Harrogate, N. Yorks. *(Great Northern Antique Fairs - 01325 380077)*

The Antique Dealers Fair of Wales, The Orangery, Margam Park, S. Wales. *(Allen Lewis Fairs - 01202 604306)*

Saturday 6th September

Antiques Fair, The Chorleywood Memorial Hall, Common Road, Chorleywood, Herts. *(Chiltern Fairs - 01753 890301)*

Antique & Collectors' Fair, The Masonic Hall, High Street, Lymington, Hants. *(Grandma's Attic Antique Fairs - 01590 677687)*

Sunday 7th September

Antiques Fair, The Centre for Epilepsy, Chalfont St Peter, Bucks. *(Chiltern Fairs - 01753 890301)*

The Malvern Antique & Collectors' Fair, The Three Counties Showground, Malvern, Worcestershire. *(County Antiques Fairs - 01278 784912)*

Antique & Collectors' Fair, The Allendale Centre, Wimborne, Dorset. *(Forest Fairs - 01202 875167)*

Antique & Collectors' Fair, The Winchester Guildhall, The Broadway, Winchester, Hants. *(Grandma's Attic Antique Fairs - 01590 677687)*

Antiques & Collectors' Fair, The Kesgrave War Memorial Hall, Twelve Acre App. off Bell Lane, Kesgrave, Ipswich, Suffolk. *(Josef's Fairs - 01473 212423/685692)*

Antique & Collectors' Fair, The Fourways Inn, Chester Road, Delamere, Near Northwich, Cheshire. *(Pine Promotions - 01565 652092)*

Antique & Collectors' Fair, The Village Hall, Corfe Castle, Dorset. *(Renaissance Fairs - 01202 319914)*

Specialist Clock, Watch, Barometer & Scientific Instrument Fair, Crawley Leisure Centre, Crawley, West Sussex. *(Right Time Clock Fairs - 01933 225674)*

Antique & Collectors' Fair, Miskin Manor, Miskin, Near Cardiff, Wales. *(David Robinson Fairs - 01222 620520)*

Antique & Collectors' Fair, The Royal Enclosure, The Racecourse, Ascot, Berks. *(Silhouette Fairs - 01635 44338)*

Regions continued

Antique & Collectors' Fair, The Exhibition Halls, Park Hall, Charnock Richard, Lancs. *(Unicorn Fairs Ltd - 0161 773 7001)*
The Sandown Park Antiques Fair, Sandown Exhibition Centre, Sandown Park Racecourse, Esher, Surrey. *(Wonder Whistle Enterprises - 0171 249 4050)*
Wednesday 10th/Sunday 14th September
The Tatton Park Decorative Antiques Fair, Tatton Park, Knutsford, Cheshire.
(Bailey Fairs - 01277 214677)
Saturday 13th September
Antique & Collectors' Fair, The Exeter Livestock Centre, Matford Park Road, Marsh Barton, Exeter, Devon. *(Devon County Antiques Fairs - 01363 82571)*
Antique & Collectors' Fair, The Romsey Show, Broadlands, Romsey, Hants. *(Forest Fairs - 01202 875167)*
Saturday 13th/Sunday 14th September
Art Nouveau & Art Deco Fair, The Kettering Leisure Village, Kettering, Northants. *(E W Services - 01933 225674)*
Antique & Collectors' Fair, The G-Mex Exhibition Centre, Manchester *(IACF Fairs - 01636 702326)*
Sunday 14th September
The Furze Hill Antiques Fair, The Banqueting Centre, Margaretting, Near Chelmsford, Essex. *(Caring for the Past - 01473 658224)*
The Brunel Clock & Watch Fair, Brunel University, Kingston Lane, Uxbridge, Middlesex. *(Mr P Dungate - 01895 834694*
Antiques Fair, The Coach House Inn, Tricketts Cross, Ferndown, Dorset. *(Forest Fairs - 01202 875167)*
Antique & Collectors' Fair, The Village Hall, (Off Sway Road), New Forest, Brockenhurst, Hants. *(Grandma's Attic Antique Fairs - 01590 677687)*
Antique & Collectors Fair, The Royal Chase Hotel, Queens Banquesting Suite, The Ridgeway, Enfield, Middlesex. *(M & S Enterprises - 0181 440 2330)*
Antique & Collectors' Fair, The Knutsford Civic Centre, Toft Road, Knutsford, Cheshire. *(Pine Promotions - 01565 652092)*
Antiques Fair, The Park Royal International Hotel, Stretton Road, Stretton, Warrington, Cheshire. *(Georgina Stevens - 01625 536926)*
Antique & Collectors' Fair, The Exhibition Halls, Park Hall, Charnock Richard, Lancs. *(Unicorn Fairs Ltd - 0161 773 7001)*
Tuesday 16th/Wednesday 17th September
The Shepton Mallet Antique & Collectors' Fair, The Royal Bath & West Showground, Shepton Mallet, Somerset. *(County Antiques Fairs - 01278 784912)*
Friday 19th/Sunday 21st September
The Holdenby House Antiques Fair, Holdenby, Northants. *(Galloway Antique Fairs - 01423 324602)*
Saturday 20th September
Antiques & Collectors' Fair, The Winter Gardens, (Seafront), Weston-Super-Mare, Avon. *(Melba Fairs - 01934 624854)*

Regions continued

Saturday 20th/Sunday 21st September
The West Midlands Antiques Fair, The Town Hall, Sutton Coldfield, W. Midlands. *(Cooper Antiques Fairs - 01249 661111)*
Sunday 21st September
Antiques Fair, The Mount Vernon Hospital, Northwood, Middlesex. *(Chiltern Fairs - 01753 890301)*
Antiques Fair, The Balmer Lawn Hotel, Brockenhurst, Hants. *(Forest Fairs - 01202 875167)*
Antique & Collectors' Fair, The Potters Heron Hotel, Ampfield, Hants. *(Grandma's Attic Antique Fairs - 01590 677687)*
Antiques Fair, The Haberdashers Askes School, Aldenham Road, Elstree, Herts. *(Harlequin Fairs - 01462 671688)*
Antique & Collectors' Fair, The Harrow Leisure Centre, Christchurch Avenue, Wealdstone, Middlesex. *(Jax Fairs - 01444 400570)*
Antique & Collectors' Fair, The Community Hall, Station Road, Woodbridge, Suffolk. *(Kyson Fairs - 01473 735528)*
Antique & Collectors Fair, The Water End Barn, Banquetting Suite, St Peters Street, St Albans, Herts. *(M & S Enterprises - 0181 440 2330)*
Antique & Collectors' Fair, The The Hatfield Red Lion, Great North Road, Near Town Centre, Hatfield, Herts. *(Oakleigh Fairs - 01279 871110)*
Antique & Collectors' Fair, The Bowdon Rooms, The Firs, Bowdon, Near Altrincham, Cheshire. *(Pine Promotions - 01565 652092)*
Antique & Collectors' Fair, The Memorial Hall, West Parley, Dorset.*(Renaissance Fairs - 01202 319914)*
Antique & Collectors' Fair, The Stakis Newport, Chepstow Road, Langstone ? *(David Robinson Fairs - 01222 620520)*
Antique & Collectors' Fair, The Abbey Hall, Abingdon, Oxon. *(Silhouette Fairs - 01635 44338)*
Antiques Fair, The Wilmslow Moat House Hotel, Altrincham, Near Wilmslow, Cheshire. *(Georgina Stevens - 01625 536926)*
Antique & Collectors' Fair, The Exhibition Halls, Park Hall, Charnock Richard, Lancs. *(Unicorn Fairs Ltd - 0161 773 7001)*
Tuesday 23rd September
Antiques Fair, The Public Hall, Southdown Road, Harpenden, Herts. *(Chiltern Fairs - 01753 890301)*
Wednesday 24th September
Antique & Collectors' Fair, The Corn Exchange, High Street, Dorchester, Dorset. *(Forest Fairs - 01202 875167)*
The International Antique & Collectors' Fair, The South of England Showground, Ardingley, Sussex. *(IACF Ltd - 01636 702326)*
Antiques & Collectors' Fair & Drive-In, The Racecourse, Newton Abbot, Devon. *(Melba Fairs - 01934 624854)*
Thursday 25th/Sunday 28th September
The Moat House Antiques Fair, King's Road, Harrogate, N. Yorks. *(Galloway Antiques Fairs - 01423 324602)*

Regions continued

Thursday 25th September/ Wednesday 1st October
The 47th Northern Antiques Fair, The Royal Baths Assembly Rooms, Harrogate, N .Yorks. *(Bailey Fairs - 01277 214677)*
Friday 26th/Sunday 28th September
The Cotswolds Oak & Country Antiques Fair, The Chavenage House, Tetbury, Glos. *(Cooper Antique Fairs - 01249 661111)*
Saturday 27th September
Antique & Collectors' Fair, The Salisbury Leisure Centre, The Butts, Hulse Road, Salisbury, Wilts. *(Devon County Antiques Fairs - 01363 82571)*
Antique & Collectors' Fair, The St. Thomas' Church Hall, top of High Street, Lymington, Hants. *(Grandma's Attic Antique Fairs - 01590 677687)*
Antique & Collectors' Fair, The Macclesfield Leisure Centre, Priory Lane, Macclesfield, Cheshire. *(Pine Promotions - 01565 652092)*
Saturday 27th/Sunday 28th September
Antique & Collectors' Fair, The Pavilion Gardens, Buxton, Derbys. *(Unicorn Fairs Ltd - 0161 773 7001)*
Sunday 28th September
Antiques Fair, The Racecourse, Windsor, Bucks. *(Chiltern Fairs - 01753 890301)*
Antiques & Collectors' Fair, The Derngate, Northampton, Northants. *(E W Services - 01933 225674)*
Antique & Collectors' Fair, The Guildhall, Salisbury, Wilts. *(Forest Fairs - 01202 875167)*
Antique & Collectors' Fair, The Lyndhurst Park Hotel, High Street, Lyndhurst, Hants. *(Grandma's Attic Antique Fairs - 01590 677687)*
Antique & Collectors' Fair, The Racecourse, Cheltenham, Glos. *(Melba Fairs - 01934 624854)*
Antique & Collectors' Fair, The Plumley Village Hall, near Knutsford, Cheshire. *(N & B Fairs - 01565 722144)*
Antique & Collectors' Fair, The Village Hall, Bashley, Hants. *(Renaissance Fairs - 01202 319914)*
Specialist Clock, Watch, Barometer & Scientific Instrument Fair, The Elmbridge Leisure Centre, Walton on Thames. *(Right Time Clock Fairs - 01933 225674)*
Antiques Fair, The Town Hall, Hungerford, Berks. *(Silhouette Fairs - 01635 44338)*
Antique & Collectors' Fair, The Exhibition Halls, Park Hall, Charnock Richard, Lancs. *(Unicorn Fairs Ltd - 0161 773 7001)*
Wednesday 1st October
Antiques Fair, The Village Hall, Long Melford, Suffolk. *(Caring for the Past - 01473 658224)*
Thursday 2nd/Sunday 5th October
The 30th Surrey Antiques Fair, The Civic Hall, Guildford, Surrey. *(Cultural Exhibitions Ltd - 01483 422562)*
Friday 3rd/Sunday 5th October
Antique & Collectors' Fair, The Bingley Hall County Showground, Stafford, Staffs. *(Bowman Antiques Fairs - 0113 284 3333)*

Regions continued

The North Yorkshire Antiques Fair, Hovingham Hall, Hovingham, Yorks. *(Cooper Antiques Fair - 01249 661111)*
The Leighton Hall Antiques Fair, Carnforth, Lancs. *(Galloway Antiques Fairs - 01423 324602)*
Saturday 4th October
Antiques Fair, The Chorleywood Memorial Hall, Common Road, Chorleywood, Herts. *(Chiltern Fairs - 01753 890301)*
Antique & Collectors' Fair, The Exeter Livestock Centre, Matford Park Road, Marsh Barton, Exeter, Devon. *(Devon County Antiques Fairs - 01363 82571)*
Antiques Fair, The Community Centre, Buckingham, Bucks . *(E W Services - 01933 225674)*
Antique & Collectors' Fair, The Masonic Hall, High Street, Lymington, Hants. *(Grandma's Attic Antique Fairs - 01590 677687)*
Antiques & Collectors' Fair, The Winter Gardens (Seafront), Weston-Super-Mare, Avon. *(Melba Fairs - 01934 624854)*
Saturday 4th/Sunday 5th October
The Autumn Little Easton Manor Antiques Fair, Little Easton, Near Great Dunmow, Essex. *(Caring for the Past - 01473 658224)*
Sunday 5th October
Antiques Fair, The Centre for Epilepsy, Chalfont St Peter, Bucks. *(Chiltern Fairs - 01753 890301)*
Antiques Fair, The Village Hall, Lewes Road, Ditchling, W. Sussex. *(Mr G Deakin - 01273 845141)*
Antique & Collectors' Fair, The Brigstock Village Hall, Bridge Street, Brigstock, Northants. *(E W Services - 01933 225674)*
Antiques Fair, The Balmer Lawn Hotel, Brockenhurst, Hants. *(Forest Fairs - 01202 875167)*
Antique & Collectors' Fair, The Winchester Guildhall, The Broadway, Winchester, Hants. *(Grandma's Attic Antique Fairs - 01590 677687)*
Antique & Collectors' Fair, The The Harlow Moat House Hotel, Southern Way, Harlow, Essex. *(Oakleigh Fairs - 01279 871110)*
Antiques & Collectors' Fair, The Fourways Inn, Chester Road, Delamere, Near Northwich, Cheshire. *(Pine Promotions - 01565 652092)*
Antique & Collectors' Fair, The Village Hall, Corfe Castle, Dorset. *(Renaissance Fairs - 01202 319914)*
Antique & Collectors' Fair, The Newhouse Country Hotel, Thornhill, Cardiff, Wales. *(David Robinson Fairs - 01222 620520)*
Antique & Collectors' Fair, The Royal Enclosure, The Racecourse, Ascot, Berks. *(Silhouette Fairs - 01635 44338)*
Antique & Collectors' Fair, The Exhibition Halls, Park Hall, Charnock Richard, Lancs. *(Unicorn Fairs Ltd - 0161 773 7001)*
Friday 10th/Sunday 12th October
The Annual Kelham Hall Antiques Fair, Kelham Hall, Near Newark, Notts. *(Bailey Fairs - 01277 214677)*
The Cheshire County Antiques Fair, Arley Hall, Near Knutsford, Cheshire. *(Cooper Antiques Fair - 01249 661111)*

Regions continued

Saturday 11th October

Antiques & Collectors' Fair, The Kesgrave War Memorial Hall, Twelve Acre App. off Bell Lane, Kesgrave, Ipswich, Suffolk. *(Josef's Fairs - 01473 212423/685692)*

Saturday 11th/Sunday 12th October

Art Nouveau & Art Deco Fair, The Kettering Leisure Village, Kettering, Northants. *(E W Services - 01933 225674)*

Sunday 12th October

The Furze Hill Antiques Fair, The Banqueting Centre, Margaretting, Near Chelmsford, Essex. *(Caring for the Past - 01473 658224)*

The Malvern Antique & Collectors' Fair, The Three Counties Showground, Malvern, Worcestershire. *(County Antiques Fairs - 01278 784912)*

Antiques Fair, The King's Arms Hotel, Christchurch, Dorset. *(Forest Fairs - 01202 875167)*

Antique & Collectors' Fair, The Allendale Centre, Wimborne, Dorset. *(Grandma's Attic Antique Fairs - 01590 677687)*

Antique & Collectors' Fair, The Community Hall, Station Road, Woodbridge, Suffolk. *(Kyson Fairs - 01473 735528)*

Antique & Collectors' Fair, The Moat House, Dupont Suite, Barnet By-pass, Borehamwood, Elstree, Herts. *(M & S Enterprises - 0181 440 2330)*

Antique & Collectors' Fair, The Knutsford Civic Centre, Toft Road, Knutsford, Cheshire. *(Pine Promotions - 01565 652092)*

Antique & Collectors' Fair, The Memorial Hall, West Parley, Dorset.*(Renaissance Fairs - 01202 319914)*

Antiques Fair, The Park Royal International Hotel, Stretton Road, Stretton, Warrington, Cheshire. *(Georgina Stevens - 01625 536926)*

Antique & Collectors' Fair, The Exhibition Halls, Park Hall, Charnock Richard, Lancs. *(Unicorn Fairs Ltd - 0161 773 7001)*

Tuesday 14th October

The Sandown Park Antiques Fair, Sandown Exhibition Centre, Sandown Park Racecourse, Esher, Surrey. *(Wonder Whistle Enterprises - 0171 249 4050)*

Wednesday 15th October

Antiques & Collectors' Fair & Drive-In, The Racecourse, Newton Abbot, Devon. *(Melba Fairs - 01934 624854)*

Wednesday 15th/Sunday 19th October

The Decorative Antiques & Fine Arts Fair, The Pavilions, Gardens Buxton, Derbys. *(Bailey Fairs - 01277 214677)*

Friday 17th/Sunday 19th October

The Stansted House Antiques Fair, Rowlands Castle, Hants. *(Galloway Antiques Fair - 01423 324602)*

Saturday 18th October

Antiques Fair, Dr Challoner's Grammar School, Amersham, Bucks. *(Chiltern Fairs - 01753 890301)*

Saturday 18th/Sunday 19th October

The 44th Luton Antiques Fair, Putteridge Bury House on the A505, Luton to Hitchin Road, Herts. *(Mr D Ball - 01525 210753)*

Regions continued

The Stafford County Antiques Fair, Sandon Hall, Sandon, Near Stone, Staffs. *(Cooper Antiques Fair - 01249 661111)*

Antique & Collectors' Fair, The Kingston Maurward House, (The Dorset College of Agriculture & Horticulture) , Dorchester , Dorset. *(Grandma's Attic Antiques Fairs - 01590 677687)*

Sunday 19th October

Antiques Fair, The Mount Vernon Hospital, Northwood, Middlesex. *(Chiltern Fairs - 01753 890301)*

Antiques & Collectors' Fair, The St Peter's School, Huntingdon, Cambs. *(E W Services- 01933 225674)*

Antiques Fair, The Coach House Inn, Tricketts Cross, Ferndown, Dorset. *(Forest Fairs - 01202 875167)*

Antiques Fair, The Haberdashers Askes School, Aldenham Road, Elstree, Herts. *(Harlequin Fairs - 01462 671688)*

Antique & Collectors Fair, The Water End Barn, Banquetting Suite, St Peters Street, St Albans, Herts. *(M & S Enterprises - 0181 440 2330)*

Antique & Collectors' Fair, The The Hatfield Red Lion, Great North Road, Near Town Centre, Hatfield, Herts. *(Oakleigh Fairs - 01279 871110)*

Antique & Collectors' Fair, The Bowdon Rooms, The Firs, Bowdon, Near Altrincham, Cheshire. *(Pine Promotions - 01565 652092)*

Specialist Clock, Watch, Barometer & Scientific Instrument Fair, The Grove Leisure Centre, Newark, Notts. *(Right Time Clock Fairs - 01933 225674)*

Antique & Collectors' Fair, The Copthorne Hotel, Culverhouse Cross, Cardiff, Wales. *(David Robinson Fairs - 01222 620520)*

Antique & Collectors' Fair, The Abbey Hall, Abingdon, Oxon. *(Silhouette Fairs - 01635 44338)*

Antique & Collectors' Fair, The Exhibition Halls, Park Hall, Charnock Richard, Lancs. *(Unicorn Fairs Ltd - 0161 773 7001)*

Tuesday 21st October

Antiques Fair, The Public Hall, Southdown Road, Harpenden, Herts. *(Chiltern Fairs - 01753 890301)*

The International Antique & Collectors' Fair, The Newark & Nottinghamshire Showground, Newark, Notts. *(IACF Fairs - 01636 702326)*

Wednesday 22nd October

Antique & Collectors' Fair, The Corn Exchange, High Street, Dorchester, Dorset. *(Forest Fairs - 01202 875167)*

Friday 24th/Sunday 26th October

The Annual Hertfordshire Antiques Fair, The Hertfordshire Conference and Exhibition Centre, Old Knebworth Lane, Stevenage, Herts. *(Bailey Fairs - 01277 214677)*

The Oxfordshire Antiques Fair, Bloxham School, Bloxham, Near Banbury, Oxon. *(Cooper Antique Fairs - 01249 661111)*

The Stonyhurst College Antiques Fair, Near Clitheroe, Lancs. *(Galloway Antique Fairs - 01423 324602)*

The Sixth East Anglian Antique Dealers Fair, Langley Park School, Loddon, Norfolk. *(Lomax Antiques Fairs - 01603 737631)*

Regions continued

Saturday 25th October
Antique & Collectors' Fair, The St. Thomas' Church Hall, top of High Street, Lymington, Hants. *(Grandma's Attic Antique Fairs - 01590 677687)*
Antique & Collectors' Fair, The Macclesfield Leisure Centre, Priory Lane, Macclesfield, Cheshire. *(Pine Promotions - 01565 652092)*

Saturday 25th/Sunday 26th October
The Cardiff Antiques Fair, The Cardiff International Arena, Cardiff, South Glamorgan *(County Antiques Fairs - 01278 784912)*

Sunday 26th October
Antiques Fair, The Racecourse, Windsor, Bucks. *(Chiltern Fairs - 01753 890301)*
Antiques & Collectors' Fair, The Derngate, Northampton, Northants. *(E W Services - 01933 225674)*
Antique & Collectors' Fair, The Harrow Leisure Centre, Christchurch Avenue, Harrow, Middlesex. *(Garden City Promotions - 0181 368 1902)*
Antique & Collectors' Fair, The Lyndhurst Park Hotel, High Street, Lyndhurst, Hants. *(Grandma's Attic Antique Fairs - 01590 677687)*
Antique & Collectors' Fair, The Newmarket Racecourse, Newmarket, Suffolk. *(IACF Fairs - 01636 702326)*
Antique & Collectors' Fair, The Racecourse, Cheltenham, Glos. *(Melba Fairs - 01934 624854)*
Antique & Collectors Fair, The Royal Chase Hotel, Queens Banquesting Suite, The Ridgeway, Enfield, Middlesex. *(M & S Enterprises - 0181 440 2330)*
Antique & Collectors' Fair, The Plumley Village Hall, near Knutsford, Cheshire. *(N & B Fairs - 01565 722144)*
Antique & Collectors' Fair, The Village Hall, Bashley, Hants. *(Renaissance Fairs - 01202 319914)*
Antiques Fair, The Town Hall, Hungerford, Berks. *(Silhouette Fairs - 01635 44338)*
Antiques Fair, The Wilmslow Moat House Hotel, Altrincham, Near Wilmslow, Cheshire. *(Georgina Stevens - 01625 536926)*
Antique & Collectors' Fair, The Exhibition Halls, Park Hall, Charnock Richard, Lancs. *(Unicorn Fairs Ltd - 0161 773 7001)*

Friday 31st October/Sunday 2nd November
The High Wycombe Antiques Fair, The Town Hall, High Wycombe, Bucks. *(Cooper Antiques Fair - 01249 661111)*
The Duncombe Park Antiques Fair, Near Helmsley, North Yorks. (*Galloway Antiques Fair - 01423 324602)*

Saturday 1st November
Antiques Fair, The Chorleywood Memorial Hall, Common Road, Chorleywood, Herts. *(Chiltern Fairs - 01753 890301)*
Antique & Collectors' Fair, The Masonic Hall, High Street, Lymington, Hants. *(Grandma's Attic Antique Fairs - 01590 677687)*

Saturday 1st/Sunday 2nd November
Antiques Fair, The Westpoint Exhibition Centre, Clyst St Mary, Exeter, Devon. *(Devon County Antiques Fairs - 01363 82571)*

Regions continued

Antique & Collectors' Fair, The Wellingborough School, Wellingborough, Northants. *(E W Services - 01933 225674)*
Antique & Collectors' Fair, The Pavilion Gardens Buxton, Derbys. *(Unicorn Fairs Ltd - 0161 773 7001)*

Sunday 2nd November
Antiques Fair, The Centre for Epilepsy, Chalfont St Peter, Bucks. *(Chiltern Fairs - 01753 890301)*
The Malvern Antique & Collectors' Fair, The Three Counties Showground, Malvern, Worcestershire *(County Antiques Fairs - 01278 784912)*
Antiques Fair, The Balmer Lawn Hotel, Brockenhurst Hants. *(Forest Fairs - 01202 875167)*
Antique & Collectors' Fair, The Winchester Guildhall The Broadway, Winchester, Hants. *(Grandma's Attic Antique Fairs - 01590 677687)*
The Glass' Collectors Fair, The National Motorcycle Museum, Birmingham, W. Midlands. *(Patricia Hier 01260 271975)*
Antique & Collectors' Fair, The Fourways Inn Chester Road, Delamere, Near Northwich, Cheshire *(Pine Promotions - 01565 652092)*
Specialist Clock, Watch, Barometer & Scientific Instrument Fair, The Elmbridge Leisure Centre Walton on Thames. *(Right Time Clock Fairs - 0193 225674)*
Antique & Collectors' Fair, The Friendly Hotel Tongwynlais, Cardiff, Wales. *(David Robinson Fairs 01222 620520)*
Antique & Collectors' Fair, The Royal Enclosure, The Racecourse, Ascot, Berks. *(Silhouette Fairs - 0163 44338)*
Antique & Collectors' Fair, The Exhibition Halls, Park Hall, Charnock Richard, Lancs. *(Unicorn Fairs Ltd 0161 773 7001)*

Wednesday 5th November
Antiques Fair, The Village Hall, Long Melford Suffolk. *(Caring for the Past - 01473 658224)*
The International Antique & Collectors' Fair, The South of England Showground, Ardingley, Sussex *(IACF Ltd - 01636 702326)*

Thursday 6th November
Antique & Collectors' Fair, The Bingley Hall Count Showground, Stafford, Staffs. *(Bowman Antique Fairs - 0113 284 3333)*

Friday 7th/Sunday 9th November
The Annual Holker Hall Antique Fair, Holker Hall Cark-in-Cartmel, Grange-over-sands, Cumbria. *(Baile Fairs - 01277 214677)*
The Leicester County Antique Fair, Prestwold Hal Near Hoton, Loughborough, Leics. *(Cooper Antique Fairs - 01249 661111)*
The 20th Edinburgh Antiques Fair, The Roxburgh Hotel, Charlotte Square, Edinburgh, Scotland *(Galloway Antiques Fairs - 01423 324602)*
The Great Northern International Antique Collectors' Fair, The Yorkshire Showground Harrogate, N. Yorks. *(Great Northern Antique Fairs 01325 380077)*

Saturday 8th November
Antiques & Collectors' Fair, The Kesgrave Wa Memorial Hall, Twelve Acre App. off Bell Lane Kesgrave, Ipswich, Suffolk. *(Josef's Fairs - 0147 212423/685692)*

Regions continued

Antiques & Collectors' Fair, The Winter Gardens, (Seafront), Weston-Super-Mare, Avon. *(Melba Fairs - 01934 624854)*

Saturday 8th/Sunday 9th November

Art Nouveau & Art Deco Fair, The Kettering Leisure Village, Kettering, Northants. *(E W Services - 01933 225674)*

Sunday 9th November

The Furze Hill Antiques Fair, The Banqueting Centre, Margaretting, Near Chelmsford, Essex. *(Caring for the Past - 01473 658224)*

Antique & Collectors' Fair, The Allendale Centre, Wimborne, Dorset. *(Forest Fairs - 01202 875167)*

Antique & Collectors' Fair, The Littledown Centre, Castle Lane (Opp New Bournemouth Hospital), Dorset. *(Grandma's Attic Antique Fairs - 01590 677687)*

Antique & Collectors' Fair, The Bushey Golf & Country Club, Banquetting Suite, The High Street, Bushey, Herts. *(M & S Enterprises - 0181 440 2330)*

Antique & Collectors' Fair, The Knutsford Civic Centre, Toft Road, Knutsford, Cheshire. *(Pine Promotions - 01565 652092)*

Antique & Collectors' Fair, The Memorial Hall, West Parley, Dorset.*(Renaissance Fairs - 01202 319914)*

Antiques Fair, The Park Royal International Hotel, Stretton Road, Stretton, Warrington, Cheshire. *(Georgina Stevens - 01625 536926)*

Antique & Collectors' Fair, The Pembrokeshire Showground, Haverfordwest, Dyfed, Wales. *(Towy Antiques Fairs - 01225 314713)*

Antique & Collectors' Fair, The Exhibition Halls, Park Hall, Charnock Richard, Lancs. *(Unicorn Fairs Ltd - 0161 773 7001)*

Tuesday 11th November

Antique & Collectors' Fair, The National Agriculture Centre, Stoneleigh, Near Kenilworth, West Midlands. *IACF Fairs - 01636 702326)*

Saturday 15th/Sunday 16th November

The Shepton Mallet Antique & Collectors' Fair, The Royal Bath & West Showground, Shepton Mallet, Somerset. *(County Antiques Fairs - 01278 784912)*

Antiques & Decorative Arts Fair, The Lordsbridge Arena, Barton, Cambs. *(E W Services - 01933 225674)*

Sunday 16th November

Antique & Collectors' Fair, The Guildhall, Salisbury, Wilts. *(Forest Fairs - 01202 875167)*

Antique & Collectors' Fair, The Village Hall, (Off Sway Road), New Forest, Brockenhurst, Hants. *(Grandma's Attic Antique Fairs - 01590 677687)*

Antiques Fair, The Haberdashers Askes School, Aldenham Road, Elstree, Herts. *(Harlequin Fairs - 01462 671688)*

Antique & Collectors' Fair, The Community Hall, Station Road, Woodbridge, Suffolk. *(Kyson Fairs - 01473 735528)*

Antique & Collectors' Fair, The The Hatfield Red Lion, Great North Road, Near Town Centre, Hatfield, Herts. *(Oakleigh Fairs - 01279 871110)*

Antique & Collectors' Fair, The Bowdon Rooms, The Firs, Bowdon, Near Altrincham, Cheshire. *(Pine Promotions - 01565 652092)*

Regions continued

Specialist Clock, Watch, Barometer & Scientific Instrument Fair, The Federation Brewery, Newcastle. *(Right Time Clock Fairs - 01933 225674)*

Antique & Collectors' Fair, Miskin Manor, Miskin, Near Cardiff, Wales. *(David Robinson Fairs - 01222 620520)*

Antique & Collectors' Fair, The Abbey Hall, Abingdon, Oxon. *(Silhouette Fairs - 01635 44338)*

Antique & Collectors' Fair, The Exhibition Halls, Park Hall, Charnock Richard, Lancs. *(Unicorn Fairs Ltd - 0161 773 7001)*

Wednesday 19th November

Antique & Collectors' Fair, The East of England Showground, Peterborough, Cambs. *(IACF Fairs - 01636 702326)*

Antiques & Collectors' Fair & Drive-In, The Racecourse, Newton Abbot, Devon. *(Melba Fairs - 01934 624854)*

Friday 21st/Sunday 23rd November

The Annual HoghtonTowers Antiques Fair, Hoghton, Preston, Lancs. *(Bailey Fairs - 01277 214677)*

The Beaulieu Antiques Fair, The Bealieu National Motor Museum, Near Brockenhurst, Hants. *(Galloway Antiques Fairs - 01423 324602)*

Saturday 22nd November

Antique & Collectors' Fair, The St. Thomas' Church Hall, top of High Street, Lymington, Hants. *(Grandma's Attic Antique Fairs - 01590 677687)*

Sunday 23rd November

The Woodbridge Antiques Fair, Melton Grange Hotel, Pytches Road, Woodbridge, Suffolk. *(Caring for the Past - 01473 658224)*

Antiques Fair, The Racecourse, Windsor, Bucks. *(Chiltern Fairs - 01753 890301)*

Antiques & Collectors' Fair, The Derngate, Northampton, Northants. *(E W Services - 01933 225674)*

Antiques Fair, The Coach House Inn, Tricketts Cross, Ferndown, Dorset. *(Forest Fairs - 01202 875167)*

Antique & Collectors' Fair, The Harrow Leisure Centre, Christchurch Avenue, Harrow, Middlesex. *(Garden City Promotions - 0181 368 1902)*

Antique & Collectors' Fair, The Potters Heron Hotel, Ampfield, Hants. *(Grandma's Attic Antique Fairs - 01590 677687)*

Antique & Collectors Fair, The Royal Chase Hotel, Queens Banquesting Suite, The Ridgeway, Enfield, Middlesex. *(M & S Enterprises - 0181 440 2330)*

Specialist Clock, Watch, Barometer & Scientific Instrument Fair, Crawley Leisure Centre, Crawley, West Sussex. *(Right Time Clock Fairs - 01933 225674)*

Antiques Fair, The Town Hall, Hungerford, Berks. *(Silhouette Fairs - 01635 44338)*

Antique & Collectors' Fair, The Exhibition Halls, Park Hall, Charnock Richard, Lancs. *(Unicorn Fairs Ltd - 0161 773 7001)*

Tuesday 25th November

Antiques Fair, The Public Hall, Southdown Road, Harpenden, Herts. *(Chiltern Fairs - 01753 890301)*

The Sandown Park Antiques Fair, Sandown Exhibition Centre, Sandown Park Racecourse, Esher, Surrey. *(Wonder Whistle Enterprises - 0171 249 4050)*

Regions continued

Wednesday 26th November
Antique & Collectors' Fair, The Corn Exchange, High Street, Dorchester, Dorset. *(Forest Fairs - 01202 875167)*
Friday 28th/Sunday 30th November
The Autumn Chester Racecourse Antiques Fair, The Racecourse, Chester, Cheshire. *(Bailey Fairs - 01277 214677)*
The Hever Castle Antiques Fair, The Pavilion, Hever Castle, Near Edenbridge, Kent. *(Cooper Antiques Fairs - 01249 661111)*
Saturday 29th November
Antique & Collectors' Fair, The Exeter Livestock Centre, Matford Park Road, Marsh Barton, Exeter, Devon. *(Devon County Antiques Fairs - 01363 82571)*
Antique & Collectors' Fair, The Masonic Hall, High Street, Lymington, Hants. *(Grandma's Attic Antique Fairs - 01590 677687)*
Antique & Collectors' Fair, The Macclesfield Leisure Centre, Priory Lane, Macclesfield, Cheshire. *(Pine Promotions - 01565 652092)*
Saturday 29th/Sunday 30th November
Antique & Collectors' Fair, The Pavilion Gardens, Buxton, Derbys. *(Unicorn Fairs Ltd - 0161 773 7001)*
Sunday 30th November
Antiques Fair, The Mount Vernon Hospital, Northwood, Middlesex. *(Chiltern Fairs - 01753 890301)*
The Midlands Clock & Watch Fair, The National Motorcycle Museum, Solihull, Near Birmingham, West Midlands. *(Mr P Dungate - 01895 834694)*
Antiques Fair, St Peter's School, Huntingdon, Cambs. *(E W Services - 01933 225674)*
Antiques Fair, The King's Arms Hotel, Christchurch, Dorset. *(Forest Fairs - 01202 875167)*
Antique & Collectors' Fair, The Lyndhurst Park Hotel, High Street, Lyndhurst, Hants. *(Grandma's Attic Antique Fairs - 01590 677687)*
Antique & Collectors' Fair, The Harrow Leisure Centre, Christchurch Avenue, Wealdstone, Middlesex. *(Jax Fairs - 01444 400570)*
Antique & Collectors' Fair, The Racecourse, Cheltenham, Glos. *(Melba Fairs - 01934 624854)*
Antique & Collectors Fair, The Water End Barn, Banquetting Suite, St Peters Street, St Albans, Herts. *(M & S Enterprises - 0181 440 2330)*
Antique & Collectors' Fair, The Plumley Village Hall, near Knutsford, Cheshire. *(N & B Fairs - 01565 722144)*
Antiques & Collectors' Fair, The The Harlow Moat House Hotel, Southern Way, Harlow, Essex. *(Oakleigh Fairs - 01279 871110)*
Antique & Collectors' Fair, The Village Hall, Bashley, Hants. *(Renaissance Fairs - 01202 319914)*
Specialist Clock, Watch, Barometer & Scientific Instrument Fair, The Grove Leisure Centre, Newark, Notts. *(Right Time Clock Fairs - 01933 225674)*
Antique & Collectors' Fair, The 'Rest', Rest Bay, Porthcawl, Wales. *(David Robinson Fairs - 01222 620520)*
Antiques Fair, The Wilmslow Moat House Hotel, Altrincham, Near Wilmslow, Cheshire. *(Georgina Stevens - 01625 536926)*

Regions continued

Antique & Collectors' Fair, The Exhibition Halls, Park Hall, Charnock Richard, Lancs. *(Unicorn Fairs Ltd - 0161 773 7001)*
Tuesday 2nd December
The International Antique & Collectors' Fair, The Newark & Nottinghamshire Showground, Newark Notts. *(IACF Fairs - 01636 702326)*
Wednesday 3rd December
Antiques Fair, The Village Hall, Long Melford Suffolk. *(Caring for the Past - 01473 658224)*
Friday 5th/Sunday 7th December
The Swinton Castle Antiques Fair, Swinton Castle Mesham, N. Yorks *(Bailey Fairs - 01277 214677)*
Saturday 6th December
Antiques Fair, The Chorleywood Memorial Hall Common Road, Chorleywood, Herts. *(Chiltern Fairs 01753 890301)*
Antique & Collectors' Fair, The Salisbury Leisure Centre, The Butts, Hulse Road, Salisbury, Wilts *(Devon County Antiques Fairs - 01363 82571)*
Antique & Collectors' Fair, The St. Thomas' Church Hall, top of High Street, Lymington, Hants *(Grandma's Attic Antique Fairs - 01590 677687)*
Sunday 7th December
Antiques Fair, The Centre for Epilepsy, Chalfont St Peter, Bucks. *(Chiltern Fairs - 01753 890301)*
The Malvern Antique & Collectors' Fair, The Three Counties Showground, Malvern, Worcestershire *(County Antiques Fairs - 01278 784912)*
Antique & Collectors' Fair, The Allendale Centre Wimborne, Dorset. *(Forest Fairs - 01202 875167)*
Antique & Collectors' Fair, The David Lloyd Riverside Club, Christchurch Road, Ringwood, Hants *(Grandma's Attic Antiques Fairs - 01590 677687)*
Antique & Collectors' Fair, The Fourways Inn Chester Road, Delamere, Near Northwich, Cheshire *(Pine Promotions - 01565 652092)*
Antique & Collectors' Fair, The Village Hall, Corfe Castle, Dorset. *(Renaissance Fairs - 01202 319914)*
Specialist Clock, Watch, Barometer & Scientific Instrument Fair, The North Bridge Leisure Centre Halifax, Yorks. *(Right Time Clock Fairs - 0193. 225674)*
Antique & Collectors' Fair, The Copthorne Hotel Culverhouse Cross, Cardiff, Wales. *(David Robinson Fairs - 01222 620520)*
Antique & Collectors' Fair, The Royal Enclosure, The Racecourse, Ascot, Berks. *(Silhouette Fairs - 0163. 44338)*
Antique & Collectors' Fair, The Exhibition Halls, Park Hall, Charnock Richard, Lancs. *(Unicorn Fairs Ltd 0161 773 7001)*
Tuesday 9th December
Antique & Collectors' Fair, The Guildhall, Salisbury Wilts. *(Forest Fairs - 01202 875167)*
Thursday 11th/Sunday 14th December
The N.E.C. Winter Antiques Fair, 'Antiques for Everyone', Hall 3, National Exhibition Centre Birmingham, West Midlands. *(Mrs Louise Goodwin Centre Exhibitions - 0121 767 2760)*

Regions continued

Friday 12th/Sunday 14th December
Antique & Collectors' Fair, The Bingley Hall County Showground, Stafford, Staffs. *(Bowman Antiques Fairs - 0113 284 3333)*
The Scone Palace Antiques Fair, Perth, Scotland. *(Galloway Antiques Fairs - 01423 324602)*
Saturday 13th December
Antiques & Collectors' Fair, The Winter Gardens, (Seafront), Weston-Super-Mare, Avon. *(Melba Fairs - 01934 624854)*
Saturday 13th/Sunday 14th December
Art Nouveau & Art Deco Fair, The Kettering Leisure Village, Kettering, Northants. *(E W Services - 01933 225674)*
Sunday 14th December
The Furze Hill Antiques Fair, The Banqueting Centre, Margaretting, Near Chelmsford, Essex. *(Caring for the Past - 01473 658224)*
Antiques Fair, The Village Hall, Lewes Road, Ditchling, W. Sussex. *(Mr G Deakin - 01273 845141)*
Antiques Fair, The Balmer Lawn Hotel, Brockenhurst, Hants. *(Forest Fairs - 01202 875167)*
Antiques & Collectors' Fair, The Community Hall, Station Road, Woodbridge, Suffolk. *(Kyson Fairs - 01473 735528)*
Antique & Collectors' Fair, The Racecourse, Cheltenham, Glos. *(Melba Fairs - 01934 624854)*
Antique & Collectors' Fair, The Moat House, Dupont Suite, Barnet By-pass, Borehamwood, Elstree, Herts. *(M & S Enterprises - 0181 440 2330)*
Antique & Collectors' Fair, The Knutsford Civic Centre, Toft ROad, Knutsford, Cheshire. *(Pine Promotions - 01565 652092)*
Antique & Collectors' Fair, The Memorial Hall, West Parley, Dorset.*(Renaissance Fairs - 01202 319914)*
Antique & Collectors' Fair, The Abbey Hall, Abingdon, Oxon. *(Silhouette Fairs - 01635 44338)*
Antiques Fair, The Park Royal International Hotel, Stretton Road, Stretton, Warrington, Cheshire. *(Georgina Stevens - 01625 536926)*
Antique & Collectors' Fair, The Exhibition Halls, Park Hall, Charnock Richard, Lancs. *(Unicorn Fairs Ltd - 0161 773 7001)*
Tuesday 16th December
Antiques Fair, The Public Hall, Southdown Road, Harpenden, Herts. *(Chiltern Fairs - 01753 890301)*
Saturday 20th December
Antiques Fair, The Community Centre, Buckingham, Bucks . *(E W Services - 01933 225674)*
Saturday 20th/Sunday 21st December
The South Cotswolds Antiques Fair, The Westonbirt School, Tetbury, Glos. *(Cooper Antiques Fairs - 01249 661111)*
Sunday 21st December
The Brunel Clock & Watch Fair, Brunel University, Kingston Lane, Uxbridge, Middlesex. *(Mr P Dungate - 01895 834694*
Antiques Fair, The Haberdashers Askes School, Aldenham Road, Elstree, Herts. *(Harlequin Fairs - 01462 671688)*
Antiques & Collectors' Fair, The Kesgrave War Memorial Hall, Twelve Acre App. off Bell Lane, Kesgrave, Ipswich, Suffolk. *(Josef's Fairs - 01473 212423/685692)*

Regions continued

Antique & Collectors' Fair, The Racecourse, Cheltenham, Glos. *(Melba Fairs - 01934 624854)*
Antique & Collectors' Fair, The The Hatfield Red Lion, Great North Road, Near Town Centre, Hatfield, Herts. *(Oakleigh Fairs - 01279 871110)*
Antique & Collectors' Fair, The Bowdon Rooms, The Firs, Bowdon, Near Altrincham, Cheshire. *(Pine Promotions - 01565 652092)*
Saturday 27th/Sunday 28th December
Antique & Collectors' Fair, The Pavilion Gardens, Buxton, Derbys. *(Unicorn Fairs Ltd - 0161 773 7001)*
Sunday 28th December
Antiques Fair, The Racecourse, Windsor, Bucks. *(Chiltern Fairs - 01753 890301)*
Antique & Collectors' Fair, The Harrow Leisure Centre, Christchurch Avenue, Harrow, Middlesex. *(Garden City Promotions - 0181 368 1902)*
Antique & Collectors' Fair, The Allendale Centre, Wimborne, Dorset. *(Grandma's Attic Antique Fairs - 01590 677687)*
Antique & Collectors' Fair, The Bushey Golf & Country Club, Banquetting Suite, The High Street, Bushey, Herts. *(M & S Enterprises - 0181 440 2330)*
Antique & Collectors' Fair, The Plumley Village Hall, near Knutsford, Cheshire. *(N & B Fairs - 01565 722144)*
Antique & Collectors' Fair, The Village Hall, Bashley, Hants. *(Renaissance Fairs - 01202 319914)*

OVERSEAS

Friday 6th/Sunday 8th June
Antique & Collectors' Fair, The South Florida Fairgrounds, West Palm Beach, Florida, USA. *(Piccadilly Promotions Inc - 813 345 4431)*
Saturday 7th/Sunday 8th June
Antique & Collectors' Fair, The Henderson Convention Centre, Henderson, Nevada, USA. *(Piccadilly Promotions Inc - 813 345 4431)*
Saturday 21st/Sunday 22nd June
Antique & Collectors' Fair, The Sarasota County Fairgrounds, Sarasota, Florida, USA. *(Piccadilly Promotions Inc - 813 345 4431)*
Friday 11th/Sunday 13th July
Antique & Collectors' Fair, The South Florida Fairgrounds, West Palm Beach, Florida, USA. *(Piccadilly Promotions Inc - 813 345 4431)*
Saturday 19th/Sunday 20th July
Antique & Collectors' Fair, The Cashman Field Centre, Las Vegas, Nevada, USA. *(Piccadilly Promotions Inc - 813 345 4431)*
Saturday 26th/Sunday 27th July
Antique & Collectors' Fair, The Sarasota County Fairgrounds, Sarasota, Florida, USA. *(Piccadilly Promotions Inc - 813 345 4431)*
Friday 17th/Thursday 23rd October
The International Fine Art & Antique Dealers Show, The Seventh Regiment Armory, Park Avenue at 67th Street, New York City, New York, USA *(Mr B Haughton - 0171 734 5491)*

Services

This section has been included to enable us to list those businesses which do not sell antiques but are in associated trades. The following categories are included.

Arts, Books, Carpets and Rugs, Ceramics, Clocks and Barometers, Consultancy, Courier, Enamel, Engraving, Fireplaces, Framing, Furniture (including reproduction), Glass, Insurance and Finance, Ivory, Jewellery and Silver, Locks and Keys, Metalwork (see also Suppliers), Photography, Reproduction, Stonework, Suppliers, Textiles, Tortoiseshell and Toys.

We would point out that the majority of dealers also restore and can give advice in this field.

Below are listed the trade associations mentioned within this section.

BAFRA -	British Antique Furniture Restorers' Assn
FTAG -	Fine Art Trade Guild
GADAR -	Guild of Antique Dealers and Restorers
GMC -	Guild of Master Craftsmen
MBHI -	Member of British Horological Institute
UKIC -	UK Institute for Conservation
CGC -	Ceramic and Glass Conservation Group
BTCM -	British Traditional Cabinet Makers
BFMA -	British Furniture Manufacturers Assn
BCFA -	British Contract Furniture Assn
ASFI -	Assn of Suppliers to Furniture Industry
GAI -	Guild of Architectural Ironmongers
MBWCG -	Member British Watch and Clockmakers Guild

ART

Armor Paper Conservation Ltd

Glebe Cottage, 2 The Green, Garsington, Oxon. OX44 9DF. Tel: 01865 361741; fax - 01865 36185. *Conservation and restoration of drawings, prints, watercolour paintings, documents and archive material on paper, parchment or vellum.*

Richard Bennett

18 Kirkgate, Thirsk, Yorks North. Tel: 01845 524085; home - same. UKIC., AABPR. 1979. Open by appointment. *Oil paintings cleaned and lined on the premises; gilt/gesso frames restored and repaired; framing.* LOC: Joins Market Place.

Paul Congdon-Clelford

14 Bostock Close, Sparsholt, Winchester, Hants. SO21 2QH. Tel: 01962 776495. ABPR, FATG, GADAR. *Conservator of oil paintings on canvas and panel; collection and delivery.*

Art continued

Claudio Moscatelli Oil Painting Restoration

46 Cambridge St., London SW1V 4QH. Tel: 0171 828 1304. Associate member Assn. British Picture Restorers. *Oil paintings cleaned, relined, retouched and varnished.*

BOOKS

Brignell Bookbinders

2 Cobbles Yard, Napier St., Cambridge CB1 1HP Tel: 01223 321280; fax - same. Society of Bookbinders Guild of Mastercraftsmen. 1982 *Book restoration, conservation, table tops, leather photo cases, journal and thesis bindings, boxes, cloth or leather.* VAT: Stan.

Books continued

The Dummy Book Company

No 1 Cow Shed, Upton Grove, Tetbury, Glos. Tel: 01666 503376. (Jonathan Eaton). TADA. View by appointment. *Manufacturers of a wide range of book-themed gifts including men's desks, desk accessories, storage hides and clocks. Faux book spines for use within the home and office.*

The Manor Bindery Ltd.

Calshot Road, Fawley, Southampton, Hampshire. SO4 1BB. Tel: 01703 894488; fax - 01703 899418. *Manufacturers of false books, either to use as a display or for cabinet makers to apply to doors and cupboards. Also book tables, decorative objects and accessories, various decorative replica book boxes. Leather library shelf edging and range of cabinets with false book doors. Individual items made to order with a book theme.*

CARPETS AND RUGS

(See also Textiles)

Barin Carpets Restoration

57a New Kings Rd., London SW6 4SE. Tel: 0171 731 0546. GMC. Conservation Register Museums and Galleries Commission. *Oriental carpets, rugs, European tapestries, Aubussons expertly cleaned, restored and lined. Expert advice, free estimates.*

The Restoration Studio

Unit 11 Kolbe House, 63 Jeddo Rd., London W12 9EE. Tel: 0181 740 4977. Member Rug Restorers Assn. *Restoration, cleaning, lining and mounting of tapestries, Aubusson carpets, kilims and all kinds of needlework.*

CERAMICS

Ceramic Restorations

Unit 15 Coppull Mill, Mill Lane, Coppull, Chorley, Lancs. PR7 5AN. Tel: 01257 792835; fax - 01257 793994. *Quality restoration of all ceramics and glassware using latest technology, experienced team undertakes restorations for individuals, trade and auction houses in UK and and Europe. Free estimates, regular collections and deliveries within London area.* VAT: Stan.

China Repairers

64 Charles Lane, London NW8 7SB. Tel: 0171 722 8407. (H. Howard and V. Baron). Est. 1952. *Specialised restorations of all pottery and porcelain; restoration courses held.*

The China Repairers

1 Street Farm Workshops, Tetbury, Glos. Tel: 01666 503551. TADA. (Mrs A Chalmers). *Long established china restorers and more recently, mirror and picture frame gilders. Awarded Royal Warrant.*

Ceramics continued

Porcelain Repairs

240 Stockport Rd., Cheadle Heath, Stockport, Cheshire. SK3 0LX. Tel: 0161 428 9599; fax - 0161 286 6702. CGCG, UKIC. Est. 1970. *Highest standard restorations of European and Oriental ceramics, especially under glaze blue and white, museum repairs, carat gilding and modelling. Cracks and crazing removed without any overpainting or glazing.*

CLOCKS AND BAROMETERS

Clive and Lesley Cobb

3 Pembroke Crescent, Hove, East Sussex BN3 5DH. Tel: 01273 772649. Listed by the Conservation Unit of the Museum and Galleries Commission. Est. 1972. *Quality, sympathetic restoration of lacquer clock cases and furniture, and painted clock dials.*

Edmund Czajkowski and Son

See entry under Furniture - BAFRA section (Lincs.)

Martin H. Dunn

Glebe Farm, Clarke's Rd., North Killingholme, South Humberside. DN40 3JQ. Tel: 01469 540901; fax - 01469 541512. Guild of Lincolnshire Craftsmen. *Clock movements and dials, brass work. Agent for several German clock movement makers.* VAT: Stan.

Richard Higgins (Conservation)

See entry under Furniture - BAFRA section (Shrops).

A.C. Layne

48 Cecil St., Carlisle, Cumbria. CA1 1NT. Tel: 01228 45019. Open 8-11.30 and 1-4. *Repairs to antique clocks and complicated watches.*

Robert B. Loomes

3 Kings Rd., Stamford, Lincs. PE9 1HD. Tel: 01780 481319. MBWCG. *British antique clock restoration - longcase, lantern and bracket. Dial restoration, brass and painted dials. Valuations. Strictly by appointment.*

Lynton Clocks and Dials

22 Norwich St., Fakenham, Norfolk. NR21 9AE. Tel: 01328 863666; fax - 01485 518650. LBHI. MWCG. *Clock repairs and restorations. Manufacturers and restorers of vitreous enamelled dials up to 12" diameter.*

William C. Mansell

24 Connaught St., London W2. Tel: 0171 723 4154. *Specialists in repair/restoration of antique clocks and vintage watches.*

Meadows and Passmore

Farningham Rd., Crowborough, East Sussex. TN6 2JP. Tel: 01892 662255; fax - 01892 662277. *Clock and barometer parts, tools and materials. Mail Order Only.*

Clocks and Barometers continued

Menim Restorations
Bow St., Langport, Somerset. Tel: 01458 252157; fax - 01458 253449. GMC. Est. 1830. *Specialists in English and French clocks, full cabinet making and horological service; French polishing.*

Newcombe and Son
89 Maple Rd., Penge, London SE20 8UL. Tel: 0181 778 0816. MBHI, GMC, Conservation Register of Museums and Galleries Commission. *Specialist in the making, repair and restoration of fine quality longcase, bracket and wall clocks. Quality clock cases made to order, barometers repaired, silvering and gilding, clock faces (including enamel) restored or repainted, brass and wooden frets, clock hands, all hand cut and finished to order, clocks bought and sold.*

Repton Clocks
Acton Cottage, 48 High St., Repton, Derbys. DE65 6GF. Tel: 01283 703657; fax - 01283 702367. MBWCMG; MBHI. Open by appointment 9-6. CL: Sat. *Antique and modern watch and clock restoration; musical box repairs; gear cutting; clocks made to order.*

Kevin Sheehan
15 Market Place, Tetbury, Glos. Tel: 01666 503099. TADA. Open 9-4.30, Sat. 10-12. *Specialist repairer of English and French 18th-19th C clocks. Written estimates given, all work guaranteed. Awarded Royal Warrant.*

Southerns
Precista House, 48/56 High St., Orpington, Kent. BR6 0JH. Tel: 01689 824318/875206; fax - 01689 870079; e-mail - 106212.3302@compuserve.com. BJA; MBWCG; Jewellery Industry Distributors Assn. *Watch and clock replacement and restoration materials; specialised tools for the horological trade.* VAT: Stan. *Trade Only.*

A.R. Webb
9 Northam Rd., Southampton, Hants. SO14 0NZ Tel: 01703 221546. Open 9-5. *Restorer of clocks and watches.*

CONSULTANCY

Athena Antiques
59 Elvetham Rd., Fleet, Hants. Tel: 01252 615526; home - same. Est. 1975. Available seven days by appointment. *Consultancy; valuations (jewellery, silver, clocks and furniture); restorations (clocks and furniture); buys at auction on commission.* LOC: Near Fleet railway station.

Curtis Associates
36 Heather Walk, Meadow View, Smallfield, Surrey. RH6 9GP. Tel: 01342 844748. Open by appointment every day 9-6. *Consultancy specialising in furnishing whole houses, financial institutions and yachts, using British antiques. Valuations; restorations.*

Consultancy continued

John Fell-Clark LAPADA
84 Ledbury Rd., London W11 2AH. Tel: 0171 229 0224; home - same. Est. 1971. By appointment. ***Valuations; restorations; consultancy and interior design; buys at auction (17th-20th C furniture and tapestries).*** **LOC: Off Westbourne Grove. VAT: Spec.**

Geoffrey Godden
3 The Square, Findon, West Sussex. Tel: 01903 873456. *Consultant and lecturer in ceramics.*

John W.L. Kitchin
13 Blenheim Gardens, Sanderstead. Surrey. CR2 9AA. Tel: 0181 657 1350. BAFRA.

Ryder-Cole and Denbigh LAPADA
129 Stormont Rd., London SW1 5EJ. Tel: 0171 228 7072; fax - 0171 978 6712. Est. 1994. Open Mon.-Fri. by appointment. ***Public relations and marketing; courier; antique sourcing service.*** **VAT: Stan.**

COURIER

Antique Tours
11 Farleigh Rise, Monkton Farleigh, Nr Bradford-on-Avon, Wilts. BA15 2QP. Tel: 0122 858527 (24 hr. answerphone); mobile - 086 489831. (C.J. Veal). Est. 1988. *Private hir chauffeur service; car tours of antique shops i the West Country, or any other area, for up t four persons; service to and from air and se ports; packing and shipping arranged. Genea logical research also undertaken.*

Personal Travel Services
25 Howard Rd., London SE25 5BU. Tel: 018 656 3207; fax - same. *Driver guided tours t major antiques fairs, multi-dealer centres an individual dealers in the UK, except Ireland. On to eight passengers can be accommodated in choice of estate car or luxury minibus. Itinerarie prepared, accommodation selected and reserve packing and shipping arranged, airport transfer undertaken.*

Neil Robson Antiques Courier Service
10 Towrise, Sulgrave, Banbury, Oxon. OX1 2SB. Tel: 01295 760045; fax - same; mobile 0385 785447. *Complete service for oversea buyers, throughout Britain and into Europ Personalised itineraries prepared covering a aspects of the trade - specialist dealers, fair markets, auctions, restorers and reproductio sources. Clients met at airport in spacious car c people carrier and accompanied throughout tri Collection, packing, shipping and documentati of goods can be arranged.*

ENAMEL

Istvan Markovits - Enameller Consultant

11 Mallard Place, Strawberry Vale, Twickenham, Middx. TW1 4SW. Tel: 0181 891 1743; mobile - 0421 622791. *Badgemakers. Worldwide restorers of enamel antique jewellery. Restorers of clock faces and ceramics.*

ENGRAVING

Edward J. Woods - Hand and Machine Engravers

2 Mill Close, Tillingham, Essex CM0 7TF. Tel: 01621 779387. GMC. Est. 1970. *Engraving for silversmiths, polishers and platers, jewellery manufacturers; chapter rings, barometer dials, etc.* VAT: Stan.

FIREPLACES

Antiques and Restoration

Old Town Hall, Antique Village, Levenshulme, Manchester, Lancs. Tel: Mobile - 0973 416537; home - 0161 431 5685. *Antique marble fireplaces, and furniture, restored and polished.*

FRAMING

Natural Wood Framing

Eight Bells Gallery, 14 Church St., Tetbury, Glos. Tel: 01666 505070. FATG. TADA. (Mark Wallington). Open 9-5. CL: Sat. *Range of contemporary and sporting art. Bespoke framing, specialising in antiques, textiles and restorations.*

FURNITURE

British Antique Furniture Restorers' Association (In county order)

BEDFORDSHIRE

Duncan Everitt - D.M.E. Restorations Ltd

1 Church St., Ampthill, Beds. MK45 2PL. Tel: 01525 405819; fax - same. BAFRA.

BERKSHIRE

Graham Childs - Alpha (Antique) Restorations

High St., Compton, Newbury, Berks. RG20 6NL. Tel: 01635 578245; mobile - 0860 575203. BAFRA. *Fine oak, walnut and mahogany. Traditional hand finishes. Veneering and inlaying. Clock cases.*

BAFRA continued

Ben Norris & Co

Knowl Hill Farm, Knowl Hill, Kingsclere, , Newbury, Berks. RG15 8NY. Tel: 01635 297950; fax - 01635 299851. BAFRA. *All aspects of furniture restoration including carving, gilding, copy chair making and architectural woodwork. BADA Dip. Excellent storage facilities.* VAT: Stan.

BUCKINGHAMSHIRE

David Hordern Restorations (Thame) Ltd.

8/9 Lea Lane, Thame Road, Long Crendon, Aylesbury, Bucks. HP18 9RN. Tel: 01844 202213; fax - 01844 202214. BAFRA. *Boulle, cabinetwork, carving, gilding, lacquer, leather, marble, marquetry, ormolu, upholstery.*

CAMBRIDGESHIRE

Ludovic Potts

Unit 1 Haddenham Business Park, Station Rd., Ely. Cambridgeshire. CB6 3XD. Tel: 01353 741537; fax - same; mobile - 0589 341671. BAFRA.

BAFRA continued

Robert Williams
Osborn's Farm, 32 Church St., Willingham, Cambs. CB4 5HT. Tel: 01954 260972. BAFRA. *Boulle, carving, clockcases, inlay work, marquetry, metalwork, painted furniture, with the emphasis on carefully cleaning and retaining old patinated surfaces. Survey and condition reports undertaken.*

CORNWALL

Graham H. Usher
Fairhope, 5 Rose Terrace, Mitchell, Cornwall. TR8 5AU. Tel: 01872 510551. BAFRA. *Restoration and courses.*

CUMBRIA

Jeremy Hall - Peter Hall & Son
Danes Rd., Staveley, Kendal, Cumbria. LA8 9PL. Tel: 01539 821633; fax - 01539 821905. BAFRA.

DERBYSHIRE

Anthony Allen Antique Restorers
Old Wharf Workshop, Redmoor Lane, New Mills, Derbys. SK22 3JL. Tel: 01663 745274. BAFRA. *Boulle, marquetry, walnut, oak, veneering restorations and upholstery.*

DEVON

Dan Bent
Newholt, Court Rd., Newton Ferrers, Plymouth, Devon. PL8 1DE. Tel: 01752 872831. BAFRA.

Tony Vernon
15 Follett Rd., Topsham, Devon. EX3 0JP. Tel: 01392 874635. BAFRA. *Furniture, cabinet making, upholstery, gilding, veneering, inlay and French polishing.*

Stevie Young
Claymore, The Workshop, Little Pit Cottage, Clyst Lydon, Nr Cullompton. Devon. EX15 2NF. Tel: 01884 277660. BAFRA.

DORSET

Michael Barrington
The Old Rectory, Warmwell, Dorchester, Dorset. DT2 8HQ. Tel: 01305 852104; fax - same. BAFRA. *18th-19th C furniture, gilding, upholstery, antique metalwork, organ casework and pipe decoration, mechanical models and toys.*

Peter Binnington
Barn Studio, Botany Farm, East Lulworth, Wareham, Dorset BH20 5QH. Tel: 01929 400224; fax - 01929 400744. BAFRA. *Restoration of period furniture and interiors, gilding and verre eglomisé, decorated surfaces.*

BAFRA continued

Richard Bolton
Athelhampton House, Dorchester, Dorset. DT2 7LG. Tel: 01305 848346. BAFRA. *All aspects of furniture restoration; residential and non-residential courses for beginners and more experienced.* A35 between Puddletown and Tolpuddle.

Peter Brazier - Court Restorations Ltd
Nash Court Farmhouse, Marnhull, Sturminster Newton, Dorset. DT10 1JZ. Tel: 01258 820255. BAFRA. *Comprehensive restoration service.*

Philip Hawkins
Glebe Workshop, Semley, Shaftesbury, Dorset. SP7 9AP. Tel: 01747 830830. BAFRA. *16th to early 18th C oak and country furniture restoration.*

S.R. Robertson
4 Burraton Yard, Poundbury Village, Dorset. Tel 01305 257377. BAFRA.

Raymond Robertson - Tolpuddle Antique Restorers
The Stables, Southover House, Tolpuddle Dorchester, Dorset. DT2 7HF. Tel: 0130 848739. BAFRA. *Furniture, clocks and barometers, marquetry, veneering and boulle work lacquer, japaning and gilding.*

ESSEX

Clive Beardall
104b High Street, Maldon. Essex. CM9 7ET. Tel 01621 857890. BAFRA.

Dick Patterson - Forge Studio Workshops
Stour St., Manningtree, Essex. CO11 1BE. Tel 01206 396222. BAFRA. *Carving, general restoration, copying and bespoke cabinet making.*

William A.J. Pigeon - Lomas Pigeon & Co. Ltd
The Workshops, Rear of 1 Beehive Lane Chelmsford, Essex. CM2 9SU. Tel: 0124 353708; fax - 01245 257706. BAFRA. *Period cabinet restoration, French polishing, traditional upholstery, desk linings, rocking horses.*

GLOUCESTERSHIRE

Keith Bawden - Restorer of Antiques
Mews Workshops, Montpellier Retrea Cheltenham, Glos. GL50 2XG. Tel: 01242 23032 BAFRA. *All period furniture, plus restoration of items made from wood, metals, porcelain, pottery fabrics, leather, ivory, papier-mâché, etc.*

Peter Campion - Uedelhoven & Campion
Rear of Well House, Gretton, Cheltenham, Glo GL54 5EP. Tel: 01242 604403. BAFRA.

BAFRA continued

Alan Hessel
The Old Town Workshop, St. George's Close, Moreton-in-Marsh, Glos. GL56 0LP. Tel: 01608 650026; fax - same. BAFRA. *Comprehensive restoration service. English and continental fine period furniture.*

Stephen Hill
5 Cirencester Workshops, Brewery Court, Cirencester, Glos. GL7 1JH. Tel: 01285 658817 (24 hr); fax - 01285 652554. BAFRA. *General furniture including oak, walnut, mahogany, 17th-19th C gilding, carving, upholstery, rush and cane seating. Furniture made by commission only.*

Colin Holcombe
54 Alcove Rd., Fishponds, Bristol, Glos. BS16 3DR. Tel: 0117 965 1299. BAFRA.

Christian Macduff Hunt - Hunt and Lomas
Village Farm Workshops, Preston Village, Cirencester, Glos. GL7 5PR. Tel: 01285 640111. BAFRA. *17th-19th C oak, mahogany, walnut, satinwood, carving.*

Donald Hunter
The Old School Room, Shipton Oliffe, Cheltenham, Glos. GL54 4JG. Tel: 01242 820755. BAFRA. *Restoration of fine antiques, cabinet making, water gilding, lacquer work, decorative finishes.*

Andrew Lelliott
6 Tetbury Hill, Avening, Tetbury, Glos. GL8 8LT. Tel: 01453 835783/832652. BAFRA. TADA. Conservation Register Museums & Galleries Commission. *Comprehensive restorations.*

Godfrey Robertson
Fourwinds, Ablington, Bibury, Cirencester, Glos. GL7 5NX. Tel: 01285 740355; fax - same. BAFRA. *General restorations, willing to work in situ if necessary.*

Angus Stewart
Sycamore Barn, Bourton Industrial Park, Bourton-on-the-Water, Cheltenham, Glos. GL54 2HQ. Tel: 01451 821611. BAFRA. *16th-18th C cabinet making, gold leafing, decorative finishes, lacquer, carving and mirror glass.*

Roy Stratton
4 Gales Court, Lechlade. Glos. GL7 3DG. Tel: 01367 253878. BAFRA.

Laurence Whitfield
The Old School, Winstone, Cirencester, Glos. GL7 7JX. Tel: 01285 821342. BAFRA.

HAMPSHIRE

Guy Bagshaw
The Old Dairy, Plain Farm, East Tisted, Alton, Hants. GU34 3RT. Tel: 01420 588362. BAFRA. *18th to early 19th C English furniture restoration. Tutored weekend courses available.*

BAFRA continued

John Hartley
The Tankerdale Workshop, The Old Forge, Village St., Sheet, Petersfield, Hants. GU32 2AQ. Tel: 01730 233792; fax - 01730 233922. BAFRA. *Comprehensive restoration and conservation service, including carving, gilding, painted furniture, lacquer, marquetry, boulle and architectural woodwork. Adviser to The National Trust.*

David C. E. Lewry
Wychelms, 66 Gorran Avenue, Rowner, Gosport, Hants. PO13 0NF. Tel: 01329 286901; fax - 01329 289964; mobile - 0385 766844. BAFRA. *17th to early 19th C furniture.*

Humphrey Sladden
Yard House, South Harting, Petersfield, Hants. GU31 5NS. Tel: 01730 825339. BAFRA.

HEREFORDSHIRE

Jeremy J. Daffern
55 The Hamlet, Stoke Edith. Herefordshire. HR1 4HQ. Tel: 01432 890740. BAFRA.

Reginald W. Dudman Antique Restorations
The Old Vicarage, Blakemere, Hereford. Herefordshire. HR2 9PY. Tel: 01981 500413. BAFRA.

HERTFORDSHIRE

John B. Carr - Charles Perry Restorations Ltd
Praewood Farm, Hemel Hempstead Rd., St Albans, Herts. AL3 6AA. Tel: 01727 853487 BAFRA.

KENT

Timothy Akers - Antique Furniture Restorations
The Forge, 39 Chancery Lane, Beckenham, Kent BR3 2NR. Tel: 0181 650 9179. BAFRA. *Restorations of 17th-19th C English furniture, longcase and bracket clocks.*

Benedict Clegg
Rear of 20 Camden Road, Tunbridge Wells. Kent TN1 2PT. Tel: 01892 548095. BAFRA.

Robert Coleman
The Oasthouse, Three Chimneys, Nr. Ashford Biddenden, Kent. TN27 8LW. Tel: 01580 29152[illegible] BAFRA. *Mahogany and walnut furniture.*

Raymond Konyn Antique Restorations
The Old Wheelwright's Shop, Brasted Forge Brasted, Westerham, Kent. TN16 1JL. Tel: 0195[illegible] 563863; fax - 01959 561262. BAFRA. *Furniture traditional upholstery, longcase and bracket cloc[illegible] cases, polishing, brass casting. Consultancy.*

BAFRA continued

Timothy Long Restoration
St. John's Church, London Rd., Dunton Green, Sevenoaks, Kent. TN13 2 TE. Tel: 01732 743368; fax - 01732 742206. BAFRA. *Cabinet restoration, French polishing, upholstery, brass and steel cabinet fittings.*

Bruce Luckhurst
The Little Surrenden Workshops, Ashford Rd., Bethersden, Kent. TN26 3BG. Tel: 01233 820589. BAFRA. *Conservation and restoration training plus comprehensive restoration service.*

Richard J. Marson - R.M. Restoration
Unit 8 Hilltop Meadows, Old London Road, Knockholt, Kent. TN14 7JW. Tel: 01959 533771. BAFRA. *Period furniture, traditional upholstery, French polishing.*

LANCASHIRE

Eric Smith - Antique Furniture Restorations
The Church, Park Rd., Darwen, Lancs. BB3 2LD. Tel: 01254 776222. BAFRA. UKIC. MA. Conservation Register Museums & Galleries Commission. *Restoration of long case clocks and furniture. Comprehensive conservation and restoration of fine furniture.*

LINCOLNSHIRE

Michael Czajkowski - Edmund Czajkowski and Son
96 Tor-o-Moor Rd., Woodhall Spa, Lincs. LN10 6SB. Tel: 01526 352895; fax - same. BAFRA. *Furniture, clocks and barometers restored, including church clocks. Veneering, marquetry, English lacquer and boulle work, carving and gilding.*

LONDON

David Battle - Phoenix Antique Furniture Restoration Ltd
96 Webber St., Waterloo, London SE1 0QN. Tel: 0171 928 3624. BAFRA. *Cabinet making, restoration and conservation work; polishing, clock cases, veneer and marquetry work, woodturning. Specialists in 17th-19th C English and Continental furniture. Collections and deliveries.*

Martin Body - Giltwood Restoration
7 Addington Square, London SE5 7JZ. Tel: 0171 703 4351. BAFRA. *Specialist conservation of fine gilded furniture and frames.*

Lucinda Compton - Compton Hall Restoration
Unit A, 133 Riverside Business Centre, Haldane Place, London SW18 4UQ. Tel: 0181 874 0762. BAFRA. *Painted furniture, papier-mâché, tôle ware, lacquer and gilding.*

BAFRA continued

William Cook
167 Battersea High St., London SW11 3JS. Tel: 0171 736 5329 or 01672 513017. BAFRA. *18th C and English period furniture.*

Marie Louise Crawley
39 Woodvale, London SE23 3DS. Tel: 0181 299 4121. BAFRA. *Painted furniture, papier-mâché, tôle ware, lacquer and gilding.*

Robert H. Crawley
75 St. Mary's Rd., Ealing, London W5 5RH. Tel: 0181 566 5074. BAFRA.

Raymond Dudman - W. Thomas Ltd.
1 Warwick Place. London. W9 2PX. Tel: 0171 286 1945. BAFRA.

Brian A. Duffy - Hope & Piaget
1K Leroy House, 436 Essex Rd., Islington, London N1 3QP. Tel: 0171 359 1400; fax - 0171 288 1515. BAFRA. UKIC.

Sebastian Giles Furniture
11 Junction Mews, London W2 1PN. Tel: 0171 258 3721. BAFRA.

Rodrigo Titian
318 Kensal Rd., London W10 5BN. Tel: 0181 960 6247; fax - 0181 969 6126. BAFRA. *Carving, gilding, lacquer, painted furniture, French polishing.*

Clifford J. Tracy
6-40 Durnford St., London N15 5NQ. Tel: 0181 800 4773/4; fax - 0181 800 4351. BAFRA. *General restorations including boulle, marquetry, leather lining, upholstery.*

Andrew White
16 Arminger Road. London. W12 7BB. Tel: 0181 749 2576. BAFRA.

MIDDLESEX

Alun Courtney Smith
45 Windmill Road, Brentford. Middlesex. TW8 0QQ. Tel: 0181 568 5249; fax - 0181 560 4017. BAFRA.

NORFOLK

David Bartram
The Raveningham Centre, Beccles Rd., Raveningham, Nr. Norwich, Norfolk. NR14 6NU. Tel: 01508 548721. BAFRA. *18th-19th C English furniture, rosewood, walnut and mahogany, inlay and turning; full cabinet making service, chair copying and upholstery.*

Michael Dolling
Church Farm Barns, Glandford, Holt. Norfolk. NR25 7JR. Tel: 01263 741115. BAFRA.

BAFRA continued

Roderick Larwood

The Oaks, Station Rd., Larling, Norfolk. NR16 2QS. Tel: 01953 717937. BAFRA. *Brass inlay, 18th to early 19th C furniture; French polishing.*

OXFORDSHIRE

Alistair J. Frayling-Cork

2 Mill Lane, Wallingford, Oxon. OX10 0DH. Tel: 01491 826221. BAFRA. *Antique and period furniture, clock cases, ebonising, wood turning, stringed instruments and brass fittings repaired.*

Clive Payne

Unit 4, Mount Farm, Churchill, Chipping Norton. Oxfordshire. OX7 6NP. Tel: 01608 658856; fax - same; mobile - 0585 770957. BAFRA.

Colin Piper - Conservation & Restoration

Highfield House, The Greens, Leafield, Witney, Oxon. OX8 5NP. Tel: 01993 878593. BAFRA.

SHROPSHIRE

Richard Higgins (Conservation)

The Old School, Longnor, Nr. Shrewsbury, Shrops. SY5 7PP. Tel: 01743 718162; fax - 01743 718022. BAFRA. LBHI. Conservation Register Museums and Galleries Commission. *Comprehensive restoration of all fine furniture and clocks, including movements and dials; specialist work to boulle, marquetry, carving, turning, cabinet and veneer work, lacquer, ormolu, metalwork, casting, glazing, polishing, upholstery, cane and rush seating. Stocks of old timber, veneers, tortoiseshell etc. held to ensure sympathetic restoration.*

SOMERSET

Stuart Bradbury - M& S Bradbury

The Barn, Hanham Lane, Paulton, Somerset. BS18 5PF. Tel: 01761 418910. BAFRA. *All aspects of antique furniture restoration.*

Nicholas Bridges

20 Newchester Cross, Merriott, Somerset. TA16 5QJ. Tel: 01460 74672. BAFRA.

Michael Durkee

Castle House, 1 Bennetts Field Estate, Wincanton, Somerset. BA9 9DT. Tel: 01963 33884. BAFRA. *Restoration, conservation and finishing of all styles of period furniture. Boulle and inlay work.*

Alan Stacey - Boxwood Antique Restorers

67 High St., Wincanton, Somerset. BA9 9JZ. Tel: 01963 33988. BAFRA. *Finest quality antique restoration and conservation. Wax polishing, French polishing, carving, metalwork, brass fittings, specialist cabinet making, tortoiseshell specialists (tea caddies, frames, brushes, etc.), ivory, shagreen, horn, mother of pearl, etc. Regular deliveries to London and surrounding areas.* VAT: Stan.

BAFRA continued

Robert Tandy Restoration

Unit 5 Manor Workshops, Manor Park, West End, Nailsea, Bristol, Somerset. BS19 2DD Tel: 01275 856378. BAFRA. *Furniture restoration especially 17th-19th C longcase clock cases; French polishing and traditional oil and wax finishing.* VAT : Stan.

SURREY

David J. Booth - A.E. Booth & Son

9 High St., Ewell, Surrey. KT17 1SG. Tel: 0181 393 5245. BAFRA. *Restorations and polishing, upholstery. Barometers, longcase clocks, mahogany and walnut.*

Glen Fraser-Sinclair - G. and R. Fraser-Sinclair & Co

11 Orchard Works, Streeters Lane, Beddington, Surrey. SM6 7ND. Tel: 0181 669 5343 or 01883 349467. BAFRA. *18th C furniture.*

Michael Hedgecoe LAPADA

21 Burrow Hill Green, Chobham, Surrey. GU24 8QS. Tel: 01276 858206; fax - same. BAFRA. ***General restorations, cabinet work, polishing, upholstery, chair making.***

Stuart Hobbs Antique Furniture Restoration

Meath Paddock, Meath Green Lane, Horley, Surrey. RH6 8HZ. Tel: 01293 782349. GMC. BAFRA. *Full restoration service for period furniture.*

John W.L. Kitchin

13 Blenheim Gardens, Sanderstead. Surrey. CR2 9AA. Tel: 0181 657 1350. BAFRA. *Consultancy only*

Simon Marsh

The Old Butchers Shop, High Street, Bletchingly. Surrey. RH1 4PA. Tel: 01883 743350; fax - 01883 744844. BAFRA.

Timothy Morris

Unit 4a, 19 St Peters St., Croydon, Surrey. CR2 7DG. Tel: 0181 681 2992. BAFRA.

Timothy Naylor

The Workshop, 2 Chertsey Rd., Chobham, Surrey. GU24 8NB. Tel: 01276 855122. BAFRA. *Antique furniture restoration.*

BAFRA continued

David A. Sayer - Courtlands Restorations
Courtlands, Park Rd., Banstead, Surrey. SM7 3EF. Tel: 01737 352429; fax - 01737 373255. BAFRA. *French and wax polishing, cabinet making, turning, carving, veneering, gilding, metal repairs, leather and 18th-19th C furniture.*

EAST SUSSEX

Maxwell Black
Brookhouse Studios, Novington Lane, East Chiltington, Lewes, Sussex East. BN7 3AX. Tel: 01273 890175. BAFRA.

WEST SUSSEX

Peter G. Casebow
Pilgrims, Mill Lane, Worthing, West Sussex. BN13 3DE. Tel: 01903 264045. BAFRA. *Period furniture, turning, marquetry, inlay, fretwork, polishing.*

Simon Paterson
74 Double Barn, West Dean, Chichester. West Sussex. PO18 0RR. BAFRA.

Noel Pepperall
Dairy Lane Cottage, Walberton, Arundel, West Sussex. BN18 0PT. Tel: 01243 551282. BAFRA. *Gilding and painted furniture a speciality.*

Albert Plumb Furniture Restoration
31 Whyke Lane, Chichester, West Sussex. PO19 2JS. Tel: 01243 789100; fax - 01243 788468. BAFRA. *Oak, walnut, mahogany and country furniture, upholstery and cabinet making.*

WILTSHIRE

William Cook
High Trees House, Savernake Forest, Nr. Marlborough. Wiltshire. SN8 4NE. Tel: 01672 513017. BAFRA.

WORCESTSHIRE

Jeffrey Hall - Malvern Studios
56 Cowleigh Road, Malvern. Worcestershire. WR14 1QD. Tel: 01684 574913; fax - 01684 569475. BAFRA.

Phillip Slater
93 Hewell Road, Barnt Green, Nr. Birmingham. Worcestershire. B45 8NL. Tel: 0121 445 4942. BAFRA.

NORTH YORKSHIRE

Lucinda Compton
Manor House, Marton-le-Moor, Ripon, North Yorks. HG4 5AT. Tel: 01423 324290. BAFRA.

BAFRA continued

T. L. Phelps - Fine Furniture Restoration
8 Mornington Terrace, Harrogate, North Yorks. HG1 5DH. Tel: 01423 524604. BAFRA. *Specialist restoration and conservation services; all cabinet work, including dining tables, large items; all veneer work; architectural woodwork; traditional hand polishing, colouring and waxed finishes.*

SOUTH YORKSHIRE

Neil Trinder
Burrowlee House, Burrowlee Rd., Hillsborough, Sheffield, South Yorks. S19 6LX. Tel: 0114 2852428/2552972. BAFRA. *Boulle, gilding, marquetry, carving, fine furniture.*

WEST YORKSHIRE

Rodney F. Kemble
16 Crag Vale Terrace, Glusburn, Nr. Keighley, West Yorks. BD20 8QU. Tel: 01535 636954/633702. BAFRA. *Cabinet restorations, clock cases, traditional hand finishes and upholstery.*

SCOTLAND

Gow Antique Restoration
Pitscandly Farm House, Forfar, by Lunanhead, Angus, Scotland. DD8 3NZ. Tel: 01307 465342. BAFRA. Accredited by Historical Scotland and the Museums and Galleries Commission. Appointment advisable. *17th-19th C English and Continental furniture. Specialist restoration of European furniture, marquetry.*

William Trist and Andrew McBain - Trist & McBain
135 St Leonard's Street, Edinburgh, Scotland. EH8 9RB. Tel: 0131 667 7775; fax - 0131 667 4333. BAFRA.

Luigi Maria Villani
Hillhead Farm, Forres, Scotland. IV36 0RT. Tel: 01309 676247. BAFRA. *Freelance restorer of antique furniture, picture and mirror frames and objets d'art; study days, tuition and advice.*

WALES

Bryan Wigington - Antique Furniture Restoration
Pembertons, 4 Hightown, Hay-on-Wye, Wales. HR3 4AE. Tel: 01497 820545 (24 hr.) BAFRA. Est. 1961. Open any time by appointment. *Furniture conservation and restoration.* LOC: Next to Post Office.

Non-BAFRA Furniture Restorers

Albion Antiques
36 Duke St., Kettering, Northants. NN16 9DY Tel: 01536 516220 (answerphone). 1980. Open by appointment. *Caning, rushing and upholstery.*

The Antique Restoration Centre
14 Suffolk Road, Cheltenham, Gloucestershire GL50 2AQ Tel: 01242 262549. Open Mon-Fri 9.30-5. *All types of restoration - all restorers BADA qualified.*

Antiques and Restoration
See under Fireplaces.

B.P.A. Antique Restorations LAPADA
Bell Passage Antiques, 36-38 High St., Wickwar, Glos. GL12 8NP. Tel: 01454 294251; fax - same. Est. 1966. *Restorers of antique and modern furniture, specialists in French and wax polishing, picture restoration, gilding, inlay and metal work. Chair copying a speciality; traditional and modern upholstery. Work carried out on site.*

D. Baker
12 Downs Rd., Folkestone, Kent. CT19 5PW. Tel: 01303 255136. Est. 1961. *Restoration of antique and fine furniture and french polishing.*

Batheaston Chairmakers Ltd. H. Lockhart Ltd.
20 Leafield Way, Corsham, Wilts. SN13 9SW. Tel: 01225 811295; fax - 01225 810501. BFMA. BCFA. *Oak reproduction furniture made from solid kiln dried timbers, antique hand finish. Extensive range of Windsor, ladderback and country Hepplewhite chairs; refectory, gateleg and other extendable tables, Welsh dressers, sideboards and other cabinet models. Trade Only.*

Belvedere Reproductions
11 Dove St., Ipswich, Suffolk. IP4 1NG. Tel: 01473 727585; fax - 01473 253229. *Suppliers of traditionally constructed and hand polished oak and fruitwood country furniture.* VAT: Stan.

Berry and Crowther
119 Wakefield Rd., Moldgreen, Huddersfield, West Yorks. HD5 9AN Tel: 01484 544229 (answerphone); fax - same. Workshop attached to Peter Berry Antiques Shop. *Fine antique restorers and conservators; restoration with traditional methods to highest standards on fine furniture, ceramics and clocks. Insurance work approved.*

Rupert Bevan
40 Fulham High St., London SW6 3LQ. Tel: 0171 731 1919; fax - same. *Gilding, carving and painting.* VAT: Stan.

A.E. Booth & Son
Crows Nest, Edgeley Rd., Barton, Torquay, Devon. TQ2 8ND. Tel: 01803 312091. *Restorations, polishing, upholstery. Barometers, longcase, mahogany and walnut.*

Furniture continued

Lawrence Brass
154 Sutherland Avenue, Maida Vale, London W9. Tel: 0122 585 2222. UKIC. Approved by the Museums and Galleries Commission. *Conservation and restoration of fine antiques, metal work, gilding and upholstery.*

Paul Bruce Antiques
Frobisher Rd., Ipswich, Suffolk. IP3 0HR. Tel: 01473 255400/233671; fax - 01473 233656. IADCC. *Makers of fine furniture in oak, mahogany and walnut. Restorations; valuations.* VAT: Stan.

Bruton Cast Ltd
Station Road Industrial Estate, Bruton, Somerset. BA10 0EH. Tel: 01749 813266; mobile - 0973 342047; fax - 01749 813266. *Quality Victorian replica furniture - mahogany, teak, pine, cast iron and Venetian style mirrors. Any item copied in exact detail and exclusive designs catered for.*

James Burrell
Upton Barn, Seavington St. Michael, Ilminster, Somerset. TA19 0PZ. Tel: 01460 240610. *17th-19th C furniture (English), European furniture, carving, clock cases, inlay work, marquetry, lacquerwork, upholstery.*

Cane and Able - Cane & Rush Restoration
The Plains, Ampton, Bury St. Edmunds, Suffolk. IP31 1HX. Tel: 01284 728097. *Specialist restorers of antique furniture, rush seating, antique cane.*

Catspaw Restoration
6 Oakley Wood Farm, Wallingford, Oxon. OX10 6QG. Tel: 01491 834987. Est. 1972. *Sympathetic restoration of antiques and decorative items.*

Clare Hall Company
The Barns, Clare Hall, Cavendish Rd., Clare, Nr Sudbury, Suffolk. CO10 8PJ. Tel: 01787 278445 fax - 01787 278803; 01787 277510 (ansaphone). Est. 1970. *Hand-made copies of floor standing and table globes. Full cabinet making especially four poster beds, etc; restoration of all antiques and upholstery.* VAT: Stan/Spec.

J.W. Crisp Antiques
1 Kingston Mews, Kingston Lane, Teddington Middlesex TW11 Tel: 0181 977 5554. Open Mon-Fri 10-4 (prior phone call advisable). *Restoration of furniture and French polishing.*

EFMA
4 Northgate Close, Rottingdean, Brighton, East Sussex. BN2 7DZ. Tel: 01273 589744; fax 01273 589745. Fed. of Sussex Industries, IDDA Inst. of Export, Inst. of Linguists. *Hand-finished reproductions in walnut, elm, myrtle, yew mahogany, satinwood. Custom-work and bespoke polishing - 18th C, Biedermeier, Victorian*

Furniture continued

mahogany dining tables. Country furniture - distressed oak and cherry refectory, gateleg and coffee tables, Windsor chairs. Tables reproduced from old timber. VAT: Stan.

D.S. Embling - The Cabinet Repair Shop

Woodlands Farm, Blacknest, Alton, Hants. GU34 4QB. Tel: 01252 794260. C&G London Inst; GMC; League of Professional Craftsmen. Est. 1977. *Antique and modern furniture restoration and repair including marquetry and veneering, French polishing, modern finishes. Parts made, wood turning, collection and delivery; insurance claim repairs.*

Everitt and Rogers

Dawsnest Workshop, Grove Rd., Tiptree, Essex. CO5 0JE. Tel: 01621 816508. GADAR. Est. 1969. *Expert antique furniture restoration.*

John Farbrother Furniture Restoration

Ivy House, Main St., Shipton-by-Beningbrough, York, North Yorks. YO6 1AB. Tel: 01904 470187. GADAR. Est. 1987. *All repairs undertaken, refinishing process from complete strip to reviving existing finish. French polishing, oil, wax and lacquers. Pressurised fluid application woodworm treatment.*

Fauld Town and Country Furniture (Division of I. & J.L. Brown Ltd.)

58 Commercial Rd.,Hereford, Herefordshire. HR1 2BP. Tel: 01432 353183; fax - 01432 275338. Est. 1972. Open 8-5, appointment advisable. *Windsor chairs, extensive range of farmhouse tables, case pieces, including dressers; all traditional reproduction.* VAT: Stan.

Andrew Foott

4 Claremont Rd., Cheadle Hulme, Cheshire. SK8 6EG. Tel: 0161 485 3559. *Sympathetic restoration and conservation of antique furniture and mercurial barometers; free advice and estimates; quality items occasionally for sale.*

Georgian Cabinets Manufacturers Ltd

Unit 4 Fountayne House, 2-8 Fountayne Rd., London N15 4QL. Tel: 0181 885 1293; fax - 0181 365 1114. Est. 1964. *Manufacturers, restorers and polishers. Large stock of inlaid furniture.* LOC: Near Seven Sisters underground, Tottenham. VAT: Stan.

Melven Glander

Tel: 01284 828429. *Restoration and repair service to furniture, woodwork, clocks and period fixtures and fittings; free estimates and advice. Collection and delivery. Upholstery arranged.*

Mark Griffin Furniture

Byrebrook Studio, Lower Farm, North Moor, Oxon. OX8 1AU. Tel: 01865 300171; fax - 01865 883454.

Furniture continued

Roland Haycraft

The Lamb Arcade,Wallingford, Oxon. Tel: 01491 839622. *All aspects of antique restorations; one-off reproductions and copying. Stringed instrument maker and restorer/repairer.*

B.R. Honeyborne

The Whyle Cottage, Pudleston, Leominster, Herefordshire. HR6 0RE. Tel: 01568 750250. Guild of Herefordshire Craftsmen. *Antique furniture restoration and restoration courses; postal service of mouldings and bracket feet.*

Michael Jeffries

3 Upper Lambridge St., Larkhall, Bath, Somerset. BA1 6RY. Tel: 01225 310417; 01225 448103. Assn. of Master Upholsterers. *Antique upholstered furniture; decorative pieces.* VAT: Stan.

Johnson Antique Restoration

43 High St., Chatteris, Cambs. PE16 6BH. Tel: 01354 692622. GADAR. *Quality French polishing, caning, basic upholstery, veneering and structural repairs. Restored antique furniture sold at antique centre.*

Julian Kelly

26a Gopsall St., London N1 5HJ. Tel: 0171 739 2949; fax - same. *Woodcarving to suit all styles. Restorations - leathering, wood turning and metal polishing.*

T. H. Kelsall (Woodcrafts)

82 Main Rd., Slyne with Hest, Lancaster, Lancs. LA2 6AU. Tel: 01524 822347. GMC, GADAR. Est. 1987. *Repair and restoration of fine antique furniture and clocks, barometers and other works. Cabinet making, carving, marquetry, inlays, veneering, turning and polishing. Replica furniture and clock cases made to order.*

Kent Traditional Furniture

Moor Lane, Grassington, North Yorks. BD23 5BD. Tel: 01756 753045; fax - 01756 752865. *Specialist in hand made solid oak furniture.*

John Lloyd

The Old Bakehouse, The Street, Bolney, West Sussex. RH17 5PG. Tel: 01444 881988. *Sympathetic restoration and conservation of English and Continental furniture; traditional hand finishing, veneering, marquetry and inlay work, carving and turning, gilding, upholstery, rush/cane work, leather lining and tooling, lock repairs and keys. Antique furniture copied or designed and made to order. Regular delivery/ collection service to London.*

David Mitchell

45 St. Michael's Rd., Bedford, Beds. MK40 2LD. Tel: 01234 359976. *Veneering, carving, turning, inlay, French polishing; oil painting restoration.*

Furniture continued

R.V. Morgan & Co
Unit 41, 26-28 The Queensway, Ponders End, Enfield, Middlesex. EN3 4SA Tel: 0181 805 0353; fax - 0181 372 9946. GADAR. 1983. Open by appointment. *Inlays, veneers, turning, carving, fretwork; furniture made to order.* LOC: Off Hertford road, off A10. VAT: Stan.

M. R. Nelms
Unit 2, Trench Farm, Tilley Green, Wem, Shrops. SY4 5PQ. Tel: 01939 235463. GADAR. *Furniture, including antique and fitted, full restoration, antique boxes and clock cases a speciality.*

Nicholas J. Newman
22 Eastcroft Rd., West Ewell, Surrey. KT19 9TX. Tel: 0181 224 3347. *Comprehensive including exterior woodwork and locks.*

Nigel Northeast Cabinet Makers
Furniture Workshops, Back Drove, West Winterslow, Salisbury, Wilts. SP5 1RY. Tel: 01980 862051; fax - 01980 863986. GADAR. Est. 1982. *Antique restoration and French polishing. New furniture made to order, chairs made to complete sets. Cane and rush seating; fire and flood damage service.* VAT: Stan.

Painted and Plastered
5 Long St., Tetbury, Glos. Tel: 01666 505808. (Tara Higgins). TADA. Open 10-5.30. *Hand painted furniture and design, hand painted furniture and accessories available, commission pieces made to order and work carried out in the home. Special painting effects, murals, trompe l'oeil and faux finishes.*

Pinewood Furniture Studio Ltd
1 Eagle Trading Estate, Stourbridge Rd., Halesowen, West Midlands. B63 3UA. Tel: 0121 550 8228; fax - 0121 585 5611. *Manufacturers of pine furniture. Special orders undertaken.* VAT: Stan.

Nathan Polley Antique Furniture Restoration
The Barn, The Chippings, Tetbury, Glos. Tel: 01666 504997. TADA. Open 9-6. *Fine furniture restoration and cabinet making. Inlay work, wood turning, French polishing and waxing. Specialists in period mahogany, walnut and early oak.*

Neil Postons Restorations
29 South St., Leominster, Herefordshire. HR6 8JQ. Tel: 01568 616677; fax - same; home - 01568 770442. UKIC. Registered with the Museums and Galleries Commission. Open 8.45-5.30, Sat. and other times by appointment. *Antique and fine furniture restorations including re-construction, veneering, carving, turning, French and wax polishing, re-upholstery, rush and cane seating.*

Furniture continued

Nicholas S. Reeve
The Old Oaks, Otley Rd., Framsden, Stowmarket, Suffolk. IP14 6HU. Tel: Mobile - 0850 817216; fax - 01473 890173. Est. 1860. *Makers of 16th-18th C oak and cherry English country period furniture.* VAT: Stan.

Riches
Wixamtree, 69 Wood Lane, Cottonend, Beds. MK45 3AP. Tel: 01234 742121. (R.J. Jennings). *Re-upholstery, repairs and re-caning.*

Signal Furniture
Swan Corner, Pewsey, Wilts. SN9 5HL. Tel: 01672 563333; fax - 01672 562391. *Suppliers of classic solid wood furniture from Java and manufacturers of custom designed pine furniture including tables, beds, chests, bookcases and desks.*

David R. Solomons and Son
14 Moss Hall Grove, London N12 8PB. Tel: 0181 446 1693; works - 0181 985 6674; fax - 0181 446 9225. British Traditional Cabinet Makers. *Manufacturers of traditional furniture especially in burr/burl elm and burr/burl walnut veneers.* VAT: Stan. *Trade Only.*

Julian Stanley Woodcarving - Furniture
Unit 5 The Sitch, Longborough, Moreton-in-Marsh, Glos. GL56 0QJ. Tel: 01451 831122; fax - same. *Fine quality copies of 16th-19th C antiques - exotic carved furniture, figure carving, portrait busts (especially in lime), mirror frames and architectural pieces of all dimensions. Gilding, upholstery, painting and polishing. Work designed and made to order. No restorations.* VAT: Stan/Spec.

Thakeham Furniture
Marehill Rd., Pulborough, West Sussex. RH20 2DY. Tel: 01798 872006. *Cabinet work, veneer repairs, wax and French polishing, turning, marquetry, carving, etc.*

Treen Antiques
Treen House, 72 Park Rd., Prestwich, Manchester, Lancs. M25 0FA. Tel: 0161 720 7244; fax - same; mobile - 0973 471185. GADAR, RFS, FHS, UKIC. Open by appointment. *Conservation and restoration of all antique furniture (including vernacular) and woodwork, with emphasis on preserving original finish. Research undertaken, housekeeping advice, environmental monitoring and all aspects of conservation. Furniture assessment and advice on purchase and sales. Courses in restoration work held on request. Listed in Bonham's Directory.*

Barry J. Wateridge
Padouk, Portsmouth Rd., Bramshott Chase Hindhead, Surrey. GU26 6DB. Tel: 01428 607235. *French polishing and antique furniture restorations.*

Furniture continued

Weaver Neave and Daughter
17 Lifford St. Putney, London SW15 1NY. Tel: 0181 785 2464. *Recaning and re-rushing of antique furniture in traditional manner with traditional materials.*

Gerald Weir Antiques
Unit 1, Riverside Industrial Park, Wherstead Road, Ipswich, Suffolk. Tel: 01473 252606; fax - 01473 214621. Open by appointment. *Suppliers of reproduction oak furniture for European markets and decorative furniture for American markets. Trade Only.*

Jonathan Wilbye
Church Green Farm, Old Church Lane, Pateley Bridge, North Yorks. HG3 5LZ. Tel: 01423 711581. *Full restoration service including all carving, inlay, turning and polishing. Longcase clock cases a speciality.*

Peter Williams Antique Furniture Restoration
Silkmill House, 4 Charlton Rd., Tetbury, Glos. Tel: 01666 502311. TADA. *Early oak, period mahogany, walnut and country furniture. Wood turning, French polishing and waxing, gold tooled leather. Insurance claims. Antiques bought and sold. Established over 25 years.*

Furniture continued

Woodside Restoration Services
Beechfield House, Woodside, Frilford Heath, Nr. Abingdon, Oxon. OX13 5QG. Tel: 01865 390588. GADAR. Est. 1968. *All general cabinet repairs and polishing. Full barometer restoration; upholstery. Some mirror repairs and decorative work.*

GLASS

Mill Lane Stained Glass Workshop
Lower House, Mill Lane, Longhope, Glos. GL17 0AA. Tel: 01452 831100. *Design, manufacture and installation of traditional stained glass windows, domestic and secular. Manufacture of traditional leaded lights, including historic and listed buildings. Repair and renovation work undertaken.*

Sargeant Restorations
21 The Green, Westerham, Kent. TN16 1AX. *Restoration and cleaning of chandeliers, lustres and candelabra.*

INSURANCE AND FINANCE

Antique & Fine Art Finance Ltd
The Malthouse, 50 Kington St. Michael, Chippenham, Wilts. SN14 6JE Tel: 01249 750701; fax - same. *Provision of finance facilities to the clients of antique and fine art dealers.*

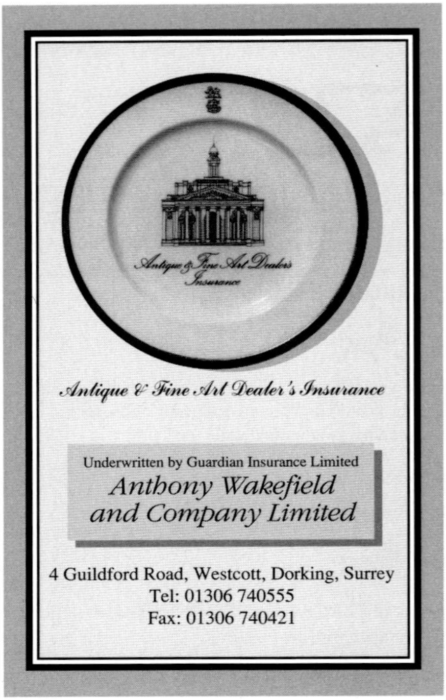

Antique & Fine Art Dealers Insurance
Antique & Fine Art Dealer's Insurance
Underwritten by Guardian Insurance Limited
Anthony Wakefield and Company Limited
4 Guildford Road, Westcott, Dorking, Surrey
Tel: 01306 740555
Fax: 01306 740421

Insurance and Finance continued

The Art and Antiques Service
Scales Barn, 1 Pearces Yard, Grantchester, Cambridge, Cambs. CB3 9NZ. Tel: 01223 846699; fax - 01223 846626; mobile - 0850 932894. *Professional valuations and insurance for probate, family division. Buying specific items or total refurbishments including architectural - fireplaces, doors. Advice on building up or scaling down collections and placing items for sale.*

Lockson Insurance Consultants
29 Broomfield St, London E14 6BX Tel: 0171 515 8600; fax - 0171 515 4866.

Minet Ltd.
Fine Arts and Jewellery Division, 66 Prescot St., London E1 8HG. Tel: 0171 481 0707; fax - 0171 488 9786. *International insurance brokers, specialising in fine arts and jewellery.*

Sneath, Kent and Stuart Ltd.
Stuart House, 53-55 Scrutton St., London EC2A 4QQ. Tel: 0171 739 5646; fax - 0171 739 2584/6467. Lloyds Insurance Brokers. *Specialists in : contemporary art galleries, fine art galleries, restorers and conservators, antique and fine art dealers, antique centres, auctioneers and valuers, "heirloom" dealers and collectors household and all risks insurances. Official brokers to LAPADA, BAFRA, Fine Art Trade Guild, IDDA, ABPA, Royal Society of Sculptors.*

Insurance and Finance continued

Anthony Wakefield & Company Ltd
4 Guildford Rd., Westcott, Dorking, Surrey. RH4 2JZ. Tel: 01306 740555; fax - 01306 740421. Members IIB. *Fine art and household insurance brokers; special terms for collectors; exclusive antique and fine art dealers policy with Guardian; exclusive Connoisseur household policy with dealers/fairs extension.*

IVORY

Boxwood Antique Restorers
See under Furniture - BAFRA Section (Somerset).

JEWELLERY AND SILVER

Goldcare
5 Bedford St., Middlesborough, Cleveland. TS1 2LL. Tel: 01642 231343. *Jewellery repair, engraving, re-stringing, stone cutting. Restoration of silver and cutlery; brass, copper, pinchbeck restoration.* VAT: Stan.

LOCKS & KEYS

Bramah Security Centres Ltd.
31 Oldbury Place, London. W1M 3AP. Tel: 0171 935 7147; fax - 0171 935 2779. Open Mon.-Fri. 8.30-5. *Keys cut to old locks; old locks opened; repair of old locks; new locks made to an old design; original Bramah locks dated. Quotation provided. Overseas work undertaken.* LOC: Near Baker Street tube station. VAT: Stan.

METALWORK

Ian Jarvis Restoration
Stable Workshop, Iken Hall, Iken, Woodbridge, Suffolk. IP12 2EP. Tel: 01728 689065. UKIC Metals Group. Est. 1988. *Cleaning, restorations and repairs to bronze and spelter figures, lamps, lanterns and general decorative metalwork. Repairs to woodwork, woodcarving and gilding.*

Allan Reeling Metal Restoration
42 Hodge Bower, Ironbridge, Shrops. TF8 7QL Tel: 01952 433031. GADAR. *Restoration and refurbishment of metal items including cleaning, repair and polishing.*

Surrey Antique Restoration
Croydon/South London area. Tel: 0181 684 1356; fax - same. *High quality restoration of metalware using traditional methods and materials. Over 2 years experience.*

PHOTOGRAPHY

Gerry Clist Photography LMPA
London NW6. Tel: 0171 624 0716; fax - 017 624 9475. *Specialising in sculptures, antiques an works of art photography - studio and location.*

REPRODUCTION STONEWORK

Hampshire Gardencraft

Rake Industries, Rake, Nr. Petersfield, Hants. GU31 5DR. Tel: 01730 895182; fax - 01730 893216. *Manufacturers of antiqued garden ornaments, troughs and pots in reconstituted stone in an old Cotswold stone finish. Many designs, catalogue available.*

SUPPLIERS

C. and A.J. Barmby

140 Lavender Hill, Tonbridge, Kent. TA9 2NJ. Tel: 01732 771590. Est. 1980. Open 9.30-4.45. *Suppliers of display stands in wire, acrylic and wood; reference books and catalogues; lamps and magnifers. Exhibitor at Alexandra Palace, Wembley, and all IACF fairs.* VAT: Stan.

The Display Stand Company Ltd

5 Rickett Street, London SW6 1RU. Tel: 0171 381 0255; fax - same. Est. 1993. Open by appointment only. *Specialist suppliers of display stands, bespoke stands for individual works of art.* VAT: Stan.

Suppliers continued

Just Bros. and Co.

Roeder House, Vale Rd.,London N4 1NG. Tel: 0181 880 2505; fax - 0181 802 0062. Member British Jewellery and Giftware Federation Ltd. Open 9-5, Fri. 9-12.30. *Reproduction presentation cases, Victoriana and traditional range of quality cases - part of largest selection in Europe. Catalogue on request.*

Lord Sheraton Ltd

18 St. George's Sq., Stamford, Lincs. PE9 2BN. Tel: 01780 66787; fax - 01780 52225. *Furniture polishes - unique formulas with pure beeswax and natural oils; 1773 furniture balsams in original and darkening, leather balsams, caretaker aerosols and dusting brushes.*

Marshall Brass

Keeling Hall Rd., Foulsham, Norfolk. NR20 5PR. Tel: 01362 684105; fax - 01362 684280. GMC. *Suppliers of quality period replica furniture fittings in brass and iron.*

Martin and Co. Ltd

119 Camden St., Birmingham, West Midlands. B1 3DJ. Tel: 0121 233 2111; fax - 0121 236 0488. ASFI, GAI. *Cabinet hardware supplied - handles, locks, hinges, castors etc. Trade Only.*

Suppliers continued

Alan Morris Wholesale

10 Coughton Lane, Alcester, Warks. B49 5HN. Tel: 01789 762800. Est. 1969. *Display stands - coated wire, plastic, acrylic and wood for plates, cups, saucers, bowls etc; plate hangers, wire and disc; jewellery boxes, polishing and cleaning cloths, peelable white labels and strung tickets. Mail order available.* VAT: Stan. *Trade Only.*

Relics

35 Bridge St., Witney, Oxon. Tel: 01993 704611. Est. 1978. Open 9-5. *Suppliers of furniture restoration material, brass castors, handles, locks, waxes and polish, upholstery and caning requisites, reproduction paints, stencils, etc. Mail order also.* LOC: Main road.

J. Shiner and Sons Ltd.

8 Windmill St. , London W1P 1HF. Tel: 0171 636 0740; fax - 0171 580 0740. *Suppliers of brass handles, castors, locks, brass grills and leathers.*

Suppliers continued

Suffolk Brass

Thurston, Bury St. Edmunds, Suffolk. IP31 3SN. Tel: 01359 233383; fax - 01359 233384. *Period replica cabinet fittings in brass and iron. One-off castings in lost wax or sand. Catalogue £5. Trade Only.*

The Victorian Ring Box Company

North Lodge, Ardpeaton, Cove, Dunbartonshire, Scotland. G84 0NY. Tel: 01436 850261; fax - same. By appointment only. *International designers, manufacturers and distributors of high quality antique style presentation boxes.*

TEXTILES

The Textile Restoration Studio

2 Talbot Rd., Bowdon, Altrincham, Cheshire. WA14 3JD. Tel: 0161 928 0020; fax - same. Registered with the conservation unit of the Museums & Galleries Commission. *Cleaning and repair of all types of antique textiles including tapestries, samplers, canvas work, beadwork, lace, costume, ecclesiastical vestments and furnishings, dolls and fans. Mail order catalogue of specialist textile conservation materials (Free - send large stamped addressed envelope). Home cleaning kits for needlework and acid-free tissue packs available to trade.*

TORTOISESHELL

Boxwood Antique Restorers

See under Furniture - BAFRA Section (Somerset).

TOYS

Robert Mullis Rocking Horse Maker

55 Berkeley Rd., Wroughton, Swindon, Wilts. SN4 9BN. Tel: 01793 813583; fax - same. British Toymakers Guild. *Full or partial restorations of antique horses, some wooden toy restoration. Traditional methods and materials used. Collection and delivery. New rocking horses made in five sizes, commissions undertaken.*

Tobilane Designs

Newton Holme Farm, Whittington, Carnforth, Lancs. LA6 2NZ. Tel: 015242 72662; home - same. Est. 1985. Open 10-5 including Sun. *Makers and restorers of a wide range of wooden toys including rocking horses and dolls' houses. Buys at auction (toys, teddies, dolls and rocking horses). Commissions accepted, replicas made.* LOC: B6254 3 miles south of Kirkby Lonsdale, between Whittington and Arkholme. VAT: Stan.

ALPHABETICAL LIST OF TOWNS AND VILLAGES WITH THE COUNTIES UNDER WHICH THEY APPEAR IN THIS GUIDE

Birkenhead, Merseyside.
Birmingham, W. Mids.
Birstwith, N. Yorks.
Bishop's Castle, Shrops.
Bishop's Stortford, Herts.
Bishops Cleeve, Glos.
Bishops Waltham, Hants.
Bishopston, Wales.
Bishopswood, Somerset.
Blackburn, Lancs.
Blackmore, Essex.
Blackpool, Lancs.
Bladon, Oxon.
Blaenau Ffestiniog, Wales.
Blairgowrie, Scotland.
Blandford Forum, Dorset.
Blandford Forum, Dorset.
Bletchingley, Surrey.
Blewbury, Oxon.
Bloxham, Oxon.
Bloxwich, W. Mids.
Blythburgh,, Suffolk.
Bodorgan , Wales.
Bognor Regis, Sussex West.
Bollington, Cheshire.
Bolton, Lancs.
Bolton-by-Bowland, Lancs.
Boroughbridge, N. Yorks.
Boscastle, Cornwall.
Boston, Lincs.
Boston Spa, W. Yorks.
Botley, Hants.
Bottisham, Cambs.
Boughton, Kent.
Bourne, Lincs.
Bournemouth, Dorset.
Bovey Tracey, Devon.
Bowness-on-Windermere, Cumbria.
Bowness-on-Windermere, Cumbria.
Brackley, Northants.
Bradfield St. George, Suffolk.
Bradford, W. Yorks.
Bradford-on-Avon, Wilts.
Bradley, N. Yorks.
Brailsford, Derbys
Bramhall, Cheshire.
Bramley, Surrey.
Brampton, Cumbria.
Brancaster Staithe, Norfolk.
Brandsby, N. Yorks.
Branksome, Dorset.
Brasted, Kent.
Braunton, Devon.
Brechin, Scotland.
Brecon, Wales.
Brentwood, Essex.
Brereton, Staffs.
Bridge of Earn, Scotland.
Bridgnorth, Shrops.
Bridlington, E. Yorks.
Bridport, Dorset.
Brierfield, Lancs.
Brighton, Sussex East.
Brinklow, Warks.
Brinkworth, Wilts.
Bristol, Glos.
Brixham, Devon.
Brixworth, Northants.
Broadstairs, Kent.
Broadway, Worcs.
Brobury, Herefs.
Brockdish, Norfolk.
Brodick and Whiting Bay, Scotland.
Bromley, Kent.
Brompton, N. Yorks.
Broseley, Shrops.
Broughton Astley, Leics.
Bruton, Somerset.
Buckland St. Mary, Somerset.
Budleigh Salterton, Devon.
Bulkington, Warks.
Bungay, Suffolk.
Bures, Suffolk.
Burford, Oxon.
Burgess Hill, Sussex West.
Burghfield Common, Berks.
Burneston, N. Yorks.
Burnham Market, Norfolk.
Burnham on Crouch, Essex.
Burnham-on-Sea, Somerset.
Burnley, Lancs.
Burscough, Lancs.
Burton-on-Trent, Staffs.
Burwash, Sussex East.
Burwell, Cambs.
Bury, Lancs.
Bury St. Edmunds, Suffolk.
Bushey, Herts.
Bushmills, Co. Antrim, N.Ireland.
Buxton, Derbys.

C

Cadeby, Leics.
Cadnam, Hants.
Caerphilly, Wales
Caistor, Lincs.
Callington, Cornwall.
Calne, Wilts.
Camberley, Surrey
Camborne, Cornwall.
Cambridge, Cambs.
Cambridge, Glos.
Camelford, Cornwall.
Canonbie, Scotland
Canterbury, Kent.
Cardiff, Wales
Carhampton, Somerset.
Carlisle, Cumbria.
Carmarthen, Wales
Carrefour Selous, Jersey, Channel Islands.
Carshalton, Surrey
Cartmel, Cumbria.
Castle Ashby, Northants.
Castle Cary, Somerset.
Castle Combe, Wilts.
Castle Douglas, Scotland
Castletown, Isle of Man
Cavendish, Suffolk
Caversham, Berks.
Cawood, N. Yorks.
Ceres, Scotland
Cerne Abbas, Dorset.
Chagford, Devon.
Chalfont St. Giles, Bucks.
Chalford, Glos.
Chalgrove, Oxon.
Chard, Somerset.
Charlton Marshall, Dorset.
Charmouth, Dorset.
Chatburn, Lancs.
Chatham, Kent.
Cheadle, Cheshire.
Cheadle Hulme, Cheshire.
Cheddleton, Staffs.
Chelmsford, Essex.
Cheltenham, Glos.
Chepstow, Wales
Cherhill, Wilts.
Chertsey, Surrey
Chesham, Bucks.
Chester, Cheshire.
Chesterfield, Derbys
Chichester, Sussex West
Chiddingstone, Kent.
Chilcompton, Somerset.
Chilton, Oxon.
Chingford, Essex.
Chippenham, Wilts.
Chipping Campden, Glos.
Chipping Norton, Oxon.
Chipping Sodbury, Glos.
Chirk, Wales
Chislehurst, Kent.
Chittering, Cambs.
Chobham, Surrey
Chorley, Lancs.
Christchurch, Dorset.
Christian Malford, Wilts.
Church Stretton, Shrops.

Churt, Surrey
Ciliau Aeron, Wales
Cirencester, Glos.
Clacton-on-Sea, Essex.
Clare, Suffolk
Claudy, Co. Londonderry, N.Ireland.
Cleobury Mortimer, Shrops.
Clevedon, Somerset.
Clitheroe, Lancs.
Clola by Mintlaw, Scotland
Clutton, Somerset.
Coalville, Leics.
Cobham, Surrey
Cockermouth, Cumbria.
Cockfosters, Herts.
Cocking, Sussex West
Codford, Wilts.
Codicote, Herts.
Codsall, Staffs.
Coggeshall, Essex.
Colchester, Essex.
Coldstream, Scotland
Coleraine, Co. Londonderry, N. Ireland.
Coleshill, Warks.
Collessie, Scotland
Collingham, Notts.
Colne, Lancs.
Colsterworth, Lincs.
Coltishall, Norfolk.
Colwyn Bay, Wales
Colyton, Devon.
Comberton, Cambs.
Congleton, Cheshire.
Consett, Durham.
Conwy, Wales
Cooden, Sussex East
Cookham, Berks.
Cookstown, Co. Tyrone, N.Ireland.
Copthorne, Sussex West
Corby Hill, Cumbria.
Corringham, Essex.
Corsham, Wilts.
Costessey, Norfolk.
Coulsdon, Surrey
Cove, Scotland
Coventry, W. Mids.
Cowbridge, Wales
Cowes, Isle of Wight
Cowfold, Sussex West
Coxley, Somerset.
Cranborne, Dorset.
Cranbrook, Kent.
Craven Arms, Shrops.
Crawley, Hants.
Crayford, Kent.
Cremyll, Cornwall.
Crewe, Cheshire.
Crewkerne, Somerset.
Crickhowell, Wales
Cricklade, Wilts.
Crieff, Scotland
Cromer, Norfolk.
Crook, Durham.
Crosby Ravensworth, Cumbria.
Cross Hills, N. Yorks.
Croughton, Northants.
Crowborough, Sussex East
Croydon, Surrey
Crudwell, Wilts.
Cuckfield, Sussex West
Culham, Oxon.
Cullompton, Devon.

D

Dalbeattie, Scotland
Danbury, Essex.
Darlington, Durham.
Dartford, Kent.
Dartmouth, Devon.
Darwen, Lancs.
Datchet, Berks.
Davenham, Cheshire.
Deal, Kent.
Debenham, Suffolk
Deddington, Oxon.
Deganwy, Wales
Denby Dale, W. Yorks.
Denny, Scotland
Derby, Derbys
Devizes, Wilts.
Didcot, Oxon.
Dingwall, Scotland
Disley, Cheshire.
Diss, Norfolk.
Ditchling, Sussex East
Doddington, Cambs.
Donaghadee, Co. Down, N.Ireland.
Doncaster, S. Yorks.
Dorchester, Dorset.
Dorchester-on-Thames, Oxon.
Dorking, Surrey
Dornoch, Scotland
Douglas, Isle of Man
Dover, Kent.
Doveridge, Derbys
Dowlish Wake, Somerset.
Driffield, E. Yorks.
Drimpton, Dorset.
Droitwich, Worcs.
Dronfield, Derbys
Drumnadrochit, Scotland
Duffield, Derbys
Dulford, Devon.
Dulverton, Somerset.
Dumfries, Scotland
Dunchurch, Warks.
Dundee, Scotland
Dunkeld, Scotland
Dunmow, Essex.
Dunsfold, Surrey
Durham., Durham.
Durrington, Sussex West
Duxford, Cambs.

E

Eachwick, Northumbs.
Eaglescliffe, Cheshire.
Earsham, Norfolk.
Easingwold, N. Yorks.
East Budleigh, Devon.
East Grinstead, Sussex West
East Hagbourne, Oxon.
East Molesey, Surrey
East Peckham, Kent.
East Pennard, Somerset.
East Rudham, Norfolk.
Eastbourne, Sussex East
Eastleigh, Hants.
Ebrington, Glos.
Eccleston, Lancs.
Edenbridge, Kent.
Edenfield, Lancs.
Edgware, Middx.
Edinburgh, Scotland
Egham, Surrey
Elgin, Scotland
Elie, Scotland
Ellesmere, Shrops.
Elton, Notts.
Ely, Cambs.
Empingham, Rutland
Emsworth, Hants.
Endmoor, Cumbria.
Enfield, Middx.
Epsom, Surrey
Ermington, Devon.
Errol, Scotland
Esher, Surrey
Eversley, Hants.
Evesham, Worcs.
Ewell, Surrey
Exeter, Devon.
Exmouth, Devon.
Exning, Suffolk
Eye, Suffolk
Eynsham, Oxon.

F

Fairford, Glos.

Holt, Norfolk.
Holt, Wales
Holywood, Co. Down, N.Ireland.
Honiton, Devon.
Horam, Sussex East
Horncastle, Lincs.
Horndean, Hants.
Horrabridge, Devon.
Horsebridge, Sussex East
Horsell, Surrey
Horsham, Sussex West
Horton, Berks.
Hoylake, Merseyside
Huddersfield, W. Yorks.
Hull, E. Yorks.
Hungerford, Berks.
Hunstanton, Norfolk.
Huntercombe, Oxon.
Huntingdon, Cambs.
Huntly, Scotland
Hursley, Hants.
Hurst, Berks.
Hurst Green, Sussex East
Hurstpierpoint, Sussex West
Hyde, Cheshire.
Hythe, Kent.

I

Ibstock, Leics.
Ickleton, Cambs.
Ilchester, Somerset.
Ilford, Essex.
Ilfracombe, Devon.
Ilkeston, Derbys
Ilkley, W. Yorks.
Ilminster, Somerset.
Inchture, Scotland
Instow, Devon.
Inverness, Scotland
Ipswich, Suffolk
Irby-in-the-Marsh, Lincs.
Ironbridge, Shrops.
Isleworth, Middx.
Islip, Northants.
Iver, Bucks.
Ixworth, Suffolk

J

Jedburgh, Scotland
Jesmond, Tyne and Wear

K

Keighley, W. Yorks.
Kelling, Norfolk.
Kelvedon, Essex.
Kempsford, Glos.
Kendal, Cumbria.
Kenilworth, Warks.
Kentisbeare, Devon.
Kesgrave, Suffolk
Kessingland, Suffolk
Keswick, Cumbria.
Kettering, Northants.
Ketton, Lincs.
Kew, Surrey
Kew Green, Surrey
Kidderminster, Worcs.
Kidwelly, Wales
Kilbarchan, Scotland
Kilham, E. Yorks.
Killamarsh, Derbys
Killearn, Scotland
Killin, Scotland
Killinghall, N. Yorks.
Kilmacolm, Scotland
Kilmarnock, Scotland
Kilmichael Glassary, Scotland
Kiltarlity, Scotland
Kincardine O'Neil, Scotland
King's Langley, Herts.
King's Lynn, Norfolk.
Kinghorn, Scotland
Kingsbridge, Devon.
Kingsley, Staffs.
Kingsthorpe, Northants.
Kingston-on-Spey, Scotland
Kingston-upon-Thames, Surrey
Kingswear, Devon.
Kingussie, Scotland
Kinross, Scotland.
Kinver, Staffs.
Kirk Deighton, N. Yorks.
Kirkby Lonsdale, Cumbria.
Kirkby Stephen, Cumbria.
Kirkcudbright, Scotland
Kirton, Lincs.
Kirton in Lindsey, Lincs.
Knaresborough, N. Yorks.
Knebworth, Herts.
Knighton, Wales
Knipton, Leics.
Knowle, W. Mids.
Knutsford, Cheshire.

L

Lake, Isle of Wight
Laleham, Surrey
Lamberhurst, Kent.
Lampeter, Wales
Lancaster, Lancs.
Landbeach, Cambs.
Lane End, Bucks.
Langford, Notts.
Langham, Norfolk.
Langholm, Scotland
Langley Burrell, Wilts.
Largs, Scotland
Lavenham, Suffolk
Leamington Spa, Warks.
Leavenheath, Suffolk
Lechlade, Glos.
Leckhampstead, Berks.
Ledbury, Herefs.
Leeds, W. Yorks.
Leedstown, Cornwall.
Leek, Staffs.
Leicester, Leics.
Leigh, Kent.
Leigh, Lancs.
Leigh, Staffs.
Leigh-on-Sea, Essex.
Leighton Buzzard, Beds.
Leiston, Suffolk
Lennoxtown, Scotland
Leominster, Herefs.
Lepton, W. Yorks.
Letchmore Heath, Herts.
Lewes, Sussex East
Lichfield, Staffs.
Limpsfield, Surrey
Lincoln, Lincs.
Lindfield, Sussex West
Lingfield, Surrey
Linlithgow, Scotland
Linton, N. Yorks.
Lisbellaw, Co. Fermanagh, N.Ireland.
Lisburn, Co. Antrim, N.Ireland.
Liss, Hants.
Little Abington, Cambs.
Little Bedwyn, Wilts.
Little Downham, Cambs.
Little Haywood, Staffs.
Little Malvern, Worcs.
Littlebourne, Kent.
Littlehampton, Sussex West
Littleton, Cheshire.
Littleton, Somerset.
Litton Cheney, Dorset.
Liverpool, Merseyside
Llandissilio, Wales
Llandudno, Wales
Llandudno Junction, Wales
Llanelli, Wales
Llanfair Caereinion, Wales
Llangollen, Wales
Llanrwst, Wales
Long Buckby, Northants.
Long Cawston, Leics.
Long Eaton, Derbys
Long Hanborough, Oxon.

Long Marton, Cumbria.
Long Melford, Suffolk
Long Preston, N. Yorks.
Long Stratton, Norfolk.
Long Sutton, Lincs.
Longridge, Lancs.
Looe, Cornwall.
Lostwithiel, Cornwall.
Loughborough, Leics.
Louth, Lincs.
Low Fell, Tyne and Wear
Low Newton, Cumbria.
Lowestoft, Suffolk
Lubenham, Leics.
Ludlow, Shrops.
Lurgan, Co. Armagh, N.Ireland.
Luton, Beds.
Lydford, Devon.
Lye, W. Mids.
Lymington, Hants.
Lyneham, Wilts.
Lynton, Devon.
Lytchett Minster, Dorset.
Lytham St. Annes, Lancs.

M

Macclesfield, Cheshire.
Maidencombe, Devon.
Maidenhead, Berks.
Maidstone, Kent.
Maldon, Essex.
Malmesbury, Wilts.
Malton, N. Yorks.
Malvern Link, Worcs.
Malvern Wells, Worcs.
Manchester, Lancs.
Manfield, N. Yorks.
Manningtree, Essex.
Mansfield, Notts.
Manton, Rutland
Mapplewell, S. Yorks.
Marazion, Cornwall.
Margate, Kent.
Market Bosworth, Leics.
Market Deeping, Lincs.
Market Harborough, Leics.
Market Rasen, Lincs.
Market Weighton, E. Yorks.
Markington, N. Yorks.
Marlborough, Wilts.
Marlesford, Suffolk
Marlow, Bucks.
Marple Bridge, Cheshire.
Martlesham, Suffolk
Masham, N. Yorks.
Matching Green, Essex.
Mathry, Wales
Maybole, Scotland
Meare, Somerset.
Medbourne, Leics.
Meigle, Scotland
Melbourne, Derbys
Melbury Osmond, Dorset.
Melksham, Wilts.
Mellor, Cheshire.
Melmerby, N. Yorks.
Menston, W. Yorks.
Merstham, Surrey
Merton, Devon.
Mevagissey, Cornwall.
Middleton Village, Lancs.
Midhurst, Sussex West
Midsomer Norton, Somerset.
Milburn, Cumbria.
Mildenhall, Suffolk
Milford, Surrey
Milford Haven, Wales
Milnthorpe, Cumbria.
Milton Keynes, Bucks.
Milton Lilbourne, Wilts.
Milverton, Somerset.
Minchinhampton, Glos.
Minety, Wilts.
Ministeracres, Northumbs.
Mirfield, W. Yorks.
Mitcham, Surrey
Mobberley, Cheshire.
Modbury, Devon.
Moffat, Scotland
Monkton, Devon.
Monmouth, Wales
Montacute, Somerset.
Montrose, Scotland
Morchard Bishop, Devon.
Morden, Surrey
Morecambe, Lancs.
Morestead, Hants.
Moreton-in-Marsh, Glos.
Moretonhampstead, Devon.
Morriston, Wales
Much Wenlock, Shrops.
Murton, Wales

N

Nantwich, Cheshire.
Narberth, Wales
Narborough, Leics.
Needham Market, Suffolk
Nelson, Lancs.
Nether Stowey, Somerset.
Nettlebed, Oxon.
New Bolingbroke, Lincs.
Newark, Notts.
Newbridge-on-Wye, Wales
Newburgh, Scotland
Newby Bridge, Cumbria.
Newcastle Emlyn, Wales
Newcastle-under-Lyme, Staffs.
Newcastle-upon-Tyne, Tyne and Wear
Newhaven, Sussex East
Newmarket, Suffolk
Newnham, Kent.
Newport, Essex.
Newport, Isle of Wight
Newry, Co. Down, N. Ireland
Newton Abbot, Devon.
Newton St. Cyres, Devon.
Newton Tony, Wilts.
Newtonmore, Scotland
Newtown, Derbys
Newtownabbey, Co. Antrim, N. Ireland.
Norham, Northumbs.
North Aston, Oxon.
North Berwick, Scotland
North Cave, E. Yorks.
North Kelsey Moor, Lincs.
North Petherton, Somerset.
North Shields, Tyne and Wear
North Walsham, Norfolk.
North Wraxall, Wilts.
Northallerton, N. Yorks.
Northampton, Northants.
Northchapel, Sussex West
Northfleet, Kent.
Northleach, Glos.
Norton, Glos.
Norton, N. Yorks.
Norwich, Norfolk.
Nottingham, Notts.

O

Oadby, Leics.
Oakham, Rutland
Oban, Scotland
Odiham, Hants.
Okehampton, Devon.
Oldham, Lancs.
Ollerton, Notts.
Olney, Bucks.
Orford, Suffolk
Ormskirk, Lancs.
Orpington, Kent.
Osbournby, Lincs.
Osgathorpe, Leics.
Otford, Kent.
Otley, W. Yorks.
Outwell, Cambs.
Oxford, Oxon.
Oxted, Surrey

P
Painswick, Glos.
Paisley, Scotland
Parkstone, Dorset.
Pateley Bridge, N. Yorks.
Patrington, E. Yorks.
Paulerspury, Northants.
Peasenhall, Suffolk
Peel, Isle of Man
Pembroke, Wales
Penkridge, Staffs.
Penn, Bucks.
Penrith, Cumbria.
Penryn, Cornwall.
Penshurst, Kent.
Penzance, Cornwall.
Pershore, Worcs.
Perth, Scotland
Peterborough, Cambs.
Petersfield, Hants.
Petworth, Sussex West
Pevensey, Sussex East
Pevensey Bay, Sussex East
Pickering, N. Yorks.
Pitlochry, Scotland
Pittenweem, Scotland
Plumley, Cheshire.
Plymouth, Devon.
Polegate, Sussex East
Pollokshields, Scotland
Pontarddulais, Wales
Pontefract, W. Yorks.
Ponterwyd, Wales
Poole, Dorset.
Portadown, Co. Armagh, N.Ireland.
Portaferry, Co. Down, N.Ireland.
Portballintrae, Co. Antrim, N.Ireland.
Porthcawl, Wales
Portree, Scotland
Portrush, Co. Antrim, N. Ireland.
Portslade, Sussex West
Portsmouth, Hants.
Portsoy, Scotland
Portstewart, Co. Londonderry, N. Ireland.
Potterne, Wilts.
Potterspury, Northants.
Poulton-le-Fylde, Lancs.
Poynton, Cheshire.
Prestbury, Cheshire.
Preston, Lancs.
Prestwick, Scotland
Princes Risborough, Bucks.
Puckeridge, Herts.
Puddletown, Dorset.
Pulborough, Sussex West
Purleigh, Essex.
Pwllheli, Wales

Q
Queen Camel, Somerset.
Queniborough, Leics.
Quorn, Leics.

R
Radlett, Herts.
Rainford, Merseyside
Rait, Scotland
Ramsbury, Wilts.
Ramsey, Cambs.
Ramsgate, Kent.
Raveningham, Norfolk.
Ravensmoor, Cheshire.
Ravenstonedale, Cumbria.
Rayleigh, Essex.
Reading, Berks.
Redbourn, Herts.
Redditch, Worcs.
Redhill, Surrey
Reepham, Norfolk.
Reigate, Surrey
Rhosneigr, Wales
Rhuallt, Wales
Richmond, Surrey
Rickmansworth, Herts.
Ridgewell, Essex.
Ringway, Cheshire.
Ringwood, Hants.
Ripley, Surrey
Ripon, N. Yorks.
Risby, Suffolk
Riverhead, Kent.
Rochdale, Lancs.
Rochester, Kent.
Rodley, Glos.
Rolvenden, Kent.
Romsey, Hants.
Ross-on-Wye, Herefs.
Rotherham, S. Yorks.
Rottingdean, Sussex East
Roxwell, Essex.
Royston, Herts.
Rugeley, Staffs.
Rumford, Cornwall.
Runfold, Surrey
Rushden, Northants.
Ruskington, Lincs.
Ruthin, Wales
Rutland Water, Rutland
Ryde, Isle of Wight
Rye, Sussex East

S
Sabden, Lancs.
Saffron Walden, Essex.
Salisbury, Wilts.
Saltaire, W. Yorks.
Saltcoats, Scotland
Samlesbury, Lancs.
Sanderstead, Surrey
Sandgate, Kent.
Sandhurst, Berks.
Sandhurst, Kent.
Sandwich, Kent.
Sarnau, Wales
Sawbridgeworth, Herts.
Sayers Common, Sussex West
Scarborough, N. Yorks.
Scarisbrick, Lancs.
Scarthingwell, N. Yorks.
Scarthoe, Lincs.
Scratby, Norfolk.
Scunthorpe, Lincs.
Seaford, Sussex East
Seaton, Devon.
Sedbergh, Cumbria.
Selkirk, Scotland
Semley, Wilts.
Settle, N. Yorks.
Sevenoaks, Kent.
Shaftesbury, Dorset.
Shaldon, Devon.
Shanklin, Isle of Wight
Shardlow, Derbys
Sharrington, Norfolk.
Sheffield, S. Yorks.
Shefford, Beds.
Shenfield, Essex.
Shenton, Leics.
Shepperton, Surrey
Sherborne, Dorset.
Sherburn in Elmet, N. Yorks.
Shere, Surrey
Sheringham, Norfolk.
Shifnal, Shrops.
Shipley, W. Yorks.
Shipston-on-Stour, Warks.
Shirley, Surrey
Shrewsbury, Shrops.
Sible Hedingham, Essex.
Sidcup, Kent.
Siddington, Cheshire.
Sidmouth, Devon.
Sileby, Leics.
Skegness, Lincs.
Skipton, N. Yorks.
Slad, Glos.
Sleaford, Lincs.
Smethwick, W. Mids.
Snainton, N. Yorks.

Snape, Suffolk
Snodland, Kent.
Solihull, W. Mids.
Somersham, Cambs.
Somerton, Somerset.
Sonning-on-Thames, Berks.
South Brent, Devon.
South Cave, E. Yorks.
South Harting, Sussex West
South Molton, Devon.
South Shields, Tyne and Wear
South Walsham, Norfolk.
Southampton, Hants.
Southborough, Kent.
Southend-on-Sea, Essex.
Southport, Merseyside
Southwell, Notts.
Southwold, Suffolk
Sowerby Bridge, W. Yorks.
Spalding, Lincs.
Spennithorne, N. Yorks.
St. Albans, Herts.
St. Andrews, Scotland
St. Annes-on-Sea, Lancs.
St Aubin, Jersey, Channel Islands
St. Austell, Cornwall.
St. Gerrans, Cornwall.
St. Helens, Isle of Wight
St. Helier , Jersey, Channel Islands
St. Ives, Cambs.
St. Ives, Cornwall.
St. Lawrence , Jersey, Channel Islands
St. Leonards-on-Sea, Sussex East
St. Margaret's Bay, Kent.
St. Martin, Guernsey, Channel Islands
St. Neots, Cambs.
St. Peter Port, Guernsey, Channel Islands
St. Sampson, Guernsey, Channel Islands
Stafford, Staffs.
Staines, Surrey
Stalham, Norfolk.
Stamford, Lincs.
Standlake, Oxon.
Stanford-le-Hope, Essex.
Stansted, Essex.
Stanton, Shrops.
Stapleford, Lincs.
Staunton Harold, Leics.
Staveley, Cumbria.
Stewarton, Scotland
Steyning, Sussex West
Stickney, Lincs.
Stiffkey, Norfolk.
Stillington, N. Yorks.
Stirling, Scotland
Stock, Essex.
Stockbridge, Hants.
Stockbury, Kent.
Stockland, Devon.
Stockport, Cheshire.
Stockton Heath, Cheshire.
Stoke by Nayland, Suffolk
Stoke Ferry, Norfolk.
Stoke-on-Trent, Staffs.
Stonehaven, Scotland
Storrington, Sussex West
Stourbridge, W. Mids.
Stow-on-the-Wold, Glos.
Stowmarket, Suffolk
Stradbroke, Suffolk
Stratford-upon-Avon, Warks.
Strathblane, Scotland
Stretton, Cheshire.
Stretton-on-Fosse, Warks.
Stretton-under-Fosse, Warks.
Stroud, Glos.
Sturminster Newton, Dorset.
Suckley, Worcs.
Sudbury, Suffolk
Suffield, Norfolk.
Sunderland, Tyne and Wear
Sundridge, Kent.
Sunningdale, Berks.
Surbiton, Surrey
Sutton, Surrey
Sutton Bridge, Lincs.
Sutton Coldfield, W. Mids.
Sutton Valence, Kent.
Sutton-on-Sea, Lincs.
Swadlincote, Derbys
Swaffham, Norfolk.
Swafield, Norfolk.
Swanage, Dorset.
Swansea, Wales
Swindon, Wilts.
Swinford, Leics.
Swinton, Lancs.
Synod Inn, Wales

T

Tacolneston, Norfolk.
Taddington, Glos.
Tadley, Hants.
Tarporley, Cheshire.
Tarvin, Cheshire.
Tarvin Sands, Cheshire.
Tattenhall, Cheshire.
Tattershall, Lincs.
Taunton, Somerset.
Tavistock, Devon.
Taynton, Oxon.
Teddington, Middx.
Teignmouth, Devon.
Telford, Shrops.
Templeton, Wales
Tenby, Wales
Tenterden, Kent.
Tern Hill, Shrops.
Tetbury, Glos.
Tetsworth, Oxon.
Tewkesbury, Glos.
Teynham, Kent.
Thame, Oxon.
Thames Ditton, Surrey
Thatcham, Berks.
Thirsk, N. Yorks.
Thorne, S. Yorks.
Thornhill, Scotland
Thornton le Dale, N. Yorks.
Ticknall, Derbys
Tillington, Herefs.
Tillington, Sussex West
Tilston, Cheshire.
Tingewick, Bucks.
Tintern, Wales
Tisbury, Wilts.
Titchfield, Hants.
Tiverton, Devon.
Tockwith, N. Yorks.
Toddington, Beds.
Todmorden, W. Yorks.
Tonbridge, Kent.
Topsham, Devon.
Torquay, Devon.
Totnes, Devon.
Tottenhill, Norfolk.
Towcester, Northants.
Trawden, Lancs.
Tregony, Cornwall.
Treherbert, Wales
Treorchy, Wales
Trevor, Wales
Tring, Herts.
Troon, Scotland
Truro, Cornwall.
Tunbridge Wells, Kent.
Tutbury, Staffs.
Tuxford, Notts.
Twickenham, Middx.
Twyford, Bucks.
Twyford, Hants.
Twyford, Norfolk.
Tynemouth, Tyne and Wear
Tywardreath, Cornwall.
Tywyn, Wales

Specialist Dealers' Index

Most antique dealers in Britain sell a wide range of goods from furniture, through porcelain and pottery, to pictures, prints and clocks. Much of the interest in visting antiques shops comes from this diversity. However, there are a number of dealers who specialise and the following is a list of these dealers. Most of them will stock a representative selection of the items found under their classification.

The name of the business, together with the area of London or the town and county under which the detailed entry can be found are given in the listing. Again we would like to repeat the advice given in the introduction that, if readers are looking for a particular item, they are advised to telephone first, before making a long journey.

CLASSIFICATIONS

Antique Centres & Markets

Georgian Village Antiques Market, London E17.
Angel Arcade, London N1.
Camden Passage Antiques Centre, London N1.
Fleamarket, The, London N1.
London Militaria Market, London N1.
Mall Antiques Arcade, The, London N1.
York Arcade, London N1.
Palmers Green Antiques Centre, London N13.
Southgate Antiques & Collectables, London N14.
Hampstead Antique and Craft Market, London NW3.
Alfies Antique Market, London NW8.
Bermondsey Antiques Market, London SE1.
Greenwich Antiques Market, London SE10.
Franklin's Camberwell Antiques Market, London SE5.
Northcote Road Antiques Market, London SW11.
Antiquarius, London SW3.
Chelsea Antique Market, London SW3.
Fulham Cross Antiques, London SW6.
Magpies, London SW6.
Bond Street Antiques Centre, London W1.
Grays Antique Market, London W1.
Arbras Gallery, London W11.
Corner Portobello Antiques Supermarket, The, London W11.
Crown Arcade, London W11.
Dolphin Arcade, London W11.
Grays Portobello, London W11.
Red Lion Market (Portobello Antiques Market), The, London W11.
Roger's Antiques Gallery, London W11.
Silver Fox Gallery, The, London W11.
Stouts Antiques Market, London W11.
World Famous Portobello Market, London W11.
Old Cinema Antique Department Store, The, London W4.
Kensington Church Street Antiques Centre, London W8.
Apple Market Stalls, London WC2.
Covent Garden Flea Market, London WC2.
London Silver Vaults, The, London WC2.
Ampthill Emporium, Ampthill, Beds.
Harrold Antique Centre, Harrold, Beds.
The Woburn Abbey Antiques Centre, Woburn, Beds.
Barkham Antique Centre, Barkham, Berks.
Hungerford Arcade, Hungerford, Berks.
Reading Emporium, Reading, Berks.
Moss End Antique Centre, Warfield, Berks.
Amersham Antiques and Collectors Centre, Amersham, Bucks.
Buck House Antique Centre, Beaconsfield, Bucks.
Marlow Antique Centre, Marlow, Bucks.
Olney Antique Centre, Olney, Bucks.
Well Cottage Antiques Centre, Princes Risborough, Bucks.
Tingewick Antiques Centre, Tingewick, Bucks.
Adrian Hornsey Ltd, Twyford, Bucks.
Antiques at. .Wendover Antiques Centre, Wendover, Bucks.
Winslow Antiques Centre, Winslow, Bucks.
Collectors Centre, Cambridge, Cambs.
Collectors' Market, Cambridge, Cambs.
Gwydir Street Antiques Centre, Cambridge, Cambs.
Hyde Park Corner Antiques (Antiques Centre), Cambridge, Cambs.
Adams Furniture Centre, Huntingdon, Cambs.
The Old Bishop's Palace Antique Centre, Little Downham, Cambs.
Fitzwilliam Antiques Centre, Peterborough, Cambs.
Hyperion Antique Centre, St Ives, Cambs.
Walpole Highway Antiques Centre, Wisbech, Cambs.
Chester Drawers Antique Centre, Chester, Cheshire.
Guildhall Fair - Chester, Chester, Cheshire.
Davenham Antique Centre, Davenham, Cheshire.
Arts and Antiques Centre, Knutsford, Cheshire.
E. R. Antiques Centre, Stockport, Cheshire.
Tarporley Antique Centre, Tarporley, Cheshire.
Waterfront Antiques Market, Falmouth, Cornwall.
Chapel Street Antiques Market, Penzance, Cornwall.
St. Austell Antiques Centre, St. Austell, Cornwall.
Carlisle Antique and Craft Centre, Carlisle, Cumbria.
Cockermouth Antiques Market, Cockermouth, Cumbria.
Belper Antiques Centre, Belper, Derbys.
The Shambles, Ashburton, Devon.
Colyton Antique Centre, Colyton, Devon.
The Antique Centre on the Quay, Exeter, Devon.
McBains of Exeter, Exeter, Devon.
The Meeting, Exeter, Devon.
The Quay Gallery Antiques Emporium, Exeter, Devon.
The Antique Centre Abingdon House, Honiton, Devon.
Newton Abbot Antiques Centre, Newton Abbot, Devon.
Barbican Antiques Centre, Plymouth, Devon.
New Street Antique Centre, Plymouth, Devon.
Sidmouth Antiques and Collectors Centre, Sidmouth, Devon.
The Furniture Market, South Molton, Devon.
Mulberry House, Topsham, Devon.
Hardy's Collectables, Bournemouth, Dorset.
Bridport Antiques Centre, Bridport, Dorset.
Charmouth Antique Centre, Charmouth, Dorset.
Colliton Antique and Craft Centre, Dorchester, Dorset.
Sherborne Antique Centre, Sherborne, Dorset.
North Quay Collector's Centre, Weymouth, Dorset.
Wimborne Antiques and Collectables Centre, Wimborne Minster, Dorset.
Battlesbridge Antique Centre, Battlesbridge, Essex.
Essex Antiques Centre, Colchester, Essex.
Trinity Antiques Centre, Colchester, Essex.
Finchingfield Antiques Centre, Finchingfield, Essex.
Kendons and Atticus Books, Grays, Essex.
Baddow Antique Centre, Great Baddow, Essex.
Townsford Mill Antiques Centre, Halstead, Essex.
Kelvedon Art and Antiques, Kelvedon, Essex.
Maldon Antiques and Collectors Market, Maldon, Essex.
Berkeley Antiques Market, Berkeley, Glos.
The Antique Centre Bristol, Bristol, Glos.
The Bristol Antiques Centre, Bristol, Glos.
St. Nicholas Markets, Bristol, Glos.
Charlton Kings Antiques Centre, Cheltenham, Glos.
Cheltenham Antique Market, Cheltenham, Glos.
Cirencester Antique Market, Cirencester, Glos.
Gloucester Antique Centre, Gloucester, Glos.
Aspley House Antiques Centre, Lechlade, Glos.
Lechlade Antiques Arcade, Lechlade, Glos.
The Swan Antiques and Crafts Centre, Lechlade, Glos.
Jubilee Hall Antiques Centre, Lechlade-on-Thames, Glos.
Antique Centre, Moreton-in-Marsh, Glos.
Windsor House Antiques Centre, Moreton-in-Marsh, Glos.
Painswick Antique Centre, Painswick, Glos.
Durham House Antiques Centre, Stow-on-the-Wold, Glos.
Fox Cottage Antiques, Stow-on-the-Wold, Glos.
The Antique and Interior Centre, Tetbury, Glos.
The Antiques Emporium, Tetbury, Glos.
Tewkesbury Antique & Curio Centre, Tewkesbury, Glos.
Dolphin Quay Antique Centre, Emsworth, Hants.
The Antiques Centre, Hartley Wintney, Hants.
Lymington Antiques Centre, Lymington, Hants.
The Folly Antiques Centre, Petersfield, Hants.
Bridge House Antique Centre, Wickham, Hants.
Samuels Spencers Antiques and Decorative Arts Emporium, Winchester, Hants.
Hereford Antique Centre, Hereford, Herefs.
Leominster Antiques Market, Leominster, Herefs.
Bushey Antique Centre, Bushey, Herts.
Hertford Antiques, Hertford, Herts.
The Herts and Essex Antiques Centre, Sawbridgeworth, Herts.
By George! Antiques Centre, St. Albans, Herts.
St. Albans Antique Market, St. Albans, Herts.
Tring Triangle Antiques Centre, Tring, Herts.
Royal Victoria Arcade, Ryde, Isle of Wight

Beckenham Antique Market, Beckenham, Kent.
The Village Antique Centre, Brasted, Kent.
Bromley Antique Market, Bromley, Kent.
Burgate Antique Centre, Canterbury, Kent.
Rastro Antiques, Canterbury, Kent.
Cranbrook Antique Centre, Cranbrook, Kent.
The Wooden Chair Antiques Centre, Cranbrook, Kent.
Malthouse Arcade, Hythe, Kent.
Sandgate Antiques Centre, Sandgate, Kent.
Noah's Ark Antique Centre, Sandwich, Kent.
The Antiques Centre, Sevenoaks, Kent.
Bradbourne Gallery, Sevenoaks, Kent.
Peppercorns Antique and Craft Centre, Sevenoaks, Kent.
Sidcup Antique and Craft Centre, Sidcup, Kent.
Tenterden Antiques Centre, Tenterden, Kent.
Barden House Antiques, Tonbridge, Kent.
Corn Exchange Antiques Centre, Tunbridge Wells, Kent.
Tunbridge Wells Antique Centre, Tunbridge Wells, Kent.
Castle Antiques Centre, Westerham, Kent.
Bolton Antique Centre, Bolton, Lancs.
King's Mill Antique Centre, Burnley, Lancs.
Antiques and Crafts Centre, Chorley, Lancs.
Bygone Times Ltd, Eccleston, Lancs.
The Assembly Rooms Market, Lancaster, Lancs.
G.B. Antiques Ltd, Lancaster, Lancs.
Lancaster Leisure Park Antiques Centre, Lancaster, Lancs.
Lancastrian Antiques & Co, Lancaster, Lancs.
The Attic Centre, Longridge, Lancs.
Antiques Village, Manchester, Lancs.
The Ginnell Gallery Antique Centre, Manchester, Lancs.
The Antique Centre, Preston, Lancs.
Preston Antique Centre, Preston, Lancs.
Walter Aspinall Antiques, Sabden, Lancs.
Boulevard Antique and Shipping Centre, Leicester, Leics.
Whitemoors Antiques and Fine Art, Shenton, Leics.
Portobello Row Antique & Collectors' Centre, Boston, Lincs.
Astra House Antiques Centre, Hemswell Cliff, Lincs.
Hemswell Antiques Centre, Hemswell Cliff, Lincs.
Great Expectations, Horncastle, Lincs.
The Lincs. Antiques Centre, Horncastle, Lincs.
Irby Antiques Centre, Irby-in-the-Marsh, Lincs.
Roundabout Antique and Craft Centre, Lincoln, Lincs.
The Louth Antique Centre, Louth, Lincs.
St. Martins Antiques Centre, Stamford, Lincs.
Stamford Antiques Centre, Stamford, Lincs.
Hoylake Antique Centre, Hoylake, Merseyside.
The Jay's Middlesex Antique Centre, Harefield, Middx.
Phelps Antiques, Twickenham, Middx.
Coltishall Antiques Centre, Coltishall, Norfolk.
Fakenham Antique Centre, Fakenham, Norfolk.
Le Strange Old Barns Antiques, Arts & Craft Centre, Hunstanton, Norfolk.
The Old Granary Antiques and Collectors Centre, King's Lynn, Norfolk.
Pine and Things, King's Lynn, Norfolk.
Cloisters Antiques Fair, Norwich, Norfolk.
Norwich Antiques Centre, Norwich, Norfolk.
St Mary's Antique Centre, Norwich, Norfolk.
St. Michael at Plea Antiques Centre, Norwich, Norfolk.
Wells Antique Centre, Wells-next-the-Sea, Norfolk.
E.K. Antiques, Finedon, Northants.
Finedon Antiques (Antiques Centre), Finedon, Northants.
The Village Antique Market, Weedon, Northants.
Antiques and Bric-a-Brac Market, Wellingborough, Northants.
Castle Gate Antiques Centre, Newark, Notts.
Newark Antiques Centre, Newark, Notts.
Portland Street Antiques Centre, Newark, Notts.
Tudor Rose Antiques Centre, Newark, Notts.
Top Hat Antiques Centre, Nottingham, Notts.
Old George Inn Antique Galleries, Burford, Oxon.
Country Markets Antiques and Collectables, Chilton, Oxon.
Chipping Norton Antique Centre, Chipping Norton, Oxon.
Deddington Antiques Centre, Deddington, Oxon.
Didcot Antiques Centre, Didcot, Oxon.
Friday Street Antique Centre, Henley-on-Thames, Oxon.
Henley Antique Centre, Henley-on-Thames, Oxon.
The Oxford Antique Trading Co, Oxford, Oxon.
TheSwan at Tetsworth, Tetsworth, Oxon.
The Lamb Arcade, Wallingford, Oxon.
Le Print Antique Centre, Woodstock, Oxon.
Span Antiques, Woodstock, Oxon.
Barnsdale Antiques Centre, Rutland Water, Rutland
Old Mill Antique Centre, Bridgnorth, Shrops.
Stretton Antiques Market, Church Stretton, Shrops.
Cleobury Mortimer Antique Centre, Cleobury Mortimer, Shrops.
Ironbridge Antique Centre, Ironbridge, Shrops.
Pepper Lane Antiques, Ludlow, Shrops.
Princess Antique Centre, Shrewsbury, Shrops.
Shrewsbury Antique Centre, Shrewsbury, Shrops.
Shrewsbury Antique Market, Shrewsbury, Shrops.
Welsh Bridge Antique Centre, Shrewsbury, Shrops.
Bartlett Street Antique Centre, Bath, Somerset.
Bath Antiques Market, Bath, Somerset.
Bath Saturday Antiques Market, Bath, Somerset.
Paragon Antiques and Collectors Market, Bath, Somerset.
Guildhall Antique Market, Chard, Somerset.
Octopus Antique Centre, Crewkerne, Somerset.
Oscars Antiques, Crewkerne, Somerset.
County Antiques Centre, Ilminster, Somerset.
Taunton Antiques Market - Silver Street, Taunton, Somerset.
Green Dragon Antiques Centre, Wincanton, Somerset.
Rugeley Antique Centre, Brereton, Staffs.
The Antique Centre, Kinver, Staffs.
The Leek Antiques Centre, Leek, Staffs.
Tudor of Lichfield Antique Centre, Lichfield, Staffs.
Antique Market, Newcastle-under-Lyme, Staffs.
Windmill Antiques, Stafford, Staffs.
Waveney Antiques Centre, Beccles, Suffolk.
Clare Antique Warehouse, Clare, Suffolk.
Debenham Antique Centre - Gil Adams Antiques, Debenham, Suffolk.
Raymond Norman Antiques/ George Norman Antiques/Jenny Norman, Eye, Suffolk.
Long Melford Antique Centre, Long Melford, Suffolk.
The Old Town Hall Antique Centre, Needham Market, Suffolk.
The Risby Barn, Risby, Suffolk.
Snape Antiques and Collectors Centre, Snape, Suffolk.
The Emporium Antiques and Collectors Centre, Southwold, Suffolk.
Wrentham Antiques Centre, Wrentham, Suffolk.
Memories, Bramley, Surrey.
Chertsey Antiques, Chertsey, Surrey.
Victoria Antiques, Coulsdon, Surrey.
Dorking Antique Centre, Dorking, Surrey.
Pilgrims Antique Centre, Dorking, Surrey.
Victoria and Edward Antiques Centre, Dorking, Surrey.
The Antiques Arcade, East Molesey, Surrey.
The Sovereign Antique Centre, East Molesey, Surrey.
Bourne Mill Antiques, Farnham, Surrey.
Farnham Antique Centre, Farnham, Surrey.
Maltings Monthly Market, Farnham, Surrey.
The Antiques Centre, Guildford, Surrey.
Haslemere Antique Market, Haslemere, Surrey.
Wood's Wharf Antiques Bazaar, Haslemere, Surrey.
Kingston Antiques Centre, Kingston-upon-Thames, Surrey.
Antiques Centre, Oxted, Surrey.
Richmond Antiques, Richmond, Surrey.
Shere Antiques Centre, Shere, Surrey.
Fern Cottage Antiques, Thames Ditton, Surrey.
Tymes Past Antiques, Battle, E. Sussex.
Brighton Antique Wholesalers, Brighton, E. Sussex.
Brighton Flea Market, Brighton, E. Sussex.
Chateaubriand Antiques Centre, Burwash, E. Sussex.

Eastbourne Antiques Market, Eastbourne, E. Sussex.
Enterprise Collectors Market, Eastbourne, E. Sussex.
The Old Town Antiques Centre, Eastbourne, E. Sussex.
Pharoahs Antiques Centre, Eastbourne, E. Sussex.
George Street Antiques Centre, Hastings, E. Sussex.
Horsebridge Antiques Centre, Horsebridge, E. Sussex.
Church Hill Antiques Centre, Lewes, E. Sussex.
Cliffe Antiques Centre, Lewes, E. Sussex.
The Emporium Antique Centre, Lewes, E. Sussex.
Lewes Antique Centre, Lewes, E. Sussex.
The Courtyard Antiques Market, Seaford, E. Sussex.
Seaford's "Barn Collectors' Market" and Studio Bookshop, Seaford, E. Sussex.
The Hastings Antique Centre, St. Leonards-on-Sea, E. Sussex.
Old House Antique Centre, Adversane, W. Sussex.
Mamie's Antiques Centre, Arundel, W. Sussex.
Tarrant Street Antique Centre, Arundel, W. Sussex.
Treasure House Antiques and Collectors Market, Arundel, W. Sussex.
Great Grooms Antique Centre, Billingshurst, W. Sussex.
Almshouses Arcade, Chichester, W. Sussex.
Chichester Antiques Centre, Chichester, W. Sussex.
Curfew Antiques Centre, Midhurst, W. Sussex.
Eagle House Antiques Market, Midhurst, W. Sussex.
Petworth Antique Market, Petworth, W. Sussex.
Anna Harrison Antiques Centre, Gosforth, Tyne and Wear
Antiques Centre, Newcastle-upon-Tyne, Tyne and Wear
Malthouse Antiques Centre, Alcester, Warks.
Bidford Antiques Centre, Bidford-on-Avon, Warks.
Dunchurch Antique Centre, Dunchurch, Warks.
The Stables Antique Centre, Hatton, Warks.
Leamington Pine and Antique Centre, Leamington Spa, Warks.
Meer Street Antiques Arcade, Stratford-upon-Avon, Warks.
Stratford Antique Centre, Stratford-upon-Avon, Warks.
The Stratford Antiques and Interiors Centre Ltd, Stratford-upon-Avon, Warks.
Windsor Place Antiques Centre, Stratford-upon-Avon, Warks.
The Old Cornmarket Antiques Centre, Warwick, Warks.
Smith St. Antiques Centre, Warwick, Warks.
Vintage Antiques Centre, Warwick, Warks.
The Warwick Antique Centre, Warwick, Warks.
Warley Antique Centre, Birmingham, W. Mids.
Falcon Antiques Centre, Stourbridge, W. Mids.
Regency Antique Trading Centre, Stourbridge, W. Mids.
The Marlborough Parade Antique Centre, Marlborough, Wilts.
King Street Curios, Melksham, Wilts.
Antique and Collectors Market, Salisbury, Wilts.
The Avonbridge Antiques and Collectors Market, Salisbury, Wilts.
Micawber's, Salisbury, Wilts.
Tubbjoys Antique Market, Wootton Bassett, Wilts.
Antiques and Curios, Worcester, Worcs.
St. Georges Antiques, Worcester, Worcs.
The Tything Antique Centre, Worcester, Worcs.
Worcester Antiques Centre, Worcester, Worcs.
Grannie's Treasures, Hull, E. Yorks.
The Ginnel, Harrogate, N. Yorks.
Grove Collectors Centre, Harrogate, N. Yorks.
Montpellier Mews Antique Market, Harrogate, N. Yorks.
Malton Antique Market, Malton, N. Yorks.
Scarthingwell Arcades, Scarthingwell, N. Yorks.
Drey Antique Centre, Sherburn in Elmet, N. Yorks.
The Emporium, York, N. Yorks.
York Antiques Centre, York, N. Yorks.
Treasure House Antiques Centre, Bawtry, S. Yorks.
Foster's Antique Centre, Rotherham, S. Yorks.
Court House Antique Centre, Sheffield, S. Yorks.
Sheffield Antiques Emporium, Sheffield, S. Yorks.
Halifax Antiques Centre, Halifax, W. Yorks.
Leeds Antiques Centre, Leeds, W. Yorks.
The Victoria Centre, Saltaire, W. Yorks.
Todmorden Antiques Centre, Todmorden, W. Yorks.
The Antique Centre, St. Peter Port, Guernsey, C. I.
Union Street Antique Market, St. Helier, Jersey, C. I.
Clola Antiques Centre, Clola by Mintlaw, Scotland
Bath Street Antiques Galleries, Glasgow, Scotland
Heritage House Antiques, Glasgow, Scotland
King's Court Antique Centre, Glasgow, Scotland
The Victorian Village, Glasgow, Scotland
Virginia Antique Galleries, Glasgow, Scotland
Ian Murray Antique Warehouse, Perth, Scotland
Rait Village Antiques Centre, Rait, Scotland
Wellfield Antique Centre, Bangor, Wales
Jacobs Antique Centre, Cardiff, Wales
The Antiques Centre, Cowbridge, Wales
Antique Market, Hay-on-Wye, Wales
Offa's Dyke Antique Centre, Knighton, Wales
Pembroke Antiques Centre, Pembroke, Wales
Swansea Antique Centre, Swansea, Wales

Antiquities

Auld, Ian, London N1.
Martin (Coins) Ltd, C.J., London N14.
Vale Stamps and Antiques, London SE3.
Symes Ltd, Robin, London SW1.
Wace Ancient Art Ltd, Rupert, London SW1.
Ede Ltd, Charles, London W1.
Hadji Baba Ancient Art, London W1.
Mansour Gallery, London W1.
Oriental Bronzes Ltd, London W1.
Seaby Antiquities, London W1.
Sheppard Ltd, Christopher, London W1.
Town Hall Antiques, Woburn, Beds.
Potter's Antiques and Coins, Bristol, Glos.
Tamblyn, Alnwick, Northumbs.
A. Burton-Garbett, Morden, Surrey.
Molly Alexander, Seaford, E. Sussex.
Hermitage Antiquities, Fishguard, Wales.

Antiquarian Books

Ash Rare Books, London EC3.
Clarke-Hall Ltd, J., London EC4.
Finney Antique Prints and Books, Michael, London N1.
Korn, M.E., London N10.
Forster, W., London N16.
Walford's - Nicholas Goodyer, London N5.
Fisher and Sperr, London N6.
East-Asia Co, London NW1.
de Lotz, P.G., London NW3.
Fawkes, Keith, London NW3.
Marks Ltd, Barrie, London NW5.
Baron, H., London NW6.
Leadlay Gallery, The Warwick, London SE10.
Rogers Turner Books, London SE10.
Allen & Co. (The Horseman's Bookshop) Ltd, J. A., London SW1.
Classic Bindings, London SW1.
Edwards, Christopher, London SW1.
Heneage Art Books, Thomas, London SW1.
Pickering and Chatto Ltd, London SW1.
Sims, Reed Ltd, London SW1.
Hünersdorff Rare Books, London SW10.
Thornton, John, London SW10.
Foster's Bookshop, Paul, London SW14.
Han-Shan Tang Books, London SW15.
Reeves Bookseller Ltd, William, London SW16.
Chelsea Rare Books, London SW3.
Greer, Robin, London SW6.
Orssich, Paul, London SW6.
Heywood Hill Ltd, G., London W1.
Holland & Holland, London W1.
Maggs Bros Ltd, London W1.
Marlborough Rare Books Ltd, London W1.
O'Shea Gallery, The, London W1.
Potter Ltd, Jonathan, London W1.
Quaritch Ltd (Booksellers), Bernard, London W1.
Russell Rare Books, London W1.
Sawers, Robert G., London W1.
Schuster, Thomas E., London W1.
Shapero Rare Books, Bernard J., London W1.
Sotheran Ltd, Henry, London W1.
Books & Things, London W11.
Demetzy Books, London W11.
Parikian, D., London W14.
Bayswater Books, London W2.
Hosains Books and Antiques, London W2.
Crawley and Asquith Ltd, London W8.

Atlantis Bookshop, London WC1.
Cinema Bookshop, London WC1.
Frew Ltd, Robert, London WC1.
London Antiquarian Book Arcade, London WC1.
Marchmont Bookshop, London WC1.
Museum Bookshop, The, London WC1.
Skoob Books Ltd, London WC1.
Skoob Two, London WC1.
Bell, Book and Radmall, London WC2.
Blackwell's, London WC2.
Drummond at Pleasures of Past Times, David, London WC2.
Foyle Ltd, W. and G., London WC2.
Pordes Books Ltd, Henry, London WC2.
Remington, Reg and Philip, London WC2.
Rota Ltd, Bertram, London WC2.
Stage Door Prints, London WC2.
Storey's Ltd, London WC2.
Tooley Adams & Co., London WC2.
Watkins Books Ltd, London WC2.
Zeno Booksellers and Publishers, London WC2.
Zwemmer, London WC2.
Marlborough Sporting Gallery and Bookshop, Hungerford, Berks.
Penn Barn, Penn, Bucks.
David Bickersteth, Bassingbourn, Cambs.
G. David, Cambridge, Cambs.
Deighton Bell and Co, Cambridge, Cambs.
Galloway and Porter Ltd, Cambridge, Cambs.
Sarah Key, Cambridge, Cambs.
Abington Books, Little Abington, Cambs.
Old Soke Books, Peterborough, Cambs.
Stothert - Antiquarian Books, Chester, Cheshire.
Lion Gallery and Bookshop, Knutsford, Cheshire.
New Street Books, Penzance, Cornwall.
Maurice Dodd Books, Carlisle, Cumbria.
Norman Kerr - Gatehouse Bookshop, Cartmel, Cumbria.
Peter Bain Smith (Bookseller), Cartmel, Cumbria.
Archie Miles Bookshop, Gosforth, Cumbria.
The Book House, Ravenstonedale, Cumbria.
R. F. G. Hollett and Son, Sedbergh, Cumbria.
Michael Moon, Whitehaven, Cumbria.
G.K. Hadfield, Swadlincote, Derbys.
Chantry Bookshop and Gallery, Dartmouth, Devon.
Exeter Rare Books, Exeter, Devon.
Honiton Old Bookshop, Honiton, Devon.
Geoffrey M. Woodhead, Honiton, Devon.
Porcupines Bookroom, Instow, Devon.
P.M. Pollak, South Brent, Devon.
Collards Books, Totnes, Devon.
Ancient and Modern Bookshop (including Garret's Antiques), Blandford Forum, Dorset.
The Dorset Bookshop, Blandford Forum, Dorset.
PIC's Bookshop, Bridport, Dorset.
Words Etcetera, Dorchester, Dorset.
Christopher Williams Antiquarian Bookseller, Parkstone, Dorset.
Antique Map and Bookshop, Puddletown, Dorset.
The Swan Gallery, Sherborne, Dorset.
Reference Works, Swanage, Dorset.
Books Afloat, Weymouth, Dorset.
Books & Bygones, Weymouth, Dorset.
J. Shotton Antiquarian Books, Prints and Coins, Durham, Durham.
Elkin Mathews, Coggeshall, Essex.
Castle Bookshop, Colchester, Essex.
Cotham Hill Bookshop, Bristol, Glos.
A.R. Heath, Bristol, Glos.
Triangle Books (inc. John Roberts Bookshop Est. 1955), Bristol, Glos.
The Wise Owl Bookshop, Bristol, Glos.
David Bannister FRGS, Cheltenham, Glos.
Michael Rayner, Cheltenham, Glos.
Ian Hodgkins and Co. Ltd, Slad, Glos.
The Coach House Bookshop, Tetbury, Glos.
Studio Bookshop and Gallery, Alresford, Hants.
Hughes and Smeeth Ltd, Lymington, Hants.
The Petersfield Bookshop, Petersfield, Hants.
H.M. Gilbert and Son, Southampton, Hants.
Peter M. Daly, Winchester, Hants.
H.M. Gilbert, Winchester, Hants.
SPCK Bookshops, Winchester, Hants.
Ross Old Book and Print Shop, Ross-on-Wye, Herefs.
H. Pordes Ltd, Cockfosters, Herts.
Wheldon and Wesley Ltd, Codicote, Herts.
Eric T. Moore, Hitchin, Herts.
Clive A. Burden, Rickmansworth, Herts.
Julia Margaret Cameron Gallery, Cowes, Isle of Wight.
Charles Dickens Bookshop, Cowes, Isle of Wight.
Ventnor Rare Books, Ventnor, Isle of Wight.
Graham Stead Antiques and Reference Books, Brasted, Kent.
The Canterbury Bookshop, Canterbury, Kent.
Chaucer Bookshop, Canterbury, Kent.
Periwinkle Press, Newnham, Kent.
Baggins Book Bazaar - The Largest Secondhand Bookshop in England, Rochester, Kent.
Baskerville Books, Tunbridge Wells, Kent.
Hall's Bookshop, Tunbridge Wells, Kent.
London House Antiques, Westerham, Kent.
Taylor-Smith, Westerham, Kent.
W.B. McCormack, Lancaster, Lancs.
Forest Books of Cheshire, Manchester, Lancs.
Gibb's Bookshop Ltd, Manchester, Lancs.
Eric J. Morten, Manchester, Lancs.
Secondhand and Rare Books, Manchester, Lancs.
Halewood and Sons, Preston, Lancs.
Preston Book Co, Preston, Lancs.
Anthony W. Laywood, Knipton, Leics.
P.J. Cassidy (Books), Holbeach, Lincs.
Golden Goose Books, Lincoln, Lincs.
Harlequin Gallery, Lincoln, Lincs.
Staniland (Booksellers), Stamford, Lincs.
C.K. Broadhurst and Co Ltd, Southport, Merseyside.
Ian Sheridan's Bookshop Hampton, Hampton, Middx.
Anthony C. Hall, Twickenham, Middx.
John Ives Bookseller, Twickenham, Middx.
Rita Shenton, Twickenham, Middx.
David Ferrow, Gt. Yarmouth, Norfolk.
Simon Gough Books, Holt, Norfolk.
Baron Art, Kelling, Norfolk.
Peter Crowe, Antiquarian Book Seller, Norwich, Norfolk.
The Scientific Anglian (Bookshop), Norwich, Norfolk.
The Tombland Bookshop, Norwich, Norfolk.
R.L. Cook, Sheringham, Norfolk.
Turret House, Wymondham, Norfolk.
The Old Hall Bookshop, Brackley, Northants.
Occultique, Northampton, Northants.
Park Book Shop, Wellingborough, Northants.
Emerald Isle Books, Belfast, N. Ireland.
The Book Shelf, Mansfield, Notts.
N.J. Doris - 'Dorisbooks', Nottingham, Notts.
E.M. Lawson and Co, East Hagbourne, Oxon.
Richard J. Kingston, Henley-on-Thames, Oxon.
Blackwell's Rare Books, Oxford, Oxon.
Thorntons of Oxford Ltd, Oxford, Oxon.
Titles - Old and Rare Books, Oxford, Oxon.
Waterfield's, Oxford, Oxon.
Goldmark Books, Uppingham, Rutland.
Candle Lane Books, Shrewsbury, Shrops.
George Bayntun, Bath, Somerset.
George Gregory, Bath, Somerset.
Patterson Liddle, Bath, Somerset.
Rothwell and Dunworth, Dulverton, Somerset.
Janet Clarke, Freshford, Somerset.
Steven Ferdinando, Queen Camel, Somerset.
Sterling Books, Weston-Super-Mare, Somerset.
Mike Abrahams Books, Lichfield, Staffs.
Images - Peter Stockham, Lichfield, Staffs.
L. Royden Smith, Lichfield, Staffs.
The Staffs Bookshop, Lichfield, Staffs.
Besleys Books, Beccles, Suffolk.
Trinders' Fine Tools, Clare, Suffolk.
Claude Cox at College Gateway Bookshop, Ipswich, Suffolk.
R.G. Archer, Lavenham, Suffolk.
R.E. and G.B. Way, Newmarket, Suffolk.
Joan Stevens, Bookseller, Yoxford, Suffolk.
Vandeleur Antiquarian Books, Epsom, Surrey.
J.W. McKenzie, Ewell, Surrey.
Thomas Thorp Bookseller, Guildford, Surrey.
Charles W. Traylen, Guildford, Surrey.
Lloyds of Kew, Kew, Surrey.
A. Burton-Garbett, Morden, Surrey.
Reigate Galleries Ltd, Reigate, Surrey.
Raymond Slack FRSA & Shirley Warren, Sanderstead, Surrey.
Elizabeth Gant, Thames Ditton, Surrey.
Holleyman and Treacher Ltd, Brighton, E. Sussex.
Colin Page Antiquarian Books, Brighton, E. Sussex.
Brian Page Antiques, Brighton, E. Sussex.
Camilla's Bookshop, Eastbourne, E. Sussex.
Roderick Dew, Eastbourne, E. Sussex.
A. & T. Gibbard, Eastbourne, E. Sussex.
Premier Gallery, Eastbourne, E. Sussex.
Howes Bookshop, Hastings, E. Sussex.
Bow Windows Book Shop, Lewes, E. Sussex.
A.J. Cumming, Lewes, E. Sussex.

Fifteenth Century Bookshop, Lewes, E. Sussex.
The Book Jungle, St. Leonards-on-Sea, E. Sussex.
Jeremy Wood Fine Art, Billingshurst, W. Sussex.
R.D. Steedman, Newcastle-upon-Tyne, Tyne and Wear.
The Stratford Bookshop, Stratford-upon-Avon, Warks.
Robert Vaughan, Stratford-upon-Avon, Warks.
Duncan M. Allsop, Warwick, Warks.
Alan Richards Brocante, Birmingham, W. Mids.
David Temperley Fine and Antiquarian Books, Birmingham, W. Mids.
Clent Books, Halesowen, W. Mids.
Clive Farahar and Sophie Dupré - Rare Books, Autographs and Manuscripts, Calne, Wilts.
Hilmarton Manor Press, Calne, Wilts.
The Military Parade Bookshop, Marlborough, Wilts.
Heraldry Today, Ramsbury, Wilts.
The Barn Book Supply, Salisbury, Wilts.
D.M. Beach, Salisbury, Wilts.
Victoria Bookshop, Swindon, Wilts.
Clent Books, Bewdley, Worcs.
Broadway Old Books (formerly Stratford Trevers), Broadway, Worcs.
Malvern Bookshop, Great Malvern, Worcs.
Antique Map and Print Gallery, Worcester, Worcs.
Andrew Boyle (Booksellers) Ltd, Worcester, Worcs.
The Great Ayton Bookshop, Great Ayton, N. Yorks.
Rievaulx Books, Helmsley, N. Yorks.
Potterton Books, Thirsk, N. Yorks.
Barbican Bookshop, York, N. Yorks.
Minster Gate Bookshop, York, N. Yorks.
O'Flynn Antiquarian Booksellers, York, N. Yorks.
Ken Spelman, York, N. Yorks.
Alan Hill Books, Sheffield, Sheffield, S. Yorks.
The Toll House Bookshop, Holmfirth, W. Yorks.
The Grove Bookshop, Ilkley, W. Yorks.
Channel Islands Galleries Ltd, St. Peter Port, Guernsey, C. I.
Geoffrey P. Gavey, Vale, Guernsey, C. I.
John Blench & Son, St. Helier, Jersey, C. I.
The Selective Eye Gallery, St. Helier, Jersey, C. I.
Thesaurus (Jersey) Ltd, St. Helier, Jersey, C. I.
Highland Antiques, Avoch, Scotland.
The McEwan Gallery, Ballater, Scotland.
McNaughtan's Bookshop, Edinburgh, Scotland.
Alan Rankin, Edinburgh, Scotland.
James Thin (Booksellers), Edinburgh, Scotland.
Marianne Simpson, Fochabers, Scotland.
Amber Antiques, Kincardine O'Neil, Scotland.
Paisley Fine Books, Paisley, Scotland.
A. and F. McIlreavy Rare and Interesting Books, St. Andrews, Scotland.
H.K. Lockyer, Abergavenny, Wales.
Maps, Prints and Books, Brecon, Wales.
Glance Back Bookshop, Chepstow, Wales.
Richard Booth's Bookshop Ltd, Hay-on-Wye, Wales.
Mark Westwood Antiquarian Books, Hay-on-Wye, Wales.
Doggie Hubbard's Bookshop, Ponterwyd, Wales.
Dylan's Bookshop, Swansea, Wales.

Arms & Armour

London Militaria Market, London N1.
Finchley Fine Art Galleries, London N12.
Laurence Corner, London NW1.
Dale Ltd, Peter, London SW1.
Spink and Son Ltd, London SW1.
Period Brass Lights, London SW7.
Blunderbuss Antiques, London W1.
Holland & Holland, London W1.
Under Two Flags, London W1.
German, Michael C., London W8.
Hales Antiques Ltd, Robert, London W8.
Trafalgar Square Collectors Centre, London WC2.
T.L.O. Militaria, Windsor and Eton, Berks.
Sundial Antiques, Amersham, Bucks.
Anthony D. Goodlad, Chesterfield, Derbys.
Rex Antiques, Chagford, Devon.
Blade and Bayonet, Bournemouth, Dorset.
Boscombe Militaria, Bournemouth, Dorset.
Sterling Coins and Medals, Bournemouth, Dorset.
M. & R. Lankshear Antiques, Christchurch, Dorset.
Nautical Antique Centre, Weymouth, Dorset.
Castle Antiques, Leigh-on-Sea, Essex.
Chris Grimes Militaria, Bristol, Gloucestershire.
Heydens Antiques and Militaria, Cheltenham, Gloucestershire.
Military Curios, HQ84, Gloucester, Gloucestershire.
Mark A. Serle (Antiques and Restoration), Lechlade, Gloucestershire.
Hampton Gallery, Tetbury, Gloucestershire.
Romsey Medal and Collectors Centre, Romsey, Hants.
Trecilla Antiques, Ross-on-Wye, Herefs.
H.S. Greenfield and Son, Gunmakers (Est. 1805), Canterbury, Kent.
J.T. Rutherford and Son, Sandgate, Kent.
Peter Ireland Ltd, Blackpool, Lancs.
Bulldog Antiques, Manchester, Lancs.
Bus Stop Curios, Manchester, Lancs.
Garth Vincent Antique Arms and Armour, Allington, Lincs.
Guns and Tackle, Scunthorpe, Lincs.
David Allan Antiques, Birkenhead, Merseyside.
Liverpool Militaria, Liverpool, Merseyside.
The Old Brigade, Kingsthorpe, Northants.
Michael D. Long - Trident Arms, Nottingham, Notts. .
English Heritage, Bridgnorth, Shrops.
Atfield and Daughter, Ipswich, Suffolk.
One Bell, Lavenham, Suffolk.
West Street Antiques, Dorking, Surrey.
Casque and Gauntlet Militaria, Farnham, Surrey.
Mark and David Hawkins, Brighton, E. Sussex.
St. Pancras Antiques, Chichester, W. Sussex.
Michael Miller, Hurstpierpoint, W. Sussex.
Steve Johnson Medals & Militaria, Newcastle-upon-Tyne, Tyne and Wear.
Arbour Antiques Ltd, Stratford-upon-Avon, Warks.
James Wigington Arms and Armour, Stratford-upon-Avon, Warks.
March Medals, Birmingham, West Midlands,.
Edred A.F. Gwilliam, Cricklade, Wilts.
Magpie Jewellers and Antiques and Magpie Arms & Armour, Evesham, Worcs.
Cairncross and Sons, Filey, N. Yorks.
Hanover Antiques, Scarborough, N. Yorks.
Adamson Armoury, Skipton, N. Yorks.
Andrew Spencer Bottomley, Holmfirth, W. Yorks.
D.W. Dyson (Antique Weapons), Huddersfield, W. Yorks.
Angus Antiques, Dundee, Scotland.
Hermitage Antiquities, Fishguard, Wales.

Art Deco

Antique Trader, The, London N1.
Oosthuizen t/a de Verzamelaar, Pieter, London N1.
Style, London N1.
Tadema Gallery, London N1.
Titus Omega, London N1.
Art Furniture, London NW1.
Beverley, London NW8.
Bizarre, London NW8.
Gallery on Church Street, The, London NW8.
Studio, The, London NW8.
Cobra and Bellamy, London SW1.
Gallery '25, London SW1.
Keshishian, London SW1.
Twentieth Century, London SW12.
Acanthus Antiques, London SW19.
Butler and Wilson, London SW3.
Gill, David, London SW3.
Purple Shop, The, London SW3.
Watson Ltd, Gordon, London SW3.
Lamp Gallery, The, London SW6.
Editions Graphiques Gallery, London W1.
Liberty, London W1.
Mayfair Gallery, London W1.
Facade, The, London W11.
Leigh, Joan, London W11.
Themes and Variations, London W11.
Haslam and Whiteway, London W8.
Jesse, John, London W8.
New Century, London W8.
Pruskin Gallery, London W8.
Deco Inspired, London WC2.
Morgan Stobbs, Windsor and Eton, Berks.
20th Century, Cambridge, Cambs.
Bizarre Decorative Arts North West, Altrincham, Cheshire.
Aldersey Hall Ltd, Chester, Cheshire.
Nantwich Art Deco and Decorative Arts, Nantwich, Cheshire.
Antique Furniture Warehouse, Stockport, Cheshire.
Maggie Mays, Buxton, Derbys.
Beaminster Antiques, Beaminster, Dorset.
Lionel Geneen Ltd, Bournemouth, Dorset.
Libra Antiques, Bournemouth, Dorset.
Bernard Weaver Antiques, Cirencester, Glos.
Ruskin Antiques, Stow-on-the-Wold, Glos.
Alexanders, Titchfield, Hants.
Delf Stream Gallery, Sandwich, Kent.
Vicary Antiques, Lancaster, Lancs.

A.S. Antique Galleries, Manchester, Lancs.
Irving Antique Toys, Manchester, Lancs.
Osiris Antiques, Southport, Merseyside.
Arbiter, Wallasey, Merseyside.
Aspidistra Antiques, Finedon, Northants.
Antiques on the Square, Church Stretton, Shrops.
Expressions, Shrewsbury, Shrops.
Moderne, Bath, Somerset.
Tara's Hall, Hadleigh, Suffolk.
Decodream, Coulsdon, Surrey.
Dorking Emporium Antiques Centre, Dorking, Surrey.
Bits and Pieces, Farnham, Surrey.
The Gooday Gallery, Richmond, Surrey.
Cockrell Antiques, Surbiton, Surrey.
Art Deco Etc., Brighton, E. Sussex.
Oasis Antiques, Brighton, E. Sussex.
Timewarp, Brighton, E. Sussex.
Witney & Airault, Brighton, E. Sussex.
Peter Hancock Antiques, Chichester, W. Sussex.
Art Deco Ceramics, Stratford-upon-Avon, Warks.
Alan Richards Brocante, Birmingham, W. Mids.
Bridge House Antiques (formerly Avenue Antiques of Hull), Beverley, E. Yorks.
Muir Hewitt Art Deco Originals, Halifax, W. Yorks.
The Rendezvous Gallery, Aberdeen, Scotland.
Montresor, Edinburgh, Scotland.
Jeremy Sniders Antiques, Glasgow, Scotland.
Rhudle Mill, Kilmichael Glassary, Scotland.
Paul Gibbs Antiques and Decorative Arts, Conwy, Wales.

Architectural Items

London Architectural Salvage & Supply Co. (LASSCo), The, London EC2.
Westland & Company, London EC2.
Townsends, London NW8.
Old Cinema Antique Warehouse, The, London SE1.
Junk Shop, The, London SE10.
Lamont Antiques Ltd, London SE10.
Thornhill Galleries Ltd. in association with A. & R. Dockerill Ltd, London SW15.
Edwards, Charles, London SW6.
Fairfax Antiques and Fireplaces, London SW6.
Thornhill Galleries Ltd, London SW6.
Architectural Antiques - Bedford, Bedford, Beds.
T. Smith, Chalfont St. Giles, Bucks.
Solopark Plc, Cambridge, Cambs.
Nostalgia Architectural Antiques, Stockport, Cheshire.
Cheshire Brick and Slate Co, Tarvin Sands, Cheshire.
The Great Northern Architectural Antique Company Ltd, Tattenhall, Cheshire.
Antique Fireplace Centre, Hartlepool, Cleveland.
W.R.S. Architectural Antiques, Low Newton, Cumbria.
Havenplan's Architectural Emporium, Killamarsh, Derbys.
Ashburton Marbles, Ashburton, Devon.
Rex Antiques, Chagford, Devon.
Fagins Antiques, Exeter, Devon.
Great Western Antiques, Torquay, Devon.
Talisman, Gillingham, Dorset.
Au Temps Perdu, Bristol, Glos.
Robert Mills Architectural Antiques Ltd, Bristol, Glos.
Cox's Architectural Reclamation Yard, Moreton-in-Marsh, Glos.
Ronson's Architectural Effects, Norton, Glos.
Architectural Heritage, Taddington, Glos.
Burgess Farm Antiques, Morestead, Hants.
"Old Cottage Things", Romsey, Hampshire,
The Pine Cellars, Winchester, Hants.
Baileys Architectural Antiques, Ross-on-Wye, Herefs.
Old Smithy, Feniscowles, Lancs.
Antique Fireplaces, Manchester, Lancs.
In-Situ Architectural Antiques, Manchester, Lancs.
Victoriana Architectural, Long Cawston, Leics.
Antique Fireplaces, Liverpool, Merseyside.
Peco, Hampton, Middx.
Crowther of Syon Lodge Ltd, Isleworth, Middx.
Architectural Heritage of Northants, Weedon, Northants.
Ball & Claw Ltd, Weedon, Northants.
Rococo Antiques and Interiors, Weedon, Northants.
Hallidays (Fine Antiques) Ltd, Dorchester-on-Thames, Oxon.
Aston Pine Antiques, Faringdon, Oxon.
The Country Seat, Huntercombe, Oxon.
Architectural Antiques and Interiors, Ludlow, Shrops.
David Bridgwater, Bath, Somerset.
Walcot Reclamation, Bath, Somerset.
J.C. Giddings, Carhampton, Somerset.
Wells Reclamation Company, Coxley, Somerset.
J.C. Giddings, Wiveliscombe, Somerset.
Anvil Antiques Ltd, Leek, Staffs.
Top of the Hill - Ceramic Search, Stoke-on-Trent, Staffs.
E.T. Webster, Blythburgh, Suffolk.
Drummonds of Bramley Architectural Antiques Ltd, Bramley, Surrey.
Antique Buildings Ltd, Dunsfold, Surrey.
The Packhouse, Runfold, Surrey.
Chancellor's Church Furnishings, Walton-on-Thames, Surrey.
Brighton Architectural Salvage, Brighton, E. Sussex.
Shiners Architectural Reclamation, Newcastle-upon-Tyne, Tyne and Wear.
Gallop and Rivers Architectural Antiques, Crickhowell, Wales.
Architectural Antiques of Moseley, Birmingham, W. Mids.
The Original Choice Ltd, Birmingham, W. Mids.
Retro Products, Lye, W. Mids.
Martin-Quick Antiques, Wolverhampton, W. Mids.
Harriet Fairfax Fireplaces and General Antiques, Langley Burrell, Wilts.
Ray Coggins Antiques, Westbury, Wilts.
Holloways, Suckley, Worcs.
Kevin Marshall's Antiques Warehouse, Hull, E. Yorks.
Old Flames, Easingwold, N. Yorks.
White House Farm Antiques, Easingwold, N. Yorks.
Robert Aagaard & Co, Knaresborough, N. Yorks.
Daleside Antiques, Markington, N. Yorks.
Andy Thornton Architectural Antiques Ltd, Halifax, W. Yorks.
Period Architectural Features and Antiques, Annahilt, Co. Down, N. Ireland.
Dunedin Antiques Ltd, Edinburgh, Scotland.
EASY - Edinburgh & Glasgow Architectural Salvage Yards, Edinburgh, Scotland.
EASY - Edinburgh and Glasgow Architectural Salvage Yards, Glasgow, Scotland.

Barometers (see also Clock Dealers)

Frost and Son Ltd, C.R., London EC1.
Capon, Patric, London N1.
Strike One (Islington) Ltd, London N5.
Rose FBHI, R.E., London SE9.
Carlton-Smith, John, London SW1.
Jillings of Belgravia, London SW1.
Philip and Sons Ltd, Trevor, London SW1.
Clock Clinic Ltd, The, London SW15.
Brocklehurst, Aubrey, London SW7.
Fielden, Brian, London W1.
Phillips Ltd, Ronald, London W1.
Stair and Company Ltd, London W1.
Old Father Time Clock Centre, London W11.
Raffety, London W11.
Raffety, London W8.
The Clock Workshop, Caversham, Berks.
Walker and Walker, Halfway, Berks.
Medalcrest Ltd, Hungerford, Berks.
The Old Malthouse, Hungerford, Berks.
M.V. Tooley, CMBHI, Chesham, Bucks.
John Beazor and Sons Ltd, Cambridge, Cambs.
Doddington House Antiques, Doddington, Cambs.
T. W. Pawson - Clocks, Somersham, Cambs.
Derek and Tina Rayment Antiques, Barton, Cheshire.
The Clock House, Hazel Grove, Cheshire.
Peter Bosson Antiques, Wilmslow, Cheshire.
Mike Read Antique Sciences, St. Ives, Cornwall.
Honiton Clock Clinic, Honiton, Devon.
Barometer World (Barometers), Merton, Devon.
Alan Jones Antiques, Okehampton, Devon
Leigh C. Extence, Teignmouth, Devon.
Good Hope Antiques, Beaminster, Dorset.
M.C. Taylor, Bournemouth, Dorset.
Tom Tribe and Son, Sturminster Newton, Dorset.
Littlebury Antiques - Littlebury Restorations Ltd, Saffron Walden, Essex.
It's About Time, Westcliff-on-Sea, Essex.
Montpellier Clocks, Cheltenham, Glos.
Saxton House Gallery, Chipping Campden, Glos.
Antony Preston Antiques Ltd, Stow-on-the-Wold, Glos.
Styles of Stow, Stow-on-the-Wold, Glos.
Vanbrugh House Antiques, Stow-on-the-Wold, Glos.
M.J. Bristow Antiques, Tetbury, Glos.
Evans and Evans, Alresford, Hants.
Clockwise, Emsworth, Hants.
Bryan Clisby Antique Clocks, Hartley Wintney, Hants.

Clockwise, Winchester, Hants.
G.E. Marsh Antique Clocks Ltd, Winchester, Hants.
Todd and Austin Antiques of Winchester, Winchester, Hants.
Barometer Shop, Leominster, Herefs.
Robert Horton Antiques, Hertford, Herts.
John Chawner, Birchington, Kent.
Michael Sim, Chislehurst, Kent.
Anthony Woodburn, Leigh, Kent.
De Tavener Antiques, Ramsgate, Kent.
Marks Antiques, Westerham, Kent.
Drop Dial Antiques, Bolton, Lancs.
Harrop Fold Clocks (F. Robinson), Bolton-by-Bowland, Lancs.
N. Bryan-Peach Antiques, Wymeswold, Leics.
Robin Fowler (Period Clocks), Aylesby, Lincs.
David J. Hansord and Son, Lincoln, Lincs.
Rita Shenton, Twickenham, Middx.
Keith Lawson Antique Clocks, Scratby, Norfolk.
The Antique Galleries, Paulerspury, Northants.
Peter Wiggins, Chipping Norton, Oxon.
Gerald E. Marsh (Antique Clocks), North Aston, Oxon.
Rosemary and Time, Thame, Oxon.
Mark Shanks, Watlington, Oxon.
R.G. Cave and Sons Ltd, Ludlow, Shrops.
Dodington Antiques, Whitchurch, Shrops.
Bath Galleries, Bath, Somerset.
David Gibson, Crewkerne, Somerset.
Bernard G. House, Wells, Somerset.
Edward A. Nowell, Wells, Somerset.
Grosvenor Clocks, Leek, Staffs.
J. de Haan & Son, Clare, Suffolk.
Ashley Antiques, Ipswich, Suffolk.
Antique Clocks by Simon Charles, Long Melford, Suffolk.
Patrick Marney, Long Melford, Suffolk.
Suthburgh Antiques, Long Melford, Suffolk.
Trident Antiques, Long Melford, Suffolk.
E. Hollander, Dorking, Surrey.
B.S. Antiques, East Molesey, Surrey.
Horological Workshops, Guildford, Surrey.
Surrey. Clock Centre, Haslemere, Surrey.
B. M. and E. Newlove, Surbiton, Surrey.
R. Saunders, Weybridge, Surrey.
Chattels Antiques, Woking, Surrey.
Chaunt House, Burwash, E. Sussex.
Baskerville Antiques, Petworth, W. Sussex.
Summersons, Hatton, Warks.
The Grandfather Clock Shop, Shipston-on-Stour, Warks.
'Time in Hand', Shipston-on-Stour, Warks.
R. Collyer, Birmingham, W. Mids.
Osborne Antiques, Sutton Coldfield, W. Mids.
P.A. Oxley Antique Clocks and Barometers, Cherhill, Wilts.
Inglenook Antiques, Ramsbury, Wilts.
Hansen Chard Antiques, Pershore, Worcs.
Time and Motion, Beverley, E. Yorks.
Lewis E. Hickson FBHI, Gilberdyke, E. Yorks.
Fulwood Antiques and The Basement Gallery, Sheffield, S. Yorks.
Muirhead Moffat and Co, Glasgow, Scotland.

Beds

Tobias and The Angel, London SW13.
And So To Bed Limited, London SW6.
Simon Horn Furniture Ltd, London SW6.
Hirst Antiques, London W11.
Old Dairy, The, London W4.
The Pine Merchants, Great Missenden, Bucks.
And So To Bed, Keswick, Cumbria.
Staveley Antiques, Staveley, Cumbria.
The Antiques Warehouse, Buxton, Derbys.
Pugh's Farm Antiques, Monkton, Devon.
Annterior Antiques, Plymouth, Devon.
Antique Bed Shop, Halstead, Essex.
Antique Four-Poster Beds, Bristol, Glos.
Morpheus - Elgin House, Tetbury, Glos.
Chatelain Antique Beds and Mirrors, Tillington, Herefs.
Old Pine Shop, Walford, Herefs.
Harriet Ann Sleigh Beds, Biddenden, Kent.
R. and J. L. Henley Antiques, Canterbury, Kent.
House Things Antiques, Hinckley, Leics.
A Barn Full of Brass Beds, Louth, Lincs.
Graham Pickett Antiques, Stamford, Lincs.
Peco, Hampton, Middx.
Rococo Antiques and Interiors, Weedon, Northants.
The Corner Cupboard, Woodford Halse, Northants.
Meadow Lane Antiques, Nottingham, Notts.
Manor Farm Antiques, Standlake, Oxon.
Gallery Antiques, Oakham, Rutland.
Swans, Oakham, Rutland.
Orlando Jones, Bath, Somerset.
Antiques Warehouse, Framlingham, Suffolk.
Goodbreys, Framlingham, Suffolk.
Sleeping Beauty Antique Beds, Brighton, E. Sussex.
The Victorian Brass Bedstead Company, Cocking, W. Sussex.
L.P. Antiques (Mids) Ltd, Walsall, W. Mids.
S.W. Antiques, Pershore, Worcs.
Penny Farthing Antiques, North Cave, E. Yorks.
Village Farm Antiques, Wykeham, N. Yorks.
Seventh Heaven, Chirk, Wales.

Brass (see Metal)

Bronzes

Furniture Vault, London N1.
Julian Antiques, London N1.
Page Oriental Art, Kevin, London N1.
Style, London N1.
Finchley Fine Art Galleries, London N12.
Lenson Smith, London NW8.
Magus Antiques, London NW8.
Tara Antiques, London NW8.
Vale Stamps and Antiques, London SE3.
Bowman, Robert, London SW1.
Franses Gallery, Victor, London SW1.
Lewis, M. and D., London SW1.
Nahum at The Leicester Galleries, Peter, London SW1.
Seago, London SW1.
Bridge, Christine, London SW13.
Kensington Sporting Paintings Ltd, London SW20.
James and Son Ltd, Anthony, London SW3.
Cooper Fine Arts Ltd, London SW6.
Tulissio De Beaumont, London SW6.
Davies Oriental Art, Barry, London W1.
Editions Graphiques Gallery, London W1.
Eskenazi Ltd, London W1.
Redford, William, London W1.
Sladmore Gallery, The, London W1.
Tryon & Swann Gallery, London W1.
Cohen and Pearce (Oriental Porcelain), London W11.
Lewis, M. and D., London W11.
Lipitch Ltd, J., London W11.
Petrou, Peter, London W11.
Walpole, Graham, London W11.
Brower Antiques, David, London W8.
Deutsch Antiques, H. and W., London W8.
Grosvenor Antiques Ltd, London W8.
Jay Antiques and Objets d'Art, Melvyn, London W8.
Jesse, John, London W8.
Jones, Howard, London W8.
Pruskin Gallery, London W8.
Wise, Mary, London W8.
Ivor and Patricia Lewis Antique and Fine Art Dealers, Peterborough, Cambs.
West End Galleries, Buxton, Derbys.
Michael Sim, Chislehurst, Kent.
Apollo Galleries, Westerham, Kent.
London House Antiques, Westerham, Kent.
Mary Cruz, Bath, Somerset.
Edward Cross - Fine Paintings, Weybridge, Surrey.
Sport and Country Gallery, Bulkington, Warks.
Richard Hagen, Broadway, Worcs.
Fettes Fine Art, York, N. Yorks.

Carpets & Rugs

Lavian, Joseph, London N4.
Wilkins, David J., London NW1.
Soviet Carpet and Art Centre, London NW2.
Orientalist, London NW5.
Franses and Sons, Robert, London NW8.
Belgrave Carpet Gallery Ltd, London SW1.
Franses Gallery, Victor, London SW1.
Franses Ltd, S., London SW1.
Heraz (David Hartwright Ltd), London SW1.
Keshishian, London SW1.
Mayorcas Ltd, London SW1.
Rare Carpets Gallery, London SW10.
Gallery Yacou, London SW3.
Perez, London SW3.
Stephenson, Robert, London SW3.
Bookham Galleries, London SW6.
Perez Antique Carpets Gallery, London SW6.
Anglo Persian Carpet Co, London SW7.
Heskia, London SW8.
Aaron Gallery, London W1.
Atlantic Bay Carpets, London W1.
Colefax and Fowler, London W1.
Eskenazi Ltd, John, London W1.
Essie Carpets, London W1.
Gallery Zadah Ltd, London W1.
John (Rare Rugs) Ltd, C., London W1.
Juran and Co, Alexander, London W1.
Kennedy Carpets, London W1.
Mayfair Carpet Gallery Ltd, London W1.
Nels Ltd, Paul, London W1.
Rabi Gallery Ltd, London W1.
Shaikh and Son (Oriental Rugs) Ltd, London W1.

Vigo Carpet Gallery, London W1.
Black Oriental Carpets, David, London W11.
Fairman Carpets Ltd, London W11.
Graham and Green, London W11.
Rezai Persian Carpets, A., London W11.
AntiqueWest Ltd, London W8.
Coats Oriental Carpets, London W8.
Sinai Antiques Ltd, London W8.
Oriental Rug Gallery Ltd, Windsor and Eton, Berks.
Clive Rogers Oriental Rugs, Wraysbury, Berks.
Peter Norman Antiques and Restorations, Burwell, Cambs.
ParvisSigaroudinia, Lisburn, Co. Antrim, N. Ireland.
White Elephant Antiques, Bowness-on-Windermere, Cumbria.
J.L. Arditti, Christchurch, Dorset.
Christchurch Carpets, Christchurch, Dorset.
Hamptons, Christchurch, Dorset.
The Collector, Barnard Castle, Durham.
Eric Pride Oriental Rugs, Cheltenham, Glos.
Anthony Hazledine, Fairford, Glos.
Town & Country Antiques, Lechlade, Glos.
Samarkand Galleries, Stow-on-the-Wold, Glos.
The Odiham Gallery, Odiham, Hants.
Oriental Rug Gallery Ltd, St. Albans, Herts.
Desmond and Amanda North, East Peckham, Kent.
Rosewood Gallery, Hadlow, Kent.
Samovar Antiques, Hythe, Kent.
The Rug Gallery, Leicester, Leics.
Country and Eastern, Norwich, Norfolk.
M.D. Cannell Antiques, Raveningham, Norfolk.
Richard Purdon, Burford, Oxon.
Thames Oriental Rug Co, Henley-on-Thames, Oxon.
Christopher Legge Oriental Carpets, Oxford, Oxon.
Tattersall's, Uppingham, Rutland.
Haliden Oriental Rug Shop, Bath, Somerset.
Bruce Tozer Rugs & Antiques, Bath, Somerset.
Michael and Amanda Lewis Oriental Carpets and Rugs, Wellington, Somerset.
The Persian Carpet Studio, Leavenheath, Suffolk.
Karel Weijand Fine Oriental Carpets, Farnham, Surrey.
Dennis Woodman Oriental Carpets, Kew, Surrey.
Lindfield Galleries - David Adam, Lindfield, W. Sussex.
Majid Amini - Persian Carpet Gallery, Petworth, W. Sussex.
A.W. Hone and Son Oriental Carpets, Birmingham, W. Mids.
London House Oriental Rugs and Carpets, Harrogate, N. Yorks.
Omar (Harrogate) Ltd, Harrogate, N. Yorks.
The Gordon Reece Gallery, Knaresborough, N. Yorks.
Ellis's, Sheffield, S. Yorks.
The Oriental Rug Shop, Sheffield, S. Yorks.
London House Oriental Rugs and Carpets, Boston Spa, W. Yorks.
Whytock and Reid, Edinburgh, Scotland.
Young Antiques, Edinburgh, Scotland.
R.L. Rose and Co, Glasgow, Scotland.
C.S. Moreton (Antiques), Inchture, Scotland.
Gallery Persia, Inverness, Scotland.
Herrald of Edinburgh, Meigle, Scotland.
Nigel Stacy-Marks Ltd, Perth, Scotland.

Cars & Carriages

T.L.O. Militaria, Windsor and Eton, Berks.
Finesse Fine Art, Weymouth, Dorset.
Fieldings Antiques, Haslingden, Lancs.
The Complete Automobilist, Baston, Lincs.
Whatnots, Strathblane, Scotland.
C.A.R.S. (Classic Automobilia & Regalia Specialists), Brighton, E. Sussex.

Chinese Art (see Oriental)

Church Furniture & Furnishings

London Architectural Salvage & Supply Co. (LASSCo), The, London EC2.
Whiteway and Waldron Ltd, London SW6.
Havenplan's Architectural Emporium, Killamarsh, Derbys.
Robert Mills Architectural Antiques Ltd, Bristol, Glos.
Kitchenalia, Longridge, Lancs.
Chancellor's Church Furnishings, Walton-on-Thames, Surrey.

Clocks & Watches

City Clocks, London EC1.
Frost and Son Ltd, C.R., London EC1.
Capon, Patric, London N1.
Julian Antiques, London N1.
Sugar Antiques, London N1.
Strike One (Islington) Ltd, London N5.
Penny Farthing Antiques, London SE1.
North London Clock Shop Ltd, London SE25.
Rose FBHI, R.E., London SE9.
Camerer Cuss and Co, London SW1.
Carlton-Smith, John, London SW1.
Harrods Ltd, London SW1.
Jillings of Belgravia, London SW1.
Somlo Antiques, London SW1.
Whyte, Philip, London SW1.
Clock Clinic Ltd, The, London SW15.
Adams Ltd, Norman, London SW3.
Big Ben Antique Clocks, London SW6.
Gutlin Clocks and Antiques, London SW6.
Brocklehurst, Aubrey, London SW7.
Page, A. & H., London SW7.
Carrington and Co. Ltd, London W1.
Garrard & Co. Ltd (The Crown Jewellers), London W1.
Lord, Frank, London W1.
Mallett and Son (Antiques) Ltd, London W1.
Mallett at Bourdon House Ltd, London W1.
Pendulum of Mayfair Ltd, London W1.
Phillips Ltd, Ronald, London W1.
Rose - Source of the Unusual, Michael, London W1.
Kleanthous Antiques Ltd, Stouts Antiques Market, London W11.
Mayflower Antiques, London W11.
Old Father Time Clock Centre, London W11.
Raffety, London W11.
Silver Fox Gallery, The, London W11.
Badger, The, London W5.
Brower Antiques, David, London W8.
Jay Antiques and Objets d'Art, Melvyn, London W8.
Raffety, London W8.
Roderick Antique Clocks, London W8.
Kettle Ltd, Thomas, London WC2.
London Silver Vaults, The, London WC2.
Pearl Cross Ltd, London WC2.
House of Clocks, Ampthill, Beds.
The Clock Workshop, Caversham, Berks.
Robert and Georgina Hastie, Hungerford, Berks.
Medalcrest Ltd, Hungerford, Berks.
The Old Malthouse, Hungerford, Berks.
Times Past Antiques, Windsor and Eton, Berks.
Wyrardisbury Antiques, Wraysbury, Berks.

M.V. Tooley, CMBHI, Chesham, Bucks.
Peter Wright Antiques, Great Missenden, Bucks.
Robin Unsworth Antiques, Olney, Bucks.
Tim Marshall Antiques, Tingewick, Bucks.
Peter Norman Antiques and Restorations, Burwell, Cambs.
John Beazor and Sons Ltd, Cambridge, Cambs.
Doddington House Antiques, Doddington, Cambs.
Mere Antiques, Fowlmere, Cambs.
Antique Clocks, Harston, Cambs.
T. W. Pawson - Clocks, Somersham, Cambs.
Anthony Baker Antiques, Alderley Edge, Cheshire.
Adams Antiques, Chester, Cheshire.
Veevers, Chester, Cheshire.
The Clock House, Hazel Grove, Cheshire.
Cranford Clocks, Knutsford, Cheshire.
Chapel Antiques, Nantwich, Cheshire.
Coppelia Antiques, Plumley, Cheshire.
Peter Bosson Antiques, Wilmslow, Cheshire.
Paul Jennings Antiques, Angarrack, Cornwall.
Little Jem's, Penzance, Cornwall.
Saint Nicholas Galleries Ltd. (Antiques and Jewellery), Carlisle, Cumbria.
Langley Antiques, Corby Hill, Cumbria.
Calvert Antiques, Endmoor, Cumbria.
David Hill, Kirkby Stephen, Cumbria.
Dragon Antiques, Duffield, Derbys.
Derbyshire Clocks, Glossop, Derbys.
Goodacre Engraving Ltd, Long Eaton, Derbys.
The Spindles, Melbourne, Derbys.
G.K. Hadfield, Swadlincote, Derbys.
Nimbus Antiques, Whaley Bridge, Derbys.
Moor Antiques, Ashburton, Devon.
Gold and Silver Exchange, Exeter, Devon.
John Nathan Antiques, Exeter, Devon.
Honiton Clock Clinic, Honiton, Devon.
Alan Jones Antiques, Plymouth, Devon.
Brian Taylor Antiques, Plymouth, Devon.
Tempus Fugit, Shaldon, Devon.
L.G. Wootton Clocks and Watches, South Brent, Devon.
Leigh C. Extence, Teignmouth, Devon.
Good Hope Antiques, Beaminster, Dorset.
M.C. Taylor, Bournemouth, Dorset.
D.J. Burgess, Parkstone, Dorset.
Tom Tribe and Son, Sturminster Newton, Dorset.
Eden House Antiques, West Auckland, Durham.
Mark Marchant (Antiques), Coggeshall, Essex.
Antique Clock Repair Shoppe, Gants Hill, Essex.
W.A. Pinn and Sons, Sible Hedingham, Essex.
David, Jean and John Antiques, Westcliff-on-Sea, Essex.
It's About Time, Westcliff-on-Sea, Essex.
Antique Corner with A & C Antique Clocks, Bristol, Glos.
Montpellier Clocks, Cheltenham, Glos.
Saxton House Gallery, Chipping Campden, Glos.
School House Antiques, Chipping Campden, Glos.
Jonathan Beech Antique Clocks, Cirencester, Glos.
Blenheim Antiques, Fairford, Glos.
Arthur S. Lewis, Gloucester, Glos.
Gerard Campbell, Lechlade, Glos.
Mick and Fanny Wright, Minchinhampton, Glos.
Jeffrey Formby Antiques, Moreton-in-Marsh, Glos.
Keith Harding's World of Mechanical Music, Northleach, Glos.
Colin Brand Antiques, Stow-on-the-Wold, Glos.
Styles of Stow, Stow-on-the-Wold, Glos.
Vanbrugh House Antiques, Stow-on-the-Wold, Glos.
M.J. Bristow Antiques, Tetbury, Glos.
Evans and Evans, Alresford, Hants.
Olive Antiques, Alverstoke, Hants.
Clockwise, Emsworth, Hants.
Cedar Antiques Limited, Hartley Wintney, Hants.
Bryan Clisby Antique Clocks, Hartley Wintney, Hants.
A.W. Porter and Son, Hartley Wintney, Hants.
Barry Papworth, Lymington, Hants.
Gaylords, Titchfield, Hants.
Twyford Antiques, Twyford, Hants.
Clockwise, Winchester, Hants.
G.E. Marsh Antique Clocks Ltd, Winchester, Hants.
Trecilla Antiques, Ross-on-Wye, Herefs.
Howards, Baldock, Herts.
Robert Horton Antiques, Hertford, Herts.
The Clock Shop - Philip Setterfield of St. Albans, St. Albans, Herts.
Country Clocks, Tring, Herts.
John Corrin Antiques, Douglas, Isle of Man.
John Chawner, Birchington, Kent.
Clockshop, Boughton, Kent.
Old Manor House Antiques, Brasted, Kent.
Michael Sim, Chislehurst, Kent.
Anthony Woodburn, Leigh, Kent.
De Tavener Antiques, Ramsgate, Kent.
Michael Fitch Antiques, Sandgate, Kent.
Nancy Wilson, Sandwich, Kent.
Aaron Antiques, Snodland, Kent.
Derek Roberts Fine Antique Clocks, Music Boxes, Barometers, Tonbridge, Kent.
B. Somerset., Tonbridge, Kent.
Aaron Antiques, Tunbridge Wells, Kent.
Hadlow Antiques, Tunbridge Wells, Kent.
Pantiles Spa Antiques, Tunbridge Wells, Kent.
The Old Clock Shop, West Malling, Kent.
Marks Antiques, Westerham, Kent.
Regal Antiques, Westerham, Kent.
Drop Dial Antiques, Bolton, Lancs.
Harrop Fold Clocks (F. Robinson), Bolton-by-Bowland, Lancs.
Fieldings Antiques, Haslingden, Lancs.
P.W. Norgrove - Antique Clocks, Haslingden, Lancs.
Boodle and Dunthorne Ltd, Manchester, Lancs.
Bulldog Antiques, Manchester, Lancs.
Brittons Jewellers and Antiques, Nelson, Lancs.
Charles Howell Jeweller, Oldham, Lancs.
H.C. Simpson and Sons Jewellers (Oldham)Ltd, Oldham, Lancs.
Hackler's Jewellers, Preston, Lancs.
Owen Antiques, Rochdale, Lancs.
Davies Antiques, Whalley, Lancs.
Lowe of Loughborough, Loughborough, Leics.
Old Timers, Swinford, Leics.
N. Bryan-Peach Antiques, Wymeswold, Leics.
Robin Fowler (Period Clocks), Aylesby, Lincs.
Grantham Clocks, Grantham, Lincs.
Wilkinson's, Grantham, Lincs.
Second Time Around, Hemswell Cliff, Lincs.
Robert Kitching, Horncastle, Lincs.
Staines Antiques, Horncastle, Lincs.
Mr Van Hefflin, Kirton in Lindsey, Lincs.
David J. Hansord and Son, Lincoln, Lincs.
Trade Antiques, Long Sutton, Lincs.
Harwood Tate, Market Rasen, Lincs.
Pinfold Antiques, Ruskington, Lincs.
Wilkinson's, Sleaford, Lincs.
Kevin Whay's Clock Shop and Antiques, Hoylake, Merseyside.
Boodle and Dunthorne Ltd, Liverpool, Merseyside.
Theta Gallery, Liverpool, Merseyside.
Weldons Jewellery and Antiques, Southport, Merseyside.
Rita Shenton, Twickenham, Middx.
As Time Goes By - Antique and Exterior Clocks, Aylsham, Norfolk.
Village Clocks, Coltishall, Norfolk.
R.C. Woodhouse (Antiquarian Horologist), Hunstanton, Norfolk.
Tim Clayton Jewellery, King's Lynn, Norfolk.
Keith Lawson Antique Clocks, Scratby, Norfolk.
Parriss, Sheringham, Norfolk.
Norton Antiques, Twyford, Norfolk.
M.C. Chapman, Finedon, Northants.
Michael Jones Jeweller, Northampton, Northants.
Hazel Cottage Clocks, Eachwick, Northumbs.
Gordon Caris, Hexham, Northumbs.
David and Carole Potter Antiques, Nottingham, Notts.
Horseshoe Antiques and Gallery, Burford, Oxon.
Hubert's Antiques, Burford, Oxon.
Jonathan Howard, Chipping Norton, Oxon.
Tuckers Country Store and Art Gallery, Deddington, Oxon.
Craig Barfoot, East Hagbourne, Oxon.
Gerald E. Marsh (Antique Clocks), North Aston, Oxon.
Laurie Leigh Antiques, Oxford, Oxon.
Rosemary and Time, Thame, Oxon.
Witney Antiques, Witney, Oxon.
Rutland Antique Clock Gallery, Oakham, Rutland.
Mytton Antiques, Atcham, Shrops.
R.G. Cave and Sons Ltd, Ludlow, Shrops.
The Curiosity Shop, Ludlow, Shrops.
Mitre House Antiques, Ludlow, Shrops.
Dodington Antiques, Whitchurch, Shrops.
John Hawley (MBHI) Antique Clocks, Badgworth, Somerset.
Bath Galleries, Bath, Somerset.
Quiet Street Antiques, Bath, Somerset.
David Gibson, Crewkerne, Somerset.
Bernard G. House, Wells, Somerset.
Edward A. Nowell, Wells, Somerset.
Edward Venn, Williton, Somerset.
Grosvenor Clocks, Leek, Staffs.
Richard Midwinter Antiques, Newcastle-under-Lyme, Staffs.
Clock House, Leavenheath, Suffolk.
Antique Clocks by Simon Charles, Long Melford, Suffolk.

Suthburgh Antiques, Long Melford, Suffolk.
Village Clocks, Long Melford, Suffolk.
Antique Clocks by Simon Charles, Sudbury, Suffolk.
Edward Manson (Clocks), Woodbridge, Suffolk.
Suffolk. House Antiques, Yoxford, Suffolk.
Simon Marsh, Bletchingley, Surrey.
E. Hollander, Dorking, Surrey.
Norfolk House Galleries, Dorking, Surrey.
Abbott Antiques, East Molesey, Surrey.
B.S. Antiques, East Molesey, Surrey.
Roger A. Davis Antiquarian Horologist, Great Bookham, Surrey.
Horological Workshops, Guildford, Surrey.
Surrey. Clock Centre, Haslemere, Surrey.
Hill Rise Antiques, Richmond, Surrey.
F. and T. Lawson Antiques, Richmond, Surrey.
B. M. and E. Newlove, Surbiton, Surrey.
S. Warrender and Co, Sutton, Surrey.
The Clock Shop Weybridge, Weybridge, Surrey.
Chattels Antiques, Woking, Surrey.
D.H. Edmonds Ltd, Brighton, E. Sussex.
Hove Antique Clocks, Brighton, E. Sussex.
Yellow Lantern Antiques Ltd, Brighton, E. Sussex.
Chaunt House, Burwash, E. Sussex.
Wm. Bruford and Son Ltd, Eastbourne, E. Sussex.
John Cowderoy Antiques, Eastbourne, E. Sussex.
Coach House Antiques, Hastings, E. Sussex.
The Old Mint House, Pevensey, E. Sussex.
Arundel Clocks, Arundel, W. Sussex.
Julian Antiques, Hurstpierpoint, W. Sussex.
Samuel Orr Antique Clocks, Hurstpierpoint, W. Sussex.
Churchill Clocks, Midhurst, W. Sussex.
Baskerville Antiques, Petworth, W. Sussex.
J. Powell (Hove) Ltd, Portslade, W. Sussex.
Thakeham Furniture, Pulborough, W. Sussex.
Peter Smith Antiques, Sunderland, Tyne and Wear.
Summersons, Hatton, Warks.
The Grandfather Clock Shop, Shipston-on-Stour, Warks.
'Time in Hand', Shipston-on-Stour, Warks.
Ashleigh House Antiques, Birmingham, W. Mids.
R. Collyer, Birmingham, W. Mids.
F. Meeks & Co, Birmingham, W. Mids.
M. Allen Watch and Clockmaker, Four Oaks, W. Mids.
Osborne Antiques, Sutton Coldfield, W. Mids.
Alan M. France, Wolverhampton, W. Mids.
Avon Antiques, Bradford-on-Avon, Wilts.
Moxhams Antiques, Bradford-on-Avon, Wilts.
P.A. Oxley Antique Clocks and Barometers, Cherhill, Wilts.
Monkton Galleries, Hindon, Wilts.
Ray Best Antiques, Newton Tony, Wilts.
Inglenook Antiques, Ramsbury, Wilts.
Salisbury Antiques Warehouse, Salisbury, Wilts.
Chris Wadge Clocks, Salisbury, Wilts.
Allan Smith Antique Clocks, Swindon, Wilts.
Broadway Clocks, Broadway, Worcs.
Hansen Chard Antiques, Pershore, Worcs.
Time and Motion, Beverley, E. Yorks.
Lewis E. Hickson FBHI, Gilberdyke, E. Yorks.
The Old Ropery Antique Clocks, Kilham, E. Yorks.
John Pearson Antique Clock Restoration, Birstwith, N. Yorks.
Milestone Antiques, Easingwold, N. Yorks.
Haworth Antiques, Harrogate, N. Yorks.
D. Mason & Son, Harrogate, N. Yorks.
Chris Wilde Antiques, Harrogate, N. Yorks.
Brian Loomes, Pateley Bridge, N. Yorks.
Cottage Antiques, Snainton, N. Yorks.
N.J. and C.S. Dodsworth, Spennithorne, N. Yorks.
B. Ogleby - St James' House Antiques, Thirsk, N. Yorks.
Eileen Quigley, Thirsk, N. Yorks.
Tomlinson (Antiques) Ltd. & Period Furniture Ltd, Tockwith, N. Yorks.
Keith Stones Grandfather Clocks, Bessacarr, S. Yorks.
Fishlake Antiques, Fishlake, S. Yorks.
F S Antiques, Sheffield, S. Yorks.
Fulwood Antiques and The Basement Gallery, Sheffield, S. Yorks.
Canterbury House, Thorne, S. Yorks.
Jeremiah's Antiques, St Helier, Jersey, C. I.
Robert Christie Antiques, Ballyclare, Co. Antrim, N. Ireland.
Timecraft, Greyabbey, Co. Down, N. Ireland.
Time & Tide Antiques, Portaferry, Co. Down, N. Ireland.
John Mann Antique Clocks, Canonbie, Scotland.
Ian Burton, Denny, Scotland.
Craiglea Clocks, Edinburgh, Scotland.
Donald Ellis incorporating Bruntsfield Clocks, Edinburgh, Scotland.
John Whyte, Edinburgh, Scotland.
West End Antiques, Elgin, Scotland.
James Forrest and Co (Jewellers) Ltd, Glasgow, Scotland.
Muirhead Moffat and Co, Glasgow, Scotland.
Silvertime, Brecon, Wales.
Past and Present, Cardiff, Wales.
Rodney Adams Antiques, Pwllheli, Wales.
Eynon Hughes Antiques, Swansea, Wales.

Coins & Medals

Rankin Coin Co. Ltd, George, London E2.
Martin (Coins) Ltd, C.J., London N14.
Eimer, Christopher, London NW11.
Dolphin Coins, London NW3.
Armoury of St. James's Military Antiquarians, The, London SW1.
Knightsbridge Coins, London SW1.
Spink and Son Ltd, London SW1.
Beaver Coin Room, London SW5.
Seaby Antiquities, London W1.
Michael Coins, London W8.
Baldwin and Sons Ltd, A.H., London WC2.
Bord (Gold Coin Exchange), M., London WC2.
Trafalgar Square Collectors Centre, London WC2.
T.L.O. Militaria, Windsor and Eton, Berks.
B.R.M. Coins, Knutsford, Cheshire.
Souvenir Antiques, Carlisle, Cumbria.
Penrith Coin and Stamp Centre, Penrith, Cumbria.
Sterling Coins and Medals, Bournemouth, Dorset.
The Treasure Chest, Weymouth, Dorset.
Robin Finnegan (Jeweller), Darlington, Durham.
J. Shotton Antiquarian Books, Prints and Coins, Durham, Durham.
Potter's Antiques and Coins, Bristol, Glos.
Butler and Co, Cheltenham, Glos.
Military Curios, HQ84, Gloucester, Glos.
Portsmouth Stamp Shop, Portsmouth, Hants.
Romsey Medal and Collectors Centre, Romsey, Hants.
The Coin and Jewellery Shop, Accrington, Lancs.
Chard Coins, Blackpool, Lancs.
Peter Ireland Ltd, Blackpool, Lancs.
Rowletts of Lincoln, Lincoln, Lincs.
Gold and Silver Exchange, Gt. Yarmouth, Norfolk.
Clive Dennett Coins, Norwich, Norfolk.
Hockley Coins, Nottingham, Notts.
Val Smith Coins and Antiques, Nottingham, Notts.
Denver House Antiques and Collectables, Burford, Oxon.
Collectors' Gallery, Shrewsbury, Shrops.
Bath Stamp and Coin Shop, Bath, Somerset.
St. Pancras Antiques, Chichester, W. Sussex.
Intercoin, Newcastle-upon-Tyne, Tyne and Wear.
Format of Birmingham Ltd, Birmingham, W. Mids.
Castle Galleries, Salisbury, Wilts.
Whitmore, Great Malvern, Worcs.
B.B.M. Jewellery and Antiques, Kidderminster, Worcs.
C.J. and A.J. Dixon Ltd, Bridlington, E. Yorks.
Coins International and Antiques International, Leeds, W. Yorks.
Cookstown Antiques, Cookstown, Co. Tyrone, N. Ireland.
The Collectors Shop, Edinburgh, Scotland.
Edinburgh Coin Shop, Edinburgh, Scotland.
A.D. Hamilton and Co, Glasgow, Scotland.
Abbey Antiques, Stirling, Scotland.
Glance Back Bookshop, Chepstow, Wales.

Dolls & Toys

Donay Antiques, London N1.
Lassalle, Judith, London N1.
Relic Antiques, London N1.
Yesterday Child, London N1.
Dolly Land, London N21.
Game Advice, London NW5.
Engine 'n' Tender, London SE25.
Victoriana Dolls, London W11.
Dolls and Toys of Yesteryear at Bow House Antiques, Hungerford, Berks.
Tim Armitage, Nantwich, Cheshire.
Rosina's, Falmouth, Cornwall.
Abbey House, Derby, Derbys.
Honiton Antique Toys, Honiton, Devon.

The Vintage Toy and Train Museum Shop, Sidmouth, Devon.
Boscombe Models and Collectors Shop, Bournemouth, Dorset.
Hobby Horse Antiques, Bridport, Dorset.
I. Westrope, Birdbrook, Essex.
Tilly's Antiques, Leigh-on-Sea, Essex.
The Doll's House, Northleach, Glos.
Park House Antiques, Stow-on-the-Wold, Glos.
Peter Pan's of Gosport, Gosport, Hants.
The Attic, Baldock, Herts.
Bridge Antiques, Wingham, Kent.
Swag, Preston, Lancs.
C. and K.E. Dring, Lincoln, Lincs.
Francis Bowers Chess Suppliers, Whaplode, Lincs.
Stiffkey Antiques, Stiffkey, Norfolk.
Granny's Attic, Nottingham, Notts.
Images - Peter Stockham, Lichfield, Staffs.
Trench Puzzles, Stowmarket, Suffolk.
Childhood Memories, Farnham, Surrey.
Elizabeth Gant, Thames Ditton, Surrey.
Bears and Friends, Brighton, E. Sussex. .
C.A.R.S. (Classic Automobilia & Regalia Specialists), Brighton, E. Sussex.
Paul Goble, Brighton, E. Sussex.
Sue Pearson, Brighton, E. Sussex.
Coach House Antiques, Hastings, E. Sussex.
Hinsdale Antiques, Lindfield, W. Sussex.
Recollect Studios, Sayers Common, W. Sussex.
Dolly Mixtures, Birmingham, W. Mids.
Robert Taylor, Four Oaks, W. Mids.
'Broadway Bears & Dolls', Broadway, Worcs.
Grannie's Parlour, Hull, E. Yorks.
Windmill Antiques, Harrogate, N. Yorks.
Fun Antiques, Sheffield, S. Yorks.
Collectors Old Toy Shop and Antiques, Halifax, W. Yorks.
Memory Lane, Sowerby Bridge, W. Yorks.
Angus Antiques, Dundee, Scotland.
Now and Then (Toy Centre), Edinburgh, Scotland.
Stockbridge Antiques and Fine Art, Edinburgh, Scotland.
Pastimes Vintage Toys, Glasgow, Scotland.
Museum of Childhood, Beaumaris, Wales.

Etchings & Engravings

Royal Exchange Art Gallery, London EC3.
Moreton Street Gallery, London SW1.
Old Maps and Prints, London SW1.
International Arts Group, London SW18.
Map House, The, London SW3.
Old Church Galleries, London SW3.
King's Court Galleries, London SW6.
Collino, Julie, London SW7.
Wyllie Gallery, The, London SW7.
Agnew's, London W1.
Editions Graphiques Gallery, London W1.
Weston Gallery, William, London W1.
Skrebowski Prints, Justin F., London W11.
Foye Gallery, Luton, Beds.
Polly Coleman Antiques, Chesterfield, Derbys.
The Lantern Shop Gallery, Sidmouth, Devon.
PIC's Bookshop, Bridport, Dorset.
Antique Map and Bookshop, Puddletown, Dorset.
Elizabeth Cannon Antiques, Colchester, Essex.
Talbot Court Galleries, Stow-on-the-Wold, Glos.
Oldfield Gallery, Portsmouth, Hants.
The Shanklin Gallery, Shanklin, Isle of Wight.
Peter Goodall, Ventnor, Isle of Wight.
P. Farmer, Chatham, Kent.
G. and D.I. Marrin and Sons, Folkestone, Kent.
London House Antiques, Westerham, Kent.
Hammond Smith (Fine Art), Leicester, Leics.
Leicestershire Sporting Gallery and Brown Jack Bookshop, Lubenham, Leics.
Graftons of Market Harborough, Market Harborough, Leics.
P.J. Cassidy (Books), Holbeach, Lincs.
The Coach House, Costessey, Norfolk.
TRADA, Chipping Norton, Oxon.
The Barry M. Keene Gallery, Henley-on-Thames, Oxon.
Elizabeth Harvey-Lee, North Aston, Oxon.
John Garner, Uppingham, Rutland.
The Mount, Woore, Shrops.
George Gregory, Bath, Somerset.
England's Gallery, Leek, Staffs.
King's Court Galleries, Dorking, Surrey.
The Court Gallery, East Molesey, Surrey.
Limpsfield Watercolours, Limpsfield, Surrey.
Reigate Galleries Ltd, Reigate, Surrey.
Palmer Galleries, Richmond, Surrey.
Boathouse Gallery, Walton-on-Thames, Surrey.
The Witch Ball, Brighton, E. Sussex.
Faringdon Gallery, Arundel, W. Sussex.
George House Gallery, Petworth, W. Sussex.
Osborne Art and Antiques, Jesmond, Tyne and Wear.
Ronald Carr, Salisbury, Wilts.
The Jerram Gallery, Salisbury, Wilts.
Heirloom & Howard Limited, West Yatton, Wilts.
Penoyre Antiques, Pershore, Worcs.
The Waverley Gallery, Aberdeen, Scotland.
The McEwan Gallery, Ballater, Scotland.
Open Eye Gallery Ltd, Edinburgh, Scotland.
Ewan Mundy Fine Art Ltd, Glasgow, Scotland.
Mainhill Gallery, Jedburgh, Scotland.
The George Street Gallery, Perth, Scotland.
Nigel Stacy-Marks Ltd, Perth, Scotland.
David Windsor Gallery, Bangor, Wales.

Fire Related Items

Rupert's Antiques, London E18.
Westland & Company, London EC2.
House of Steel Antiques, London N1.
Julian Antiques, London N1.
Amazing Grates - Fireplaces Ltd, London N2.
Antique Shop (Valantique), The, London N2.
Tsar Architectural, London N7.
Victorian Fireplace Co, London NW1.
Acquisitions (Fireplaces) Ltd, London NW5.
Townsends, London NW8.
Bartlett, Nigel A., London SE1.
Main Street Antiques, London SE10.
Oddiquities, London SE23.
Under Milkwood, London SE24.
Ward Antiques, London SE7.
Fireplace, The, London SE9.
Poulter and Son, H.W., London SW10.
Thornhill Galleries Ltd. in association with A. & R. Dockerill Ltd, London SW15.
Wandle's Workshop, Mr, London SW18.
Wilson Ltd, O.F., London SW3.
Crotty and Son Ltd, J., London SW6.
Fairfax Antiques and Fireplaces, London SW6.
Hollingshead and Co, London SW6.
Old World Trading Co, London SW6.
Thornhill Galleries Ltd, London SW6.
Buckle (Antique Fireplaces), Ruby, London W2.
Chiswick Fireplace Co., The, London W4.
Architectural Antiques, London W6.
Architectural Antiques - Bedford, Bedford, Beds.
The Fire Place (Hungerford) Ltd, Hungerford, Berks.
Sundial Antiques, Amersham, Bucks.
Grosvenor House Interiors, Beaconsfield, Bucks.
Ann Roberts Antiques, Congleton, Cheshire.
Pillory House, Nantwich, Cheshire.
Nostalgia Architectural Antiques, Stockport, Cheshire.
Antique Fireplaces, Tarvin, Cheshire.
Antique Fireplace Centre, Hartlepool, Cleveland.
Hearth and Home, Penrith, Cumbria.
Wooden Box Antiques, Woodville, Derbys.
Ashburton Marbles, Ashburton, Devon.
Antique Fireplace Centre, Plymouth, Devon.
Dodge and Son, Sherborne, Dorset.
Antique Metals, Coggeshall, Essex.
Au Temps Perdu, Bristol, Glos.
Flame and Grate, Bristol, Glos.
Oldwoods, Bristol, Glos.
Period Fireplaces, Bristol, Glos.
Cox's Architectural Reclamation Yard, Moreton-in-Marsh, Glos.
Baileys Architectural Antiques, Ross-on-Wye, Herefs.
Victorian Fireplace, Canterbury, Kent.
Old Smithy, Feniscowles, Lancs.
Antique Fireplaces, Manchester, Lancs.
Colin Blakey Fireplaces, Nelson, Lancs.
Carrcross Gallery, Scarisbrick, Lancs.
Pine Antiques, St. Annes-on-Sea, Lancs.
Britain's Heritage, Leicester, Leics.
David Allan Antiques, Birkenhead, Merseyside.
Antique Fireplaces, Liverpool, Merseyside.
Peco, Hampton, Middx.
Crowther of Syon Lodge Ltd, Isleworth, Middx.
Marble Hill Gallery, Twickenham, Middx.
Stiffkey Antiques, Stiffkey, Norfolk.
Rococo Antiques and Interiors, Weedon, Northants.
Blacksmiths Forge, Balderton, Notts.
Key Antiques, Chipping Norton, Oxon.
Hallidays (Fine Antiques) Ltd, Dorchester-on-Thames, Oxon.
Aston Pine Antiques, Faringdon, Oxon.
Walcot Reclamation, Bath, Somerset.
Rickett & Co. Antiques, Shepperton, Surrey.
Brighton Architectural Salvage, Brighton, E. Sussex.

L.E. Lampard and Sons, Horsham, W. Sussex.
Shiners Architectural Reclamation, Newcastle-upon-Tyne, Tyne and Wear.
Grate Expectations (Fireplaces), Washington, Tyne and Wear.
Architectural Antiques of Moseley, Birmingham, W. Mids.
The Original Choice Ltd, Birmingham, W. Mids.
Tudor House Antiques, Halesowen, W. Mids.
Old Flames, Easingwold, N. Yorks.
Robert Aagaard & Co, Knaresborough, N. Yorks.
Chimney Piece Antique Fires, Sheffield, S. Yorks.
Chapel House Fireplaces, Holmfirth, W. Yorks.
Mews Antique and Reproduction Fireplaces & Architectural Salvage, Belfast, N. Ireland.
Period Architectural Features and Antiques, Annahilt, Co. Down, N. Ireland.
Burning Embers, Aberdeen, Scotland.
EASY - Edinburgh & Glasgow Architectural Salvage Yards, Edinburgh, Scotland.
T. and J. W. Neilson Ltd, Edinburgh, Scotland.
EASY - Edinburgh and Glasgow Architectural Salvage Yards, Glasgow, Scotland.
The Renaissance Furniture Store, Glasgow, Scotland.
Flame 'n' Grate, Barry, Wales.
Back to the Wood, Cardiff, Wales.
Kings Fireplaces, Antiques and Interiors, Cardiff, Wales.

Frames

Mason Gallery, Paul, London SW1.
Wiggins and Sons Ltd, Arnold, London SW1.
Milne Ltd, Nigel, London W1.
Mitchell Ltd, Paul, London W1.
Whately, Rollo, London W1.
Daggett Gallery, London W11.
Lacy Gallery, London W11.
Skrebowski Prints, Justin F., London W11.
Skrebowski Prints, Justin F., London WC2.
The Fairhurst Gallery, Norwich, Norfolk.
Rob Dixon Fine Engravings, Culham, Oxon.
Looking Glass of Bath, Bath, Somerset.
Victoria C - The Antique Gallery (Potterne), Potterne, Wilts.
W. Greenwood (Fine Art), Burneston, N. Yorks.
Coulter Galleries, York, N. Yorks.

Furniture - Continental (mainly French)

Westland & Company, London EC2.
Charlton House Antiques, London N1.
Gridley, Gordon, London N1.
Relic Antiques, London N1.
Tapsell Antiques, London N1.
Lenson Smith, London NW8.
Hirschhorn, Robert E., London SE5.
Aaron (London)Ltd, Didier, London SW1.
Antiquités, London SW1.
Blanchard (London) Ltd, London SW1.
Ciancimino Ltd, London SW1.
Hamilton Ltd, Ross, London SW1.
Hermitage Antiques plc, London SW1.
Hobbs, Carlton, London SW1.
Howe, Christopher, London SW1.
Jeremy Ltd, London SW1.
Lewis, M. and D., London SW1.
Rogier Antiques, London SW1.
Hastie, Rupert, London SW10.
Kerr Antiques Ltd, Thomas, London SW10.
McVeigh & Charpentier, London SW10.
Rendlesham Antiques, London SW10.
Coleman Antiques, Simon, London SW13.
Jorgen Antiques, London SW15.
Adams Room Antiques, London SW19.
No. 12, London SW3.
Prides of London, London SW3.
Wilson Ltd, O.F., London SW3.
275 Antiques, London SW6.
Arabesque Antiques, London SW6.
Brown Ltd, I. and J.L., London SW6.
Cavendish Antiques, Rupert, London SW6.
Fabre Antiques, Nicole, London SW6.
Greenwood, Judy, London SW6.
Hurford Antiques, Peter, London SW6.
Lewin, London SW6.
Mathers Antiques, Megan, London SW6.
Napier Ltd, Sylvia, London SW6.
Pauw Antiques, M., London SW6.
Alan Ltd, Adrian, London W1.
Bernheimer Ltd, Konrad O., London W1.
Blairman and Sons Ltd., H., London W1.
Howard Antiques, London W1.
Mallett at Bourdon House Ltd, London W1.
Partridge Fine Arts plc, London W1.
Pelham Galleries Ltd, London W1.
Redford, William, London W1.
Toynbee-Clarke Interiors Ltd, London W1.
Turpin Ltd, M., London W1.
Barham, P.R., London W11.
Barham Antiques, London W11.
Canonbury, London W11.
Curá Antiques, London W11.
Di Michele Antiques, E. and A., London W11.
Lewis, M. and D., London W11.
Lipitch Ltd, J., London W11.
Mankowitz, Daniel, London W11.
Martin Antiques, Robin, London W11.
Oakstar Ltd, London W11.
Rostrum Antiques, London W11.
Marshall Gallery, London W14.
Bornoff, Claude, London W2.
Alan Ltd, Adrian, London W8.
Brower Antiques, David, London W8.
Harris, Jonathan, London W8.
Jay Antiques and Objets d'Art, Melvyn, London W8.
Reindeer Antiques Ltd, London W8.
Stodel, Jacob, London W8.
Teignmouth and Son, Pamela, London W8.
Youll's Antiques, Hungerford, Berks.
Country Furniture, Windsor and Eton, Berks.
Ulla Stafford Antiques, Windsor and Eton, Berks.
Phoenix Antiques, Fordham, Cambs.
Ivor and Patricia Lewis Antique and Fine Art Dealers, Peterborough, Cambs.
David H. Dickinson, Bramhall, Cheshire.
Adams Antiques, Chester, Cheshire.
Richmond Galleries, Chester, Cheshire.
Antique Furniture Warehouse, Stockport, Cheshire.
West End Galleries, Buxton, Derbys.
Francis De Aquilar, Cullompton, Devon.
Pilgrim Antiques, Honiton, Devon.
Sextons, Kentisbeare, Devon.
Pugh's Farm Antiques, Monkton, Devon.
Colystock Antiques, Stockland, Devon.
Lionel Geneen Ltd, Bournemouth, Dorset.
Georgina Ryder, Frampton, Dorset.
Talisman, Gillingham, Dorset.
Millers Antiques Kelvedon, Kelvedon, Essex.
Old Barn Antiques, Matching Green, Essex.
Gloucester House Antiques Ltd, Fairford, Glos.
Elizabeth Parker, Moreton-in-Marsh, Glos.
Craig Carrington Antiques, Painswick, Glos.
Annarella Clark Antiques, Stow-on-the-Wold, Glos.
Antony Preston Antiques Ltd, Stow-on-the-Wold, Glos.
Geoffrey Stead, Stow-on-the-Wold, Glos.
The Decorator Source, Tetbury, Glos.
Anne Fowler, Tetbury, Glos.
Gales Antiques, Tetbury, Glos.
Artemesia, Alresford, Hants.
Cedar Antiques Limited, Hartley Wintney, Hants.
David Lazarus Antiques, Hartley Wintney, Hants.
Phoenix Green Antiques, Hartley Wintney, Hants.
Charles Wallrock - Wick Antiques, Lymington, Hants.
Millers of Chelsea Antiques Ltd, Ringwood, Hants.
I. and J.L. Brown Ltd, Hereford, Herefs.
Great Brampton House Antiques Ltd, Hereford, Herefs.
Robin Lloyd Antiques, Ross-on-Wye, Herefs.
Samovar Antiques, Hythe, Kent.
Dench Antiques, Sandgate, Kent.
Henry Baines, Southborough, Kent.
Flower House Antiques, Tenterden, Kent.
Sparks Antiques, Tenterden, Kent.
Claremont Antiques, Tunbridge Wells, Kent.
Up Country, Tunbridge Wells, Kent.
Apollo Galleries, Westerham, Kent.
Bridge Antiques, Wingham, Kent.
Park Galleries Antiques, Fine Art and Decor, Bolton, Lancs.
J. Green and Son, Queniborough, Leics.
Robin Cox Antiques, Ketton, Lincs.
David J. Hansord and Son, Lincoln, Lincs.
J. and R. Ratcliffe, Lincoln, Lincs.
Moor Pine, North Kelsey Moor, Lincs.
Graham Pickett Antiques, Stamford, Lincs.
Ron Green, Towcester, Northants.
Ball & Claw Ltd, Weedon, Northants.
Helios & Co (Antiques), Weedon, Northants.
Ashton Gower Antiques, Burford, Oxon.
Jonathan Fyson Antiques, Burford, Oxon.
Gateway Antiques, Burford, Oxon.
Bugle Antiques, Chipping Norton, Oxon.
Summers Davis Antiques Ltd, Wallingford, Oxon.
Witney Antiques, Witney, Oxon.
Swans, Oakham, Rutland.
Doveridge House of Neachley, Albrighton (Neachley), Shrops.
Hall's Antiques, Ash Priors, Somerset.
Jadis Ltd, Bath, Somerset.

Pennard House Antiques, Bath, Somerset.
Pennard House, East Pennard, Somerset.
Gilbert & Dale, Ilchester, Somerset.
Suffolk. Antique Connection, Stoke by Nayland, Suffolk.
Heath-Bullocks, Godalming, Surrey.
Marryat, Richmond, Surrey.
Ripley Antiques, Ripley, Surrey.
Wych House Antiques, Woking, Surrey.
Dermot and Jill Palmer Antiques, Brighton, E. Sussex.
Ruddy Antiques, Brighton, E. Sussex.
Graham Lower, Flimwell, E. Sussex.
John Botting Antiques, Horam, E. Sussex.
Delmas, Hurst Green, E. Sussex.
Lennox Cato, Lewes, E. Sussex.
Graham Price Antiques Ltd, Polegate, E. Sussex.
Julian Antiques, Hurstpierpoint, W. Sussex.
T.G. Wilkinson Antiques Ltd, Petworth, W. Sussex.
Sayer Antiques, Warnham, W. Sussex.
Apollo Antiques Ltd, Warwick, Warks.
Alan Richards Brocante, Birmingham, W. Mids.
L.P. Antiques (Mids) Ltd, Walsall, W. Mids.
Ghiberti Antiques and Fine Art, Wolverhampton, W. Mids.
Kimber & Son, Wolverhampton, W. Mids.
Avon Antiques, Bradford-on-Avon, Wilts.
Moxhams Antiques, Bradford-on-Avon, Wilts.
Edward Marnier Antiques, Tisbury, Wilts.
Obelisk Antiques, Warminster, Wilts.
Kimber & Son, Malvern Link, Worcs.
Norwood House Antiques, Killinghall, N. Yorks.
Charlotte and John Lambe, Belfast, N. Ireland.
Whytock and Reid, Edinburgh, Scotland.
Aldric Young, Edinburgh, Scotland.
Jeremy Sniders Antiques, Glasgow, Scotland.
Ship Street Galleries, Brecon, Wales.

Furniture - Country (for 16th-17th C, see also Oak)

At the Sign of the Chest of Drawers, London N1.
Lewis Antiques, Michael, London N1.
Rookery Farm Antiques, London N1.
This and That (Furniture), London NW1.
Hirschhorn, Robert E., London SE5.
Rogier Antiques, London SW1.
Furniture Cave, The, London SW10.
Young Antiques, Robert, London SW11.
Coleman Antiques, Simon, London SW13.
Yesterday's Antiques, London SW14.
Brown Ltd, I. and J.L., London SW6.
Sampson Antiques Ltd, Alistair, London W1.
Seligmann, M. and D., London W8.
Alan Hodgson, Great Shefford, Berks.
Ivy House Antiques, Great Shefford, Berks.
Jack Harness Antiques, Marlow, Bucks.
Pine Reflections, Princes Risborough, Bucks.
Tim Marshall Antiques, Tingewick, Bucks.
Simon and Penny Rumble Antiques, Chittering, Cambs.
A.P. and M.A. Haylett, Outwell, Cambs.
Olwyn Boustead Antiques, Chester, Cheshire.
Farmhouse Antiques, Chester, Cheshire.
Richmond Galleries, Chester, Cheshire.
Peter Bunting Antiques, Hyde, Cheshire.
Adams Antiques, Nantwich, Cheshire.
Antiques and Curios, Ravensmoor, Cheshire.
Oak Room, Stockport, Cheshire.
Daphne's Antiques, Penzance, Cornwall.
Anvil Antiques, Cartmel, Cumbria.
Maggie Tallentire Antiques, Cartmel, Cumbria.
Langley Antiques, Corby Hill, Cumbria.
David Hill, Kirkby Stephen, Cumbria.
Mortlake Antiques, Kirkby Stephen, Cumbria.
Utopia Antiques Ltd, Low Newton, Cumbria.
Winton Hall Antiques, Winton, Cumbria.
Lewis Antiques, Bakewell, Derbys.
Byethorpe Furniture (Brian Yates Antiques), Barlow, Derbys.
Rex Antiques, Chagford, Devon.
Cobweb Antiques, Cullompton, Devon.
Francis De Aquilar, Cullompton, Devon.
G. Mounter, Dulford, Devon.
Wickham Antiques, Honiton, Devon.
Sextons, Kentisbeare, Devon.
Pugh's Farm Antiques, Monkton, Devon.
Alan Jones Antiques, Plymouth, Devon.
Barrington Antiques, Tiverton, Devon.
The Ark Antiques & Design, Topsham, Devon.
Fine Pine Antiques, Totnes, Devon.
The Collector, Barnard Castle, Durham.
English Rose Antiques, Coggeshall, Essex.
Dean Antiques, Colchester, Essex.
Julia Bennet (Antiques), Dunmow, Essex.
Lennard Antiques, Sible Hedingham, Essex.
Denzil Verey, Barnsley, Glos.
J. and R. Bateman Antiques, Chalford, Glos.
John P. Townsend, Cheltenham, Glos.
Waterloo Antiques, Cirencester, Glos.
Woodminster Antiques, Cirencester, Glos.
Gloucester House Antiques Ltd, Fairford, Glos.
Outhouse Antiques, Kempsford, Glos.
Anthony Sampson, Moreton-in-Marsh, Glos.
Annarella Clark Antiques, Stow-on-the-Wold, Glos.
Keith Hockin (Antiques) Ltd, Stow-on-the-Wold, Glos.
Huntington Antiques Ltd, Stow-on-the-Wold, Glos.
The Chest of Drawers, Tetbury, Glos.
Day Antiques, Tetbury, Glos.
Fifty-One Antiques Et Cetera, Tetbury, Glos.
Anne Fowler, Tetbury, Glos.
Gales Antiques, Tetbury, Glos.
Westwood House Antiques, Tetbury, Glos.
Close Antiques, Alresford, Hants.
Airdale Antiques, Hartley Wintney, Hants.
Cedar Antiques Limited, Hartley Wintney, Hants.
Phoenix Green Antiques, Hartley Wintney, Hants.
Hursley Antiques, Hursley, Hants.
Burgess Farm Antiques, Morestead, Hants.
Millers of Chelsea Antiques Ltd, Ringwood, Hants.
Elizabeth Viney, Stockbridge, Hants.
The Pine Cellars, Winchester, Hants.
I. and J.L. Brown Ltd, Hereford, Herefs.
Robin Lloyd Antiques, Ross-on-Wye, Herefs.
Singleton Antiques, Ross-on-Wye, Herefs.
M. and J. Russell, Yazor, Herefs.
Anne Barlow Antiques, Letchmore Heath, Herts.
Tim Wharton Antiques, Redbourn, Herts.
Old Bakery Antiques, Brasted, Kent.
Dinah Stoodley, Brasted, Kent.
Michael Pearson Antiques, Canterbury, Kent.
The Pedlar's Pack, Hadlow, Kent.
Henry Baines, Southborough, Kent.
Jackson-Grant Antiques, Teynham, Kent.
Claremont Antiques, Tunbridge Wells, Kent.
Phoenix Antiques, Tunbridge Wells, Kent.
Up Country, Tunbridge Wells, Kent.
Kitchenalia, Longridge, Lancs.
Davies Antiques, Whalley, Lancs.
Quorn Pine and Decoratives, Quorn, Leics.
Audley House, Osbournby, Lincs.
Graham Pickett Antiques, Stamford, Lincs.
Sinclair's, Stamford, Lincs.
Holt Antique Centre, Holt, Norfolk.
Sue Miller Antiques and Collectables, Langham, Norfolk.
Antiques, West Haddon, Northants.
Paul Hopwell Antiques, West Haddon, Northants.
Horseshoe Antiques and Gallery, Burford, Oxon.
Swan Gallery, Burford, Oxon.
Bugle Antiques, Chipping Norton, Oxon.
Key Antiques, Chipping Norton, Oxon.
Dorchester Antiques, Dorchester-on-Thames, Oxon.
Wychwood Antiques, Taynton, Oxon.
Windrush Antiques, Witney, Oxon.
Witney Antiques, Witney, Oxon.
Ark Antiques, Bishop's Castle, Shrops.
Antique Corner, Ludlow, Shrops.
G. & D. Ginger Antiques, Ludlow, Shrops.
Marcus Moore Antiques, Stanton, Shrops.
Dodington Antiques, Whitchurch, Shrops.
No. 7 Antiques, Woore, Shrops.
Lansdown Antiques, Bath, Somerset.
Acorn Antiques, Dulverton, Somerset.
Gilbert & Dale, Ilchester, Somerset.
Milverton Antiques, Milverton, Somerset.
J.C. White, Milverton, Somerset.
Times Past, Somerton, Somerset.
Tilly Manor Antiques, West Harptree, Somerset.
Johnson's, Leek, Staffs.
Guillemot, Aldeburgh, Suffolk.
Mole Hall Antiques, Aldeburgh, Suffolk.
Noel Mercer Antiques, Long Melford, Suffolk.
Oswald Simpson, Long Melford, Suffolk.
Peasenhall Art and Antiques Gallery, Peasenhall, Suffolk.
Suffolk. Antique Connection, Stoke by Nayland, Suffolk.
Stubcroft Period Furnishings and Restorations, Stradbroke, Suffolk.
Suffolk. House Antiques, Yoxford, Suffolk.
Stoneycroft Farm, Betchworth, Surrey.
Cobham Galleries, Cobham, Surrey.
Christopher's Antiques, Farnham, Surrey.
Elm House Antiques, Merstham, Surrey.
Mollie Evans, Richmond, Surrey.
Anthony Welling Antiques, Ripley, Surrey.
Hadlow Down Antiques, Hadlow Down, E. Sussex.

John Bird Antiques, Lewes, E. Sussex.
Pastorale Antiques, Lewes, E. Sussex.
Graham Price Antiques Ltd, Polegate, E. Sussex.
Park View Antiques, Wadhurst, E. Sussex.
Antiquities, Arundel, W. Sussex.
Michael Wakelin and Helen Linfield, Billingshurst, W. Sussex.
Alexander Antiques, Henfield, W. Sussex.
West Street Antiques & Presents, Midhurst, W. Sussex.
Angel Antiques, Petworth, W. Sussex.
J.C. Tutt Antiques, Petworth, W. Sussex.
Down Memory Lane, Atherstone, Warks.
King's Cottage Antiques, Leamington Spa, Warks.
L.P. Antiques (Mids) Ltd, Walsall, W. Mids.
Combe Cottage Antiques, Castle Combe, Wilts.
Monkton Galleries, Hindon, Wilts.
Annmarie Turner Antiques, Marlborough, Wilts.
Ray Coggins Antiques, Westbury, Wilts.
The Antique Pine & Country Furniture Shop, Driffield, E. Yorks.
Bill Bentley, Harrogate, N. Yorks.
Elaine Phillips Antiques Ltd, Harrogate, N. Yorks.
York Cottage Antiques, Helmsley, N. Yorks.
Crambe Antioques, Malton, N. Yorks.
Northern Antiques Company, Norton, N. Yorks.
Pateley Bridge Antiques, Pateley Bridge, N. Yorks.
Roy Precious, Settle, N. Yorks.
Settle Antiques Agency, Settle, N. Yorks.
E. Thistlethwaite, Settle, N. Yorks.
Coach House Antiques, Whitby, N. Yorks.
Ruth Ford Antiques, York, N. Yorks.
Fishlake Antiques, Fishlake, S. Yorks.
Fagin & Co., Todmorden, W. Yorks.
Moyallon Antiques, Portadown, Co. Armagh, N. Ireland.
Tim Hardie Antiques, Edinburgh, Scotland.
Cwmgwili Mill, Carmarthen, Wales.
Havard and Havard, Cowbridge, Wales.
Gallop and Rivers Architectural Antiques, Crickhowell, Wales.
Michael Lloyd, Henllan, Wales.
Country Antiques (Wales), Kidwelly, Wales.
Islwyn Watkins, Knighton, Wales.
Jim and Pat Ash, Llandeilo, Wales.
Heritage Restorations, Llanfair Caereinion, Wales.
Kim Scurlock, Swansea, Wales.
Audrey Bull, Tenby, Wales.

Furniture - Georgian

Bedford plc, William, London N1.
Chapman Antiques, Peter, London N1.
Dome Antiques (Exports) Ltd, London N1.
Furniture Vault, London N1.
Gridley, Gordon, London N1.
Inheritance, London N1.
Restall Brown and Clennell Ltd, London N1.
Tapsell Antiques, London N1.
Vane House Antiques, London N1.
Finchley Fine Art Galleries, London N12.
Henham (Antiques), Martin, London N2.
Gould and Julian Gonnermann Antiques, Betty, London N6.
Regent Antiques, London NW1.
Gillingham Ltd, G. and F., London NW2.
Beckman Antiques, Patricia, London NW3.
Wainwright, David and Charles, London NW3.
Camden Art Gallery, London NW8.
Harvey Antiques and Decoration, Patricia, London NW8.
Wellington Gallery, London NW8.
Antiques Pavilion, The, London SE1.
Old Cinema Antique Warehouse, The, London SE1.
Tower Bridge Antiques, London SE1.
Junk Shop, The, London SE10.
Relcy Antiques, London SE10.
Hirschhorn, Robert E., London SE5.
Antique Warehouse, London SE8.
Anno Domini Antiques, London SW1.
Batstone Decorative Antiques, Hilary, London SW1.
Bly, John, London SW1.
Ciancimino Ltd, London SW1.
Fernandes and Marche, London SW1.
General Trading Co Ltd, London SW1.
Hamilton Ltd, Ross, London SW1.
Harrods Ltd, London SW1.
Hawksmoor, London SW1.
Hotspur Ltd, London SW1.
Howe, Christopher, London SW1.
Humphrey-Carrasco, London SW1.
Jeremy Ltd, London SW1.
Johnson, Lucy, London SW1.
Jones, Peter, London SW1.
Pairs Antiques Ltd, London SW1.
Priest Antiques, Michael, London SW1.
Tillman Ltd, William, London SW1.
Westenholz Antiques Ltd, London SW1.
Brown Antiques, Alasdair, London SW10.
Furniture Cave, The, London SW10.
Hastie, Rupert, London SW10.
Mallord Street Antiques, London SW10.
Dining Room Shop, The, London SW13.
McDonald, Joy, London SW13.
Seale Antiques, Jeremy, London SW13.
Jorgen Antiques, London SW15.
Marsh and Son, A.V., London SW15.
Baxter and Sons, H.C., London SW16.
Adams Room Antiques, London SW19.
Adams Ltd, Norman, London SW3.
Apter Fredericks Ltd, London SW3.
Courtney Ltd, Richard, London SW3.
Dickson and Lesley Rendall Antiques, Robert, London SW3.
Foster, Michael, London SW3.
Fredericks and Son, C., London SW3.
Godson and Coles, London SW3.
James and Son Ltd, Anthony, London SW3.
Keil Ltd, John, London SW3.
Lipitch Ltd, Michael, London SW3.
Lipitch Ltd, Peter, London SW3.
Pettifer Ltd, David, London SW3.
Prides of London, London SW3.
Saunders Antiques, Charles, London SW3.
Wright Antiques Ltd, Clifford, London SW3.
Antique and Modern Furniture Ltd, London SW5.
Arabesque Antiques, London SW6.
Bookham Galleries, London SW6.
Clay, John, London SW6.
Cochrane Antiques, Fergus, London SW6.
Floyd Ltd, George, London SW6.
George d'Epinois, London SW6.
HRW Antiques (London) Ltd, London SW6.
Hurford Antiques, Peter, London SW6.
King Antiques, Eric, London SW6.
Kreckovic, L. and E., London SW6.
Lewin, London SW6.
Marriott Ltd, Michael, London SW6.
Martin-Taylor Antiques, David, London SW6.
Mathers Antiques, Megan, London SW6.
Ossowski, London SW6.
Pauw Antiques, M., London SW6.
Rogers & Co, London SW6.
Toth, Ferenc, London SW6.
Vaughan, London SW6.
Blairman and Sons Ltd., H., London W1.
Cheneviere Fine Arts, Antoine, London W1.
Colefax and Fowler, London W1.
Fielden, Brian, London W1.
Fortnum and Mason plc, London W1.
Halcyon Days, London W1.
Jefferson Ltd, Patrick, London W1.
Leuchars and Jefferson, London W1.
Mallett and Son (Antiques) Ltd, London W1.
Partridge Fine Arts plc, London W1.
Pendulum of Mayfair Ltd, London W1.
Phillips Ltd, Ronald, London W1.
Scarisbrick and Bate Ltd, London W1.
Stair and Company Ltd, London W1.
Toynbee-Clarke Interiors Ltd, London W1.
Turpin Ltd, M., London W1.
Aalders, Michael, London W11.
B. and T. Antiques, London W11.
Britannia Export Antiques, London W11.
Butchoff Antiques, London W11.
Davidson, Michael, London W11.
Fox, Judy, London W11.
Lipitch Ltd, J., London W11.
Mankowitz, Daniel, London W11.
Martin Antiques, Robin, London W11.
Morse and Son Ltd, Terence, London W11.
Oakstar Ltd, London W11.
Rostrum Antiques, London W11.
Stanton, Louis, London W11.
Wainwright, David and Charles, London W11.
Weaver, Trude, London W11.
Marshall Gallery, London W14.
Aberdeen House Antiques, London W5.
Badger, The, London W5.
Terrace Antiques, London W5.
Thomson Ltd, Murray, London W6.
Bardawil, Eddy, London W8.
Barnet Antiques, London W8.
Cattanach, Anne-Marie, London W8.
Harman Antiques, Robert, London W8.
Lewis and Lloyd, London W8.
Major (Antiques) Ltd, C.H., London W8.
Reindeer Antiques Ltd, London W8.
Rolleston Antiques Ltd, Brian, London W8.
Sandberg Antiques, Patrick, London W8.
Teignmouth and Son, Pamela, London W8.
Fluss and Charlesworth Ltd, London W9.
Paris Antiques, Ampthill, Beds.
Pilgrim Antiques, Ampthill, Beds.
Guy Roe Antiques, Ampthill, Beds.
S. and S. Timms Antiques Ltd, Ampthill, Beds.
David Ball Antique Furnisher, Leighton Buzzard, Beds.
Town Hall Antiques, Woburn, Beds.
John A. Pearson Antiques, Horton, Berks.
Bow House Antiques, Hungerford, Berks.

Robert and Georgina Hastie, Hungerford, Berks.
Roger King Antiques, Hungerford, Berks.
Medalcrest Ltd, Hungerford, Berks.
The Old Malthouse, Hungerford, Berks.
Widmerpool House Antiques, Maidenhead, Berks.
Cavendish Fine Arts - Janet Middlemiss, Sonning-on-Thames, Berks.
John Connell - Wargrave Antiques, Wargrave, Berks.
Eton Antiques Partnership, Windsor and Eton, Berks.
Shirley Hayden Antiques, Windsor and Eton, Berks.
Peter J. Martin, Windsor and Eton, Berks.
Ulla Stafford Antiques, Windsor and Eton, Berks.
Times Past Antiques, Windsor and Eton, Berks.
The Cupboard Antiques, Amersham, Bucks.
June Elsworth - Beaconsfield Ltd, Beaconsfield, Bucks.
Grosvenor House Interiors, Beaconsfield, Bucks.
Period Furniture Showrooms, Beaconsfield, Bucks.
The Spinning Wheel, Beaconsfield, Bucks.
Fenlan, Olney, Bucks.
John Overland Antiques, Olney, Bucks.
Country Furniture Shop, Penn, Bucks.
Wendover Antiques, Wendover, Bucks.
Peter Norman Antiques and Restorations, Burwell, Cambs.
Jess Applin Antiques, Cambridge, Cambs.
John Beazor and Sons Ltd, Cambridge, Cambs.
Mere Antiques, Fowlmere, Cambs.
Quayside Antiques, St Ives, Cambs.
Anthony Baker Antiques, Alderley Edge, Cheshire.
Sara Frances Antiques, Alderley Edge, Cheshire.
Lostock Antiques, Altrincham, Cheshire.
David H. Dickinson, Bramhall, Cheshire.
Adams Antiques, Chester, Cheshire.
Olwyn Boustead Antiques, Chester, Cheshire.
Melody's Antique Galleries, Chester, Cheshire.
Moor Hall Antiques, Chester, Cheshire.
John Titchner & Sons, Chester, Cheshire.
Glynn Interiors, Knutsford, Cheshire.
John Titchner and Sons, Littleton, Cheshire.
The Mulberry Bush, Marple Bridge, Cheshire.
David Bedale, Mobberley, Cheshire.
Rex Boyer Antiques, Nantwich, Cheshire.
Chapel Antiques, Nantwich, Cheshire.
Wyche House Antiques, Nantwich, Cheshire.
Coppelia Antiques, Plumley, Cheshire.
Hole in the Wall Antiques, Stockport, Cheshire.
Page Antiques, Stockport, Cheshire.
Margaret Bedi Antiques, Billingham, Cleveland.
Ruby Snowden Antiques, Yarm, Cleveland.
John Bragg Antiques, Lostwithiel, Cornwall.
Ken Ashbrook Antiques, Penzance, Cornwall.
Pydar Antiques and Pine, Truro, Cornwall.
Victoria Antiques, Wadebridge, Cornwall.
Anthemion - The Antique Shop, Cartmel, Cumbria.
Anvil Antiques, Cartmel, Cumbria.
Jennywell Hall Antiques, Crosby Ravensworth, Cumbria.
Calvert Antiques, Endmoor, Cumbria.
Alexander Adamson, Kirkby Lonsdale, Cumbria.
Haughey Antiques, Kirkby Stephen, Cumbria.
Mortlake Antiques, Kirkby Stephen, Cumbria.
Townhead Antiques, Newby Bridge, Cumbria.
Winton Hall Antiques, Winton, Cumbria.
Pamela Elsom - Antiques, Ashbourne, Derbys.
Chappell's Antiques & Fine Art, Bakewell, Derbys.
Martin and Dorothy Harper Antiques, Bakewell, Derbys.
Lewis Antiques, Bakewell, Derbys.
Water Lane Antiques, Bakewell, Derbys.
Antique Exporters U.K, Brailsford, Derbys.
The Antiques Warehouse, Buxton, Derbys.
The Penny Post Antiques, Buxton, Derbys.
Hackney House Antiques, Chesterfield, Derbys.
Ian Morris, Chesterfield, Derbys.
Dragon Antiques, Duffield, Derbys.
Wayside Antiques, Duffield, Derbys.
N. and C.A. Haslam, Grassmoor, Derbys.
Shardlow Antiques Warehouse, Shardlow, Derbys.
Sam Savage Antiques, Ticknall, Derbys.
Nimbus Antiques, Whaley Bridge, Derbys.
Wooden Box Antiques, Woodville, Derbys.
Gravelly Bank Pine Antiques, Yeaveley, Derbys.
Moor Antiques, Ashburton, Devon.
J. Collins and Son, Bideford, Devon.
John Prestige Antiques, Brixham, Devon.
David J. Thorn, Budleigh Salterton, Devon.
Rex Antiques, Chagford, Devon.
Cullompton Old Tannery Antiques, Cullompton, Devon.
Mills Antiques, Cullompton, Devon.
Bramble Cross Antiques, Honiton, Devon.
Roderick Butler, Honiton, Devon.
L.J. Huggett and Son, Honiton, Devon.
Lombard Antiques, Honiton, Devon.
Pilgrim Antiques, Honiton, Devon.
Upstairs, Downstairs, Honiton, Devon.
Sextons, Kentisbeare, Devon.
W. J. Woodhams, Shaldon, Devon.
Philip Andrade, South Brent, Devon.
Extence Antiques, Teignmouth, Devon.
Bygone Days Antiques, Tiverton, Devon.
The Ark Antiques & Design, Topsham, Devon.
Past and Present, Totnes, Devon.
Anthony James Antiques, Whimple, Devon.
Colin Rhodes Antiques, Yealmpton, Devon.
Good Hope Antiques, Beaminster, Dorset.
Strowger of Blandford, Blandford Forum, Dorset.
Lionel Geneen Ltd, Bournemouth, Dorset.
Sainsburys of Bournemouth Ltd, Bournemouth, Dorset.
Peter Stebbing, Bournemouth, Dorset.
David Mack Antiques, Branksome, Dorset.
Zona Dawson Antiques, Charlton Marshall, Dorset.
Hamptons, Christchurch, Dorset.
Tower Antiques, Cranborne, Dorset.
Michael Legg Antiques, Dorchester, Dorset.
Legg of Dorchester, Dorchester, Dorset.
John Walker Antiques, Dorchester, Dorset.
Dodge and Son, Sherborne, Dorset.
Heygate Browne Antiques, Sherborne, Dorset.
Antiquatat Antiques, Wimborne Minster, Dorset.
Brown's Antiques, Barnard Castle, Durham.
Joan and David White Antiques, Barnard Castle, Durham.
Alan Ramsey Antiques, Darlington, Durham.
Eden House Antiques, West Auckland, Durham.
Revival, Abridge, Essex.
Swan Antiques, Baythorne End, Essex.
Lindsell Chairs, Coggeshall, Essex.
Dean Antiques, Colchester, Essex.
Julia Bennet (Antiques), Dunmow, Essex.
Michael Beaumont Antiques, Hempstead, Essex.
Millers Antiques Kelvedon, Kelvedon, Essex.
G.T. Ratcliff Ltd, Kelvedon, Essex.
Thomas Sykes Antiques, Kelvedon, Essex.
Richard Wrenn Antiques, Leigh-on-Sea, Essex.
Clive Beardall Antiques, Maldon, Essex.
Old Barn Antiques, Matching Green, Essex.
Stone Hall Antiques, Matching Green, Essex.
West Essex Antiques, Matching Green, Essex.
Brown House Antiques, Newport, Essex.
F.G. Bruschweiler (Antiques) Ltd, Rayleigh, Essex.
The Interior Design Shop, Saffron Walden, Essex.
Hedingham Antiques, Sible Hedingham, Essex.
W.A. Pinn and Sons, Sible Hedingham, Essex.
Barton House Antiques, Stanford-le-Hope, Essex.
Harris Antiques (Stansted), Stansted, Essex.
Linden House Antiques, Stansted, Essex.
White Roding Antiques, White Roding, Essex.
Andrew Lelliott, Avening, Glos.
Antique Corner with A & C Antique Clocks, Bristol, Glos.
Robin Butler, Bristol, Glos.
No. 74 Antiques and Collectables, Bristol, Glos.
H.W. Keil (Cheltenham) Ltd, Cheltenham, Glos.
Latchford Antiques, Cheltenham, Glos.
Triton Gallery, Cheltenham, Glos.
Swan Antiques, Chipping Campden, Glos.
Forum Antiques, Cirencester, Glos.
Hares, Cirencester, Glos.
Rankine Taylor Antiques, Cirencester, Glos.
Patrick Waldron Antiques, Cirencester, Glos.
Waterloo Antiques, Cirencester, Glos.

Bernard Weaver Antiques, Cirencester, Glos.
Blenheim Antiques, Fairford, Glos.
Mark Carter Antiques, Fairford, Glos.
A.J. Ponsford Antiques, Gloucester, Glos.
Lemington House Antiques, Moreton-in-Marsh, Glos.
Elizabeth Parker, Moreton-in-Marsh, Glos.
Anthony Sampson, Moreton-in-Marsh, Glos.
Craig Carrington Antiques, Painswick, Glos.
Acorn Antiques, Stow-on-the-Wold, Glos.
Duncan J. Baggott, Stow-on-the-Wold, Glos.
Baggott Church Street Ltd, Stow-on-the-Wold, Glos.
Colin Brand Antiques, Stow-on-the-Wold, Glos.
Christopher Clarke Antiques Ltd, Stow-on-the-Wold, Glos.
Fosse Way Antiques, Stow-on-the-Wold, Glos.
Roger Lamb Antiques & Works of Art, Stow-on-the-Wold, Glos.
Little Elms Antiques, Stow-on-the-Wold, Glos.
Antony Preston Antiques Ltd, Stow-on-the-Wold, Glos.
Priests Antiques, Stow-on-the-Wold, Glos.
Queens Parade Antiques Ltd, Stow-on-the-Wold, Glos.
Stow Antiques, Stow-on-the-Wold, Glos.
Styles of Stow, Stow-on-the-Wold, Glos.
Vanbrugh House Antiques, Stow-on-the-Wold, Glos.
Ball and Claw Antiques, Tetbury, Glos.
Breakspeare Antiques, Tetbury, Glos.
The Chest of Drawers, Tetbury, Glos.
Gales Antiques, Tetbury, Glos.
Morpheus - Elgin House, Tetbury, Glos.
Porch House Antiques, Tetbury, Glos.
Berkeley Antiques, Tewkesbury, Glos.
Gainsborough House Antiques, Tewkesbury, Glos.
Prichard Antiques, Winchcombe, Glos.
Close Antiques, Alresford, Hants.
Butterfly Pine, Botley, Hants.
Nicholas Abbott, Hartley Wintney, Hants.
Andwells, Hartley Wintney, Hants.
Antique House, Hartley Wintney, Hants.
Deva Antiques, Hartley Wintney, Hants.
David Lazarus Antiques, Hartley Wintney, Hants.
Millon Antiques, Hartley Wintney, Hants.
Phoenix Green Antiques, Hartley Wintney, Hants.
Lita Kaye of Lyndhurst, Lyndhurst, Hants.
Monaltrie Antiques, Odiham, Hants.
Cull Antiques, Petersfield, Hants.
Millers of Chelsea Antiques Ltd, Ringwood, Hants.
L. Moody, Southampton, Hants.
Elizabeth Viney, Stockbridge, Hants.
Gasson Antiques and Interiors, Tadley, Hants.
Gaylords, Titchfield, Hants.
J.W. Blanchard Ltd, Winchester, Hants.
Burns and Graham, Winchester, Hants.
Mary Roofe Antiques, Winchester, Hants.
Great Brampton House Antiques Ltd, Hereford, Herefs.
John Nash Antiques and Interiors, Ledbury, Herefs.
Serendipity, Ledbury, Herefs.
Farmers Gallery, Leominster, Herefs.
Jeffery Hammond Antiques, Leominster, Herefs.
Robson Antiques, Walford, Herefs.
Anthony Butt Antiques, Baldock, Herts.
Ralph and Bruce Moss, Baldock, Herts.
The Windhill Antiquary, Bishop's Stortford, Herts.
Michael Gander, Hitchin, Herts.
Hanbury Antiques, Hitchin, Herts.
Phillips of Hitchin (Antiques) Ltd, Hitchin, Herts.
Tom Salusbury Antiques, Hitchin, Herts.
J.N. Antiques, Redbourn, Herts.
Tim Wharton Antiques, Redbourn, Herts.
New England House Antiques, Tring, Herts.
Collins Antiques (F.G. and C. Collins Ltd.), Wheathampstead, Herts.
Michael Armson (Antiques) Ltd, Wilstone, Herts.
John Corrin Antiques, Douglas, Isle of Man.
David Barrington, Brasted, Kent.
Peter Dyke, Brasted, Kent.
Keymer Son & Co. Ltd, Brasted, Kent.
Roy Massingham Antiques, Brasted, Kent.
Tilings Antiques, Brasted, Kent.
Conquest House Antiques, Canterbury, Kent.
Chislehurst Antiques, Chislehurst, Kent.
Michael Sim, Chislehurst, Kent.
Chevertons of Edenbridge Ltd, Edenbridge, Kent.
Alan Lord Antiques, Folkestone, Kent.
John Jackson, Hythe, Kent.
Samovar Antiques, Hythe, Kent.
Deo Juvante Antiques, Rochester, Kent.
J.D. and R.M. Walters, Rolvenden, Kent.
Christopher Buck Antiques, Sandgate, Kent.
Dench Antiques, Sandgate, Kent.
Finch Antiques, Sandgate, Kent.
Michael Fitch Antiques, Sandgate, Kent.
Freeman and Lloyd Antiques, Sandgate, Kent.
James Porter Antiques, Sandwich, Kent.
Nancy Wilson, Sandwich, Kent.
Steppes Hill Farm Antiques, Stockbury, Kent.
Sutton Valence Antiques, Sutton Valence, Kent.
Flower House Antiques, Tenterden, Kent.
Garden House Antiques, Tenterden, Kent.
Sparks Antiques, Tenterden, Kent.
Jackson-Grant Antiques, Teynham, Kent.
The Pantiles Antiques, Tunbridge Wells, Kent.
Pantiles Spa Antiques, Tunbridge Wells, Kent.
Phoenix Antiques, Tunbridge Wells, Kent.
John Thompson, Tunbridge Wells, Kent.
Up Country, Tunbridge Wells, Kent.
Apollo Galleries, Westerham, Kent.
Brazil Antiques, Westerham, Kent.
Anthony J. Hook, Westerham, Kent.
London House Antiques, Westerham, Kent.
Marks Antiques, Westerham, Kent.
Taylor-Smith, Westerham, Kent.
Laurens Antiques, Whitstable, Kent.
Tankerton Antiques, Whitstable, Kent.
Silvesters, Wingham, Kent.
E.W. Webster, Bickerstaffe, Lancs.
Park Galleries Antiques, Fine Art and Decor, Bolton, Lancs.
Brun Lea Antiques (J. Waite Ltd), Burnley, Lancs.
K.C. Antiques, Darwen, Lancs.
The Baron Antiques, Manchester, Lancs.
Bulldog Antiques, Manchester, Lancs.
Luigino Vescovi, Morecambe, Lancs.
Brooks Antiques, Nelson, Lancs.
Alan Grice Antiques, Ormskirk, Lancs.
Frederick Treasure Ltd, Preston, Lancs.
S.C. Falk, Rochdale, Lancs.
Old Bakehouse Antiques and Gallery, Broughton Astley, Leics.
Withers of Leicester, Hoby, Leics.
Corry's, Leicester, Leics.
Walter Moores and Son, Leicester, Leics.
Lowe of Loughborough, Loughborough, Leics.
Abbey Antiques, Market Harborough, Leics.
J. Stamp and Sons, Market Harborough, Leics.
Ken Smith Antiques Ltd, Narborough, Leics.
David E. Burrows, Osgathorpe, Leics.
J. Green and Son, Queniborough, Leics.
Mill on the Soar Antiques Ltd, Quorn, Leics.
Paddock Antiques, Woodhouse Eaves, Leics.
Clive Underwood Antiques, Colsterworth, Lincs.
Seaview Antiques, Horncastle, Lincs.
Laurence Shaw Antiques, Horncastle, Lincs.
Staines Antiques, Horncastle, Lincs.
David J. Hansord and Son, Lincoln, Lincs.
J. and R. Ratcliffe, Lincoln, Lincs.
Harwood Tate, Market Rasen, Lincs.
Pinfold Antiques, Ruskington, Lincs.
Dawson of Stamford, Stamford, Lincs.
Graham Pickett Antiques, Stamford, Lincs.
St. George's Antiques, Stamford, Lincs.
St. Mary's Galleries, Stamford, Lincs.
Underwoodhall Antiques, Woodhall Spa, Lincs.
V.O.C. Antiques, Woodhall Spa, Lincs.
Stefani Antiques, Liverpool, Merseyside.
Colin Stock, Rainford, Merseyside.
Decor Galleries, Southport, Merseyside.
Tony and Anne Sutcliffe Antiques, Southport, Merseyside.
Yarnall Antiques, Wallasey, Merseyside.
Helen Horswill Antiques and Decorative Arts, West Kirby, Merseyside.
Kathleen Mann - The Other Shop, Harrow, Middx.
Tobias Jellinek Antiques, Twickenham, Middx.
Ivy House Antiques, Acle, Norfolk.
A.E. Bush and Partners, Attleborough, Norfolk.
M. and A. Cringle, Burnham Market, Norfolk.
Anne Hamilton Antiques, Burnham Market, Norfolk.
Market House, Burnham Market, Norfolk.
Eric Bates and Sons, Coltishall, Norfolk.
Roger Bradbury Antiques, Coltishall, Norfolk.
A.E. Seago, Cromer, Norfolk.
Anne Hamilton Antiques, East Rudham, Norfolk.
Peter Howkins, Gt. Yarmouth, Norfolk.
Peter Robinson, Heacham, Norfolk.
Arthur Brett and Sons Ltd, Norwich, Norfolk.
Nicholas Fowle Antiques, Norwich, Norfolk.

John Howkins Antiques, Norwich, Norfolk.
Echo Antiques, Reepham, Norfolk.
Leo Pratt and Son, South Walsham, Norfolk.
Stalham Antique Gallery, Stalham, Norfolk.
Norton Antiques, Twyford, Norfolk.
T.C.S. Brooke, Wroxham, Norfolk.
M.E. and J.E. Standley, Wymondham, Norfolk.
Berengar Antiques, Barnwell, Northants.
Simon Banks Antiques, Finedon, Northants.
C B Antiques, Finedon, Northants.
M.C. Chapman, Finedon, Northants.
Huntershield Antiques, Flore, Northants.
Christopher Jones at Flore House, Flore, Northants.
F. and C.H. Cave, Northampton, Northants.
The Antique Galleries, Paulerspury, Northants.
Reindeer Antiques Ltd, Potterspury, Northants.
Boadens Antiques, Hexham, Northumbs.
Hallstile Antiques, Hexham, Northumbs.
Hedley's of Hexham, Hexham, Northumbs.
James Miller Antiques, Wooler, Northumbs.
E.M. Cheshire, Bingham, Notts.
Rectory Bungalow Workshop, Elton, Notts.
Antiques and General Trading Co, Nottingham, Notts.
Meadow Lane Antiques, Nottingham, Notts.
Pegasus Antiques, Nottingham, Notts.
David and Carole Potter Antiques, Nottingham, Notts.
Strouds (of Southwell Antiques), Southwell, Notts.
Benson Antiques and Gallery, Benson, Oxon.
Ashton Gower Antiques, Burford, Oxon.
Burford Antique Centre, Burford, Oxon.
Gateway Antiques, Burford, Oxon.
Hubert's Antiques, Burford, Oxon.
Anthony Nielsen Antiques, Burford, Oxon.
David Pickup, Burford, Oxon.
Swan Gallery, Burford, Oxon.
Zene Walker, Burford, Burford, Oxon.
Rupert Hitchcox Antiques, Chalgrove, Oxon.
Georgian House Antiques, Chipping Norton, Oxon.
Hallidays (Fine Antiques) Ltd, Dorchester-on-Thames, Oxon.
The Faringdon Antique Centre, Faringdon, Oxon.
La Chaise Antique, Faringdon, Oxon.
Richard J. Kingston, Henley-on-Thames, Oxon.
The Country Seat, Huntercombe, Oxon.
Willow Antiques and The Nettlebed Antique Merchants, Nettlebed, Oxon.
Michael and Jane de Albuquerque, Wallingford, Oxon.
Chris and Lin O'Donnell Antiques, Wallingford, Oxon.
Mike Ottrey Antiques, Wallingford, Oxon.
Summers Davis Antiques Ltd, Wallingford, Oxon.
Cross Antiques, Watlington, Oxon.
Stephen Orton Antiques, Watlington, Oxon.
Mark Shanks, Watlington, Oxon.
Colin Greenway Antiques, Witney, Oxon.
Joan Wilkins Antiques, Witney, Oxon.
Windrush Antiques, Witney, Oxon.
Witney Antiques, Witney, Oxon.
Thistle House Antiques, Woodstock, Oxon.
Churchgate Antiques, Empingham, Rutland.
Old Bakery Antiques, Empingham, Rutland.
Gallery Antiques, Oakham, Rutland.
Swans, Oakham, Rutland.
T.J. Roberts, Uppingham, Rutland.
Robert Bingley Antiques, Wing, Rutland.
Doveridge House of Neachley, Albrighton (Neachley), Shrops.
Mytton Antiques, Atcham, Shrops.
D.W. and A.B. Bayliss, Ludlow, Shrops.
R.G. Cave and Sons Ltd, Ludlow, Shrops.
M. and R. Taylor (Antiques), Ludlow, Shrops.
Teme Valley Antiques, Ludlow, Shrops.
Valentyne Dawes Gallery, Ludlow, Shrops.
F.C. Manser and Son Ltd, Shrewsbury, Shrops.
Marcus Moore Antiques, Stanton, Shrops.
Brian James Antiques, Telford, Shrops.
L. Onions - White Cottage Antiques, Tern Hill, Shrops.
Dodington Antiques, Whitchurch, Shrops.
Hall's Antiques, Ash Priors, Somerset.
Alderson, Bath, Somerset.
G.A. Baines of Bath, Bath, Somerset.
Beau Nash Antiques, Bath, Somerset.
Lawrence Brass, Bath, Somerset.
Geoffrey Breeze, Bath, Somerset.
John Croft Antiques, Bath, Somerset.
Mary Cruz, Bath, Somerset.
Andrew Dando, Bath, Somerset.
Frank Dux Antiques, Bath, Somerset.
Jadis Ltd, Bath, Somerset.
Montague Antiques, Bath, Somerset.
Francis O'Dwyer Antiques, Bath, Somerset.
Quiet Street Antiques, Bath, Somerset.
T.E. Robinson, Bath, Somerset.
M.G.R. Exports, Bruton, Somerset.
J.C. Giddings, Carhampton, Somerset.
Guy Dennler Antiques, Dulverton, Somerset.
C.W.E. and R.I. Dyte Antiques, Highbridge, Somerset.
West End House Antiques, Ilminster, Somerset.
Edward A. Nowell, Wells, Somerset.
Tilly Manor Antiques, West Harptree, Somerset.
Edward Venn, Williton, Somerset.
J.C. Giddings, Wiveliscombe, Somerset.
John Hamblin, Yeovil, Somerset.
Milestone Antiques, Lichfield, Staffs.
Richard Midwinter Antiques, Newcastle-under-Lyme, Staffs.
Browse, Stafford, Staffs.
The Potteries Antique Centre, Stoke-on-Trent, Staffs.
Armson's of Yoxall Antiques, Yoxall, Staffs.
Thompson's Gallery, Aldeburgh, Suffolk.
Saltgate Antiques, Beccles, Suffolk.
Denzil Grant Antiques, Bradfield St. George, Suffolk.
Country House Antiques, Bungay, Suffolk.
Foord Antiques and Restoration, Bures, Suffolk.
Peppers Period Pieces, Bury St. Edmunds, Suffolk.
Cavendish Rose Antiques, Cavendish, Suffolk.
J. de Haan & Son, Clare, Suffolk.
F.D. Salter Antiques, Clare, Suffolk.
C. & A.C. Bigden Antiques, Debenham, Suffolk.
Ian Collins Antiques, Debenham, Suffolk.
English and Continental Antiques, Eye, Suffolk.
Randolph, Hadleigh, Suffolk.
Ashley Antiques, Ipswich, Suffolk.
Hubbard Antiques, Ipswich, Suffolk.
J. and J. Baker, Lavenham, Suffolk.
Warrens Antiques Warehouse, Leiston, Suffolk.
Roger Carling and Tess Sinclair, Long Melford, Suffolk.
Charles Antiques, Long Melford, Suffolk.
Sandy Cooke Antiques, Long Melford, Suffolk.
The Court Antiques, Long Melford, Suffolk.
Alexander Lyall Antiques, Long Melford, Suffolk.
Suthburgh Antiques, Long Melford, Suffolk.
Martlesham Antiques, Martlesham, Suffolk.
Mary Palmer Antiques, Stradbroke, Suffolk.
Stubcroft Period Furnishings and Restorations, Stradbroke, Suffolk.
Napier House Antiques, Sudbury, Suffolk.
Antique Furniture Warehouse, Woodbridge, Suffolk.
Simon Carter Gallery, Woodbridge, Suffolk.
David Gibbins Antiques, Woodbridge, Suffolk.
Hamilton Antiques, Woodbridge, Suffolk.
Anthony Hurst Antiques, Woodbridge, Suffolk.
Sarah Meysey-Thompson Antiques, Woodbridge, Suffolk.
A.G. Voss, Woodbridge, Suffolk.
J.C. Heather, Woolpit, Suffolk.
Suffolk. House Antiques, Yoxford, Suffolk.
Susan Wells Antiques, Yoxford, Suffolk.
John Anthony Antiques, Bletchingley, Surrey.
Simon Marsh, Bletchingley, Surrey.
Howard Blay Antiques, Dorking, Surrey.
Dorking Desk Shop, Dorking, Surrey.
Dorking Emporium Antiques Centre, Dorking, Surrey.
Hampshires of Dorking, Dorking, Surrey.
Harman's Antiques, Dorking, Surrey.
Harvey's Period Decor, Dorking, Surrey.
Holmwood Antiques, Dorking, Surrey.
Mayfair Antiques, Dorking, Surrey.
Norfolk House Galleries, Dorking, Surrey.
Elaine Saunderson Antiques, Dorking, Surrey.
Surrey. Antiques, Dorking, Surrey.
Thorpe and Foster Ltd, Dorking, Surrey.
West Street Antiques, Dorking, Surrey.
A. E. Booth & Son, Ewell, Surrey.
Christopher's Antiques, Farnham, Surrey.
Heytesbury Antiques, Farnham, Surrey.
Heath-Bullocks, Godalming, Surrey.
Bookham Galleries, Great Bookham, Surrey.
Bow Antiques Ltd, Haslemere, Surrey.

M. J. Bowdery, Hindhead, Surrey.
Oriel Antiques, Hindhead, Surrey.
Glencorse Antiques, Kingston-upon-Thames, Surrey.
I.O.U. (Interesting, Old & Unusual), Lingfield, Surrey.
Elm House Antiques, Merstham, Surrey.
Michael Andrews Antiques, Milford, Surrey.
F.G. Lawrence and Sons, Redhill, Surrey.
The Gallery, Reigate, Surrey.
Antique Mart, Richmond, Surrey.
The Chair Set - Antiques, Richmond, Surrey.
Hill Rise Antiques, Richmond, Surrey.
F. and T. Lawson Antiques, Richmond, Surrey.
Marryat, Richmond, Surrey.
Roderic Antiques, Richmond, Surrey.
J. Hartley Antiques Ltd, Ripley, Surrey.
Ripley Antiques, Ripley, Surrey.
Sage Antiques and Interiors, Ripley, Surrey.
Cockrell Antiques, Surbiton, Surrey.
B. M. and E. Newlove, Surbiton, Surrey.
Clifford and Roger Dade, Thames Ditton, Surrey.
Ian Caldwell, Walton-on-the-Hill and Tadworth, Surrey.
Church House Antiques, Weybridge, Surrey.
R. Saunders, Weybridge, Surrey.
Weybridge Antiques, Weybridge, Surrey.
Country Antiques, Windlesham, Surrey.
Alexandria Antiques, Brighton, E. Sussex.
Brighton Antique Wholesalers, Brighton, E. Sussex.
David Burkinshaw, Brighton, E. Sussex.
P. Carmichael, Brighton, E. Sussex.
Alan Fitchett Antiques, Brighton, E. Sussex.
Dudley Hume, Brighton, E. Sussex.
Patrick Moorhead Antiques, Brighton, E. Sussex.
Michael Norman Antiques Ltd, Brighton, E. Sussex.
Ben Ponting Antiques, Brighton, E. Sussex.
Yellow Lantern Antiques Ltd, Brighton, E. Sussex.
Dycheling Antiques, Ditchling, E. Sussex.
Aspidistra Antiques, Forest Row, E. Sussex.
Hadlow Down Antiques, Hadlow Down, E. Sussex.
John Botting Antiques, Horam, E. Sussex.
Lennox Cato, Lewes, E. Sussex.
Cliffe Gallery Antiques, Lewes, E. Sussex.
Renée and Roy Green, Lewes, E. Sussex.
The Old Mint House, Pevensey, E. Sussex.
Trade Wind, Rottingdean, E. Sussex.
Bragge and Sons, Rye, E. Sussex.
Herbert Gordon Gasson, Rye, E. Sussex.
Rye Antiques, Rye, E. Sussex.
The Old House, Seaford, E. Sussex.
Aarquebus Antiques, St. Leonards-on-Sea, E. Sussex.
Ringles Cross Antiques, Uckfield, E. Sussex.
Bygones, Angmering, W. Sussex.
Michael Wakelin and Helen Linfield, Billingshurst, W. Sussex.
Antique Shop, Chichester, W. Sussex.
Gems Antiques, Chichester, W. Sussex.
David Foord-Brown Antiques, Cuckfield, W. Sussex.
Richard Usher Antiques, Cuckfield, W. Sussex.
Hinsdale Antiques, Lindfield, W. Sussex.
N. and S. Callingham Antiques, Northchapel, W. Sussex.
Baskerville Antiques, Petworth, W. Sussex.
J. Du Cros Antiques, Petworth, W. Sussex.
Richard Gardner Antiques, Petworth, W. Sussex.
Granville Antiques, Petworth, W. Sussex.
William Hockley Antiques, Petworth, W. Sussex.
Red Lion Antiques, Petworth, W. Sussex.
T.G. Wilkinson Antiques Ltd, Petworth, W. Sussex.
J. Powell (Hove) Ltd, Portslade, W. Sussex.
Thakeham Furniture, Pulborough, W. Sussex.
Loewenthal Antiques, Tillington, W. Sussex.
Wilsons Antiques, Worthing, W. Sussex.
Ian Sharp Antiques, Tynemouth, Tyne and Wear.
Yesterdays, Leamington Spa, Warks.
The Grandfather Clock Shop, Shipston-on-Stour, Warks.
Apollo Antiques Ltd, Warwick, Warks.
Fynewood Antiques, Warwick, Warks.
Patrick and Gillian Morley Antiques, Warwick, Warks.
James Reeve, Warwick, Warks.
Don Spencer Antiques, Warwick, Warks.
Westgate Antiques, Warwick, Warks.
Ashleigh House Antiques, Birmingham, W. Mids.
Peter Clark Antiques, Birmingham, W. Mids.
Bob Harris and Sons, Antiques, Birmingham, W. Mids.
John Hubbard Antiques and Fine Art, Birmingham, W. Mids.
The Old Bakehouse, Birmingham, W. Mids.
Geoffrey Hassall Antiques, Solihull, W. Mids.
Thomas Coulborn and Sons, Sutton Coldfield, W. Mids.
Ghiberti Antiques and Fine Art, Wolverhampton, W. Mids.
Kimber & Son, Wolverhampton, W. Mids.
Martin-Quick Antiques, Wolverhampton, W. Mids.
Avon Antiques, Bradford-on-Avon, Wilts.
Mac Humble Antiques, Bradford-on-Avon, Wilts.
Moxhams Antiques, Bradford-on-Avon, Wilts.
Paul Nash Antiques, Bradford-on-Avon, Wilts.
Town and Country Antiques, Bradford-on-Avon, Wilts.
Harley Antiques, Christian Malford, Wilts.
Matthew Eden, Corsham, Wilts.
Robin Shield Antiques, Cricklade, Wilts.
Turpin's Antiques, Little Bedwyn, Wilts.
Andrew Britten Antiques, Malmesbury, Wilts.
The Antique and Book Collector, Marlborough, Wilts.
Cook of Marlborough Fine Art Ltd, Marlborough, Wilts.
Robert Kime Antiques, Marlborough, Wilts.
Alan Jaffray, Melksham, Wilts.
Rupert Gentle Antiques, Milton Lilbourne, Wilts.
Ray Best Antiques, Newton Tony, Wilts.
Victoria C - The Antique Gallery (Potterne), Potterne, Wilts.
Derek Boston Antiques, Salisbury, Wilts.
Robert Bradley, Salisbury, Wilts.
Edward Hurst Antiques, Salisbury, Wilts.
Salisbury Antiques Warehouse, Salisbury, Wilts.
Edward Marnier Antiques, Tisbury, Wilts.
Bishopstrow Antiques, Warminster, Wilts.
Obelisk Antiques, Warminster, Wilts.
A.J. Romain and Sons, Wilton, Wilts.
Barnt Green Antiques, Barnt Green, Worcs.
Fenwick and Fenwick Antiques, Broadway, Worcs.
H.W. Keil Ltd, Broadway, Worcs.
Miscellany Antiques, Great Malvern, Worcs.
Kimber & Son, Malvern Link, Worcs.
Penoyre Antiques, Pershore, Worcs.
Lower House Fine Antiques, Redditch, Worcs.
Bygones by the Cathedral, Worcester, Worcs.
Bygones (Worcester), Worcester, Worcs.
M. Lees and Sons, Worcester, Worcs.
Priory Antiques, Bridlington, E. Yorks.
David K. Hakeney Antiques, Hull, E. Yorks.
Houghton Hall Antiques, Market Weighton, E. Yorks.
Galloway Antiques, Boroughbridge, N. Yorks.
Anthony Graham Antiques, Boroughbridge, N. Yorks. .
St. James House Antiques, Boroughbridge, N. Yorks.
R.S. Wilson and Sons, Boroughbridge, N. Yorks.
Simon Greenwood Antiques, Burneston, N. Yorks.
Milestone Antiques, Easingwold, N. Yorks.
Elm Tree Antiques, Flaxton, N. Yorks.
Bernard Dickinson, Gargrave, N. Yorks.
R.N. Myers and Son, Gargrave, N. Yorks.
Armstrong, Harrogate, N. Yorks.
Bryan Bowden, Harrogate, N. Yorks.
Derbyshire Antiques Ltd, Harrogate, N. Yorks.
Garth Antiques, Harrogate, N. Yorks.
Haworth Antiques, Harrogate, N. Yorks.
David Love, Harrogate, N. Yorks.
Charles Lumb and Sons Ltd, Harrogate, N. Yorks.
Walker Galleries Ltd, Harrogate, N. Yorks.
Weatherell's of Harrogate Antiques and Fine Arts, Harrogate, N. Yorks.
Chris Wilde Antiques, Harrogate, N. Yorks.
Windmill Antiques, Harrogate, N. Yorks.
Sturman's Antiques, Hawes, N. Yorks.
Milton J. Holgate, Knaresborough, N. Yorks.
John Thompson Antiques, Knaresborough, N. Yorks.
Ings House Antiques, Linton, N. Yorks.
Trade Antiques - D.D. White, Manfield, N. Yorks.
Daleside Antiques, Markington, N. Yorks.
Aura Antiques, Masham, N. Yorks.
Sigma Antiques and Fine Art, Ripon, N. Yorks.

Browns Antiques, Scarborough, N. Yorks.
Anderson Slater Antiques, Settle, N. Yorks.
Corn Mill Antiques, Skipton, N. Yorks.
Cottage Antiques, Snainton, N. Yorks.
N.J. and C.S. Dodsworth, Spennithorne, N. Yorks.
B. Ogleby - St James' House Antiques, Thirsk, N. Yorks.
Eileen Quigley, Thirsk, N. Yorks.
Tomlinson (Antiques) Ltd. & Period Furniture Ltd, Tockwith, N. Yorks.
Garth Antiques, Whixley, N. Yorks.
Robert Morrison and Son, York, N. Yorks.
Julie Goddard Antiques, Sheffield, S. Yorks.
Peter James Antiques, Sheffield, S. Yorks.
A.E. Jameson and Co, Sheffield, S. Yorks.
Bingley Antiques, Haworth, W. Yorks.
Peter Berry Antiques, Huddersfield, W. Yorks.
Coopers of Ilkley, Ilkley, W. Yorks.
Barleycote Hall Antiques, Keighley, W. Yorks.
Geary Antiques, Leeds, W. Yorks.
Windsor House Antiques (Leeds) Ltd., Leeds, W. Yorks.
Park Antiques, Menston, W. Yorks.
The Titus Gallery, Shipley, W. Yorks.
Victoria Antiques, Alderney, Alderney, C. I.
Mark Blower Antiques, St. Martin, Guernsey, C. I.
Grange Antiques, St. Peter Port, Guernsey, C. I.
St. James's Gallery Ltd, St. Peter Port, Guernsey, C. I.
Robert Christie Antiques, Ballyclare, Co. Antrim, N. Ireland.
Dunluce Antiques, Bushmills, Co. Antrim, N. Ireland.
ParvisSigaroudinia, Lisburn, Co. Antrim, N. Ireland.
MacHenry Antiques, Newtownabbey, Co. Antrim, N. Ireland.
Furney Antiques and Interiors, Donaghadee, Co. Down, N. Ireland.
Downshire House Antiques, Newry, Co. Down, N. Ireland.
McCabe's Antique Galleries, Newry, Co. Down, N. Ireland.
Time & Tide Antiques, Portaferry, Co. Down, N. Ireland.
Antiques and Fine Art Gallery, Warrenpoint, Co. Down, N. Ireland.
Forge Antiques, Lisbellaw, Co. Fermanagh, N. Ireland.
K.O. Hagan, Claudy, Co. Londonderry, N. Ireland.
Colin Wood (Antiques) Ltd, Aberdeen, Scotland.
William Young Antiques & Fine Art, Aberdeen, Scotland.
T.W. Beaty, Beattock, Scotland.
Coldstream Antiques, Coldstream, Scotland.
The Antiquarian, Dumfries, Scotland.
Westport Fine Art, Dundee, Scotland.
Dunkeld Interiors, Dunkeld, Scotland.
Laurance Black Ltd, Edinburgh, Scotland.
Bruntsfield Antiques, Edinburgh, Scotland.
Dunedin Antiques Ltd, Edinburgh, Scotland.
Georgian Antiques, Edinburgh, Scotland.
London Road Antiques, Edinburgh, Scotland.
Stockbridge Antiques and Fine Art, Edinburgh, Scotland.
Whytock and Reid, Edinburgh, Scotland.
Aldric Young, Edinburgh, Scotland.
Greycroft Antiques, Errol, Scotland.
Gow Antiques, Forfar, Scotland.
Albany Antiques, Glasgow, Scotland.
Butler's Furniture Galleries Ltd, Glasgow, Scotland.
Muirhead Moffat and Co, Glasgow, Scotland.
C.S. Moreton (Antiques), Inchture, Scotland.
Kilmacolm Antiques Ltd, Kilmacolm, Scotland.
QS Antiques and Cabinetmakers, Kilmarnock, Scotland.
Rhudle Mill, Kilmichael Glassary, Scotland.
Miles Antiques, Kinross, Scotland.
Harper-James, Montrose, Scotland.
Newburgh Antiques, Newburgh, Scotland.
Crossroads Antiques, Prestwick, Scotland.
Waverley Antiques, Upper Largo, Scotland.
Ship Street Galleries, Brecon, Wales.
K.W. Finlay Antiques, Ciliau Aeron, Wales.
Bulmer's, Cowbridge, Wales.
Havard and Havard, Cowbridge, Wales.
Renaissance Antiques, Cowbridge, Wales.
Furn Davies Partnership, Holt, Wales.
Kidwelly Antiques, Kidwelly, Wales.
J. and R. Langford, Llangollen, Wales.
Peter Thomas Antiques, Narberth, Wales.
Castle Antiques, Newcastle Emlyn, Wales.
Water Street Antiques, Newcastle Emlyn, Wales.
Rodney Adams Antiques, Pwllheli, Wales.
Eynon Hughes Antiques, Swansea, Wales.
Barn Court Antiques, Templeton, Wales.
Clareston Antiques, Tenby, Wales.
F.E. Anderson and Son, Welshpool, Wales.

Furniture - Oak (prior to 1700)

Wainwright, David and Charles, London NW3.
Hirschhorn, Robert E., London SE5.
Johnson, Lucy, London SW1.
Furniture Cave, The, London SW10.
Young Antiques, Robert, London SW11.
McDonald, Joy, London SW13.
Apter Fredericks Ltd, London SW3.
Booth, Joanna, London SW3.
Sampson Antiques Ltd, Alistair, London W1.
Stanton, Louis, London W11.
Wainwright, David and Charles, London W11.
Fenlan, Olney, Bucks.
Pine Reflections, Princes Risborough, Bucks.
Tim Marshall Antiques, Tingewick, Bucks.
Simon and Penny Rumble Antiques, Chittering, Cambs.
Melody's Antique Galleries, Chester, Cheshire.
Peter Bunting Antiques, Hyde, Cheshire.
Adams Antiques, Nantwich, Cheshire.
Rex Boyer Antiques, Nantwich, Cheshire.
Pillory House, Nantwich, Cheshire.
Hole in the Wall Antiques, Stockport, Cheshire.
Oak Room, Stockport, Cheshire.
Anvil Antiques, Cartmel, Cumbria.
Maggie Tallentire Antiques, Cartmel, Cumbria.
Langley Antiques, Corby Hill, Cumbria.
Jennywell Hall Antiques, Crosby Ravensworth, Cumbria.
Kendal Studios Antiques, Kendal, Cumbria.
Shire Antiques, Newby Bridge, Cumbria.
Antiques of Penrith, Penrith, Cumbria.
Winton Hall Antiques, Winton, Cumbria.
Beedham Antiques Ltd, Bakewell, Derbys.
Michael Goldstone, Bakewell, Derbys.
Robert Byles, Bampton, Devon.
Rex Antiques, Chagford, Devon.
Cullompton Old Tannery Antiques, Cullompton, Devon.
Wickham Antiques, Honiton, Devon.
Alan Jones Antiques, Okehampton, Devon.
Colystock Antiques, Stockland, Devon.
Colin Rhodes Antiques, Yealmpton, Devon.
Brown's Antiques, Barnard Castle, Durham.
The Collector, Barnard Castle, Durham.
Grant's Antiques, Barnard Castle, Durham.
Julia Bennet (Antiques), Dunmow, Essex.
C. and J. Mortimer and Son, Great Chesterford, Essex.
Michael Beaumont Antiques, Hempstead, Essex.
Millers Antiques Kelvedon, Kelvedon, Essex.
Freemans Antiques, Roxwell, Essex.
Lennard Antiques, Sible Hedingham, Essex.
Andrew Lelliott, Avening, Glos.
Robin Butler, Bristol, Glos.
J. and R. Bateman Antiques, Chalford, Glos.
School House Antiques, Chipping Campden, Glos.
Swan Antiques, Chipping Campden, Glos.
William H. Stokes, Cirencester, Glos.
Woodminster Antiques, Cirencester, Glos.
Mark Carter Antiques, Fairford, Glos.
Gloucester House Antiques Ltd, Fairford, Glos.
Duncan J. Baggott, Stow-on-the-Wold, Glos.
J. and J. Caspall Antiques, Stow-on-the-Wold, Glos.
Keith Hockin (Antiques) Ltd, Stow-on-the-Wold, Glos.
Priests Antiques, Stow-on-the-Wold, Glos.
Arthur Seager Antiques, Stow-on-the-Wold, Glos.
Day Antiques, Tetbury, Glos.
Westwood House Antiques, Tetbury, Glos.
Close Antiques, Alresford, Hants.
Quatrefoil, Fordingbridge, Hants.
Cedar Antiques Limited, Hartley Wintney, Hants.
Elizabeth Viney, Stockbridge, Hants.
P. and S.N. Eddy, Leominster, Herefs.
Hubbard Antiques, Leominster, Herefs.
Robin Lloyd Antiques, Ross-on-Wye, Herefs.
Singleton Antiques, Ross-on-Wye, Herefs.
M. and J. Russell, Yazor, Herefs.
Dobson's Antiques, Abbots Langley, Herts.
Tim Wharton Antiques, Redbourn, Herts.
Collins Antiques (F.G. and C. Collins Ltd.), Wheathampstead, Herts.
R. Kirby Antiques, Acrise, Kent.
Dinah Stoodley, Brasted, Kent.

Michael Pearson Antiques, Canterbury, Kent.
Douglas Bryan, Cranbrook, Kent.
Old English Oak, Sandgate, Kent.
Henry Baines, Southborough, Kent.
Jackson-Grant Antiques, Teynham, Kent.
Cowden Antiques, Tunbridge Wells, Kent.
The Baron Antiques, Manchester, Lancs.
Lowe of Loughborough, Loughborough, Leics.
Robin Cox Antiques, Ketton, Lincs.
J. and R. Ratcliffe, Lincoln, Lincs.
Audley House, Osbournby, Lincs.
Sinclair's, Stamford, Lincs.
St. Mary's Galleries, Stamford, Lincs.
Tobias Jellinek Antiques, Twickenham, Middx.
Pearse Lukies, Aylsham, Norfolk.
Arthur Brett and Sons Ltd, Norwich, Norfolk.
Nick Goodwin Exports, Guilsborough, Northants.
Doric Antiques, Upper Boddington, Northants.
Paul Hopwell Antiques, West Haddon, Northants.
E.M. Cheshire, Bingham, Notts.
Antiques and General Trading Co, Nottingham, Notts.
Horseshoe Antiques and Gallery, Burford, Oxon.
Anthony Nielsen Antiques, Burford, Oxon.
Swan Gallery, Burford, Oxon.
Bugle Antiques, Chipping Norton, Oxon.
Key Antiques, Chipping Norton, Oxon.
Willow Antiques and The Nettlebed Antique Merchants, Nettlebed, Oxon.
Windrush Antiques, Witney, Oxon.
Witney Antiques, Witney, Oxon.
G. & D. Ginger Antiques, Ludlow, Shrops.
Marcus Moore Antiques, Stanton, Shrops.
L. Onions - White Cottage Antiques, Tern Hill, Shrops.
Stuart Interiors (Antiques) Ltd, Barrington, Somerset.
Lawrence Brass, Bath, Somerset.
Frank Dux Antiques, Bath, Somerset.
Milverton Antiques, Milverton, Somerset.
Times Past, Somerton, Somerset.
Tilly Manor Antiques, West Harptree, Somerset.
Barry M. Sainsbury, Wincanton, Somerset.
John Nicholls, Leigh, Staffs.
Richard Midwinter Antiques, Newcastle-under-Lyme, Staffs.
Denzil Grant Antiques, Bradfield St. George, Suffolk.
Peppers Period Pieces, Bury St. Edmunds, Suffolk.
C. & A.C. Bigden Antiques, Debenham, Suffolk.
Ian Collins Antiques, Debenham, Suffolk.
J. and J. Baker, Lavenham, Suffolk.
Noel Mercer Antiques, Long Melford, Suffolk.
Oswald Simpson, Long Melford, Suffolk.
Suthburgh Antiques, Long Melford, Suffolk.
Trident Antiques, Long Melford, Suffolk.
Simon Carter Gallery, Woodbridge, Suffolk.
Hamilton Antiques, Woodbridge, Suffolk.
Anthony Hurst Antiques, Woodbridge, Suffolk.
Suffolk. House Antiques, Yoxford, Suffolk.
Stoneycroft Farm, Betchworth, Surrey.
Howard Blay Antiques, Dorking, Surrey.
Sage Antiques and Interiors, Ripley, Surrey.
Anthony Welling Antiques, Ripley, Surrey.
B. M. and E. Newlove, Surbiton, Surrey.
R. Saunders, Weybridge, Surrey.
E. and B. White, Brighton, E. Sussex.
Graham Lower, Flimwell, E. Sussex.
Herbert Gordon Gasson, Rye, E. Sussex.
Rye Antiques, Rye, E. Sussex.
Monarch Antiques, St. Leonards-on-Sea, E. Sussex.
John H. Yorke Antiques, St. Leonards-on-Sea, E. Sussex.
Park View Antiques, Wadhurst, E. Sussex.
L.E. Lampard and Sons, Horsham, W. Sussex.
Down Memory Lane, Atherstone, Warks.
King's Cottage Antiques, Leamington Spa, Warks.
The Grandfather Clock Shop, Shipston-on-Stour, Warks.
James Reeve, Warwick, Warks.
Mac Humble Antiques, Bradford-on-Avon, Wilts.
Monkton Galleries, Hindon, Wilts.
Turpin's Antiques, Little Bedwyn, Wilts.
A.J. Romain and Sons, Wilton, Wilts.
H.W. Keil Ltd, Broadway, Worcs.
R.N. Myers and Son, Gargrave, N. Yorks.
Bill Bentley, Harrogate, N. Yorks.
Derbyshire Antiques Ltd, Harrogate, N. Yorks.
Elaine Phillips Antiques Ltd, Harrogate, N. Yorks.
York Cottage Antiques, Helmsley, N. Yorks.
Pateley Bridge Antiques, Pateley Bridge, N. Yorks.
Roy Precious, Settle, N. Yorks.
Coach House Antiques, Whitby, N. Yorks.
Joan Frere Antiques, Drumnadrochit, Scotland.
Strathspey Gallery, Grantown-on-Spey, Scotland.
Cwmgwili Mill, Carmarthen, Wales.
Peter Thomas Antiques, Narberth, Wales.

Furniture - Pine

Rupert's Antiques, London E18.
At the Sign of the Chest of Drawers, London N1.
Islington Antiques, London N1.
Lewis Antiques, Michael, London N1.
Rookery Farm Antiques, London N1.
Trader Antiques, London N13.
Home to Home, London N6.
This and That (Furniture), London NW1.
Main Street Antiques, London SE10.
Under Milkwood, London SE24.
Abbott Antiques and Country Pine, London SE26.
Furniture Cave, The, London SW10.
Remember When, London SW13.
Yesterday's Antiques, London SW14.
Woodentops Country Furniture, London SW18.
Bishops Park Antiques, London SW6.
Old Pine and Painted Furniture, London SW6.
Pine Mine (Crewe-Read Antiques), The, London SW6.
Beech Antiques, Nicholas, London SW8.
Andy's All Pine, London W14.
Old Dairy, The, London W4.
Antique Pine Ltd, London W5.
Terrace Antiques, London W5.
The Pine Parlour, Ampthill, Beds.
Willow Farm Pine Centre, Harlington, Beds.
Alan Hodgson, Great Shefford, Berks.
Ivy House Antiques, Great Shefford, Berks.
T. Smith, Chalfont St. Giles, Bucks.
For Pine, Chesham, Bucks.
The Pine Merchants, Great Missenden, Bucks.
Bach Antiques, Lane End, Bucks.
Jack Harness Antiques, Marlow, Bucks.
Pine Antiques, Olney, Bucks.
Pine Reflections, Princes Risborough, Bucks.
Tingewick Antiques Centre, Tingewick, Bucks.
Cambridge Pine, Bottisham, Cambs.
Abbey Antiques, Ramsey, Cambs.
The Edge Antiques, Alderley Edge, Cheshire.
Richmond Galleries, Chester, Cheshire.
Pine Too, Congleton, Cheshire.
Steven Blackhurst, Crewe, Cheshire.
Chapel Antiques, Nantwich, Cheshire.
Antiques and Curios, Ravensmoor, Cheshire.
Pine and Period Furniture, Grampound, Cornwall.
Pinewood Studios, Penzance, Cornwall.
Blackwater Pine Antiques, Truro, Cornwall.
Pydar Antiques and Pine, Truro, Cornwall.
Ben Eggleston Antiques, Long Marton, Cumbria.
Utopia Antiques Ltd, Low Newton, Cumbria.
The Barn, Buxton, Derbys.
Friargate Pine and Antiques Centre, Derby, Derbys.
Tanglewood, Derby, Derbys.
Pine Antiques Workshop, Doveridge, Derbys.
Michael Allcroft Antiques, Hayfield, Derbys.
Wooden Box Antiques, Woodville, Derbys.
Gravelly Bank Pine Antiques, Yeaveley, Derbys.
W.G. Potter and Son, Axminster, Devon.
Robert Byles, Bampton, Devon.
Petticombe Manor Antiques, Bideford, Devon.
Cobweb Antiques, Cullompton, Devon.
Cullompton Old Tannery Antiques, Cullompton, Devon.
G. Mounter, Dulford, Devon.
The Old Dairy - Antiques & Bygones, Honiton, Devon.
Annterior Antiques, Plymouth, Devon.
Colystock Antiques, Stockland, Devon.
King Street Curios, Tavistock, Devon.
Barrington Antiques, Tiverton, Devon.
Fine Pine Antiques, Totnes, Devon.
Antiques and Furnishings, Bournemouth, Dorset.
Victorian Parlour, Bournemouth, Dorset.
Hardy Country, Melbury Osmond, Dorset.
Overhill Antique and Old Pine Warehouse, Poole, Dorset.
Pine on the Green, Sherborne, Dorset.
Hay Green Antiques, Blackmore, Essex.
English Rose Antiques, Coggeshall, Essex.

Partners in Pine, Coggeshall, Essex.
Dean Antiques, Colchester, Essex.
The Stores, Great Waltham, Essex.
Churchgate Antiques, Sible Hedingham, Essex.
Fox and Pheasant Antique Pine, White Colne, Essex.
Denzil Verey, Barnsley, Glos.
Oldwoods, Bristol, Glos.
Relics - Pine Furniture, Bristol, Glos.
Bed of Roses, Cheltenham, Glos.
John P. Townsend, Cheltenham, Glos.
Campden Country Pine Antiques, Chipping Campden, Glos.
Waterloo Antiques, Cirencester, Glos.
Europa Antiques, Moreton-in-Marsh, Glos.
Ronson's Architectural Effects, Norton, Glos.
Kelly Antiques, Rodley, Glos.
Country Homes, Tetbury, Glos.
Morpheus - Elgin House, Tetbury, Glos.
Pinecrafts, Bishops Waltham, Hants.
Butterfly Pine, Botley, Hants.
C.W. Buckingham, Cadnam, Hants.
Bakers Country Furniture, Crawley, Hants.
Airdale Antiques, Hartley Wintney, Hants.
Burgess Farm Antiques, Morestead, Hants.
Smith & Sons, Ringwood, Hants.
The Pine Cellars, Winchester, Hants.
Old Pine Shop, Walford, Herefs.
Dobson's Antiques, Abbots Langley, Herts.
Country Life Antiques, Bushey, Herts.
Frenches Farm Antiques, King's Langley, Herts.
Galerias Segui, Cowes, Isle of Wight.
Harriet Ann Sleigh Beds, Biddenden, Kent.
Antique and Design, Canterbury, Kent.
Pine and Things, Canterbury, Kent.
Penny Lampard, Headcorn, Kent.
Traditional Pine Furniture, Hythe, Kent.
Old English Pine, Sandgate, Kent.
Claremont Antiques, Tunbridge Wells, Kent.
Richard Moate Antiques, Woodchurch, Kent.
Treasures of Woodchurch, Woodchurch, Kent.
Ann and Peter Christian, Blackpool, Lancs.
Enloc Antiques, Colne, Lancs.
Kitchenalia, Longridge, Lancs.
Pine Antiques, St. Annes-on-Sea, Lancs.
House Things Antiques, Hinckley, Leics.
Victoriana Architectural, Long Cawston, Leics.
Country Pine Antiques, Market Bosworth, Leics.
Abbey Antiques, Market Harborough, Leics.
Richard Kimbell Ltd, Market Harborough, Leics.
David E. Burrows, Osgathorpe, Leics.
Quorn Pine and Decoratives, Quorn, Leics.
R. A. James Antiques, Sileby, Leics.
Robert J. Kent Antiques, Frampton West, Lincs.
Bell Antiques, Grimsby, Lincs.
Kate, Hemswell Cliff, Lincs.
Moor Pine, North Kelsey Moor, Lincs.
Andrew Thomas, Stamford, Lincs.
Allens Antiques - Pine Furniture, Stapleford, Lincs.
Richard Kimbell, Enfield, Middx.
Valtone Pine, Hampton, Middx.
Earsham Hall Pine, Earsham, Norfolk.
Heathfield Antiques, Holt, Norfolk.
Heathfield Country Pine, Holt, Norfolk.
Holt Antique Centre, Holt, Norfolk.
M.D. Cannell Antiques, Raveningham, Norfolk.
Echo Antiques, Reepham, Norfolk.
Nick Goodwin Exports, Guilsborough, Northants.
Laila Gray Antiques, Kingsthorpe, Northants.
The Country Pine Shop, West Haddon, Northants.
The Corner Cupboard, Woodford Halse, Northants.
Bailiffgate Antique Pine, Alnwick, Northumbs.
Haydon Bridge Antiques, Haydon Bridge, Northumbs.
Ministeracres Pine & Oak, Ministeracres, Northumbs.
Jack Spratt Antiques, Newark, Notts.
Harlequin Antiques, Nottingham, Notts.
Tuckers Country Store and Art Gallery, Deddington, Oxon.
Aston Pine Antiques, Faringdon, Oxon.
The Faringdon Antique Centre, Faringdon, Oxon.
Ark Antiques, Bishop's Castle, Shrops.
St. George's Antiques, Telford, Shrops.
Lansdown Antiques, Bath, Somerset.
Pennard House Antiques, Bath, Somerset.
Antique and Country Pine, Crewkerne, Somerset.
Hennessy, Crewkerne, Somerset.
Pennard House, East Pennard, Somerset.
Westville House Antiques, Littleton, Somerset.
Milverton Antiques, Milverton, Somerset.
Bay Tree House Antiques, Weston-Super-Mare, Somerset.
Burton Antiques, Burton-on-Trent, Staffs.
Justin Pinewood Ltd, Burton-on-Trent, Staffs.
Country Cottage Interiors, Kingsley, Staffs.
Anvil Antiques Ltd, Leek, Staffs.
Gemini Trading, Leek, Staffs.
Roger Haynes - Antiques Finder, Leek, Staffs.
Johnson's, Leek, Staffs.
Guillemot, Aldeburgh, Suffolk.
Joyce Hardy Pine and Country Furniture, Hacheston, Suffolk.
Orwell Pine Co Ltd, Ipswich, Suffolk.
Carlton Road Antiques, Lowestoft, Suffolk.
Mildenhall Antiques, Mildenhall, Suffolk.
House of Christian, Ash Vale, Surrey.
Cherub Antiques, Carshalton, Surrey.
Cherub Antiques, Mitcham, Surrey.
The Packhouse, Runfold, Surrey.
Yesterdays Pine, Shere, Surrey.
Euro-Pine, Sutton, Surrey.
Chancellor's Church Furnishings, Walton-on-Thames, Surrey.
Richard Kimbell Antiques, Windlesham, Surrey.
The Venture, Woking, Surrey.
Hadlow Down Antiques, Hadlow Down, E. Sussex.
John Bird Antiques, Lewes, E. Sussex.
Cliffe Gallery Antiques, Lewes, E. Sussex.
Bob Hoare Pine Antiques, Lewes, E. Sussex.
Pastorale Antiques, Lewes, E. Sussex.
Graham Price Antiques Ltd, Polegate, E. Sussex.
Ann Lingard - Rope Walk Antiques, Rye, E. Sussex.
Park View Antiques, Wadhurst, E. Sussex.
Antiquities, Arundel, W. Sussex.
English Interiors, Balcombe, W. Sussex.
Squire's Pantry Pine and Antiques, Cowfold, W. Sussex.
Red Lion Antiques, Petworth, W. Sussex.
Stewart Antiques, Petworth, W. Sussex.
Northumbria Pine, Whitley Bay, Tyne and Wear.
Cottage Pine Antiques, Brinklow, Warks.
Hague Antiques, Leamington Spa, Warks.
Pine and Things, Shipston-on-Stour, Warks.
The Old Bakehouse, Birmingham, W. Mids.
Tudor House Antiques, Halesowen, W. Mids.
North Wilts Exporters, Brinkworth, Wilts.
Crudwell Furniture, Crudwell, Wilts.
Pillars Antiques, Lyneham, Wilts.
Cross Hayes Antiques, Malmesbury, Wilts.
Sambourne House Antiques, Minety, Wilts.
Ray Coggins Antiques, Westbury, Wilts.
St. James Antiques, Little Malvern, Worcs.
Antique Warehouse, Worcester, Worcs.
Antiques and Pine, Worcester, Worcs.
The Antique Pine & Country Furniture Shop, Driffield, E. Yorks.
Imperial Antiques, Hull, E. Yorks.
Pieter Plantenga, Market Weighton, E. Yorks.
L.L. Ward and Son, Brandsby, N. Yorks.
Country Pine Antiques, Brompton, N. Yorks.
Heathcote Antiques, Cross Hills, N. Yorks.
Fox's Antique Pine, Easingwold, N. Yorks.
Milestone Antiques, Easingwold, N. Yorks.
The Main Pine Co, Green Hammerton, N. Yorks.
Michael Green Traditional Interiors, Harrogate, N. Yorks.
Havelocks, Harrogate, N. Yorks.
Westway Pine, Helmsley, N. Yorks.
The Emporium, Knaresborough, N. Yorks.
Daleside Antiques, Markington, N. Yorks.
Kindon Antiques Ltd, Melmerby, N. Yorks.
Northern Antiques Company, Norton, N. Yorks.
Settle Antiques Agency, Settle, N. Yorks.
Ruth Ford Antiques, York, N. Yorks.
St. John Antiques, York, N. Yorks.
Fishlake Antiques, Fishlake, S. Yorks.
Farmhouse Antiques, Great Houghton, S. Yorks.
A Maze of Pine and Roses, Mapplewell, S. Yorks.
Peter James Antiques, Sheffield, S. Yorks.
Sheffield Pine Centre (inc. Canterbury Place Antiques), Sheffield, S. Yorks.
Aberford Antiques Ltd, Aberford, W. Yorks.
Manor Barn, Addingham, W. Yorks.
Cottingley Antiques, Bradford, W. Yorks.
K.L.M. & Co. Antiques, Lepton, W. Yorks.
Cottage Antiques, Pontefract, W. Yorks.
Memory Lane, Sowerby Bridge, W. Yorks.
Cottage Antiques (1984) Ltd, Walsden, W. Yorks.

The Pine Collection, St. Peter Port, Guernsey, C. I.
Hearth and Home, Belfast, N. Ireland.
Moyallon Antiques, Portadown, Co. Armagh, N. Ireland.
Herbert Gould and Co., Holywood, Co. Down, N. Ireland.
K.O. Hagan, Claudy, Co. Londonderry, N. Ireland.
Homes, Pubs and Clubs, Coleraine, Co. Londonderry, N. Ireland.
Times Past Antiques, Auchterarder, Scotland.
London Road Antiques, Edinburgh, Scotland.
West of Scotland Antique Centre Ltd, Glasgow, Scotland.
QS Antiques and Cabinetmakers, Kilmarnock, Scotland.
Old Pine Furniture and Jouet, Kiltarlity, Scotland.
Mostly Pine, Kingussie, Scotland.
Alton House Antiques, Moffat, Scotland.
Abbey Antiques, Stirling, Scotland.
The Furniture Cave, Aberystwyth, Wales.
Back to the Wood, Cardiff, Wales.
Heritage Antiques and Stripped Pine, Cardiff, Wales.
The Pot Board, Carmarthen, Wales.
Pine Corner Antiques, Haverfordwest, Wales.
Barn Antiques, Lampeter, Wales.
Jim and Pat Ash, Llandeilo, Wales.
Heritage Restorations, Llanfair Caereinion, Wales.
R. and S. M. Percival Antiques, Ruthin, Wales.
Kim Scurlock, Swansea, Wales.
Granny Midge's Emporium, Wrexham, Wales.

Furniture - Victorian (1830-1901) (see also Shipping Furniture and Period Furniture to the Trade)

Blake - Old Cottage Antiques, P., London E11.
Georgina's Antiques, London E17.
Bushwood Antiques, London N1.
Chapman Antiques, Peter, London N1.
Dome Antiques (Exports) Ltd, London N1.
Furniture Vault, London N1.
Graham Gallery, The, London N1.
Inheritance, London N1.
Newland Antiques, Chris, London N1.
Restall Brown and Clennell Ltd, London N1.
Ross Antiques, Marcus, London N1.
Finchley Fine Art Galleries, London N12.
Gould and Julian Gonnermann Antiques, Betty, London N6.
Home to Home, London N6.
Crouch End Antiques, London N8.
Solomon, London N8.
Regent Antiques, London NW1.
Gillingham Ltd, G. and F., London NW2.
Beckman Antiques, Patricia, London NW3.
Wainwright, David and Charles, London NW3.
Camden Art Gallery, London NW8.
Just Desks, London NW8.
Wellington Gallery, London NW8.
Antique Warehouse, London SE1.
Antiques Pavilion, The, London SE1.
Oola Boola Antiques London, London SE1.
Tower Bridge Antiques, London SE1.
Junk Shop, The, London SE10.
Relcy Antiques, London SE10.
Whitfield Antiques, Robert, London SE10.
Allen Antiques Ltd. World Wide Antique Exporters, Peter, London SE15.
Black Cat, The, London SE20.
Abbott Antiques and Country Pine, London SE26.
Ward Antiques, London SE7.
Antique Warehouse, London SE8.
Batstone Decorative Antiques, Hilary, London SW1.
Bly, John, London SW1.
General Trading Co Ltd, London SW1.
Hamilton Ltd, Ross, London SW1.
Harrods Ltd, London SW1.
Hawksmoor, London SW1.
Hotopf Antiques, William, London SW1.
Howe, Christopher, London SW1.
Humphrey-Carrasco, London SW1.
Lewis, M. and D., London SW1.
McClenaghan, London SW1.
Pairs Antiques Ltd, London SW1.
Westenholz Antiques Ltd, London SW1.
Brown Antiques, Alasdair, London SW10.
Overmantels, London SW11.
Seale Antiques, Jeremy, London SW13.
Fowle, A. and J., London SW16.
Chelsea Bric-a-Brac Shop Ltd, London SW19.
Prides of London, London SW3.
Antique and Modern Furniture Ltd, London SW5.
275 Antiques, London SW6.
Arabesque Antiques, London SW6.
Clay, John, London SW6.
Cochrane Antiques, Fergus, London SW6.
Edwards, Christopher, London SW6.
HRW Antiques (London) Ltd, London SW6.
King Antiques, Eric, London SW6.
Kreckovic, L. and E., London SW6.
Lewin, London SW6.
Martin-Taylor Antiques, David, London SW6.
Mathers Antiques, Megan, London SW6.
Rogers & Co, London SW6.
Alan Ltd, Adrian, London W1.
Arenski, London W11.
Barham, P.R., London W11.
Barham Antiques, London W11.
Benchmark, London W11.
Britannia Export Antiques, London W11.
Fox, Judy, London W11.
Graham and Green, London W11.
Lewis, M. and D., London W11.
Morse and Son Ltd, Terence, London W11.
Myriad Antiques, London W11.
Wainwright, David and Charles, London W11.
Weaver, Trude, London W11.
Quest Antiques, London W13.
Marshall Gallery, London W14.
Craven Gallery, London W2.
Edge, Jacqueline, London W2.
Old Dairy, The, London W4.
Aberdeen House Antiques, London W5.
Badger, The, London W5.
Terrace Antiques, London W5.
Thomson Ltd, Murray, London W6.
Alan Ltd, Adrian, London W8.
Harman Antiques, Robert, London W8.
Haslam and Whiteway, London W8.
Lewis and Lloyd, London W8.
Teignmouth and Son, Pamela, London W8.
Paris Antiques, Ampthill, Beds.
Pilgrim Antiques, Ampthill, Beds.
Guy Roe Antiques, Ampthill, Beds.
S. and S. Timms Antiques Ltd, Ampthill, Beds.
David Ball Antique Furnisher, Leighton Buzzard, Beds.
J. Denton (Antiques), Luton, Beds.
Manor Antiques, Wilstead (Wilshamstead), Beds.
Town Hall Antiques, Woburn, Beds.
Bow House Antiques, Hungerford, Berks.
Roger King Antiques, Hungerford, Berks.
Medalcrest Ltd, Hungerford, Berks.
Hill Farm Antiques, Leckhampstead, Berks.
Widmerpool House Antiques, Maidenhead, Berks.
John Connell - Wargrave Antiques, Wargrave, Berks.
Addrison Bros, Windsor and Eton, Berks.
Eton Antiques Partnership, Windsor and Eton, Berks.
Shirley Hayden Antiques, Windsor and Eton, Berks.
Peter J. Martin, Windsor and Eton, Berks.
Times Past Antiques, Windsor and Eton, Berks.
The Cupboard Antiques, Amersham, Bucks.
June Elsworth - Beaconsfield Ltd, Beaconsfield, Bucks.
Period Furniture Showrooms, Beaconsfield, Bucks.
The Spinning Wheel, Beaconsfield, Bucks.
Fenlan, Olney, Bucks.
John Overland Antiques, Olney, Bucks.
Robin Unsworth Antiques, Olney, Bucks.
Country Furniture Shop, Penn, Bucks.
Tingewick Antiques Centre, Tingewick, Bucks.
Jess Applin Antiques, Cambridge, Cambs.
Comberton Antiques, Comberton, Cambs.
Mere Antiques, Fowlmere, Cambs.
Sydney House Antiques, Wansford, Cambs.
Sara Frances Antiques, Alderley Edge, Cheshire.
Lostock Antiques, Altrincham, Cheshire.
Olwyn Boustead Antiques, Chester, Cheshire.
Moor Hall Antiques, Chester, Cheshire.
John Titchner & Sons, Chester, Cheshire.
W. Buckley Antiques Exports, Congleton, Cheshire.
Glynn Interiors, Knutsford, Cheshire.
John Titchner and Sons, Littleton, Cheshire.
The Mulberry Bush, Marple Bridge, Cheshire.
Rex Boyer Antiques, Nantwich, Cheshire.
Chapel Antiques, Nantwich, Cheshire.
Wyche House Antiques, Nantwich, Cheshire.
Coppelia Antiques, Plumley, Cheshire.
Antiques Import Export UK, Stockport, Cheshire.
Hole in the Wall Antiques, Stockport, Cheshire.
Limited Editions, Stockport, Cheshire.
Page Antiques, Stockport, Cheshire.
Margaret Bedi Antiques, Billingham, Cleveland.
John Bragg Antiques, Lostwithiel, Cornwall.

Ken Ashbrook Antiques, Penzance, Cornwall.
Pydar Antiques and Pine, Truro, Cornwall.
Victoria Antiques, Wadebridge, Cornwall.
Pink Cottage Antiques, Widegates, Cornwall.
Anthemion - The Antique Shop, Cartmel, Cumbria.
Calvert Antiques, Endmoor, Cumbria.
Haughey Antiques, Kirkby Stephen, Cumbria.
Mortlake Antiques, Kirkby Stephen, Cumbria.
Chappell's Antiques & Fine Art, Bakewell, Derbys.
Water Lane Antiques, Bakewell, Derbys.
The Antiques Warehouse, Buxton, Derbys.
Maggie Mays, Buxton, Derbys.
The Penny Post Antiques, Buxton, Derbys.
Hackney House Antiques, Chesterfield, Derbys.
Ian Morris, Chesterfield, Derbys.
Wayside Antiques, Duffield, Derbys.
N. and C.A. Haslam, Grassmoor, Derbys.
Sam Savage Antiques, Ticknall, Derbys.
Wooden Box Antiques, Woodville, Derbys.
Gravelly Bank Pine Antiques, Yeaveley, Derbys.
Moor Antiques, Ashburton, Devon.
Petticombe Manor Antiques, Bideford, Devon.
John Prestige Antiques, Brixham, Devon.
Mills Antiques, Cullompton, Devon.
Pennies, Exeter, Devon.
Bramble Cross Antiques, Honiton, Devon.
House of Antiques, Honiton, Devon.
L.J. Huggett and Son, Honiton, Devon.
Lombard Antiques, Honiton, Devon.
Upstairs, Downstairs, Honiton, Devon.
Pugh's Farm Antiques, Monkton, Devon.
W. J. Woodhams, Shaldon, Devon.
Philip Andrade, South Brent, Devon.
Bygone Days Antiques, Tiverton, Devon.
The Ark Antiques & Design, Topsham, Devon.
Great Western Antiques, Torquay, Devon.
Past and Present, Totnes, Devon.
Anthony James Antiques, Whimple, Devon.
Woodbury Antiques, Woodbury, Devon.
Colin Rhodes Antiques, Yealmpton, Devon.
Richard Dunton Antiques, Bournemouth, Dorset.
Victorian Chairman, Bournemouth, Dorset.
David Mack Antiques, Branksome, Dorset.
Zona Dawson Antiques, Charlton Marshall, Dorset.
Hamptons, Christchurch, Dorset.
Tower Antiques, Cranborne, Dorset.
Michael Legg Antiques, Dorchester, Dorset.
Heygate Browne Antiques, Sherborne, Dorset.
Joan and David White Antiques, Barnard Castle, Durham.
Nichol and Hill, Darlington, Durham.
Alan Ramsey Antiques, Darlington, Durham.
Eden House Antiques, West Auckland, Durham.
Revival, Abridge, Essex.
Swan Antiques, Baythorne End, Essex.
Hay Green Antiques, Blackmore, Essex.
Nicholas Salter Antiques, Chingford, Essex.
Argentum Antiques, Coggeshall, Essex.
Lindsell Chairs, Coggeshall, Essex.
Argyll House Antiques, Felsted, Essex.
John Burls, Great Oakley, Essex.
Michael Beaumont Antiques, Hempstead, Essex.
Flowers Antiques, Ilford, Essex.
Colton Antiques, Kelvedon, Essex.
Tilly's Antiques, Leigh-on-Sea, Essex.
Clive Beardall Antiques, Maldon, Essex.
Old Barn Antiques, Matching Green, Essex.
Stone Hall Antiques, Matching Green, Essex.
West Essex Antiques, Matching Green, Essex.
Brown House Antiques, Newport, Essex.
F.G. Bruschweiler (Antiques) Ltd, Rayleigh, Essex.
Bush Antiques, Saffron Walden, Essex.
The Interior Design Shop, Saffron Walden, Essex.
Hedingham Antiques, Sible Hedingham, Essex.
Harris Antiques (Stansted), Stansted, Essex.
Linden House Antiques, Stansted, Essex.
It's About Time, Westcliff-on-Sea, Essex.
White Roding Antiques, White Roding, Essex.
Antique Corner with A & C Antique Clocks, Bristol, Glos.
Bristol Guild of Applied Art Ltd, Bristol, Glos.
No. 74 Antiques and Collectables, Bristol, Glos.
Latchford Antiques, Cheltenham, Glos.
Past & Present, Cheltenham, Glos.
Swan Antiques, Chipping Campden, Glos.
E.C. Legg and Son, Cirencester, Glos.
Patrick Waldron Antiques, Cirencester, Glos.
Mark Carter Antiques, Fairford, Glos.
Berry Antiques, Moreton-in-Marsh, Glos.
Grimes House Antiques & Fine Art, Moreton-in-Marsh, Glos.
Lemington House Antiques, Moreton-in-Marsh, Glos.
Elizabeth Parker, Moreton-in-Marsh, Glos.
Acorn Antiques, Stow-on-the-Wold, Glos.
Christopher Clarke Antiques Ltd, Stow-on-the-Wold, Glos.
Queens Parade Antiques Ltd, Stow-on-the-Wold, Glos.
Styles of Stow, Stow-on-the-Wold, Glos.
Ball and Claw Antiques, Tetbury, Glos.
Balmuir House Antiques, Tetbury, Glos.
The Chest of Drawers, Tetbury, Glos.
Porch House Antiques, Tetbury, Glos.
Berkeley Antiques, Tewkesbury, Glos.
Butterfly Pine, Botley, Hants.
Antique House, Hartley Wintney, Hants.
Phoenix Green Antiques, Hartley Wintney, Hants.
Plestor Barn Antiques, Liss, Hants.
Charles Wallrock - Wick Antiques, Lymington, Hants.
Affordable Antiques, Portsmouth, Hants.
The Gallery, Portsmouth, Hants.
L. Moody, Southampton, Hants.
Gasson Antiques and Interiors, Tadley, Hants.
Gaylords, Titchfield, Hants.
J.W. Blanchard Ltd, Winchester, Hants.
Cabbages & Kings, Winchester, Hants.
Warings of Hereford Antiques, Hereford, Herefs.
John Nash Antiques and Interiors, Ledbury, Herefs.
Serendipity, Ledbury, Herefs.
Jeffery Hammond Antiques, Leominster, Herefs.
Anthony Butt Antiques, Baldock, Herts.
Hanbury Antiques, Hitchin, Herts.
Phillips of Hitchin (Antiques) Ltd, Hitchin, Herts.
Tom Salusbury Antiques, Hitchin, Herts.
J.N. Antiques, Redbourn, Herts.
New England House Antiques, Tring, Herts.
Collins Antiques (F.G. and C. Collins Ltd.), Wheathampstead, Herts.
Michael Armson (Antiques) Ltd, Wilstone, Herts.
John Corrin Antiques, Douglas, Isle of Man.
Royal Standard Antiques, Cowes, Isle of Wight.
Hayter's, Ryde, Isle of Wight.
Courtyard Antiques, Brasted, Kent.
Peter Dyke, Brasted, Kent.
Keymer Son & Co. Ltd, Brasted, Kent.
Roy Massingham Antiques, Brasted, Kent.
Graham Stead Antiques and Reference Books, Brasted, Kent.
Conquest House Antiques, Canterbury, Kent.
Chislehurst Antiques, Chislehurst, Kent.
Chevertons of Edenbridge Ltd, Edenbridge, Kent.
Lawton's Antiques, Folkestone, Kent.
Alan Lord Antiques, Folkestone, Kent.
John Jackson, Hythe, Kent.
Samovar Antiques, Hythe, Kent.
Charles International Antiques, Maidstone, Kent.
Newnham Court Antiques, Maidstone, Kent.
Northfleet Hill Antiques, Northfleet, Kent.
Deo Juvante Antiques, Rochester, Kent.
J.D. and R.M. Walters, Rolvenden, Kent.
Dench Antiques, Sandgate, Kent.
Finch Antiques, Sandgate, Kent.
Michael Fitch Antiques, Sandgate, Kent.
Nancy Wilson, Sandwich, Kent.
Steppes Hill Farm Antiques, Stockbury, Kent.
Colin Wilson Antiques, Sundridge, Kent.
Sparks Antiques, Tenterden, Kent.
Kentdale Restorations, Tunbridge Wells, Kent.
Linden Park Antiques, Tunbridge Wells, Kent.
The Pantiles Antiques, Tunbridge Wells, Kent.
Pantiles Spa Antiques, Tunbridge Wells, Kent.
Phoenix Antiques, Tunbridge Wells, Kent.
Up Country, Tunbridge Wells, Kent.
Brazil Antiques, Westerham, Kent.
Anthony J. Hook, Westerham, Kent.
Marks Antiques, Westerham, Kent.
Taylor-Smith, Westerham, Kent.
Laurens Antiques, Whitstable, Kent.
Tankerton Antiques, Whitstable, Kent.
Silvesters, Wingham, Kent.
Brun Lea Antiques (J. Waite Ltd), Burnley, Lancs.
Folly Antiques, Clitheroe, Lancs.
Cottage Antiques, Darwen, Lancs.

K.C. Antiques, Darwen, Lancs.
L. Booth Antiques and Reproductions, Freckleton, Lancs.
The Baron Antiques, Manchester, Lancs.
Bulldog Antiques, Manchester, Lancs.
Premiere Antiques, Manchester, Lancs.
Prestwich Antiques Ltd, Manchester, Lancs.
Luigino Vescovi, Morecambe, Lancs.
Brooks Antiques, Nelson, Lancs.
The Odd Chair Company, Preston, Lancs.
Frederick Treasure Ltd, Preston, Lancs.
Carrcross Gallery, Scarisbrick, Lancs.
House Things Antiques, Hinckley, Leics.
Withers of Leicester, Hoby, Leics.
Corry's, Leicester, Leics.
Walter Moores and Son, Leicester, Leics.
Abbey Antiques, Market Harborough, Leics.
J. Stamp and Sons, Market Harborough, Leics.
Ken Smith Antiques Ltd, Narborough, Leics.
J. Green and Son, Queniborough, Leics.
Mill on the Soar Antiques Ltd, Quorn, Leics.
Paddock Antiques, Woodhouse Eaves, Leics.
Clive Underwood Antiques, Colsterworth, Lincs.
Pilgrims Antiques Centre, Gainsborough, Lincs.
Grantham Furniture Emporium, Grantham, Lincs.
Seaview Antiques, Horncastle, Lincs.
Laurence Shaw Antiques, Horncastle, Lincs.
Staines Antiques, Horncastle, Lincs.
C. and K.E. Dring, Lincoln, Lincs.
Graham Pickett Antiques, Stamford, Lincs.
Sinclair's, Stamford, Lincs.
St. George's Antiques, Stamford, Lincs.
The Antique Shop, Sutton Bridge, Lincs.
Underwoodhall Antiques, Woodhall Spa, Lincs.
V.O.C. Antiques, Woodhall Spa, Lincs.
Stefani Antiques, Liverpool, Merseyside.
Colin Stock, Rainford, Merseyside.
Decor Galleries, Southport, Merseyside.
Tony and Anne Sutcliffe Antiques, Southport, Merseyside.
Yarnall Antiques, Wallasey, Merseyside.
Kathleen Mann - The Other Shop, Harrow, Middx.
Ivy House Antiques, Acle, Norfolk.
A.E. Bush and Partners, Attleborough, Norfolk.
Brancaster Staithe Antiques, Brancaster Staithe, Norfolk.
Brockdish Antiques, Brockdish, Norfolk.
M. and A. Cringle, Burnham Market, Norfolk.
Eric Bates and Sons, Coltishall, Norfolk.
A.E. Seago, Cromer, Norfolk.
Peter Howkins, Gt. Yarmouth, Norfolk.
Peter Robinson, Heacham, Norfolk.
Norfolk Galleries, King's Lynn, Norfolk.
Old Coach House, Long Stratton, Norfolk.
Eric Bates and Sons, North Walsham, Norfolk.
Nicholas Fowle Antiques, Norwich, Norfolk.
John Howkins Antiques, Norwich, Norfolk.
Echo Antiques, Reepham, Norfolk.
Leo Pratt and Son, South Walsham, Norfolk.
Stalham Antique Gallery, Stalham, Norfolk.
Jubilee Antiques, Tottenhill, Norfolk.
M.E. and J.E. Standley, Wymondham, Norfolk.
Brackley Antiques, Brackley, Northants.
Aspidistra Antiques, Finedon, Northants.
Simon Banks Antiques, Finedon, Northants.
F. and C.H. Cave, Northampton, Northants.
The Corner Cupboard, Woodford Halse, Northants.
Haydon Bridge Antiques, Haydon Bridge, Northumbs.
Boadens Antiques, Hexham, Northumbs.
Hallstile Antiques, Hexham, Northumbs.
Hedley's of Hexham, Hexham, Northumbs.
James Miller Antiques, Wooler, Northumbs.
Blacksmiths Forge, Balderton, Notts.
Rectory Bungalow Workshop, Elton, Notts.
Fair Deal Antiques, Mansfield, Notts.
Harlequin Antiques, Nottingham, Notts.
Meadow Lane Antiques, Nottingham, Notts.
David and Carole Potter Antiques, Nottingham, Notts.
Strouds (of Southwell Antiques), Southwell, Notts.
Benson Antiques and Gallery, Benson, Oxon.
Ashton Gower Antiques, Burford, Oxon.
Burford Antique Centre, Burford, Oxon.
Gateway Antiques, Burford, Oxon.
Hubert's Antiques, Burford, Oxon.
Anthony Nielsen Antiques, Burford, Oxon.
David Pickup, Burford, Oxon.
Zene Walker, Burford, Burford, Oxon.
Rupert Hitchcox Antiques, Chalgrove, Oxon.
Georgian House Antiques, Chipping Norton, Oxon.
Hallidays (Fine Antiques) Ltd, Dorchester-on-Thames, Oxon.
The Faringdon Antique Centre, Faringdon, Oxon.
La Chaise Antique, Faringdon, Oxon.
Richard J. Kingston, Henley-on-Thames, Oxon.
The Country Seat, Huntercombe, Oxon.
Willow Antiques and
The Nettlebed Antique Merchants, Nettlebed, Oxon.
Michael and Jane de Albuquerque, Wallingford, Oxon.
Chris and Lin O'Donnell Antiques, Wallingford, Oxon.
Cross Antiques, Watlington, Oxon.
Stephen Orton Antiques, Watlington, Oxon.
Mark Shanks, Watlington, Oxon.
Colin Greenway Antiques, Witney, Oxon.
Joan Wilkins Antiques, Witney, Oxon.
Bees Antiques, Woodstock, Oxon.
Thistle House Antiques, Woodstock, Oxon.
Old Bakery Antiques, Empingham, Rutland.
Gallery Antiques, Oakham, Rutland.
Swans, Oakham, Rutland.
T.J. Roberts, Uppingham, Rutland.
Robert Bingley Antiques, Wing, Rutland.
Doveridge House of Neachley, Albrighton (Neachley), Shrops.
Mytton Antiques, Atcham, Shrops.
Hodnet Antiques, Hodnet, Shrops.
D.W. and A.B. Bayliss, Ludlow, Shrops.
M. and R. Taylor (Antiques), Ludlow, Shrops.
Valentyne Dawes Gallery, Ludlow, Shrops.
F.C. Manser and Son Ltd, Shrewsbury, Shrops.
Roushill Antiques Warehouse, Shrewsbury, Shrops.
Brian James Antiques, Telford, Shrops.
Hall's Antiques, Ash Priors, Somerset.
The Antiques Warehouse, Bath, Somerset.
Geoffrey Breeze, Bath, Somerset.
Mary Cruz, Bath, Somerset.
Kingsley Gallery, Bath, Somerset.
Montague Antiques, Bath, Somerset.
Francis O'Dwyer Antiques, Bath, Somerset.
M.G.R. Exports, Bruton, Somerset.
J.C. Giddings, Carhampton, Somerset.
Guy Dennler Antiques, Dulverton, Somerset.
C.W.E. and R.I. Dyte Antiques, Highbridge, Somerset.
West End House Antiques, Ilminster, Somerset.
Selwoods, Taunton, Somerset.
Tilly Manor Antiques, West Harptree, Somerset.
John Hamblin, Yeovil, Somerset.
Gilligans Antiques, Leek, Staffs.
Milestone Antiques, Lichfield, Staffs.
Richard Midwinter Antiques, Newcastle-under-Lyme, Staffs.
Browse, Stafford, Staffs.
Manor Court Antiques, Stoke-on-Trent, Staffs.
The Potteries Antique Centre, Stoke-on-Trent, Staffs.
Old Chapel Antique & Collectables Centre, Tutbury, Staffs.
Thompson's Gallery, Aldeburgh, Suffolk.
Saltgate Antiques, Beccles, Suffolk.
Country House Antiques, Bungay, Suffolk.
Peppers Period Pieces, Bury St. Edmunds, Suffolk.
Cavendish Rose Antiques, Cavendish, Suffolk.
J. de Haan & Son, Clare, Suffolk.
C. & A.C. Bigden Antiques, Debenham, Suffolk.
English and Continental Antiques, Eye, Suffolk.
Halesworth Antiques Market, Halesworth, Suffolk.
A. Abbott Antiques, Ipswich, Suffolk.
Ashley Antiques, Ipswich, Suffolk.
Ixworth Antiques, Ixworth, Suffolk.
Warrens Antiques Warehouse, Leiston, Suffolk.
Roger Carling and Tess Sinclair, Long Melford, Suffolk.
Charles Antiques, Long Melford, Suffolk.
The Court Antiques, Long Melford, Suffolk.
Alexander Lyall Antiques, Long Melford, Suffolk.
Carlton Road Antiques, Lowestoft, Suffolk.
Mildenhall Antiques, Mildenhall, Suffolk.
Mary Palmer Antiques, Stradbroke, Suffolk.
Napier House Antiques, Sudbury, Suffolk.
Hamilton Antiques, Woodbridge, Suffolk.

Anthony Hurst Antiques, Woodbridge, Suffolk.
Lambert's Barn, Woodbridge, Suffolk.
A.G. Voss, Woodbridge, Suffolk.
J.C. Heather, Woolpit, Suffolk.
Wrentham Antiques, Wrentham, Suffolk.
Susan Wells Antiques, Yoxford, Suffolk.
House of Christian, Ash Vale, Surrey.
Dorking Desk Shop, Dorking, Surrey.
Dorking Emporium Antiques Centre, Dorking, Surrey.
Harman's Antiques, Dorking, Surrey.
Harvey's Period Decor, Dorking, Surrey.
Holmwood Antiques, Dorking, Surrey.
Mayfair Antiques, Dorking, Surrey.
Surrey. Antiques, Dorking, Surrey.
West Street Antiques, Dorking, Surrey.
A. E. Booth & Son, Ewell, Surrey.
The Antiques Warehouse, Farnham, Surrey.
Christopher's Antiques, Farnham, Surrey.
Bookham Galleries, Great Bookham, Surrey.
Bow Antiques Ltd, Haslemere, Surrey.
M. J. Bowdery, Hindhead, Surrey.
Oriel Antiques, Hindhead, Surrey.
Glencorse Antiques, Kingston-upon-Thames, Surrey.
I.O.U. (Interesting, Old & Unusual), Lingfield, Surrey.
Elm House Antiques, Merstham, Surrey.
Michael Andrews Antiques, Milford, Surrey.
F.G. Lawrence and Sons, Redhill, Surrey.
The Gallery, Reigate, Surrey.
Antique Mart, Richmond, Surrey.
Hill Rise Antiques, Richmond, Surrey.
Marryat, Richmond, Surrey.
Roderic Antiques, Richmond, Surrey.
Sage Antiques and Interiors, Ripley, Surrey.
Cockrell Antiques, Surbiton, Surrey.
B. M. and E. Newlove, Surbiton, Surrey.
Brocante, Weybridge, Surrey.
Church House Antiques, Weybridge, Surrey.
Olde Forge Antiques, Weybridge, Surrey.
Weybridge Antiques, Weybridge, Surrey.
Country Antiques, Windlesham, Surrey.
Bexhill Antique Exporters, Bexhill-on-Sea, E. Sussex.
The Old Mint House, Bexhill-on-Sea, E. Sussex.
Alexandria Antiques, Brighton, E. Sussex.
Ashton's Antiques, Brighton, E. Sussex.
Brighton Antique Wholesalers, Brighton, E. Sussex.
P. Carmichael, Brighton, E. Sussex.
Alan Fitchett Antiques, Brighton, E. Sussex.
Dudley Hume, Brighton, E. Sussex.
Patrick Moorhead Antiques, Brighton, E. Sussex.
Ben Ponting Antiques, Brighton, E. Sussex.
Ruddy Antiques, Brighton, E. Sussex.
Dycheling Antiques, Ditchling, E. Sussex.
Timothy Partridge Antiques, Eastbourne, E. Sussex.
Aspidistra Antiques, Forest Row, E. Sussex.
Hadlow Down Antiques, Hadlow Down, E. Sussex.
Coach House Antiques, Hastings, E. Sussex.
John Botting Antiques, Horam, E. Sussex.
Cliffe Gallery Antiques, Lewes, E. Sussex.
The Old Mint House, Pevensey, E. Sussex.
Graham Price Antiques Ltd, Polegate, E. Sussex.
Trade Wind, Rottingdean, E. Sussex.
Rye Antiques, Rye, E. Sussex.
The Old House, Seaford, E. Sussex.
Aarquebus Antiques, St. Leonards-on-Sea, E. Sussex.
Nicholas Cole Antiques, St Leonards-on-Sea, E. Sussex.
Bygones, Angmering, W. Sussex.
Peter Francis Antiques, Arundel, W. Sussex.
Richard Usher Antiques, Cuckfield, W. Sussex.
Keith Atkinson Antiques, East Grinstead, W. Sussex.
Hinsdale Antiques, Lindfield, W. Sussex.
N. and S. Callingham Antiques, Northchapel, W. Sussex.
Baskerville Antiques, Petworth, W. Sussex.
J. Du Cros Antiques, Petworth, W. Sussex.
Richard Gardner Antiques, Petworth, W. Sussex.
Red Lion Antiques, Petworth, W. Sussex.
J. Powell (Hove) Ltd, Portslade, W. Sussex.
Wilsons Antiques, Worthing, W. Sussex.
Renaissance Antiques, Tynemouth, Tyne and Wear.
Ian Sharp Antiques, Tynemouth, Tyne and Wear.
Down Memory Lane, Atherstone, Warks.
Yesterdays, Leamington Spa, Warks.
Tim Harrison Wholesale Exports, Stratford-upon-Avon, Warks.
Apollo Antiques Ltd, Warwick, Warks.
Fynewood Antiques, Warwick, Warks.
John Goodwin and Sons, Warwick, Warks.
Patrick and Gillian Morley Antiques, Warwick, Warks.
James Reeve, Warwick, Warks.
Don Spencer Antiques, Warwick, Warks.
Archives, Birmingham, W. Mids.
Peter Clark Antiques, Birmingham, W. Mids.
Bob Harris and Sons, Antiques, Birmingham, W. Mids.
John Hubbard Antiques and Fine Art, Birmingham, W. Mids.
The Old Bakehouse, Birmingham, W. Mids.
Nicholas Green's Antiques, Coventry, W. Mids.
Retro Products, Lye, W. Mids.
Geoffrey Hassall Antiques, Solihull, W. Mids.
Brett Wilkins Antiques, Wednesbury, W. Mids.
Golden Oldies, Wolverhampton, W. Mids.
Kimber & Son, Wolverhampton, W. Mids.
Martin Taylor Antiques, Wolverhampton, W. Mids.
Mac Humble Antiques, Bradford-on-Avon, Wilts.
Calne Antiques, Calne, Wilts.
Robin Shield Antiques, Cricklade, Wilts.
Andrew Britten Antiques, Malmesbury, Wilts.
Cross Hayes Antiques, Malmesbury, Wilts.
The Antique and Book Collector, Marlborough, Wilts.
Cook of Marlborough Fine Art Ltd, Marlborough, Wilts.
Alan Jaffray, Melksham, Wilts.
Ray Best Antiques, Newton Tony, Wilts.
Derek Boston Antiques, Salisbury, Wilts.
Salisbury Antiques Warehouse, Salisbury, Wilts.
Edward Marnier Antiques, Tisbury, Wilts.
Bishopstrow Antiques, Warminster, Wilts.
Isabella Antiques, Warminster, Wilts.
Obelisk Antiques, Warminster, Wilts.
K. and A. Welch, Warminster, Wilts.
Barnt Green Antiques, Barnt Green, Worcs.
Carlton Antiques, Great Malvern, Worcs.
Miscellany Antiques, Great Malvern, Worcs.
S.W. Antiques, Pershore, Worcs.
Lower House Fine Antiques, Redditch, Worcs.
Antiques and Interiors, Worcester, Worcs.
M. Lees and Sons, Worcester, Worcs.
Priory Antiques, Bridlington, E. Yorks.
David K. Hakeney Antiques, Hull, E. Yorks.
Houghton Hall Antiques, Market Weighton, E. Yorks.
Penny Farthing Antiques, North Cave, E. Yorks.
The Old Copper Shop and Post House Antiques, South Cave, E. Yorks.
Galloway Antiques, Boroughbridge, N. Yorks.
Anthony Graham Antiques, Boroughbridge, N. Yorks. .
St. James House Antiques, Boroughbridge, N. Yorks.
R.S. Wilson and Sons, Boroughbridge, N. Yorks.
Simon Greenwood Antiques, Burneston, N. Yorks.
Milestone Antiques, Easingwold, N. Yorks.
Elm Tree Antiques, Flaxton, N. Yorks.
Garth Antiques, Harrogate, N. Yorks.
Haworth Antiques, Harrogate, N. Yorks.
David Love, Harrogate, N. Yorks.
Chris Wilde Antiques, Harrogate, N. Yorks.
Windmill Antiques, Harrogate, N. Yorks.
Sturman's Antiques, Hawes, N. Yorks.
Norwood House Antiques, Killinghall, N. Yorks.
Milton J. Holgate, Knaresborough, N. Yorks.
Reflections, Knaresborough, N. Yorks.
John Thompson Antiques, Knaresborough, N. Yorks.
Ings House Antiques, Linton, N. Yorks.
Trade Antiques - D.D. White, Manfield, N. Yorks.
Sigma Antiques and Fine Art, Ripon, N. Yorks.
Browns Antiques, Scarborough, N. Yorks.
Anderson Slater Antiques, Settle, N. Yorks.
Corn Mill Antiques, Skipton, N. Yorks.
B. Ogleby - St James' House Antiques, Thirsk, N. Yorks.
Eileen Quigley, Thirsk, N. Yorks.
Farmhouse Antiques, Great Houghton, S. Yorks.
Fulwood Antiques and The Basement Gallery, Sheffield, S. Yorks.
Julie Goddard Antiques, Sheffield, S. Yorks.
Peter James Antiques, Sheffield, S. Yorks.
N.P. and A. Salt Antiques, Sheffield, S. Yorks.

Paul Ward Antiques, Sheffield, S. Yorks.
Aberford Antiques Ltd, Aberford, W. Yorks.
Joan's Antiques, Denby Dale, W. Yorks.
Bingley Antiques, Haworth, W. Yorks.
Peter Berry Antiques, Huddersfield, W. Yorks.
Barleycote Hall Antiques, Keighley, W. Yorks.
The Antique Exchange, Leeds, W. Yorks.
Geary Antiques, Leeds, W. Yorks.
Windsor House Antiques (Leeds) Ltd., Leeds, W. Yorks.
Park Antiques, Menston, W. Yorks.
The Titus Gallery, Shipley, W. Yorks.
Victoria Antiques, Alderney, Alderney, C. I.
St. James's Gallery Ltd, St. Peter Port, Guernsey, C. I.
The Country Antiques, Antrim, Co. Antrim, N. Ireland.
Robert Christie Antiques, Ballyclare, Co. Antrim, N. Ireland.
Charlotte and John Lambe, Belfast, N. Ireland.
Dunluce Antiques, Bushmills, Co. Antrim, N. Ireland.
ParvisSigaroudinia, Lisburn, Co. Antrim, N. Ireland.
Moyallon Antiques, Portadown, Co. Armagh, N. Ireland.
Downshire House Antiques, Newry, Co. Down, N. Ireland.
McCabe's Antique Galleries, Newry, Co. Down, N. Ireland.
Time & Tide Antiques, Portaferry, Co. Down, N. Ireland.
Antiques and Fine Art Gallery, Warrenpoint, Co. Down, N. Ireland.
Forge Antiques, Lisbellaw, Co. Fermanagh, N. Ireland.
K.O. Hagan, Claudy, Co. Londonderry, N. Ireland.
Colin Wood (Antiques) Ltd, Aberdeen, Scotland.
William Young Antiques & Fine Art, Aberdeen, Scotland.
Highland Antiques, Avoch, Scotland.
Mansfield Antiques, Ayr, Scotland.
T.W. Beaty, Beattock, Scotland.
Coldstream Antiques, Coldstream, Scotland.
The Antiquarian, Dumfries, Scotland.
Westport Fine Art, Dundee, Scotland.
Dunkeld Antiques, Dunkeld, Scotland.
Dunkeld Interiors, Dunkeld, Scotland.
Laurance Black Ltd, Edinburgh, Scotland.
Bruntsfield Antiques, Edinburgh, Scotland.
Alan Day Antiques, Edinburgh, Scotland.
Dunedin Antiques Ltd, Edinburgh, Scotland.
Georgian Antiques, Edinburgh, Scotland.
Tim Hardie Antiques, Edinburgh, Scotland.
London Road Antiques, Edinburgh, Scotland.
Whytock and Reid, Edinburgh, Scotland.
Young Antiques, Edinburgh, Scotland.
Pringle Antiques, Fochabers, Scotland.
Gow Antiques, Forfar, Scotland.
Albany Antiques, Glasgow, Scotland.
Butler's Furniture Galleries Ltd, Glasgow, Scotland.
Kilmacolm Antiques Ltd, Kilmacolm, Scotland.
QS Antiques and Cabinetmakers, Kilmarnock, Scotland.
Rhudle Mill, Kilmichael Glassary, Scotland.
Miles Antiques, Kinross, Scotland.
Newburgh Antiques, Newburgh, Scotland.
A.S. Deuchar and Son, Perth, Scotland.
Strachan Antiques, Pollokshields, Scotland.
Crossroads Antiques, Prestwick, Scotland.
The Furniture Cave, Aberystwyth, Wales.
Ship Street Galleries, Brecon, Wales.
Plough House Interiors, Chepstow, Wales.
K.W. Finlay Antiques, Ciliau Aeron, Wales.
North Wales Antiques - Colwyn Bay, Colwyn Bay, Wales.
Havard and Havard, Cowbridge, Wales.
Renaissance Antiques, Cowbridge, Wales.
Furn Davies Partnership, Holt, Wales.
Kidwelly Antiques, Kidwelly, Wales.
Barn Antiques, Lampeter, Wales.
Jeremiah Antiques, Llandissilio, Wales.
Collinge Antiques, Llandudno Junction, Wales.
J. and R. Langford, Llangollen, Wales.
Castle Antiques, Newcastle Emlyn, Wales.
Water Street Antiques, Newcastle Emlyn, Wales.
R. and S. M. Percival Antiques, Ruthin, Wales.
Eynon Hughes Antiques, Swansea, Wales.
Kim Scurlock, Swansea, Wales.
Barn Court Antiques, Templeton, Wales.
Clareston Antiques, Tenby, Wales.
All Old Exports Ltd., Treherbert, Wales.
Steven Evans Antiques, Treorchy, Wales.
Romantiques, Trevor, Wales.

Garden Furniture, Ornaments & Statuary

London Architectural Salvage & Supply Co. (LASSCo), The, London EC2.
Westland & Company, London EC2.
Gridley, Gordon, London N1.
House of Steel Antiques, London N1.
Edwards, Charles, London SW6.
Pauw Antiques, M., London SW6.
Mallett at Bourdon House Ltd, London W1.
Myriad Antiques, London W11.
Seago, London SW1.
Napier Ltd, Sylvia, London SW6.
Teger Trading and Bushe Antiques, London N4.
Old Cinema Antique Warehouse, The, London SE1.
Batstone Decorative Antiques, Hilary, London SW1.
Wainwright, David and Charles, London NW3.
275 Antiques, London SW6.
Bridgwater, David, London W9.
Cheshire Brick and Slate Co, Tarvin Sands, Cheshire.
The Great Northern Architectural Antique Company Ltd, Tattenhall, Cheshire.
Haughey Antiques, Kirkby Stephen, Cumbria.
Townhead Antiques, Newby Bridge, Cumbria.
Talisman, Gillingham, Dorset.
Wiffen's Antiques, Parkstone, Dorset.
The Collector, Barnard Castle, Durham.
I. Westrope, Birdbrook, Essex.
Julia Bennet (Antiques), Dunmow, Essex.
Ronson's Architectural Effects, Norton, Glos.
Duncan J. Baggott, Stow-on-the-Wold, Glos.
Architectural Heritage, Taddington, Glos.
Jardinique, Greatham, Hants.
Jimmy Warren Antiques, Littlebourne, Kent.
Folly Antiques, Clitheroe, Lancs.
Crowther of Syon Lodge Ltd, Isleworth, Middx.
Berengar Antiques, Barnwell, Northants.
Reindeer Antiques Ltd, Potterspury, Northants.
The Country Seat, Huntercombe, Oxon.
Willow Antiques and
The Nettlebed Antique Merchants, Nettlebed, Oxon.
John Garner, Uppingham, Rutland.
David Bridgwater, Bath, Somerset.
Walcot Reclamation, Bath, Somerset.
Drummonds of Bramley Architectural Antiques Ltd, Bramley, Surrey.
Heath-Bullocks, Godalming, Surrey.
Sweerts de Landas, Ripley, Surrey.
The Packhouse, Runfold, Surrey.
Brighton Architectural Salvage, Brighton, E. Sussex.
Dermot and Jill Palmer Antiques, Brighton, E. Sussex.
John Bird Antiques, Lewes, E. Sussex.
Lennox Cato, Lewes, E. Sussex.
Architectural Antiques of Moseley, Birmingham, W. Mids.
The Old Bakehouse, Birmingham, W. Mids.
Matthew Eden, Corsham, Wilts.
Holloways, Suckley, Worcs.
White House Farm Antiques, Easingwold, N. Yorks.

Glass

Ketley Antiques, Carol, London N1.
Highgate Antiques, London N6.
Magus Antiques, London NW8.
Wilkinson plc, London SE6.
Galerie Moderne Ltd, London SW1.
Hotopf Antiques, William, London SW1.
Sattin Ltd, Gerald, London SW1.
Bridge, Christine, London SW13.
Dining Room Shop, The, London SW13.
Barnes Antiques, R.A., London SW15.
West - Cobb Antiques Ltd, Mark J., London SW19.
Burne (Antique Glass) Ltd, W.G.T., London SW20.
Newby (A.J. & M.V. Waller), H.W., London SW8.
Goode and Co (London) Ltd, Thomas, London W1.
Sheppard Ltd, Christopher, London W1.
Wilkinson plc, London W1.
Harbottle, Patricia, London W11.
Mercury Antiques, London W11.
Phillips and Sons, E.S., London W11.
Tomkinson Stained Glass, London W11.
Craven Gallery, London W2.
Denton Antiques, London W8.
Hayhurst Fine Glass, Jeanette, London W8.
Peter Shepherd Antiques, Hurst, Berks.
Cavendish Fine Arts - Janet Middlemiss, Sonning-on-Thames, Berks.
Berks Antiques Co Ltd, Windsor and Eton, Berks.
Antiques, Marazion, Cornwall.
Brownside Coach House, Alston, Cumbria.
Alexander Adamson, Kirkby Lonsdale, Cumbria.

Elizabeth and Son, Ulverston, Cumbria.
Martin and Dorothy Harper Antiques, Bakewell, Derbys.
Mary Payton Antiques, Chagford, Devon.
A & D Antiques, Blandford Forum, Dorset.
Peter Stebbing, Bournemouth, Dorset.
Quarterjack Antiques, Sturminster Newton, Dorset.
Richard Wrenn Antiques, Leigh-on-Sea, Essex.
Robin Butler, Bristol, Glos.
Potter's Antiques and Coins, Bristol, Glos.
Latchford Antiques, Cheltenham, Glos.
Rankine Taylor Antiques, Cirencester, Glos.
Grimes House Antiques & Fine Art, Moreton-in-Marsh, Glos.
Acorn Antiques, Stow-on-the-Wold, Glos.
Denys Sargeant, Westerham, Kent.
Jack Moore Antiques and Stained Glass, Trawden, Lancs.
Keystone Antiques, Coalville, Leics.
Liz Allport-Lomax, Coltishall, Norfolk.
Sue Miller Antiques and Collectables, Langham, Norfolk.
Dorothy's Antiques, Sheringham, Norfolk.
Laurie Leigh Antiques, Oxford, Oxon.
Joan Wilkins Antiques, Witney, Oxon.
Bees Antiques, Woodstock, Oxon.
Frank Dux Antiques, Bath, Somerset.
Abbey Antiques, Glastonbury, Somerset.
Somervale Antiques, Midsomer Norton, Somerset.
C. and R. Scattergood, Burton-on-Trent, Staffs.
Mary Palmer Antiques, Stradbroke, Suffolk.
Pat Golding, Arundel, W. Sussex.
David R. Fileman, Steyning, W. Sussex.
Ray Best Antiques, Newton Tony, Wilts.
Delomosne and Son Ltd, North Wraxall, Wilts.
Dragon Antiques, Harrogate, N. Yorks.
York Cottage Antiques, Helmsley, N. Yorks.
Dunluce Antiques, Bushmills, Co. Antrim, N. Ireland.
Brian R. Bolt Antiques, Portballintrae, Co. Antrim, N. Ireland.
Fine Antique Glass, Abernyte, Scotland.
Forsyth Antiques, Perth, Scotland.
Gallery One, Perth, Scotland.

Glass Domes

"Get Stuffed", London N1.
Old Father Time Clock Centre, London W11.
John Burton Natural Craft Taxidermy, Ebrington, Glos.
Heads 'n' Tails, Wiveliscombe, Somerset.

Icons (see Russian Art)

Islamic Art

Spink and Son Ltd, London SW1.
Aaron Gallery, London W1.
Emanouel Corporation (UK) Ltd, London W1.
Hadji Baba Ancient Art, London W1.
Mansour Gallery, London W1.
Mohamed Ltd, Bashir, London W1.
Axia Art Consultants Ltd, London W11.
Hosains Books and Antiques, London W2.
Clive Rogers Oriental Rugs, Wraysbury, Berks.
Dennis Woodman Oriental Carpets, Kew, Surrey.

Japanese Art (see Oriental)

Jewellery (see Silver & Jewellery)

Lighting

Davidson Antiques, Carlton, London N1.
Lemkow, Sara, London N1.
Turn On Lighting, London N1.
Antique Shop (Valantique), The, London N2.
Winchmore Antiques, London N21.
Malik and Son Ltd, David, London NW10.
B.C. Metalcrafts Ltd, London NW9.
Oddiquities, London SE23.
Wilkinson plc, London SE6.
Batstone Decorative Antiques, Hilary, London SW1.
Blanchard (London) Ltd, London SW1.
Hermitage Antiques plc, London SW1.
Hobbs, Carlton, London SW1.
Howe, Christopher, London SW1.
Jeremy Ltd, London SW1.
Lion, Witch and Lampshade, London SW1.
McClenaghan, London SW1.
Rogier Antiques, London SW1.
Poulter and Son, H.W., London SW10.
Allegra's Lighthouse Antiques, London SW19.
Burne (Antique Glass) Ltd, W.G.T., London SW20.
275 Antiques, London SW6.
Arabesque Antiques, London SW6.
Bangs, Christopher, London SW6.
Cochrane Antiques, Fergus, London SW6.
Crotty and Son Ltd, J., London SW6.
Edwards, Charles, London SW6.
Edwards, Christopher, London SW6.
Greenwood, Judy, London SW6.
Hollingshead and Co, London SW6.
Lamp Gallery, The, London SW6.
Napier Ltd, Sylvia, London SW6.
Old World Trading Co, London SW6.
Pauw Antiques, M., London SW6.
Tulissio De Beaumont, London SW6.
Vaughan, London SW6.
Wray's Lighting Emporium, Christopher, London SW6.
Period Brass Lights, London SW7.
Sitch and Co. Ltd., W., London W1.
Stair and Company Ltd, London W1.
Turpin Ltd, M., London W1.
Jones Antique Lighting, London W11.
Marshall Gallery, London W14.
Davighi, N., London W6.
Crick Chandeliers, Mrs. M.E., London W8.
Denton Antiques, London W8.
Cohn, George and Peter, London WC1.
Manor Antiques, Wilstead (Wilshamstead), Beds.
Temple Lighting (Jeanne Temple Antiques), Milton Keynes, Bucks.
Starlight, Wansford, Cambs.
The Edge Antiques, Alderley Edge, Cheshire.
The Lantern Shop, Sidmouth, Devon.
Antique Metals, Coggeshall, Essex.
Government House, Cheltenham, Glos.
H.W. Keil (Cheltenham) Ltd, Cheltenham, Glos.
Triton Gallery, Cheltenham, Glos.
J. and J. Caspall Antiques, Stow-on-the-Wold, Glos.
Antony Preston Antiques Ltd, Stow-on-the-Wold, Glos.
Queens Parade Antiques Ltd, Stow-on-the-Wold, Glos.
Fritz Fryer Antique Lighting, Ross-on-Wye, Herefs.
Magic Lanterns, St. Albans, Herts.
P. Farmer, Chatham, Kent.
Denys Sargeant, Westerham, Kent.
Prestwich Antiques Ltd, Manchester, Lancs.
The Stiffkey Lamp Shop, Stiffkey, Norfolk.
Barclay Antiques, Headington, Oxon.
Ian McCarthy, Clutton, Somerset.
Odeon Antiques, Leek, Staffs.
Post House Antiques, Bletchingley, Surrey.
Rickett & Co. Antiques, Shepperton, Surrey.
Timewarp, Brighton, E. Sussex.
Libra Antiques, Hurst Green, E. Sussex.
David R. Fileman, Steyning, W. Sussex.
The Incandescent Lighting Company, Leamington Spa, Warks.
Delomosne and Son Ltd, North Wraxall, Wilts.
Inglenook Antiques, Ramsbury, Wilts.
Penoyre Antiques, Pershore, Worcs.
Lower House Fine Antiques, Redditch, Worcs.
Old Flames, Easingwold, N. Yorks.
'Bobbins' Wool, Crafts, Antiques, Whitby, N. Yorks.
Fine Antique Glass, Abernyte, Scotland.
Berland's of Edinburgh, Edinburgh, Scotland.
Eklektikos Antiques Centre, Edinburgh, Scotland.

Maps & Prints

Ash Rare Books, London EC3.
Clarke-Hall Ltd, J., London EC4.
Boutique Fantasque, London N1.
Finney Antique Prints and Books, Michael, London N1.
Lassalle, Judith, London N1.
MacDonnell, Finbar, London N1.
Totteridge Gallery, The, London N20.
Centaur Gallery, London N6.
Mulder, Frederick, London NW3.
Denham Gallery, John, London NW6.
Gallery Kaleidoscope, London NW6.
Leadlay Gallery, The Warwick, London SE10.
Addison-Ross Gallery, London SW1.
Artemis Fine Arts Limited, London SW1.
Douwes Fine Art Ltd, London SW1.
Hartnoll, Julian, London SW1.
Mason Gallery, Paul, London SW1.
Mendez incorporating Craddock and Barnard, Christopher, London SW1.
Old Maps and Prints, London SW1.
Parker Gallery, The, London SW1.
Parkin Fine Art Ltd, Michael, London SW1.
Sotheran Ltd, Henry, London SW1.
Bloxham (Fine Art) Ltd, John, London SW11.
Barnes Gallery, The, London SW13.
International Arts Group, London SW18.
Chelsea Rare Books, London SW3.
Gallery Lingard, London SW3.
Hoppen Ltd, Stephanie, London SW3.
Map House, The, London SW3.
Old Church Galleries, London SW3.
20th Century Gallery, London SW6.
King's Court Galleries, London SW6.
Marriott Ltd, Michael, London SW6.
Orssich, Paul, London SW6.

Trowbridge Gallery, London SW6.
Burlington Gallery Ltd, London W1.
Cazalet Ltd, Lumley, London W1.
Edmunds, Andrew, London W1.
Fritz-Denneville Fine Arts Ltd, H., London W1.
O'Shea Gallery, The, London W1.
Potter Ltd, Jonathan, London W1.
Schuster, Thomas E., London W1.
Schuster Gallery, The, London W1.
Shapero Rare Books, Bernard J., London W1.
Somerville Ltd, Stephen, London W1.
Sotheran Ltd, Henry, London W1.
Blackburn, Norman, London W11.
Lassalle, Patrick, London W11.
Skrebowski Prints, Justin F., London W11.
Bayswater Books, London W2.
Connaught Galleries, London W2.
Campbell Gallery, The Lucy B., London W8.
Crawley and Asquith Ltd, London W8.
Austin/Desmond Fine Art, London WC1.
Franks, J.A.L., London WC1.
Frew Ltd, Robert, London WC1.
London Antiquarian Book Arcade, London WC1.
Print Room, The, London WC1.
Grosvenor Prints, London WC2.
Jackson, Lee, London WC2.
Skrebowski Prints, Justin F., London WC2.
Stage Door Prints, London WC2.
Storey's Ltd, London WC2.
Tooley Adams & Co., London WC2.
Witch Ball, The, London WC2.
Graham Gallery, Burghfield Common, Berks.
TheStudio Gallery, Datchet, Berks.
Jaspers Fine Arts Ltd, Maidenhead, Berks.
Grove Gallery, Windsor and Eton, Berks.
Omniphil Prints, Chesham, Bucks.
Penn Barn, Penn, Bucks.
Medina Antiquarian Maps and Prints, Winslow, Bucks.
Benet Gallery, Cambridge, Cambs.
The Lawson Gallery, Cambridge, Cambs.
Sebastian Pearson Paintings Prints and Works of Art, Cambridge, Cambs.
Moor Hall Antiques, Chester, Cheshire.
Richard A. Nicholson, Chester, Cheshire.
Lion Gallery and Bookshop, Knutsford, Cheshire.
Harper Fine Paintings, Poynton, Cheshire.
J. Alan Hulme, Waverton, Cheshire.
John Maggs, Falmouth, Cornwall.
Archie Miles Bookshop, Gosforth, Cumbria.
Kendal Studios Antiques, Kendal, Cumbria.
R. F. G. Hollett and Son, Sedbergh, Cumbria.
Cavendish House Gallery, Ashbourne, Derbys.
Polly Coleman Antiques, Chesterfield, Derbys.
Medina Gallery, Barnstaple, Devon.
Medina Gallery, Bideford, Devon.
New Gallery, Budleigh Salterton, Devon.
Mary Payton Antiques, Chagford, Devon.
Chantry Bookshop and Gallery, Dartmouth, Devon.
The Lantern Shop Gallery, Sidmouth, Devon.
Birbeck Gallery, Torquay, Devon.
The Artist Gallery, Bournemouth, Dorset.
PIC's Bookshop, Bridport, Dorset.
Words Etcetera, Dorchester, Dorset.
F. Whillock, Litton Cheney, Dorset.
Antique Map and Bookshop, Puddletown, Dorset.
The Swan Gallery, Sherborne, Dorset.
The Treasure Chest, Weymouth, Dorset.
J. Shotton Antiquarian Books, Prints and Coins, Durham, Durham.
Castle Bookshop, Colchester, Essex.
Simon Hilton, Dunmow, Essex.
Newport Gallery, Newport, Essex.
Cleeve Picture Framing, Bishops Cleeve, Glos.
Alexander Gallery, Bristol, Glos.
Cotham Hill Bookshop, Bristol, Glos.
David Cross (Fine Art), Bristol, Glos.
Triangle Books (inc. John Roberts Bookshop Est. 1955), Bristol, Glos.
David Bannister FRGS, Cheltenham, Glos.
Steven D. Bartrick, Gloucester, Glos.
Kenulf Fine Arts, Stow-on-the-Wold, Glos.
Talbot Court Galleries, Stow-on-the-Wold, Glos.
Vanbrugh House Antiques, Stow-on-the-Wold, Glos.
Studio Bookshop and Gallery, Alresford, Hants.
Hughes and Smeeth Ltd, Lymington, Hants.
The Petersfield Bookshop, Petersfield, Hants.
Oldfield Gallery, Portsmouth, Hants.
Bell Fine Art, Winchester, Hants.
Printed Page, Winchester, Hants.
Brobury House Gallery, Brobury, Herefs.
Coltsfoot Gallery, Leominster, Herefs.
Farmers Gallery, Leominster, Herefs.
Ross Old Book and Print Shop, Ross-on-Wye, Herefs.
Moreden Prints, Yatton, Herefs.
Eric T. Moore, Hitchin, Herts.
Clive A. Burden, Rickmansworth, Herts.
James of St Albans, St. Albans, Herts.
Julia Margaret Cameron Gallery, Cowes, I. of Wight.
Galerias Segui, Cowes, I. of Wight.
The Shanklin Gallery, Shanklin, I. of Wight.
Ventnor Rare Books, Ventnor, I. of Wight.
Marlborough House Antiques, Yarmouth, I. of Wight.
The Canterbury Bookshop, Canterbury, Kent.
Chaucer Bookshop, Canterbury, Kent.
Leadenhall Gallery, Canterbury, Kent.
Cranbrook Gallery, Cranbrook, Kent.
The Print Room Gallery, Deal, Kent.
G. and D.I. Marrin and Sons, Folkestone, Kent.
The China Locker, Lamberhurst, Kent.
Periwinkle Press, Newnham, Kent.
Langley Galleries, Rochester, Kent.
London House Antiques, Westerham, Kent.
Forest Books of Cheshire, Manchester, Lancs.
Halewood and Sons, Preston, Lancs.
Leics Sporting Gallery and Brown Jack Bookshop, Lubenham, Leics.
P.J. Cassidy (Books), Holbeach, Lincs.
Golden Goose Books, Lincoln, Lincs.
Harlequin Gallery, Lincoln, Lincs.
Lyver & Boydell Galleries, Liverpool, Merseyside.
The Hampton Hill Gallery, Hampton Hill, Middx.
The Coach House, Costessey, Norfolk.
David Ferrow, Gt. Yarmouth, Norfolk.
The Haven Gallery, Gt. Yarmouth, Norfolk.
Baron Art, Holt, Norfolk.
In the Picture (The Golf Collection), Holt, Norfolk.
Baron Art, Kelling, Norfolk.
Crome Gallery and Frame Shop, Norwich, Norfolk.
Peter Crowe, Antiquarian Book Seller, Norwich, Norfolk.
Right Angle, Brackley, Northants.
Savage Fine Art, Haselbech, Northants.
Park Book Shop, Wellingborough, Northants.
Park Gallery, Wellingborough, Northants.
Jane Neville Gallery, Aslockton, Notts.
TRADA, Chipping Norton, Oxon.
Rob Dixon Fine Engravings, Culham, Oxon.
The Barry M. Keene Gallery, Henley-on-Thames, Oxon.
Elizabeth Harvey-Lee, North Aston, Oxon.
Magna Gallery, Oxford, Oxon.
Sanders of Oxford Ltd, Oxford, Oxon.
Churchgate Antiques, Empingham, Rutland.
The Old House Gallery, Oakham, Rutland.
Marc Oxley Fine Art, Uppingham, Rutland.
The Mount, Woore, Shrops.
Patterson Liddle, Bath, Somerset.
Trimbridge Galleries, Bath, Somerset.
Michael Lewis Gallery, Bruton, Somerset.
Julian Armytage, Crewkerne, Somerset.
House of Antiquity, Nether Stowey, Somerset.
Richard Joslin Galleries, Taunton, Somerset.
The Bournemouth Gallery Ltd, Lichfield, Staffs.
Besleys Books, Beccles, Suffolk.
Suthburgh Antiques, Long Melford, Suffolk.
King's Court Galleries, Dorking, Surrey.
Vandeleur Antiquarian Books, Epsom, Surrey.
Reigate Galleries Ltd, Reigate, Surrey.
Palmer Galleries, Richmond, Surrey.
Leoframes, Brighton, E. Sussex.
The Witch Ball, Brighton, E. Sussex.
A. & T. Gibbard, Eastbourne, E. Sussex.
Murray Brown, Pevensey Bay, E. Sussex.
Helgato, St. Leonards-on-Sea, E. Sussex.
Ivan R. Deverall, Uckfield, E. Sussex.
Baynton-Williams, Arundel, W. Sussex.
The Antique Atlas, East Grinstead, W. Sussex.
The Antique Print Shop, East Grinstead, W. Sussex.
George House Gallery, Petworth, W. Sussex.
Julia Holmes Antique Maps and Prints, South Harting, W. Sussex.
Osborne Art and Antiques, Jesmond, Tyne and Wear.
Janice Paull Antiques, Kenilworth, Warks.
Robert Vaughan, Stratford-upon-Avon, Warks.
Eastgate Fine Arts, Warwick, Warks.
Woodland Fine Art, Alvechurch, W. Mids.
Carleton Gallery, Birmingham, W. Mids.
D.M. Beach, Salisbury, Wilts.

Bracebridge Gallery, Astwood Bank, Worcs.
Broadway Old Books (formerly Stratford Trevers), Broadway, Worcs.
Gandolfi House, Malvern Wells, Worcs.
Antique Map and Print Gallery, Worcester, Worcs.
Houghton Hall Antiques, Market Weighton, E. Yorks.
The Great Ayton Bookshop, Great Ayton, N. Yorks.
Country Connections (Esk House Arts), Grosmont, N. Yorks.
McTague of Harrogate, Harrogate, N. Yorks.
Minster Gate Bookshop, York, N. Yorks.
O'Flynn Antiquarian Booksellers, York, N. Yorks.
Alan Hill Books, Sheffield, Sheffield, S. Yorks.
The Grove Bookshop, Ilkley, W. Yorks.
Oakwood Gallery, Leeds, W. Yorks.
C.I. Galleries Ltd, St. Peter Port, Guernsey, C.I.
Geoffrey P. Gavey, Vale, Guernsey, C.I.
John Blench & Son, St. Helier, Jersey, C.I.
Grange Gallery and Fine Arts Ltd, St. Helier, Jersey, C.I.
The Selective Eye Gallery, St. Helier, Jersey, C.I.
Thesaurus (Jersey) Ltd, St. Helier, Jersey, C.I.
Phyllis Arnold Gallery Antiques, Greyabbey, Co. Down, N. Ireland.
The Waverley Gallery, Aberdeen, Scotland.
The McEwan Gallery, Ballater, Scotland.
Calton Gallery, Edinburgh, Scotland.
The Carson Clark Gallery. Scotia Maps - Mapsellers, Edinburgh, Scotland.
Alan Rankin, Edinburgh, Scotland.
A. and F. McIlreavy Rare and Interesting Books, St. Andrews, Scotland.
H.K. Lockyer, Abergavenny, Wales.
David Windsor Gallery, Bangor, Wales.
Maps, Prints and Books, Brecon, Wales.
Manor House Fine Arts, Cardiff, Wales.
Glance Back Bookshop, Chepstow, Wales.
Glance Gallery, Chepstow, Wales.
Philip Davies Fine Art, Swansea, Wales.

Metalware/work

Heritage Antiques, London N1.
House of Steel Antiques, London N1.
Lemkow, Sara, London N1.
Young Antiques, Robert, London SW11.
Chelsea Bric-a-Brac Shop Ltd, London SW19.
Bangs, Christopher, London SW6.
Place Antiques, Peter, London SW6.
Casimir Ltd, Jack, London W11.
Von Pflugh Antiques, Johnny, London W11.
Walpole, Graham, London W11.
Manor Antiques, Wilstead (Wilshamstead), Beds.
Christopher Sykes Antiques, Woburn, Beds.
The Fire Place (Hungerford) Ltd, Hungerford, Berks.
Berks Metal Finishers Ltd, Sandhurst, Berks.
Peter J. Martin, Windsor and Eton, Berks.
Sundial Antiques, Amersham, Bucks.
Albert Bartram, Chesham, Bucks.
Phoenix Antiques, Fordham, Cambs.
A.P. and M.A. Haylett, Outwell, Cambs.
The Antique Shop, Chester, Cheshire.
Antiques and Curios, Ravensmoor, Cheshire.
Shire Antiques, Newby Bridge, Cumbria.
Pamela Elsom - Antiques, Ashbourne, Derbys.
Martin and Dorothy Harper Antiques, Bakewell, Derbys.
Water Lane Antiques, Bakewell, Derbys.
Roderick Butler, Honiton, Devon.
Morchard Bishop Antiques, Morchard Bishop, Devon.
Alan Jones Antiques, Okehampton, Devon.
Philip Andrade, South Brent, Devon.
Peter Stebbing, Bournemouth, Dorset.
J.B. Antiques, Wimborne Minster, Dorset.
Antique Metals, Coggeshall, Essex.
Richard Wrenn Antiques, Leigh-on-Sea, Essex.
William H. Stokes, Cirencester, Glos.
J. and J. Caspall Antiques, Stow-on-the-Wold, Glos.
Christopher Clarke Antiques Ltd, Stow-on-the-Wold, Glos.
Country Life Antiques, Stow-on-the-Wold, Glos.
Keith Hockin (Antiques) Ltd, Stow-on-the-Wold, Glos.
Huntington Antiques Ltd, Stow-on-the-Wold, Glos.
Arthur Seager Antiques, Stow-on-the-Wold, Glos.
Prichard Antiques, Winchcombe, Glos.
Cedar Antiques Limited, Hartley Wintney, Hants.
Monaltrie Antiques, Odiham, Hants.
Cull Antiques, Petersfield, Hants.
Elizabeth Viney, Stockbridge, Hants.
P. and S.N. Eddy, Leominster, Herefs.
Hubbard Antiques, Leominster, Herefs.
Michael Gander, Hitchin, Herts.
Two Maids Antiques, Biddenden, Kent.
Dinah Stoodley, Brasted, Kent.
James Porter Antiques, Sandwich, Kent.
E.W. Webster, Bickerstaffe, Lancs.
House Things Antiques, Hinckley, Leics.
V.O.C. Antiques, Woodhall Spa, Lincs.
Peter Robinson, Heacham, Norfolk.
Arthur Brett and Sons Ltd, Norwich, Norfolk.
M.D. Cannell Antiques, Raveningham, Norfolk.
Huntershield Antiques, Flore, Northants.
Rococo Antiques and Interiors, Weedon, Northants.
Antiques, West Haddon, Northants.
E.M. Cheshire, Bingham, Notts.
Jonathan Fyson Antiques, Burford, Oxon.
Horseshoe Antiques and Gallery, Burford, Oxon.
Anthony Nielsen Antiques, Burford, Oxon.
Key Antiques, Chipping Norton, Oxon.
Mike Ottrey Antiques, Wallingford, Oxon.
Joan Wilkins Antiques, Witney, Oxon.
Witney Antiques, Witney, Oxon.
Alderson, Bath, Somerset.
Brian and Caroline Craik Ltd, Bath, Somerset.
Ian McCarthy, Clutton, Somerset.
Bernard G. House, Wells, Somerset.
Tilly Manor Antiques, West Harptree, Somerset.
Peppers Period Pieces, Bury St. Edmunds, Suffolk.
J. and J. Baker, Lavenham, Suffolk.
Oswald Simpson, Long Melford, Suffolk.
Suffolk House Antiques, Yoxford, Suffolk.
Anthony Welling Antiques, Ripley, Surrey.
Rickett & Co. Antiques, Shepperton, Surrey.
Wellers Restoration Centre, Eastbourne, E. Sussex.
Rye Antiques, Rye, E. Sussex.
Park View Antiques, Wadhurst, E. Sussex.
Michael Wakelin and Helen Linfield, Billingshurst, W. Sussex.
J. Du Cros Antiques, Petworth, W. Sussex.
Retro Products, Lye, W. Mids.
Avon Antiques, Bradford-on-Avon, Wilts.
Town and Country Antiques, Bradford-on-Avon, Wilts.
Combe Cottage Antiques, Castle Combe, Wilts.
Monkton Galleries, Hindon, Wilts.
Harriet Fairfax Fireplaces and General Antiques, Langley Burrell, Wilts.
Turpin's Antiques, Little Bedwyn, Wilts.
Rupert Gentle Antiques, Milton Lilbourne, Wilts.
Ray Best Antiques, Newton Tony, Wilts.
H.W. Keil Ltd, Broadway, Worcs.
Ryefield House Antiques, Bradley, N. Yorks.
Bill Bentley, Harrogate, N. Yorks.
Garth Antiques, Harrogate, N. Yorks.
Charles Lumb and Sons Ltd, Harrogate, N. Yorks.
Elaine Phillips Antiques Ltd, Harrogate, N. Yorks.
York Cottage Antiques, Helmsley, N. Yorks.
Aura Antiques, Masham, N. Yorks.
Eastgate Antiques, Pickering, N. Yorks.
E. Thistlethwaite, Settle, N. Yorks.
Garth Antiques, Whixley, N. Yorks.
Minster Antiques, York, N. Yorks.
Geary Antiques, Leeds, W. Yorks.
Unicorn Antiques, Edinburgh, Scotland.
Tim Wright Antiques, Glasgow, Scotland.

Miniatures

Lavender (Antiques) Ltd, D.S., London W1.
Phillips Ltd, S.J., London W1.
Deutsch Antiques, H. and W., London W8.
Wendover Antiques, Wendover, Bucks.
Simon Brett, Moreton-in-Marsh, Glos.
Michael Sim, Chislehurst, Kent.
Regal Antiques, Westerham, Kent.
Gough Bros. Art Shop and Gallery, Bognor Regis, W. Sussex.
Arden Gallery, Henley-in-Arden, Warks.

Mirrors

Julian Antiques, London N1.
Tapsell Antiques, London N1.
Anno Domini Antiques, London SW1.
Fernandes and Marche, London SW1.
Ossowski, London SW1.
Overmantels, London SW11.
McDonald, Joy, London SW13.
Adams Ltd, Norman, London SW3.
James and Son Ltd, Anthony, London SW3.
Lipitch Ltd, Peter, London SW3.
Wright Antiques Ltd, Clifford, London SW3.
275 Antiques, London SW6.
House of Mirrors, London SW6.
Hurford Antiques, Peter, London SW6.

James, P.L., London SW6.
Through the Looking Glass Ltd, London SW6.
Toth, Ferenc, London SW6.
Fielden, Brian, London W1.
Stair and Company Ltd, London W1.
Turpin Ltd, M., London W1.
Oakstar Ltd, London W11.
Simpsons - Bespoke Carvings, London W14.
Howard, Valerie, London W8.
Through the Looking Glass Ltd, London W8.
Doddington House Antiques, Doddington, Cambs.
Triton Gallery, Cheltenham, Glos.
Stow Antiques, Stow-on-the-Wold, Glos.
Balmuir House Antiques, Tetbury, Glos.
Chatelain Antique Beds and Mirrors, Tillington, Herefs.
The Windhill Antiquary, Bishop's Stortford, Herts.
Ashton Gower Antiques, Burford, Oxon.
Tattersall's, Uppingham, Rutland.
Looking Glass of Bath, Bath, Somerset.
Quiet Street Antiques, Bath, Somerset.
Molland Antique Mirrors, Leek, Staffs.
J. de Haan & Son, Clare, Suffolk.
Susan Wells Antiques, Yoxford, Suffolk.
The Gallery, Reigate, Surrey.
Dermot and Jill Palmer Antiques, Brighton, E. Sussex.
Julian Antiques, Hurstpierpoint, W. Sussex.
Victoria C - The Antique Gallery (Potterne), Potterne, Wilts.
Penoyre Antiques, Pershore, Worcs.
W. Greenwood (Fine Art), Burneston, N. Yorks.

Musical Instruments, Boxes & Literature

St. Peters Organ Works, London E2.
Boxes and Musical Instruments, London E8.
Freeman, Vincent, London N1.
Bingham, Tony, London NW3.
Haas (A. and M. Rosenthal), Otto, London NW3.
Talking Machine, London NW4.
Baron, H., London NW6.
Morley and Co Ltd, Robert, London SE13.
Reeves Bookseller Ltd, William, London SW16.
Beare, John and Arthur, London W1.
Biddulph, Peter, London W1.
Pelham Galleries Ltd, London W1.
Mayflower Antiques, London W11.
Travis and Emery, London WC2.
Times Past Antiques, Windsor and Eton, Berks.
Mill Farm Antiques, Disley, Cheshire.
Bruntsfield Antiques, Edinburgh, Scotland.

Oil Paintings

Royal Exchange Art Gallery, London EC3.
Chapman Antiques, Peter, London N1.
Graham Gallery, The, London N1.
Swan Fine Art, London N1.
Finchley Fine Art Galleries, London N12.
Henham (Antiques), Martin, London N2.
Stewart - Fine Art, Lauri, London N2.
Totteridge Gallery, The, London N20.
Centaur Gallery, London N6.
Lummis Fine Art, Sandra, London N8.
Barkes and Barkes, London NW1.
Gunter Fine Art, London NW2.
Miller Fine Arts, Duncan R., London NW3.
Newhart (Pictures) Ltd, London NW3.
Denham Gallery, John, London NW6.
Gallery Kaleidoscope, London NW6.
Camden Art Gallery, London NW8.
Drummond/Wrawby Moor Art Gallery Ltd, Nicholas, London NW8.
Harvey Antiques and Decoration, Patricia, London NW8.
Greenwich Gallery, The, London SE10.
Relcy Antiques, London SE10.
Aaron (London)Ltd, Didier, London SW1.
Ackermann & Johnson, London SW1.
Addison-Ross Gallery, London SW1.
Åmell Ltd, Verner, London SW1.
Antiquus, London SW1.
Beetles Ltd, Chris, London SW1.
Brisigotti Antiques Ltd, London SW1.
Carritt Limited, David, London SW1.
Cato, Miles Wynn, London SW1.
Chaucer Fine Arts Ltd, London SW1.
Cohen, Edward, London SW1.
Cox and Company, London SW1.
Dickinson Ltd, Simon, London SW1.
Douwes Fine Art Ltd, London SW1.
Eaton Gallery, London SW1.
Frost and Reed Ltd (Est. 1808), London SW1.
Gregory Gallery, Martyn, London SW1.
Hamilton Ltd, Ross, London SW1.
Harrods Ltd, London SW1.
Hartnoll, Julian, London SW1.
Hawksmoor, London SW1.
Hazlitt, Gooden and Fox Ltd, London SW1.
Hermitage Antiques plc, London SW1.
Hobbs, Carlton, London SW1.
Hull Gallery, Christopher, London SW1.
Hunter Fine Art, Sally, London SW1.
Innes Gallery, Malcolm, London SW1.
Johns Ltd, Derek, London SW1.
MacConnal-Mason Gallery, London SW1.
Mall Galleries, The, London SW1.
Mason Gallery, Paul, London SW1.
Mathaf Gallery Ltd, London SW1.
Matthiesen Fine Art Ltd., London SW1.
Moreton Street Gallery, London SW1.
Morrison, Guy, London SW1.
Nahum at The Leicester Galleries, Peter, London SW1.
Pairs Antiques Ltd, London SW1.
Paisnel Gallery, London SW1.
Parker Gallery, The, London SW1.
Parkin Fine Art Ltd, Michael, London SW1.
Polak Gallery, London SW1.
Portland Gallery, London SW1.
Priest Antiques, Michael, London SW1.
Rich & Michael Rich, Steven, London SW1.
Simon Fine Art Ltd, Julian, London SW1.
Spink and Son Ltd, London SW1.
Thomson - Albany Gallery, Bill, London SW1.
Trafalgar Galleries, London SW1.
Valls Ltd, Rafael, London SW1.
Valls Ltd, Rafael, London SW1.
Van Haeften Ltd, Johnny, London SW1.
Waterman Fine Art Ltd, London SW1.
Whitford Fine Art, London SW1.
Clark & Co, Jonathan, London SW10.
Collins and Hastie Ltd, London SW10.
Gallery on Lots Road, London SW10.
Hollywood Road Gallery, London SW10.
Offer Waterman and Co. Fine Art, London SW10.
Park Walk Gallery, London SW10.
Pawsey and Payne, London SW10.
Bloxham (Fine Art) Ltd, John, London SW11.
Alton Gallery, London SW13.
Barnes Gallery, The, London SW13.
New Grafton Gallery, London SW13.
Few, Ted, London SW17.
International Arts Group, London SW18.
Curzon Gallery, The David, London SW19.
Kensington Sporting Paintings Ltd, London SW20.
Campbell Picture Frames Ltd, John, London SW3.
Denny Ltd, Colin, London SW3.
Gallery Lingard, London SW3.
Hoppen Ltd, Stephanie, London SW3.
Pettifer Ltd, David, London SW3.
20th Century Gallery, London SW6.
Cavendish Antiques, Rupert, London SW6.
Cooper Fine Arts Ltd, London SW6.
Edwards, Charles, London SW6.
Spink, John, London SW6.
Valcke, François, London SW6.
Collino, Julie, London SW7.
Taylor Gallery, The, London SW7.
Wyllie Gallery, The, London SW7.
Agnew's, London W1.
Bernheimer Ltd, Konrad O., London W1.
Browse and Darby Ltd, London W1.
Burlington Paintings Ltd, London W1.
Colnaghi & Co Ltd, P. and D., London W1.
Connaught Brown plc, London W1.
d'Offay, Anthony, London W1.
Editions Graphiques Gallery, London W1.
Fine Art Society plc, The, London W1.
Fritz-Denneville Fine Arts Ltd, H., London W1.
Gage (Works of Art) Ltd, Deborah, London W1.
Gibson Fine Art Ltd, Thomas, London W1.
Green, Richard, London W1.
Hahn and Son Fine Art Dealers, London W1.
Lane Fine Art Ltd, London W1.
Lefevre Gallery, The, London W1.
Maas Gallery, London W1.
MacConnal-Mason Gallery, London W1.
Mallett Gallery, London W1.
Marlborough Fine Art (London) Ltd, London W1.
Messum, David, London W1.
Miles Gallery, Roy, London W1.
Mitchell and Son, John, London W1.
Mould Ltd, Anthony, London W1.
Noortman, London W1.
O'Nians, Hal, London W1.
Partridge Fine Arts plc, London W1.
Patterson Fine Arts Ltd, W.H., London W1.
Pyms Gallery, London W1.
Somerville Ltd, Stephen, London W1.
Spink Leger Pictures, London W1.
Stoppenbach and Delestre Ltd, London W1.
Thuillier, William, London W1.
Tryon & Swann Gallery, London W1.
Walpole Gallery, London W1.
Waterhouse and Dodd, London W1.
Weiss Gallery, The, London W1.

Wildenstein and Co Ltd, London W1.
Wilkins and Wilkins, London W1.
Williams and Son, London W1.
Aalders, Michael, London W11.
Addison Fine Art, London W11.
Arenski, London W11.
Butchoff Antiques, London W11.
Caelt Gallery, London W11.
Curá Antiques, London W11.
Daggett Gallery, Charles, London W11.
Fleur de Lys Gallery, London W11.
Graham Gallery, Gavin, London W11.
Lacy Gallery, London W11.
Milne and Moller, London W11.
Philp, London W11.
Piano Nobile Fine Paintings, London W11.
Skrebowski Prints, Justin F., London W11.
Stern Art Dealers, London W11.
Von Pflugh Antiques, Johnny, London W11.
Garratt (Fine Paintings), Stephen, London W14.
Marshall Gallery, London W14.
Igel Fine Arts Ltd, Manya, London W2.
Aberdeen House Antiques, London W5.
Ealing Gallery, London W5.
Baumkotter Gallery, London W8.
Crawley and Asquith Ltd, London W8.
Dare, George, London W8.
Leask Ward, London W8.
Sabin Galleries Ltd, London W8.
Austin/Desmond Fine Art, London WC1.
Skrebowski Prints, Justin F., London WC2.
Baroq at Brindleys, Heath and Reach, Beds.
Foye Gallery, Luton, Beds.
Woburn Fine Arts, Woburn, Beds.
Graham Gallery, Burghfield Common, Berks.
Phillips and Sons, Cookham, Berks.
TheStudio Gallery, Datchet, Berks.
John A. Pearson Antiques, Horton, Berks.
Jaspers Fine Arts Ltd, Maidenhead, Berks.
The Coworth Gallery, Sunningdale, Berks.
Grove Gallery, Windsor and Eton, Berks.
H.S. Wellby Ltd, Haddenham, Bucks.
Penn Barn, Penn, Bucks.
Cambridge Fine Art Ltd, Cambridge, Cambs.
The Lawson Gallery, Cambridge, Cambs.
Sebastian Pearson Paintings Prints and Works of Art, Cambridge, Cambs.
Baron Fine Art, Chester, Cheshire.
Harper Fine Paintings, Poynton, Cheshire.
Margaret Bedi Antiques, Billingham, Cleveland.
T.B. and R. Jordan (Fine Paintings), Eaglescliffe, Cleveland.
Copperhouse Gallery - W. Dyer & Sons, Hayle, Cornwall.
Tony Sanders Penzance Gallery and Antiques, Penzance, Cornwall.
Myles Varcoe, Tywardreath, Cornwall.
Peter Haworth, Beetham, Cumbria.
The Gallery, Penrith, Cumbria.
R. F. G. Hollett and Son, Sedbergh, Cumbria.
Cavendish House Gallery, Ashbourne, Derbys.
Kenneth Upchurch, Ashbourne, Derbys.
Charles H. Ward, Derby, Derbys.
J. Collins and Son, Bideford, Devon.
Medina Gallery, Bideford, Devon.
New Gallery, Budleigh Salterton, Devon.
Mill Gallery, Ermington, Devon.
Honiton Fine Art, Honiton, Devon.
Skeaping Gallery, Lydford, Devon.
Gordon Hepworth Fine Art, Newton St. Cyres, Devon.
Michael Wood Fine Art, Plymouth, Devon.
The Lantern Shop, Sidmouth, Devon.
Bygone Days Antiques, Tiverton, Devon.
Birbeck Gallery, Torquay, Devon.
Stour Gallery, Blandford Forum, Dorset.
Hants Gallery, Bournemouth, Dorset.
Brandler Galleries, Brentwood, Essex.
Neil Graham Gallery, Brentwood, Essex.
S. Bond and Son, Colchester, Essex.
Simon Hilton, Dunmow, Essex.
C. and J. Mortimer and Son, Great Chesterford, Essex.
John Burls, Great Oakley, Essex.
Thomas Sykes Antiques, Kelvedon, Essex.
Newport Gallery, Newport, Essex.
David Lloyd Gallery, Purleigh, Essex.
Reddings Art and Antiques, Southend-on-Sea, Essex.
Galerie Lev, Woodford Green, Essex.
Cleeve Picture Framing, Bishops Cleeve, Glos.
The Priory Gallery, Bishops Cleeve, Glos.
Alexander Gallery, Bristol, Glos.
David Cross (Fine Art), Bristol, Glos.
David Howard, Cheltenham, Glos.
H.W. Keil (Cheltenham) Ltd, Cheltenham, Glos.
Manor House Gallery, Cheltenham, Glos.
Triton Gallery, Cheltenham, Glos.
School House Antiques, Chipping Campden, Glos.
P.J. Ward Fine Paintings, Cirencester, Glos.
Gerard Campbell, Lechlade, Glos.
Astley House - Fine Art, Moreton-in-Marsh, Glos.
Astley House - Fine Art, Moreton-in-Marsh, Glos.
Berry Antiques, Moreton-in-Marsh, Glos.
Grimes House Antiques & Fine Art, Moreton-in-Marsh, Glos.
Southgate Gallery, Moreton-in-Marsh, Glos.
Nina Zborowska, Painswick, Glos.
Baggott Church Street Ltd, Stow-on-the-Wold, Glos.
Cotswold Galleries, Stow-on-the-Wold, Glos.
The John Davies Gallery, Stow-on-the-Wold, Glos.
The Fosse Gallery, Stow-on-the-Wold, Glos.
Fosse Way Antiques, Stow-on-the-Wold, Glos.
Kenulf Fine Arts, Stow-on-the-Wold, Glos.
Roger Lamb Antiques & Works of Art, Stow-on-the-Wold, Glos.
Arthur Seager Antiques, Stow-on-the-Wold, Glos.
Balmuir House Antiques, Tetbury, Glos.
Brian Sinfield - Compton Cassey Gallery, Withington, Glos.
Antique House, Hartley Wintney, Hants.
Corfields Ltd, Lymington, Hants.
Robert Perera Fine Art, Lymington, Hants.
The Petersfield Bookshop, Petersfield, Hants.
Lacewing Fine Art Gallery, Romsey, Hants.
Bell Fine Art, Winchester, Hants.
Webb Fine Arts, Winchester, Hants.
Farmers Gallery, Leominster, Herefs.
Countrylife Gallery, Hitchin, Herts.
Carole Thomas (Fine Arts), Hitchin, Herts.
The Shanklin Gallery, Shanklin, I. of Wight.
Peter Dyke, Brasted, Kent.
Michael Sim, Chislehurst, Kent.
Francis Iles, Rochester, Kent.
Langley Galleries, Rochester, Kent.
Alexandra's Antiques, St. Margaret's Bay, Kent.
Sundridge Gallery, Sundridge, Kent.
Sparks Antiques, Tenterden, Kent.
Nicholas Bowlby, Tunbridge Wells, Kent.
Graham Gallery, Tunbridge Wells, Kent.
Pantiles Spa Antiques, Tunbridge Wells, Kent.
Apollo Galleries, Westerham, Kent.
London House Antiques, Westerham, Kent.
Charnley Fine Arts, Longridge, Lancs.
Fulda Gallery Ltd, Manchester, Lancs.
St. James Antiques, Manchester, Lancs.
Owen Antiques, Rochdale, Lancs.
Henry Donn Gallery, Whitefield, Lancs.
P. Stanworth (Fine Arts), Cadeby, Leics.
Corry's, Leicester, Leics.
Leics Sporting Gallery and Brown Jack Bookshop, Lubenham, Leics.
Graftons of Market Harborough, Market Harborough, Leics.
Lincoln Fine Art, Lincoln, Lincs.
Lyver & Boydell Galleries, Liverpool, Merseyside.
Ailsa Gallery, Twickenham, Middx.
The Coach House, Costessey, Norfolk.
The Haven Gallery, Gt. Yarmouth, Norfolk.
Baron Art, Holt, Norfolk.
Baron Art, Kelling, Norfolk.
The Bank House Gallery, Norwich, Norfolk.
Crome Gallery and Frame Shop, Norwich, Norfolk.
The Fairhurst Gallery, Norwich, Norfolk.
Mandell's Gallery, Norwich, Norfolk.
The Westcliffe Gallery, Sheringham, Norfolk.
Staithe Lodge Gallery, Swafield, Norfolk.
Norton Antiques, Twyford, Norfolk.
Coughton Galleries Ltd, Arthingworth, Northants.
Berengar Antiques, Barnwell, Northants.
Right Angle, Brackley, Northants.
Castle Ashby Gallery, Castle Ashby, Northants.
Savage Fine Art, Haselbech, Northants.
Dragon Antiques, Kettering, Northants.
Clark Galleries, Towcester, Northants.
Ron Green, Towcester, Northants.
Bryan Perkins Antiques, Wellingborough, Northants.
Haydon Bridge Antiques, Haydon Bridge, Northumbs.
Haydon Gallery, Haydon Bridge, Northumbs.
Boadens Antiques, Hexham, Northumbs.
Jane Neville Gallery, Aslockton, Notts.
Anthony Mitchell Fine Paintings, Nottingham, Notts.
Benson Antiques and Gallery, Benson, Oxon.
H.C. Dickins, Bloxham, Oxon.
Horseshoe Antiques and Gallery, Burford, Oxon.

Hubert's Antiques, Burford, Oxon.
The Stone Gallery, Burford, Oxon.
Swan Gallery, Burford, Oxon.
Georgian House Antiques, Chipping Norton, Oxon.
Tuckers Country Store and Art Gallery, Deddington, Oxon.
Hallidays (Fine Antiques) Ltd, Dorchester-on-Thames, Oxon.
The Barry M. Keene Gallery, Henley-on-Thames, Oxon.
Thames Gallery, Henley-on-Thames, Oxon.
Churchgate Antiques, Empingham, Rutland.
Fine Art of Oakham, Oakham, Rutland.
The Old House Gallery, Oakham, Rutland.
John Garner, Uppingham, Rutland.
Gallery 6, Broseley, Shrops.
Teme Valley Antiques, Ludlow, Shrops.
Valentyne Dawes Gallery, Ludlow, Shrops.
Wenlock Fine Art, Much Wenlock, Shrops.
F.C. Manser and Son Ltd, Shrewsbury, Shrops.
Haygate Gallery, Telford, Shrops.
The Mount, Woore, Shrops.
Hall's Antiques, Ash Priors, Somerset.
Adam Gallery, Bath, Somerset.
Beau Nash Antiques, Bath, Somerset.
Mary Cruz, Bath, Somerset.
Trimbridge Galleries, Bath, Somerset.
The Court Gallery, Nether Stowey, Somerset.
Richard Joslin Galleries, Taunton, Somerset.
Nick Cotton Fine Art, Watchet, Somerset.
Sadler Street Gallery, Wells, Somerset.
Tim Everett, West Buckland, Somerset.
England's Gallery, Leek, Staffs.
Richard Midwinter Antiques, Newcastle-under-Lyme, Staffs.
Thompson's Gallery, Aldeburgh, Suffolk.
The Fortescue Gallery, Ipswich, Suffolk.
J. and J. Baker, Lavenham, Suffolk.
Charles Antiques, Long Melford, Suffolk.
Trident Antiques, Long Melford, Suffolk.
Equus Art Gallery, Newmarket, Suffolk.
Peasenhall Art and Antiques Gallery, Peasenhall, Suffolk.
Simon Carter Gallery, Woodbridge, Suffolk.
The Falcon Gallery, Wortham, Suffolk.
Suffolk House Antiques, Yoxford, Suffolk.
Cider House Galleries Ltd, Bletchingley, Surrey.
Cobham Galleries, Cobham, Surrey.
The Whitgift Galleries, Croydon, Surrey.
The Court Gallery, East Molesey, Surrey.
Jenny Asplund Fine Art, Esher, Surrey.
Heytesbury Antiques, Farnham, Surrey.
Glencorse Antiques, Kingston-upon-Thames, Surrey.
Bourne Gallery Ltd, Reigate, Surrey.
The Gallery, Reigate, Surrey.
Roland Goslett Gallery, Richmond, Surrey.
F. and T. Lawson Antiques, Richmond, Surrey.
Marryat, Richmond, Surrey.
Piano Nobile Fine Paintings, Richmond, Surrey.
Cedar House Gallery, Ripley, Surrey.
Sage Antiques and Interiors, Ripley, Surrey.
B. M. and E. Newlove, Surbiton, Surrey.
Boathouse Gallery, Walton-on-Thames, Surrey.
Edward Cross - Fine Paintings, Weybridge, Surrey.
Willow Gallery, Weybridge, Surrey.
Stephen Welbourne, Brighton, E. Sussex.
John Day of Eastbourne Fine Art, Eastbourne, E. Sussex.
Premier Gallery, Eastbourne, E. Sussex.
Stewart Gallery, Eastbourne, E. Sussex.
Delmas, Hurst Green, E. Sussex.
Murray Brown, Pevensey Bay, E. Sussex.
E. Stacy-Marks Limited, Polegate, E. Sussex.
Molly Alexander, Seaford, E. Sussex.
Peter Francis Antiques, Arundel, W. Sussex.
Susan and Robert Botting, Billingshurst, W. Sussex.
Lannards Gallery, Billingshurst, W. Sussex.
Jeremy Wood Fine Art, Billingshurst, W. Sussex.
Gough Bros. Art Shop and Gallery, Bognor Regis, W. Sussex.
The Canon Gallery, Petworth, W. Sussex.
George House Gallery, Petworth, W. Sussex.
T.G. Wilkinson Antiques Ltd, Petworth, W. Sussex.
Wilsons Antiques, Worthing, W. Sussex.
Anna Harrison Fine Antiques, Gosforth, Tyne and Wear.
MacDonald Fine Art, Gosforth, Tyne and Wear.
Osborne Art and Antiques, Jesmond, Tyne and Wear.
The Dean Gallery Ltd, Newcastle-upon-Tyne, Tyne and Wear.
Ian Sharp Antiques, Tynemouth, Tyne and Wear.
Sport and Country Gallery, Bulkington, Warks.
Arden Gallery, Henley-in-Arden, Warks.
Colmore Galleries Ltd, Henley-in-Arden, Warks.
Fine-Lines (Fine Art), Shipston-on-Stour, Warks.
Astley House - Fine Art, Stretton-on-Fosse, Warks.
Woodland Fine Art, Alvechurch, W. Mids.
Ashleigh House Antiques, Birmingham, W. Mids.
John Hubbard Antiques and Fine Art, Birmingham, W. Mids.
Kestrel House Antiques and Auction Salerooms, Birmingham, W. Mids.
Robert Withers Paintings, Halesowen, W. Mids.
Oldswinford Gallery, Stourbridge, W. Mids.
Driffold Gallery, Sutton Coldfield, W. Mids.
Robin Shield Antiques, Cricklade, Wilts.
D.M. Beach, Salisbury, Wilts.
The Jerram Gallery, Salisbury, Wilts.
Salisbury Antiques Warehouse, Salisbury, Wilts.
Ian J. Brook, Antiques and Picture Gallery, Wilton, Wilts.
Bracebridge Gallery, Astwood Bank, Worcs.
Richard Hagen, Broadway, Worcs.
Hay Loft Gallery, Broadway, Worcs.
Haynes Fine Art of Broadway, Broadway, Worcs.
Haynes Fine Art of Broadway
Picton House Galleries, Broadway, Worcs.
John Noott Galleries, Broadway, Worcs.
Malvern Arts, Great Malvern, Worcs.
Gandolfi House, Malvern Wells, Worcs.
The Highway Gallery, Upton-upon-Severn, Worcs.
James H. Starkey Galleries, Beverley, E. Yorks.
Steven Dews Fine Art, Hull, E. Yorks.
Houghton Hall Antiques, Market Weighton, E. Yorks.
Galloway Antiques, Boroughbridge, N. Yorks.
Anthony Graham Antiques, Boroughbridge, N. Yorks .
W. Greenwood (Fine Art), Burneston, N. Yorks.
Garth Antiques, Harrogate, N. Yorks.
Sutcliffe Galleries, Harrogate, N. Yorks.
Walker Galleries Ltd, Harrogate, N. Yorks.
Reflections, Knaresborough, N. Yorks.
Gary K. Blissett, Long Preston, N. Yorks.
Talents Fine Arts Ltd, Malton, N. Yorks.
Rose Fine Art and Antiques, Ripon, N. Yorks.
Roy Precious, Settle, N. Yorks.
BennettRichard, Thirsk, N. Yorks.
Garth Antiques, Whixley, N. Yorks.
Coulter Galleries, York, N. Yorks.
Fulwood Antiques and The Basement Gallery, Sheffield, S. Yorks.
Hibbert Brothers Ltd, Sheffield, S. Yorks.
E. Carrol, Bingley, W. Yorks.
Oakwood Gallery, Leeds, W. Yorks.
Thirkills Antiques, Leeds, W. Yorks.
The Titus Gallery, Shipley, W. Yorks.
Todmorden Fine Art, Todmorden, W. Yorks.
Robin Taylor Fine Arts, Wakefield, W. Yorks.
Mark Blower Antiques, St. Martin, Guernsey, C.I.
C.I. Galleries Ltd, St. Peter Port, Guernsey, C.I.
St. James's Gallery Ltd, St. Peter Port, Guernsey, C.I.
Geoffrey P. Gavey, Vale, Guernsey, C.I.
Grange Gallery and Fine Arts Ltd, St. Helier, Jersey, C.I.
The Selective Eye Gallery, St. Helier, Jersey, C.I.
I.G.A. Old Masters Ltd, St. Lawrence, Jersey, C.I.
The Bell Gallery, Belfast, N. Ireland.
Dunluce Antiques, Bushmills, Co. Antrim, N. Ireland.
Antiques and Fine Art Gallery, Warrenpoint, Co. Down, N. Ireland.
Atholl Antiques, Aberdeen, Scotland.
The Rendezvous Gallery, Aberdeen, Scotland.
The Waverley Gallery, Aberdeen, Scotland.
Colin Wood (Antiques) Ltd, Aberdeen, Scotland.
William Young Antiques & Fine Art, Aberdeen, Scotland.
Paul Hayes Gallery, Auchterarder, Scotland.
Highland Antiques, Avoch, Scotland.
Mansfield Antiques, Ayr, Scotland.
The McEwan Gallery, Ballater, Scotland.
Westport Fine Art, Dundee, Scotland.
Laurance Black Ltd, Edinburgh, Scotland.
Bourne Fine Art Ltd, Edinburgh, Scotland.

Calton Gallery, Edinburgh, Scotland.
Tom Fidelo, Edinburgh, Scotland.
Malcolm Innes Gallery, Edinburgh, Scotland.
John Mathieson and Co, Edinburgh, Scotland.
Open Eye Gallery Ltd, Edinburgh, Scotland.
The Scottish Gallery, Edinburgh, Scotland.
Aldric Young, Edinburgh, Scotland.
Young Antiques, Edinburgh, Scotland.
The Roger Billcliffe Fine Art, Glasgow, Scotland.
Ewan Mundy Fine Art Ltd, Glasgow, Scotland.
Scottish Art Heritage, Glasgow, Scotland.
Mainhill Gallery, Jedburgh, Scotland.
Kilmacolm Antiques Ltd, Kilmacolm, Scotland.
Newburgh Antiques, Newburgh, Scotland.
The Fitzroy Gallery (formerly The McIan Gallery), Oban, Scotland.
Gallery One, Perth, Scotland.
The George Street Gallery, Perth, Scotland.
Nigel Stacy-Marks Ltd, Perth, Scotland.
St. Andrews Fine Art, St. Andrews, Scotland.
Abbey Antiques, Stirling, Scotland.
David Windsor Gallery, Bangor, Wales.
Michael Webb Fine Art, Bodorgan, Wales.
Manor House Fine Arts, Cardiff, Wales.
Philip Davies Fine Art, Swansea, Wales.
Thicke Galleries, Swansea, Wales.
Barn Court Antiques, Templeton, Wales.
Welsh Art, Tywyn, Wales.

Oriental Art

Nanwani and Co, London EC3.
Chancery Antiques Ltd, London N1.
Hart and Rosenberg, London N1.
Inheritance, London N1.
Japanese Gallery, London N1.
Li, Wan, London N1.
Mitchell Antiques Ltd, Laurence, London N1.
Page Oriental Art, Kevin, London N1.
Ross Antiques, Marcus, London N1.
Tapsell Antiques, London N1.
East-Asia Co, London NW1.
Henderson, Milne, London NW6.
Magus Antiques, London NW8.
B.C. Metalcrafts Ltd, London NW9.
Day Ltd, Shirley, London SW1.
Lawrence Ltd, Clare, London SW1.
Sainsbury & Mason, London SW1.
Spink and Son Ltd, London SW1.
Napier Ltd, Sylvia, London SW6.
Rankin and Ian Conn, Daphne, London SW6.
Bernheimer Ltd, Konrad O., London W1.
Brandt Oriental Art, London W1.
Davies Oriental Art, Barry, London W1.
de Biolley Oriental Art, Jehanne, London W1.
Eskenazi Ltd, London W1.
Eskenazi Ltd, John, London W1.
Hall, Robert, London W1.
Hawthorn Ltd, Gerard, London W1.
Moss Ltd, Sydney L., London W1.
Oriental Bronzes Ltd, London W1.
Pitcher Oriental Art, Nicholas S., London W1.
Robinson, Jonathan, London W1.
Sampson Antiques Ltd, Alistair, London W1.
Speelman Ltd, A & J, London W1.
Toynbee-Clarke Interiors Ltd, London W1.
van Beers Oriental Art, Jan, London W1.
Wrigglesworth, Linda, London W1.
Cohen and Pearce (Oriental Porcelain), London W11.
M.C.N. Antiques, London W11.
Nanking Porcelain Co, London W11.
Van Vredenburgh Ltd, Edric, London W11.
AntiqueWest Ltd, London W8.
Baker Oriental Art, Gregg, London W8.
Berwald Oriental Art, London W8.
Brower Antiques, David, London W8.
Coats Oriental Carpets, London W8.
Cohen & Cohen, London W8.
Deutsch Antiques, H. and W., London W8.
J.A.N. Fine Art, London W8.
Japanese Gallery, London W8.
Kemp, Peter, London W8.
Leask Ward, London W8.
Marchant & Son, S., London W8.
McPherson, Robert, London W8.
Santos, A.V., London W8.
Sinai Antiques Ltd, London W8.
Clive Rogers Oriental Rugs, Wraysbury, Berks.
Glade Antiques, Marlow, Bucks.
Gabor Cossa Antiques, Cambridge, Cambs.
Highland Antiques, Stockport, Cheshire.
David L.H. Southwick Rare Art, Kingswear, Devon.
Brian Taylor Antiques, Plymouth, Devon.
Mere Antiques, Topsham, Devon.
Lionel Geneen Ltd, Bournemouth, Dorset.
Sandy's Antiques, Bournemouth, Dorset.
Oriental Gallery, Moreton-in-Marsh, Glos.
Art-Tique, Tetbury, Glos.
Artemesia, Alresford, Hants.
Oriental Rug Gallery Ltd, St. Albans, Herts.
Michael Sim, Chislehurst, Kent.
John Jackson, Hythe, Kent.
Mandarin Gallery, Riverhead, Kent.
Flower House Antiques, Tenterden, Kent.
M.D. Cannell Antiques, Raveningham, Norfolk.
The Country Seat, Huntercombe, Oxon.
F.C. Manser and Son Ltd, Shrewsbury, Shrops.
Peter Wain, Woore, Shrops.
Haliden Oriental Rug Shop, Bath, Somerset.
Hyndford Antiques, Brighton, E. Sussex.
Patrick Moorhead Antiques, Brighton, E. Sussex.
Brian Page Antiques, Brighton, E. Sussex.
Gensing Antiques, St. Leonards-on-Sea, E. Sussex.
Ringles Cross Antiques, Uckfield, E. Sussex.
Heirloom & Howard Limited, West Yatton, Wilts.
Paul M. Peters Antiques, Harrogate, N. Yorks.
Another World, Edinburgh, Scotland.
Albany Antiques, Glasgow, Scotland.
Jean Megahy, Glasgow, Scotland.
Amber Antiques, Kincardine O'Neil, Scotland.

Paperweights

Coleman, Garrick D., London W11.
Coleman, Garrick D., London W8.
Sweetbriar Gallery, Helsby, Cheshire.
Portique, Bournemouth, Dorset.
Todd and Austin Antiques of Winchester, Winchester, Hants.
The Stone Gallery, Burford, Oxon.
David R. Fileman, Steyning, W. Sussex.
Antiques and Fine Art, Crieff, Scotland.

Photographs & Equipment

Jubilee Photographica, London N1.
Vintage Cameras Ltd, London SE26.
Bayswater Books, London W2.
Classic Collection, London WC1.
Jessop Classic Photographica, London WC1.
Medina Gallery, Barnstaple, Devon.
Medina Gallery, Bideford, Devon.
Peter Pan's Bazaar, Gosport, Hants.

Pottery & Porcelain

Hart and Rosenberg, London N1.
Huntley, Diana, London N1.
Ketley Antiques, Carol, London N1.
Mitchell Antiques Ltd, Laurence, London N1.
Oosthuizen, Jacqueline, London N1.
Finchley Fine Art Galleries, London N12.
Henham (Antiques), Martin, London N2.
Highgate Antiques, London N6.
Manheim (Peter Manheim) Ltd, D.M. and P., London N6.
Klaber and Klaber, London NW3.
Clark Antiques, Gerald, London NW7.
Collector, The, London NW8.
Magus Antiques, London NW8.
Amor Ltd, Albert, London SW1.
Galerie Moderne Ltd, London SW1.
Hamilton Ltd, Ross, London SW1.
Johnson, Lucy, London SW1.
Le Pavillon de Sèvres Ltd, London SW1.
Lewis, M. and D., London SW1.
Sattin Ltd, Gerald, London SW1.
Long, Stephen, London SW10.
Young Antiques, Robert, London SW11.
Barnes Antiques, R.A., London SW15.
Oosthuizen, Jacqueline, London SW3.
Rogers de Rin, London SW3.
Newby (A.J. & M.V. Waller), H.W., London SW8.
Goode and Co (London) Ltd, Thomas, London W1.
Harcourt Antiques, London W1.
Haughton Antiques, Brian, London W1.
Sampson Antiques Ltd, Alistair, London W1.
Venners Antiques, London W1.
Fox, Judy, London W11.
J. and B. Antiques, London W11.
Lewis, M. and D., London W11.
Mercury Antiques, London W11.
Nanking Porcelain Co, London W11.
Schredds of Portobello, London W11.
Badger, The, London W5.
Harold's Place, London W5.
Dixon, Tony, London W6.
Atkins, Garry, London W8.
Brower Antiques, David, London W8.
Davies Antiques, London W8.
Dennis, Richard, London W8.
Deutsch Antiques, H. and W., London W8.
Grosvenor Antiques Ltd, London W8.
Hope and Glory, London W8.
Horne, Jonathan, London W8.
Howard, Valerie, London W8.
Jellicoe, Roderick, London W8.
Jones, Howard, London W8.
Kemp, Peter, London W8.
Libra Antiques, London W8.

London Antique Gallery, London W8.
Manners, E. and H., London W8.
Oliver-Sutton Antiques, London W8.
Seligmann, M. and D., London W8.
Sewell (Antiques) Ltd, Jean, London W8.
Spero, Simon, London W8.
Stobo, Constance, London W8.
Stockspring Antiques, London W8.
Wise, Mary, London W8.
Anchor Antiques Ltd, London WC2.
Baroq at Brindleys, Heath and Reach, Beds.
Cobblers Hall Antiques, Toddington, Beds.
Cavendish Fine Arts - Janet Middlemiss, Sonning-on-Thames, Berks.
Berks Antiques Co Ltd, Windsor and Eton, Berks.
Ulla Stafford Antiques, Windsor and Eton, Berks.
Gabor Cossa Antiques, Cambridge, Cambs.
Cottage Antiques, Cambridge, Cambs.
Abbey Antiques, Ramsey, Cambs.
Sydney House Antiques, Wansford, Cambs.
Lostock Antiques, Altrincham, Cheshire.
Aldersey Hall Ltd, Chester, Cheshire.
The Antique Shop, Chester, Cheshire.
Cameo Antiques, Chester, Cheshire.
Made of Honour, Chester, Cheshire.
Watergate Antiques, Chester, Cheshire.
Little Collectables, Congleton, Cheshire.
The Mulberry Bush, Marple Bridge, Cheshire.
Imperial Antiques, Stockport, Cheshire.
Ruby Snowden Antiques, Yarm, Cleveland.
Antiques, Marazion, Cornwall.
Clock Tower Antiques, Tregony, Cornwall.
Alan Bennett, Truro, Cornwall.
Saint Nicholas Galleries Ltd. (Antiques and Jewellery), Carlisle, Cumbria.
Souvenir Antiques, Carlisle, Cumbria.
Brian Blakemore - Dower House Antiques, Kendal, Cumbria.
Kendal Studios Antiques, Kendal, Cumbria.
Alexander Adamson, Kirkby Lonsdale, Cumbria.
Netherley Cottage Antiques, Milburn, Cumbria.
Jane Pollock Antiques, Penrith, Cumbria.
Kenneth Upchurch, Ashbourne, Derbys.
De-Vine Antiques, Bakewell, Derbys.
David J. Thorn, Budleigh Salterton, Devon.
Mary Payton Antiques, Chagford, Devon.
The Old Brass Kettle, Moretonhampstead, Devon.
The Lantern Shop, Sidmouth, Devon.
Philip Andrade, South Brent, Devon.
Charterhouse Antiques, Teignmouth, Devon.
Mere Antiques, Topsham, Devon.
Birbeck Gallery, Torquay, Devon.
Richard Dunton Antiques, Bournemouth, Dorset.
Box of Porcelain, Dorchester, Dorset.
Heygate Browne Antiques, Sherborne, Dorset.
Reference Works, Swanage, Dorset.
Grant's Antiques, Barnard Castle, Durham.
Domino Antiques, Barling Magna, Essex.
Bush House, Corringham, Essex.
Argyll House Antiques, Felsted, Essex.
John Burls, Great Oakley, Essex.
Castle Antiques, Leigh-on-Sea, Essex.
Richard Wrenn Antiques, Leigh-on-Sea, Essex.
Bush Antiques, Saffron Walden, Essex.
Barton House Antiques, Stanford-le-Hope, Essex.
Harris Antiques (Stansted), Stansted, Essex.
Julian Tatham-Losh, Andoversford, Glos.
Antique Corner with A & C Antique Clocks, Bristol, Glos.
No. 74 Antiques and Collectables, Bristol, Glos.
Stuart House Antiques, Chipping Campden, Glos.
Swan Antiques, Chipping Campden, Glos.
Woodminster Antiques, Cirencester, Glos.
Berry Antiques, Moreton-in-Marsh, Glos.
Chandlers Antiques, Moreton-in-Marsh, Glos.
Mrs M.K. Nielsen, Moreton-in-Marsh, Glos.
Acorn Antiques, Stow-on-the-Wold, Glos.
Colin Brand Antiques, Stow-on-the-Wold, Glos.
Martin House Antiques, Stow-on-the-Wold, Glos.
Dolphin Antiques, Tetbury, Glos.
Fifty-One Antiques Et Cetera, Tetbury, Glos.
Tetbury Gallery, Tetbury, Glos.
Muriel Lindsay, Winchcombe, Glos.
Goss and Crested China Centre and Goss Museum, Horndean, Hants.
Lita Kaye of Lyndhurst, Lyndhurst, Hants.
Lane Antiques, Stockbridge, Hants.
Anne Barlow Antiques, Letchmore Heath, Herts.
Tilings Antiques, Brasted, Kent.
W.W. Warner (Antiques) Ltd, Brasted, Kent.
Serendipity, Deal, Kent.
Alan Wood, Gravesend, Kent.
Owlets, Hythe, Kent.
Amherst Antiques, Riverhead, Kent.
Kent Cottage, Rolvenden, Kent.
Beaubush House Antiques, Sandgate, Kent.
Delf Stream Gallery, Sandwich, Kent.
Aaron Antiques, Snodland, Kent.
Steppes Hill Farm Antiques, Stockbury, Kent.
Pantiles Spa Antiques, Tunbridge Wells, Kent.
Old Corner House Antiques, Wittersham, Kent.
Roy W. Bunn, Barnoldswick, Lancs.
Park Galleries Antiques, Fine Art and Decor, Bolton, Lancs.
Cottage Antiques, Darwen, Lancs.
Clare's Antiques and Auction Galleries, Garstang, Lancs.
Village Antiques, Manchester, Lancs.
The Antique Shop, St. Annes-on-Sea, Lancs.
Paddock Antiques, Woodhouse Eaves, Leics.
Staines Antiques, Horncastle, Lincs.
J. and R. Ratcliffe, Lincoln, Lincs.
The Strait Antiques, Lincoln, Lincs.
Underwoodhall Antiques, Woodhall Spa, Lincs.
Ivy House Antiques, Acle, Norfolk.
Liz Allport-Lomax, Coltishall, Norfolk.
Roger Bradbury Antiques, Coltishall, Norfolk.
Isabel Neal Cabinet Antiques, Coltishall, Norfolk.
Peter Robinson, Heacham, Norfolk.
Richard Scott Antiques, Holt, Norfolk.
Sue Miller Antiques and Collectables, Langham, Norfolk.
Malcolm Turner, Norwich, Norfolk.
Dorothy's Antiques, Sheringham, Norfolk.
Leo Pratt and Son, South Walsham, Norfolk.
T.C.S. Brooke, Wroxham, Norfolk.
Peter Jackson Antiques, Brackley, Northants.
R. and M. Nicholas, Towcester, Northants.
Felton Park Antiques, Felton, Northumbs.
Hedley's of Hexham, Hexham, Northumbs.
Melville Kemp Ltd, Nottingham, Notts.
David and Carole Potter Antiques, Nottingham, Notts.
Swan Gallery, Burford, Oxon.
Bees Antiques, Woodstock, Oxon.
The Old House Gallery, Oakham, Rutland.
T.J. Roberts, Uppingham, Rutland.
Micawber Antiques, Bridgnorth, Shrops.
Tudor House Antiques (Bill Dickenson), Ironbridge, Shrops.
Teme Valley Antiques, Ludlow, Shrops.
Peter Wain, Woore, Shrops.
David and Sally March Antiques, Abbots Leigh, Somerset.
Andrew Dando, Bath, Somerset.
Quiet Street Antiques, Bath, Somerset.
M. Wood, Bishopswood, Somerset.
Dowlish Wake Antiques, Dowlish Wake, Somerset.
West End House Antiques, Ilminster, Somerset.
Milestone Antiques, Lichfield, Staffs.
Eveline Winter, Rugeley, Staffs.
Five Towns Antiques, Stoke-on-Trent, Staffs.
The Potteries Antique Centre, Stoke-on-Trent, Staffs.
Top of the Hill, Stoke-on-Trent, Staffs.
Ceramic Search, Stoke-on-Trent, Staffs.
Derby Cottage Collectables, Exning, Suffolk.
J. and J. Baker, Lavenham, Suffolk.
Oswald Simpson, Long Melford, Suffolk.
John Read, Martlesham, Suffolk.
David Gibbins Antiques, Woodbridge, Suffolk.
Red House Antiques, Yoxford, Suffolk.
Suffolk House Antiques, Yoxford, Suffolk.
Susan Wells Antiques, Yoxford, Suffolk.
Churt Curiosity Shop, Churt, Surrey.
Decodream, Coulsdon, Surrey.
Dorking Emporium Antiques Centre, Dorking, Surrey.
Church Street Antiques, Godalming, Surrey.
Antiques Arcadia, Richmond, Surrey.
Susan Becker, Walton-on-Thames, Surrey.
Brocante, Weybridge, Surrey.
Patrick Moorhead Antiques, Brighton, E. Sussex.
Yellow Lantern Antiques Ltd, Brighton, E. Sussex.
Stewart Gallery, Eastbourne, E. Sussex.
Southdown Antiques, Lewes, E. Sussex.
Leonard Russell, Newhaven, E. Sussex.
Herbert Gordon Gasson, Rye, E. Sussex.
Peter Francis Antiques, Arundel, W. Sussex.
Pat Golding, Arundel, W. Sussex.

Gems Antiques, Chichester, W. Sussex.
David Foord-Brown Antiques, Cuckfield, W. Sussex.
Richard Gardner Antiques, Petworth, W. Sussex.
William Hockley Antiques, Petworth, W. Sussex.
Ian Sharp Antiques, Tynemouth, Tyne and Wear.
Coleshill Antiques and Interiors Ltd, Coleshill, Warks.
Janice Paull Antiques, Kenilworth, Warks.
Burman Antiques, Stratford-upon-Avon, Warks.
H. and R.L. Parry Ltd, Sutton Coldfield, W. Mids.
Pendeford House Antiques, Wolverhampton, W. Mids.
Moxhams Antiques, Bradford-on-Avon, Wilts.
Antiques - Rene Nicholls, Malmesbury, Wilts.
Ray Best Antiques, Newton Tony, Wilts.
Heirloom & Howard Limited, West Yatton, Wilts.
Bygones by the Cathedral, Worcester, Worcs.
Bygones (Worcester), Worcester, Worcs.
John Edwards Antiques, Worcester, Worcs.
M. Lees and Sons, Worcester, Worcs.
Long Tran Antiques, Worcester, Worcs.
Worcester Antiques Centre, Worcester, Worcs.
The Crested China Co, Driffield, E. Yorks.
Houghton Hall Antiques, Market Weighton, E. Yorks.
Ryefield House Antiques, Bradley, N. Yorks.
Bryan Bowden, Harrogate, N. Yorks.
David Love, Harrogate, N. Yorks.
York Cottage Antiques, Helmsley, N. Yorks.
Ings House Antiques, Linton, N. Yorks.
Country Collector, Pickering, N. Yorks.
Nanbooks, Settle, N. Yorks.
Anderson Slater Antiques, Settle, N. Yorks.
Caedmon House, Whitby, N. Yorks.
Farmhouse Antiques, Great Houghton, S. Yorks.
Muir Hewitt Art Deco Originals, Halifax, W. Yorks.
Peter Berry Antiques, Huddersfield, W. Yorks.
Grange Antiques, St. Peter Port, Guernsey, C.I.
St. James's Gallery Ltd, St. Peter Port , Guernsey, C.I.
The Country Antiques, Antrim, Co. Antrim, N. Ireland.
Dunluce Antiques, Bushmills, Co. Antrim, N. Ireland.
Clifford J. Auld Antiques (Old Cross Antiques), Ashfield, Co. Down, N. Ireland.
Downshire House Antiques, Newry, Co. Down, N. Ireland.
McCabe's Antique Galleries, Newry, Co. Down, N. Ireland.
Steeple Antiques, Ceres, Scotland.
Collessie Antiques, Collessie, Scotland.
Laurance Black Ltd, Edinburgh, Scotland.
Bruntsfield Antiques, Edinburgh, Scotland.
Present Bygones, Edinburgh, Scotland.
Young Antiques, Edinburgh, Scotland.
Tim Wright Antiques, Glasgow, Scotland.
Strathspey Gallery, Grantown-on-Spey, Scotland.
Elm House Antiques, Haddington, Scotland.
Miles Antiques, Kinross, Scotland.
Herrald of Edinburgh, Meigle, Scotland.
Harper-James, Montrose, Scotland.
Newburgh Antiques, Newburgh, Scotland.
Waverley Antiques, Upper Largo, Scotland.
Howards of Aberystwyth, Aberystwyth, Wales.
Paul Gibbs Antiques and Decorative Arts, Conwy, Wales.
Bulmer's, Cowbridge, Wales.
Manor House Antiques, Fishguard, Wales.
Hebbards of Hay, Hay-on-Wye, Wales.
Islwyn Watkins, Knighton, Wales.
Deco on the Dee, Llangollen, Wales.
J. and R. Langford, Llangollen, Wales.
Passers Buy (Marie Evans), Llangollen, Wales.
West Wales Antiques, Murton, Wales.
Magpie Antiques, Swansea, Wales.
Clareston Antiques, Tenby, Wales.
Castle Antiques, Usk, Wales.

Prints (see Maps & Prints)

Rugs (see Carpets)

Russian/Soviet Art

Soviet Carpet and Art Centre, London NW2.
Hermitage Antiques plc, London SW1.
Andipa & Son Icon Gallery, Maria, London SW3.
Richardson and Kailas Icons, London SW6.
Cheneviere Fine Arts, Antoine, London W1.
Ermitage Ltd, London W1.
Miles Gallery, Roy, London W1.
Wartski Ltd, London W1.
Temple Gallery, London W11.
Mark Gallery, The, London W2.
Mir Russki, Linlithgow, Scotland.
The Fitzroy Gallery (formerly The McIan Gallery), Oban, Scotland.

Scientific Instruments

Finchley Fine Art Galleries, London N12.
Burness Antiques and Scientific Instruments, Victor, London SE1.
Laurie Antiques, Peter, London SE10.
Relcy Antiques, London SE10.
Jillings of Belgravia, London SW1.
Mercer (Chronometers) Ltd, Thomas, London SW1.
Philip and Sons Ltd, Trevor, London SW1.
Watts, Captain O.M., London W1.
Delehar, Peter, London W11.
Mayflower Antiques, London W11.
Von Pflugh Antiques, Johnny, London W11.
Gould at Ocean Leisure, Gillian, London WC2.
Middleton, Arthur, London WC2.
Christopher Sykes Antiques, Woburn, Beds.
Malcolm Frazer Antiques, Cheadle, Cheshire.
Cremyll Antiques, Cremyll, Cornwall.
Mike Read Antique Sciences, St. Ives, Cornwall.
Alan Jones Antiques, Plymouth, Devon.
Branksome Antiques, Branksome, Dorset.
Mayflower Antiques, Harwich, Essex.
The Chart House, Shenfield, Essex.
Chris Grimes Militaria, Bristol, Glos.
Country Life Antiques, Stow-on-the-Wold, Glos.
Wessex Medical Antiques, Portsmouth, Hants.
Barometer Shop, Leominster, Herefs.
Michael Sim, Chislehurst, Kent.
Hadlow Antiques, Tunbridge Wells, Kent.
David J. Hansord and Son, Lincoln, Lincs.
Turret House, Wymondham, Norfolk.
Bernard G. House, Wells, Somerset.
Patrick Marney, Long Melford, Suffolk.
Roy Arnold, Needham Market, Suffolk.
Principia Arts and Sciences, Marlborough, Wilts.
Minster Antiques, York, N. Yorks.
Time & Tide Antiques, Portaferry, Co. Down, N. Ireland.

Sculpture

Centaur Gallery, London N6.
Miller Fine Arts, Duncan R., London NW3.
Tara Antiques, London NW8.
Hirschhorn, Robert E., London SE5.
Bowman, Robert, London SW1.
Chaucer Fine Arts Ltd, London SW1.
Day Ltd, Shirley, London SW1.
Hazlitt, Gooden and Fox Ltd, London SW1.
Seago, London SW1.
Whitford Fine Art, London SW1.
Clark & Co, Jonathan, London SW10.
Barnes Gallery, The, London SW13.
Few, Ted, London SW17.
Tulissio De Beaumont, London SW6.
Agnew's, London W1.
Alan Ltd, Adrian, London W1.
Browse and Darby Ltd, London W1.
Cazalet Ltd, Lumley, London W1.
Colnaghi & Co Ltd, P. and D., London W1.
d'Offay, Anthony, London W1.
Editions Graphiques Gallery, London W1.
Eskenazi Ltd, London W1.
Fine Art Society plc, The, London W1.
Gibbs Ltd, Christopher, London W1.
Jefferson Ltd, Patrick, London W1.
Sladmore Gallery, The, London W1.
Stoppenbach and Delestre Ltd, London W1.
Curá Antiques, London W11.
Milne and Moller, London W11.
Petrou, Peter, London W11.
Philp, London W11.
Piano Nobile Fine Paintings, London W11.
Van Vredenburgh Ltd, Edric, London W11.
Wolseley Fine Arts plc, London W11.
Alan Ltd, Adrian, London W8.
Simon Hilton, Dunmow, Essex.
Quatrefoil, Fordingbridge, Hants.
Lacewing Fine Art Gallery, Romsey, Hants.
London House Antiques, Westerham, Kent.
Robin Cox Antiques, Ketton, Lincs.
Pearse Lukies, Aylsham, Norfolk.
Arthur Brett and Sons Ltd, Norwich, Norfolk.
The Barry M. Keene Gallery, Henley-on-Thames, Oxon.

David Bridgwater, Bath, Somerset.
Bruton Gallery, Bath, Somerset.
Tim Everett, West Buckland, Somerset.
Equus Art Gallery, Newmarket, Suffolk.
Piano Nobile Fine Paintings, Richmond, Surrey.
Apollo Antiques Ltd, Warwick, Warks.
Patrick and Gillian Morley Antiques, Warwick, Warks.
The Jerram Gallery, Salisbury, Wilts.
Fettes Fine Art, York, N. Yorks.
Calton Gallery, Edinburgh, Scotland.
The Roger Billcliffe Fine Art, Glasgow, Scotland.
Mainhill Gallery, Jedburgh, Scotland.

Shipping Goods & Period Furniture for the Trade

Skeel Antique Warehouse, Keith, London N1.
Crispin Antiques, Ian, London NW1.
Regent Antiques, London NW1.
Antique Trade Warehouse, London SE1.
Antique Warehouse, London SE1.
Oola Boola Antiques London, London SE1.
Penny Farthing Antiques, London SE1.
Tower Bridge Antiques, London SE1.
Fredericks and Son, J.A., London W1.
Secondhand Alley, Shefford, Beds.
Tavistock Antiques, St. Neots, Cambs.
R. Wilding, Wisbech, Cambs.
W. Buckley Antiques Exports, Congleton, Cheshire.
Paul Jennings Antiques, Angarrack, Cornwall.
Ben Eggleston Antiques, Long Marton, Cumbria.
Antique Exporters U.K, Brailsford, Derbys.
Michael Allcroft Antiques, Newtown, Derbys.
Shardlow Antiques Warehouse, Shardlow, Derbys.
John Prestige Antiques, Brixham, Devon.
G. Mounter, Dulford, Devon.
Fagins Antiques, Exeter, Devon.
McBains of Exeter, Exeter, Devon.
Sextons, Kentisbeare, Devon.
Richard Dunton Antiques, Bournemouth, Dorset.
Wiffen's Antiques, Parkstone, Dorset.
Jo Patterson Antiques, Crook, Durham.
Alan Ramsey Antiques, Darlington, Durham.
Barton House Antiques, Stanford-le-Hope, Essex.
Bristol Trade Antiques, Bristol, Glos.
Cabbages & Kings, Winchester, Hants.
Alan Lord Antiques, Folkestone, Kent.
Charles International Antiques, Maidstone, Kent.
Sutton Valence Antiques, Maidstone, Kent.
Sutton Valence Antiques, Sutton Valence, Kent.
West Lancs. Antique Exports, Burscough, Lancs.
The Antique Shop, Edenfield, Lancs.
P.J. Brown Antiques, Haslingden, Lancs.
R.J. O'Brien and Son Antiques, Manchester, Lancs.
G.G. Exports, Middleton Village, Lancs.
Tyson's Antiques, Morecambe, Lancs.
John Robinson Antiques, Wigan, Lancs.
Streetwalker Antiques Warehouse, Barton-on-Humber, Lincs.
Grantham Furniture Emporium, Grantham, Lincs.
Seaview Antiques, Horncastle, Lincs.
Michael Brewer, Lincoln, Lincs.
C. and K.E. Dring, Lincoln, Lincs.
Trade Antiques, Long Sutton, Lincs.
G & J Crowson, Skegness, Lincs.
Bridge Antiques, Sutton Bridge, Lincs.
Old Barn Antiques Warehouse, Sutton Bridge, Lincs.
Kensington Tower Antiques Ltd, Liverpool, Merseyside.
The Original British American Antiques, Liverpool, Merseyside.
Swainbanks Ltd, Liverpool, Merseyside.
Theta Gallery, Liverpool, Merseyside.
Molloy's Furnishers Ltd, Southport, Merseyside.
Tony and Anne Sutcliffe Antiques, Southport, Merseyside.
Sheila Hart and John Giles, Aylsham, Norfolk.
Pearse Lukies, Aylsham, Norfolk.
Eric Bates and Sons, Coltishall, Norfolk.
Old Coach House, Long Stratton, Norfolk.
John Roe Antiques, Islip, Northants.
R.E. Thompson, Long Buckby, Northants.
Bryan Perkins Antiques, Wellingborough, Northants.
James Miller Antiques, Wooler, Northumbs.
T. Baker, Langford, Notts.
Fair Deal Antiques, Mansfield, Notts.
Newark Antiques Warehouse, Newark, Notts.
Meadow Lane Antiques, Nottingham, Notts.
Mitre House Antiques, Ludlow, Shrops.
Francis O'Dwyer Antiques, Bath, Somerset.
M.G.R. Exports, Bruton, Somerset.
Pennard House, East Pennard, Somerset.
T.M. Dyte Antiques, Highbridge, Somerset.
The Treasure Chest, Highbridge, Somerset.
J.C. Giddings, Wiveliscombe, Somerset.
Burton Antiques, Burton-on-Trent, Staffs.
Cordelia and Perdy's Antique Junk Shop, Lichfield, Staffs.
Armson's of Yoxall Antiques, Yoxall, Staffs.
Goodbreys, Framlingham, Suffolk.
A. Abbott Antiques, Ipswich, Suffolk.
Antique Furniture Warehouse, Woodbridge, Suffolk.
Laurence Tauber Antiques, Surbiton, Surrey.
Euro-Pine, Sutton, Surrey.
Bexhill Antique Exporters, Bexhill-on-Sea, E. Sussex.
The Old Mint House, Bexhill-on-Sea, E. Sussex.
Ashton's Antiques, Brighton, E. Sussex.
Attic Antiques, Brighton, E. Sussex.
Lloyd Williams - Antique Anglo Am Warehouse, Eastbourne, E. Sussex.
The Old Mint House, Pevensey, E. Sussex.
J. Powell (Hove) Ltd, Portslade, W. Sussex.
Peter Smith Antiques, Sunderland, Tyne and Wear.
Renaissance Antiques, Tynemouth, Tyne and Wear.
Tim Harrison Wholesale Exports, Stratford-upon-Avon, Warks.
Magpie House, Hockley Heath, W. Mids.
Smithfield Antiques, Lye, W. Mids.
Grannies Attic Antiques, Smethwick, W. Mids.
Brett Wilkins Antiques, Wednesbury, W. Mids.
Martin Taylor Antiques, Wolverhampton, W. Mids.
North Wilts Exporters, Brinkworth, Wilts.
Calne Antiques, Calne, Wilts.
Harley Antiques, Christian Malford, Wilts.
Pillars Antiques, Lyneham, Wilts.
Cross Hayes Antiques, Malmesbury, Wilts.
Sambourne House Antiques, Minety, Wilts.
K. and A. Welch, Warminster, Wilts.
Geoffrey Mole/Antique Exports, Hull, E. Yorks.
Pearson Antiques, Hull, E. Yorks.
Trade Antiques - D.D. White, Manfield, N. Yorks.
Tomlinson (Antiques) Ltd. & Period Furniture Ltd, Tockwith, N. Yorks.
Roger Appleyard Ltd, Rotherham, S. Yorks.
Philip Turnor Antiques, Rotherham, S. Yorks.
Dronfield Antiques, Sheffield, S. Yorks.
Gilbert and Sons, Sheffield, S. Yorks.
N.P. and A. Salt Antiques, Sheffield, S. Yorks.
North Bridge Antiques, Halifax, W. Yorks.
Times Past Antiques, Auchterarder, Scotland.
Imrie Antiques, Bridge of Earn, Scotland.
Neil Livingstone, Dundee, Scotland.
George Duff Antiques, Edinburgh, Scotland.
Georgian Antiques, Edinburgh, Scotland.
Narducci Antiques, Largs, Scotland.
A.S. Deuchar and Son, Perth, Scotland.
Narducci Antiques, Saltcoats, Scotland.
Charlotte's Wholesale Antiques, Cardiff, Wales.
Michael Lloyd, Henllan, Wales.
Anne and Colin Hulbert (Antiques and Firearms), Swansea, Wales.
All Old Exports Ltd., Treherbert, Wales.
Steven Evans Antiques, Treorchy, Wales.

Silver & Jewellery

Rankin Coin Co. Ltd, George, London E2.
Finecraft Workshop Ltd, London EC1.
Harris (Jewellery) Ltd, Jonathan, London EC1.
Hirsh Ltd, London EC1.
Joseph and Pearce Ltd, London EC1.
McKay, R.I., London EC1.
Ullmann Ltd, A.R., London EC1.
Nanwani and Co, London EC3.
Searle and Co Ltd, London EC3.
Eclectica, London N1.
Graham Gallery, The, London N1.
Hart, Rosemary, London N1.
Hatcher, Sherry, London N1.
Laurie (Antiques) Ltd, John, London N1.
Oosthuizen, Jacqueline, London N1.
Little Curiosity Shop, The, London N21.
Delieb Antiques, London NW11.
Corner Cupboard, The, London NW2.
Silver Belle, London NW8.
Creek Antiques, London SE10.
Vale Stamps and Antiques, London SE3.
A.D.C. Heritage Ltd, London SW1.
Bourdon-Smith Ltd, J.H., London SW1.
Cobra and Bellamy, London SW1.
Cornucopia, London SW1.

Davis (Works of Art) Ltd, Kenneth, London SW1.
Dickenson Fine Silver Ltd, Alastair, London SW1.
Franklin, N. and I., London SW1.
Kojis Antique Jewellery Ltd, London SW1.
Longmire Ltd (Three Royal Warrants), London SW1.
Sattin Ltd, Gerald, London SW1.
Boodle and Dunthorne Ltd, London SW3.
Hardy and Co, James, London SW3.
Leslie, Stanley, London SW3.
McKenna and Co, London SW3.
Merola, London SW3.
Oosthuizen, Jacqueline, London SW3.
Schell, Christine, London SW3.
Watson Ltd, Gordon, London SW3.
Harris, Nicholas, London SW6.
Levene Ltd, M.P., London SW7.
Page, A. & H., London SW7.
Antrobus Ltd, Philip, London W1.
Armour-Winston Ltd, London W1.
Asprey plc, London W1.
Bennett, Paul, London W1.
Bentley & Co Ltd, London W1.
Bond Street Silver Galleries, London W1.
Boodle and Dunthorne Ltd, London W1.
Bull (Antiques) Ltd
JB Silverware, John, London W1.
Carrington and Co. Ltd, London W1.
Cronan Ltd, Sandra, London W1.
Davis Ltd, A. B., London W1.
Demas, London W1.
Editions Graphiques Gallery, London W1.
Ermitage Ltd, London W1.
Garrard & Co. Ltd (The Crown Jewellers), London W1.
Griffin Antiques Ltd, Simon, London W1.
Hadleigh Jewellers, London W1.
Hancocks and Co, London W1.
Harris and Son (London) Ltd, S.H., London W1.
Harvey and Gore, London W1.
Hennell of Bond Street Ltd. Founded 1736 (incorporating Frazer and Haws (1868) and E. Lloyd Lawrence (1830)), London W1.
Holmes Ltd, London W1.
Inglis, Brand, London W1.
Johnson Walker & Tolhurst Ltd, London W1.
Lacloche Freres, London W1.
Lavender (Antiques) Ltd, D.S., London W1.
Marks Antiques, London W1.
Milne Ltd, Nigel, London W1.
Moira, London W1.
Ogden Ltd, Richard, London W1.
Phillips Ltd, S.J., London W1.
Richards and Sons, David, London W1.
Rose - Source of the Unusual, Michael, London W1.
Silver Fund Ltd, The, London W1.
Tessiers Ltd, London W1.
Wartski Ltd, London W1.
Bexfield Antiques, Daniel, London W11.
Britannia Export Antiques, London W11.
Central Gallery (Portobello), London W11.
Freeman, J., London W11.
Kleanthous Antiques Ltd, Stouts Antiques Market, London W11.
Portobello Antique Store, London W11.
Schredds of Portobello, London W11.
Silver Fox Gallery, The, London W11.
Smith and Gerald Robinson Antiques, Colin, London W11.
Craven Gallery, London W2.
McAleer, M., London W2.
Cooke Antiques Ltd, Mary, London W8.
Deutsch Antiques, H. and W., London W8.
Green's Antique Galleries, London W8.
Hampson and Lewis, London W8.
Jesse, John, London W8.
Jones, Howard, London W8.
Lev (Antiques) Ltd, London W8.
Sinai Antiques Ltd, London W8.
Nortonbury Antiques, London WC1.
Shrubsole Ltd, S.J., London WC1.
Kettle Ltd, Thomas, London WC2.
London Silver Vaults, The, London WC2.
Pearl Cross Ltd, London WC2.
Silver Mouse Trap, The, London WC2.
Styles Silver, Hungerford, Berks.
Turks Head Antiques, Windsor and Eton, Berks.
Buckies, Cambridge, Cambs.
Pembroke Antiques, Cambridge, Cambs.
Attic Gallery, Wisbech, Cambs.
D.J. Massey and Son, Alderley Edge, Cheshire.
Cameo Antiques, Chester, Cheshire.
Kayes of Chester, Chester, Cheshire.
Lowe and Sons, Chester, Cheshire.
Veevers, Chester, Cheshire.
Watergate Antiques, Chester, Cheshire.
The Clock House, Hazel Grove, Cheshire.
D.J. Massey and Son, Macclesfield, Cheshire.
Highland Antiques, Stockport, Cheshire.
Imperial Antiques, Stockport, Cheshire.
A. Baker and Sons, Warrington, Cheshire.
Little Jem's, Penzance, Cornwall.
Alan Bennett, Truro, Cornwall.
Saint Nicholas Galleries Ltd. (Antiques and Jewellery), Carlisle, Cumbria.
The Silver Thimble, Kendal, Cumbria.
Jane Pollock Antiques, Penrith, Cumbria.
Elizabeth and Son, Ulverston, Cumbria.
Mark Parkhouse Antiques and Jewellery, Barnstaple, Devon.
Timothy Coward Fine Silver, Braunton, Devon.
David J. Thorn, Budleigh Salterton, Devon.
Gold and Silver Exchange, Exeter, Devon.
Brian Mortimer, Exeter, Devon.
John Nathan Antiques, Exeter, Devon.
Boase Antiques, Exmouth, Devon.
J. Barrymore and Co, Honiton, Devon.
Otter Antiques, Honiton, Devon.
Charterhouse Antiques, Teignmouth, Devon.
Extence Antiques, Teignmouth, Devon.
Beaminster Antiques, Beaminster, Dorset.
G.B. Mussenden and Son Antiques, Jewellery and Silver, Bournemouth, Dorset.
Geo. A. Payne and Son Ltd, Bournemouth, Dorset.
R.E. Porter, Bournemouth, Dorset.
Portique, Bournemouth, Dorset.
Peter Stebbing, Bournemouth, Dorset.
Batten's Jewellers, Bridport, Dorset.
D. J. Jewellery, Parkstone, Dorset.
Greystoke Antiques, Sherborne, Dorset.
Henry Willis (Antique Silver), Sherborne, Dorset.
Georgian Gems Antique Jewellers, Swanage, Dorset.
Heirlooms Antique Jewellers and Silversmiths, Wareham, Dorset.
Robin Finnegan (Jeweller), Darlington, Durham.
Argentum Antiques, Coggeshall, Essex.
Elizabeth Cannon Antiques, Colchester, Essex.
Grahams of Colchester, Colchester, Essex.
J. Streamer Antiques, Leigh-on-Sea, Essex.
Richard Wrenn Antiques, Leigh-on-Sea, Essex.
Gostick Hall Antiques, Newport, Essex.
Harris Antiques (Stansted), Stansted, Essex.
Whichcraft Jewellery, Writtle, Essex.
Grey-Harris and Co, Bristol, Glos.
Kemps, Bristol, Glos.
Greens of Cheltenham Ltd, Cheltenham, Glos.
Martin and Co. Ltd, Cheltenham, Glos.
Scott-Cooper Ltd, Cheltenham, Glos.
Swan Antiques, Chipping Campden, Glos.
Walter Bull and Son (Cirencester) Ltd, Cirencester, Glos.
Rankine Taylor Antiques, Cirencester, Glos.
Mick and Fanny Wright, Minchinhampton, Glos.
Olive Antiques, Alverstoke, Hants.
Squirrel Collectors Centre, Basingstoke, Hants.
A.W. Porter and Son, Hartley Wintney, Hants.
Barry Papworth, Lymington, Hants.
Meg Campbell, Southampton, Hants.
Parkhouse and Wyatt Ltd, Southampton, Hants.
Robin Howard Antiques, Titchfield, Hants.
Warings of Hereford Antiques, Hereford, Herefs.
Abbey Antiques - Fine Jewellery & Silver, Hemel Hempstead, Herts.
Bexfield Antiques, Hitchin, Herts.
Forget-me-Knot Antiques, St. Albans, Herts.
Stuart Wharton, St. Albans, Herts.
J. and H. Bell Antiques, Castletown, I. of Man.
R. J. Baker, Canterbury, Kent.
Owlets, Hythe, Kent.
Amherst Antiques, Riverhead, Kent.
Steppes Hill Farm Antiques, Stockbury, Kent.
Chapel Place Antiques, Tunbridge Wells, Kent.
Glassdrumman Antiques, Tunbridge Wells, Kent.
Pantiles Spa Antiques, Tunbridge Wells, Kent.
Andrew Smith Antiques, West Malling, Kent.
The Coin and Jewellery Shop, Accrington, Lancs.
Kenworthys Ltd, Ashton-under-Lyne, Lancs.
Ancient and Modern, Blackburn, Lancs.
Mitchell's (Lock Antiques), Blackburn, Lancs.
Chard Coins, Blackpool, Lancs.
Leigh Jewellery, Leigh, Lancs.
Snuff Box, Lytham St. Annes, Lancs.
Boodle and Dunthorne Ltd, Manchester, Lancs.
Cathedral Jewellers, Manchester, Lancs.
St. James Antiques, Manchester, Lancs.
Brittons Jewellers and Antiques, Nelson, Lancs.
Charles Howell Jeweller, Oldham, Lancs.

H.C. Simpson and Sons Jewellers (Oldham)Ltd, Oldham, Lancs.
Keystone Antiques, Coalville, Leics.
Corry's, Leicester, Leics.
Letty's Antiques, Leicester, Leics.
Stanley Hunt Jewellers, Gainsborough, Lincs.
Pilgrims Antiques Centre, Gainsborough, Lincs.
Wilkinson's, Grantham, Lincs.
Mr Van Hefflin, Kirton in Lindsey, Lincs.
Rowletts of Lincoln, Lincoln, Lincs.
James Usher and Son Ltd, Lincoln, Lincs.
G & J Crowson, Skegness, Lincs.
Wilkinson's, Sleaford, Lincs.
Dawson of Stamford, Stamford, Lincs.
St. Mary's Galleries, Stamford, Lincs.
C. Rosenberg, Heswall, Merseyside.
Kevin Whay's Clock Shop and Antiques, Hoylake, Merseyside.
Boodle and Dunthorne Ltd, Liverpool, Merseyside.
Edward's Jewellers, Liverpool, Merseyside.
Stefani Antiques, Liverpool, Merseyside.
H.S. Walne, Southport, Merseyside.
Weldons Jewellery and Antiques, Southport, Merseyside.
Bond Street Antiques (inc. Jas. J. Briggs Est. 1820), Cromer, Norfolk.
Market Place Antiques, Fakenham, Norfolk.
Barry's Antiques, Gt. Yarmouth, Norfolk.
Folkes Antiques and Jewellers, Gt. Yarmouth, Norfolk.
Peter Howkins, Gt. Yarmouth, Norfolk.
Wheatleys, Gt. Yarmouth, Norfolk.
Tim Clayton Jewellery, King's Lynn, Norfolk.
Albrow and Sons Family Jewellers, Norwich, Norfolk.
Clive Dennett Coins, Norwich, Norfolk.
Leona Levine Silver Specialist, Norwich, Norfolk.
Maddermarket Antiques, Norwich, Norfolk.
Oswald Sebley, Norwich, Norfolk.
James and Ann Tillett, Norwich, Norfolk.
Thomas Tillett & Co, Norwich, Norfolk.
Parriss, Sheringham, Norfolk.
Michael Jones Jeweller, Northampton, Northants.
Boadens Antiques, Hexham, Northumbs.
Melville Kemp Ltd, Nottingham, Notts.
Barclay Antiques, Headington, Oxon.
Thames Gallery, Henley-on-Thames, Oxon.
Reginald Davis Ltd, Oxford, Oxon.
Payne and Son (Goldsmiths) Ltd, Oxford, Oxon.
MGJ Jewellers Ltd., Wallingford, Oxon.
Churchgate Antiques, Empingham, Rutland.
English Heritage, Bridgnorth, Shrops.
Teme Valley Antiques, Ludlow, Shrops.
Cruck House Antiques, Much Wenlock, Shrops.
Hutton Antiques, Shrewsbury, Shrops.
The Little Gem, Shrewsbury, Shrops.
F.C. Manser and Son Ltd, Shrewsbury, Shrops.
Abbey Galleries, Bath, Somerset.
Bladud House Antiques, Bath, Somerset.
D. and B. Dickinson, Bath, Somerset.
E.P. Mallory and Son Ltd, Bath, Somerset.
Castle Antiques, Burnham-on-Sea, Somerset.
Beach Antiques, Clevedon, Somerset.
Winston Mac (Silversmith), Bury St. Edmunds, Suffolk.
A. Abbott Antiques, Ipswich, Suffolk.
Temptations, Ashtead, Surrey.
T. M. Collins, Dorking, Surrey.
Hebeco, Dorking, Surrey.
E. Hollander, Dorking, Surrey.
Pauline Watson, Dorking, Surrey.
Cry for the Moon, Godalming, Surrey.
Tramp Jewellers, Guildford, Surrey.
Glydon and Guess Ltd, Kingston-upon-Thames, Surrey.
Horton's, Richmond, Surrey.
Lionel Jacobs, Richmond, Surrey.
S. Warrender and Co, Sutton, Surrey.
Church House Antiques, Weybridge, Surrey.
Not Just Silver, Weybridge, Surrey.
Harry Diamond and Son, Brighton, E. Sussex.
James Doyle Antiques, Brighton, E. Sussex.
D.H. Edmonds Ltd, Brighton, E. Sussex.
Paul Goble, Brighton, E. Sussex.
The Gold and Silversmiths of Hove, Brighton, E. Sussex.
Douglas Hall Ltd, Brighton, E. Sussex.
Hallmarks, Brighton, E. Sussex.
The House of Antiques, Brighton, E. Sussex.
Harry Mason, Brighton, E. Sussex.
S.L. Simmons, Brighton, E. Sussex.
Wm. Bruford and Son Ltd, Eastbourne, E. Sussex.
Trade Wind, Rottingdean, E. Sussex.
Rye Antiques, Rye, E. Sussex.
Aarquebus Antiques, St. Leonards-on-Sea, E. Sussex.
Peter Hancock Antiques, Chichester, W. Sussex.
Westbourne Antiques, Westbourne, W. Sussex.
Rathbone Law Antiques, Worthing, W. Sussex.
Sovereign Antiques, Gateshead, Tyne and Wear.
Davidson's The Jewellers Ltd, Newcastle-upon-Tyne, Tyne and Wear.
Intercoin, Newcastle-upon-Tyne, Tyne and Wear.
Owen's Jewellers, Newcastle-upon-Tyne, Tyne and Wear.
Coleshill Antiques and Interiors Ltd, Coleshill, Warks.
MPA Warwick Ltd, Gaydon, Warks.
Jean A. Bateman, Stratford-upon-Avon, Warks.
Howards Jewellers, Stratford-upon-Avon, Warks.
Russell Lane Antiques, Warwick, Warks.
Westgate Antiques, Warwick, Warks.
Peter Clark Antiques, Birmingham, W. Mids.
Maurice Fellows, Birmingham, W. Mids.
Rex Johnson and Sons, Birmingham, W. Mids.
Piccadilly Jewellers, Birmingham, W. Mids.
H. and R.L. Parry Ltd, Sutton Coldfield, W. Mids.
Hardwick Antiques, Walsall, W. Mids.
Nicholls Jewellers and Antiques, Walsall, W. Mids.
Cross Keys Jewellers, Devizes, Wilts.
Cross Keys Jewellers, Marlborough, Wilts.
JonathanGreen Antiques, Salisbury, Wilts.
Howards of Broadway, Broadway, Worcs.
Magpie Jewellers and Antiques and Magpie Arms & Armour, Evesham, Worcs.
B.B.M. Jewellery and Antiques, Kidderminster, Worcs.
Lower House Fine Antiques, Redditch, Worcs.
Bygones by the Cathedral, Worcester, Worcs.
Bygones (Worcester), Worcester, Worcs.
Lesley Berry Antiques, Flamborough, E. Yorks.
Country Antiques, Boroughbridge, N. Yorks.
D. Mason & Son, Harrogate, N. Yorks.
Ogden of Harrogate Ltd, Harrogate, N. Yorks.
Christopher Warner, Harrogate, N. Yorks.
Mary Milnthorpe and Daughters Antique Shop, Settle, N. Yorks.
Barbara Cattle, York, N. Yorks.
Golden Memories of York, York, N. Yorks.
Robert M. Himsworth, York, N. Yorks.
John Mason Jewellers Ltd, Rotherham, S. Yorks.
Canterbury House, Thorne, S. Yorks.
Geoff Neary (incorporating Fillans Antiques Ltd), Huddersfield, W. Yorks.
Jack Shaw and Co, Ilkley, W. Yorks.
Keighleys of Keighley, Keighley, W. Yorks.
Aladdin's Cave, Leeds, W. Yorks.
Coins International and Antiques International, Leeds, W. Yorks.
Grange Antiques, St. Peter Port, Guernsey, C.I.
The Country Antiques, Antrim, Co. Antrim, N. Ireland.
Dunluce Antiques, Bushmills, Co. Antrim, N. Ireland.
Brian R. Bolt Antiques, Portballintrae, Co. Antrim, N. Ireland.
Clifford J. Auld Antiques (Old Cross Antiques), Ashfield, Co. Down, N. Ireland.
Old Priory Antiques, Greyabbey, Co. Down, N. Ireland.
Timecraft, Greyabbey, Co. Down, N. Ireland.
Cookstown Antiques, Cookstown, Co. Tyrone, N. Ireland.
Sinclair's Antique Gallery, Belfast, N. Ireland
McCalls (Aberdeen), Aberdeen, Scotland.
McCalls Limited, Aberdeen, Scotland.
William Young Antiques & Fine Art, Aberdeen, Scotland.
Wildman's Antiques, Dalbeattie, Scotland.
Joseph Bonnar, Jewellers, Edinburgh, Scotland.
Goodwin's Antiques Ltd, Edinburgh, Scotland.
Montresor, Edinburgh, Scotland.
Royal Mile Curios, Edinburgh, Scotland.
John Whyte, Edinburgh, Scotland.
West End Antiques, Elgin, Scotland.
James Forrest and Co (Jewellers) Ltd, Glasgow, Scotland.
A.D. Hamilton and Co, Glasgow, Scotland.
Jeremy Sniders Antiques, Glasgow, Scotland.

Tim Wright Antiques, Glasgow, Scotland.
Kilmacolm Antiques Ltd, Kilmacolm, Scotland.
Amber Antiques, Kincardine O'Neil, Scotland.
Mir Russki, Linlithgow, Scotland.
Harper-James, Montrose, Scotland.
Forsyth Antiques, Perth, Scotland.
Gallery One, Perth, Scotland.
Hardie Antiques, Perth, Scotland.
Old St. Andrews Gallery, St. Andrews, Scotland.
Abbey Antiques, Stirling, Scotland.
Jones and Dyson, Ann Evans, Bangor, Wales.
Hazel of Brecon, Brecon, Wales.
Silvertime, Brecon, Wales.
Alexander Antiques, Cardiff, Wales.
Cronin Antiques, Cardiff, Wales.
Gold and Silver Shop, Gorseinon, Wales.
Tortoiseshell Antiques, Henllan, Wales.
Cartrefle Antiques, Mathry, Wales.
James Allan, Swansea, Wales.
Audrey Bull, Tenby, Wales.

Sporting Items & Associated Memorabilia

Mallard Billiards, London N1.
Risky Business, London NW8.
Holland & Holland, London W1.
Arnold Sporting Antiques, Sean, London W11.
World Famous Portobello Market, London W11.
Sir William Bentley Billiards (Antique Billiard Table Specialist Company), Hungerford, Berks.
Warboys Antiques, Warboys, Cambs.
Yesterday Tackle and Books, Bournemouth, Dorset.
John Burton Natural Craft Taxidermy, Ebrington, Glos.
Simon Brett, Moreton-in-Marsh, Glos.
Hamilton Billiards & Games Co., Knebworth, Herts.
Garden House Antiques, Tenterden, Kent.
Irving Antique Toys, Manchester, Lancs.
The Spinning Wheel, Southport, Merseyside.
Manfred Schotten Antiques, Burford, Oxon.
Billiard Room Antiques, Chilcompton, Somerset.
Academy Billiard Company, West Byfleet, Surrey.
Burman Antiques, Stratford-upon-Avon, Warks.
James Wigington Arms and Armour, Stratford-upon-Avon, Warks.
Grant Fine Art, Droitwich, Worcs.
Fun Antiques, Sheffield, S. Yorks.
Old St. Andrews Gallery, St. Andrews, Scotland.
Old Troon Sporting Antiques, Troon, Scotland.

Sporting Paintings & Prints

Swan Fine Art, London N1.
Relcy Antiques, London SE10.
Ackermann & Johnson, ,London SW1.
Addison-Ross Gallery, London SW1.
Frost and Reed Ltd (Est. 1808), London SW1.
Innes Gallery, Malcolm, London SW1.
Mason Gallery, Paul, London SW1.
Collins and Hastie Ltd, London SW10.
Kensington Sporting Paintings Ltd, London SW20.
Old Church Galleries, London SW3.
Burlington Gallery Ltd, London W1.
Green, Richard, London W1.
Holland & Holland, London W1.
Lane Fine Art Ltd, London W1.
O'Shea Gallery, The, London W1.
Sabin Ltd, Frank T., London W1.
Tryon & Swann Gallery, London W1.
Connaught Galleries, London W2.
Iona Antiques, London W8.
Grosvenor Prints, London WC2.
Marlborough Sporting Gallery and Bookshop, Hungerford, Berks.
Julian Tatham-Losh, Andoversford, Glos.
Coltsfoot Gallery, Leominster, Herefs.
G. and D.I. Marrin and Sons, Folkestone, Kent.
Leics Sporting Gallery and Brown Jack Bookshop, Lubenham, Leics.
In the Picture (The Golf Collection), Holt, Norfolk.
Paul Hopwell Antiques, West Haddon, Northants.
Jane Neville Gallery, Aslockton, Notts.
Sally Mitchell's Gallery, Tuxford, Notts.
H.C. Dickins, Bloxham, Oxon.
John Garner, Uppingham, Rutland.
Julian Armytage, Crewkerne, Somerset.
Equus Art Gallery, Newmarket, Suffolk.
Vandeleur Antiquarian Books, Epsom, Surrey.
Julia Holmes Antique Maps and Prints, South Harting, W. Sussex.
Burman Antiques, Stratford-upon-Avon, Warks.
Country Connections (Esk House Arts), Grosmont, N. Yorks.
Paul Hayes Gallery, Auchterarder, Scotland.
Malcolm Innes Gallery, Edinburgh, Scotland.
Strathspey Gallery, Grantown-on-Spey, Scotland.

Stamps

Argyll Etkin Gallery, London W1.
Michael Coins, London W8.
Franks, J.A.L., London WC1.
Gibbons, Stanley London WC2.
Avalon Post Card and Stamp Shop, Chester, Cheshire.
Penrith Coin and Stamp Centre, Penrith, Cumbria.
Portsmouth Stamp Shop, Portsmouth, Hants.
Denver House Antiques and Collectables, Burford, Oxon.
Jeremy's (Oxford Stamp Centre), Oxford, Oxon.
A.J. Saywell Ltd. (The Oxford Stamp Shop), Oxford, Oxon.
Collectors' Gallery, Shrewsbury, Shrops.
Bath Stamp and Coin Shop, Bath, Somerset.
Corridor Stamp Shop, Bath, Somerset.
Edinburgh Coin Shop, Edinburgh, Scotland.
Glance Back Bookshop, Chepstow, Wales.

Tapestries, Textiles & Needlework

Gumb, Linda, London N1.
Lavian, Joseph, London N4.
Franses and Sons, Robert, London NW8.
Gallery of Antique Costume and Textiles, London NW8.
Batstone Decorative Antiques, Hilary, London SW1.
Franses Ltd, S., London SW1.
Graham, Joss, London SW1.
Heraz (David Hartwright Ltd), London SW1.
Keshishian, London SW1.
Mayorcas Ltd, London SW1.
Smyth - Antique Textiles, Peta, London SW1.
Rare Carpets Gallery, London SW10.
Antiques and Things, London SW11.
Kilim Warehouse Ltd, The, London SW12.
Garrow, Marilyn, London SW13.
Tobias and The Angel, London SW13.
Booth, Joanna, London SW3.
Stephenson, Robert, London SW3.
Arabesque Antiques, London SW6.
Greenwood, Judy, London SW6.
Lunn Antiques, London SW6.
Perez Antique Carpets Gallery, London SW6.
Heskia, London SW8.
Atlantic Bay Carpets, London W1.
Eskenazi Ltd, John, London W1.
Gallery Zadah Ltd, London W1.
John (Rare Rugs) Ltd, C., London W1.
Juran and Co, Alexander, London W1.
Nels Ltd, Paul, London W1.
Pelham Galleries Ltd, London W1.
Vigo Carpet Gallery, London W1.
Wrigglesworth, Linda, London W1.
Cook, Sheila, London W11.
Fairman Carpets Ltd, London W11.
Mankowitz, Daniel, London W11.
Charleville Gallery, London W14.
Coats Oriental Carpets, London W8.
Horne, Jonathan, London W8.
Robert and Georgina Hastie, Hungerford, Berks.
Made of Honour, Chester, Cheshire.
Joyce and Rod Whitehead, Chester, Cheshire.
Penzance Antiques and Furnishings, Penzance, Cornwall.
Martin and Dorothy Harper Antiques, Bakewell, Derbys.
The House that Moved, Exeter, Devon.
The Honiton Lace Shop, Honiton, Devon.
The Lace Shop, South Molton, Devon.
Georgina Ryder, Frampton, Dorset.
Maureen Morris, Saffron Walden, Essex.
The Stuffed Dog Antiques, Berkeley, Glos.
Anthony Hazledine, Fairford, Glos.
Huntington Antiques Ltd, Stow-on-the-Wold, Glos.
Meg Andrews, Harpenden, Herts.
Two Maids Antiques, Biddenden, Kent.
The Lace Basket, Tenterden, Kent.
Farmhouse Antiques, Bolton-by-Bowland, Lancs.
20th Century Frocks, Lincoln, Lincs.
Mansions, Lincoln, Lincs.
Audley House, Osbournby, Lincs.
Country and Eastern, Norwich, Norfolk.
The Barn, Collingham, Notts.
Witney Antiques, Witney, Oxon.
Clutter, Uppingham, Rutland.
Antique Linens and Lace, Bath, Somerset.
Ann King, Bath, Somerset.
Susannah, Bath, Somerset.
Bruce Tozer Rugs & Antiques, Bath, Somerset.

Faded Elegance, Dulverton, Somerset.
Richard Midwinter Antiques, Newcastle-under-Lyme, Staffs.
Tara's Hall, Hadleigh, Suffolk.
Oswald Simpson, Long Melford, Suffolk.
Sarah Meysey-Thompson Antiques, Woodbridge, Suffolk.
Heytesbury Antiques, Farnham, Surrey.
John Bird Antiques, Lewes, E. Sussex.
Patrick and Gillian Morley Antiques, Warwick, Warks.
Avon Antiques, Bradford-on-Avon, Wilts.
Emma Hurley Antiques and Textiles, Warminster, Wilts.
Penny Farthing Antiques, North Cave, E. Yorks.
Simon Greenwood Antiques, Burneston, N. Yorks.
London House Oriental Rugs and Carpets, Boston Spa, W. Yorks.
Real Macoy, Keighley, W. Yorks.
Lawn and Lace, Mirfield, W. Yorks.
Echoes, Todmorden, W. Yorks.
Present Bygones, Edinburgh, Scotland.
Townhouse Antiques, Walkerburn, Scotland.
Tortoiseshell Antiques, Henllan, Wales.

Taxidermy

"Get Stuffed", London N1.
Curios, London N19.
Yesterday Tackle and Books, Bournemouth, Dorset.
Castle Antiques, Leigh-on-Sea, Essex.
John Burton Natural Craft Taxidermy, Ebrington, Glos.
Heads 'n' Tails, Wiveliscombe, Somerset.
The Enchanted Aviary, Bury St. Edmunds, Suffolk.

Tools (including Needlework & Sewing)

Old Tool Chest, The, London N1.
Ye Little Shoppe, Modbury, Devon.
Thomas and Pamela Hudson, Cirencester, Glos.
Mark A. Serle (Antiques and Restoration), Lechlade, Glos.
Norton Antiques, Twyford, Norfolk.
Ark Antiques, Bishop's Castle, Shrops.
David Bridgwater, Bath, Somerset.
Sheila Cooper t/a Sheila Smith Antiques, Bath, Somerset.
Peppers Period Pieces, Bury St. Edmunds, Suffolk.
Trinders' Fine Tools, Clare, Suffolk.
Roy Arnold, Needham Market, Suffolk.
Tortoiseshell Antiques, Henllan, Wales.

Toys (see Dolls)

Trade Dealers (see Shipping Goods)

Treen

Halcyon Days, London EC3.
Young Antiques, Robert, London SW11.
Halcyon Days, London W1.
Seligmann, M. and D., London W8.
Cobblers Hall Antiques, Toddington, Beds.
Phoenix Antiques, Fordham, Cambs.
A.P. and M.A. Haylett, Outwell, Cambs.
Shire Antiques, Newby Bridge, Cumbria.
Baggott Church Street Ltd, Stow-on-the-Wold, Glos.
Huntington Antiques Ltd, Stow-on-the-Wold, Glos.
Country Homes, Tetbury, Glos.
Day Antiques, Tetbury, Glos.
Prichard Antiques, Winchcombe, Glos.
Millers of Chelsea Antiques Ltd, Ringwood, Hants.
Elizabeth Viney, Stockbridge, Hants.
Mary Roofe Antiques, Winchester, Hants.
Two Maids Antiques, Biddenden, Kent.
E.W. Webster, Bickerstaffe, Lancs.
Audley House, Osbournby, Lincs.
Antiques, West Haddon, Northants.
The Barn, Collingham, Notts.
Brian and Caroline Craik Ltd, Bath, Somerset.
Guillemot, Aldeburgh, Suffolk.
Foord Antiques and Restoration, Bures, Suffolk.
Peppers Period Pieces, Bury St. Edmunds, Suffolk.
J. Du Cros Antiques, Petworth, W. Sussex.
Moxhams Antiques, Bradford-on-Avon, Wilts.
Combe Cottage Antiques, Castle Combe, Wilts.
Annmarie Turner Antiques, Marlborough, Wilts.
Fenwick and Fenwick Antiques, Broadway, Worcs.
Bill Bentley, Harrogate, N. Yorks.
Michael Green Traditional Interiors, Harrogate, N. Yorks.
Brian R. Bolt Antiques, Portballintrae, Co. Antrim, N. Ireland.
Islwyn Watkins, Knighton, Wales.

Vintage Cars (see Carriages and Cars)

Watercolours

Royal Exchange Art Gallery, London EC3.
Boutique Fantasque, London N1.
Finney Antique Prints and Books, Michael, London N1.
Finchley Fine Art Galleries, London N12.
Stewart - Fine Art, Lauri, London N2.
Totteridge Gallery, The, London N20.
Centaur Gallery, London N6.
Lummis Fine Art, Sandra, London N8.
Barkes and Barkes, London NW1.
Gunter Fine Art, London NW2.
Newhart (Pictures) Ltd, London NW3.
Gallery Kaleidoscope, London NW6.
Greenwich Gallery, The, London SE10.
Beetles Ltd, Chris, London SW1.
Cato, Miles Wynn, London SW1.
Douwes Fine Art Ltd, London SW1.
Frost and Reed Ltd (Est. 1808), London SW1.
Gregory Gallery, Martyn, London SW1.
Hunter Fine Art, Sally, London SW1.
Moreton Street Gallery, London SW1.
Old Maps and Prints, London SW1.
Paisnel Gallery, London SW1.
Parkin Fine Art Ltd, Michael, London SW1.
Polak Gallery, London SW1.
Spink and Son Ltd, London SW1.
Thomson - Albany Gallery, Bill, London SW1.
Waterman Fine Art Ltd, London SW1.
Collins and Hastie Ltd, London SW10.
Gallery on Lots Road, London SW10.
Hollywood Road Gallery, London SW10.
Park Walk Gallery, London SW10.
Pawsey and Payne, London SW10.
Bloxham (Fine Art) Ltd, John, London SW11.
Alton Gallery, London SW13.
International Arts Group, London SW18.
Curzon Gallery, The David, London SW19.
Campbell Picture Frames Ltd, John, London SW3.
Chelsea Rare Books, London SW3.
Denny Ltd, Colin, London SW3.
Gallery Lingard, London SW3.
Green and Stone, London SW3.
Hoppen Ltd, Stephanie, London SW3.
Pettifer Ltd, David, London SW3.
20th Century Gallery, London SW6.
Coopér Fine Arts Ltd, London SW6.
Spink, John, London SW6.
Collino, Julie, London SW7.
Agnew's, London W1.
Connaught Brown plc, London W1.
Editions Graphiques Gallery, London W1.
Fine Art Society plc, The, London W1.
Maas Gallery, London W1.
Mallett Gallery, London W1.
Mitchell and Son, John, London W1.
O'Nians, Hal, London W1.
Piccadilly Gallery, London W1.
Somerville Ltd, Stephen, London W1.
Spink Leger Pictures, London W1.
Waterhouse and Dodd, London W1.
Daggett Gallery, Charles, London W11.
Milne and Moller, London W11.
Skrebowski Prints, Justin F., London W11.
Garratt (Fine Paintings), Stephen, London W14.
Ealing Gallery, London W5.
Crawley and Asquith Ltd, London W8.
Dare, George, London W8.
Spero, Simon, London W8.
Kendall, The English Watercolour Gallery, Beryl, London W9.
Abbott and Holder, London WC1.
D'Orsai Ltd, Sebastian, London WC1.
Skrebowski Prints, Justin F., London WC2.
Baroq at Brindleys, Heath and Reach, Beds.
Charterhouse Gallery Ltd, Heath and Reach, Beds.
David Ball Antique Furnisher, Leighton Buzzard, Beds.
Foye Gallery, Luton, Beds.
Knight's Gallery, Luton, Beds.
Graham Gallery, Burghfield Common, Berks.
Marlborough Sporting Gallery and Bookshop, Hungerford, Berks.
Jaspers Fine Arts Ltd, Maidenhead, Berks.
Grove Gallery, Windsor and Eton, Berks.
J. Manley, Windsor and Eton, Berks.
Grosvenor House Interiors, Beaconsfield, Bucks.
Images in Watercolour, Chalfont St. Giles, Bucks.
Windmill Fine Art, High Wycombe, Bucks.
Angela Hone Watercolours, Marlow, Bucks.
Penn Barn, Penn, Bucks.
Medina Antiquarian Maps and Prints, Winslow, Bucks.
Cambridge Fine Art Ltd, Cambridge, Cambs.
Sebastian Pearson Paintings Prints and Works of Art, Cambridge, Cambs.

Baron Fine Art, Chester, Cheshire.
Richard A. Nicholson, Chester, Cheshire.
St. Peters Art Gallery, Chester, Cheshire.
Harper Fine Paintings, Poynton, Cheshire.
Margaret Bedi Antiques, Billingham, Cleveland.
T.B. and R. Jordan (Fine Paintings), Eaglescliffe, Cleveland.
Copperhouse Gallery - W. Dyer & Sons, Hayle, Cornwall.
Tony Sanders Penzance Gallery and Antiques, Penzance, Cornwall.
Myles Varcoe, Tywardreath, Cornwall.
St. Breock Gallery, Wadebridge, Cornwall.
Peter Haworth, Beetham, Cumbria.
The Gallery, Penrith, Cumbria.
Cavendish House Gallery, Ashbourne, Derbys.
Kenneth Upchurch, Ashbourne, Derbys.
Charles H. Ward, Derby, Derbys.
J. Collins and Son, Bideford, Devon.
Medina Gallery, Bideford, Devon.
Chantry Bookshop and Gallery, Dartmouth, Devon.
Mill Gallery, Ermington, Devon.
Honiton Fine Art, Honiton, Devon.
Skeaping Gallery, Lydford, Devon.
Michael Wood Fine Art, Plymouth, Devon.
The Lantern Shop, Sidmouth, Devon.
Bygone Days Antiques, Tiverton, Devon.
Stour Gallery, Blandford Forum, Dorset.
Hants Gallery, Bournemouth, Dorset.
The Swan Gallery, Sherborne, Dorset.
Domino Antiques, Barling Magna, Essex.
Brandler Galleries, Brentwood, Essex.
Neil Graham Gallery, Brentwood, Essex.
S. Bond and Son, Colchester, Essex.
Richard Iles Gallery, Colchester, Essex.
Simon Hilton, Dunmow, Essex.
Newport Gallery, Newport, Essex.
David Lloyd Gallery, Purleigh, Essex.
Reddings Art and Antiques, Southend-on-Sea, Essex.
Galerie Lev, Woodford Green, Essex.
Cleeve Picture Framing, Bishops Cleeve, Glos.
The Priory Gallery, Bishops Cleeve, Glos.
Alexander Gallery, Bristol, Glos.
David Cross (Fine Art), Bristol, Glos.
David Howard, Cheltenham, Glos.
Manor House Gallery, Cheltenham, Glos.
School House Antiques, Chipping Campden, Glos.
Astley House - Fine Art, Moreton-in-Marsh, Glos.
Nina Zborowska, Painswick, Glos.
The John Davies Gallery, Stow-on-the-Wold, Glos.
The Fosse Gallery, Stow-on-the-Wold, Glos.
Kenulf Fine Arts, Stow-on-the-Wold, Glos.
Roger Lamb Antiques & Works of Art, Stow-on-the-Wold, Glos.
Studio Bookshop and Gallery, Alresford, Hants.
Antique House, Hartley Wintney, Hants.
J. Morton Lee, Hayling Island, Hants.
Corfields Ltd, Lymington, Hants.
The Petersfield Bookshop, Petersfield, Hants.
Lacewing Fine Art Gallery, Romsey, Hants.
Bell Fine Art, Winchester, Hants.
Brobury House Gallery, Brobury, Herefs.
Coltsfoot Gallery, Leominster, Herefs.
Countrylife Gallery, Hitchin, Herts.
Carole Thomas (Fine Arts), Hitchin, Herts.
Galerias Segui, Cowes, I. of Wight.
The Shanklin Gallery, Shanklin, I. of Wight.
Cranbrook Gallery, Cranbrook, Kent.
Judith Peppitt, Harrietsham, Kent.
John Jackson, Hythe, Kent.
Periwinkle Press, Newnham, Kent.
Francis Iles, Rochester, Kent.
Langley Galleries, Rochester, Kent.
Sundridge Gallery, Sundridge, Kent.
Nicholas Bowlby, Tunbridge Wells, Kent.
Graham Gallery, Tunbridge Wells, Kent.
Apollo Galleries, Westerham, Kent.
Old Corner House Antiques, Wittersham, Kent.
Fulda Gallery Ltd, Manchester, Lancs.
Hammond Smith (Fine Art), Leicester, Leics.
Graftons of Market Harborough, Market Harborough, Leics.
Lincoln Fine Art, Lincoln, Lincs.
Lyver & Boydell Galleries, Liverpool, Merseyside.
The Hampton Hill Gallery, Hampton Hill, Middx.
Marble Hill Gallery, Twickenham, Middx.
The Coach House, Costessey, Norfolk.
The Haven Gallery, Gt. Yarmouth, Norfolk.
Crome Gallery and Frame Shop, Norwich, Norfolk.
The Fairhurst Gallery, Norwich, Norfolk.
Mandell's Gallery, Norwich, Norfolk.
The Westcliffe Gallery, Sheringham, Norfolk.
Staithe Lodge Gallery, Swafield, Norfolk.
Norton Antiques, Twyford, Norfolk.
Coughton Galleries Ltd, Arthingworth, Northants.
Right Angle, Brackley, Northants.
Savage Fine Art, Haselbech, Northants.
Dragon Antiques, Kettering, Northants.
Haydon Bridge Antiques, Haydon Bridge, Northumbs.
Haydon Gallery, Haydon Bridge, Northumbs.
Anthony Mitchell Fine Paintings, Nottingham, Notts.
John Harrison Fine Art, Aston Tirrold, Oxon.
Benson Antiques and Gallery, Benson, Oxon.
H.C. Dickins, Bloxham, Oxon.
The Burford Gallery, Burford, Oxon.
Horseshoe Antiques and Gallery, Burford, Oxon.
The Stone Gallery, Burford, Oxon.
Wren Gallery, Burford, Oxon.
Tuckers Country Store and Art Gallery, Deddington, Oxon.
The Barry M. Keene Gallery, Henley-on-Thames, Oxon.
Fine Art of Oakham, Oakham, Rutland.
The Old House Gallery, Oakham, Rutland.
Marc Oxley Fine Art, Uppingham, Rutland.
Gallery 6, Broseley, Shrops.
Teme Valley Antiques, Ludlow, Shrops.
Cruck House Antiques, Much Wenlock, Shrops.
F.C. Manser and Son Ltd, Shrewsbury, Shrops.
Haygate Gallery, Telford, Shrops.
The Mount, Woore, Shrops.
Hall's Antiques, Ash Priors, Somerset.
Adam Gallery, Bath, Somerset.
Trimbridge Galleries, Bath, Somerset.
The Court Gallery, Nether Stowey, Somerset.
Richard Joslin Galleries, Taunton, Somerset.
Coach House Gallery, Wedmore, Somerset.
Sadler Street Gallery, Wells, Somerset.
England's Gallery, Leek, Staffs.
Richard Midwinter Antiques, Newcastle-under-Lyme, Staffs.
Thompson's Gallery, Aldeburgh, Suffolk.
The Fortescue Gallery, Ipswich, Suffolk.
J. and J. Baker, Lavenham, Suffolk.
Equus Art Gallery, Newmarket, Suffolk.
Peasenhall Art and Antiques Gallery, Peasenhall, Suffolk.
Simon Carter Gallery, Woodbridge, Suffolk.
The Falcon Gallery, Wortham, Suffolk.
Suffolk House Antiques, Yoxford, Suffolk.
Cobham Galleries, Cobham, Surrey.
The Court Gallery, East Molesey, Surrey.
Jenny Asplund Fine Art, Esher, Surrey.
Barbara Rubenstein Fine Art, Godalming, Surrey.
Glencorse Antiques, Kingston-upon-Thames, Surrey.
Limpsfield Watercolours, Limpsfield, Surrey.
Bourne Gallery Ltd, Reigate, Surrey.
The Gallery, Reigate, Surrey.
Roland Goslett Gallery, Richmond, Surrey.
F. and T. Lawson Antiques, Richmond, Surrey.
Marryat, Richmond, Surrey.
Palmer Galleries, Richmond, Surrey.
Cedar House Gallery, Ripley, Surrey.
Sage Antiques and Interiors, Ripley, Surrey.
Margaret Melville Watercolours, Staines, Surrey.
Boathouse Gallery, Walton-on-Thames, Surrey.
Edward Cross - Fine Paintings, Weybridge, Surrey.
Stephen Welbourne, Brighton, E. Sussex.
John Day of Eastbourne Fine Art, Eastbourne, E. Sussex.
Premier Gallery, Eastbourne, E. Sussex.
Molly Alexander, Seaford, E. Sussex.
Faringdon Gallery, Arundel, W. Sussex.
Sussex Fine Art, Arundel, W. Sussex.
Susan and Robert Botting, Billingshurst, W. Sussex.
Lannards Gallery, Billingshurst, W. Sussex.
Jeremy Wood Fine Art, Billingshurst, W. Sussex.
Gough Bros. Art Shop and Gallery, Bognor Regis, W. Sussex.
The Antique Print Shop, East Grinstead, W. Sussex.
The Canon Gallery, Petworth, W. Sussex.
George House Gallery, Petworth, W. Sussex.
Wilsons Antiques, Worthing, W. Sussex.
Anna Harrison Fine Antiques, Gosforth, Tyne and Wear.
MacDonald Fine Art, Gosforth, Tyne and Wear.
Osborne Art and Antiques, Jesmond, Tyne and Wear.

The Dean Gallery Ltd, Newcastle-upon-Tyne, Tyne and Wear.
Ian Sharp Antiques, Tynemouth, Tyne and Wear.
Sport and Country Gallery, Bulkington, Warks.
Arden Gallery, Henley-in-Arden, Warks.
Colmore Galleries Ltd, Henley-in-Arden, Warks.
Fine-Lines (Fine Art), Shipston-on-Stour, Warks.
The Loquens Gallery, Stratford-upon-Avon, Warks.
Woodland Fine Art, Alvechurch, W. Mids.
Ashleigh House Antiques, Birmingham, W. Mids.
John Hubbard Antiques and Fine Art, Birmingham, W. Mids.
Kestrel House Antiques and Auction Salerooms, Birmingham, W. Mids.
The Windmill Gallery, Birmingham, W. Mids.
Robert Withers Paintings, Halesowen, W. Mids.
Oldswinford Gallery, Stourbridge, W. Mids.
Driffold Gallery, Sutton Coldfield, W. Mids.
D.M. Beach, Salisbury, Wilts.
The Jerram Gallery, Salisbury, Wilts.
Ian J. Brook, Antiques and Picture Gallery, Wilton, Wilts.
Richard Hagen, Broadway, Worcs.
Hay Loft Gallery, Broadway, Worcs.
Haynes Fine Art of Broadway, Broadway, Worcs.
Picton House Galleries, Broadway, Worcs.
John Noott Galleries, Broadway, Worcs.
Malvern Arts, Great Malvern, Worcs.
Gandolfi House, Malvern Wells, Worcs.
The Highway Gallery, Upton-upon-Severn, Worcs.
James H. Starkey Galleries, Beverley, E. Yorks.
Anthony Graham Antiques, Boroughbridge, N. Yorks .
W. Greenwood (Fine Art), Burneston, N. Yorks.
Garth Antiques, Harrogate, N. Yorks.
McTague of Harrogate, Harrogate, N. Yorks.
Walker Galleries Ltd, Harrogate, N. Yorks.
Gary K. Blissett, Long Preston, N. Yorks.
Talents Fine Arts Ltd, Malton, N. Yorks.
Rose Fine Art and Antiques, Ripon, N.Yorks.
Bennett, Richard, Thirsk, N. Yorks.
Garth Antiques, Whixley, N. Yorks.
Coulter Galleries, York, N. Yorks.
Fulwood Antiques and The Basement Gallery, Sheffield, S. Yorks.
Peter James Antiques, Sheffield, S. Yorks.
E. Carrol, Bingley, W. Yorks.
The Titus Gallery, Shipley, W. Yorks.
Robin Taylor Fine Arts, Wakefield, W. Yorks.
C.I. Galleries Ltd, St. Peter Port, Guernsey, C.I.
Geoffrey P. Gavey, Vale, Guernsey, C.I.
The Bell Gallery, Belfast, N. Ireland.
Phyllis Arnold Gallery Antiques, Greyabbey, Co. Down, N. Ireland.
The Rendezvous Gallery, Aberdeen, Scotland.
The Waverley Gallery, Aberdeen, Scotland.
The McEwan Gallery, Ballater, Scotland.
Calton Gallery, Edinburgh, Scotland.
Malcolm Innes Gallery, Edinburgh, Scotland.
John Mathieson and Co, Edinburgh, Scotland.
Young Antiques, Edinburgh, Scotland.
The Roger Billcliffe Fine Art, Glasgow, Scotland.
Ewan Mundy Fine Art Ltd, Glasgow, Scotland.
Scottish Art Heritage, Glasgow, Scotland.
Mainhill Gallery, Jedburgh, Scotland.
Newburgh Antiques, Newburgh, Scotland.
The George Street Gallery, Perth, Scotland.
Nigel Stacy-Marks Ltd, Perth, Scotland.
St. Andrews Fine Art, St. Andrews, Scotland.
David Windsor Gallery, Bangor, Wales.
Michael Webb Fine Art, Bodorgan, Wales.
Manor House Fine Arts, Cardiff, Wales.
Philip Davies Fine Art, Swansea, Wales.
Thicke Galleries, Swansea, Wales.
Barn Court Antiques, Templeton, Wales.

Wholesale Dealers (see Shipping Goods)

Wine Related Items

Johnson Collection, The Hugh, London SW1.
Harbottle, Patricia, London W11.
Christopher Sykes Antiques, Woburn, Beds.
Bacchus Antiques - In the Service of Wine, Cartmel, Cumbria.
Robin Butler, Bristol, Glos.
Neil Willcox, Twickenham, Middx.
Bacchus Gallery, Petworth, W. Sussex.

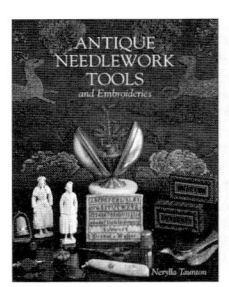

Dealers' Index

In order to facilitate reference to dealers both the names of the individuals and their business names are indexed separately, i.e. the name of their shop or business, as well as the towns and counties under which they appear. Thus A.E. Jones and C. Smith of High Street Antiques will be indexed under

Jones, A.E., Town, County
Smith, C., Town, County
and High Street Antiques, Town, County

This year we have combined the Centres and Markets Dealers' Index with the main index and the same rules apply. Also where the title of the market is the same as the town under which it appears, the name of the town is not shown again.

A

B

C

D

F

G

H

I

J

K

L

M

N

O

P

Q

R

S

T

Wyche House Antiques, Nantwich, Cheshire.
Wychwood Antiques, Taynton, Oxon.
Wycliffe Antiques, Ginnel, The, Harrogate, Yorks North
Wylie, Mrs M., Hindhead, Surrey.
Wyllie Gallery, The, London SW7.
Wyllie, J.G., London SW7.
Wyncoll, Craig, Grays Antique Market, London W1.
Wynsave Investments Ltd, Hungerford, Berks.
Wyrardisbury Antiques, Wraysbury, Berks.

X

XS Baggage, Antiquarius, London SW3.

Y

Yacobi, C.B. and C, Bond Street Antiques Centre, London W1
Yamamoto, Matsuko, Bond Street Antiques Centre, London W1.
Yandell, Mrs A., Cambridge, Cambs.
Yang, Chris, Stouts Antique Market, London W11.
Yang, Grays Antique Market, London W1.
Yardy, S., London W14.
Yarnall Antiques, Wallasey, Merseyside.
Yarnall, Richard and Joy, Wallasey, Merseyside.
Yarrow, J.B., North Petherton, Somerset.
Yates, A., Chipping Campden, Glos.
Yates, Mr, Nottingham, Notts.
Yates, Mrs D., York, N. Yorks.
Yates, S., Quorn, Leics.
Ye Little Shoppe, Modbury, Devon.
Ye Olde Saddlers Shoppe, Horrabridge, Devon.
Yealland, J. M., Caversham, Berks.
Year Dot, Leeds, W. Yorks.
Yellow Lantern Antiques Ltd, Brighton, E. Sussex.
Yendell, J.M., Bampton, Devon.
"Yester-year", Iver, Bucks.
Yesterday Child, London N1.
Yesterday Tackle and Books, Bournemouth, Dorset.
Yesterday's Antiques, London SW14.
Yesterday's Pine, Carlisle Antique and Craft Centre, Cumbria
Yesterdays Pine, Shere, Surrey.
Yesterdays, Bollington, Cheshire.
Yesterdays, Leamington Spa, Warks.
Yestertime Antiques, St. Georges Antiques, Worcester, Worcs.
Yesteryear, Glasgow, Scotland.
Yesteryears, Almshouses Arcade, Chichester, Sussex West.
Yew Tree Antiques, Four Elms, Kent.
Yorca Antiques, Durham House Antiques Centre, Stow-on-the-Wold, Glos.
York Antiques Centre, York, N. Yorks.
York Arcade, London N1.
York Cottage Antiques, Helmsley, N.Yorks.
York Whiting, The Furniture Cave, London SW10.
York, G., Honiton, Devon.
York, T.O. and J., Quorn, Leics.
Yorke Antiques, John H., St. Leonards-on-Sea, E. Sussex.
Yorke, J.H., St. Leonards-on-Sea, E. Sussex.
Yosir, Grays Antique Market, London W1
Youde, Malcolm, Tarvin Sands, Cheshire.
Youll's Antiques, Hungerford, Berks.
Youll, B., Hungerford, Berks.
Young and Son (Antiques), John, Keswick, Cumbria.
Young Antiques & Fine Art, William, Aberdeen, Scotland.
Young Antiques, Edinburgh, Scotland.
Young Antiques, Robert, London SW11.
Young, A.J. and A.R., Deal, Kent.
Young, Aldric, Edinburgh, Scotland.
Young, J., Sheffield, S. Yorks.
Young, K.J., Cove, Scotland.
Young, Mavis, Newton Abbot Antiques Centre, Devon
Young, Michael, The Mall Antiques Arcade, London N1.
Young, Mr. M. and Mrs G., Wareham, Dorset.
Young, T.C., Edinburgh, Scotland.

Z

Zacaroli, Stephen, Worcester, Worcs.
Zakoji, Miss E., Antiquarius, London SW3
Zborowska, Nina, Painswick, Glos.
Zeitgeist, Kensington Church Street Antiques Centre, London W8.
Zeno Booksellers and Publishers, London WC2.
Zentner, F., London WC1.
Zoakee, Helen, Grays Antique Market, London W1
Zoil, S., London SW18.
Zwemmer, London WC2.

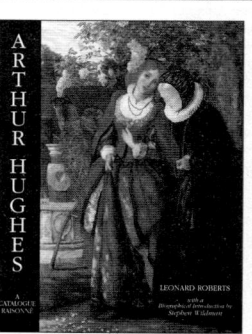

STOP PRESS

Bedfordshire

Luton

S & J Acquisitions

28 Hitchin Rd.(Sylvia and Jo Holdstock). Est. 1992. Open 12-3, Sat. 11-4. CL: Wed., Fri. and Sun. except by appointment. SIZE: Medium. *STOCK: Antiques for the garden, 18th-19th C; decorative artifacts for pubs etc, farming bygones and kitchenalia; all £5-£400.* LOC: From M1, junction 10 (Luton Airport), follow town centre signs, Hitchin Rd. adjacent to railway station.. PARK: Easy. TEL: 01582 451507; home - 01582 415834.

Suffolk

Wickham Market

Greystone Antiques

87 High St. (M. W. & L. D. Turner). Est. 1989. Open Fri., Sat., and Sun. am, other times prior telephone call advisable. SIZE: Small. *STOCK: Victorian and Edwardian pine and satin walnut, £100-£300; Art Deco clocks and figures, £80-£120; enamel stoves, £100-£400.* PARK: Market Sq. TEL: 01728 746654.

Scotland

Stanley (Perthshire)

Coach House Antiques Ltd

Charleston.PH1 4PN. (John Walker). Est. 1971. Open by appointment. SIZE: Medium. *STOCK: Period furniture, from 1760, from £200; decorative items, 18th-19th C, from £50: garden furniture, 19th C, from £100.* LOC: 9 miles north of Perth off A9. Take first slip road to Lungarty and Stanley, continue 2 miles through Stanley village, sign at end of the road 'Charleston'. PARK: Easy. TEL: 01738 828627; home - same. SER: Valuations; restorations; buys at auction (furniture). VAT: Spec.

Gilberts

Charleston. PH1 4PN. (Nicola Gilbert). ISVA. Est. 1996. Open by appointment. SIZE: Medium. *STOCK: Decorative furniture and objects, 19th C, £50-£500; needleworks including samplers and bedspreads.* LOC: 9 miles north of Perth off A9. Take first slip road to Lungarty and Stanley - continue 2 miles through Stanley village, Charleston Farm, set back in fields. PARK: Easy. TEL: 01738 828627; home - same. SER: Valuations; buys at auction (decorative items).

FOR A NEW OR SUBSTANTIALLY ALTERED ENTRY USE THIS FORM

Please complete and return this form; there is no charge

NAME OF SHOP ....

ADDRESS OF SHOP ....

....
full address including actual county (not postal area)

Name (or names) and initials of proprietor(s) ....
(Mr/Mrs/Miss/or title)

Previous trading address (if applicable) ....

....

State whether 'Trade Only' (Yes or No) ....

BADA (Yes or No) .... LAPADA (Yes or No) ....

Year Established .... Resident on premises (Yes or No) ....

OPENING HOURS: (One entry, e.g. '9.30—5.30' if open all day or part day. Two entries, e.g. '9.30—1.00, 2,00—5.30' if closed for lunch)

Please put 'CLOSED' and 'BY APPT.' where applicable

	Morning	Afternoon
Sunday	....	....
Monday	....	....
Tuesday	....	....
Wednesday	....	....
Thursday	....	....
Friday	....	....
Saturday	....	....

SIZE OF SHOWROOM

Small (up to 600 sq.ft.) ....

Medium (600 to 1,500 sq.ft.) ....

Large (over 1,500 sq.ft.) ....

HOW TO GET TO YOUR SHOP (BUSINESS)

Brief helpful details from the nearest well-known road:

....

....

....

....

OF WHAT DOES YOUR STOCK CHIEFLY CONSIST?

(A) Please list in order of importance	(B) Approximate period or date of stock	(C) Indication of price range of stock eg £50—£100 or £5—£25
1. (Principal stock)		
2.		
3.		

IS PARKING *OUTSIDE* YOUR SHOP (BUSINESS) Easy (Yes or No) ....

TELEPHONE NUMBER: Business ....

Home ....
(only if customers can ring for appointments outside business hours)

V.A.T. scheme operated — Standard/Special/Both ....

SERVICES OFFERED:

Valuations (Yes or No) ....

Restorations (Yes or No) ....

Type of work...

Buying specific items at auction for a commission (Yes or No) ....

Type of item...

FAIRS:

At which fairs (if any) do you normally exhibit? ....

....

....

CERTIFICATION:

The information given above is accurate and you may publish it in the Guide. I understand that this entry is entirely free.

Signed..

Date..

ENGLISH COUNTY BOUNDARIES

Map showing county boundaries of England. For county boundary details of Northern Ireland, Scotland and Wales see maps at start of relevant sections.